The Middle East
A HISTORY

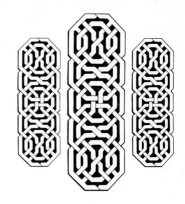

The Middle East

A HISTORY
THIRD EDITION

Sydney Nettleton Fisher
Professor Emeritus
THE OHIO STATE UNIVERSITY 88 — 43

ALFRED · A · KNOPF   NEW YORK

THIS IS A BORZOI BOOK
PUBLISHED BY ALFRED A. KNOPF, INC.

Third Edition

98765432

Library of Congress Cataloging in Publication Data

Fisher, Sydney Nettleton, 1906–
    The Middle East.

    Bibliography: p.
    Includes index.
    1. Near East—History.   2. Near East—History—
20th century.   I. Title.
DS62.F5 1979   956   78-17852
ISBN 0-394-32098-0

Cover & text design by Deborah Payne
Manufactured in the United States of America

Preface
to the Third Edition

In the ten years since the publication of the second edition of this work, major events have transpired in every one of the Middle Eastern states that affect their internal political, social, and economic patterns. These developments have had their impact on the relations between and among these states. At the same time, international forces in distant sectors of the world have had a bearing on Middle Eastern life. To attempt to record these changes in any meaningful and intelligent way has required the addition of a number of pages in chapters dealing with the history of the several countries since the end of World War II. In turn, the increased coverage has necessitated cutting and eliminating material throughout the entire volume in order that its length not become too unwieldy.

The chapters embracing the long period prior to World War II were not touched in the second edition, published in 1969, and, consequently, stood as originally written, largely in 1954 and 1955. The amount of new scholarship that has appeared in the last twenty-five years is almost beyond belief when one begins to review it. No field or period of history has been ignored in research, study, and writing by the increasing number of scholars. Therefore, a full revision was demanded. Updating the contents of the previous edition in the light of new knowledge and understanding has been enjoyable though challenging.

In view of the growing importance and influence of Iran over the last two decades, it seemed fitting to develop more of the historical growth of that country between the fifteenth and the twentieth century. Sections have been added to chapters covering those years as well as a new chapter dealing with the decades from the middle of the nineteenth century to World War I. Likewise the material on Egypt from the time of the British occupation to World War I has been expanded into a separate chapter. Also the old chapter on Arabia has been divided into two: one on Saudi Arabia; and the other on all the other states of the Arabian peninsula.

In all the varied aspects of this revision, students and colleagues have been generous and helpful in their corrections and suggestions. Without all their aid and encouragement this revision could not have been completed. The forbearance of my family has been wonderful throughout this seemingly unending task.

Worthington, Ohio   SYDNEY NETTLETON FISHER

v

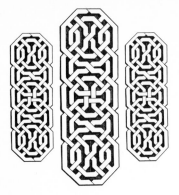

Preface
to the Second Edition

Since 1959, when this text first appeared, the Middle East has experienced many events and developments of considerable significance for the world and for the area. Furthermore, new evidence and information of the past have been revealed by documents, memoirs, statements, and scholars.

In this revision, an attempt has been made to update the material since 1958, to include some of the details of the crisis of the summer of 1967, and to change and correct other statements as required by recent studies and publications.

I wish to thank the various individuals who over the past decade have pointed out errors and omissions and have offered other views for consideration. Some of these have been incorporated in the several reprintings of the first edition and others are included in this revision. I am especially indebted to Mr. James Saeger of Lehigh University for aiding in the preparation of additions to the bibliographical references.

Worthington, Ohio   SYDNEY NETTLETON FISHER

Preface
to the First Edition

For the last two thousand years and more the West has been drawn to, involved in, and fascinated by the culture, religion, resources, and politics of the Middle East. First the Greeks, then the Romans, later the Western Europeans, and now the Americans are discovering the Middle East and its peoples. Historically, the area has been labeled the Orient, the East, the Levant, or the Near East; at present the most widely used term is the Middle East.

The United States, because of her great power and world position since the end of World War II, finds herself concerned with the contemporary problems of the Middle East. In general, Americans of today, many of whom have just become cognizant of the existence of the Middle East, find numerous aspects of its life and affairs quite unintelligible. This is particularly true when these complexities are expressed in the various and often conflicting pronouncements of propagandists for the Arabs, the Israelis and Zionism, the imperialists, the oil companies, the internationalists, the isolationists, the various nationalisms of the Middle East, and all sundry interests.

The attempt of this volume has been to present a brief account of the contemporary Middle Eastern scene so that the beginning college student or general reader can place the area in its proper setting and perspective. Many of the present situations and problems cannot be appreciated or evaluated properly without a knowledge and comprehension of the past, since the contemporary civilization of the Middle East probably has deeper and more significant roots in its past culture and experience than many other civilizations.

With this in mind, it was deemed advisable to begin the story, after a short introduction, with the life of the prophet Muhammad and the revolutionary changes that he made upon the society of his time. From this point the narrative has been carried forward, changing the central locus of the scene from Medina to Damascus to Baghdad to Asia Minor to Istanbul and back to the Arab lands as the fortunes of the area have developed, and at the same time examining each era more in detail as the present is approached.

Certain technicalities have been simplified for the beginner. The titles of many positions, past and present, have been translated into English equivalents in order not to confuse the reader with strange words or tire his eyes with unfamiliar combinations of letters and words. The transliteration of

Middle Eastern proper names has always presented difficulties. In Western literature pertaining to the Middle East, one can find the name of the Prophet rendered as Muhammad, Mohammed, Mohammad, Mohamed, Mahomet, Mehmed, Mehmet, Mehemet, and several other ways. In this book, Muhammad has been used for Arabs, Mehmed for Turks, and Mohammed for some others when individuals spelled the name in that fashion. For most words a spelling has been employed that would render them and their pronunciation most easily adopted by American readers. Where names of places or people have acquired a widely accepted Western spelling, those forms have been used.

Since almost every volume concerning detailed or specialized aspects of Middle Eastern life and affairs contains considerable bibliographical material, and because of the excellent and wide coverage provided in Richard Ettinghausen's *A Selected and Annotated Bibliography of Books and Periodicals in Western Languages dealing with the Near and Middle East with Special Emphasis on Mediaeval and Modern Times* (The Middle East Institute, Washington, D.C., 1952 and 1954), the inclusion of an extensive bibliography has not been felt necessary. The bibliographical entries at the end of the chapters have been supplied to indicate to the beginning student where easily accessible additional material on particular subjects may be obtained. These titles are suggested to serve as second steps for inquiring students who wish to dig more deeply into the many topics discussed only summarily in this text.

In gathering material for this volume it has been necessary to refer to a wide range of books, produced after years of diligent research and study by several generations of scholars in various lands. All will recognize my debt to these; students familiar with the literature of the diverse aspects of Middle Eastern history will appreciate my indebtedness to scholars of other years. This text could not have been written without their labors.

Through the years it has been my good fortune to obtain a closer knowledge of many aspects of Middle Eastern affairs and society through personal conversations and correspondence with many individuals concerned with that area of the world. Without mentioning names, I wish to thank them for the contributions they have made, sometimes unknowingly, to this text. Specifically I desire to pay tribute to inspiring teachers and mentors who have given me a better understanding of general and detailed problems and periods of Middle Eastern history. They are Frederick B. Artz of Oberlin College; Dr. Edgar J. Fisher of Amherst, Virginia; the late Albert Howe Lybyer of the University of Illinois; Philip K. Hitti and the late Walter Livingston Wright, Jr., of Princeton University; and Paul Wittek of the University of London.

In addition to these I am under deep obligation to my colleagues Professors William F. McDonald and John R. Randall for their criticism and aid in regard to certain chapters. Also, Dr. Halford L. Hoskins of the Library of Congress and Professor George G. Arnakis of the University of Texas read the entire volume, offered valuable suggestions, and caught numerous errors and slips. Dr. J. Merle Rife, State University, Indiana, Pennsylvania, was most helpful in assisting in the compilation of the bibliographical references.

However, any faults in fact or judgment which remain are my sole responsibility. Further recognition is due The Ohio State University Graduate School for assistance in the preparation of the manuscript.

This text could not have been prepared without the tolerance and cooperation of my entire family, which has lived with the manuscript for several years.

Worthington, Ohio   SYDNEY NETTLETON FISHER

Contents

ish Administration; The Jewish Agency; The Passfield White Paper; Economic Advances; Peel Report; Civil War; Transjordan; References.

List of Maps
by Theodore R. Miller

The Middle East
A HISTORY

Chapter 1

Geographic Prologue

Geography

Since the end of World War II the term *Middle East* has referred to that area of the world comprising the present political states of Lebanon, Syria, Israel, Jordan, Iraq, Saudi Arabia, Kuwayt, Bahrayn, Qatar, the United Arab Amirates, Oman, South Yemen, Yemen, Egypt, Sudan, Turkey, and Iran. In addition, *Middle East* is employed as a cultural designation for a society and civilization found not only in that region but also to a certain degree in a number of adjacent localities such as Afghanistan, Pakistan, Libya, Tunisia, Algeria, and Morocco.

Two geographic features of the Middle East have been significant in all periods of history. Its location has given it an important, sometimes strategic, position between Africa and Eurasia, and between the Mediterranean world and the Asia of India and the Far East. Nations, tribes, traders, armies, and pilgrims—peoples on the move—have traversed the Middle East, finding the land bridge convenient and along the way discovering the wealth of the area and the civilization of its people.

The second important geographic feature is the relative magnitude of the Middle East. Arabia, the central land mass of the Middle East, embraces an area about the same size as that of the United States east of the Mississippi River plus Texas and California. The southern shore facing the Indian Ocean from Aden to Muscat is as far as from New Orleans to Boston; on the west, the Red Sea is as wide as Lake Erie is long, and the distance from Aden to Port Said is nearly the same as from New York to Denver. Northward from Arabia proper to the Turkish frontier is another 400 miles. When Egypt, Iran, and Turkey are added, the area becomes equivalent to that of the continental United States.

Stretching out 2,000 miles westward in a narrow band from the mouth of the Nile River to the Atlantic Ocean lies North Africa, a cultural part of the Middle East since the end of the seventh century. Moreover, this delimitation of the Middle East has omitted Turkestan, Afghanistan, and Pakistan, with such historic cities as Bukhara, Samarkand, Kabul, and Lahore. Thus, the physical size of the Middle East becomes impressive to Europeans and Americans who are accustomed to seeing these areas in the framework of maps of Asia and Africa.

Physiography

The geologic characteristics of the Middle East show a wide variety of land features, ranging from great bodies of water to low-lying land and swampy regions to rough mountain areas. Over the past 7,000 years or so there seems to have been no important physiographical change except that the deltas of most of the rivers have grown and extended the land seaward. In western Turkey, for example, camels and cattle now graze on the flood plain of the Meander River in front of the ancient walls of Miletus and Priene, in the exact spot where the Persian fleet vanquished the Greeks five centuries before Christ.

Arabia, in general, is a tilted plateau, slanting upward from the northeast to the southwest with a sharp drop in Yemen from 12,000 feet down to the Red Sea. Central Turkey and central Iran are elevated plateaus, in places reaching an altitude of 8,000 feet. Rugged mountains dominate Middle Eastern geography. From a high center in northwestern Iran in the neighborhood of Mount Ararat, mountain ranges up to 18,000 feet in altitude branch out in several chains: the Elburz group running eastward south of the Caspian Sea; the Zagros system, a wide series of ranges protruding in a southeasterly direction to Afghanistan and India; and the famed Taurus mountains, pushing southwestward to the Mediterranean and separating the Anatolian plateau from Arabia.

Rivers have played an important role in society and have deeply influenced the development of civilization in the Middle East. Two are fabled and basic in the history of the area: the Nile and the Tigris-Euphrates. Flowing from central Africa and Abyssinia, the Nile passes through a relatively flat region in the Sudan until it reaches the cataract zone north of Khartoum, where a gorge has been cut. Below Aswan, the Nile flows through a well-developed valley about six miles wide to Cairo, where the delta begins. In August the river starts to rise in Egypt, reaching its peak in September, eighteen feet above the low of April and May. Annually some 110 million tons of sediment, rich in mineral substances, are carried into Egypt, and until the completion of the Aswan Dam in 1970, more than half of this silt reached the delta.

The other great river system, the Tigris-Euphrates, rises in the highlands of eastern Turkey. Winter snowfall feeds both streams, which turn and twist through precipitous and narrow defiles emptying out upon the plateau plains of Syria and Kurdistan. Rushing southward, they converge upon Baghdad but meet only about 230 miles farther on where they form the Shatt al-Arab, which flows gently for about 75 miles to the Persian Gulf. The fall in the river beds between Asia Minor and Baghdad is very marked, producing a swift current with strong erosive powers. The rivers are at their lowest in September and October but begin to rise appreciably in December, reaching a flood stage of about eighteen feet in April for the Tigris and, until recently, about eleven feet in May for the Euphrates. In 1973 Syria completed the first stage of the large Euphrates Dam, and Turkey finished the great Keban Dam on the Euphrates. These structures will control much of the flooding, generate electric power, and extend the arable lands in both countries. Within historic times silt from the Tigris and the Euphrates and two Iranian tributaries of the former—the Karkeh and the Karun—filled in the Persian Gulf from near the site of Baghdad to the present shoreline. No longer a tributary, the Karkeh is dissipated at the present time in the marshes of lower Mesopotamia.

One of the most renowned and romantic geographic spots of the Middle East has been the straits that form the waterway from the Black Sea to the Aegean Sea. At the northern end is the present-day Bosphorus, a sixteen-mile strait varying in width from nearly two miles to 547 yards at the narrowest point. Everywhere the channel is deep, 400 feet in spots, and the drop-off at the edge is so sharp that vessels requiring considerable draft may tie up at many places along the shore and unload directly upon the adjacent road. On a point of land where the Bosphorus empties into the Sea of Marmara stands one of the great cities of the Middle East—variously known as Byzantium, Constantinople, or Istanbul. Dotted with a number of islands, the Sea of Marmara is 60 miles wide and extends some 125 miles southwestward to the Dardanelles. This historic passage, often called the Hellespont, is 25 miles long and is wider than the Bosphorus, varying from 2.5 miles to 4.5 miles at its southern end, where it empties into the Aegean. These three bodies of water, collectively known through the years as the Straits, separate Europe from Asia yet serve as a strong connecting link between East and West. Economically, politically, and strategically, the Straits have been important throughout all history.

Climate

During the fourth glacial period, some 25,000 years ago, when much of Europe and northern Asia was covered with an ice sheet, the Middle East and the Sahara regions were moist and dotted with lakes and seas, a well-watered wooded land abounding with game. As the ice receded, the desert area between the tropic and the temperate zones appeared. Little change, however, has occurred in the climate of the Middle East in the last 5,000 years.

Rainfall along the shores of the Mediterranean, Black, and Caspian seas comes for the most part during the winter months. Many areas receive an average annual fall of thirty inches. (As one progresses inland, however, the average drops appreciably; Egypt and the plateaus of Arabia, Iran, and eastern Turkey have a desert climate.) Moreover, the rains are not only seasonal but almost capricious. Damascus has an average annual rainfall of about ten inches, but four inches have been known to fall in one morning. The mountainous areas of eastern Turkey and Iran receive more moisture, but here, too, winter is the wet season, with much of the precipitation occurring in the form of snow. The one exception to the winter rain pattern is the monsoon region of southern and southwestern Arabia, which gets most of its rainfall in the months of July, August, and September.

Temperatures depend upon latitude and altitude, and winter in the mountains of Arabia can be quite bitter. Summer temperatures in Egypt,

Arabia, Iran, and the interior of Turkey are hot, over 100° F. during the day, but nights are cool everywhere except in some of the lower valleys where the humidity is high.

Flora and Fauna

Wood has been a prized building material and the principal fuel in the Middle East from the beginning of history until the advent of coal and oil, and over the last 5,000 years a process of deforestation has denuded most of the land. Some stands of oak, beech, pine, juniper, and boxwood remain on the slopes of the Elburz Mountains, in east Asia Minor, and of the Lebanon Mountains. Elsewhere the land would be bare but for cypresses in cemeteries and gardens and poplars along streams and irrigation ditches.

It has been estimated that unconcern about land conservation over the last 5,000 years has resulted in the destruction of 90 percent of the forest and topsoil resources of the Middle East. But absence of concern cannot be said to exist with respect to the cultivation of edible flora of the area. Wheat, barley, rye, broad beans, lentils, onions, leeks, garlic, figs, grapes, melons, pomegranates, pears, plums, apples, peaches, apricots, almonds, walnuts, olives, and dates are the principal foods developed from the native vegetation of the area.

Domestication of native animals of the Middle East probably began about the same time that the land was beginning to be cultivated. In what order it is difficult to tell, but at some very early time the dog (probably first), sheep, goat, pig, ox, and ass were tamed and used for work or to provide food and clothing. Domesticated horses and camels were introduced into the area from farther east in Asia in the second millennium before Christ. As the forests became scarcer, the pig was replaced by more economical all-purpose animals like the ox, goat, and sheep; and the arrival of the camel made habitation in the desert possible and facilitated Middle Eastern nomadism in Arabia proper.

The waters teem with fish. The Caspian has long been noted for its sturgeon and caviar. The Black Sea and the Bosphorus abound in tuna, mackerel, and herring of many excellent varieties. And the eastern Mediterranean, fed by the vegetable matter of the Nile, has been through the centuries an attractive and productive spot for fish of all kinds, although the dam at Aswan is reducing the number of fish.

Resources

The significant natural resources of the Middle East have been, and still are, the availability and interrelationship of water, soil, sun, plants, and animals, allowing for a propitious agricultural life. Other natural resources are the excellent clays with which the bricks, pots, and finer ceramics of many cultures have been fashioned. Mountains, lava extrusions along the geologic faults, and rock formations laid bare by river erosion have provided extensive quarries for basalt, granite, marble, porphyry, sandstone, and limestone.

Gold, silver, copper, and iron occur in easily workable ores, and their ready utilization marked the end of the Neolithic age. The presence of other metals such as tin and nickel with copper led the way to the development of bronze and brass. Deposits of these metals have been worked almost continuously up to the present, and the output has been of considerable value in the economy and life of the area. In the twentieth century other metals have come to the fore. Chromium and manganese are found in sizable deposits; and small amounts of antimony, molybdenum, mercury, and cobalt are available. Coal and lignite exist in considerable amounts in Turkey and Iran, but only in recent years have these beds been exploited.

The greatest of the natural resources of the Middle East of the twentieth century, beyond land and water, is oil. Small fields have been located in Turkey, Egypt, Syria, and Israel, but the large ones are those of Khuzistan in Iran, those of Mosul-Kirkuk in Iraq, those along the Persian Gulf in Saudi Arabia, Kuwayt, Bahrayn, Qatar, the shaykhdoms of the Persian Gulf, and Oman, and those in Libya and in Algeria. No one yet knows the full extent of the oil reserves of the Middle East; but its known reserves alone far outstrip those of any other oil-producing region, and the presence of this natural resource is rapidly changing the world importance of the Middle East.

People

The Middle East, blest with a warm climate, a fertile soil, native animals and plants suitable for food, waters available for controlled irrigation, and varied mineral resources, was thus an area of the world favorable for the propagation of the human race, for the increase in standards of living, and for the growth of an organized society.

Although anthropologists, archaeologists, and geneticists have yet to unravel the twisted and indistinct story of life and the wanderings of prehistoric *Homo sapiens* in the Middle East, it seems quite certain that around 15,000 B.C., as the fourth glacial period terminated, the well-watered regions of Arabia and the Sahara were inhabited by people of Mediterranean race. Then, through ten millennia of the Mesolithic age, as the ice cap was retreating to Scandinavia, Arabia and the Sahara became desiccated and their inhabitants moved northward and seaward. Some in east Africa became the ancestors of the Hamites of Egypt; others in Arabia clung to the shores of the Persian Gulf or moved to the southern highlands. The latter became known to the world as Semites. In addition, significant pockets of Mediterranean peoples remained along the shores of that sea, and evidences of their settlements are being found in Palestine, Israel, Lebanon, Syria, and Turkey. Another branch of the Mediterranean group lived on the Iranian plateau, where much domestication of plants and animals took place. As these peoples moved with their advanced cultures into other parts of the Middle East and into Europe, the Neolithic age was born.

With the advent of Neolithic *Homo sapiens* into valleys of the Indus, the Tigris-Euphrates, the Nile, the Jordan, and rivers of the south-central plateau of Asia Minor, Middle Eastern and Western civilization had its beginnings. Because the annual flooding of rivers renewed the soil with the silt it deposited, Neolithic agriculturists could continue to cultivate the same fields year after year, generation after generation. Even a partial nomadism became unnecessary; a stable, stationary society evolved. Records accumulated and history in the Middle East began.

REFERENCES: Chapter 1

Ariens-Kappers, C. U. *An Introduction to the Anthropology of the Near East in Ancient and Recent Times.* Amsterdam: N. V. Noordhollandsche Uitgeversmaatschappij, 1934. A study of the physical anthropology of the Middle East.

Clawson, Marion, Hans H. Landsberg, and Lyle T. Alexander. *The Agricultural Potential of the Middle East.* New York: American Elsevier, 1971. A Rand Corporation study that gives information on soil, water, and climatic resources; on farm structure, crop and livestock output, rural community services, and manpower; and the potential for the year 2000.

Coon, Carleton S. *Caravan: The Story of the Middle East.* New York: Holt, 1951. An excellent anthropological introduction to the Middle East, written in a style easily understood by the beginning student. The author was an outstanding authority in anthropology, especially as it relates to the Middle East. For many years he was a curator of the museum of the University of Pennsylvania.

Dewdney, J. C. *Turkey: An Introductory Geography.* New York: Praeger, 1971. Sound and current.

Fisher, W. B. *The Middle East: A Physical, Social and Regional Geography.* London: Methuen, 1971. The only volume of its kind. Authoritative yet easily read by the beginner in the field of geography of Middle Eastern studies. This is the sixth edition, which adds a chapter on Sudan and updates economic and statistical material.

———— (ed.). *The Land of Iran. The Cambridge History of Iran,* vol. 1. Cambridge, Eng.: Cambridge University Press, 1968. A complete study of the geography, geology, geomorphology, climate, soils, vegetation, mammals, minerals, and the like, in Iran, including early humans in Iran, pastoralism, nomadism, and social anthropology.

Ginsburg, Norton S. (ed.). *The Pattern of Asia.* New York: Prentice-Hall, 1958. Seven chapters on the geography of the Middle East are written by John R. Randall.

Oxford Regional Economic Atlas: The Middle East and North Africa. Prepared by the Clarendon Press and *The Economist.* New York: Oxford University Press, 1957.

Pitcher, Donald Edgar. *An Historical Geography of the Ottoman Empire: From the Earliest Times to the End of the Sixteenth Century, with Detailed Maps to Illustrate the Expansion of the Sultanate.* Leiden: Brill, 1972. Emphasis is on political geography with thirty-six excellent colored maps and an extensive index of names and their equivalents in different languages.

Roolvink, R. *Historical Atlas of the Muslim Peoples.* Amsterdam: Djambatan, 1957. An excellent collection of historical maps showing events since 612 B.C. Harvard University Press is the American agent.

Chapter 2

Pre-Islamic Politics and Society in the Middle East

The Rise of Civilization

Scholars have debated for two centuries whether Western civilization began first in the Nile valley or in Mesopotamia along the Tigris-Euphrates River. However, archaeologists are now discovering that significant Protoneolithic cultures were independently developed in north Syria at Ras Shamra and in Palestine in the Jordan valley, especially at Jericho about the year 9000 B.C., the so-called Natufian culture; in northern Iraq at Karim Shabir, Zawi Chemi, and Shanidar of the Zagros region around 8900 B.C., the Shanidar culture; and in the south-central plateau of Asia Minor north of the Taurus range at Çatal Hüyük and Hacilar in the general region around Konya some time before 7000 B.C. There is general agreement that these Protoneolithic and Neolithic populations of the Middle East were descended from Paleolithic and Mesolithic inhabitants of the area. Botanists and geneticists have shown that in these upland regions and perhaps in other foothills of western Asia between the Mediterranean and the Himalayas edible grasses, like wheat and barley, and herd animals, such as sheep, goats, and cattle, had their natural habitats. Small sheltered groups of people learned to cultivate and domesticate these natural resources and established settled societies. Eventually, large towns were built and defended, and civilizations with art forms, religious practices, foreign trade, and social and political norms appeared.

Only when agricultural skills and social techniques had been developed adequately could the complex problems of living on great riverine plains be solved. Just how and where the transitions occurred has not yet been determined, but they undoubtedly took place slowly over several millennia. In any case, in two centers of highly evolved urban civilizations along the Nile and the Tigris-Euphrates it can be shown that each culture arrived in the area already in a transitional stage from the Neolithic age to the Early Bronze age, that each brought with it domesticated plants and animals (many of which were of common origin), but that each in its new habitat developed an urban civilization largely autochthonous in character.

Somewhat before the year 4000 B.C. the Sumerian people arrived at one of the mouths of the Tigris-Euphrates River. Where they came from has not been determined with any exactitude, but they were an Asianic type of the

Mediterranean race speaking a language wholly unrelated to any known tongue. There in the Tigris-Euphrates valley, Sumerian city-states evolved with society divided into technological-social classes—nobility, priests, traders, farmers, and artisans—divisions that have persisted as constant factors in all Middle Eastern civilizations. Shortly thereafter other peoples from the shores and watered places of Arabia were drawn to the prosperous Sumerian cities. They spoke a language belonging to the Semitic family, the basic tongue arising in the Arabian peninsula. Thus, very early in history, the Sumerians became a mixed people.

Farther north along the middle Euphrates about the beginning of the third millennium B.C., Semites, probably from the desert, founded the state of Akkad. For a thousand years the Sumerian and the Semitic states were ardent rivals. Cities such as Lagash, Akkad, and Ur each had its day and then passed the scepter to another. At times Mesopotamia was united to confront a third force—the Elamites, a non-Semitic ethnic group from Elam (Susa) on the Karkeh River. The Sumerian element in the area, however, was politically submerged by the union of all of Mesopotamia under the Amorite (Semitic) Hammurabi of Babylon about the year 1700 B.C.

At approximately the same time that the Sumerians appeared in Mesopotamia, Hamites began to develop a civilization along the Nile. Some came from eastern Africa, and others from North Africa; the Hamitic tongue of the early Egyptians was a blending of the two. The nature of the land, the annual flooding of the Nile, the local presence of copper (which began to be worked about 3000 B.C.), and the relative isolation of the Nile valley by the surrounding deserts were conducive to the establishment of an absolute monarchy and a flourishing culture.

Early in the second millennium B.C. Indo-Europeans from eastern Europe and western Asia began a southward movement, exerting population pressures upon the whole of the Middle East. In a succession of thrusts, these intruders with bronze and iron weapons and horses and camels pushed ahead of them into the Middle East such non-Indo-Europeans as the Kassites and the Hyksos. The Kassites came down with horses from the Zagros Mountains to rule Mesopotamia through most of the second millennium B.C.; and the Hyksos came with their horse-drawn chariots to rule Egypt for two centuries beginning about 1800 B.C. Later, genuine Indo-European waves brought Hittites, Armenians, Achaean and Dorian Greeks, Philistines, Medes, Persians, Macedonians, Parthians, Romans, and Sasanids. Between these invasions and conquests of the northmen, Hamite rulers reappeared in Egypt, and Semitic tribes such as Amorites, Assyrians, Arameans, Canaanites, Phoenicians, Hebrews, Nabateans, Palmyrenes, and Ghassanids moved from the Arabian peninsula to establish states in Mesopotamia, Syria, or Palestine.

Each group of invaders, at the time of its arrival upon the Middle Eastern scene and in its first contact with Middle Eastern civilization, was leading a nomadic or pastoral life. The transition to an organized life on the Middle Eastern pattern of greater specialization and division of labor produced

THE EARLIEST CIVILIZATIONS
OF THE MIDDLE EAST
AND THE
MIGRATIONS OF PEOPLES, 1500-200 B.C.

turmoil and strains, but the transition was always made successfully within the span of a few generations so that a continuity prevailed and civilization was ever victorious. Each group added something in religion, the art of writing, metallurgical skills, political organization, transportation, irrigation, or astronomy, and within a brief period the knowledge was disseminated over the entire area.

Ancient Empires

By the beginning of the first millennium B.C. the Middle East was rapidly becoming one cultural region, and a number of efforts were made to unite the area politically. Throughout the second millennium B.C. the Egyptian pharaohs sought and from time to time held control of Syria and Palestine. Mesopotamian kings, however, vied with the pharaohs for these provinces; and from that age until the present the Syrian coast has been able to maintain its independence only when both Egypt and Mesopotamia have been weak or evenly matched.

One of the great empires controlling a major part of the Middle East was that of the Assyrians, whose capital was at Nineveh on the upper Tigris in Mesopotamia. Iron weapons, a disciplined army, a tight bureaucracy, and iron battering rams mounted on wheels gave the Semitic Assyrians such an advantage in the seventh century B.C. that Nineveh held sway from Sinai to the Caspian Sea and from the Persian Gulf to the plains of central Asia Minor. However, overextension of the empire and exhausting battles, coupled with luxury, indolence, and unwise taxation, weakened the army and the government, with the result that Nineveh with its palace and great library was sacked by Iranians in league with another Semitic group which established its capital at Babylon on the Euphrates. Comprising the full Fertile Crescent from Sinai to the Persian Gulf, this new Chaldean empire won fame from its "hanging gardens," from the Babylonian captivity of the Hebrews, and from such names as Nebuchadnezzar and Belshazzar.

Upon the fall of Nineveh the unity of the Middle East was destroyed until the Persians, a small group of Iranians from the southeastern end of the Zagros range, reunited the areas of the previous Assyrian empire and added Greek Asia Minor, Byzantium, Thrace, the Nile valley to the Sudan, Afghanistan, Baluchistan, the Punjab, Bactria, and Sogdiana. With the establishment of the Persian Empire in the sixth century B.C. Semitic rule in the Middle East was crushed for over a thousand years. It was not until the rise of the Arabs under the banners of Islam that the Indo-Europeans lost their hegemony.

Checked at Marathon in 490 B.C. and at Thermopylae a decade later, the Persians maintained their power in the Middle East by an imperial system of government that skillfully combined local autonomy with centralized authority and responsibility. This form of government fashioned by the Persians was adopted in most essentials by succeeding rulers for over 2,000 years and established a governmental pattern that became accepted as a part of Middle Eastern civilization. The twenty-three provinces, or satrapies, of the Persian Empire were organized along lines of nationalities, and local independence was real to a considerable degree. Taxes and loyalty were the important requirements; a governor (satrap), a general, and a secretary, each reporting independently to the royal residence (Susa, Babylon, or Persepolis), preserved Persian rule.

Another secret of Persian success was the advancement of communications and transportation. Good roads from the frontier to the heart of the empire were kept open under constant repair and surveillance. The old canals between the Nile and the Red Sea were repaired so that the Phoenicians, the stalwarts of the Persian fleet, could sail directly from the Persian Gulf to the Mediterranean. In the end, however, the old story was repeated: the emperors grew decadent; the traveling inspectors of the empire became careless; and corruption, inefficiency, and incompetence developed.

Alexander and the Greeks

In the fourth century B.C. a new Indo-European people related to the Greeks began their ascent to power under Philip of Macedon. By the use of heavier armor and the integration of cavalry and the Macedonian phalanx, Greece was subjected to his rule. But Greece captured the mind and spirit of his son, Alexander, perhaps through his private tutor, the famed Aristotle. The campaigns and conquests of Alexander the Great and the creation of his vast Greek empire have been retold through the ages by countless poets, romantics, and historians of many lands and races.

After defeating the Persian army in 334 B.C., the young Alexander, only twenty-two years old, swept all before him. Asia Minor, Syria, Palestine, Egypt, Mesopotamia, Iran, and India to the Indus had been conquered and consolidated into an empire before his death in 323. Alexander had hoped to unify the entire Middle East into one lasting empire. He married an Asian princess and commanded his army officers to follow his example. But his untimely death left only his chief generals to battle for the empire, which they eventually divided: Ptolemy in Egypt, Antigonus in Asia Minor, Antipater and Cassander in Macedonia and Greece, Seleucus in Asia, and a number of lesser officers in scattered corners of the Middle East.

Following the breakup of Alexander's empire, the Middle East fell heir to a century of international political anarchy and intermittent wars; yet it enjoyed a period of vast trade and wealth as well as many decades of important intellectual and artistic activity. It was the apogee of the brilliant Hellenistic age, which persisted for two centuries more until the last vestige of Ptolemaic rule in Egypt had ended with Cleopatra's suicide and the Nile valley became a Roman province.

The Roman Empire and Its Successors

At the invitation of Egypt, Rhodes, and Pergamum, Rome became the arbiter of Middle Eastern affairs, and naval disarmament agreements turned the Mediterranean into a vast Roman lake. Except for the Tigris-

Euphrates area the Middle East had virtually fallen into a state of vassalage
to Rome. Transformed into Roman provinces, the Middle East was subjected to Roman rule until the emperor Constantine transferred his capital
eastward to the shores of the Bosphorus. From the establishment of Constantinople in A.D. 330 to the defeat of Emperor Heraclius by the Arab
armies in 638, the Roman provinces of the Middle East were important
parts of the Byzantine Empire.

The eastern provinces—Mesopotamia and Iran—fell away from the
Seleucids, and early in the second century B.C. the great Parthian Empire
was established in Iran by Mithridates I. Seleucia-on-the-Tigris was taken;
and before the century closed, all territory east of the Euphrates had been
seized by the Parthian King of Kings, who built his royal palace at Ctesiphon on the east bank of the Tigris opposite Seleucia. The Parthian power
rested on its nomadic Scythian cavalry and on the reaction against Hellenism, even though the kings knew Greek and had Greek tragedies performed at their court. The Parthians defeated the Romans, and Augustus
recognized Parthian dominion over all of Mesopotamia. When Marcus
Aurelius destroyed Seleucia, the center of Greek culture in Parthia, any
further expansion of Greek influence upon the East was doomed.

Internal weakness, however, brought the downfall of the Parthian kings
at the hands of a more national Iranian family, the Sasanids. The founder
of the dynasty was a devotee of Zoroaster, and the fire cult was vigorously
advanced, becoming the official religion of the empire. Wars with the Romans and Byzantines found the religious differences as important as the
rivalries of empire.

From their main residence at Ctesiphon the Sasanids time and again
harried the Byzantine provinces of Syria and Asia Minor. After the fifth
century, when Christianity was tolerated and the Nestorian Church had
become widespread in the Sasanid Empire, particularly in Mesopotamia,
the conflicts with Constantinople were more imperial in nature. Belisarius,
Justinian's general, checked the Sasanids temporarily, but they sacked
Aleppo and Antioch and forced upon the Byzantine emperor a peace treaty
whereby no Christian proselytizing would be permitted in their empire.
Peace, however, was not realized and exhausting campaigns were resumed
under Justinian's successors.

A powerful Sasanid army erupted into Syria in 613, destroying the
Church of the Holy Sepulcher in Jerusalem, pillaging Damascus, and plundering and massacring everywhere. An Iranian army conquered Egypt in
619, and another captured the cities of Chalcedon and Chrysopolis across
from Constantinople. Evil days appeared for the Byzantines, but the tide
turned. Between 622 and 628 Heraclius, the new Byzantine emperor, conducted three brilliant campaigns and even succeeded in driving the Sasanids from Egypt and Syria. But the wars and the ensuing destruction left
both empires weakened. Syria, Egypt, and Mesopotamia were ripe for
picking by the new vigorous Muslim Arabs in the next decade.

Pre-Islamic Civilization in the Middle East

For nearly a thousand years the Semitic and Persian Middle East had been subjected to the influence and the forced cultivation of Greek, Hellenistic, Roman, and Byzantine civilizations. Although it would be possible to point out distinguishing characteristics of each of these four civilizations and to show how each evolved from its predecessor, they form one continuous cultural experience and development in the history of the Middle East.

First and foremost among the changes was the adoption of Greek by the educated and by the leaders of society as the language of government, philosophy, literature, and sophisticated communication. Greek colonists—merchants, soldiers, and government officials—settled in most of the Middle Eastern cities and founded many new Greek cities like Antioch in Syria and Alexandria in Egypt. Intellectually and artistically the Middle East appeared as one world. Greek philosophies and Greek science became universal throughout the area, although many leaders were not of Greek stock, and much of the philosophy and science was not Greek in origin or inspiration.

Roman rule ended the internecine warfare of the Alexandrian successor states and brought a more bountiful material life to the cities of the Middle East. The remains of the almost countless theaters, temples, baths, and public buildings that dot the Middle East today are silent witnesses of the populous, thriving, and wealthy cities of that age. However, in governing the Middle East the Romans were more crassly materialistic, more ruthlessly extortionate, and more heedlessly arrogant than previous foreign rulers.

Even Roman military might, the Roman genius for efficiency, and administrative skill could not control the Middle Eastern hate for the Romans. On one occasion the population rose in Asia Minor and slaughtered 100,000 Romans. In the states of the Middle East, natives who adopted Greek and Roman ways in speech, dress, food, religion, and manners were detested and shunned by the others. As the years passed, the Hellenistic states became less and less Greek, conforming more faithfully to the age-old patterns of life in the Middle East. The Ptolemies appeared as pharaohs, and the Seleucids lived as Assyrian and Persian monarchs. Jesus of Nazareth spoke Aramaic, not Greek. St. Paul was a learned Jew with a Greek and Roman education, but his conversion to Christianity exemplified a rejection of foreign ideologies.

For all the show of Greek and Roman civilization in the cities of Syria and Egypt, Hellenism and Romanism rested very lightly on the common peoples of the Middle East. Under the rule of the Byzantine emperors the reassertion of Middle Eastern patterns was accelerated in Syria and Egypt. Asia Minor, with such ancient cities as Miletus, Sardis, Ephesus, and Pergamum, which had participated in Greek cultural development long before the age of Alexander, had not been a part of the empires of the Middle East except that of the Persians. Thus, the Roman province of Asia (western Asia

Minor) exhibited a Hellenistic life more Greek and Roman and less Oriental than did Syria or Egypt.

Christianity

The new contribution that came to the cultural stream of the Middle East with Byzantine dominion was Christianity, which received recognition as the official religion of the empire. In Hellenistic and Roman periods people were groping for a philosophy of life and a religion that would answer some of the problems of those rapidly changing and turbulent days. Faith in the power or protection of the Olympian gods had largely disappeared by the time of Alexander. The educated neglected the gods and pursued the philosophies fashioned by Plato and Aristotle. Other philosophic systems followed: Cynicism, Epicureanism, Skepticism, and Stoicism. Each of these had its advocates and its followers, but each was more negative than positive. They were intellectual shelters where sensitive and distressed souls might take refuge from a materialistic and heartless society.

To the masses these philosophies were meaningless. The formation of a world state deprived one of a sense of identity with a city-state and its protecting god. As helpless individuals in a large empire, people needed a savior. They therefore turned to the mystery cults of Asia, which spread widely and had a devoted and numerous following.

Magic and astrology had such a vogue that the latter quite destroyed astronomy for many centuries. By some secret formula a person might force the hand of a god to alter one's fate somehow or open up a shortcut to fortune. But the mystery cults were far more influential. Here the individual, by witnessing and participating in an esoteric ritual, was initiated into the mysteries of life and death, god and immortality. As the savior-god had lived and died and risen again, so the lonely and helpless individual, living in a tumultuous and materialistic world, might win eternal salvation by personal union with the god.

The most important of these religions of the Hellenistic world was that of the triplex of Sarapis-Osiris, Anubis-Horus, and Isis. Sarapis was a Greek Osiris, ruler of all, and his son Anubis led the souls of the dead to immortal life. Isis, however, was above Fate and she freed her adherents from the dominion of Fate and of death. Moreover, being a woman—one who was a wife and a mother and one who had suffered—she appealed to the female half of the population. The ritual of initiation comprised a purification by water, a journey through dark places of the underworld comparable to that of Osiris between the time of his death and resurrection, and a final appearance in holy robes and in a full panoply of light before the whole congregation. From that moment onward the member's soul was godlike and secure from earthly forces.

In the second century A.D. the greatest change in the Middle East came with the rise and spread of Christianity. Taking many of the positive and uplifting tenets of Judaism, of the Greek philosophies, and of the Oriental cults, Christianity added two vital factors which were largely absent in

Hellenism and Romanism: Christ offered immortality to all; and His creed was based on love of humanity.

Early Christianity appealed almost solely to urban Hellenistic society, the language of the church being Greek exclusively. After Christianity obtained official favor and adoption, the Byzantine state rapidly developed into a synthesis of Hellenism, Orientalism, and Christianity and a syncretism of the political power of the state and the religious authority of the church.

The union of autocracy and theocracy in the Byzantine state—the so-called Caesaro-papism of Constantinople—ensured the permanent alienation of the masses in the Middle Eastern provinces. As new doctrines from the Middle East were branded heresies by the state-dominated church councils—Nicaea (325), Ephesus (431), and Chalcedon (451)—separate native Christian churches evolved. Aramaic, its Syriac dialect, and Ethiopic became liturgic languages. Byzantine Constantinople could not force her type of Christianity upon the Middle Eastern peoples.

The Nestorian Church presented a dualism of good and evil not far distant from Zoroastrian doctrines, a fact which may explain its acceptance in Mesopotamia and Iran. Monophysite Christianity certainly embodied some of the Egyptian ideas of human divinity. Heresies flourished in non-Greek areas of the Byzantine Empire and served as basic factors in the almost complete lack of resistance and even passive cooperation of the Middle Eastern provinces at the time of the conquests by the Muslim Arabs. Links with the Semites from the desert proved stronger than those with Christian Constantinople.

The Arabs

In the first half of the seventh century the Arabs, another Semitic nation, under the banners of a new religion descended upon Syria, Egypt, Mesopotamia, and Iran—the chief regions of the civilized Middle East. Coming from an area little touched by the mainstreams of Middle Eastern life, the Arabs seemed to be a new and different force to the peoples of that age.

The Arabs were the last group of Semites to leave the shores and deserts of Arabia. Their chief difference from other Semites lay in the fact that they did not sever their connections with their past abode. The Arabs lived along the shores of Arabia, in the southern highlands of Arabia where there was some rainfall, and in the scattered oases and around the meager water holes that remained in Arabia as the fourth glacier receded. These desert inhabitants—farmers and shepherds—were numerically small and insignificant until the advent of the camel about 1200 B.C. The peculiar characteristics of this beast made nomadic life in the desert possible and profitable. The camel was as revolutionary to life in Arabia at that time as oil and the motor vehicle have been in the twentieth century. The camel people became lords of the desert. Above all, the camel welded town and desert life in Arabia into one integrated society, each dependent upon the other.

The use of the camel, moreover, eased many difficulties of the transit trade between India and the Mediterranean. Camel caravans began

THE MIDDLE EAST

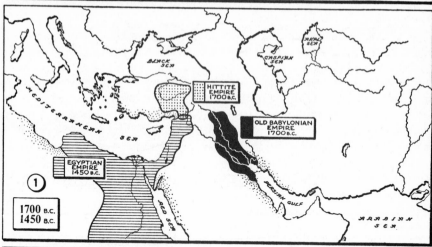

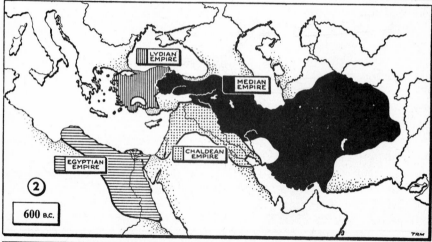

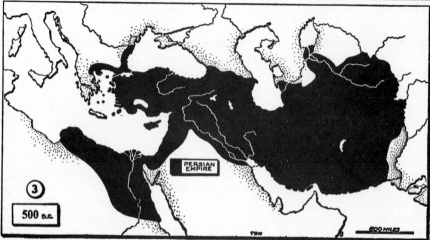

THE MIDDLE EAST

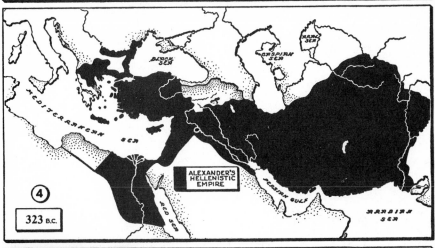

ALEXANDER'S HELLENISTIC EMPIRE

④ 323 B.C.

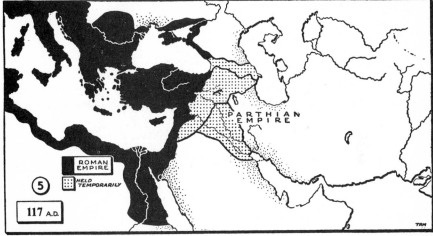

ROMAN EMPIRE

HELD TEMPORARILY

PARTHIAN EMPIRE

⑤ 117 A.D.

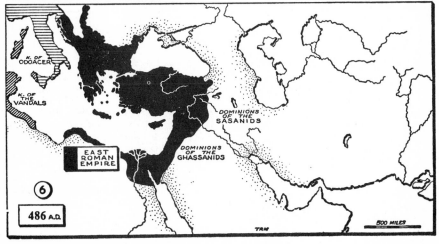

K. OF ODOACER

K. OF THE VANDALS

EAST ROMAN EMPIRE

DOMINIONS OF THE SASANIDS

DOMINIONS OF THE GHASSANIDS

⑥ 486 A.D.

500 MILES

to carry spices and incense along the Hadhramaut to Yemen and thence to Mecca, the Hijaz, Damascus, and the Mediterranean. Other trade routes connected Mecca with towns on the Euphrates and the Persian Gulf. Cities prospered, small kingdoms were established, and civilization advanced, as demands of the Hellenistic, Roman, and Sasanid worlds expanded.

Arabian Society

Arabia in the sixth century, the time of the birth of Muhammad the Prophet, was being affected increasingly by events in surrounding states. During Justinian's precarious détente with the Sasanids, Constantinople could obtain her Eastern luxury goods by way of the Black Sea, the Caucasus, Iran, and Turkestan. The tariffs imposed along this route, however, were sufficient to enhance overland trade from Yemen to Syria and the Byzantine markets. With the end of the détente and resumption of war, virtually all Eastern goods passed through western Arabia and the Hijaz. Mecca, Muhammad's native city, stood at the crossroads of caravan routes from Yemen to Syria and from Abyssinia to Mesopotamia, and possessing a permanent spring and an ancient sacred shrine, the Meccans dominated the Hijaz and all of the expanse of territory along the Red Sea.

To understand Muhammad's actions and ideas and his sense of values as well as the Meccan response to his preaching, it is profitable to examine briefly the economic, political, social and religious forces current in his day in the Hijaz and in Mecca.

Mecca was a commercial city and a growing financial center. It had originated as an entrepôt, but by the end of the sixth century, Meccan merchants were buying and selling wares in all of the markets from Yemen to Damascus. Mercantile wealth was turning to financial speculation and investment. (There is little evidence of local industry in Mecca or the Hijaz. There were orchards and cereal production at al-Taif, and dates grew at the oasis of Medina; but Mecca was set in the midst of barren land.)

Nomads—Bedouins, or desert Arabs—dwelt with their herds in the neighborhood of Mecca. Moving about in search of pasturage, they enjoyed a free, open, precarious existence; yet they were exceedingly jealous of their rights and the ownership of the desert over which they roamed. Brigandage to them was perfectly legitimate, whether upon oases or caravans. The Bedouins were good fighters, and when the advent of the North Arabian saddle greatly enhanced their raiding abilities, merchants, cities, and agriculturists often bought protection in the form of tribute. Between city and nomad an interdependence developed, and the welfare and station of the nomad in the Hijaz improved with the growing prosperity and population of Mecca.

In Muhammad's time the Kuraysh tribe of Arabs dominated life in Mecca. The Kuraysh were north Arabians who had controlled affairs in Mecca for more than a century, although families from the older inhabitants still lived in the city. The tribe had split into a dozen or more clans, which were grouped into two federations. Muhammad's clan was the Hashim, so named for his great-grandfather. Other notable clans were Makhzum, Abd Shams, al-Muttalib, Taym, and Adi. The last three belonged to the same federation as did the Hashim. The other two were the most powerful clans of Mecca in Muhammad's day.

Membership in a clan was based on kinship through the male line. Security of person and property was a clan responsibility; violation of either was a cause for reprisal by the clan. An irresponsible member was usually disowned by the clan and consequently became a kind of social, political, and economic outcast.

Manly virtues were still largely those related to desert nomadism—"bravery in battle, patience in misfortune, persistence in revenge, protection of the weak, defiance of the strong." Other admirable qualities were generosity, hospitality, loyalty, and fidelity. The man with honor and moral excellence was the man who exhibited the possession of these characteristics and who with judgment demonstrated his capacity to govern his life by them.

Government in Mecca was simple, direct, unorganized, and exceedingly democratic. An assembly of chiefs and leading men of the clans met as a council, but each clan was independent and could go its own way. Individuals within a clan might differ with the majority and act accordingly but were sure to find such action difficult and the results uncomfortable. Unanimity of clan action had to be achieved by personal negotiation among the leaders who commanded respect because of wealth, wisdom, and strength of character. A few offices possessed privileges, sometimes with opportunities for profit, such as control over the water of the sacred well or supplying sustenance to pilgrims.

Political affairs in the foreign field taxed the skill and ingenuity of the Meccan leaders, for the Arabs were buffeted by the contest between the Byzantine and Sasanid empires. Eastern Arabs were satellites of Iran, and such Arabs as the Ghassanids east of the Jordan were on the Byzantine side. Upon the development of an Iranian-sponsored rule in Yemen, Meccan commerce from south Arabia northward to Byzantine Syria became a touchy enterprise. But Meccan neutrality and diplomatic and economic shrewdness consolidated the caravan trade from the south into the hands of the Makhzum and Abd Shams clans.

Previously, the Hashim clan had operated caravans north to Syria, but in Muhammad's time it began to lose that monopoly. Hashim, Muhammad's great-grandfather, had obtained from the Byzantine ruler protection for Meccan merchants and their goods in Syria. To complement this arrangement Hashim organized what some have labeled the "Commonwealth of Mecca." He and his successors secured a novel partnership with hitherto hostile Bedouin tribes in the northern and central areas of Arabia whereby, through a sharing of the profits between Meccan merchants and leaders of the tribes, as well as the hiring of the tribes to escort the caravans, Meccan commerce prospered as never before. Other factors in strengthening the

Meccan trade position were the innovations of joining poor members of Meccan families to their rich brethren and of including some Bedouin goods in merchandise marketed in Mecca and in Syria. Furthermore, many Meccan leaders married daughters of prominent Bedouin leaders. Thus, beginning with Hashim many groups developed a common interest in the Meccan trade enterprise.

Society in Mecca was reeling from the strains of this swift transition. Not only had the emphasis among the Kuraysh shifted from tribe to clan membership, with intense rivalry developing among clans, but individualism within a clan was growing at a quickening tempo. Business partnerships were being formed across clan lines. And the leaders and powerful men of Mecca were successful businessmen and capitalists, who did not always live by the long-accepted Arab standards of manliness and honor. Common material interests seemed to be replacing common blood in the determination of kinship in the new Mecca. Social maladjustment resulted from the failure of the new economic life to accommodate itself to the old moral values of Arab life.

Pagan Mecca had numerous gods and goddesses, most of whom possessed abstract characteristics. Stones, trees, and other objects were venerated as places in which these deities were thought to reside. Magic and superstition were inextricably interwoven in this paganism, but belief in the gods had begun to fade in Muhammad's time.

A more forceful religion was that which was bound up with the belief in the immortality of the tribe and clan. Honor, bravery, generosity, and the other manly virtues were possessions that ensured the survival of the tribe. Fate was believed to govern life in only a few ways, determining, for instance, one's provisions, the length of life, sex, and happiness. Otherwise individuals controlled their own destiny. It was not quite the same for the desert Arab, however, for life in the desert was so precarious that it seemed to be governed by some unfathomable law or whim of a force beyond one's control or responsibility. Since everything in one's life was considered transient, the fate of the individual was unimportant. There was no belief in personal immortality; immortality rested with the tribe.

Finally, in Mecca a conception of monotheism was evolving. The Arab word *Allah* was derived from the words *al-ilah,* meaning "the god." Allah, then, was The God, The Supreme God; and Muhammad in using this word did not have to give his audiences any explanation. The idea, evidently, was in the air at Mecca, though undoubtedly the understanding of monotheism was vague and ill-defined in Meccan minds. The source of monotheism in Mecca and surrounding Arabia is an interesting question for speculation and has been debated by scholars at great length. Judaism and Christianity have had their champions, and certainly the Meccans had had ample opportunities to become acquainted with each of these religions. Evidence from the words of Muhammad would indicate, however, that the sources were laymen rather than learned religious men.

The important point is that Muhammad and Meccan society were not entirely unfamiliar with monotheistic thoughts. Obviously from the course of events that followed they were ready for these thoughts to be organized and marshaled into a systematic religion for them—a religion that was distinctly Arab in character. That was the great work and accomplishment of Muhammad.

REFERENCES: Chapter 2

Akurgal, Ekrem. *Ancient Civilizations and Ruins of Turkey: From Prehistoric Times Until the End of the Roman Empire.* Translated from the Turkish by John Whybrow and Mollie Emre. Istanbul: Mobil Oil Türk, 1970. Probably the best handbook guide for this period of history in Turkey. Full of sketches, drawings, and photographs.

Alkim, U. Bahadir. *Anatolia I: From the Beginnings to the End of the 2nd Millennium B.C.* Translated from the French by James Hogarth. Cleveland: World, 1968. This book has fine illustrations and an excellent descriptive survey of the Stone Age, Minoan civilization, the Chalcolithic period, the Early Bronze Age of Troy, Miletus and Ephesus, Assyrian colonies, and the Hittite period, showing connections between Asia Minor and Mycenaean developments.

Breasted, James H. *A History of Egypt from the Earliest Times to the Persian Conquest.* 2d ed. New York: Scribner, 1912. Still the best comprehensive account of ancient Egypt.

Bulliet, Richard W. *The Camel and the Wheel.* Cambridge, Mass.: Harvard University Press, 1975. Discusses the domestication of the camel, its various uses, and how it displaced the wheel in transportation in the Middle East and North Africa. The author contends that the development of the North Arabian saddle made possible the Arab conquests and expansion.

Childe, Vere Gordon. *New Light on the Most Ancient Near East.* 4th ed. London: Routledge & Kegan Paul, 1952. A fundamental synthesis of the culture of Mesopotamia and Egypt.

Hitti, Philip K. *History of Syria Including Lebanon and Palestine.* New York: Macmillan, 1951. An excellent portrayal of the development of Syria, particularly of the period preceding the coming of the Arabs.

Jackh, Ernest (ed.). *Background of the Middle East.* Ithaca, N.Y.: Cornell University Press, 1952. Chapters 7, 8, and 9 by Edgar Alexander are valuable in explaining the development of Christianity into Western, Eastern, and Oriental branches.

Johnson, Allan C., and Louis C. West. *Byzantine Egypt: Economic Studies.* Princeton, N.J.: Princeton University Press, 1949. This volume sheds light on the economic importance of Egypt to the Byzantine Empire and to the entire Middle East in the two or three centuries before the Arab conquest.

Mellaart, James. *Çatal Hüyük: A Neolithic Town in Anatolia.* New York: McGraw-Hill, 1967. A fascinating and well-illustrated account of an excavated town in Asia Minor containing twelve levels, or ages, the earliest dating from 7000 to 8000 B.C.

————. *Earliest Civilizations of the Near East.* London: Thames and Hudson, 1965. An authoritative survey.

Metzger, Henri. *Anatolia II: First Millennium B.C. to the End of the Roman Period.* Translated from the French by James Hogarth; London: Cresset Press, 1969. Excellent illustrations and fine descriptions of the land of Urartu, Phrygia, Lycia, and Lydia, the Greek colonial period, and Hellenistic and Roman remains.

O'Leary, DeLacy. *Arabia Before Muhammad*. London: Kegan Paul, 1927. The standard work on the Arabs and Arabia before the birth of Islam.

Olmstead, Albert T. E. *The History of the Persian Empire: Achaemenid Period*. Chicago: University of Chicago Press, 1948. The standard cultural, political, and religious history.

Tarn, W. W., and G. T. Griffith. *Hellenistic Civilization*. 3rd ed. London: Arnold, 1952. A profound summary and synthesis of Middle Eastern culture and life in the centuries following the death of Alexander the Great.

Vasiliev, A. A. *History of the Byzantine Empire, 324–1453*. Madison: University of Wisconsin Press, 1952. The standard history of the Byzantine Empire, especially regarding political and military matters.

Part One

The Rise and Spread of Islam

Chapter 3

Muhammad: His Life and Leadership

"There is no God but Allah, and Muhammad is His Prophet." The acceptance of this statement as the fundamental truth of life identifies all who follow the teachings of Muhammad. Allah is the God worshiped by Jews and Christians. But who was this man Muhammad?

It has been said that Muhammad was the only great prophet born in the full light of history. However, the first biography of Muhammad was not written until he had been dead for one hundred years; at least four others were compiled during the second century after his passing. It is from these sources that the traditional accounts of Muhammad's life have come, and recent investigations have shown that these early biographies were somewhat fictionalized. Nevertheless, modern students have been able to sift out some of the stories and have established many points. By analyzing words and phrases of various early accounts of his life and the lives of his contemporaries and by studying social, economic, political, religious, and anthropologic aspects of the society in which he moved, they have been able to reconstruct most of Muhammad's life so as to make it reasonable and understandable.

Muhammad was a mortal human being; he never professed otherwise and always emphasized this point to his followers, indicating that he would die like any other man. Nevertheless, as the founder of a great religion, he was revered as a most holy man even within his own lifetime. It is not strange, then, to find his biographies, written five or six generations later, full of fabricated and supernatural incidents to show his spirituality and his virtues. Perhaps this traditional figure has been more important than the real one in fashioning the culture and civilization of the Middle East from his day to our own.

Muhammad's Early Life

In the year A.D. 570 or 571, or perhaps as late as 580, there was born in Mecca to the Hashim family of the Kuraysh tribe a male child who was given the name of Muhammad, meaning "highly praised." His family was not one of the wealthier or more powerful of the city; neither was it of the poorest or lowliest class. His father, Abdallah, died before he was born; and his mother died when Muhammad was about six years old. First, as a father-

less boy, and then as an orphan, his lot was not easy. His paternal grandfather, Abd al-Muttalib, cared for and protected him. Upon his grandfather's
death Muhammad became the ward of his uncle Abu Talib.

From many of Muhammad's statements it is apparent that his uncle was
not a prosperous man and that they lived in modest circumstances. Evidently there was no opportunity for Muhammad in any of the businesses
of his uncles; and without any capital from his father, a job had to be found
for him outside the family circle. Such a post was located with the rich
widow, Khadijah, of a distantly related family. She had been married twice
—once to a Makhzumi—and had children from each marriage.

Khadijah was older than Muhammad, some say as much as fifteen years;
and certainly her social position in Mecca was far superior to his. She was
an astute businesswoman and continued her husbands' commercial activities. At what age Muhammad began working for her, exactly what he did,
and how old he was when she asked him to marry her are uncertainties. The
story of her prososal is probably factual. In Mecca it was not the usual
custom for the woman to propose; but in this instance, on account of her
wealth, her better social class, and her position as employer, it would not
have been unlikely. This step altered Muhammad's life very greatly and at
this point he becomes a clearer historical personage.

Muhammad had already gained recognition as a successful trader and
skilled administrator and this marriage reinforced his reputation. He and
Khadijah had four daughters who grew to maturity and several sons, all of
whom died in infancy. Khadijah died about A.D. 619, but as long as she lived,
Muhammad had no other wife, a situation which may have resulted from
the differences in their social and economic positions. Although he continued to act as Khadijah's commercial agent after their marriage, giving him
a security heretofore lacking, Muhammad now had means and a definite
position in the society of Mecca.

His Call

In the Middle East, from time immemorial, it has been the custom for men
who have some means and who are troubled intellectually and emotionally
by the cares and ills of society to retreat to some lonely spot to think and
to find answers for problems of the day. Muhammad, after his marriage,
began to follow this practice.

One day in the year 610 Muhammad must have had a sudden and unusual
experience in the form of thoughts flooding upon him and arranging themselves in a clear and definite order. In the language and understanding of
his time it was a revelation, and he readily accepted it as such. (This day is
celebrated each year by the faithful as The Night of Power toward the end
of Ramadan, the month of fasting.) Probably occurring in a cave on one of
the hillsides outside Mecca, the message commanded Muhammad to
preach the Truth to his fellow Meccans. This was his call.

Beginning with this first revelation, Muhammad on frequent occasions
heard voices from within him. Certainly he fully believed in the verses that

THE EASTERN MEDITERRANEAN AND THE MIDDLE EAST, 600 A.D.

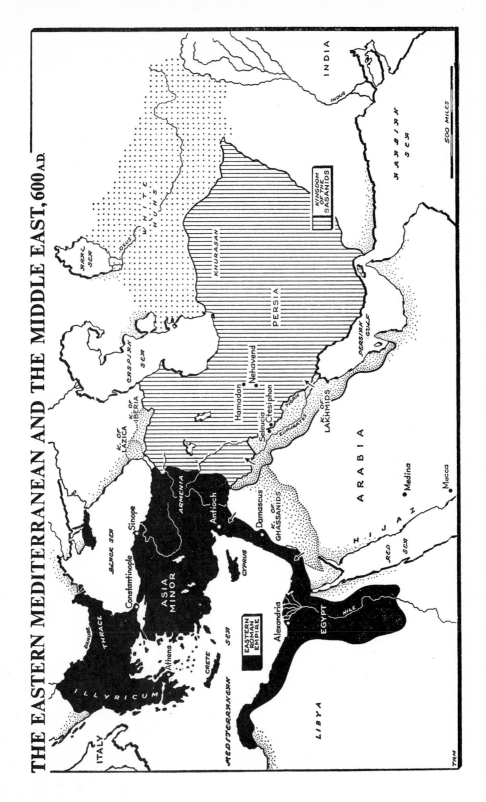

KINGDOM OF THE SASANIDS

EASTERN ROMAN EMPIRE

INDIA

INDUS

ARABIAN SEA

500 MILES

WHITE HUNS

OXUS

ARAL SEA

KHURASAN

PERSIA

CASPIAN SEA

K. OF IBERIA

K. OF LAZICA

Hamadan

Nehavend

Seleucia

Ctesiphon

TIGRIS

EUPHRATES

K. OF LAKHMIDS

PERSIAN GULF

ARMENIA

Antioch

Damascus

K. OF GHASSANIDS

ARABIA

HIJAZ

Medina

Mecca

RED SEA

BLACK SEA

Sinope

Constantinople

ASIA MINOR

CYPRUS

THRACE

DANUBE

Athens

CRETE

Alexandria

EGYPT

NILE

MEDITERRANEAN SEA

ITALY

ILLYRICUM

LIBYA

TRM

29

seemed to come to him. He was his first convert. The voices only spoke ideas that he had heard others repeat or that he had contemplated in more objective moods. There can be no real doubt of his own sincerity and conviction.

With respect to religion, Muhammad had grown up a pagan in the pagan society of Mecca. One of his sons, Abd Manaf, bore a pagan name. Muhammad believed in spirits and devils, recognized evil omens, and frequently used the mysterious oaths, the rhymed prose, and the verbiage of the typical Arab soothsayer. Mecca was a holy place, famed for the Kaaba, the earthly abode of many gods. And the Kuraysh had a special relationship and certain responsibilities to this abode.

Mecca and the Hijaz, however, were experiencing at this time a gradual trend toward a more intellectual religion. (Muhammad was not the only prophet to appear in Arabia or the Hijaz in that century. One of Khadijah's cousins already had been preaching, and some of his ideas were not much different from those later espoused by Muhammad.) Moreover, the ideas and teachings of Judaism and Christianity had spread and become known in Mecca through slaves, pilgrims, and traders as the city grew more prosperous and its life more settled. Repeatedly, Muhammad referred to Judaism and Christianity, and to demonstrate the truth of his own utterance and revelations he claimed agreement with those older faiths. Although Muhammad never showed the ability to read anything other than the most simple writing, he was familiar with many of the ideas and perhaps some of the ecclesiastical tracts of the Monophysite sect of Christians in Syria.

Preaching and Converts

At first Muhammad presented quite a simple religion. God was represented as all-powerful, as good, and as loving every individual. Created existence was transitory; the Creator was permanent. But God in creating humans implanted in them moral responsibility for themselves and, particularly, for their fellows. There would be a final judgment on the Day of Resurrection. Pure individuals were those who were grateful to God, worshiped Him, appealed to God for the forgiveness of sin, offered prayers frequently, helped their fellows, avoided all forms of cheating, led chaste lives, and had cleansed themselves from love of wealth. Such persons, then, would recognize the goodness and power of God and their dependence upon God. This was Islam—the surrender to God—and the pious who thus purified themselves became Muslims.

At first, Muhammad really had no idea of founding a new religion. The heavenly truths had been revealed to him and duty compelled him to remind the Arabs of Mecca of these truths in order to save them from divine wrath on the approaching Day of Judgment. And in the beginning his preaching brought no firm opposition. His first converts were in his own household: his wife Khadijah, his cousin Ali, and Sayd, a former slave. The most important of the others were Abu Bakr, Umar, al-Zubayr, Abd al-

Rahman, Saad, Talhah, and Uthman. Some of the early converts were younger sons of influential men of the leading families and clans of Mecca. The father of one was the most prominent financier in Mecca; another's father had been a religious leader prior to Muhammad's time; and two were nephews of the head of the Makhzum clan, the wealthiest and dominant family among the Kuraysh. The majority, however, were young men of no great social standing. Some had neither family nor clan ties, and the families of others had ceased for one reason or another to afford them protection.

To characterize this group the terms "young men" and "weak people" are the most appropriate. Early Islam was a movement of young people, mostly well under forty years old and from the middle class of Mecca. They were individuals who felt their positions to be inferior when they compared their wealth and influence with the fortunes and power of those at the top.

Such a generalization certainly implies that economic, social, and political conditions in Mecca had a hand in fostering the development and growth of Islam. At least for several decades before Muhammad's call, life in Mecca had been changing. The rapid growth of commerce and a money economy had widened the gap between rich and poor and between the influential and their dependents. Wealth and the life of a merchant promoted individualism as contrasted to family and clan solidarity. Kinship of money was supplanting that of blood, a substitution that did not satisfy the less "successful." Nomadic manly virtues were hardly those to be esteemed in a mercantile society. Old ideals of generosity, honor, the moral responsibilities of family and clan, and the group's accountability for trespasses of its members were seriously challenged in the evolving individualistic society. Seemingly, anything could be obtained through money and power.

Muhammad and his early converts, however, were not consciously frustrated men seeking solace in religion. In these first days they were conservatives preaching against the abandonment of the old virtues. Nevertheless, Muhammad did recognize individualism as a permanent aspect of society. The Last Judgment concerned individuals; for it was said that on the Day of the Last Judgment "one shall have no influence on behalf of another." Salvation came from taking care of poor relatives, making sure of the well-being of orphans, and being generous to the poor. For the rich it meant sacrificing and cooperating with the poor.

Muhammad began his public preaching about the year 613. While his ideas concerning monotheism were still ill-defined, he made a public pronouncement that al-Lat, al-Uzza, and Manat, three goddesses from the old Arab pantheon, were lesser celestial beings who could intercede for one with God. Traditionally this admission has been called "the satanic verses," for after reflection Muhammad renounced the utterance as the work of the devil. There has been much speculation and contention over this incident. Most likely, Muhammad was attempting to gain a wider following from the more influential Meccans.

Persecution

Upon the denial in 615 of any special powers for these pagan goddesses, Muhammad and Islam entered a new period of development. Monotheism evolved and was plainly recognized. Opposition and persecution began. Muslims were subjected to tongue-lashing and all manner of verbal insults. Garbage was dumped at their doors. Unprotected individuals were beaten, as were Kuraysh Muslims by their fellow clansmen. Economic pressure was exerted by refusal to pay debts and by a severe boycott that greatly reduced the fortunes of many, including Muhammad's closest friend, Abu Bakr.

Abu Jahl, the head of the Makhzum clan, declared economic war upon the Muslims and asserted that every one of them would be ruined financially. He coaxed and threatened Abu Talib, Muhammad's uncle and the leader of the Hashim clan, to abandon Muhammad. Failure in this approach led to the formation of an alliance of all the Kuraysh clans to pursue an economic boycott of the Hashim clan and its closest ally, the al-Muttalib clan. There were to be no business dealings and no intermarriage with any member of either clan.

This open economic break had long been brewing, and the controversy over Muhammad offered the excuse. Apparently during this break the Hashim maintained their own caravans to Syria and withstood the pressure. After two years the grand alliance was dissolved and the economic sanctions lapsed, since they had proved unsuccessful in destroying Muhammad. In fact, they had tended to increase the financial and economic hegemony of the Makhzum clan over the others.

More significant was the verbal assault, which indicated the opinions held by those in opposition. They scoffed at the idea of the Day of Last Judgment and ridiculed Muhammad's preaching of the resurrection of the body after it had moldered in the grave. They kept asking scornfully: "When is the Hour?" Muhammad's conviction that God was One and only One and that all idolatry was evil disturbed Meccan society because to a considerable degree this meant forsaking the religion of the forefathers. Muhammad tried to counter this with the contention that he was following in the footsteps of the religion of Abraham and the prophets of old and thus that Muslims were only regaining the old Arab religion.

The opposition jeered at Muhammad's claim to prophethood, calling him a magician, a soothsayer, a poet possessed by spirits, even a madman. If God had desired to reveal the Truth, they asserted sarcastically, He would have selected someone more important than Muhammad for this role. And why was not the full revelation made all at one time? How else could Muhammad explain the driblets of revelation except that he and some assistants were busy making up the verses!

Traditionally, the opposition to Muhammad by the leaders of Mecca centered around his preaching of the unity of God and his rejection of the use of idols. More likely, they objected to his cardinal message that the rich, meaning Meccan and Bedouin leaders, should help the poor among them, fearing that the adoption and practice of these beliefs would alienate the

Bedouin tribes and ruin Mecca as a flourishing commercial center. Abu Jahl, the most ambitious financier of Mecca, recognized the threat of Islam and its philosophy to his way of life and realized that widespread acceptance would give the leadership of the city to Muhammad. He felt that it would destroy the "Commonwealth of Mecca," whereas Muhammad believed that only this course would save and preserve it. Other leaders, whose positions seemed beyond jeopardy, regarded Muhammad as an innovator who was disrupting the political and social development of Mecca. Because of the rapid social evolution of Mecca many were cognizant of the disintegration of the old political, social, economic, and intellectual values. Muhammad sought to preserve and adjust these values through religion. Step by step, however, he was led by the opposition to establish a new religion.

The ending of the economic boycott in 619 possibly was interpreted as the harbinger of acceptance and success. But one incident after another quickly dashed such optimism and brought Muhammad close to the breaking point. Khadijah died, and then his uncle and protector, Abu Talib, followed her. Abu Lahab, another uncle, who now became the leader of the Hashim, refused to continue protection. Several years had elapsed since any important person had accepted Islam. Signs indicate that Muhammad began to suffer from a kind of mental depression and fatigue. There was no Muslim in Mecca with sufficient stature to offer him protection. How easily Islam could have perished! The only alternative was to leave the city.

Flight to Medina

Muhammad first visited the neighboring town of al-Taif to explore the possibilities of establishing residence and the headquarters of Islam there. He was met with a quick rebuff and upon leaving was stoned. Several of the nomadic tribes around Mecca were approached but without success.

Some 200 miles to the north and east lay the town of Yathrib—later called Medina by the Muslims. Yathrib comprised an area of twenty square miles of date oases, fertile lands, and scattered settlements. Numerous tribes occupied quarters of the town and had been engaged in bloody and exhausting civil war, in part over the limited cultivated lands of Yathrib. The most important clans were Aws, Khazraj, Nadir, Kurayzah, and Kaynuka, of which the last three adhered to the Jewish faith.

During the pilgrimage of 620 and following the rebuff at al-Taif, Muhammad discussed Islam with several pilgrims of the Khazraj tribe of Yathrib and raised the question of asylum. Next year additional people from Yathrib participated in the pilgrimage and more discussions occurred. One of Muhammad's trusted supporters returned with them, and converts were obtained from every important family except one. In the pilgrimage of 622 seventy-five Muslims from Yathrib came to Mecca and there made the famous Pledge of al-Akabah to protect Muhammad and to recognize him as a prophet to whom disputes were to be referred. Furthermore, there was some understanding concerning the migration of the Muslims, including

Muhammad, from Mecca to Yathrib and the establishment of an alliance between Muslims and the people of Yathrib. Later additions to the pledge in the so-called Constitution of Medina granted Muhammad sufficient authority to form the Commonwealth of Medina. (Why these pagan Arabs from Yathrib so readily accepted Muhammad and the others has aroused much speculation. One probable reason was that Yathrib was painfully experiencing the evolution of the mores of a nomadic society to those of a settled life, and Islam offered the possibility of a united community of people free of political rivalry and the continual feuding of the many clans. Moreover, in addition to Muhammed, whose business acumen was well established, Yathrib would be acquiring some seventy Meccans who were also experts in trade.)

As soon as agreement had been reached, Muhammad urged all Muslims to go to Yathrib. Over a period of weeks they left secretly in small groups until only Muhammad, Abu Bakr, Ali, and a handful of Muslims remained in Mecca. After all who planned to migrate had gone, Muhammad and Abu Bakr slipped away at night, hid in a nearby cave for a couple of days until the search for them had been relaxed, and then proceeded to Yathrib. On September 24, 622, they were joyously greeted at the outskirts of the city which has ever since been called Medina—"The City."

This migration—Hijrah—was a dangerous move on the part of the Muslims, for they were abandoning the protection of their families and their city for the untested protection of strangers. Almost overnight their position was so changed that the Hijrah came to mark the new era. The Muslim calendar A.H. 1 begins on July 16, 622, the first day of the year in which the Hijrah occurred. In Mecca, Muhammad and the preaching of Islam had failed to alter society or to break down either the growing individualism or the family ties. In Medina, Muhammad immediately became the acknowledged political and social leader as well as the religious head of a compact community.

Residence in Medina placed new demands upon Muhammad's diplomatic and executive talents. He could count definitely on the full support of the Muhajirun—the "emigrants" from Mecca—and the converts of Medina—called Ansar, or "helpers." Old feuds, however, could be rekindled quickly. The Jews soon began to quiz and mock Muhammad because their knowledge of the Old Testament was far superior. He had expected that they would testify to the validity of his message, but they could not accept an Arab as the Messiah. Upon their rejection Muhammad forsook the older established religions of the Middle East and began to identify Islam as a new faith. By taking over Abraham and the God of the Meccan shrine and by adopting many of the ceremonies with respect to the sanctuary in Mecca, Muhammad molded his new religious concepts with the old and gave Islam a distinct Arab cultural flavor. This aspect came to be emphasized with the beginning of his Medinese residence.

For protection and sustenance Muhammad created a new kind of brotherhood between every two emigrants. Also, every emigrant was assigned one Medinese as a special brother and protector. The problems and the affairs of the Muslim community were to be brought before God and Muhammad, whose judgments had to be obeyed. Herein lay the basis for the establishment of Muslim theocracy. God was Muhammad's Guide and Protector and the disobedient would suffer the agonies of hell.

In the first days following the Hijrah the Muslims had adopted several of the Jewish rites. One prayed facing Jerusalem; midday prayers and Jewish fast days were observed; and Friday, market day as well as the Jewish day of preparation, became the Muslim day of public prayer. Later, when relations with the Medinese Jews became tense, Muhammad turned away from some of the Jewish forms. In worship the faithful faced the sanctuary in Mecca; the annual pilgrimage to Mecca was prescribed for Muslims; and a period of fasting—the month of Ramadan—was ordered.

Conflict with Mecca

During the winter of the first year in Medina, Muhammad and his followers were busy establishing their new homes. When spring and summer came and the rich caravans began to pass northward toward Syria, armed Muslim bands from Medina menaced the Meccan merchants. No booty was taken, and the caravans were so well protected that these incidents served only as reconnaissance missions. However, the need to provide a livelihood for the expatriates of Mecca forced Muhammad to direct attacks upon the passing caravans. It was a normal expediency in Arabia.

Late in 623 a handful of Muslims under orders from Muhammad surprised a small Meccan caravan on the road between Mecca and al-Taif. One Meccan was killed, two were held for ransom, and much booty was captured. Nevertheless, sentiment in Medina was divided. The Medinese had promised the emigrants from Mecca protection from attack but had not agreed to let their city serve as a base of operations against Mecca. The success of the venture, however, invited other and larger expeditions.

Muhammad decided to ambush the main caravan of the Kuraysh upon its return from Syria. Muhammad himself led the band of 305 with over 70 camels and 2 horses to waylay the caravan under Abu Sufyan, the head of the powerful Umayyad family. At Badr, twenty miles southwest of Medina, Muhammad was challenged by a force of some 800 or 900 armed Meccans. The fighting was fierce and bloody, but the smaller force of Muslims was victorious. As a battle it was hardly more than a minor fracas. Muhammad lost 14 men; the Meccans had 50 killed and 50 captured. The Muslim booty consisted of 14 horses, 115 camels, coats-of-mail, and other pieces of military equipment. But the significance of the Battle of Badr was such that some have called it one of the decisive battles of history. To the Muslims it was a miracle, positive proof that God was supreme.

Henceforth Muhammad was a marked man, for the news of this victory traveled quickly to every tribe and tent of Arabia. Moreover, the battle set the stage and the pattern of the future: a fifth of all booty was assigned to Muhammad to be allotted to the needy or used by the state. The Commonwealth of Medina now became a real possibility. From the moment of victory there could be no peace until the supremacy between pagan and Muslim Meccans was decided. Within two decades Muslims came to appreciate the momentousness of this battle; those who had participated in it were the "nobility of Islam"; and a cloak that had been worn at the Battle of Badr was a most distinguished robe of honor.

This victory by no means guaranteed to Muhammad a straight and easy path to his now clearly recognizable goal of control over Mecca and the incorporation of all its inhabitants into his Muslim community. Indeed, although the battle showed the Muslims that such a goal was attainable, it also revealed to the leaders of Mecca the ambition of Muhammad and goaded them into a real effort to annihilate the Muslim community.

Muhammad, taking advantage of his success, moved to consolidate his position. Alliances were made with a number of neighboring Bedouin tribes, the first steps toward the new commonwealth. The Kaynuka tribe, the weakest of those adhering to the Jewish faith, was driven from Medina. In 625, however, Abu Sufyan, the new leader of Mecca since the death of Abu Jahl on the battlefield of Badr, set forth with an army of 3,000 for revenge. Electing to meet the enemy outside the city at the foot of the hill of Uhud, the Muslims appeared at first to be winning but were subsequently overrun in the flank and rear by the Meccan cavalry. In the melee Muhammad was wounded but managed to establish a position on the slopes of Uhud. Torn with dissension as usual, the Meccan army neither pursued the Muslims nor pressed on to Medina. Two years later, Abu Sufyan returned again with an even larger army. Forewarned, Muhammad ordered a wide ditch dug in front of the less protected sides of Medina. After a fortnight's siege, bad weather, persistent quarrels, and the disaffection of some of the nomad allies led to the withdrawal of the Meccans, who claimed that the Muslim trench was a dishonorable artifice to which no Arab would resort. The Battle of the Ditch joined with Badr and Uhud to make the three battles where lines were drawn between the pagan and Muslim Kuraysh. The battles were in some measure part of a civil war. Participants on each side were well known to the other. Old slights and grudges were remembered, and emotions and the spirit of vengeance ran high.

Following each of these failures by pagan Mecca, Muhammad moved quickly to solidify the Medina community. When the Medinese Jews failed to hide their delight over the Uhud misadventure, the Muslims attacked the Jewish Nadir clan and drove them from Medina to Khaybar. After the third battle the last Jewish tribe of Medina, the Kurayzah, was expelled, and its lands and possessions seized. Citizens of Medina who, until now, had neither accepted Islam nor recognized Muhammad as their leader joined the Muslim band. This meant that by the end of 627 Muhammad had established Medina as a united community with one religion as its cohesive force.

The next spring Muhammad was advised that some of the men of Mecca wished to arrange peace with the Muslims. With this information Muhammad called for an advance upon Mecca during the month of a minor pilgrimage. His Bedouin allies would not join him, and Mecca sent forth an armed force to contest his entry. A compromise was reached stipulating that the Muslims might participate freely in the lesser pilgrimage the following year, and marking Muhammad's first success in his peaceful conquest of Mecca. Later that year the Muslims captured the fertile oasis of Khaybar, largely inhabited by Jews. This acquisition made the Muslims wealthy, since the lands were most productive. The inhabitants were not exiled but remained on their lands, paying yearly taxes to the conquerors and establishing a precedent for the years and centuries to come.

Victory

In March 629 Muhammad led more than a thousand of his men into Mecca to perform the rites of the lesser pilgrimage as agreed upon the previous year. A number of Meccans joined him, recognizing in Muhammad the coming leader. Two of the most redoubtable military figures of Islam were among those who joined: Amr ibn al-As and Khalid ibn al-Walid. Even Abu Sufyan in secret negotiations tried to adjust to the inevitable.

As more Bedouin tribes joined the Muslims, Muhammad began to insist that they accept Islam and become an integral part of the community rather than serve merely as political allies. However, the sense of completeness and fulfillment of the Muslim community was lacking so long as Mecca did not recognize Muhammad as the leader and refused to accept Islam. Mecca was the site of the Kaaba, the religious sanctuary and holy shrine designated by Muhammad. It had also been the home of the leaders of the Muslim community. Without Mecca, the prosperous trade in Arabia which had been seriously curtailed by Muhammad's battles would be difficult to revive.

An insignificant incident brought Muhammad and the Muslims to Mecca to do battle in 630. Hardly anyone in Mecca was disposed to fight, however. Abu Sufyan came out from the city to pay homage to Muhammad and received amnesty for all who would submit. Upon entering the city Muhammad gave gifts to everyone and demanded only the destruction of all idols in Mecca. He had merged his commonwealth with that of Mecca.

Muhammad's astuteness in politics and diplomacy was revealed by his decision not to settle again in Mecca but to return to his adopted city of Medina. The Kuraysh were a proud people and it had not been easy for them to acknowledge Muhammad as the leader. He did not tarry long to remind them too plainly of their new position. Moreover, the rapid spread of Islam and the increasing numbers of Muslims were presenting a multitude of problems. For a time in 631 division and opposition erupted to the point that one group withdrew and established its own house of prayer. A rather unsuccessful campaign occurred in Transjordan, and missions went as far as Bahrayn and Oman. There were small Muslim groups to be found in all parts of Arabia, but many still denied that Muhammad was God's messenger. (In all areas where Muslim political authority had penetrated,

Christians, Jews, and Parsis were tolerated on condition that they concede political rule to the Muslims.)

Muhammad could now see that Arabia was rapidly becoming one great united religious community—a community where religion rather than blood, language, customs, or economics held the people together and a community where there were no distinctions among the believers except that of the degree of piety. He understood that many Arabs professed Islam, not because they submitted to the will of God, but because they feared not being a Muslim or because they wanted the political, social, and economic advantages of being one. Consequently, the commandments began to turn more to social and political matters and stressed to a much lesser degree forms of worship and religious ideas that had been revealed in the Meccan and early Medinese prophecies.

Although Mecca acknowledged Muhammad as its leader, the great host of visitors to the Kaaba in the month of the great pilgrimage were still pagan Arabs. Perhaps because of a possibility of dishonor, Muhammad declined to go on the great pilgrimage in 631 and sent Abu Bakr at the head of 300 Muslims. Ali, Muhammad's cousin and son-in-law, was deputized to announce that after four months no pagan would be permitted to participate in a pilgrimage to Mecca and that all alliances of a political nature between Muslims and other Arab tribes would be revoked if Islam were not accepted. Muhammad's authority and Muslim power were such that no trouble arose from these pronouncements, although later developments indicated that compliance was hardly voluntary.

Thus the stage was set for Muhammad to lead the initial reformed pilgrimage in March 632. Only Muslims would be present, and the veneration for Muhammad would be complete. Since Muhammad died soon after this pilgrimage, it has been called the Farewell Pilgrimage; and the events of the occasion are buried deeply in later accretion and tradition. Muhammad eliminated many of the purely pagan aspects from the ceremonious rites that had been performed at the Meccan sanctuary. His every move and act have been described and followed by devout pilgrims. He knew the significance of this first solidly Muslim pilgrimage; and in his address, as leader, he must have said something like, "Today I have perfected your religion and completed my favors for you and chosen Islam as a religion for you."

Three days later he departed for Medina and in less than three months (June 8, 632) he died from an ordinary fever. He had no male heir, and no provision had been made for a successor as leader of the Muslim community-state. Genuine bewilderment reigned in Medina. For a whole day his body lay disregarded. It was finally buried under the floor of the hut of Aishah, one of his wives.

The personality and private life of Muhammad remain to be considered. In general his tastes were quite simple. There is no evidence that his standard of living changed greatly upon the successes and the growth of the Muslim community. Perhaps the only significant change was in regard to marriage. After Khadijah died, Muhammad married several times. At one

time he had nine wives. Without question, his favorite was the daughter of
Abu Bakr, Aishah, whom he married soon after the Hijrah while she was
still a child. His disposition to all was kindly and gentle, and he made no
distinction in his treatment of people. The frailties of human nature were
well appreciated, and Muhammad never expected too much from his converts. When he found wrongdoing, he upbraided the culprits for their
actions but he was lenient and cautious in his interdicts.

Most outstanding, however, were Muhammad's personality and character. The loyalty and compliance rendered naturally and generously to
Muhammad by his companions in Mecca and Medina stemmed from the
magnetism of his being. His display of a sense of justice and his revelation
of religious truth centered the attention of the citizens of Medina upon him.
His converts, from first to last, testified to something special and nigh irresistible in his nature. Lacking this quality, Muhammad's stand as a prophet
of God would surely have been ignored by the worldly citizens of Mecca.

REFERENCES: Chapter 3

Cragg, Kenneth. *The Event of the Qur'an: Islam in Its Scripture.* London: Allen &
Unwin, 1971. A religious biography of Muhammad and his inner development as
it is unfolded in the Koran.

Hodgson, Marshall G. S. *The Venture of Islam: Conscience and History in a World
Civilization.* Vol. 1. *The Classical Age of Islam.* Chicago: University of Chicago
Press, 1974. The first volume of a three-volume work (over 1,600 pages in all)
covering the history of Islamic civilization. Written in a verbose and difficult style
this volume also covers in great detail pre-Islamic society. The author, who died
in 1968, portrays the new social order established by Muhammad and carries the
story to the middle of the tenth century. It is rich in discussions of religious
thought, philosophy, and literary developments.

ibn Ishaq, Muhammad. *The Life of Muhammad.* Edited by Abd al-Malik ibn Hi-
sham. Translated with an introduction and notes by Alfred Guillaume. New York:
Oxford University Press, 1955. Ibn Ishaq was born about 705 and died in 767 in
Baghdad. His work is the earliest known biography of the Prophet. The original
is lost but remains in the edited version by ibn Hisham, who died in Egypt in 833.
This is the source of most traditional accounts of Muhammad's life.

Muir, William. *The Life of Mohammad from Original Sources.* Edited by T. H.
Weir. Edinburgh: Grant, 1923. A full account of the life of the Prophet, including
most of the traditional stories and incidents attributed to his life without, however, much sifting or critical appraisal. Yet, it is a useful biography of the traditional Muhammad.

Rodinson, Maxime. *Mohammed.* Translated by Anne Carter. New York: Pantheon,
1971. The author uses a psychological approach in analyzing stories and events
to explain and interpret his life.

Shaban, M. A. *Islamic History, A.D. 600–750 (A.H. 132): A New Interpretation.* Cambridge, Eng.: Cambridge University Press, 1971. This is a most significant volume
giving many new ideas about developments during this formative period in the
Middle East. It does not give details of events but tries to shed light on forces
behind them.

Watt, W. Montgomery. *Muhammad at Mecca.* Oxford: Clarendon Press, 1953. A
thorough and scholarly treatment of the life of the Prophet up to the time of his

departure for Medina. Based on wide research, the volume discusses the theology and the social milieu in which Muhammad was reared and illuminates the period of his preaching and revelation.

———. *Muhammad at Medina.* Oxford: Clarendon Press, 1956. A sequel to the above. This volume depicts Muhammad as the leader of a community where he served as the religious, political, social, and military head.

Chapter 4

The Establishment of the Muslim State

The Caliphate

Muhammad's position as a prophet of God precluded the nominating of a successor, even though his other roles as head of the state, chief judge, sole legislator, and commander in chief of the armed forces did warrant some such forehandedness. Muhammad had sought counsel and taken advice from his companions as situations demanded. Within minutes after his death his three most frequent and trusted counselors agreed that Abu Bakr should be the leader of the Muslims. Muhammad's closest friend, Abu Bakr had led the prayers in the mosque and presided over the gatherings of Muslims in the last days when the Prophet had been too ill to perform these functions of leadership. When news of his death spread through the city, the native Medinese nominated one of their own as head of the community; but the Meccan Kuraysh prevailed upon all to accept Abu Bakr as their commander. The following day in the mosque, even before Muhammad was laid to rest, the assembled citizens swore allegiance to Abu Bakr as the successor of Muhammad.

This outcome was neither unusual nor startling. Chiefs in Mecca and Medina, as well as in Arab tribes, were chosen by the heads of families meeting more or less openly. Leadership often passed to another within the same family, but without any idea of inheritance or of legal claim; the power and prestige of a family prejudiced the decision in its favor. In this instance Abu Bakr commanded the support of the Muslims who had emigrated to Medina, and that element won the election for Abu Bakr. Other aspirants would have been from the Makhzumi or Umayyad families of Mecca, from a prominent family of Medina, or perhaps from Muhammad's immediate family; but the election of one of these would have been based on factors other than Islam. Authority passing into the hands of Abu Bakr, one of Muhammad's close companions, meant the survival of the Muslim community.

Khalifat Rasul Allah—"Successor of the Apostle of God"—was the name frequently used to describe Abu Bakr and his position. Abu Bakr probably used it himself, although not as a title. From this appellation came the title *khalifa* ("caliph"), used for centuries in the Muslim world. It implied the assumption of all the duties and prerogatives exercised by Muhammad except those connected with his role as prophet. The caliph was head of the state, supreme judge, leader in public worship, and commander in chief of the army. If he did not actually occupy the pulpit in the mosque, the sermon was delivered in his name. His name appeared on coins. And it was he whom Muslims revered.

Abu Bakr

Abu Bakr, about three years younger than Muhammad, had probably been the first convert outside the immediate family. A prosperous merchant from one of the lesser Kuraysh families and blindly devoted to Muhammad and Islam, Abu Bakr maintained his position of great respect because of a gentle and genial personality coupled with a clear head in matters of judgment and advice. It was a fortunate election in that Abu Bakr pursued Muhammad's ways and thoughts. No innovator, he succeeded in holding together the remarkable and talented men who had risen to prominence in this new society.

The first significant task facing the new leadership was to maintain the degree of centralization in Arabia already established by Muhammad. Except for Medina, Mecca, and a few other nearby places thoroughly controlled by the Muslims of Medina, most Arabs questioned the political and fiscal authority of Medina. Some even denounced Islam, seizing the end of personal allegiance to Muhammad as an opportunity to cast off the yoke of submission. Transition from the Commonwealth of Mecca to the Commonwealth of Medina had strained the loyalties of many Arab tribes and certainly had disrupted trade, in some cases to the point of ruin.

Abu Bakr met the challenge with the vigor and fire of the Prophet. Khalid ibn al-Walid, a most fortunate choice, subdued the tribes of central Arabia, many of which had not given their allegiance to Muhammad. Encouraged, other Muslim generals suppressed revolts and more thoroughly established Islam throughout Arabia, including Bahrayn, Oman, Yemen, and Hadhramaut. Treating the vanquished and renegade with mercy, Abu Bakr in less than a year had subjugated most of Arabia and restored the commonwealths of Medina and Mecca as one.

Indirectly, the complete Islamization of the Hijaz and the domination of the Arabian peninsula by the Muslims led, in the year 633, to military expeditions into Syria and Iraq. Since fighting among Muslims was contrary to the principles of the new society and since raiding was an economic necessity in Arabia as well as the natural occupation of most Arab tribes, ventures into adjacent lands were inevitable. With little cognizance on the part of Medina, Khalid finished the conquest of northeastern Arabia and then, joining some loyal Muslim tribes, spilled over into the Sasanid lands in Iraq, taking Hirah, a city west of the Euphrates and almost on a line with modern Baghdad.

For the men of Mecca and Medina, Syria was far more important than Iraq. Their caravans went there; it was more accessible; and to them it was a land flowing with milk and honey. The Syrian expedition was thus a calculated raiding campaign. Three forces of 3,000 men each, led by Amr ibn al-As and Yazid ibn Abu Sufyan, defeated the Byzantine governor of Palestine near the Dead Sea and destroyed his fleeing troops near Gaza in February 634. To oppose the fresh Byzantine levies Abu Bakr ordered Khalid to cross the desert from Iraq to Syria. Appearing almost miraculously, Khalid, as the supreme commander of the united Arab forces, defeated the Byzantine army in July 634, in the historic battle at Ajnadayn, thus opening all of Palestine to the Muslims.

The news of this victory reached Abu Bakr on his deathbed. His passing, however, hardly caused a ripple across Arabia, for Umar immediately assumed the power of leadership that he had been exercising behind the scenes. Recognition and fealty were given to Umar publicly and voluntarily by all. But the caliphate of Abu Bakr must not be considered as a brief empty interlude between two glorious periods nor should Abu Bakr be seen as a shallow, colorless figure. He made the important distinction between state property and the privy purse of the ruler, even though this action irreconcilably alienated Muhammad's daughter Fatimah. Perhaps most important, when war booty was first coming to Medina from outside of Arabia, Abu Bakr held fast to Muhammad's dictum on the spoils of war—all true believers, whether at the front or at home in Arabia, had equal rights.

Umar

Umar's accession to the caliphate marked the opening of a ten-year administration of an energetic and brilliant man, then only forty-three years old, whom Muslims consider the second founder of Islam. An early convert, Umar, like Abu Bakr, belonged to one of the less important families of Mecca. Leadership in the hands of Umar signified that Muslim aspects of the community continued. Umar, in fact, strengthened Islam with many religious decrees and renewed the theocratic state of Muhammad's time.

The affairs most pressing upon Umar at his accession were the military adventures in Iraq and Syria. At that very moment the brilliant Bedouin general al-Muthanna, commander of the Muslim armies in Iraq, was in Medina pleading for reinforcements, even though he had just defeated the Sasanid army at Babylon. He begged that troops be raised among the Arab tribes guilty of apostasy upon Muhammad's death, rightly judging that, however moribund Sasanid society and government might be, surrender to the Arabs would not be without a struggle.

Although the lifting of the ban against apostates brought streams of warriors into Iraq, superb Iranian generalship, the use of elephants, the size of the armies, and the wealth available to the Sasanid kings more than matched the ardor and gallantry of al-Muthanna's tribesmen. Ravaging far and wide, even to the gates of Ctesiphon, the Arab forces acquired vast herds and immense stores of grain; yet they had to retire from Iraq into the western desert when faced by an organized Iranian army under royal leadership.

Umar soon recognized that to hold Iraq and secure its borders it would

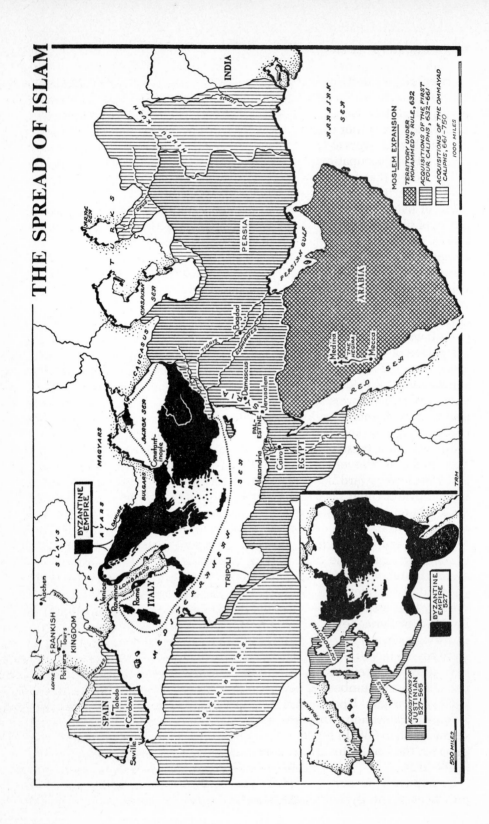

THE SPREAD OF ISLAM

MOSLEM EXPANSION

TERRITORY UNDER MOHAMMED'S RULE, 632

ACQUISITIONS OF THE FIRST FOUR CALIPHS, 632–661

ACQUISITIONS OF THE OMMAYAD CALIPHS, 661–750

1000 MILES

BYZANTINE EMPIRE

ACQUISITIONS OF JUSTINIAN 527–565

BYZANTINE EMPIRE 527

500 MILES

be necessary to destroy the main Iranian army and reduce the capital at Ctesiphon. A major force was gathered, and in a decisive four-day battle at Kadisiyah in 637 General Rustem's Iranian army was routed. Ctesiphon capitulated, and other battles consolidated the lands bordering on the Tigris and Euphrates rivers as far north as Mosul. These years saw the permanent conquest and occupation of Mesopotamia.

The booty that fell to the Arabs suddenly showered great wealth and unknown luxuries upon the simple nomad, altering immeasurably his standards of living. After the Battle of Kadisiyah each soldier received 6,000 pieces of silver; the jewels alone from Rustem's body were valued at 70,000 pieces. At the fall of Ctesiphon each of the 60,000 soldiers received 12,000 pieces. Gold became as common as silver; and fabulous objects, such as a life-size silver camel with rider of gold or a golden horse with trappings of gold, emeralds for teeth, and its neck set with rubies, became the prizes of the day. One Bedouin who sold a beauteous maiden for 1,000 pieces of silver was chided by another for having sold her for so little. The excuse offered was that he had not known any sum larger than ten hundred. From the palace of Ctesiphon the army sent to Umar the royal banquet carpet, measuring 105 by 90 feet and portraying a landscape. The ground was represented by gold and the paths were silver; meadows were made of emeralds; streams were cascades of pearls; trees, flowers, and fruits were depicted by diamonds, rubies, and other precious stones. Some suggested that the carpet be kept as a trophy; but when many pointed out that earthly goods were but passing things, the carpet was cut into pieces.

Over the next several years Muslim parties raided Khuzistan, took Sus, and advanced toward Isfahan. Iranian forces rallied at Hamadan; but with the removal of Umar's ban on advances into Iran, Muslims overran that land from one end to the other. In the ten years of Umar's caliphate Muslim armies had in an almost unbelievable sweep conquered Iraq and Iran. They repeatedly crushed armies that only a few years previously had been able to stand up against the best of Byzantine soldiers. This success was even more remarkable considering that other Arab armies at the same time were engaged in conquering Syria, Mesopotamia, and Egypt.

Umar's accession to the caliphate did not change Muslim activities in Palestine or Syria. Several Arab forces converged upon Damascus in 635, and after a siege of more than six months the city capitulated to Khalid. The emperor Heraclius, not willing to cede Syria to the invader, gathered a large army of Greeks, Armenians, Syrians, and Ghassanid Arabs (Christian); but he, too, succumbed to Khalid, in the summer of 637 at the decisive Battle of Yarmuk. Upon receiving the news of this disaster Heraclius left Syria and Palestine to the Muslims; north Syria fell in 637 and Jerusalem surrendered in 638. In the next two years Arab tribes entered the al-Jazirah between the Euphrates and the Tigris in the north and ruled that vast and fertile area.

Conclusively, in only four years, the Muslims had occupied these fair provinces of the Byzantine Empire. Mountains to the north discouraged further advance into Byzantine lands or the vigorous pursuit of the emperor's armies. Arab generals and many tribes, however, finding repose galling, looked for new adventures. Amr ibn al-As, who had traded in Egypt in earlier days, decided upon an expedition in that direction. Although Alexandria, the second city of the Byzantines and an important naval base, was strongly tied to Constantinople by sea routes, the loss of Syria and Palestine cut off Egypt from the empire. The chief granary of Constantinople and one of the richest and most populous areas of the Middle East, Egypt was very inviting to an ambitious general like Amr. Umar gave his assent to the campaign, but reluctantly. Amazed at the extent of the territory already occupied by his armies, he was fearful lest they be spread too thinly.

Leaving Palestine by the historic route along the coast, Amr with 4,000 men entered Egypt late in 639 and captured Pelusium (al-Farma), not far from the modern Port Said. Amr then moved toward the apex of the Nile delta, taking Heliopolis, Babylon (near modern Cairo), and most of the eastern delta area before the summer flooding of the Nile prohibited military operations for the next several months. Joined by a larger Arab contingent under one of the Companions of the Prophet ("those who knew Muhammad"), Amr moved on Alexandria and forced its surrender in the autumn of 641. It was a great and rich metropolis, whose public buildings, harbor facilities, and defense walls and towers were a cause of wonder to the desert Arab.

To protect his position Amr pushed on westward into Cyrenaica and even received tribute from Berber tribes around Tripoli. Egypt, from Alexandria up the Nile to a point well beyond modern Cairo, was now a Muslim possession, thus completing the circle of conquests under Umar. During his caliphate, Iran, Iraq, Syria, Palestine, and Egypt became parts of the Muslim world. They, together with Arabia, are still today the heartland of Islam.

Problems of Adminstration

These conquests alone would have assured Umar the position of second founder of Islam. But Umar's orders regarding the occupation and administration of the new territories were equally important in setting the Muslim pattern that has persisted to the present. Except in some parts of Syria and a few other places the people of the conquered provinces continued to work and live as they had for centuries, generally with the advantage of paying less in tribute than the former rulers had taxed them. Armies were destroyed and administrators either departed or were employed in similar capacities by the Muslims, but most inhabitants were hardly touched.

Indeed, in some instances, Arab domination was not only tolerable but welcome. In Syria and Palestine urbanites had acquired a Hellenistic affectation and many of them, especially in Syria, left with the defeated Byzantine armies; but the rural peoples had retained contact with the desert Arab, thus easing the transition to Arab rule. In Iraq, Sasanid rule had been a foreign rule, and native tribes rejoiced in the Sasanid defeats. In Iran, however, the Arab was never wholly accepted and the rapidity of the Muslim conquest can be attributed to the collapse of the royal government and the momentary inability of the Iranian people to organize a resistance.

In Syria, Palestine, and Egypt heavy imperial taxes and the arrogant, high-handed attitude of officials from Constantinople embittered the provinces. More aggravating and more emotional were the religious persecutions inflicted upon local Christians. The orthodox Council of Chalcedon in the year 451 condemned the Monophysite doctrine of Egypt and Syria according to which divinity and humanity make one compound nature in Christ. This Monophysite heresy was persecuted savagely by many emperors without success, until Heraclius, under whose rule these provinces were lost to Islam, tried to effect a compromise by supporting the Monothelite doctrine that Christ had two natures in one person with one will. In Syria and Egypt the churches were ardently Monophysite; in Egypt that faith assumed a patriotic coloration which persists today in the Coptic church. Thus, when it became apparent that Muslim rule meant religious freedom as well as lower taxes, the Arabs had little difficulty in obtaining cooperation from the local peoples. Since at this time Muslims paid no taxes, this toleration of taxpaying Christians and Jews is the origin of the often repeated but little understood Muslim formula of the three-way choice—Islam, taxes, or death—offered to conquered peoples.

Except in Iran the armies of occupation were held aloof from the established urban centers as much as possible. Umar, distressed at the soft appearance and paleness of some of the troops occupying Iraq and quartered in old Ctesiphon, ordered that camps be placed in the open near the desert. Later camp cities were established in each of the newly won provinces— Basrah in lower Iraq, Kufah in central Iraq, Jabiyah in Syria, Ramlah in Palestine, and Fustat (Cairo) in Egypt.

In Syria Muslim soldiers and local Arabs took over partially deserted towns and some lands whose owners, being Byzantine supporters, had departed. Some 20,000 of the former moved into Hims and Damascus, but the latter were more numerous. Jealousy and strife arose over available houses and lands, so much so that Umar visited Syria and made an even-handed redistribution among everyone.

In all the conquered territories governors were appointed to collect taxes and maintain order. Only a handful of administrators accompanied the governors, and, in general, bureaus of government were manned by previous officials. Non-Muslims could not bear arms and were subject to their own laws, a practice that established Islamic society as one of the most tolerant of all ages and developed into the famous millet, or self-administered religious community, system of the Ottoman Empire. Arabs from Arabia were not permitted to own agricultural lands in conquered territory. Under the Umayyads this injunction evolved into a system of land ownership and rights of tenancy which still prevails in the Middle East. Considering all aspects of life, the conquered peoples of the Middle East were disturbed very little by Muslim occupation; and civilization proceeded to absorb and modify the new increment.

Many other developments occurred during Umar's caliphate. Arabia was declared a holy land, and all non-Muslims were forced to leave, although by this time few remained who did not profess Islam. Even today this decree obtains; and the presence of non-Muslims in Arabia is regarded by the devout as evidence of the forbearance of the rulers of Arabia. With wealth from victories pouring in, the character of Mecca and Medina began to change. There was great building activity, particularly in Medina, where apartments were needed for retired soldiers, administrators, and others who flocked to the capital city as well as for the old inhabitants whose wealth had now greatly increased.

Umar enunciated again Muhammad's policy that although prisoners and movable property belonged to the soldiers who won them, land and taxes from conquest belonged to the whole Muslim community, and one-fifth of all income from conquered territory was to be forwarded to Medina. To facilitate distribution among the Muslims, Umar had a census taken in Arabia and a register (*diwan*) made of the sum each was to receive each year from the public treasury. The list included Muslims of all ranks, from Aishah and the Prophet's family down to the lowliest women and children of non-Arab warriors. Aishah received 12,000 dirhams (a silver coin); Companions of the Prophet 5,000; and a child of the lowliest, 200.

Perhaps Umar's regulation of the calendar best showed the belief that a new state and society had been born. Numbering the new era with the Prophet's emigration to Medina, Umar decreed that Muslim dating should be counted as so many years after the Hijrah and that he had become caliph in the year A.H. 13.

As the years went by and wealth and opportunity grew, Umar had more and more difficulty with his provincial governors and their administrations. Since he had no power to enforce his will, the governors were nearly independent. Consequently, the required one-fifth of the income from conquered lands was not always forthcoming; Syria, in fact, never sent any. Among the leaders of Islam, Umar was only first among equals. This was especially true in the camp cities of Kufah and Basrah, inhabited by many nomad warriors who were proud, hardy, political Muslims, resentful of Kuraysh rule. Al-Mughirah, Umar's governor of Basrah, was a brilliant, tough, scheming, licentious native of al-Taif, just the sort of rough-and-ready genius that a new city would require. But when caught in adultery, the protests from Basrah were so vociferous that he was recalled to Medina for trial. Although he escaped punishment by slipping through a legal loophole, Umar relieved him of his post. Later al-Mughirah was able to wangle the appointment to Kufah. He retained this appointment for many years, augmenting its power and scope until he became one of the most powerful men in the Muslim world.

In 644 at the very height of Umar's power and prestige he was assassinated at worship in the mosque of Medina by an Iranian Christian slave who had a personal grudge to settle. On his deathbed Umar selected six leading notables of Medina, all ex-Meccans, to choose his successor and directed his own son to wait upon them. Shortly after he had been buried beside Muhammad and Abu Bakr, the notables, probably on the basis of seniority and a pledge to follow the policies and practices of Umar, selected Uthman ibn Affan, who ruled as caliph from 644 to 656. Another leading candidate popular with the older Medinese families was Muhammad's cousin, Ali, who was passed by because he would not promise to follow in Umar's footsteps.

Uthman

Uthman was a member of the very prominent and powerful Umayyad family of the Kuraysh. Noted for his mild manner and piety, his only distinction as a Muslim leader was having been a respected Companion of the Prophet. His three predecessors had belonged to lesser Kuraysh families, as had most of the emigrants to Medina. Perhaps it was because of this that they had ignored the traditional Arab policy of nepotism and regarded all Muslims as members of one community and one brotherhood. This new social philosophy was one of the revolutionary aspects of Islam.

Although Uthman was seventy when he became caliph and not particularly energetic, he nevertheless sought greater control over the provinces. He was fortunate to have at his command within his own clan a number of vigorous governors and generals to carry forward the banners of Islam. His brother Abdallah was appointed governor of Egypt with financial and civil control, while the conquering Amr was left as commander of the Muslim army. Outraged, Amr immediately repaired to Medina and refused to serve, with the acid remark: "To be over the army and not over the revenue was like holding the cow's horns while another milked her." Abdallah carried on campaigns for booty to the west and south. His armies held Benghazi and Tripoli, ravaged Tunisia, and raided Nubia for slaves. But Abdallah's great contribution was the development of a Muslim fleet, which in 652 repulsed a Byzantine armada before it could attack Alexandria.

In Syria, Uthman had as governor his shrewd and aggressive cousin Muawiyah ibn Abu Sufyan, one of the greatest administrators in Muslim history. Umar had appointed him governor of Damascus; and as other governorships in Syria fell vacant they were added to Muawiyah's territory until under Uthman he became the powerful ruler of all of Syria. He rebuffed a large Byzantine army in 647 and in subsequent years sent raiding parties into Asia Minor. He, too, built a fleet, took Cyprus in 649, ravaged the island of Rhodes, and in 655 in conjunction with Abdallah's ships destroyed a large part of the Byzantine navy off the Lycian coast.

Other cousins of Uthman were appointed as governors of Kufah and Basrah and they led Arab armies during these years in Iran, continuing to fan out eastward. Fars was fully subdued by 650; Khurasan was taken in 651; inroads were made into Armenia in 652; and before the end of Uthman's caliphate, raiding expeditions reached Balkh, Kabul, and Ghazna.

Even though the caliph might not be personally aggressive, the valor, might, and leadership of the Muslim army and navy were no longer questioned in the Middle East. The growing problem was the impact of the new empire upon the Muslim community which had so recently emerged from Arab society. Most of the original emigrants who still lived were now notables and exceedingly wealthy. One, reputedly, had 1,000 slaves and a palace in each of the great cities; another left a fortune of 400,000 dinars; and many had villas in Mecca and Medina or in the hills nearby.

A second and new generation was coming to full manhood. The amusements and luxuries of Alexandria, Damascus, Ctesiphon, and the camp cities of Basrah, Kufah, and Fustat were tempting. Wine, women and gambling were the undoing of many. Gone were days when, as Aishah easily recalled, Muhammad considered wheat bread a rare treat and usually made a meal of dates or milk but never had the luxury of both at the same time. Sumptuous living, however, was neither the sole difficulty nor the root of the other evils. Personal politics, power, and prestige began to eat at the vitals of Muslim society, and certainly Uthman was not strong enough to stem the process. Probably no one could have halted it.

Muslim Political Parties

Three political parties were developing in the Islamic world. The first considered itself the party of Muhammad. Led by members of the less important families of Mecca, it was composed of those who had established the Muslim community. Abu Bakr and Umar had been members of this party; and in most circles Ali, as the husband of Muhammad's daughter Fatimah, was looked upon as the leader. The strength of the party, legitimists as they are sometimes called, lay in Egypt and Iraq.

Leaders of the second party were members of the Umayyad family and their associates among the Kuraysh. It had been one of the two wealthiest and leading Meccan families in the pre-Islamic period—a family that had bitterly attacked Muhammad and had led the campaigns against the Muslims in Medina. Uthman was an Umayyad, as were Muawiyah, Abdallah in Egypt, and Marwan, who served as Uthman's executive secretary in Medina. Though latecomers to Islam, they possessed great managerial talent and were rapidly surging to the fore in administering the empire. Umar had used them and controlled them; but the legitimists contended that the Umayyads controlled Uthman through their great power and wealth in Syria.

The third party was composed of Arab soldiers who had joined the Muslims just before or after Muhammad's death. They outnumbered the other two parties, but they were unorganized and their leaders did not have the prestige of the Kuraysh. Yet, it was their swords that had been the instruments responsible for the rapid expansion of Islam, and since Islam acknowledged no distinctions among peoples or individuals, they resented the inferior political position forced upon them. The third party had followers everywhere, but their forces were concentrated in Arabia and the two great military cities in Iraq.

Having lost the election that followed Umar's death, the legitimists carped at Uthman for his policies and caviled at his inaction. He was censured for enlarging the square around the Kaaba in Mecca and for rebuilding and embellishing the mosque in Medina. Even his standardization of the Koran (still the canonical text today) was attacked, many feeling that he had no superior religious insight or authority for such an undertaking. But the most severe criticism was leveled at him for appointing so many members of the Umayyad family to high office, for embezzling state properties, and for distributing unjustly the spoils of war. His political opponents claimed that he was reverting to the old order of Arab society where blood ties had ruled. Muhammad had preached earnestly to create a unitary Muslim community wherein all members would be brothers and where social, economic, and political equality would prevail; yet after a dozen years the traditional Arab predilection for the family reasserted its consuming role. From that day to the present it remains as one of the persistent sores upon Middle Eastern society.

Malcontents across the empire fed on the stories and rumors regarding the sale of positions and the power and wealth of favorites. Supporters of Ali in Kufah first raised the banners of revolt. When a band of revolutionaries from Egypt arrived in Medina and surrounded Uthman's residence, the caliph would not permit an army to be raised in his defense and commanded Muawiyah not to come to his rescue. After a siege of several months in 656 the rebels stormed the palace and murdered Uthman, the first dagger being struck by Abu Bakr's son. Anarchy reigned for a week in Medina until a group of notables, under pressure from the rebels from Egypt, elected Ali to the caliphate and restored order.

Ali

Ali, Muhammad's cousin, adopted son, and son-in-law, was a pious and esteemed Muslim, who as an individual soldier in his younger days had shone as one of the great heroes of Muslim battles. He had already been disappointed three times in not being elected caliph, and he may have known of the move to kill Uthman. Generally throughout the Muslim world he was recognized as the caliph; and the new governors appointed by him were accepted everywhere except in Syria, where Muawiyah refused to resign. There were, however, many individuals who did not acknowledge Ali as caliph, largely because of jealousy or shock over the murder of Uthman.

Disgruntled elements among the legitimists aided by Aishah, who bitterly hated Ali, hatched a rebellion in Mecca on the pretext that Ali had implicated himself by not punishing the regicides. Ali led his army from Medina, which from that day to the present ceased to be the residence of any caliph, and defeated the insurgents near Basrah in the renowned Battle of the Camel (so-called because the fighting swirled around Aishah on her camel). In this first battle of Muslim against Muslim neither booty nor reprisal against the vanquished was taken. Many illustrious Companions of the Prophet were killed. Aishah was captured but was permitted to return to Medina, where she lived on for twenty-two years in her apartment, under the floor of which Muhammad, Abu Bakr, and Umar had been buried.

Denouncing Ali as the confrere of the murderers of the caliph, Muawiyah withheld his fealty and met Ali's forces at Siffin on the banks of the Euphrates in northern Syria in 657. In the midst of battle, fighting between Muslims was dramatically halted upon agreement that the contest would be decided by referring to the Koran. Arbitration was unsuccessful; Muawiyah refused to accept Ali as caliph, and Ali would neither abdicate nor consider Muawiyah governor of Syria. Each force, however, retired from the field, and a stalemate ensued.

Following the Battle of the Camel, Ali had made his capital at Kufah. His episode with Muawiyah was, in part, a revival of the age-old and persistent rivalry between Syria and Iraq for dominance in the Middle East. It was also a struggle between the Umayyad Kuraysh and the Arab tribes of the desert for supremacy. The immediate quarrel between the two was over the policy of immigration of Arab tribes into new provinces. Under Uthman, Muawiyah had been able to keep Syria closed to this rather unruly element, thereby forcing Iraq to absorb most of the exodus. Ali, seeking a solution for Iraq's population pressure, proposed opening Syria. Muawiyah and his Syrians objected violently and were willing to fight to preserve their province and keep out the mass of immigrants.

At the Battle of the Camel so many of the legitimist party perished that it disappeared from the annals of Islam, leaving Ali, in Kufah, at the mercy of the dominant tribes party. In fact, some members took the name Kharijites ("Seceders") and revolted against Ali in protest against his willingness to arbitrate and his propensity for appointing relatives and close Kuraysh friends to high office. Ali destroyed their force in 659, but was assassinated in 661 by a Kharijite in Kufah on the way to prayers. Hasan, Ali's eldest son, was declared caliph in Kufah; but Muawiyah was recognized as caliph in Damascus. A few months later Hasan reached an agreement with Muawiyah and retired on a royal pension to the pleasures of his palace in Medina. Muawiyah, thenceforth, was accepted throughout the Muslim Empire as the sole caliph, and the center of the state shifted to Damascus.

Thus ended the so-called republican and democratic era of the caliphate wherein the rulers were elected or chosen for reasons other than birth or military might. Throughout most of this period Medina still served as the capital of the Muslim world, and the leaders of society had known the Prophet personally. It was an Arab state; the conquered provinces had not yet conquered their rulers. With the transfer of the seat of authority to Damascus and the caliphate to Muawiyah of the Umayyad family, a new era was born.

REFERENCES: Chapter 4

References at the end of the preceding chapters relate to this chapter as well.

Arnold, Thomas W. *The Caliphate.* Oxford: Clarendon Press, 1924. A careful discussion of the formation and history of the rule of the Muslim state.

Brockelmann, Carl. *History of the Islamic Peoples.* New York: Putnam, 1947. A general survey of the Islamic period of the Middle East, written by an outstanding German scholar.

Frye, R. N. (ed.). *The Cambridge History of Iran.* Vol. 4. *The Period from the Arab Invasion to the Saljuqs.* London: Cambridge University Press, 1975. Seven scholarly chapters on the history of Iran during this period, followed by excellent chapters by outstanding scholars on social organization, visual arts, numismatics, exact and life sciences, religion, philosophy, sects and heresies, and literature.

Hitti, Philip K. *History of the Arabs from the Earliest Times to the Present.* London: Macmillan, 1953. The standard text of the history of the Arab peoples up to the sixteenth century. The remaining four centuries are treated very briefly. Professor Hitti is a native of Lebanon who was professor of Oriental languages and literature at Princeton University for many years.

Lewis, Bernard. *The Arabs in History.* London: Hutchison's University Library, 1950. A concise account of the rise of the Arab people, emphasizing the broad economic movements through the ages and correlating these developments with historical processes among the Arabs.

Muir, William. *The Caliphate: Its Rise, Decline, and Fall, from Original Sources.* Edinburgh: Grant, 1915. Although this volume is outdated in its critical analysis of the sources, it still contains a full and useful running account of the earliest days of the founding of the Muslim state.

Shoufani, Elias. *Al-Riddah and the Muslim Conquest of Arabia.* Toronto: University of Toronto Press, 1975. A new study of the wars in Arabia upon the death of Muhammad, showing that tribes of the Najd revolted against paying tribute or taxes to Medina and that Arabia was far from united at the time of the Prophet's death.

Chapter 5

Islam

The accession of Muawiyah inaugurated a period of Umayyad and Syrian domination of Islam during which the Hellenistic philosophy and theology of Egypt and Syria rapidly effected a revolution within Islamic thought and practice. Almost immediately the new concepts and dogmas gave birth to numerous Muslim sects; and under the Umayyads the unity of theology, as well as of politics, was forever lost in the Muslim world.

After 660 the various Muslim schools of law, theologies, customs, and practices deviated and multiplied until the simple straightforward conceptualism of Islam was lost and the masses found the exact nature of their religion difficult to determine. Furthermore, rapidity of expansion and multifold conversions admitted to Muslim society many whose knowledge of Islam was limited to a few platitudinous phrases. Throughout all these divergencies and vicissitudes there remained, nevertheless, considerable similarity. The central belief of all variants retained the simple religion preached by Muhammad.

Acceptance of monotheism was the most important facet of religion to Muhammad. To be a Muslim it was sufficient to profess the unity of God and to admit Muhammad as His messenger. God had ninety-nine names, each with a related attribute. The mere recitation of these indicates Muhammad's conception of God: omniscient, omnipotent, the Judge, the Mighty, the Creator, merciful, compassionate, self-subsistent, forgiving, magnificent, everlasting, most generous, and most high.

Of the infinite qualities of God, Muhammad constantly stressed everlastingness. God was the Creator of creation and existed through all eternity. All people were His creatures and He "misleads whom He will and guides whom He will." Fear of God and the Day of Judgment was particularly emphasized in Muhammad's early days to impress materialistic Meccan society; but Muhammad also visualized God as a loving, bountiful, and forgiving Protector, "closer to a man than his own jugular vein." A third important attribute of God was mystical in nature: He was termed the Light of the Heavens and of the Earth. In later centuries theologians developed this quality into various organized mysticisms which served as powerful forces in the spread and influence of Islam.

The Koran

The basis for Muhammad's views of God and religion and for the central belief of Muslims of every sect rested upon the Koran ("lecture" or "recitation"), the collection of Muhammad's revelations. Consisting of 114 chapters, called *surahs,* made up of 6,236 verses (77,934 words), the earliest versions were assembled soon after Muhammad's death. Some of the revelations had been written down in his later years by his secretaries; other revelations were only remembered word for word by his companions. Tradition has it that after a battle in which many reciters of the Koran perished, Abu Bakr ordered the full Koran to be committed to parchment so that it would not be lost. Later Uthman established the copy held in Medina as the true Koran. In the tenth century the text, as it now stands, was adopted from seven different readings which evolved because of the lack of vowels and diacritical marks in the Arabian script.

Except for the first, which is a short prayer, the chapters were arranged according to length, so that the later but longer Medinese chapters are located at the beginning. In total length it is about two-thirds that of an Arabic version of the New Testament.

Muslims regard the Koran as the word of God, transmitted to Muhammad by the angel Gabriel; and for many centuries they considered that the Koran contained all knowledge of any value. It furnished the basis for law in the Islamic world for all Muslims; like a modern constitution, it was the skeleton of the legal and judicial systems. It also prescribed a pattern of daily individual and community living which distinguishes Islamic culture from all others. Since no official translation was made until modern times, Koranic Arabic served as a common language and a bond for all Muslims from one end of the world to the other. The Koran was the schoolbook, and committing it to memory was standard practice for children everywhere. The very sound of the Arabic words stirs the emotions; read silently, the Koran loses much of its power.

The major part of the Koran is concerned with God: His attributes are cited, His powers proclaimed, and the individual's relations to Him defined. Associated with a vivid explanation of the Day of Judgment are portrayals of the resurrection, paradise and hell, and angels and devils. Religious and ethical paths for one to follow in life are sometimes presented directly, almost as codes and commandments; but for the most part they are contained in parables and stories, many of which have been taken from the Old and New Testaments and their associated literature. Adam, Noah, Abraham, Joseph, Moses, David, Solomon, Elijah, Job, Zachariah, John the Baptist, Mary, and Jesus are all set forth, not in any special historical sense but to verify that God rewards the righteous and punishes the wicked.

A perusal of the Torah, the Bible, and the Koran discloses a number of very similar passages. Surah 21, verse 105, is identical to Psalm 37, verse 9: "For evil doers shall be cut off; but those that wait upon the Lord, they shall inherit the earth." The Christians of Constantinople and the West branded

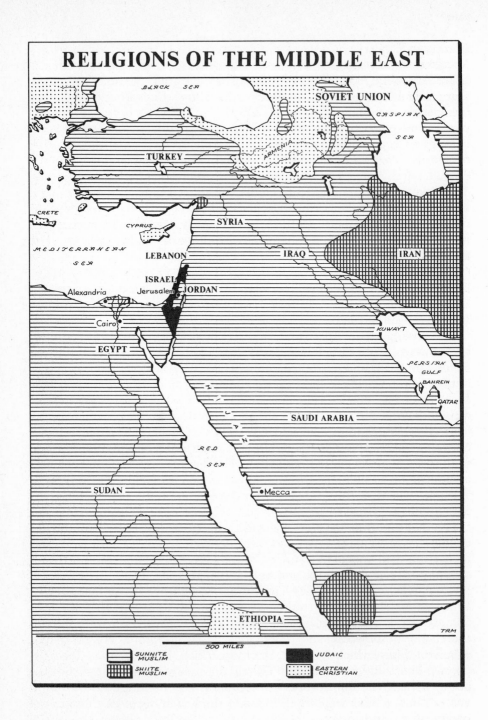

RELIGIONS OF THE MIDDLE EAST

BLACK SEA

SOVIET UNION

CASPIAN SEA

TURKEY

ARMENIA

CRETE

CYPRUS

SYRIA

MEDITERRANEAN SEA

LEBANON

IRAQ

IRAN

ISRAEL
Jerusalem JORDAN

Alexandria

Cairo

EGYPT

KUWAYT

PERSIAN GULF

BAHREIN

QATAR

SUDAN

RED SEA

SAUDI ARABIA

Mecca

ETHIOPIA

TRM

500 MILES

SUNNITE MUSLIM

SHIITE MUSLIM

JUDAIC

EASTERN CHRISTIAN

Islam as a Christian heresy—a castigation which led to the abhorrence of Muslims and an exaggeration of the differences between Christianity and Islam. In reality, Judaism and its two offshoots, Christianity and Islam, have a great deal in common. The dissimilitude is more in language, style, and form than in substance. Through each of these three religions runs a strong message of personal salvation for righteous individuals. This message of hope gives to the individual a sense of significance and equality that is not ordinarily available in cultures where other religions prevail.

Traditions

Following the Prophet's death it became obvious that his revelations did not provide an answer to every problem that arises in daily life. Muhammad had recognized, at least after he became the ruler of Medina, that decisions he made publicly were obeyed in the same measure that the revelations of God's will were obeyed. Muhammad always distinguished carefully between spiritual and secular affairs and spoke most explicitly concerning God's word. God's word was law; Muhammad's words were only guides to lead to a wise and holy life.

As the years slipped by leaving fewer and fewer Muslims who knew from their own memories what Muhammad had said and done, great collections of his comments and deeds were considered vital for following his precedents. Traditions *(hadith)* by the hundreds of thousands appeared; from these has come much of the common law of Islam, called *sunnah* ("custom"). Each of the different sects and parties that developed in Islam accepted certain hadith and rejected others as forgeries to prove the correctness of the party's views, no matter whether the contention affected militarism or pacifism, predestination or free will, mysticism or realism, asceticism or worldliness.

By the second or third century after the Hijrah, hadith had become very intricate in response to the philosophical and theological demands of the scholars of the time. In the early days of Islam, hadith had comprised the simple, unvarnished ideas and stories that Muhammad had voiced or that his friends had repeated word for word. They are of varied topics, for Muhammad had definite opinions on all types of subjects. On one occasion he said: "God curse the woman who wears false hair and the woman who ties it on." When Aishah acquired a pictured cushion, Muhammad exploded: "Verily, the makers of these pictures will be severely punished on the Day of Resurrection." On slavery he remonstrated: "A slave must not be given a task which he is unable to perform." Muhammad sometimes perceived the difference between legality and righteousness, as when he observed: "Of the things which are lawful the most hateful to God is divorce." In a similar vein he declared: "There is no man who receives a bodily injury and forgives the offender but God will exalt his rank and diminish his sin." Having been an orphan, Muhammad was always concerned with such unfortunates and proclaimed: "The best house amidst the Muslim community is that which contains an orphan who is well treated,

58 The Rise and Spread of Islam

and the worst is that wherein an orphan is wronged." Perhaps best known is the attitude Muhammad held toward usury and moneylenders. In commenting on persons paying or charging usurious rates of interest, he averred: "They are equally culpable." Among Muslims one of his oft-quoted commands indicated Muhammad's view that his religion was a matter for everyday life: "No monkery in Islam!"

Dogmas

Muhammad was not a systematic theologian. But shortly after his death Muslim theologians and philosophers classified Muhammad's faith into three fundamentals: religious beliefs *(iman)*, religious duties *(ibadat)*, and good works *(ihsan)*.

First and foremost, of course, is the belief that God is One and has all of the attributes ascribed to Him by Muhammad. It has never been clear, however, how the attribute of omnipotence ought to be interpreted, and this problem has engendered controversy among Muslims from the days of the first caliphs to the present. In the early unaffected period, God's omnipotence meant without intricate debate that the individual is completely subordinate to God and can do nothing unless God permits it. Yet all persons are responsible for what they do and will be rewarded or punished accordingly. Muhammad preached incessantly on this point and declared that people would fall into evil ways if they did not believe in God.

Muhammad and the first Muslims referred so frequently to the Day of Judgment and the Resurrection that belief in these two has become one of the significant aspects of Islam. When the cataclysmic day comes, each individual's faith and deeds will be weighed, one's body will rise, and either enter paradise or be cast into hell. Martyrs for the faith do not wait for the Judgment Day but immediately enter paradise. Paradise is clearly described as a beautiful garden by a flowing river where the blessed rest on silken couches, partake of heavenly food and drink, and are entertained by dark-eyed maidens and wives of perfect purity. The terrors of hell are beyond description. Waters are boiling; sinner's bellies are filled with molten brass. Into this fiery hell go the unbelieving, the covetous, and those who worship other gods.

Another basic point in the religious belief of Muslims is the role played by angels *(jinn)*. Heaven and earth are populated by these invisible spirits who serve as God's messengers and record one's deeds. Gabriel is recognized as the leading angel and the spirit who brought the Koran to Muhammad. Rebellious jinn are devils, and like humans will be cast into hell on the Last Day. The leading devil is one who at the time of creation did not worship Adam and who continues to seduce people into evil ways until the Resurrection.

Muslims believe that God has sent many human messengers to teach the world His ways and that the last and greatest was Muhammad. The Koran specifically mentions twenty-eight prophets: four are Arabs; one is Greek (Alexander the Great); three (Zachariah, John the Baptist, and Jesus) come from the New Testament; and the remainder come from the Old Testament. The most important are Adam, Noah, Abraham, Moses, and Jesus. The last is Muhammad, whom God sent as the "Seal" of all. Prophets did not perform miracles except on special occasions when God gave them these powers. Divine revelation was granted to Moses in the Jewish Torah, to David in the Psalms, to Jesus in the Gospels, and to Muhammad in the Koran, which was his only miracle. All of them preached salvation through the recognition that God is One.

Muslims are to accept and believe all of these scriptures, for they are the word of God and they corroborate each other. The final word of God, the Koran, attests the revelations in the other scriptures, clarifies all previous uncertainties, and brings perfect Truth. The Koran is believed to be eternal and uncreated; its earthly reproduction is identical in language and spelling to the heavenly original, every word and letter of which are sacred and divine.

Duties

The second essential in Islam as taught by Muhammad comprised religious duties. These are actions less obligatory than those of faith; but their performance required and constituted the individual's recognition of the omnipotence of God. These duties have usually been termed the "five pillars" of Islam; they are the easiest to observe and, unfortunately for many uninformed non-Muslims and even for some Muslims, these five pillars have been mistaken for the true religious substance of Islam.

The first and foremost pillar is the open profession of faith. Often reduced to the Koranic formula "No god but God and Muhammad is the messenger of God," this declaration is used throughout a Muslim's life and suffices to ensure one's acceptance as a nominal Muslim.

Muhammad emphasized prayer as the second obligation for Muslims. The Koran mentions directly no set ritual for prayer, but bids the faithful to pray frequently. Before Muhammad's death it had become customary for Muslims to pray formally five times daily: daybreak, noon, midafternoon, sunset, and nightfall. A Muslim prays at these times wherever one may be, but it is preferable to pray in unison with others and in a mosque if possible, with one acting as leader and the others standing in rows behind, all facing Mecca. Each prayer is composed of a certain number of bows: two at daybreak, three at sunset, and four at the other times. Each bow consists of seven distinct acts: (1) placing the open hands at each side of the head and repeating, "God is most great"; (2) standing upright with the left hand over the right and repeating the opening prayer of the Koran and at least one other Koranic passage; (3) bending from the hips and touching the knees with the hands; (4) straightening up, saying, "God listens to the one who praises Him"; (5) falling to the knees and prostrating oneself with the forehead touching the ground; (6) sitting on the haunches; and (7) a second prostration. Most Muslim prayers are concerned with God and His attributes, and devout Muslims pray frequently at other times during the day and night. Certain events such as burials, eclipses, serious decisions, and religious celebrations demand specially prescribed prayers. The Friday noon prayer is the great congregational prayer wherein a sermon *(Khutbah)* is usually delivered. At first the sermon was delivered by Muhammad, then by the caliph or his representative, and now by a learned Muslim, who also offers a prayer on behalf of the ruling head of the state.

At the time of prayer one must be in a state of purity, which is determined in various ways. Usually before prayers, simple purity, as defined in the Koran, is achieved by washing the hands and arms to the elbows, the face, and the feet up to the ankles. In the absence of water, sand may be used.

Of all the features of Islam, prayer in its public form has been the most constant democratizing force. Side by side at prayer are common soldier and general, prince and pauper, merchant and holy man. No distinction is made and the proudest individual falls to his knees and humbly and reverently prostrates himself in complete obeisance in the presence of the omnipotence and omniscience of God.

The third pillar of Islam is almsgiving. Muhammad at first regarded giving to the poor and needy as a personal atonement and a means of salvation. Sometime in the Medinese period of his prophecy almsgiving was regularized to become a 2.5 percent voluntary tax on all produce and revenue of each Muslim. Termed *zakah,* the proceeds were used to support the poor, to erect religious buildings, and to help defray government expenses. In later years when states were much weaker, it was not possible to collect alms on any such basis and it became solely a free-will offering. Alms are also to be given generously for various religious and human charities such as mosques, hospitals, poorhouses, and schools. Likewise, beggars and the destitute are never turned away from the door empty-handed. On the Day of Judgment in a Muslim's book of deeds will be recorded the alms given.

Fasting, the fourth pillar of Islam, was enjoined upon all Muslims by Muhammad, and in the Medinese era he designated Ramadan (the ninth lunar month) as a month of fasting. From the very first flush of dawn to nightfall, food, drink, medicine, and smoke are not to pass the lips; bleeding, application of leeches, and sexual intercourse are also forbidden. At various times and places in history Muslims who have failed to observe Ramadan have been beaten. Fasting is considered the best means of expiating one's sins of the year.

The fifth pillar of Islam, that of the pilgrimage to Mecca *(hajj),* stands as the symbol of Muslim unity. In pre-Islamic times there existed a holy month of pilgrimage to the sanctuary in Mecca; Muhammad continued this custom. It was a maxim that each Muslim, man and woman, should participate in the pilgrimage each year if possible. Later, as the Muslim world grew, it became too arduous for many to go from Iraq, Syria, and Egypt; and when Islam had spread to India and Spain, the pilgrimage became obligatory only once in a lifetime and only for those who could afford it. Occurring in the twelfth month *(Dhu'l-Hijjah),* the pilgrimage ritual is celebrated on certain days by elaborate and involved rites at the Kaaba in Mecca and at other sacred spots in the neighborhood. Since Muhammad's Farewell Pilgrimage in 632, non-Muslims have not been permitted to be present in Mecca during the pilgrimage; and in general they are forbidden entry into the city at all times.

Throughout the entire course of Muslim history the pilgrimage has been a most valuable unifying force within Islamic civilization. Pilgrims have come to Mecca from the four corners of the Muslim world. There, on the way, and in returning the interchange of philosophical and theological dogmas, the gaining of geographical and economic knowledge, the exchange of seeds and agricultural products, and the interplay of political forces and ideas have been factors in maintaining a common Muslim culture among the diverse peoples embracing Islam.

To some Muslims a sixth pillar of Islam has been added: that of holy war (jihad). Many consider that every Muslim bears the duty to expand the frontiers of Islam, by force if necessary, until the entire world has been won. In recent centuries, however, it has not been a vital force among Muslim people.

Virtues

It might well be thought that after professing the religious beliefs of Islam and performing the various duties of a Muslim, the circle of religion had been completed. In addition, however, the Koran imposes upon all a course of right living, thus giving a religious character to private and public morality. From the virtues he extolled, Muhammad emerges as a moralist and something of a puritan. The Koran limits the number of wives to four, and then adds: "But if you fear that you will act unjustly among them, then marry only one." There are many other commandments that raised the status of women in Arabian society. Settlements are required to be made upon a woman if she is divorced; a widow can marry whomever she wishes; and the burying alive of daughters is prohibited.

Murderers are promised burning in hell; and earthly penalties are imposed for homicide, stealing, fraud, perjury, and libel. Injunctions are delivered against gambling, usury, and monopolistic practices. The use of wine and the eating of pork are forbidden. An interdiction is imposed upon making statues, pictures, puppets, and any representation of animate objects, because God is the creator of all things and human beings should not try to imitate His works. Moreover, idolatry is most sinful, and the making of images is only one step removed from worshiping other gods. Most of these declarations of right living are injunctions against practices that were common in the pagan and hedonistic society of Mecca.

In view of the comprehensive scope of Islam with respect to religious beliefs, religious duties, and virtues, Muhammad must be regarded as a very successful prophet and reformer. Muhammad found Mecca, as one writer has well expressed it, a "materialistic commercial" city "where lust of gain and usury reigned supreme, where women, wine, and gambling filled up the leisure time, where might was right, and widows, orphans, and the feeble were treated as superfluous ballast." Muhammad, practically a no-body in so many of the things that counted in Mecca, brought to his people and those of Mecca a knowledge of God and a way of salvation that changed the life and philosophy of all Arabia. Since Islam required individual belief and morality, the tribal and family morality of pre-Islamic Arabia was replaced by the personal responsibilities of the individual Muslim as a member of the universal Muslim brotherhood.

REFERENCES: Chapter 5

References at the end of Chapters 3 and 4 relate to this chapter as well.

Bell, Richard. *The Qur'an. Translated, with a Critical Re-arrangement of the Surahs.* 2 vols. Edinburgh: Clark, 1937, 1939. One of the very best translations, fully edited and annotated with many cross references.

Cragg, Kenneth. *The Mind of the Qur'an: Chapters in Reflection.* London: Allen & Unwin, 1973. Shows how the Koran became the mold for forming Islamic society, for transforming pagan Arabs into a monotheistic community, and for shaping typical Islamic attitudes.

Farah, Caesar E. *Islam: Beliefs and Observances.* Woodbury, N.Y.: Barron's Educational Series, 1968. A concise statement of the life and preaching of Muhammad, the Koran, the beliefs and obligations of Islam, the many sects, practices, and Islam in the modern world.

Gibb, H. A. R. *Mohammedanism: An Historical Survey.* London: Oxford University Press, 1953. This little volume in The Home University Library of Modern Knowledge, no. 197, is probably the best short account and discussion of Islam in any language. The style is simple and direct, the language is readily understood, and the scholarship is beyond reproach.

Guillaume, Alfred. *The Traditions of Islam: An Introduction to the Study of the Hadith Literature.* Oxford: Clarendon Press, 1924. An important monograph on hadith and its significance in the development of tradition as a part of Islamic belief and ritual.

Jeffery, Arthur. *The Qur'an as Scripture.* New York: R. F. Moore, 1952. Important for the study of Islam and the Koran.

Tritton, A. S. *Muslim Theology.* London: Luzac, 1947. The basic principles are well presented in this volume and the variants are explained.

Watt, W. Montgomery. *Free Will and Predestination in Early Islam.* London: Luzac, 1948. An excellent presentation of this dichotomy in the philosophy of the Muslim world.

———. *What Is Islam?* New York: Praeger, 1968. A survey of the background of Islam, the historical perspective, the work of religious intellectuals, and the Islamic world-view.

Chapter 6

The Spread and Organization of the Muslim Empire Under the Umayyads

The death of Ali left no serious rival to Muawiyah and his leadership over all Muslims. Proclaimed caliph at Jerusalem in 661, Muawiyah established Damascus as his chief residence and seat of government. Until his death nineteen years later he managed the provinces through energetic, capable, and forceful governors, who tried to maintain a strong discipline over the proud and turbulent Arab soldiery. In Iraq, however, the crowded garrison cities and determined leaders declared their autonomy so vigorously that Muawiyah wisely acquiesced and challenged them only when feasible. Muslim soldiers held the province and the Sasanid governmental lands as theirs by right of conquest and rarely sent any part of the income to Damascus.

At home Muawiyah ruled confidently and nobly as the first among equals. He discussed policies of state with the notables about him, frequently explaining the course of government publicly from the pulpit of the mosque. In truth, his power rested upon the personal loyalty of the Syrian army, which was the strongest and best organized of any in the state. More and more he built an administration in the Romano-Byzantine tradition; less and less was he the tribal Arab shaykh governing purely on a personal basis. He was the first Muslim ruler to execute a fellow Muslim for political reasons.

Five years before his death Muawiyah induced the leaders of the empire to recognize his son Yazid as his successor. Thereupon, Yazid was taken to Medina and Mecca to have those holy cities accept him as the next caliph. This procedure was definitely a Roman custom, and the haughty Muslim aristocracy of Medina, declaring the step to be a sinful innovation, refused to render the requested homage. Essentially, this method of succession made the position of caliph an hereditary one, or at least a family prerogative, and overtly established the Umayyad Empire, which lasted until 750. Twice during the period there was a question who the next caliph would be; and once a serious contender arose outside of the Umayyad family.

In general and by comparison with other ruling families the Umayyads produced talented, competent caliphs. They were much maligned by later Muslim historians, who wrote under the patronage of the succeeding dynasty and who depicted the Umayyads as hard-riding, wine-bibbing, luxury-loving, worldly-minded usurpers of the caliphate. But the Umayyads

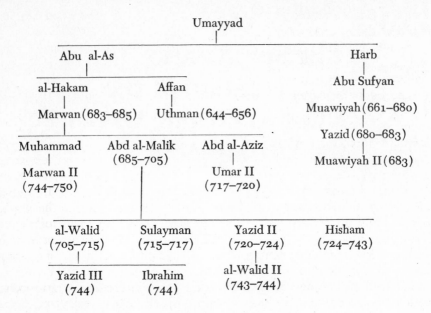

THE UMAYYAD CALIPHATE

organized the Muslim state into a more centralized force that once again carried forward the banners of Islam into distant places. They were hard-hitting realists who to meet existing and evolving situations could not always follow the principles of government and law being formulated by theologians and jurists in the holy city of Medina.

Campaigns Against Byzantium

The nearest and greatest rival power of the Umayyad state was the Byzantine Empire; the nearest and richest land for the Muslims to raid was Asia Minor. Battles with Byzantine forces were not novel experiences for Muawiyah. As governor of Syria he had driven Byzantine armies from north Syria, twice defeated Byzantine fleets, and occupied Cyprus. Muawiyah's army exploited the weakness of the rule from Constantinople by annual summer excursions through the passes into Asia Minor as far north as Caesarea (Kayseri). After he became caliph his forces roamed far and wide over Anatolia; one Muslim general wintered in 668 at Chalcedon (Kadiköy) across the Bosphorus from Constantinople. That spring Muawiyah sent a fleet to support the land force and attack Constantinople, but the land and sea walls of the city proved too great a barrier for the Arabs. From this campaign has come the legendary hero Abu Ayyub (Eyub), who died and was buried near the walls of Constantinople. The standard-bearer of the Prophet, the then aged Abu Ayyub had accompanied the soldiers to stimulate their enthusiasm. His remains, discovered in 1453 when the Turks were storming the walls, have been entombed in a mosque-mausoleum near the Golden Horn, where the Ottoman sultans were girded with the sword of their authority.

The raising of the siege of Constantinople upon Muawiyah's death did not presage the relaxing of Muslim pressure on the Byzantine Empire. Another assault upon Constantinople was launched by the caliph Sulayman, who subscribed to the legend that Constantinople would be taken by the bearer of a prophet's name. His brother Maslamah, supported by land and sea forces, occupied both shores of the Bosphorus and held a tight siege of Constantinople for fourteen months. In 717, however, he was foiled by Greek fire and the brilliant defenses of the new emperor, Leo the Isaurian (a Syrian from Marash) and by the ravages of disease, hunger, and an unusually severe winter. At the same time the new caliph, Umar II, strongly opposed to all expansionist policies, ordered the siege lifted and the Muslim forces withdrawn. Several generations elapsed before the Muslims appeared again before the walls of Constantinople, which always proved too thick and too strong for the Arabs to penetrate without the aid of gunpowder.

Had Constantinople been taken in 717, the subsequent course of European history might well have been greatly altered. The road to Italy and western Europe through the Balkans would have been traversed almost unimpeded; and once in western Europe, these Muslim generals would have effected a union with their brothers-in-arms coming by way of North Africa and Spain.

North Africa and Spain

The records do not disclose any planned pincers movement on Europe by the Umayyads, although simultaneously with their last attacks upon Constantinople the greatest westward movement of Islam was being executed. Amr, governor of Egypt, sent a Muslim force westward into North Africa, the object being Tunisia and Algeria *(Ifrikiyah)*, and Morocco *(Maghrib)*. A camp city built in 670 at Kayrawan in Tunisia served as headquarters to subdue Berber tribes and the coastal cities dependent upon Constantinople. Toward the end of the century Byzantine rule over the coast was terminated by a cooperative army-fleet maneuver which drove the Greeks from Carthage. Appointed governor of Africa in 708, Musa ibn Nusayr consolidated North Africa from Egypt to the Atlantic and added greatly to his military force by recruiting new armies from among the Berber tribesmen.

One of Musa's Berber lieutenants led a small reconnoitering band across the Strait of Gibraltar in 710 and returned easily with such valuable booty that Tarik, the fabled Berber lieutenant in command at Tangier, crossed on his celebrated raid in the early summer of 711 with several thousand men, mostly Berbers, and established a base on the strong height which still is called Tarik's mountain—*Jabal Tarik,* or Gibraltar. Crushing the Visigothic forces of Spain, Tarik fanned out northward at will. Málaga, Cordoba, and

Toledo fell; and by winter Tarik found himself master of half of Spain with an almost unlimited amount of booty at his disposal.

Scolding Tarik for acting independently, Musa joined his heroic hench-man in 712. Within two years Spain had been overrun by Muslim forces. The highlands of Leon, Aragon, and the Asturias were occupied; and from Galicia, Musa looked down upon the waters of the Atlantic and the Bay of Biscay. At this point a messenger ordered Musa to appear before the caliph in Damascus. Accompanied by Tarik, Musa made the long trek overland and presented to the court his trophies and many Visigothic nobles and maidens. Shortly thereafter a new caliph stripped Musa of his wealth and degraded him, perhaps because of fear or jealousy of Musa's great popu-larity. Musa died in poverty a few years later in the Hijaz, a strange fate for one who had opened Europe to the Muslims.

Within six or seven years the conquest of Spain was completed. The Arabs called the province al-Andalusia ("Land of the Vandals") and it, or some part of it, remained a Muslim land for almost eight centuries. The Arab-Berber-Muslim (Moorish) culture left its indelible mark upon Spain, which in turn had a profound influence upon Islamic society. The speed and ease with which Spain was conquered indicated that it was in a state of near anarchy, waiting for a positive force to enter the vacuum. Ruling in a most oppressive and tyrannical fashion and attempting to convert all Jews to Christianity by force, the Visigoths had always been at odds with the Romano-Spanish peoples, who looked upon their Teutonic masters as bar-barians.

As in Syria, Iraq, and Egypt, the Muslims fought not against the native inhabitants but only against the armies of the rulers. Spain was taken so quickly that in many towns and cities no Arab or Berber forces could be spared for garrison duty; and since Muslim administrators were usually not available, native Jews were left in charge.

Ignoring the nonexpansionist policy of Umar II, one of Musa's successors crossed the Pyrenees in 718 and plundered France as far as Nîmes. Two years later Arab-Berber invaders seized Narbonne on the Mediterranean and established an arsenal and base for operations north of the Pyrenees. Predatory columns rode out of Narbonne every year, terrorizing the coun-tryside and carrying off rich booty, especially from the treasures of churches and convents. The greatest of these expeditions was the renowned foray of 732 led by the governor of Spain, Abd al-Rahman. Defeating the Duke of Aquitaine near the Garonne, Abd al-Rahman burned churches in Bordeaux and outside of Poitiers. The raiders turned back from their northward course only after the loss of their leader in the determined and bloody resistance put up by Charles Martel in the celebrated but indecisive Battle of Tours. Never again did an organized expedition of Muslims approach so near to Paris, but Muslim forces did succeed in taking Avignon in 734 and several years later sacked Lyons.

Although Narbonne was not abandoned until 759 the Arab-Berbers of Spain never fashioned a real hold upon southern France because of their lack of manpower, the distance from Damascus, and a running feud between Berber and Arab which led to violent insurrection in North Africa and Spain. Conversions to Islam among the Berbers were so extensive as to compromise the relationship between conquerors and vanquished in North Africa. Arabs looked down upon the Berbers, who upon becoming Muslims anticipated equality with the proud Arab. When the expected treatment was not forthcoming, rebellion burst out everywhere. From 734 to 742 North Africa was in flames from one end to the other. Berbers claimed that they were given semiarid plateau lands in Spain while the Arabs acquired all of the fertile areas.

In addition, factional strife among the Arabs existed at every turn. Political, religious, and family quarrels were at this moment rocking the Islamic world from the Pyrenees to the Indus, making incursions beyond well-established frontiers wholly ineffective. Furthermore, rivalry developed between Arabs from Arabia and the Syrian army sent to subdue Berber uprisings; their bickerings with the Arab governors and lords of Toledo and Cordoba were interminable. From the time of the Battle of Tours to the landing of the Umayyad prince in Spain in 755, the term of the governorship of Spain averaged twelve months. With such turmoil, uncertainty, and anarchy permanent conquests in France were impossible.

Expansion in Asia

While the Umayyads were extending Islam westward into North Africa and Spain, a similar expansion carried Muslim rule to the Indus River and the frontiers of China. Becoming viceroy of the eastern lands of the caliphate in 695, al-Hajjaj, a schoolmaster of al-Taif, gave his govenor of Khurasan several thousand Arab troops to establish a strong base at Marw. (These were added to the 50,000 Arabs from Kufah and Basrah that Muawiyah had sent to settle in the oases around Marw in 671 to relieve the population pressures of those cities.) From there he crossed the Amu Darya River (known then as the Oxus) and in a series of brilliant campaigns brought Transoxiana under Muslim domination. Balkh, Bukhara, and Samarkand in Turkestan, and Khiva were subdued between 705 and 712 and soon became Islamic strongholds; Buddhist temples and monasteries were destroyed. Native Turkish rulers were left in charge of civil affairs, although Muslim tax collectors and military inspectors represented the imperial authority. A generation later another caliph sent an Arab general to Transoxiana as far as Kashgar to reconquer the area and bring the Turkish rulers, some of whom had accepted Islam, again under caliphal authority.

Further south, al-Hajjaj's son-in-law was authorized to lead a column toward India. Taking Makran, he occupied Baluchistan and subdued Sind. Daybul and Haydarabad became Muslim, and Multan in the Punjab was conquered. Muslim control along the Indus was permanent. Steady conversion to Islam soon made this northwestern corner of India an important part of the Muslim world and laid the foundations for the modern Islamic state of Pakistan.

Fiscal Developments

This second wave of Muslim expansion under the Umayyads brought to a head certain economic and fiscal problems which had been developing at an accelerated pace. From the time of the Hijrah, Muslims were subject to a small tax to support their poor and unfortunate brethren, but there was no general taxation. Toward the end of the seventh century, with Arabs scattered over the face of the earth and conversions among conquered non-Arab peoples growing by leaps and bounds, questions of state annuities to worthy Muslims, land ownership, and taxation arose to vex one caliph after another and ignited serious disturbances in Muslim society.

Besides the state's share of booty, which in the Umayyad era was very sizable, the principal source of revenue came in taxes from land and subject peoples. Each free non-Muslim was required to pay for his protection a poll tax *(jizyah)* of four, two, or one dinar, according to his wealth and position. Land taxes were far more complex. In the days of the earliest conquests Muslims (Arabs) were forbidden to possess land outside of Arabia proper. Domain lands of ousted Byzantine and Sasanid governments and vacant lands fell to the caliph as agent for the Muslim community, and the income went into provincial coffers, with all surplus supposedly being forwarded to Damascus. Ownership of other land was not changed, and in most cases the taxes *(kharaj)* remained the same and were collected by the same agents. As Arab Muslims acquired properties in Syria, Iraq, and other provinces outside Arabia, freedom from land taxes usually prevailed. The state leased domain land to Muslim Arabs, who bought and sold the rights so that the land had the appearance of private property. Consequently, Arab laws governing landownership and tenure adhered generally to Byzantine, Persian, and more ancient practices and customs, thereby assuring to tillers of the soil throughout the Middle East a continuity which changed only imperceptibly until the great land reforms following World War II.

As the number of non-Arab Muslims increased through conversion, many deserted the land for the city in the expectation of living on state annuities as Arabs did. They paid no taxes on the land left behind in the village and ceased to pay the poll tax. This disastrously affected the treasuries, especially in North Africa, Iraq, and Khurasan.

Furthermore, in order to eliminate increasing resentment of non-Arab Muslims and to prevent incipient revolutions in several of the provinces, Umar II decided to free Muslims, irrespective of origin or state, from paying poll and land taxes. The result was a lowering of revenues that upset the fiscal system of the government beyond the point of toleration. Caliph Hisham withdrew the order and instituted the policy, generally permanent in Muslim lands ever since, that although poll taxes "fell off" upon conversion to Islam, land taxes did not. At that time in the provinces these tax measures were considered by non-Arab Muslims, the principal landowners, to be very inequitable. Great disaffection led to civil war in North Africa and proved to be a major factor in the overthrow of the Umayyad regime by the troops from Iraq and Khurasan.

Social Organization

As the Arabs and the native inhabitants of the conquered territories began to coalesce to form Umayyad civilization, there arose four social classes: Muslim Arabs; Muslim non-Arabs; non-Muslim free persons (Christians, Jews, Zoroastrians); and slaves.

The Arab was the aristocrat of the Muslim world, and the Kuraysh claimed to be the noblest. Wherever Islam spread, Arabs regarded themselves as the rightful leaders of society, and at first only they could live in the new garrison cities such as Kayrawan, Cairo, and Kufah. Although Islam taught the equality of all believers and disavowed family connections in favor of religious ties, Muslim Arabs everywhere retained pride in their lineage: clan and tribe feelings ran high, and marriage between an Arab woman and a non-Arab man was considered a serious misalliance. In the Umayyad period all Arabs were enrolled upon the imperial registry, each receiving regular payments from the state treasury on the theory that the receipts of the Muslim community were divided among all its members. In practice the Arabs acted as if it were decreed that the Arab minority would rule the non-Arab majority, Muslims as well as non-Muslims.

By the opening of the eighth century the non-Arab Muslims, often called clients *(mawali)*, outnumbered the Arab Muslims in all parts of the Umayyad Empire except Arabia. Moreover, the masses in North Africa, Egypt, Iraq, and Khurasan had been converted so rapidly that revenues in those provinces had dropped very conspicuously. Rarely were these converts accepted as equals by the Arabs and usually they attached themselves to an Arab tribe or family (thus the nomenclature "clients"). Yet the converts were in many instances trained and educated individuals with skills not possessed by many Arabs. Several generations later, because of the universality of the Arabic language and considerable intermarriage, the pure Arab of Arabia who had migrated to conquered territory had been lost in the welter of peoples, all of whom participated in the common culture and practices of that particular section of the Middle East. In Syria and Iraq, where most of the Arabs settled, non-Arab Muslims were absorbed quickly, and the new society became Arab. In more distant lands such as Iran, India, Morocco, and Spain the few ruling Arabs dominated society only temporarily. The non-Arab Muslims soon engulfed their rulers, and Iranian, Indian, and Berber-Moorish characteristics triumphed.

Non-Muslims—Jews, Christians, Zoroastrians, pagan Berbers, and a few scattered others—were called *dhimmis* and were recognized legally as second-class subjects. They were judged almost entirely in their own courts in accordance with their own laws and were permitted to worship in their own way and to live their personal lives as they wished. They were, nevertheless, greatly circumscribed in matters of civil rights and community affairs. Non-Muslims could not bear arms; instead, they paid taxes, as has already been discussed. They were subject to many distinctive regulations concerning dress, styles of coiffures, types of saddles, and manner of riding.

Finally, the *dhimmis* could neither hold public office nor give evidence in court against a Muslim.

At the bottom of the social ladder were the slaves. Slavery in the Middle East was as old as time itself; and although Muhammad openly condemned it, saying that manumission was pleasing in the sight of God, he declared the practice legal. In Islamic society no Muslim could be enslaved; acceptance of Islam, however, did not give a slave freedom. Children of a slave woman remained slaves unless the owner of the slave accepted them as his children. Marriage between master and slave was not permissible, although concubinage was. A concubine who presented her master with children could not be sold, was accorded special recognition as the mother of his children, and gained her freedom upon his death.

Slave trading was a very active and profitable business in the Middle East under the Umayyads. Most slaves were acquired as booty in victorious campaigns and successful raiding expeditions, but many were purchased through regular slave channels. Greeks, Armenians, Turks, Kurds, Spaniards, Goths, Iranians, black Africans, and Berbers predominated; but slaves were of every color and description. Prices rose and fell with the supply. Most Arab Muslims possessed several slaves, and the wealthy frequently counted theirs in the thousands.

Political Administration

When Muawiyah became sole caliph, his first task was to effect a systematic administration for the empire. Obviously following the example and practices of the East Roman Empire current in Syria and even using much of its personnel, Muawiyah organized his government along three main functional or departmental lines: political and military affairs; tax collection; and religious administration, including courts and endowments.

Outside Syria-Palestine, which was governed directly by the caliph in Damascus, the empire was divided under the Umayyads into five great states, each with a viceroy appointed by the caliph: (1) Kufah, which included all of Iraq and the Muslim lands farther east; (2) the Hijaz, which took in central Arabia and Yemen; (3) al-Jazirah, comprising the northern lands between the Euphrates and the Tigris, eastern Asia Minor, Armenia, and the Caucasus; (4) Egypt; and (5) Africa, which ran from Cyrenaica to the Atlantic and the Pyrenees.

The army as well as the civil administration in each lesser province acted upon the authority of a governor, and all were directed by and responsible to the viceroy. Local expenses were defrayed from taxes collected in the provinces, only the tax balances being forwarded to Damascus. Toward the end of the Umayyad regime when administration began to weaken, viceroys and provincial governors built up great personal fortunes by neglecting to forward the full balance to the caliph. Viceroys even remained in Damascus, hiring agents to go to the provinces to perform irksome functions. Frequently, special officers were sent directly by the caliph to collect taxes and to be responsible solely to him rather than to the viceroy, who always resented the implied lack of confidence. (It was a step such as this that aroused the enmity of Amr in Egypt toward the caliph Uthman.)

As the empire expanded, problems of trained and loyal personnel, of communications, and of money came to the fore. The number of qualified Arabs was too small to fill the positions required to keep the government functioning. In Syria, Iraq, and Egypt Muawiyah retained the services of most of the government employees he found there upon the conquest. These employees used Greek, Persian, and Coptic in their records. Not until the time of Abd al-Malik was the process of supplanting these civil servants with Arabic-speaking officers begun. By the end of the Umayyad era, however, government affairs were recorded in Arabic, and clerks were Arabic-speaking and usually Muslim in faith.

At the time of the conquest the Byzantine and Sasanid empires were largely on a money economy with gold, silver, and copper coins in wide circulation. The Muslims took these over as media of exchange, sometimes with a phrase from the Koran stamped on. True Muslim-Arabic coins, first minted at Damascus in the reign of Abd al-Malik, were similar in value to coins already in circulation. The gold ones were called dinars after the Roman denarius; the silver, dirhams, from the Greek drachma.

Muslim judges *(kadis)* for the various cities of the empire were usually chosen by the provincial governors and were responsible to them. Since these judges were concerned only with the Muslims, there was little occasion for judges in the villages at this time. Caliphs, generals, viceroys, and governors also held court and handed out justice personally in matters pertaining to political and governmental affairs. Judges, who served as guardians for orphans and incompetents and as managers of religious foundations, were selected from those trained in theology and canon law.

As long as Muawiyah lived, his firm hand checked the factious spirit of the Arabs. However, the two great tribal parties of the Arabs, which existed certainly for a century or two before the advent of Islam, persisted even though submerged throughout the period of the first caliphs. Muhammad refused to recognize the differences and Umar was most intolerant of any display of partisanship. Under the Umayyads with the rule of Abd al-Malik and his ruthless viceroy, al-Hajjaj, party strife touched a high point and influenced every aspect of political life in all parts of the empire.

Reminiscent of the famous Blues and Greens of the Byzantine Empire, the rivalry of the Arab parties was always keen and often bitter. These party rivalries were frequently family affairs, and each group went by a variety of names depending upon what particular family was dominant at any given time and place. One main division was called the South Arabian party. Its members argued that the disintegration of economic and political life in the region of Yemen—perhaps capped by the breaking of the Marib Dam—had forced them to migrate northward and settle on the confines of the desert east of the Jordan and the Dead Sea. Claiming common descent from Kahtan (Joktan of the Book of Genesis), they affected a culture superior to others. The other party, North Arabians, had been nomadic in character and believed that its families came from the central and northern areas of Arabia. Calling their common ancestor Adnan, the North Arabians were clearly the Ishmaelites of the Bible.

Between the two parties any differences of language, culture, and physiognomy had long since disappeared; only legend and rivalry remained to perpetuate the factions. Nevertheless, the feuding between the two was very real, as is attested by the oft-repeated incident of the two-year war in Damascus that was touched off just because a member of one party stole a watermelon from a garden belonging to a member of the other party.

Beginning with Abd al-Malik until the downfall of the Umayyads, differences between the two parties became fixed upon two central issues, one political and one social. The first was the question of military campaigns of expansion. The South Arabians, or Yemenis as they were then termed, were opposed to these campaigns, and when Sulayman, a Yemeni sympathizer, became caliph in 715, he tolerated only expeditions that would consolidate frontiers. His attack on Constantinople was necessitated by Byzantine problems on the northern frontier; his withdrawal in the east and his humbling of Musa were examples more indicative of his policy. Umar II, a staunch supporter of this nonexpansionist view, stopped every campaign in 717 when he became caliph. His successors, however, were all expansionist North Arabians, or Qaysites as they called themselves, and al-Hajjaj lieutenants were reappointed to high positions. They believed that the social and economic ills of the empire, such as pressures for equality, taxation, fiscal policies of stipends for all Arabs, and civil disturbances caused by some Arabs' refusing to go on campaigns, could be met by expansion on the frontiers, which would occupy the soldiers and avert civil wars, at the same time bringing in booty for soldier and imperial treasury alike.

The social problem was over assimilation—the granting of full civil rights to non-Arab Muslims. Yemenis believed that Islam recognized equality between Arab, Iranian, Berber, Egyptian, and all Muslims, and that the caliph should lead the state and society to this end. The Qaysite view, on the other hand, held that Arabs formed a special elite. In general, Yemenis, as exemplified by Sulayman and Umar II, felt that successful rule could be effected only by the consent and cooperation of those ruled. Qaysites relied upon authority, force, and favoritism to maintain order and peace. (In spite of their views concerning equal rights, the Yemenis excluded non-Arabs from their leadership, as did, of course, the Qaysites. For example, Abd al-Malik raised thirteen sons, but only the six born of Arab mothers could be considered as possible successors; even the capable Maslamah was ineligible because his mother was non-Arab.)

Under Muawiyah rebellious forces among Muslims never had an opportunity to show their colors. However, upon the death of Ali's son Hasan, who had relinquished his caliphate in Kufah to make way for Muawiyah, Hasan's brother Husayn became the head of the house of Ali. He remained at peace with the Umayyads until Muawiyah's death, then, refusing to recognize Yazid as successor and caliph, he and others from the families of Muhammad's early Companions rebelled openly. Husayn set out for Kufah with a meager force and at Karbala was surrounded and cut down by Umayyad supporters on the tenth of Muharram, A.H. 61 (October 10, 680). Although at the time it caused hardly a ripple across the Muslim body politic, his death was later celebrated by the Shiite sect of Muslims, which came to regard Husayn and his brother Hasan as martyrs for the faith. Karbala has become a most holy spot, and frequently a kind of passion play is enacted on the tenth of Muharram.

Husayn's martyrdom left the opposition to the Umayyads in a very weakened position. When Medina, the center of remaining opposition, surrendered to Yazid's army, the rebels sought the protection of the supposed inviolability of the Holy City but were pursued by the Syrian forces. In the midst of siege operations, which shattered the Kaaba and broke the mysterious Black Stone, news of Yazid's death led the Syrian army to withdraw. The North Arabian party in Mecca thereupon openly supported a certain Ibn al-Zubayr, who was recognized as caliph throughout Arabia, Iraq, Egypt, al-Jazirah, and even in parts of Syria. Had he been willing to transfer his residence to Damascus, it is possible that all Muslims would have accepted his rule. Instead, Ibn al-Zubayr's followers were defeated by the South Arabians on the field of Marj Rahit in Syria and Marwan, Muawiyah's cousin and formerly executive secretary to Caliph Uthman, took power. Nine months later Marwan was dead, and the task of reuniting the state fell to his son Abd al-Malik. In 692, eight years later, a Syrian army led by al-Hajjaj defeated Ibn al-Zubayr after a six-month siege of Mecca and thus ended the second Muslim civil war.

This violent struggle of the Umayyads with Husayn and Ibn al-Zubayr was more than a personal or dynastic struggle; it was even more than a bitter outbreak of political party rivalry. In the first instance, the lesser families and clans of the Kuraysh of Mecca still resented and begrudged the power and dominance that the Umayyad clan had possessed in the decades just prior to the Hijrah. Added to this jealousy was indignation over the fact that Umayyads had opposed Muhammad almost to the very end; in fact, Muawiyah's father had driven Muhammad and the Muslims from Mecca. That Abu Sufyan's sons and family should inherit Muhammad's mantle was more than the Prophet's Companions could stomach.

More serious in the long run was the moving of the center of the state to Syria. It was inevitable that the wealth and worldliness of that Roman province would effect a marked transformation of the simple Arab life. Visitors from Arabia were shocked at the elegance and pomp of the Damascus court and were scandalized by the flow of wine, the singing girls, and the devotion to the chase exhibited there. All these seemed far removed from the teachings of Muhammad. As the wealth and power of the ruling society increased, idleness, pleasure seeking, and disregard for Muslim virtues multiplied. It was often told, for example, that Caliph Yazid drank wine daily and had a pet monkey which would become drunk along with him. Caliph al-Walid drank only every other day, whereas Hisham drank wine only on Fridays. The prize went to al-Walid II who enjoyed swimming in a pool of wine, drinking as he swam.

Such antics and the neglect of strict Muslim precepts fanned the propaganda fires of all malcontents of Islam. Shiite and Kharijite parties flourished in Iraq, Iran, and Khurasan. Iraq took umbrage over Syrian rule. In a sense it revived the old enmity between East and West exemplified in the wars of the Sasanid and Byzantine empires. Shiites, who held the view that the mantle of the Prophet rightfully belonged to the family of Muhammad and Ali and objected to the idea that might makes right, formed the nucleus of the opposition. At this time they were joined by the Kharijites, Muslim anarchists, who objected to all authority and maintained that a council of state rather than any caliph should rule over Muslims.

The third subversive party was that of the Abbasids, led first by Muhammad, a great-grandson of al-Abbas, who in turn was an uncle of the Prophet. This Muhammad circulated the story that one of Ali's grandsons on his deathbed had transferred the rights of the Alids (followers of Ali) to the Abbasid family. Beginning about the year 740, Abbasids posed as the leaders of the House of Hashim—Alid as well as Abbasid—and from their headquarters south of the Dead Sea gathered under their standard all anti-Umayyads of Islam. The Umayyads should have seen the handwriting on the wall when many Arabs in Syria, finding life too comfortable, refused to answer the call to arms, forcing Marwan II to depend upon Qaysite forces from al-Jazirah.

The most valuable support to Alids and Abbasids came from Arab and non-Arab Muslims of Iran and Khurasan, who in a restored national vigor objected to an inferior position, demanded the equality preached in Islam, and rebelled against Marwanid policies of expansion and authoritarian rule. The organizational structure of the Umayyad Empire was decaying rapidly. An atmosphere of petty, vicious, and sometimes murderous rivalry surrounded the court; and in every corner of the empire there was strife between the two Arab parties. Such violent partisanship, coupled with the Sybarite life of many Arab leaders, invited rebellion everywhere and played into the hands of non-Arab Muslims. The Abbasids utilized these factors to the full in their propaganda in the east and gathered Iranians, Khurasanians, Shiites, Alids, and all the malcontents around their banner, for which they chose the Prophet's color of black. The Umayyad's and Alid's banners were white; that of the Kharijites, red.

In June 747 Abu al-Abbas, a great-great-grandson of al-Abbas, raised the standard of revolt, and under his Iranian agent a band of Iranians, Khurasanians, and South Arabians took the city of Marw. Iraq fell in 749, and Abu al-Abbas was recognized in Kufah as caliph. Marwan II met the rival force early in 750 on the bank of the Zab, a tributary of the Tigris. The great Abbasid victory there opened all Syria, and Damascus surrendered in April 750. At an infamous banquet near Jaffa some eighty Umayyads were murdered; other members of the family were hunted from one end of the empire to the other in an Abbasid attempt to extirpate the entire Umayyad tribe. Among the few who escaped was Hisham's grandson, Abd al-Rahman, who made his way to Spain and established the great Umayyad caliphate of Cordoba.

Abu al-Abbas moved the capital of Islam from Damascus to Kufah, establishing Iraq as the center of the Abbasid empire. The East had been triumphant over the West.

REFERENCES: Chapter 6

Volumes cited at the end of Chapter 4 are pertinent to this chapter.

Coulson, N. J. *Succession in the Muslim Family.* London: Cambridge University Press, 1971. A detailed study of the Islamic law of inheritance, in both classical and present times.

Dennett, D. C. *Conversion and the Poll Tax in Early Islam.* Cambridge, Mass.: Harvard University Press, 1950. This volume deals with one of the most vexatious problems of the Umayyads.

Fahmy, Aly Mohamed. *Muslim Naval Organisation in the Eastern Mediterranean from the Seventh to the Tenth Century A.D.* 2d ed. Cairo: National Publication and Printing House, 1966. A detailed study of the naval centers in Egypt, Syria, Crete, and Africa with a chapter on shipbuilding materials. Contains a thorough discussion of organization of navies, including expenditures, taxes, recruitment of sailors, and a full description of all types of ships.

Gibb, H. A. R. *The Arab Conquests in Central Asia.* London: Royal Asiatic Society, 1923. Readable and based on original sources.

Glubb, John B. *The Great Arab Conquests.* Englewood Cliffs, N.J.: Prentice-Hall, 1964. A military history by an English general with long experience in the Middle East, especially in Jordan.

von Grunebaum, Gustave E. *Medieval Islam: A Study in Cultural Orientation.* Chicago: University of Chicago Press, 1946.

Lane-Poole, Stanley. *A History of Egypt in the Middle Ages (600–1500).* London: Methuen, 1901. Still useful and authoritative.

————. *The Mohammedan Dynasties.* London: Constable, 1894. A standard work which gives a brief account of each ruling family and lists the members and the date of their lives.

Shaban, M. A. *The 'Abbasid Revolution.* Cambridge, Eng.: Cambridge University Press, 1970. The volume is a detailed account of the Arab conquest of Iran and Khurasan from the time of Uthman to the Abbasid victory. It shows a fine picture of Arab society in Khurasan and highlights the importance of assimilation between Arabs and Iranians.

Watt, W. Montgomery. *The Formative Period of Islamic Thought.* Edinburgh: Edinburgh University Press, 1973. A detailed study of Islamic ideas from the death of Muhammad to the year 945 and the triumph of Sunni thought and practice. This important work closely relates the effect of this development of ideas and beliefs upon the political events.

Chapter 7

The Flowering of the Muslim World Under the Abbasids

The destruction of the Umayyads marked the opening of a new era in Muslim development. With the establishment of the Abbasid family in the caliphate the center of Islam shifted eastward to the Tigris-Euphrates valley. Since Arabia proper had become less significant in power and wealth, Damascus with its interior lines of communication and transport no longer held an advantage as the capital of such an empire. Iraq was more productive than Syria or Egypt and profited from extensive trade with India, China, the Indies, and central Asia, whereas commerce languished in the Mediterranean and Europe. The markets of India and China were fabulous and their industry was varied; the decaying economy of the West, except for Spain and Constantinople, was yielding rapidly to the demands of a self-subsistent agricultural life.

As has been pointed out, the Abbasids had shrewdly capitalized on the many grievances that various factions held against the Umayyads and, in an adroit propaganda campaign throughout Islam, had posed as the champion of each disgruntled group. However, hardly was Abu al-Abbas, the first of the line, seated on the throne than he openly showed the insincerity of Abbasid promises. Though he surrounded himself with theologians and pretended to take their advice, positions of authority and power were filled by Abbasids or by trusted family agents. A new governmental official, the chief executioner, always stood near the caliph's throne. Alids were ignored; Kharijites, who had generally opposed the Umayyads, received little consideration; viceroys, generals, and ministers who became too wealthy or too popular were executed. Abbasid rulers governed more imperiously than their predecessors, and beheadings were the order of the day. Indeed, so many Umayyad governors and leaders who had engineered the Abbasid revolution were liquidated in the first years of the new regime that later scholars, to follow the Alid practice of giving honorific or regnal titles to the caliphs, assigned to Abu al-Abbas the name al-Saffah ("the bloodletter").

It was at the end of Abu al-Abbas's reign, however, that the true installation of the new empire occurred with the ascension to the caliphate in 754 of Abu al-Abbas's brother Abu Jafar. This ancestor of the next thirty-five caliphs took the sobriquet al-Mansur (meaning "rendered victorious") setting the precedent of honorific titles or surnames for Abbasid rulers.

Like many of the Abbasids that followed, al-Mansur pursued and destroyed rival caliphs from the Alid, or Shiite, party. On one occasion, when his troops had gone to Medina to disperse disloyal Shiites, al-Mansur discovered that his personal safety was in question, especially since his residence lay so close to hostile Kufah. The danger led him to build a new capital at the village of Baghdad, where a personal bodyguard of several thousand was on hand at all times. This new circular fortress-palace of al-Mansur grew within a few decades into the fabled luxury-filled city of Baghdad, which has thrilled the imagination of peoples from the Atlantic to the Pacific.

Again like many of the Abbasids that followed, al-Mansur had to face a struggle that eventually sapped the strength and effectiveness of the Abbasid government: the question of succession to the throne. To obtain the recognition for his son al-Mahdi, al-Mansur gave prodigious bribes to his cousin, who had been named to the line of succession by al-Saffah. Nonetheless, al-Mahdi's elder son and designated heir, Musa al-Hadi, was almost passed over by the generals and court ministers in favor of his more popular younger brother, Harun al-Rashid. The court intrigues involving the accession of later caliphs grew more direct and perfidious as time passed. By the close of the ninth century the question of the succession overshadowed every act of the caliph and dominated the thoughts of the court. By the tenth century caliphs were removed, blinded, and turned out into the streets to beg.

Succession to the caliphate and the rivalry between the Abbasids and the Alids were not, of course, the only internal struggles of the Abbasid government. Simultaneously, issues concerning theology and jurisprudence (which will be examined in the following chapter) added fuel to the political fires, while differences in governmental philosophy complicated the political jockeying at the Abbasid court almost from the beginning until the rule of al-Mamun and his immediate successors. The religious scholars preached that the life of state and society should be based on the Koran and the normal practice of traditional Arab society; whereas the other main contestants for the caliph's ear, the civil secretaries and governing officials, looked for a political structure tending toward absolutism so that their decisions would be enforced. The latter group desired the "guidance of an inspired or charismatic leader"; the former sought security in the "collective wisdom of a charismatic community." Caliph al-Mamun looked in vain for a compromise between these two factions.

The Glory of Baghdad
During the great first century of the Abbasid caliphs Baghdad was the hub of the universe. Officially named Madinat al-Salam (the "City of Peace"), Baghdad was a circular garrison fortress, situated on the west bank of the Tigris near a canal connecting with the Euphrates. The central area had a mosque and a green-domed palace with an audience hall 130 feet in height and was surrounded by a wall, a deep moat, and two thick outer brick walls.

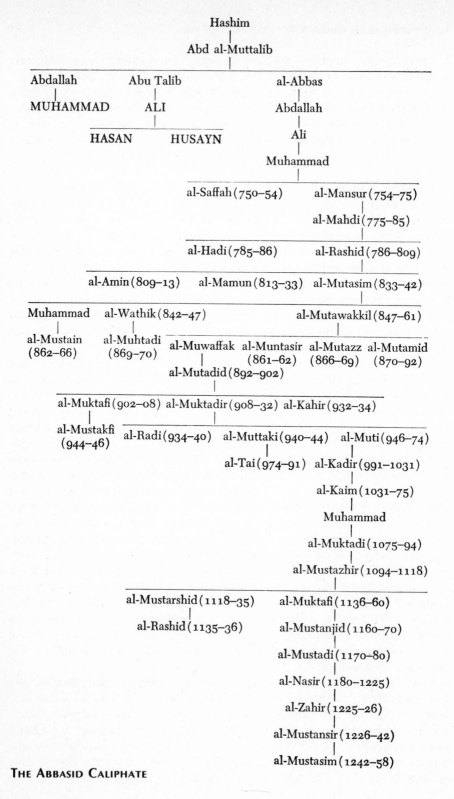

Hashim
|
Abd al-Muttalib

Abdallah   Abu Talib   al-Abbas
| | |
MUHAMMAD   ALI   Abdallah
|
HASAN   HUSAYN   Ali
|
Muhammad
|

al-Saffah(750–54)   al-Mansur(754–75)

al-Mahdi(775–85)

al-Hadi(785–86)   al-Rashid(786–809)

al-Amin(809–13)   al-Mamun(813–33)   al-Mutasim(833–42)

Muhammad   al-Wathik(842–47)   al-Mutawakkil(847–61)

al-Mustain   al-Muhtadi   al-Muwaffak al-Muntasir al-Mutazz al-Mutamid
(862–66)   (869–70) | (861–62) (866–69) (870–92)
                       al-Mutadid(892–902)

al-Muktafi(902–08) al-Muktadir(908–32) al-Kahir(932–34)

al-Mustakfi   al-Radi(934–40) al-Muttaki(940–44) al-Muti(946–74)
(944–46)

al-Tai(974–91) al-Kadir(991–1031)

al-Kaim(1031–75)

Muhammad

al-Muktadi(1075–94)

al-Mustazhir(1094–1118)

al-Mustarshid(1118–35)   al-Muktafi(1136–60)

al-Rashid(1135–36)   al-Mustanjid(1160–70)

al-Mustadi(1170–80)

al-Nasir(1180–1225)

al-Zahir(1225–26)

al-Mustansir(1226–42)

al-Mustasim(1242–58)

THE ABBASID CALIPHATE

Numerous other luxurious palaces for princes and ministers of state were erected, and beyond these rose the busy metropolis of the Muslim world.

The setting of the Abbasids in the lavish fortress capital of Baghdad ensured that their rule would follow the pattern of the Persian and Oriental monarchies of earlier days. In comparison to the unabashed prodigality of royal life in Baghdad and to the difficulty an ordinary Arab had in approaching the caliph, the rule of the Umayyads seemed the essence of frugality and simplicity.

The wealth and magnificence of the court of al-Rashid were world renowned in his own day, and through the tales of *The Arabian Nights* the splendors of his court and life in Baghdad have captured popular fancy in all ages. The center of display was, of course, the palace of the caliph, where Zubaydah, al-Rashid's favorite wife, held sway. She insisted that all dishes be made of gold and the tapestries be studded with precious gems. She outfitted several hundred of her most attractive maidservants as pageboys (a fashion that was soon all the rage in Baghdad), largely to amuse her son and to divert his affections from a favorite eunuch. At a festival celebrating the marriage of a prince, a thousand matched pearls were showered upon the couple as they sat upon a jewel-encrusted mat of gold.

In Baghdad, the wheel of fortune turned easily. This aspect of Abbasid rule was exemplified in the life of Khayzuran, al-Rashid's mother. Given as a slave to al-Mahdi, she became his favorite; and her sons were recognized at an early age as the heirs to the throne. Khayzuran had her family brought to court (perhaps from Yemen); her father was given a prominent position; and her sister married a prince whose daughter was the famous Zubaydah. Before Khayzuran died she held vast properties bringing in an annual income of more than 160 million dirhams. Her power at court was inestimable, and the preference of the generals and courtiers for al-Rashid over al-Hadi was stimulated considerably by her acknowledged favor for the former. (Although Khayzuran's fortunes seemed to have steadily improved, wealth, position, and favor in Baghdad were always precarious, as the sudden fall of many favorites and advisers attested.)

At the court any word or act of flattery, a song or poem that pleased, or a deed well done was rewarded handsomely: 60,000 dinars tossed to the singer of a pleasant tune with complimentary lines; 100,000 dirhams to a poet who beguiled at the right moment; a landed estate to an entertainer or a dancer! For a sonnet extolling al-Rashid on a trivial occasion a poet was given 5,000 gold pieces, a robe of honor, ten Greek slave girls, and a horse from the imperial stables.

From the four corners of the known world came royal embassies bearing gifts and seeking the caliph's favor. Most publicized of these, at least in the West, was the mission sent by Charlemagne in 797 to secure greater safety for Frankish pilgrims to the Holy Land and to get Abbasid aid against Umayyad Spain and the Byzantine Empire. No mention of this embassy has been found in Eastern sources, and there is little evidence that it ever accomplished any of its aims. Still, the trophies brought back from the journey, the most fantastic being an elephant, so magnified the incident for the West that Baghdad and Arabia became romantic, incredible, and fabulous places and Harun al-Rashid a person in some far-off never-never land.

Intellectual interests of the Abbasids, hand in hand with imperial munificence, produced a great cultural flowering. The learning of the Greco-Romans, the Iranians, and the Hindus was translated into Arabic and assimilated into Muslim culture. Arabic became the common language not only for theology and jurisprudence but for philosophy, science, and the humanities. History, political treatises, literature, poetry, and etiquette came largely from Iran; astronomy and mathematics, from India; philosophy, medicine, and science, from Greece. By the middle of the ninth century the main works of Aristotle, Plato, Euclid, Ptolemy, Hippocrates, and Galen had been translated into Arabic and were well known the length and breadth of the Islamic world. Royal patronage set the stage for translations and the expansion and dissemination of knowledge. Every prince, governor, and high official followed the same course and became, on a lesser scale, a patron of scholars.

Administrative Organization

The Khurasani soldiery was the power that had raised the Abbasids to the caliphate; and for several generations a Khurasan bodyguard maintained imperial authority in Baghdad and elsewhere. Eastern, or Iranian, influences grew apace at the court. After the building of Baghdad, Iranian dress, manners, and techniques spread quickly throughout the empire, especially in fashionable society. Foremost among the Iranian introductions was the rank and office of vizir *(wazir)*. The Umayyads had had advisers and ministers heading various departments of the government. Under the Abbasids, however, there arose the office of chief minister, the vizir, who became the alter ego of the caliph. The vizir's power was almost unlimited and the office was frequently handed down from father to son.

The first family of vizirs was the famous Barmakids of the second half of the eighth century. Khalid ibn Barmak, son of a Buddhist chief priest of Balkh, held the confidence of al-Saffah and al-Mansur. Although a Shiite in faith, Khalid served as minister of finance and then as governor, became a general, and acted as guardian of al-Rashid. Khalid amassed a great fortune; on one occasion he was forced to pay 3 million dirhams of taxes which as governor he had not forwarded to Baghdad. His son Yahya served al-Mahdi as vizir but fell into disfavor and was imprisoned by al-Hadi.

The apogee of Barmakid fortunes was reached under al-Rashid. Yahya became the first true grand vizir, issuing orders and managing the empire with great skill and profit. His sons al-Fadl and Jafar also exercised unlimited power. The son al-Fadl followed in his father's footsteps as governor and vizir, while Jafar became al-Rashid's boon companion and confidant. The Barmakids lived in a sumptuous manner, and their generosity to their own favorites and clients became proverbial throughout the Arabic-speaking world. Yahya, however, was distressed by Jafar's personal and intimate relationship with al-Rashid, fearing that it would bring disaster. The family was, after all, Iranian and Shiite and could not hope for social, political, or religious equality with the Abbasids. In 803, without warning, Jafar was beheaded, undoubtedly because he had used al-Rashid's friendship to impinge too far upon royal prerogatives; Yahya, al-Fadl, and two others were imprisoned; and the Barmakid fortune—palaces, lands, and some 30 million dinars in cash—was confiscated.

Other families of viziers rose and fell, and with them rival generals and armies. Under the Abbasids, generals were always a significant factor in obtaining the throne. Following al-Rashid's reign, intense rivalry arose between two of his offspring, the voluptuary al-Amin, son of the famed Zubaydah, and the more serious and steady al-Mamun, son of an Iranian slave girl. The latter had the better generals, and marching from his base in Marw with the full support of the Iranian army, he attacked Baghdad and beheaded his caliph brother. Although al-Mamun ruled illustriously for twenty years, generals henceforth decided the succession to the throne. The rulers al-Mamun and al-Mutasim, al-Rashid's son by a Turkish slave girl, brought Turkish slaves to Baghdad and Samarra (al-Mutasim's capital) in such numbers that the chief of the Turkish bodyguard became the actual ruler of the state and acquired the title *sultan* ("he-with-authority").

After the middle of the ninth century the Abbasid caliphs rapidly receded into the background as puppet rulers. Powerful captains in the eastern and western provinces seized authority and established independent Muslim states. The unity of Islam, which had already been cracked in the 750s by the establishment of the Umayyad state in Spain, was completely shattered with the advent of the ruling military bodyguard of the Abbasids.

Economic Life

The bases of Abbasid wealth rested upon agriculture and a century of relatively capable, honest, and stable administration of the provinces. Caliph al-Mansur established such a vigilant and judicious system of government throughout the empire and enforced such thrift that it took more than a century of profligate largesse to dislocate the economy of the state. In Iraq the ancient canal system was operated so efficiently and extended to such a degree that productivity rose to a peak never matched in any period of its long history. In that same century imperial revenues from Egypt, Syria, and Iran showered great wealth upon the ruling circles and the inhabitants of the capital cities.

As a natural corollary to this organized agriculture and governmental stability, a flourishing commerce and, for that age, an advanced technical industry arose. The great preponderance of Islamic commerce was in the nature of "domestic" trade. Caravans plied the trade routes from the Indus to the Pyrenees, distributing the wares of each province throughout the empire and exchanging manufactures of Iran for those of Egypt, carpets of Tabaristan for paper of Baghdad. Handsome profits were realized, but great fortunes were as easily lost.

The bulk of Muslim "foreign" trade was with the Far East. From Baghdad and Basrah, Muslim merchants carried their goods by sea to China, India, and the Archipelago, but the main route to China lay overland through Samarkand. Trade with Italy, France, and Germany, or with Constantinople, Russia, and Scandinavia, was undoubtedly profitable. It seemed so trivial, however, that Muslim traders left it for the most part to Christian and Jewish itinerants. Goods from the Middle East were too expensive and too refined for barbarous Western tastes, and the West had little to offer in exchange.

Concurrent with the rich agriculture and brisk commerce of the Abbasid empire, there developed an active industry in every province. Artisan traditions of the ancient Middle East had never perished, and under a relatively secure political system these industries revived and expanded. Textiles of linen, cotton, silk, and wool were the most important. Although each area produced high-quality fabrics of many types, every city or province excelled in some particular pattern or technique; carpets from Bukhara, silk kerchiefs from Kufah, linens from Egypt, damask from Damascus, and brocades from Shiraz gained world renown. Special skills were often localized, and families guarded trade secrets, which were passed on as prized possessions from father to son through the centuries.

The science of paper making was acquired from China, and by the tenth century, paper mills existed in Iran, Iraq, and Egypt. In the twelfth century one was built in Spain. Fine glass was produced in Egypt, and the glass industry of old Phoenicia still survived along the Syrian coast. The ceramic industry in the Middle East reached back into the most distant past, and the Abbasid era created some of the finest potteries and glazed tile. Samarkand, Rayy, Baghdad, and Damascus won fame for their decorated porcelains and their fine blues, greens, and turquoise shades. Middle Eastern artisans were equally skilled in the shaping, working, and hammering of metals: iron, steel, copper, brass, silver, and gold. Other industries of great note manufactured fine soaps, dyes, perfume, jewelry, leather, inlaid and decorated wood, and enamelwork on wood and metal.

The Middle East in the eighth and ninth centuries utilized many of the arts and techniques of handicraft of China, India, Iran, and the East Roman Empire, and those of the early civilizations of Greece, Egypt, and Mesopotamia. The synthesis of these gave great life to Muslim industry, which was regarded in Europe as the marvel of the ages. The slow movement of Middle Eastern know-how across the Mediterranean and over the Pyrenees gave rise to the development of similar handicrafts in Europe.

The Abbasid championing of non-Arab elements within the Muslim Empire promoted a rapid Arabization of the empire. Iranians, Berbers, Syrian Christians, Copts, and others began to speak Arabic in their daily living. Science, philosophy, literature, and books of knowledge from other cultures and tongues were rendered into Arabic. And an Arab civilization evolved in which poets, scholars, musicians, merchants, soldiers, viziers, and concubines considered themselves cultural Arabs and little heed was given to parentage or birthplace.

Although Arab civilization came to prevail in the Abbasid era from the borders of China to the Pyrenees, there was never more than a fleeting political unity. The theological views of the followers of Ali were never modified, and as time passed, more and more religious sects arose to battle against authority. Social and economic ills disturbed the empire periodically. Ambitious and not too loyal soldiers sought to carve out their own principalities. Centered upon a land area, communications and transportation over most of the empire were costly, slow, and tedious. Distant provinces were difficult to control; and, as caliphs grew less and less concerned with the grueling task of governing, even nearer provinces flaunted the wishes of the Abbasid rulers. When Abbasid caliphs degenerated into mere puppets in the hands of generals of the bodyguard, governors and soldiers in the provinces readily declared their independence.

Local rulers, however, followed the common patterns of Abbasid government and administration, and Muslim-Arab civilization continued to prevail. Political loyalties might differ as more often than not religious doctrines did; but artists, men of letters, scientists, merchants, and travelers were as much at home in Cordoba as in Cairo, Baghdad, or Samarkand. Provincial governors, even those who were not independent, imitated as sumptuously as they could the court at Baghdad. From India to Spain were built artistic palaces and impressive mosques where petty princes lived in the grand manner among poets, scholars, artists, soldiers, dancing slaves, and fawning courtiers.

Spain and North Africa

Abd al-Rahman, grandson of Caliph Hisham, escaped from Abbasid vengeance, and, making his way in disguise through Syria, Egypt, and North Africa, reestablished the Umayyad dynasty in Spain in 756. First as amirs and then in the tenth century as caliphs the rulers maintained at Cordoba a court that enjoyed an eminence that rivaled its contemporary in Baghdad. Many distinguished scholars, scientists, and literati of the Muslim world flourished under their patronage. At its zenith in the tenth century, Cordoba had 500,000 inhabitants, 700 mosques, 300 public baths, and a royal palace comprising 400 rooms which ranked second only to those at Baghdad and Constantinople in size and splendor.

Umayyad power, however, commenced to deteriorate toward the middle of the tenth century. As with the Abbasids in Baghdad, the palace guard seized control; and Muslim Spain disintegrated into smaller states (Seville, Málaga, Toledo, Saragossa, and Granada) under the leadership of various families. In the eleventh century resurgent Christian Spain began a drive that ended in 1492 with the capitulation of the sultan of Granada, the last Muslim ruler in Spain. Though Muslim law and government were terminated, the deportation of the Spanish Muslims (Morescos) was not enforced until a special edict was issued in 1609 by Philip III.

In 788 Idris ibn Abdallah, a descendant of Ali, established an independent Shiite regime in Morocco. From their capital at Fez the Idrisids ruled Morocco for two centuries, firmly implanting Islam in that corner of Africa before succumbing to the Umayyads of Cordoba. In the middle of the eleventh century a religious military brotherhood, the Murabits (Almoravides), swept out from an island in the Senegal, conquering Algeria, Morocco, and southern Spain and establishing Marrakesh and Seville as their capitals. But the luxuries, vices, and complexities of civilization prepared the way for the submission of the Murabits in the twelfth century to the Muwahhids (Almohades), a band of Muslim reformers originating in the Atlas region of Morocco. The Muwahhids toppled Spain too, and within a decade overpowered Algeria, Tunisia, and Tripoli. Then they were driven from Spain in 1212. A half century later their capital, Marrakesh, was taken by Berber tribes, and they disappeared from the scene.

Harun al-Rashid appointed Ibrahim ibn al-Aghlab governor of Africa in 800. The latter, however, declared his independence, and for a century the Aghlabids ruled as free amirs from Kayrawan in Tunisia. Their fleets ravaged the coasts of Italy and France, seizing Malta, Sicily, and Sardinia. The great mosque of Kayrawan was built by the Aghlabids and soon became for western Muslims a venerated shrine, next in importance and holiness to Mecca, Medina, and Jerusalem. But in 909 the Aghlabids were engulfed by a Shiite uprising which placed on the throne one who claimed to be a descendant of Fatimah, the Prophet's daughter.

Meanwhile, beginning with the middle of the ninth century, a succession of clever governors and two short-lived Turkish dynasties, Tulunids and Ikhshidids, ruled Egypt independent of Abbasid dominion. In the second half of the tenth century Egypt was conquered by the Fatimids of North Africa, who took the title of caliph and transferred their capital from Kayrawan to the newly constructed city of Cairo.

Under the Tulunids and Ikhshidids and to a greater extent under the Fatimids the Egyptian court and its society experienced a prosperity and a great burst of accomplishment in commerce, art, letters, and learning. No longer did even a part of the produce or taxes of Egypt flow to Baghdad. Though Shiite in faith, Fatimid Egypt participated greatly in the artistic and intellectual endeavors of the Muslim world; many great works of early medieval Muslim art and architecture still extant in Egypt date from the Tulunid and Fatimid periods.

The Tulunids had added Syria to their realm and established a naval base at Acre, and the Ikhshidids had acquired the Hijaz and Yemen. Thus, at their height about the year 1000 the Fatimids ruled all of the western Muslim world except Spain: the Fatimid caliph's name was mentioned in the Friday prayers from the Atlantic to the Euphrates. However, because of idle rulers and foreign slave armies the Fatimid empire began to break up early in the eleventh century. To a considerable degree it was this disintegration which permitted the handfuls of Western knights called Crusaders to penetrate, capture, and hold the Christian Holy Land and the Syrian littoral in the twelfth and thirteenth centuries.

The Eastern Provinces

East of Baghdad the Abbasid empire was likewise succumbing to the laxity of the caliph's rule and falling into the hands of aggressive soldiers and politicians who founded ephemeral dynasties. In the ninth century the Tahirids and Saffarids extended their sway from Marw to the frontiers of India. In the tenth century the Samanids seized all of Khurasan, but settled in Transoxiana, establishing Bukhara as their capital and Samarkand as the leading city of the state. Culture continued to flourish under Samanid rule, and the new forces were quickly assimilated, as illustrated by the Samanid ruler who invited the young Ibn Sina (Avicenna) to Bukhara and gave him free run of the state library. Under the Samanids, Firdawsi wrote his first poetry, marking the rebirth of Persian literature. From the Muslim conquest to the Samanid period, Arabic had been the language used everywhere by scholars and men of letters; this new era signaled the advent of the brilliant works of Muslim Iran.

From the bodyguard of the Samanids a Turkish slave, Alptigin, rose through the ranks to govern Khurasan. Fleeing from the Samanid domain, he captured Ghaznah and established the famed Ghaznawid empire of Afghanistan and the Punjab. The most eminent of the family was Alptigin's grandson Mahmud, who led nearly a score of expeditions into India and in the eleventh century laid the foundations of the permanent Islamization of north and northwest India. Loot from Hindu temples gave him the material strength to destroy the Samanids and extend his state to include most of the eastern provinces of the Muslim world. Although a vestige of the Ghaznawid empire remained at Lahore until 1186, decline followed rapidly upon the death of Mahmud in 1030. Muslim independent states in India broke away, and Buwayhid Iranians and Seljuk Turks appeared in western areas of the Ghaznawid empire.

In Baghdad itself the authority of the Abbasid caliph vanished almost completely. Only the appellation remained. Turkish captains of the bodyguard deposed caliphs at will; at one time three blind ex-caliphs were beggars on the streets of Baghdad. Taking the title *amir al-umara* (literally, "commander of commanders," but better, "prince of princes"), the de facto ruler imprinted his name on coins and insisted that his name be coupled with the puppet caliph in the Friday prayers.

Toward the middle of the tenth century a Shiite Iranian, Ibn Buwayh, entered Baghdad with a strong army and was recognized by the caliph as the commander of commanders. Making and unmaking caliphs openly, the Buwayhids of Shiraz took various titles such as king *(malik)* or king of kings *(malik al-muluk* or *shahanshah)* and ruled over what remained of the Abbasid state. They beautified their city and brought to it many learned men. For a century Shiraz rivaled Baghdad, Ghaznah, Bukhara, Cairo, and

Cordoba in culture and splendor. But in the eleventh century Buwayhid fought against Buwayhid for the position of king and in the end fell easy prey to the Turks riding in from the east.

The Turks

Turkish nomads from the Kirghiz steppes of Turkestan wandered into the Transoxiana region and became partially settled there toward the middle of the tenth century. Their chieftain, or khan, under the Samanids was Seljuk. For three centuries his dynasty played such an outstanding role in the Muslim world from Syria eastward and so dominated the Turkish elements of society that even today Muslim Turks of that age bear the name of Seljuk Turks.

The true founder of the dynasty, Seljuk's grandson Tughril, ascended to power rapidly in Khurasan. Defeating the Ghaznawids and ejecting the Buwayhids from Iran, Tughril entered Baghdad with an army in 1055; he was recognized King of the East and the West and *al-Sultan*. Henceforth, Seljuk rulers adopted "sultan" as their official title.

Tughril's nephew Alparslan followed as sultan and succeeded in gathering within his domain the vast lands of the Muslim world from the frontiers of China to the Mediterranean. Having expanded into Armenia and taken the Byzantine emperor prisoner in the decisive Battle of Manzikert in 1071, Alparslan opened Asia Minor to his Turkish nomads. His horsemen camped on the shores of the Sea of Marmara and lay astride the commercial and pilgrim routes of Asia Minor. His son Malikshah pushed westward and southward, taking Damascus and Jerusalem and threatening Fatimid Egypt. When he made Baghdad his capital, the old imperial city of the Abbasids became once again the hub of the eastern Muslim universe and recaptured much of its abandoned glory.

The political genius through the reigns of Alparslan and Malikshah was Nizam al-Mulk, their principal vizir. A cultured and versatile Iranian, Nizam al-Mulk founded the renowned Nizamiyah, an academy in Baghdad, and wrote the *Siyasatnamah,* a scholarly monograph on the science of government. Nizam also revised the calendar and is perhaps best known in the Western world as the patron of the Persian astronomer-poet Umar Khayyam.

Any semblance of unity among the Seljuks vanished in 1092 upon the death of Malikshah and the assassination of Nizam al-Mulk. In prior years there had been numerous civil wars among members of the family; upon the demise of these two leaders the breakup into petty Seljuk states was immediate. One son succeeded to the sultanate in Baghdad. A brother held Damascus and Aleppo, although these cities were soon seized by different sons. A cousin ruled Asia Minor from Konya; others possessed Jerusalem, Edessa, Mosul, Diyarbakir, and Amasya. Soon afterward the appearance of the Crusaders from the West disrupted Seljuk rule in Syria even further, though the main branch of the dynasty maintained its hold upon Baghdad until 1194.

The death of Malikshah and the collapse of the Seljuk state definitely heralded for medieval times the end of a Muslim political entity strong enough and sufficiently organized to dominate the Middle East. Under the rule of Malikshah a merchant could travel alone unmolested with his goods from Samarkand to Aleppo. But within a few years intraregional political anarchy and its disastrous social and economic chaos lured the Crusader eastward. Not until the appearance of the Turks from their strong base on the Bosphorus in the sixteenth century did the Middle East again experience a stable political existence.

REFERENCES: Chapter 7

Titles mentioned at the end of Chapters 2, 4, and 6 contain material significant for this chapter.

Abbott, Nabia. *Two Queens of Baghdad: Mother and Wife of Harun al-Rashid.* Chicago: University of Chicago Press, 1946. Not only does this volume detail the lives of Khayzuran and Zubaydah, but it is full of the color and life of Baghdad in the eighth and ninth centuries.

Arberry, A. J. *Shiraz: Persian City of Saints and Poets.* Norman, Okla.: University of Oklahoma Press, 1960. A colorful story of a city of artists and intellectuals.

Brown, L. Carl (ed.). *From Medina to Metropolis: Heritage and Change in the Near Eastern City.* Princeton, N.J.: Darwin Press, 1973. A collection of eleven essays on cities and their architectural planning, structure, and utility in the Middle East from medieval times to the present.

Fischel, Walter J. *Jews in the Economy and Political Life of Mediaeval Islam.* New York: Ktav, 1969. The role of some Jews as important figures at Abbasid, Fatimid, and Ilkhan courts, as well as many persecutions and oppressions.

Frye, Richard N. *Bukhara: The Medieval Achievement.* Norman, Okla.: University of Oklahoma Press, 1965. An authoritative account of one of the great cities of central Asia.

Goitein, S. D. *A Mediterranean Society: The Jewish Communities of the Arab World in the Documents of the Cairo Geniza.* Vol. 1. *Economic Foundations.* Berkeley: University of California Press, 1967. The first of three monumental volumes to study the life and works of Jews in the Arab world during the Middle Ages.

Hodgson, Marshall G. S. *The Venture of Islam: Conscience and History in a World Civilization.* Vol. 2. *The Expansion of Islam in the Middle Periods.* Chicago: University of Chicago Press, 1974. The author discusses the establishment of an international Islamic civilization, showing the widening social and economic implications of the Islamic world, its intellectual traditions, Sufism, Persian literary culture, the visual arts, and the coming of the Mongols.

Lane, Edward William. *Arabian Society in the Middle Ages: Studies from the Thousand and One Nights.* London: Chatto and Windus, 1883. Although an old book, it contains much of value for this period.

Lapides, Ira (ed.). *Middle Eastern Cities: A Symposium on Ancient, Islamic, and Contemporary Middle Eastern Urbanism.* Berkeley: University of California Press, 1969. Seven important papers by leading authorities.

Le Strange, Guy. *Baghdad During the Abbasid Caliphate.* London: Oxford University Press, 1924. An interesting description of the great city at its height.

Philby, H. St. John B. *Harun al-Rashid.* London: Appleton-Century-Crofts, 1934. An important biography by a British Orientalist who became a convert to Islam and served as an adviser at the court of the kings of Saudi Arabia.

Richards, D. S. (ed.). *Islam and the Trade of Asia.* Philadelphia: University of Pennsylvania Press, 1970. Contains fifteen papers presented at Oxford in 1967 by well-known scholars such as Charles Issawi, G. F. Hudson, and Maxime Rodinson.

Sykes, Percy M. *A History of Persia.* 2 vols. London: Macmillan, 1930. A standard volume for the medieval period of Iran.

Udovitch, Abraham L. *Partnership and Profit in Medieval Islam.* Princeton, N.J.: Princeton University Press, 1970. A study of Muslim commercial arrangements for the early medieval period.

Chapter 8

Muslim Theology and Law

Theology

The uncomplicated, direct, and ethical religion preached by Muhammad appealed to the untutored Arab of Mecca and Medina and to the unlettered nomad of the desert. In general, it was easily adjusted to the needs of the theocratic state under Muhammad and the Companions who immediately followed him at Medina.

Upon the spread of Islam and Muslim rule beyond Arabia and the establishment of regimes based on military power, Muhammad's theocracy faced unforeseen conditions. Succeeding generations of Muslims were exposed to the intellectualized philosophies current in the acquired provinces and developed a finely drawn Islamic theology.

Though the political capital of Islam was transferred to Damascus and then to Baghdad, Medina maintained its ascendancy as a center of Muslim theology for several centuries. Opinions not subscribed to by the doctors of Medina were declared to be in serious error. Divergent views led to the formation of groups branded as heretical by the Medinan theologians.

At the time of the disputation between Ali and Muawiyah the Kharijites broke away, rejecting the concept of compromise that Ali proposed. They believed that might does not make right and that only God can judge among people. They nevertheless professed their way of life to be the right way, and when they quoted the Koran, "be patient until God judges between us," they meant that the fight should be continued until God granted them victory. The Kharijites were against both Ali and Muawiyah and opposed the growing organized structure of society in which they were being enveloped. Coming from a nomadic background, they found settled life in large groups alien to their spirits. Shortly thereafter the Kharijites hardened into a sect that held that good works are the measure of faith and the only path to salvation. They also insisted upon pursuing openly and literally the commandment to preach to all persons a righteous life and to restrain them, by the sword if necessary, from doing evil.

Laxity of life in Damascus induced others to uphold belief in the adequacy of inherent faith in attaining personal salvation. In essence, these Murjites, as they were termed, were opposites of Kharijites, for they readily accepted rulers whose conduct was sinful. They held that faith is not impaired by sin, that persons, as long as they profess God's unity, should not be judged because of their sins (unless they worship idols), but should be accepted as believers. In the first two centuries of Islam the Murjites' concern was to preserve the unity of the Muslim community. Rebuked by Medina, they eased their ethics to political accommodation under the Umayyads and found their redemption in the doctrine of predestination. When the Abbasid revolution approached, Murjites supported the Umayyad claim to the caliphate, but once the Abbasids had won, they found no reason to oppose them.

In the formative period of Muslim theology those between these two extremes were known as Mutazilites. By the time of Harun al-Rashid, Mutazilites, accepting the doctrine of free will, were entangled in Aristotelian and Hellenistic Christian philosophies and engaged in adjusting Islam to Greek logic. Adhering to rationalism, free will, and philosophical theology in the ninth century, they lost acceptance when Muslim theology was pronounced in the tenth century by al-Ashari of Baghdad and fixed in the early twelfth century by al-Ghazzali (Algazel) of Khurasan.

A myriad of theological questions appeared, several arising over and over again. Foremost was the question of God's omnipotence in relation to human responsibility or, as it devolved to the religious plane, the problem of predestination and free will. The second great problem related to the nature of the Koran: Was it uncreated and eternal or was it created? The third troublesome subject centered upon the nature of God and His attributes. If God could hear, see, and speak, was not His unity in doubt?

Mutazilites held that if God rendered punishment for deeds that had been predetermined, He would be an unjust God, and that therefore the human being does have free will. They professed that the Koran had been created by God and that between God and His creation, the human being, there is no resemblance. On other points Mutazilites believed that God does not forgive the grave sinner except after repentance, and being just, He punishes all persons equally. They stood between Kharijites and Murjites with regard to the Umayyads and their sins, saying that judgment should not be rendered. On the question of one's duty to judge others, they asserted that one should command one's fellows to follow the right path. Wrongful actions should be forbidden—which meant that armed revolt against an unjust ruler was justified when there was a chance of success.

According to al-Ashari, the apparent contradiction embodied in the concepts of predestination and free will was explained by the doctrine that human beings are responsible for their actions but only because God has willed it. For al-Ashari the Koran was preexistent and eternal; the words or expressions were created and revealed by the angels to the Prophet only as guides to the eternal Word. The apparent contradiction between the unity of God and His other, more human attributes referred to in the Koran was explained by the dogma that God is One and Eternal, but that His existence is not the same as existence in the world. Thus, these attributes are real but divested of all anthropomorphism.

Many other points in theology were established by al-Ashari, including the dogma that right and wrong are what they are because God declared them to be so, and that God could inflict pain in this world or in the next without being unjust.

Even al-Ashari, however, was cursed by the religious men of Medina, because they considered his theology too rationalistic and too far removed from the Islam of Muhammad. Asharite scholastics remained unpopular in Baghdad until the advent of al-Ghazzali, whose writing and teaching united the modified Greek logic and philosophy of al-Ashari with Muhammad's religion to create a faith that has remained the basis of the mainstream of Islam to the present day.

The Science of Tradition
When the word of the Koran did not appear to give the answer to some specific problem, the divines of Medina and the pious throughout Islam looked for guidance in the words and actions of Muhammad or in those which he had allowed. Arab tribes were devoted to traditions and normal practice, and custom *(sunnah)* was a powerful force in their lives. In the new community established by Muhammad and severed from many tribal customs, the life of Muhammad served as the touchstone for proper Muslim thought and conduct.

Early in Muslim history great collections of the statements and deeds of Muhammad were made. Aishah was the source of several thousand; and Medina, where a great many Companions resided, became the center of the compilations. Each saying was called a hadith, or a tradition; and the whole body of these traditions was known as the hadith. When forgeries appeared, each hadith acquired an introduction giving its full pedigree of transmission. Scholars developed a science with respect to these traditions to establish which were authentic and which spurious. Each sect of Islam, each lawyer, and each theologian chose the most suitable traditions on which to base some contention or press a point.

The first written collections were instigated for judicial ends, and each city had its own. By the ninth century the collections and literature on the subject were growing so voluminous that the science of hadith evolved. The author al-Bukhari, who died in 870, published his collection under the title *al-Sahih ("The Genuine")*. Containing over 7,000, it was generally pronounced the most authoritative source of tradition. One of the largest collections was that of Ibn Hanbal, who assembled nearly 30,000 to form a corpus of tradition that served as the basis of his law code. Each major Muslim city or province eventually adopted as standard practice the collected traditions of one of the noted theologians.

Acceptance of a body of traditions in time established for Islam the Muhammad Sunnah, a new customary, or common, law. Attachment to these traditions by any Muslim community identified its members as following the Islamic Sunnah and thus gave them the name of Sunnites.

Muslim Law

Early Muslims, pious and devout, perceived hardly any difference between law and religion. Only God knew the perfect law, and coexisting with Him was natural law, comprising right and justice. Islam, then, was the ideal system, and its law pointed the "path" *(shariah)* to an individual's salvation; divine law recognized good and evil. Law preceded the state, which existed only to enforce the law. If the state failed to enforce the law, the state's validity ceased. The caliph as head of the state was charged principally with the enforcement of law. Divine law was inexorable and unchanging, allowing no consideration for time or place. Muslims living beyond the pale of Islam still were bound by the law. Law upheld the common good of the community and served individual interests only when these conformed to those of the Muslim community as a whole. Islamic law had to be observed in good faith and sincerity; duplicity and dissimulation were repudiated.

The Muslim system of law grew largely from two roots: the Koran and the traditions. Caliphs and their judges, even in Medina, discovered early, however, that the Koran and the traditions were not explicit with respect to many situations with which they had to deal. In the absence of a definite statement, judges and lawyers resorted to the use of analogy *(kiyas)* to some instance in the Koran or the traditions in deciding a case brought before them. Although the strictest judges did not practice analogy, on the grounds that it allowed too much to human judgment, it was, nevertheless, adopted widely in the eighth century as a legal aid, and from precedent to precedent became an integral part of the shariah. In the same century Malik ibn Anas, a jurist-theologian of Medina, compiled a book of traditions that incorporated many of the local juridical customs and practices. This procedure introduced the institution of public consensus *(ijma)*, which at first was reserved to Medina.

In the next generation al-Shafii drew together these several elements and expanded consensus to include the Muslim community at large. In thus establishing Sunni Islam, al-Shafii was instrumental in advancing the idea in law of following the "idealized practice as recognized by representative scholars." Questions of law were to be resolved ultimately through the four fundamental principles: the Koran; the traditions, or Sunnah; analogy; and consensus. Al-Shafii's general doctrine became widely accepted, with the modification of restricting consensus to that of scholars rather than to the whole community. The inclusion of consensus in the principles of the shariah established the classical Sunni theory of the roots of jurisprudence and enabled Islam through the centuries to adapt its institutions to a changing world.

Another additional source of Muslim law has been private opinion *(ray)*. Private opinion was never quite accepted as a fifth principle of the shariah, but it was widely practiced. Early caliphs employed it extensively until bitter complaints that human legislation corrupted divine law forced its abandonment. Nevertheless, most caliphs and later rulers were compelled by administrative necessity to issue laws and decrees that were sanctioned almost wholly by opinion. Such laws and regulations were later termed *Kanuns,* from the Greek and Latin word. Thus, Muslim canon law meant civil and secular law, whereas Islamic divine law was the equivalent of Western canon law.

Four Sunni Schools

The Sunni jurists accepted the five roots of the shariah but differed as to which traditions were genuine and as to the weight that ought to be allowed to analogy, consensus, and opinion in establishing a viable Muslim code of law. At the time of al-Mansur it was suggested that he codify and enforce the diverse laws in the empire. Local particularism, however, won the day, and numerous systems prevailed among the Muslims. Since the eleventh century four principal schools of legal practice have been recognized as permissible by the Sunnites, and law schools such as the al-Azhar in Cairo have carried instruction in all four rites.

In point of development the earliest school was the Hanafite. Abu-Hanifah, legal scholar of Kufah and Baghdad, held a tolerant view on the use of analogy and consensus and particularly emphasized the value and necessity of private opinion and judgment on the part of those administering the law. By the eleventh century, however, a strong conservative movement closed the door on further innovations in the matter of juridical opinions. Judges, henceforth, could allow only opinions previously rendered and were required to adhere closely to the Hanafite teachings. The Hanafite rite was the established procedure followed in the Ottoman Empire, parts of India, and central Asia.

Historically, the second orthodox school was the Malikite. Malik ibn Anas of Medina, who died in 795, codified the traditions of Islam and acknowledged the authority of the consensus of the Medina community. Malikite jurists, however, never equivocated in their stand against general consensus, private opinion, and the broad use of analogy. The Malikite school was accepted in Spain, and still prevails in North Africa and eastern Arabia.

Next to the Hanafite school in general acceptance has been that of the Shafiite. The jurist al-Shafi studied under Malik in Medina and taught in Baghdad and Fustat (Cairo), where he died in 820. The Shafiite rites permitted wider use of consensus than did those of the Malikites, and al-Shafi asserted that consensus was the safest and highest legislative authority in Islam. The Shafiite school dominates legal practice in Palestine, Lower Egypt, eastern Africa, western and southern Arabia, parts of India, and the East Indies.

The Hanbalite school was the fourth and smallest among the orthodox schools. Its founder, Ahmad ibn Hanbal, a student of al-Shafi, rebelled against the teachings of his master. The Hanbalites accepted neither private opinion nor analogy and scorned the use of consensus. They maintained that the only valid basis of Muslim law, besides the Koran, was the traditions. For his refusal to disavow his views Ibn Hanbal was beaten and persecuted by al-Mamun and al-Mutasim. Despite Ibn Hanbal's apparent personal appeal, as suggested by the 500,000 who attended his funeral in Baghdad in 855, Hanbalism was too rigid to be popular or practical over the centuries and had only scattered followers in Syria and Iraq. After the Ottoman conquest the doctrine perished, to be revived in the eighteenth century by the Wahhabis in central Arabia, where the Hanbalite rites are still observed.

In addition to the four principal codes of law, another body of law evolved from a court practice of submitting the summary of involved and important cases to a learned jurist, as a consultant, for an opinion known as a fatwa, while the opinion giver was called a mufti. Fatwas, which presented the legal issues and indicated the proper decision, were later collected and used as guides to the courts in rendering judgments. Until the advent of the Ottoman Empire, muftis more or less remained free from control or restraint by the government.

Rationalism

In essence, all of these jurist-theologians were attempting to fashion a system of law by a synthesis of Islamic truths and the highly refined and developed rationalism of the Greek philosophers. In the Umayyad period those favoring the introduction of Hellenistic logic into Muslim theology were called Mutazilites. The arguments regarding the nature of God and the Koran rocked the empire. The debates lasted for several centuries, and the particular views of each caliph determined which opinion flourished at any given time. Hisham put to death several who preached the doctrines of the created Koran and of free will. Caliph al-Mamun persecuted all but Mutazilites and ruthlessly suppressed all who did not support free thought. Caliph al-Mutawakkil ousted the Mutazilites. Eventually, theologians under al-Ashari and the learned founders of the schools of religious law brought the controversy to rest.

The great philosophic efforts, however, had the effect of taking Islam away from the people and ran the danger of destroying it as a practical religion. People desired a living experience of God, not a metaphysical or conceptual discussion of religion. To the simple Muslim, God was a personage always near at hand. One could talk to God, as a Bedouin's prayer in a time of drought attested: "O God of the devotees, what is the matter with us and You? You used to give us water—What has possessed You? Do send rain down on us. Exert Yourself!"

Asceticism and Mysticism

In the first years after Muhammad piety in Islam took the form of asceticism. In a manner similar to the practices of holy men in Christian Syria and Mesopotamia pious Muslims seeking knowledge of God and salvation for themselves adopted and preached asceticism. Prayer, fasting, solitary meditations, and prolonged vigils would lead the soul to God. Poverty, humility, patience, repentance, and silence in this world would save believers seeking godliness from eternal chastisement and permit them to come into the presence of God, to taste the unalloyed and unabated joys of paradise, and to abide therein to eternity.

In spite of a waning of ascetic tendencies in the Abbasid period, the traits and virtues of asceticism remained strong forces among Muslims across the centuries. Sultans, generals, rich merchants, judges, and scholars might not adopt ascetic practices themselves, but they usually paid open deference, sometimes approaching veneration, to those who did.

Toward the end of the eighth century, mysticism entered into Islam with a great impetus. Theology and philosophy had never affected the masses, and after the first half of the ninth century the majority of the literate community found little of interest in the hairsplitting of the scholastics. For religious experience they turned to mysticism. Knowledge of God was to be achieved by the inner light of the individual soul, not by the intellectual methods of the philosopher.

Mysticism spread over Islam, bringing into the creed of the Koran and the preaching of Muhammad all the quietism and occult practices and beliefs of the East: Buddhist stories, Hindu monism, Zoroastrian dualism, Gnostic ideas from Iraq, and miracles from the Gospels. The second coming of Christ became the doctrine of the coming of the Mahdi, the rightly-guided one, who would bring complete victory to Islam.

The essence of mysticism was love, an ecstatic communion with the divine, and final absorption into the godhead. Nothing existed but God. To know and love God and to be united with Him, without any thought of reward or salvation, was an emotional means of purifying the soul. God was eternal beauty and the path leading to Him was love. The mystic sought to lose the self in life with God. The process of comingling self with God could best be achieved by love and thought of God and a unifying of the senses which might be exercised as one. A mystic poet has expressed the thought in these lines:

> *My eye conversed whilst my tongue gazed;*
> *My ear spoke and my hand listened;*
> *And whilst my ear was an eye to behold everything visible,*
> *My eye was an ear listening to song.*

Until the twelfth century, popular preachers who based much of their message on and won their wide appeal through mysticism were despised by philosophers and theologians and were frequently adjudged guilty of heresy. Then, as al-Ashari had made rationalism and Islamic theology compatible, so al-Ghazzali led the learned and pious doctors and jurists to accept mysticism.

Appointed professor at the Nizamiyah at Baghdad in 1091, al-Ghazzali had the court and the scholars at his feet, and for four or five years his fame spread far and wide. Apparently secure for life, some sort of personal admonition flashed through him; he abandoned everything to become a mendicant mystic. After about a decade of wandering, contemplation, and writing, he returned to society and taught at the Nizamiyah at Nishapur. His great contribution, largely through his writings, vitalized Islam by making personal experience and emotion a part of religion. Islam began to live again for the ordinary man.

Fraternal Orders

At the time of the appearance of mysticism a holy man was called a *sufi*, meaning "one garbed in wool." Sufis preached to the masses, and as pious men, mystics, and often occultists lived a life of example for those to whom they were appealing. (It was evidently as a Sufi that al-Ghazzali spent his years of abdication.) Without question the conversion to Islam of the Berber tribesmen of North Africa, the fellaheen of Egypt, and the masses in many of the Muslim lands of today was the accomplishment of the Sufis.

For several centuries Sufism was an unorganized movement throughout Islam, an entirely individual pursuit. Certain Sufis obtained a devoted following, but partisanship was usually personal. Before the end of the tenth century, however, groups of Sufis formed compact brotherhoods. The master Sufi (a *shaykh, baba,* or *pir*) was the teacher and initiated disciples into the order. The members (dervishes), by study, ritual, and piety, proceeded up the ladder of the order until they were ready to leave to establish a branch center.

A master's residence was called a *ribat, khangah,* or *tekkeh.* By the thirteenth century thousands of such lodges dotted the Muslim landscape from Morocco to India. Each order had its own peculiar ritual and liturgy *(dhikr).* Some were elaborate and others simple; but all were mystical efforts to reach God. In addition to the master and the dervishes most fraternities had hundreds, sometimes thousands, of lay members, who went about their normal occupations in city or town. At stated times they met at the lodge to observe their ceremonies. A few of the orders increased the mystical stimulus by an accompaniment of music or by dancing or whirling.

It was not possible to know how many different orders existed at any one time; new splinter fraternities were springing into being and others disappearing at regular intervals. One of the strongest and best known was the Kadiriya, which had its center in Baghdad and spread throughout Islam. More conservative than most, its members have been noted for their philanthropy and humility. Morocco, parts of Spain, and North Africa yielded to the grip of the militant and strict Murabit and Muwahhid orders. The fanatical Rifaiya have been famed for glass-eating, fire-walking, and self-mortification. In Turkey the two best-known orders were the Bektashi, to which most of the Ottoman janissaries belonged, and the Mevlevis, whose members were popularly called whirling dervishes because of certain aspects in their ritual. In eastern Anatolia and Iran there was the Nakhshbandiya order, and in India the Chishti and Kalandari orders were established.

As a great social and religious development the significance of the fraternal orders lay in the members' extensive participation in the spread and popularization of Islam, resulting in the majority of the people in North Africa, Sudan, Asia Minor, central Asia, certain parts of India, and Indonesia becoming converted to Islam. In this process, much to the horror and disapproval of Muslim theologians and lawyers, local beliefs and religious customs were grafted upon the original doctrines to form a popular Islam. In most instances, therefore, popular Islam in different parts of the world became exceedingly diverse in form and practice and far removed from the teachings of either Muhammad or Muslim theologians. Only the barest fundamentals and the simplest of externals were retained.

Shiism

Differences of opinion and belief have always been accepted in Islam. Variations in practice and doctrine among the four Sunni legal systems, the many conflicting interpretations of tradition in vogue throughout the Muslim world, and the confusing welter of exotic ideas rampant in popular Islam have made a definitive imputation of heresy difficult to verify on purely theological grounds.

Until comparatively recently rulers throughout the world usually persecuted subjects whose religion was at marked variance with theirs. Nonetheless, Islam was exceedingly tolerant, as the treatment of Christians and Jews testifies, and the caliphs permitted many types of religious deviation. In general, deviation became a serious matter only when religious doctrines denied to the caliph the right of his position and his power. Therein lay the true seeds of heresy.

Following the death of Ali and the ascension of the Umayyads, die-hard Alids contended that caliphs were usurpers and that the imamate, as they called the caliphate, should be lodged in the house of Ali and Fatimah. For more than two centuries intermittent political and military attempts were made by the Shiites (the partisans, or sect, of Ali) to unseat the caliph. Failing in this, the Shiites developed an intricate theology, engendering many dogmas repugnant to Sunni Islam.

The Shiite faith held that Ali had been the legitimate *imam* ("leader") and that the imamate was rightfully transmitted to his descendants. Ali had been given an esoteric power to interpret the Koran, a knowledge that was handed in turn on to his sons and grandsons. (Later some extremists even professed that God's revelations had been intended for Ali but that the angel Gabriel had mistakenly given them to Muhammad.) Ali's descendants, therefore, ruled by a divine right that was handed down to them from Adam; they were infallible, impeccable, and certainly beyond human censure.

The Shiite heresy has been divided into numerous sects since the eighth century. The majority, the Twelvers, adhered to the faith that there was a succession of twelve imams to Muhammad al-Muntazar ("The Expected"), who disappeared in a cave to return as the savior (Mahdi) of humanity. In his absence the law and the creed were interpreted by scholars who acted merely as agents of the hidden imam. Thus, in law, the Shiites accepted only

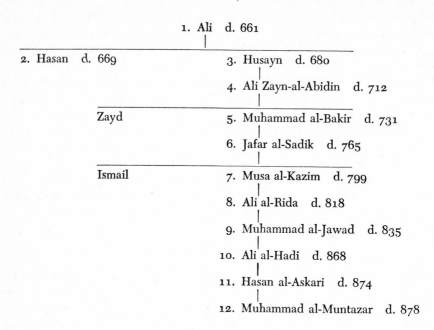

THE TWELVE IMAMS

the Koran, those traditions narrated by a recognized imam, and a scholar's or judge's personal opinion when it could be upheld by tradition or precedent established by an imam. Analogy and consensus were rejected.

Aside from petty ritualistic differences which through the centuries were greatly exaggerated in the minds of all Muslims, the chief peculiarities of these schismatics—Twelvers, or Imamis—were the allowance of temporary marriage and the practice of dissimulation. The former virtually legalized prostitution. The latter permitted Shiites to deny their faith to avoid persecution when caliphs and Sunnites attacked them for disavowing caliphal authority. In the twentieth century the majority of Muslims in Iran and southern Iraq are Shiites of the Twelver persuasion.

The most conservative of the Shiites are found in Morocco and Yemen. In its political organization Morocco became Shiite; yet her theology and law were strictly Sunnite. In Yemen is the sect called Zaydi, which has recognized the series of imams. The Zaydis, however, allow for no supernaturalism in their theology and have no esoteric dogmas. The founder of their sect was Zayd, a grandson of the martyred Husayn.

On the other extreme of the Shiite sect there have been a score or more of divergent heterodoxies. Of these the sect of the Ismailis, or Seveners, has had the greatest following. They regarded Ismail as the rightful seventh and last imam. At first Jafar al-Sadik named Ismail, his eldest son, as successor; but because Ismail imbibed wine freely, Jafar designated another son, Musa, as successor. The Seveners rejected this substitution as impossible, arguing that the imam was incapable of erring and that drinking wine did not therefore affect him or the succession. Seven became a sacred and mystical number as in the Pythagorean system. The emanence of the universe came in seven steps: God, universal mind, universal soul, matter, space, time, and earth and the human being.

The Ismailis were masters of organization and tactics. Sent out by the true founder, Abdallah ibn Maymun, from Salamyah in northern Syria, missionaries traveled through the Muslim world preaching that the language of the Koran was an occult veil covering an inner and true meaning which could be revealed only to the adept. Initiation of the novice proceeded in seven graded degrees, wherein was divulged secret knowledge such as transmigration of souls, the divinity of Ismail, and the coming of the Mahdi. The son of the real founder of the Ismaili sect established his rule in North Africa early in the ninth century. His successors, the Fatimids, ruled much of the western portion of the Muslim world.

Cults and Sects
Two effluences of the Ismailis in medieval times were the communistic Karmatians and the notorious Assassins. Led by Hamdan Karmat in the ninth century, the former sect was a revolutionary group which supported itself from a common fund contributed to by all, practiced the community of property and wives, and considered proper the shedding of the blood of any opposition, even Muslim. A Karmatian state was established on the western shore of the Persian Gulf and kept the whole area in bloody turmoil. In 930 the Karmatians raided Mecca and carried off the sacred Black Stone from the Kaaba.

The Assassins were founded in Iran by Hasan ibn al-Sabbah, who studied Ismaili rites and doctrine in Fatimid Egypt and then returned to his home as a missionary. In 1090 he established near Kazwin in the Elburz Mountains his fortified monastery of Alamut, which became the residence of the grand master of the order. Below him were priors and propagandists; at the lowest rank stood the *fidais,* who risked death for the faith. Their familiar name, Assassins, was derived from *hashshashun*, the Arabic word for hashish, which they used in their fearless raids from mountain fortresses. Adopting values based vaguely on Ismaili theology, the Assassins freed themselves from dogmas and prophets and were encouraged "to believe nothing and dare all." Exact information is lacking, however, because their records and books were destroyed in 1256 when Hulagu razed Alamut.

Spreading westward, the Assassins converted the Turkish prince of Aleppo in the twelfth century and held numerous castles in north Syria. The most famous Assassin master was Rashid-al-Din Sinan of Masyad, who as the *shaykh al-jabal* became for the Crusaders and thence to the West "The Old Man of the Mountain." The assassination of the famous vizir Nizam al-Mulk in 1092 was the first in a series of assassinations of prominent individuals which struck terror through Islam. The western branch of the order was eliminated by Baybars, the Mamluk sultan of Egypt in 1272.

Other Ismaili sects were the Nusayris, or Alawites, of northern Syria and the Druzes of Lebanon, Syria, and Jordan. The Nusayris were devotees of the eleventh imam but nevertheless adhered to the main tenets of the Seveners. They looked upon Ali as the incarnation of God and possessed a liturgy with many Christian borrowings. The Druze sect was an eleventh-century splinter group from Fatimid Egypt. Its members settled in the Lebanon mountain region, where they developed an elaborate ritual and a pattern of life distinctive even in minor detail. Both the Druze and the Nusayri maintained strict secrecy with respect to their faith and practices; even today mystery shrouds their beliefs and ceremonies.

Probably the best-known Ismaili in the twentieth century was the incomparable Agha Khan III of Bombay, London, Paris, and the Riviera, who traced his descent through the last grand master of the Assassins at Alamut to the seventh imam. Regarded as infallible and impeccable by his followers in Syria, India, Oman, and Zanzibar, he received a tenth of their revenues.

In addition to the sects and divisions of these branches of Islam already described, there have been and are at least forty or fifty more. Perhaps the most different are the Yazidis of Syria, who follow much of the theology of the Ismailis but assign the divine attributes to the Umayyad caliphs Yazid and Marwan.

Thus, the plain unvarnished revelations of the Prophet Muhammad and the simple direct philosophy of his preaching passed through the fires of Greek logic, Hellenistic Christianity, and Persian dualism to evolve a finely drawn legalistic and intellectual theology, a highly charged supernatural recondite religion, or a semiascetic mysticism. The apocryphal words of Muhammad have apparently been fulfilled: When told that there were seventy-two varieties of Christianity, the Prophet was supposed to have said that Islam would have seventy-three!

REFERENCES: Chapter 8

References for Chapters 1, 3, 5, 6, and 7 relate to the subject matter of this chapter.

Afnan, Soheil M. *Avicenna: His Life and Works.* London: Allen & Unwin, 1958.

Arnold, Thomas, and Alfred Guillaume (eds.). *The Legacy of Islam.* London: Oxford University Press, 1931. Two chapters, "Philosophy and Theology" by Alfred Guillaume and "Law and Society" by David de Santillana, contain valuable material on the subject discussed in this chapter.

Dodge, Bayard. *Al-Azhar: A Millennium of Muslim Learning.* Washington, D.C.: Middle East Institute, 1961. An excellent and appreciative study of the great Muslim university in Cairo.

Gibb, H. A. R. *Studies in the Civilization of Islam.* Boston: Beacon Press, 1962.

Hodgson, Marshall G. S. *The Order of Assassins.* The Hague: Mouton, 1955. A thorough analysis of this well-known minority sect of Islam, which flourished from 1090 to 1256.

Hourani, George F. *Islamic Rationalism: The Ethics of 'Abd al-Jabbar.* Oxford: Clarendon Press, 1971. An integration of the work of Abd al-Jabbar on monotheism and theodicy into the larger framework of knowledge of medieval Islam. Abd al-Jabbar was an early-eleventh-century Mutazilite. His work was found in a library in Yemen in 1951 and showed that rationalism, voluntarism, and opposition to ethical positivism of theistic and legalistic Islam ran deeper than had been thought.

Khadduri, Majid. *The Islamic Law of Nations: Shaybani's Siyar.* Baltimore: Johns Hopkins Press, 1966. An insight into an eighth-century treatise on international law.

————. *War and Peace in the Law of Islam.* Baltimore: Johns Hopkins Press, 1955. The fundamental nature of the Islamic state and law is explored; and the classical Muslim attitudes toward foreign policy, international trade, warfare, treaties, and neutrality are examined.

Lewis, Bernard. *The Assassins: A Radical Sect in Islam.* New York: Weidenfeld & Nicolson, 1967. A study of the first large-scale political terrorist group in history. Well researched, well written, authoritative.

————. *The Origins of Isma'ilism.* Cambridge, Eng.: Cambridge University Press, 1940. Still the best study of this important sect.

Liebesny, Herbert J. *The Law of the Near and Middle East: Readings, Cases and Materials.* Albany, N.Y.: State University of New York Press, 1974. A systematic treatment of the subject from early to modern times with translations of documents, histories, commentaries, and modern law codes as well as representative cases decided by courts in Middle East countries. Dr. Liebesny is one of the recognized authorities on Middle Eastern law.

Makarem, Sami Nasib. *The Druze Faith.* Delmar, N.Y.: Caravan Books, 1974. An authoritative book on the creed and origins of this sometimes secretive sect of Islam.

Rosenthal, E. I. J. *Political Thought in Medieval Islam.* Cambridge, Eng.: Cambridge University Press, 1958. A first-rate book in paperback.

Salem, Elie Adib. *Political Theory and Institutions of the Khawarij.* Baltimore: Johns Hopkins Press, 1956. A thorough combing of Arab sources on these puritan predecessors of the Wahhabis. It is an objective study showing the favorable position the Khawarij accorded women.

Schacht, Joseph. *An Introduction to Islamic Law.* New York: Oxford University Press, 1964. The best book in the field and more than an introduction, for the author sheds new light on the importance of al-Shafii.

Schimmel, Annemarie. *Mystical Dimensions of Islam.* Chapel Hill: University of North Carolina Press, 1975. This is a synthesis of Sufi theory and practice, its history, psychological and social significance, and literary output, as described in original texts and interpreted by scholars from East and West. An authoritative work of a high standard.

Trimingham, J. Spencer. *The Sufi Orders of Islam.* Oxford: Clarendon Press, 1971. A comprehensive treatment of this mystic movement.

Watt, W. Montgomery. *Muslim Intellectual: A Study of al-Ghazali.* Edinburgh: University of Edinburgh Press, 1963. A full study of this great theological philosopher.

Wensinck, A. J. *The Muslim Creed: Its Genesis and Historical Development.* London: Cass, 1965. A reprinting of a 1932 classic with very good chapters on the Kharijites, Qadarites, Mutazilites, and other Muslim groupings and sects to show the scope of Muslim creed.

Chapter 9

Muslim Culture

The Arabs burst from the cities of the Hijaz and the deserts of Arabia into the complex Greco-Roman civilizations of Syria and Egypt, into the cultured valleys of India, and into the refined society of Mesopotamia and Iran. Everywhere they demonstrated a remarkable genius for assimilating various attributes of these native cultures and blending them with their own to form a new and varied Muslim culture. Belief in the oneness of God, acceptance of Muhammad as His prophet, and the Arabic language became the significant distinguishing characteristics of Islamic culture. After a few centuries even Arabic did not remain universal.

Philosophy

The emergence of the Mutazilites indicated that Greek logic was studied during the Umayyad era. Not until the reign of al-Mamun, however, was the bulk of Hellenistic thought and science translated into Arabic. Beginning with a majority of the works of Aristotle and Plato, translators soon rendered almost the whole of Hellenic and Hellenistic philosophies into Arabic. It was upon this base that Arabian philosophy was erected.

The earliest of the prominent Arab philosophers was al-Kindi (Alkindius), born in Kufah in the first half of the ninth century. He excelled in the study of optics, chemistry, medicine, and music; but above all he was a philosopher. A Neoplatonist of the school of Plotinus and Porphyry, al-Kindi also imbibed the ideas of Aristotle and Plato. He intermingled philosphy and theology, holding that the world of intelligence is supreme. Immortality results from having the correct knowledge of God and the universe. A century later al-Farabi (Alpharabius), a Turk from Transoxiana, blended Aristotelian, Platonic, and Sufi thought. He presented his philosophy in a political science treatise by describing a model city where the ruler was a moral and intellectual being and the happiness of all was the governing force. However, al-Farabi shocked Muslims by claiming that the world was not created and had no beginning.

Arabian philosophers better known to the Western world were Ibn Sina (Avicenna) and Ibn Rushd (Averroes). The former, called by the Arabs "the shaykh and the prince of the learned," was born in 980 in a village near Bukhara. An Ismaili Iranian, Ibn Sina lived as a young man at the Samanid library of Bukhara, where he acquired an encyclopedic knowledge of medicine, mathematics, astronomy, and philosophy. Since he was able to write concisely, yet in a popular style, Ibn Sina's numerous works on these diverse subjects had a wide vogue among Muslims and greatly influenced the advancement of philosophic thought in medieval Europe. Pursuing Aristotelian philosophy, Ibn Sina developed and passed on to the Western schoolmen the notion that there are two intelligibles—the concept of an object such as a chair, and the pursuant or logical concept of a chair in relation to its abstract universal concept. He taught that the idea of a chair existed before the chair was created, that in each chair existed the idea of chair, and that from many chairs came the idea of chair. Such logic resembled the later thoughts of Abélard and were in part taken over by Albertus Magnus and his pupil Saint Thomas Aquinas.

Ibn Rushd, the Malikite Muslim judge and philosopher, lived in Cordoba, Seville, and Marrakesh during the Muwahhid regime. He wrote in the fields of philosophy, medicine, mathematics, law, and theology. As the last of the classical Muslim philosophers of Spain, he built on the systems of al-Farabi, Ibn Sina, and his fellow countrymen Ibn Bajjah (Avempace) and Ibn Tufayl. He declared that active human reason and possible reason or knowledge are one and present in everyone. Although differing considerably on this point, Ibn Rushd and Aquinas advanced philosophies that were remarkably parallel. Ibn Rushd's commentaries on Aristotle were more popular in Christian Europe than they were in the Muslim world.

From Aristotle, Plato, and other Greek philosophers the Muslim scholars, writing in Arabic, created an Arabian school of philosophy which had a profound and recognized influence upon Christian philosophers of medieval Europe. More significant to the Middle East, however, was their permanent popularity throughout the Muslim world. Summaries, treatises, and commentaries on these philosophers and scores of others less well known were widely read and discussed; public and private libraries bulged with books on metaphysics, cosmology, and philosophy.

Medicine

Muhammad supposedly declared that there exist two sciences: the science of God and the science of the human—theology and medicine. Consequently, throughout the period of medieval Islam most Muslim philosophers and scientists were students of medicine; frequently they were also practicing physicians. Muslims first became aware of medical knowledge at the Damascus court of the Umayyads, through their Greek, Syrian, and Iranian physicians, whose skills were based almost exclusively on works of Greek scientists. A few Greek or Syriac treatises were translated into Arabic, and the Alexandrine medical school was transferred, part to Antioch and part to Harran in Iraq.

The great strides in medicine, however, were taken under the Abbasid rule in Baghdad. Medical works of Galen, Hippocrates, and Paul of Aegina and the materia medica of Dioscorides were translated into Arabic. Seven of Galen's books, lost in the original Greek, were preserved in Arabic. Several schools of medicine developed, and a physician took state examinations to obtain a license to practice his profession. In the year 931 there were 860 physicians registered in Baghdad; they swore to work for the benefit of humanity and for the relief and cure of the sick and not to give deadly medicines. Jails as well as traveling clinics for the poor were supported by the state and hospitals, an Iranian innovation, were introduced into the Muslim world by Harun al-Rashid. The Seljuk Turkish sultan Malikshah had with him on most of his campaigns a mobile hospital, carried on forty camels. Pharmacists were also examined and licensed, and schools of pharmacy and drugstores were established. In 776 Jabir ibn Hayyan compiled the first Arabic pharmacopoeia.

In 765 the Nestorian Jurjis ibn Bakhtishu, dean of the academy of medicine of Jundishapur (Shahabad in southwestern Iran), came to the court of al-Mansur to cure the caliph's stomach ailment. Fortunes were made by court physicians, who passed on their professional skills and practices as valued possessions from father to son for generations. Ibn Bakhtishu's grandson understood psychiatry; he cured, through a form of hypnosis, one of al-Rashid's slave girls of hysterical paralysis by pretending to disrobe her publicly. Descendants of Ibn Bakhtishu served the Abbasid court for nearly three centuries.

The arrival of physicians from Jundishapur opened the way for medical investigations beyond the works of the ancient Greeks, and the ninth century in Baghdad was a period of many advances in medical knowledge. Ibn Masawayh dissected apes and wrote a monograph on ophthalmology. The compendium by Thabit ibn Kurra of Harran discussed general hygiene. It stated causes, symptoms, and treatment for diseases of the skin and every part of the body from head to foot. Infectious diseases were classified; fractures and dislocations were described; and the importance of climate, food, diet, and sex was explained.

The most ingenious Muslim physician was al-Razi (Rhazes), chief of the Baghdad hospital during the first quarter of the tenth century. Considered the best original mind and clinician of the Middle Ages, he developed the use of seton in surgery, treated bladder and kidney stones, and presented the first clinical report on smallpox. He had some 120 monographs on medicine and surgery to his credit. His *al-Hawi,* a comprehensive medical encyclopedia, was translated into Latin in 1279 and first printed in 1486 under the title *Continens.* A contemporary, al-Majusi (Haly Abbas), wrote on childbirth, the capillary system, and dietetics, and also compiled a materia medica.

The most famous Muslim medical work was *al-Kanun,* written in the eleventh century by Ibn Sina (Avicenna) of Bukhara. Encyclopedic in character, it showed the advances of Muslim knowledge and the originality of Ibn Sina in this field. Among other things, it explained the contagious nature of tuberculosis, showed that disease could be spread through water, recognized pleurisy, diagnosed bilharziasis, and described 760 different drugs.

Largely replacing the works of Galen and al-Razi, *al-Kanun* was the chief medical book of the Middle East and western Europe from the twelfth to the seventeenth century. Gerard of Cremona translated it into Latin, and it ran through sixteen printed editions before the end of the fifteenth century.

Muslim Spain possessed superior physicians and surgeons. The ablest surgeon was Abu al-Kasim (Abulcasis) of Cordoba. He practiced the art of crushing bladder stones, cauterized wounds, and advocated dissection and vivisection. His surgical writings were translated by Gerard of Cremona and became the surgical manual at the medical schools of Salerno, Montpellier, and other European centers. In Seville, Ibn Zuhr (Avenzoar), vizir and court physician to the Muwahhid rulers, carried on the family profession and found time to write six medical works, of which the most valuable is on therapeutics and diet. At the time of the Black Death in the middle of the fourteenth century the Muslim physicians of Granada, Ibn al-Khatib and Ibn Khatima, recognized its contagious character; and in their treatises they noted that a patient's symptoms were identical to those of the person from whom he had been infected. Although religious law denied contagion, Ibn al-Khatib held that "experience, investigation, the evidence of the senses and trustworthy reports" established without a doubt the reality of infection from the afflicted.

Building on Greek and Persian sources, the galaxy of Muslim physicians pushed the frontiers of medicine forward. Their practice, monographs, and compendiums demonstrated originality and ingenuity. The diversity and number of their works, translated into Latin and eventually printed, further established the place of Muslim physicians in the history of medical science. Evidence of their actual skill was attested by the eagerness with which the Crusaders sought the services of Muslim doctors. Part of the progress originated in the popularity and fashionable reputation enjoyed by medical knowledge. Since the chief avocation of countless leading Muslims was medicine and the study of its lore, every medical genius was encouraged to reach the pinnacle of his ability and capacity.

Mathematics
Arab scholars also found mathematics an attractive and useful science, especially in company with astronomy and astrology. By far the greatest achievement of the Arab mathematicians was the adoption and wide use of "Arabic numerals." It is not known whether they were brought from India or developed locally. In any case, the use of these numerals, including the use of zero and the placing of the digit in a series to denote units, tens, hundreds, and so on, made "everyday arithmetic" possible and simplified calculations, enabling Arabs to take the square and cube roots of numbers. The word "cipher" was taken directly from the Arabic *shifr*, meaning "empty."

Building on Indian and Greek works, Middle Eastern scholars advanced mathematical knowledge very considerably. In the ninth century al-

Khwarizmi of Khurasan did a study on numerals which later circulated in the West. Through his name came the word "algorism." He wrote on the solution of quadratic equations; and from part of the title of one of his books was derived the word "algebra" (*al-jabr*—"integration").

In the same century three sons of a Baghdad astronomer worked on the measurement of plane and spherical surfaces, while the geometrician Thabit ibn Kurra developed new propositions and studied irrationals. The Iranian al-Battani (Albategnius) was the first to present ideas on trigonometric ratios. Toward the end of the tenth century another Iranian, Abu al-Wafa of Baghdad, established the formula in trigonometry for the addition of angles. Through a simple geometric process al-Karaji was able to determine the sum of successive numbers raised to the third power $(1^3 + 2^3 + 3^3 \ldots + n^3)$; with great skill al-Kashi of Samarkand did the same for successive numbers raised to the fourth power $(1^4 + 2^4 + 3^4 \ldots + n^4)$. By using the intersection of a hyperbola and a circle, Sijzi gave the solution to the problem of the trisection of an angle.

One of the most distinguished mathematicians was the Iranian poet Umar al-Khayyam. He advanced far beyond al-Khwarzimi, establishing procedures for the solution of cubic and quadrinomial equations and developing analytical geometry in numerous ways to the same level achieved much later by Descartes. The last great medieval mathematician of the Middle East was the Iranian Nasir-al-Din al-Tusi, who assembled his laboratory at Maraghah in northwestern Iran under the patronage of Hulagu Khan. Here he wrote his famous *Treatise on the Quadrilateral* and carried on his brilliant studies in the field of spherical trigonometry.

Thus, besides assimilating and transmitting to posterity the mathematics of the ancients, Middle Eastern savants made many original contributions in the practical and theoretical branches of the subject. The widespread use of numerals gave arithmetic an everyday value. Algebra became an exact science, and solid foundations were laid in the fields of analytical geometry and plane and spherical trigonometry. Through Spain and Sicily most of these ideas passed at an early date to the Western world, where they contributed to the scientific advancement of Europe.

Astronomy

From mathematics it was an easy step to astronomy, especially since in the construction of any mosque it was always necessary to fix the *kibla* (the direction of Mecca) in order to build the *mihrab* (the prayer niche). Furthermore, since astrology and horoscopy were much pursued and the latitude and longitude of one's birthplace determined one's horoscope, the movement of the stars was significant.

When al-Mansur decided to build his new palace in Baghdad, the Iranian astronomer Naubakht was employed to draw the plans. Shortly thereafter, Mauka, an Indian astronomer, introduced the court to *Sindbind*, an Indian treatise on astronomy. This treatise was translated into Arabic by al-Fazari, who was also familiar with the Pahlawi astronomical tables compiled in the Sasanid period. A few decades later Ptolemy's *Quadripartitum* was translated. Muslim astronomy thus started from Greek, Iranian, and Indian contributions.

Many palaces in Baghdad had private astronomical observatories. The main professional observatories were at Jundishapur and Baghdad. It was from the latter that scientists at the time of al-Mamun went to the plain of Sinjar to determine the length of a degree of latitude. Walking north and south until the pole star rose or sank a degree (thus assuming the earth to be round), they took the mean distance for one degree. From this they calculated the diameter of the earth to be about 6,500 miles and the circumference roughly 20,400 miles. This made the Mediterranean 52° in length, improving upon Ptolemy's 62°. The precession of the equinoxes was well understood. Rather exact astronomical tables and calendars with a compendium were prepared by al-Farghani (Alfraganus) of Transoxiana in the ninth century. These were translated into Latin in the twelfth century and were still used and valued by Regiomontanus and Melanchthon.

Thabit ibn Kurra determined the altitude of the sun and computed the length of the solar year; al-Battani (Albategnius) recorded his observations on the appearance of the new moon, the inclination of the ecliptic, the length of the tropic and sideral year, and eclipses of the sun. Abu Mashar (Albumasar) of Baghdad, although chiefly concerned with astrology, wrote on the relation between the rising and setting of the moon and the laws of the tides. The astronomer al-Biruni at Ghaznah in Afghanistan proposed the idea that the earth rotates on its axis and reckoned quite accurately latitudes and longitudes for every important city in the Middle East. Umar al-Khayyam, who was a better astronomer than poet, arranged for Sultan Malikshah at the Naysabur observatory a calendar with an error of only one day in 5,000 years.

In the west al-Zarkali (Arzachel) of Toledo invented an astrolabe, on which he wrote a treatise later used by Copernicus. Near Cordoba a century later lived the great astronomer al-Bitruji (Alpetragius), who computed the length of the Mediterranean and found it to be 42° of longitude, a nearly correct measurement. He advanced the idea of diurnal movements of the earth and explained the movement of the stars by the turning of the earth on its axis as well as by its circling about the sun.

One of the finest observatories was established by Hulagu at Maraghah, where the scientist Nasir-al-Din al-Tusi developed the most precise instruments in medieval times. He greatly perfected the armillary sphere and constructed a mural quadrant and a solstitial armilla. Because of his excellent equipment his *Ilkhanian Tables* were long regarded as the most exact of astronomical tables.

The Arabic names of many stars and constellations and the Arabic origin of such words as "azimuth," "nadir," and "zenith" vouch for the brilliance of the Middle Eastern astronomers and the acceptance of their contributions by the West. One can only wonder if Columbus would have had the courage to set sail westward for India and Cathay had he known the size of the earth as determined by al-Bitruji.

Sciences

In addition to medicine, mathematics, and astronomy, the medieval Middle Easterners investigated all of the basic physical and natural sciences. It is not possible here to detail the various advances made in each science. Works on botany existed, chiefly in connection with drugs for the pharmacist and physician. Zoological studies were made, some for use by veterinarians. (Arabs were always interested in horses.) The Arab al-Masudi, who died about 957 in Cairo, discussed earthquakes, described windmills, and advanced a theory of evolution. In his book on geology Ibn Sina suggested several postulates about earthquakes, winds, climate, and geologic sedimentation.

However, the greatest strides in the other sciences were taken in chemistry and physics. Chemistry was studied mostly in connection with alchemy. Even the word affirms the Arabic origins of that science. The Arabic term is *al-kimiya,* which was probably derived from an ancient Egyptian word meaning "black." Even in antiquity the science had a reputation as "black magic."

Alchemy was founded on the belief that all metals are basically the same and that it is possible to transmute one to another. Further, it was believed that gold is the purest form of metal and that some substance exists that can transform baser metals into gold. Throughout the Muslim world countless individuals engaged in the search for this substance and the technique of its use. Celebrated philosophers and physicians gave their time and genius to the quest. One of these men, al-Razi, distinguished volatile and nonvolatile bodies and classified all matter as vegetable, animal, or mineral. Others in their research determined the specific weights of stones and metals.

The greatest chemist, or alchemist, was Jabir ibn Hayyan (Geber), who lived in Kufah toward the end of the eighth century. Jabir advocated experimentation and recognized the importance of confirming by careful observation theories resting only on previous writings and hypotheses. He was able to prepare arsenious oxide, lead acetate, sulphide of mercury, and sal ammoniac, the last of which had been unknown to the Greeks. Jabir presented new and improved methods of evaporation, filtration, sublimation, melting, crystallization, and distillation. Jabir's works were translated into Latin in the twelfth century by Robert of Chester and Gerard of Cremona and proved to be the foundation of Western alchemy and chemistry. The Arabic origin of such words as "alkali," "alcohol," "antimony," and "alembic" and "aludel" (parts of the older typical apparatus for distilling) gives an inkling of Western dependence upon Middle Eastern discoveries in this branch of science.

In physics the widest interest lay in theoretical and applied mechanics as related to problems of irrigation and the flow of water. Water wheels and clocks were built in many cities of the Middle East, some of the water clocks being exceedingly ingenious in design. In the twelfth century al-Khazine of Marw observed the greater density of water when it was nearer the center of the earth.

The most significant developments in physics, however, were in the field of optics. Many prominent scientists of the age investigated the subject. The most outstanding was al-Hasan ibn al-Haytham (Alhazen), who flourished in Cairo at the time of the Fatimids. In his book *On Optics* he refused to accept Euclid's and Ptolemy's theory that the eye emits visual rays; instead he advanced the theory that vision is due to the impact of light rays. Experimenting with reflection and optic illusions, he studied refraction through spherical segments filled with water. In another work, *On Light*, he proposed that light is fire reflected at the spheric limit of the atmosphere; and from observing phenomena at twilight he reckoned the atmosphere to be about ten miles high. In what was probably the first recorded observation of the camera obscura, he noticed during eclipses the semilunar shape of the sun's image on a wall opposite a fine hole in a window shutter. Ibn al-Haytham's studies greatly influenced, through translation, the works of Roger Bacon, Vitellio, Kepler, and Leonardo da Vinci.

Geography

The religious precept of a pilgrimage to Mecca once in a lifetime undoubtedly led to a persistent urge among many in medieval Islamic lands to travel and see the world. Because geographic data were needed by these travelers, and because some travelers and traders, sometimes after twenty years of travel, wrote detailed books on where they had been and what they had seen, geography became one of the most popular pursuits of the Middle Ages.

Before the end of the ninth century Ptolemy's *Geography* had been translated into Arabic, and Muslim geographers always had difficulty in freeing themselves from some of the ancients' concept of the world. The scientist al-Khwarizmi, at al-Mamun's command, prepared a great map of the earth and a companion text which was used by geographers until the fourteenth century. Largely following Ptolemy, al-Khwarizmi pictured the world encircled by a continuous ocean from which the Sea of Rum (Mediterranean) and the Sea of Fars (Indian Ocean) branched to separate the land of the earth, which was divided into seven climate zones. The western prime meridian of longitude ran through the Canary Islands, and all east and west directions came from the "world cupola" located in India at Arin (Ujjayini).

Fortunately, the conservative and classical geographers, whose views upheld the Koran, were ignored by travelers and sailors who recognized irregular coasts strewn with gulfs and peninsulas and stated that the Indian Ocean, in certain directions, has no limit. The tales of these voyagers came down through the ages as the stories of Sindbad the Sailor. They described

China in the ninth century and Russia in the tenth. Their road books were a mine of historical topography and economic and political geography. The tenth-century scholar was frequently on the move. The greatest globe-trotter was al-Masudi, who visited most of the countries of Asia, Zanzibar, and most of North Africa. His thirty-volume work became one of the two recognized geographical encyclopedias of the medieval period. Other travelers and geographers left numerous works, many with special merit for their colored maps of separate countries and areas. One of the last discerning voyagers was Ibn Battutah of Morocco. Living in the fourteenth century, he was on the move for nearly three decades. He made four pilgrimages to Mecca and visited China, Ceylon, Constantinople, and central Africa.

The most noted geographer of the Muslim world was al-Idrisi (Edrisi), born in Ceuta in 1100 and for many years the chief geographer for King Roger II at Palermo in Sicily. In his writings and discourses (in Arabic) he summed up the ideas and contributions of Ptolemy, al-Khwarizmi, and al-Masudi. Using silver, al-Idrisi constructed for his patron a celestial sphere and a disclike map of the earth. It is interesting that the latter distinctly showed the source of the Nile to be a lake in central Africa.

The last eminent Muslim geographer was Yakut ibn Abdallah al-Hamawi, a Greek slave from Asia Minor who was educated and given his freedom by his Hamawi owner. Before his death at Aleppo in 1229 Yakut compiled his famous *Mujam al-Buldun,* a vast encyclopedia of geographical information. Arranged alphabetically, it summed up the whole fund of knowledge to his day in this field and thus became an invaluable source book for all scholars.

Agriculture

The Arabs were not farmers, and to engage in agricultural work was beneath the dignity of free men in Arabia. But moving into the rich agricultural lands of Iraq, Syria, and Egypt, they quickly learned the value of efficient cultivation of the soil. As the native populations of these provinces and other fertile areas, such as Spain and Sogdiana, were converted to Islam, Muslims were engaged directly in agriculture. Accordingly, the governing classes, the landowners, and the actual farmers were concerned with agricultural progress.

In the Middle East in historic times the prime factor in agriculture has been water. Problems of irrigation and canal-building were not private affairs, and everywhere rulers paid strict attention to digging, reopening, and repairing water channels. Under Muslim governments gardens flourished, with many different plants, vegetables, and fruit trees being propagated. The Arabs had known numerous varieties of dates, and families treasured their own species with favored qualities of flavor, sweetness, and moisture. The same interest and care was given to all produce of the land as Islam spread into new areas and new crops were grown. Middle Easterners usually took keen pride in their gardens and land. Their own peaches or apricots, cotton or sugar cane, melons or squashes were always something quite special. They were interested in improving the quality, and they took specimens wherever they went. On pilgrimages to Mecca they usually carried seeds and cuttings to exchange for others from distant lands. Thus, the best varieties were distributed far and wide. Into Spain on the distant edge of the Islamic world was introduced the cultivation of cotton, sugar cane, oranges, apricots, peaches, and rice. One of the best-known gardens of the world was that of the Generalife (*jannat al-arif*—"the inspector's paradise") near the Alhambra.

With the date palm and fruit trees, the technique of controlled pollenization was known and frequently practiced with special and prized varieties.

The Crusaders learned to value Middle Eastern agriculture and acquired a taste for many of its products. Yet it was largely through Sicily and Spain that agricultural knowledge and skills passed to Christian Europe.

Poetry

In pre-Islamic Arabia poetry was a favorite vehicle of expression. Epic and lyric poetry abounded. A talented poet was highly esteemed, and the cultured person was one who appreciated fine poetry and could recite an endless quantity of verse. Muhammad found much of this poetry distasteful, since the virtues extolled and the way of life suggested were not those of Islam. But Islam was unable to eradicate the love of verse inherent in Middle Eastern peoples.

The advent of the Umayyad regime set the stage for the return of poetry to its pre-Islamic popularity. The poet Umar wrote with charming grace of free and erotic love, and his directness and simplicity influenced generations of Arab poets. Singers and entertainers found his style well suited to their ballads. His contemporary Jamil, however, wrote of platonic love and honored chaste and faithful passion. Lyric poetry reached its height in the Majnun-Layla romance. The author-hero of the Layla tribe became mad *(majnun)* because of his burning passion for a lady whose father compelled her to marry another. The deranged lover roamed the world seeking his beloved. Ever after, Majnun Layla was the typical hero of unrequited-love poems throughout the Middle East.

In addition, there reappeared in the Umayyad period many writers of eulogistic and epic poetry of the pre-Islamic style. Noted for their dissolute language and political invective, these panegyrists pleased their patrons; but their poetry was more revealing of the life and morals of the age than deserving of a niche in world literature.

With the coming of the Abbasids and the court's move to Iraq and Baghdad the poets followed. Persian influence and rich caliphal patronage introduced an elegance and a licentiousness unknown in Umayyad poetry. One of the first poets in this period was Bashshar ibn Burd, whose paeans of love were so popular and so apt for singing that al-Mahdi had him executed in

783 for endangering public morals. The boon companion of Harun al-Rashid was the sparkling and lusty Abu Nuwas, whose libidinous poetry is typified by his verse:

> *Ho! a cup, and fill it up, and tell me it is wine.*
> *For I will never drink in shade if I can drink in shine!*
> *Curst and poor is every hour that sober I must go,*
> *But rich am I whene'er well drunk I stagger to and fro.*
> *Speak, for shame, the loved one's name, let vain disguise alone:*
> *No good there is in pleasures o'er which a veil is thrown.*

Poetry, however, was not all wine, women, and song. Abu al-Alahiyah raised his voice against the lascivious and frivolous verses of his contemporaries and sang the praises of a moral and ascetic life. Unmindful of the reproaches, al-Rashid pensioned him generously.

At the court and in wealthy society poetry was on the lips of all, and every elegant household had its poet. The immediate material rewards were great, as was, consequently, the quantity of verse, much of it ephemeral doggerel or limerick eulogizing the patron or adorning the moment. Since the golden days of Baghdad the poetry of that classical age has retained its favored position among educated Arabic-speaking Middle Eastern peoples.

In the West the best-known poet was Ali ibn Hazm of eleventh-century Cordoba, whose platonic love verses, collected in an anthology called *Tawq al-Hamamah (The Dove's Necklace),* have been much translated. Much more significant was the indigenous development of the *zajal* and the *muwashshah* (the ballad and folk song) of Muslim Spain, which were popularized and spread by wandering minstrels. The epoch of the troubadour in northern Spain, Italy, and France was largely dependent upon this Spanish development; the idealization of the lady and love found in the troubadour songs was a Christian characterization of themes prevalent in Arabic lyrics of the Muslim world.

At the other end of the Muslim world in the province of Fars and especially in Shiraz, there arose the school of Persian poets. As an outgrowth of national feeling Firdawsi, who died in 1020, presented his *Shahnamah,* or great national epic, to Mahmud of Ghaznah. No poetry has ever stirred the soul of the Iranian people as has Firdawsi's *Shahnamah;* even today one can hear illiterate camel-drivers reciting national legends and history from Firdawsi's poetry with great emotion.

The Persian poet best known outside of Iran is, of course, Umar al-Khayyam, whose *Rubaiyat,* through FitzGerald's unrivaled rendering into English, has come in the West to be regarded as the epitome of Middle Eastern poetry. His quatrains expressed the cultured sophistry of twelfth-century Nishapur and were merely the product of the idle moments of this illustrious mathematician.

Besides Firdawsi, the other poets regarded as truly gifted by Iranians were Nizami, whose romantic *Five Treasuries* were exceptionally popular and whose rendition of the Majnun-Layla theme was depicted in countless miniatures; Jalal al-Din al-Rumi, the mystic poet who founded the Mawlawi (Mevlevi) dervish order and died at Konya in Asia Minor in 1273; Sadi of Shiraz, another mystic whose *Gulistan* ("Rose Garden") and *Bustan* ("Orchard") were among the most favorite poems of Iran; and the fourteenth-century Hafiz, the master of Persian lyricists, a materialist yet a mystic, whose love for the shady gardens, the wine and women, and the laughter-loving people of Shiraz was shown in his *Diwan,* or *Collection of Odes.*

Literature
For the most part the classical literature of the medieval Middle East consisted of the writings of famous philosophers, theologians, geographers, historians, and men of like interests. Belles-lettres, prose fiction, and drama were not so highly regarded among the Arabs; not until the tenth century did Persian contacts influence the general taste to produce Arabic literature of this type. Affected and ornate to the Westerner and embellished with philological curiosities, rhymed prose emphasized elegant form over substance. In Muslim Spain a type of anecdote, frequently introducing a moral lesson through the adventure of some dashing hero, became the prototype of the Spanish picaresque novel. In his rhetorical tales al-Hariri of Basrah (1054–1122) criticized rather subtly the existing social order.

Superb, however, were a number of delightful anthologies—each one partly a treasury of poetry, literature, and history and partly the original work of the compiler. Today they serve as invaluable sources for the study of Muslim civilization. Two outstanding examples are the twenty-volume *Kitab al-Aghani (Book of Songs)* gathered by Abu al-Faraj al-Isfahani, who died in 967 in Aleppo, and *al-Iqd al-Farid (The Unique Necklace)* by Ibn Abd Rabbih, who died in 940 in Cordoba.

Of all the literature of the Middle East the most colorful, fanciful, and noteworthy through many centuries has been *The Arabian Nights.* Taking the core of the stories and names of leading characters from an old Persian collection, al-Jahshiyari in the first half of the tenth century in Iraq blended local color and current episodes and romances of the courts of al-Rashid, al-Mamun, and the other spirited caliphs to produce the great *Alf Laylah wa Laylah (One Thousand and One Nights).* Its present form was achieved in the fourteenth century in Mamluk Egypt. In the nineteenth century, excellent English translations were made by Edward W. Lane, John Payne, and Sir Richard F. Burton.

History
Middle Eastern peoples have always been mindful of their own history, the Muslims not excepted. The epic poetry of pre-Islamic days related the history of the tribes and families of Arabia, and the collecting and arranging of the hadith soon after the death of Muhammad definitely preserved a great deal of historical material. To the early Muslims the break with their immediate past appeared so sharp and complete that several generations

passed before they began the process of examining their own chronicles. The caliph Muawiyah in Damascus commanded the preparation of a *Book of Kings and History of the Ancients,* but only so that he himself might pursue kingly ways.

By the middle of the eighth century, historical works began to attract the attention of Muslim scholars. The first known biography of the Prophet was composed by Ibn Ishak, who died in 767. In the ninth century, accounts of the early battles of Islam, tales of the astonishing Arab expansion, and biographical dictionaries of historical figures appeared. The two best were those of al-Hakam (an Egyptian), the story of the conquest of Egypt, North Africa, and Spain, and of al-Baladhuri (an Iranian), a full narrative of Muslim expansion.

The lengthy and more formal histories of the Middle East produced in the medieval era were numerous and varied. Every century and court had professional chroniclers. One of the more noted was al-Tabari (838–923), who traveled widely and studied at many important Muslim centers. A most prolific writer for more than forty years, al-Tabari left a monumental historical chronicle incorporating data sifted from innumerable monographs. His contemporary from Baghdad, al-Masudi, dealt with the same material but treated the unfolding of civilizations topically instead of chronologically as al-Tabari had done. Written after years of travel had taken the author nearly everywhere, al-Masudi's work ran to thirty volumes.

Probably the best known of Muslim historians has been the Tunisian Ibn Khaldun (1332–1406). A citizen of the Muslim world, he studied and held important political positions in Fez, Granada, Algeria, and Cairo. His history of the Muslim states and peoples was a significant contribution to knowledge, especially the sections regarding North Africa. But Ibn Khaldun's fame rested on his history's first volume, entitled *Mukaddamah (Prolegomena),* in which he presented his philosophy of the development of civilization and explained how the historian should record and study the interrelated forces of society. Since he considered the factors of climate, geography, economics, and culture, Ibn Khaldun can be called the first modern historian.

Education
In the early days of the Muslim Empire the ruling Arabs held that a man was educated if he learned to read and write, to use the bow and arrow, and to swim. A man should be taught courage, endurance, justice, hospitality, honesty, manliness, generosity, and respect for women. Among the conquered peoples schools of various types and grades existed, and in general they attained high proficiency in their intellectual skills. By the opening of the eighth century most leading Muslims employed tutors or owned slaves to teach their children. The only education available for the masses was that which could be obtained from Koran readers in the mosques.

In the Abbasid period the number of elementary schools increased, so that many children were taught to read and write. The curriculum centered upon the Koran and allied religious texts, and memory achievement was the goal. Children of wealthy and prominent families continued to get rigorous and comprehensive private instruction. It was still not easy to acquire an advanced education, although to make one's way about the Muslim world in quest of the great teacher was less arduous than in earlier days. Various academies existed, some with endowments; but they were unorganized and did not furnish any systematic education.

The first university to be established under Islam was the University of Cordoba, founded by Abd al-Rahman III in the middle of the tenth century. Enlarged and placed upon a more solid financial basis by al-Hakam, Cordoba gathered professors and attracted students from every Muslim land. Professorial chairs were endowed, and fellowships were granted to advanced students. One of the most famous of the Islamic universities was the al-Azhar University in Cairo, founded by the Fatimid caliph al-Aziz in the latter part of the tenth century. Through the centuries al-Azhar maintained a reputation for scholarship and a high quality of education, especially in the fields of theology and law. Today it still draws thousands of students from every quarter of Islam.

A bureau for translation, a library, and an observatory in al-Mamun's House of Wisdom in Baghdad served as a kind of collegiate institution; but the honor of creating the first center of learning in the east fell to Nizam al-Mulk, the ingenious eleventh-century vizir. His Nizamiyah in Baghdad was duplicated within a few years throughout the Muslim world by similar institutions called *madrasahs*. In the leading cities of Islam each of the larger mosques included a *madrasah*, where law, philosophy, history, and the sciences were taught. Memory work predominated as in most educational establishments in all civilizations throughout the ages. But the need for thinking and the obligation to show the relation between the ideas they imparted and the ethical and social requirements of society were recognized by noted Muslim teachers.

Architecture
One feature of Muslim civilization that has always impressed visitors has been the mosque and its accompanying minaret. The house of the urban Arab in Muhammad's time was almost invariably a simple enclosure, usually square, with a few huts placed in a rather haphazard way along the edge. The first mosque was none other than the house of Muhammad. Before he died it assumed a public character, for here the followers congregated to pray with Muhammad and to hear his revelations, sermons, and instructions. Along one side palm trunks were set up and covered with palm leaves as a protection from the sun. Muhammad first used to lean against a trunk when he spoke; later he stood on a piece of a palm trunk. Some pointer indicated the direction of Mecca so that prayers could be made facing that holy city. Bilal stood on some roof top to call the Muslims to prayer or to a community meeting. Thus were established the essentials of a mosque.

As the Arabs and Muslims expanded into other lands, they employed local masons, carpenters, stonecutters, and other craftsmen in the building of mosques. Consequently, skills, techniques, and materials differed from place to place. But the fundamentals of a congregational mosque remained unchanged. A large part of the mosque area was an open courtyard, usually with a fountain where ablutions could be performed and sometimes with a narrow covered arcade on three sides. On the fourth side was the mosque proper. In most mosques in Syria, Egypt, North Africa, Spain, and Iraq the mosque proper consisted of a system of arches supported by piers or columns arranged in series of parallel aisles and upholding domes, vaults, and either a flat or a gabled wooden roof. Where the dome covered a square chamber or area, the transition from the arch was made by the use of squinches or spherical triangular pendentives. Stilted and horseshoe arches appeared early in the development of Islamic architecture, largely because the available cut columns taken from older structures were not long enough to hold the roof at the desired height. At Cordoba this problem was met by a series of columns and arches superimposed upon another series.

At one or more of the corners of the enclosure there stood a minaret. First appearing at the mosque in Damascus, it was a square towerlike structure from which the call to prayer was given. Round or pencil-shaped minarets did not develop until late in the medieval period, although circular ziggurat-type minarets are known to have existed in ninth-century Iraq and Iran.

In the wall of the mosque on the side toward Mecca the mihrab, or niche, was usually constructed to indicate the exact direction of the Holy City. This was particularly helpful in converted churches, since they were often not correctly oriented. A wooden or marble pulpit *(minbar)* was a necessary piece of furniture of a congregational mosque, enabling the imam who delivered the Friday sermon to be seen and heard by all. The façade encasing the main portal of the mosque enclosure as well as the inner façade around the doorway to the mosque itself came in time to be elaborately decorated, taking on the appearance of an external mihrab. Semidomes, vaults, arcatures, stalactite corbeling, marble paneling, and molding surrounded these entrances and made peerless approaches for the mosques. In Iran and the east some mosques had lofty and imposing portals showing an unmistakable influence of ancient structures of Persepolis and Ctesiphon upon Muslim architecture.

The exterior and interior decoration of the mosques was based upon matched and quartered panels of marble, porphyry, and other types of stone, different-colored stones being used in alternate courses in the walls or in alternate voussoirs in the arches. Capitals, spandrils, and other spaces were often covered with finely carved geometric and floral patterns; and in many instances the walls were given color, warmth, and depth by the use of plain or figured tiles. One of the most frequent and pleasing patterns employed in stone, wood, or ceramics was that composed of highly stylized

Arabic letters, almost invariably a verse from the Koran. Human and animal figures were forbidden by the Koran and their use in decoration rarely appeared in a mosque, although the prohibition was often disregarded in objects of secular use.

Some of the imposing mosques of the Middle East that date from the early medieval period are the Umayyad mosque of Damascus, begun in 705; the Mosque of Ibn Tulun in Cairo, finished in 879; the Great Mosque of Kayrawan, built about 743; the Mosque of Karawiyn of Fez, begun in 859 and finished in 1135; the Great Mosque of Cordoba, begun in 785 (now the cathedral); the Friday Mosque of Isfahan, built about 760; and the Mosque of Sultan Ala-al-Din of Konya, built in 1220.

Although mosques and great mausoleums have been the most permanent of Middle Eastern edifices of the medieval period, various books contain descriptions of numerous libraries, hospitals, bazaars, palaces, forts, shrines, and palatial public baths in Baghdad and other cities. Probably the most widely known sacred building in the Muslim Middle East is the revered *Kubbat-al-Sakhra* ("The Dome of the Rock"), often popularly referred to as The Mosque of Umar. An annular structure, it was begun in 685 by Caliph Abd al-Malik to cover and enshrine the spot from where, according to legend, Muhammad made his nocturnal journey to heaven. Termed the oldest extant Muslim place of worship except for the Kaaba in Mecca, it comprises an octagon surmounted by a dome which rests upon an interior circle of piers and columns. The space between the inner circle and the octagonal wall was too wide to be spanned by beams, necessitating an intermediate octagon of arches borne by piers and columns. Thus was formed two rings which were used for ceremonial circumambulation. Originally the upper part of the exterior was covered with marble and gold mosaics, but these were replaced with the decorated tiles that are now there. The style of the building was a composite of Syrian, Roman, and Byzantine traditions and contained a number of novel adaptations. The style, however, was followed in later Muslim architecture only in technical and decorative details and not as a general model for other structures.

The Minor Arts
In the whole field of the so-called minor arts Muslims in the medieval period carried on the skills and techniques of antiquity in a notable fashion. Far ahead of western Europe in each of the minor arts, at least until the High Renaissance of the fifteenth century, the Middle East produced outstanding rugs, silk and cotton textiles, leatherwork, fine glass, highly glazed ceramics of many types, shapes, and varieties, and exquisite pieces in gold, silver, copper, brass, and bronze, many of the pieces heavily inlaid with other metals or encrusted with precious gems. The illumination of manuscripts and the painting of miniature pictures developed into a fine and precise art. Skilled penmanship produced a calligraphy so graceful and so pleasing that later Western artists frequently employed strips of Arabic script in their own decorations. The expertness of the Middle Eastern artist in the me-

dium of enamel inlay upon metal was manifest to the Crusaders, so much so that many terms used in describing color (enamelwork) in armorial bearings and in heraldry were derived from Arabic words.

One striking evidence of the real unity of the Muslim world between the seventh and thirteenth centuries was the ease and extent of exchange of knowledge and movement of individuals. Such a circulation dictated a considerable universality of Muslim civilization, and the minor arts are an excellent illustration. From Marrakesh and Toledo on the west to Samarkand in the east, each of the great cities boasted reputable craftsmen and artists in all of the arts. For centuries Byzantine Constantinople was the only comparable center outside of the Muslim world.

The Seclusion of Women

By the tenth century the role of wealthy, middle-class, and urban women in the family and in society had undergone a marked change. The veil, seclusion, and segregation of the sexes were practiced by Muslims and by many non-Muslims in the Middle East. Their origin and the reasons for their introduction are not certain, but the best indications point to Byzantine civilization as the main influence. With the general and wide acceptance of concubinage and its excesses, the rank of the actual wife was greatly elevated. Slave girls might sing, dance, and entertain quite openly and freely for the guests of their masters; wives never. Thus, the veil and seclusion grew as a protection and a mark of distinction. However, the freedom and the public life of women such as enjoyed by Aishah, Khayzuran, and Zubaydah disappeared, not to return to the Muslim world until the twentieth century.

Recreation

The great mass of people in the medieval Middle East, as in all other regions and in other periods except for the present, had neither time nor energy for recreation and entertainment. People of moderate means as well as the wealthy and the leaders of society in the Middle East enjoyed poetry and music. Although Muhammad had castigated music as one of the devil's handmaidens, song and music from various instruments were exceedingly popular. Accomplished musicians were praised, highly rewarded, and accepted as companions in high society. Slaves with musical talent and training commanded high prices. The elite themselves sometimes performed, and al-Rashid's brother Ibrahim was regarded as a truly accomplished musician.

The Middle Eastern gentleman relaxed at home or at a public bath which served as his club. Baghdad in its heyday boasted several thousand such establishments. After soaking and steaming and a vigorous massage the patron might sip cool sherbet, listen to music, and engage in a game of dice, backgammon, or chess. Chess was an ancient Indian game which came to

Christian Europe by way of Iran and the Muslims. The word "chess" is a corruption of the Persian *shah*, "checkmate," of *shah mat* ("the king is dishonored"). "Rook" is the Persian *rukh*, or the dreaded roc described by Sindbad the Sailor. In Spain, the piece known in English as "bishop" is called *el alfil* from the Arabic *al-fil* ("the elephant"). And the modern "queen" has evolved from a piece that Chaucer called "fers," which was the Arabic *al-firzan* ("the counselor").

Outdoor sports were many; favorites were archery, javelin-throwing, fencing, polo, and a ball game that may have been the ancestor of tennis. Hunting with its allied sports of hawking and falconry was much in vogue in the Umayyad and Abbasid eras. Caliphs and generals organized great hunts in which thousands participated in driving the game into confined quarters where the hunters could shoot the quarry without much effort. However, certain wild game at close range frequently provided a dangerous and exciting sport, sometimes depicted in painting and ceramic decoration. The art of falconry was greatly refined, and there were numerous books on the subject.

The most royal of all sports in the Middle East was horse racing. In ancient Iran, in Greece, and in Roman and Byzantine times racing was the sport of kings and the favorite of the masses. The Arabs loved and prized horses; and the Muslim rulers quickly took to racing their horses in Syria, Iraq, and Egypt, as the Byzantine and Sasanid governors were doing when the Arabs appeared on the scene. Caliphs had their own stables, and al-Rashid apparently evidenced great pleasure when his horses won their races. Betting, though unlawful by Koranic injunction, accompanied horse racing, as it did all sports for that matter, and made the races and games more exciting. Pedigrees and an interest in the breeding of horses advanced to the point where eastern horses were recognized and valued everywhere as Arabian horses.

From the foregoing survey of the many aspects of Muslim culture and its development in the medieval period it can be adduced that the permanence of Muslim culture must be credited to the wisdom of Muhammad and the Islamic leaders during the formative years of their empires. They appropriated and adapted from other civilizations and societies valuable ideas, experiences, and skills to create the new Muslim civilization. No civilization has been able to endure for long or to pursue any dynamic course when isolated either geographically or intellectually. Progress has been accelerated by the exchange of knowledge among people and cultures; the greater the exchange, the faster the acceleration. Although the Muslim empires were always politically unstable, any investigation of Muslim society reveals a continuing progress until the havoc and chaos following in the wake of the Mongol invasions of the thirteenth century brought upon the whole Middle Eastern society a penury and a despair from which it is only now in the twentieth century escaping.

REFERENCES: Chapter 9

Among the volumes already cited, those of particular value for this chapter are in Chapters 4, 5, 7, and 8.

Ahmed, Munir-ud-Din. *Muslim Education and the Scholar's Social Status up to the 5th Century Muslim Era in the Light of Ta'rikh Baghdad.* Zurich: Verlag Der Islam, 1968. A great deal of data about scholars.

Arberry, Arthur J. *Classical Persian Literature.* New York: Macmillan, 1958. A thorough discussion of the great classics.

Ardalan, Nader, and Laleh Bakhtiar. *The Sense of Unity: The Sufi Tradition in Persian Architecture.* Chicago: Chicago University Press, 1973. A beautiful book showing the place and effect of Sufi thought in Iranian architecture.

Atiyeh, George N. *Al-Kindi, the Philosopher of the Arabs.* Rawalpindi: Islamic Research Institute, 1966. A full study of the philosopher and an annotated list of his works.

Boer, Tjitze J. de. *History of Philosophy in Islam.* Translated by E. R. Jones. London: Luzac, 1903.

Briggs, Martin S. *Muhammadan Architecture in Egypt and Palestine.* Oxford: Clarendon Press, 1924. A thorough survey of the field.

Browne, E. G. *Arabian Medicine.* Cambridge, Eng.: Cambridge University Press, 1921. Excellent.

———. *A Literary History of Persia.* 4 vols. Cambridge, Eng.: Cambridge University Press, 1928. The standard work on this subject, and one that relates to political and social developments.

Creswell, K. A. C. *Early Muslim Architecture: Umayyads, Early 'Abbasids and Tulunids.* 2 vols. Oxford: Clarendon Press, 1932–1940. An essential work for a study of the subject.

———. *A Short Account of Early Muslim Architecture.* Baltimore: Penguin, 1958. A brief survey of his earlier works, covering Umayyad, Abbasid, and Tulunid periods and discussing works in Jerusalem, Cordoba, Kayrawan, and Samarra.

Dodge, Bayard (ed. and trans.). *The Fihrist of al-Nadim: A Tenth-Century Survey of Muslim Culture.* 2 vols. New York: Columbia University Press, 1970. A translation of a compendium of all knowledge written in the tenth century by al-Nadim from newly found manuscripts.

———. *Muslim Education in Medieval Times.* Washington, D.C.: The Middle East Institute, 1962. An unusual and scholarly work.

Fakhry, Majid. *A History of Islamic Philosophy.* New York: Columbia University Press, 1970. A substantial comprehensive history of Islamic theoretical philosophy, theology, and mysticism. Concentrates on metaphysics, ignores politics, and touches on ethics only lightly. A profound analysis of Neoplatonic philosophy and the theosophy of the Sufis.

Gibb, H. A. R. *Arabic Literature: An Introduction.* London: Oxford University Press, 1926. Contains a good bibliography of available translations.

———. (transl.). *The Travels of Ibn Battuta (A.D. 1325–1354).* 3 vols. Cambridge, Eng., and New York: Cambridge University Press, 1958, 1962, 1972. A native of Tangier, Ibn Battutah set out as a pilgrim as a young man and traveled in nearly all the Muslim countries of his time and beyond to the Black Sea area, China, south Asia, Spain, and west Africa.

Giffen, Lois Anita. *Theory of Profane Love Among the Arabs: The Development of the Genre.* New York: New York University Press, 1971. A study of the extensive theoretical writings in medieval Arabic on interhuman love: first, on the essence and nature of love; and second, on its various phases.

Grabar, Oleg. *The Formation of Islamic Art.* New Haven: Yale University Press, 1973. The author's treatment is very sensitive, his insights are thought-provoking, and his expression superb. It is full of conceptual contributions. He defines the originality and uniqueness of Islamic art. A most important work.

Grube, Ernst J. *The World of Islam.* New York: McGraw-Hill, 1966. Landmarks of Islamic art.

Grunebaum, Gustave von. *Islam: Essays in the Nature and Growth of a Cultural Tradition.* New York: Barnes & Noble, 1961. Important in linking Islam and culture.

———— (ed.). *Unity and Variety in Muslim Civilization.* Chicago: University of Chicago Press, 1955. A symposium by sixteen specialists showing the impact certain well-established cultures had upon Muslim culture when the latter was forcefully imposed upon the former.

Gurgani, Fakr-ud-Din. *Vis and Ramin.* Translated by George Morrison. The Persian Heritage series. New York: Columbia University Press, 1972. An eleventh-century Persian love poem on the theme of the Parthian legend of love. Both Sa'adi and Hafiz were influenced by this work.

Hill, Derek. *Islamic Architecture and Its Decoration: A Photographic Survey.* Introductory text by Oleg Grabar. London: Faber & Faber, 1964. Excellent pictures and interpretive descriptions and analysis.

Kritzeck, James (introduction and commentaries). *Anthology of Islamic Literature from the Rise of Islam to Modern Times.* New York: Holt, Rinehart and Winston, 1964. Discusses all forms of literature from the Koran and early commentaries to political science writings, history, stories, and Karagöz.

Levey, Martin. *Early Arabic Pharmacology: An Introduction Based on Ancient and Medieval Sources.* Leiden: Brill, 1973. Focuses on materia medica and therapeutics, beginning with pre-Islamic pharmacology.

Levy, Reuben. *Persian Literature: An Introduction.* Oxford: Oxford University Press, 1923. Excellent for the beginner.

————. *The Social Structure of Islam.* Cambridge, Eng.: Cambridge University Press, 1957. A thorough study and analysis of all aspects of society in the Islamic world from the earliest times to the present.

Lewis, Bernard, and P. M. Holt (eds.). *Historians of the Middle East.* New York: Oxford University Press, 1962. A most important work.

Margoliouth, D. S. *Lectures on Arabic Historians.* Calcutta: University of Calcutta, 1930.

Nasr, Seyyed Hossein. *Science and Civilization in Islam.* Cambridge, Mass.: Harvard University Press, 1968. A discussion of the development of science, technology, and scientific methodology in medieval Islam.

Nicholson, R. A. *A Literary History of the Arabs.* Cambridge, Eng.: Cambridge University Press, 1930. Gives the reader an excellent view of the many types of Arab poetry and prose before 1000 A.D.

Peters, F. E. *Aristotle and the Arabs: The Aristotelian Tradition in Islam.* New York: New York University Press, 1968. A study of the synthesis of Hellenism and Islam and of the Arab's reception, adaptation, and assimilation of Aristotelianism.

Pope, Arthur Upham. *An Introduction to Persian Art Since the Seventh Century A.D.* New York: Scribner, 1931. Well written and amply illustrated by an authority for the beginner, but interesting also to the specialist in the field of Middle Eastern studies.

Ibn al-Razzaz al-Jazari. *The Book of Knowledge of Ingenious Mechanical Devices.* Translated and annotated by Donald R. Hill. Boston: Reidel, 1973. A faithful translation of the Arabic treatise on machines written in 1206 by an engineer who worked for the Artuqid princes of Diyarbakir.

Rescher, Nicholas. *The Development of Arabic Logic.* Pittsburgh: University of Pittsburgh Press, 1964. A very useful compendium of biographical and bibliographical data on logic and other cultural fields.

Richmond, Ernest Tatham. *The Dome of the Rock in Jerusalem: A Description of Its Structure & Decoration.* Oxford: Clarendon Press, 1924. A complete description of this historic shrine.

Rosenthal, Franz. *The Herb: Hashish Versus Medieval Muslim Society.* Leiden: Brill, 1971. A kind of source book for the sociology of hashish usage in Islam. It is a collection of law, poetry, custom, philology, medicine, and natural history as they deal with hashish and its use.

————. *Knowledge Triumphant: The Concept of Knowledge in Medieval Islam.* Leiden: Brill, 1970. An examination of the workings of the conception of knowledge in Islamic theology and religious science, in education, and in general culture.

Stern, S. M., Albert Hourani, and Vivian Brown (eds.). *Islamic Philosophy and the Classical Tradition.* Columbia, S. C.: University of South Carolina Press, 1972. These are papers dealing with Arabic Aristotelianism, Islamic ethics, and scholastic theology.

Ibn Tufayl. *Hayy Ibn Yaqzan.* Translated by Lenn Evan Goodman. New York: Twayne, 1972. A twelfth-century story of a child reared in solitude on a desert isle, illustrating the struggle between philosophy and mysticism.

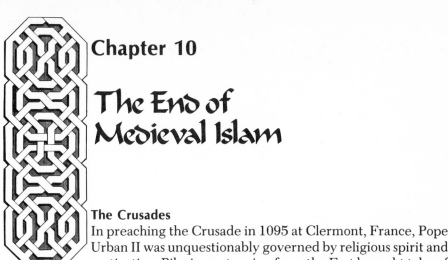

Chapter 10

The End of Medieval Islam

The Crusades

In preaching the Crusade in 1095 at Clermont, France, Pope Urban II was unquestionably governed by religious spirit and motivation. Pilgrims returning from the East brought tales of the woe that recent Seljuk conquests had inflicted upon them in Asia Minor and Syria. They also reported that disunity and internecine warfare among the petty Muslim states of Syria and their leaders would make possible a victorious assault by Christian knights of Europe. Furthermore, the desperate appeal sent by Alexius Comnenus, emperor of Constantinople, promised the cooperation of the Byzantine army and fleet.

Western feudal Christendom had developed economically, socially, politically, and psychologically to a degree that it could outfit and send a temporary expeditionary force overseas. The success this force might achieve stemmed from the power vacuum and political chaos that descended upon the Middle East after the death of Sultan Malikshah.

Gathering at Constantinople as an advance base, the Crusaders, almost always called Franks by Middle Easterners, departed for the Holy Land in the spring of 1097. Taking by force Iznik (Nicaea) in June and Eskishehr (Doryleum) in July, the main Frankish army won Antakya (Antioch) after many heroic and emotional incidents and a nine-month siege. By an inland route the Crusaders began the investing of Jerusalem on June 7, 1099, and successfully stormed the walls on July 15. Later that year the first victory on the coast was scored at Ascalon, and in the ensuing decade one after another of the coastal cities of the Levant fell to the merchant fleets of Pisa, Venice, and Genoa.

Shortly after the conquest of the Holy City, Godfrey of Bouillon became the Baron and Defender of the Holy Sepulchre and the titular head of the kingdom of Jerusalem. Other prominent Crusaders scattered along the coast to become the count of Edessa, prince of Antioch, and count of Tripoli, these newly created principalities being held as fiefs of Jerusalem. Merely extensions of feudal Europe, these four little Crusader states along the Mediterranean littoral were the so-called Latin kingdoms of the East. Most of the Crusaders returned home as soon as the first victories were won, and those who stayed on were continuously hard-pressed to retain their possessions. In fact, they would have been lost at an early date had not an uninterrupted stream of knights appeared from the West and had not the merchant cities of the western Mediterranean maintained fleets in the Levant.

Eventually the kingdom of Jerusalem was extended eastward across the Dead Sea and southward in a narrow tongue of land to touch the Gulf of Akaba. In the north the county of Edessa reached eastward to the headwaters of the Tigris. Elsewhere, the Franks clung close to the coast, in some places holding a strip barely ten to fifteen miles wide. They never gained possession of such cities as Aleppo, Homs, or Damascus.

The great majority of Western successes sprang from the complete disunity of the Muslim rulers. The amirs of Syria were delighted by the Crusaders' defeat of the Seljuks in Asia Minor; and during the siege of Antioch emissaries from Egypt proposed a combination of the Crusaders and the Fatimid caliph against the Turks. It becomes tiresome to record the alliances made by Muslim princes with the Latins against fellow Muslims, or alliances made by Franks with Muslim amirs against fellow Crusader feudal lords.

Before a decade had passed only a newly arrived naïve Crusader carried the religious spirit and fervor that had launched the First Crusade. In the Middle East the Latin knight reverted to the search for fiefs and the constant fighting that he had known in the West. That he could do this and feel at home in Syria and Palestine in the twelfth century was a result of the political chaos already present at his arrival. Nevertheless, the more advanced civilization of the Middle East began to influence the more barbarous Westerners. Latin nobles emulated the ways and adopted the higher standard of living of Middle Eastern ruling classes, thus opening the way for some of the knowledge of the East to find its way to western Europe and hasten the coming of the Renaissance.

Baghdad and the eastern Seljuk sultans were hardly perturbed by the inroads of the Crusaders, especially since the latter succumbed within a few years to the general preexisting political pattern of the Middle East. Resistance to the West awaited the appearance of a vigorous leader capable of creating an extensive Muslim state that might serve as a base for an attack upon the Franks.

Such a man was the blue-eyed Zangi, Turkish lord of Mosul. Consolidating the northern arc of the Fertile Crescent from Mosul to Aleppo into one Muslim state, Imad-al-Din Zangi stormed and took Edessa in 1144, an act that touched off the so-called Second Crusade. Although such notables as Louis VII of France and Conrad III of Germany participated, the chief effect of this expedition was to bring fresh recruits to ward off other blows and hold the line.

The Zangid principality subsequently augmented its power as the Seljuk rule in Baghdad and the Fatimid power in Cairo waned. Zangi's son added Damascus to his state, conquered all of the county of Edessa, and wrested territory from Antioch and Tripoli. By-passing the Franks in Jerusalem, his armies forced the Fatimid caliph of Egypt to surrender control of that fair

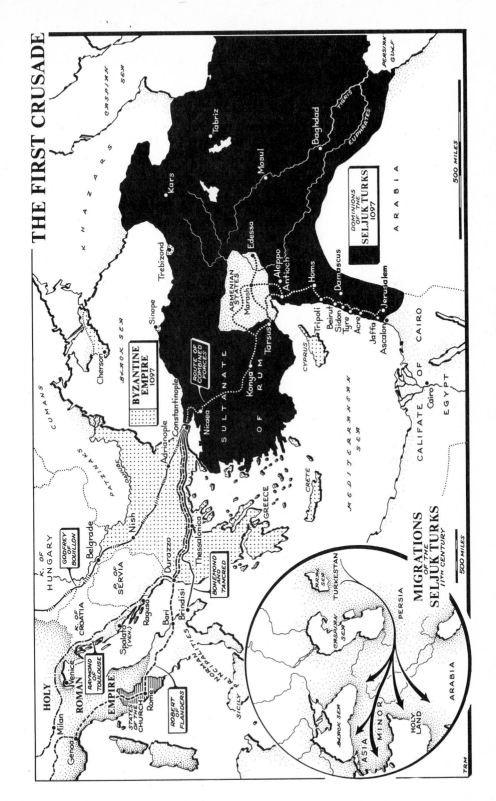

THE FIRST CRUSADE

BYZANTINE EMPIRE
1097

DOMINIONS OF THE
SELJUK TURKS
1097

ROUTE OF
COMBINED
FORCES

MIGRATIONS
OF THE
SELJUK TURKS
11TH CENTURY

500 MILES

125

Muslim province to a Zangid lieutenant, Salah-al-Din Yusuf ibn Ayyub (Saladin).

Of Kurdish stock, Salah-al-Din sought to unify Islam and destroy the Crusaders. In 1171 he refused to recognize the Fatimid (Shiite) caliph and restored Egypt to the Sunnite creed. Upon the end of the Zangids, Salah-al-Din seized Syria, went on to take Mosul and northern Iraq, and eventually was accepted as the sultan of the Hijaz, Nubia, and North Africa as well.

Turning upon the Franks, Salah-al-Din wiped out the cream of the knights' armies at the Battle of Hittin on July 4, 1187. This victory enabled him to retake Jerusalem and all of the principal cities except Antioch, Tripoli, and Tyre.

Jerusalem's fall initiated the Third Crusade, which gave rise to more romantic episodes in the history and literature of Islam and Christendom alike than any of the other Crusades. Philip Augustus, Frederick Barbarossa, and Richard the Lion-Hearted could not recapture Jerusalem; but after a fabulous siege of two years Acre (Akka) fell to Richard. When the demanded ransom was not forthcoming, Richard decreed the execution of the garrison of 2,700. This was in sharp contrast to Salah-al-Din's clemency following the fall of Jerusalem, when all who were not ransomed were set free.

Pursuant to the victory at Acre, Richard suggested the marriage of his sister and Salah-al-Din's brother. Jerusalem was to be a wedding gift, and general peace was to be arranged between Frank and Muslim. The marriage did not occur, but an armistice was concluded, leaving a narrow coastal area in possession of the Latins.

Salah-al-Din died the next spring, and upon his passing the usual political dismemberment developed. One son held Damascus; others governed at Cairo and Aleppo. A brother, the Saphadin of Western chroniclers, ruled Transjordania and conquered Syria and Egypt. Upon his death division and anarchy again ruled the Ayyubids until their own slaves and the Mongols destroyed them.

The recurring Muslim turmoil played into the Westerners' hands, enabling them to retake Beirut, Tiberias, Ascalon, and Jerusalem (1229). However, quarrels of Venetian against Genoese, Templar against Hospitaler, and baron against baron prevented lasting achievements. Salah-al-Din's nephew forced the Latins to abandon Damietta in Egypt, where they had landed in realization of the significance of Egypt and the Red Sea in their commerce with India and the East. Nevertheless, he made friendly treaties with the Italian city-states, entertained and discussed theology with St. Francis of Assisi, and gave Jerusalem to Frederick II.

Jerusalem was taken in 1244 by a band of Turks; Louis IX's crusade to Egypt fell victim to the plague in 1249; and in that same year the Ayyubid family in Egypt was supplanted by Turkish generals from its slave army. A new era in Muslim history was emerging—the Mamluk (slave) period. Baybars, the fourth Mamluk sultan, captured Palestine and moved northward along an inland route to take Antioch. His successor continued the drive against the Latin state, and in 1291 another Mamluk took Acre. This was the signal for the remaining Crusader towns of Beirut, Sidon, and Tyre to surrender. An episode in the history of the Middle East had ended.

As significant events influencing the development of civilizations and the destiny of humanity, the Crusades have been greatly overrated. Nineteenth-century romanticists dramatized them and enlarged their role far beyond the actual facts. Most of the Crusaders remained in the Middle East such a short time and were so poorly prepared psychologically and educationally that they profited little from the experience. Of the few who resided in the Middle East for any length of time only the rare knight was fain to exchange the rich and interesting life in his new abode for the dull monotony on his former estate in the West.

Trade between East and West in the Mediterranean did, however, increase markedly. Italian merchants now had for the first time a paying eastbound cargo: Crusaders. This reduced the cost of Eastern goods in Western markets. Furthermore, returning Crusaders created an expanded Western market for Eastern goods, since even those who remained in the Middle East only a brief time did acquire a taste for Oriental foods and a preference for its superior manufactured goods such as textiles, cutlery, metal wares, and leather goods. However, the main channels of Muslim influence upon western Europe were Sicily and Spain. Perhaps the flow through those areas was accelerated as a result of the Crusades and the returning Crusaders' awakened consciousness, if not appreciation, of a foreign civilization obviously richer than their own.

The effects upon the Middle East were much less significant. Its people became convinced that the Westerner was a ruthless soldier, semibarbarous in nature, ignorant, and uncivilized. Even today Syrian mothers frighten their children when they misbehave by threatening them with "Richard the Lion-Hearted will get you." For centuries, Crusaders' castles dotted the landscape, but these never altered in any measurable degree the architecture of the Levant. The Middle East was politically disunited when the Crusaders arrived; it was still in fragments when they departed. In the interim, to be sure, the Ayyubids united the Muslims from the Nile to the Tigris. But this had no relationship to the Crusades; it was only an example of the recurring pattern of centralizing and decentralizing political forces continually at work in the area. In general it can be said that the Crusaders were more destructive than constructive, and that the Middle East was poorer because of the experience.

The Mongol Invasions

In the thirteenth century as the Crusades were waning, devastation rode in upon the Muslim world from the east. Born about 1160 in the neighborhood of Lake Baikal, Genghiz Khan, ruler over Mongol nomads and the self-styled Scourge of God, consolidated in his hands the military might of the tireless Mongol warriors. Shortly after the opening of the thirteenth century, Genghiz and his hordes moved westward to Iran, conquering all lands in their path. Bukhara, Samarkand, Marw, Nishapur, Hamadan,

Maraghah, and many other centers of civilization were stormed and sacked. Inhabitants were slain by the hundreds of thousands, perhaps millions.

Iraq, Syria, and provinces in the west were spared by Genghiz's death in 1227 and by the subsequent division of the empire among his sons. But his sons and grandsons and other Mongol khans maintained the great empire. Pressure continued upon the Middle East. The Seljuk Turks in Asia Minor were defeated in a ruinous battle in 1243, and the Mongols levied tribute upon them. Under Mangu, the third successor to the position of supreme khan, a great expedition moved westward under the direction of Mangu's younger brother Hulagu. Starting from Karakorum in 1252 to rid the world of the Assassins and to destroy the Abbasid caliphate, Hulagu Khan razed Alamut, the Assassin headquarters. Baghdad's turn came in 1258. Following a siege of several months, the city fell and was given over completely to the troops for a week. Destruction continued for a month. The Mongols then proceeded westward as far as Damascus but were halted by Baybars, the Mamluk sultan of Egypt, in an historic battle in 1260 at Ayn Jalat, near Nazareth. Egypt was spared Mongol violence; and Baybars pressed his victory, freeing Syria from Mongol control.

The Mongols in their conquests helped themselves to whatever they wanted and destroyed the rest, not knowing what to do with it. They could not garrison the cities adequately; they were pagans; and they neither understood nor appreciated the cultures and civilizations of the peoples they conquered. The effects of the devastation wrought by the Mongols is only now in the twentieth century being mended. Millions of peoples perished; cities vanished; canals silted and irrigation ceased; lands became barren and deserted; government disintegrated; civilization foundered; and life returned to the bare essentials. Through the previous ages conquering armies and peoples had come and gone—Medes, Persians, Sasanids, Greeks, Romans, Byzantines, and Arabs—and customs, religions, knowledge, and culture had been modified, developed, and altered. But through all this time the Middle East had never suffered such a cataclysmic and paralytic shock as it received from the Mongol invasions.

Mamluk Rule in Egypt

Untouched by the Mongol devastation, Egypt suddenly became the great stronghold of Muslim civilization, even though she herself had just entered into the strangest epoch of her long history.

Upon the death of the Ayyubid sultan in 1249 one of his widows seized power with the support of a Turkish slave general whom she married. When she later had him murdered in his bath, she was beaten to death by his slave soldiers. The rule of Egypt then passed briefly to his son and then to other slave generals, one after another until 1517 when Egypt was conquered by the Ottomans. This long period of two and a half centuries of Egyptian history was termed the Mamluk ("slave") era. Until 1390 the Mamluks were mostly Turkish and Mongol in origin, and they went by the name of Bahri ("river") Mamluks. Between 1390 and 1517 they were generally Circassians and were known as the Burji ("citadel") Mamluks.

Begun by the later Ayyubids as a slave army and bodyguard of foreign origin, the Mamluks evolved into a self-perpetuating slave military oligarchy. The recruit was purchased, usually in an eastern slave market, by the agent of a slave general or officer and rigorously trained in the arts of war. As he developed and progressed toward the top, he in turn made new purchases. A score of generals or amirs at the summit intrigued and battled for supremacy, though nominally electing the successor to the late Mamluk sultan. Many never bothered to learn Arabic and were Muslims in name only. Aloof from the native Egyptians, whom they despised, the Mamluks oppressed their subjects unmercifully.

Although frequently illiterate, the Mamluk sultans were always crafty, and some of them were capable organizers and redoubtable generals. Nevertheless, their lives were fearfully uncertain, the average reign of the forty-seven Mamluk sultans being less than six years. The most resourceful, and one of the most enduring, Sultan Baybars, not only turned back the Mongols in Palestine but also cracked the strength of the Crusaders in Syria. Understanding diplomacy and statecraft, he established friendly relations with Sicily, Aragon, and Seville, sent envoys to the Byzantine emperor, and made an alliance with the Kipchak Turks of the Volga River basin (his own birthplace) against the Mongols of Iran and Mesopotamia. Bringing from Damascus a refugee scion of the Abbasid family, Baybars originated the practice of having an Abbasid in Cairo as titular caliph without actual power. Such caliphs resided there up to the time of the Ottoman conquest, and their presence gave to Mamluk rulers a mark of legal recognition throughout Islam.

Under the Mamluk regime feudalism spread in Egypt. Since late Roman rule in the Middle East certain practices of feudalism had been present, and many of these were accepted by the Muslim conquerors. But in the tenth and eleventh centuries, as the power of the Abbasid governments declined, army generals, captains, and cavalrymen were assigned provinces and estates from which they collected taxes for their own support. For these privileges and benefits they were expected to serve the caliph or sultan, usually in a military capacity. Gradually all of the land of Egypt was granted to Mamluk officers who had to support, equip, and assure the service of a number of soldiers, the number depending upon their rank and the size of the grant.

Destruction of the Medieval Muslim World

Simultaneously with the development of Middle Eastern feudalism came the spread of a self-subsistent manorial economy. As the uncertainties of government mounted and the difficulties of transportation and communication increased, industry and commerce were depressed and the money economy was greatly weakened. Political anarchy and civil wars destroyed the controls over the nomads within the Middle East and the perpetual battle between the Desert and the Sown was resumed, hastening the advent of a manorial economy. The Middle Eastern Muslim lands entered into this new era piecemeal over a long period of time. In the middle of the eleventh century the Beni Hillal and the Beni Sulaym, Arab tribes transplanted to Upper Egypt, ravaged Libya and Tunisia and sacked the holy city of Kayrawan, leaving that part of North Africa in the desolate state that in large part persists today.

The major portion of the Middle East under the Mongol Empire was split into a variety of provinces. Government and wealth moved eastward. From time to time in the century following the conquests of Hulagu, peace among Genghiz Khan's descendants allowed for passage of traders and travelers such as Marco Polo and Ibn Battutah. But the persistent military violence, direct or threatened, stunted the growth of a middle class. Moreover, in 1368 the founder of the Ming dynasty in China conquered the Mongols and closed the trade routes from central Asia into China, diverting all commerce with the Mediterranean to the route through the Arabian Ocean, the Red Sea, and Egypt.

The final blows to the highly developed Muslim culture and civilization of the medieval period in Mesopotamia, central and eastern Asia Minor, and parts of Iran were administered by the Mongolian Turks. For a quarter of a century, 1380–1405, the east was in turmoil because of the eruption of the Mongolian Turks led by Timur Leng ("Timur the Lame," or Tamerlane). Son of a Turkish chieftain who revolted against a descendant of Genghiz Khan, Timur first won control of Transoxiana, which served as a base for expansion, both eastward and westward. In 1380 his hordes began the conquest of Afghanistan, Iran, and Kurdistan. In rapid succession he captured Baghdad, Isfahan, Delhi, Aleppo, Damascus, Ankara, and Smyrna. Timur's death in 1405 and the subsequent anarchy among his heirs brought relief to the Middle East; but the majority of the middle class had disappeared, and much of the desolation wrought at his hands was never repaired. His most notorious custom was the construction of pyramids of human heads after the sacking of cities; at Aleppo 20,000 heads were built into such markers. Schools, mosques, and libraries were destroyed, and only the walls of the famed Umayyad mosque in Damascus were left. Skilled artisans and their families were deported to Samarkand; many ancient skills that had survived through the ages were now lost forever.

In the wake of this barbarian tide three states remained in the Middle East: a fragmentized Iran; a broken and reduced Ottoman state; and the wealthy, firmly organized, corrupt Mamluk state of Egypt. Fifteenth-century affairs in the Middle East revolved around the economic, political, and international problems and interrelationships of these three powers.

The Ottoman Turks
The fortunes of the Ottoman state are considered in more detail elsewhere in this volume. Here it is sufficient to point out that the Ottoman state was reunited by Sultan Mehmed I within fifteen years after the debacle of his

father at Ankara. The process of building an empire by adding provinces in the Balkans and Asia Minor was resumed, with Constantinople falling to Sultan Mehmed II in 1453. Following that world-renowned event, the Ottomans in their expansion southward and eastward came into conflict with Iranians and Mamluks. Mehmed II in 1473 turned back Uzun Hasan of Iran, and Selim I soundly trounced Shah Ismail, clearing Anatolia of most of the Iranian sympathizers and fellow heretics. Under Mehmed II border disputes flared between Turkey and Syria and between the satellites of the Mamluks and the Ottomans. In the 1490s Bayezid II was engaged in seven campaigns against the Mamluks. The latter won technical decisions in each case; but twenty years later (1517) Selim I and his army marched victoriously into Cairo, reducing the Mamluk state to an Ottoman province and carrying off the last puppet Abbasid caliph to Istanbul.

Iran

Iran in 1409 came under the rule of Timur's son Shah Rukh, who attempted to rebuild Herat and Marw and to establish a peaceful and prosperous regime. The succeeding Timurids, however, battled among themselves to such an extent that they were unable to control the Turkish nomadic tribes of the area. New groups and families arose to divide Iran and to render her impotent in the struggle for power in the Middle East. Raids by Uzbeg tribes in Transoxiana and the absence of trade to the east led the center of population and importance to shift westward.

In the Caucasus and the highlands of eastern Anatolia, Turkish tribes under the leadership of the Kara Koyunlu ("Black Sheepmen") seized control of Armenia and Azerbayjan. For a time after the death of Timur the Kara Koyunlu ruled Baghdad and established Tabriz as their capital, building the famous "Blue Mosque" there. Other Turkish tribes in an Ak Koyunlu ("White Sheepmen") federation were established in Armenia and northern Mesopotamia with Diyarbakir as their capital. The pinnacle of Ak Koyunlu power came under Uzun Hasan, who ruled all of Iran from 1467 until his death in 1478. Married to a daughter of the Greek emperor of Trebizond, Uzun Hasan through his in-laws was approached by Venice to fight Venetian battles against the Ottomans. The envoy, Caterino Zeno, successfully persuaded Uzun Hasan. However, he found Mehmed II a formidable foe, especially since Venice made no move to engage the Ottomans in another quarter.

After the death of Uzun Hasan the Ak Koyunlu state rapidly disintegrated, preparing the ground for the rise of the more native Safavi dynasty under Shah Ismail.

Egypt

The trade of the Far East and India passed to Europe through the Red Sea and to the Mediterranean either by way of Egypt or by the historic caravan routes in the Hijaz to Transjordan, Damascus, Beirut, Aleppo, and Alexandretta. The Mamluk Empire, therefore, possessed a strong, almost monopo-

listic, control over East-West trade. The steady growth of this trade in the
fifteenth century together with the natural productivity of the Nile valley
and the skilled artisan manufactures of Egypt gave to the Mamluk-Arab
society a brilliance unrivaled in any other Arab land. What cultural life and
quest for knowledge remained in the Arab world found refuge and patronage in Cairo and Alexandria. Although originality had passed, science and
literature were cultivated by students and supported by the court and the
wealthy. The greatest activity was in the construction of mausoleum-
mosques. Of these the most outstanding was that of Sultan Kaitbay, who
died in 1495. Noted for its alternate red and white stone courses, the
mosque-tomb-school has a stately high dome over the tomb chamber. The
exterior of the dome is covered by an elaborate geometric pattern inter-
spaced with intricate floral designs. The minaret, in several stories, is one
of the most handsome in Cairo. The arched gallery of the second floor of
the school reminds one of the arched loggias of Venice.

Yet, despite all the trade and wealth and the escape from invasion and
devastation, society and civilization in Egypt were artificial and decadent.
Government was uncertain. Mamluk sultan succeeded Mamluk sultan with
frequency and violence. In the fifteenth century there were twenty-two
changes of sultan; on one occasion there were three sultans in a single year.
The system of training Mamluk officers and soldiers broke down, and the
quality of new slaves deteriorated as the difficulty of purchasing slaves in
the Volga and the Black Sea areas increased. Law became the whim of the
ruler, and the ruling class was beyond the law. Graft, corruption, and inefficiency within the Mamluk order mushroomed. As land revenues declined,
government officials grew more venal.

Between native Arab-Egyptian and Mamluk the chasm widened; the
community of interests ceased. Personal insult was added to exploitation
and civil degradation until the Mamluk, although a coreligionist, was
loathed by the native Egyptian. Nevertheless, rich merchants flourished in
Cairo. In the middle of the fifteenth century there were reported to be at
least 200 merchants worth a million ducats each and over 2,000 worth
100,000 ducats each. The presence of such wealth gave Cairo an aura of
prosperous strength that misled most European visitors.

The Mamluk Empire included the Hijaz and Syria as well as Egypt, the
outlying provinces being held through semiautonomous amirs. These satellites to the north were tied to Cairo loosely when the sultan was weak; and
frequently at such moments the amirs played the dangerous game of flirting
with the reviving Ottoman state or with whatever prince ruled in Iran.
Border disputes were inevitable, and in 1485 when a war broke between
rivals for the throne of Dhu-al-Kadr, Ottoman sultan Bayezid II backed one
contender while Mamluk sultan Kaitbay supported the other. Six campaigns followed. At one time the Ottomans occupied Aleppo; at other times
Mamluk generals penetrated Anatolia as far as Kayseri. Before the war
ended, the commanding Ottoman general was twice captured and carried
in chains to Cairo. The Mamluks won the battles but could not achieve

victory, and in 1491 peace was arranged through the efforts of an envoy from Tunisia.

Within a decade after this successful defense of the distant frontiers of the state Mamluk good fortune was irretrievably lost. The Portuguese rounded Africa and strongly established themselves in the Indian trade, since they could afford to pay higher prices for goods than the Arabs could. In 1502 the Portuguese attempted to block the Gulf of Aden to prevent ships from entering the Red Sea. Portuguese ships threatened the port of Jidda on the Red Sea, and in 1506 the Portuguese occupied and fortified the Island of Socotra near the entrance to the Gulf of Aden. Syria alone had spices to export, and the Mamluk sultan Kansawh al-Ghawri began the construction of a fleet on the Red Sea. His efforts, however, were too little and too late. The small Mamluk fleet was destroyed in 1509 by the Portuguese under their able Admiral Albuquerque. Bayezid II of Turkey sent timber and armament for thirty ships, but to no avail. The trade was lost, and the Egyptian economy collapsed. The coinage was debased as revenues declined. Living standards fell, and the Mamluk government disintegrated.

It was upon such a hopeless scene that the Ottoman sultan Selim I appeared when he arrived in Syria. The Mamluk sultan brought his army to Aleppo to threaten the rear and flank of Selim, who was engaged with Shah Ismail of Iran. Selim turned quickly, crossed the Taurus mountains, and routed the Mamluk rabble at Marj Dabik in August, 1516. Twenty years previously the Mamluk army was well paid and well equipped, but the force before the Ottomans here was a sullen, dispirited, and unpaid mob using obsolete armament, whereas Ottoman armies had powerful cannons that could destroy most fortifications. Selim proceeded southward taking all of Syria with ease; cities such as Damascus, Tripoli, and Beirut surrendered peacefully.

Cairo was taken by assault in January 1517, and the last Mamluk sultan, Tumanbay, was seized and hanged. Egypt became an Ottoman province, and the puppet caliph, al-Mutawakkil, was taken to Istanbul. With Selim I's departure from Egypt the center of the Middle East politically, economically, and culturally shifted to Istanbul and the Ottoman Empire. An age had wearily come to an end. Although Turkish sultans, Turkish generals, and Turkish slaves had been ruling in Arab countries for several centuries, the future now belonged to a Turkish rule that identified itself as Turkish and based its power on Turkish people.

REFERENCES: Chapter 10

Many volumes already cited bear upon this chapter, including several in Chapters 4, 6, and 7.

Ayalon, David. *Gunpowder and Firearms in the Mamluk Kingdom*. London: Valentine, Mitchell, 1956. An important work, referring to the Ottoman and Safavid armies as well.

Barthold, V. V. *Turkestan Down to the Mongol Invasion*. London: Luzac, 1928. The standard work on central Asia from the seventh to the thirteenth century.

Boyle, J. A. (ed.). *The Saljuq and Mongol Periods.* The Cambridge History of Iran, vol. 5. Cambridge, Eng.: Cambridge University Press, 1968. Beginning with the political and dynastic history of Iran from 1000 to 1217, the volume describes the internal structure of the Seljuk empire and its religion. It continues with a discussion of the Il-Khans, the Ismaili state, and the Mongols. Chapters on poetry and prose, the arts, and sciences are most useful.

Ehrenkreutz, Andrew S. *Saladin.* Albany, N. Y.: State University of New York Press, 1972. A study of his liquidation of the Fatimid dynasty in Egypt, the establishment of his house as a princely family, and the unification of Egypt and Syria; it indicates that the Crusades were a small side issue.

Fulcher of Chartres. *A History of the Expedition to Jerusalem, 1095–1127.* Edited by Harold S. Fink. Translated by Frances Rita Ryan. Knoxville: University of Tennessee Press, 1970. A handsome volume judiciously edited.

Gibb, H. A. R. *The Damascus Chronicle of the Crusades, Extracted and Translated from the Chronicle of Ibn al-Qalanisi.* London: Luzac, 1965.

Glubb, John Bagot. *Soldiers of Fortune: The Story of the Mamluks.* London: Hodder & Stoughton, 1973. An account from Arab chronicles of the military rule of Egypt and Syria from 1250 to 1517 by a military slaveocracy of largely Turkish origins. A detailed account of the rivalry for power among the cliques and various military contingents and the utter ruthlessness of the process.

Lapidus, Ira Marvin. *Muslim Cities in the Later Middle Ages.* Cambridge, Mass.: Harvard University Press, 1967.

Abu-Lughod, Janet. *Cairo: 1001 Years of the City Victorious.* Princeton, N.J.: Princeton University Press, 1971. The first five chapters cover the period from 969 to 1798; the second part deals with the nineteenth and early twentieth centuries; the third part is contemporary.

Riley-Smith, Jonathon. *The Knights of St. John in Jerusalem, 1050–1310.* New York: St. Martin's Press, 1968. A study using the full archives of the order, giving a survey of the political history, an account of the internal organization, and a detailed report of their properties and problems of living in the Middle East.

Runciman, Steven. *A History of the Crusades.* 3 vols. Cambridge, Eng.: Cambridge University Press, 1951–58. Thorough and readable. Largely from the Western point of view.

Wolff, Robert Lee, and Harry W. Hazard (eds.). *A History of the Crusades.* Vol. 2. *The Later Crusades (1189–1311).* Philadelphia: University of Pennsylvania Press, 1962.

Ziadeh, Nicola A. *Damascus Under the Mamluks.* Norman, Okla.: University of Oklahoma Press, Norman, 1964.

Part Two

The Ottoman Empire

Chapter 11

The Byzantine Empire

Establishment of the State

A prominent student of Byzantine history has defined the Byzantine Empire as "the Roman Empire in its Christian form." If this is true, then its history must begin with the era of the Emperor Constantine and his building of the city of Constantinople on the site of ancient Byzantium.

Except for a period in the thirteenth century when Latin knights of the Fourth Crusade occupied it, Constantinople was the hub of the Eastern Roman Empire until its fall to the Turks in 1453. Thus, the Roman Empire under Christianity endured for more than eleven centuries—centuries that witnessed, especially in Constantinople, the preservation and propagation of the Christian faith and its theology; the knowledge of the Hellenistic and Roman ages; the art and architecture of the ancient world; the artisan skills of Greece, Rome, and the Orient; and many techniques of government discovered through centuries of Roman rule.

In establishing a new capital for the empire Constantine placed his chief residence closer to the populous part of the empire and in a better situation for the defense of the Balkan provinces. Moreover, he was able to break more completely with obsolete paraphernalia of government in Rome. His reforms, and those of Diocletian before him, were easier to sustain in a new location.

In Constantinople the emperor was the accepted absolute monarch with power strictly centralized in his hands. Except in a very few provinces civil and military powers were separated, and a regular civil service system for the various bureaus of government was expanded on a basis of merit and seniority. The University of Constantinople was created to further the dissemination and advance of Hellenistic culture.

Finally, but perhaps first in significance, was Constantine's recognition of Christianity, his participation in Christian affairs to the extent of calling the first general council of the Christian Church at Nicaea in 325, and his use of the emperor's power to try to achieve uniformity in Christian doctrine. Constantine's action resulted in the union of Church and state and the interdependence of emperor and patriarch that is known as the Caesaropapism of the Byzantine Empire.

From the first days, therefore, the Byzantine state embodied imperial tradition, Christian orthodoxy, and Hellenistic culture—forces that gave direction to government, religion, and literature in Constantinople for a thousand years.

Political History

Following Constantine, more than seventy emperors or empresses graced the imperial throne of Constantinople before its fall in 1204 to Fourth Crusaders. A relatively large number of these rulers were capable leaders; many were outstanding. Theodosius I (r. 379–395) made Christianity the official and sole religion of the empire. Theodosius II (r. 408–450) published the code of Roman law bearing his name and constructed the storied land walls of Constantinople, which stretch from the Sea of Marmara five miles to the Golden Horn. Without a doubt this formidable barrier on countless occasions saved the imperial city, and therefore the empire, from northern barbarians and the Arabs.

Justinian I (r. 527–565), an Illyrian, and his empress Theodora (r. 527–548) have enjoyed fame through the ages. Many of their structures still stand in Istanbul, the noblest of which are the incomparable Church of Hagia Sophia and the majestic aqueducts north of the city. Equally celebrated were the Justinian codes of laws, compiled and digested by a commission of leading jurists and law professors. Remaining the foundation of law through the years in the Byzantine Empire, these codes appeared in Italy in the twelfth century and served as the basis for the reintroduction of Roman law in the West. Probably the main reason for publication of the laws was Justinian's need for rigorous control of the empire and efficient collection of taxes to provide funds for his military campaigns in North Africa, Italy, and Spain.

The next gifted emperor, Heraclius (r. 610–641), an Armenian and son of the governor of Carthage, is often called the creator of the medieval Byzantine period. He was the first to use officially the title Basileus, and it was under him that Greek became the official language of the empire. Upon his accession he found the empire in a disturbed and debilitated condition, with Slavs and Sasanids threatening its existence. By reuniting Church and state, by revitalizing the army and navy, and by reinstituting strict economy, Heraclius defeated the Iranians in a series of brilliant campaigns and freed Syria and Egypt from Sasanid control. However, the financial strain of these wars and the cost in manpower left the Basileus unable to meet the Muslim Arabs in a favorable posture, and the recovered provinces were lost to Islam in Heraclius' last days.

During the remainder of the seventh century the frontiers contracted, and the economy of the state materially weakened. Muslim armies ravaged Asia Minor, camped on the shores of the Sea of Marmara, and took to the sea in the eastern Mediterranean. But the empire was preserved by the accession of Leo III (r. 717–740), an Isaurian from Marash in the region of the Taurus mountains. Besides shielding the empire from Eastern onslaughts, the Isaurian advanced Heraclius' administrative system of themes, which were provinces where the military general *(strategos)* was also governor. Thus, they were military districts, although judges and other civil officials did submit their accounts directly to the central administration. At first only a few were organized in this manner, but by the time of the Fourth Crusade thirty-eight provinces had been transformed into themes, the most important of which were in Asia Minor facing the Muslims.

A contemporary of Charlemagne and Harun al-Rashid, the Empress Irene (r. 797–802) captured the imagination of many ages. The Greek wife of Leo the Isaurian's grandson and the power behind the throne of her son for twenty years, Irene blinded her son and ruled alone as *emperor* until overthrown by a revolution. She recognized Charlemagne as Holy Roman Emperor, paid tribute to Harun al-Rashid, and gave her support to factions in the capital that opposed Isaurian iconoclastic policy. The first two actions were indicative of the decline of Byzantine power. The third disclosed the deep-seated religious division that persisted in the empire. Many with Monophysite tendencies, especially those from eastern reaches of the empire, objected to icons, images, pictures, and in particular representations of the Virgin Mary in church services and decorations. Leo III, over the protests of many bishops and monastics in Constantinople, forbade the use of icons, an act pleasing to the soldiery of his eastern themes. Irene made a political alliance with orthodox churchmen, and for their favor in her struggle for imperial position and power she pursued orthodox doctrines of anti-iconoclasm.

Evil days again fell upon the Byzantine Empire until the ascent of Basil the Macedonian (r. 867–886). Maintaining its supremacy until 1056, the Macedonian dynasty led the empire during one of the more brilliant periods of its long life. Basil, of humble origin, rose from the imperial stables, where his superb physique and feats of prowess attracted the attention of the emperor. Soon co-ruler, Basil I took the next step and had his patron murdered. Nevertheless, he and his successors, particularly Basil II (r. 976–1025), were capable emperors, republishing old codes of laws, restoring harmony in the Church, and pursuing a vigorous defense of the state against Arabs and Bulgarians.

From the death of Basil II until the fall of Constantinople to the Fourth Crusaders in 1204, a series of calamities befell the Byzantine state, reducing its effective power to an alarming degree. Beginning in the tenth century, transformation of the rural society and economy proceeded relentlessly and sometimes rapidly. The free peasant and the free landholding soldier, especially in Asia Minor, were disappearing as a result of the expansion of great estates held by the landed aristocracy and the Church. Heavy taxes, bad weather, famine, and insecurity caused the peasants to lose their lands to powerful lords. The stronger the magnates became, the more certain they were to obtain privileges, reduced taxes, and many other concessions from the central authorities. In turn, these events weakened the Byzantine fiscal position, lowered the available supply of loyal soldiers, and created a powerful class in the provinces able and eager to threaten or overthrow an unwary or uncooperative emperor. By the middle of the tenth century, emperors began to issue decrees to halt this process of aggrandizement but to no avail.

When the strong hand of Basil II was removed, intense rivalry between the landed military aristocrats of the provinces and the powerful capital bureaucrats flared into the open for competition for the throne. The latter group controlled the central administration, the imperial navy, the troops around the emperor, and the finances of the empire. In their party were included a number of aristocratic families, many senators, most of the cultured segments of society, and almost all the important administrators. From 1025 until 1057 the civilian government thwarted some thirty rebellions and exiled, executed, or blinded a long list of generals who had mounted these insurrections. But the bureaucracy, looking for compliant emperors, found for the most part those "ill, old, or dominated by women and the eunuchs, and concerned only with enjoying the pleasures of their office."

In 1057 Isaac Comnenus, an Anatolian general, led his allied military magnates to attack Constantinople. Aided by the patriarch and the guilds of the city and by some of the aristocratic bureaucrats, including the Ducas family, he became emperor. When Comnenus fell ill two years later, Constantine Ducas rejoined the civilian party to oust the generals. In another eight years a civilian split enabled the generals to recapture the throne and install Romanus IV Diogenes as emperor.

Since the main strength of the great Anatolian families lay in their control of the armies stationed in their midst, the bureaucrats had set out to dismantle these local troops by withholding financial support from them, dismissing competent generals, and terminating obligations of various groups that owed military service. This was done at a time when Seljuk Turks were pressing on the frontiers in the east and others were invading the Balkans. The result was an increasing use of foreign mercenary troops. When Isaac Comnenus attacked Constantinople in 1057, for example, one-fifth of his army was Russian and two-fifths were Norman; by the reign of Romanus IV Diogenes the chief reliance everywhere was upon foreign mercenaries. The difficulty with such forces was their lack of loyalty. In addition to the ease with which they changed sides, these mercenaries (their number included Kurds, Turks, Armenians, Arabs, English, Germans, Iranians, and others) frequently ravaged the Anatolian countryside, held towns for ransom, and invariably reduced the flow of taxes to the imperial treasury. The economy of the empire sagged and the power of the state ebbed as the rival parties for political power, in spite of all consequences and at all costs, vied for supremacy.

With the accession of Alexius I Comnenus to the throne in 1081 the generals began a reign that lasted until the fall of Constantinople in 1204. During that time two dynasties—the Comneni and the Angeli—ruled the empire. Of these, the Comneni (1081–1185) was the more illustrious, perhaps because it held the throne throughout most of the period of the Crusades.

Civil wars continued unabated with generals and leading families feuding among themselves and seeking to establish semiindependent fiefdoms. Not least among these rivals were former mercenary leaders, many of them Normans and Turks. Typical of some of these foreign adventurers, though active a few years earlier, was Roussel of Bailleul, who rebelled and established an independent principality in Anatolia, levying taxes on towns, crushing a Byzantine army of other mercenaries at Sakarya, and marching to the Bosphorus, where he burned the cities opposite Constantinople. Alexius I found himself between Turk on the east and Frank on the west, hardly knowing which to fear the more. His daughter Anna Comnena has left a most interesting account of the arrival of the First Crusade at Constantinople; the contrast in culture and civilization of the two Christian societies of her day was sharply drawn.

Unfortunately for the Comneni, during their last days there was a large influx of Latins into Constantinople. Many influential government positions were given to them, much to the displeasure of the local bureaucracy. A French noblewoman, Mary of Antioch, served as regent for her son Alexius II (1180–1183) and became so much the target of public hatred that a pleasing scoundrel, Andronicus I, stirred up the capital to murder Latins quite indiscriminately and to sell others into captivity. As one author says, "the seed of the fanatic enmity between West and East, if not planted, was watered." Two decades later Constantinople finally fell to Venetians and Fourth Crusaders, an act that ended the true Byzantine Empire. What later passed for that empire proved to be only a shell of its former power, grandeur, and significance.

The Church

Before discussing this later phase of the empire, it may be well to study a few institutions of society as they were at the height of Byzantine glory, for their forms persevered into the weak last days and even beyond into the Ottoman period. The strongest and most vital arm of the emperor was the Christian Church. After the demise of paganism in the fourth century the capital, the Balkans, Greece, and Asia Minor were devoted in their support and loyalty to the Church. Its tight organization with the patriarch at its hierarchical apex gave powerful support or presented determined opposition to the emperor and government. Consequently, the emperor always tried to control the selection of the patriarch and reckoned with his views. As many as one hundred monastic or holy orders had cloisters in Constantinople, and the members had a profound influence upon the religious views of the populace. Frequently the government found it necessary to follow doctrines espoused by the populace, even though other dogmas were preferable for reasons of imperial policies. Whenever an emperor compromised with heresy to mollify a distant province or the army in some Asian theme or entered into an understanding with the papacy regarding the universal Christian Church, the orthodox voice of the capital was heard.

In a way the Church resembled an administrative department of the government, and the patriarch acted as a minister of state in charge of religion. A dynamic emperor chose, appointed, and dismissed patriarchs; an energetic patriarch bent weak emperors to his will. It was this interrelationship that has been called Caesaro-papism, but at most times the emperor was supreme and the Church was subordinate to the state.

Agriculture and Industry

After the loss of Egypt to the Arabs, Constantinople and cities of the empire were supplied with necessary sustenance by Asia Minor, Thrace, and the Balkans. The lot of the peasant was hard, and few envied him his life. Yet he seldom lacked food, clothing, or shelter, and famines were rare. Land was fundamental to the economy, and livestock such as oxen greatly increased productivity of the land and peasant. Monasteries in the capital and elsewhere possessed numerous estates which provided monks with their living. This would indicate that agriculture in the Byzantine Empire was not at the low level of a subsistence economy. One bought and held land for the money income which it produced.

Although agriculture was the mainstay of the empire, industry and commerce gave it wealth and luxury. In the great cities of the empire compact populations were engaged to a considerable degree in manufacturing articles of everyday use. Many, too, produced luxury goods of great value which were used in rituals and services of thousands of churches and monasteries and which were vital to the pageantry of the imperial court. Sumptuous living was much enjoyed; and the wealth of silk fabrics, gold brocades, jewelry, reliquaries, enameled wares, fine glassware, and all the precious and refined luxury of the medieval age dazzled Western visitors. Crafts and skills of Roman and Hellenistic artisans prevailed for a thousand years in the Byzantine world, making it almost as much an industrial society as it was agricultural.

Trade

The most active commercial city of the Byzantine Empire, Constantinople was filled with warehouses, depots, caravansarais, banks, moneychangers, and all aids and agents for promotion of foreign and domestic commerce. Trade from the Black Sea area and most of Russia centered upon Constantinople. Goods from the Far East and western Asia passed down the Bosphorus to quays on the Golden Horn. Surplus produce—manufactures and raw materials—of the empire gravitated to the capital for exchange and transshipment. Ships plied regularly between Constantinople and Cherson, Trebizond, Salonica, Venice, Amalfi, and Genoa. A standard tax of 10 percent, levied on all imports and exports, brought to the imperial government a large part of its revenue. Italian cities, however, found it possible to obtain tariff concessions from the emperors; Alexius I permitted Venetian merchants a remission of taxes on goods exported from Constantinople in return for their "policing" the Adriatic, which they already controlled, and for carrying imperial cargoes if requested. The Comneni later granted a concession of 6 percent in the export-import tariff for Genoese and Pisan merchants trading in the empire.

Commerce in certain goods was forbidden: soap could not be imported; and gold, raw silk, court ceremonial robes, unsewn fabrics, and salt fish could not be exported. Industry and commerce were strictly regulated by the government. Controls were exercised over prices, quality and quantity produced or imported, profits, locations of business, labor conditions, and movement of workers.

Guilds

Implementation of these controls was effected by individual guilds—industrial, commercial, and financial—which were highly organized and fully developed before A.D. 900. Most guilds were granted special privileges and certain monopolies, making membership in the respective guild a great advantage in any business or trade. To some extent guilds were restrictive in character. At times they were repressive, and they were always conservative. Yet they prevented speculation and collusion, protected rights of individuals in local and distant markets, and performed many social and legal functions for members. The state appointed heads of the guilds, and by minutely regulating their activities, controlled the economy of the state.

Through the ages and up to the present, writers have maligned the Byzantine Empire, its civilization, and particularly its rulers. Intrigue, court politics and so-called palace revolutions, the sharp business acumen of the merchants, and the mercenary character of some aspects of its life have led historians to use the word "byzantine" in a malicious and derogatory manner. Nevertheless, a close objective study of Byzantine records reveals a fully civilized society which possessed an efficient government and excellent public services, which was managed and directed by an educated and sophisticated bureaucracy, and which was protected by an army of high tactical ability. At a time when western Europe was semibarbaric, inhabitants of the Byzantine Empire were enjoying literature, philosophy, urban social culture, and a much higher standard of living.

The Crusades

In 1071 when Emperor Romanus IV Diogenes was defeated by Alparslan at the Battle of Manzikert near Lake Van in eastern Asia Minor, the rout was so complete that Asia Minor became overrun with Turkish bands. Within a few years they were encamped on the shores of the Bosphorus across from Constantinople. Food supplies and raw materials, revenues, commerce, trade routes, and manpower supplies were lost; this further contraction of the empire spelled its doom.

However shocking this major defeat in 1071 may have been, it had been in the making for the half century since the death of Basil II. For more than a decade prior to Manzikert the armed battles to control Constantinople had denuded the Anatolian provinces of their military might, opening the way for Turkish invaders who sacked Kayseri and pillaged the entire countryside around Malatya. When Romanus IV Diogenes marched out to meet Alparslan, not only was his military equipment woefully inferior but half of his soldiers were merely untrained city youths and the other half were unreliable mercenaries. On his way to battle he had to subdue his own unruly Germans; he also attacked Armenians at Sivas because they had been so merciless toward the Greeks there. In the heat of the battle Andronicus Ducas, leader of the contingent of bureaucrats in the emperor's army, spread the word that Romanus was being defeated and withdrew his men. Turkish forces, witnessing the anarchy, attacked the Byzantine army in flight and captured the emperor. Never before had an emperor fallen into the hands of "barbarians"!

The humiliation of Manzikert accelerated the fragmentation of society. When the Turks set Romanus IV free, war erupted between him and Michael VII Ducas, cousin of the treacherous Andronicus, further destroying military power in Anatolia and creating a power vacuum. Petty independent states sprang up everywhere: Normans in Bithynia; Seljuk Turks at Nicaea; Armenians in the southeast; and Turkoman tribes everywhere. Before the able general Alexius I Comnenus seized the imperial throne in 1081 several contenders had relied on Turkish armies in their battles against each other. These actions and the encouragement of Alparslan to Turkoman tribes to invade Anatolia brought Turkish sieges of many walled towns and the general ravaging of the countryside in every corner of Anatolia.

At last Alexius I Comnenus sent out a desperate call to Western Christendom for aid. The Crusades were the response; but they did more harm than good. Italian merchants traveled in the Crusaders' vanguard and, as soon as the Latin states were founded, they arranged to carry their Oriental trade through Syria, frequently by-passing Constantinople. The West expended little sentiment over the Byzantine Empire, as the infamous Fourth Crusade demonstrated. The fall of Constantinople to Venetian merchants and soldiers in 1204 terminated abruptly the Byzantine Empire, and its society and civilization collapsed. The Orthodox Church was Latinized; monasteries disappeared; wealth of the churches was carried off; the university closed; learning and literature vanished; books and libraries were lost; and works of art were destroyed. Original works of Praxiteles, Aristotle, Aeschylus, and others, known to have existed in Constantinople in 1204, were never found or heard of after that catastrophe.

The flight of the Byzantine court and ruling classes from Constantinople in 1204 had the immediate effect of producing several independent Greek principalities in the Byzantine provinces. Shortly, the fragmentation was reduced to three: Trebizond on the Black Sea coast in eastern Asia Minor; Nicaea in Bithynia in northwestern Asia Minor; and Arta and Salonica in Epirus and Thrace. At Nicaea, Theodore Lascaris, husband of an Angeli princess, gathered many of the old aristocracy and had the patriarch crown him emperor, thereby gaining a prestige never enjoyed by his two rivals.

Meanwhile, the Latin empire of Constantinople hardly had a chance. Fraught with internal feuding and largely deserted by the West, the Crusaders were hemmed in by the Bulgarian kingdom and the Greeks of Epirus and Nicaea. Finally in 1261 Michael Palaeologus, a general who usurped the Lascaris throne, overthrew the Latins and reestablished the Byzantine state in Constantinople.

The End of Byzantine Rule

From 1261 to 1453 Byzantine rule held in Constantinople; but it cannot justly be regarded as a restoration of the Byzantine Empire. It was never more than a Greek kingdom, and for the final half century nothing more than the capital city itself. The old empire was broken beyond repair. Furthermore, simultaneously with the expulsion of the Latins from Constantinople the invasions of Genghiz Khan and his grandson Hulagu destroyed the Seljuk Empire of Asia Minor which in the absence of Byzantine authority had come to control much of Anatolia. Thus, this sector of the Middle East was groping for new leadership, and adjustment of the balance of power to new conditions became inevitable. Upon the ruins of these two empires a new Ottoman state arose.

The Palaeologi tried to maintain a style of imperial government unjustified by the extent of their actual domain. Only a small part of northwestern Asia Minor remained in their hands, and the Balkans were held by Bulgarian and Serbian rulers. Land revenue was extremely low. Indeed, with so much of Far Eastern trade passing to western Europe through Mamluk Egypt the imperial crown jewels had to be pawned in Venice.

One mediocre ruler succeeded another; palace poverty and intrigue spawned civil wars and revolutions. Toward the middle of the fourteenth century the poor rose in Constantinople and Adrianople and massacred the aristocracy and the rich. In Salonica the populace had a peoples' republic for seven years. Interminable strife also marked the history of the Church. The Palaeologi, in their desperation for aid, repeatedly made and accepted bids to subordinate the Orthodox Church to the pope and his authority. Monks, churchmen, and the people always objected, and religious unity with the West was continually being postponed or abandoned.

In foreign affairs, the Greek state of Constantinople, in addition to negotiations and agreements with the papacy over church matters, was confronted with the rising dynamic Ottoman Turks in Asia Minor and the Bulgars and Serbs in the Balkans. In 1355 Stefan Dushan, at the head of an extensive Balkan Serbian empire bounded by the Aegean, the Adriatic, and the Danube, seized Adrianople. Perhaps only his sudden death saved Constantinople.

Foreign and transit trade of Constantinople fell into the hands of Venetians and Genoese. From their docks and counting houses of Galata, a suburb across the Golden Horn from Constantinople, the latter yearly grew more powerful and more insolent in their dealings with the Palaeologi. Since the Genoese possessed numerous ports and stations on the shores of the Black Sea and the Sea of Azov, many old Greek trading families of Constantinople found themselves excluded from their traditional haunts.

The most spectacular group of foreigners that came to the Byzantine state was the mercenary Catalan Grand Company of soldiers under the leadership of Roger de Flor. No longer could the state afford a regular standing army; only when a crisis arose or a threat appeared could an army be supported. Roger, a German by birth, and his Spanish company of 10,000, including wives, mistresses, and children, were hired in 1302 to combat the mounting aggression of the Turks. The emperor, however, was soon more terrified of the Catalans than he was of the Turks and successfully plotted Roger's murder.

In the century and a half preceding the fall of Constantinople international politics in the Byzantine area consisted almost entirely of constantly shifting alliances and realignments among the Byzantine successor states, of which the Greek state was only one. Greek emperors made friends with Turkish princes of Asia Minor against the Ottomans. However, when Venetians and Serbs banded together to seize Constantinople, Orhan, the Ottoman ruler, was given the hand of Theodora, the daughter of John VI Cantacuzenus, as partial inducement to bring his forces across the Dardanelles into Europe to defend Thrace from that combination. A rival emperor in alliance with the Genoese drove the Ottomans back to Asia and sent his predecessor to a monastery, where he spent the rest of his days writing his brilliant memoirs. Deposed by his own son and the Genoese, the new emperor called for Ottoman support, which returned him victoriously to Constantinople in 1379.

From that time on Ottoman sultans were deeply involved in Byzantine affairs. Emperors frequently recognized sultans as their suzerains, sent their sons as hostages to the Ottoman court, and sometimes led the Turkish fleet on adventures into the Black Sea. Sultans plotted palace revolutions in Constantinople, and emperors sponsored rivals to the sultan's throne and intrigued with Turkish principalities against the Ottomans. Manuel II and Mehmed I personally discussed affairs from their respective galleys on the European shores of the Bosphorus and then crossed to the Asiatic side for a picnic, although the emperor did not descend from his galley. When an emperor died childless in 1448, Murad II approved the selection of Constantine XI, whose niece married Mehmed II.

Genoese, Venetians, Serbs, Bulgars, Greeks, and Ottomans were the active groups in the Straits area of the Middle East in that epoch, their religious and linguistic differences proving not to be significant barriers to political or economic partnerships. A blending of social patterns and institutional structures was proceeding so naturally that contemporary observers who were familiar with the situation showed no burning concern over the thought that the Ottomans might take Constantinople and the Straits. Little fear was evidenced that an Ottoman society and government on the Golden Horn would be very different from the Greek state. Life, trade, government, and religion would go on much the same. The Ottomans showed every indication of being as much European as they were Asian.

From a Byzantine point of view the debacle in Asia Minor following the Mongol invasions nurtured a new Turkish principality under the leader Osman. Within a few decades the northwestern section of Asia Minor came under Ottoman control. ("Ottoman" was an Italian corruption of "Uthman," just as "Osman" was a Turkish corruption of "Uthman.") And for the remainder of the century Ottoman activity was centered in Europe. At first the Ottomans were invited and hired by Byzantine emperors to fight in battles against Serbs, Bulgars, and Italians or for one faction of Palaeologi against another. Later they settled in Europe, and before the close of the fourteenth century they had become masters of Thrace, Macedonia, Bulgaria, and parts of Serbia. Constantinople was isolated but obtained a fifty-year reprieve from Timur's crushing defeat of the Ottomans at the Battle of Ankara in 1402.

For fifty years Constantinople was all that remained of the Byzantine Empire. That it did not fall to the Ottomans after their state was re-created under Mehmed I can be credited almost wholly to its superb defensive position. With water on three sides and the marvelous Theodosian Wall between the Golden Horn and the Sea of Marmara making the fourth side, the inhabitants of Constantinople felt secure. Any attacker had seemingly insurmountable obstacles to overcome.

By building the famous castles on the European shore of the Bosphorus in 1452 Mehmed II was able to blockade Constantinople by sea. Control of the Balkans gave him complete freedom to mass an army equipped with heavy artillery before the land walls in the spring of 1453. The plight of the city was obvious to all. When the walls were breached and his army transported from the Bosphorus over the hills of Pera to the Golden Horn, the fate of Constantinople was sealed. Constantine XI died vaingloriously on the walls; Muslim prayers were said in Hagia Sophia; and bells tolled in Europe. The once great and vigorous Byzantine Empire finally succumbed of old age after a long and painful illness. The young Ottoman Empire ushered in a new day for the great imperial site on the Bosphorus.

REFERENCES: Chapter 11

Volumes cited at the end of Chapters 2 and 10 are also important for this chapter.

Arnakis, G. Georgiades. "Captivity of Gregory Palamas by the Turks and Related Documents as His Historical Sources." *Speculum*, 26 (January 1951): 104–118. A short but illustrative picture of the early relationship between the Turks and the Byzantines.

Barker, Ernest (ed.). *Social and Political Thought in Byzantium, from Justinian I to the Last Palaeologus.* New York: Oxford University Press, 1957.

Diehl, Charles. *Byzantium: Greatness and Decline.* Translated by Naomi Walford. New Brunswick, N.J.: Rutgers University Press, 1957. The first English translation of the French classic. It is also the first volume in the Rutgers Byzantine series and contains a fine bibliographical essay by Peter Charanis.

————. *History of the Byzantine Empire.* Translated by George B. Ives. Princeton, N.J.: Princeton University Press, 1925. An important work by the great French Byzantinist.

Kostof, Spiro. *Caves of God: The Monastic Environment of Byzantine Cappadocia.* Cambridge, Mass.: MIT Press, 1972. A fine account of the Christian monuments and art in the famed troglodyte region of Cappadocia in Asia Minor. Forty-five excellent illustrations.

Obolensky, Dimitri. *The Byzantine Commonweath: Eastern Europe, 500–1453.* New York: Praeger, 1971. An excellent study of the Balkan and eastern European relations to Constantinople under the Byzantine emperors. Important for religious, social, economic, and cultural relations.

Ostrogorsky, George. *History of the Byzantine State.* Translated from the German by Joan Hussey. Rev. ed. New Brunswick, N.J.: Rutgers University Press, 1969. A one-volume history which is one of the very best of its kind, with many excellent illustrations and a great number of source references. It follows the political history in a chronological order but also contains much insight on religious, economic, social, and regional developments.

Van Milligen, Alexander. *Byzantine Churches in Constantinople: Their History and Architecture.* London: Macmillan, 1912. Detailed and well illustrated.

————. *Byzantine Constantinople: The Walls of the City and Adjoining Historical Sites.* London: Murray, 1899. Out of date, but still the best.

Vryonis, Speros, Jr. *Byzantium and Europe.* London: Thames and Hudson, 1967. A concise survey of Byzantine history by the leading scholar, with great insight into the complete life in the empire. One hundred and twenty-nine illustrations, several maps, and a superb simulated aerial view of the city of Constantinople showing the walls, locations of buildings, highways, monuments, and the surrounding seas.

————. *The Decline of Medieval Hellenism in Asia Minor and the Process of Islamization from the Eleventh through the Fifteenth Century.* Berkeley: University of California Press, 1971. Without question this work is a great landmark in scholarship and has altered the concepts of developments in later Byzantine times and the Turkish rule in Asia Minor. The author uses Greek, Turkish, Russian, Balkan, and Western sources with great understanding.

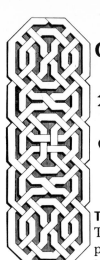

Chapter 12

Early Turkish States of Asia Minor

Turkish Penetration of Asia Minor

The Battle of Manzikert in 1071, wherein Alparslan completely routed the Byzantine army, ranks as a decisive historical event: it opened Asia Minor to Turkish settlement. Suleiman, one of Alparslan's distant cousins, was assigned responsibility for the Seljuk frontier facing the Byzantine Empire. Within ten years Turkish forces fanned out over Asia Minor and established themselves so solidly that Suleiman could choose Nicaea, a western city, as his capital. Smyrna was taken, and Turks occupied towns and villages along the Asian shore of the Sea of Marmara.

The ease with which the Turks invested Asia Minor suggests that a vacuum existed and that some Turks were conditioned already to exploit the opportunity. Emperors of the Ducas dynasty taxed the Anatolian provinces heavily and withdrew financial support and governmental privileges from frontier districts. March warriors *(akritoi)* and Armenian areas were disaffected, and gave the emperors little aid. After the humiliation of Manzikert these groups deserted the empire. When Suleiman entered Asia Minor, he found numerous Armenian principalities asserting their independence. To the serfs he gave freedom from all dues. Many *akritoi* had already joined their arms with those of Turkish frontier warriors *(ghazis)* in overrunning Asia Minor—in effect opening Anatolia for the entry of Suleiman, his Seljuk cohorts, other Turkish princely dynasties such as the Danishmendids, Shaddadids, and Artukids, and independent Turkomans by the tens of thousands.

Alparslan never expected to conquer Asia Minor; his victory at Manzikert was a maneuver to guarantee his right flank while he subdued Syria and Egypt. Suleiman, whose father had been guilty of treason, was sent partially as an exile; but he looked upon the post as a fortuitous opportunity to gather a loyal army and following with which he might return victorious to the main Seljuk state. However, Suleiman and his Seljuk organization did not conquer Anatolia; many Turkish tribes and bands infiltrated the provinces and settled upon the land. The Seljuk family only systematized the conquest but never controlled all of it.

Since the seventh-century era of great victories and Muslim expansion the Taurus mountains and Armenian highlands of eastern Asia Minor had

served as an effective boundary between Christendom and Islam. Armies
of each raided and penetrated across frontiers into lands of the other, but
no extensive change in the line occurred. On each border semiautonomous
provinces arose to attract adventurers, outcasts, heretics, fanatics, and the
unemployed from each society. Muslims called them *ghazis*, "warriors of
the faith"; to the Byzantines they were *akritoi*. Together they comprised
a typical body of freethinkers and freebooters, forming one society with one
culture, even though nominally part were Christian and part were Muslim.

Prior to the Battle of Manzikert, Turkish bands plundered Asia Minor,
even such cities as Sivas, Kayseri, and Konya. Afterward Anatolia was fully
opened to the ghazis, who for more than a century had been chiefly Turkish
in origin and language. As they scattered over the land, great numbers of
Turkish nomadic tribes found the roads and passes inviting. These peoples,
traditionally called Turkomans or Yuruks, were identical in blood, and
nearly so in dialect, to Seljuks and their Turkish adherents or to Turkish
ghazis. In fact, nomadic Turks were staunch allies of organized Turkish
forces. One day a Turkoman would be peacefully tending his flocks or
threshing his grain, and the next he might be lending his sword to Seljuk
or ghazi in furthering the conquest of Asia Minor.

Seljuk Turks of Rum

The First Crusade infused Byzantine forces with a new strength to stem the
Turkish tide. Nicaea was retaken, and western sections of Asia Minor were
restored to Byzantine control. Central and eastern Anatolia remained Turkish, and ghazi Turkish at that. Ruling in Baghdad, Syria, and Iran, the Seljuk
family took cognizance of this new province of Islam and sent Suleiman to
reign over that land. Since little power accompanied him and no prestige,
his authority in Asia Minor was only nominal. As long as he and his heirs
contented themselves with dreams of winning power and favor only in the
older Muslim world, the local Turks tolerated them. Turkish ghazi, Turkoman, and Seljuk Turk united against Byzantines and Crusaders. Kilij Arslan
II, Suleiman's great-grandson, recognized that his opportunity lay only in
Asia Minor and thus emphasized a policy of creating an empire centered
upon Konya. With this new intention began the Seljuk kingdom of Rum
(Asia Minor).

Turkish ghazi bands were sensitive to every change and immediately
challenged the new Seljuk ambition. Chief among these was the Danishmend ghazi family, long the recognized ghazi leader of Anatolia. Claiming
descent from Ghazi Seyyid Battal, a Muslim frontier hero of legendary
fame, the Danishmends made Sivas their headquarters and held sway from
the Taurus mountains to the Black Sea, even holding at one time or another
such strong points as Ankara, Amasya, Kayseri, and Malatya. The Danishmends, like other ghazi states, never developed much governmental apparatus and lived mainly from booty taken on raids beyond the frontier.
When Byzantine forces under the Comneni organized their frontiers, ghazi
raids became less profitable, and Turkish bands began to attack each other.

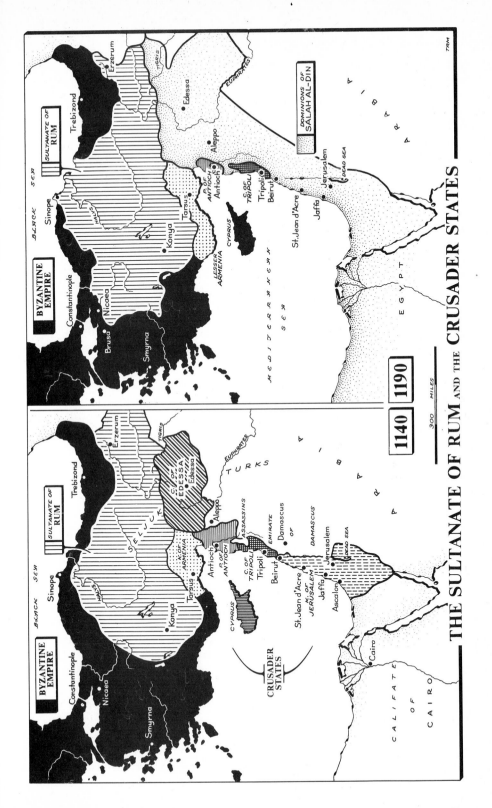

THE SULTANATE OF RUM AND THE CRUSADER STATES

1140 1190

300 MILES

Map for 1190 (top):

BLACK SEA

SULTANATE OF RUM

BYZANTINE EMPIRE

Erzerum
Trebizond
Sinope
Edessa
EUPHRATES
TIGRIS
Constantinople
Nicaea
Brusa
Smyrna
HALYS
Konya
Tarsus
LESSER ARMENIA
CYPRUS
Aleppo
P. OF ANTIOCH
Antioch
C. OF TRIPOLI
Tripoli
Beirut
St. Jean d'Acre
Jaffa
Jerusalem
DEAD SEA
MEDITERRANEAN SEA
EGYPT
ARABIA

DOMINIONS OF SALAH AL-DIN

TRM

Map for 1140 (bottom):

BLACK SEA

SULTANATE OF RUM

BYZANTINE EMPIRE

Erzerum
Trebizond
Sinope
EUPHRATES
TIGRIS
TURKS
Constantinople
Nicaea
Smyrna
HALYS
SELUK
Konya
Tarsus
K. OF ARMENIA
CYPRUS
Aleppo
C. OF EDESSA
Edessa
P. OF ANTIOCH
Antioch
ASSASSINS
EMIRATE OF DAMASCUS
Damascus
C. OF TRIPOLI
Tripoli
Beirut
St. Jean d'Acre
Jaffa
Ascalon
K. OF JERUSALEM
Jerusalem
DEAD SEA
MEDITERRANEAN SEA
CRUSADER STATES
CALIFATE OF CAIRO
Cairo

151

At this crucial point in Anatolian development Kilij Arslan II became lord and master of the Turks of Rum. The true founder of the Seljuk dynasty in Asia Minor, he ruled from 1155 to 1192, subduing Danishmend ghazis, fighting against Zangids over the frontier between Syria and Anatolia, and obtaining from Emperor Manuel Comnenus recognition as the commanding and responsible Turkish lord of Asia Minor. Because of the great prestige adhering to the Seljuk name, Konya attracted learned Muslim divines to teach in its schools; mystics, dervishes, and poets frequented its court. The Seljuks established Muslim financial administration throughout their state and built mosques, mausoleums, and caravansarais in the high Muslim style, imposing remains of which may still be seen in Konya, Sivas, Kayseri, and other cities of Anatolia.

Yet the Seljuk state displayed a mixed and varied culture, and centralization of government was never more than a goal to attain. As Seljuk authority was extended, Kilij Arslan II assigned governorships to his twelve sons, who declared their independence in their father's declining years.

Ghazi independence in Anatolia was never crushed by the Seljuks; its spirit and viewpoint remained a political and social force with which Seljuk sultans continually had to reckon. Seljuks made peace with Byzantine emperors; and on one occasion Kilij Arslan was welcomed and entertained

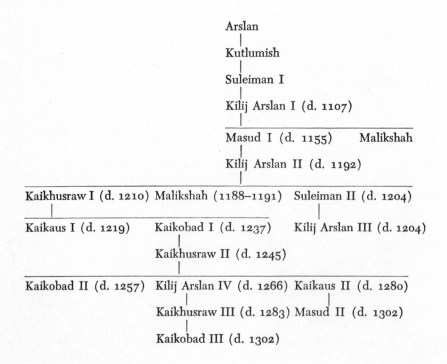

SELJUK DYNASTY OF RUM

royally by Emperor Manuel I in Constantinople, much to the consternation of the ghazi element. To receive Christian renegades at the court in Konya and give them responsible positions or to possess Christian women in the harem and have a Christian mother were understandable, but to fraternize with Christian potentates was unthinkable. Christian churches and monasteries remained in many urban centers, even owing their allegiance to the patriarch in Constantinople. The mixed culture prevailed in rural areas, in former ghazi districts, and definitely at the frontiers toward the Byzantine Empire. In certain Turkish circles criticism of Kilij Arslan's soft policy was so significant that a small success over Manuel was trumpeted as proof of the Seljuk ardor in extending Islam.

But Kilij Arslan nor, in fact, any Seljuk or Danishmend prince could control Turkomans in Anatolia, and they penetrated every corner of the land, constantly raiding Byzantine lands even to the point of capturing and leveling towns. The process of Turkification and Islamization of the population was proceeding. Some Greeks fled westward; others were killed or enslaved; many became Muslims and gradually turned to speak Turkish. Manuel I Comnenus conducted campaigns in various parts of western Anatolia, killing Turkomans by the thousands. In turn, Turkoman bands entered Byzantine territories to the north, carrying off the inhabitants in like numbers and selling them on slave markets in Mamluk Syria and Egypt. Manuel then set out to destroy the Seljuk state. In 1176 in a mountain pass at Myriocephalum west of Konya he met Kilij Arslan's forces. Already crippled by the constant raiding of his immense baggage train and harassed by Turkomans, "numerous as the locusts," who realized the emperor had come to drive them from their valley and upland pasturages, the emperor's army was destroyed. Though the sultan offered a generous peace which the emperor accepted, the significance of this battle, almost equal to that of Manzikert, was obvious. Manuel and his successors gave up any idea of reconquering Asia Minor, and the Seljuk sultans henceforth felt secure from any serious attack from Constantinople. After Myriocephalum, the Seljuks, other Turkish rulers, ghazi bands, and Turkomans controlled Asia Minor except for a small district around Trebizond on the Black Sea coast and the area between Brusa, Nicaea, and Constantinople.

Thus, through most of the century from 1150 to 1250 the Seljuk sultanate of Konya, or Rum, shone brightly. Muslim and Christian traders frequented its markets, and a considerable share of Far Eastern trade passed through the area to enrich various treasuries. Schools were crowded and the arts flourished. Armenian stonecutters, Iranian tile decorators, Persian poets, and Arab calligraphers practiced their crafts and were much appreciated. Ghazis settled down, Turks became villagers, communities were established, and life and people in central and eastern Asia Minor in the course of 150 years grew increasingly homogeneous in every aspect.

Nevertheless, frontier marches were never fully consolidated within the culture of the central provinces of the Seljuk state. Brothers, cousins, and nephews of sultans were in continual rebellion and usually found support or refuge among frontier warriors, from whom the Seljuk sultans never commanded complete obedience. Unreformed ghazis could not comprehend Seljuk peace treaties with Christian emperors and did not accept the idea of coexistence in any part of Asia Minor.

Peace and a more settled life quickly produced many effects of population pressures. Another blow to ghazi life and economy fell when Seljuk sultans ceased sending out raiding parties. More and more, warfare in Anatolia was only among contestants for the sultanate of Konya. Then, early in the thirteenth century, Turks, nomadic families and tribes, soldiers, princes, bureaucrats, dervishes, artisans, and scholars began drifting into Anatolia in swelling numbers. Mongols, under the leadership of Genghiz Khan and his heirs, drove them westward, and Seljuks encouraged these displaced persons to settle on the frontiers.

A complicating factor of significant proportions for the Seljuks and the frontier marches resulted from the fall of Constantinople to the Fourth Crusade. With their capital moved to Nicaea, Byzantine emperors gave full attention to Anatolia and its defenses. Ghazi aggressions suddenly met sterner resistance; frontier lines became rigid; and the growing Turkish population was ready to burst its bounds.

That the land was in a state of ferment was demonstrated by a movement in 1239 against Kaikhusraw II led by Baba Ishak, a holy man and mystic who protested against the luxurious life of the sultan and his court. To a considerable degree it was a revolt of seminomadic Turkomans and warriors against the sedentary Seljuk townsmen. The sultan suppressed this socioreligious outbreak unmercifully, but in so doing forever alienated the allegiance of ghazi Turks and Turkomans of Anatolia. Martyrdom of the holy Baba at the hands of Christian and Norman mercenaries ensured the wide and permanent acceptance of his heretical doctrines throughout Asia Minor.

Mongol Invasion

No sooner was Baba Ishak's resistance movement driven underground than Kaikhusraw II was confronted by Mongol invasions. Erzerum was taken, and at the fateful Battle of Kozadagh in 1243 the Seljuk armies were crushed. Sivas fell, Kayseri was sacked and its population slaughtered. Upon the sultan's sudden death two years later, Seljuk independence was extinguished. Kilij Arslan IV journeyed eastward to Karakorum, where he observed the election of Kuyuk as the great khan of the Mongols and where his position as Seljuk sultan of Rum was confirmed.

All Seljuk rulers, thenceforth, were only puppets or vassals of the Mongols. At the time of Kilij Arslan IV's appointment the amount of yearly tribute was set, and from its size the fiscal extortion by the Mongols became apparent. Later the Mongol Hulagu divided Muslim Anatolia in two, giving everything east of the Kizil Irmak to Kilij Arslan IV and assigning the land west of that river to his brother Kaikaus II. The latter conspired with the Mamluks of Egypt and fled to Constantinople to the home of his uncles. (His mother was the daughter of a Greek priest of that city.)

In the face of such actions and because of obvious weakness, all respect for Seljuk rulers by other Turks of Anatolia vanished. Since Mongol rulers never had the time or interest to establish their authority firmly in Asia Minor, their invasion, followed by an immediate withdrawal, politically fragmentized Turkish Anatolia. Each Turkish prince was suddenly on his own, and every Turkoman followed his own whim. Almost simultaneously the Byzantine emperors regained Constantinople and became involved immediately in Balkan affairs. Their Asian provinces were neglected. Turkish ghazis and Turkoman tribes discovered not only that the restraining hand of the Seljuk sultan could be ignored but also that Byzantine frontiers could be easily penetrated.

Turkification of Asia Minor

Within a few years Asia Minor, except for a small northwestern corner, was overrun by Turkish forces. The eastern half of the Seljuk state remained for many decades under Mongol authority and continued to render tribute to the great khan. In the western half, however, and in the newly acquired more westerly areas Turkish independence was openly declared and easily maintained.

The greatest strides in the transformation of Asia Minor from a Greek and Armenian Christian society to a Turkish Muslim land were made in this epoch. Throughout the twelfth and thirteenth centuries and on into the fourteenth constant pressure was exerted on every aspect of Christian life and society. Initially, the vicious strife between Byzantine factions pulled the military forces toward Constantinople and opened the way for Turkoman and Seljuk infiltration. Decisive victories for Muslim armies, continual battles and marches across the land by hungry soldiers and rapacious mercenaries, sacking of cities, and scorched-earth policies generated massacres, flight, enslavement, plague, and famine. The majority who remained were filled with insecurity and a sense of helplessness.

As the various areas fell into Turkish hands, certain factors made it fairly easy to assume the customs and manners of the victors. In the first place, non-Muslims were discriminated against in many ways with regard to dress and life and unquestionably they were second-class subjects. Converts, on the other hand, escaped discrimination—as well as many taxes. Furthermore, Christian communities became leaderless at a time of great psychological and economic crisis. Consequently, whole villages turned Muslim overnight.

The Seljuk state and Turks in general tolerated Christians and the Church. But Muslims were favored, and Islamic institutions were supported generously. Within a few decades Asia Minor was blanketed with mosques, *medressehs* (advanced schools), hospitals, rest homes, caravansarays, and even halfway houses for converts to Islam. Most of these were endowed by leading Turks or by the state from confiscated Christian church and monastic estates, usually the income from Christian villages. Christian communities cut off from support and communication with bishops and the patriarch found penury and isolation too difficult to face for long. Christianity had been defeated; victorious, affluent Islam was nigh irresistible. Moreover, Anatolia was saturated by Sufis and dervishes who preached a mystical popular Islam that reached the people. They pressed conversion to Islam and presented a kind of religious syncretism that equated Islamic practices and holy men to those of the Christians. The twelve apostles became the twelve imams and the Trinity came to consist of God, Muhammad, and Ali. This phenomenon of cultural change continued in Asia Minor until the mid-fifteenth century when the Ottoman Turks captured Constantinople, recognizing the patriarch as subject to the sultan, and in essence institutionalizing and protecting the Church as a part of the state. As a consequence, Christian communities could look to the patriarch and bishops without fear of reprisal and the Church hierarchy felt responsible for its flock throughout the Ottoman domain.

Turkish States

Although each Turkish principality had individual characteristics, two general types appeared: Turkoman, and ghazi. Few of the former left much of a mark on the pages of history. The Torgud and Warsak tribes of the Taurus mountains maintained their independence until the sixteenth century but never had more than nomadic states and governments. Other Turkoman groups from Malatya to Antalya on the Mediterranean formed principalities which with the passing of time assumed the way of life of ghazi states. The leaders, for whom the states were named, however, never adopted the title ghazi. The more permanent of these states were Teke-eli at Antalya, Ramazan at Tarsus and Adana, and Dhu-al-Kadr (Sulkadr) at Diyarbakir, Malatya, and Elbistan.

From the ghazi states arose the political and social patterns that dominated Asia Minor and Turkish life for several centuries. Countless ghazi leaders created independent baronies in the wake of the Mongol demolition of the Seljuk state. Gradually, energetic leaders consolidated numerous petty holdings into sizable ghazi principalities, or amirates. At the time, the one founded by Osman near Eskishehir was quite insignificant. Other more important and more extensive amirates were Menteshe at Milas and Mughla; Sarukhan at Manisa; Aydin at Aydin; Karaman at Laranda, Karaman, and eventually Konya; Karasi at Bergama; Isfendiyar at Kastamonu; and Hamid between Antalya and Konya. Another principality of considerable importance in connection with the development of the Ottoman state was that of Kermian (Germian) at Kutahya. Never calling themselves ghazis, Kermian rulers were more typical of the Seljuk rulers, but they were allied with the ghazi states around them. Eventually the state founded by Osman conquered or annexed all the others.

Since records are scanty, the political evolution in this period of Anatolian history has remained confused and uncertain. Perhaps the oldest of these states was established in the extreme southwestern corner of Asia Minor by Menteshe, who came there by sea from the Seljuk winter residence and naval base at Antalya. Menteshe, his sons, and followers took to sea raids and could be called ghazi pirates. The dismantling of the Byzantine fleet for economic reasons led many Byzantine sailors to join the Menteshe forces, which were then able to take the island of Rhodes and raid coastal areas almost at will. The Knights of St. John, however, expelled the ghazi corsairs from Rhodes about 1310 and denied them easy access to the Aegean Islands.

Soon the Menteshe amirate was eclipsed by that of Aydin, built on the site of the ancient Greek city of Tralles on a tributary of the Meander River. Ensconced in the hinterland around Smyrna, Ghazi Aydin combined the strength of land and sea ghazis. He took Smyrna—Turks called it Izmir— and led his raiders to Greek and Thracian coasts, returning richly laden with booty. His fame spread, and volunteers appeared in camp from amirates far and near. In 1344 an active alliance of Venice, Cyprus, Rhodes, and the pope defeated the Aydin ghazis and retook Smyrna. The Aydin amirs, however, remained independent until the end of the fourteenth century, when Ottoman forces subdued the amirate.

Karamania, situated in the foothills of the Taurus mountains southwest of Konya and originally a ghazi state, offered the most persistent opposition to the Ottomans. Arising among the partisans of Baba Ishak, Karaman was the son of a Sufi mystic. The demise of the Seljuk state, nevertheless, encouraged the Karamans to assume Turkish leadership and to move to Konya as the Seljuk heirs. In so doing they lost many ghazi characteristics and acquired qualities of older and more catholic Muslim governments. These latter qualities gave greater stability and permanence to the organization of the state, and enabled the Karamans to maintain their independence from the Ottoman Empire until the beginning of the sixteenth century.

Other ghazi amirates of Anatolia were similar to these three, and that established by Osman at Sögüt had few attributes different from usual ghazi traditions upheld in these principalities. Ibn Battutah, the fourteenth-century Moroccan globetrotter, visited Asia Minor and left a record of his impressions of these amirates. Entertained at the courts of many, he reserved no special tribute for Orhan, Osman's son, and in no way singled out the Ottomans for the fame that was to be theirs.

Ghazi Society

One may well ask what were these ghazi traditions and attributes? Foremost, a ghazi state possessed as the reason for its existence a duty to battle against the infidel. It consisted of a band of dedicated warriors who rode out on raids beyond the frontiers of Islam, bringing back rich plunder which in most instances gave economic viability to the group. Although ghazis held fiefs of land, the state collapsed when raids were unsuccessful. Ghazis were equal socially and politically; aristocracy was derived from actions and leadership rather than from blood. It was a typical frontier society. To become a ghazi, however, was not an automatic step. One had to prove his worth by deeds and by evidence of character. In a ghazi state, society was organized into several classes or corporations, the ghazi group being the highest.

Another feature of ghazi life was recognition and acceptance of the *futuwwa*, a set of rules by which the virtuous life should be lived. In fact, ghazi brotherhoods were organized on this moral and ethical base. Mutual fidelity among the membership was particularly emphasized. Likewise, almost every ghazi brotherhood recognized a spiritual leader; in most cases this leader was a mystic, dervish, or Sufi, so ghazis usually adhered to some dervish order. Frequently a badge or special headgear would be worn to distinguish ghazis from other individuals.

A ghazi, then, was one who had a sense of belonging to a separate and distinct corporation of individuals whose main occupation was military conquest. In a world of confusion and a period of political disintegration the ghazi movement flourished. But ghazi states found that raids eventually ceased, whereupon the states withered because life was not devised on a solid internal economy. To make the transition required more administrative apparatus than ghazis possessed. This problem confronted the Ottomans constantly in their meteoric path across Anatolia and the Balkans. The success with which they solved this continuing problem determined, in considerable measure, the permanent or ephemeral character of Ottoman conquests. This theme is more or less central in the understanding and explanation of the rise and spread of the Ottoman state.

REFERENCES: Chapter 12

Material can be found in Chapters 2, 4, 7, 10, and 11.

Birge, John K. *A Guide to Turkish Area Study.* Washington, D.C.: American Council of Learned Societies, 1949. An indispensable bibliography.

Cahen, Claude. *Pre-Ottoman Turkey: A General Survey of the Material and Spiritual Culture and History, c. 1071–1330.* Translated from the French by J. Jones-Williams. London: Sidgwick & Jackson, 1968. A very important work by an outstanding scholar. Dealing with the coming of the Seljuks, it contains a full description of society and the institutions developed in Asia Minor. This is followed by a section of thirteen chapters covering the area during the Mongol period.

Gibbons, Herbert A. *The Foundation of the Ottoman Empire.* Oxford: Clarendon Press, 1916. The first book to tackle the problem; still useful.

Kissling, E. J., F. R. C. Bagley, N. Barbour, J. S. Trimingham, H. Braun, and H. Hartel. *The Muslim World: A Historical Survey.* Pt. 2. *The Last Great Muslim Empires.* Translation and adaptations by F. R. C. Bagley. Leiden: Brill. 1969. A good text covering from the end of the Mongol period to the nineteenth century.

Langer, William L., and Robert P. Blake. "The Rise of the Ottoman Turks and Its Historical Background." *American Historical Review,* 27 (April 1932): 468–505. An important article.

Le Strange, Guy. *Mesopotamia and Persia Under the Mongols in the Fourteenth Century* A.D. London: Royal Asiatic Society, 1903.

Rice, Tamara Talbot. *The Seljuks in Asia Minor.* New York: Praeger, 1961. An architectural history.

Sümer, Faruk, Ahmet E. Uysal, and Warren S. Walker (trans. and eds.). *The Book of Dede Korkut: A Turkish Epic.* Austin: University of Texas Press, 1972. A fine translation of the great tenth-century epic Turkish tale and song from medieval Turkish courts. Called by some the greatest monument of Turkish literature.

Ünsal, Behçet. *Turkish Islamic Architecture in Seljuk and Ottoman Times, 1071–1923.* London: Tiranti, 1959. The author discusses geographical, historical, physical, and cultural conditions affecting Turkish architecture. Describes mosques, *medressehs*, inns, markets, palaces, illustrating different kinds of materials and types of construction and comparing Turkish architects.

Vryonis, Speros. "Seljuk Gulams and Ottoman Devshirmes." *Der Islam, Zeitschrift für Geschichte und Kultur des Islamischen Orients,* 41 (October 1965): 224–252. This is a very basic article showing how the system developed and operated, what the slaves became, and whence they had come.

Chapter 13

Ottoman Origins and Early Institutions

Ottoman Origins

Osman, founder of the Ottoman state, was the son of Ertogrul, a Turkish frontier warrior who possessed the land of Sögüt as a fief, given by one of the later Seljuk sultans. An insignificant place and an extreme outpost on the frontier, Sögüt was not particularly desirable. Nothing of certainty is known about Ertogrul's ancestry or background, but he must not have been very outstanding or he would have commanded a more important assignment. Probably he was one of the countless seminomadic Turkomans looking for a place in Anatolia.

Like any other frontier warrior *(ujbey)*, Ertogrul led raiding excursions into Byzantine territory, but he bequeathed to his son Osman little more than the original fief of Sögüt. Moreover, the conquest and absorption of neighboring villages and fortified places began only in the 1280s. This was presumably after Osman had married Malkhatun, the daughter of a certain Shaykh Edebali, who adhered to one of the mystical or Sufi sects common to those frontiers. It was probably he who introduced Osman to the ghazi corporation and gave him the moral and ethical ideas of the *futuwwa*.

In any case, Osman as a leader of ghazis began to acquire by capture or alliance a number of small towns such as Eskishehir, Inönü, Bilejik, and Yenishehir. Between 1300 and 1320, using Yenishehir as a base, Osman and his ghazis seized the countryside west of the Sakarya River as far south as Eskishehir and the Kermian amirate, and west and north to Uludagh (Mount Olympus) and the Sea of Marmara. Yet they were not strong enough or sufficiently well equipped to take the walled towns of Brusa, Nicaea, and Nicomedia. Not until Osman was on his deathbed in 1326 did his ghazis, under the leadership of his son Orhan (Orkhan in old Turkish spelling), take Brusa, which surrendered without a struggle after several years of siege.

The fall of Brusa was the signal for Byzantine collapse in that corner of Asia Minor. Orhan occupied Nicaea in 1331 and Nicomedia in 1337. Later he dispossessed the quarreling sons of the amir of Karasi and placed Ottoman rulers over Bergama (Pergamum) and other towns of that amirate. Thus by 1345 the Ottoman state included the entire northwestern corner of Asia Minor from the Aegean to the Black Sea.

Several factors prepared the way and assisted in this accelerating growth of the Ottoman state. No doubt the personality and spirit of Osman counted heavily in forging a firm and successful band. Certainly his men and his lieutenants were loyal and devoted to him. At first Osman was placed in an exposed position between and near fortified areas within one day's sail from Constantinople. Even though emperors were weak and consumed with constant intrigues, they possessed sufficient determination to resist Turkish attacks until the fourteenth century. Thereafter, Byzantine force weakened rapidly, and such towns as Brusa and Nicaea were summarily abandoned to their fate.

A most important element in the growth of Ottoman forces was the policy of welcoming any and all fighting men who would join in advancing the ghazi cause. Köse Mikhal, a Greek renegade, became one of Osman's favorite comrades, and his descendants, as the Mikhaloglu, held prominent positions through centuries of Ottoman history. In 1305 some of the Catalan Company joined the Ottoman camp; defeated Mongol raiders, given clemency, fell in with the men under Orhan; and many disillusioned Greek soldiers defending Brusa became Muslims and fought as Ottomans after that city capitulated. Fighting men from Kermian, Karasi, and other Turkish and ghazi amirates flocked to the Ottomans as their successes multiplied.

However, in the first half century under Osman and Orhan, Ottoman expansion was gradual enough to permit the organization of some governmental administration. Moreover, the Muslim world was in such disorder that Muslim artisans, merchants, bureaucrats, theologians, jurists, fiscal experts, teachers, and scribes were attracted by seemingly unlimited opportunities in this new frontier Muslim state. Schools of theology were built in Bursa and Iznik (Turkish names for Brusa and Nicaea) soon after their capture, and Bursa long remained the center of learning and philosophical discussion for the Ottomans.

Furthermore, the immigrant artisans and merchants formed corporations known as *akhis*. Somewhat like European guilds, these akhis were closely knit bodies subscribing to specific *futuwwa* very similar to the ghazi code of honor. A close alliance and understanding between ghazi and akhi gave to Ottoman society an economic strength lacking in other ghazi states. But the early arrival of Muslim lawyers and theologians *(ulema)* tempered the ghazi crusading fervor, and Orhan accepted the older Muslim practice of allowing Christians and Jews to live in a Muslim land by paying taxes and special tribute. Thus at an early date social and economic disturbances in towns passing into Ottoman hands were largely minimized. Life went on in much the same way with considerable intermingling of people. Orhan himself married Nilufer, a daughter of the Greek lord of a captured town. Taronites, Orhan's Greek physician, felt very comfortable and much at home among the Ottomans.

By the middle of the fourteenth century Orhan had become amir of a sizable state facing the historic Straits and Europe beyond. Silver coins were minted, and a lively trade developed in such prosperous towns as Bursa, Iznik, Izmid (Nicomedia), and Bergama. The Ottoman state assumed a place as an important powerful component in the political, diplomatic, and military turbulence concomitant with the decline of an obsolete empire.

Ghazis were long accustomed to raiding parties in Thrace and Macedonia. Orhan and his men became allies of Emperor John VI Cantacuzenus in 1345 to fight against his rival Emperor John V Palaeologus. Part of Orhan's bargain was the privilege of plundering; another part was the hand in marriage of Theodora, Cantacuzenus' daughter. Six thousand Ottomans ravaged the hinterland of Constantinople and the Black Sea coast and were instrumental in taking Adrianople. Similarly, every year thereafter Ottoman soldiers practiced their profession in Thrace and the Lower Balkans, amassing fortunes in booty.

Ottomans in Europe

In these same years the Black Death struck. Reaching Constantinople first in 1347, it spread in following years through the Balkans and to the maritime towns and cities of the Aegean and the Straits and on to Europe, leaving dislocation and terror everywhere. It ended all talk of a crusade to crush the Ottomans or to regain Constantinople again for the Franks. No soldier would go to the East! The Black Death made victories for the Ottomans much easier in Europe.

In 1354 a severe earthquake demolished the walls of Gallipoli on the European shore of the Dardanelles. Ottoman forces in Europe rushed into Gallipoli, asserting that God had given it to them. Orhan refused to return it to his father-in-law and sent Ottomans there to colonize the city, much of whose population had been carried off by the Black Death.

From this first bridgehead in Europe, Ottomans stormed over eastern Thrace, seizing all areas between the Aegean and the Black seas except, of course, the imperial city of Constantinople. Adrianople opened its gates in 1362 to Murad, third in the Ottoman line of rulers, and for nearly a century that city (which the Turks call Edirne) stood as the Ottoman European capital.

Murad I, the younger son of Orhan and Nilufer, followed in his father's footsteps, vigorously pushing one campaign after another northward and westward into the Balkans. Rival emperors of Constantinople, Serbian and Bulgarian tsars, independent princes of Greece, the city-states of Venice and Genoa, popes, and Crusaders kept the Balkans in such a constant turmoil and confusion that Murad in his expeditions never had to worry about facing a consolidated offensive and usually had several Christian allies in his camp.

Under Murad's leadership (r. 1360–1389) Ottoman armies and raiders succeeded in conquering most of Bulgaria, Macedonia, and parts of Serbia to Lake Ochrida, including Widin, Sofia, Monastir, and Nish. During the crushing defeat of the Serbs in the Battle of Kossovo in 1389, Murad lost his own life but sealed the doom of independence for any Christian Balkan state and securely established the Ottoman position in southern Europe.

Likewise, Murad made extensive advances in Asia. He took Ankara and by a combination of prestige, power, money, and diplomacy nearly doubled his Anatolian possessions. Marriage of his son Bayezid to the daughter of the Kermian amir brought the town of Kutahya as a dowry. Murad forced the amir of Hamid to "sell" most of his domain and will the balance to the Ottomans. Campaigns were launched against Karamania and Teke, but with little success, because ghazis were unwilling to fight against those whom they considered to be "warriors of the faith." In these Anatolian campaigns Murad's most loyal supporters were contingents of his Slavic allies and mercenaries.

When Bayezid I succeeded to the Ottoman sultanship on the field of Kossovo, he inherited a state that in the brief span of two generations had grown from a petty principality to a dominant power stretching from the Danube to the Taurus mountains. The Black Death, political anarchy in Europe and Asia, religious fervor, and a search for booty on the part of the ghazis may have accounted for some of the rapidity of the development. Credit, however, should also be given to the dynamic personalities, the administrative talents, and the driving genius of Orhan and Murad.

Ottoman Army

Among the Ottomans the army, its organization, and its recruitment were matters of prime importance. Under Osman criers went through the villages announcing that anyone who wished to participate in a raid should meet at a given place at a specified time. Orhan, however, organized the army. Traditionally he did this on the counsel and under the supervision of his brother Ala al-Din Ali and a maternal relative Kara Khalil Chendereli. The latter was probably of akhi membership and has usually been considered to have had some formal education. Moreover, in the wars of Orhan and Murad closer contacts with the Byzantine military provided examples from which the Ottoman army obtained useful suggestions.

The army was organized on a basis of units of 10, 100, and 1,000 men, with a responsible officer over each group. This was as true of irregular infantry (*azab*) and volunteer horsemen and cavalry scouts (*akinji*) as it was of regular feudal cavalry (*sipahis*) and the newly formed janissaries (*yeni cheri*). Officers of the immediate family and entourage of the Ottoman ruler were placed in overall charge of the armies. Evrenos Bey, a Greek from Karasi, became chief of the European frontier and always led the feudal sipahis, while Köse Mikhal was responsible for the scouts. Suleiman Pasha, Orhan's eldest son, was the first to be commander in chief (*beylerbey*) of the troops in Europe.

The institution of the janissaries held a special place in Ottoman annals. The origin of this corps has been much debated. Their role in innumerable Ottoman victories through several centuries was so prominent that many authors have sought for some special beginning or at least for the name of their brilliant innovator. In a Muslim state, even in the time of the Prophet, the ruler as the embodiment of the state usually received one-fifth of the booty of war. Since human beings had long been valuable prizes of success-ful campaigns and since their lot was invariably one of slavery, Ottomans under Orhan and Murad found more slaves on their hands than they knew how to employ in customary tasks. Moreover, the market for slaves in surrounding areas was slack. The answer was to turn them into soldiers to fight for their captors.

Caliphs and sultans in the past had slave bodyguards, and in contempo-rary Egypt the ruling cliques, the Mamluks, were slaves. Seljuk rulers had slaves *(gulams)* by the thousands who were trained as soldiers, led their armies, and rose to become high officials. Most of them were Greek youths of Anatolia taken as prisoners or levied as a tribute from the Greek subjects. Youths captured in battle were kept as slaves by the Ottoman sultans as well. Nominally converted to Islam, they were banded together and trained as special corps in the army about the sultan. Their name, *yeni cheri* ("new soldier"), was corrupted to "janissary" by Europeans, who learned to fear these soldiers and stand in awe of their discipline, their esprit de corps, and their prowess with arms. Many younger captives were "farmed out" for a number of years to Ottoman feudal officers as apprentices. During these years they learned some Turkish, which became the Ottoman lingua franca, and they grew, were toughened, and became adept in the skills of fighting. To assimilate the janissaries into the Ottoman ranks as soldiers and as people was not difficult. Most of these captives were Greeks, Armenians, Serbs, and Bulgars, and were hardly different, socially, racially, or culturally, from many of those free renegades who voluntarily became ghazis and Otto-mans.

In the days of Murad I the janissaries probably did not exceed 3,000 in number. They were paid a small daily wage and did not marry while active as soldiers. Living together in barracks, drilling, training, and being garbed alike gave the janissaries the status of a standing army more than a century before standing armies became the European practice. Some were cavalry; most were infantrymen; others were members of a specially honored left-handed guard. Many rose through the ranks and became high officers and trusted civil officials; a few were beheaded for dishonesty or disobedience. Before a century passed, only those who became regular infantrymen were known as janissaries. Other ranks and other corps had their own special designations.

Another important factor contributing to Ottoman successes was the development of sipahis, who answered the need for regular cavalry, for colonization of newly won lands, and for local provincial administration. Adapting Seljuk, Arab, and Byzantine feudal practices, Ottoman rulers rewarded ghazis and fighting men with grants of land from which they derived their living. Actual dispensation of land was made by the com-mander on the field. Greater valor resulted in larger fiefs. The smallest unit granted was a *timar,* to which additional fields were joined as more service was rendered. When lands held were sufficient to produce revenue to outfit more than five horsemen, the *timarji* became a *zaim* and his holding was termed a *ziamet*. Still-larger grants were called *khass*, but these were reserved for special officers such as governors and commanding generals.

Each year when a campaign was announced, sipahis left their estates and appeared equipped to fight under the immediate leadership of a local officer whom they elected. This feudal cavalry not only was the main force of the Ottoman armies but also was engaged almost continually in raids beyond the frontier. Sons went along on campaigns with their fathers and learned the profession of arms. They were eligible to inherit their fathers' trade and were usually awarded at least a part of the family fief. By settling and rearing families on the land, the feudal cavalry served as the first Ottoman colonizers and administrators of new territories.

Running strongly through the ranks of the Ottoman feudal cavalry until the end of the sixteenth century was the ghazi spirit and ideology. In certain areas where the frontier was long a battleground, as in Bosnia, northern Epirus, the Albanian mountains, Macedonia, and Thrace, a ghazi society emerged similar to those of earlier ghazi frontier areas in Anatolia. A thorough admixture of Ottoman warriors with local populations occurred, giving rise in the Balkans to Greek-, Serb-, and Albanian-speaking Muslims.

Bayezid I

Seizing the reins of government on the field of Kossovo in 1389, Bayezid I avenged his father's death with victory over the Serbians. Then, even before nightfall, he consolidated his personal position by ordering that his only brother, Yakub, be strangled. Yakub had fought valiantly at Kossovo and had served his father well and loyally, not only in battle but also as governor of several provinces. Having the example of bitter and destructive rivalries of the Byzantine imperial family before him, however, Bayezid judged that bowstringing his brother was for the best. He attempted to legalize this action by Koranic reference, with such success that practices of this kind became standard and legal procedure for a new sultan to take upon accession to the throne and prevailed in the Ottoman family for 250 years.

With the rise of modern nationalism Kossovo was to become the symbol among the Serbs for lost national identity and for subjection, but in 1389 no great ill-feeling seemed to be generated. The Serbian royal princess Despina was married to the victorious Bayezid, who became devoted to her; and Serb levies and contingents remained extremely loyal to Bayezid throughout his reign. In succeeding years Ottoman forces raided Bosnia and Hungary, even crossing the Danube, and Bayezid brought greater numbers of Ottomans into Europe, especially into Thrace.

Indeed, beginning in 1391 all of Thrace was occupied up to the very walls of Constantinople: the city was virtually blockaded from the land side. A full investiture of Constantinople was outlined and a full blockade planned. On the Asian side of the Bosphorus at Anadolu Hisar fortifications were constructed in 1393. Bayezid attempted to close the Bosphorus and the Dardanelles to ships destined for the imperial city. But attacks, first in Europe and later in Asia, saved Constantinople for half a century.

Sigismund, later Holy Roman Emperor but then only king of Hungary, was concerned over successful Ottoman aggressions. He therefore invaded Bulgaria in 1392 and captured the fortress of Nicopolis, only to withdraw within a few months before a large Ottoman force. The following year Bayezid judged it necessary to eject his Bulgarian vassal, whose capital, Tirnovo, fell before the onslaughts of Bayezid's son Suleiman. Suleiman followed the victory by fortifying Silistria, Widin, and Nicopolis. These actions, in addition to the creation of an Ottoman navy which began depredations in the Adriatic, led Europe to heed Sigismund's loud cries for a crusade.

The romantic and fateful crusade of Nicopolis of 1396 was the result. Nobles from England, France, Germany, Flanders, and Burgundy, laden with wine and women, joined as if on a picnic. Leadership went to Jean de Nevers, grandson of the king of France, who appeared with Sigismund and Hungarian and Wallachian armies before Nicopolis. They foolishly charged the center of the Ottoman forces, commanded personally by Bayezid, who had left the siege of Constantinople to meet the knights of Europe. Utterly outmaneuvered, the flower of Western nobility fell on the battlefield of Nicopolis, and thousands were captured. Those under twenty years of age were taken for the janissary corps or the sultan's court. One of these— Johann Schiltberger—after twenty-five years returned to his Bavarian home and wrote a valuable historical account of his experiences. Many, like Jean de Nevers, were held for ransom. And others as ordinary slaves were impressed to row in the galleys. This first serious encounter between Europeans and Ottomans had brought disaster to the former and vetoed for several decades any thought of a crusade on their part.

A follow-up campaign deep into Europe was feared by Venice, but Bayezid turned his attention instead to Greece. Ottoman armies overran Thessaly, penetrated the Peloponnesus, and captured towns and smaller cities. Ottomans were settled in the northeastern corner of the Peloponnesus, then called Morea, and fiefs were handed out in northern Greece. But fortified cities such as Athens, Salonica, Nauplia, Coron, and Modon that could still be supplied from the sea were, like Constantinople, beyond Ottoman reach.

Bayezid's involvements in Europe and the investment of Constantinople did not deter him from campaigns in Asia Minor. Without question, one of his burning ambitions was to unite under his rule, contrary to ghazi tradition, all Muslim lands of Asia Minor and perhaps of the entire Middle East. Although this idea paralleled naturally the common phenomena of expansion and unification attendant upon the rise and growth of a new state, Bayezid's haughty manner and ruthless tactics spelled his ruin.

In rapid succession between 1390 and 1397 Ottoman forces, frequently led by Bayezid in person, captured and annexed old ghazi and Turkoman amirates such as Aydin, Sarukhan, Menteshe, Teke, Karaman, and Isfendiyar and seized the areas of Kayseri, Sivas, Samsun, and Sinop. The dispossessed princes, instead of being commissioned with Ottoman responsibilities to weld them into the Ottoman people, fled with revenge in their hearts to the court of Timur Leng (Tamerlane).

Acquisition of Aydin and Menteshe brought experienced ghazi sailors to the Ottoman state, and in 1390 the first Ottoman navy was formed. Ships harried the coasts of Greece and descended upon various islands of the Aegean, and an embargo was declared on grain ships destined for Rhodes, Lemnos, Lesbos, and Chios.

With Bayezid engaged in subduing Bulgaria and in besieging Constantinople, the Karaman leaders judged that a revolt might be successful. However, Bayezid transferred his troops to Asia with amazing speed and destroyed the Karamans in front of Bursa. He did this so completely and so quickly that his soldiers dubbed him Yilderim ("Lightning").

Except for a few walled towns like Constantinople and Athens, Bayezid Yilderim was now lord and master of the land from the Adriatic and the plains of Hungary to the Euphrates. In barely a decade he had doubled his Asian possessions and gained recognition as lord of the Balkans. In 1395 he held court at Serres; Serbian princes and Byzantine emperors rendered homage. The uncomplicated Ottoman state of Osman and Orhan had vanished, and the rulers were no longer humble and unaffected.

Trade

The extension of the Mongol Empire into Asia Minor in the thirteenth century had established profitable trade routes, especially for Chinese and Persian silks, through Tabriz to Erzerum and Sivas and then branching off to Konya or Constantinople. At the same time Arab merchants brought spices, sugar, and Indian fabrics to Aleppo or by sea to Antalya. From these entrepôts the goods were carried to Konya and thence to the principal markets of Anatolia and to Constantinople. In the fourteenth century with the disintegration of the Mongol state and the rise of the Ottomans more and more of this trade found its way to Bursa, which by the year 1400 had become the most important trading city in Anatolia. As Bayezid extended his rule in Asia Minor, merchants could travel safely from Tabriz and Aleppo to Bursa where merchants from Venice, Genoa, Florence, Pisa, and Lucca (the center of European silk industry) bought their supplies.

The Ottomans were always interested in commerce and industry and the akhi groups were influential members of their society. Ibn Battutah noted in 1333 that Orhan, because he held Bursa, was the richest Turkish ruler in Anatolia. And as early as 1340 Orhan had built a bazaar and an enclosed market in Bursa where valuable goods could be safely stored and sold. Again, even before the Ottomans took Adrianople, they had concluded commercial treaties with the Genoese to facilitate their merchant trade in Bursa. Such interests as these had greatly aided the Ottoman successes.

Political and Social Development

In the time of Murad I the government began to grow; under Bayezid expansion was rapid and very noticeable. Its organization by religious leaders and graduates of the schools of Bursa and Iznik introduced more efficiency and rigidity in administration. At the same time evolution of the post of grand vizir in the hands of Kara Khalil Chendereli, later known as Khair al-Din Pasha, aroused considerable opposition and much unhappiness among ghazi feudal soldiers, accustomed for generations to great freedom.

Dismay also stemmed from Bayezid's dreams of empire. In 1394 he sent an embassy to the caliph in Egypt requesting to be invested with the title sultan of Rum. Even Bayezid's grandfather had used that title, and evidently it was commonly applied to Bayezid. Yet he wished recognition from the older Muslim world. Numerous Turkoman amirates of Asia Minor that he engulfed looked upon him as a tyrant and spread treasonable ideas at every turn. Few true ghazis participated in his Asian campaigns; Bayezid learned that in operations against fellow Muslims he could be sure only of his janissaries and contingents sent by his European Christian vassals. Many Muslims in Asia could hardly escape questioning Bayezid's own faith when he led Christain soldiers against Muslim soldiers.

There were other ways in which Bayezid's actions alienated his subjects. The ghazi cultural background of Ottoman leaders left them open for many innovations, and with a medley of individuals appearing among them eclecticism developed. Discussions among religious leaders of various sects within the Ottoman state led to proposals for a common religion from a composite of Islam, Judaism, and Christianity. Undoubtedly this trend can be seen in the names of Bayezid's younger sons—Musa (Moses), Isa (Jesus), and Mehmed (Muhammad). Other sons were Ertogrul (Turkish name), Mustafa (Muslim mysticism), Kasimir (Balkan Christian), and Suleiman (Solomon).

Even more objectionable were Bayezid's personal habits. Increasingly, he took on the ways of Balkan and Byzantine rulers and nobles. Manners and dress changed; court ceremony became more elaborate. Many ghazis still remembered the ease with which they could approach Orhan and contrasted the simplicity of Orhan's establishment to the complexity of Bayezid's. Bayezid, though brilliant and energetic at first, fell under the spell of grandeur and sumptuous living. He became addicted to wine and sodomy, both of which scandalized the Ottomans. His harem was large and he began to follow in the footsteps of the caliphs of old. Even the increase in the number of his sons (Osman had only two, Orhan three, and Murad three) would indicate a devotion to his harem, an institution not mentioned in connection with either Osman or Orhan.

Defeat at Ankara

This dissatisfaction and unrest among Bayezid's subjects, especially the Muslims, and the presence of many Anatolian émigré amirs in the entourage of Timur induced the latter to lead an incursion into Anatolia. In addition, Bayezid had invaded territory beyond the Euphrates to the Tigris and given indications of ambitions in Syria, thereby threatening Timur's vassals. After Bayezid ignored letters from Timur inviting him to mend his ways, Timur marched into Asia Minor.

Surprisingly overconfident, Bayezid moved leisurely to meet the threat. In the face of so great a danger he organized a huge hunting party, wasting valuable time and tiring his men. The contest came in 1402 at Ankara, where only the janissaries and the Christian vassals of the Balkans stood fast. Bayezid, a prisoner, was brought before Timur, who honored him until his haughtiness became insufferable. Within a few weeks he died of humiliation, and his body was returned to Bursa, the chief Ottoman burial site.

Following his great victory, Timur marched across Anatolia to Smyrna on the Aegean. He showed little desire to hold Anatolia directly, however. Ottoman conquests in Europe and the early holdings of Osman and Orhan in Asia were divided among Bayezid's remaining sons: Suleiman, Musa, Isa, and Mehmed. Kasimir for some reason was never considered; Ertogrul had been tortured to death earlier by Timur; and Mustafa disappeared at the Battle of Ankara. Anatolian amirates taken by Murad and Bayezid were restored to their previous hereditary families.

Bayezid had a dream of empire, but it was shattered at Ankara. The Ottoman family was left in possession of those of its holdings which were considered legitimate. Bayezid's sons and all other amirs of Anatolia swore allegiance to Timur and became his vassals. Three years later when Timur died, the amirs of western Asia Minor renounced all dependence upon the Timurids, and Anatolia was left as it had been before the invasion except for the breakup of the Ottoman domain among Bayezid's four heirs. If there was to be an Ottoman Empire, it was yet to be fashioned.

REFERENCES: Chapter 13

Volumes cited at the end of Chapters 11 and 12 are important for this chapter.

Alderson, A. D. *The Structure of the Ottoman Dynasty.* Oxford: Clarendon Press, 1956. An important volume on the Ottoman family and the lives of the individual sultans.

Creasy, Edward S. *History of the Ottoman Turks: From the Beginning of Their Empire to the Present Time.* London: Bentley, 1877. Based on the many-volume history of the Ottoman Empire by Joseph von Hammer-Purgstall, which though uncritical and out of date is still one of the most extensive works in any language.

Davison, Roderic H. *Turkey.* Englewood Cliffs, N.J.: Prentice-Hall, 1968. A fine paperback volume by an outstanding scholar incorporating up-to-date research on the early Turks down to the time of publication.

Eversley, G. J. S., and Valentine Chirol. *The Turkish Empire from 1288 to 1922.* London: Unwin, 1923. A standard work carefully done.

Inalcik, Halil. *The Ottoman Empire: The Classical Age, 1300–1600.* Translated from the Turkish by Norman Itzkowitz and Colin Imber. New York: Praeger, 1973. A thorough study of the early empire by the outstanding Ottoman scholar. In addition to political history, the author discusses administration, law, economic and social life, culture, and fanaticism in a most enlightened way.

Itzkowitz, Norman. *Ottoman Empire and Islamic Tradition.* New York: Knopf, 1973. This is an excellent introduction to the Ottoman Empire by a well-known scholar. Deals with the early history leading to the formation of the empire.

Lane-Poole, Stanley, E. J. W. Gibb, and Arthur Gilman. *The Story of Turkey.* New York: Putnam, 1888. Still a fine one-volume work.

Schiltberger, Johannes. *The Bondage and Travels of Johann Schiltberger, a Native of Bavaria, in Europe, Asia, and Africa, 1396–1427.* Translated from the German and edited by J. Buchan Telfer, with notes by P. Bruun, from the Heidelberg manuscript published by K. F. Neumann. London: The Hakluyt Society, 1879. A fascinating account of life in the Ottoman state by a young page who was captured at the battle of Nicopolis in 1396 and became a janissary, serving in the sultan's army for twenty years. Valuable for first-hand observations.

Stanford, Shaw. *History of the Ottoman Empire and Modern Turkey.* Vol. 1. *Empire of the Gazis: The Rise and Decline of the Ottoman Empire, 1280–1808.* Cambridge: Cambridge University Press, 1976. This is an outstanding contribution by a leading scholar in the field. He analyzes the many forces in Asia Minor that produced the Ottoman Empire and relates the seeds that led to its decline.

Wittek, Paul. *The Rise of the Ottoman Empire.* London: Royal Asiatic Society, 1938. A masterful work by the most eminent authority in the field. This study is a kind of landmark in the subject.

Chapter 14

The Winning of the Ottoman Empire

Mehmed I Reunites the State

The capture of Sultan Bayezid I at the Battle of Ankara in 1402 left the remaining Ottoman provinces to be apportioned among his sons. Timur recognized Mehmed, probably the youngest, as governor of Amasya, his residence under his father. Isa was designated as lord of Bursa. Suleiman, the eldest and formerly governor at Manisa, went to Edirne and ruled the Ottoman possessions in Europe. Musa, taken prisoner by Timur, was placed on parole to the Kermian family at Kutahya. Shortly afterward he was authorized to take his father's body to Bursa for burial and was then sent to the court of his brother Mehmed.

The transitory character of Timur's conquest permitted the four sons to quarrel among themselves over their patrimony. At first Mehmed and Musa teamed up against Suleiman and Isa, striking their first blows in Asia. With Mehmed's compliance Musa drove Isa from Bursa. Fleeing to Constantinople, Isa was encouraged by Suleiman, himself under pressure from Musa, to make a bid to regain his city. He was, however, beaten by Mehmed and vanished from the scene.

Meanwhile, having escaped from the Ankara disaster with Ali Pasha Chendereli and the leader of the janissaries, Suleiman arrived at Edirne, European headquarters for the Ottoman family. With the richest part of the state in his hands and supported by his father's chief ministers, Suleiman in 1403 claimed to be ruler of the Ottomans. But Mehmed and Musa refused to acknowledge his supremacy.

Rivalry among the three brothers endured for a decade. Its genesis was Bayezid I's killing of his own brother on the field of Kossovo. But competition among Suleiman, Musa, and Mehmed also arose from the factionalism in Ottoman politics that emerged from their father's attempts to consolidate and centralize the state.

The imperial clique found its candidate in Suleiman. Supported by the Chendereli and Evrenos families, by the governmental machinery in Edirne, and by the janissaries who survived the rout at Ankara, Suleiman reigned until 1411. Treaties with the Venetian doge and the Byzantine emperor recognized him as Ottoman ruler and facilitated trade and commerce in Europe, affairs in which the Chendereli family was personally interested. Suleiman failed, however, in his campaigns to dislodge Musa and Mehmed from Bursa.

With the aid of discontented Serbs and Wallachians, Musa carried the struggle against Suleiman to Eurpoe in 1410, engaging him in battle between Edirne and Constantinople. Unsuccessful in the first attempt, Musa caught Suleiman the next year in a surprise raid upon Edirne and killed him as he was fleeing to Constantinople. Ibrahim Chendereli, the Evrenos family, and the court immediately transferred their loyalty to Musa, who was now recognized as lord of Europe. Mehmed remained supreme in Asia Minor.

Besides Balkan vassals and Ottoman European officialdom, Musa was supported by a freethinking religious coterie pursuing a theological eclecticism popular at that time. As chief judge in Ottoman European territories he appointed one of its leaders, Shaykh Bahr al-Din Mahmud ibn Kadi Simavna, who held views leading toward a socialistic society and a union of Judaism, Christianity, and Islam. Some years later Shaykh Bahr al-Din led an unsuccessful socialist rebellion against the state, and in the mid-sixteenth century his views were still being preached by one of his descendants.

Musa was an energetic individual and sent out raiding parties into Greece and as far into Europe as Carinthia. The siege of Constantinople that had been lifted upon the coming of Timur into Anatolia was resumed. Strangely, Mehmed aided the emperor against his brother. Musa's revolutionary tendencies and his open favoring of the common people drove many of his supporters among high officials and the wealthy such as Ibrahim Chendereli over to Mehmed, who carried on an active campaign for allies among high-placed Ottoman feudal lords in Europe. Most of these went over to Mehmed; and in 1413 Edirne fell to Mehmed, who caught up with Musa near Sofia. Musa perished, and his body was returned with honor to Bursa to be buried beside his grandfather.

Mehmed now reigned alone and all Ottomans paid him homage. Having first governed in Amasya, heartland of the old Danishmend ghazi district, Mehmed professed the ghazi way of life and throughout remained its champion. With the favor of this powerful faction, essentially the military foundation of the state, propaganda for him among frontier raiders and Ottoman colonists in Europe took root easily. Mehmed in their eyes represented the "good old days" of Osman and Orhan.

In looking for factors in the success of Mehmed, the role of his tutor *(lala)* cannot be disregarded. As was customary, Mehmed was sent as a boy to govern a province and learn the art of ruling. A high state dignitary accompanied the prince "to advise" in all matters. In this instance the tutor was Bayezid Pasha, an Albanian by birth and a war captive retained by Murad and raised at court. Bayezid Pasha proved to be an outstanding general and a devoted slave to Mehmed, winning battles, organizing campaigns, and above all leading Mehmed to the task of reuniting the Ottoman state. Bayezid Pasha was one of the very first of a new type of high Ottoman official who in his attachment to his masters, the Ottoman family, showed his proclivity for a strongly centralized state.

Most important, in strongly identifying himself with Anatolia and the old ghazi way of life, Mehmed avoided the mistakes of his father and his brother Suleiman in their European and Balkan manners. He chose for his wife a daughter of the amir of Dhu-al-Kadr, a Turkoman amirate of the Syrian frontier. Known as Chelebi ("Gentleman"), Kurushji ("Wrestler"), or Pahlevan ("Champion"), Mehmed grew to be revered by the Ottomans for his gentleness, integrity, and modesty.

Expansion in Asia

There were in Asia Minor many Turks, however, who were not considered Ottomans and who did not accept the idea of one united state or acquiesce in its rule. Although forces from Karamania and Dhu-al-Kadr fought with Mehmed when he ousted his brother Isa from Bursa, the Karaman prince, always the prime Ottoman rival in Anatolia, beseiged Bursa when Mehmed was destroying Musa in Rumeli. (The European part of the Ottoman state was always Rumeli—the land of the Romans, i.e., Byzantines.) The Karamans were defeated in 1414, but their state was not conquered. In the same year Mehmed dealt with an adventurer from Izmir by name of Junayd, who had in turn supported Bayezid I, Isa, Mehmed, Suleiman, and Musa. Junayd gathered strength from Aydin and the coastal areas around Izmir, but recognized his defeat before any battle occurred. According to the standard practice of assigning European positions to dispossessed Anatolians, Mehmed magnanimously gave Junayd the governorship of Nicopolis on the Danube.

Except for the states of Karaman, Dhu-al-Kadr, and Isfendiyar, Turkish families recognized the dominant position of the Ottomans in central and western Anatolia. The disruption of society resulting from Timur's invasion and continued by the civil wars of Bayezid's sons generated many religious and mystical sects in Asia Minor. A number of dervish orders founded by holy men from Iran date their origin from this period. Social disorders, too, were not unknown. In 1416 Bayezid Pasha had to raise levies from most of Anatolia to quell in the peninsula north of Izmir a socioreligious revolutionary movement led by the mystic Bahr al-Din, one-time European army judge under Musa.

As a genuine ghazi, Mehmed could not ignore Europe and the great conquests there. Furthermore, the manner in which the Balkans were acquired made Rumeli produce far greater revenue for the Ottoman government than did Anatolia. Any slackening of the sultan's activity in Europe always brought on financial repercussions. Mehmed intervened in Wallachia, built fortresses north of the Danube, and encouraged ghazi raids in Hungary, Bosnia, and Styria.

After Junayd's defeat Mehmed gathered a fleet to clear Venetian pirates from the Aegean Islands and the Izmir coast. Venice sent ships to protect her vassals, and Admiral Loredano broke Mehmed's fleet off Gallipoli in

1416. Peace, however, was soon negotiated, and Mehmed refused to resume the attack that his father and brothers had begun upon Constantinople.

One other episode marred the peace and harmony of Mehmed's rule. In 1419 one who claimed to be Mustafa, the son of Bayezid I who disappeared at the Battle of Ankara, arose in Europe, obtaining immediate support from the Wallachians and the scoundrel Junayd in Nicopolis. When Mehmed defeated the pretender and Junayd, they received asylum in Salonica. Later they were sent by the governor to the emperor in Constantinople, who held them for Mehmed.

Unquestionably, Mehmed reestablished Ottoman unity approximately to the extent that it had existed in his father's time. But an Ottoman empire was not yet created. There remained Constantinople, geographic and economic center of the area. Without the power emanating from its position, an empire could not be. Mehmed made no attempt upon it. Friendly relations with the emperor in times of distress induced him to refuse to entertain any designs upon the city. Nonetheless, his early death from a stroke in 1421 may have saved the city from attack.

Murad II

The idea of the continuity of the state and the sultan's relationship to governmental power had so grown that Mehmed's closest advisers, of whom Bayezid Pasha was one, concealed his death for forty days until his son and successor Murad II, arrived in Edirne from Amasya to take charge. Nearly eighteen years old, Murad had resided with his advisers and tutors at Manisa before being moved to Amasya and had participated in the campaign against Bahr al-Din. At the time of his father's death Murad had one surviving brother, Mustafa, who was thirteen years old. Afraid that Murad would kill him as Bayezid had strangled Yakub, Mustafa fled from his Anatolian governorship with his tutors to the protection of the Karaman family in Konya.

Murad surrounded himself with representatives of old Ottoman families such as Chendereli, Evrenos, Timurtash, and Mikhaloglu and with leaders of the new courtiers like Bayezid Pasha, although this latter group was less numerous. At the very outset of Murad's reign the perfidious Byzantine emperor freed the old pretender Mustafa, who circulated in Rumeli gathering supporters, chief among whom was none other than Junayd, again governor of Nicopolis. This Mustafa and his supporters defeated and killed Bayezid Pasha, seized Gallipoli with the emperor's aid, and invaded Anatolia. Murad rallied and drove them back to Europe. In 1422 Genoese cooperation in transporting his troops across the Straits permitted him to catch and kill the pretender and the rebels in Edirne.

Murad raged at the emperor for his duplicity and ordered resumption of the siege of Constantinople. With prodigious effort, much enthusiasm, and the use of breaching cannon for the first time in Ottoman history, Murad and his soldiers stormed the walls. After two months of failure Murad lifted the siege to meet a new threat in Asia Minor: Byzantine diplomacy with the Karamans had brought Murad's brother Mustafa from his refuge in Konya to an unsuccessful attack upon Bursa.

Though Mustafa was caught and hanged, Murad never resumed the attack upon Constantinople. The emperor agreed to pay the Ottomans a yearly tribute of 30,000 ducats and surrender all territory outside the walls except for areas that fed the aqueducts of the city. In Anatolia, Murad judiciously alternated between diplomacy and force. A slight engagement with the amir of Isfendiyar ended when Murad married the amir's daughter and obtained possession of the copper mines in that region. The Karaman amir sued for peace, and Menteshe and Teke recognized Murad's suzerainty. Peace with Karamania, however, was never sure; and whenever Murad became deeply engrossed or embarrassed in Europe, war with the princes of Konya became imminent and sometimes necessary.

Murad's greatest efforts were expended in Europe, and there lay his greater gains. In 1430 Salonica was taken after a long struggle from Venice, which had purchased the city from the Byzantine emperor. Ottoman pressure was maintained in the Morea, northern Epirus, Albania, Bosnia, Serbia, Hungary, and Wallachia. Upon the accession to the throne of Hungary, Ladislaus, king of Lithuania and Poland, dissident elements—Serbs, Wallachians, Hungarians, and Bosnians—banded their arms together and invaded Ottoman territory. In 1443 under the leadership of John Hunyadi, Sigismund's illegitimate son, the invaders won numerous strongholds, were victorious at Nish and Sofia, and brought Murad to the edge of ruin. The Karamans chose this moment for an attack, and it is important to note that Murad himself fought the enemy in Asia and sent trusted generals to the European front.

Nevertheless, Murad concluded an honorable peace with King Ladislaus in 1444 at Szeged, each promising not to invade the other's territory for ten years. Murad had defeated the Karamans, and Hunaydi realized that the Ottoman army, with Murad at its head and the janissaries included, would be quite a different body from the feudal army that he had met the previous year. Murad gave up suzerainty over Wallachia and Serbia and ransomed his son-in-law for 60,000 ducats.

Ottoman Society and Culture

Evidently Murad felt that he had made peace with the world in Europe and Asia and that the time was propitious for retirement from active rule. He was forty years old and had been sultan for twenty-three years. His two older sons having died, Murad abdicated in favor of his fifteen-year-old third son, Mehmed, who went to Edirne with Khalil Pasha Chendereli as grand vizir and Molla Khusraw of the Warsak Turkoman tribe as chief judge. Murad himself withdrew to his favorite residence in Manisa, where he intended to live in ease and peace with poets, mystics, theologians, and men of letters. He wished to pursue the *futuwwa*, the ideal life, modestly studying and writing in quiet contemplation.

It was the time of an incipient Turkish renaissance. The Turkish language, as spoken at the Ottoman court and in western Anatolia, became a medium of cultured expression. Konya, Kutahya, and Bursa in Asia Minor and Edirne in Europe were its centers; its patrons were the Karaman, Kermian, and Ottoman families and their courts. Heretofore, Persian and Arabic were the languages of poetry, records, and education. But Turkish was growing more popular. Umur Bey, a son of Timurtash Pasha, instructed a poet whom he patronized to use as many Turkish words as possible in his verses.

Many Persian and Arabic works were translated into Ottoman Turkish, and such poets as Shaykhi, Kemal Ummi, Eshrefoglu, Rumi, Husami, Shemsi, and Nedimi were held in high esteem. Sufis, mystics, and holy men (or *shaykhs* as they were known in Anatolia) were numerous and earnestly venerated. The most revered in Bursa from the time of Bayezid I until his death in 1430 was Amir Sultan, a native of Bukhara in Turkestan. The shrine built over his tomb indicated his popularity and the honor rendered him by the Ottomans.

Ottoman history was first cultivated under Murad, when a "romantic" movement arose. Until this time Ottoman chronicles were sagas of ghazis and their great deeds. Under Murad there developed a new and formal Ottoman history, which included illustrious ancestors going back to the most noble of Turkish tribes—the Oghuz tribe. Beautiful tales were written of Osman's ancestors riding with 400 horsemen into Asia Minor from Turkestan and plunging into a battle they witnessed. Naturally bringing victory to the side they aided, they were richly rewarded with fiefs. In this manner the Ottomans received their start! It must be remembered that at the time of Murad's retirement 150 years had passed since Osman's first conquests, and that in a new and rapidly evolving society not many men could relate the exploits of their great-great-great grandfathers.

Murad's intellectual and cultural concerns were reflected in the education of his children. He employed as teachers for the princes the most enlightened and distinguished scholars of the state. Many had important army or administrative positions. Included with the princes in the palace school were other boys, some of whom were captives of war or sons of distinguished vassals of the sultan. Murad desired not only to educate his own sons to their responsibilities but also to train other youths in discipline, integrity, and moral values that might serve state and sultan intelligently and faithfully. Proof of the value and thoroughness of this school was first demonstrated visibly in the education and ability of Murad's son Mehmed.

Military Developments

For a few months all went well in the Ottoman state. Murad had retired to Manisa, and the boy Mehmed II was surrounded by advisers and teachers at Edirne. But the Hungarians broke the peace of Szeged in the autumn of 1444, perhaps thinking that the treaty with Murad was invalidated by his retirement and that victory would be possible against a boy ruler. Murad was recalled from his retirement and crushed the invaders near Varna. King Ladislaus and Cardinal Julian, who had insisted upon breaking the treaty against Hunyadi's admonitions, lost their lives.

Ottomans now easily overran Serbia and Bosnia. Since Ottomans were tolerant of all forms of Christianity whereas Hungarians in their brief sway had begun to impose Latin rites upon Serbian and Bosnian churches, many fortresses opened their gates to Murad.

With this affair apparently settled, Murad abdicated a second time in 1445 and returned to Manisa. It was not long, however, before an open demonstration of rebellion against Mehmed II by the janissaries brought Murad back to active rule in Edirne. The ringleaders were executed, imprisoned, or exiled from the capital, and the sultan's authority was fully restored.

This episode was a harbinger of future grave difficulties that Ottoman sultans would experience with janissary and other imperial troops, who were becoming hardened ruthless professional soldiers. Simply educated, reared and trained exclusively for warfare, and not too well paid because of the expectation that they would be richly rewarded from plunder won on campaigns, the janissaries felt their power and importance and were easily induced to demand favors of many kinds. Between them and older Ottomans—feudal cavalry and old family administrators like those closest to Murad—rivalry was keen and often bitter.

In this connection Murad about 1430 reinstituted for the janissary corps a draft *(devshirmeh)* procedure originated in the reign of Murad I. Every few years army officers toured the Anatolian and Balkan rural districts, conscripting Christian boys between the ages of ten and fifteen. These youths from Greece, Macedonia, Albania, Serbia, Bosnia, Herzegovina, Bulgaria, and all parts of Anatolia were brought to Edirne. As slaves of the sultan they were parceled out among court officers, the feudatory, and the sultan himself. The draftees from the Balkans were sent to Asia Minor and vice versa. After a few years of growth, toughening, Islamization, and Turkification in language and customs they were returned to Edirne, where they received military training and were assigned to a janissary barracks. The more favored were attached to the palace; the very best attended the princes' school, whereupon any position in the state was open to them. At first employed to augment the ranks of the janissaries when wars and raids failed to yield sufficient captives, the draft was justified as another form of taxation for the subject communities, analogous to poll taxes except they paid taxes in boys! More significant was the fact that the most vigorous and capable youths were being removed from their villages and raised as Ottomans. Some observers remarked that this policy helped to keep the Christian population in subjection by drawing away future leaders. Some families turned to Islam rather than lose their sons.

It was also the custom for vassal Christian princes to send a son or two as hostages to the sultan's court. Various defeated Balkan leaders were permitted to retain their lands, but sent their sons to be reared as Ottomans.

One such hostage was George Kastriota, who with his three brothers was sent to Murad II. Renamed Iskender (Alexander), he was educated in the princes' school, served in various responsible posts under Murad, but deserted in 1443. Skanderbeg, as he was now called, returned to his native Albania; and there for twenty-five years he led resistance movements and guerrilla warfare against Murad and Mehmed II, with whom he had gone to school.

After the janissary revolt of 1445 was put down, Murad did not again retire but engaged in campaigns in Europe. Twice he entered Albania in pursuit of Skanderbeg. In 1448 he drove Hunyadi out of Serbia, defeating him on the plains of Kossovo. Murad also campaigned in Greece and the Peloponnesus, seizing Corinth and Patras. Early in 1451 the aged warrior (about fifty years old) died in Edirne. The young Mehmed, now grown to manhood, when apprised in Manisa of his father's death, supposedly leaped on his horse and raced to Edirne to take charge.

Mehmed II

In some ways Mehmed II's character was an extension of his father's. Since he had the benefits of the princes' school, his mind was well trained. He knew literary Turkish, Arabic, Persian, and Greek and was able to converse in ordinary Serbian and Italian. He enjoyed poetry and was familiar with the classical poetry of Iran, Greece, and Rome. Mehmed was an accomplished poet himself and gathered about him poets from the four corners of the Muslim world. As a student he read philosophy and was much taken with writings of the Stoics and the Peripatetics. He loved history, particularly biographies of Alexander the Great and the Caesars. The study of war and of everything associated with war, such as strategy, supplies, munitions, and topography, aroused his interest greatly. Every Ottoman, even of the royal family, had a trade—perhaps because of the akhi heritage—and Mehmed was an accomplished gardener. Later, between campaigns and for relaxation, he worked in the gardens of the royal palace.

With regard to administration, however, Mehmed was quite unlike his father. Thoroughness and efficiency combined with great energy and promptness became the order of the day whenever Mehmed was present. Delay and procrastination were foreign to his nature. In many respects Murad had not been very businesslike in his administration, and Mehmed spent the first year of his reign reorganizing governmental departments. The treasury, in particular, was tightened up; many tax officials were forced to straighten their accounts, whereupon they were dismissed. The entire administration of the royal palace was surveyed, registers of the troops scrutinized, and soldiers' pay increased. Some provincial governors were removed, others were promoted. Mehmed's criteria for determining an individual's fitness for holding a position were his knowledge and his sense of diplomacy and justice. One unhappy episode was the ordering that his only brother, an infant, be drowned in his bath, thus perpetuating the custom begun by Bayezid I. Years later Mehmed decreed that whoever of his sons seized the throne should execute his brothers.

Capture of Constantinople

With the coming of 1452 Mehmed began his plans for taking Constantinople. Munitions were gathered: armor, bows, arrows, mortars, cannon, balls, gunpowder, timbers, and war articles of every sort. At Gallipoli a fleet was assembled and new ships built. Mehmed and his officers studied every inch of the terrain along the land walls of Constantinople and for miles around in every direction. To control the Bosphorus he ordered the construction of a fortress on its European shore opposite the fortifications built on the Asian side half a century earlier by his great-grandfather. Erected just above the narrowest point of the Bosphorus, these three formidable towers (called Rumeli Hisar) were connected with heavy walls and formed a castle harboring cannon whose range controlled the passage of the Bosphorus. Mehmed's admiral, Baltaoglu, gathered the fleet at a small inlet, now called Balta Liman, just north of the fortress to participate in the siege of Constantinople. An enormous bronze siege cannon, so large the soldiers called it an "apparatus," was cast. It possessed greater power and could hurl a large stone ball weighing 1,200 pounds farther and with greater force than any known at that time.

The true attack upon Constantinople (or Stambul, as the citizens called their city) began in April 1453. About 170,000 of the best soldiers that Mehmed could muster were assembled for the assault. The fleet numbered between 300 and 400 ships, but even these were unable to control the Straits completely. A squadron of 5 Genoese ships brought slight relief to the beleaguered city by eluding Baltaoglu, who was relieved of his command for this blunder and properly bastinadoed, until the janissaries protested.

For fifty-four days cannon balls pounded the land walls of the city. The sea walls were bombarded by the fleet, but the walls along the Golden Horn could not be reached. Mortars from the shores of the Bosphorus did sink some Greek ships on the Golden Horn, but a heavy chain from Galata to Constantinople effectively closed the Horn to Mehmed's ships. Not to be thwarted, Mehmed constructed a greased wooden runway from the shore of the Bosphorus at Dolma Bakche up the hill of Beyoglu (Pera) and down the slope to the Golden Horn at Kasim Pasha. Sixty-seven ships of the Ottoman fleet were hauled up over the incline and slid down to the Golden Horn, from where they threw their stone cannon balls on the city walls.

Cut off completely and bombarded from every side, the defenders of Constantinople resisted the attacks valiantly. The Genoese and other Italians in Galata and Pera gave no assistance, and most of the 50,000 inhabitants of the once great city acted supremely indifferent to their fate, perhaps because Emperor Constantine in desperation called for aid from the West and announced submission to the pope in exchange for promises of soldiers. A few came, but help was entirely inadequate. The citizenry

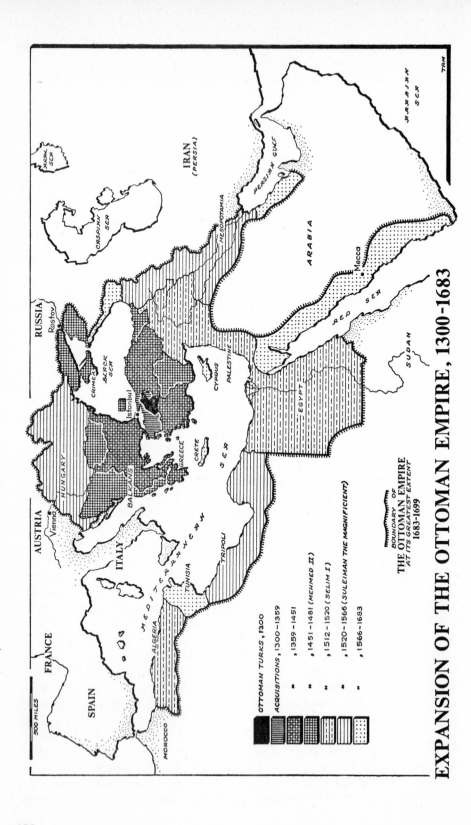

EXPANSION OF THE OTTOMAN EMPIRE, 1300-1683

BOUNDARY
OF
THE OTTOMAN EMPIRE
AT ITS GREATEST EXTENT
1683-1699

OTTOMAN TURKS, 1300

ACQUISITIONS, 1300-1359
      "   , 1359-1451
      "   , 1451-1481 (MEHMED II)
      "   , 1512-1520 (SELIM I)
      "   , 1520-1566 (SULEIMAN THE MAGNIFICIENT)
      "   , 1566-1683

500 MILES

FRANCE

SPAIN

MOROCCO

ALGERIA

TUNISIA

TRIPOLI

ITALY

AUSTRIA

Vienna

HUNGARY

BALKANS

GREECE

CRETE

CYPRUS

RUSSIA

Rostov

BLACK SEA

CRIMEA

Istanbul

MEDITERRANEAN SEA

AEGEAN SEA

CASPIAN SEA

ARAL SEA

IRAN
(PERSIA)

MESOPOTAMIA

PALESTINE

EGYPT

ARABIA

RED SEA

SUDAN

Mecca

PERSIAN GULF

ARABIAN SEA

preferred Ottoman rule to Latin rule and Muslim tolerance to Roman intolerance.

A stupendous assault near the Gate of St. Romanos (Top Kapu) was launched on May 29, 1453; cannon fire breached the walls, and the city was taken. Following the universal custom of that age, the conquering troops had complete license in the city, except that no public buildings could be touched. On the third day Mehmed entered the city, and the plundering ceased. He went to Hagia Sophia, where prayers were said. He then quickly turned to the problem of the city that the Ottomans have always called Istanbul. A governor was appointed; inhabitants were encouraged to remain by exempting them from taxes and by giving them back their houses; the sultan ransomed many on condition that they would stay; the army was disbanded; and Mehmed returned to Edirne, his capital.

The economic, military, and cultural effects of the capture of Constantinople have usually been exaggerated. Later centuries developed a myth that the fall of Constantinople blocked the trade routes to the Far East, thereby forcing the Age of Discoveries and the voyages of Columbus. According to another legend, the fall of Constantinople resulted in the migration of Greek monks and manuscripts to Italy, thus initiating the Renaissance. One story has related that the fall of Constantinople removed the Balkan bastion, at once enabling the Ottoman Turks to conquer the whole peninsula of southeast Europe. All three of these myths have been exploded by careful examination of historical development. Yet even today these tales are repeated and found in modern books.

Nevertheless, the emotional impact of the fall of Constantinople on the people of the fifteenth century should not be minimized. To Christian Europe, and especially to the West, the great imperial city had fallen. In a sense the Roman Empire had come to an end. Heretofore the Turks had been raiding "unknown and uncertain" areas, but Constantinople was a real place in Western thinking. Everywhere there was talk of a crusade; but of course, it was only talk.

To Muslims the fall of Constantinople was a great and glorious achievement. Islamic rulers and armies had attempted it many times in the past. To them Constantinople was the majestic city of imperial tradition, whose conquest had always been a goal of the great caliphs. Now a new Muslim state had accomplished the impossible, and consequently Mehmed II received great acclaim and respect throughout the East.

To the Ottomans it was the conquest of the natural capital and center of their state. Since the time of Bayezid I its incorporation in the state had been a logical and necessary step, but it had been long in coming. Its acquisition served as the keystone in creating the Ottoman Empire.

REFERENCES: Chapter 14

References in Chapters 11, 12, and 13 are important for this chapter.

Cook, M. A. (ed.). *Studies in the Economic History of the Middle East from the Rise of Islam to the Present Day.* London: Oxford University Press, 1970. All the articles are by major authors: nine on the medieval period, six on the early modern period, and twelve on the nineteenth and twentieth centuries. Many of the articles explore new ideas.

Kritovoulos. *History of Mehmed the Conqueror.* Translated by Charles T. Riggs. Princeton, N.J.: Princeton University Press, 1954. A contemporary account by a Greek in the service of the Ottomans.

Kuran, Aptullah. *The Mosque in Early Ottoman Architecture.* Chicago: University of Chicago Press, 1968. Develops the idea that the basic unit in early Ottoman architecture was the domed square. Describes, pictures, and shows plans of the early mosques in Amasya, Bursa, Edirne, and Iznik, as well as in Istanbul. Scholarly and authoritative.

Pears, Edwin. *The Destruction of the Greek Empire and the Story of the Capture of Constantinople.* New York: Longmans, Green, 1903. Carefully written from Greek and Western sources by a British lawyer who resided in Istanbul for more than forty years.

Runciman, Steven. *The Fall of Constantinople, 1453.* Cambridge, Eng.: Cambridge University Press, 1969. A paperback edition of a first-rate book published in 1965. The author, a recognized scholar, has scoured the sources and presented in great detail and with much understanding a very readable and reliable account of the taking of the city.

Chapter 15

Building the Ottoman Empire

Consolidation of the Empire

Beyond taking Constantinople, Mehmed II, always called Fatih ("The Conqueror") by his subjects, extended the periphery of his empire only moderately. Campaigns and wars were scheduled almost every year, but in the main they consolidated the Ottoman possessions, rounded out frontiers, and built the empire. Operations were conducted in the Balkans and Asia Minor and from Venice and southern Italy to Iran and the Crimea. Affairs of any one area always involved those of others; and Mehmed never was able to isolate his many international and domestic problems to deal with one at a time. Moreover, Venetian envoys were plotting at every court to swell the number of his enemies and bring his downfall.

Ottoman campaigns, colonization, and government had been proceeding in the Balkans for a century. Nonetheless, Ottoman rule was still not effective in several regions, and many provinces that were tied to the Ottomans by a kind of vassalage or alliance were not integrated units of the state. Bosnia and Serbia remained under local rulers who were subservient to the sultans. Whenever opportunity arose, rebellion was in the air. Mehmed set his campaign in 1456 for the stronghold of Belgrad, hoping that its fall would give him a tighter grip on central and lower Danube regions and lessen the danger of Serbian revolt.

The heroic effort failed, however, just as the walls were breached and as victory seemed in his grasp. Since vast quantities of munitions, especially cannon, were abandoned in the hasty retreat, no major campaign could be undertaken anywhere the following year. Instead, colorful festivities to celebrate the circumcision of his two older sons, Bayezid and Mustafa, were arranged in Edirne, with distinguished visitors and envoys from many countries attending.

Pressure on the Balkans, however, was maintained continuously. In the next decade Serbia and Bosnia were subjected to Ottoman rule and organized as regular imperial provinces. Wallachia and Moldavia were forced to become allies. Skanderbeg was checked in Albania, and the fortresses of Elbasan, Kroia, and Skodra were taken. After Skanderbeg's death in 1478 Albania and Herzegovina became provinces of the empire. Greece and the

Peloponnesus, except for a few Venetian ports of call such as Coron and Modon, were conquered, and some of the lands were parceled out as fiefs.

Mehmed also pursued a vigorous policy in Asia Minor. The most resistant foe had always been the Karaman dynasty. In 1464 Mehmed directed a large force against them, and in 1466 at the Battle of Larenda, Karaman opposition was broken. Later Cilicia was acquired; and as his reign closed, Mehmed became involved in family quarrels of the Dhu-al-Kadr of Diyarbakir. The entire Mediterranean coast of Asia Minor was now in Ottoman hands.

Since Istanbul and the Straits were now Ottoman, Mehmed moved eastward, hoping to control the Black Sea shores. Sinop with its adjacent copper resources was taken from the last of the Isfendiyar, who received fiefs in Europe. That same year (1461), with the cooperation of the navy from Gallipoli, Mehmed forced the surrender of the Greek emperor of Trebizond, thus obliterating the last remnant of the Byzantine Empire.

These activities led the Ottomans into conflict with Ak Koyunlu, who dominated Iran, Armenia, and eastern Asia Minor. Venetian ambassadors traveled to the court of Uzun Hasan at Tabriz and encouraged war against Mehmed. Although Venice was concerned with Eastern trade, the main consideration was to lessen Ottoman pressure upon Venice and her European territory. Mehmed collected a mighty army including his two sons, Mustafa and Bayezid, his grand vizir, and Gedik Ahmed Pasha, a burly general who had risen from the ranks of the ordinary janissaries. He defeated Uzun Hasan in 1473 near Erzinjan in eastern Asia Minor. Next the Crimea, which was ruled by Turkish khans, came under Ottoman aegis, and the important commercial city of Kaffa (the modern Feodosiya) on the Straits between the Black Sea and the Sea of Azov was taken from the Genoese. Except for the coast between the Crimea and the Danube, the Black Sea was now an Ottoman lake.

Although Venetian envoys professed friendship for Mehmed, conflict between Venice and the Ottoman Empire was almost inevitable. To ensure control of the Aegean coast of Anatolia and safeguard Ottoman ventures into the Morea it was necessary to incorporate into the empire the Aegean Islands, particularly Chios, Lemnos, Lesbos (Mytilene), and Euboea (Negroponte). This was particularly important because Venetians and pirates used these islands and their numerous harbors as bases to harry the Ottoman coast and hold up trade. Mehmed's fleet, therefore, captured these islands along with Cephalonia in the Ionian Islands; and for fifteen years (1463–1478) he was at war sporadically with Venice. Pressure on Venetian outposts along the Dalmatian coast was constant, and ghazis from Albania and Bosnia kept alarms sounding on St. Mark's Square. In 1477 Ottoman raiders overran Friuli and descended to the Italian plain north of Venice. At night Venetian senators from the roof of St. Mark's could see Ottoman camp fires and burning villages as far as the banks of the Piave. When autumn came the Ottomans returned home laden with booty. Venice concluded peace with Mehmed and recognized his island acquisitions.

In 1480 an Ottoman army under Gedik Ahmed Pasha crossed the Adriatic from Epirus and took Otranto on the heel of the Italian peninsula, thus establishing a bridgehead for the conquest of Italy. Gedik Ahmed wintered there, but upon Mehmed's sudden death in May 1481 the expedition to Otranto was withdrawn, never to be launched again. Simultaneously (1480) Mesih Pasha led an unsuccessful attack upon the Knights of St. John on the island of Rhodes. Just before he died Mehmed had gathered an army in Anatolia, but his sudden death in camp came before he or his line of march had revealed his destination.

The conqueror was dead. Secrecy was maintained in the Ottoman Empire until a successor could mount the throne. Bells pealed in Europe when the news arrived. There was no doubt anywhere that a great man had died.

Settlement of Istanbul

Never recovering from the devastation wrought by the Fourth Crusade, and gradually strangling economically after the first Ottoman crossing to Europe, Constantinople when it fell in 1453 was only a half-populated city, and had been depressed and dying slowly for more than two centuries. Many buildings were empty and in various stages of decay. From the very outset Mehmed was concerned with repopulating the city. For twenty days he tarried in Istanbul, freeing many prisoners allocated to him, encouraging others to remain, and exempting many from taxation for various lengths of time. The Christian population, as in most Ottoman cities, was never subjected to the *devshirmeh.* In almost every conquest in later years inhabitants of this town and that were ordered to move to Istanbul, frequently settling old vacant districts and giving their names to sections of the city such as Aksaray and Karaman.

When Mehmed "Fatih" entered the city, he learned that the patriarch was dead. Appreciating the need for the election of a new patriarch and understanding the security and stability that such a move would give the Greek community, not only of Istanbul but of the entire empire, Fatih indicated confidence in George Scolarius, who had long been popular with the Greeks of the city and in disfavor with the last Byzantine emperor because he headed the anti-Roman faction. Duly elected, Scolarius took the name Gennadius. Mehmed feted him, recognized him as patriarch and leader of the Christians in Istanbul, and ordered the vizir and officers to accord him proper respect. Gennadius was also charged with responsibility for the obedience, conduct, and life of the Greek people and their relationship to the Ottoman government. Thus in many ways Greek Christians were encouraged to reside in Istanbul and allowed to live according to their own ways and laws as long as they did not infringe upon or come into conflict with the administration of the government and the lives of Muslim subjects. In like manner Mehmed II recognized the Armenian patriarch and the Jewish grand rabbi of Istanbul as the leaders of their respective communities.

Public buildings were reserved for the state, and many churches were converted into mosques. The outstanding example was Justinian's great church Hagia Sophia which became the Muslim Aya Sofya. Since the decline in population had left many empty churches and chapels, the conversion of the churches worked little hardship upon the Greek inhabitants. Another site was designated for the erection of a new mosque; and a series of surrounding structures, for schools, hospitals, and poor relief. (The new mosque was badly damaged by an earthquake in the eighteenth century, and the present Fatih Mosque is of later construction and design.)

Fatih chose as his residence the Monastery of the Pantocrator in the old Forum of Theodosius, the most populous part of the city and today the site of the University of Istanbul. Various additions were made to the monastery, which he occupied for about twelve years whenever in Istanbul. In 1459 he chose a new spot for his quarters, and here in 1465 was completed a new palace which remained the chief domicile of sultans until the nineteenth century. The old palace, Eski Saray, became the abode of the harem until the time of Suleiman I; thereafter for three centuries it was a home for wives, daughters, and harems of previous sultans. The new palace, Yeni Saray, was erected on the site of the fortress of ancient Byzantium on the point of land between the Golden Horn and the Sea of Marmara. Facing the entrance to the Bosphorus, it was the most natural and beautiful spot in the city for an imperial residence. It was soon called popularly Top Kapu Saray ("Cannon Gate Palace") because of the heavily fortified gate at the tip of the point of land. The whole area enclosed by walls was soon known everywhere by its Italian name, Seraglio; it was famed for its many splendid buildings and large number of inhabitants. Yet Fatih passed winters, summers, and many seasons at the palace in Edirne or at family lodges in Bursa, Demotika, and other cities of the empire. Edirne remained the favorite summer headquarters of sultans until the eighteenth century.

The Palace School
In the years of Mehmed's reign full integration of the empire with governors for all provinces appointed by the sultan, along with expansion of the state, its growing complexity, and diversity of population, augmented the need for trained personnel to operate the government. Murad II had faced a similar problem and had resolved it by placing the most promising of his young slaves in the school beside his own sons. Mehmed met the crisis by creating the Palace School of Istanbul. It was first established at the old palace, but was later transferred to the Seraglio, where it maintained continuous operation until the twentieth century. Students, called pages, were selected after a very careful screening from the boys between ten and fourteen years old among war captives and those drafted from Christian provinces. At the Palace School they received a thorough secular education in languages, literature, music, law and theology, military science, mathematics, philosophy, governmental administration, taxation, finance, physical training, personal conduct, sports, and manual training. Only the very

best lasted through the ten to twelve rigorous years of the course; those unable to continue drew governmental positions commensurate to their abilities.

Graduates were appointed to administrative posts in various departments of the government. They were pledged to secrecy about the school and life of the inner palace where they had lived. The instructional staff was drawn from the finest teachers in mosque schools of Bursa, Edirne, and Istanbul and from high administrative offices of the government. Physique was considered important; weight-lifting and carrying heavy loads were practiced to such a degree that many students developed the strength to carry 700 or 800 pounds for as many paces. It was thought fitting that each should learn a trade in case he should some day have to earn a living as a craftsman. All in all, a tremendous spirit was induced into the students; graduates of the Palace School formed a firmly knit group that stood apart in their conduct and loyalty to the sultanship. Trained by one sultan, they often served his son or held the government together until a successor was determined. These "courtiers," as Western observers and envoys termed them, were reported to be more cultured, more faultless in their courtesy, more devoted to their master, and more skilled in their operation of the government than the courtiers and advisers of any Western king or emperor. At the time of the great success, efficiency, and strength of the Ottoman government, the entire system was based on merit. Merit alone brought appointment to government office and subsequent promotions and favors. When factors other than merit began to have weight, the government stagnated.

Bayezid and Jem
Mehmed II left two sons. Bayezid, aged thirty-three, was governor of Amasya, the old ghazi center. Jem, aged twenty-one, was governor of Konya, the former Seljuk capital. Since Amasya was eight days' ride from Istanbul whereas Konya was only four, the younger son had an advantage in obtaining control of the central administration. But the janissaries, the pages of the palace, and the government officials who were slaves of the sultan and graduates of the Palace School preferred Bayezid. Mehmed's last grand vizir, however, belonged by birth to the old Muslim aristocracy of Anatolia and was partial to Jem. He tried to conceal Fatih's death, secretly dispatched couriers to Jem, and moved to isolate Istanbul until Jem's arrival. However, Mehmed's death became known, whereupon the slave officials and the janissaries seized control, murdered the grand vizir, impaled his messengers to Jem, and awaited Bayezid's appearance. They chose the latter because they considered his residence of twenty-five years or more at Amasya as wedding him to the ghazi tradition, of which they were fast becoming the heirs. Moreover, recognizing the so-called law of fratricide, Bayezid cleverly attached through marriages and political friendship several potent figures of the government hierarchy to his candidacy. Jem was supported by the conservative Muslim community of Asia Minor. His chief

difficulty was his comparative youth; Bayezid for years had been gathering his party for the eventual day, and Bayezid's eldest son was already, with his preceptors, governor of Manisa.

To break through the cordon of officers blocking the gate to the palace, Bayezid pledged a handsome gift of money to every janissary, declared an amnesty for all plundering and crimes committed in the period of interregnum, and, most significant, agreed to appoint to the vizirship only men from the soldier-palace-slave group.

Jem with forces from Karaman and Konya occupied Bursa and challenged Bayezid for the throne. Gedik Ahmed was recalled from Otranto and with the army that Mehmed had gathered defeated Jem, who fled to Egypt whence he made the holy pilgrimage to Mecca. Bayezid offered him a princely income if he would live peacefully in Jerusalem, but Jem returned in 1482 and made a second vain attempt at the throne. Escaping to the protection of the Knights of St. John of the island of Rhodes, he was held in custody by them and used to obtain a favorable treaty of peace with the Ottomans. Bayezid agreed to pay 40,000 ducats a year as long as Jem remained in captivity. The knights subsequently moved him to their castles in France, where he fell into the hands of Charles VIII. Later Jem was presented to the pope, then was borrowed by Charles in 1494, from Pope Alexander VI, ostensibly to participate in a crusade against the Ottomans. Jem, however, died of a fever in Naples early the next year. His body was finally obtained by Bayezid and interred at Bursa.

Wars of Bayezid II

Between 1482 and 1495 Bayezid's fear of his brother's return somewhat restricted him in foreign activities. Yet the organization of the Ottoman state was conditioned to aggressive expansion. When campaigns were not in progress, feudal sipahi, janissaries, and the court became uneasy. During these years, therefore, a number of expeditions along the Dalmatian coast and into Hungary, Styria, and Carinthia were undertaken. Although these raids were usually indecisive, they were rewarding in plunder. Akkerman on the Black Sea at the mouth of the Dniester River was taken and Wallachia and Moldavia were subdued.

In this early period of Bayezid's reign war broke out with the Mamluk sultans of Egypt. Dynastic difficulties among the Dhu-al-Kadr involved Egyptians and Ottomans in a border dispute. In 1484 after aid and asylum had been given to Jem, open war broke out. Despite six sizable campaigns wherein the Ottoman army and fleet participated, Bayezid was not able to retain Adana; and his leaders were captured repeatedly by the Mamluks. The peace concluded in 1491 left Egypt in possession of the disputed border areas; but since Turkoman and non-Ottoman forces in southern Anatolia were suppressed by Ottoman armies, no difficulties appeared for two decades.

Following Jem's death Bayezid pursued a more aggressive policy in the West. The tempo of Ottoman raids along the Dalmatian coast increased;

Sinop, Gallipoli, Lepanto, Valona, and Preveza rang with the noise of carpenters, coopers, and caulkers constructing war galleys and ships of all
kinds. When war broke out with Venice in 1499, Ottomans took Modon and
Coron in the Peloponnesus and defeated the Venetian fleet in a great sea
engagement at Navarino. Peace was not concluded until Andrea Gritti and
Bayezid's viziers came to terms in 1503. The war further eclipsed Venetian
power in Greece and the eastern Mediterranean, and Ottoman sea power
became strongly established. Thereafter in Bayezid's reign contingents of
the Ottoman navy raided every Mediterranean shore, and Ottoman admirals and captains followed the pattern of the old ghazi corsairs.

The end of the war with Venice marked the rise of a new figure on the
Ottoman frontier, Shah Ismail of Iran, who kindled a religio-national enthusiasm in the peoples of Iran and eastern Asia Minor. Claiming descent
from the Prophet Muhammad, Ali, and the seventh imam on the paternal
side and from Ak Koyunlu Turks and Byzantine emperors on the other,
Ismail united Iranians, Turks, and heterodox followers of Ali in devotion to
his mystical being. Ismail (often called the Great Sufi) became shah in 1503
and pronounced Shiism as the official doctrine of his realm. Political agents
—Sufis and shaykhs—permeated Asia Minor, concentrating in mountainous
areas of the east, south, and southwest. Ismail's propaganda was effective in
the provinces of Teke, Karaman, and Dhu-al-Kadr, among the Warsak and
Torgud tribes of the Taurus regions, and in Anatolia, where his followers
were called *kizilbash* ("red head") because of the red hats they wore.

Muslims of the Ottoman Empire were not thoroughly orthodox; Bayezid
was a philosopher by nature and enough of a mystic that one of his nick-
names was Sufi; and the janissaries as well as Bayezid and many court
officers belonged to the Bektashi dervish order which entertained many
heretical creeds. Despite or perhaps because of these facts the Ottomans
could not permit the subversive ideas of a foreign monarch free rein within
their state. Minor skirmishes occurred near Diyarbakir in 1502, and Ismail
protested that his followers were prevented from visiting him. Although
envoys traveled back and forth, Bayezid kept Ismail's ambassador isolated
and under strict surveillance for fear the janissaries might be corrupted.
Armies were assembled in 1508 and stationed in Anatolia to face Ismail in
Harput and Diyarbakir, but no battle ensued. Difficulties arose in eastern
Iran compelling Ismail to transfer his attentions, whereas Bayezid had no
taste for war because Ismail had so many sympathizers.

Shah Ismail's doctrines proved popular however, and open revolt developed in 1511 under the leadership of Karabiyik, an eastern shaykh using the
pseudonym Shah Kuli. Starting in Antalya and Teke, Shah Kuli besieged
and took Konya, seized Kutahya (Ottoman Anatolian army headquarters),
and impaled the Ottoman commander in chief. However, he was subsequently killed near Kayseri in a battle against an army that included 4,000
janissaries under the grand vizier and three Ottoman princes. With their
leader gone, the heretics scattered, and the rebellious problem subsided,
only to come to a violent head a few years later under Bayezid's successor.

Selim's Succession

After the end of the Venetian war Bayezid suffered poor health and was often carried on a stretcher so that the troops might see him. With each illness his sons and grandsons became exceedingly nervous about the future. Of his eight sons, only three remained in 1511: Korkud at Manisa; Ahmed at Amasya; and Selim, the youngest, at Trabzon. Each was jockeying for advantages and seeking favors and strategic appointments for friends and sons. The janissaries and the soldiers preferred Selim, since he was the most energetic and devoted to warfare. Bayezid and the high officials advanced Ahmed as the solid administrator. The poets, philosophers, and theologians supported Korkud, for he was one of them.

From Trabzon, Selim moved his forces to Kaffa, where his son Suleiman was governor. Then with the support of the khans of the Crimea he brought his army toward Edirne. Assuaged with appointment over Semendra in the Balkans, Selim held his hand for immediate action should Bayezid suddenly die, as his French doctors were predicting. When Bayezid and his close advisers began granting vast authority and prodigious sums of money to Ahmed, Selim seized Edirne. Bayezid could find no officer to drive Selim from his prize. Meanwhile, to gain friends in Anatolia, Ahmed had turned heretic and donned the red hat of the *kizilbash.* Upon this development the staunchly orthodox Bayezid called Selim to Istanbul in 1512 and abdicated in his favor. A month later Bayezid died while en route to retirement in the palace at Demotika, where he had been born.

For thirty-one years Bayezid, a peace-loving, scholarly, and contemplative philosopher, had governed the Ottoman Empire. Never attacking a neighboring state without provocation, he spent years in organizing the administration of the government for the well-being of the state, and incidently its inhabitants. He took great interest in the Palace School, often quizzing the students himself. Trade flourished, with merchants from Venice, Genoa, Florence, and Ragusa thronging to Istanbul. Bayezid was exceedingly tolerant of other religions, and more than 100,000 Jews came to Istanbul, Izmir, Edirne, and Salonica when they were driven from Spain in 1492. Yet he was strict with Muslims. His father's unorthodox ways disturbed him, and one of Bayezid's first acts as sultan was to clear from the palace the pictures of his father and court officials painted by Gentile Bellini. He sold them in the bazaar.

Selim I (nicknamed Yavuz, meaning "stern" or "inflexible") gave a munificent bonus to each soldier, as had become the custom in securing the throne. But he entered the palace by a side gate in order not to bow openly to their demands. The facts were that he held only Rumeli with Istanbul, Ahmed controlling most of Anatolia from his seat at Amasya. When Selim had marched his army to Edirne in the previous year, Ahmed had occupied Bursa and camped not far from the Bosphorus. He went back to Amasya only upon the insistence of Bayezid, who pointed out that Selim had returned to the Crimea and Kaffa.

Upon Selim's enthronement Ahmed sent his son to take Bursa. Selim instantly crossed to Asia and carried the attack against Ahmed, who resisted with political guile and force until the following spring, when he was defeated and strangled. Meanwhile five of Selim's nephews and his brother Korkud were similarly disposed of. Because Ahmed had obtained considerable support from the *kizilbash* of Anatolia, Selim decided to curb the growth of the sect, particularly since it was popular in the difficult mountainous and frontier areas of Teke, Karaman, and Diyarbakir. Late in 1513 Selim stationed troops and agents in all parts of the empire. Lists of active heretics were drawn up, and at a given notice about 40,000 were cut down. By transporting others to Europe, Selim hoped that he had settled the religious problem of Asia Minor.

War Against Iran

In this ferocious act Selim recognized the role of Shah Ismail in Asia Minor, who was supported by *kizilbash* and regarded by many in Anatolia as a holy saint. Following Ismail's interference in affairs of Dhu-al-Kadr, and along Ottoman frontiers, Selim sent the fleet with his commissariat to Trabzon, with several thousand janissaries, the grand vizir, and feudal troops of Rumeli and Anatolia, supported by batteries of cannon, he marched eastward. Shah Ismail scorched the earth as he retreated; Selim's soldiers murmured as they were driven on. But Selim would not turn back. In August 1514 at Chalderan, northeast of Lake Van not far from the foot of Mount Ararat, Selim's cannon turned the tide. Ismail fled, leaving even his harem to be captured.

Although the victory at Chalderan momentarily settled Selim's problems on his eastern frontier, in no way did it destroy the new state arising in Iran or eliminate the Safavid dynasty and its spreading of Shiite Islam.

Establishment of the Safavids in Iran

As the Mongol state declined in the late thirteenth and fourteenth centuries, many Turkoman tribes became autonomous, each constituting a virtual state within a state; and at the same time numerous Sufi orders appeared, each quite independent from the next. Like the later Mongol kings, the Turkoman tribes and most of the Sufi orders converted to Shiism, Sufi leadership thus becoming hereditary and powerful not only as religious leaders but as commanders of the warriors of the faith.

One Sufi order in Ardebil was called Safavid after its first leader, Safi, who died in 1334. (As has been mentioned, their name *kizilbash*, or "red head," was derived from the hat they adopted as a distinctive mark—a scarlet cone-shaped affair with twelve scallops, or gores, one for each of the twelve imams.) In time, seven powerful Turkoman tribes of western Iran and eastern Asia Minor, accepting Shiism, supported this Safavid order and became instrumental in its rise to power. In 1490 Safi's descendant, Shaykh Haydar, was killed in battle, leaving a three year old son, Ismail. Within a few years the leadership of the order fell to him. With the indispensable aid of Turkish *kizilbash* tribes, Ismail defeated the prince of Shirvan, took Armenia and Azerbayjan in 1501, and proclaimed himself shah in Tabriz in 1503. The next year he seized most of the Tigris–Euphrates basin, including Mosul and Diyarbakir, and ruled over western Iran. In 1508 he occupied Baghdad and most of Iraq.

As leader of the Safavid religious order, Ismail regarded himself as, and was accepted as, the absolute agent of God. He was worshiped during his lifetime as a saint who possessed supernatural attributes and who, consequently, was invincible: his subjects prostrated themselves before him as before God. His state, from the very first, was based on the principles of Shiism and his task in Iran was to clear "the flower-garden of religion of the chaff and rubbish of insubordination." Wherever his rule spread, the choice was fixed: conversion to Shiism or death. Though most Iranians had been Sunni Muslims, Ismail's cruelty in enforcing his edict, coupled with his policy of confiscating properties of Sunnites, expropriating endowments of Sunni orders, and executing or exiling Sunni religious leaders, changed Iran into a Shiite state by the time of his death in 1524. His power was based on the support of the Turkish tribal leaders, held by a mystical allegiance and tied to urban populations who were devotees of the Safavids. The tribal and Sufi leaders, together, could be called a kind of religious fraternity. With economic patterns of urban life shifting into Shiite hands, a permanent interest in the Safavid dynasty occurred and peace and prosperity were sought. In return for soldiers and revenue, each *kizilbash* chief was given a province as a fief, with the power of life and death over its populace and the obligation to convert all to Shiism.

Claiming descent from Muhammad and Ali on his father's side and from Sasanid, Byzantine, and Turkoman princes on his mother's side, Ismail established a theocratic militaristic state in western Iran with his principal strength in the province of Gilan. Expanding eastward, he annexed Khurasan and successfully waged war against the Uzbegs, killing their chieftain in 1510. Having controversies with Bayezid II over Shiite *kizilbash* followers in southern Anatolia, Cilicia, and especially in the Taurus mountain area, Ismail had the Uzbeg chieftain's skin stuffed with straw and sent to Bayezid II as a warning. (In an even more typically macabre gesture Ismail had that same victim's skull rimmed with gold and set with jewels, using it as his favorite drinking cup.)

In order to establish the true faith, Ismail felt it necessary to maintain well-organized political power. To this end a governing apparatus of three main divisions was formed: military, religious, and bureaucratic. At first no sharp distinction in the ruling establishment existed between military and civilian officers: all were members of the monarch's household. (The only real distinction was that most of the military were Turkish and most of the civilian force Iranian.) As political centralization gained momentum, the reins of government were gathered into the hands of Ismail's associates and officials. At the top of the hierarchy stood the viceroy *(wakil)*, who exercised both temporal and spiritual authority. He took a leading role in political affairs, acted as a military commander, and influenced the selecting of other officials. The initial viceroy, appointed in 1501, was Ismail's tutor, a *kizilbash* Turkoman leader. However, his replacement in 1508 was an Iranian, as were succeeding viceroys, a fact deeply resented by the *kizilbash* Turkish leaders. In the midst of a battle against the Uzbegs in 1512, the *kizilbash* forces deserted, guaranteeing the defeat and death of the viceroy. After another viceroy was killed in the battle of Chalderan in 1514, the position was limited to supervision of the bureaucracy and the temporal administration. Next in line stood the commander in chief *(amir al-umara)*, a post that was originally held by the viceroy and that, in addition to controlling the military, had considerable influence in administrative and political matters. In 1509 Ismail chose an obscure officer for this post in an obvious move to weaken the power of the Turkoman leaders. Naturally there developed among these officials a great deal of rivalry for power and for Ismail's favor, and the strains between the Turkish forces and the Iranian elements were constantly felt.

When Selim seized the Ottoman throne in Istanbul in 1512, he became involved in the raging quarrel in Anatolia over the heretical *kizilbash* tribes. Finding the quasi-divine adoration showered upon Ismail intolerable, Selim set out to destroy him. At Chalderan the superiority of janissary discipline, muskets, and Ottoman artillery over swords, spears, and bows and arrows was demonstrated. Most of the outstanding Turkoman *kizilbash* leaders and many high Iranian officials were killed. Ismail's spirit was crushed; it is said that he never smiled again. And he began to drink excessively. Henceforth the Turkoman leaders no longer accepted Ismail's claim of supernatural powers. But with Selim seizing Kurdistan, Diyarbakir, and Marash, and wiping out *kizilbash* rebellion in Anatolia, their ties with those regions were severed; they had no choice but to remain and give lip service to Ismail. Ismail never again led troops into battle and he virtually withdrew from conduct of state affairs. He tried to put civilians into positions of trust and power in order to break the might of the *kizilbash* leaders but he could not control all the provinces, especially Khurasan, and only after his death in 1524 did the full extent of the decline of the ruling institution become apparent.

Because Ismail's son, Tahmasp, was a boy of only ten years, Turkoman leaders were able to regain their power. But after a decade Tahmasp established his personal authority, civilian rule as set by Ismail became dominant, and the Safavid state survived. Though it appeared to be a theocracy, the Sufi organization was unsuccessful in penetrating or subverting the administrative system of the Safavid government. During this period in Iran the main lines of monarchy were worked out, the capital was fixed in the north and west of the state, and Shiism became the established official religion. In a sense the Safavid state was almost an adequate heir to the Sasanid Empire in its absolutist administrative and cultural ideals.

The Conquest of Egypt

With Shah Ismail's defeat, Selim began to use the title shah and sometimes *shahinshah* ("king of kings"), or *padishah* ("father of kings"). More important, the balance of power among the three eastern Muslim states—Iran, Egypt, and the Ottomans—was fully upset in favor of the last. Ismail wrote to the Mamluk sultan for aid against Selim. In 1516 the Mamluks, feigning peace, marched into Syria in full force. Having been kept well informed by Ottoman agents, Selim as usual took the offensive, crushing the Mamluk army at Marj Dabik, north of Aleppo. Again it was a victory of artillery, and muskets, in the hands of a well-disciplined, well-paid, and well-supplied army over swords, spears, and bows and arrows in the hands of an undisciplined, unpaid, and disloyal motley force. Aleppo, Damascus, Beirut, and other cities opened their gates to the Ottomans. Ottoman governors were appointed everywhere, but little else was changed. Taxes continued to be farmed; the amirs of the Lebanon Mountains became only nominal vassals; and Jews and Christians were treated well. Tariffs were reduced from 20 to 5 percent; pilgrim fees in Jerusalem were cut to an insignificant sum; and Selim established an annual grant of 500 ducats to the Franciscan brothers of the Holy Sepulchre in Jerusalem.

By January 1517 Selim and his army were on the outskirts of Cairo, which they stormed and took after several days of fighting. Selim was now sultan from the Danube to the cataracts of the Nile. Shah Ismail hastened to congratulate him on his new territories, and from every side of the Middle East the Ottoman Empire was recognized as the dominant power.

A quarter of a century earlier the Mamluk power had defeated the Ottomans in several campaigns over successive years. Now Selim took their measure with little difficulty and captured the Mamluk Empire in one campaign. Between these two events the Portuguese rounded Africa and cut the trade routes that passed through Syria and Egypt. The Mamluk government was impoverished and could no longer meet its commitments or protect the state. Evidence of this condition began to appear late in the reign of Bayezid II and progressed rapidly in the years before the conquest. Yet it is not certain that Selim would have attacked had not the Mamluk sultan attempted to interfere in Ottoman affairs with Iran.

Back in Istanbul by midsummer 1518 after an absence of two years, Selim faced the question of the caliphate. At Aleppo the puppet Abbasid caliph al-Mutawakkil, whom the Mamluks brought along on the expedition, fell into Selim's possession. Selim took the caliph to Istanbul, where he was charged with embezzlement of trust funds and confined to Yedi Kuli, the state prison. Much later, in 1543, he was permitted to return to Cairo, where he died. It has been claimed that he transferred his caliphal authority to the Ottoman ruling family before he departed; and in later years the Ottoman sultans based their use of the title caliph and the exercise of its power on this incident.

In Selim's long absence his only son, Suleiman, wielded power in Edirne; Piri Pasha, the great admiral, managed Istanbul; and Bursa was governed by Hersekoglu Ahmed Pasha, several times grand vizir and cavalry officer under Mehmed II and Bayezid II. Even under such able guidance the affairs of state suffered and the treasury was depleted. Selim remained in Edirne and Istanbul, straightening out accounts, collecting back taxes, and preparing a navy adequate for an attack upon Rhodes. However, cancer struck him in the spring of 1520 and he died that autumn.

Selim I

Selim Yavuz was a controversial figure. *Yavuz* means "good," "just," "stern," "inflexible," "ferocious"; and he was all of those. He massacred 40,000 heretics in his land. Vizirs and generals lost their heads at seemingly the slightest failure. A standard curse came to be, "May you become Selim's vizir!" He was an excellent general, a brilliant poet, and a skillful administrator. His court supported philosophers, historians, theologians, and literary figures of many kinds. His tastes were simple; he read widely, slept little, and was uninterested in his harem. Some attributed his moods to an addiction to opium, but there is no evidence that he used the drug before cancer troubled him.

In Selim's brief reign of eight years Ottoman territory increased greatly —almost exclusively in Asia at the expense of other Muslim states. Dominating the Middle East, the Ottoman Empire became the outstanding Muslim Empire of the area, heir of the medieval Umayyad and Abbasid empires and ruler of the Muslim holy lands. These acquisitions were a determining factor in the process of orientalizing the Ottoman Empire. Selim's sole male heir Suleiman reigned over the Ottomans for forty-six years. Longer than any heretofore among his forefathers, Suleiman's rule brought the Ottoman Empire and the life of its people to the pinnacle of power and luster. The fabric of society and the sources of power and wealth, however, were well fixed by the time of Selim's death. The eminence of Suleiman's period rested on the firm building of his ancestors.

REFERENCES: Chapter 15

Works mentioned at the end of Chapters 7, 10, 12, 13, and 14 relate to this chapter.

Armajani, Yahya. *Iran.* Englewood Cliffs, N.J.: Prentice-Hall, 1972. For a short one-volume history of Iran, it is rich in detail and has a sound feeling for Iranian culture.

Aslanapa, Oktay. *Turkish Art and Architecture.* New York: Praeger, 1971. Full of fine illustrations and a complete bibliography, including many articles. It covers Ottoman mosques, castles, baths, glass, textiles, metalworking, calligraphy, bookbinding, and so on. Also deals with pre-Islamic Turkish art, Tulunid art in Egypt, and Ghaznevid, Seljuk, Turkish Mamluk, and other Turkish pre-Ottoman art and architecture. This is a first-rate book in every detail.

Cook, M. A. *Population Pressure in Rural Anatolia, 1450–1600.* London Oriental series, vol. 27. London: Oxford University Press, 1972. A thorough examination of population trends during the period and its effects. Discusses the Jelali uprisings. Penetrating.

Davis, Fanny. *The Palace of Topkapi in Istanbul.* New York: Scribner, 1970. A detailed study which shows all the latest materials on the palace and is well-illustrated. Scholarly and popular.

Fisher, Sydney Nettleton. *The Foreign Relations of Turkey, 1481–1512.* Urbana, Ill.: University of Illinois Press, 1948. Deals with the period of the reign of Bayezid II.

Goodwin, Godfrey. *A History of Ottoman Architecture, with 4 Colour Plates and 521 Illustrations, Including 81 Plans.* Baltimore: Johns Hopkins Press, 1971. One of the outstanding works of its kind, covering the periods before Bursa, Bursa, Edirne, Istanbul including Sinan's works, baroque, and with an excellent chapter on the Ottoman house.

Grey, Charles (trans. and ed.). *A Narrative of Italian Travels in Persia in the Fifteenth and Sixteenth Centuries.* The Hakluyt Society *Works,* Vol. 49, London, 1873. A collection of many interesting voyages, two important ones being those of Caterino Zeno and Giovan Maria Angiolello.

Hodgson, Marshall G. S. *The Venture of Islam: Conscience and History in a World Civilization.* Vol. 3. *The Gunpowder Empires and Modern Times.* Chicago: University of Chicago Press, 1974. This volume emphasizes the period from about 1500 to the time of Napoleon. The nineteenth century is covered inadequately and the twentieth century is considered as a kind of afterthought. Written in a most difficult style and poorly organized.

Jelavich, Charles, and Barbara Jelavich. *The Balkans in Transition: Essays on the Development of Balkan Life and Politics Since the Eighteenth Century.* Hamden, Conn.: Archon, 1974. Papers from a conference held in 1960. Includes important contributions by Stanford Shaw of UCLA (on Ottoman government and society of the sixteenth and seventeenth centuries, especially its structure), Wayne Vucinich of Stanford (on social life and customs of the Ottomans in the Balkans), and Traian Stoianovich of Rutgers (on the relation of social life and structure to politics).

Lewis, Bernard. *Istanbul and the Civilization of the Ottoman Empire.* Norman, Okla.: University of Oklahoma Press, 1963. A brilliant survey of the city at its heyday.

Mihailović, Konstantin. *Memoirs of a Janissary.* Translated from the Czech by Benjamin Stolz, with historical commentary and notes by Svat Soucek. Ann Arbor: University of Michigan, 1975. This volume contains the Czech original along with the translation. The author was a Serb who, after being captured at Novo Brdo in 1455 by the Ottomans, took part in the siege of Belgrad in 1456 and then was captured at Zvečaj in 1463. The original in Serb has been lost but exists in Polish and Czech manuscripts. Very interesting and illuminating.

Miller, Barnette. *Beyond the Sublime Porte: The Grand Seraglio of Stambul.* New Haven, Conn.: Yale University Press, 1931. An authoritative account of this great, historic monument.

————. *The Palace School of Muhammed the Conqueror.* Cambridge, Mass.: Harvard University Press, 1941. A thorough and well-written exposition of this important institution of the Ottomans.

Ramazani, Rouhollah K. *The Foreign Policy of Iran, 1500–1941: A Developing Nation in World Affairs.* Charlottesville: University Press of Virginia, 1966. The author's analysis is lucid and his interpretations are sound and perceptive. The period before 1800 is dealt with very briefly.

Richards, Gertrude Randolph Bramlette (ed.). *Florentine Merchants in the Age of the Medici. Letters and Documents from the Selfridge Collection of Medici Manuscripts.* Cambridge, Mass.: Harvard University Press, 1932. An excellent view of the economic relations between Turkey and the Middle East and Italy, especially Florence, and an insight into some of the problems of doing business in the Ottoman Empire of that day.

Ross, E. Denison. "The Early Years of Shah Ismail, Founder of the Safavi Dynasty." *Journal of the Royal Asiatic Society,* n.s., vol. 28 (1896). An important work.

Runciman, Steven. *The Great Church in Captivity: A Study of the Patriarchate of Constantinople from the Eve of the Turkish Conquest to the Greek War of Independence.* Cambridge, Eng.: Cambridge University Press, 1968. The author contends that under the sultans the patriarch became a lay ruler of a state within a state and that the church endured as a great spiritual force.

Savory, Roger M. "The Principal Offices of the Safawid State During the Reign of Isma'il I(907–30/1501–24)." *Bulletin* of the School of Oriental and African Studies, University of London, vol. 23, pt. 1(1960), 91–105. This is an important article discussing the power of the first Safavid ruler and the organization of the top echelon of his government.

Simsar, Muhammed Ahmed. *The Waqfiyah of 'Ahmed Paša.* Philadelphia: University of Pennsylvania Press, 1940. A fine translation with notes on a perpetual trust established in 1511 by Ahmed Hersekoglu Pasha, who was the son of the last duke of Herzegovina and who became officer and vizir under Mehmed II, Bayezid II, and Selim I. It gives an insight into prices, administrative details, and customs of the time.

Stripling, George William Frederick. *The Ottoman Turks and the Arabs, 1511–1574.* Urbana, Ill.: University of Illinois Press, 1942. Although published earlier, this is a sequel to the reference by Fisher, above, and covers the reigns of Selim I, Suleiman, and Selim II and the conquests of Syria, Egypt, and Iraq.

Sumner-Boyd, Hilary, and John Freely. *Strolling Through Istanbul: A Guide to the City.* Istanbul: Redhouse Press, 1972. One of the very best guides to the city with all sorts of interesting anecdotes.

Chapter 16

Institutions of the Ottoman Empire

The Sultan

At the head of the Ottoman Empire and at the pinnacle of the various social strata stood the sultan. In the West his government was called the Sublime Porte, presumably because edicts and decisions emanated from the principal gate of the palace, called the Gate of Felicity. The sultan's authority was derived from the military power that he controlled, from the reverence and obedience that his subjects gave him, and from the constitutional position of caliph that was held after Selim I's conquest of Egypt.

All military power was under his command. Whether slaves, feudal cavalry, irregular infantry, or sailors of the fleet, all were supposed to obey his orders. Not that they always did, of course. Feudal cavalry groups frequently went on unauthorized raids into Christian lands, often to the embarrassment of the sultan. On numerous occasions the army insisted upon abandoning long and arduous campaigns which took them from the pleasures of Edirne and Istanbul during winter months or from their homes in the provinces. And the janissaries always demanded bonuses and concessions from the sultan upon his accession to the throne.

Nevertheless, the armed services were generally loyal, and certainly they were more obedient than similar forces in western Europe were to their kings and emperors. Upholding the sultan was the long ghazi tradition of his leadership; no other family possessed the prestige of the Ottoman dynasty. Moreover, the slave status of most of the commanding officers and the nature of their rearing gave the sultan such a hold over their lives that deviation from his wishes was risky.

Although Ottoman sultans avoided use of the title caliph, those following Selim I wielded the powers of that position. The sultan was head of the Islamic state, defender of the faith, and executor of sacred law. Muslims rendered obedience to him. Indirectly, Christians did likewise, since the sultan appointed and invested the Greek patriarch and ordered church officials and laymen to obey him.

In general Ottomans followed the law and jurisprudence of Muslim Arabs. Four distinct bodies or sources of law existed. Foremost and supreme over the other three stood sacred law *(shariah)*. (The Ottoman interpretation of sacred law followed that of the orthodox Hanafite school.) Sultan, judges, and lawyers were bound by sacred law, and to ignore it invited disaster. Second stood *kanuns,* or published decrees of sultans, which were either administrative in character or supplementary to sacred law. Kanuns, for example, dealt with intricate ceremonial law of the Ottoman government and with feudal, military, financial, criminal, and police law. Last in the strata of law were *adet* and *urf.* Adet was customary law as observed by Turks from time immemorial, by Ottomans, and by peoples conquered by them. Thus, adet in Bosnia might be different from adet in the Morea, and both might be different from adet in Ankara. Urf was the sovereignty or will of the ruling sultan and might contravene adet. Kanuns could change adet and urf and could annul or amend other kanuns. Sacred law was inviolable.

The great institutions of the state, established either by sacred law or kanuns, were accepted as emanating from God or from the sultan's supreme will; in no sense were they considered to flow from the desires of the people. In examining governmental institutions of the Ottoman Empire it becomes apparent that over the 600 years of the empire's existence the structure and procedures of government were not necessarily identical from one century to the next. Ceremonial forms may have often remained the same, but the power, realities, relationships, and even the character of the personnel varied from period to period. All the personnel and their families can be said to have belonged to the "ruling class."

At the time of the accession of Suleiman there were four principal divisions of government: the palace services; the military-governing administration; the scribal-financial bureaucracy; and the religious-judicial establishment. In theory and in practice the sultan was over all of these and the officials in each were directly or indirectly answerable to him. In common parlance they were referred to as belonging to the military *(askeri)* class, and many went on campaigns with the sultan, even if they were not trained to fight. This terminology was used to differentiate them from the *rayah* class—those Turks, Muslims, and non-Muslims who did not belong to the Ottoman service and system. The leaders and upper echelons in these four branches of government were, certainly, the elite of state and society. Furthermore, all members of these branches, except those of the religious establishment, were by law slaves of the sultan, though in actual practice many were not.

The Palace Services

Since the sultan was the supreme head of the government with absolute power, the center of the government was wherever he happened to be. Thus his household, the palace, gained a special significance and power through the influence that could be exercised upon him. Technically, individuals of the "ruling class" with the exception of the feudatory enjoyed membership in the sultan's court and were expected to be a part of his retinue on ceremonial occasions and sometimes in camp. More specifically, the court consisted of the harem, the Inside Service, and the Outside Service.

Until about 1540 there were relatively few in the harem, which was quartered in the Old Palace in Istanbul or in the palaces in Edirne and Demotika. It formed a palace within a palace and included consorts of the sultan, female servants of the court, and girls in training, who upon reaching the age of twenty-five were married to court officers unless they had moved up the well-defined hierarchy in the harem. The greatest lady of the harem was the sultan's mother *(sultana valideh);* after her came the mother of the sultan's first-born son, and then mothers of other sons. Numbering about 200 and guarded by 40 black eunuchs, the harem was transferred to the Great Palace in 1540; the Old Palace still housed elderly and retired women of the harem.

Functionaries who took care of the sultan's personal affairs comprised the Inside Service, which was divided into five groups, chambers, or halls: inner (royal bedchamber); treasury; commissariat; great hall; and small hall. Chief of the entire Inside Service was the general of the gate, a white eunuch. He was invariably a high state dignitary, who served also as grand master of ceremonies for the palace, director in chief of the Palace School, and confidential agent of the sultan. Chief administrators of the halls and their immediate assistants were white eunuchs, who numbered about fifty in the sixteenth century.

Aside from the white eunuchs, members of the halls were called pages and were young men usually chosen from the elite of the captives and tribute children. The great and small halls were divisions of the Palace School; and pages in the other halls were serving a kind of postgraduate internship in administering affairs of the sultan and his palace. Usually the pages served in one of these halls for four to eight years, the best then moving to one of the other halls of the Inside Service for further training and service. Those who did not obtain advancements joined the sultan's cavalry at various levels or received other suitable appointments. After four or eight more years in one of the three specialized chambers, the pages remained as officials in the Inside Service or were appointed as provincial governors, high officers in the janissary corps or cavalry, or as officials in the Outside Service or another principal branch of government. Once a page was promoted to a position outside the inner palace, he never returned.

Whereas the Inside Service controlled the relations of the sultan's life within the palace, the Outside Service coordinated his relations with life in the world outside. However in the first part of the sixteenth century, demarcation lines between the Outside Service and other branches of government were not sharply drawn; at least there is no evidence that individuals in this service made any real distinction among the branches. Since all the high officials serving the sultan at this time were in the Outside Service, it could be called "the court"; most European observers thought of it as such and regarded its members as the sultan's courtiers.

In the Outside Service the most important official for the military-governing administration was the grand vizir; others were the remaining vizirs; commanders of the janissaries and the sultan's cavalry divisions; generals of the armies when not on campaigns; officers responsible for the palace security, discipline, and protocol; the kitchen service; gardeners; tent-pitchers; masters of the hunt; equerries; officers of supply; the treasurer; record keepers; the personal bodyguard; learned associates of the sultan; and all other top officials who made the government function. The learned associates of the sultan were members of the religious-judicial establishment, constituted by the sultan's religious teacher and adviser, preachers, muezzins, chanters, readers, astrologers, physicians, and surgeons. The bodyguard was drawn from sons of high officials, choice graduates from the Inside Service, and veteran janissaries—in all about 400 men. Many palace guards were responsible officials, and to that group belonged ambassadors and executioners. The treasurer and record keepers were members of the scribal-financial bureaucracy, which was just beginning to form at this time. Others tended the palace gardens or rowed the sultan's caïques on Bosphorus excursions. Boys destined for the ordinary ranks of the janissaries frequently served as helpers in the Outside Service.

At the time of Suleiman I the sultan's court with its three services numbered in the neighborhood of 10,000 persons. Earlier Ottoman sultans lived more simply; several accounts of public ceremonies in mosques and other places report that it was difficult to distinguish the sultan from his attendants. Probably in the court of Murad II and certainly in that of Mehmed II, magnificence in ceremony appeared. After the conquest of Constantinople, Mehmed II introduced into his bodyguard a company of 100 halberdiers, copied in arms, costumes, and manners from the Byzantine emperor's bodyguard. By the middle of the sixteenth century, rituals and functions of each section of the services became so elaborate and rigid that a law of ceremonies was drawn, and observance of details involving procedure equaled in importance the fulfilling of duties.

Until the reign of Suleiman I the court and its personnel seldom trespassed upon the direct field of government and administration. The court served the personal needs of sultan and palace. Insofar as court officers and chamberlains had direct access to the sultan, they could be influential persons whose favor was eagerly sought. To have a friend highly placed at court was a precious asset.

The Military-Governing Administration

The administrators in the sixteenth century who ran the government and the army were usually products of the Inside Service of the palace, the great majority, from the end of Mehmed II's reign through most of the following century, being chiefly recruited, though not entirely so, from the tribute and captive children. At the top was the vizir, or chief minister; later, when four ministers had the title of vizir, one was designated first vizir, or under Suleiman I, grand vizir. The sultan delegated his political and executive

authority only to his vizirs. When they were in the provinces or on campaign they could even impose the death penalty. The grand vizir by the
law of Mehmed II had power greater than all other men and was in all
matters the sultan's absolute deputy. In ceremonies and meetings he took
his place before all others. He was also entrusted with the sultan's personal
seal (the taking away of which signaled dismissal from office). Murad I had
appointed the first such vizir from one of the prominent Ottoman families.
Murad II chose vizirs from the religious-judicial establishment and from the
army. Mehmed II picked them from the graduates of the Palace school and
from Ottoman families of Anatolia, but from the accession of Bayezid II
until late in the sixteenth century all were from some part of the palace
service.

The vizirs, under the chairmanship of the grand vizir, made up a council,
or divan, with whom the sultan conferred on matters of state. Other members of the divan, also often called vizirs, were the head of the janissaries;
two *kadiaskers,* or chief judges—one for Anatolia and one for Rumeli; two
defterdars, or treasurers, again one each for Anatolia and Rumeli; the chief
nishanji, or secretary of state; and the chief admiral of the navy. (Since
judges were members of the religious-judicial establishment, their responsibilities will be described later.)

The divan met with the sultan for several hours every Saturday, Sunday,
Monday, and Tuesday to decide all matters of government. Analogous to a
modern cabinet meeting but also bearing some resemblance to a supreme
court, the divan meeting served as a kind of union and capstone to the
several branches of the Ottoman government. However, by the time of
Mehmed II the sultan, rather than attending divan meetings himself, would
after each session receive the divan members in the room behind the
Sublime Porte to listen to and consider their decisions. The head of the
janissaries, since he was responsible directly and only to the sultan, entered
first, conducted his business, then left. Next to meet with the sultan were
the chief judges. On their departure all the others entered, delivered their
reports, then exited, leaving the grand vizir to give his account and to
obtain confirmation of the day's business.

It was a rule that no one, not even the other vizirs, could be privy to the
grand vizir's dealings with the sultan and to their secret decisions. Yet there
were many checks on the authority of the grand vizir, for he was obliged
before making any important decision to consult with the other members
of the divan. Failure to abide by this procedure was an important factor in
the dismissal and execution of the grand vizir Ibrahim in 1536. In addition,
the heads of the janissaries, the treasury, and the judiciary also dealt directly
with the sultan. (As stated by Mehmed II, not a single penny would enter
or leave the treasury unless the head of the treasury ordered it.) On after-
noons after a divan meeting, the grand vizir, the judges, and the head of
the treasury held council meetings in their residences to discuss the business of their own offices. One other item of note was the custom, even the
compulsion, of vizirs and other officials to maintain a household similar to

that of the sultan, with the number of slaves, pages, and aides usually dictated by the position. Rustem Pasha, one of Suleiman's grand viziers, had 1,700 slaves at the time of his death.

By the middle of the sixteenth century the core of the Ottoman army was the janissary corps, numbering over 10,000. They were commanded by an *aga* (general) who was directly responsible to the sultan. Usually this aga was an officer trained in the palace, although sometimes he rose from the ranks like other janissary officers. In addition to the ordinary janissaries there were a number of specialized units, including the *solak* guard, 150 of the best bowmen who marched on the left (solak) side of the sultan on campaigns; other superior janissaries were regularly advanced to special posts in the sultan's service.

The regular cavalry, generally called *sipahis* of the Porte to distinguish it from the feudal cavalry, or *sipahis*, was drawn principally from the ordinary janissaries and the pages of the palace. A few of the feudal cavalry, however, were rewarded with admission to the regular cavalry. One special battalion was a kind of Foreign Legion, consisting of non-Ottoman Turks, Kurds, Arabs, Christian renegades, and horsemen from sources outside the sultan's court.

The Ottomans gave special attention to the technical services; and all European observers at that time marveled at the equipment, food, transport, and roads provided for Ottoman armies. Most important were the artillery corps and ordnance services which cast cannon and manufactured gunpowder. These branches more than any other brought victory after victory to Ottoman armies.

Beginning with Murad II, the navy became an effective division of the armed services. Development of sea power advanced reign by reign until under Selim I and Suleiman I the navy applied its force everywhere in the Mediterranean. Ships were built at many different ports from the Black Sea to the Adriatic. Venetian master shipbuilders along with Greek and Turkish builders, frequently working by flares at night, kept the navy in fighting trim. Commanded by the Kapudan Pasha, who ranked with the viziers, the navy was manned by experienced seafaring men from North African coasts and the eastern Mediterranean area.

Fleets of 300 to 400 ships, as large and as well armed as those of Spain, France, or Venice, were maintained at all times. In peaceful years Ottoman sea captains, many of them Greek or Italian renegades, sailed on their own responsibility and often turned to piracy against Christian Europe in much the same fashion as ghazis on land raided Carinthia and Styria.

One of the superior segments of the Ottoman army came from the provinces and from fief holders. Whenever a campaign was announced, the governor of each province assembled the feudal cavalry, which until the end of the sixteenth century matched any cavalry of western Europe. Each holder of a *timar* or *ziamet* came with a predetermined number of knights in his entourage. They elected their own immediate leaders, although their provincial commander *(sanjakbey)* was an appointee of the sultan (after the time of Murad II, frequently a graduate of the Palace School). Prior to the period of Suleiman I supreme command of the feudal cavalry rested on the shoulders of two generals—the beylerbey of Anatolia and the beylerbey of Rumeli. (At a later time additional beylerbeys were designated for areas such as Syria, Hungary, and Baghdad.) These two generals acted as vizirs, attended meetings of the divan when convenient, and commanded the wings of the army in battle. They rewarded the brave directly with fiefs and meted out punishment to laggards.

Other branches of the armed forces were the *akinjis* and the *azabs*. The former were irregular, unpaid, volunteer cavalrymen who answered the call to arms in hopes of booty or the gift of a fief for valor. *Azabs* were similar to *akinjis* except that they were foot soldiers. Usually in any battle *akinjis* and *azabs* were used as front-line troops to absorb the first shocks of contact with the enemy.

The Scribal-Financial Bureaucracy

Every official of the government had his private secretary, a corps of scribes, and personal bureaucrats commensurate with the tasks involved. Most of the private secretaries became indispensable and influential with their superiors, drafting laws, and advising on matters of state. On a broader base, however, three main branches of the bureaucracy evolved into the executive office of the divan, the chancery, and the treasury. In the early days individuals manning these offices had usually come from the palace, but by the middle of the sixteenth century most were recruited from the families of Ottoman officials and their clients and from sons and relatives of members of the bureaucracy. Clerks entered the bureaus as apprentices and learned on the job, often simultaneously taking courses at mosque medressehs to enhance their knowledge of law and religious sciences. Promotions in the bureaus came at regular intervals (usually four years), and diligent and intelligent clerks could work their way to the top. Changing from one bureau to another was possible but unlikely except when one had reached a fairly high position.

The divan had a secretarial staff, and as time passed, a regular bureau under a bureau head *(reis)* was formalized to draw up and execute the approved orders to governors and officials of the state. The head of this bureau, in turn, became called the *reis al-kuttab,* ("chief scribe") or first secretary of the grand vizir, and in later centuries became a minister of state and foreign minister. The chancellor *(nishanji),* who was a member of the divan, checked on all appointments to office, kept records of salaries, and recorded all ordinances and commands of the sultan, the divan, the vizirs, and other officials, affixing the seal of authority and the sultan's signature to official documents. The chancellor had personal access to the sultan, was responsible only to him, and in his public capacity could be judged only by him. The treasurer *(defterdar)* collected state income, ascertained its sources, and was charged with accounting for all receipts and expenditures of the central government. Until the time of Mehmed II collection of taxes was administered directly by the treasury, but difficulties and leakages in collections led to a system of tax farming. The Ottoman Empire was greatly decentralized financially; provincial governments collected and spent their own funds; and the religious establishment was supported by revenues from properties granted as endowments and not always funneled through the treasury. Total revenue for the central government in the 1520s has been estimated at from 6 million to 8 million ducats, a sum that compared quite favorably with incomes of contemporary governments of western Europe. The treasurer, like the chancellor, was a member of the divan and responsible only to the sultan. There were checks on him and his office; in 1595 two clerks of the treasury were hanged for accepting bribes and six others were dismissed. However, when it was suggested that the treasurer be tried on similar charges, the sultan rejected the idea on the grounds that the treasurer acts on the sultan's authority.

In addition to these main departments of government, there were a number of others, including the mint, the customs bureaus, commissionerships, governors in the provinces, courts, and endowments that developed bureaucracies of their own. Consequently there were thousands of secretaries and scribes in the Ottoman Empire in the sixteenth century—as evidenced by the tons of records in the archives in Istanbul and elsewhere.

The Religious-Judicial Establishment

Parallel with the three main branches of government already described stood the purely Muslim branch. In many ways it was quite separate from the others but never fully independent of them. Since Islam was the religion of the government (with the sultan responsible for the enforcement of Islamic law) and all officials were Muslims, every aspect of government was touched by the religious-judicial establishment, whose personnel at the top levels often moved to other branches of government, particularly from the religious-judicial group into the others. Functionally, this establishment had three main divisions: religion, education, and law.

Since Islam has no priesthood, no clergy, and no monks, it has always been difficult to describe Muslim religious personnel in Western terms. Teachers in all schools and others who had passed through schools beyond the primary grades were classified as the learned *(ulema)*. Other purely religious members of the Muslim group were preachers, mosque caretakers, muezzins, professional leaders of prayers in mosques, dervishes, and sharifs and sayyids. Mosque endowments provided for regular attendants and leaders in mosque activities on a full-time basis. Dervishes were for Islam what monks, hermits, and begging friars were for Christianity; they preached holy wars, spread heresies, and inspired emotional public demonstrations. Sharifs and sayyids traced their descent from Hasan and Husayn, grandsons of the Prophet, wore green turbans, and had numerous personal prerogatives. One was always the sultan's standard-bearer *(mir-alem)* and ranked above all officers of the army.

Every mosque, large and small, had a primary, or reading, school, where pupils studied reading, writing, Arabic, and the Koran. Schools of higher learning called *medressehs* taught grammar, logic, metaphysics, rhetoric, geometry, and astronomy. Advanced *medressehs* gave courses in law and theology. Students in *medressehs* were partially supported by religious endowments; those in law were completely subsidized. *Medressehs* were numerous throughout the empire, and in Istanbul every sizable mosque had one or more attached to it. Fatih's mosque had eight, Suleiman's five, the former being the most prestigious in the empire until the more advanced latter were founded. Each stage of a *medresseh* education was rigidly graded; those who finished a *medresseh* belonged to the learned class. A graduate received a degree, called *danishmend* ("talisman"), and became qualified to teach in a primary school. Further study raised the *danishmend* holder to higher ratings which permitted him to be a professor *(muderris)* in a *medresseh* or a jurist or judge.

The learned who completed law courses of *medressehs* usually received appointments first as a *muderris,* then as a judge (kadi), and finally as a legal counselor (mufti), or as an assistant in the office of one of these. In every city and large town the sultan appointed a judge who exercised juridical control over the surrounding territory. Slaves of the sultan, sharifs, and sayyids had their own judges and courts. Except in cases that involved Muslims, foreigners and non-Muslims were subject to their own laws. Sanjakbeys, beylerbeys, and vizirs also administered justice in their courts except in cases involving sacred law. The hierarchy of judges was based on five carefully classified grades, and advancement proceeded from one grade to another. Each judge had a sizable staff of assistants and scribes. *Medresseh* professors were well paid and judges usually received three or more times as much.

At the top of the system of judges were two *kadiaskers*—one for Europe and one for Asia—who nominated all judges of the empire. Appeals progressed from court to court, and sentences were executed by the civil authorities. Although each judge had a special title, all were generally referred to as kadis, and *molla* was the title of respect enjoyed by all.

Associated with the judge of every city was a mufti who had finished the regular law course of a *medresseh* and who was assigned to interpret sacred law for the judge and high government officials. Appointed for life, the muftis remained private citizens; in legal and juridical matters they had no initiative of action. When a judge, or even a private citizen, was faced with a legal problem, he submitted the question in point to the mufti for legal opinion. The mufti examined the law and gave his answer, a *fetva,* which usually settled the case for the judge or helped the private citizen in his pending lawsuit. In Istanbul the mufti ranked above the judge; and since the sultan and vizirs might pose important questions vital to the life of the whole empire, he became a very significant official. Mehmed II added to the mufti's dignity by conferring upon him the title Shaykh al-Islam, "Leader of Islam," and in ceremonies he took precedence over the grand vizir.

The Muslim establishment within the Ottoman Empire, from the Shaykh al-Islam and the sultan's personal *hoja* (teacher) to the lowliest *naib* (village judge) and teacher in a mosque primary school, welded the empire together under one type of education and one body of law. Any Muslim child, if he studied hard and passed the various examinations, might rise in the ranks, just as fighting men and the sultan's slaves advanced on merit in their branches.

Poverty was no barrier but important friends or relatives did help. Perhaps one-third of the land of the empire was set aside as endowment for various religious activities. These endowments, or *vakf*, were gifts of sultans and private individuals for support of some specific mosque, library, school, almshouse, hospital, bridge, inn, or fountain. The imperial treasury actually handled the funds; but the Shaykh al-Islam, the grand vizir, or an official close to the sultan was usually designated as trustee. The donor often stipulated in the deed of transfer that his own descendants should be administrators of the endowment. Slaves of the sultan found this method a convenience in providing perpetual and inalienable income for their sons and descendants. Furthermore, since official members of the Muslim establishment were exempt from taxation and since their properties were not subject to confiscation, these families had many financial advantages and formed a kind of privileged class.

Non-Muslim Subjects

Following the arrival of Muslim ulema in the Ottoman state at the time of Sultan Orhan, Ottomans grew tolerant of non-Muslims in the fashion of the older Muslim world. Christian and Jewish groups were given their religious and cultural freedom; many Balkan communities preferred such autonomy under the Ottomans to the religious and cultural restrictions and persecutions suffered under Hungarian and Hapsburg rule.

When the settlement of Istanbul was made in 1453, Mehmed II, in recognizing the election of Gennadius as patriarch of the Orthodox Church, pursued the custom of Byzantine emperors in confirming the election of patriarchs. He also acknowledged the practice, already well established in the Ottoman state, of permitting Christians to retain the independence of their religious community. Likewise, Mehmed II recognized Jewish and Armenian Gregorian communities.

These three separate religious groups were called *millets*, which meant a community or nation of people with a particular religion within the Ottoman Empire. Each *millet* or nation had the legal right to use its own language, develop its own religious, cultural, and educational institutions, collect taxes and render them to the imperial treasury, and maintain courts for trying members of the nation in all cases except those involving public security and crime. Each *millet* had a leader who was responsible to the sultan for the payment of taxes from the *millet* and for the good behavior and loyalty of members of his community. To some degree all non-Ottoman

Muslims belonged to a kind of fourth *millet,* a Muslim *millet,* but these were under the care of the religious-judicial establishment and the other branches of the government. In a way these four *millets* stood alongside the Ottoman *millet* which was organized into the four branches.

Foreigners

Further paralleling these *millets* as part of the empire were groups of foreigners, chiefly merchants residing in Istanbul. Each group lived under provisions of a formal treaty drawn up between the sultan and the foreign authority. Even Bayezid I, Mehmed I, and Murad II had agreements with Ragusa, Venice, and Genoa. Mehmed II, Bayezid II, and Selim I had regular treaties with Ragusa, Hungary, Genoa, Milan, Venice, Florence, the pope, Naples, and the Knights of St. John on the island of Rhodes. Suleiman I had one with France.

The general tenor of these treaties was exemplified in the Treaty of 1503 between Bayezid II and Venice. Among other things, the sultan agreed that a Venetian consul *(bailo)* might come to Istanbul with his family and reside there for three years. Although Venetians could live in certain designated cities of the empire for one year and although the sultan agreed to be reasonable in extending their residence, they could travel about only with the consul's permission. The consul should settle all cases and disputes between Venetians; and Venetian testimony was recognized as valid in courts of Christian and Jewish Ottoman subjects. In criminal cases Venetians were guaranteed justice in regular Ottoman courts. That same year in a similar treaty with the king of Hungary, an article provided that commercial clauses would be valid for subjects of certain other states, including the Holy Roman Empire, France, England, Spain, Portugal, and Poland, upon proper ratification of the treaty by the king of the respective state.

These treaties recognizing certain rights and obligations for European residents in the Ottoman Empire were based on the assumption that since Christians could not avail themselves of Muslim sacred law, they would have to live by their own Christian laws. However, in later years when the balance of power between western Europe and the Ottoman Empire shifted to favor the former, such arrangements evolved into the famous capitulatory treaties, which gave nationals of other governments an apparent privileged position in the Ottoman Empire and frequently allowed foreign governments untold influence over vital policies of the Sublime Porte.

REFERENCES: Chapter 16

In addition to general studies on Middle Eastern history and Muslim institutions, references in Chapters 12, 13, 14, and 15 are of particular importance.

Birge, John Kingsley. *The Bektashi Order of Dervishes.* Hartford, Conn.: Hartford Seminary Press, 1937. A significant work by a careful scholar on the origin and development of this order and its relationship to the leaders and various strata of Ottoman society.

De Busbecq, Ogier G. *Turkish Letters.* Translated by Edward S. Forster. Oxford: Clarendon Press, 1927. De Busbecq was imperial ambassador to the Porte for many years; his observations were singularly objective and discerning.

Gibb, H. A. R., and Harold Bowen. *Islamic Society and the West: A Study of the Impact of Western Civilization on Moslem Culture in the Near East.* Vol. 1 (in two parts). *Islamic Society in the Eighteenth Century.* London: Oxford University Press, 1950 and 1957. A detailed and penetrating study of Ottoman institutions as they existed in the eighteenth century and as they had evolved from earlier forms since the fourteenth century.

Itzkowitz, Norman. "Eighteenth Century Ottoman Realities." *Studia Islamica,* 41 (1962): 73–94. A very important article examining the structure and institutions of the government of the Ottoman Empire from the sixteenth to the nineteenth century, opening new ideas. It is a revision of the ideas put forth by Professor A. H. Lybyer. Recently there have been challenges to Professor Itzkowitz's revision.

Knolles, Richard. *The Generall Historie of the Turkes, from the First Beginning of that Nation to the Rising of the Othoman Familie: With all the Notable Expeditions of the Christian Princes Against Them. Together with the Lives and Conquests of the Othoman Kings and Emperours . . .* London, 1603. This is still the most extensive and longest Ottoman history in the English language, written by an Englishman, long a resident in Turkey. There are many later editions.

Lybyer, Albert Howe. *The Government of the Ottoman Empire in the Time of Suleiman the Magnificent.* Cambridge, Mass.: Harvard University Press, 1913. A thorough examination of the institutions of the Ottomans. A pioneer study in this field.

Chapter 17

The Ottoman Empire as a World Power

Suleiman I

The government of the Ottoman Empire was so well organized, regulated, and staffed under Mehmed II, Bayezid II, and Selim I and the number of intelligent, trained, and disciplined officers, pages, and students in the palace was so great that the government could function well without much direction from the sultan. And since Selim I left only one son, the transfer of authority in 1520 generated no stress and no factious activities at the Porte. His son, Suleiman, moreover, was born in the year A.H. 900, the opening year of the tenth century of Islam, and was the tenth of his dynasty. Because of these portentous beginnings his subjects believed that he was destined to rule over a great part of the world.

In this favorable setting the youthful Suleiman appeared as a magnificent sovereign, certainly the match of his equally youthful contemporaries Charles V, Francis I, and Henry VIII. Suleiman reigned for forty-six years. During those years the Ottoman Empire, built on solid foundations by his predecessors, reached its height in power, wealth, and brilliance. Accordingly, Suleiman, called The Magnificent by Europeans and Kanuni ("The Lawgiver") by his own people, has been regarded as a majestic figure among the galaxy of distinguished rulers of all ages.

During the latter years of Bayezid II's reign Suleiman, then a lad of fifteen or so, was assigned as governor of Bolu. But after strong protests by his uncle Ahmed he was transferred to Kaffa in the Crimea, where his mother, daughter of a Tartar khan, had been reared. After his father seized the throne Suleiman was called to govern Istanbul, while Selim fought against brothers and nephews in Asia Minor. Suleiman governed Edirne again during his father's long wars in Iran and Egypt. Only upon Selim's return to Istanbul in 1517 was Suleiman sent to rule the province around Manisa in western Anatolia. Thus Suleiman attended the pages' school in Istanbul and resided for more than five years at the palaces of Istanbul and Edirne. In addition, he had nearly six years of experience as provincial governor, surrounded by teachers, advisers, and graduates of the famous Palace School. No prince of his time had better training or more practical preparation for the responsibility of ruling a great empire. He was a refined gentleman of the Renaissance.

Belgrad and Rhodes

Suleiman passed the first winter of his reign becoming acquainted with his elevated position; and since Piri Pasha continued as grand vizir, no sharp break in governmental personnel occurred. When spring came, Suleiman met the demand for action by choosing Belgrad for the campaign of 1521. At Sofia he gathered his army and supplies, including 3,000 camels carrying ammunition and 30,000 laden with grain. At least 10,000 wagonloads of grain were requisitioned locally, and 300 cannon were brought up the Danube from Istanbul.

As expected, there was little opposition from Europe. Charles V was not only busily engaged preparing for war against Francis I but also deeply involved with Luther and imperial problems. The cream of Hungarian nobility, meanwhile, was at Bratislava celebrating the marriage of King Louis to Mary of Hapsburg, Charles V's sister. Nevertheless, Belgrad offered a valiant defense, its garrison holding out for three weeks. Ottoman cannon, implanted on an island in the Danube, demolished a part of the inner fortress and ended all resistance late in August. Many Serbs were transplanted to the outskirts of Istanbul, where the Belgrad Forest still remains as testimony to this important victory which opened the Hungarian plains and the upper Danube basin to the Ottomans.

The following year Suleiman assembled his forces in Asia for the heralded attack upon the island of Rhodes. Rhodes lay six miles off the coast of Asia Minor astride the sea route from Istanbul to Alexandria, and since the conquest of Egypt the Knights of St. John had continually harassed Ottoman trade. Frequently, Ottoman prisoners were slaughtered, contrary to the provisions of the treaty concluded with Bayezid II, who regarded the knights as professional pirates and cutthroats.

Rhodes was a highly fortified port, and large contingents of knights from many European commanderies of the order arrived to defend the citadel. Venice sent her fleet, but to protect Cyprus! Massing 300 ships and 100,000 men, Suleiman led the attack. It lasted from July until December. Thousands of stone cannon balls of prodigious size bombarded the walls, and a few rudimentary explosive shells were hurled into the town. Effective attacks were launched in conjunction with sapping and mining operations against the walls, but the cost in men on each side was beyond reason. Since Pope Adrian VI's finances and Charles V's victory that spring over Francis I precluded any aid from reaching the knights, they surrendered on Christmas Day 1522. They were allowed to depart with all mercenary soldiers and townsmen who desired to leave. Those who remained were unmolested, were guaranteed full civil rights, and were freed from taxation for five years.

Suleiman's Court

The fall of Rhodes and Belgrad consolidated fully into Ottoman hands the Middle East, or the Levant as it was called in the West. For the following three summers Suleiman remained in Edirne, Istanbul, or their environs enjoying peace. He loved the gardens of the palace, and one of his greatest pleasures was boating on the Bosphorus and the Sea of Marmara. Frequently he would be rowed across to the Asian shore to walk in his gardens there.

It was also during these years that a Russian slave girl named Khurrem caught his fancy. Known generally to posterity as Roxelana, meaning "the Russian," she soon captivated Suleiman completely, became his legal wife, and dominated him until her death in 1558. Suleiman's mother ruled his harem until her death in 1533; after that date Roxelana forced her way into political affairs. Her chief rival, Gulbahar, a Montenegrin slave girl and mother of Suleiman's oldest living son, Mustafa, departed to Manisa in 1534 in the company of her son when he was established there as governor. Roxelana bore Suleiman three children: Selim, Bayezid, and a daughter, Mihrimah. Suleiman had two other sons who grew to manhood: Mehmed, who was older than Selim; and Jihangir, a hunchback. Competition in the harem for Suleiman's affections and intense rivalry among the mothers for the advancement and protection of their sons brought dismay and affliction upon Suleiman and the government in later days.

At this same time Piri Pasha, the grand vizir, retired on a handsome pension, and Suleiman advanced to the grand vizirate his favorite and boon companion, Ibrahim. The son of a Greek sailor of Parga on the Adriatic coast, Ibrahim had been captured by pirates and sold to a lady of Manisa, who gave her slave an excellent education. As a prince in Manisa, Suleiman recognized Ibrahim's talents, enjoyed his violin playing, and brought him to Istanbul as chief falconer and head of the pages of the inner chamber (royal bedchamber). Instead of advancing the second vizir, who fully expected the promotion because of his meritorious conduct during the siege of Rhodes, Suleiman appointed the youthful Ibrahim to the post vacated by Piri Pasha, and also to the office of beylerbey of Rumeli. For the following thirteen years Ibrahim governed the empire, year by year relieving Suleiman of more of the tiresome duties of ruling. He even took the title of Seriasker-Sultan ("commander in chief of the armies" with the power of sultan). He dined with Suleiman, was with him at all hours, and even slept in the sultan's apartments. Between 1523 and 1536 no policy of state was reached without Ibrahim's consideration and approval.

Unfortunately, Ibrahim's rapid advancement to chief of the royal bedchamber and then to grand vizir ran counter to the system of promotions based on merit and service. There could be no question that Ibrahim was a brilliant and successful administrator and adviser. Still, others who had proved their abilities through service were passed over by the sultan's personal favorite. Thus, early in Suleiman's reign the personalities of Roxelana and Ibrahim and their roles at the palace sowed the seeds of harem influence and personal favoritism that proved so disastrous in succeeding centuries.

The first demonstration of Ibrahim's genius came in Egypt. The second vizir in 1523 had asked for and received as a consolation the governorship of Egypt. Within months after his arrival in Cairo he was deeply involved in treason and was murdered in his bath by loyal Ottomans. Other revolts by Arab tribes and Mamluks led Suleiman to commission Ibrahim to go to Egypt for six months to inaugurate a more stable regime. Finances, administration, law, and trade procedures were thoroughly overhauled. The Ottoman pasha was also given more responsibility, although landholders still had direct access to the sultan and considerable local autonomy. The arrangement cleverly tied Ottoman authority to Egyptian independence, producing a system that worked well enough to last for nearly four centuries.

The Siege of Vienna

But the janissaries and palace troops grew restless under the long inactivity and the paucity of booty that Suleiman's repose enforced upon them. Stringent measures in 1525 along with a few well-placed executions were required to quell a janissary riot that could easily have grown into a serious rebellion. Immediately, preparations for a major campaign were unfurled. Following the disastrous Battle of Pavia in 1525 the French begged Suleiman to join in a war against Charles V. All summer Suleiman and his vizirs debated whether a campaign up the Danube beyond Belgrad or one into Transylvania would be better.

In April 1526 the choice fell on the former, and Suleiman, Ibrahim, and other vizirs set out from Istanbul with 100,000 men and several hundred cannon. In July, Peterwardein was taken by Ibrahim. Early in August the Ottomans crossed the Drava and moved toward Mohacs, where a crushing victory opened all of Hungary. Early in September, Buda surrendered to Suleiman, and two weeks later Pest on the east bank of the Danube was burned. The following day Suleiman and his army began the long trek homeward, reaching Istanbul in the middle of November.

But the expedition into Hungary, even with its exciting battles, ended only as a magnified raid. Suleiman did not possess adequate manpower to garrison such distant cities as Budapest and Mohacs. No lands were handed out as fiefs to Ottoman officers; and Hungary remained a political vacuum.

Subsequently, John Zapolya, duke of Transylvania, occupied Budapest and was crowned king of Hungary. Then Ferdinand of Hapsburg, archduke of Austria, defeated Zapolya at Tokay in 1527 and became Hungarian king. In desperation Zapolya turned to the Ottomans. Through the suave diplomacy of the Venetian-Ottoman Ludovico Gritti, Ibrahim's business partner, Suleiman moved in 1529 to oust the Austrians from Hungary. Not until the middle of May did the army leave Istanbul, and continuous drenching rains impeded its march. The larger cannon had to be abandoned along the way. Mohacs was reached only in mid-August; Budapest, a month later. Soon afterward *akinjis* penetrated into Austria like swarms of locusts, and the attack upon Vienna opened on September 29. Although Ferdinand had all summer to meet the threat, forces to defend Vienna assembled less than a week before the siege began.

Mining operations, assaults, countermining, and sorties raged day after day. On October 12, 1529, mines seriously damaged the walls, and infantry attacks almost succeeded. Both sides grew weary, however, and on the fifteenth the Ottomans retired. To the defenders of Vienna it seemed miraculous, for they were on the point of surrender. In truth, the retreat was forced by the grumbling of the janissaries, indicating that they wished to reach Edirne and Istanbul before winter. Ferdinand, unable to pursue the retiring Ottomans, recognized Suleiman's hold upon Hungary in a peace treaty in 1533.

Vienna had not been taken by Suleiman because his communications were so extended that his forces could not be effective. Incessant rains in the Balkans and in Austria made the long marches arduous and the hauling of the heavy cannon that took Belgrad almost impossible. The army left Istanbul only after the mud dried late in April and insisted upon returning before the winter rains began in December. Neither the janissaries nor the feudal cavalry would campaign in the winter. Vienna was thus beyond Ottoman reach, although Christendom failed to appreciate the full facts of the sultan's limitations.

Naval Activities

While Suleiman was engaged in Hungary combating the Hapsburgs, the French looked to him as a useful ally in their struggle against Charles V. Two French embassies reached Istanbul in 1525, both pleading for aid against the king of Spain. But the wily Francis called upon Suleiman only as a last stratagem in war against Charles. In 1530 he quickly dropped the Ottomans and cooperated with Charles against them, sending a dozen French galleys with Andrea Doria's fleet to attack Algeria. But again in 1535, with the vagaries of political and diplomatic fortunes, French envoys pursued Suleiman to the Caucasus to secure Ottoman aid against Charles. No commitments were made, but ambassadors were exchanged on a more permanent basis, and in the following year a treaty was signed giving the French recognition and status similar to that accorded Venice and other Italian city-states for the residence and trade of their nationals in the Ottoman Empire. However, since the French king never ratified the treaty, it did not become effective.

Relations with the French and Hapsburgs inevitably led the Ottomans to extend their interests to the entire Mediterranean. Ottoman navies had existed before the fall of Constantinople and had grown in competence. Mehmed II was able in 1480 to support an expedition across the Adriatic to the heel of Italy. Under the great sea captain Kemal during the reign of Bayezid II, Ottoman sea power came of age, controlled the eastern Mediterranean, and repeatedly plundered the shores of Spain. Under Suleiman the navy occupied and added much of North Africa to the empire.

While Selim I was conquering Egypt, Aruj Barbarossa and his more famous brother Khair al-Din appeared in Tunis to lead the fleets against Christian Europe. Their father was an Ottoman fief-holder from Rumeli who had settled on the island of Mytilene following its conquest by Mehmed II, and they followed the sea-ghazi tradition prevalent along that coast for more than two centuries. After retaking Algiers, Aruj lost his life in an assault upon Tlemcen. Thereupon Khair al-Din, who inherited his brother's sobriquet Barbarossa, sent word that he would consent to Selim's overlordship in exchange for aid and official position. Appointed beylerbey of Algiers and North Africa with absolute authority to rule those provinces and to raise and organize a janissary army, Barbarossa exercised Ottoman power in the Mediterranean until his death in 1546. His ships raked the coasts of Spain and maintained unceasing pressure upon Charles V. Barbarossa's men were of all nationalities, thus truly Ottoman; but his personal bodyguard was composed exclusively of Spanish renegades.

In 1533 Suleiman summoned Khair al-Din to Istanbul, where with much fanfare he was reappointed beylerbey of Algiers and given a fleet of eighty-four ships, many of which were built under his supervision. He regarded himself as a veritable sea ghazi, and on this occasion visited the tomb of Jelal al-Din Rumi in Konya to obtain the blessings of this patron saint of all ghazis. After ravaging the coast of southern Italy in a manner long remembered, Barbarossa descended upon Bizerta and became master of Tunis.

Such a victory could not be left unchallenged. The following year Charles V and Andrea Doria, employing a large fleet and a powerful army, dislodged the Ottomans from Tunis. But Barbarossa escaped with a score of his ships to Algiers to pillage Minorca and the coast of Valencia. Thence he proceeded with his loot, which included 6,000 prisoners and 2 rich Portuguese caravels, to Istanbul—where Suleiman appointed him Kapudan Pasha and made him responsible for all naval activities.

No important naval conquests graced the remainder of Suleiman's reign. Spanish attacks upon Algiers were beaten off, and Ottoman pirate ghazis raided and plundered from one end of the Mediterranean to the other. They visited the Canary Islands, and the English ambassador in Spain complained to Queen Elizabeth in 1562 that North African pirates had seized three English ships near Cadiz, making off with more than 100,000 ducats. After the treaty with France in 1536, French ships frequently cooperated with Ottoman fleets in the western Mediterranean. In the winter of 1543 the harbor and town of Toulon were given over entirely to Barbarossa, his ships, and men; the inhabitants gladly moved out to avoid unpleasant incidents. After Khair al-Din died in 1546 his role was admirably filled by Turgut (Dragut), Piale Pasha, Uluj Ali (a Calabrian by birth), and Khair al-Din's son Hasan. Tripoli was stormed and became the headquarters of Turgut who was named its beylerbey. The strategic island of Jerba off the eastern coast of Tunisia fell to Piale Pasha, who had sailed out to prevent Philip II's fleet from recovering Tripoli.

In 1565 Suleiman sent Piale with 200 ships and a landing force of nearly 30,000 men to take the island of Malta from the Knights of St. John, whom he had driven from Rhodes more than forty years earlier. After several months of costly and fruitless assaults upon the island fortresses, the Ottomans withdrew. Curiously, the Christian forces made no attempt to follow up this failure. Ottoman supremacy upon the Mediterranean continued for many years after Suleiman's death.

Eastern Campaigns

On several occasions in the early years of Suleiman's reign there were difficulties with the shah of Iran. The Ottoman court, being Sunnite, looked with contempt upon the Shiites of the East. They also feared any successes of these heretics, for devotees lived in various parts of the Ottoman Empire. Although Selim I had beaten Shah Ismail and killed thousands of heretics in Anatolia, border chieftains in eastern Asia Minor vacillated in their loyalty from Tabriz to Istanbul and back to Tabriz again as advantages shifted from one to the other. Such changing allegiance brought conflict between the two great empires and perpetuated minor border engagements.

The first Eastern campaign conducted personally by Suleiman was in 1534. Ibrahim led the advance contingents into Tabriz, Suleiman reaching the Iranian capital weeks later. Not being able to come to grips with Shah Tahmasp, they moved southward and captured Baghdad. There Suleiman passed the winter, arranging the administration of this new addition to his empire. Suleiman then sacked and fired Tabriz. He returned to Istanbul early in 1536, having been gone for eighteen months.

A decade later Shah Tahmasp's brother appeared at the Porte, seeking help in a bid for the Iranian throne. Suleiman left Istanbul in 1548, recaptured Tabriz, wintered in Aleppo, and spent all of 1549 pillaging cities and pursuing the elusive Tahmasp, who never dared risk a battle.

Again in 1553, perhaps believing that the Ottomans were fully engaged in Europe, Tahmasp adopted an aggressive policy toward the Porte and seized Erzerum. Rustem Pasha, the grand vizir, headed a large army to halt the Iranians. However, the army, particularly the janissaries, disliked him; they began to mutter that if Suleiman were too old to lead them his eldest living son, Prince Mustafa, should. Egged on by Roxelana, who was plotting for the favored position for one of her sons, Suleiman took the field, then summoned Mustafa to Eregli, where he had three mutes strangle his son. Suleiman again wintered at Aleppo and spent 1554 subjugating the lands east of the Euphrates. Then, recognizing the futility of trying to hold these Eastern conquests, the Porte arranged a peace that allowed the Ottomans to retain Iraq, including Baghdad, and a port on the Persian Gulf.

Suleiman also took an interest in developments in the Red Sea area and along the shores of the Arabian Sea. Salman, an ex-pirate, led an Ottoman force that plundered Yemen and Aden in 1525. Thirteen years later an Ottoman admiral sailed from Suez, installed loyal governors in Aden and Yemen, and then passed on to the Malabar coast, where he landed and unsuccessfully besieged Diu. Suleiman also found that the Portuguese blocked the exit from the Persian Gulf, in part nullifying his capture of Baghdad and Basrah. When the famous geographer–sea captain Piri Pasha failed to oust the Portuguese from the Straits of Hormuz, he was beheaded for cowardice. His successors were likewise unsuccessful in driving them from Hormuz. Nonetheless, the Ottomans retained control over the Persian Gulf, Aden, Yemen, and the Red Sea.

Hungary Again

Suleiman, like other rulers of his time, had too many irons in the fire to press his Eastern campaigns vigorously. In the latter half of his reign he became involved again in Hungary, occupying Budapest in 1541 and for the first time merging Hungary directly into his empire. His officers were installed in all territories between the Danube and the Theiss. Some twenty-five provinces were formed, each with a governor under the beylerbey of Budapest (Ofen). As always in the Ottoman state, the Magyar people continued to live and worship as they had in the past.

Ferdinand of Austria tried to retaliate, but his siege of Budapest failed. Peace treaties were signed in 1547; each party retained the lands in his possession, and Austria paid a tribute of 30,000 ducats a year to the Porte. The Hapsburgs, however, violated the peace; and in 1552 Suleiman's second vizir captured fortress after fortress and incorporated the Banat of Temesvar into the empire. Only a minor fortress of Sziget in Hungary remained. Busbecq, the noted commentator on Suleiman's court and the imperial ambassador at the Porte, arranged a renewal of the peace in 1561.

Maximilian II succeeded his father, Ferdinand, in 1564. He, too, refused to pay the tribute and attacked Ottoman territory. When governors clamored for support in 1566, Suleiman set forth on his seventh campaign into Hungary. He was over seventy years of age, and being no longer able to ride a horse, he traveled in a carriage. Pointing for Erlau, the troops were deflected to reduce the fortress at Sziget, where a Croatian count had killed one of Suleiman's favorite officers. Situated on lowlands near the Danube, Sziget was surrounded by marshes and lakes. Dry weather prevailed, however, and Sziget fell on the evening of September 5 with the explosion of a huge mine under the walls. That same night—the eve of the consolidation of Hungary, the fulfilment of the conquest that had begun with the fall of Belgrad in his first year of campaigning—Suleiman died.

Suleiman's Family and Friends

Mehmed Sokolli, the grand vizir, kept Suleiman's death a secret for over three weeks, while a messenger went to Kutahya to summon Selim to the succession. Suleiman had had eight sons, but only one outlived him. Three died as small children in the first years of his reign. Mehmed, who was Suleiman's favorite, died in 1543 at the age of twenty-one. The fate of Mustafa, the son of Roxelana's chief harem rival, has already been narrated; and his brother, Jihangir the hunchback, committed suicide upon learning of Mustafa's death. The remaining two, Selim and Bayezid, were Roxelana's sons. Selim, the elder, drank to excess and was given to intrigue. The soldiers preferred Bayezid, who resembled Suleiman and who was probably the choice of Suleiman and Roxelana.

Each brother had a following at court, and rivalry between the two was intense. Selim and his friends employed every means to advance his power, even daring to risk forging and intercepting letters between Bayezid and his father. Especially after Roxelana's death in 1558, Selim's fortunes were watched over by Rustem Pasha. The latter was the husband of Roxelana's daughter Mihrimah, who had as much power over her father as her mother did. Civil war between the brothers broke out in 1559. Suleiman ordered the provincial governors in Asia Minor to give active support to Selim, who was then victorious in a battle near Konya. Bayezid wrote to Suleiman asking to be forgiven, but the letter never reached his father. Fleeing to the court of Shah Tahmasp, Bayezid became the source of much diplomatic correspondence. Eventually on the payment of 400,000 ducats he and his four sons were turned over to Suleiman's agent, who executed all of them. Thus, when Suleiman died, there remained of his sons only Selim the Drunkard—a fat, fun-loving, and debauched person.

Another unhappy personal incident of Suleiman's reign involved his companion and grand vizir Ibrahim. After he was appointed to office in 1523, Suleiman grew to depend upon him for nearly every important decision. Before Suleiman designated Khair al-Din Barbarossa beylerbey of Algiers, Barbarossa had to proceed to Aleppo to secure the blessing and approval of Ibrahim. For the first Iranian campaign Ibrahim was named *seriasker* and at times appropriated the title sultan. Presumably, Suleiman came to feel that Ibrahim was amassing too much power. One evening in 1536 Ibrahim dined as usual with Suleiman and retired for the night to his customary place in Suleiman's apartments. The next morning his strangled body was found outside the palace. No explanation was ever given. His immense wealth reverted to the crown, since he was Suleiman's slave. In later years Suleiman tried to avoid promoting officers too rapidly or elevating them too obviously over the heads of their seniors.

Imperial Problems

The relationship between Suleiman and Ibrahim and its calamitous end were symptomatic of the rapidly changing scene in and about the government. The expansion into eastern Asia Minor, Syria, and Egypt by Selim I was followed without much breathing space by Suleiman's conquests in Serbia, Hungary, North Africa, and Mesopotamia. The result was that in two decades the empire experienced an astonishing increment not only of power and wealth but also of responsibilities.

More and more provinces were created with a proportionate increase in the number of governors, judges, tax collectors, and clerks. The janissary corps was doubled in size. Wealth poured into Istanbul; and high officers of the court, personally interested in money even in the days of Murad II, adopted a life of sumptuous pomp and splendor. (To celebrate the circumcision of Mustafa, Mehmed, and Selim in the summer of 1530, high dignitaries gathered in Istanbul for festivities that lasted three weeks.) Each vizir had a magnificent court of his own, modeled after that of his master. Each had his own slaves, whom he trained and employed for his own interests. Ibrahim even established a school. Mehmed Sokolli, the grand vizir at the time of Suleiman's death, had become Suleiman's slave when Iskender Chelebi, the chief treasurer, was executed and his property confiscated in 1534. Ayas Pasha, Ibrahim's successor as grand vizir and a slave of Albanian origin, lived in the grand manner. At his death from the plague it was cryptically noted that there were 40 cradles at one time at his palace and that he left 120 children!

As governmental administration became vaster and more complex, favoritism, corruption, and intrigue multiplied. The situation was abetted by the haphazard growth of Ottoman law and legal procedures. Suleiman, therefore, issued numerous new laws and revamped and codified old laws in a vain attempt to regularize his administration. (It is on the basis of this legal activity that he has been known in Ottoman history as Suleiman Kanuni—"the Lawgiver.") Many laws related to matters of inheritance, salary, rank, and ceremony for officers of the court. Market and guild regulations were modified; criminal laws were developed; and in 1532 there was arranged a full Egyptian law code, almost a constitution, based on the decrees and settlements made by Ibrahim while he had been there in 1524. One of the greatest collections of laws was that fashioned in 1530 for the feudal class to eliminate confusion and end the growing corruption. The granting of all fiefs was changed from the hands of the beylerbey to those of the sultan. A sipahi or a prospective sipahi received a note from the beylerbey, but had to appear at the Porte to obtain his confirmation.

Suleiman's revenues were greater than those of any of the contemporary monarchs in Europe. Income was derived from many sources. Since the Ottomans usually followed the customs that were practiced in a province before its conquest, the sources varied from province to province. Tithes on land, poll taxes, special taxes on lands of non-Muslims, trade, animals, produce, markets, mines, confiscations, escheat, and booty annually brought Suleiman about 12 million ducats. Even so, Suleiman, like each of the European monarchs, was often hard-pressed for funds; and in his later years he forced gifts from his officers upon their appointment to a higher position, a practice that unfortunately opened the door to venality.

Selim II

Throughout his reign of eight years Selim II retained his father's last grand vizir, Mehmed Sokolli, who administered the government and might well be called the actual ruler. Virtually afraid of his grand vizir, Selim generally deferred to him and to other high officials of proven abilities, though at times he embarrassed Sokolli by acting on the advice of an old tutor. Selim was highly emotional and sensitive, and a truly gifted poet. But he was also self-centered. He was unaware of how the court and the soldiers felt toward him and lived in the company of and was easily influenced by fawning courtiers and unscrupulous adventurers, of which there was a goodly number at the Porte.

Since Sokolli continued as grand vizir throughout Selim's reign and on into that of his successor, there was no break in governmental procedure or policy, although there was some difficulty at the onset. Selim and his personal friends erred in not comprehending the power and fearlessness of the janissaries; and at first they declined to give the customary accession donations to the soldiers. Complaints, demands, and a show of force followed until Selim promised the money.

Otherwise, the course of events proceeded as it had under Suleiman. Piale Pasha took the island of Chios from the Genoese; Bosnian sipahi raided Carniola; ambassadors came and went; peace was signed with Austria and Poland; and Yemen was subjected. An ambitious project was undertaken in 1569: forces were sent to conquer Astrakhan at the mouth of the Volga River; meanwhile, engineers and excavators started digging a canal to connect the Don and the Volga at a point where they are only about thirty miles apart. The purpose was to enable ships and military supplies to be sent to the Caspian Sea and to support attacks upon Iran. The garrison at Astrakhan withstood the storm, however, and an army under Prince Serebinoff drove away the workmen on the canal. The enterprise was abandoned and peace between Muscovy and the Porte was reestablished.

Sokolli had a similar dream of cutting a waterway across Suez, but affairs in Yemen and Arabia and then Selim's insistence upon war against Venice for the conquest of Cyprus postponed the work. Lala Mustafa, Selim's tutor who had intrigued and plotted so successfully to destroy Bayezid, obtained command of the war against Venice. The beylerbey of Anatolia and many governors were ordered to support him. Three naval contingents assisted when the attack began in 1570. The ports fell and the whole island of Cyprus was subdued at heavy cost by midsummer of 1571. Cyprus became a unified part of the empire (and Selim could now command the entire output of Cypriote wine of which he was so fond).

The attack on Cyprus and the extraordinary naval preparations of the Ottomans not only alarmed Venice but instigated the formation of a redoubtable naval league which included Spain, Venice, Savoy, the pope, and the Knights of Malta. Commanded by Don Juan of Austria, the Christian fleet met the Ottomans at the Gulf of Lepanto in October 1571. A furious battle ensued with the Ottomans losing over 200 ships and many men. The allied fleets suffered less, and victory was theirs. To the Ottomans and the East the Battle of Lepanto was a severe loss in a long series of naval engagements. However, a new fleet was built that winter in the naval yards of Gallipoli and Istanbul; and by the spring of 1572 the Ottoman naval position was largely repaired. To the Christians, however, it had seemed a notable victory; it gave them courage and proved that the Ottomans were not invincible upon the sea. Nevertheless, they failed to follow up the victory, and their combined fleets were scattered. By spring of the following year it was too late. A new Ottoman navy was ready.

Peace between Venice and the Porte was never officially broken, and in 1573 a new treaty was signed in which Venice not only recognized the loss of Cyprus but agreed to pay the Ottomans the cost of the war. Don Juan did, however, act to drive the Ottomans from the harbor and city of Tunis, part of which was occupied by Uluj Ali while the conquest of Cyprus was underway. Tunis now joined Algiers and Tripoli as Ottoman strongholds on the north shore of Africa and remained an Ottoman possession until the nineteenth century.

Whether the decay and weakening of the Ottoman Empire would have become noticeable under Selim had he lived longer is difficult to determine. In any case, late in 1574 Selim was inspecting a new bath at the palace; and to protect himself from any dampness of the fresh plaster, drained an entire bottle of Cypriote wine. Being slightly unsteady, he fell on the damp floor, and died a few days later from a brain concussion. His death, followed a year later by the assassination of Mehmed Sokolli, terminated an era in Middle Eastern history. The glory of the empire and its augmentation soon turned into stagnation and decline. The powerful and dynamic Ottoman Empire gradually gave way to the weak and corrupt state that the rising centralized monarchies and nation states of Europe found so tempting.

Shah Tahmasp I of Safavid Iran

When the despondent Ismail died in 1524, he was succeeded by his eldest son, Tahmasp, a lad of ten years. Though Ismail had been trying for more than fifteen years to elevate Iranian elements in the state and subordinate domineering *kizilbash* Turkoman tribal leaders, the *kizilbash* gained power after his death and held it for a decade. However, civil war among the Turkoman tribes kept the state in turmoil until Tahmasp subdued the rebellions and ended the strife by establishing an Iranian viceroy in 1533.

When Suleiman threatened Iran over her support of various Turkoman chiefs, Tahmasp in vain sent envoys to Hungary and Charles V for cooperation. In 1534 the Ottomans, led by Suleiman, invaded, sacking Tabriz and Gilan, and capturing Baghdad. Another campaign occurred in 1548 when Tahmasp's brother induced the Ottomans to send an invading army that seized Azerbayjan. Peace was arranged in 1555, but the shah did not retain Tabriz or Baghdad because his forces were inadequate to defeat the main Ottoman army. Nevertheless, although the lack of artillery and muskets was a critical disadvantage to Tahmasp, distances from Istanbul, difficult terrain, problems in the Danube basin and the Mediterranean, and the psychology of Ottoman fighting men made it equally unlikely for Ottoman forces to reach Tahmasp and impose a settlement. Thus, Tahmasp was able to enforce his rule from the Tigris to Transoxiana and from the Persian Gulf to both sides of the Caspian Sea.

Within the Safavid state great strife raged over the competition between *kizilbash* Turkomans and non-Turkish Iranian populace. Shah Tahmasp attempted, as his father had before him, to find an alternative to the power of unreliable *kizilbash*. Nearly every province was held as a fief by one of their leaders, and their incomes and retainers gave an independence difficult to offset. Between 1540 and 1544 Tahmasp sent four expeditions to

Georgia, bringing back 30,000 prisoners, most of whom were boys to be trained as *gulams* to serve in his army or to be trained as governing administrators. The girls served as concubines whose sons also entered the shah's service. This policy of creating a Georgian and Circassian counterweight to the *kizilbash* in the end proved disastrous as civil war broke out between them in 1572 as Tahmasp grew old and feeble. His many sons and their mothers began to intrigue for the succession. Two leading candidates were Prince Suleiman, whose mother was a Circassian, and Prince Haydar, whose mother was Georgian. In the end the *kizilbash* declared they would support sons of Turkish mothers only.

In 1576 Tahmasp was poisoned by Haydar's mother, but the *kizilbash* had the power to put Ismail, his fourth son, on the throne, for his mother was a Turkoman. Having been incarcerated for twenty-five years by his father, he was half mad and given to drink and drugs. He killed all the royal princes except Prince Muhammad Khudabanda who was nearly blind and not considered a threat. Ismail executed many *kizilbash* leaders who had supported his brothers and finally gave orders to have his sole remaining brother executed. Before the deed could be committed, however, poison was mixed one night in 1577 with Ismail's usual juice of opium poppy and Indian hemp, and he was found dead in the morning. After placing Muhammad on the throne (since he had a Turkoman mother), the *kizilbash* were thwarted for eighteen months by the new shah's ambitious Iranian wife until she was assassinated.

Shah Muhammad Khudabanda ruled as a kind of puppet in Turkoman hands for ten years until 1587, when he was overthrown and killed by Turkoman leaders who had seized Qazvin, the capital, and put his sixteen-year-old-son, Abbas, on the throne. Ruling for forty-one years, Abbas ushered in a new age in Iranian history. By 1587 the religious zeal for the Safavid rule had been frittered away, and over the century the shah's position as the head of a secular state dominated. There had been a gradual change and evolution under Tahmasp with acceptance of the idea of a central government. He strengthened the government by moving the capital from Tabriz to Qazvin which was safer from Ottoman assault. Moreover, Shiite doctrinal unity had been achieved to a great extent, making religion much less of an emotional issue. One could now recognize the consolidation of Safavid Iran into a state of considerable permanence.

Ottoman Architecture
In this illustrious period of Ottoman history the most viable and lasting evidence of its greatness and magnificence was the galaxy of majestic mosques that still silhouette the skyline of Istanbul from every quarter. Sultans, grand viziers, kapudan pashas, princes and princesses, ladies of the harem, and *validehs*—all built impressive mosques and tombs to memorialize themselves. Most of the prominent mosques of the empire, and of Istanbul in particular, date from the sixteenth century. A few Byzantine churches were converted at the time of the conquest or shortly thereafter,

but of these only Hagia Sophia was outstanding. A few mosques were erected before the close of that century, but the score of great ones comprised a series which began with the mosque of Sultan Bayezid II (completed about 1500), and ended with the Blue Mosque of Sultan Ahmed I (1617).

The simplest style and form, exemplified in the mosque of Sultan Selim I in Istanbul, consisted of a plain square building carrying one large dome. The transition between square and circle was accomplished by flat and spherical triangular pendentives.

The second type of imperial mosque was evolved in the mosques of Bayezid II and Suleiman I. These mosques showed that Ottoman architects studied Hagia Sophia, saw its grandeur, and appreciated its solution of the problem of building a domed open square or rectangular structure suitable for congregational worship. In these two mosques, the great rectangle was roofed by a large dome on spherical pendentives which effected the transition from the dome to the four broad pointed arches resting upon four piers. The dome was abutted longitudinally by semidomes fitted to their rectangles by pendentives or small semidomes, which in Suleimaniyeh were anchored to their corners by stalactite pendentives. The pendentives confused the eye and thereby hid the awkwardness, thus serving much the same function as the colored mosaics of the Byzantines. The strong buttresses in the lateral walls were admirably concealed by external porches. In some details the influences of Italian Renaissance architecture were also evident.

The architect Sinan was the master of the age and he contended that his early Shahzade mosque in memory of Suleiman's son Mehmed was the work of an apprentice; his later mosque of Suleiman, the work of a journeyman, and Sultan Selim II's mosque in Edirne, completed in 1574, the work of a master. In Shahzade, Sinan presented a new style aimed at opening the entire edifice into one congregational hall so that every worshiper could see the mihrab. The great mosque of Sultan Ahmed I followed the same principle and achieved its goal by replacing the small domes of the lateral aisle by one large semidome. The central dome at Ahmed was supported by large circular piers. Upon entering Ahmed, one noticed immediately that the whole area was unified and that the central space was vaster than in Hagia Sophia.

At the mosque of Sultan Selim II in Edirne, Sinan developed another type of imperial mosque. The dome, thirty-one meters across, was supported by an octagon of arches, pendentives of stalactite corbels, and eight sturdy paneled piers which Sinan called "elephant feet." Again, as in Suleimaniyeh, the buttresses were hidden by external porches.

The internal centers of the domes were usually decorated with flowered and calligraphic frescoes, and the walls were embellished by panels of colored and veined marble or colored ceramic tiles. The Ottomans were more conscious of esthetic external lines and composition than Byzantine builders, and this accounts for the architectural evolution that gave to the Istanbul horizon its splendor of domes and slender minarets.

Ottoman Literature

The sixteenth century led in architectural achievement; but it was also a brilliant period of Ottoman literary activity. Suleiman had a strong historical feeling; he emphasized the parallelism of Mehmed II and Constantine and equated himself to Justinian. Like Justinian, Suleiman was lawgiver and law codifier, builder of remarkable religious edifices and aqueducts, leader of armies, and generous patron of scholars and men of letters.

A quarter of the eminent Ottoman poets and writers belonged to the period of Suleiman and Selim II. Poetry and history were the outstanding forms of literary effort. Suleiman kept a historical diary which has proved of unique value in studying his reign; and both sultans were accomplished poets, Suleiman writing under the nom de plume Muhibbi. The shining lyric poet of that age and perhaps of the Turkish language of all ages was Abd al-Baki.

Historians flourished. Their works were sometimes general in scope and sometimes specific, describing only one phase or incident of the period. Ramazan wrote of the capture of Rhodes; Kemalpashazade narrated the victorious campaign of Mohacs. One of the most revered of Ottoman historians appeared late in the sixteenth century in the person of Saad al-Din. Tutor of Suleiman's grandson Murad III, he wrote and compiled *The Crown of Histories,* which covered in numerous volumes the gamut of Ottoman history. Continued by Saad al-Din's son, for several centuries it dominated concepts of Ottoman development from the earliest times to his own day.

Progress in the Ottoman Empire in the sixteenth century was typical of that in other Mediterranean and European countries. Selim I was a harsh, brilliant, demanding, energetic tyrant, who set the governmental machinery in motion toward momentous conquest. Suleiman was a dignified, orderly, just, conscientious, and artistic soldier and gentleman, who gave the Ottoman Empire a sense of distinction and cultural urbanity. Selim II was a talented, irresponsible, emotional, dissolute drunkard, who hastened the decay of the state.

REFERENCES: Chapter 17

Most titles already cited for the chapters discussing the Ottoman Empire are relevant to this chapter. Especially noteworthy are those in Chapters 7, 12, 13, 14, 15, and 16.

Carswell, John, and C. J. F. Dowsett. *Kutahya Tiles and Pottery from the Armenian Cathedral of St. James, Jerusalem.* 2 vols. London: Oxford University Press, 1972. This work contains, in addition to the tiles of the Jerusalem cathedral, a general history of Kutahya ceramics from the fifteenth to the nineteenth century, showing interrelationships of Iznik, Rhodian, and Kutahya potteries. It now seems that much of what museums label as Iznik ware may be really Kutahya.

Erdmann, Kurt. *Seven Hundred Years of Oriental Carpets.* Berkeley: University of

California Press, 1970. Contains 286 plates from various world wide collections by the late directory of Islamic department of the Berlin Museums.

Gibb, E. J. W. *A History of Ottoman Poetry.* 6 vols. London: Luzac, 1900–1909. This is the standard work.

Guilmartin, John Francis, Jr. *Gunpowder and Galleys: Changing Technology and Mediterranean Warfare at Sea in the Sixteenth Century.* London: Cambridge University Press, 1974. A masterful study on ships, provisions, sea battles, and their influence on the politics and economies of the Ottoman Empire, Venice, and other Italian states. A very significant work.

Holt, Peter. *Egypt and the Fertile Crescent, 1516–1922.* Ithaca, N.Y.: Cornell University Press, 1966. Valuable for the Ottoman settlement and problems and government in all Arab lands from the sixteenth to the twentieth century. Authoritative.

Hurewitz, J. C. *The Middle East and North Africa in World Politics: A Documentary Record.* Vol. 1. *European Expansion, 1535–1914.* New Haven, Conn.: Yale University Press, 1975. The first volume of the three-volume revision and expansion of his earlier work. Contains 70 more documents and 325 more pages. Indispensable for scholars working in the field of Middle East and North African studies.

Kortepeter, Carl Max. *Ottoman Imperialism During the Reformation: Europe and the Caucasus.* New York: New York University Press, 1972. A study of how the political units in the great span between Europe and the Caucasus got along with each other and Ottoman relationships to them all.

Liebetrau, Preben. *Oriental Rugs in Colour.* New York: Macmillan, 1963.

Lillys, William, Robert Reiff, and Emel Esin. *Oriental Miniatures: Persian, Indian, Turkish with Introduction and Notes.* Rutland, Vt.: Tuttle, 1965. A well-illustrated survey of the miniatures of these three cultures.

Merriman, R. B. *Suleiman the Magnificent, 1520–1566.* Cambridge, Mass.: Harvard University Press, 1944. An adequate summary of the life of the great sultan. Largely written about the year 1900 by Professor Archibald Cary Coolidge, the manuscript was only slightly revised by the author.

Savory, Roger M. "The Principal Offices of the Safawid State During the Reign of Tahmasp I (930–84/1524–76)." *Bulletin* of the School of Oriental and African Studies, University of London, 24, pt. 1 (1961): 65–85. This article gives a picture of the personnel in Tahmasp's court and their rivalries.

Shaw, Stanford J. *The Financial and Administrative Organization and Development of Ottoman Egypt, 1517–1798.* Princeton, N.J.: Princeton University Press, 1962. Basically this is a study of Egyptian revenues and their relationship to the Ottoman treasury, showing how they made possible the Ottoman drive to Vienna and control of the Mediterranean.

Stoye, John. *Siege of Vienna.* New York: Holt, 1965. A detailed account.

Stratton, Arthur. *Sinan.* New York: Scribner, 1972. A narrative biography which depicts the court society of the time more than it does the life of the great architect Sinan.

Unesco World Art Series. *Turkey: Ancient Miniatures.* New York: New York Graphic Society, 1961. This is a beautiful volume reproducing miniatures from the manuscript on the circumcision of the sons of Sultan Murad III and many other manuscripts from all periods of Turkey, done under the supervision of Richard Ettinghausen.

Vogt-Goknil, Ulya. *Living Architecture: Ottoman.* Photographs by Eduard Widmer. Fribourg: Office du Livre, 1965. Pictures and explanatory descriptions of mosques and the complexes about them, baths, caravansarays, and so on.

Chapter 18

A Century of Stagnation and Decay in the Ottoman Empire and Iran

Privilege, Indolence, and Corruption

The death of Selim II in 1574 ushered in a century and a quarter of disgraceful Ottoman history. A dozen sultans ruled during the period. Four were under sixteen years old when they succeeded to the throne, and most of the rest were undisciplined young men. The wealth, splendor, and ease of the court sapped their energy and morals. The Ottoman political system, which had developed with an absolute sultan as the keystone of the arch of power, sagged badly and began to crumble.

The causes of this obvious change are difficult to pinpoint. The character of Selim II or the influence of Ibrahim and Roxelana has frequently been described as a cancerous development that brought the downfall. Others have ascribed the collapse to an evolving process discernible for a number of years. Certainly, seeds of decay were nurtured for several decades and the causes of the decline were varied and profound. Since its earliest days the Ottoman state supported itself in considerable part from raids and conquest. As frontiers in Europe were extended, the enemy increased in number, and campaign costs became staggering. The booty obtained hardly met expenses, and little was left for palace extravagances which continued nevertheless.

The shift in world trade from the Mediterranean to the Atlantic permitted the Ottomans to take a weakened Egypt. But in the end, this shift brought a marked decline in Ottoman revenues from international trade. Simultaneously, Europe and the Mediterranean world were experiencing a continuing monetary inflation. Government income never quite met expenditures, and most contemporary monarchs were plagued with unbalanced budgets.

In the last two decades of Suleiman's life and in the reigns of Selim II and his successors finances were always straitened. Without loot from beyond the frontiers coming into Istanbul it was difficult to maintain the magnificence to which all had grown accustomed. To make up for this loss of revenue officials were obliged to give liberal sums to the sultan upon promotions. With the reign of Murad III the sultan obtained bribes for appointments, and by the time of Sultan Ibrahim there was open trafficking in

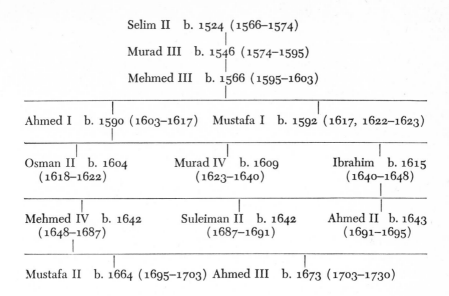

Selim II   b. 1524 (1566–1574)

Murad III   b. 1546 (1574–1595)

Mehmed III   b. 1566 (1595–1603)

Ahmed I   b. 1590 (1603–1617)   Mustafa I   b. 1592 (1617, 1622–1623)

Osman II   b. 1604   Murad IV   b. 1609   Ibrahim   b. 1615
   (1618–1622)   (1623–1640)   (1640–1648)

Mehmed IV   b. 1642   Suleiman II   b. 1642   Ahmed II   b. 1643
   (1648–1687)   (1687–1691)   (1691–1695)

Mustafa II   b. 1664 (1695–1703) Ahmed III   b. 1673 (1703–1730)

offices at the Porte. Such corruption quickly filtered down to the lowliest
official.

As a result of the conquests of Selim I and Suleiman I and the doubling
of the size of the empire, administrative problems became more and more
difficult. As the work of governing increased to overwhelming proportions,
the sultan left more affairs of state to the grand vizir. Suleiman threw over
most of the work to Ibrahim and began to defer to him in policy decisions.
Later sultans frequently were unwilling to perform any onerous duties as
head of the state and gave themselves up to a life of total voluptuousness
and frivolity. Meanwhile, vizirs, beylerbeys and leading officers drew unprecedented power into their hands. Beginning with Selim II's son Murad
III, the sultans gave high office and substantial authority to their favorites,
who were usually ill fitted for the jobs to be done. As long as Mehmed
Sokolli lived, he tried unsuccessfully to prevent this trend, but after his
assassination in 1579 the favorites held full sway.

Equally damaging to affairs of state were the influence and even the
actual formulation of policies by women of the palace. Murad III was controlled by his mother and by his harem favorite, Sultana Safiye Baffo, who
actually ruled the empire while her son Mehmed III occupied the throne.
Daughter of the Venetian governor of Corfu and from the noble Baffo
family, Safiye had been captured by corsairs and presented to Suleiman,
who in turn gave her to his grandson. For a time Murad was so faithful to
Safiye that his mother and sister, the wife of Sokolli, fretted over her undue
power and made presents of pretty and clever slaves to distract Murad's
attention. In at least one respect they were obviously successful: Murad
fathered over 100 children, of whom 20 sons and 27 daughters survived
him.

Another enervating and corrupting practice developed upon the accession of Ahmed I in 1603. Unlike his father, who had had his own nineteen brothers strangled, Ahmed allowed his insane brother, Mustafa, to live closeted in the palace. Henceforth, the usual practice was to immure brothers and sons in the palace, the eldest male of the dynasty succeeding upon the death or abdication of the sultan. Ibrahim, for example, was so frightened when the vizirs came to announce his accession that he barricaded the doors and refused to let them enter until they brought the dead body of his brother.

The sultans were surrounded by fawning officials and courtiers, truckling women and slaves, jugglers, wrestlers, musicians, buffoons, dwarfs, eunuchs, soothsayers, astrologers, and servile literati. They usually found it impossible to differentiate the important from the petty and frequently were of a mentality that bordered upon derangement. Mustafa I was, in fact, quite mad, and Ibrahim's reign of eight years was one long series of wild caprices. Among many other things, the latter disrupted divan meetings, on one occasion calling out the grand vizir to purchase some carts of firewood for the harem kitchens. Ibrahim had a great passion for furs and commanded that the floors and walls of his apartments be carpeted and covered with sable.

In such an atmosphere intrigue flourished. Personal spies, agents, forgeries, intercepted letters, perjury, and malicious gossip became acknowledged techniques of government. Apparently the executions of Suleiman's sons, Mustafa and Bayezid, resulted from machinations in the palace. Another evil of Ottoman society sprang from the slave system in the army and government. Separated from family and country at an early age, soldiers and officials of the court were trained to be loyal to the sultan and to serve him. Wealth, high office, and the sultan's favor were the rewards; the irresolute found the emoluments irresistible and were governed by mercenary motives. Earlier Venetian envoys had remarked on the eagerness of Bayezid II's vizirs for rich presents and pouches of ducats. When the sultans could no longer command true respect from their slaves, officers, and bureaucrats, venality ruled, the power and services of the state degenerating rapidly.

The degradation of sultans, high officers of the state, and the military invited insubordination and rebellion from the rank and file of the armed forces. By the time of Mehmed II the janissaries and sipahis of the palace were already headstrong bodies that had to be placated by monetary donations at festivals and, especially, at accessions of new sultans. The janissaries ordered the retirement of Bayezid II and frequently dictated policies in Suleiman's time. Beginning with the reign of Murad III, soldiers often stormed the palace to demand the head of a particular official, usually one who was obnoxious or corrupt and whose rapacity or incompetence inflicted hardship and injury upon them. Once this type of action proved successful, ambitious officials through clever propaganda instigated movements among the troops to remove rivals.

Equally debilitating were civil wars between different branches of the services and open revolts of garrisons or local forces in the provinces. Bad blood developed between the janissaries and the sipahis of the court. In the reign of Murad III warfare broke out in the streets of Istanbul. Under Mehmed III the janissaries, at the bidding of Safiye Baffo, broke the insubordination of the sipahis. Wishing to weaken the power of the janissaries, Osman II entered into war against Poland with the purpose of thinning the janissaries' ranks; he then intended to set out for Anatolia to gather an army of Kurds and Turkomans to fight the janissaries, a project that led to his dethronement and murder.

The saddest chapter in seventeenth-century Ottoman history was the sixteen-year period embracing the reign of Ibrahim and the minority of Mehmed IV. Ibrahim, a voluptuary of the lowest type, commissioned a trusted woman of the harem to make the rounds of Istanbul baths to seek out special beauties and describe their charms. Her master then contrived to install the more comely in his harem. No person and no property were secure against Ibrahim; he even seduced the daughter of the shaykh al-Islam. In 1648 the janissaries and ulema, led by the shaykh al-Islam, deposed Ibrahim as unfit to rule and placed his seven-year-old son on the throne. Ten days later when the sipahis rioted in his favor, the executioners were sent to his cell. For eight years the Ottoman Empire was the scene of "court intrigue, military insubordination and violence, judicial venality, local oppression and provincial revolt." Ibrahim's mother was murdered, and chaos descended upon Istanbul. Sultana Tarkhan, Mehmed IV's mother, saved the day for her son by appointing an old, experienced, and honest official (Mehmed Köprülü) as grand vizir with absolute power and authority.

With all the evil developments appearing in the Ottoman Empire there persisted evidence of a remarkable devotion to the government and a substantial body of capable, trained, and right-minded officials. Even before the advent of Köprülü there were flashes of old Ottoman vigor. Murad IV was cast in the same mold as his ancestor Selim I, the conqueror of Egypt. At Murad's accession the treasury was empty, the coinage debased, and the soldiery of Istanbul unruly and lawless. His mother had talent and energy and preserved the sultan's authority for several years until he became of age. In 1632 the sipahis rose in revolt, camped for three days in the hippodrome, and called for the heads of seventeen high officials, including the shaykh al-Islam and the grand vizir. The sipahis were appeased, but more heads were demanded. For two months terror reigned at the Porte. Murad perceived that his own turn might easily come unless he acted swiftly. Gathering a few faithful officers and obtaining the full support of the janissaries and the judges, he seized and executed the leaders of the rebellious sipahis and through vigorous measures restored a semblance of order and government to Istanbul and the provinces.

Twice Murad personally led expeditions eastward in Asia Minor. The second time, in 1638, he reconquered Baghdad from the Iranians, personally performing prodigious feats with his sword. As the years progressed, however, he grew hardened to the presence of the executioner. Frequently through mere caprice he removed someone's head, perhaps just for crossing the road in front of him. Furthermore, he took to excessive drinking bouts which undermined his rugged physique and carried him to the grave at the age of twenty-eight.

The Fundamentals of Decline

The foregoing account of the hedonism and corruption that pervaded the upper reaches of the state might well lead one to explain the decline of the empire in terms of a Turkish proverb current at the time: "The fish stinks from the head." However, sultanic rot was not the entire story.

Until about the 1580s, life and society in the Ottoman Empire, especially in Istanbul and the central provinces, seemed to be stable and secure. Incomes were assured, and prices were constant; food and goods were abundant; and optimism reigned. With this confidence and well-being, the population had increased over the century—40 percent in villages, 80 percent in towns and cities. The influx of people into cities was altering their character to the extent that rootless and volatile elements stood ready to respond to emotional situations, introducing a demoralizing instability and doubt.

Likewise, a smugness and an opposition to all innovation arose among so many of the ulema that education faltered and there developed an antipathy to inquiring theology and intellectual sciences. Those supporting innovation in thought or belief were anathematized by popular preachers from Istanbul pulpits. Song, coffee, tobacco, and intellectual sciences were attacked in the same breath with luxury, lax morals, and injustice, all as factors undermining religious faith. An uprising led by these preachers was quelled by Mehmed Köprülü, who exiled the rabble rousers. Murad III built an observatory in Galata in 1577 for astrological purposes but, with instruments as fine as any in Europe, the scientists used it for astronomy. Shortly thereafter an outbreak of the plague was attributed to God's vengeance against those who had penetrated His secrets. The shaykh al-Islam petitioned the sultan to have it dismantled and without waiting, the janissaries leveled it to the ground. Fanaticism and stagnation triumphed along with anti-intellectualism.

At the same time conquests ceased. For centuries the Ottomans had expanded on schedule with the body politic living sumptuously on the conquests. But now Austria, Russia, Iran, the western Mediterranean, and North Africa were proving too removed, and campaigns in those areas too costly, to be pressed fully. When the conquests ended, not only did the elite find new incomes not forthcoming but the central government discovered many of the distant provinces a continuing expense. Treasury reports showed that empire was not a paying proposition.

Compounding this problem was the fact that the increasing military sophistication of European forces created a growing need for improved Ottoman manpower and weaponry. Between Suleiman's accession to the throne and the end of the century, the janissaries increased from 8,000 to 38,000 and the sipahis from 5,000 to 21,000. Under Suleiman many native-born Turks entered these corps, and janissaries were allowed to marry so that by 1600 their grandsons were in the service. Spirit and merit were less significant. Moreover, with the population pressures, the central and provincial governments formed new troops, called *sekbans*, who had to be trained in the use of firearms. Money had to be found to pay the salaries of the larger armies, at a time when income was declining. When payless days arrived the *sekbans* ravaged the countryside. Joined by other malcontents, they, under the name of *jelalis*, menaced Anatolia from one end to the other for many years beginning in 1595. Kara Yaziji led 20,000 of these *jelalis* in 1598, capturing Kayseri, Tokat, and Urfa. These rampages left many dead and large areas deserted as people fled to Iraq, Iran, and Syria. Government troops finally gained control and inaugurated the policy of stationing salaried and privileged janissary contingents in the province. Almost immediately the janissaries joined the merchants, the guild masters, and the ulema in the upper class. They amassed great fortunes by tax-farming extortions, acquiring vast tracts of land and forcing villagers to become sharecroppers. From this janissary infusion came the local dynastic families that dominated the provinces in the eighteenth century, weakening the central government still more.

If not the root causes of all these changes of fortune, as some economic historians contend, at least major complicating factors were the massive influx of gold and silver into Europe from Africa and America, the ensuing monetary and price inflation, and the failure of the Porte to adopt a mercantile economy. The biggest impact of these changes came in the 1580s, producing tremors felt throughout the next century. Silver began to flood the market. In 1510, 1 gold coin equaled 54 silver ones, in 1580, still only 60; but by 1590 it took 120 silver coins to buy 1 gold coin, and by 1640, 250. Within twenty years wheat and meat tripled in price. People on fixed incomes—government officeholders, judges, janissaries, sipahi, endowment-holders—were ruined unless they turned to bribery and corruption. For the central government it was fully as disastrous. In 1534 the treasury had an income of 5 million gold ducats, but by 1591 it was only half that, for taxes were levied in silver. Domestically, the government tried to hold down prices in the face of tremendous increases in Europe. The resulting price differentials stimulated the smuggling of significant quantities of wheat, copper, wool, silk, and other raw and basic materials from the empire, producing local shortages and even greater inflation. Because of the enormous profits to be had, large tax farms conveniently located for this clandestine trade began to be oriented to an agrarian regime better suited to this massive commercialization. Local industries were not as capitalistic as the new European textile and metallurgical enterprises, and within a few years export of silk cloth from Bursa and mohair fabrics from Ankara ceased. The balance of trade was reversed.

Against new Western mercantilist policies the Porte clung to an international free market, concerned only with providing the home market with an abundance of necessities. It encouraged imports and discouraged exports, prohibiting the export of certain commodities for fear of domestic shortages. It saw no danger in extending capitulations to foreigners to the point that by 1600 Europeans controlled the carrying trade even between Mediterranean ports of the empire. When Europeans were ridding themselves of trade medievalisms, the Ottomans embraced traditional forms more zealously. In cultural, political, religious, social, and economic matters, the Ottomans were still convinced of their own superiority.

External Affairs: Europe, the Mediterranean, and the East

Even though there were occasional upsurges of reform and governmental strength and even though Europe was convulsed by bitter struggles such as the Thirty Years' War, external affairs of the empire fell moribund. For leaders at the Porte, however, it was campaigning as usual. Major ghazi raids north from Hungary were trumpeted as softening tactics preceding the main offensive in 1593, even in face of the perilous condition of the treasury. The Hapsburgs were granting special privileges to Ottoman refugees along the Croatian frontier and creating an erratic situation that called for correction. The Ottomans were unequal to the task, however, and a kind of inconclusive border warfare ensued, Hapsburg intrigues against Ottoman suzerainty in Wallachia, Moldavia, and Transylvania lost steam, and the great victory of Ottoman arms in 1596 at Mezökeresztes kept the Hapsburgs at bay. With each side worn-out, peace was signed in 1606 at Zsitva-Torok on the basis of the status quo. This was the first time an Ottoman peace treaty had been negotiated outside the empire; and it was the first time the Hapsburg ruler was recognized as a fellow emperor who did not have to pay tribute. He did, however, make a single cash contribution of 200,000 Dutch guldens. Fortunately for the Ottomans, whose depleted treasury would have made further military engagements precarious, the Thirty Years' War soon engulfed the Hapsburgs.

The question of the security of the eastern Mediterranean was important and perennial. Wheat, barley, rice, sugar, and other vital supplies came from Egypt, as did an annual surplus revenue, sometimes amounting to half a million ducats. With Venice threatening the routes from Egypt because of her use of the new broadsided tall ships, one of which was the match of ten Ottoman ships, the Porte sought to capture Crete from Venice, and war began in 1643. In June 1656 one in a series of inept admirals, Kenan Pasha, whose only recommendation was his position as son-in-law of the sultan's mother, led the fleet out of the Dardanelles to total destruction. Venice occupied Tenedos and Lemnos and blockaded the Straits, failing to land on the Gallipoli peninsula only because of the fortuitous presence of an Ottoman force about to leave for the north. Istanbul was in panic: prices of foodstuffs soared, and property values slumped as many fled for Anatolia.

The shaykh al-Islam, who had blessed the venture, was dismissed and fled to Bursa where he was assassinated.

Ottoman weakness showed in other quarters as well. English and Dutch pirates had begun to operate in the Red Sea in 1613 and Ottoman forces in the Persian Gulf and Indian Ocean became ineffective. Cossacks in the north raided at will on the Black Sea, burning Sinop in 1614 and Yeniköy on the Bosphorus in 1625. Meanwhile the sultans increasingly lost their hold on North Africa, which came to grant hardly more than the nominal gesture toward the caliph.

From 1578 to 1639 the Ottomans had repeated military adventures in the East. Aid from the Crimean khan kept them at Darband on the Caspian, and Kars was converted into a fortress and Eastern base in 1579. Baghdad, Mosul, and all of Mesopotamia were formally annexed in 1586, and a favorable treaty in 1590 with Iran left Tabriz in Ottoman hands. But by 1603 Shah Abbas I had reorganized his army and had added cannon cast in Iran by the English Sherley brothers. Taking the offensive while the Ottomans were still engaged in Hungary, he captured Tabriz, much of the Caucasus, and Kars. In 1623 another Ottoman army was crushed and Abbas took Baghdad and the rest of Mesopotamia. By the middle of the next decade, however, Murad IV had sufficiently revitalized the Ottoman army to take Erivan and to recapture Baghdad in 1638. The peace that was arranged in 1639 settled Eastern affairs for many years, leaving Baghdad, Mesopotamia, and Kars to the sultan and Azerbayjan to the shah.

Resurgence Under the Köprülüs

The problems of state seemed beyond solution. But Mehmed Köprülü assumed office in 1656 with a ruthless determination to cleanse the government. In five years of his grand vizirate some 30,000 officers, officials, judges, and theologians were executed for acts contrary to the interests of the sultan. His son Ahmed Köprülü succeeded to the post and remained grand vizir until his death in 1676. Restoration of law and order under these two vizirs revealed that the strength of the state had not been sapped beyond repair.

Although Mehmed IV gave himself up completely to hunting and to the harem, he remained steadfast in his support of the Köprülüs. In 1663 an army gathered at Edirne to settle the Hungarian frontier. Mehmed placed the battle standard in the hands of Ahmed Köprülü, who then led the largest force assembled since the campaigns of Suleiman I to Belgrad and beyond. However, Ahmed Köprülü was repulsed at the renowned Battle of St. Gothard in Austria.

Ahmed Köprülü then turned his attention to the island of Crete. In 1645 Ibrahim had ordered its conquest because Maltese pirates seized several Ottoman ships and took them to Crete under the shelter of the Venetian rulers. But Candia, the ancient Knossos, resisted sporadic Ottoman assaults for twenty years; to the Porte it became like a running sore. Köprülü conducted a three-year siege of Candia until it fell in 1669; and Crete, in Venetian hands since the Fourth Crusade, became an Ottoman possession.

Next the scene shifted to Galicia, Podolia, and the Ukraine. Cossacks of the Dneiper and the Bug threw off their Polish yoke; joining the Tartars of the Crimea, they sought the protection of the Porte. When the cossack hetman came to Istanbul in 1672, he received a two-horsetail standard from Köprülü and was named sanjakbey of the Ukraine. Poland protested; and the grand vizir led an army that captured Kamenets and Lvov (Lemberg), forcing Poland to surrender Podolia and the Ukraine and to pay an annual tribute of 220,000 ducats. Several more campaigns followed, and a treaty in 1676 incorporated Podolia and the Ukraine into the empire.

Three days after the signing of this treaty Ahmed Köprülü died. Unfortunately, Mehmed IV filled his place with his court favorite, Kara Mustafa. In 1683 he organized the last attack upon Vienna. Early in the spring the ambitious Kara Mustafa gathered more than 200,000 men and marched north through Belgrad, reaching Vienna in the middle of July. For two months the army mined and bombarded the walls of Vienna, which were defended by Count Starhemberg and a force of only 11,000 men. As September approached, the weakness of Vienna and the depletion of its garrison were obvious. The janissaries felt confident that Vienna would fall and fretted that the grand vizir did not order a full assault upon the walls. But Kara Mustafa held back, hoping that the city would surrender: if it did, its wealth would be his, whereas if the soldiers took the city by storm, it would be theirs to loot. He meanwhile ignored the information that King John Sobieski of Poland was approaching with an army of 70,000 to relieve the city. When Sobieski encamped on the heights outside Vienna, Kara Mustafa virtually dismissed his presence as a threat. The debacle occurred on September 12, 1683, with only a small portion of the Ottomans escaping. Kara Mustafa was subsequently executed by the sultan for incompetence.

Retreat from Vienna

In the next four years one calamity after another descended upon the empire. Venetians under generals Morosini and Otto von Königsmarck captured the Morea, Corinth, and Athens. In the siege of Athens the Ottoman defenders made their last stand on the Acropolis, which von Königsmarck shelled, exploding the Parthenon which was serving as a powder magazine. The Austrian forces pursued the victory at Vienna, took Budapest, and seized Hungary. In 1687 the loss of Mohacs so infuriated the Ottoman soldiers that they forced Mehmed's deposition and placed his next younger brother on the throne as Suleiman II. The new sultan, who had been incarcerated in the palace for forty-five years and had passed his time in study, did not know how to cope with the situation. Janissaries and sipahis rioted in Istanbul, partially sacked the city, and completely dislocated the administration. Belgrad fell in 1688; Widin and Nish, in 1689

Vienna in 1529 and at Lepanto in 1571. But the calamities of the seventeenth century left their mark upon the finances and institutions of Ottoman society, especially upon the military. Governorships were given to court favorites and estates were left vacant so that the income would devolve upon the governor. Governorships were sold to new courtiers every two or three years, and a succession of grasping rulers led to desolation in the provinces. When the call for a campaign was sounded, the feudal sipahis hid on their estates or bribed the commanding officer to excuse them. Only the poorest and weakest appeared for duty. At one time a census was ordered, compelling all sipahis in Europe to register in order to expose unfit and fraudulent fief-holders. Unfortunately, the inspectors were so incompetent that they could not distinguish a soldier from a pastry cook, and no one was caught. The number and quality of sipahis so declined that by the eighteenth century there were only 25,000. Since few were equipped with up-to-date firearms and came unattended, they were relegated to digging trenches and hauling cannon.

The degeneration of the janissaries, the sipahis of the court, and palace soldiers was no less deplorable. Captive boys and renegades diminished in numbers as the seventeenth century progressed; and the drafting of Christian boys from Balkan and Anatolian villages ceased entirely during the reign of Murad IV. Ahmed Köprülü in his attempt to restore the vigor of the state reinstituted the program and collected 3,000 boys in 1675, but the policy was dropped after his death. Sons and grandsons of janissaries and court officials joined the ranks; even jugglers, acrobats, and other unsuited persons were rewarded by membership in the privileged bands. Worst of all was the ignoring of merit in questions of promotion, for it meant that officers were not necessarily skilled in military affairs. Many janissaries had other occupations and were members of the corps only on payday. European commanders in the seventeenth century observed the mediocre leadership of Ottoman armies and outmaneuvered them time and time again. By the beginning of the eighteenth century the janissaries had become an ill-disciplined, oddly equipped, turbulent gang, more dangerous at the palace and on the streets of Istanbul and Edirne than against aggressors at the frontiers.

After the loss of Nish in 1689 Suleiman II recognized the desperate plight of his empire and appointed as grand vizir Mustafa Köprülü, brother of the late Ahmed Köprülü. The genius of the Köprülü family ran strong in the new grand vizir. He instituted financial measures that made it possible to assemble an army and regain Nish, Semendra, and Belgrad. Köprülü attempted again the following summer to drive the Austrians further back but lost his life in battle.

The energy of Mustafa II brought a series of minor Balkan victories; but when faced by Prince Eugene of Savoy in 1697 at Zenta the Ottoman companies were crushed, and Hungary and the lands north of Belgrad were lost forever. Meanwhile, the city of Azov surrendered to Peter the Great of Russia after repeated attacks.

Treaty of Karlowitz

In the face of these reverses Mustafa called to the vizirate Husayn Köprülü, who listened to the offers of mediation advanced by Lord Paget, English ambassador to the Porte. For a number of years prior to 1697 Austria was engaged with France in the war of the Palatinate, but the peace of Ryswick freed the Hapsburgs to press their advantage over the decaying Ottoman state. Nevertheless, the courts and armies of Europe were nervously awaiting the momentarily expected death of the childless king of Spain and the anticipated war between the Hapsburgs and Bourbons for that throne. The English, who wished to free their Austrian ally from any possible distraction from the Ottoman quarter, pressed Husayn Köprülü for peace.

After much preliminary correspondence, negotiators met at Karlowitz north of Belgrad in modern Yugoslavia. Under the chairmanship of Lord Paget, the Ottoman minister of foreign affairs and representatives of the Netherlands, Austria, Venice, Poland, and Russia agreed on a general principle that each power should retain what it possessed. Peace was signed in 1699. In addition, the sultan reiterated that he would give his Christian subjects consideration and protection, as he always had. Venice gave up Athens, but retained the Morea and Dalmatia. Austria obtained Transylvania and Hungary with the exception of the Banat of Temesvar. Poland received the provinces of Kamenets and Podolia. As for Russia, only a two-year truce was signed; England wished to keep the Porte occupied with Russia to prevent Ottoman arms from supporting the French in the forthcoming struggle over Spain. Russian envoys, however, came to the Porte and agreed to the treaty of Istanbul in 1700, drawn up on the basis of their Karlowitz armistice.

Karlowitz marks a definite period in Middle Eastern history, especially in the relations of the Porte and Europe. First, it was a treaty with European states arranged by and participated in by one or more nonbelligerent powers, thereby acknowledging that all European states were rightfully concerned with questions of the Middle East. It recognized the interest and importance of the tsars with respect to the Ottoman Empire and the Middle East. The treaty and the negotiations preceding it indicated the entrance of the sultan's Christian subjects into the diplomatic pouches of European foreign offices.

At the peace conference of Karlowitz, European emissaries carried on their negotiations largely through the Ottoman minister's Greek interpreter and assistant, Alexander Mavrocordatos, and carried away the erroneous impression that he was chief of the delegation. But his presence and evident role signified the change that was transpiring in the Ottoman government and its civil service. For a century the great majority of Ottoman officials had been Turks at least of the second and third generations. Many were not educated in the palace and their schooling was less secular than in previous generations. To be sure, they called themselves Ottomans, were proud of that distinction, and had a background and training quite different from most Turks living in Asia Minor. Yet more and more they became dependent upon Christian subjects, chiefly Greeks residing in Istanbul, for secretaries, interpreters, and counselors. After Karlowitz it was not incorrect to speak of the Ottoman Empire as the Turkish empire.

As for Europe, Karlowitz ended the fear of an Ottoman invasion of central Europe and opened an avenue for further aggressions toward Istanbul and the Straits. When Europe was engaged in its own internal struggles, Turkish forces were able to win victories, but from the beginning of the eighteenth century, Ottoman armies and navies were no match for first-rate European soldiers. No longer was the Ottoman Empire a grave military question. As one writer aptly put it, her importance became diplomatic.

Shah Abbas the Great of Isfahan

When the *kizilbash* chieftains left Herat for Qazvin in 1587 to install Abbas on the Safavid throne, the Uzbeg tribes invaded and captured Herat. Shah Abbas met them at Meshed, but crucial rebellions of local princes in his western provinces demanded his immediate return. With the combined forces of local *kizilbash* tribes and an army improvised from Georgian prisoners and held together by his personal leadership, Abbas was able to put down a very serious uprising in Shiraz and soon had central Iran pacified. The Ottoman attack in the west could not be thwarted, however; and by the peace of 1590 with Murad III, Tabriz, some Caspian ports, and surrounding areas were ceded.

During the following seven years Abbas consolidated his position and power, his initial step being the destruction of *kizilbash* forces. Their leaders were killed and their provinces and lands confiscated. With the income from these holdings plus the funds of the royal household Abbas formed a standing army of 10,000 horsemen and 20,000 foot soldiers from prisoners and slaves from Armenia and Georgia. In addition to this strengthening of manpower, Abbas significantly improved his firepower. In 1597 Sir Anthony, Sir Robert, and Sir Thomas Sherley, along with twenty-six other Englishmen, arrived in Isfahan, the new capital, to discuss trade and an alliance against the Turks and the Dutch. They helped Abbas train musketeers and taught his men how to cast cannon. Within a few years Abbas had a force of 12,000 artillery men equipped with 500 brass and bronze cannon with which he effectively challenged the Ottoman armies as well as dissidents within his own state. A new corps of 12,000 mounted musketeers was raised from the peasantry and another 10,000 Georgian prisoners were added to the army. Throughout his reign Abbas continued the policy of turning prisoners of war into soldiers: on one occasion 20,000 Armenians were taken from the region of Erzerum and pressed into service; on another, an expedition into Georgia in 1617, 130,000 prisoners were taken and moved into his state in various areas and capacities.

Beginning in 1597 Abbas began to clear the frontiers of challengers. He drove the Uzbegs from Meshed, Herat, and Khurasan and moved eastward to Balkh. To defend Khurasan he transported thousands of Kurdish horsemen and their families to the frontier, establishing them so securely that many of their descendants still reside in that area. War against the Ottomans erupted in 1601, as already narrated, and Tabriz, Erivan, and Kars were recaptured. With the decline of the Ottomans, Abbas took Kurdistan and Shirvan from Ahmed I and in 1623 recaptured Baghdad, Mosul, and Diyarbakir, restoring to Iran the territories held at the time of Shah Ismail. On other fronts Abbas defeated the Moguls, taking Kandahar; seized the island of Bahrayn in the Persian Gulf; and with British aid drove the Portuguese from Hormuz in 1622, founding the important trading post of Bandar Abbas. When Shah Abbas died in 1629, his land was at peace and prospering. In contrast, the Ottoman Empire was declining, Russia was experiencing her Time of Troubles, and the Moguls in India were losing hold of that country.

Administration and Trade Under Abbas
By the year 1600 Shah Abbas had established his authoritarian rule over most of the provinces of Iran. Warfare was relegated to the frontiers and was fought by professional soldiers. The administration of the provinces was overseen by royal governors, all of whom were subservient to the royal will. Like Allahvardi Khan, governor of Fars and one of Abbas's first appointees, many of these officials were slaves. In due course, more than a fifth of the central government came from the *gulam* ranks. Each city had its mayor, responsible for taxes and civil order. The numerous craft guilds were strictly regulated, their chief masters meeting with the mayor once a month to debate taxes and matters of general concern.

Abbas had a special concern for commerce, domestic and foreign. To connect all major cities throughout the land, Abbas provided a network of roads that every 20 miles or so had a secure caravansaray where several caravans could spend the night safe from marauders. With regard to the silk trade, which was important and highly profitable, Abbas showed similar initiative. Since Armenian communities were basic in the silk trade, with one of their centers at Julfa on the Aras River in Azerbayjan, Abbas imported 3,000 Armenian families and created New Julfa for them on the outskirts of Isfahan, exempting them from various taxes, and permitting them to elect their own mayor. A monopoly over the silk trade was established and these Armenians ran it for him. To exploit European enthusiasm for fine porcelain from China, Abbas brought 300 Chinese potters to Isfahan to supply pottery in the Chinese style. Not only was an additional export developed but an important tradition was established, for the most skillful and resourceful potters since the seventeenth century have been in Isfahan.

It was not long before Iranian goods were highly esteemed and their quality and artistry became legendary. Among the more important were silk and wool carpets and textiles of all types, porcelains, miniature paintings, enamelwork, glassware, dyes, jewelry, lacquered and inlaid woods, bookbindings, leather goods, gold and silver plates, vases, and fine steel swords. Since many of these items were the product of court workshops, they were of a design and workmanship that were nearly always superb and could be afforded only by the most wealthy. Such examples of these artifacts that have survived are found in the leading museums of the world or in the hands of private collectors.

Undoubtedly the best-known articles have been the Persian carpets. The finest of these carpets were made in court workshops for the court and the wealthiest patrons, few if any being exported. In their manufacture only materials of the highest quality were employed. Sheep were specially bred for their delicate wool and were tended like children so that their wool would never be soiled or roughened. Even the water for washing the wool was important. Court painters designed the carpets, generally employing refined stylized motifs that incorporated gardens, animals, and pools. Great carpet factories were located at the time of Abbas at Kerman, Joshaghan, Shustar, Herat, Hamadan, Tabriz, and Karabagh, but most cities and provinces produced fine carpets which were much in demand, especially in Europe. Rugs manufactured for export, though of a lesser quality, were nevertheless rich in color, design, and fabrication, most coming from workshops closely allied to the court. However, even the carpet-weaving of nomads and villagers followed the highest traditions.

Skills in other manufactures and arts were also highly developed. Velvets, brocades, and embroideries were produced with the greatest care and exquisite design, and the finest pieces of these materials were, of course, very costly. Painting and the decorative arts were of a highly intricate style that displayed a keen sense of blending floral and geometric patterns to create a pleasing whole. The pierced and repoussé work of goldsmiths and silversmiths has hardly been surpassed. Potters learned how to decorate their wares in many colors, often firing seven or more colors at once on large tiles.

The Splendor of Isfahan

The internal stability established by Shah Abbas the Great encouraged a great increase in trade, raised levels of production, opened wider avenues of opportunity for many, and assured a great prosperity for all. At the court in Isfahan the resulting wealth transformed the style of life to a scale of lavishness seldom seen. European visitors gave nearly incredible descriptions of the dazzling opulence: Abbas on his throne surrounded by several hundred courtiers clothed in gold and silver with an array of gray, scarlet, yellow, green, plum, blue, and maroon silks embroidered with the rarest of jewels. What Abbas lacked in terms of the size of his palaces he made up for in number—over 100 in Isfahan alone. Each of these palaces was a masterpiece of design and decoration, as can be seen from Ali Kapu and Chahil Sutun, which still stand.

In the center of Isfahan, Abbas laid out a great open "square," 560 yards by 174 yards and surrounded by magnificent buildings, which served as the site for polo—the popular sport of the courtiers at that time—horse races, fireworks displays, and other spectacles. On one side of the square was Ali Kapu, on a lovely pavilion in which Abbas liked to lounge with his courtiers and watch the festivities of the square. On another side was the imperial mosque, Masjid-i-Shah, the masterpiece of Safavid architecture. An impressive pointed archway more than eighty feet high led to an inner courtyard surrounded by a graceful two-storied arcade. Opposite the entrance was another portal leading to the mosque proper, whose walls carried a large dome, the exterior of which was covered by exquisite tiles with arabesque patterns in dark blue and green on a sky-blue background. On another side of the area was a great covered bazaar with a monumental arched entrance. The dome of the imperial mosque served as a landmark of the center of the heavily walled city, which had 600,000 inhabitants and boasted 1,802 caravansarays, 162 mosques, 273 public baths, and 48 colleges and academies. Isfahan with its rich verdure, pools, and watercourses was a flower-lover's paradise, its gardens displaying roses, jasmine, stocks, lilies, irises, pansies, sweet williams, larkspurs, sweet sultans, poppies, narcissus, and many others in every variety and shade. Abbas himself laid out the gardens, planned the buildings, and even gave detailed instructions to the workmen.

Decline and End of Safavid Rule

For more than a hundred years following his death, Abbas the Great's Safavid heirs succeeded to the throne, all their reigns equally odious. Had it not been for the strength of administration, the quality of many of the governors and officials, the vitality of the commerce, the general peace and prosperity, and the weakness of the forces beyond the frontiers, the dynasty and the state might well have disappeared.

The seeds of this decline might be said to have been sown by Abbas himself. Because he could brook no rival and feared the popularity of his own sons, he had had his eldest executed and the other two blinded, making them ineligible to rule. In addition, he instituted the insidious practice of keeping the royal princes as indulged prisoners within the palace, in the company of women and servants who satisfied their every sensual whim. Catapulted to the throne after years of sheltered pampering, their incompetence and incorrigibility were compounded by the influence of scheming, ignorant women and fawning, unscrupulous slave officials. Often naive and upright when ascending the throne, a young shah would be intentionally corrupted with drink and perverted by court attendants to enable them to rule without his interference.

Consequently, upon his death in 1629, Abbas was succeeded by a seventeen-year-old grandson, Shah Sufi, whose debauchery was thoroughgoing. He murdered his mother, a sister, his favorite wife, army generals, provincial governors, and many of the court officials. Nevertheless, the government under Sufi did have the strength and will to repel Uzbeg incursions into Khurasan and suppress rebellions in Gilan, although the Moguls repossessed Kandahar and the Ottomans retook Baghdad.

Sufi was followed by his nine-year-old son, Abbas II, who started with real promise and at the age of sixteen showed vigor and flashes of his great-grandfather's character by leading an army in the recapture of Kandahar and by conciliating the Uzbeg chiefs. Shortly, however, he turned to drink and sensualities, murdering many around him. Upon his death from excesses at thirty-three in 1668, he was succeeded by his seventeen-year-old son who first took the title Sufi II but because of illness and the foreboding omen of Cossack raids in Shirvan was recrowned the following year as Shah Suleiman. He reigned (it could not be said that he ruled) for twenty-six long years, dying in 1694. A drunkard and a voluptuary, he thought little about the state: once, when told that the Turks were about to attack, he replied that it made no difference to him, as long as he could keep Isfahan. He was weak and vicious, especially when inebriated, and had many of the generals and government officials executed, leaving more of the administration to his palace cronies, who were only too happy to step into the vacuum the shah was creating. When he died in 1694 he had already executed his eldest son and left the choice between his other sons to the eunuchs and courtiers of the palace. They chose Husayn. Having been shut up in the harem of the palace for twenty-six years, Husayn was ignorant, superstitious, extremely credulous, and easily influenced—just the kind of shah the courtiers desired.

Subject to excessive piety, Husayn inaugurated his reign by prohibiting the use of wine: he had all the wine jars in the palace broken and would not permit the Armenians who controlled the wine trade to sell in Isfahan. As a youth he had become a partisan of religious teachers and leaders, or *mullahs,* so much so that many jokingly called him Mullah Husayn. Through all, Husayn's piousness was never lost. In 1706 he organized a pilgrimage to the holy shrine at Qum, the site of the family tombs. Over 60,000 accompanied him on this outing, the tents and pavilions of his retinue stretching out for more than six miles along the country road. This venture proved so enjoyable that the next year he went with an equal number of retainers on the 600-mile pilgrimage to Meshed, remaining there a whole year. The extravagance of this expedition not only emptied the treasury but ruined all the provinces through which it passed.

Thanks to an aunt who prevailed upon him to permit her to drink in the palace, Husayn did not remain abstemious for long. Soon wine flowed freely everywhere. Husayn became licentious, and his agents were constantly on the lookout for attractive faces to kidnap for his harem. Unable to curb his lavish habits and faced with the mounting cost of maintaining a standing army with cannon and muskets, Husayn's ministers had to find additional income. The most convenient means was to squeeze more revenue from the provinces. Under Sufi I and Abbas II many provinces had been transferred to the royal household and their governorships sold to court favorites, who reimbursed themselves by gouging the inhabitants. Upon the raiding of Kandahar by Baluchis, Husayn sent a Georgian general as the new governor in 1703. He turned out to be exceedingly harsh and rapacious, very energetic and clever, and adopted such severe measures against the Ghalzai Afghan inhabitants that they rose in revolt under Mir Ways and in 1709 killed the Georgian governor and most of his retinue. Husayn sent an army from Isfahan in 1711 to destroy Mir Ways, but being ill-paid and divided by jealousies among three different components, it was routed in front of the walls of Kandahar. Mir Ways thus became an independent ruler, calling himself regent of Kandahar.

In 1715 Mir Ways was succeeded by his sixteen-year-old son Mahmud, an ambitious youth who took the offense and began to attack the shah's kingdom, advancing to a point only nine miles from Isfahan. The battle for Isfahan was joined in March 1722, with Mahmud occupying the Armenian suburb of New Julfa and investing the city. After a six-month siege which saw 60,000 inhabitants killed by starvation or epidemics, and 20,000 killed in fighting, Husayn surrendered. In a humiliating ceremony Husayn went out to Mahmud's headquarters and there, with his own hands, took from his turban the imperial plume of heron's feathers set with jewels—the sign of sovereignty—placed it on Mahmud's head, and bade him rule in peace.

During the siege Tahmasp, one of Husayn's older sons, escaped from Isfahan and made his way to Qazvin, where he was recognized as Shah Tahmasp II. Affairs were not favorable, however. The Ottomans seized Tiflis, Tabriz, and Hamadan; Peter the Great of Russia, outfitting a fleet on the Caspian, took Shirvan and Gilan, and compelled Tahmasp II to sign a treaty in July 1722, ceding to Russia Darband, Baku, Gilan, Astarabad, and Mazandaran in exchange for Peter's commitment to drive the Afghans from Isfahan. When Mahmud learned of the proposed Russian incursion to place Tahmasp II back on the throne in Isfahan, he had all the members of the Safavid family assembled in the palace courtyard; he and two of his friends then hacked them to death, except for Husayn and two small children whom Husayn shielded with his own body. Mahmud was rapidly growing insane and died in 1725, being succeeded by his cousin Ashraf. The Ottoman armies meanwhile pressed forward into Iran, asserting that they planned to restore the Safavids to their rightful possessions. Ashraf thereupon had Husayn executed and sent his head to the Ottoman commander to forestall his need to attack Isfahan.

Meanwhile Tahmasp II gathered an army in Mazandaran in 1727, being supported by Fath Ali Khan, the chief of the Qajar tribe, and Nadir Kuli Khan of the Afshar tribe, each bringing several thousand experienced soldiers. They marched into Khurasan and recaptured Meshed and Herat from the Abdali Afghans in 1729; along the way Nadir Khan murdered his rival, Fath Ali, and thus became the sole commander of the royal army. The next year Nadir routed the Afghans under Ashraf, expelling them from Isfahan and Shiraz. Tahmasp II returned as shah to Isfahan but gave powers of taxation and independent control to Nadir. In 1732 Nadir dethroned him and sent him as a prisoner to Khurasan, where he was later killed. Nadir put Tahmasp's infant son on the throne as Abbas III, but the child died in 1736 and Nadir assumed the title shah, the powers of which he had been holding for several years. Safavid rule had ended.

REFERENCES: Chapter 18

Works important to this chapter are also found in Chapters 7, 12, 13, 14, 15, 16, and 17.

Bayerle, Gustav. *Ottoman Diplomacy in Hungary.* Bloomington, Ind.: Indiana University Press, 1972. There are 107 documents (in Hungarian with English summaries) written by pashas of Buda to Austrian officials and the emperor around 1590. They throw considerable light on the relations between the two great powers at the time.

Heyd, Uriel. *Ottoman Documents on Palestine, 1552–1615.* London: Oxford University Press, 1960. Valuable source material by an outstanding Israeli scholar.

Lockhart, Laurence. *The Fall of the Safavi Dynasty and the Afghan Occupation of Persia.* New York: Cambridge University Press, 1958. Deals largely with the eighteenth century. Excellent.

O'Kane, John (trans.). *The Ship of Sulaiman.* The Persian Heritage series. New York: Columbia University Press, 1972. A Persian story about an embassy from Shah Suleiman in the last half of the seventeenth century from Isfahan to the king of Siam. A significant contribution to Asian commercial, economic, and diplomatic history.

Rycaut, Paul. *History of the Turkish Empire, 1623–1677.* Two volumes in one. London: Clabell & Roper, 1680. A detailed account by an eyewitness.

———. *The Present State of the Ottoman Empire.* London: Clabell & Roper, 1686. Really a third volume to the reference cited above.

Wright, Walter Livingston, Jr. *Ottoman Statecraft: The Book of Counsel for Vezirs and Governors of Sari Mehmed Pasha, the Defterdar, Turkish Text with Introduction, Translation, and Notes.* Princeton, N.J.: Princeton University Press, 1935. This is the translation of a book written by a Turkish ex-official pointing out the weaknesses and evils in the Ottoman system and the sources of its corruption.

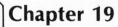

Chapter 19

The Decline and Retreat of the Ottoman Empire

Weak Sultans

The sultans of the eighteenth century were weak figures, unequal to the vicissitudes facing the empire. To cope with the corruption, inefficiency, incompetence, harem intrigue, vested interests, and indolence of the court, will power was required; to comprehend the policies of state, training and education were important. Each of the sultans, however, came to the throne after decades of confinement; none had opportunity to learn the art of statecraft or to develop an effective personality. Usually his mother or the harem favorite dominated the government; and though clever and forceful, these women lacked the experience to conduct the business of government.

Ahmed III was frivolous and lighthearted, interested in birds and his tulip gardens. Fortunes were spent on festivals and illuminations for the women of the court. Mahmud I loved literature and surrounded himself with second-rate poets and men of letters. The rest of his energy was devoted to building mosques, palaces, kiosks, and other structures of questionable utility. Osman III, Mustafa III, and Abdul Hamid I were well along in years when they ascended the throne; and they proved to be mild, ineffectual rulers. The last may at least be commended for the freer life he permitted his nephew Selim, the heir apparent; for with Selim's accession in 1789 the more vigorous attempts at reform that marked the nineteenth century began.

Wars with Russia and Austria

Austria and Venice contested the power of the Ottomans in the seventeenth century; and the latter's role fell in the eighteenth century to Russia. Although Karlowitz ceded Azov and about eighty miles of hinterland, Tsar Peter was not satisfied. The Black Sea, the Straits—an outlet to the Mediterranean which would mean freer commerce with the West—and, most important, Tsargrad (Constantinople) all beckoned the Russians on against the Ottomans. In one sense Russia could never be fully admitted to the polity of Europe as long as control over these waterways and the seat of empire were denied to the tsars.

After the defeat at Pultava in 1709 Charles XII of Sweden fled to Turkey, where he induced Ahmed III to heed the pleas of the Crimean khan for an

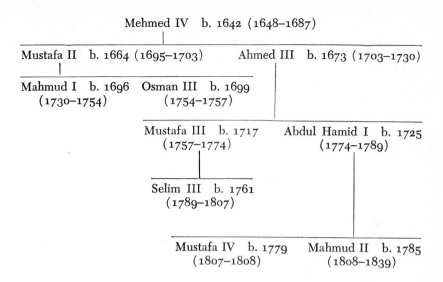

Mehmed IV b. 1642 (1648–1687)

Mustafa II b. 1664 (1695–1703)   Ahmed III b. 1673 (1703–1730)

Mahmud I b. 1696   Osman III b. 1699
  (1730–1754)   (1754–1757)

Mustafa III b. 1717   Abdul Hamid I b. 1725
  (1757–1774)   (1774–1789)

Selim III b. 1761
  (1789–1807)

Mustafa IV b. 1779   Mahmud II b. 1785
  (1807–1808)   (1808–1839)

expedition against Russia. When Peter led his army across the Pruth in 1711, he fell into an Ottoman trap. To escape he accepted the famous surrender of the Pruth, which returned Azov to the sultan, razed all fortresses in the neighborhood, and relinquished the right to have Russian ships in the Black Sea. Ahmed III dismissed the grand vizir for agreeing to such easy terms when the Ottoman army might have destroyed Peter and crushed the Russians for decades.

Peace with Russia and Austria freed the Ottomans to regain their possessions lost to Venice at Karlowitz. Using some naval clashes as a pretext, the grand vizir swept Venice from the Peleponnesus and the islands of the Archipelago in 1715 and proceeded to attack Venetian towns along the Adriatic. These victories enticed Austria to break with the Porte. Prince Eugene won several smashing engagements, capturing Temesvar and Belgrad. Britain, as eager as ever to mediate peace, arranged the treaty of Passarowitz of 1718, which ceded to Austria all the conquered territory but permitted the Ottomans to retain the lands taken from Venice.

Further aggression against Turkey was suspended for more than a decade, until Austria and Russia formed an alliance and acted together. The latter overran the Crimea, captured Azov, and demanded the sultan's lands from the Danube to the Caucasus. The Porte refused, and Austria entered the fray. When a Turkish resurgence in 1739 pushed the fighting back to the walls of Belgrad, the Marquis de Villeneuve, French ambassador to the Porte, skillfully engineered the amazing treaty of Belgrad, which returned that city to Turkey. Even though Russia, too, won great victories, she gained little: an unfortified Azov and permission to trade in the Black Sea area on condition that goods be carried on Turkish ships. For thirty-five years after the treaty the sultans rested in peace, and the growing weakness of the Ottomans was unrevealed. In fact, by "depriving" the Ottomans of military experience and the necessity for new arms for a full generation, the treaty of Belgrad accelerated the decline.

Treaty of Capitulations

As reward for the brilliant mediation of the Marquis de Villeneuve at Belgrad and through his continued representations at the Porte, France obtained in 1740 the renowned Treaty of Capitulations. France and England, and to a lesser extent the Netherlands, had valuable commercial interests in the Middle East. Ottoman wars with Venice, Austria, and Russia disturbed their trade, a factor that animated English and Dutch mediation at Karlowitz and Passarowitz.

The trading privileges that the French enjoyed under the Mamluk sultans in Egypt since the treaty obtained in 1251 by Saint Louis were reconfirmed by Suleiman in 1528; and a regular treaty with France was concluded, though never formally ratified, in 1536, a treaty similar to those made with Venice, Florence, Naples, and Hungary, by Mehmed II and Bayezid II. The French treaty was reaffirmed in 1569, 1581, 1597, 1604, and 1673. Again in 1740 the new treaty of eighty-two articles obtained by de Villeneuve reiterated the chief points of previous treaties.

The significant points of the treaty of 1740, to which almost all similar treaties of later dates with foreign states refer, granted Frenchmen the right to travel and trade in any part of the Ottoman Empire. Frenchmen and their goods were exempted from all forms of taxation except ad valorem import and export duties which were set in article 37 at 3 percent. The French ambassador and consuls were recognized as having full jurisdiction over Frenchmen in the Ottoman Empire, and no Frenchman could be arrested by an Ottoman officer except in the presence of a French consular official. The French were allowed to possess and erect churches of their own and worship freely, special considerations being made for French pilgrims and monks in the Holy Land. The property of Frenchmen in the Ottoman Empire fell upon death to the French consul, who administered the estate of the deceased according to French law. Moreover, heirs were permitted to acquire and remove their inheritance.

Most important was the article that gave France the privilege of enrolling under her flag and her protection Portuguese, Sicilians, Catalans, Anconans, and others who had no ambassador or consul at the Porte. All Roman Catholics were considered and treated as Frenchmen, giving them a very special consideration among Christians in the Ottoman Empire. Furthermore, France and other nations which had such an article in their treaties (England, Austria, the Netherlands, and later Russia) could sell *barats* to Ottoman subjects—usually Greeks, Armenians, Jews, and Balkan Christians—extending trading privileges to holders of such documents. As a result of these provisions a large portion of the exterior trade of the Ottoman Empire was exempt from all control by the Porte.

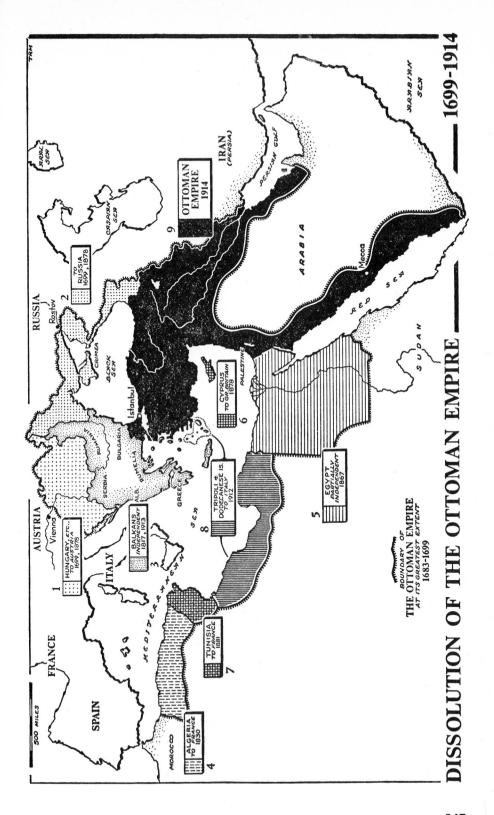

DISSOLUTION OF THE OTTOMAN EMPIRE

1699-1914

BOUNDARY OF
THE OTTOMAN EMPIRE
AT ITS GREATEST EXTENT
1683-1699

1 HUNGARY, ETC.,
TO AUSTRIA
1699, 1878

2 TO
RUSSIA
1699, 1878

3 BALKANS
INDEPENDENT
1817, 1913

4 ALGERIA
TO FRANCE
1830

5 EGYPT,
PARTIALLY
INDEPENDENT
1867

6 CYPRUS
TO GR. BRITAIN
1878

7 TUNISIA
TO FRANCE
1881

8 TRIPOLI &
DODECANESE IS.
TO ITALY
1912

9 OTTOMAN
EMPIRE
1914

SPAIN
FRANCE
MOROCCO
ITALY
AUSTRIA
Vienna
RUSSIA
Rostov
CASPIAN SEA
ARAL SEA
TURKESTAN
CRIMEA
BLACK SEA
SERBIA
RUMANIA
BULGARIA
ALB. RUMELIA
GREECE
Istanbul
AEGEAN SEA
IRAN
(PERSIA)
MEDITERRANEAN SEA
PALESTINE
ARABIA
Mecca
PERSIAN GULF
RED SEA
SUDAN

500 MILES

Treaty of Kuchuk Kainarji

Upon the termination of the Seven Years' War in 1763 the powers of Europe were free to turn their attentions to Poland and the Ottoman Empire. They were, however, compelled to weave these ambitions into the general European diplomatic fabric. When Frederick II and Catherine II signed their "unholy alliance," agreeing to cooperate with respect to Poland and the Ottoman Empire, England acquiesced in the partition of Poland and refused to oppose Catherine's designs upon the Ottoman Empire. However, Louis XV sent Vergennes as ambassador and Baron de Tott as military adviser to strengthen the Porte's position against Russian pressure. Upon the advice of Vergennes, Mustafa III unwisely rushed headlong into war against Russia in 1768, when his demands with respect to Poland were not met. Since the Turkish armies were quite unprepared, the Russians occupied Jassy and Bucharest and within two years held all of Moldavia and Wallachia.

Meanwhile a Russian fleet, directed by John Elphinston, sailed unmolested from the Baltic to the Aegean where Count Orloff assumed command. His raids upon the coasts aroused Greek hopes, but eventually left the inhabitants at the mercy of the Turkish soldiers and disillusioned with the Russians. Orloff proceeded to win a victory at Chios and destroyed the Ottoman fleet. Nonetheless, Elphinston's plea to force the Dardanelles and storm Istanbul was ignored, until Baron de Tott had repaired the fortifications sufficiently to thwart Orloff's attempt. Foiled, Orloff seized Lemnos, only to be driven off by an Ottoman admiral commanding a crew quickly mustered from the streets of Istanbul. Orloff sailed off to Egypt to threaten the Porte from that direction.

Russian successes in the Danubian provinces excited the Austrians in 1771 to sign a secret treaty of assistance with the Porte, pledging military support if the Russians crossed the Danube. Informed of this maneuver by the English ambassador, Berlin prevented war between Austria and Russia by speeding the partition of Poland among the three neighbors and simultaneously inducing Catherine to relinquish her conquests on the Pruth and the Danube. Partition of the Ottoman Empire was saved by the sacrifice of Poland! Desultory fighting came to a halt in 1774 upon the signing of the treaty of Kuchuk Kainarji.

This famous treaty was a landmark in Russo-Ottoman relations for nearly a century and a half. The sultan regained possession of Bessarabia, Moldavia, Wallachia, and the Greek islands, and Catherine's hold on Azov and the political but not the religious independence of the Crimean Tartars were confirmed. Navigation on the Danube was freed, and the Black Sea was opened to Russian shipping; but an Ottoman fort controlled the entrances of the Bug and the Dnieper on the Black Sea. A permanent Russian ambassador was accepted at the Porte; and Russian consuls could be stationed wherever the tsar thought necessary. The right of Russian pilgrimages to holy places was admitted, and permission to build a Russo-Greek church in the Galata section of Istanbul was granted.

Of particular significance for the future were articles 12 and 14, which stated in vague terms that the sultan promised to protect the Christian religion in his empire. More important, Russia as a "neighboring and sincerely friendly Power" could offer the sultan representations in behalf of his Christian subjects and could speak in favor of Bessarabia and the Danubian provinces. These two articles served Russia in the nineteenth century as useful wedges in her ambitions in the Balkans and the Straits.

Peace of Jassy

The actions and diplomacy of Austria were pursued to prevent Russia from gaining an advantageous position over the Ottoman Empire. As soon as the sultan agreed to the terms of Kuchuk Kainarji, Austria delivered her demand for the province of Bukovina as a reward for nonbelligerency during the Russian war. When Vienna ordered the occupation, the Porte recognized its helplessness and ceded Bukovina to the Hapsburgs.

For a decade and a half the sultan was left in peace, while Russia and Austria discussed the problems and possibilities of further Ottoman disintegration. By the treaties of Ainali Kavak in 1779 and 1784 Russia's role in selecting the khan of the Crimea for the "independent" Tartars was conceded, and the fate of the Crimea established by annexation in 1783. Yet the "Greek project" of Catherine II and Joseph in 1782 marked the first specific design for partitioning the Ottoman Empire. Austria would obtain Serbia, Bosnia, Herzegovina, Dalmatia, and various fortresses on the Danube; Venice's share was to be the Morea, Crete, and Cyprus; France was to be rewarded with Egypt and Syria; and Russia would be favored by a Christian kingdom of Dacia under Prince Potemkin to include Bessarabia, Moldavia, and Wallachia. And if Istanbul were taken, a Greco-Russo-Byzantine empire would be re-created under the emperorship of Catherine's grandson, appropriately named Constantine. War broke in 1787. Austria and Russia won initial victories; but international complications in Europe and serious internal disorders in the Hapsburg realm enabled the Porte to obtain the peace of Sistova with Austria (1791) and the peace of Jassy with Russia (1792). The former returned the frontier to the status quo ante, but the latter allowed Russia to advance her frontier to the Dniester River.

The second (1793) and third (1795) partitions of Poland, the death of Catherine II (1796), and the outbreak of the French Revolution gave Selim III (1789–1807) a relief from European aggression. Napoleon's rise naturally implicated the Ottoman Empire in the wars and diplomacy of that era. Incidents and circumstances of those affairs, however, fall more into the pattern of nineteenth-century European imperialism in the Middle East. The radical upsetting of the balance of power in the world, especially in Europe after 1815, was reflected in European intrigue and activities at the Porte. Meanwhile, significant changes transpired in the Ottoman Empire to weaken the state still further and to sweep the entire Middle East to the brink of complete disintegration into petty political units.

The Phanariotes

One of the more baneful developments at the Porte was the insidious avarice of the so-called Phanariotes. In the seventeenth century the residence of the patriarch was established in a district bordering the Golden Horn, taking its name Phanar from the Greek word meaning "lighthouse." Earlier, most Greeks who served the sultan had become Ottomans, but by the end of the seventeenth century it was no longer necessary for Greeks to adopt Islam to hold office. Out of this circumstance grew the term *Phanariot*, used to designate a Greek or Hellenized Christian in Ottoman service.

The ascendancy of the Phanariotes took place gradually in the last half of the seventeenth century. Alexander Mavrocordatos, who studied law at Bologna and medicine at Padua and who published learned works in Italian, became attached to the Köprülü family as a secretary. He then moved to the position of chief interpreter *(terjuman)* of the minister of foreign affairs *(reis effendi)*. As such, he became known in the West as dragoman of the Porte. Alexander served as principal negotiator in drafting the treaty of Karlowitz, and his descendants held high posts in the Ottoman service for more than a century. In fact, all Phanariotes of distinction in the eighteenth century either had Mavrocordatos blood in their veins or had wives of that family. From the Phanariotes came patriarchs, bishops, dragomans of the Porte, ambassadors, and governors of Moldavia and Wallachia from 1714 to 1821.

Of these posts, the most lucrative and therefore the most expensive to purchase were the governorships of Moldavia and Wallachia. Consequently, Phanariot governors *(hospodars)* found it necessary to sell every office and favor, ruling over their subjects in a fashion identical to that of the sultan in Istanbul. By the end of Phanariot rule Rumanian peasants had fallen to an estate lowlier than any in the Balkans. Certainly, the tone of society in Bucharest and Jassy was more corrupt and cynical than in Belgrad, Sofia, or Athens.

Yet the Danubian principalities remained the larder of Istanbul. Wheat, butter, cheese, honey, wax, lumber, horses, and livestock of every sort were sent to Istanbul. More than 500,000 head of sheep moved every year. As the production of Anatolia became less available the Danubian provinces assumed greater importance as an imperial granary, especially after the loss of the Crimea. Certain portions were requisitioned by the palace; and trade remained in the hands of Armenians, Jews, and Greeks. The evils of Phanariot rule were augmented by the frequent wars of the eighteenth century fought on Danubian soil and by four Russian occupations which increased the misery of the peasants by their wholesale requisitioning, by their spread of epidemics, and by the plundering and havoc of their ill-disciplined troops.

Perhaps because Rumanians under Phanariot rule were governed by Christian princes, the Danubian principalities were much freer from the political and financial control of the Porte than most provinces of the empire. However, by the middle of the eighteenth century the process of disintegration had reached a point where any energetic and ambitious governor could build up his own independent military, political, and economic power and defy the commands of the sultan.

Rebellious Provinces

To describe each one of these petty lords and to relate the incidents of his rise to power and his local tyrannies would be monotonous and superfluous. In Europe the best known were Ali Pasha of Janina, who ruled Epirus from 1788 to 1822, and Osman Pasvanoglu of Widin, who terrorized the lower Danube from Belgrad to the sea. Both recognized the Porte's suzerainty and occasionally sent tribute to the sultan; yet each regularly defied the central government and entered into diplomatic relations with European powers.

The most famous of the quasi-independent lords in other parts of the empire were the beys and deys (rulers) of the Barbary states of North Africa. Even in the sixteenth century at the heyday of the sultan's power, the authority of the Porte in Algiers, Tunis, and Tripoli was never very imposing. In the eighteenth century, North African corsairs recognized the sultan's overlordship only to the extent of sending him an annual token gift.

With respect to the weakening of central government and the Porte's loss of revenue, the more significant developments of the eighteenth century occurred in Egypt, Syria, Iraq, and Anatolia. The Mamluk system was never fully eradicated by Selim I or Suleiman's Ibrahim Pasha, and once the reins from Istanbul were loosened, it flourished again. Ali Bey directed Egypt on an independent course, and Count Orloff made overtures to him following the Russian fiasco in the Greek islands. From 1749 to 1831 Iraq was in the hands of another Mamluk dynasty, and Mosul was held for more than a century by the Jalili family. The al-Azm family ruled in Damascus; other families held Jerusalem; and Aleppo was so torn with strife and civil wars that between 1765 and 1785 hundreds of villages disappeared.

The most adventurous career was that of Ahmed al-Jezzar (Ahmed "the Butcher"). Of Bosnian origin, he obtained his nickname from his ruthless tactics when he was employed by Ali Bey of Egypt. Gaining the favor of Istanbul, he became pasha of Sidon and Acre, augmenting his territory later to include Damascus. Ahmed al-Jezzar Pasha maintained a private army of Albanians, Moroccans, and fellow Bosnians, built a fleet, established monopolies, made commercial agreements with Western merchants, and created an efficient governmental organization.

Even in Anatolia an identical situation prevailed in the eighteenth century. *Dereh beys* ("valley lords"), who were leaders of local families, seized power; and the central government was compelled to appease their whims in order to obtain any recognition of authority or any compliance with respect to law, taxes, and military support.

Search for Reform

Beset by foreign powers and enfeebled by internal political dissolution, the empire somehow persisted. In Istanbul and other cities the many trade and craft guilds served as a powerful bonding agent, giving individuals a sense of security and a definite place in society. (There were even guilds for prostitutes and pickpockets!) Guild members found their lives regulated by their guild, experienced their social life in the guild, and had their contacts with government almost exclusively through guild leadership. In the countryside, landowners avoided political association as much as possible, and peasants were concerned only with their landlords. Simple village life was the chief aim of the majority.

Nevertheless, many Ottomans perceived that the state was stagnating and predicted that the future of the empire was surely doomed unless reforms were undertaken. Ex-officials of the government wrote treatises deploring practices that inevitably led to corruption and inefficiency. Notable essays on these points appeared in 1616, 1630, 1657, 1725, and 1777; each of them condemned most emphatically the practice of selling offices and recounted specific abuses by every official from the sultan down to the lowliest scribe. In a book written in 1725 a former imperial treasurer prescribed as a remedy a return to the higher ethical and moral values that had prevailed two centuries earlier in the reign of Suleiman.

No reforms could be initiated with any hope of success unless supported by the sultan. In fact, it was necessary that reforms should come from the hands of the sultan himself! Many sultans of the eighteenth century desired reforms but did not know how to inaugurate them. Selim III, who succeeded to the throne in 1789, introduced many innovations and hoped to change the course of affairs from further decay to progress and growth. But a reorientation of the government demanded the labors of many dedicated souls who understood Ottoman conditions in relation to the developments and advances unfolding in other parts of the world. There were still many devoted patriots in the Ottoman Empire, but the Enlightenment in western Europe failed to touch them.

Anarchy in Iran

Tahmasp II suffered several reversals at the hands of the Ottoman armies in 1731 and ceded Tiflis, Erivan, Nakhshivan, Shamakha, and Daghestan to the Porte. This truce being thought disgraceful, Tahmasp was removed from the throne by his commander in chief, Nadir, in 1732, and exiled to Khurasan. After some further losses to the Turks, Nadir managed to revitalize his forces and effect the recovery of Tiflis and Erivan. Following the death of Peter the Great the Russians evacuated Gilan, Baku, and Darband, allowing Nadir to be crowned shah in 1736 and to place his capital at Meshed, not far from where he had been a poor shepherd boy of the Afshar tribe.

Nadir owed his position to the strength of his army and his ability to lead. For several decades the state's economy had been worsening. Taxes on the peasants had doubled, excise taxes had greatly increased, and internal trade had been impaired by the anarchy within the upper echelons of government. A standing army with artillery and muskets had become so expensive that the only way Nadir could keep his regime in funds was through expansion and conquest. First he successfully pressed the Bakhtiyari chieftains in the southwest to accept his rule, many of them enrolling their armies under his banner. In 1738 he took Kandahar after having laid siege to it for over a year with an army of 80,000 men.

Nadir, now called the Great Afshar, proceeded to Ghazni, Kabul, and through the Khyber Pass to India. Here he began to find rich stores of money with which to support his army. In 1738 he took Peshawar and moved on to meet the Mogul emperor at the Battle of Karnal, sixty miles from Delhi. Victory allowed him to proceed triumphantly into Delhi where Muhammad, the emperor, handed over his immense wealth, most of which Nadir carried off to his treasure house at Kalat near Meshed. (The most famous trophy in this loot was the peacock throne, built of gold and covered with priceless pearls and jewels, which ever since Nadir's acquisition of it has been the throne for the ruler of Iran. Another well-known prize was the Kuh-i-Nur diamond, later stolen by an Afghan general after Nadir's death and now adorning the British crown.) Since Muhammad was a Turk, Nadir treated him as an equal and left him as the ruler of India.

On his return he occupied Herat, and in 1740 invaded the lands of the Uzbegs, taking Bukhara and Khiva. In 1744 he subdued the districts of Shirvan, Shiraz, and Astrabad with severity; and in 1745 his forces defeated an Ottoman army advancing from Kars, with its artillery and military stores falling to Nadir, who then concluded peace at Kurdan with Mahmud I. But the state that Nadir had begun to fashion was crumbling. A military adventurer, Nadir never considered the relationship between military means and political ends. He administered the state poorly, and coordination between military and civilian forms of power was nonexistent. By the time of his assassination in 1747 he had become a bloody tyrant who marked his triumphs by having his victims' skulls stacked into high pyramids.

Immediately upon Nadir's murder, his composite army broke up into segments under various tribal groupings and leaders. For the better part of the following half century Iran suffered under a frightful anarchy among contenders for the throne. The land was rife with massacres and wholesale blindings. When Kerman fell to Aga Muhammad, for instance, he ordered that 20,000 pairs of eyes be presented to him! Under the rule of Karim Khan of Zand, who maintained his capital at Shiraz, there was a hiatus to this savagery. Karim had a sense of humor, was kind, upheld justice, and gave Iran two decades of calm and internal peace. But upon Karim's death in 1779 absolute confusion again engulfed Iran, with cities falling to one attacking force after another, in many cases suffering devastation that was felt up to the twentieth century. In 1794 Aga Muhammad, the leader of the Qajar tribe which had been one of the *kizilbash* tribes to support Shah Ismail in 1500, won out over all rivals, and his chief residence of Tehran became the capital of Iran. This shah, who had been castrated at the age of five by Nadir's nephew, established a Qajar rule that held sway in Iran until 1921.

REFERENCES: Chapter 19

Important for this chapter are books cited in Chapters 7, 12, 13, 14, 15, 16, 17, and 18.

Abu Hakima, Ahmad Mustafa. *History of Eastern Arabia, 1750–1800: The Rise and Development of Bahrain and Kuwait.* Beirut: Khayats, 1965. An understanding and thorough work.

Algar, Hamid. *Religion and State in Iran. 1785–1906.* Berkeley: University of California Press, 1970. Explains the relationships between spiritual and temporal powers within the sociopolitical system of Iran. A significant work important in the understanding of the functioning of society in the nineteenth century.

Anderson, M. S. *The Eastern Question, 1774–1923: A Study in International Relations.* London: Macmillan, 1966. A detailed study of European diplomacy as it related to the Ottoman Empire.

Angell, James Burrill. "The Turkish Capitulations." In *Selected Addresses.* New York: Longmans, Green, 1912. A good introduction to the problems involved.

Fisher, Alan W. *The Russian Annexation of the Crimea, 1772–1783.* Cambridge, Eng.: Cambridge University Press, 1970. Based on Russian and Ottoman archival materials, this work shows that the idea of Russian liberation of the Crimea was a myth.

Itzkowitz, Norman, and Max Mote (trans. and annotators). *Mubadele: An Ottoman-Russian Exchange of Ambassadors.* Chicago: University of Chicago Press, 1970. The reports and diaries of the two ambassadors going to Istanbul and Moscow for formal ratifications of the treaty of Kuchuk Kainarji, 1775–1776. Very interesting, illuminating respective court life and problems of travel.

Miller, William. *The Balkans: Roumania, Bulgaria, Servia and Montenegro: With New Chapter Containing Their History from 1896 to 1922.* London: Unwin, 1923. A fair summary of the histories of each of these peoples.

———. *The Ottoman Empire, 1801–1913.* Cambridge, Eng.: Cambridge University Press, 1913. The introduction contains a summary of the decline of the Ottomans.

Montagu, Mary Wortley. *Letters.* London: Cape, 1934. Lady Mary accompanied her husband to Turkey on a diplomatic mission in 1717–1718. Her letters, though sometimes doubtful as to accuracy, are interesting reading and give a valuable record.

Olson, Robert W. *The Siege of Mosul and Ottoman-Persian Relations, 1718–1743: A Study of Rebellion in the Capital and War in the Provinces of the Ottoman Empire.* Bloomington, Ind.: Indiana University Press, 1975. The author not only considers the Ottoman-Iranian relations but also includes extensive material on the political, social, and economic problems of the Ottoman Empire in the first half of the eighteenth century.

Pallis, Alexander. *In the Days of the Janissaries.* London: Hutchinson, 1951. A good account of the janissaries in their later days.

Rafeq, Abdul-Karim. *The Province of Damascus, 1723–1783.* Beirut: Khayats, 1966. A detailed work that reveals the decline of the Ottoman regime.

Ravndal, G. Bie. "Capitulations." In *Modern Turkey: A Politico-Economic Interpretation, 1908–1923, Inclusive, with Selected Chapters by Representative Authorities,* Eliot Grinnel Mears, ed. New York: Macmillan, 1924. Written by an American consular officer, this work reflects the operations of the capitulations during the twentieth century.

Salibi, K. S. *The Modern History of Lebanon.* New York: Praeger, 1965. From the seventeenth century to the present, the author covers the period of the eighteenth and nineteenth centuries in considerable detail with a brief summary of the period since World War I.

Sanjian, Avedis K. *The Armenian Communities in Syria Under Ottoman Dominion.* Cambridge, Mass.: Harvard University Press, 1965. An examination of groups of Armenians often overlooked.

Searight, Sarah. *The British in the Middle East.* New York: Atheneum, 1970. Accounts of British travelers from the middle of the sixteenth century to World War I.

Seton-Watson, R. W. *A History of the Roumanians from Roman Times to the Completion of Unity.* Cambridge, Eng.: Cambridge University Press, 1934. A good summary of the history of the Danubian provinces under the Phanariotes.

Shaw, Stanford J. *The Financial and Administrative Organization and Development of Ottoman Egypt, 1517–1798.* Princeton, N.J.: Princeton University Press, 1962. The most significant study of Ottoman imperialism in the Arab world.

————. *Between the Old and New: The Ottoman Empire Under Sultan Selim III. 1789–1807.* Cambridge, Mass.: Harvard University Press, 1971. A comprehensive description of the political and diplomatic affairs of Selim III's reign and an analysis of the internal and external forces working upon him.

Shay, Mary Lucille. *The Ottoman Empire from 1720 to 1734 as Revealed in Despatches of the Venetian Baili.* Urbana, Ill.: University of Illinois Press, 1944. A study of diplomacy.

Sumner, B. H. *Peter the Great and the Ottoman Empire.* Oxford: Blackwell's, 1949.

Thomas, Lewis V. *A Study of Naima.* Edited by Norman Itzkowitz. New York: New York University Press, 1972. A perceptive study of the life, ideas, and contributions of the great Ottoman historian and chronicler of the late seventeenth and early eighteenth centuries. Edited after Professor Thomas's death by his pupil.

Weber, Shirley H. *Voyages and Travels in the Near East to 1801.* Princeton: School of Classical Studies at Athens, 1953. Dr. Weber was librarian at the Gennadion in Athens where he had access to a wide variety of travel books.

Part Three

European Imperialism in the Modern Middle East

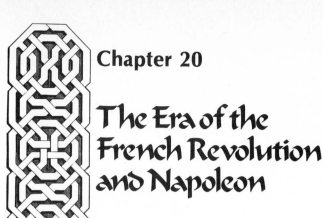

Chapter 20

The Era of the French Revolution and Napoleon

Selim's Reforms

In the month preceding the convening of the Estates General at Versailles which ushered in the French Revolution, Selim III was girt with the sword of Osman, and a new era in Ottoman history opened. Selim took his position seriously and desired to restore the power of court and governmental authority. That he thought of himself as a reformer in a modern sense or regarded the changes that he sought in terms of progress is doubtful. But he did understand that techniques pursued in Russia and the West had unquestionably placed great power in the hands of the ruler and his government.

In 1789 Selim was about twenty-seven years old and had studied more widely than most of his immediate predecessors. At first, wars with Austria and Russia tied his hands. The French Revolution, however, dissipated the attention of the European powers, gave the Ottoman Empire a few years of respite from Western imperialism, and offered Selim an unexpected opportunity to show his true character.

In the central government Selim sought to curb the arrogant powers and often treasonable intrigues of the grand vizir by reorganizing the imperial divan to consist of twelve ministers and by commanding that it be consulted on all important measures. Specialized commissions and advisory councils, each for a particular matter, were formed, and the divan ministers were ordered to consider their recommendations. One of the greatest difficulties in administering any reform was the lack of officials who thought of their position as anything but an opportunity for personal profit at the expense of the state and the people.

In the provinces Selim found that his word received little heed and foresaw that reforms would prove ineffectual unless a thorough transformation could be carried out in the army. The janissaries and standing cavalry had degenerated into virtual worthlessness; the training and weapons of all were hopelessly obsolete. Following the peace of Jassy, Selim recruited Omar, a Turk who had served as a lieutenant in the tsar's army. The sultan commissioned him as an aga and gave him a corps of 600 men, who were outfitted in the current European military garb and trained in European tactics. When Selim suggested to the divan that the janissaries adopt similar

uniforms and be drilled in the same manner, he was able to appease mutineers only by withdrawing the request.

Selim instituted similar reforms in the old army units by reorganizing the
financing of the army and giving the administrative and financial duties of
the commanders to other officers, thus allowing the agas to concentrate on
military aspects of their leadership. Fortunately, the historic interest which
French governments had shown in the commerce and diplomacy of the
Ottoman Empire since the days of Francis I did not evaporate with the
French Revolution and its nationalism. In 1796 the Directory sent General
du Bayet as ambassador to the Porte, presenting as the customary gift to the
sultan several of the latest pieces of artillery and munitions. In his suite were
artillerymen and army engineers to advise in the use and manufacture of
the new pieces and drill sergeants from French infantry and cavalry regiments to reorganize and train a new Ottoman army.

Called Nizam-i-Jedid (Army of the New Order), this force had come into
being about 1792, almost accidentally, and grew slowly, first hardly more
than a toy for Selim's amusement. Aided by the French and others who saw
a chance to create a force with real firepower, the first regiment was joined
by a second in 1799, as a result of the French invasion of Egypt, and by a
third in 1800. By 1801 there were over 9,000 men and 27 officers in the new
army; in 1807 there were 23,000 men and 1,600 officers. But because of the
rapidity of this expansion, training and discipline were superficial, and
many of the troops were idle much of the time. Since a majority of the
recruits (yamaks) came from villages of Anatolia or along the Black Sea
coast, they were unaccustomed to a regulated and confining life; they
became unruly and took to plundering Istanbul suburbs. The janissaries
refused to adopt any "Christian" devices and objected to serving alongside
the Nizam-i-Jedid. Thus these troops played only a token role in the 1806
and 1807 campaigns against the Serbs and Russians, leaving the main
fighting to the ineffective janissaries and sipahis.

Selim encouraged the founding of schools, especially engineering academies, which he felt were necessary adjuncts to any military reform. He
started a small one near Eyub to train his own companions and servants, and
in 1793, incorporating the old artillery school, opened the Imperial Land
Engineering School. Within four years there were eighty students enrolled.
The Imperial Naval Engineering School, begun two decades earlier, now
included courses in naval architecture at the insistence of the French naval
architect Le Brun, who was employed by Selim until 1804. The arsenal was
improved, and by 1798, 45 naval vessels had been launched, including 3
large ships of the line, the greatest one being the *Selimiye*, 153 feet long
with cannon on 3 decks. In all, there were 20 ships of the line and 25 frigates
with an armament of 2,156 cannon and 40,000 sailors. The navy could
compete with European fleets whereas the army could not. At Tophane a
cannon foundry was built and a new gunpowder plant set up north of

Istanbul where supplies of good quality were manufactured. Other scattered technical improvements included the founding of the naval school of medicine and the reintroduction of printing establishments which made possible the printing of mathematical and technical books, some translated from Western sources.

There is no evidence, however, that Selim understood the need for social, economic, and political reforms to support these military and technical changes. To improve Turkish foreign policy, permanent Ottoman embassies were accepted at London, Paris, Vienna, and Berlin where a number of young Turks were sent to learn about Western society and diplomacy. He issued orders to reduce the number of officials in every office, doing away with many who did no work. Selim increased taxes, debased the coinage, seized private property, and melted down all gold and silver utensils, sending the bullion to the mint. But these measures were merely palliative, leading to inflation, hunger, and, ultimately, economic disaster. In Istanbul laws to regulate costumes of persons according to creed, profession, trade, and position were openly flouted. To reduce violence and disorder on the streets, Selim demanded that laws be enforced, including those regarding dress, and even went out in disguise to catch offenders himself. Another attempt to bring law and order to the capital and to reduce its burgeoning population was an edict to cut down on the number of taverns and coffeehouses, to forbid the building of any new hotels or lodging houses, and to send idlers back to their villages. When grain became scarce, Selim socialized the supply and the trade: bakers had to buy their grain, and sell their bread, at fixed prices. In addition, bread had to be standardized in content, size, and quality. This measure was followed by a similar one for coffee. However, neither decree lasted very long, failing, as did many of Selim's reforms, from his personal weakness and lack of determination. Unfortunately, the direction of these activities lapsed entirely when General Bonaparte invaded Egypt.

Napoleon Invades Egypt

The sultan's authority in Egypt had been only nominal for nearly a century. Selim I and Suleiman had exercised considerable power in Cairo, Alexandria, and the delta, but they had not destroyed the Mamluk bands. In fact, lands in Egypt were parceled out to Mamluks to control and manage for the state. As the power of the Porte waned, Mamluks grew wealthy and independent. At various periods in the eighteenth century, Mamluk groups in Egypt defied the sultan's orders and refused to remit taxes to Istanbul. Ali Bey achieved a predominance over other Mamluks in 1769, when he became governor of Cairo and declared his independence from the Ottomans. When Ali was murdered, other Mamluks seized power. At this point an Ottoman fleet and army occupied Alexandria and Rosetta. However, even more rapacious Mamluks rose to rule when the Turks departed; and

Europeans openly disparaged any hope of maintaining residence much longer in Egypt.

Ostensibly, General Bonaparte invaded Egypt to destroy the Mamluks, who were proving so troublesome to his ally Sultan Selim III. However, Bonaparte's real objectives are shrouded in mystery even today. Claims have been put forward that the French looked upon the campaign as an attack upon Britain and the route to India, which the French had so recently surrendered to England, and believed that the possession of Egypt would widen the French sphere in the Mediterranean and offset the loss of India. In view of Napoleon's known regard for the importance of Istanbul, perhaps he intended to take Egypt and thence move upon Istanbul, the Balkans, and Austria.

In any case, Bonaparte gathered his army at Toulon; and accompanied by engineers, historians, archaeologists, architects, mathematicians, chemists, and Egyptologists, he set sail in May 1798 to take Malta and Egypt. He landed on July 1, took Alexandria on July 2, and defeated the Mamluks at the famous Battle of the Pyramids outside Cairo on July 21. His fleet, however, was destroyed by Lord Nelson at Aboukir Bay; his line of supply was thus cut and his freedom of action impeded.

Since Egypt was a province of the Ottoman Empire, the attack brought a declaration of war from the Porte, which joined with England and Russia in a coalition against France. Selim gave Ahmed al-Jezzar command of the army in Syria, and a fleet and army were collected at Rhodes for the relief of Egypt. Napoleon, having decided to carry the battle to the Turks, marched on Syria in 1799 in the hope that discontented Muslim Arabs, Druzes in Lebanon, and Christians in Syria would rise against the Turks. He took Gaza and Jaffa, where in cold blood he murdered 2,000 Turkish prisoners. But al-Jezzar, with reinforcements landed by an English squadron, held off Napoleon's attack at Acre. Repulsed there, Napoleon hurried to Egypt to meet a landing of Turkish infantry and cavalry at Aboukir Bay. These he drove into the sea, regaining mastery of Egypt. He then deserted his troops and sailed for France, where he executed his famous coup d'état.

The French forces remaining in Egypt were not conquered or evacuated until 1801. Several Turkish expeditions, in collaboration with an English army and naval squadron, forced the surrender of the French and gave them a guarantee of safe-conduct home. British forces held Egypt and prevented the several local competing factions from open warfare until the peace of Amiens in 1802 required the departure of the British. At that point Muhammad Ali, leader of one of the Ottoman factions, took advantage of the prevailing political and military anarchy and set the course of his meteoric ascent. His rise was of great significance for the Middle East, but it separated to a very marked degree the affairs of the Nile from those of the Straits and the Porte.

At the time that the peace of Amiens was concluded, agreement was reached between Selim III and Napoleon. The capitulations were restored for Frenchmen; and Napoleon sent General Brune and, later, General Sebastiani as ambassadors to the Porte. Selim was also at peace with England, Russia, and Austria. Trade revived in Ottoman ports, and shipping was brisk on the Black Sea and the Bosphorus. The Russians and British, however, used every device to offset French influence and to gain the Porte as an ally for their European policies.

Uprising in Serbia

Upon the general establishment of peace in Europe, Selim expected to proceed with his reforms, but calamity befell him in Serbia. The treaty of Sistova had provided for the return of Belgrad and its environs to the sultan; but it also stipulated that the janissaries, who previously ruled the area in a most ferocious manner, would not be permitted to return. Selim's new governor gave Serbia the most peaceful, prosperous, and enlightened rule she had known for nearly a century. However, to appease Pasvanoglu Pasha of Widin, Selim agreed to the return of the janissaries to Belgrad in 1799. Murdering the enlightened governor, four janissary leaders defied Selim's authority and divided Serbia among themselves. Outrage upon Christian and Muslim people followed outrage, until there occurred the famous uprising of 1804 against janissary rule.

Aided by Austrian arms and led by Kara George, Serbian insurgents were successful in destroying the janissaries. Selim sought to reestablish Ottoman rule in Belgrad, but the Serb leaders insisted that the terms of settlement be supervised by an Austrian commissioner. Selim declared he could not consent to foreign interference in domestic affairs, and Austria refused to break the treaty of Sistova. When the Serbs then turned to Russia for recognition, the Porte sent troops against the rebels. Victorious, the Serbs organized a provisional autonomous regime and again defeated the Turks. In 1806 the outbreak of war between Turkey and Russia induced the latter to aid Serbia, clearing Ottoman arms from the entire province. Thereupon Serbian affairs became a part of the European tangle of international diplomacy and power politics.

In the midst of this uprising realignment in Europe had its repercussions on the Golden Horn. When England formed the Third Coalition against France in 1805, General Sebastiani succeeded in obtaining Selim's sympathy for the French. But the Porte renewed the peace with Russia upon threats of war and invasion. It was only after Austerlitz and Jena that Selim felt able to declare openly for the French. At this time he removed the two pro-Russian governors of Wallachia and Moldavia, replacing them with pro-French officials. When Russia invaded the Danubian provinces in 1806, the Turks declared war and closed the Straits to Russian ships. Britain cooperated with her ally by assembling a squadron near the mouth of the Dardanelles and insisting that Selim expel Sebastiani from Istanbul and open the Straits. Upon Selim's refusal Admiral Duckworth led the fleet through the Dardanelles into the Sea of Marmara to lie near Istanbul. With

Russian troops invading Moldavia, the Porte considered a peremptory rebuff of Admiral Duckworth unwise. While the sultan's ministers spun out the negotiations, Sebastiani and military engineers hurriedly repaired the defenses of the Straits. Duckworth's intelligence advised withdrawal before escape became impossible, and the British retired from their foolhardy venture.

Overthrow of Selim

Napoleon's victories in central Europe and the defeat of the Russians at Friedland in 1807 strengthened the Turkish position. Meanwhile the appearance of 500 French cannoneers to defend the Straits from further escapades served to bring Selim closer to an open alliance with the French. However, a change of equipment for the garrisons on the Bosphorus incited the janissaries to demand the dismissal of the divan. And since payments due them were in arrears, the janissaries overturned their soup kettles, the traditional sign of revolt. The ensuing uprising by unruly and idle janissary trainees precipitated Selim's deposition and the elevation of his cousin Mustafa IV in May 1807. Formal charges against Selim were that he incited revolution by military innovations and that he had fathered no children after more than seventeen years of rule.

As has been indicated, Selim did not possess the resolute will and ruthlessness necessary to cope with the turbulence of the age. Surrounded by self-seeking, dishonest, insubordinate, and often traitorous officials, his every act was thwarted to the point where he came to realize that his only hope was to play one faction against another. Each suggested innovation jeopardized some vested interest, the most perceptibly threatened group being the janissaries whose distress brought his downfall. The masses were agitated over prices and by fears of uprisings in many of the provinces. French and Russian promises and threats kept everyone on edge, and the presence of a growing number of Europeans in influential positions introduced a pervasive leaven that disturbed the political elite. Selim's removal from office was nearly inevitable.

Mustafa IV was a mild and ineffectual person, the puppet of those who had overthrown Selim. Although the French officers and technicians were dismissed, the new sultan sent Napoleon a present of ten fine horses to indicate friendship for France—an amity that led to a truce between Russia and Turkey. The truce, however, was disastrous for Mustafa and the rebellious janissaries, since it freed the Ottoman armies on the Danube. An Ottoman army of Bosnians and Albanians, commanded by Bayraktar, governor of Ruschuk, marched on Istanbul and camped near the capital. Bayraktar called many leaders to his camp and in July 1808 moved upon the city and the palace. Before Bayraktar's men could force the gates, Mustafa executed Selim and gave orders for the strangling of his own brother Mahmud. The insurgents, however, imprisoned Mustafa and placed on the throne Mahmud II, who had been hidden in an empty furnace of the palace.

Mahmud II and the Napoleonic Wars

Mahmud II gave the office of grand vizir to Bayraktar, and the movement for reform proceeded along the lines drawn by Selim. After the organization of a new Europeanized army Bayraktar permitted his Bosnians and Albanians to return home. Thereupon the janissaries rose up and destroyed Bayraktar. Civil war raged in the streets of Istanbul for a week, with serious fires, explosions, and chaos, during which Mustafa was executed. Mahmud, now the sole surviving male of the Ottoman dynasty, was fairly safe; but friends of the janissaries controlled the government, and military reforms were out of the question.

Shortly after Admiral Duckworth fled to the more open seas of the Aegean in 1807 Turkey adhered to Napoleon's Continental Blockade, and the Straits were closed to English commerce. But Russian failure to withdraw from Moldavia, as promised, incited the Hapsburgs to mediate the breach between the Porte and England, since England was most likely to withstand the advances of a Franco-Russian combination. These maneuvers resulted in 1809 in the famous treaty of the Dardanelles between the Ottoman Empire and Great Britain. Turkey withdrew the decrees against British commerce, and England recognized the ancient orders with respect to the Straits. Until the Napoleonic invasion of Egypt the Straits were always closed to all warships when the Ottoman Empire was at peace. The new treaty only restated the ancient principle.

The French and Russians were furious; and the tsar sent his troops to the Danube, taking Silistria, Ruschuk, Nicopolis, and Sistova. These victories were valueless, however, because in 1811 the break with Napoleon was foreseen and operations in the Balkans came to a halt. Luckily for Russia, the treaty of Bucharest was signed a month before the French attack on Russia was launched. If this had not been the case, the Porte might have obtained better terms. Mahmud II dismissed the grand vizir and executed the negotiators for giving Bessarabia to the tsar.

The treaty abandoned the Serbs to the sultan who pledged that Serbs could manage their own internal affairs. The Russian regiment left Belgrad, and the Turks attempted to rule the province. Although Kara George departed, a new leader, Milosh Obrenovitch, continued the Serbian revolt. The Congress of Vienna in 1815 allowed the Serbs to retain their arms and gave them a voice in the management of their own government through an elected parliament. The sultan's suzerainty over Serbia was hardly more than a legal fiction, as most of the taxes that the Serbs collected remained in Serbia. At the congress, Turkey urged that Bessarabia be returned; but Vienna was unconcerned, and the treaty of Bucharest stood. This indicated that the relations between Russia and Turkey with respect to the use of the Straits returned to the ancient rule and that the treaties of 1798 and 1805 were indirectly rescinded. Likewise, no contrary stipulation was raised at the congress concerning the treaty of the Dardanelles, which established the relations of Turkey and England and which, curiously enough, recognized that Turkey might be simultaneously a belligerent in the Black Sea and a neutral state in the Mediterranean.

From all appearances, therefore, the Ottoman Empire in 1815 successfully weathered the wars and cataclysms of the French Revolution and Napoleon. Bessarabia was lost; a semiautonomous regime was legalized in Belgrad; and two sultans were slain by military revolts. But little change resulted in the internal organization of the empire. Nonetheless, the seeds of nationalism and reform were sown by wide movements of men and ideas, and a growth in commerce raised incentives to a new high.

The Ottoman Empire was on the threshold of a new century and a new life.

The Qajar Dynasty in Iran

Aga Muhammad Shah of the Qajar tribe, who won out in 1794 over other rivals for the throne of Iran following the demise of Karim Khan of Zand in 1779, had as a child been enslaved and castrated. Subsequently freed, he had gained ascendency in the leading Qajar tribe as a young man and then passed many years as a political hostage at the court of Karim Khan. In the commotion over Karim's death Aga Muhammad made his way to Tehran, where he organized a force, drove the Russians from Ashraf in 1781, and had so strengthened his position that by the fall of Kerman in 1794 major resistance to Qajar rule was eliminated in the central Iranian lands.

Aga Muhammad, attacking the Georgians and their Russian allies, took Tiflis and Erivan. When the Russians marched with 40,000 men in 1796 and occupied Baku and Darband, his position would have been quite hopeless had not Catherine the Great's death that year brought about a Russian withdrawal. He managed to pacify Kurdistan and subdued parts of Khurasan and fortified it against Uzbeg forays, at the same time seizing all the jewels of the late Shah Rukh.

Aga Muhammad was generally recognized to have had four passions: power, avarice, revenge, and hunting, the greatest being power. He has been described as a "conniving, vindictive, cruel, and stingy misanthrope." Widely cursed in Iran by his own people, he was murdered by his personal servants in 1797.

Aga Muhammad had chosen as his successor his nephew Fath Ali. Governor at Shiraz at the time of his uncle's assassination, Fath Ali hastened to Tehran by forced marches while a Qajar general held the throne for him. Scions of the Afshar and Zand tribes made bids for the throne, but Fath Ali had an army and the throne which gave him sufficient edge to overwhelm them. Whenever a Qajar shah died, and even prior to the Qajars, several contenders, within and outside the royal family, always battled for the imperial turban and plunged the state into disorder. Two centuries earlier the central government's acquisition of artillery and muskets gave the opposition little chance, but at the outset of the nineteenth century many forces and contingents in Iran possessed these weapons and could seriously question any designated heir. Eventually, however, the throne passed more peacefully, even though the government's army was largely on paper. British and Russian contingents more or less guaranteed a regular succession, since they preferred the status quo.

The monarchy was an outstanding feature of Iran, and the shah's word was law, final at the court and within the central government. If he made prudent decisions, the state prospered; if he made unfortunate ones, all suffered. But Iran was not truly unified: there was no social cohesion, and the absolutism of the shah was a delightful myth. Within the royal family and among the elite there remained almost complete self-interest and self-indulgence, with little sense of nation and even less concern for the welfare of Iran. In addition, the cleft between Turk and Tajik (old Iranian stock) reached such proportions that some even predicted dismemberment of the state. Each faction was inordinately proud and each despised the other.

The shah had power over the central government and some authority over taxation but his capricious actions were made tolerable throughout Iran by corruption, distance, and inefficiency. Corruption speaks for itself. There were no railroads in Iran until after World War I and between the urban centers of the central provinces there were vast stretches of hostile or barren countryside controlled by nomadic and seminomadic tribes which the central government in Iran found impossible to bridle until the advent of the airplane and helicopter after World War II. Inefficiency was everywhere, and outside of Tehran the government "did little beyond collecting revenue."

The general population in Iran in the nineteenth century hated the Qajars and on the whole looked to their religious leaders for inspiration and guidance. The ulema held considerable power for several reasons. Shiite theology allowed more leeway for the ulema and religious judges to interpret the Koran and the traditions and gave rulings by religious jurists on legal and political matters a force often greater than those made by Qajar officials. The ulema frequently mediated confrontations arising between cities and provinces, since the central government could not manage such an arduous task. Even Fath Ali Shah, an avowed tyrant, maintained a close and lasting association with many of the ulema and welcomed, at times, their participation in governmental matters. He knew that an appearance of piety was useful and sometimes necessary. The ulema also possessed great wealth, derived from the taxes that all Shiites were obligated to pay directly to them as well as from rich endowments scattered across the land. Another factor in the power wielded by the ulema was that the recognized center of Shiite thought and jurisdiction lay in centers in Ottoman Mesopotamia outside of Iran and beyond the reach of Qajar power.

Diplomacy During the French Revolution and Napoleon in Iran
For Fath Ali and his ministers Russian power and aggression engendered apprehension throughout his entire reign. During the French Revolution and the Napoleonic Wars in Europe, French, British, and Russian envoys

and military missions journeyed to Tehran vying for Iranian favors and alliances. The French were always looking for aid against the British in India, and the British were cajoling Iran to stand firm against France. The Russians sometimes were allies of the French and usually opposed the influence of the British. After Napoleon had been defeated, the British had a greater interest in Iranian policies, since to a certain degree India's northwest frontier was more peaceful when Iran blocked Russia and held the Afghans in check.

Until 1805 British missions to Tehran and Fath Ali's to Bombay discussed relations with the Afghans. French approaches in 1805 proposed that Fath Ali sever his undertakings with the British and invade India with French support. At the same time an alliance against Russia was suggested with the idea of French aid in regaining Georgia from Russia. Sent to France to undertake negotiations, Prince Reza caught up with Napoleon at Tilsit and signed the treaty of Finkenstein in May 1807. By its terms Iran pledged to declare war on Great Britain, to incite the Afghans to attack India, and to grant French troops right of passage across Iran; the French meanwhile recognized Iran's right to Georgia, agreeing "to compel Russia to relinquish Georgia," and committed a military mission to Tehran. General Claude Gardane and seventy officers and technicians soon arrived to train the Iranian army along European lines.

Sorely disappointed by the treaty of Tilsit because it contained no mention of Iran, Fath Ali did not declare war against Great Britain. In 1809 the British envoy presented the shah with an exceptionally large diamond and signed a treaty that promised an annual subsidy to Iran as long as Great Britain was at war with Russia and pledged a mission of British officers to train the Iranian army. General Gardane was given his passport to leave and the British sent a fine contingent of officers. One in particular, Captain Henry Lindsay Bethune, an artillery officer who was six feet eight inches tall, so captivated the Iranians that he remained there for many years and became commander in chief of the Iranian army. The shah sent one of the princes to London to learn how the substantial subsidy was to be paid and from these negotiations the treaty of Tehran of 1814 was signed. According to this treaty all alliances between Iran and European powers hostile to Great Britain were null and void; Iran agreed to induce the rulers of Bukhara and other places to prohibit armies from marching against India; frontiers between Iran and Russia were to be determined by Iran, Russia, and Great Britain; and a large subsidy was to be given each year to Iran by the British minister resident in Tehran. Frequently called the Definitive Treaty, this arrangement was the basis of relations between the two countries for many years.

The previous year the treaty of Gulistan, signed with the Russians, ceded Georgia, Baku, Shirvan, and other areas in the Caucasus, with the stipulation that Iran would have no navy on the Caspian Sea, and committed Russia to support Prince Abbas for succession to the throne. Vagueness in the treaty of Gulistan led to border warfare and in 1827 the Russians captured Erivan and Tabriz. The important treaty of Turkumanchai of 1829 gave Erivan and certain indemnities to Russia and, most significant, gave Russians capitulatory rights in Iran, rights that soon were extended to other Europeans.

Reform in Iran

Even before the Gardane mission arrived in Iran, Prince Abbas as governor of Azerbayjan had been reorganizing the Iranian army along European lines. Russian officers were employed to train the soldiers of this "new army," the Nizam-i-Jadid, who were recruited on a permanent basis with fixed pay, disciplined and dressed as European troops, and equipped with modern weapons. They were similar to the New Army of Selim III in Istanbul, and the ulema in Iran objected to them just as those in the Ottoman Empire had. (Prince Abbas drilled with the new soldiers but had to do so in private so that his religious faith would not be questioned.) French officers replaced the Russians in 1808, only to be replaced in turn by the British, who continued in the role of military advisers for several decades. Prince Abbas began many other reforms in Tabriz and was most energetic in improving the systems of taxation and justice. These changes represented the first elements of Westernization and modernization in the social structure of Iran. Unfortunately, Abbas fell ill and died suddenly in 1833 to be followed the next year by his father, Shah Fath Ali. Thus, in 1834, Prince Abbas's son Prince Muhammad, who had been residing at Isfahan, was urged by the British and Russian ambassadors to proceed to Tehran and take the throne. Supported by troops from both countries and a large financial grant from Great Britain, he ascended as Muhammad Shah. The new shah's grandfather, Shah Fath Ali, at his death had left 53 sons, 46 daughters, and 784 grandchildren. The number of his progeny and the length of his white beard were his claims to fame. With so many uncles and cousins, Muhammad Shah would have had difficulty in surviving the bitter rivalry had it not been for the aid of the British and the staunch support of General Sir Henry Lindsay Bethune.

REFERENCES: Chapter 20

Among volumes already cited, those of particular value for this chapter are in Chapters 7, 12, 13, 16, and 19.

Eton, William. *A Survey of the Turkish Empire.* London: Cadell & Davies, 1799. An interesting and useful contemporary account.

Fasa'i, Hasan-e. *History of Persia Under Qajar Rule.* A translation by Heribert Busse of *Farsnama-ye Naseri.* New York: Columbia University Press, 1972. This is a detailed native account of the Qajar dynasty and rule to 1882. Factual, anecdotal, and illuminating.

Ghurbal, Shafik. *The Beginnings of the Egyptian Question and the Rise of Mehemet Ali: A Study in the Diplomacy of the Napoleonic Era Based on Researches in the British and French Archives.* London: Routledge, 1928. By an Egyptian scholar.

Kelly, J. B. *Britain and the Persian Gulf, 1795–1880.* Oxford: Clarendon Press, 1968. A monumental work of the first order dealing with the British interest and activities on all sides of the Gulf during this period.

Ma'oz, Moshe. *Ottoman Reform in Syria and Palestine, 1840–1861.* London: Oxford University Press, 1968. A well-balanced description of political, social, and religious conditions from the end of Egyptian occupation to the death of Abd al-Aziz. Excludes Mount Lebanon. Excellent.

Polk, William L. *The Opening of South Lebanon, 1788–1840.* Cambridge, Mass.: Harvard University Press, 1963. A detailed and comprehensive study.

Puryear, Vernon J. *Napoleon and the Dardanelles.* Berkeley: University of California Press, 1951. A comprehensive work on the diplomacy of the Middle East during the period of the French Revolution and Napoleon.

Shupp, Paul F. *The European Powers and the Near Eastern Question, 1806–1807.* New York: Columbia University Press, 1931. Based on English and French archival material.

Temperley, Harold W. V. *England and the Near East.* Vol. 1. *The Crimea.* London: Longmans, Green, 1936. An indispensable work covering the years from 1808 to 1854.

Weber, Shirley H. *Voyages and Travels in the Near East, XIX Century.* Princeton, N.J.: American School of Classical Studies at Athens, 1952. A continuation of his volume cited in chapter 19.

Chapter 21

Mahmud II: Nationalism and Reform

The Greek Revolution

One of the exciting legacies of the French Revolution to the Middle East was the rise of the Greek nation. Eighteenth-century liberal Europeans wished to emulate ancient Greek society and culture; they particularly admired Greek political ideas. Therefore, when Greeks came into contact with Europeans at the turn of the century, they were impressed with their own heritage and fostered an intellectual and literary renaissance of significant proportions in all Greek communities from Odessa to Marseilles. Before 1820 over 3,000 different books had been published in modern Greek. These included not only translations of the important works of Voltaire, Schiller, Goethe, Alfieri, and Montesquieu but also renditions of the ancient Greek classics into a form which modern Greeks could read and understand.

The two outstanding Greek intellectual patriots were Rhegas and Adamantios Koraes, each of whom traveled and studied in Europe. Rhegas, in his Greek version of the *Marseillaise,* roused his countrymen to arms and aided them in forming a society to raise money and munitions to cast off the Turkish yoke. Following Plato and Rousseau, Koraes held that every form of bad citizenship was an injustice. He also asserted that every bad citizen was a Turk at heart. In addition to hating Turks and carrying Western ideas to the Greeks, he glorified the heroic deeds of ancient Greeks and advanced the reconstruction of modern Greek by condemning foreign words and abandoning colloquialisms and barbarisms that had crept into the ancient tongue.

The labors of these patriots would have been fruitless had it not been for the Greek Church, which preserved the identity of the Greek community, and for Greek schools, everywhere present to train churchmen and incidentally to teach many to read and write Greek. As Greeks became prosperous, they founded more schools, and many pursued advanced studies in Italy and France. After the fall of Venice in 1797 the Greek cultural center moved to Vienna, where a Greek press published books and newspapers that circulated wherever Greeks went.

The decay of the Ottoman government gave rise to many outlaw bands in the mountains of Greece. Known as *klephts,* these brigands posed as Robin Hoods attacking Turks and helping Greeks. They fired the Greek spirit and created a nucleus of Greeks familiar with the handling of weapons. Also, as in antiquity, many Greeks were drawn to the sea and foreign commerce; and their knowledge of the ways and languages of the Middle East proved extremely beneficial in trade between Ottoman and Mediterranean ports. During the Napoleonic Wars they reaped enormous profits flying the Turkish or Russian flag in the Black Sea and the Turkish or other flags in the Mediterranean as conditions demanded.

In 1814 a group of Greeks in Odessa founded a secret band named Philike Hetaeria ("Friendly Society") to organize a rising against the Turks. Similar to contemporary European secret societies, the Philike Hetaeria grew so rapidly with the commercial depression after 1815 that over 200,000 were initiated by 1820. Its members could not be restrained; and in 1821 Alexander Ypsilantis, a distinguished Phanariot Greek and a general in the Russian army who had lost his right hand at the battle of Kulm, unfurled the banner of revolt.

He crossed the Pruth River from Russian Bessarabia into Turkish Moldavia. This was not the most propitious spot to launch a Greek revolution, since the native Rumanians hated Greeks far more than they did Turks. Turks in Galatz and Jassy were impaled. Bankers were blackmailed. The Great Powers, at that moment convening at Ljubljana (Laibach) to suppress a Neapolitan uprising, induced Russia to strike Ypsilantis's name from Russian army rolls and disown the adventure. When a Turkish army drove him from Bucharest, he shamelessly deserted his followers and fled to Hungary.

Within a few weeks of the crossing of the Pruth, the revolution was in full swing in the Peloponnesus. From Kalamata to Patras to Corinth, Turks—men, women, and children—were massacred and the population of surrendered towns put to the sword. When Tripolitsa, the Turkish capital, fell, over 8,000 Turks were butchered. (Many modern wealthy Greek families acquired their fortunes in the sack of the city.) Athens, except for the Acropolis, fell, as did Mesolonghi and other towns on the northern shore of the Gulf of Corinth. Immediately the Turks fought back; on Crete and some of the Aegean islands reprisals and counterreprisals were common.

The rebellions in the Danubian provinces and the Peloponnesus led Mahmud II to take action against suspected Hetaeriaists in Istanbul. A number of leading Phanariotes were executed, and on Easter Sunday the Greek patriarch was hanged from the gate of his residence. Of all the Aegean islands, Chios with its famous mastic gardens was the most wealthy, and its inhabitants showed no interest in the uprisings on the mainland. Early in 1822, however, Greek adventurers took over the island against the wishes of the Chiotes. Thereupon, a Turkish admiral landed. Greek sailors counterattacked in vain. The Turks leveled villages, put Chios to the torch, and massacred nearly 25,000 Greeks, scattering the rest to all parts of the world. Shortly thereafter, Turks surrendered the Acropolis in Athens on the pledge that their lives would be spared. The promise was not kept.

One of the factors that had led to the first successes of these uprisings was Mahmud's decision to settle some scores with Ali, the rebellious pasha of

Janina. Indeed because Ottoman forces were weak and dispersed, Mahmud's withdrawal of the best of his soldiers to subdue Ali virtually ensured success. A strange mixture of eighteenth-century European enlightenment, Oriental splendor, and devotion to ancient Greek literature, Ali had ruled as a benevolent tyrant for thirty years, corresponding with Napoleon and negotiating with British governors of the Ionian islands. In 1820 Mahmud sent an army to Epirus to bring in his head. During this campaign the Turkish garrisons in Athens, Tripolitsa, and other Greek towns were reduced to the barest minimum, leaving the towns defenseless against a popular uprising. When, however, Ali Pasha's head and those of his sons and grandsons were exhibited on a silver platter outside the sultan's palace in Istanbul in 1822, Mahmud's forces had better success against the Greeks. The sultan's forces were considerably spent, but the Greeks were torn already with dissension.

Intervention by Egypt and the Powers

The Powers looked upon the Greek activities with uncertainty and considerable misgivings, but philhellenic committees in England and France compelled their governments to take an interest in Greek affairs. Furthermore, the Greek provisional government obtained in 1824 the first of a series of loans from British bankers, a move that guaranteed a continuing interest from London. Considerable romantic publicity accompanied the enlistment of veteran European soldiers, especially philhellenes. The most famous of these was Lord Byron, whose death in 1824 at Mesolonghi created more sentiment for the Greek revolution than any other single event in the long struggle.

In 1824 Mahmud commissioned his powerful vassal of Egypt, Muhammad Ali, to aid in suppressing the insurrection. His son Ibrahim was appointed governor of the Peloponnesus and set out to subjugate his new charge. He landed at Modon in 1825, captured Navarino, and proceeded to establish his authority by fire and sword. Meanwhile an Ottoman army subdued western Greece, took Mesolonghi, and recaptured Athens. Greek independence seemed very doubtful.

The victories of Mahmud's lieutenants hastened the intervention of the Powers. Various preliminary discussions suggesting local Greek autonomy led to the treaty of London, signed in 1827 by England, Russia, and France. In this treaty the three demanded an armistice from Turkey and the Greeks and the mediation of any differences. Since Mahmud refused to declare an armistice, Admiral Codrington was ordered to intercept, with cannon balls if necessary, all supplies and reinforcements destined for Ibrahim. The famous Battle of Navarino on October 20, 1827, completely shattered Ottoman naval forces, and a French army compelled Ibrahim to withdraw.

Russian interests in Greece were tied to the affairs of Serbia and the Danubian provinces. Even before Nicholas I agreed to the London treaty, an ultimatum had been delivered to the Porte demanding cession of Kars and other eastern provinces; evacuation of Moldavia and Wallachia, whose governors would be elected for seven-year terms by the native aristocracy and could be removed only upon Russian consent; and immediate autonomy for Serbia. On the last day of grace Mahmud accepted the terms, which were incorporated in the convention of Akkerman of 1826.

After the destruction of the Ottoman navy at Navarino, Russia could not resist taking advantage of Turkish weakness. A peculiar kind of war was declared in 1828: Russia became a belligerent in the Balkans and the Black Sea but remained a neutral in the Mediterranean. One army advanced in the Caucasus with considerable success, taking Ardahan, Bayezid, and Erzerum; another under General Diebitsch took Varna and Burgas on the Black Sea, crossed the Balkans, and entered Edirne.

Treaty of Adrianople

Upon the advice of Prussian and British envoys Mahmud sought peace. Diebitsch was in collaboration with the Russian fleet, which was divided between the Black Sea and the Aegean; and it appeared that nothing could prevent him from occupying Istanbul. The treaty of Adrianople (Edirne) of 1829 reestablished the frontiers much as they were before the war. The Straits were open again to Russian trade. The Danubian provinces no longer had to supply corn, wood, and mutton to the sultan's government; only the annual tribute to the Porte was continued. Governors held their posts for life and ruled in consultation with native assemblies. The ties with Turkey were reduced to a minimum, and Russia moved into the vacuum.

Other provisions of the treaty stipulated that the articles of the convention of Akkerman should be put into immediate effect. Another article declared that Turkey adhered to a second treaty of London which England, France, and Russia had concluded earlier in 1829 and which established a Greek state. In consequence of its inclusiveness the treaty of Adrianople was an important landmark in Balkan development as well as in the relationship of the Ottoman Empire to the great European states.

Destruction of the Janissaries

Although the duke of Wellington erred in thinking that the treaty foretold the imminent collapse of the Ottoman Empire, the treaty did materially change the balance of power in the Balkans and in the Middle East. An event of vaster proportions and ramifications, however, preceded the treaty and was in part responsible for it. In 1826 Mahmud destroyed the janissaries. For more than 300 years sultans found the janissary corps unruly; and since the beginning of the seventeenth century these soldiers frequently vetoed policies of state, and grand vizirs were beheaded at their behest. Through the eighteenth century several of the sultans contrived to modernize the army and equip the janissaries with more efficient weapons, but each scheme was successfully rebuffed. Since the sultan's authority in the provinces was continually snubbed by recalcitrant governors, a reliable standing army had to be created before he could reassert his power. The modernization of the army became even more urgent as Ottoman units met with Austrian and Russian regiments, to which they compared adversely.

Selim lost his life in the attempt to modernize the army. Mahmud plotted more warily. Although Ali Pasha of Janina, Ahmed al-Jezzar of Syria, and Muhammad Ali of Egypt possessed competent standing armies, the sultan depended upon janissaries and feudal levies. The lesson of Murat, who cleared the streets of Madrid in 1808 with cannon and grapeshot, was not lost upon Mahmud. Ottoman artillery was carefully improved, and more than 14,000 artillerymen were gathered in Istanbul. When the blow was readied, Mahmud had the loyalty of the artillerymen, the grand vizir, the shaykh al-Islam, the chief of the janissaries, and a sizable force of Anatolian levies stationed at Uskudar across the Bosphorus.

In 1826 Mahmud forced the divan to order some janissaries to drill in European fashion. The revolution broke, as was expected. The artillery mowed down the janissaries as they charged the palace and then shelled their barracks into a mass of ruins, burying 4,000 beneath the rubble. Victory was followed up in the provinces, where janissaries were hunted down and either exterminated or completely scattered. New troops were ordered to be assembled, and Mahmud planned to organize and train an army of 40,000. Although the Russian attacks in 1828 and 1829 were launched before the new troops were trained and weakened them permanently as the Russians had hoped, Mahmud rid his state of an anachronism that had considerably retarded the process of change in the empire. It was a first step in destroying the power of the governors in outlying provinces and in rebuilding the centralized control that had proved so effective in the fifteenth and sixteenth centuries. Other reforms could now occur.

Muhammad Ali and Mahmud II
But there was hardly any time for sound reform. Peace was no more than established when Mahmud faced rebellion and serious attack by Muhammad Ali, his vassal in Egypt. The actions of this dynamic newcomer affected Mahmud's empire profoundly, particularly in its relationship to the Powers.

For lending aid to the sultan, Muhammad Ali had been given an outright promise of Crete and of the governorship of the Peloponnesus for his son Ibrahim. The latter promise did not materialize, however, because the Powers established the kingdom of Greece; and Crete by itself was inadequate. Therefore, Muhammad Ali turned his eyes on the Barbary Coast. But French action in Algeria in 1830 diverted his attention to Syria, which he requested for Ibrahim in lieu of the Peloponnesus. Since some reward in Syria was originally offered for the Greek adventure, this request seemed appropriate. When Mahmud refused, Muhammad Ali invaded Syria on the pretext that such action would coerce Abdallah of Acre to subserve the sultan and would chastise him for harboring Egyptian conscript dodgers and practicing the arts of extortion upon Egyptian merchants.

Ibrahim meanwhile waged a combined land and sea attack upon Acre, which finally fell in 1832 after a prolonged siege and several bloody assaults.

Mahmud hardly lifted a finger to aid Abdallah; Ibrahim easily routed a Turkish army collected near Homs; and in rapid succession Damascus, Aleppo, Adana, and Konya were occupied by the Egyptian army. Up to this point the Powers were unconcerned; France even looked with favor upon the expansion of Muhammad Ali's territory. When Ibrahim defeated the main Turkish army near Konya and pushed on to Kutahya, however, Mahmud grew frantic and begged the Powers to rescue him. Metternich refused; England was involved in parliamentary reform and Belgian affairs; France had strong ties with Muhammad Ali. Only Russia responded. Early in 1833 a Russian fleet anchored in the Bosphorus, and 14,000 Russian marines landed to protect Mahmud from his vassal and to guarantee the concessions and treaties the Russians had obtained from the Porte since 1774.

Meanwhile Russian and Ottoman envoys in Cairo were discussing peace terms, while French diplomatic and consular agents were pressing Mahmud to accept some of the Egyptian demands. Compromises were effected, and the convention of Kutahya was signed. Syria, including Damascus and Aleppo, was assigned to Muhammad Ali upon condition that he pay an annual tribute; he was also to retain Adana, which would give him easy access to the Taurus passes and Anatolia. Ibrahim's troops were recalled from Anatolia. The Russian fleet and troops, however, postponed their departure from the Bosphorus. Two days before they reembarked from the Bosphorus village of Hunkiar Iskelesi, where they had encamped, a treaty was signed that shocked the other European powers and achieved for Russia a long-sought goal. The treaty of Hunkiar Iskelesi of 1833 was a straightforward alliance between Russia and Turkey, providing for perpetual friendship, peace, and mutual assistance. The provocation lay in a secret article, which did not remain unknown very long, stating that upon Russian request the sultan would close the Straits to the extent of "not allowing any foreign vessel of war to enter therein, under any pretext whatsoever." Although diplomats questioned the significance of the secret article, the value of Hunkiar Iskelesi to Russia, and the objection of the Powers, rested on the right of Russia to interfere in Turkish affairs "to the exclusion of the alliance and intervention of the Powers."

Mahmud's Reforms
Whereas England and France recognized immediately the advantage won by Russia and initiated action to recoup their losses, Mahmud used the peace he had so dearly purchased to carry forward the reform of his government. Destruction of the janissaries and the formation of new troops, termed Muslim Soldiers, were only publicized aspects of his military innovations. The abolition of feudalism ruined the cavalry and levies upon which sultans had greatly depended and which had proved valuable for Mahmud. Income from fiefs now went directly to the treasury, and officers of the sultan enlisted recruits from these areas. The best sipahis were enrolled in four new squadrons of cavalry and the rest were pensioned. Hel-

muth von Moltke and a group of Prussians participated in training Turkish officers; other Turkish officers studied at Woolwich in England. Military and medical colleges were opened in 1830; and a national militia was organized in 1834 to give rudimentary training in the provinces. Connected with these colleges and previously established engineering schools were primary and secondary schools where a regular secular education was given to prepare students properly for advanced training. Mahmud in 1824 declared a primary education compulsory for all, but means for carrying out this decree never materialized. The best primary-secondary school was the one attached to the medical college at Galatasaray. With instruction given in Turkish and French, it became the precursor of one of the more influential forces for the education of leaders of the country in the latter part of the nineteenth century. Another important preparatory school with instruction in Turkish and French was connected with a newly established school of military sciences.

Since the ulema had opposed previous attempts at reform, Mahmud silenced the more irresponsible of them. In 1826 he gave an office building to the shaykh al-Islam and created it as a regular department of government with its own staff of bureaucrats; courts for Muslim subjects came under its authority. However, the appointment of teachers and the control of schools passed to the new Ministry of Education and the selection of judges and the administration of law went to a Ministry of Justice. Even more damaging to the ulema's power was the creation of the Ministry of Pious Foundations to which was given the income of all religious and charitable endowments. This ministry collected the funds and paid out what was needed to the various foundations, placing the remainder in the treasury. Dervish orders were attacked. Bektashi leaders were exiled and the order's buildings and properties confiscated. Actually this latter decree was never fully executed; dervish houses remained in the possession of Bektashis in most parts of the empire, even in Istanbul, until the twentieth century. The fez was adopted as the headgear for government officials. The frock coat was also adopted. And within a few years the fez, the frock coat, trousers, and black leather boots became the standard dress in urban centers. When the shaykh al-Islam objected, Mahmud removed him, giving public notice of his earnestness in these matters.

Changes in the military were the means to strengthen and reorganize the government. The independent local lords (dereh beys) in Anatolia were checked, Iraq was subdued in 1831, and other governors began to feel and respect the sultan's authority. To a certain extent the war with Egypt resulted from Mahmud's desire to project his power into every corner of the realm. As a further curb on local rulers, governors were forbidden to execute anyone without referring the case to Istanbul. This removal of the death sentence from a governor's whim gave people throughout the empire a deeper sense of security.

In addition to ministries already cited, two bureaus within the office of the grand vizir were cut off and formed into two ministries: Foreign Affairs, and Civil Affairs. Upon this development the grand vizir ceased being the supreme and all-powerful deputy of the sultan and became a prime minister, for a number of years holding this title instead of that of grand vizir. Even when the latter title was restored, the grand vizir remained merely chairman of the Council of Ministers. One of the more important innovations came after the Greek revolution when Greek Phanariotes were no longer trusted to serve as translators and interpreters for Foreign Affairs. Within a few years a translation bureau was attached to the Ministry of Foreign Affairs, and officials in this bureau became significant members of the government, many later in the century rising to be grand vizirs. Every department of government was staffed by better-trained civil servants. Better salaries lessened bribery, and more attention was given to promotion on merit. Many sinecures were abolished and much governmental red tape was eliminated.

To a significant degree the changes that were instituted came as a result of closer contact with the West. The first steamship arrived in the Golden Horn in 1828, and within a few years regular schedules were established between Istanbul and western Mediterranean ports. The time of a trip from France was cut from a month to twelve days. Thus the 1830s saw an influx of Western visitors, merchants, and missionaries joining Istanbul to the West as nothing previously had ever done. As a result, European techniques of government were studied and employed in many ways.

The end of the wars with Russia and Egypt left Turkey almost bankrupt. Foreign observers commented on the great wealth and bountiful produce of the country but inefficiency in the collection of taxes reduced the sultan to penury. Under new procedures the central government assumed direct responsibility and sent out its own agents or tax farmers, thereby reducing the number of hands through which the taxes passed. New roads improved trade, and Muslims were encouraged to enter business by the abolition of the Court of Confiscations in which the government seized the property of an exiled or condemned individual. Creditors henceforth felt less personal danger in pressing the government and its high officials for the payment of debts. In general these measures were effective. By the end of Mahmud's reign European consular officials were reporting that the empire had progressed remarkably in the preceding twenty years.

Mahmud also recognized the stimulus to reform that a general circulation of books and newspapers would generate. Presses were established in Istanbul and Izmir, publishing with those of Muhammad Ali in Egypt several thousand books in Turkish and Arabic between 1830 and 1840. The military and medical colleges introduced many young Turks to French and German and opened to them the eighteenth- and nineteenth-century liberal ideas contained in the literature of those languages. French newspapers were founded in Izmir in the 1820s; and in 1832 the first Turkish newspaper, *Takvimi-Vekayih*, appeared in Istanbul with official support from Mahmud.

The Ottoman Empire found in Mahmud a sultan whose high ability in the craft of ruling broke the conservative and reactionary grip held by special interest groups upon the government and society. In later decades of the nineteenth century the progress of reform might seem slow and uncertain. Yet after Mahmud's changes a return to the old order was impossible, and a liberalizing forward-looking movement prevailed.

REFERENCES: Chapter 21

Works containing material pertinent to this chapter are cited in Chapters 12, 13, 18, 19, and 20.

Bailey, Frank Edgar. *British Policy and the Turkish Reform Movement: A Study in Anglo-Turkish Relations, 1826–1853.* Cambridge, Mass.: Harvard University Press, 1942. Written largely from the British point of view.

Chaconas, Stephen George. *Admantios Korais: A Study in Greek Nationalism.* New York: Columbia University Press, 1942. A thorough study of this famous Greek patriot.

Crawley, C. W. *The Question of Greek Independence.* Cambridge, Eng.: Cambridge University Press, 1930. An instructive monograph on the Greek revolution.

Grunwald, Kurt. *Türkenhirsch: A Study of Baron Maurice de Hirsch, Entrepreneur and Philanthropist.* Jerusalem: Israel Program for Scientific Translations, 1966. The chapter on the financing and building of the Oriental Railway to Istanbul, completed in 1888, is a fascinating story of intrigue, deals, and diplomacy. There are also good chapters on Hirsch's interest in and philanthropy for Zionism.

Hershlag, Z. Y. *Introduction to the Modern Economic History of the Middle East.* Leiden: Brill, 1964. A lengthy survey of the economy of the area before World War I, followed by five sections covering the economy as it stood at the end of World War I. Also included are studies of the economy between the two wars in Turkey, Iran, Egypt, and the mandated territories. Many tables.

Issawi, Charles (ed.). *The Economic History of the Middle East, 1800–1914.* Chicago: University of Chicago Press, 1966. A useful collection of essays by outstanding scholars.

Keddie, Nikkie (ed.). *Sufis, Scholars and Saints: Muslim Religious Institutions Since 1500.* Berkeley: University of California Press, 1972. A fine collection of articles dealing with the learned and popular aspects of Islam in various parts of the Muslim world. An important book by leading scholars.

Koprulu, Fuat. *On the Way to Democracy.* The Hague: Mouton, 1964. A fine interpretation by a leading Turkish historian and political leader.

Lewis, Bernard. *The Emergence of Modern Turkey.* London: Oxford University Press, 1961. An account of the development of Turkey in the nineteenth century that is first-rate, especially in its treatment of the Young Turks and Kemal's reforms and in its analysis of the decade of the 1950s.

Lewis, Geoffrey. *Turkey.* New York: Praeger, 1960. A standard work that is very reliable.

Puryear, Vernon John. *France and the Levant from the Bourbon Restoration to the Peace of Kutiah.* Berkeley: University of California Press, 1941. A history of diplomacy in the Middle East for the period.

Shaw, Stanford J., and Ezel Kural Shaw. *History of the Ottoman Empire and Modern Turkey*, Vol. II, *Reform, Revolution, and Republic: The Rise of Modern Turkey, 1808–1975.* Cambridge, Eng.: Cambridge University Press, 1977. This very substantial volume touches upon every aspect of change and growth in the Ottoman Empire and Turkey over these years. It is especially strong in explaining the governmental structure that developed in the nineteenth century and in relating it to the events of the times.

Yale, William. *The Near East: A Modern History.* Ann Arbor: University of Michigan Press, 1958. Good for the nineteenth century.

Chapter 22

Muhammad Ali and the Development of Modern Egypt

Rise of Muhammad Ali

Nineteenth-century Egypt was the creation of Muhammad Ali, who must be recognized as one of the great rulers of his age. In 1798 when Selim III raised an army to send to Egypt against Napoleon, the governor of Kavalla in Thrace supplied 300 men, the second in command being Muhammad Ali, probably of Albanian descent and then about twenty-nine years old. (His name as spelled here follows the form used in Egypt and the Arab world. In Turkish he was called Mehmed Ali, as he referred to himself; the British rendering was Mehemet Ali.)

He had been engaged in the tobacco trade, but his latent political talent was soon manifested in Egypt. The peace of Amiens in 1802 and the British evacuation of the Nile found Muhammad Ali responsible for several thousand Albanian and Bosnian troops. At the moment three major powers existed in Egypt: the Ottoman pasha, who ruled in the name of the sultan; the Mamluks, who held landed estates and were hopelessly split in jealous factions; and the Albanians. The people of Cairo constituted a weak fourth.

Muhammad Ali played his cards extremely well. When the British left Egypt in 1803, he sided with the Mamluks and drove the Turkish governor from Cairo. Muhammad Ali then turned one Mamluk faction against another. Finally, with the aid of the Cairo populace, he chased the Mamluks into the desert and deposed the new governor who had just arrived from Istanbul, becoming himself recognized as governor by the citizens of Cairo. When in 1806 Muhammad Ali accepted the honor and asserted his full submission to Selim, the latter appointed him pasha of Egypt.

Affairs in Europe in 1807 pushed Turkey into the French camp; since Muhammad Ali persisted in his loyalty to the Porte, a British expeditionary force was landed at Alexandria. In league with Mamluk remnants, the British occupied Alexandria, but were defeated at Rosetta and withdrew. After the treaty of Tilsit, which threw England and Turkey into each other's arms, Britain renounced all designs upon Egypt, leaving the Mamluks to shift for themselves. Muhammad Ali was now the actual as well as the titular ruler of Egypt.

Finances cramped him severely. On several occasions Muhammad Ali's own Albanians, their pay considerably in arrears, shot at him as he passed in the streets of Cairo. War and the successive passage of troops in Lower

Egypt reduced the delta to barrenness. In previous administrations taxes and levies supported an Egyptian army, but Muhammad Ali found little to levy upon, and taxes proved quite insufficient. Consequently, in 1808 he ordered a survey of all landholdings and confiscated properties with irregular titles. Later he seized land grants upon which payments to the state were in arrears, abolished the ancient system of land tenure, and expropriated the remaining fiefs (*iltizams*). Even exemptions for lands belonging to religious institutions were rescinded and their lands surveyed to be sure none escaped.

As land taxes increased, Muhammad Ali turned his attention to commerce and established a government monopoly on the export of grain. In several of these years the Nile valley possessed the only exportable surplus available to the British fleet and Wellington's army in Spain. Demand was brisk, and profits in the grain trade often reached 500 percent. Frequently, Muhammad Ali accepted cotton goods and small manufactures in exchange for grain, thus gaining from a two-way trade as well as improving his relations with the British.

Muhammad Ali's power and the loyalty of his troops rose in direct proportion to his improved finances. One long-standing score remained to be settled, not only for himself but for the authority of his suzerain, the Ottoman sultan. The Mamluks, particularly those holding fiefs in Upper Egypt, had never been fully subjected, defying one Ottoman governor after another. For several years Muhammad Ali threatened, cajoled, and attacked them. His entreaties induced many to settle at Giza across from Cairo; and at the ceremonies of the investiture of his son as pasha of Jidda in 1811 they were tricked into entering the citadel of Cairo, where the Albanian soldiers slaughtered them. A year later another thousand were executed in Upper Egypt.

Arabia and the Sudan
Organization of the finances of Egypt and destruction of the Mamluk power enabled Muhammad Ali to consider widening his rule. For many decades the Porte was troubled by attacks and depredations of the Saudi tribe of Arabia. In the middle of the eighteenth century Muhammad ibn Saud became converted to the teachings of Muhammad ibn Abd al-Wahhab, a native of Nejd who had studied in Damascus and Baghdad. Returning home, the latter grew convinced of the necessity of eliminating from Muslim practices the pagan superstitions that had become prevalent among the desert Arab tribesmen. He also felt compelled to destroy the philosophic subtleties and the worldly deviations that had crept into Islam over the ages and to restore Islam to the pure, original, and simple form as pronounced by the Prophet, and as set forth in the Hanbali doctrines, one of the four Sunni Muslim law schools.

Muhammad ibn Saud and his descendants, armed with the Wahhabi faith, spread their rule over many tribes in Arabia, pillaging Shiite and Sunnite shrines. Their seizure of the Hijaz during the Napoleonic Wars disrupted

Meccan pilgrimages, and the Porte entreated Muhammad Ali to drive them from Medina and Mecca. In 1811 his son Tusun headed an expedition to subdue and annex the Hijaz. Not until 1818, however, under the firm and courageous leadership of Muhammad Ali's able son Ibrahim, did the superior equipment and discipline of the Egyptian troops turn the scales against the Saudi-Wahhabi forces.

Ibrahim was named governor of the Hijaz and Ethiopia, the latter consisting then of a few Red Sea ports which served as outlets for the Sudan as much as for Abyssinia. Muhammad Ali looked upon the Sudan as a boundless area full of gold, precious stones, and slaves. He also believed that he could develop a fine army from stalwart black slaves from the Sudan, thereby securing independence from his unruly Albanians. An expedition went southward in 1820 under Ismail, another of his sons. Sennar and El Obeid were taken; and within six years the country was pacified and the modern city of Khartoum founded.

Greek Expedition

The experiment with regard to an army of Sudanese slaves proved a total failure. An attempt was made at Aswan under the direction of a French officer, Colonel Sève, who as Suleiman Pasha served Muhammad Ali loyally for more than twenty years. But disease and fatalities among the Sudanese constrained him to build an army around Egyptian soldiers and Turkish and European officers. Over 30,000 Egyptian peasants were sent to Aswan, where in a short time they were drilled into effective soldiers. Meanwhile, Muhammad Ali assembled a fleet. One ship mounting sixteen guns was built at Suez; others were bought in Bombay, Genoa, Venice, Marseilles, and the Greek islands.

While these developments were in process, the Greek revolution turned the eastern Mediterranean into a nest for Greek pirates. In 1822 Mahmud II offered the governorship of Crete to Muhammad Ali, if he would subdue it. After Muhammad Ali had taken Crete, Mahmud bestowed upon him the overlordship of the Peloponnesus on like terms. Under Ibrahim's command 16,000 men and a navy of 63 ships left Alexandria in 1824 to clear the Aegean of the Greek pirate-nationalist navy. Various islands were attacked and plundered, Muhammad Ali replacing his losses with new ships from France and Italy; he even bought some from Greek shipbuilders. Ibrahim and Suleiman Pasha landed in Greece in 1825; but that adventure was extremely costly for Muhammad Ali: his fleet was ruined, and his trained and disciplined army returned to Egypt starved and crippled.

Conquest of Syria

But Muhammad Ali was not a ruler to be discouraged easily. From his ready income provided by the changed tax base he rapidly reconstituted an army. And by 1829 the new self-sufficient naval arsenal at Alexandria, under the direction of de Cerisy, a French naval engineer from Toulon, had begun to turn out frigates, corvettes, and other men-of-war. For a time Muhammad

Ali dallied with French suggestions to cooperate in the destruction of the dey of Algiers, but he tired of French indecision and came to realize that such an excursion would render him a French vassal. Syria was far more inviting, especially since its four districts were pledged to him as payment for his undertaking in Greece. Using a variety of excuses, Muhammad Ali sent Ibrahim against Acre, which fell in May 1832. He then turned upon Turkish forces, speedily entered the Beylan pass south of Alexandretta, and marched northward to the outskirts of Konya. Ibrahim's devastating victory at Konya carried him on to Kutahya, where peace between Mahmud and his rebellious viceroy was concluded in 1833. Crete, Egypt, Syria, Adana, and Tarsus were assigned to Muhammad Ali, for which he agreed to pay a tribute of £150,000 a year to Istanbul.

Ibrahim governed Syria for eight years. A distinguished Syrian has written that these years "may be regarded as the beginning of the modern age for the country." Taxes were regularized, justice was more sure for people of all religions, commerce was encouraged, privileges for foreigners were less abused, education was stimulated, law and order were more prevalent. Ibrahim proved to be more of an Arab than he was a Turk, and ideas of a revival of an Arab state to include all Arabs were circulated.

The resolute rule that Muhammad Ali created in Egypt was also attempted in Syria. Had it been given a longer period of trial, it might have succeeded. Conscription, however, was resisted; the new taxes were hated; and rebellion faced Ibrahim on several occasions. A strong army was an absolute necessity for Muhammad Ali and Ibrahim; and Mahmud was rebuilding an army while European officers were training new Turkish regiments. Since the governorships of Egypt, Syria, and Crete were granted for only one year at a time, and since there were constant disputes over tribute, Muhammad Ali considered maintenance of an ever-ready army a prime requisite for his own safety. When, therefore, European governments urged abandonment of conscription in Syria, reduction of his armaments by half, and withdrawal of his troops from Syria, Muhammad Ali gladly agreed, but on condition that Mahmud grant him hereditary title to his territories and that the Powers guarantee him against aggression.

Receiving no agreement to such conditions, Muhammad Ali decided to declare his independence. Before this could be done, however, Ottoman forces invaded Syria and were destroyed at Nazib by Ibrahim in June 1839. Five days later Mahmud II died, and before July was out the Turkish fleet deserted to join the Egyptians at Alexandria. Muhammad Ali was now master of the situation, and the Porte prepared to surrender to his demands of hereditary vassalage for all territories then in his possession. However, a joint note from Austria, England, France, Prussia, and Russia informed the sultan that they were concerned with developments within the Middle East and recommended that no action be taken on Muhammad Ali's claims without their approval. The British feared that Russia would call into operation provisions of the hated treaty of Hunkiar Iskelesi or that France through Muhammad Ali would dominate Syria and Egypt and control all routes from the Mediterranean to India. The British, therefore, preferred a united action to Russian or French unilateral steps. Fortified with this backing, the Porte informed Muhammad Ali of European concern and awaited the decision of the Powers. In the end Lord Palmerston prevailed upon Russia, Prussia, and Austria to sign the treaty of London in 1840. This treaty was a diplomatic defeat in the Levant for Louis Philippe's government. It allowed Muhammad Ali the hereditary governorship of Egypt if he agreed to the settlement within twenty days, and a lifetime rule over south Syria if he agreed in ten days. Otherwise, the four powers would blockade Egypt and defend the integrity of the Ottoman Empire.

Since Muhammad Ali refused to budge, the only recourse was force. British agents in Lebanon and Syria raised a rebellion against Ibrahim, while a combined British-Austrian fleet landed troops at Beirut and captured Acre. Muhammad Ali was forced to recall Ibrahim from Syria and accept British terms. Egypt was left as a hereditary province to Muhammad Ali and his heirs. Since communications were slow and the arrangements complex, it was not until July 1841 that the Porte confirmed him in the hereditary position in Egypt and granted him authority to make military appointments below the rank of general. France agreed to the terms and returned to the concert of European powers in their concern with affairs of the Middle East.

Organization of Egypt

The defeats of 1840 and the diplomatic negotiations of 1841 gave Muhammad Ali full political power in Egypt but left him an old and broken man. However, in his declining years, Europe learned to appreciate his numerous accomplishments. As Muhammad Ali's representative, Ibrahim was feted in France and England; Muhammad Ali himself was invited to London, but the old man ventured only to Istanbul and his birthplace, Kavalla. He lapsed into senility in 1847 and died two years later.

For forty years Muhammad Ali had ruled Egypt, and every phase of life and society had interested him at one time or another. He had created a new government and developed a cabinet with ministers of war, navy, agriculture, finance, commerce and foreign affairs, education, and security. Real power, however, had never slipped from the hands of the Pasha, as Muhammad Ali was always known. In the 1830s councils of notables were appointed to discuss governmental affairs. Western travelers were greatly impressed. But the Pasha never intended that his rule be other than that of a benevolent despot.

The trade monopoly for grain was extended to include cotton, tobacco, and indigo, although the British terminated the monopoly system in 1838 when a new commercial treaty for the entire Ottoman Empire was concluded with Mahmud II. Revision of the tax laws and methods of collection, confiscations of Mamluk holdings, attacks upon endowments, and other acquisitions of land brought the state—that is, Muhammad Ali—control by 1840 of more than half the cultivable land in Egypt. Though he had given vast tracts to various members of his extended family by the time of his death, the ruling family fully controlled the domestic market. (Some termed Egypt Muhammad Ali's farm.) Through the various state enterprises, the import trade was strongly affected by his policies, and for more than a decade he enjoyed a monopoly over imports as well as exports. By the treaties of 1840 and 1841 Muhammad Ali was forced to recognize the Ottoman sultan as his suzerain and to agree to abide by the sultan's laws, especially the capitulations held by the Great Powers. Since taxes were paid in kind, the Pasha's government continued to be the principal participant in the export trade; and most foreign merchants in Alexandria did not object after Muhammad Ali agreed to offer his goods at public auction to export houses. Corn and rice were introduced. In many areas steam pumps and better canals allowed summer irrigation, enabling the fellaheen to double the yield by growing two crops a year. Great attention was given to the science of irrigation. Swamp lands were drained, old canals opened, and new ones built. North of Cairo a great barrage was constructed to raise canal levels, especially in years of scanty floods. However, since the engineering work was not too sound, it proved ineffective until rebuilt in the 1880s.

The age of Muhammad Ali in Egypt coincided with the first industrial surge in western Europe, and the Pasha became convinced of the value of such a program for his land. He imported textile plants and built sugar factories. But technical knowledge, suitable labor, and supplies of coal and iron were lacking; even before Muhammad Ali died, the failure to industrialize Egypt was apparent.

Two other of his successful endeavors were sanitation and education. Great plagues raged every year; and annual deaths from cholera and bubonic plague sometimes rose to 10 percent of the population. A more effective quarantine was organized, and the foreign consuls in Alexandria were appointed to a board of sanitation, which was given ample funds and absolute authority. After 1840 visitations of these diseases were restricted and health conditions in general were improved. The marked increase in the population was largely attributed to advances in agriculture and the absence of epidemics.

The first schools established were for the military—infantry, cavalry, engineers, navy, and artillery. Most of the instructors in these schools were French; and boys were sent to study in France, Italy, and England. In 1833, however, the Polytechnic School was founded with a staff comprised almost entirely of Egyptian teachers. Soon preparatory schools to feed the Polytechnic were organized in Cairo and Alexandria. A medical college was established by Clot Bey, a French doctor long in the Pasha's service. In connection with the schools a government press was set up at Bulaq near Cairo; most of its publications were translations of European technical works. Newspapers printed in both Arabic and French not only gave urban society access to Western ideas but also made Egypt a leader in the intellectual life of the Arab world.

Muhammad Ali was impatient and tried to change society rapidly without a sufficient supply of sympathetic officials. His innovations were too hurried and too shallow to endure. He once commented toward the end of his life that he had found Egypt "utterly barbarous" and that he had tried to make some improvement. Alexandria was transformed into a Mediterranean city resembling Marseilles, Genoa, and Naples. Construction of the great Mahmudiyah Canal brought all Nile trade and traffic from Cairo to Alexandria and turned the latter into a boom town. Its population increased from 15,000 in 1805 to 150,000 in 1847. Since many of its inhabitants were Europeans, Alexandria became one of the most cosmopolitan cities of the world. During his reign, Muhammad Ali had given Egypt the first constructive leadership in centuries and sown the seeds for the establishment of a national state. Incredibly, this was done without incurring any debts.

Unfortunately, much of Muhammad Ali's work was undone by his successor, his grandson Abbas Pasha. A conservative, traditional Turkish gentleman who had headed an army in Syria under Ibrahim, Abbas Pasha disliked Europeans and resented the presence of the large number of them in Egypt; but he also realized that his interests paralleled those of the British. He shunned Frenchmen and permitted many of his grandfather's innovations to lapse. Factories were abandoned, trade monopolies abolished, and schools closed. Aggressive policies were curtailed, and the army was halved. Although a British firm constructed the first railway between Alexandria and Cairo, French agents seeking to build the Suez Canal were unable to receive a hearing. (In exchange for the railway concession the British aided Abbas Pasha in having set aside for Egypt certain provisions of the Ottoman penal code of 1851, which had transferred to Istanbul death-penalty authorizations.) Upon Abbas Pasha's murder in 1854, authority passed to his uncle Said, Muhammad Ali's favorite son, who surrounded himself with Frenchmen.

The Suez Canal
In Said's youth he had formed a friendship with Ferdinand de Lesseps, son of the French political agent in Egypt, and within four months after his accession Said granted his friend a broad concession to construct the Suez Canal. Officially promulgated in 1855, the news touched off a long diplomatic imbroglio. The British government opposed the scheme, believing that it would impair British commercial advantages with the Orient and that it would inevitably create an Egyptian question for European diplomacy. Because it was involved at the moment in the Crimean War, the Porte could ill afford to antagonize England and thus did not accord the project the necessary ratification.

In 1856 an international commission of engineers surveyed the land and reported on the proposal, setting an estimate of £6 million as a maximum cost. In a detailed concession given to the Compagnie Universelle du Canal Maritime de Suez, three types of shares of stock were authorized. Preference shares, which enjoyed 15 percent of the net profits of the company, went to Said for granting the concession and for furnishing the labor required to dig the canal. Founder shares, which received 10 percent of the net profits, were held by the organizers or were given without cost to influential personages. And 400,000 ordinary shares sold for 500 francs each.

Until 1858 Napoleon III seemed unconcerned, but when the subscription lists were opened for the ordinary shares, his views changed. It is believed that de Lesseps gave a substantial number of founder shares to influential members of his court, if not to the emperor and empress themselves. When the books were closed, 207,111 shares had been bought in France, and 96,517 in Egypt (92,136 by Said). Some 85,500 shares reserved for nationals of England, Russia, Austria, and the United States remained unsold. Although Said warned that construction of the canal should not begin until approved in Istanbul, digging started in April 1859. The British protested vigorously over the use of forced labor and were able to keep the sultan from ratifying the concession. Notwithstanding the fact that Said took up the balance of unsubscribed shares, little work had been accomplished when Said died in 1863 and Ismail, Ibrahim's oldest living son, became governor.

Ismail was thirty-three years old. He had been educated in Paris at the École d'État-Major and had gone for Said on missions to Turkey, France, and the Vatican. At his accession Ismail accepted the commitments concerning the canal, and by 1866 the British no longer opposed it. Under pressure from Napoleon III the Porte gave its authorization. Ismail paid an indemnity for not supplying forced labor, and the construction proceeded rapidly. When it was finished in 1869, Ismail spent £1 million on the opening ceremonies. Empress Eugénie was the guest of honor among 6,000 guests including the Emperor of Austria and the crown prince of Prussia. Verdi's *Aida*, composed for this event, was performed in Cairo at the opera house built for the occasion.

For the first several years the canal operated at a loss, and the company was perilously close to bankruptcy. However, traffic increased, the canal showing profits continuously after 1875. Ismail and Egypt, nevertheless, did not benefit from it. The cost of the canal to Said and Ismail was estimated at £11.5 million, for which Egypt received no return. To a considerable extent this was because Ismail was a spendthrift and impractical.

From the beginning, two questions confronted the company. The original concession authorized a charge of 10 francs a ton for passage. To settle how a ship's tonnage should be calculated an international conference was held in 1873 at Istanbul. The conference also set a higher schedule of rates until traffic and profits should warrant a reduction. Increasing commerce gradually reduced the dues, and by 1906 the charge per ton was only 7.75 francs. The concession also stipulated that the canal would be open, without any preferential treatment, to merchant vessels of every flag. During the Egyptian crisis of 1881 and 1882 the British closed the canal for four days, and navigation by warships was debated. A conference in Istanbul in 1888 attended by Austria, France, Germany, Great Britain, Italy, the Netherlands, Russia, Spain, and Turkey agreed to the Constantinople convention, which declared that the canal should "always be free and open, in the time of war as in time of peace, to every vessel of commerce or of war, without distinction of flag." Britain signed with reservations which she did not relinquish until 1904.

Ismail's Rule
From the moment of Ismail's accession in 1863 until his deposition in 1879 life at the court in Egypt was sumptuous: money flowed like the waters of the Nile. Ismail showered munificent gifts upon all, and his trips to Europe and Istanbul were lavish in every detail. Presents to the sultan on the order of £1 million and a diamond-encrusted solid-gold dinner service were not unusual. Ismail possessed a charismatic personality which dispelled all opposition; and his use of flattery and urbane suavity earned him the acclaim of Europe. Shortly after Ismail's accession, Sultan Abd al-Aziz visited him in Egypt, being the first Ottoman sultan to come to Cairo since its capture in 1517. (It should be pointed out that these two rulers, who resembled each other in many ways, were cousins, their mothers being sisters.) In 1866–1867 Ismail visited Istanbul, where through princely gifts he won the title khedive and recognition of the succession to the Egyptian throne by the law of primogeniture. At the same time, for the doubling of his tribute he was allowed to strengthen his army, coin money, and bestow decorations and titles on his own. In 1869 he was received, entertained, and decorated by the crowned heads of Europe. However, Ismail was rapidly falling into the clutches of unscrupulous moneylenders and European bankers.

At Ismail's accession Egypt had a foreign debt of £3 million and a domestic debt of £4 million. Thirteen years later it had a foreign debt of £68 million and a domestic debt of £30 million. Of this, nearly 35 percent was incurred in the form of discounts and commissions, putting the rates on the "verge of fraudulence." Interest charges mounted to £5 million per annum, more than half the total annual revenue of the government. Ismail flogged the fellaheen to increase taxes and sought new sources of income. In 1874 he sold his 176,602 ordinary shares of Canal stock to the British government for nearly £4 million. (He had previously sold 1,040 shares to French capitalists.) But this only delayed the day of reckoning, which came in 1876 when Ismail ceased payment on his bills and debts.

Before detailing Ismail's bankruptcy his reign should be examined to provide a balance against his financial profligacy by acknowledging his imagination and leadership in lifting Egypt into the modern world—for Egypt in 1880, the end of Ismail's rule, was a far cry, indeed, from the Egypt of 1860.

Perhaps the most apparent change during Ismail's reign was the Europeanization of urban Egypt. By 1880 more than 100,000 Europeans were living in Cairo and Alexandria. The leading citizenry of Egypt meanwhile was sending most of its sons to Europe to be educated. Ismail's fondness for saying that Egypt was a part of Europe was not without foundation. And, in fact, it was the Europeanized elite, participating in government, education, and general culture, who maintained his drive and aims and sustained and improved upon most of his works.

In government Ismail inaugurated in 1866 the Assembly of Delegates, made up of seventy-five members elected for three-year terms. Though only a quasi-parliamentary body, the assembly, most of whose members came from a new class of wealthy and influential headmen, served Ismail as a kind of constitutional shield to offset the Turkish elite that was evolving from the privileged army-officer and government-official classes. It also served as a potential means of impressing French and British bankers. Until 1875 the assembly meetings were superficial and under Ismail's thumb, but then the financial crisis emboldened the members to criticize foreign financial powers and to demand ministerial responsibility for the assembly. In a session in 1876 it requested an explanation of government operations and suggested that the assembly supervise government expenditures. The assembly's increasing assertiveness in 1878 brought foreign pressure on Ismail, and in 1879 he dissolved the assembly. The delegates, continuing to meet unofficially in various members' homes, formed a nucleus of leaders who showed the way to a nationalist cause in years to come.

Long-staple cotton had been introduced in 1821 from the Ethiopian-Sudanese border, and Muhammad Ali had eagerly spread its cultivation. By 1850, 35 million pounds were being grown annually. During the American Civil War production soared from 59 million to 250 million pounds per year, and the price increased by 400 percent to a total of over £25 million. At all levels everyone hastened to profit from this bonanza, but with the end of the war, prices tumbled, and peasants were thrown into a miserable condition of mortgage foreclosures and usurious indebtedness. Village headmen improved their influence and prosperity throughout these times by lending to their bankrupt neighbors. Their dominance in the assembly, formed at a time of peasant hardship and depression, was not just a coincidence. Since cotton was a cash crop, it tended to destroy the old communal economy of the village; and in steps under Said and Ismail, family proprietorship with an individualistic economy began to prevail. The state monopoly over agricultural products was terminated, and in 1871 Ismail gave full right of ownership to villages. Still, with heavy taxes a peasant flight from the land persisted. Big estates flourished and were subject to taxation only after 1854, though at a lower rate. Village headmen, however, remained important in the political, economic, and social life of the country, and their sons, no longer exempt from conscription under Said, began to improve the quality of the rank and file in the army and even to change its character as higher ranks were opened to them. Large estates, swollen by abandoned lands, were owned by the khedivial family and the elite of the Turkish officials. Yet there was a certain fluidity in ownership caused by personal mismanagement and indebtedness and the fractioning of landholdings under Muslim laws of inheritance. Undoubtedly all Ismail's policies and actions, including the building of the Ibrahimiyya Canal from the Nile River at Assyut northward and the bringing of over a million acres of new land under cultivation, were efforts to increase his income; nevertheless, they did benefit the whole nation, as the population growth of a million during his sixteen years of rule testified.

In the sphere of international affairs Ismail had certain autonomous rights granted by several decrees from the Porte. In addition to the ability to contract loans, Ismail could negotiate with foreign governments, but only through consuls, never ambassadors. As a part of the Ottoman Empire, Egypt was subject to the capitulatory treaties with other states, chiefly European. Abused by traders and all foreigners, the treaties practically assured that law cases were settled by diplomatic pressure rather than on a basis of merit or justice. The number (100,000 in 1875) and the variety of foreign nationals residing in Egypt made cases of one foreigner against another difficult to adjudicate. However, to obtain agreement for any change from seventeen different consular jurisdictions seemed impossible. In 1862 a circular sent to all consulates providing for the abridgment of the capitulations to permit the arrest and questioning of foreign nationals received no reply. In 1867 Ismail's foreign minister, Nubar Pasha, proposed a mixed court staffed by Egyptians and foreign judges which would administer codes of law to be drawn up by an international commission on the basis of French law. It would deal with civil and criminal cases, with jurisdiction reserved by the consuls only over their own nationals. This reform bid was rejected by France; others accepted in varying degrees; and negotiations dragged on. Eventually a conference in Istanbul in 1873 authorized the Mixed Courts and the six law codes that they would apply. France finally agreed the next year, and the courts began in 1875 with a majority of foreign judges and the French language used in all proceedings. Judges, Egyptian and foreign, were appointed by the khedive, although foreigners were nominated by participating governments which agreed to recognize judgments of these courts. (Judge Farman of New York was nominated by President Grant and served for many years.) Establishment of the Mixed Courts, however, weakened the government and frequently frustrated its operation. They did not end the capitulations but modified them in an important way.

Ismail's boldest venture was the extension of Egyptian rule into the Sudan. Muhammad Ali had conquered parts of the region, and in 1842 the sultan had recognized him as governor general of the Sudan. During the middle of the century under Abbas and Said, interest lapsed, the only activities with regard to the Sudan being along the Red Sea and involving conflict with Ethiopia over ports like Suakin and Massawa. The Ottoman government ceded these to Ismail in 1865, and he set up a new southern province with Fashoda on the White Nile as its capital. Ismail was Europeanized to the extent of considering Egypt as a participant in the partitioning of Africa, and he devised ambitious schemes of expanding Egypt to the equator and including all of the basin of the White Nile. In 1869 he declared that steps were being taken to end the slave trade in the Sudan and sent the British explorer Sir Samuel Baker to govern equatorial Sudan. Under Ismail's aegis Sir Samuel led expeditions to the equatorial lakes district that resulted in the attachment of Bahr al-Ghazal to the Sudan. His successor, General Charles George Gordon, led two unsuccessful forays against Ethiopia in 1875 and 1876 but had more luck curtailing the slave trade. In fact, he was so successful in the latter endeavor as to disturb the local economy and dislocate the principal preoccupation of local leaders. Gordon departed with many of his European assistants in 1877, and upon Ismail's deposition in 1879 the Sudan was left in a state of near anarchy. Without financial resources from Cairo, the mild Egyptian replacement was no match for the uprising led by Muhammad Ahmad of Dongola, who declared himself Mahdi in 1881.

Ismail in his European travels partook of the social and cultural life and insisted upon creating a similar society in Egypt. Hardly any facet escaped his attention. His improvements in the cities and towns brought residential quarters, squares, and parks along with water service, gas supplies, and street lighting. Societies were organized for archaeology, music, and poetry, for the construction of libraries (the Khedivial Library in 1870) and museums (the Egyptian Museum in 1863) for the advancement of Egyptology, and in 1875 the Khedivial Geographical Society for African exploration. In 1868 Ismail opened a comedy theater in Cairo and brought European companies to perform theatricals such as he had seen in Paris. The next year the Cairo Opera House was opened with a performance of *Rigoletto* followed by the première of *Aïda* in December 1869. At the same time two theaters were built in Alexandria. Newspapers were encouraged and the famous daily *Al-Ahram* began in 1876.

Above all else, Ismail believed firmly that education would turn his state and people around. Western influences and culture had been weakened under Abbas, who banished some educators to Khartoum. Although they returned during Said's rule, education did not come into its own until the advent of Ismail. A ministry of education was established, separate from the military, and headed at times by Ali Pasha Mubarak, a great scholar and vigorous administrator. A law of 1868 created a state system of education, which set up the first school for girls five years later. Specialized schools were started for lawyers, engineers, and administrators; Teachers College was founded in 1872; and the renowned School of Languages was reopened under the direction of Rifaa Tahtawi, a great scholar and author who was to inspire many of the leaders of Egyptian public life for the following half century.

There is no question that Ismail was exceedingly extravagant. He had little understanding of the value of money: it was merely a ready commodity for obtaining what he wanted. For years European bankers had been anxious to loan him funds for his many whims and projects. But the capitulations practically condemned Egypt to the penurious role of an agriculturally based economy which in the period following the Crimean War and the

American Civil War reduced Egypt to a level of relative inferiority. Universal hard times in the mid-1870s found Ismail bankrupt; further loans were impossible to obtain at any price, and state revenues were inadequate.

To extricate himself from bankruptcy Ismail conducted a losing battle against European bondholders, "unofficial" government officials, commissions of inquiry, and consuls general. Seeking aid from the British, he accepted a mission led by Steven Cave to investigate Egyptian finances. The Cave report recommended a control commission over Egyptian finances to approve future loans. At this juncture Ismail suspended all payments on loans, whereupon British and French creditors appointed representatives to negotiate for new arrangements with Ismail. In 1876 the entire debt was unified, and Ismail agreed to set up the Caisse de la Dette Publique with four members representing the British, French, Italian, and Austrian creditors. These fund directors (the British member was Major Evelyn Baring of the Baring banking family and later Lord Cromer) supervised all revenues and expenditures in Egypt, channeling 60 percent of the revenues to pay off the debt and enabling the servicing of the debt to be met fully in 1877. But Ismail had been forced in 1876 to appoint dual controllers: Major Baring for the British and M. de Blignières for the French. The controllers could attend cabinet meetings, demand information, give advice, and report to their diplomatic representatives in the event advice was ignored. They became the real rulers of Egypt. On the findings of an international commission of inquiry a law was enacted squeezing the debt down to £85 million and reserving £4.5 million of the annual government income for the budget. All excess income, then estimated at £4 million, was to be employed to retire the debt. Unfortunately for the future development of Egypt, expanding revenues resulting from increased productivity and hard work or from inflation would not benefit Egyptians or improve services of the government. Since the controllers were duty-bound to guard the revenue and pay off the debt, they could hardly fail to be unpopular with the Egyptians, to whom their regime appeared unduly oppressive.

The commission of inquiry demanded that Ismail accept a civil list for himself and his family and the idea of ministerial responsibility. Moreover, an international cabinet was installed with Nubar Pasha as prime minister, Mr. Rivers Wilson (a member of the commission) as finance minister, and M. de Blignières as minister of public works, and with many Europeans serving in the various offices at generous salaries. Times were hard everywhere; government expenditures were greatly curtailed; and the Nile flooding of 1877–1878 was exceedingly low, drastically reducing crop yields. The crisis encouraged independent activity of the Assembly of Delegates, military conspiracies, press agitation, and the formation of national secret societies, some of which were probably encouraged by Ismail.

In 1879 Nubar Pasha and Rivers Wilson were mobbed in Cairo by a group of army officers whose pay had just been cut in half, and they were saved only by Ismail's personal intervention. Ismail then dismissed Nubar Pasha and the international ministry, eventually appointing in its place an all-

Egyptian cabinet of his choice under Sharif Pasha. With a great deal of national constitutional enthusiasm arising, Ismail defied Europe. He summoned the consuls general to confront them with the discontent of the Assembly of Delegates, the disaffection of the army, and the disquiet of the public. A draft constitution of forty-nine articles was submitted to the assembly, giving among other things full control of finances to the assembly. There was great jubilation all around when the assembly accepted the constitution. The British and the French, however, were determined that Ismail be deposed. Threats of independent action on the part of Bismarck heartened the European powers to persuade the sultan in Istanbul to send a telegram on June 26, 1879, addressed to the "former" Khedive Ismail informing him that rule had passed to his son Muhammad Tawfik. Following the failure of his appeal through the press, Ismail left for Italy. He died in Naples in 1895.

European Intervention

Soon after Ismail's deposition a crisis developed over the question of Egyptian autonomy under laws decreed by the Porte as against subservience to the European powers as represented by French and British officials. Authority passed to the revived dual controllers, who naturally cut expenditures to the bone. The size of the army was reduced; many officers were retired; civil budgets and personnel were pared. Yet a sizable number of foreign administrators came in at inordinate salaries. Opposition quickly formed in Egypt. The evolution of society under Ismail had brought four parties to the fore: a weak reactionary party led by Riaz Pasha; a vigorous Islamic modernist party developed by Muhammad Abdu; a constitutional party of wealthy Europeanized Egyptian landowners organized by Sharif Pasha from membership in the assembly and from other groups (this party was later called the Helwan group after its meeting place); and an army group composed of pure Egyptians in the lower officer echelons and inspired by Colonel Ahmad Urabi. Only Riaz's party acquiesced in the foreign dual control, preferring it to any of the Egyptian groups. The army was the most violent in its opposition, because high-ranking officers were Turks or Circassians and the dual control did not remove these officers to the extent that it curbed the rise of native Egyptians.

When in January 1882 England and France presented a joint note to the khedive protesting the formation of a constitutional government, the army partly gained control of the cabinet. England and France had to occupy the country or give up the dual control. Nationalist excesses in Alexandria served as the pretext. A change in the French government, however, altered French policy; and England alone intervened. The English occupied Egypt in July 1882 to overthrow Urabi and reestabilsh European control. Alexandria was shelled; the British navy occupied Port Said, Ismailia, and Suez; and in September, British troops won the Battle of Tel al-Kebir and took Cairo. At this point rebellion in Egypt collapsed.

REFERENCES: Chapter 22

Readings for this chapter are also found in Chapters 7, 13, 19, 20, and 21.

Abu-Lughod, Ibrahim. *Arab Rediscovery of Europe: A Study in Cultural Encounters.* Princeton, N.J.: Princeton University Press, 1963. A study of the Arab travelers and students in Europe, especially Paris, in the century after Napoleon. Shows the importance not only of their experiences and development there but also discusses the impact of books printed in Arabic about their life and travels in Europe.

Amin, Osman. *Muhammad 'Abduh.* Translated by Charles Wendell. Washington, D.C.: American Council of Learned Societies, 1953. A short biography of the great reformer of Egypt.

Arkell, A. J. *A History of the Sudan to 1821.* London, Athlone Press, 1961. This is an expanded version of a valuable work first published in 1955.

Baer, Gabriel. *Egyptian Guilds in Modern Times.* Jerusalem: The Israel Oriental Society, 1964. An important contribution.

————. *A History of Landownership in Modern Egypt, 1800–1950.* New York: Oxford University Press, 1962. A most important work.

Blunt, Wilfrid S. *Secret History of the English Occupation of Egypt.* London: Unwin, 1907. Written by a long-time resident of Egypt who was a friend of many of the leading Egyptian nationalists and sympathetic to their aspirations.

Brinton, Jasper Y. *The Mixed Courts of Egypt.* Rev. ed. New Haven: Yale University Press, 1968. The first edition appeared in 1930. This revised edition has added three new chapters on the stages of the termination of the courts and a final evaluation.

Cleland, Wendell. *The Population Problem in Egypt: A Study of Population Trends and Conditions.* Lancaster, Pa.: Science Press, 1936. An analysis of births and deaths over thirty years and an inquiry into the Malthusian theory as it pertains to Egypt.

Collins, Robert O., and Robert L. Tignor. *Egypt and the Sudan.* Englewood Cliffs, N.J.: Prentice-Hall, 1967. This is a very useful volume in the Modern Nations in Historical Perspective series, which covers Egypt and the Sudan, each separately, from earliest times to the present, with emphasis on the nineteenth and twentieth centuries. Since the authors are acknowledged authorities in their specialties, the study is very reliable.

Dodwell, Henry. *The Founder of Modern Egypt: A Study of Muhammad 'Ali.* Cambridge, Eng.: Cambridge University Press, 1931. Lacks much that has been presented by recent scholarship, but still serves as a good summary.

Farnie, D. A. *East and West of Suez: The Suez Canal in History, 1854–1956.* Oxford: Clarendon Press, 1969. A monumental work, derived from a vast range of Western-language sources.

Gray, Richard. *A History of the Southern Sudan, 1839–1889.* New York: Oxford University Press, 1961. A major contribution to the historiography of the modern Sudan.

Hill, Richard. *Slatin Pasha.* London: Oxford University Press, 1965. An account of one of the European adventurers in the Sudan.

Hoskins, Halford L. *British Routes to India.* New York: Longmans, Green, 1928. A masterful study of the Middle East from the mid-eighteenth century to the twentieth century, particularly as it related to European interests.

Huseyn Efendi. *Ottoman Egypt in the Age of the French Revolution.* Cambridge, Mass.: Harvard University Press, 1964.

Landau, Jacob M. *Jews in Nineteenth-Century Egypt.* New York: New York University Press, 1969. A study of the internal organization and external relationships of the Jewish community and its extensive growth in the nineteenth century.

Landes, David S. *Bankers and Pashas: International Finance and Economic Imperialism in Egypt.* Cambridge, Mass.: Harvard University Press, 1958. A case study of private banking in Egypt in the 1860s discussing the fortunes of Edouard Dervieu et Cie. of Alexandria in the first years of the reign of Ismail.

Lane, E. W. *Manners and Customs of the Modern Egyptians.* New York: Dutton, 1923. A significant work.

Marlowe, John. *A History of Modern Egypt and Anglo-Egyptian Relations, 1800–1956.* Hamden, Conn.: Archon, 1965. A useful survey.

———. *World Ditch: The Making of the Suez Canal.* New York: Macmillan, 1964. A careful study of the building of the canal.

Owen, E. R. J. *Cotton and the Egyptian Economy, 1820–1914: A Study in Trade and Development.* Oxford: Clarendon Press, 1969. A stimulating and scholarly analysis of the Egyptian economy. Discusses the question of income distribution.

Rivlin, Helen Anne B. *The Agricultural Policy of Muhammad Ali in Egypt.* Cambridge, Mass.: Harvard University Press, 1961. An outstanding work which considers the entire economy of Egypt and the relationship of Muhammad Ali's agricultural policy to his reign.

Rodkey, Frederick S. *Turco-Egyptian Question, 1832–41.* Urbana, Ill.: University of Illinois, 1924. A diplomatic account.

Schonfield, Hugh J. *The Suez Canal: In Peace and War, 1869–1969.* Coral Gables, Fla.: University of Miami Press, 1969. This volume covers the first century of the canal, including the June War of 1967, and adds to the author's *The Suez Canal in World Affairs* (1952) and *The Suez Canal* (1939).

Vatikiotis, P. J. *The Modern History of Egypt.* New York: Praeger, 1969. A fine detailed work on nineteenth- and twentieth-century Egypt. Shows the historical continuity in Egyptian society and reveals the ways that Islam and the Arabic language have shaped Egyptian society. Strong on social and intellectual movements in the rise of Egyptian nationalism.

Wakefield, Gordon. *Egypt.* New York: Walker, 1967. A well-organized and well-balanced synthesis of Egyptian history from the earliest times to the present, with emphasis on the latter.

Weigall, Arthur E. P. Brome. *A History of Events in Egypt from 1798 to 1914.* London: Blackwood, 1915. Still a useful outline.

Wright, L. C. *United States Policy Toward Egypt, 1830–1914.* New York: Exposition Press, 1969. Helpful in understanding Egypt's strategic international importance.

Young, George. *Egypt.* New York: Scribner, 1927. A valuable survey.

Chapter 23

European Ambitions and Diplomacy in the Middle East

European Interests

Throughout the nineteenth century, Russia, England, Austria, and France maintained a continuing interest in affairs of the Ottoman Empire. Toward the end of the century Germany became the fifth major European power involved in imperialism in the Middle East.

Dynastic aggrandizement at the expense of the Ottomans motivated Austrian and Russian conquests in the eighteenth century. The Hapsburgs desired Hungary, Transylvania, Dalmatia, and Serbia; and at the turn of the century they would have pushed southward in the Balkans had not the Napoleonic Wars absorbed their full strength. Metternich recognized the importance of Istanbul and the weakness of the Ottoman Empire, but advocated the preservation of its integrity, since Austria was unable to expect a major portion from any partition scheme. He opposed rescuing the Greeks for fear that even a modicum of Greek independence would redound in more freedom for Serbs and other national groups within the Austrian Empire. Austria was also apprehensive lest Russia gain advantages in the Balkans, control Istanbul and the Straits, and flank Austria dangerously from the south.

France thought of the Ottoman Empire in terms of commerce, imperial geopolitical strategy, diplomacy, military and naval alliances, culture, and tradition. The merchants of Marseilles, who were engrossed in trade in every port of the Levant, were most instrumental in obtaining the great treaty of capitulations from the Porte in 1740. France was interested in empire and commerce in India and farther Asia in addition to her interests in North Africa and the Mediterranean. The land mass of the Middle East lay astride the routes to the Orient. Since England rivaled France in the East, whichever power gained secure access to Middle Eastern routes could threaten and block the communications of the other. For this reason Muhammad Ali of Egypt appeared to be an excellent ally, and the French cultivated him and his successors assiduously.

In the realm of diplomacy the French endeavored to sway the Porte toward a course amicable to France and tried to get the sultan to view international affairs through the eyes and words of the French ambassador.

The heroic age of the Crusades gave the French a historic interest in the Middle East and the French king still possessed the right to defend the Holy Places. Broadly interpreted, this right meant the privilege of interfering in all events of the Middle East. As a kind of corollary to these interests, the French believed fervently that penetration of their culture and use of their language in the Middle East would indissolubly tie its people to French views and create a sympathetic and understanding bond of everlasting friendship.

British interest in the Middle East began during the reign of Elizabeth I, but remained almost exclusively commercial until the Napoleonic era. In the nineteenth century, especially after the treaty of Adrianople (Edirne), a changing emphasis in trade and a shifting European balance of power won over Britain to the maintenance of Turkey as a means of blocking Russian egress into the Mediterranean. This policy impelled England to oppose partition of the Ottoman Empire and to pursue a positive course to strengthen the sultan's government. Moreover, profitable markets in the Middle East stimulated the British to cultivate the friendship of the Turks. Sir Stratford Canning—later Viscount de Redcliffe—combined these varied British interests into a unified approach to the Porte. His words and instructions had a statesmanlike quality, respected and esteemed by the Turks. The populace of Istanbul referred to him as The Great Ambassador.

Russia proved the most consistent and persistent enemy of the Ottoman Empire in the eighteenth and nineteenth centuries. The tsars and tsarinas dreamed of gaining Istanbul and reestablishing a Christian empire in the city of Constantine. Joined to this ambition was the belief that control of navigation through the Straits for commerce and war was an absolute necessity to complete the full sovereignty of Russia. Means to these ends, but eventually ends in themselves, were interests in the Holy Land; concern over the welfare, security, and friendship of all Christians in the Ottoman Empire; and creation of friendly Christian satellite states in the Balkans and the Caucasus.

Although war and peace recurred intermittently between Russia and the Ottoman Empire, the first notable landmark of their relationship in the nineteenth century was fixed by the famous treaty of Kuchuk Kainarji of 1774. A number of subsequent treaties concluded between the two states —Ainali Kavak in 1779, Jassy in 1792, Istanbul in 1798 and in 1805, Bucharest in 1812, and Akkerman in 1826—confirmed the concessions granted by the Porte but without greatly augmenting them. The treaty of Adrianople, however, altered the status quo. It gave Russia an increased role in the Balkans and served definite notice to the European powers that Russian policy might not be averse to an immediate dissolution of the Ottoman Empire. But the dangers for Russia in such a policy alarmed Count Nesselrode and Nicholas I, who advocated the presence of a weak Turkish neighbor as a safer course. Partition would mean certain prizes for England and France in the Middle East, a development that could only be hostile to Russian interests.

Nicholas therefore accepted in 1833 the invitation to protect the Ottoman Empire against attack by Muhammad Ali and sent Count Orloff with a fleet and marines to the Bosphorus to defend the helpless Mahmud. Orloff was a superb diplomat, and after thwarting Muhammad Ali but before the armed forces departed he obtained the famous treaty of Hunkiar Iskelesi. Important territorial concessions might have been wrung from Mahmud at this time, but Nicholas did not presume that Russia was strong enough to face the certain hostility of England, France, and Austria to such a unilateral action.

Diplomats and political leaders immediately sensed the gravity of Hunkiar Iskelesi. Even with one secret clause, it was a simple short treaty proclaiming a defensive alliance between the two states and promising aid to each other in case of need. In particular, Turkey declared anew the "ancient rule of the Ottoman Empire" and the closing of the Straits to all warships. The chief import of the treaty, however, lay in its affirmation of friendship, which indicated the direction in which the weathervane of Ottoman diplomacy turned.

Commerce and Trade

Lord Ponsonby, British ambassador, set about immediately to redress the balance and win the favor of the Porte, a task in which his success was demonstrated in 1838 by the signing of the important and advantageous commercial convention of Balta Liman, a significant blow to Russian favoritism. British traders were permitted to import goods upon payment of an ad valorem duty of 5 percent; upon the export of Turkish goods a duty of 12 percent was charged. Furthermore, monopolistic practices were abolished on goods exported from the empire. This provision specifically included Egypt. The most important result of the arrangement was the ability, henceforth, of British merchants to carry on foreign trade at the same rates as applied to Ottoman nationals. Since British firms had a wider organization and were not subject to Ottoman taxation, the convention soon proved to be a blow to Turkish traders.

Again, articles of the Balta Liman convention did not in themselves bestow upon Great Britain any marked position in the Middle East. France, the Netherlands, and other nations were accorded identical treatment before the year was out. In following years, however, when Muhammad Ali reasserted his position against the sultan, the British were instrumental in removing the unilateral approach to the Straits question as contained in Hunkiar Iskelesi. They substituted the concerted five-power settlement of the Straits and Middle Eastern problems contained in the London conventions of 1840 and 1841. The earlier of these dealt with the affairs of Muhammad Ali, Syria, and Egypt. Even that convention, however, contained articles emphasizing that any occupation within the Straits by foreign armed forces to protect the sultan from Muhammad Ali had to be only temporary and "not derogate in any degree from the ancient rule of the Ottoman Empire."

The following year the convention among Great Britain, Austria, France, Prussia, Russia, and Turkey reaffirmed the ancient rule, mentioning the Bosphorus as well as the Dardanelles. Each European signatory was thus committed to defend the sultan's sovereignty over the Straits and to prohibit warships from entering those waters while the sultan was at peace. With the expiration of Hunkiar Iskelesi that autumn no European state had any special privilege that others did not possess. Europe recognized that the treaties of Kuchuk Kainarji, Akkerman, and Adrianople were still valid and that Russia enjoyed specified rights in the Balkans and among certain Christian groups throughout the empire. But in the Straits and at the Porte no nation had a treaty advantage or position of favor over another.

The convention of Balta Liman marked a definite upsurge in commerce between Turkey and Western Europe. After 1846 and the repeal of the corn laws in England, the grain trade with the Ottoman Empire and especially with the Danubian provinces rose to unprecedented heights. Within a few years Britain was obtaining as much grain from Turkey as she was from Russia (a development that should not be ignored in considering the factors leading to the Crimean War). General trade between Turkey and England increased as well. Opium, raisins, currants, figs, olive oil, silk, mohair, wool, cotton, sheep, and carpets were bought by British merchants in Istanbul, Izmir, Beirut, Alexandria, Aleppo, Trabzon and Salonika. Britain sold textiles and manufactured goods in increasing volume as her purchases mounted. In 1827 British exports to the Ottoman Empire were about £500,000; by 1845 they had jumped to £2,210,000; in 1849 they were £2,400,000. Britain's imports from the Middle East in this period were nearly as great as her exports and were expanding no less rapidly.

The trade of France, the Netherlands, Prussia, and Austria in the Middle East also developed, though not as markedly as that of Britain. Marseilles remained an important trading city for the Levant, and Austrian trade with the Balkan provinces improved as transport developed along the Danube. Growing industrial areas in Western Europe found in the Middle East a source of foodstuffs and raw materials that could be obtained in exchange for the products of the new machines of the West. The trade, however, seriously affected handicraft industries in the Middle East, largely substituting machine-made textiles of Western Europe for local homespun cloth. Many an Eastern village suddenly experienced an economic crisis from which it never recovered.

Use of machines and new types of power made it possible for the West to forge far ahead of the Middle East in matters of material welfare and wealth; and the imbalance of power and prestige of Western industrialized states over the agricultural Middle Eastern areas became more preponderant with each decade. The Ottoman Empire speedily developed into an economic colony of Western Europe. The privileges known as capitulations hastened the process and fastened the bonds more securely.

The Capitulations

Originally given to foreign merchants in the fifteenth century in order to encourage commerce with Christian states, the capitulations indicated procedures, laws, regulations, and responsibilities of nationals of a state residing and trading in the Ottoman Empire. With great increases in trade in the nineteenth century and shifting power relationships, the capitulations became exceedingly onerous for Turkey. With the support of their governments foreigners took advantage of every loosely worded phrase, and all significant trade within the Ottoman Empire devolved into foreign hands. Any Turkish subject who wished to enter the field sought means by which he could become a foreigner in his own country. This step was done by securing from a consul or ambassador of a foreign country—for a consideration—a document called a *barat*, which conferred upon the holder the rights of a national of that country as expressed in the capitulatory treaty. Since *barats* were frowned upon in the nineteenth century, outright sale of citizenship and passports was practiced openly by the unscrupulous and winked at by the punctilious ambassadors. Consequently, in Ottoman ports Greeks, Jews, Armenians, and Levantines were often nationals of some European state even though neither they nor any of their ancestors had ever set foot on their "native land." Furthermore, their children and their children's descendants, though born within the Ottoman Empire, retained foreign citizenship.

Three facets of the capitulations were particularly important: law, taxes, and tariffs. Foreigners had the right to be tried in their own consular courts, where laws of their own country prevailed. Since Turkish government officials frequently relied upon the advice of powerful European ambassadors, consuls could usually have criminal cases against their nationals dropped. No foreigner could be arrested or held by Turkish police, unless an official from his consulate was present. This regulation meant that most misdemeanors by foreigners were ignored or glossed over by the Turkish authorities to avoid difficulties, arguments, and awkward situations.

Foreigners were exempt from local taxes and were thus able to conduct local business with less interference from the government and at a lower cost than Turkish subjects. The sultan found it impractical to increase many business taxes, since the result was only deleterious to Turkish nationals.

Important export tariffs were established by the capitulations and could not be changed except by consent of each party in a specific treaty. Since each treaty also contained a "most favored nation" clause, it was necessary to change all treaties in concert to make any successful change at all: to get all to agree was virtually impossible. Because Turkey was not strong enough to defy all the Great Powers at once and denounce all treaties simultaneously, tariffs in Turkey in the nineteenth century moved only in the direction of free trade. Such a situation made possible the commercial exploitation of the weak Middle East by the powerful Western nations. No relief could be expected until the capitulations were abrogated; and to this the Powers would not give their consent because of the benefits their nationals derived with respect to residence, law, and taxes, as well as to trade.

Religious Issues

Into this picture of the capitulations was injected an additional feature: religion. Oddly enough, the reasons for many of the so-called capitulatory articles were religious. Mehmed II, after conquering Constantinople, recognized the native Orthodox Greek religious community and soon thereafter the Armenian and Jewish communities as special legal entities, called *millets.* In a parallel way, various foreign national communities such as Venetians, Florentines, Genoese, and French, each under a designated representative, were recognized by the capitulations as "national *millets.*" Frequently a treaty, like the French treaty of 1740, permitted a foreign community to adopt other nationals whose governments possessed no treaty with the Porte.

The most extraordinary extension came with assertions in the French treaty of 1740 and the treaty of Kuchuk Kainarji in 1774 that Roman Catholics were under the protection of the French and Orthodox Christians under the aegis of the tsar. In subsequent negotiations the Porte pressed for its understanding that only the respective clergy were included, but France and Russia held that the entire communities were embraced. The extension of foreign interest, therefore, had a widening concern in Ottoman domestic affairs; and, coupled with the ancient *millet* system, it led to an identification of creed with nationality, making nationalism synonymous with religion.

Prior to the treaty of Adrianople and the recognition of Greek independence there were still only three *millets* in the Ottoman Empire. But by 1914 there were seventeen, and almost all enjoyed the sponsorship of a foreign government. Not entirely responsible for this movement but certainly encouraging it were the foreign missionaries and Bible societies. Christian missionaries from Europe had labored in the Middle East for centuries; and Roman Catholic churches, convents, hospices, and missions were well established in the Levant before the nineteenth century. The great drive in the Middle East, however, began during the Napoleonic Wars and has carried through to the present. Russian, Polish, Austrian, Prussian and German, Danish, Dutch, French, Italian, British, Canadian, and American mission groups of many denominations established schools, churches, hospitals, printing presses, orphanages, and a variety of other service groups to carry the Christian message and Western concepts of society to Middle Eastern peoples. Completely unsuccessful in converting Muslims, they concentrated their efforts upon the indigenous Christian groups. With respect to the Muslims they philosophized that they might Christianize them by first Westernizing them.

Individual missionaries and home societies supporting them were entirely sincere in their goals and made many noble sacrifices in their work.

Their governments, however, often subsidized them for ulterior aims and gave direction to their work for political ends. Russia and England, for instance, competed for the Armenians, and neither wished to see American missionaries enter the field. Missionaries always were regarded as an advance guard in the process of imperialism—political and economic—and the *millet* system lent itself wonderfully to the business of expanding a national influence.

The European powers quarreled and competed for the minds and souls of the Christian population of the Middle East and the expected advantages of religious and missionary patronage. Through the efforts of Sir Stratford, Protestants in the Ottoman Empire were recognized as a *millet* in 1850. This move was certainly warranted; yet it could hardly do other than favor British interests, since the French had the Roman Catholics and Russia the Orthodox.

The greatest rivalry occurred in the Holy Land between the Russians and the French. Since medieval times Latin monks and clerics had attended the shrines and Holy Places in Bethlehem, Jerusalem, and Nazareth. The capitulatory treaty of 1740 confirmed the right of the French government to protect these churchmen and accorded them certain privileges, one of which was possession of the key to the main door of the Church of the Nativity in Bethlehem. Since almost every treaty or convention signed by the Porte with any European state contained equal recognition, the true legal situation was entirely confused by the middle of the nineteenth century.

Orthodox churchmen dated their rights to control and protect the Holy Sepulchre from the seventeenth century. They protested against the French rights, claiming that they were false and had been wrung from the sultan when Orthodox support had been weak. Whatever the rights may have been, few Latin pilgrims visited the Holy Land in the eighteenth and nineteenth centuries, whereas crowds of Orthodox traveled thousands of miles to pray at the Holy Sepulchre or the Grotto of the Holy Manger in Bethlehem. Russian pilgrims, Russian monks, and generous monetary gifts from the Russian tsar and his government descended upon Palestine. Only a few Frenchmen evinced any interest, and most of these were moved by romanticism and visited Jerusalem to paint pictures or write poetry. Latin privileges, therefore, lapsed through neglect and default. In 1808 the Church of the Holy Sepulchre was ruined by fire. The Orthodox under the direction of the patriarch of Istanbul rebuilt it, levying a tax on all Orthodox Christians in the Ottoman Empire for the purpose. Even Mahmud II made a generous donation.

Beginning about 1840 there was a rising crescendo in France over the Holy Land and the position of the Latin Church therein. Nurtured by the ultramontanists, Latins complained that Greeks had stolen a silver star engraved with the arms of France and infixed over the Holy Manger, protested that Latins were permitted to enter only by a side door, and alleged that Latins were discriminated against in all Holy Places. In 1842 when the cupola of the Church of the Holy Sepulchre needed repair, a great commotion arose over which sect should enjoy the privilege. Actual fighting broke out in 1847, and at Christmastime in Bethlehem, Latin and Greek monks attacked each other with candlesticks and crosses at the Church of the Nativity. The pasha of Jerusalem posted sixty soldiers inside the Church of the Holy Sepulchre to prevent disorders and bloodshed.

In 1843 the usual practice of having the Greek patriarch of Jerusalem reside in Istanbul had been parted with when the newly elected Cyril, who had been bishop of Lydda and the Russian candidate, chose to live in Jerusalem, where he received callers and entertained with dignity and great splendor. As a countermove Pope Pius IX in 1847 ordered the Latin patriarch of Jerusalem, who for centuries never resided in his see, to live there and combat the influence and prestige of the Orthodox.

The Crimean War

With the election of Louis Napoleon as president of France followed by his coup d'état in 1852, rivalry between Russia and France at the Golden Horn and in the Holy Land became acute. Each insisted upon historic rights over the Holy Places; and in the process Nicholas insulted Napoleon by addressing him as *bon ami* instead of *mon frère*. The Porte confounded the issue by sending a note to the French acceding to their demands for changes, at the same time issuing a royal decree to the patriarch in Istanbul assuring that no changes would be made. The matter now stood as one of personal and national honor and a question of religion upon which compromise was difficult. Since the royal decree was never publicly read and thus never fully legal, the Russians felt that they had been duped by the sultan and the French. Consequently, it was the tsar who took the initial overt action.

Prince Mensikov arrived at the Porte in 1853 with explicit instructions to deliver Russia's demands. As drawn up by Nesselrode, points to be insisted upon were full restoration and public recognition of Orthodox privileges and prerogatives in the Holy Land; Russian right to repair the cupola of the Church of the Holy Sepulchre (which meant the construction of a Russian-type bulbous dome which Latins would never countenance); special treaty or convention with Russia again guaranteeing for an indefinite future full privileges for all Orthodox Christians in the empire and reacknowledging the tsar's obligations to protect them as recorded in previous decrees and treaties (Kuchuk Kainarji, Jassy, and Adrianople); rejection of French ascendancy and restriction of other Christian communities that worked to damage Russian influence; and conclusion of a secret defensive alliance with Russia.

For weeks Mensikov intrigued, bullied, and bribed to obtain the Russian program. Settlement was reached on the first two items: both Orthodox and Latins would receive concessions at the Holy Places, and the sultan would repair the Church of the Holy Sepulchre, following the plans of its original construction. But Mensikov's ultimatums and Russian mobilization along the Pruth did not intimidate the sultan's government. Gestures were made to placate Mensikov, but Abdul Mejid refused to accede to the demands regarding protection of Orthodox Christians. To do so was in the view of the imperial divan tantamount to giving Russia the right to govern between 10 million and 12 million inhabitants of the Ottoman Empire.

Undoubtedly the Porte was encouraged in this stand by the known attitude of Napoleon and by the confidence held for the British ambassador Lord Stratford de Redcliffe, who was reappointed to his post and returned early in 1853. His appearance in the midst of the crisis and his revelation to Abdul Mejid that the British cabinet had authorized him to call up the British fleet from Malta stiffened Turkish resistance.

Nicholas ordered the crossing of the Pruth and occupation of the Danubian provinces. The British and French sent their Mediterranean squadrons to Besika Bay, just outside the Dardanelles. Still there were no declarations and no intention of war. The Porte sent a note to European diplomats convening at Vienna, stressing the sultan's peaceful sentiments, and also forwarded copies of recent decrees granting anew in perpetuity the ancient privileges to Orthodox Christians. Turkish feelings now ran high; and this note was regarded as the final appeasement. At Vienna, however, the Powers substituted their own version of a settlement, which stated that France and Russia would guarantee the status quo regarding Christians in the Ottoman Empire. Bolstered and excited by the recent arrival of a large Egyptian fleet at the Golden Horn, the Turks rejected the Vienna note. Meanwhile the war party in Istanbul fanned the emotions of the populace by calling for the ousting of the Russians from Moldavia. Thereafter events moved rapidly, and Lord Stratford de Redcliffe was unable to prevent a Turkish declaration of war.

Nevertheless, Europe and the leading statesmen did not want war. Although Nicholas pledged that Russia would not interfere in Ottoman internal affairs, the British cabinet instructed Sir Stratford to acquiesce to French insistence on bringing the fleets to the Bosphorus, in part because the autumn gales made Besika Bay an impossible anchorage. With supreme effort Sir Stratford obtained a promise from the Ottoman council of ministers to abstain from any hostile act for two weeks. Unaware of this pledge, Omar Pasha attacked the Russians on the Danube, and war began. Inconsequential Turkish successes were obtained on the Danube and in the Caucasus; but real victory was won by the Russians when the Turkish navy was destroyed off Sinop on the Black Sea coast. Nicholas was satisfied. But the British and French governments sent their combined fleets into the Black Sea to inform Nicholas that all Russian ships must withdraw to the harbor at Sevastopol. This was more than Russian honor could accept, and the British and French ambassadors in St. Petersburg were handed their passports.

No European power was prepared to participate in, much less to allow, the partition of the Ottoman Empire. Russia and England had had an entente to that effect ever since Nicholas's verbal agreement with Lord

Aberdeen in 1844. Russia, however, blundered into a difficult position over the religious controversy. Since neither Nicholas nor Nesselrode ever bothered to read the treaty of Kuchuk Kainarji, they never understood how much they were demanding of the Porte. Russia followed her time-honored procedure of occupying the Danubian provinces, a step that sent the British and French fleets to the Bosphorus to ensure the security of Turkey. In the spring of 1854 Austria and Prussia joined in the concert against Russia by requesting assurances of the integrity of Turkey. When Austria mobilized her forces, the tsar's army retired behind the Pruth; Nicholas was not prepared to face all Europe, and war should have terminated then. Disturbances in Serbia were quelled, and British and French troops occupied Athens to "put some sense in the heads of King Otto and his Queen" and force the Greeks to abandon their attack upon Turkey. But sentiment in England and France, on the streets and in the governments, was for further war.

Since a treaty of alliance had already been consummated by Britain, France, and Turkey, the sultan followed suit. There is no need to relate the episodes of the Crimean War here, since it was a European rather than a Middle Eastern war. About 7,000 Turkish soldiers, nearly 10 percent of the allied army, fought before Sevastopol. Ottoman monetary debts to English and French bankers mounted as costs mushroomed. Cholera weakened the armies more than did battles, but the will to fight persisted. Nicholas died in February 1855; peace overtures failed; and war continued until the fall of Sevastopol to the allies in September and the fall of Kars to the Russians in November. Austria suggested peace, which was speedily concluded at Paris in March 1856 after less than five weeks of discussion.

Results of the War

The treaty of Paris with two additional conventions solemnly declared that the Ottoman Empire was a European power. In a separate treaty England, France, and Austria agreed to respect, defend, and guarantee its independence and integrity. Special vassalage status was conferred upon Wallachia and Moldavia; and navigation upon the Danube and Black Sea was made free and unrestricted under the administration of a commission composed of the signatories. The Black Sea was neutralized and demilitarized; except for small, defined coastal police vessels for Russia and Turkey, warships were banned. Equally important was European acceptance of a new reform edict already promulgated by Abdul Mejid, guaranteeing many reforms for Christians.

Although the peace treaty returned the Middle East, broadly speaking, to the status quo ante bellum, the war had profound effects upon the Middle East and its development. Moreover, war brought the Middle East to the attention of a great many Europeans; for the battles and incidents of the Crimean War were discussed in the newspapers more vividly than those of any previous war. For the first time Europe became fully conscious of the

Near East, as it was then called; and events there were regarded by the general public as of prime importance.

The modern state of Rumania was born at Paris in 1856. The victors decided that a stronger and more independent rule for the Danubian principalities would serve as a better buffer between Turkey and Russia. Britain feared the breakup of the Ottoman Empire and secured the establishment of an anomalous fiction called the United Principalities of Moldavia and Wallachia. Eventually the natural desire of the two peoples for union was permitted, and in 1866 Rumanian leaders chose young Prince Charles of Hohenzollern as their Prince Carol. Rumania had taken a further step toward independence, and thereafter her development touched the course of Middle East affairs only indirectly.

The Lebanon

While issues on the Danube were testing the friendship of the recent allies of the Crimean War, a series of bloody events in Syria and Lebanon furnished another pretext for forging the pattern of European intervention in internal problems of the Middle East. After the ejection of Ibrahim from Syria a political vacuum arose in Lebanon, or the Mountain as it was usually called. Since the time of Napoleon, Amir Bashir Shehab had ruled the Mountain from his palace, Bayt-al-Din, with ruthless calculation. His staunch loyalty to Ibrahim, however, compelled the Porte to replace him in 1840 with an incompetent nephew. Maronites and Druzes soon fell to fighting. European pressure elicited a pacification from the sultan in 1843: the northern regions of the Mountain were governed by a Maronite, supported by the French; the southern portion was left to the Druzes, who were favored by the British.

An uneasy peace and prosperity reigned for a decade in Lebanon. However, a new and weak governor in the Maronite district, installed in 1854, permitted feudal lords to abuse villagers; and population pressures were felt keenly. In 1857 a kind of social upheaval was effectively crushed; and in 1860 a similar phenomenon in the Druze district, where many of the peasants were Maronites, so roused French anxieties that the Powers, under a protocol, permitted Napoleon to send a force of 6,000 to restore order to the Mountain. The Porte, however, had the situation in hand before the French arrived; and a European commission under Lord Dufferin drew up a statute at Beirut for autonomous rule in Lebanon. Signed by Abdul Mejid in 1861, it provided for an Ottoman Christian governor appointed with consent of the Powers. He was to have full executive power and was to be assisted by a central administrative council composed of members of all important religious groups. Feudal law ended, and a separate police force and judiciary were created. The first governor, Daud Pasha, an Armenian Catholic, proved exceptionally able as a diplomat and administrator; and the rule under the statute, redrawn in 1864, remained in effect until modified by the French mandate in 1920.

Ottoman Finances

While better government was being established in the Mountain of Lebanon, the same could not be said for the central government on the Golden Horn. One of its most unfortunate developments, which concerned the Powers and which they both condoned and abetted, was the contracting of foreign loans. Beginning with the Crimean War, the Ottoman government contracted loans to meet extraordinary expenses of the army and navy. As has been pointed out, the financial structure and tax system of the empire were antiquated even before the war; and for years the sultan had borrowed locally to satisfy current expenses. Tax anticipations were, therefore, hopelessly inadequate for a loan of the size needed in 1854. Guaranteed by the Egyptian tribute, a £3 million loan was handled in London at 6 percent interest with the issue price set at 80. Another loan the next year for £5 million was floated in London at only 4 percent interest with an issue price of nearly 103, the interest being guaranteed by the British and French governments.

Once the habit was fixed, loans were contracted almost every year, with Istanbul customs duties, tobacco and salt taxes, sheep taxes, and various revenues pledged as security. By 1875 Ottoman foreign debts had risen to £200 million bearing annual charges of £12 million. The total revenue of the government stood at £22 million. Either bankruptcy or government reorganization was in order, but European moneylenders could not bring themselves to terminate such a golden bonanza. Even in 1874 there was a loan of £40 million issued at 43.5!

Although these loans were made chiefly in London and Paris, no idea of annexing the Ottoman Empire to the British or French empire was entertained. Money was seeking investment, and issue prices ran interest rates well over 10 percent. As long as confidence could be maintained, bankers had little difficulty in floating bonds, and profits were enormous. When one grand vizir balked at taking a loan, Palmer, a British banker, used his influence to replace him for a more willing borrower. Bankers in Galata, the commercial district of Istanbul, made current loans to the government or discounted its bills at ruinous rates. When a sizable amount accumulated, the debt was consolidated into a bond issue and sold to greedy small investors in England and France with the approval of their governments. Furthermore, the Russian ambassador encouraged the growing indebtedness, perhaps as a development rushing headlong toward the dissolution of the empire.

The theory of the right of European governments to intervene in Ottoman affairs grew with the series of loans. Commissioners were appointed to investigate spending of funds and the financial feasibility of the loans and to supervise the collection of the moneys designated as security for the loans. But there is ample evidence that intervention remained only theoretical. On October 6, 1875, the Ottoman government announced, in face of a large budget deficit, that only half the amounts due on foreign bonds would be paid in cash. The balance was to be met by five-year bonds bearing 5 percent interest. The end had come.

The growing financial crisis affected every part of the empire. The burden of the foreign debt left the treasury a diminishing sum to meet expenses of government. Officials who went unpaid resorted to corrupt practices, while the government adopted harsher methods of taxation. Peasants everywhere were squeezed, and provinces stirred with an uneasy patience. The most serious rebellion burst in Bosnia.

Balkan Problems

From their mountain retreats descendants of Muslim Slavic ghazis of earlier days resisted innovations of a new age. In 1831 they fought Mahmud's reforms. European disturbances in 1848 and unrest among the Serbs again provoked the Bosnians to rebel. This time they were subdued in 1850 by Omar Pasha, a Croat by birth, who established a new Bosnian capital at Sarajevo. Financial difficulties called for rigid collection of taxes in Bosnia in 1875, even though there had been a scanty harvest the previous year. Revolt throughout Herzegovina and other Balkan areas erupted over the stringent measures. Montenegrins and Serbs sympathetically transformed the revolt into an open declaration of war in July 1876.

Before formal hostilities began, the insurgents had tasted considerable success—and pan-Slavs in Russia, Serbia, and Austria were jubilant. Russian Red Cross units appeared in Bosnia; and General Chernayeff of Russia turned up in Serbia as a newspaper correspondent. Austria sent a note to the Porte and then to the Powers, hoping reforms in Bosnia would isolate the revolt and forestall Russian intervention. Failure to find a solution carried the problem to Berlin in 1876. Bismarck, Andrassy, and Gortchakov, faced with the murder of the French and German consuls in Salonika and riots in Istanbul, proposed an armistice for two months, a commission, relief, and sundry other measures. Upon Britain's refusal of the Berlin memorandum, Alexander II and Franz Josef met at Reichstadt to discuss division of Ottoman territories in Europe, should Turkish arms be defeated by the Balkan peoples, as everyone expected.

Disraeli, however, was still the enigma, and the presence of the British fleet at Besika Bay added to the uncertainty about his intentions. At this juncture news of Bulgarian massacres jolted Europeans. The Balkan revolt was spreading to Bulgarian districts; and an irregular militia perpetrated a horrible massacre upon the villagers of Batak, who were preparing to join in the uprising. Perhaps 5,000 individuals out of 7,000 in Batak were killed. Reports from newspaper correspondents, describing many shocking incidents, appeared in London papers. Disraeli, without any official confirmation, set them aside as "coffeehouse babble." When reports were verified by the British embassy and by Schuyler of the American legation, who went into the area upon the insistence of Dr. Washburn of Robert College, Gladstone and the Liberal opposition took Disraeli severely to task. For the next two years the Eastern question was subjected to the most partisan politics witnessed in England in many decades. The controversy seemed to preclude any possibility of British objectivity on the subject.

Because of the high emotion aroused in British politics by the Bulgarian atrocities, Russia and Austria considered the moment propitious for a change in the Balkan status quo and perhaps for a fulfillment of their Reichstadt agreement. The Porte still declined the proffered armistice; and Turkish armies defeated the Serbs, especially when the latter were led by Russians. Annihilation of Serbia was imminent. Serbia asked the Powers to intervene, and Russia gave the Porte forty-eight hours to arrange an armistice. When this was granted, a conference of the Powers met to discuss peace between Serbia and the Porte and to review the future of European Turkey. A distinguished assemblage of statesmen convened at Istanbul two days before Christmas 1876. Lord Salisbury, secretary of state for India, represented England and followed the instructions of Beaconsfield (Disraeli had accepted an earldom), advocating the status quo in Serbia and Montenegro, similar regimes for Bosnia and Herzegovina, a reorganization in Bulgaria, and general reform everywhere. But Sir Henry Elliot, British ambassador at the Porte, encouraged Midhat Pasha, the grand vizir, to resist by assuring him that public sentiment in England would never permit the Russian will to be imposed upon Turkey.

The Constantinople conference, as Europe termed it, was rudely shocked on its opening day by the sultan's proclamation of a full-drawn constitution, providing for a bicameral legislature, a responsible cabinet, freedom of the press, compulsory education, and a reformed judiciary. Midhat Pasha and Sir Henry Elliot had been discussing the constitution for more than a year, and this moment was regarded as most appropriate for its announcement. With a constitution in hand and the friendship of the British, the Porte refused to accede to the Powers, and the conference broke up in January 1877. Peace was signed directly between Serbia and Turkey in February upon the basis of the status quo, and the Powers signed a puerile protocol in London stating that they would watch the enactment of proposed Turkish reforms and act in concert for the protection of Balkan Christians.

Russo-Turkish War

Russia had several hundred thousand men mobilized along the Pruth. Either she would obtain a firmer promise for the Balkans and Turkish demobilization or war would follow. Russian demobilization without diplomatic success would be humiliating, and private conversations with Beaconsfield caused the Russians to believe that he would not object to a small Russo-Turkish war that did not threaten Istanbul and the Straits. At first, Turkish resistance softened, since Sir Henry Elliot's recall was interpreted as a repudiation of his Turkophil views. Elliot, however, was replaced by Sir Henry Layard of Nineveh fame, who much earlier had been confidential agent and "outrider" for the great Lord Stratford de Redcliffe; and the Porte quickly regained its aplomb and hardihood toward Russian demands. Russia declared war on April 24, 1877.

Russia believed she had squared herself with Austria and Germany and reasoned from Beaconfield's public utterances that Britain would protest only if the Straits were threatened. Bismarck rightly opined that Russia would find Turkey tougher than supposed. No one expected the war to last very long, because neither contestant had any ready cash, and loans did not materialize. The Turkish navy dominated the Black Sea. But Rumania deserted Turkey, declared full independence, and aided Russia. Crossing Rumania, the Russians passed the Danube and appeared to be on their way to Edirne and Istanbul. Then Osman Pasha dug in near Plevna in Bulgaria, resisting the Russian siege from July until December. Meanwhile, Ottoman arms were defeated at Kars by a Russian general, in Herzegovina by the Montenegrins, and at Nish by the Serbs. Turkey threw herself upon the mercy of the European concert. Russia, Rumania, Serbia, and Montenegro, however, continued the war, occupying Edirne on January 20, 1878. Muslims fled before the advancing armies, since cossacks and Balkan armies were as brutal in their atrocities as Turkish irregulars had been at Batak.

The Russian lines approached Istanbul, and Grand Duke Nicholas placed his headquarters at the village of Yeshilköy (San Stefano), only ten miles from the Turkish capital. Part of the British fleet was ordered up from Besika Bay to Istanbul and anchored off Büyük Ada (Principo). Excitement ran high, and London music halls rang with the song

> We don't want to fight:
> But, by jingo, if we do,
> We've got the men, we've got the ships,
> And, we've got the money too.

Sultan Abdul Hamid begged the British to withdraw to Besika Bay, since the Russians threatened to counter by an entry into Istanbul. After the fleet left, the treaty of San Stefano was signed on March 3, 1878, recognizing the independence of Montenegro, Serbia, and Rumania, each of which received considerable territory at Ottoman expense. Bosnia and Herzegovina obtained autonomous rule; and Russia acquired Batum, Kars, and eastern Anatolia up to Trabzon and Erzerum. Bulgaria was created as a large self-governing Christian principality from the Aegean to the Black Sea and westward to Albania, including Edirne but not Salonika. As a final blow 300 million rubles (roughly £30 million) was set as an indemnity for Turkey to pay to Russia.

The Congress of Berlin

Almost before the ink dried, objections arose. Rumania and Serbia felt slighted, Austria was ignored, and the creation of "Big Bulgaria" produced a storm. Greece, Serbia, Rumania, and Montenegro protested, and representatives of Albanian groups petitioned to be heard. British and Austrian opposition demanded a settlement of the Eastern question by the concert of Europe. At Berlin there gathered on June 13, 1878, a galaxy of statesmen, foreign ministers, and diplomatic stars such as had not met since the Congress of Vienna. Bismarck, Beaconsfield, Salisbury, Gortchakov, Shuvalov, Andrassy, Waddington, Corti, and many lesser lights each vied for personal prestige while advancing the interests of his own particular state. The main policy, however, was settled between Shuvalov and Salisbury in London in May, with only the details remaining. A month later the treaty was signed. At the same time the Anglo-Turkish convention of June 4, 1878, ceding the administration of Cyprus to Britain, was announced.

The treaty of Berlin reduced the "Big Bulgaria" of the treaty of San Stefano to a small autonomous principality, where the prince would be chosen by an assembly of Bulgarian notables and confirmed by the Porte. A province of Eastern Rumelia was constructed, where the governor-general was appointed by the sultan with consent of the Powers. Although Turkey could maintain troops and erect fortresses there, the police force was to be drawn from the native population. Commissions and constitutions were to be enacted for the remaining Ottoman provinces in Europe. Rumania, Montenegro, and Serbia became independent kingdoms; and Austria-Hungary occupied and administered Bosnia and Herzegovina. Navigation of the Danube was to be supervised by a commission. Ardahan, Kars, and Batum were given to Russia, and the provisions of the treaty of Paris of 1856 regarding the Black Sea and the Straits were preserved. Finally, Turkey pledged religious liberty and civil equality for the sultan's subjects in Europe and Asia alike.

The dignitaries rejoiced when they signed the treaty, because a troublesome question had been handled without a major war. Although each official felt he had done reasonably well for his country, special interests at home attacked him for having compromised on their points. As he defended his position and claimed diplomatic victories for himself, opposing statesmen in other countries claimed greater successes lest their people believe that they had been bested in the bargaining. Soon no one was satisfied, and Bismarck, who posed as "the honest broker," complained that his role was not an enviable one.

Because of recrimination and jealous rivalry generated among the Powers as an aftermath, a number of the clauses of the treaty were not carefully followed by the Porte. Nevertheless, European ambitions and diplomacy with respect to the Near and Middle East were momentarily less rampant. Soon, however, an epoch opened when a new and modern European imperialism discovered with consternation the rising nationalism of many Middle Eastern peoples—Arabs, Armenians, Iranians, and Turks, each with many variants.

REFERENCES: Chapter 23

All of the references in the preceding chapter relate to this chapter. In addition to these, others cited in Chapters 19 and 20 are pertinent.

Arnakis, G. C. *American Consul in a Cretan War: William J. Stillman.* Austin, Texas: Center for Neo-Hellenic Studies, 1966. This is an edited and annotated edition of

The Cretan Insurrection of 1866–8 by Mr. Stillman, who was sympathetic to the uprising and urged American intervention.

Blaisdell, Donald C. *European Financial Control in the Ottoman Empire: A Study of the Establishment, Activities and Significance of the Ottoman Public Debt.* New York: Columbia University Press, 1929. The most complete picture of this extraordinary episode of Ottoman history.

Chapman, Maybelle K. *Great Britain and the Bagdad Railway, 1881–1914.* Northampton, Mass.: Smith College, 1948. A late reappraisal of the diplomatic rivalries and the complications in the Middle East with special reference to the railroad.

Earle, Edward Mead. *Turkey, the Great Powers and the Baghdad Railway: A Study in Imperialism.* New York: Macmillan, 1923. A classic.

Finnie, David H. *Pioneers East: The Early American Experience in the Middle East.* Cambridge, Mass.: Harvard University Press, 1967. Stops with 1950 and is concerned with all American activities from those of diplomats to those of navy men, shipbuilders, scholars, and missionaries.

Grabill, Joseph L. *Protestant Diplomacy and the Near East: Missionary Influence in American Policy, 1810–1927.* Minneapolis: University of Minnesota Press, 1971. The great bulk of this outstanding and thoroughly researched book deals with the period around World War I.

Greaves, Rose Louise. *Persia and the Defense of India.* New York: Oxford University Press, 1959. British and Russian policy in the nineteenth century.

Harik, Iliya. *Politics and Change: Lebanon, 1711–1845.* Princeton, N.J.: Princeton University Press, 1968. This study explains the peculiar political base of modern Lebanon.

Howard, Harry N. *The Problem of the Turkish Straits.* Washington, D.C.: Department of State, 1947. A thumbnail survey by an outstanding scholar. Very useful.

Jelavich, Barbara. *The Ottoman Empire: The Great Powers and the Straits Question, 1870–1887.* Bloomington, Ind.: Indiana University Press, 1973. Concentrates on Ottoman-European relations.

Puryear, Vernon J. *England, Russia and the Straits Question, 1844–1856.* Berkeley: University of California Press, 1931. A thorough study.

———. *International Economics and Diplomacy in the Near East, 1834–1853.* Stanford: Stanford University Press, 1935. The relationship of these topics is discussed with a wealth of material.

Sarkissian, A. O. *History of the Armenian Question to 1885.* Urbana, Ill.: University of Illinois Press, 1938. A thorough investigation and study of diplomatic and political issues involved.

Seton-Watson, R. W. *Disraeli, Gladstone, and the Eastern Question: A Study in Diplomacy and Party Politics.* London: Macmillan, 1935. Important for the English interests during the latter half of the nineteenth century.

Shotwell, James Thomson, and Francis Deak. *Turkey at the Straits: A Short History.* New York: Macmillan, 1940. A concise diplomatic account.

Sousa, N. *The Capitulatory Regime of Turkey: Its History, Origin, and Nature.* Baltimore: Johns Hopkins Press, 1933. A survey from 1535 to 1923.

Stavrou, Theofanis G. *Russian Interests in Palestine, 1882–1914: A Study of Religious and Educational Enterprise.* Thessaloniki: Institute for Balkan Studies, 1963. Mostly a study of the Russian Orthodox Palestine Society.

Tibawi, A. L. *American Interests in Syria, 1800–1901: A Study of Educational, Literary, and Religious Works.* London: Oxford University Press, 1966. Deals with greater Syria and compares the work of Americans with that of other foreign groups.

———. *British Interests in Palestine, 1800–1901.* London: Oxford University Press, 1961. The relations of the British consulate with British missionaries.

Wilson, Arnold T. *The Persian Gulf: An Historical Sketch from the Earliest Times to the Beginning of the Twentieth Century.* London: Allen & Unwin, 1928. A commercial and political history.

———. *The Suez Canal: Its Past, Present and Future.* London: Oxford University Press, 1939. Interesting and useful.

Chapter 24

From Tanzimat
to the Constitution

Hatt-i Sharif of Gulhaneh

The reforms of Mahmud II were conceived not so much in the spirit of the French Revolution and eighteenth-century European enlightenment as in the pattern of governmental changes enacted by Louis XIV and Napoleon Bonaparte to strengthen and widen the authority of the central regime. Destruction of the janissaries had been the primary requirement, and upon their abolition a more effective and responsive army was developed, and other changes introduced. Disobedient and unmanageable provincial governors succumbed one after another to the force of the new Mahmud. From his desire to enforce the subservience of Muhammad Ali, however, issued the disastrous defeats of 1832–1833 and 1839. In the latter struggle Mahmud's reconstituted army and navy were lost. Mahmud died on July 1, 1839, leaving his sixteen-year-old son, Abdul Mejid, to face military defeat and to be saved by the colloquy of the Powers.

The new sultan had only a scanty, informal education and felt most at home in the company of eunuchs and women of the palace. Yet he apparently had a kindly disposition toward his subjects and wished for their well-being. Since his view of the world, his own country, and human society hardly extended beyond the palace walls, his understanding of the problems of his empire and their solution was extremely rudimentary. His misconceptions, uncertainties, and personal whims led to constant shifts of grand viziers and other ministers, frequently at the instigation of powerful ambassadors at the Porte.

Four months after his accession Abdul Mejid declared the Hatt-i Sharif ("Illustrious Rescript"), ushering in a new political era for the Middle East. Before all the notables, dignitaries, and grandees of the empire and the ambassadors gathered in the Gulhaneh ("Rose Pavilion") at the palace, Reshid Pasha, foreign minister, read this imperial decree. It abolished capital punishment without a trial; guaranteed justice to all with respect to life, honor, and property; and supported the establishment of the Supreme Council of Judicial Ordinances to frame laws as well as a new penal code against which no infringements would be tolerated because of personal rank or influence. Mixed tribunals, composed of Muslims and non-Muslims, were formed to handle commercial cases involving foreigners. Most significant, testimony by a Christian against a Muslim was made admissible in the courts. The second reform measure of the Hatt-i Sharif of Gulhaneh ended the system of tax farming and instituted the collection of taxes by government officials. Finally, methods of army recruitment and length of service were to be reviewed by the imperial military council, and new procedures were promised to ensure regularity and impartiality for all parts of the state. It was also embodied in the decree that its provisions pertained to all subjects, irrespective of religion or sect.

One of the more lasting effects of the Hatt-i Sharif was its endorsement and call for the development of the Supreme Council of Judicial Ordinances, which Mahmud II had instituted the year before as a substitute for a legislative body. A special building was erected in the compound of the offices of the grand vizir for the use of this ten-member council, which was to consider legislation on any subject and propose acts to the grand vizir and the council of ministers. The members of the Supreme Council were high officials of the government and were well paid to ensure their devotion to the position and their independence. However, although these members were appointed by the sultan, the positions were usually reserved for favorites of the grand vizir and his disciples. As a legislative body the council was thus fully controlled by the executive. Though this new council worked hard and seriously and until 1856 met every day except Thursdays, it became overworked, and matters before it were often delayed as much as a full year before they reached the agenda.

The Hatt-i Sharif was the Porte's demonstration to Europe that the Ottoman Empire was capable of self-preservation and reorganization to withstand pressures from non-Turkish groups for independence or autonomous rule. Its issuance made enactment of the London treaties of 1840 and 1841 concerning the Straits and the integrity of the Ottoman Empire appear more reasonable and just, thus easing British adherence to the settlement. Whether Reshid, who had served as ambassador for four years in London and Paris, recognized the value and appeal that statements in the Hatt-i Sharif would generate in European capitals and brought them forth as a brilliant diplomatic coup or whether he had drunk deeply of the liberal political philosophies current in Paris has been much debated. In any case, Reshid in this act committed himself to a more liberal regime. Though sometimes weak in holding to a course and often personally corruptible, he became the advocate of reform and was thoroughly pro-British in his leanings.

Though the Hatt-i Sharif was endorsed by the grand vizir, the shaykh al-Islam, and the sultan, the new spirit was soon curbed. As soon as the Powers decided to drive Muhammad Ali back to Egypt and preserve the Turkish empire, reaction set in. Reshid had introduced a new penal code, based somewhat on French models, but after he fell from office in 1841 over discussions of the new commercial code which eventually was decreed in 1850, the course of reform took a different direction. Under Riza Pasha, a conservative court favorite and commander in chief of the army, a more rigorous conscription among Muslims was effected and some foreign officers were hired. (Christians were excluded from the conscription.) The regular army, *nizam,* and the reserve, *redif,* were increased to nearly half a million; regulars served from three to four years. The currency situation was greatly improved by withdrawing most of the paper money in circulation and introducing a silver coinage, of which the twenty-piaster piece came popularly to be called a *mejidiyeh.* Government officials who went out to collect taxes proved so incompetent that peasants—Muslims and Christians alike —clamored for a return to tax farmers as the lesser of two evils. Consequently, the new commercial code was suspended.

Tanzimat
Reshid returned to office as foreign minister in 1845 and became grand vizir the following year. Immediately, he set about to reestablish the forward movement of the Hatt-i Sharif of Gulhaneh by initiating *Tanzimat,* a movement for reorganization along the lines of pure and tolerant Muslim practices. His friends and supporters, Ali and Fuad, strove to organize education on a more formal and widespread basis. The University of Istanbul was created in 1846 to coordinate the various colleges of medicine, agriculture, naval science, government administration, and veterinary medicine launched earlier by Mahmud and Abdul Mejid, but many delays and difficulties postponed its effective organization. A special council appointed to study the needs of secondary education recommended universal, compulsory, and free education, with free textbooks. Six schools providing such education were operating by 1851, but the drive collapsed because of lack of funds and the return of reactionary leaders.

Sir Stratford Canning returned to England in the autumn of 1846, not to resume his post in Istanbul until 1848. While he was absent, Reshid fell from office, but regained power when Sir Stratford invited the sultan to reappoint his reforming minister. There was no question about the influence of the Great Ambassador, and some of Reshid's successes and the various developments in the government revealed Sir Stratford's hand. The Tanzimat period, however, resulted not from foreign intervention but from internal pressures and growth. With the great increases in British commerce in the Middle East occurring in the 1840s, Reshid, who was friendly with the West and who pushed changes at the Porte favorable to England and France, naturally found an eager ally in the British ambassador.

The truer Tanzimat spirit was manifested in the growing number of Turks who were educated in the West or in a Western manner and who thus became more secular in their outlook. The best evidence of this growth was the plethora of newspapers, journals, and books that appeared in the decade preceding the Crimean War. Politics, history, biography, and philosophy were popular subjects; and new ideas awakened the younger generation. Everywhere in Europe revolts against conservatism and the old order were stirring; and Turkey, on the edge of Europe, felt some of this movement. Ever growing nationalist sentiment among Greeks, Armenians, Bulgarians, and others could not fail to arouse some Turkish patriotism, too. But a nationalist drive among the Turks existed only in an embryonic form in Istanbul and not at all in the provinces.

Some of Reshid's reforms were extended beyond the capital and appeared in measures regarding equal justice, withdrawal of capital punishment from the hands of local governors, and creation of local assemblies elected to advise the governor and give their consent before he could take action. Since assemblies were usually composed of wealthy, influential notables and conservatives, they prevented changes from being adopted and were frequently in collusion with the governor. They did, however, check the prevalence of arbitrary local government. In addition to provincial assemblies, the grand vizir checked on actions of the governor by sending out commissioners to inspect a province and receive petitions from local groups. He could also create for each governor a council, similar to the Council of Ministers to the grand vizir, or he might call provincial delegates to Istanbul to advise him on any matter. In 1845, for example, two representatives from each provincial assembly of notables were so summoned, staying for two months to discuss taxes, roads, and agricultural problems and finally making recommendations to the Supreme Council of Judicial Ordinances.

In 1851 Sir Stratford Canning reported from Istanbul that he had abandoned all hope for reform and development of a modern European-type state in Turkey. About him he saw venal government officials and recognized that Reshid, his favorite, had himself become corrupt, appointing incompetent and notorious persons to high office. The following year he left for England, never expecting to return. (His elevation to the peerage was little solace for his depressed feeling.)

The Great Ambassador did not, however, comprehend the slowness and stealth by which society changes. Communication with Western Europe was affecting an ever widening circle of Turkish people, especially the youth. As their number increased they found encouragement in one another and resisted pressures from older generations to conform to accepted political, social, and intellectual norms.

In 1840, Europeans who had not been in Istanbul for twenty years commented that the changes that had transpired during those two decades were so momentous as to alter beyond restoration the physical, social, political, economic, and intellectual situation. By 1850 the Tanzimat spirit had rooted itself permanently in Istanbul society. No longer was the government or the state solely an instrument for the sovereign to collect revenue, raise armies, and administer justice; matters of education, public works, and economic development were of equal concern to the rulers. This "reordering" spirit was also manifest in the modernization of law, diplomacy, government administration, and education. A secular attitude was injecting new ideas of law and education into the Muslim as well as into the non-

Muslim communities: the individual was coming to be regarded as such rather than as a member of a group. Although many Muslims still rebelled at the idea, Ottomanism, promising equality for all subjects, was beginning to have a sizable following. The sign that this movement had obtained some permanence came when the Supreme Council of Judicial Ordinances stated: "The real aim of the Tanzimat is to abolish tyranny and abuses, and to give to people and subjects security and comfort."

The Supreme Council of Judicial Ordinances seemed cumbersome, so in 1854 it was split into a Tanzimat Council and a Supreme Council. The Supreme Council retained the juridical functions; to it were appointed, in 1856, a Greek Ottoman official, a Jewish banker, an Armenian Catholic who was director of the mint, and a Gregorian Armenian from the family of the director of the imperial powder works. Though closely tied to the administration they represented the non-Muslim communities. The Tanzimat Council was authorized to consider legislation on any subject it wished, to receive and act upon proposals submitted to it from any source, and, above all, "to complete and extend the reforms of the Tanzimat." This Council was first headed by Ali Pasha and was composed of the highest and most esteemed officials. No law or ordinance could become effective until it had been discussed by the Tanzimat Council and approved by the Council of Ministers. It was very active in legislative matters and it enacted new legislation for various councils, ministries, departments, schools, and state organizations.

In 1861 the two councils were merged again into the Supreme Council of Judicial Ordinances, organized into administrative, legislative, and judicial divisions. Finally, in 1868, it was replaced by a Council of State with Midhat Pasha as its first president and a Judicial Council headed by Jevdet Pasha. The latter had fourteen members, including two Armenians, a Greek, a Bulgarian, and Muslims from various areas of the empire. This council served as a court of appeals for cases arising from new, Westernized civil laws, but not from religious laws, as these were handled by millet courts.

The first Council of State, appointed with great flourish by Abdul Aziz, had thirty-eight members; eight were from the provinces and eleven were non-Muslims—four Armenian Catholics, three Greek Orthodox, two Jews, one Gregorian Armenian, and one Bulgarian Orthodox. Because the Council of State and its five committees were not to interfere with the executive or the courts, some authorities have seen it as "a parliament in embryo." In any case, under Midhat's leadership many innovations were introduced, including the standardization of weights and measures under the metric system, regulations on mining, a new nationality law, a lending bank for small businesses, and a reorganization of public instruction. Unfortunately, Midhat and Ali Pasha, the grand vizir, quarreled continuously; their conflict ended only when Midhat was appointed governor of Baghdad.

Hatt-i Humayun

The process of change was accelerated greatly by the Crimean War. The presence in Istanbul of large numbers of British, French, and Italian soldiers, government officials, merchants, journalists, and tourists had marked social repercussions upon the Turks. Contacts between East and West had not been so widespread in many generations, and the quantities of money expended by the Allies in Turkey gave to many Turkish families the opportunity of satisfying their desire for European travel, study, books, and ideas. A European education became the fashion; every young man of a good or ambitious family was sent to Paris, Geneva, London, or some other center to assimilate as much Western culture as possible. The movement eventually transformed the Ottoman Empire, but the results were not immediately evident.

England, France, and Sardinia were allied to the Ottoman Empire during the Crimean War and were ostensibly fighting for the empire's preservation. Before the Treaty of Paris could be completed and the public in Western Europe satisfied that the Turkish state was worth saving, a new reform document had to be issued. This was the Hatt-i Humayun ("Imperial Rescript") of February 18, 1856, which reendorsed the Hatt-i Sharif of Gulhaneh and the Tanzimat. But it was far more specific in its details and certainly more extensive in scope than previous reform measures.

The imperial decree was in the main concerned with the Christian population of the empire; it granted them the rights and privileges that the Muslim community possessed or, at least, imagined that it enjoyed. Patriarchs and heads of communities *(millets)* were appointed for life, and through self-chosen assemblies each community controlled its own temporal administration. Freedom of worship was declared, and no one could be compelled to change religion. Religion or nationality could not be a hindrance to holding public office, employment by the state, entry into a school, or service in the army.

In matters of justice and court procedures, commercial and criminal cases between Muslims and non-Muslims and among non-Muslims of different sects were referred to mixed tribunals whose proceedings were open to the public. Corporal punishment was outlawed and reform of the penitentiary system pledged. Equality of taxes and army service among the various religious groups were pronounced, and a full new law regarding military service was promised "with as little delay as possible." Foreigners were henceforth permitted to own, purchase, and dispose of real property in the sultan's realm.

A budget for the state would be drawn up each year; banks and other financial institutions formed; and concrete steps taken to reform the monetary and financial systems of the empire. Roads and canals were envisaged. Commerce and agriculture were to be encouraged. Schools for every community were authorized. And every means was to be sought for the empire "to profit by the science, the art, and the funds of Europe."

On paper the Hatt-i Humayun contained the essentials necessary for a strong revival. To put the decree to work, however, required the backing and valiant service of more people than were available. Moreover, the Hatt-i Humayun ignored the rising tide of nationalism among non-Muslims and failed to appreciate the effect of foreign residents upon the millet system. The capitulations in the Ottoman Empire, including Egypt, gave political, social, and economic privileges to foreign nationals, individuals and groups. Non-Turkish Ottoman nationals were similarly disposed; they wanted all the privileges of living in the Ottoman Empire with none of the responsibilities. Through their schools and literature these nationalists accepted the dictum that people could only enjoy the greatest happiness when governing themselves. Thus the Hatt-i Humayun, in spite of the efforts of such men as Fuad, Ali, and Midhat Pashas, was doomed to failure almost from the beginning. Too many others were opposed to it. The wars in Europe from 1859 to 1871 that accompanied the unification of Italy and Germany and the reforms and reorganizing plans that occupied Alexander II of Russia allowed the Ottoman Empire to follow her own political course. This meant preserving the *status quo*.

Bankruptcy

Since there were not enough Ottomans sincerely and deeply dedicated to a new order, the last days of the broken Abdul Mejid and the entire reign of his weak brother, Abdul Aziz (1861–1876) were marked by disappointment. The few who preached modernization and the development of Turkey's natural resources were almost completely silenced by those who mismanaged affairs of state, lived on corruption, and assured the political stagnation of the realm. In 1867 Abdul Aziz visited Paris and London in the company of his nephews Murad and Abdul Hamid and his Foreign Minister Fuad Pasha. He returned home full of the desire for reform. But he was so lacking of perspicacity that he only reorganized his court to follow the etiquette witnessed in Europe and constructed more palaces and triumphal arches in the style seen in the West.

Instead of reform, Turkey rushed precipitously into bankruptcy. Between 1854 and 1875 one billion dollars was borrowed from Western Europe; at the end of that period almost nothing remained to show for such a vast sum—except debts. The tax system grew antiquated, and the increasing national income hardly augmented the tax income. To meet the rising cost of everything and to pay for the extravagances of Abdul Mejid and Abdul Aziz more loans were contracted and bonds floated in the money markets of the West. At the same time Turkey had a yearly excess of imports over exports. Since the 1830s the balance had been met by shipments of bullion; hard money in Turkey was being rapidly debased or replaced by paper currency. After the Crimean War unfavorable trade balances were largely offset by loans, since much of the governmental expenditure directly responsible for the loans was made internally. The great bulk of Turkish imports were consumer goods, however, and loans did not bring in the capital goods which in the end might have expanded Turkish productivity and facilitated repayment of the loans. Although the Porte recognized the need and right of British and French supervision over the spending of loans, the commissions and councils remained ineffective, supinely watched the "supreme operation rathole," and frequently encouraged it by reporting favorably on the basic wealth of Turkey and the financial soundness of the country!

Obviously, the process could not continue indefinitely. In October 1875 the grand vizir, Mahmud Nedim, perhaps influenced by the Russian ambassador, announced Turkey's insolvency by declaring that obligations could not be honored in full. This statement opened the door to a new era of wide European control of the Ottoman Empire to be ushered in a few years later. The approaching bankruptcy served to tighten the tax screws upon the provinces and brought open revolt in Bosnia and Herzegovina. The general repercussions and consequences in Europe of these disturbances have been discussed in the preceding chapter. But it should not be considered that these events had no effect upon internal Turkish affairs as well.

Ali and Fuad Pashas under Abdul Aziz

The widening influence of Western European books and ideas upon political affairs was more and more noticeable in Ottoman circles after the Crimean War, as many Turks visited and studied in Western centers. Young Ottoman Turks aped French poetry, art, philosophy, and social forms; nationalism was discussed instead of religion; and Persian elegance of phrasing became outmoded. French manners, liberalism, urbanity, and sophistication became the fashion. The effect, however, that this group had upon Ottoman society and the state as a whole was at this moment almost nil. Its day came a generation later.

Until Reshid Pasha died early in 1858 he had been for twenty years the most commanding figure in the Ottoman government, having held all the high offices at one time or another. As was the custom, he found young, talented men in the government service, "protected" them, and advanced them to higher positions if their views dovetailed with his. Two, Mehmed Emin Ali Pasha and Kechejizade Mehmed Fuad Pasha came to be regarded as Reshid's disciples and his successors. Both were "liberals," reformers, and Freemasons, and together they dominated the Ottoman government for fifteen years following the Hatt-i Humayun. Both were born in 1815, and for the decade from 1861 to 1871 one was always foreign minister while the other was usually grand vizir.

Ali Pasha, the son of an Istanbul shopkeeper, entered government service as a clerk at the age of fifteen, moved into the famed translation bureau in 1833, went to Vienna where he improved his French as secretary in the embassy in 1836, became ambassador to London in 1841, foreign minister in 1846, and grand vizir in 1852 at the age of thirty-seven. By that time he had already been governor of two provinces and, in 1854, had been named the first president of the newly created Tanzimat Council. During the Crimean War he served as foreign minister, and then in 1855 as grand vizir.

In 1856 he attended the Paris Peace Conference as the Turkish plenipotentiary. When Reshid Pasha died in 1858, Ali was named grand vizir again. He was to be, variously, and sometimes simultaneously, grand vizir, foreign minister, and minister of the interior for the next sixteen years.

A small, frail person who spoke hardly above a whisper, Ali Pasha knew when to be silent and possessed complete self-control; he could hear the most startling news without a "flicker in his expression." He was a hard worker and honest, although it was supposed that he received a sizable "gift" from Khedive Ismail in 1866. Ali, as an Ottoman leader, endeavored to uphold order in the state, to assure prosperity for all, and to initiate required and gradual changes in government and society. A moderate and cautious liberal, he proposed—to no avail—the opening of all public offices to all subjects. He believed in mixed schools where Muslims and Christians could study together, and hoped for the development of a citizenry of fully equal Ottomans. He was, however, opposed to the introduction of an elected constitutional government, arguing that the people were not sufficiently educated for that.

The only rival permitted in Ali Pasha's circle was his fellow moderate liberal, Fuad Pasha, who teamed so well with Ali yet differed from him in so many ways. Fuad, who belonged to a well-known Istanbul family, was the son of a famous poet and literary innovator. He was graduated from Galatasaray medical school, where instruction was in French, and then served in the army medical corps. His fluency in French was such that his witticisms in that language became famous throughout Europe. Entering the translation bureau in 1837, he soon became its highest officer. In 1840 he began a three-year stint as secretary to the embassy in London. Fuad conducted special negotiations for the Porte in Spain, Russia, and Egypt, and then in 1852 assumed the office of foreign minister, a post he was to hold on five separate occasions. He served terms as grand vizir, the first in 1861.

Fuad was tall, handsome, loquacious, forgiving, enterprising, and much more westernized in his habits and manners than was Ali. Nevertheless, Fuad was devoted to the service of the Ottoman state and felt that its preservation was his first and most important duty. Though somewhat of a dilettante in most branches of knowledge and often quite superficial in world affairs, he strongly believed that to survive Turkey would have to change her political and civil institutions to keep pace with progress in Europe. Noting that Islam was out of date in some respects, he argued that it was not a closed system and could accept new truths no matter whence they came. He recognized and moved to dampen the growing nationalisms in the Balkans by calling for an Ottoman equality, with liberties for all non-Muslims. To overcome the weakness and irresponsibility of Abdul Aziz, Fuad urged that the grand vizir and the council of ministers be free from interference from the sultan and his coterie at the palace.

Fuad, Ali, and Reshid were the guiding hands of the Tanzimat period. Though others might carp at them for pushing for changes too slowly or sometimes not at all, they recognized that politics is the "art of the possible" and that their ideas and hopes were being suffocated by the overwhelming ignorance and inertia about them. Under the leadership of these three statesmen, many changes were introduced into the Ottoman system. They never did resolve how these changes could be debated or legislated; they frequently aired ideas for parliaments, elected or appointed, but generally feared them.

Young Ottomans

The reorderings of the Ottoman state discussed above were only part of the total efforts and changes introduced by Ali and Fuad Pashas. Conservative, staunchly Islamic sectors of society opposed anything that even resembled Westernism. On most occasions Abdul Aziz and the palace sympathized with the supporters of the *status quo,* so that Ali and Fuad had to be on their guard at every turn. There were, as well, those who chafed at the slow progress exhibited by the leaders. By the mid-1860s quite a number of young Turks and many non-Muslims had studied in Europe, where the political turmoil and revolutions of 1848 and the unification movements in Italy and Germany had stirred European students and, in turn, those from the Ottoman Empire. Young army officers, medical students, junior government officials, sons of wealthy pashas, and many others took to the newspapers to criticize the shortcomings of the government's ministers. Following the terminology of such groups in Italy, France, and elsewhere, Europeans labeled them all Young Turks.

One band, the Patriotic Alliance, formed in 1865, and by 1867 as the New Ottomans, began to be noted by Ali and Fuad, perhaps because of its vitriolic attacks. Never more than a hundred or so altogether, the literature they left behind made them more important a generation later than they were in their own day. Nevertheless, they were noticed, their papers were shut down, and their leaders exiled or appointed to posts distant from Istanbul. Almost all had come from prominent office-holding families and many had held positions in the translation bureau. Foremost among them was Namik Kemal, whose father was court astronomer (astrologer). Namik Kemal was a clerk for a time in the translation bureau but left that for journalism, writing for a number of different papers and editing a journal, *Representation of Opinions.* A poet and an Ottoman patriot, he made the words "freedom" and "fatherland" popular in Istanbul. Later, in 1873, his play *Vatan (Fatherland)* created such a fervent stir that it was shut down by the government and Kemal was exiled. He was an idealist immersed in the ideas of Western Liberalism, in the abstractions of many nineteenth-century political image makers, yet he wrote as an Ottomanist with such emotion as to keep his Ottoman audiences spellbound. In the spring of 1867 the government gave Kemal a minor appointment at Erzerum.

Another leader of the Patriotic Alliance was Mehmed, son of the minister of posts and the nephew of Mahmud Nedim Pasha, who became grand vizir in the 1870s. A third was Ayetallah, who came from a wealthy family with a large *yali* (villa) on the Bosphorus where the group's founders frequently met.

In 1867 the Patriotic Alliance became the New Ottomans. It was a year of crises and agitation in Istanbul, of incidents that weakened the government in the eyes of Ottoman patriots. The granting of limited autonomy in Lebanon, the withdrawal of the Turkish garrison from Belgrad, concessions to Montenegro—these led to vicious attacks upon Ali and Fuad. Uprisings in Crete and appeasement of the Cretans by Istanbul infuriated the New Ottomans, who lashed out at the "diumvirate" as being shallow, blind, and traitorous.

Abdulhamid Ziya joined Namik Kemal and the others in the onslaught, turning his pen and influence against Ali, with whom he had a personal quarrel. An admirer of Western science and Persian poetry, Ziya was an Ottoman patriot who veered toward agnosticism. In the spring of 1867 he was exiled to Cyprus.

Ali Suavi was another who loved Ottoman and Turkish society. He was a man of humble origins who had attended traditional schools, had taught in secondary schools in Bursa and in the Bulgarian province and went on to become a fiery preacher. Patronized by prominent officials, Suavi assailed the government by delivering nationalist harangues in Istanbul's mosques. Early in 1867 he started a newspaper, *Intelligencer,* in which he praised Turkish racial qualities. He excited the capital when rumors circulated that Suavi was engaged in a plot to kill Ali Pasha. Thereupon, Suavi was sent by the government on a trip along the Black Sea coast and told to remain at Kastamonu.

One of the more curious of the New Ottomans was Prince Mustafa Fazil, Khedive Ismail's younger brother, who spent most of his time in Istanbul enjoying the immense wealth produced by his estates in Egypt. Until 1866, when the laws of succession in Egypt were changed to primogeniture, Mustafa Fazil had been the heir to the khediviate. At one time he had been minister of education and in 1863–1864 minister of finance. Exiled to France in 1864, he visited Napoleon III who supported his return to Istanbul as a member of a special treasury council. Quarreling bitterly with Fuad over treasury problems, he was exiled again in 1866. Khedive Ismail obtained the primogeniture decree during Fazil's absence from the capital. Thereupon, Mustafa Fazil became the patron of most Turkish dissidents and exiles.

From Paris he sent a critical letter to Abdul Aziz, 50,000 copies of which were printed and circulated clandestinely in Istanbul. Beginning, "Sire, That which enters the palace of princes with the greatest difficulty is the truth," it cataloged in vivid and uncompromising phrases the ills of the Ottoman empire: depopulation; decline in Turkish virility; moral degeneration; ruin of morale; intellectual decay; financial crises; absence of industrial, agricultural, and commercial development; and the staggering prevalence of injustices and of exactions by subordinate officials inadequately controlled. Everywhere could be found "tyranny, ignorance, misery, and corruption." Islam could not be held solely responsible for this deplorable situation, for Christianity was just as fatalistic. Comparing the situation and conditions with pre-1789 France, Fazil noted caustically that Ottoman society, irrespective of sect, was divided into "those who oppress without restraint, and those who are oppressed without pity," and ended with the emotional plea, "Sire, Save the Empire by transforming it! Save it by giving it a Constitution!"

Confronted by the many crises of 1867, Ali and Fuad tightened the reins and exiled the polemicists to distant provinces. Ali Suavi, Ziya, Namik Kemal, and other New Ottomans escaped from Turkey, met in Italy, and proceeded to Paris. Encouraged and financed by Mustafa Fazil they published newspapers and journals, which they sent to Istanbul through the French post office. When Abdul Aziz visited Paris that summer, the French government forced the New Ottomans to leave, and many went to London. Returning to Paris, they formally organized the New Ottoman Society and Ali Suavi began to publish his *Intelligencer,* financed by Fazil.

In 1867, Mustafa Fazil once again regained Abdul Aziz's favor, returned to Istanbul, and set up a sizable fund to support the New Ottoman Society. However, the New Ottomans began to fall apart almost immediately. Mustafa Fazil objected to Suavi's Islamic proclivities and withdrew his subsidy from the paper. Ziya and Namik Kemal published a new journal, *Liberty,* from London in 1868, but Fazil held back its subsidy when it began to attack Ali and the Ottoman government. By 1869 each member of the New Ottomans had broken with the rest. Khedive Ismail literally bought Ziya, who returned from Europe in 1872 and, still in Ismail's pay, became second secretary to Abdul Aziz. Namik Kemal returned to Istanbul in 1870, where he continued a career of writing and publishing critical articles against the regime until he was exiled to Cyprus in 1873 on the production of his play *Vatan.* Mustafa Fazil joined the government of Ali Pasha, first as minister of state, then finance minister, and, until 1872, as minister of justice. He died in 1875 in the midst of yet another crisis. The New Ottomans were completely scattered.

Midhat Pasha and the Constitution

Another group of men did find in their study of the West political institutions and practices that, in their eyes, would greatly benefit Turkey. Their leader was Midhat Pasha, a first-rate administrator in provincial government, devoted to reform, and an open enemy of corruption. After his success in quelling two different outbreaks of brigandage in the Balkans, he was appointed governor of Nish. Conditions became relatively so salutary in Nish that Midhat was recalled in 1864 to Istanbul, where with Fuad and Ali Pashas he drew up a new law of the provinces. The law reorganized the empire into twenty-eight large provinces *(vilayets)* and provided for mixed tribunals for cases involving Christians and Muslims and for assemblies of notables to counsel the governor. Yet, since final authority and the power of appointing the governor rested in the hands of the sultan or his advisers, the quality and type of administration enjoyed by a province depended almost wholly upon the governor's personality. One foreign observer bitingly remarked that it seemed to him as if the sole reason for the existence of the Ottoman Empire was to enable forty or fifty wealthy Turkish families and a like number of wealthy Armenian, Greek, and Jewish bankers to wring from the peasants the product of their toil.

The energetic Midhat returned to Bulgaria where for a few years he served as governor of the new Province of the Danube. He built roads, bridges, railroads, orphanages, schools, hospitals, banks, agricultural cooperatives, and stagecoach routes. Even more important was his establishment of law and order and his just treatment of the Christian population. On the other hand, Midhat Pasha refused to condone revolutionary action and ruthlessly suppressed several outbursts of nationalism aimed at self-government and independence.

In rapid succession following the Bulgarian assignment Midhat served on the imperial council of state, governed the province of Iraq, became grand vizir for three months in 1871, held the governorship of Salonika, and then retired to private life in Istanbul. The government of the Ottoman Empire had been disintegrating since the death, in 1869, of Fuad Pasha and, in 1871, of Ali Pasha. The moderating influence of the French had almost disappeared with France's defeat in the Franco-Prussian War in 1871. The whims and vacillations of Abdul Aziz could not fill the political vacuum. The financial collapse under Grand Vizir Mahmud Nedim and violent uprisings in the Balkans, with their corollary of European intervention, heartened Midhat Pasha to engineer the deposition of the incompetent Abdul Aziz and install his nephew, Murad V, on May 30, 1876. In August Murad had a nervous breakdown and was replaced by his brother Abdul Hamid II.

Nine years before, Abdul Hamid had accompanied his uncle and the liberal Fuad Pasha on their European tour. It was generally believed from the impressions he made and from the knowledge he supposedly acquired that his accession to the throne augured well for a liberal progressive regime. Midhat Pasha's designation as grand vizir was also interpreted throughout the Ottoman Empire and in Europe as an indication of the new governmental steps to be taken.

Midhat Pasha disappointed very few, for on December 23, 1876 Abdul Hamid proclaimed the constitution that Midhat and others had been formulating since the deposition of Abdul Aziz. Accepted with great rejoicing among the liberals of Istanbul, the constitution provided for a cabinet and an elected parliament and gave proportional representation to all nationalities according to the European form. It reaffirmed that all subjects of the sultan were equal, regardless of race or creed. Freedom of religion, education, and the press, and equality of taxation were guaranteed.

Parliament held two sessions in a chamber in the Ministry of Justice. But the outbreak of war with Russia enabled Abdul Hamid in February 1878 to prorogue parliament and quietly ignore the constitution. A year before,

Midhat Pasha had been summarily placed aboard a ship in the harbor and exiled to Europe. By the end of the war and the settlement at the Congress of Berlin, Abdul Hamid and his reactionary cabal had the government well in hand. In 1883 Midhat and several of his liberal compatriots were strangled in the dungeons of al-Taif, near Mecca, in Arabia. Modernization through parliamentary action died quietly. Political stagnation continued for another generation.

REFERENCES: Chapter 24

Almost all volumes concerned with the Middle East in the nineteenth century relate to subjects discussed in this chapter. Of special significance are those found in Chapters 8, 12, 13, 18, 19, 20, 21, 22, and 23.

Davison, Roderic H. *Reform in the Ottoman Empire, 1856–1876.* Princeton, N.J.: Princeton University Press, 1963. First-rate study of ideas and forces in the Ottoman Empire.

Devereux, Robert. *The First Ottoman Constitutional Period: A Study of the Midhat Constitution and Parliament.* Baltimore: Johns Hopkins Press, 1963. This work, with those by Roderic H. Davison and Şerif Mardin, makes a fine trilogy.

Emin (Yalman), Ahmed. *The Development of Modern Turkey as Measured by Its Press.* New York: Columbia University Press, 1914. An excellent work, which surveys advances since 1830.

Foster, William. *England's Quest of Eastern Trade.* London: A. C. Black, 1933. Although this book reaches back to the seventeenth century, it is strong on the trading developments of the nineteenth century.

Frye, Richard N. (ed.). *Islam and the West: Proceedings of the Harvard Summer School Conference on the Middle East, July 25–27, 1955.* The Hague: Mouton, 1956. Excellent chapters on the development of secularism and the role of Islam in Turkey.

Hamlin, Cyrus. *Among the Turks.* New York: Robert Carter & Bros., 1878. Dr. Hamlin was the founder of Robert College and lived in Turkey from the 1830s until the 1870s.

Heyd, Uriel. *The Foundations of Turkish Nationalism.* London: Harwell Press, 1950.

Lane-Poole, Stanley. *The Life of the Right Honorable Stratford Canning, Viscount Stratford de Redcliffe.* 2 vols. London: Longmans, Green, 1888. In any study of the Middle East of the nineteenth century the life of this great ambassador cannot be disregarded.

Mardin, Şerif. *The Genesis of Young Ottoman Thought: A Study in the Modernization of Turkish Political Ideas.* Princeton, N.J.: Princeton University Press, 1962. The best study of early Turkish nationalism.

Midhat, Ali Haydar. *The Life of Midhat Pasha.* London: J. Murray, 1903. A fine biography of the great Turkish statesman, written by his son.

Pears, Edwin. *Forty Years in Constantinople, 1873–1915.* New York: Appleton, 1916. Sir Edwin was a British lawyer in Constantinople and corresponded with several London newspapers. He was a keen observer and often knew inside details of events.

Polk, William R., and Richard L. Chambers (eds.) *Beginnings of Modernization in the Middle East: The Nineteenth Century.* Chicago: University of Chicago Press, 1968. Twenty papers by distinguished scholars on the many facets of change in the nineteenth-century Middle East.

Prime, E. D. G. *Forty Years in the Turkish Empire; or, Memoirs of Rev. William Goodell, D. D., Late Missionary of the A.B.C.F.M. at Constantinople.* New York: Robert Carter & Bros., 1876. The life of one of the first American missionaries, who came to Constantinople in 1831 and remained there until 1865. The volume was written by his son-in-law from material in journals and letters.

Washburn, George. *Fifty Years in Constantinople.* Boston: Houghton Mifflin, 1909. Dr. Washburn, the second president of Robert College, retired in 1903. He was influential in Ottoman affairs in Bulgaria.

Chapter 25

Abdul Hamid II and Despotism

Bulgaria

The strange events of the summer of 1876, which brought the deposition first of Abdul Aziz and then of his nephew Murad V, and resulted in the accession of Abdul Hamid II, were symptomatic of the general unrest pervading the entire empire. Nowhere was this uneasy state of affairs more evident than in Bulgaria. So thoroughly had the Bulgarian area been dominated by the Turkish government, Ottoman feudal lords, and Greek clergy that many travelers passing through that region were not even aware that a Bulgarian people existed. By the 1830s, however, enzymes of nationalism took effect; and Bulgarian schools, history, language, folklore, and national consciousness began to develop rapidly. Not least in importance in this growth were the opening of the area commercially, the marketing of wheat, flour, lumber, and attar of roses in western Europe, and the migration of Bulgarians to Odessa, Istanbul, Moscow, and the West.

In discussing Bulgarian nationalism, recognition must be given to the important advancements and indirect encouragement resulting from Midhat Pasha's benevolent rule. Education, economic prosperity, and personal security improved markedly in the 1860s, culminating in 1870 in the creation of the Bulgarian Exarchate, which included most of the Province of the Danube. Headed by an autonomous Exarch, the Bulgarian Church stimulated the nationalist movement and turned Macedonia, still a part of the Ottoman Empire, into a battleground between Bulgars and Greeks. While the Turks stood over the two parties and tried to preserve peace and order, Bulgarian political nationalists organized revolutionary societies in Bucharest and brought agents and literature into the province to maintain the nationalist spirit at fever pitch. Further unrest and agitation arose in the Bulgarian province by the forced settlement in the 1860s of 10,000 Crimean Tartars and many more Circassians from Russia. The latter, in particular, terrorized peasants and kept villages in a state of perpetual siege.

The situation in Bulgaria became tragic in 1876. Discontent in Bosnia and Herzegovina burst into a revolution, and Russian volunteers streamed across the Balkans to join the rebels. In the autumn of 1875 the Porte announced interest payments on its bonds could not be met in full. Apparently pressed to the wall, the Ottoman government reacted desperately against the Bulgarian uprising by sending wild Circassians and an ill-disciplined militia to pacify the area. Massacres followed; villages were destroyed; and British newspapers informed the world of what was happening.

International events set in motion by these disturbances have been discussed: the Constantinople Conference of Ambassadors, the Russo-Turkish War, the Treaty of San Stefano, and the Congress of Berlin. Equally important for Europe and far more significant for the Middle East were domestic events in the Ottoman Empire. In May 1876 theological students *(softas)* demonstrated against Abdul Aziz on the streets of Istanbul, obtaining, as had been done so frequently in preceding centuries, the dismissal of the grand vizir and the Shaykh al-Islam.

Accession of Abdul Hamid II

Two political parties were in formation. One was distinctly liberal, progressive, and Western in its desire for constitutional government, fiscal reforms, and economic progress looking toward industrial and commercial development. The other was conservative, corrupt, and composed of self-seeking, ambitious, ruthless, and narrow-minded men. The liberals were now led by Midhat Pasha and Husayn Avni Pasha, since Reshid, Fuad, and Ali Pashas were dead; the conservatives soon fell under the sway of Damad Mahmud Jelal al-Din and Redif Pasha.

The populace of Istanbul awoke on the morning of May 31, 1876 to find a new sultan on the throne. Midhat and Husayn Avni, with a handful of followers and the cooperation of the fleet and a few soldiers, had deposed the extravagant Abdul Aziz and enthroned Murad V. The liberal ministers were retained, and two immensely popular liberal journalists and onetime New Ottomans, Ziya and Namik Kemal, became the sultan's private secretaries. The reactionary party held its fire as Midhat proceeded to draft a constitution that would introduce responsible parliamentary and cabinet government to the Ottoman Empire.

Unfortunately for the Middle East, Murad proved mentally unstable. The suddenness and circumstances of his accession quite unnerved him, as any hitch in the plot on that fateful night or a subsequent reversal of the coup would have meant his execution. A few days later Abdul Aziz committed suicide. Ten days later a crazed officer broke into a cabinet meeting and assassinated four officials, including two ministers. These incidents tipped the balance and Murad became incapable of governing. Affairs of state stood still, until in August Midhat deposed Murad in favor of Abdul Hamid II.

The latter promised to support the liberal party and to retain Ziya and Namik Kemal as his private secretaries. Abdul Hamid, however, had much more sympathy for the party of Damad Mahmud Jelal al-Din. Although Abdul Hamid never appointed the liberals as his secretaries, he did make Midhat grand vizir and promulgated the constitution. As soon as the conference of Powers adjourned from Istanbul, however, Midhat was called to the palace, placed aboard the sultan's yacht, and carried away to Italy and exile. Parliament met in March 1877, but Abdul Hamid obtained its adjournment after a few weeks and, in February 1878, prorogued it and completely shelved the constitution. Until 1908 the constitution was printed each year in the official register, but remained ignored in every respect. The war with Russia served as the excuse for its suppression and became the pretext for Abdul Hamid to rule as the complete autocrat.

Ottoman Public Debt Administration

The suspension of the payment of half of the interest due on Ottoman bonds in 1875 was a potent factor in producing the accession and removal of Murad in 1876. It is not clear whether bankruptcy was the cause or only a symptom of the failure of the Ottoman government to keep pace with the changing society of the Middle East. But in any case, bankruptcy, followed so closely by defeat in the war with Russia, compelled Abdul Hamid and his ministers to resort to measures not consonant with complete sovereignty.

On December 20, 1881, Abdul Hamid issued an imperial decree (Decree of Muharram) legalizing an arrangement with bondholders' groups whereby about £191 million of the external debt of the empire was consolidated and reduced to £106 million. Furthermore, revenues from salt and tobacco monopolies, stamp taxes, excise taxes on fish, spirits, and silk, and other income from Bulgaria and Cyprus were assigned for debt liquidation. The Council of Administration of the Ottoman Public Debt was devised as an authorized body to collect and disburse revenues and taxes on behalf of the bondholders. The Council consisted of seven members: five represented British and Dutch, French, Italian, German, and Austrian bondholders; one was nominated by the Ottoman Bank, which was British- and French-controlled; and one was appointed by the sultan. Largely the work of the British ambassador, Goschen, an international banker, this Decree of Muharram regularized Ottoman finances and reestablished the sultan's credit. Without the Ottoman Public Debt Administration the considerable economic progress of Turkey in the period between 1880 and 1914 could not have transpired.

Within a few years after its inception the Ottoman Public Debt Administration became more than merely a collecting and banking agency. Under its direction, tobacco smuggling decreased and improvements were made in silk culture. Meanwhile, more efficiency and less corruption in the collection of taxes augmented revenues. Slowly, debts began to be liquidated and, even more important, Ottoman credit was rehabilitated so that railways could be built and many Western innovations installed. In almost every case in which Ottoman credit or public operation was involved, an agreement provided that the Ottoman Public Debt Administration should act for the government. Thus, by 1900 many railways in Turkey were supervised by the Public Debt Administration, and railway bonds became the administration's obligations. It was so successful and in such good repute that the government itself used the organization to collect various unassigned taxes, such as those on valona and opium.

Although foreigners staffed the branches of the Debt Administration in the beginning, establishing its procedures and its good reputation, as the years passed more Ottoman subjects were employed. In 1912 only 169 agents were foreigners, whereas Ottoman nationals in the administration numbered 5,625 full-time and 3,250 part-time employees. The pay was better in its service than in governmental departments and the money certainly came more regularly. Not only did the Debt Administration attract a much higher caliber of personnel than did the government, but the training and experience acquired proved exceedingly valuable in later years when many Debt Administration employees offered their talents to the Ottoman government and its successors. In 1903 a supplemental decree was issued reconsolidating several old series of bonds and distributing some new series. Important for the Ottoman government was the added stipulation that two thirds of all revenues above a fixed point were to be transferred to the government. This provision meant that improved economic conditions in Turkey would be reflected in the receipts of the public treasury, permitting better services by the government.

Sometimes the Ottoman Public Debt Administration served as an instrument of economic imperialism and, by its strength, sometimes as a political force. By and large, however, it was characterized by its restraint. It recognized that the interests of the bondholders would be best served by an improved economy. That its existence impinged upon Ottoman sovereignty there could be no doubt, and Turkish nationalists found it particularly offensive. But even the Young Turks in their revolt in 1908 were not strong enough to force its demise. The Kemalists, however, although they never denied the validity of the Ottoman debts, refused categorically to entertain even the idea of foreign intervention as indirectly implied in the Debt Administration. The Ottoman Public Debt Administration died quietly in 1923, when the Treaty of Lausanne omitted all reference to it.

Suppression of the Constitution

Through the early decades of the life of the Debt Administration, when it was proving its value and maintaining the credit of the empire, Abdul Hamid was rapidly destroying the reputation and strength of his realm by his tyranny and ignorance. When informed that a constitutional sovereign followed the dictates of his ministers, his natural predilection for absolutism surged to the fore. Midhat Pasha was strangled in the dungeons of Arabia and illustrious Turks died in exile or in the inhospitable spots to which they were consigned. Surrounded by adventurers and sycophants, Abdul Hamid lived constantly in mortal terror of his subjects. He refused to occupy the splendid palaces of his predecessors and took refuge at Yildiz, which he enhanced and rebuilt and then protected by a double encircling wall. Cunning and suspicious, he had spies everywhere. He employed General von der Goltz of Germany to train the army. Colonel Baker of England was engaged to organize a police force for the empire. Fine new ships for the navy were ordered in England, France, and the United States but they rusted in the Golden Horn. Abdul Hamid was intolerant and failed to understand the world development of his time. Suggestions were ignored, and Turks with ideas for governmental improvements were sometimes found in weighted sacks in the Bosphorus.

Yet, changes and improvements in government and society did proceed, and Abdul Hamid was not categorically opposed to reform. In 1879, after he suspended Parliament, he appointed the minister of justice, "Kuchuk" Mehmed Said Pasha, as grand vizir, with the idea and hope that Said would meet the pressing problems of the empire in a more traditional fashion. As minister of justice Said had reorganized that ministry and had tightened and improved legal procedures in all the nonreligious courts. He had also attempted to exercise some control over the mixed courts in which cases between foreigners and Ottoman subjects were tried. Foreign governments objected so successfully, however, that the latter attempt was dropped.

While minister of justice, Said Pasha had written a memorandum to Abdul Hamid proposing financial reforms to strengthen the state and improve the army; administrative reforms to end the drift toward local autonomy; and educational reforms to achieve greater allegiance to Abdul Hamid from his Muslim subjects. By this initiative Said Pasha became grand vizir, a post he held eight different times, six under Abdul Hamid, two under the Young Turks.

In 1880, Said, in a more lengthy memorandum, stressed the importance of an improved and greatly extended educational system as the key to better administration of the empire, to the just application of laws, to a more efficient army, and to increased state revenues from a more beneficent economy. Throughout the provinces the number of elementary and secondary schools was greatly increased and teacher training schools were established, and in 1883 a special education tax was introduced to support these schools. Said opened a school for training civil servants for the government; it had a modernized curriculum and boarding facilities for students from the provinces. Eighteen new professional schools or faculties were founded in Istanbul, teaching law, finance, fine arts, commerce, civil engineering, veterinary medicine, police work, and tariffs. Finally, the Imperial University in Istanbul opened in 1900.

Said Pasha also understood the need to adjust the Ottoman system to the realities of Europe, which were pressing upon the empire. The decimal system of measurement was adopted in 1881, and in 1882 the Istanbul Chamber of Commerce was created to aid Ottoman merchants in meeting the impact of Western business practices and policies. After 1885, however, Said Pasha had difficulty in overcoming Abdul Hamid's suspicion of innovation; Said's power waned, and his later terms as grand vizir were of short duration.

Effects on the Press

In such an uncertain atmosphere the press had a difficult time. In the 1860s several Turkish newspapers were launched, most of which were liberal in their attitudes toward government. Shinasi, Ziya, Namik Kemal, and Ali Suavi were the most noteworthy and capable editors and writers. But newspaper work meant "patriotic martyrdom," since editors and popular authors were almost invariably exiled and newspapers were suspended frequently. Ziya died a broken man in 1880 in Adana; Namik Kemal followed in 1887; and Ali Suavi was executed for his part in a plot against Abdul Hamid in 1878. Many writers lived and published their works abroad and sent them into Turkey through the protection of the various foreign post offices established by the states of Europe under the Capitulations.

Yet the work of the press went indefatigably on, educating the literate population to developments and thoughts in the outside world. Ebuzzia Tevfik, one of Namik Kemal's close friends, published a host of European classics and many valuable works by Turkish authors. He also edited a fortnightly magazine which copied the style and general content of the English *Fortnightly Review* and brought a Western point of view on many subjects. Other newspapers carried in serial form translations of European books. Many books appeared as single publications. Over three hundred were published in 1890, many of them exciting French novels that introduced Turks to a very different world. Abdul Hamid controlled the press and suspended opposition papers as they appeared. But he did not have enough spies to police the entire empire; consequently, the verbal and printed attacks upon him could not be wholly suppressed. Wherever Turks gathered in the absence of Abdul Hamid's agents, the discussion gravitated quickly to bemoaning the tyrannical state of affairs and the apparent helplessness to do anything about it.

Two other authors, Tevfik Fikret and Ahmed Midhat, left their marks during those decades of Abdul Hamid's stultifying influence. Tevfik Fikret, whose writings flowered later under the Young Turks, was editor from 1895 to 1901 of the *Servet-i Funun (Treasury of Science)*, which at first was an illustrated scientific and literary supplement to an Istanbul evening newspaper and then an independent periodical. A pictorial news magazine on the model of the French *L'Illustration,* it was directed to the educated elite and contained articles on biography, art, science, and literature. Because of censorship and the strict prohibition even of indirect political comment, Fikret and other authors attacked social ills through fictional writing and introduced Turkish readers to European cultural and intellectual life.

The most prolific author of the period was Ahmed Midhat, the son of a humble cloth merchant of Istanbul. Educated by his elder brother in a simple elementary school, Ahmed Midhat entered government in the civil service, which he left in 1871 at the age of twenty-seven to be a printer and a writer. He fell in with the New Ottomans and found himself deported to Rhodes for four years, returning with most of the exiles upon the deposition of Abdul Aziz. In 1877 he published a book vindicating Abdul Hamid's accession and title to the throne, an act that won for him the directorship of the state printing press and, subsequently, numerous official positions. For the next thirty-one years this acquiescent mediocrity made a great contribution to the development of Turkish society.

Ahmed Midhat edited a daily newspaper, *Interpreter of Truth*, that had a weekly supplement distributed to the students of the nation's elementary schools. Most of the stories, serials, articles, and features were written or translated by Ahmed Midhat, who at the same time was writing books, more than 150 in all, on history, ethics, religion, philosophy, and science, as well as producing many works of fiction modeled after contemporary European authors. He also wrote, in fourteen volumes, separate histories of European countries and a three-volume world history. These were the first serious efforts to give the ordinary Turkish reader a view of history beyond the Islamic world. Because Ahmed Midhat did not possess outstanding style or distinction and had little originality, men of literary talent, such as Tevfik Fikret and Namik Kemal, were contemptuous of his work and deprecated the volume of his output. Yet his prodigious outpouring of books, periodicals, and newspapers—particularly those for schoolchildren—probably did more to change the outlook of the Turkish people, preparing them for a more secular and European world, than did the work of any other author.

The spreading of Western thought in Ottoman schools swelled the ranks of the discontented, most of whom fled as exiles to Western Europe. Strangely enough, Abdul Hamid continued to found many schools and even supplied the students with pocket money in hopes they would remain loyal to their patron. Such, of course, was not the case; thrown together from every class of society, they became militant and dissatisfied. Perhaps because the teachers in the medical and military schools had had European experience, their students were the most unsettled of all. In pursuing their studies many were exposed to French or German, which immediately opened to them the ideas of nineteenth-century Europe. As a result, army officers and medical men from 1900 until recent times held positions of political leadership in Turkey all out of proportion to their numbers in society.

The Armenian Question

Abdul Hamid became odious to many Turks. Most Europeans and his non-Turkish subjects called him the "Red Sultan," or "Abdul the Damned." In large measure such appellations resulted from his treatment of the Armenians. As national aspirations stirred Serbs, Greeks, Rumanians, and Bulgars, so Armenians were moved in the latter half of the nineteenth century. Encouraged by the Russian government and stimulated by European and American missionaries, the three Armenian religious communities— Gregorian, Catholic, and Protestant—and their respective educational institutions worked to develop national consciousness. Perhaps because confidential representations regarding Armenian cultural autonomy within

Turkey were allowed at the Congress of Berlin, political societies flourished. Visions of an independent Armenia were also provided by revolutionary committees in Russia and the United States. The tsars promoted these hallucinations but steadfastly refused to become involved, since similar experiences in Bulgaria had not proved remunerative.

Abdul Hamid became frightened of the Armenian situation. He feared that six or more eastern provinces forming the Armenian highlands, where most of the Armenians were concentrated, and Little Armenia, or Cilicia, might become separated from the empire. To subdue the people, break their spirit, and forestall the possibility of an Armenian state, violent attacks upon the villages and shocking massacres were perpetrated intermittently from 1894 to 1897. Outrages occurred in Yozgat, Erzinjan, Kharput, Sivas, Marash, Urfa, and many other places, even in Istanbul. In all, perhaps one hundred thousand Armenians lost their lives.

These atrocities had a very deep effect upon Turkey. The few revolutionary societies were wiped out; Armenians were entirely cowed; and most thoughtful Turks were genuinely depressed by their government's action. Charitable foreign aid societies provided some relief, but emigration appeared to be the only solution. Economic life in many areas was disrupted. The British, French, Italian, and American governments protested in vain. Newspapers, magazines, churches, and lecture halls told and echoed to stories of the "Terrible Turks." As a result, for several decades Western governmental and diplomatic actions in Turkey were guided to a considerable degree by unfriendly public opinion in the West.

Crete
The regime's despotic nature affected Crete also. The quality of government on Crete varied greatly, since the distance of the island from Istanbul and the remoteness of certain parts of it left governors considerable autonomy. A small uprising occurred in 1841, and demands by local assemblies for reforms multiplied after the Hatt-i Humayun was issued. In the 1860s the better educated subscribed to Greek nationalism, the first outburst from union with Greece taking place in 1866. Desultory fighting and Ottoman countermeasures persisted until 1870. Although emotions aroused in Athens affected Greek politics, Athens recognized that its lack of preparation for war forbade overt actions against Turkey.

In 1885, upon the union of Eastern Rumelia and Bulgaria, the concentration of European naval units at Suda Bay in Crete placed a damper on Greek preparations for war against the Ottomans and discouraged Cretan enthusiasts for union with Greece. Nonetheless, disorders of various origins and intensities continued to maintain the tension. In 1896 and 1897, after bloody battles on the streets of Canea between Greeks and Turks brought matters to a head, Prince George of Greece cut off Turkish reinforcements and the Powers occupied Canea. Boiling national sentiment in Athens compelled the king to initiate a war against Turkey. Although the king hoped the Powers would prevent it, they held off. The "Thirty Days' War," better known as the Greco-Turkish War of 1897, was a series of Greek disasters. Only the intervention of the Powers saved Athens from a Turkish occupation. The Peace of Istanbul, which restored the boundaries, placed a heavy indemnity upon Greece. Not until the end of 1898 did Europe effect a settlement in Crete by recognizing Prince George as High Commissioner under the suzerainty of the sultan. The Turkish minority emigrated from Crete gradually; by 1908, when union with Greece was finally achieved, less than 10 percent of the population was Muslim.

Macedonia

Armenia and Crete were enough to keep the Porte embroiled with the European Powers and to stampede Abdul Hamid into innumerable unwise and bloody decisions. It was the complex affairs of Macedonia, however, that sealed his fate and substantiated the charge that the Balkans were the powder keg of Europe. Populated by Turks, Bulgars, Greeks, Serbs, Albanians, Rumanians, and many other groups, Macedonia became the focus of the chauvinistic nationalisms rampant in the Balkans for several decades prior to World War I. A proviso of the Bulgarian Exarchate, permitting churches in Macedonia a choice between Greek and Bulgarian affiliation, touched off the explosion. Balkan nationalism erupted. Nationalistic schools, scholarships, newspapers, and books, as well as raids, village burning, kidnapping, and assassination were among the tactics employed to achieve nationalist ends.

A Macedonian committee purporting to advance a movement of "Macedonia for the Macedonians" was formed in Sofia. It suggested the organization of an autonomous Macedonia with its own government at Salonika. The obvious intention was a repetition of the Eastern Rumelia episode and the union within five years of Macedonia and Bulgaria. The proposition was rejected by all except the Bulgarians, and Macedonia was consigned to disorder and chaos. Turkish police forces and the imposition of martial law were unable to cope with the situation. In 1903 the Mürzstag Program, suggested by the Powers, went into effect. Accordingly, the British, French, Italians, Austrians, and Russians each policed an area. Although some regions were excluded from the agreement, European control was sufficiently successful to induce the Powers in 1908 to extend the Mürzstag Program for another six years.

Berlin to Baghdad Railway

It should be noted that Germany did not participate in the pacification of Macedonia. Until this era German imperial interests in the Ottoman Empire were negligible. Bismarck regarded the area as worthless to Germany, and his exertions were designed only to keep Russia and Austria from fighting each other. One German banking firm was involved in the Ottoman bankruptcy in 1881 and was duly represented as a minor interest on the Council of the Ottoman Public Debt Administration. But with the accession of William II, Germany's role changed. General von der Goltz began to advise the Ottoman army in 1883, and the army was equipped with good Mauser rifles. In 1888 Baron Hirsch's Oriental Railway was completed through to Istanbul, while a newly formed German syndicate, the Anatolian Railway Company, was granted a concession to construct a railroad from the Bosphorus to Ankara. Supported by the *Deutsche Bank,* the line to Ankara was in operation by 1893. Another contract assured a branch from Eskishehir to Konya, which was completed in 1896.

The German penetration of Anatolia increased, as the value of German exports to Turkey grew 350 percent and Turkish exports to Germany jumped over 700 percent. German salesmen were everywhere. The *Deutsche Levante Linie* established direct steamship service between Hamburg, Bremen, and Istanbul. In 1889 and again in 1898 William II paid official visits to Istanbul; on the latter trip he went to Jerusalem and Damascus where he uttered the famous speech promising Muslims that the German emperor would be their friend. Oriental studies became popular in Germany, and Dr. Kiepert, the famous cartographer, surveyed Anatolia. But above all else, German interests focused upon railroad concessions, which blossomed into the much-publicized Berlin-to-Baghdad venture.

Abdul Hamid, the Porte, army leaders, and officials of the Ottoman Public Debt Administration favored building railroads to all parts of the empire. They fancied that railroads would unify the empire and bring the central government more effective power and authority over outlying regions. More of the untold mineral resources of Anatolia and Arabia would be developed, guaranteeing a burgeoning prosperity. The military posture of the state would be improved and independence protected. Although railroads were costly enterprises, it was believed that the advantageous results would amply repay the effort and monies expended.

The fondest dream encompassed building a railroad from the Bosphorus to the Persian Gulf. In 1886 Abdul Hamid proposed such an undertaking to Leland Stanford, of the United States, but Stanford was too engrossed in building American transcontinental railroads to accept. British and French companies already had built and were operating several lines connecting Izmir with the Anatolian hinterland, when in 1888 the Anatolian Railway Company took over the British railroad from Haydar Pasha on the Bosphorus to Izmit and extended it to Ankara.

These railroad concessions usually called for a Turkish subsidy to the construction firm, a guarantee of a minimum annual revenue, or both. For extending the line to Ankara, the sultan assured the Anatolian Railway Company at least 15,000 francs per kilometer annual revenue. This money was to come from the taxes of several provinces, the collection of these taxes being assigned to the Debt Administration. In 1896, when the German line reached Konya, other railroads in Asiatic districts were the Izmir-Aydin, the Izmir-Kassaba-Afyon-Karahisar, the Mersin-Adana, the Jaffa-Jerusalem, and the Beirut-Damascus-Aleppo lines. The government naturally desired to link these together and push on to Mesopotamia and the Persian Gulf. Austrian, Russian, French, British, and German capitalists and entrepreneurs all were anxious to obtain the concession, and each presented plans and offers for construction. But only the German plans met the requirements of the Porte and the Ottoman Public Debt Administration.

Abdul Hamid insisted that the railroad should not approach the Mediterranean, where gunfire from enemy fleets could interrupt traffic. The Germans, therefore, proposed to proceed from Konya to Adana, then through the Amanus range eastward to the valley of the Tigris near Mosul, and down the river to the Persian Gulf. This plan was more expensive than others, but militarily more secure. Actually, British and French capitalists accepted the idea that the concession would be awarded to the Germans, and their governments were fully satisfied. Agreements were reached among the three groups in 1899. In that year Lord Curzon arranged for Britain to conduct all foreign relations for the Shaykh of Kuwayt; this permitted England to block the railroad's best terminus on the Persian Gulf.

On March 18, 1902, Abdul Hamid issued an imperial decree giving the concession for the Baghdad road to the Anatolian Railway Company. A year later a revised convention established the Baghdad Railway Company as the actual builder and owner, arranged the financing, and enabled engineers to start construction of the first two hundred kilometers. The Ottoman Empire paid 275,000 francs per kilometer for building the railroad, guaranteed 4,500 francs per kilometer annual gross operating receipts, granted mineral rights twenty kilometers on each side of the right of way, exempted from taxation all construction material imported, and gave numerous minor benefits to the company.

When British capitalists refused because of adverse public sentiment to participate equally with German and French interests, 10 percent of the Baghdad Railway Company stock was subscribed to by the Ottoman government, 10 percent by the Anatolian Railway Company, and the remaining 80 percent by a syndicate (French, German, Austrian, Italian, and Swiss) formed by the *Deutsche Bank.*

The necessary bonds were floated and construction began. In October 1904 the first section was opened. The terrain crossed was not difficult; building cost less than was expected and profits were high. In 1906 the Porte arranged with the Powers for a slight increase in tariffs to pay for further extensions. New loans were provided in 1908, but because of the Young Turk Revolution, it was not until 1909 that a construction company was organized to undertake the second leg across the Taurus and Amanus ranges. Certain bridges and tunnels in the Taurus Mountains were still not finished at the outbreak of war in 1914. Thus, a through route to northern Iraq or Syria was not opened to traffic until the post-World War I period.

The railways to Ankara and to points beyond Konya brought an agricultural revolution to Anatolia. In districts penetrated by these roads new settlements were formed, produce marketed, and new lands cultivated. The companies initiated irrigation projects and agricultural training centers to stimulate traffic on their railroads; in these details the Germans were the most efficient and thorough. By 1910 mileage guarantees for annual receipts were no longer necessary and railroads were paying profits into the Ottoman treasury. Simultaneously, German business and banking penetration between 1899 and 1908 was facilitated and encouraged by railroad interests.

By opening up vast areas to world commerce the railroads improved local economic conditions and gave many Middle Eastern districts their first touch with the West. There was a distinct possibility that these developments might effect a real recuperation for the "sick man" of Europe. The railroads also brought German imperialism, which the Middle East actually found to be a relief from British and French colonialism. Usually Germans were more tactful and considerate of Turkish feelings and were more willing to do things in a Turkish fashion. But German inroads into the Middle East frightened the British, who after 1904 and 1907 convinced the French and Russian governments to cooperate with them in trying to block German aspirations for a *Drang nach Osten*. Without question, the Baghdad railway project and its ramifications were significant in developing the European climate that led to World War I.

REFERENCES: Chapter 25

Many readings touch upon this chapter. Those cited in Chapters 12, 13, 19, 20, 22, 23, and 24 are of particular value.

And, Metin. *A History of Theatre and Popular Entertainment in Turkey.* Ankara: Forum Yayinlari, 1964. An important paperback on a little-known subject.

Anderson, J. N. D. *Islamic Law in the Modern World.* New York: New York University Press, 1959.

Berkes, Niyazi. *The Development of Secularism in Turkey.* Montreal: McGill University Press, 1964. The most profound and stimulating book on this subject to appear, and one that no student can overlook.

Buxton, Charles R. *Turkey in Revolution.* London: T. F. Unwin, 1908. Written by a man who was in Turkey during the Revolution of 1908.

Edib, Halidé. *Memoirs.* New York: Century, 1926. The life of a Western-educated Turkish woman.

Eliot, Charles N. E. *Turkey in Europe.* London: E. Arnold, 1908. Particularly strong on the Balkans and Macedonia.

Haddad, William, and William L. Ochsenwald (eds.). *Nationalism in a Non-National State: The Dissolution of the Ottoman Empire.* Columbus, Ohio: Ohio State University Press, 1977. This volume contains a series of essays on the development of nationalism in the nineteenth and twentieth centuries in the Balkan and Arab provinces of the empire. Each has been written by a specialist for that region.

Mears, Eliot Grinnell (ed.). *Modern Turkey, A Politico-economic Interpretation, 1908–1923, Inclusive, With Selected Chapters by Representative Authorities.* New York: Macmillan, 1924. A collection of essays written by excellent observers who were long resident in Turkey. One entitled "Levantine Concession-Hunting," by Mears, is most revealing of this type of financial imperialism.

Papadopoulos, George S. *England and the Near East, 1896–1898.* Thessaloniki, Greece: Institute for Balkan Studies, 1969. A detailed study of the basic changes in British policy in the Ottoman Empire during the Salisbury administration.

Pears, Edwin. *Life of Abdul Hamid.* London: Constable, 1917. A good biography by an English barrister who was resident in Istanbul throughout the reign of Abdul Hamid II.

Ramsaur, Ernest E., Jr. *The Young Turks.* Princeton, N.J.: Princeton University Press, 1957. The best volume in any language on this topic, especially on the period before 1908. Based on many letters and communications from leading Young Turks.

Chapter 26

The Young Turks

Secret Societies

The Young Turk Revolution of 1908 was a natural reaction to oppression, absolutism, and corruption in the regime of Abdul Hamid II. Added to this was the development and growing Westernization of certain portions of the empire and the consequent effect of contemporary European ideas upon Turkish youth. At various times in the nineteenth century dissident Ottomans lived in exile in Europe and dreamed of governmental reformation at home. Many saw a temporary fruition of these hopes in the ousting of Abdul Aziz and in Midhat's constitution of 1876. When Abdul Hamid's true nature was divulged, hardy characters plotted revolution.

In 1889, at the Istanbul Imperial Military Medical College, a group of students led by an Albanian, Ibrahim Temo, organized a secret society, the Committee of Progress and Union. Membership spread to the Military Academy, the Naval Academy, the Artillery and Engineering School, the Veterinary School, and the Civil College. Similar to the Carbonari societies in Italy, of which Temo had learned in Brindisi, Progress and Union subscribed to nationalist ideas and reforms as suggested in the zealous writings of Namik Kemal, Ziya, and Shinasi.

Abdul Hamid heard of the committee through his secret agents and took reprisals against the students and school officials. Nonetheless, the committee flourished, gathering new recruits from each succeeding class at the various schools. By 1896 more important elements of Ottoman society dominated the committee, and it attracted members who had belonged to such earlier groups of rebellious spirits as the New Ottomans and Young Turks.

Committee members who escaped to Europe made common cause with other Ottoman malcontents. The best-known of these was Ahmed Riza, whose newspaper, *Meshveret (Deliberation)* became the committee's official organ. At the same time, Murad Bey, a history teacher at the Civil College who had once been an employee of the Ottoman Public Debt Administration, fled to Paris and published a more popular newspaper, *Mizan (Balance)*. These two papers, which obtained easy entrance into the empire through foreign post offices, gathered a considerable following.

Membership in Progress and Union became widespread, but rumor exaggerated its number to the point at which Abdul Hamid took fright and even the members themselves believed a coup d'état might be possible, although the committee's program denounced violence or any thought of overthrowing the reigning family; it preached reform, rejected slavish Westernization, advocated Ottoman nationalism, and opposed the intervention of European powers as a substitute for Ottoman authority. But a series of arrests nipped in the bud the society's coup planned for August 1896. Abdul Hamid, curiously enough, only sent the leaders to remote parts of the empire, whence they slipped away to Paris and Geneva. The latter city became the headquarters of the committee under the presidency of Murad Bey. The program was reduced to the simple formula that all evils of the Middle East stemmed from Abdul Hamid. Remove him, restore the constitution, and all would be well. But the wily sultan, promising a general amnesty and agreeing to listen to arguments for reform, enticed Murad Bey to Istanbul and in 1897 shattered the Committee of Progress and Union.

Abdul Hamid's triumph was only fleeting. In 1899 his nerve was badly shaken by the escape to Paris of his brother-in-law and two nephews. Prince Sabah al-Din, a son of Abdul Hamid's sister, convened in Paris in 1902 the first congress of Ottoman Liberals, which held as its high objective the restoration of the constitution of 1876. Prince Sabah al-Din championed a nationalist idea that included all peoples of the empire—a federation of Turks, Arabs, Greeks, Armenians, Kurds, Macedonians, Albanians, Jews, and others. In the pages of *Meshveret,* on the other hand, nationalism meant an Ottomanization process in which all divergent groups would become Ottoman Turks.

Turkish or Ottoman dissidents and exiles in Paris and Geneva kept hopes alive for a thorough change in the Ottoman government and a consequent revitalization of the Middle East. But they could hardly produce a revolution, not even a mild coup d'état. That had to come from within; Abdul Hamid, however, had cleverly crushed the Committee of Progress and Union. Nevertheless, the problems of Turkish society remained constant, and new revolutionary groups sprang up faster than he could cut them down.

Every class at the Military Academy was infected with the virus of revolution, and at the General Staff Academy in 1905 Mustafa Kemal was arrested as a revolutionary agitator on the very day he was commissioned. Later, when released and stationed in Damascus, he organized *Vatan* (Fatherland), a secret revolutionary society, among officers of the Fifth Army Corps in Syria. Because Macedonia and its cosmopolitan center of Salonika were susceptible to revolutionary propaganda, Kemal journeyed there surreptitiously to organize branches of Fatherland among officers of the Third Army Corps. In Salonika the society came to be called Fatherland and Liberty, and it merged with another group before Kemal arranged his transfer there in 1907.

The other group in Salonika, the Ottoman Society of Liberty, included in its earliest membership Talat Bey, Rahmi Bey, Fethi Bey, and Colonel Jemal Bey. Absorbing Fatherland and Liberty, it spread rapidly throughout European Turkey, with major centers at Monastir, Uskub, Drama, and Edirne. Ismet Bey was the leader at Edirne. Pledged to overthrow Abdul Hamid and establish a just government, the Ottoman Society of Liberty drew to its ranks liberal and freethinking Turks, especially Bektashis, Melamis, and Freemasons. When army officers fraternized with their European colleagues stationed in Macedonia, pursuant to the Mürzstag Program of 1903, they compared their own unfavorable lot and arrears in pay with the pleasant life of European officers.

In 1907 fugitives from Salonika won over Ahmed Riza in Paris to the possibility of armed revolution. Abdul Hamid's enemies joined then in a second congress of Ottoman Liberals, at which even an Armenian revolutionary society was represented. After this meeting the Paris and Macedonia groups merged under the name Society of Union and Progress and set up a permanent committee to implement the program adopted by the congress—opposition to the Ottoman government in every way possible.

The Revolution

The real revolution began in the Middle East, not in Paris. Army mutinies became frequent in 1906, largely because of miserable conditions and arrears in pay. When rebellions were seen to bring immediate improvements, many more occurred in 1907, with civilians joining to protest against corrupt officials in Erzerum, Bitlis, Izmir, and even in Istanbul. Beginning in June 1908, mutinies broke out in Macedonia; an officer whom Abdul Hamid had sent to investigate was shot and wounded on June 11 at Salonika, the same day that Nicholas II of Russia and Edward VII of England met at Reval to arrive at some method of reform in Macedonia that might end the anarchy. Both events hastened the action. Majors Enver and Niyazi and other officers of the Third Army Corps took to the hills around Resne and officers and agents of the sultan were assassinated. General Shemsi Pasha, who had been sent to crush the rebellion, was shot dead by members of the Society of Union and Progress in broad daylight outside the main post office in Monastir. This act galvanized many units of the society and the Third Army Corps in Macedonia to demand the restoration of the constitution. Messages from scores of cities and towns poured into Istanbul and meetings of soldiers and civilians proclaimed the constitution. On July 23 came the fateful telegram announcing that the Third Army Corps would march on Istanbul to enforce the reproclamation of the constitution.

The army threat was the telling blow. On that evening, July 23, 1908, Abdul Hamid restored the constitution and ordered elections for members of the Chamber of Deputies. A liberal grand vizir, Said Pasha, was appointed, and on July 25 the Istanbul press and citizens rejoiced over the good, though unexpected, news. Abdul Hamid bowed to the force of the demands and rode with the popular tide. But he did not surrender.

The summer of 1908 was spent in preparing for the elections and read-justing government ministries in accordance with the wishes of the commit-tee of the Society of Union and Progress. The committee's program called for the sultan's deposition. The society, however, had never cultivated the masses, and the popular cries in the capital were: "Long Live the Constitu-tion," "Long Live the Sultan," and "Down with the Spies." Abdul Hamid went to Aya Sofya mosque for his public prayers on the first Friday after the revolution and received much adulation from the throngs that gath-ered. He was fostering the view that he was happy over the turn of events! The committee was not fooled, but recognized that it did not have the force or following to depose him. In fact, no member of the committee or promi-nent member of the society even became a cabinet minister. It was be-lieved then that a certain skill, mystique, and rearing were required for conducting a minister's office, qualifications that none of the committee members possessed. Said Pasha soon proved unsympathetic to their aspira-tions, and Abdul Hamid, following their wishes, appointed Kiamil Pasha grand vizir on August 6.

The committee publicly declared its support of Kiamil and his cabinet. Now the government and the committee controlled state affairs; the palace was isolated. Kiamil announced his program of reform on August 16 and, unable to wait for elections and the convening of parliament, set out to convert the Ottoman Empire into a twentieth-century centralized state.

On December 17, 1908, in the chambers near Aya Sofya where Midhat's parliament had met thirty-one years earlier, Abdul Hamid, accompanied by five of his sons and in the presence of the notables of the empire and foreign representatives, opened parliament and gave a speech from the throne. Major religious and national groups of the empire were represented and various political views were in evidence. Attending were 147 Turks, 60 Arabs, 27 Albanians, 26 Greeks, 14 Armenians, 4 Jews, 5 Bulgars, 4 Serbs, and 1 Vlach. The best-organized group was the Macedonia-Salonika branch of Union and Progress, but it was far from having complete control of the situation. Ahmed Riza, their distinguished publicist from Paris, was chosen president of the Chamber of Deputies and served as a valuable figurehead for the anonymous members of the committee of the society.

Members of parliament coalesced into three political groups. In addition to Union and Progress, there were the Liberal Unionists of Ismail Kemal, Prince Sabah al-Din, and Hassan Fehmi. The Liberal Unionists believed the solution to the ills of the empire could be found in creating a loosely federated state of locally autonomous nationalist provinces. The third group was the reactionary Muslim Association, which supported pan-Is-lamism and firm adherence to religious law. Union and Progress, however, showed its power in February 1909 by causing the downfall of the grand vizir on a motion of no confidence when he appointed, without consulta-tion with the committee, his friends as minister of war and minister of marine.

Failure of the Counterrevolution

The counterrevolution struck on April 13, 1909, and leading members of Union and Progress went into hiding. Developing spontaneously among soldiers of the First Army Corps in Istanbul, the cries were: "Down with the Constitution," "Down with the Committee," and "Long Live the Sacred Law." Abdul Hamid gave his blessing to the counterrevolution, and a new grand vizir took office. The Young Turks of the Revolution, as they were called, were inexperienced in government and few in number. Moreover, they harbored the illusion that the proclamation of the constitution and the announcement of just, efficient, honest, and rational government would erase all the evils in the Middle East, and that all good people would rise up and usher in the promised day. But it did not happen. Soldiers' pay was no better, and general conditions remained about the same. The people of the Middle East were not prepared to abandon the mental attitudes of the millet system or to tolerate equality among Turk, Greek, Armenian, Bulgar, Jew, Arab, Albanian, and the other people of the empire. "Under the same blue sky we are all equal; we glory in being Ottomans." These oft-quoted words of Enver, one of the committee members who later rose to fame, stirred emotions but were not accepted as fact.

The committee of Union and Progress, however, acted decisively. Mahmud Shevket Pasha, commander of the Third Army Corps in Macedonia, was invited to march on Istanbul to defend the constitution. When he arrived at Yeshilköy on April 23, he proposed to parliament, which was holding a rump session there, the declaration of martial law, punishment for mutineers, and full obedience to him. His terms were accepted; on April 25, Istanbul was occupied, and order was restored in five hours. In an executive session on April 27, parliament deposed Abdul Hamid, having obtained a favorable *fetva* from the Shaykh al-Islam. The new sultan, Mehmed V, was a mild gentleman who had been born in 1844 and who declared he had not read a newspaper in the last twenty years. He had been completely surrounded by his brother's spies and minions—even the ladies of his harem—and had lost all initiative. He was the perfect constitutional monarch for the Young Turks.

Italian War

The task before the Young Turks would have staggered the most experienced administrators. Internal problems commanded the highest priority, but foreign affairs and war rose to occupy the minds of the committee and consumed the meager funds available. Europe feared that the Young Turk regime would restore vigor to the empire. Contemplated acts of aggression should be made at once. On October 5, 1908, Prince Ferdinand of Bulgaria cut all ties with the sultan and took the title of Tsar. On October 6 Austria-Hungary announced annexation of Bosnia and Herzegovina. That same day Crete revolted and declared union with Greece. None of these acts was surprising or momentous for the Ottoman government; these territorial losses had been all but written off several years previously. Politically, however, they were hard blows against the prestige of the Young Turks and were factors in the counterrevolution of April 1909.

A far greater shock was delivered by the Italian ultimatum of September 28, 1911, demanding that Turkey not object to an Italian military expedition to Libya. Turkey declared war on Italy immediately. Although the Turks were driven from the coastal towns of Tripoli and Benghazi, guerrilla warfare continued in the interior. Italy then occupied Rhodes and the Dodecanese Islands and shelled the Dardanelles. Sentiment ran high in Turkey. People refused to eat macaroni, and the Young Turks closed the Straits. When England and Russia protested, the Straits were reopened, but peace seemed difficult to arrange. Enver Bey and Fethi Bey, both prominent members of Union and Progress and military attachés in Berlin and Paris respectively, along with other officers of later distinction like Mustafa Kemal, made their way with difficulty to Libya, where they organized and for a time led a resistance movement among the Sanussi tribes.

An Ottoman victory was hopeless; and when it appeared that the Balkan states were plotting a common war against Turkey, the Ottomans hastily signed the Treaty of Ouchy on October 18, 1912. Under the terms of the treaty Turkey withdrew from Libya; Italy, from the Aegean Islands. Italy agreed to assume a share of the Ottoman debt and the authority of the caliph was recognized in Libya. Italy, however, refused to evacuate her island conquests, claiming Turkey continued to incite Arab warfare in Libya.

The Committee of Union and Progress

Shortly after the deposition of Abdul Hamid in 1909 the Society of Union and Progress held a party congress in Salonika and established a central executive committee that remained active until the party was dissolved at the end of World War I. From its headquarters in Salonika it ruled the party and, when the party was in power, the government and the ministers. After 1912, when the Balkan wars broke out, the central executive committee sat in Istanbul and there dictated to the membership.

The many activities of the Union and Progress party began to tell on its popularity. Even before the defeat by the Italians, the party's control of parliament weakened, and to forestall a defeat in the Chamber of Deputies the Young Turks had Mehmed V dissolve the chamber and call for a new election. The new chamber was also closed in August 1912, when radical young leaders of Union and Progress attacked a cabinet composed of men of more experience and prestige. Two ministries largely representing the Liberal Unionist party followed. The latter, however, succumbed to a coup d'état by the Union and Progress party in January 1913, when extremists rebelled at surrendering Edirne to the Balkan states. From that moment until the end of World War I leaders of Union and Progress maintained firm control over the government.

The desires of the Young Turks flowed out in every direction. Their intention was to examine all the institutions of their society, changing any that had become anachronistic. Javid Bey, Young Turk minister of finance, reorganized his department with the aid and advice of Charles Laurent of France. Sir Richard F. Crawford of England advised the customs bureau. General Liman von Sanders headed a German mission to transform the army under the direction of Enver Pasha. British Admirals Gamble and Limpus reformed the navy. French Count Roubilant formed a new gendarmery. And Count Ostorog, a French Pole, was employed for a short time to suggest means of introducing secular law without prejudicing the Sacred Law. In education and social services Young Turk reformers took the helm. Ziya Gökalp, Tevfik Fikret, Mehmed Amin, Halidé Edib, Fuad Köprülü, and many others devoted their energies and talents to improving education.

Stimulated by their studies in the West or by their reading of Western books in the original or in translation, these Young Turks sought to improve the well-being and ameliorate the lives of the great mass of Ottoman subjects. They deplored the poor existence in Turkey, suffered in their souls with the people, and wished to give pride, dignity, and an energetic determination to the nation. They wanted to create a national consciousness. They were, after all, nationalists. In the Middle East, however, society lacked homogeneity. Racial origins were many, but the ages had mixed them completely. There were religions by the score. Languages and dialects were so diverse that young British consular officers coming to Istanbul had to take lessons in Turkish, Greek, Persian, Arabic, Armenian, and Russian! And rural and urban cultures and manners were so foreign to each other that no common grouping appeared to be possible.

Nationalism

Ziya Gökalp and his friends debated these problems of their budding nationalism and at various times emphasized one factor over another. Because of the complexities three main types of nationalism developed: Ottomanism, pan-Islamism, and pan-Turanism. Ottomanism possessed the greatest attraction in the earlier days of the revolution. It was recognized that origins were mixed, and as good nineteenth-century European liberals and radicals they minimized and scoffed at religion. Language was less of a barrier as Turkish had long been the *lingua franca* of the Ottoman Empire. It was easy to note that genteel Turks had manners similar to well-bred Greeks and Armenians and that peasants and artisans were alike in many respects. Ottomanism was fashionable; thus, the bold rejoicing of all groups and nations when the revolution came in 1908.

But fundamental views and historic feelings soon triumphed. Usually most non-Turks in the Chamber of Deputies voted as a bloc in opposition to the Turks. So-called programs for Ottomanization were branded as attempts to Turkify all others. Such moves eventually provoked a revolt in Albania, where the tribes resisted fiercely. Equality in the army, holding government posts, and paying taxes went against the customs and views of too many groups in the empire to be accepted voluntarily very long. As soon as Ottomanism was advocated and practiced overtly, differences were highlighted and proved insurmountable.

The next move was toward religion and pan-Islamism. Throughout the nineteenth century there were drives to seek rapport among Muslim states and peoples and to strengthen the position of the empire by building wider support for the caliph. Missions were sent to Kabul, and Abdul Hamid subsidized Jamal al-Din al-Afghani in his work in Egypt and Syria of preaching for reform in Islam. Many Young Turks in their nationalist enthusiasm found great satisfaction in pan-Islamic dreams. Unfortunately, these reveries, when translated into reality, encouraged all manner of harshness, discrimination, and persecution for non-Muslims and freethinkers. Full responsibility for the atrocious massacres of Armenians in Cilicia in 1909 was never ascertained, but some blame should probably be shouldered by both the Young Turks and the reactionary elements, each of whom had strong pan-Islamic tendencies. The stringent and reactionary measures of a pan-Islamic nature adopted by the Union and Progress party from April 1909 to July 1912 led, at least in part, to its downfall.

The third form of nationalism appeared in pan-Turanism, which espoused the union or federation of all Turkish peoples as far eastward as Central Asia and recognized kinship to Finns, Hungarians, Tartars, and many Turkish tribes in Russia. The main efforts of the pan-Turanists were devoted to the policy of Turkification of all non-Turks and to the arduous task of instilling a national feeling among all classes of Turks within the Ottoman Empire, especially in Istanbul and Anatolia. To accomplish the latter task Union and Progress created an institution called *Türk Ojak* (Turkish Hearth), which sponsored lectures on diverse subjects in a program of adult education aimed at developing a national consciousness.

Albania and the Balkan Wars

The non-Turkish communities bitterly resisted the young Turks' Turkification drives. In several districts in Asia Minor trouble arose with Greeks and Armenians, whose boycotts and attacks caused serious dislocations of commerce. Many Arabs became disillusioned. Revolts broke out in Yemen and Asir, and Arab nationalist societies were formed in Baghdad, Damascus, and Beirut. In part these Arab societies were made up of Arab members of Union and Progress, Fatherland, and other Young Turk revolutionary societies.

The most violent storm broke in Albania, when in the process of Turkification the government took steps to enforce a decree forbidding the possession of arms. Albanians also objected to a census, taxes, and the drafting of young men to serve in Yemen (which was always called the graveyard of Ottoman armies). The Albanian rebellion was quelled early in 1911 after diplomatic intervention by Montenegro and a grant of considerable local autonomy.

Concessions to the Albanians, however, aroused hopes among other nationalities; the Macedonians particularly hoped for the establishment of a regime similar to the one in Eastern Rumelia. These concessions also excited the ambitions and jealousies of officials in Greece, Bulgaria, Serbia, and Montenegro. The Young Turks, nevertheless, pushed their policies of centralization of government, thus keeping the provinces at the boiling point. Although the Liberal Unionists achieved ascendancy in Istanbul during the last half of 1912, their proposals of decentralization came too late. The Balkan states declared war on the Turks in October.

The Powers, sensing that a Balkan league was being formed to attack Turkey, had previously notified the Balkan governments that no aggrandizements won as a result of aggression would be countenanced. Ignoring the warning, Bulgaria, Greece, Serbia, and Montenegro agreed on the division of Macedonia; within a month after the start of war these allies overran all of European Turkey north of the Chatalja lines protecting Istanbul, except for Edirne, Skodra, and Janina. The effects of the reorganization of the Balkan armies in the preceding decade surprised the Great Powers, which accepted the fact that the status quo could not be enforced.

In December an armistice was signed and the five belligerents met in London to negotiate peace. The Balkan allies demanded the cession of Edirne as their price. When it became apparent that Kiamil Pasha, the grand vizir, and the Liberal Unionists were willing to pay the price, Enver Bey and about two hundred members of Union and Progress staged a successful coup d'état. They assassinated the minister of war, Nazim Bey, and returned the radical party to power. In February 1913 war was resumed. In rapid succession Janina, Edirne, and Skodra fell to Greek, Bulgarian, and Montenegrin forces. Meanwhile, the Greek navy defeated the Turkish forces outside the Dardanelles and occupied a number of the Aegean islands.

In April a second armistice was arranged, and a peace treaty was signed in London on May 30, 1913. Turkey ceded to the victors all her European possessions north of a line from Enos on the Aegean to Midia on the Black Sea and consigned to the Powers financial, judicial, commercial, and nationalist questions arising from the transfer of territory and the division of the loot among the Balkan states. The establishment of Albania upon the insistence of the Great Powers goaded Greece and Serbia to demand a revision of their previous understandings with Bulgaria. Failure to reach agreement brought war between Bulgaria and Serbia on June 30, 1913. Greece, Montenegro, and then Rumania entered the war against Bulgaria. On July 15, 1913, Turkey invaded Thrace and Enver Bey reoccupied Edirne. The Treaty of Bucharest ended this Second Balkan War in August, although a separate settlement in Istanbul between Turkey and Bulgaria, which restored Edirne to Turkey, was not drawn up until September.

The Triumvirate

The Balkan Wars were over and the Young Turks had lost almost all Ottoman possessions in Europe. From a long-range point of view this was probably a happy development, as it removed a heavy drain upon Turkish resources. At the moment, though, it gave power to the radical wing of the Young Turks. Following their coup d'état in January 1913, Mahmud Shevket Pasha became grand vizir. But his assassination in June and the succeeding grand vizirate of Said Halim Pasha, a mild and weak Egyptian prince, permitted the reins of government to fall into the hands of a triumvirate of Young Turks: Talat, Enver, and Jemal.

Talat Bey was born of a poor family near Edirne and began work as a telegraph operator in the government office at Salonika. Possessed of a brilliant mind, he was one of the organizers of the revolutionary movement in Macedonia and served as minister of interior in several cabinets of the Young Turks. He was a dedicated man who stayed poor and remained modest in character and habits throughout his career. Ruthless in his tactics, he made a distinction between personal and national morality, believing that many acts that would be entirely immoral and cruel if perpetrated by and for an individual were perfectly moral if performed in the interests of the state. Polite and exceedingly considerate, he never forgot his humble origins.

Enver Bey came from a lower-middle-class family and received a military education. Catapulted to public attention by his defiance of Abdul Hamid and his flight to the Macedonian hills in the first stage of the revolution in 1908, Enver loved the heroics of Turkish nationalism and won fame in the war in Libya against Italy. He was a man of action and quick decisions. As an attaché in Berlin, Enver fell under the spell of Prussian militarism and thoroughly believed in the superiority and invincibility of the German military machine. He, more than any other, brought Turkey into World War I as a German ally. As he rose to power, he became vain and more distant—a development that many of his former friends and admirers deplored. As one remarked: "Enver Pasha has destroyed Enver Bey." An advocate of pan-Turanism, Enver died in 1922 pursuing this policy in Turkestan.

Jemal Pasha, who became minister of the navy, was an early member of the Society of Union and Progress. He came from an old Ottoman family and had been a pan-Islamist, but in the days of the triumvirate he became an ardent Turkish nationalist. The weakest of the three, Jemal served as a kind of policeman for the Young Turks, maintaining discipline and holding the faltering in line.

To the day of the entry of Turkey into World War I, or more properly until the arrival of the *Göben* and the *Breslau* in the Bosphorus, the triumvirate ruled Turkey with a strong hand. Disobedient party members were punished, opponents were eliminated, and uncertainty and terror returned to Turkish government circles.

REFERENCES: Chapter 26

Many references mentioned for the four preceding chapters are important for this chapter; in addition those of particular note are in Chapters 12, 13, 18, 19, and 20.

Abbott, G. F. *Turkey, Greece and the Great Powers.* London: R. Scott, 1916. A lengthy report on the problems of the Balkans and Turkey during the first decade of the twentieth century.

Ahmad, Feroz. *The Young Turks: The Committee of Union and Progress in Turkish Politics, 1908–1914.* Oxford, England: The Clarendon Press, 1969. The most thorough work on the politics of the Young Turk Revolution from 1908 to 1914. The committee, it points out, did not hold absolute power during this period and was able to adapt to altering circumstances.

Berkes, Niyazi (trans. and ed.). *Turkish Nationalism and Western Civilization: Selected Essays of Ziya Gökalp.* New York: Columbia University Press, 1959. An important source for the thought of the founder of Turkish nationalism.

DeNovo, John A. *American Interests and Policies in the Middle East, 1900–1939.* Minneapolis: The University of Minnesota Press, 1963. A thorough work that includes all aspects of American interests.

Gordon, Leland J. *American Relations with Turkey, 1830–1930, An Economic Interpretation.* Philadelphia: University of Pennsylvania Press, 1932. Particularly good on the period before World War I and American dollar diplomacy in Turkey.

Helmreich, E. C. *The Diplomacy of the Balkan Wars, 1912–1913.* Cambridge, Mass.: Harvard University Press, 1938. Basic for this topic.

Kazamias, Andreas M. *Education and the Quest for Modernity in Turkey.* Chicago: University of Chicago Press, 1966. Especially important for the twentieth century.

Kushner, David. *The Rise of Turkish Nationalism, 1876–1908.* London, Frank Cass, 1977. This is a brief study of the intellectual origins of Turkish nationalism as it grew in the last decades of the nineteenth century.

Seton-Watson, R. W. *Rise of Nationality in the Balkans.* London: Constable, 1917. Important for the Balkan Wars.

Waugh, Telford. *Turkey, Yesterday, To-Day, and To-Morrow.* London: Chapman & Hall, 1930. A useful work that includes many facts about the prewar period.

White, Wilbur W. *The Process of Change in the Ottoman Empire.* Chicago: University of Chicago Press, 1937. Discusses the impact of the West on this area in the nineteenth century, country by country.

Chapter 27

British Occupation of Egypt and the Sudan

Lord Cromer in Egypt

The British army occupied Cairo and took control of Egypt in September 1882. The British administration presumed that its occupation would be of short duration, hoping to return the khedive to the position he held before the shelling of Alexandria and then to withdraw. But the British cabinet recognized that certain aspects of Egyptian society needed to be stabilized before evacuation was possible. To this end Lord Dufferin, British ambassador to the Porte, was sent to Egypt in November to advise the khedive in reestablishing his authority and in arranging for "the well-being of all classes of the population." Dufferin found Egypt in chaos. The cabinet had fallen and Khedive Tawfik, frightened and vindictive, had asked Sharif Pasha to form a new government. Almost immediately this new government was humiliated by the British. A Colonel Urabi, who had surrendered to the British at the Battle of Tel al-Kebir, had been turned over to the khedive for trial. Urabi was found guilty of treason and sentenced to be executed, but the British intervened and insisted instead that he be exiled to Ceylon. Riaz Pasha, the Minister of the Interior, resigned in bitterness over the affront, but Sharif Pasha and Tawfik quietly acquiesced.

Lord Dufferin spent seven months forcing the changes in the Egyptian government that the British trusted would then enable them to withdraw. First the army and the police were reorganized in order to guarantee freedom of passage through the Suez Canal—which had been the reason for the British intervention. A new Egyptian army, provisionally set at 6,000, was created under General Sir Evelyn Wood as *Sirdar* (Commander in Chief), with a number of British officers serving in various high posts. The British army of occupation was cut from 12,000 to 9,500, the intention being to withdraw it entirely as soon as the new Egyptian forces could be trained. In the cities a police force of 2,000 was formed, commanded by Europeans.

The British believed that financial reforms were the second step to ensure stability and tranquility. The Dual Control, terminated by the occupation, was replaced with a single British financial adviser, who in reality became fiscal master of Egypt. Also Dufferin placed a British adviser in those key ministries whose recommendations had the force of commands and suggested cutting the staffs and reducing the proportion of highly paid Europeans. In the provinces he revived the Commission for the Reform of Native Tribunals and civil and criminal codes, based on Napoleonic codes, were adopted, and in 1883 a system of lower courts and courts of appeal was decreed with forty Belgian and Dutch judges installed in conjunction with a British general prosecutor. The system was extended to Upper Egypt in 1889, by which time most of the foreign judges had resigned.

Lord Dufferin was also instructed to see to "the establishment of institutions favourable to the prudent development of liberty," a fond hope of many English liberals. On May 1, 1883, two days before Lord Dufferin's departure, the khedive decreed that there should be a four-to-eight member advisory council elected in each province and convoked by each governor; a twenty-six member Legislative Council (ten members appointed by the khedive, the remainder elected by the provincial councils) that could examine and debate proposed legislation but could only make suggestions to the government; and a General Assembly, consisting of eighty members (eight ministers, the Legislative Council, and forty-six delegates from the provinces), whose chief function was to approve or disapprove new tax levies.

One of Lord Dufferin's more lasting reforms was the bringing in of Colonel Colin Scott-Moncrieff and other engineers as irrigation advisers to the Ministry of Public Works in 1883. They set to work to rehabilitate the old Nile Barrage built by Muhammad Ali at the apex of the delta. In 1884, after the barrage was restored, the cotton yield was 30,000 tons greater than in the previous year. With cotton at £35 per ton this increased Egypt's cotton income by over £1 million; the cost of the renovation had been only £26,000. Cromer recognized the significance of such operations and in 1885 asked the London Conference for £1 million for irrigation projects. Scott-Moncrieff and his group thereupon improved the Ibrahimiyya and other canals, making perennial irrigation and two or three crops a year standard agricultural practice in many parts of Egypt. Scott-Moncrieff also paid the workers on these projects and abolished forced labor under the lash of the *kurbash* (rhinoceros-hide bullwhip).

Between 1896 and 1903 Sir William Willcocks supervised the building of a dam at Aswan (which was heightened in 1912 and again in 1930) and a satellite barrage at Asyut, which by 1905 made perennial cropping possible for over a quarter of a million acres in Middle and Upper Egypt, guaranteed water for summer irrigation, and assured a high cotton yield in Lower Egypt. Greatly increased revenues from these improvements were largely responsible for the public and private profits that made the British occupation of Egypt acceptable to the Great Powers and their bondholders and tolerable to the Egyptian people.

With the framework for a new regime in place, Lord Dufferin returned to his post in Istanbul. In September 1883, Sir Evelyn Baring returned to Egypt as the British Agent and Consul General. Elevated to the peerage as

Lord Cromer in 1892, he ruled Egypt autocratically until his retirement in 1907.

Britain's position in regard to the khedive, the Ottoman suzerain, and the other Powers was never clearly defined. No formal machinery for control was established. The capitulations remained, as did the mixed courts, the Public Debt Fund, and the Law of Liquidation. Khedive Tawfik continued as ruler, the cabinet and the ministries functioned, local administration governed the cities and provinces, and the courts and judiciary performed their duties. The ultimate power of decision, however, resided in the British agent, who usually exercised it through a British adviser to a specific minister or through a British general or controlling officer. This indirect rule was facilitated by an unspoken alliance fashioned early between Lord Cromer and Tawfik, in which Egyptian ministers and governors either followed the advice of the British agent or forfeited their posts. Lord Cromer and his British advisers and officials determined and administered trade policies, agriculture, communications, irrigation, health, and foreign affairs in addition to Egypt's army and finances. Education failed to fit into any program. The illiteracy of the masses was hardly touched; yet the number receiving a secondary education without any technical or proficient skill was so far beyond the need that many Egyptians became dangerously frustrated.

Several prime ministers served under Cromer: Sharif Pasha, until he refused advice on the Sudan; Nubar Pasha, who held office several times but always quarreled over internal administrative affairs and local government; Riaz Pasha, a strong administrator who resigned over control of the Egyptian courts; and Mustafa Pasha Fahmi, who served the longest continuous period and who was so subservient to the British that he caused promising Egyptians to join societies and political parties whose first principle was nationalistic and anti-British.

The British occupation only worsened the financial chaos. Until 1885 the situation was desperate. The French, embittered by Britain's unilateral occupation and the abolition of the Dual Control, used every device possible to embarrass the British and to prevent any amelioration of Egypt's financial prostration. Revenues such as railway and telegraph receipts, customs duties, port fees at Alexandria, and proceeds from khedivial estates, allotted by the Law of Liquidation to the Fund for debt payments, continued to be collected, but funds for the administration of government and payment of tribute to the Porte were insufficient. By the end of 1883 government workers' salaries were in arrears and the floating current debt of £4 million had doubled. British proposals to reduce interest payments on the debt, lower the rate of amortization, and transfer some funds to pay for administration were vetoed by the French through the Fund.

Finally, at a London conference in 1885 agreement was reached to float an internationally guaranteed loan to pay off the current debt, to reduce interest payments and debt amortization, and to provide for Egyptian irrigation needs. Any surplus funds annually accruing to the Fund were to be divided equally between the administration and debt funding; a German and a Russian member were to be added to the governing board of the Fund; and the situation was to be reviewed again if the Egyptian administration was not solvent by 1888. Although it was touch and go through 1887, Cromer and his capable financial adviser, Sir Edgar Vincent, made ends meet and avoided an international investigation. By 1889 the Egyptian treasury began to show surpluses.

With Egypt's finances seemingly adjusted the British turned to the thorny problem of withdrawal from the country. Badgered from every side—and especially by France—to set a definite date and equally encouraged by Cromer to be vague on this issue, England sent Sir Henry Drummond-Wolff to Cairo and Istanbul in 1885 to conclude a withdrawal agreement in concert with the sultan and with the approval of the Powers. The French and Russians protested so strenuously against British proposals that Abdul Hamid failed to ratify a convention. As a result, the British position in Egypt remained anomalous until 1914.

Meanwhile, British imperial strategy shifted its focus to Cairo and Suez from Istanbul and the Straits where German influence was mounting. British withdrawal from Egypt was now pushed to some nebulous future. However, the Powers and the trading nations of Europe needed an understanding of the status of the Suez Canal. Consequently, a meeting was called in Istanbul in 1888 at which the Constantinople Convention, as previously outlined, was signed. Though Lord Cromer secretly railed at the many disabilities suffered by Egyptians, the international position of Egypt under the suzerainty of the Ottoman Empire and the control of Great Britain remained virtually unchanged until World War I.

Khedive Abbas Hilmi II vs. Lord Cromer

When Riaz Pasha resigned as prime minister in 1891, he was replaced by Mustafa Pasha Fahmi. An elegant Turk, weak in resolve, gentlemanly, honest, hardworking, an ally of Ismail, a friend of Urabi, and devoted to Tawfik, Fahmi continued as prime minister until Cromer's retirement in 1907. Affairs moved so smoothly during Fahmi's stewardship that Cromer allowed that he was almost bored. With imports and exports on the rise, treasury surpluses building up, and the cabinet and khedive docile, the British occupation appeared to be succeeding. Then, in January 1892, Tawfik fell ill and died. His son and successor, Abbas Hilmi II, not quite eighteen years old, was studying at the Princes' Academy in Vienna and was an untested and unknown figure. Cromer realized that the "alliance" had been broken; he would have to start afresh to educate the new khedive to reality.

From his French tutor, Abbas had gained French ideas: liberalism, free political discussion, and Anglophobic proclivities. Coming to Cairo as the khedive's European secretary, the tutor, Rouiller, encouraged Abbas to show independence of Cromer and evidently suggested that France would aid the new khedive to get rid of the British. Thereafter, Abbas was friendly toward the French and showed a strong dislike for the British. The firman of his authorization from the Porte busied the new khedive in the first few months of his rule, as Abdul Hamid had neglected to include the Sinai peninsula in Abbas's territory. Cromer was intensely disturbed over this omission, jeopardizing the Suez Canal as it did, and fully supported Abbas in the final drafting in favor of Egypt.

This episode led Cromer to call Abbas a "gentlemanlike and healthily-minded boy" whose judgment appeared "to be singularly sound for so very young a man." A few months later, however, Cromer was calling Abbas a foolish youth, for Abbas had decided to replace the seriously ill Fahmi with a prime minister of his own choosing, and offered the post to Tighrane Pasha, Nubar's son-in-law, an Armenian Christian. Cromer, knowing that Tighrane was unfriendly to the British, insisted that a Muslim be appointed instead. A few months later, Abbas dismissed the kowtowing Fahmi and appointed in his place Fakhri Pasha, a former minister of justice who had crossed Cromer on more than one occasion. Cromer exploded because Fakhri had been appointed without consultation with the British. London cabled Abbas that England could not "sanction the proposed nomination." Cromer recommended Riaz Pasha as prime minister and forced Abbas to declare that he "would always most willingly adopt British advice."

Suddenly Abbas became a hero to many of the budding Egyptian nationalists, who saw in him a young and vigorous voice for "Egypt for the Egyptians." Abbas now had the sympathies of the Egyptian people and especially of the Egyptian army, but timidity and caution kept him in subjugation. Moreover, in 1894 he discovered that the army might hail him at one moment but abandon him in a contest of will with the British. Abbas, with Mahir Pasha, undersecretary of state for war, and Kitchener, who had now become Sirdar of the Egyptian army, were making a tour of inspection in Upper Egypt. At Wadi Halfa, on the frontier, Abbas remarked disparagingly to Kitchener on the performance of the troops. Kitchener took offense, accused Abbas of criticizing British officers, and demanded a public apology. Sensing this as a suitable opportunity to put Abbas in his place, Cromer supported Kitchener's stand. Abbas was forced to publish a retraction of his remarks and had to fire Mahir Pasha after Cromer hinted that British public opinion when fully informed would likely insist on deposing the khedive. The Egyptian army would not, and could not, in view of all the British officers in dominant positions, act to support Abbas against British rule.

Abbas Hilmi II and Egyptian Nationalism

For support in his opposition to British occupation, Abbas then turned to the Egyptian nationalists, who had been increasing in number and influence. Cromer, never worried very much about Egypt's educated minority, had permitted a free press to exist. Now, a number of teachers and writers, most of whom had studied or lived in Europe, were espousing Egyptian patriotism.

Egyptian nationalists began to appear early in the nineteenth century. One of the first advocates was Rifaa Rafi al-Tahtawi, who had studied at Cairo's al-Azhar University and then in 1826 was sent by Muhammad Ali to Paris as the religious guardian of a group of Egyptian students. He remained there for five years, learning precise French and reading widely, including the works of Voltaire, Condillac, Rousseau, and Montesquieu. From 1831 until his death forty years later al-Tahtawi taught two generations of Egyptian students and wrote many significant books, among them, *Guiding Truths for Girls and Youths* and *The Paths of Egyptian Hearts in the Joys of the Contemporary Arts.* These works championed the love of Egypt but pointed out that Egypt's destiny could not be attained until the ulema were modernized and the schools offered a more secular education.

Many other writers contributed to the intellectual and ideological ferment in Egypt in the time of Said and Ismail. One was Jamal al-Din al-Afghani, who lived, taught, and conspired in Cairo from 1871 to 1879. A Shiite from Iran, he posed as a Sunnite from Afghanistan (in Afghanistan he claimed to be a Turk). He had studied in Iraq and lived in Afghanistan and Istanbul before coming to Cairo upon Riaz Pasha's offer of a government subsidy. Jamal al-Din's life can be summed up in a phrase recently used as the title of a book about him, *An Islamic Response to Imperialism.* In Egypt he found a coterie of devotees who were swept up by his compelling personality, his lucid and persuasive presentation of ideas, and the innovation and dedication of his beliefs. He argued that when the Muslim community returned to the truth of Islam, society would cease to be weak; only then would there be a regeneration. Jamal al-Din believed that the essence of Islam was identical to that of modern rationalism and that the outward trappings of Islamic scholasticism had shackled Muslim philosophers. He held that Islam came from God and was exalted above the universe. He believed also in reason, that one should use one's mind freely to know and test all. Furthermore, every mind was capable of providing the individual with self-respect and a sense of equality. Lastly, Jamal al-Din was convinced that Islam was an active way of life; it was not a passive resignation to whatever might come but a responsible activity in doing the will of God.

These preachings, which were debated privately in closed circles, were heady stuff. They were aimed against Christian imperialistic attacks upon Islamic societies and against Westernizing influences and materialism. Jamal al-Din al-Afghani was a pan-Islamist who desired to reform Islam by means of education and to adapt Islam to the conditions of modern life. He did not see how this could be done without revolution, the political unity of the Muslim world, and freedom from foreign domination. Wherever he went, whether in Syria, Egypt, Turkey, or Iran, he vigorously stirred the minds and imaginations of Muslims to react in defense of an embattled Islamic society and against its debasement by Christian Europe. He became so influential in Egypt that the government asked him to leave. The remainder of his life was spent in Iran, France, England, and the Ottoman Empire.

Some of his most effective writing was done in Paris for devotees who flocked to his side when they were in exile. He died in 1897.

Jamal al-Din's most illustrious pupil was Muhammad Abdu, a peasant from Lower Egypt who had a distinguished career as a mystic, journalist, judge, and teacher. Differing from his mentor, Muhammad Abdu deplored the use of violence and believed that true reforms came only by a gradual process. He advocated a reform of Islam that would return it to its earliest, purest dogma, permitting a more flexible interpretation of its precepts than was allowed in the Cairo of his day. Muhammad Abdu, like Urabi Pasha, wished to free the people of Egypt from despotic rule and to institute a more democratic society. He also worked for the development of Arabic into a more unified tongue, attempting to draw newspaper Arabic and the spoken vernacular together and bring both nearer to classical Koranic Arabic.

Abdu supported the Urabi movement, was an active member of the Nationalist Party (al-Hizb al-Watani), and was exiled along with Urabi. He found his way to Paris to join al-Afghani; together they edited a shortlived but influential pan-Islamic journal, The Indissoluble Bond (al-Urwa al-Wuthqa). At Cromer's urging, Abdu was allowed by Tawfik to return to Egypt in 1888. He was appointed a judge in a local court and in 1899 became Grand Mufti of Egypt, a post he retained until his death in 1905. In France Abdu had concluded that Egypt's poverty-stricken traditional society could neither mount a successful revolution nor drive out the British. Henceforth he taught that reason and the pragmatic accommodation of Islam to the modern world must supersede customary practice and belief; one should adopt what is reasonable and just for society.

Abdu and Cromer respected each other and met frequently, often at the home of Princess Nazli Fazil, who was the daughter of Prince Mustafa Fazil, Ismail's next younger brother and a prominent New Ottoman. Abdu recognized Egypt's need of a benevolent despot and probably would have supported Cromer had he been an Egyptian. Cromer backed Abdu against the vindictiveness of Tawfik and Abbas, who thus disliked and distrusted Abdu, Abbas even going so far as accusing him of having sold out to the British. Abbas circulated such rumors about Abdu that only after Abdu's death was he fully accorded his rightful honors as a patriot, scholar, teacher, judge, and reformer.

Another prominent nationalist, a contemporary and sometimes rival of Muhammad Abdu, was Ali Yusuf. As a teacher at al-Azhar University he preached reform in much the same vein as did Abdu, but without the philosophical and intellectual substance. In 1889, through the encouragement of Riaz Pasha, whose home he frequented, Ali Yusuf founded al-Muayyad (The Supporter), a newspaper financed by the anti-English element, which within a few years became the leading pro-Egyptian journal. Ali Yusuf was a good journalist and his articles were always Muslim-oriented and even pro-Ottoman. When Abbas II became khedive he befriended Ali Yusuf, subsidized the newspaper, and often took him on his travels. Naturally, *al-Muayyad* supported Abbas in his attempts to become independent of Cromer. In 1907 Ali Yusuf formed, under Abbas's patronage, the nationalist Party of Constitutional Reform, commonly called *al-Dusturiyya,* which died in 1911 with Ali Yusuf. Ali Yusuf was a conservative, orthodox nationalist who wanted Egypt governed by Egyptians. However, he doomed his movement by tying it to Abbas, for Abbas's surrender to Cromer had turned most Egyptian nationalists against him by 1905.

No nationalist was more fiery than Mustafa Kamil. Coming from the new educated class, he entered the School of Law in 1891 at the age of seventeen, then attended the newly opened French School of Law, and went on to France where he was graduated in law in 1894. He had been introduced to many prominent Egyptian leaders at the home of Ali Pasha Mubarak, and in Paris, supplied with funds from Abbas, he became acquainted with leading French literary figures who displayed this genuine Egyptian nationalist in order to disprove British claims that their occupation was fully approved of by the Egyptians. Returning to Egypt in 1896 he spent the remaining twelve years of his life agitating for Egyptian national independence. A spellbinding orator who fired audiences with his ideals and ideas, Mustafa Kamil pleaded with all Egyptians of whatever origin or religion to unite into one nationalistic force to eliminate ignorance and to support the khedive as a rallying point against the occupation. His slogans, such as, "Had I not been born an Egyptian, I would have wished to become one," instilled in his followers a love of Egypt and a pride in her past glories. Kamil worked to erase the defeatism and the sense of inferiority that the capitulations and the occupation had generated. In 1900 he founded the radical newspaper, *al-Liwa (The Standard),* and gathered nationalists about him informally, calling them *al-Hizb al-Watani,* The Nationalist Party, which did not become an organized party until 1907. Something of a pan-Islamist, whose goal was to achieve Islamic liberation of Egypt from alien rule and autonomy within the Ottoman empire under the caliph, he accused the British of impairing the authority of the khedive, destroying Arabic as the language of the educated, depriving Egypt of the Sudan, exploiting Egyptian agriculture, excluding Egyptians from top government positions, and stultifying Islam to secure the British position in India. Cromer called him a fanatic.

The Anglo-Egyptian Sudan

Throughout the nineteenth century the governing forces in Egypt maintained a lively interest in the Sudan. Muhammad Ali sent an expedition into that area in 1820, and in 1842 the sultan recognized him as governor-general of the Sudan. During the middle of the century the chief activities with regard to the Sudan consisted of conflicts with Abyssinia over such Red Sea ports as Massawa. At the time of Ismail's ouster from office, affairs in the Sudan were beginning to be difficult to manage.

In 1881 Muhammad Ahmad of Dongola proclaimed himself to be the Mahdi, the religious leader sent to complete the work of the Prophet. When revolt broke out about 150 miles south of Khartoum in the province of Kordofan, affairs in Egypt were so chaotic and finances so desperate that the Sudan was left to herself. However, in 1883 Khedive Tawfik sent Colonel Hicks to head the Egyptian army in the Sudan. He and his rabble conscript army were cut to pieces by the forces of the Mahdi, and Sir Evelyn Baring upon his arrival in Egypt insisted upon complete withdrawal from the Sudan, largely for financial reasons. Gordon was then sent in 1884 to arrange for the evacuation of Khartoum, but he delayed the operation and received almost no direct aid from Cairo. In 1885 Khartoum fell to the Mahdi, and Gordon and his men were slain.

For the following decade the Sudan was abandoned to the Mahdi, and Wadi Halfa became the frontier post of Egypt. In the 1890s the Italian war in Eritrea and French pressure upon Abyssinia led the British to consider the reconquest of the Sudan. Kitchener took Dongola in 1896. Two years later, with the support of some Indian troops, two English brigades, a cavalry regiment, and an artillery battery, he moved up the Nile, taking Omdurman and Khartoum, and completely routing the Mahdi's forces. In 1899 the Sudan Convention was consummated in Cairo, establishing what soon came to be known as the Anglo-Egyptian Sudan. Theoretically it was a condominium, but the Egyptian voice in ruling the Sudan remained only nominal. Military and civil power was vested in a governor-general chosen by the British. Egyptian law was not valid in the Sudan, nor were the mixed tribunals extended there. Import duties were not levied on goods coming from Egypt, and the slave trade was prohibited. Firearms and spiritous liquors were outlawed in accordance with the Brussels Act of 1890, which governed the traffic of such items in certain parts of Africa. Consular agents of other powers could be accredited in the Sudan only upon the consent of the British government. Although the British and Egyptian flags were flown side by side over all public buildings, no one ever doubted which power ruled the Sudan.

Taba and Dinshwai

Though nationalist attacks in the press made life more difficult for Cromer, he expected that greatly improved economic conditions would blunt the campaigns of the educated few who mounted the opposition and would allay the antagonisms of the Egyptian masses. Events seemed to be working in his favor and dashing the hopes of Abbas, Kamil, Ali Yusuf, Abdu, and others. Kitchener had secured the Anglo-Egyptian condominium over the Sudan. Meanwhile, there had been an inconclusive showdown between Kitchener and French officers at Fashoda, where each side raised the Egyptian flag and referred the settlement of the disagreement to Europe. Egyptians were disappointed by the Anglo-French Declaration of 1899, in which the French gave in to the British. This anguish was intensified by the Anglo-French Agreement of 1904, part of the Entente Cordiale, stating quite frankly that the French accepted the indefinite postponement of British evacuation and would not object to freeing Egypt from most of the

financial restrictions imposed on her by the Fund. Two years later, however, three inflammatory incidents rekindled the nationalist fires, setting
the stage for Cromer's retirement.

In January 1906 Ottoman forces landed at Taba, a desert spot near the
head of the Gulf of Akaba, and established a post there. The British protested that Taba was in the territory of Egypt but the Porte disagreed,
arguing that Taba was in the Sinai peninsula and that it was a part of Syria.
Mustafa Kamil, pan-Islamist Ali Yusuf, and other Egyptian editors came out
strongly in support of the sultan and bitterly attacked Cromer and the
British for trying to humiliate the caliph and Islam. Cromer considered the
pro-Turkish clamor only another anti-British outcry. Istanbul succumbed to
a British ultimatum to delimit the frontier in Egypt's favor.

Almost before the Taba affair was concluded the students at the School
of Law, ardent followers of Kamil, went out on strike, the first demonstration of its kind in Egypt. In the end Cromer had to arbitrate the matter.
By 1908 student strikes and disturbances became ordinary occurrences.

Then, in May 1906, the Dinshwai Affair altered irrevocably the course of
political life in Egypt. A group of British officers went to Dinshwai, a village
near Tanta, to shoot pigeons, a favorite sport of theirs. Neglecting to obtain
permission from the village headman, they greatly antagonized the villagers, who regarded the pigeons as their domesticated birds. A fire broke out,
a fracas developed, a gun went off, a village woman was shot, British officers
were mauled and one died from heat exhaustion, and a peasant was beaten
to death before order was restored. The British judged that stern measures
were needed and set up at Cromer's insistence a special tribunal to try the
Dinshwai villagers on charges of murder. Composed of Butros Pasha Ghali,
the minister of justice, the British judicial adviser, the British vice-president
of the courts, the Egyptian president of the native courts, and a British army
judge, the special tribunal handed down the verdict: thirty-one villagers
were found not guilty and released; two were sentenced to life imprisonment; one was given fifteen years; six received seven years; three were
given one year and fifty lashes; five received fifty lashes; and four were
condemned to death by hanging. Punishments were carried out immediately, in public view, in the village. The severity of the judgment stunned
Egypt and shocked Europe. Kamil wrote an article for *Le Figaro* in Paris
and George Bernard Shaw wrote the play, *John Bull's Other Island.* For
many Egyptians this naked display of power was the birth of nationalism.
It led to the formation of political parties. Mustafa Kamil set up the Nationalist Party; Ali Yusuf founded the Party of Constitutional Reform; and followers of Muhammad Abdu organized the Party of the Nation, or of the
People, *Hizb al-Umma.* All these parties urged the institution of representative government in Egypt, replacement of European officials by Egyptians, and transfer of criminal jurisdiction over foreigners from consular
courts to the mixed courts. None of the parties demanded immediate British departure. Though Cromer secured the appointment of Saad Zaghlul,
a leading member of *al-Umma,* as minister of education, Cromer's style of

governing Egypt now was outmoded and he resigned on March 28, 1907. Kamil, on the occasion, wrote in his paper that Cromer had negated the khedive's authority, had seized the Sudan with Egyptian men and money and then stripped Egypt of any influence there, had denied Egyptians any power at home, had insulted Islam, had forced Egyptians to be governed by Englishmen, had impugned Egyptian nationalism, and had converted Egypt into a British colony. Kamil's condemnation was widely accepted not only in Egypt but in England and throughout the world.

Sir Eldon Gorst and Lord Kitchener

Even in 1906, the year of crises, no threat of a nationalist uprising surfaced. To be sure, the newspapers *al-Liwa* and *al-Muayyad,* mouthpieces of the Nationalist and Constitutional Parties, sharpened their attacks and received aid from Abbas. This alliance of nationalists and the palace against the British raised more fears in London than in Cairo, for the great majority of educated Egyptians supported the People's Party, *al-Umma,* a moderate group under the leadership of Ahmad Lutfi al-Sayyid, the scholarly editor of the party's newspaper, *al-Jarida.* The leaders of *al-Umma,* although desirous of a British departure, recognized that Cromer had found chaos, financial ruin, and general frustration upon his arrival and within a decade had established financial equilibrium, organized an orderly and a tolerably efficient government, and instituted considerable justice in the administration and the courts. For this they were thankful. Life was not bad enough to warrant a revolt.

To replace Cromer, London sent Sir Eldon Gorst, who had been in Egyptian government service from 1886 to 1904. Gorst had instructions to win over Abbas, with whom he had once been friendly, and thus break the alliance between the palace and the nationalists. He had been assigned to Egypt with the recognition that a more liberal policy was needed and that he should prepare Egypt for self-rule.

Gorst began by opening up more administrative positions for Egyptians and by trying to share the formulation of policy with them. Most English officials in Egypt resented the change; Gorst got rid of the more unsympathetic ones. He extended the power of the provincial councils by giving them control over local education, trade schools, public markets, and some police, but would not consider the nationalists' call for true legislative institutions and a constitution, even though the Turks got one in 1908. Gorst did alienate the nationalists from Abbas by deferring to the khedive on almost all minor matters. Following Kamil's death in 1908, *al-Liwa,* under a new editor, the unprincipled rabble-rouser Shaykh Shawish, was so vitriolic in its attacks on Gorst, Abbas, and the government that the old press law was revived in 1909, *al-Liwa* was prosecuted, and Shawish was exiled. But the new alliance between the palace and the British Agency cost Gorst the support of the moderate nationalists and *al-Umma,* for they considered the unbridled authority of Abbas to be as dangerous as that of the British.

In 1908 Mustafa Pasha Fahmi bowed to pressure on all sides and resigned as prime minister. Gorst had found him difficult; the nationalists considered him a British straw man; and *al-Umma* and his son-in-law Saad Zaghlul encouraged him to desert the British. In his place Gorst installed Butros Pasha Ghali, a Copt. For the nationalists a worse choice could not have been found. As a minister Butros had signed the Anglo-Egyptian condominium over the Sudan and as a judge he had sat at the Dinshwai trial. He was instrumental in getting the press law reactivated and had exiled Shawish. Also, in 1909, the Suez Canal Company, whose concession ran until 1969, offered to pay the Egyptian government a million pounds a year to extend the concession an additional forty years. Many thought this to be an attractive proposition and, urged on by *al-Umma* leaders and by Gorst Butros requested the Legislative Council's approval. The debate over the extension was most vehement; Butros was accused of selling Egyptian property and perpetrating a dishonorable arrangement. In February 1910, before it was rejected, a young fanatic assassinated Butros.

These events broke Gorst's spirit; overcome by ill health he returned to England, where he died in 1911. He was replaced by Lord Kitchener, who had served with distinction in Egypt in various capacities from 1883 to 1899. Kitchener has been characterized as "an extremely able and ambitious soldier, overbearing, tactless, very much aware of his own importance, and without very much sense of humor."

Kitchener's appointment presaged the end of Gorst's liberalizing experiment. With international tensions mounting rapidly,—the Italian invasion of Tripoli, Balkan wars, other war scares and naval rivalries, and diplomatic maneuvers between the Triple Entente and the Triple Alliance—London wanted serenity and security in Egypt. Kitchener had no faith in Abbas's loyalty, dealt with him harshly, and wanted to depose him. But Kitchener's instructions, though stressing a return to order, enjoined him not to reverse Gorst's policies leading to more self-rule. He approached many of the leaders of the People's Party and worked with them in creating in 1913 a new Legislative Assembly that joined together the old Legislative Council and General Assembly. Sixty-six of the new legislature's members were elected publicly; its effective head was an elected vice-president; most of the members were prosperous landowners; and the People's Party held a majority.

In 1912 Kitchener, who disliked Saad Zaghlul, managed a petty quarrel that provoked Zaghlul into resigning from the cabinet. After a few months a minor post that Zaghlul wanted became vacant—the leadership of a student mission in Europe—but Kitchener refused to appoint him. Instead, Zaghlul ran for a seat in the Legislative Assembly, with a program for attaining justice in the courts, spreading public education, and increasing freedom of the press. He was the most popular figure in the campaign and had the backing of the bar association, the People's Party, the Nationalist Party, and the khedive, the last being noteworthy, for up to that time Abbas had refused Zaghlul any appointment.

In the elections in 1913 Zaghlul won handsomely and was popularly designated as the natural leader of the opposition. By an overwhelming vote the Assembly elected him its Vice-President (the President was appointed by the government). Within three months Zaghlul's popularity and his leadership in the Assembly made the prime minister's position untenable. Abbas and Kitchener then agreed that Mustafa Pasha Fahmi, Zaghlul's father-in-law, should be the new prime minister. When Kitchener questioned Fahmi it came to light that he intended within a matter of months to sweep from office all the ministers of the cabinet who "had been most loyal" to the British and to "install men devoted to Saad Zaghlul." Consequently, Fahmi was ruled out and Husayn Rushdi was named to form a cabinet, which remained in office until the end of World War I. Kitchener's adviser in the ministry of the interior noted at the time that cabinet ministers were not supported by the khedive and were timid in opposing the Assembly for fear of being branded unpatriotic. The adviser warned Kitchener that in the future "the success and even the existence of Egyptian Cabinets" depended upon the will of the Legislative Assembly. The Assembly adjourned on June 7, 1914; it was scheduled to meet again on November 1.

During the summer Kitchener became minister of war in London; Abbas Hilmi, who was in Istanbul, was not permitted to return to Cairo; and martial law was invoked in Egypt. In December Great Britain declared a protectorate over Egypt and the Sudan. Kitchener's mission as British agent had failed. By 1914 the efficiency of British officials in Egypt could be legitimately questioned, for their effectiveness had long ago been dissipated by the fact that they were not Egyptians. General resistance and noncooperation should have led British policy makers to realize that a more effective rule could have been maintained by Egyptian personnel. But Lord Kitchener hated politics and politicians and bravely faced a difficult task that he believed could be accomplished only if done under his orders. The problems the British were to experience in the post-World War I period were coming rapidly to the fore even before 1914. Only the outbreak of war and subsequent strong military occupation prevented Egyptian nationalists from openly attacking the British position. Such action was reserved for the time the war would be over.

REFERENCES: Chapter 27

Works cited at the end of Chapters 4, 7, 19, 20, 22, 23, 24, 25, and 26 are valuable for this chapter.

Abbas, Mekki. *The Sudan Question: The Dispute over the Anglo-Egyptian Condominium, 1884–1951.* London: Faber, 1952. Written by a Sudanese, it is neither pro-British nor pro-Egyptian.

'Abd al-Rahim, Muddathir. *Imperialism and Nationalism in the Sudan: A Study in Constitutional and Political Development, 1899–1956.* New York: Oxford University Press, 1969. A constitutional study of the peculiar relationships of the Sudan with Egypt and Britain. It is the most comprehensive study of the Anglo-Egyptian Sudan.

Adams, C. C. *Islam and Modernism in Egypt.* London: Oxford University Press, 1933. An analysis of one of the great problems of Egypt. In some ways it is a study of the thought of Muhammad Abdu. Though dated it is still useful.

Ahmed, Jamal Mohammed. *The Intellectual Origins of Egyptian Nationalism.* London: Oxford University Press, 1960. A fine account of the intellectual ferment preceding the British occupation and a commentary on Abdu's views on the value of religion.

Baer, Gabriel. *Studies in the Social History of Modern Egypt.* Chicago: University of Chicago Press, 1969. A study of how twentieth-century events have involved Egyptians in a new political experience.

Berque, Jacques. *Egypt: Imperialism and Revolution* (Jean Stewart, trans.). New York: Praeger, 1972. A description of the rise and decline of British power in Egypt, or the interrelated processes of colonization and decolonization, 1882–1952.

Boyle, Clara. *Boyle of Cairo.* Kendal, England: Titus Wilson, 1965. A biography of Lord Cromer's influential Oriental secretary, drawing on Boyle's papers.

Cromer, Evelyn Baring. *Modern Egypt.* 2 vols. London: Macmillan, 1908. Cromer's account of his rule in Egypt.

Holt, P. M. *The Mahdist State in the Sudan, 1881–1898: A Study of Its Origins, Development and Overthrow.* Oxford: Clarendon Press, 1958.

Keddie, Nikki R. *An Islamic Response to Imperialism: Political and Religious Writings of Sayyid Jamal ad-Din "Al-Afghani."* Berkeley: University of California Press, 1968. After a short biography and analysis of al-Afghani, there follows translations of some of his important works.

———. *Sayyid Jamal ad-Din "Al-Afghani": A Political Biography.* Berkeley: University of California Press, 1972. A definitive biography of the almost legendary political activist and publicist.

Kedourie, Elie. *Afghani and Abduh, An Essay on Religious Unbelief and Political Activism in Modern Islam.* London: Frank Cass, 1966. A concise study of the relationship of these two men and their beliefs.

Kerr, Malcolm A. *Islamic Reform: The Political and Legal Theories of Muhammad Abduh and Rashid Rida.* Berkeley: University of California Press, 1966. An account of how the efforts of these men to put new life into existing Islamic doctrines failed because they were unable to use classical constitutional and legal theories.

Lloyd, George Ambrose L. *Egypt Since Cromer.* 2 vols. London: Macmillan, 1933–1934. Lord Lloyd was an official in Egypt.

Magnus, Philip. *Kitchener, Portrait of an Imperialist.* New York: Dutton, 1958. A sympathetic treatment.

Marlowe, John. *Arab Nationalism and British Imperialism.* New York: Praeger, 1961. The first chapters deal with the earlier period while the later ones discuss events to 1956.

———. *Cromer in Egypt.* New York: Praeger, 1970. Based on British documentary sources. Covers Egyptian finances and British negotiations with other European powers as well as the details of Cromer's administration.

Rifaat, Mohammed. *The Awakening of Modern Egypt.* London: Longmans, Green, 1947. Although it covers the period since 1798, it is strong on the development of nationalism.

Rowlatt, Mary. *Founders of Modern Egypt.* New York: Asia Publishing House, 1962. This is a very well researched and thoughtful volume on the life and character of Muhammad Abduh and the military activity of Urabi.

al-Sayyid, Afaf Lutfi. *Egypt and Cromer: A Study in Anglo-Egyptian Relations.* New York: Praeger, 1968. The nationalist movement and the British reaction to it. The author had access to many private papers of nationalist leaders.

Tignor, Robert L. *Modernization and British Colonial Rule in Egypt, 1882–1914.* Princeton, N.J.: Princeton University Press, 1966. A very fair evaluation written in a clear and orderly fashion.

Wingate, Ronald. *Wingate of the Sudan.* London: J. Murray, 1955. An important work on the life and activities of one of the leading British officials in the Sudan.

Zayid, Mahmud Y. *Egypt's Struggle for Independence.* Beirut: Khayats, 1965. Contains two fine chapters on the history of Egypt in the nineteenth century, going as far as 1914, and material on the 1920s and 1930s. The author taught history at the American University of Beirut.

Chapter 28

Arab Nationalism

The Role of Education

At the opening of the twentieth century the twin questions of an Arab nationalism separate and distinct from Ottomanism or Egyptian patriotism and the formation of an independent Arab nationalist state were in the minds of only a very few. But the nationalist movement and feelings surrounding it were already reaching a degree of development that could burst at any moment into the full light of world attention. The activities and speeches of Muhammad Ali and his son Ibrahim stirred a few to think in terms of a truly Arab state. During the years of Egypt's occupation of Syria a few sparks of Arab nationalism were struck, and upon Ibrahim's withdrawal and the return of Ottoman rule Beirut and Damascus became centers of nascent Arab nationalism.

In Syria the leading role in revitalizing Arab intellectualism was first played by Western educators. Although Jesuits had arrived in the seventeenth century to teach in Maronite and Catholic communities, little rejuvenation of Arab thought occurred until 1820, when American Presbyterian missionaries landed in Beirut. The latter organized schools almost immediately. The Catholics now increased their energies to compete with the American Protestants, and Ibrahim furthered the educational drive by establishing many elementary schools for boys on the model of those in Egypt. Girls' schools were also opened. In 1834 Americans set up a printing press in Beirut. Soon a training college for teachers was founded in Lebanon. In 1866 the Syrian Protestant College of Beirut opened its doors. Later, as the American University, it played an important role in training young people (Muslim and Christian alike) from every corner of the Arab world. Almost simultaneously, Catholic missionaries, largely from France, settled in Syria in great numbers, and schools spread from Beirut to Damascus, Aleppo, and many other towns. In 1875 the University of St. Joseph in Beirut opened; it would educate many outstanding leaders of Syrian national and cultural life.

Numerous writers, thinkers, and teachers influenced the growth of Arab nationalism. Three of them were Christian Arabs from Lebanon. Nasif al-Yaziji taught Arabic near Beirut until his death in 1871. His masterly writings in Arabic pioneered a style, manner, and vocabulary suitable for expressing the life and ideas of the modern world and paved the way for an Arabic renaissance.

Butrus al-Bustani, a Maronite, as was al-Yaziji, assisted American Protestant missionaries in translating the Bible into Arabic. His dictionary, encyclopedia, and the many Arabic language periodicals he wrote and published helped to create a modern Arabic prose able to present the concepts of contemporary thought in language simple enough for use in newspapers; he is the father of so-called newspaper Arabic. Butrus also founded the National School, where studies were secular and based on national rather than religious principles.

The third Lebanese Christian was Jurji Zaydan, whose historical novels, modeled on those of Sir Walter Scott, built the modern romantic Arab image of the Arab past.

Complementing the endeavors of these pioneers was the Society of Arts and Sciences, established in 1847 to engender a spirit of inquiry into the sciences and a literary revival of the Arabic tongue. The Jesuits, not to be outdone, organized the Oriental Society in 1850. Because Christian missionaries participated in these two groups, Muslim Arabs refused to join. However, upon the exclusion of the foreign influence in 1857 the Syrian Scientific Society was born. Its members included Muslims and Christians of all sects. They all took pride in being Arabs. From this society came Nasif al-Yaziji's son Ibrahim's famous *Ode to Patriotism,* a secret revolutionary incitement to Arab insurgence.

In Egypt a similar educational and literary renaissance, explained in the previous chapter, was under way. The famous Bulaq Press, started in Cairo in 1822, printed over 300 books in Arabic, Turkish, and Persian before 1850. It gave to Cairo the distinction of being a literary center and drew there many intellectuals from every part of the Arab world. Without the printing press Arab nationalism and the regeneration of the Arab people would have progressed very slowly. Books were published in ever-growing volume and newspapers sprang up in the leading cities. An incomplete tally in 1913 showed 118 Arabic language newspapers in the Ottoman Empire, excluding Egypt.

In the last half of the nineteenth century Arabic presses in several cities were publishing original works and many translations of European books, and these were circulating readily in all parts of the Arab world. From French North Africa to British India, ideas of patriotism, nationalism, Islamic reform, and modernization were being developed in a unifying pattern to free Arab minds from concepts stemming from and contingent upon Western Christian imperialism. Intellectuals and publicists were traveling back and forth to Istanbul, Beirut, Damascus, Baghdad, Cairo, Tunis, and Algiers, gathering converts to new viewpoints. Every event had an impact everywhere, two of the greatest being the Dinshwai Affair and the Young Turk Revolution.

With the accession of Abdul Hamid as Ottoman sultan, clandestine societies multiplied in the Arab provinces. A Beirut secret society posted placards preaching patriotism and declaring the aims of the society to be: the independence of Syria, including Lebanon; Arabic as the national language; an end to censorship; freedom of expression; and the exclusive use of locally recruited units in local military service. In Egypt, however, local autonomy freed Arab nationalism from the sultan's surveillance. Cairo and Alexandria became centers for national exhortation; Egypt, along with France and Switzerland, became a haven for exiled Arab nationalists.

One of these exiles was Abd al-Rahman Kawakibi of Aleppo, who wrote *Umm al-Qura*, a humorous yet penetrating anthology on the future of Islamic society, and *The Attributes of Tyranny*, published anonymously in Cairo. Together they analyzed the decrepit world of Islam, especially Arab society. Kawakibi attacked the ignorance of the masses and the obscurantism of the theologians who dominated the educational field. He was also one of the first to separate Arab national revival from pan-Islamism.

The Birth of Arab Nationalism

For centuries leaders and intellectuals in the Middle East had felt the East to be superior to the West. After the Napoleonic Wars economic, cultural, and social contacts between the Middle East and Western Europe expanded greatly and the wealth and power of Europe gave it a dominance. Middle Easterners were shaken by the new perception they had of the West. Nineteenth-century nationalists such as Nasif al-Yaziji and Butrus al-Bustani put their faith in an educational revival as a means of catching up. Differences between Arabs and Turks were barely considered. The Middle Eastern culture and Islam, its central theme, were regarded as the valid bases of the society that had produced the wondrous ages of the past. Accepting the fact that Arabic was the language of religion and Turkish the language of government and politics, the early nationalist thinkers supported both Islam and the Ottoman way of life as being fundamentally sound and superior to that of the West. Conservative Ottomanists, such as Tanzimat reformers Rifaa Rafi al-Tahtawi, the Egyptian patriot, and Ahmad Faris al-Shidyaq, who published an Arabic newspaper in Istanbul, wrote that it would be necessary only to borrow certain things from the West, such as the natural and physical sciences, and the gap would close.

As the years passed and the obvious gap between the strength and development of the East and the West widened, questions began to be raised about various aspects of Middle Eastern life and culture. New polemicists such as al-Afghani and his pupil Muhammad Abdu asserted that Islam was in a deplorable condition because over the centuries society had corrupted true primitive Islam, and as a consequence Muslims had been unable to continue their remarkable progress. They believed that primitive Islam had demanded that Muslims exercise reason and examine the bases of faith. Aware of Guizot's dictum that Europe began to progress with the advent of Protestantism, they drew an analogy and insisted that the Middle East must return to primitive Islam in order to become truly modern. Among these modernist Ottomans were Muhammad Rashid Rida, whose periodical, *al-Manar,* advanced these theories to the full; and Adib Ishaq, a Lebanese Christian and associate of al-Afghani and Abdu in Cairo, who avowed that Islam was the essential element in the fabric of Middle Eastern society and culture, and that in the end patriots such as he would "expunge the shameful innovations," to lead the East to its past greatness as the cradle of religion and civilization. None of these reformers was prepared to overturn the Ottoman caliph-sultan.

Political changes led the way for conservative Ottomanism to become modernist Ottomanism, which in turn was transformed into Arabism. Ibrahim al-Yaziji, Rida, Kawakibi, and Nadrah Matran were Arab nationalists who met the Islamists by proclaiming that Islam was only one of the infinite glories of the Arab nation. They cried out against bigotry and fanaticism and called for ejecting foreigners and alien influences from the Arab scene. After the Turkish and Iranian revolutions of 1908 it became more apparent that Ottomanism and Pan-Islamism were no substitutes for Arab nationalism, though many Arab leaders clung to these ideologies until the end of World War I.

The Young Turks and Arab Nationalism

The program of the Young Turks before the counterrevolution in 1909 appealed to many Arab leaders, who saw in it the destruction of Abdul Hamid's tyranny. They fully subscribed to the Ottoman program of the Society of Union and Progress because they translated it to mean decentralization of the empire and equality of Arab with Turk. Abdul Hamid had exiled many Young Turks to Damascus, Jerusalem, and Baghdad. Along with many unhappy Turkish army officers languishing in these remote parts, the rising Arab nationalists looked upon the Turkish liberal struggle as their fight, too.

In the early days of the Revolution there was much cooperation between the Young Turks and the Arabs. The Young Turks insisted that Abdul Hamid designate Sharif Husayn of the Hashimite family Governor of the Hijaz, Keeper of the Holy Places, and Prince of Mecca. Although Husayn had resided quietly for fifteen years in Istanbul as a kind of hostage, Abdul Hamid astutely judged the man to have ambitions to rule an independent Arab state and warned the Young Turks of the folly of their recommendation. In September 1908, however, Abdul Hamid acquiesced and appointed Husayn to the post. In the same month Istanbul witnessed the inauguration, with much ceremony, of The Ottoman Arab Fraternity, an Arab society to defend the Ottoman constitution, promote the welfare of Arabs, and "foster the observance of Arab customs."

Hardly had the society been started when the Union and Progress party suppressed it. After the counterrevolution of 1909, centralization of government, Turkification, and disallowance of all local customs and tradition contrary to Turkish practice became veiled objectives of the Young Turks. As non-Turkish political societies were suppressed, the Arabs, among others, went underground. Here, then, was the birth of passionate and uncompromising Arab nationalism.

Arab Societies

As usual, a welter of societies and parties sprang into being not only among the Arabs in Istanbul, but also among those in Damascus, Beirut, Baghdad, Aleppo, and other Arab cities. An important one in Istanbul was the Literary Club, which almost immediately took the place of The Ottoman Arab Fraternity. The successor disavowed political activities; it posed as a meeting place, library, and clubhouse for Arabs living at the capital, and as a center for Arab travelers. But it was impossible, of course, to prevent Arabs, sitting relaxed in the clubhouse, from discussing political philosophy as it pertained to the Arab situation. Within a short time the club's membership reached the thousands, and branches were located throughout Syria and Iraq, a testimony to growing Arab consciousness.

The second important open group was The Ottoman Decentralization party, established in Cairo in 1912 by experienced Arab public figures. Its objectives were to mobilize Arab public opinion and impress upon the Young Turks the need to organize the new Ottoman Empire on a more federal basis. The group's headquarters remained safely in Cairo, although branches calling themselves reform societies were located in Iraq and Syria and maintained close contact with the Literary Club in Istanbul. The Decentralization party stressed party machinery and enjoyed partial success during the last half of 1912 when the Union and Progress party was out of power.

One interesting secret society was called *al-Kahtaniya*. (Kahtan was a legendary ancestor of the Arabs.) It advocated the creation of a dual Turko-Arab empire, much like the Austro-Hungarian Empire, in which "unity" of the two peoples could be attained by "separation." As the Turkish leaders of Union and Progress showed their hands and guided affairs definitely along paths of Turkification, aspirations for a Turko-Arab accommodation died. With these hopes went *al-Kahtaniya*.

Suppression by the Turks drove many Arabs abroad. As did the Turks a decade earlier, they flocked to Paris. Already Arabs were active there. In 1904 Najib Azuri had founded the League of the Arab Fatherland, and in 1907 he had set up his paper, *Arab Independence*. In 1911 the Arab refugees formed The Young Arab Society, better known as *al-Fatat* (Youth). A secret society, *al-Fatat* rejected the idea of any integration within the empire and worked for full Arab freedom and independence. It became the most widespread and effective force among Arabs, moving its headquarters to Damascus in 1914.

In view of these activities and the general Arab enthusiasm they evinced, the Young Turks adopted more stringent measures to combat them. A committee of reform, which gathered in Beirut in 1913, publicly announced a program for Arab home rule and won such wide acclaim that the

Young Turks suppressed it. After shops and offices in Beirut closed, and newspapers went into mourning, the committee's leaders were arrested. Under the leadership of *al-Fatat* a congress of Arabs was held in Paris. Attended by twenty-four delegates representing many Arab parties, the congress adopted the platforms of the Decentralization party and the committee of reform. The results of the congress were ostensibly accepted by the Young Turks; an imperial decree in 1913 incorporated the declarations as stated policy in the Arab provinces. However, the reforms remained unenforced, and the Arabs believed they had been duped.

Partially in reply, an Arab, Major Aziz Ali al-Misri of the Ottoman general staff, initiated a new society called The Covenant *(al-Ahd)*. Aziz Ali had been a member of Union and Progress in Salonika before 1908 and had won honors during the march on Istanbul in 1909, during a military mission to Yemen in 1910, and during the war against Italy in Libya. The Covenant was comprised exclusively of army officers and became for the military what The Young Arab Society was for civilians. It had many members in Beirut, Damascus, and Baghdad. In 1914 the Young Turks arrested Aziz Ali without warning. Charged with treason in Libya, he was tried, found guilty, and condemned to death. Public opinion became so indignant, especially in Egypt, that the British protested to the Porte. Aziz Ali was pardoned and sailed for Egypt as a public hero, to lead The Covenant from Cairo. Any hope that the Young Turk leaders had for Arab cooperation and participation was now completely dispelled. Ottomanism and pan-Islamism for Arab leaders disintegrated in the face of an obvious and understandable drift to Turkish nationalism shown in the actions of the radical Young Turks.

The Arab Princes

The Turks not only had difficulty with Arab nationalists and their many patriotic societies, they discovered that Arab governors and semiautonomous rulers employed every means to gain independent positions. Unsuccessful expeditions were sent to bring Imam Yahya of Yemen and Muhammad ibn al-Idrisi of Asir to heel. Tiring of the continual drain on resources, the Young Turks reached an accord with the two, granting them many powers and a liberal subsidy. In eastern Arabia the Young Turks found their support of the Rashid family unavailing against Abd al-Aziz ibn Saud, who drove the Turks and their allies from the rich province of al-Hasa in 1913.

Had it not been for the Hijaz Railway, which connected Syria with Medina, the Young Turks' authority over Sharif Husayn would also have vanished. A Turkish garrison stationed at Mecca rendered overt revolution foolhardy without considerable strength and careful planning. Early in 1914 Prince Abdallah, Husayn's second son, an Arab member of the Ottoman parliament, hinted vaguely to the British as he passed through Cairo that his father would be open to suggestions and assistance from them for rebellion against the Turks. These overtures, very discreet in nature, indicated that Husayn was considering a treaty similar to that which the British had with Arab princes and shaykhs in the Persian Gulf area. Such treaties provided for British recognition of the Arab ruler's independence from the sultan, protection, and a pension in exchange for British conduct of all foreign relations, friendship with Britain, and permission for a British resident minister to live at the court.

Suspicion that Husayn was harboring these intentions drifted back to Istanbul, where the Young Turks acted to limit his authority. Governorship of the Hijaz was assigned to another, who arrived in Mecca to destroy Husayn. In the spring of 1914 the Turks understood that Husayn had consolidated his position with the tribes of the Hijaz, and to forestall a violent insurrection the new governor was ordered to make peace. At a public ceremony in Mecca the unfortunate governor humbled himself and kissed the hem of Sharif Husayn's robe.

It was not clear that any connection existed between the actions of Husayn, al-Idrisi, Imam Yahya, and Ibn Saud on the one hand and the revolutionary societies of the Ottoman Arab world on the other. Foreign governments were friendly to the Arabs, and partly to counter the growing influence of the Germans with the Young Turks, British and French officials in Beirut and Egypt gave encouragement to Arab societies. British and French consuls general received delegations of Arab nationalists. A delegation from Damascus, visiting Lord Kitchener in Egypt, suggested that Britain annex Syria to Egypt, giving it a separate administration.

In 1913 an Arab conference was held at Mohammerah in Iran to advance the independence of Iraq. Attended, among others, by the Shaykhs of Kuwayt and Mohammerah and Sayid Talib Pasha of Basrah, it exhorted the Arabs to work together to drive out the Turks. Another conference was called for 1914 at Kuwayt, with additional invitations going to Sharif Husayn, Abd al-Aziz ibn Saud, Ibn Rashid of the Shammar tribes, and Shaykh Ajaymi of the Muntafik tribes. It never met, however, because of rivalries and jealousies among these Arab leaders. Therein lay the weakness of the Arab movement.

When the war began in 1914 the Young Turk triumvirate realized that defection in Arab provinces was likely and that the loyalty of Arab officers was highly questionable. Yet Enver, Talat, and Jemal hoped that the natural Arab proclivity for dissension would save the day. Their hope was justified. The secret societies of officers and nationalists in the urban centers were opposed to the autocratic rule of kings and suspected them of princely ambitions. Equally apprehensive were the various princes, each of the other. With such fears prevalent, united action from all groups and factions was unlikely. The Ottoman Empire was saved for the moment. But it was only a question of time before Arab nationalism would flare into the open. World War I and the disturbances, confusion, and promises it brought hastened the day of Arab revolt.

REFERENCES: Chapter 28

Works cited at the end of Chapters 20 and 22 are valuable for this chapter. In addition there are those in Chapters 4, 7, 19, 23, 24, 25, and 26.

Antonius, George. *The Arab Awakening: The Story of the Arab National Movement.* New York: Hamilton, 1938. This is the fundamental work on this topic.

Binder, Leonard. *The Ideological Revolution in the Middle East.* New York: Wiley, 1964. An attempt to explain and analyze the various nationalist and protest movements in the Arab Middle East since the middle of the nineteenth century. In nine different essays the author comments on Egyptian nationalism, the Ba'ath ideology, Nasserism, and the relationships between nationalism and Islam.

Cleveland, William L. *The Making of an Arab Nationalist: Ottomanism and Arabism in the Life and Thought of Sati' al-Husri.* Princeton, N.J.: Princeton University Press, 1971. The life of an Ottoman Arab who chose to be an Arab nationalist after World War I.

Dawn, C. Ernest. *From Ottomanism to Arabism: Essays on the Origins of Arab Nationalism.* Urbana: University of Illinois Press, 1973. Shows the most subtle aspects of the Arab revolt and its relationship to Arab nationalism and brings out many of the misconceptions about it. Also discusses the Hashimite family in the Hijaz and its leadership in the Arab revolt.

von Grunebaum, Gustave E. *Modern Islam: The Search for Cultural Identity.* Los Angeles: University of California Press, 1962. A concise and complete survey of recent movements and ideas within Islam.

Halpern, Manfred. *The Politics of Social Change in the Middle East and North Africa.* Princeton, N.J.: Princeton University Press, 1963. A thought-provoking book covering the revolution that has been under way in this area for several decades.

Hourani, Albert H. *Arabic Thought in the Liberal Age, 1798–1939.* New York: Oxford University Press, 1962. Brilliant, authoritative treatment of Arabic thought and Arab nationalism.

————. *Syria and Lebanon, A Political Essay.* London: Oxford University Press, 1946. The earlier chapters give a clear picture of the rise of Arab nationalism.

al-Husry, Khaldun S. *Three Reformers: A Study in Modern Arab Political Thought.* Beirut: Khayats, 1966. An account of the ideas of al-Tahtawi, Khair al-Din al-Tunisi, and al-Kawakibi.

Izzeddin, Nejla. *The Arab World, Past, Present, and Future.* Chicago: Regnery, 1953. The sections on the awakening of the Arabs in modern times are exceedingly well done.

Kritzeck, James. *Modern Islamic Literature.* New York: Holt, Rinehart & Winston, 1970. Covers the period since 1800.

Saleh, Zaki. *Mesopotamia (Iraq), 1600–1914.* New York: Albert Daub, 1958. Mostly British foreign affairs.

Sharabi, Hisham. *Arab Intellectuals and the West: The Formative Years, 1875–1914.* Baltimore: Johns Hopkins Press, 1970. Explains the intellectual and ideological background of modernization and transformation in the Arab world.

Tibawi, A. L. *A Modern History of Syria including Lebanon and Palestine.* New York: St. Martin's, 1969. A history of geographical Syria from the closing decades of the eighteenth century to 1921; thereafter, the history of Lebanon and Palestine is not included.

Waines, David. *The Unholy War: Israel and Palestine, 1897–1971*. Wilmette, Ill.: Medina University Press International, 1971. An account of the struggle between Zionists and Palestinians.

Zeine, Zeine N. *Arab-Turkish Relations and the Emergence of Arab Nationalism*. Beirut: Khayats, 1958. A basic study by an eminent scholar and professor at the American University of Beirut.

————. *The Struggle for Arab Independence: Western Diplomacy and the Rise and Fall of Faisal's Kingdom in Syria*. Beirut: Khayats, 1960. This is a fine continuation of the above work.

Chapter 29

Vnrest in Iran and the Revolution of 1907 and 1908

Shah Muhammad

Upon the death of Shah Fath Ali of Qajar in 1834 the throne passed to his twenty-eight-year-old grandson, Muhammad. Two of Muhammad's uncles refused to recognize him and moved to contest the throne. However, the British and Russian ministers in Iran cooperated to fund Muhammad's armed supporters and General Sir Henry Lindsay Bethune led a force that assured him the throne.

The new shah appointed his tutor, Haji Mirza Aghasi, as chief minister, a post he held throughout Muhammad's rule. Aghasi had studied under the famous sufis of the time and, before coming to Tabriz to tutor Prince Abbas's sons, had been a wandering dervish. One English observer called him lewd, ignorant, fanatic, and avaricious, noting that "his words and actions are strongly tinctured with real or affected insanity." The shah believed that Aghasi could perform miracles and had "direct and frequent communications with the divinity."

Throughout his reign the shah and his minister favored sufis and sufism against the established, conservative ulema, a natural preference, considering the fact that the ulema always treated the Qajars as usurpers. The shah's subjects found themselves caught between the realities of monarchical power and the doctrinal conceptions of the religious authority of the ulema, a conflict that was never resolved.

By enhancing sufism Shah Muhammad strengthened the state and the central government. He proceeded to remove many types of cases from religious courts, subjected provincial governors to closer scrutiny from Tehran, continued military reforms, banned torture as a means of punishment and a device for obtaining information, and abolished the slave trade. An abstainer, he prohibited the sale of alcohol as well.

The Qajars considered Herat to be the capital of Khurasan and thus a rightful part of their realm, and in 1836 Shah Muhammad set out with an army to regain it from Afghanistan. The British tried to dissuade him from the campaign as they felt it would open Afghanistan and the approaches to India to Russian interference. The British minister accompanied the shah on the expedition and attempted to mediate the differences; the Russians egged Muhammad on to battle. An English artillery officer successfully contrived Herat's defense even though such intervention was contrary to the Definitive Treaty of 1814. The shah was so enraged that after peace was arranged in 1838 he dismissed all British officers in Iran.

Trade was improving and conditions in general were bettered when Shah Muhammad died in 1848. Had it not been for the rise of a new, somewhat revolutionary religious movement that was attracting numerous adherents, the shah would have ended his days in peace.

Babism
Babism began in Shiraz with the preaching and teaching of Sayyid Ali Muhammad, a twenty-five-year-old native of that city who had spent his youth in religious study, first as a conservative Shiite and then as a sufi. In 1844, the millennium of the disappearance of the Twelfth Imam, his followers hailed him as the *Bab,* or Gate, between the world of the flesh and that of the spirit. Only through him, the Bab, was the Twelfth Imam in touch with the world. He assumed the role of "point of manifestation of the divine essence of the world" and called for universal peace, improvement of the life of women, destruction of all class distinctions, and a society that followed the spirit rather than the letter of religion.

Iran was witnessing considerable spiritual and intellectual unrest at the time. For more than a generation numerous religious leaders had been preaching about the return of the Twelfth Imam and the coming regeneration of the world. These *imamis* looked upon the Bab as one who would lead Iran on a spiritual plane to combat the menacing and powerful guns, ships, and materialism of the world outside.

At the time of Shah Muhammad's death the Bab was imprisoned in Tabriz and had been interrogated by the crown prince. To all questions he replied, "I do not know; I cannot say," and then repeated hackneyed religious phrases and spiritual exclamations. He was accused of claiming prophethood and of being addicted to bang and hashish. That year, the Bab and his followers seceded from Islam.

In 1850 Shah Nasir al-Din, experiencing a serious insurrection by a religious group thought to be devotees of the Bab, on the road between Tehran and Tabriz, ordered the Bab put to death. Sanctions for the execution were first obtained from three Muslim religious leaders, to counter any popular demonstrations.

Two years after the Bab had been executed, a member of the sect attempted to assassinate the shah. As a consequence about forty thousand Babists were massacred throughout Iran. Some leaders of the new religion escaped from Iran to establish two branches of the faith: one became headquartered in Turkey but died out by the end of the century; the other developed in Europe and the United States under the name of Bahaism and thrives today.

First Years of Shah Nasir al-Din
When Shah Muhammad died in 1848 the customary disturbances and family rivalries were held in check by British and Russian officers. The British

legation in Tehran induced a local council of notables to form a regency council for the sixteen-year-old Prince Nasir al-Din while he made his way from Tabriz. Shah Nasir al-Din appointed his tutor Mirza Taqi Khan as first minister. Taqi was the son of the cook of a high government official who had given him a fine education. Prior to his elevation to his high post, Taqi had been in Erzerum, where he had learned about the Tanzimat. He had also participated in a mission to St. Petersburg, where he saw quite a different world. Taqi became known as a man of stern integrity who possessed great zeal for reform. Naturally, the palace courtiers and the queen mother, who dominated the harem, disliked him more than they had Aghasi. With an empty treasury and a serious revolt in Khurasan Taqi faced a difficult situation.

Though Taqi's predecessor was superstitious and even irrational at times, he was aware of the economic and agricultural changes creeping across the land. Aghasi recognized that cotton, opium, silk, dried fruits, and nuts had become cash crops in foreign markets, tempting the landlords to press their peasants severely in order to garner huge profits from Russian and British merchants. Land now produced wealth in addition to the high social status it had previously conferred. Taqi extended this policy and became the merchants' friend. He built the great bazaar in Tehran and encouraged the growth of a mercantile class.

In these years three politically active classes arose beneath the royal court. There was the old elite, landed aristocratic nobles who, though generally ignorant, relied for their power on inherited privileges, extortion, intrigue, treachery, and dissimulation. The second class was the clergy, who controlled the courts, justice, morals, education, religion, and even the very level and nature of thought in Iran. They had accumulated wealth and vast landholdings. The third class was the new merchants, many of whom had traveled to Istanbul, Odessa, Cairo, Bombay, Calcutta, and Canton, and brought home not only wealth but ideas of a wider world. They relied on money to attain influence.

In suppressing the rebellion in Khurasan, Taqi formed an army of soldiers whose pay was not in arrears. Believing that the clergy should not participate in politics, he sent the army to Tabriz in 1850 and carried off the chief religious figure. But Taqi had gone too far, and in 1851 Nasir al-Din was induced by the clergy, the court, and his mother to dismiss the chief minister and to acquiesce in his murder shortly thereafter.

Taqi was replaced by Mirza Agha Khan Nuri, a vindictive mediocrity who was wily in managing diplomacy and public affairs for his own advantage. Nasir al-Din was never happy with him. Filled with remorse for having executed "the wisest man" in the state, the Shah retired to his harem. His rule became based on fear rather than consent, and the shrewd divines and crafty self-seeking elite allied against him.

With the Crimean War weakening the Russian position, Agha Khan forced the recall of the Russian minister and manipulated affairs so that the

British minister offended him and had to leave. Agha Khan could now follow independent policies, attacking and occupying Herat. The British retaliated by sending a naval force, cavalry, and artillery from India into the Persian Gulf, taking Bushire, Khurramshahr, and the island of Kharg. In 1857, at the conclusion of the Crimean War, Nasir al-Din's envoy in Paris negotiated a settlement with the British. By the terms of the treaty Iran withdrew from Herat and recognized it as a part of Afghanistan and the British evacuated the Iranian territories they had occupied in the Persian Gulf. The treaty also assigned special commercial privileges to the British and gave standard capitulatory rights to British nationals in Iran. The following year Nasir al-Din dismissed Agha Khan and refused to appoint anyone to that post, declaring that he himself would govern.

The Age of Concessions

The government in Tehran might not have persisted through the century, were it not that the British and the Russians in Iran competed against each other for the favors of Nasir al-Din and his ministers. Incompetent administrators remained in high office for lengthy periods, transportation was primitive, distances were great between principal cities, and several parts of the country were nearly autonomous. The clergy opposed the shah's government in Tehran and in every province; the strife between the religious community and the state was constant. Every innovation was resisted, and preachers easily inflamed the populace against those who ruled.

With Iran at peace Nasir al-Din made a trip in 1870 to the Shiite holy places in Iraq. He was escorted about by Prince Husayn Khan, the Iranian ambassador in Istanbul, and met Midhat Pasha, then governor of Baghdad, with whom he discussed programs being introduced to modernize the Ottoman state. Husayn accompanied the shah back to Tehran, where he became first minister and dominated the government for the next two years. The journey to Iraq was so pleasant that Nasir al-Din subsequently made three visits to Europe, nearly bankrupting the Iranian treasury. The shah was impressed with the display of vast wealth in Europe, which he believed was a kind of money tree from which power and great comfort were derived. He returned home convinced that more money in Iran would turn the country into a prosperous modern state similar to those he saw in Europe.

The building of telegraph lines across Iran, in the main to connect London to India, played an important role in opening Iran to the modern world. The first line was merely a toy to impress the shah, but within a few years Tehran was connected with several parts of the state. The rights to the international lines were sold to English companies beginning in 1862, and a local line, alongside the international ones, carried Iranian messages. No longer was Iran isolated.

The shah and the ministers, always short of funds, soon learned that

Europeans would pay handsome sums in ready cash and give enormous bribes for one privilege, right, concession, or opportunity after another. In 1873, before leaving for Europe, the shah granted to Baron Julius de Reuter a seventy-year economic concession for the development of Iran's economy and industry. So much clamor against this monopolistic concession was raised in all sectors of society in Iran and in Russia as well, that obstacles were placed in de Reuter's way to prevent his compliance with the contracts. The money guarantees accrued to the shah, the bribes were kept, and Russia and the populace were satisfied by the concession's termination and appeased by the dismissal of Prince Husayn Khan as first minister. But concession hunting continued.

In 1888 Sir Henry Drummond-Wolff arrived in Tehran as the new British minister. He intended to open the Karun river to international steamer traffic to meet Russian railroad competition in the north. Sir Henry gave the shah a written guarantee that England would "prevent any infringement of the integrity" of Iran by any other power and would "make earnest representations" against any foreign attack upon the shah. With this guarantee against Russian actions, the shah issued a decree opening the Karun river to commercial steamers of all nations. Following this coup, Wolff helped his friend de Reuter salvage from his old concession the right to establish the Imperial Bank of Persia, which for sixty years would have the right to issue notes of legal tender in Iran and to engage in any operations on its own account or for others in the fields of finance, commerce, and industry.

Russian influence, however, was not completely negated. On the shah's second trip to Europe he saw the crowds of Russian soldiers not yet demobilized after the Congress of Berlin and was frequently escorted by smart looking Russian cossacks. He requested the tsar to send some Russian military instructors to Iran to reform and improve the army. Colonel Domantovich arrived in Tehran early in 1879 and before the summer was out he presented to the shah a brilliantly dressed and trained cossack brigade. For a number of years its leadership was rather desultory but under Colonel Kosogovskii in 1894 it became again a disciplined and effective instrument of Russian pressure in Iran, lasting until 1921. Furthermore Russia had a letter from Nasir al-Din in 1887 engaging Iran not to give any concession for building a railroad or a waterway without consulting Russia.

Pressure for railroad building in Iran became so intense that in 1890 Ali Asghar Khan agreed to the Russian minister's demand that no railroad would be built on Iranian territory for the next ten years. British complaints soon subsided; in 1900 the convention was renewed and no railways were built in Iran prior to World War I.

The Tobacco Concession and Its Aftermath

Prices for agricultural products and raw materials fell dramatically throughout the world after the mid-1870s, producing financial crises in many countries. Iran suffered too. The amount of wheat exported in 1894 was eight times what it had been a quarter of a century before, but the price had fallen so much that the total receipts for the wheat exports remained the same.

It was no different for other exported commodities. Everyone worked harder and more efficiently, but income did not improve. Simultaneously, with the opening up of the country, imports doubled and tripled and their prices increased markedly. Year by year the government, the shah, public officials, wealthy merchants, and the clergy found it more difficult to make ends meet. Aside from the element of greed, fundamentally the idea behind the granting of most of the concessions to Europeans was to try to consolidate and centralize the economy and to entice foreign capital and expertise to develop the resources of the state. The hope of attracting foreign capital was one motive for the shah's trips to Europe. Unfortunately, the entire process was riddled with corrupt practices and managed by unscrupulous adventurers. Iran was being sold bit by bit to foreigners.

In England in the summer of 1889, Wolff had introduced the shah to a Major Talbot, who asked for the monopoly to buy, sell, and manufacture tobacco in Iran for fifty years. Generous bribes were handed to the shah, Ali Asghar Khan, and others, and Talbot pursued the shah back to Tehran, where the concession was given in March 1890. The company to be formed would pay the Iranian treasury £15,000 and 25 percent of its net profits annually; in return the company would control the entire traffic in tobacco —even members of the tobacco sellers' guilds would have to obtain permits from the company to engage in local trade. For many this would mean selling their tobacco to the company and then buying it back.

The Imperial Tobacco Corporation of Persia bought the concession from Talbot and set out to implement the monopoly. By 1891 a campaign was organized against the government and concentrated on the tobacco issue, for of all the concessions granted to foreign capital this one touched the most people directly. Jamal al-Din al-Afghani, who had returned to Iran in 1889 upon the shah's invitation, was one of the leaders. Jamal al-Din so aroused the shah's ire by preaching openly against the government and the shah that he had to take sanctuary *(bast)* in the shrine of Shah Abd al-Aziz outside Tehran. From there he continued his attack, scattering leaflets throughout the capital, until Nasir al-Din ordered him removed from the shrine, thus violating sanctuary. He was deposited across the Ottoman frontier.

But the eviction did not end the crisis. Revolt was threatened in Shiraz, Tabriz, Isfahan, Meshed, and other cities, and some property was damaged. Merchants rebelled; warnings of violence against those who used tobacco spread across the land; Prince Masud in Isfahan indicated he could not stop the public outcry or force the sale of tobacco; and some merchants burned their entire stock rather than sell it to the company. Religious leaders petitioned the shah against the monopoly, stating that the Koran prohibited infidels to have control over Muslims, and accused the shah of selling Muslims like slaves to the Christians. When the British manager of the monopoly arrived in Shiraz word was spread that this newly arrived infidel was responsible for Jamal al-Din's expulsion. Soldiers had to dispel the crowds of protesters in several cities, and some people were killed. A religious decree, promulgated by Shirazi, the leading Shiite divine at the holy places in Iraq, calling upon all Muslims to abstain from smoking, was, to everyone's amazement, observed everywhere in Iran. Even the shah's wives refused to smoke! On December 25 there were rumors of a holy war to be declared if the concession were not withdrawn in two days. Three days later the shah canceled the concession. This popular victory over the government and the shah by the religious and city leaders made further movements of this nature possible. Moreover, a massive loan to the government to pay indemnities arising from the cancelation of the tobacco concession opened the door to many more such loans in the following decade, leading Iran closer to the brink of bankruptcy and dissolution.

In the midst of the tobacco crisis Russian nationals obtained concessions for insurance companies, lumbering, and other endeavors. One of the more important privileges granted Russia was permission to open the Discount and Loan Bank of Persia, which, in fact, was a branch of the Russian ministry of finance and part of the Central Bank of Russia. Without real stockholders or a need to show a profit, the bank made loans on easy terms to princes, officials, divines, and merchants; by 1900 it was said that Russia had nearly bought off the ruling elite.

For the next few years there was a standoff between England and Russia in their diplomatic and economic maneuvers in Iran. Each was afraid of the other. Russian activity centered in the north while the British dominated the south. Pessimism was the paramount mood even in high circles in Iran, and as the shah's energy and interest waned, "graft, bribery, theft reached incredible proportions." Prince Masud repeatedly stated that after the shah died he would take the southern half of the state and Crown Prince Muzaffar al-Din would take the northern half. The shah's brother suggested that Iran was like "a lump of sugar in a glass of water" gradually melting away. Apparently there were no trustworthy courts of justice, no roads, no stable currency, and since the shah's third son as commander in chief neglected and robbed the troops the army was a mere rabble. It seemed hopeless as the shah continued "selling appointments and marrying new wives after his wont." In desperation the first minister, Ali Asghar Khan, even suggested to the British minister that England bribe the shah to reform! What the outcome might have been remains uncertain, for on May 1, 1896, Nasir al-Din was assassinated by Jamal al-Din al-Afghani's servant and follower at the Shah Abd al-Aziz shrine, where his master's sanctuary had been violated.

Muzaffar al-Din Shah and the Constitution
That same day the Russians and the British recognized Muzaffar al-Din as the new shah and made arrangements to escort him to Tehran. He ordered Ali Asghar Khan to remain as prime minister, and the new shah's brothers

pledged their loyalty and obedience to Muzaffar. The transfer of power was the most peaceful in Iran in more than a century.

Muzaffar al-Din was a sickly, uneducated, good-natured forty-three-year-old prince who was bored and baffled by governmental affairs and preferred the company of his wives, astrologers, and chance favorites. His first thought after his enthronement was a trip to Europe, supposedly for his health.

Ali Asghar Khan, prime minister for more than a decade of hard times, had collected so many enemies that they were able to prevail upon the weak shah to dismiss him. His replacement lasted nine months, and after a year under yet another, the shah begged Ali Asghar Khan to return to his post. The difficulty was money—without it the shah could not travel in Europe. Payments to the troops and the salaries of most officials were at least six months in arrears, and the new ministers were unskilled in the ways of Iranian administration. It was said the minister of taxation "took no bribes, which was thought foolish, and he gave none, which was thought wicked." Only Ali Asghar Khan was considered able to end the chaos. Back in office his first act was to reorganize the customs posts and offices in Tabriz and Kermanshah with Belgian officials in charge, and to take a loan from Russia. After paying Iran's debts Muzaffar al-Din and his retinue set out for Europe, visiting several health spas for his kidney ailment. By the time he arrived back in Tehran the treasury was again empty. The natural recourse was another loan.

To many, the financial and economic conditions in Iran in the autumn of 1902 seemed intolerable, worse than ever before. With troubles brewing at home and in the Far East with Japan, Russia was unwilling to make further loans and the Discount and Loan Bank was tightening the screws on merchants and others. Joseph Naus, a Belgian, Iran's director of customs, worked out a new commercial agreement with Russia, lowering the tariff on many imports from Russia and giving Russia a powerful grip on Iran's finances. All tariffs on cotton cloth were removed, thereby ruining most Iranian cloth manufacturers. The court was in a turmoil with rumors that the shah would be overthrown and that Ali Asghar Khan's influence had vanished. After the shah ordered a pension of £ 3,000 a year plus a big lump sum payment for the court astrologer because he had saved the shah's life when the shah dreamed he was drowning, Ali Asghar Khan lost his temper and said he had "raised large sums to pay for the Shah's tours and toys, but must protest paying for his dreams." In September a new prime minister was named: the cruel Prince Abd al-Majid, Muzaffar al-Din's son-in-law and grandson of Fath Ali Shah. Ali Asghar Khan went on a world tour.

A change in prime ministers was not a cure for the ills of Iran. Agitation by the clergy and popular preachers against the ministers and the arrogant efficiency of the Belgian customs officials was easily blunted by Abd al-Majid, for the central government was much stronger in 1903 than it had been in 1890 at the time of the tobacco affair.

In 1905 several bazaar merchants in Tehran were publicly flogged by the authorities for raising the price of sugar. Immediately, the merchants closed the bazaar and went on strike. The government ordered them to open the shops or have all their goods confiscated. Thereupon, about 2,000 merchants, joined by preachers and religious leaders, took sanctuary at the Imperial Mosque, the traditional form of protest in Iran, then fled to the shrine of Shah Abd al-Aziz, six miles outside of Tehran. Supported by Ali Asghar Khan and the crown prince, they insisted upon the removal of Abd al-Majid and other ministers, the ousting of the governor of Tehran, the dismissal of Joseph Naus and the Belgians from the customs offices, and the convening of a "House of Justice," to be composed of merchants, landowners, and the clergy. In January 1906 the shah acceded to their demands and they returned to Tehran.

In the spring, amid further turmoil, the shah had a stroke. Authority was weakened and responsibility diffused. Recognizing that sanctuary in mosques and shrines was no longer being respected, fifty merchants and divines took sanctuary at the British legation on July 19, 1906. Within a fortnight some 14,000 protesters were camping in the legation garden. Giant cauldrons were brought in to prepare food. Russia did not protest, and the British tolerated the invasion. Abd al-Majid was dismissed, and the shah, after being nudged by the British, on August 5 called for a representative assembly. On Septemper 17, 1906, the shah signed the imperial decree calling for parliamentary elections. It appeared that Iran had taken a step toward democracy, pushed not by an armed intervention or a revolution but by passive resistance.

Elections were held early in October. Not waiting for the representatives from the provinces, the successful candidates from Tehran met on October 7, 1906, to write a constitution and enact basic laws for a legislative body. The shah had, by this time, recovered sufficiently to return to the capital to open the assembly *(Majlis)*, although a minister had to read his speech from the throne. A new prime minister, Prince Nasrullah Khan, found the treasury empty, tax returns at a low ebb, salaries unpaid for six months, and sentiment in the majlis utterly opposed to any loan. Inexperienced and at his wit's end, he even wrote a letter to the disgraced former prime minister Ali Asghar Khan asking for suggestions on solving the dilemma. In the end the majlis voted unanimously to float a loan internally.

On December 30, 1906, the constitution was signed by Shah Muzaffar al-Din, Prime Minister Nasrullah, and Crown Prince Muhammad Ali, who had come to the capital two weeks before, since all knew that the shah was dying. The constitution, in fifty-one articles, provided for an elected majlis of sixty representatives from Tehran, including four from the court and four divines, and one hundred to one hundred forty representatives from the provinces, all to serve two-year terms, and a senate of sixty members, half to be elected and half appointed by the shah. The majlis was the dominant body and would control finances and foreign affairs. The British applauded the formation of the constitution; the Russians found it distasteful. The crown prince, an open Russophile who even spoke Russian, frankly loathed it. Shah Muzaffar al-Din died January 8, 1907, and Muhammad was crowned as shah on January 19. With an enemy on the throne the constitution's future was in jeopardy.

Shah Muhammad Ali and the Counterrevolution

Had the majlis been well organized by skillful leaders with a modicum of political experience, a representative government under a constitution might have succeeded in managing Iranian affairs and found a way to avoid bankruptcy and constant turbulence. As the members elected in the provinces joined the majlis, however, it became less and less coherent. Few thought of defending any aspect of the old government, and rival leaders quarreled over old antagonisms. A member of a prominent Tehran family was elected president of the majlis and gathered friends and hangers-on around him. His personal enemy led the opposition. Most of the members from Tabriz were radical in their views as they had been affected by revolutionaries fleeing from Russia. Political cliques or societies *(anjuman)* formed in every locality to influence events; some felt that the majlis was the largest anjuman of all. Within a few months even local anjumans split —in Tabriz between senior and junior clergy and in Meshed between merchants and shrine officials. The majlis sitting in Tehran could not enforce authority in the provinces, but it prevented local governors from doing so. Local anjumans defied the majlis, the central government, and the local administration. Land taxes went unpaid and no one collected road tolls. Smuggling prevailed. One force in the provincial cities that remained was that of the divines, who had been opposed to all governments for centuries. They had always claimed they represented justice since they dispensed holy law while the government with its laws symbolized injustice, an idea that played a decisive role in the thinking of the anjumans. Bankruptcy was never admitted, and the Belgian customs regime continued to operate under a new head, frequently turning over revenues to ministers rather than to the banks that had made loans. When the finance minister made his report to the majlis, itemizing necessary expenditures, the majlis authorized him to borrow the required funds from the National Bank, which, however, did not exist. It was generally recognized that no government could function without cooperating with the majlis, but it became apparent that the majlis had difficulty functioning at all.

In March 1907, when bankruptcy was near, all agreed that Ali Asghar Khan, the ingenious, detested negotiator of the two Russian loans, should be invited back from his repose in Switzerland. He nearly had arranged a loan with Russian, French, German, and British backing when on August 31, 1907, he was assassinated by a radical anjuman member from Tabriz. This blow eventually led to the demise of the majlis.

The constitutionalists suffered a second fatal injury the very same day with the signing of the Anglo-Russian Convention in St. Petersburg. In part, the document set aside the northern portion of Iran, including Tabriz, Tehran, Kermanshah, Isfahan, Yazd, and Meshed, as a sphere of influence

for Russia, and a small, southeastern portion from the Afghanistan border
to the Persian Gulf near Bandar Abbas as a British zone; neither power
would be paramount in the land in between the two zones. London was
more concerned with the security of India than with any interests in Iran.
Russia obtained a free hand, which the constitutionalists in Tehran considered deplorable and dishonorable. Prince Abd al-Qasim Khan, who soon
succeeded Ali Asghar Khan, could not comprehend how his British friends
could abandon efforts for political regeneration in Iran after all their encouraging words. From that day British ministers and officials in Tehran
were treated rudely by the Russians and their messages and suggestions
ignored.

With a "palsied tranquility" circulating in Tehran, Hartwig, the Russian
minister, set about to strengthen the power of the shah. Muhammad Ali,
though he swore three times to uphold the constitution, never intended to
tolerate it for long. Late in the spring, Bizot, a new financial adviser from
France, advocated a tax on tea and sugar to meet the budget deficit. The
British and Russians vetoed it, but it stirred such a commotion the shah
suggested that Russian forces be called in to prevent riots. Prince Masud,
long a friend of the British, led a split of the Qajars against this move and
allied himself with many members of the majlis. At this juncture a delegation from Tehran asked the shah to remove from his court all those opposed
to the constitution. The shah left the capital, gathered his forces, and with
Russian approval moved on Tehran on June 23, 1908, where a cossack
brigade bombarded the Majlis building, arrested many leaders, and executed three of them. As a score or more fled to the British legation for
sanctuary, Hartwig ordered the cossacks to surround the legation; to the
humiliation of the British many majlis members seeking sanctuary were
kept back. Shah Muhammad Ali, hand in hand with the Russians, was now
the absolute ruler of Iran.

Shah Muhammad Ali Abdicates

The shah's victory gave him control of the government in Tehran but it also
handed him full responsibility for the country's dire problems. His close
friends took over the various ministries and filled their pockets as rapidly
as possible to pay personal debts incurred over the years they had not been
in control. Pressed to find a loan, Bizot received the same message from the
Russians and British as before—reform the finances first.

Throughout Iran it was anarchy that reigned, rather than Muhammad
Ali. The shah did not have much control or influence outside of Tehran.
Religious leaders dominated the local anjumans and city councils. In Tabriz
the anjumans and constitutionalists revolted and gradually ruled the entire
city. The shah, with the support of the Russians, besieged Tabriz for nine
months without much success until Russian troops surrounded and invaded
the city in April 1909. Rebellious forces by this time held Meshed, Isfahan,
and Rasht, and the entire south had slipped away. In Isfahan, power had

been seized by Najaf Quli Khan, chief of the Bakhtiyari tribes, whom the shah had tried to remove. In league with the anjumans, Najaf Quli Khan revived the constitutional drive and set out with his forces for Tehran. Russian revolutionary refugees, Armenian nationalists, and many local anjumans and notables under the nominal leadership of the shah's former army commander at Tabriz, Muhammad Vali Khan, killed the governor of Rasht and took over.

The shah's party in Tehran, along with British and Russian diplomats, failed to grasp the magnitude or the temper of the opposition. The Bakhtiyari from the south joined the forces from the north to encircle Tehran, which fell on July 15, 1909. The constitution was restored; Muhammad Ali abdicated and took sanctuary in the Russian legation. Granted a pension of £16,666, he left Tehran in September with four children, a harem of ten, and a party of forty and settled in Odessa, where the Russian government found him an ample villa. Eventually, six of his staunchest henchmen were tried and executed.

Constitutional Government, 1909–1911

A few days after Muhammad Ali abdicated, his twelve-year-old son took the throne as Ahmad Shah. Prince Ali Reza Khan, the aged and trusted head of the Qajar family, was named regent. Weeping when taken from his parents, Ahmad promised that he would be a good shah. In Tehran the leaders designated a directory to serve until constitutional government could be reestablished.

Elections for the second majlis were held August 17, 1909, but it did not convene until mid-November. Officially opened by the young shah in the presence of the regent, cabinet, diplomatic corps, clergy, princes, notables and merchants, it contained sixty-five delegates; others joined as they arrived in Tehran. In September a general amnesty was declared and new British and Russian ministers presented their credentials. Constitutionalism (*mashrutiyat*) was supported by nationalists of all hues and at first even by most of the clergy who had been opposed to rule by any shah and who wanted government to follow Muslim law (*mashruiyat*), which they equated with *mashrutiyat*. As weeks passed the two groups separated and the majlis divided into Social Moderates and Social Democrats. The latter believed in the separation of temporal and religious power, compulsory conscription, universal education, and land reform; the former, the majority, were more evolutionary in their ideas and supported the clergy, the nobility, and the landowners who had opposed Shah Muhammad Ali.

Russian troops never withdrew from the northern provinces; in 1910 there were still several thousand stationed from Tabriz to Khurasan. The leaders of the cabinet repeatedly complained to the British minister, who explained that his hands were tied and that they should make their peace with the Russians. Russian demands were greater than any Iranian minister could meet. When word went out that Iran needed a sizable loan, representatives of various European bankers appeared in Tehran to negotiate, suggesting 5 or 6 percent interest rates and reasonable terms. Whenever a loan neared consummation, however, Russia appealed to the British, who easily negated it. Russia evidently intended to thwart any independence on the part of Tehran until Iran's leaders recognized the overriding position of Russia in every aspect of their affairs.

In July 1910 a new cabinet under Prince Hasan Khan, with a more radical composition of Social Democrats, was sworn in. However, its activities were hampered by even more radical nationalists who began to assassinate moderate leaders. With Russian approval these extreme anjumans were attacked, dispersed, and driven from Tehran.

The regent died in September 1910, and after considerable tension between Democrats and Moderates, the latter's candidate, Abd al-Qasim Khan, was elected regent, though he would not return from Europe until the following March. A new cabinet in which Moderates prevailed was formed, with Muhammad Vali Khan again as prime minister.

On November 5, 1910, Germany and Russia signed the Potsdam Agreement, wherein Germany acknowledged the Russian sphere of influence in Iran. Russia, with thousands of troops in northern Iran, enjoyed an even freer hand now. The Iranian leaders in Tehran who looked for aid against their overpowering neighbor to the north grew more discouraged.

In 1911 W. Morgan Shuster, an American who had had financial experience in the Philippines, was hired to be financial adviser to the government. Neither Russia nor England was ever pleased with Shuster's presence in Tehran, and they acted to make his position untenable. Shuster took the view that the Iranian government had employed him to organize and reform the finances and the treasury and he tried to be loyal and faithful to his charge. He believed that the majlis and the cabinet were important and virtuous forces in Iran and that the foreign influences were iniquitous. Favoring the Democrats and disappointing the Bakhtiyari, Shuster pressed the majlis to adopt a law establishing the Office of Treasurer-General to collect and disburse all revenues, and to appoint him Treasurer-General. Russia foresaw the possibility of Iranian emancipation through these financial reforms and fought against them. The Russian legation announced that the Belgian customs officials would not be subject to the Treasurer-General's control and that because of disorders Russia might have to take over the customs herself. It was an open declaration of war against Shuster. Finding loans impossible to arrange, as the British and Russians openly warned any banker who showed signs of giving one, Shuster began to collect taxes from notables in Tehran who had not paid their taxes in years. Many of these now sided with the cabinet members and foreign legations against the American.

During the summer of 1911 Iran was torn asunder. In the middle of July ex-shah Muhammad Ali and two of his brothers, with Russian aid and British acquiescence, crossed the Caspian Sea. Met by Turkoman supporters, they seized control of the province of Mazandaran. As word spread through the country of the landing many provinces revolted against Tehran and declared for Muhammad Ali. Before the end of July the cabinet of Muhammad Vali fell and a new one under Najaf Quli Khan, dominated by the Bakhtiyari forces, took office. Loyal government troops defeated the ex-shah in October; Muhammad Ali remained in a small village in the north until he returned to Russia in March 1912. The government's army, which the cabinet and the majlis had put in the field, was financed in part by funds collected and transmitted to it by Shuster. That autumn, on a slight pretext, the Russians invaded Iran. A Russian ultimatum on November 29, 1911, demanded the dismissal of Shuster and stipulated that the Tehran government could not hire foreigners without Russian approval. The Russians also wanted Iran to pay the cost of the Russian invasion. Najaf Quli Khan was ready to comply, but the majlis voted to reject the ultimatum. The cabinet fell. Twelve thousand Russian troops captured Tabriz, Rasht, and Anzali and prepared to take Tehran. The ousted cabinet, however, expelled the majlis from its building on December 24, 1911. The majlis did not meet again until January 1915. Shuster was fired the next day.

The Strangling of Persia

When Shuster returned to America in 1912 he wrote a book about his experiences in Iran, entitled *The Strangling of Persia*. This phrase was accepted widely, and the term has been given to the period extending from Shuster's dismissal to the outbreak of World War I. Shuster's departure was a blow to the Democrats from which they never recovered. Bakhtiyari leaders controlled the government, and their chieftain ruled from behind the scenes. Over the next three years a series of prime ministers proceeded through that office. Many Bakhtiyari khans received lucrative provincial governorships and ministries. The state disintegrated rapidly; local authority soon superseded central rule. Roads were unsafe, and the company that had the concession on the Karun river and overland traffic to Shiraz had to pay local brigands for protection. Trade came to a standstill in many provinces. Leading officials preyed on the government treasury.

In March 1912 the Russian government gave up on Muhammad Ali and attempted to disburse his sympathizers gathered at Meshed. The city was bombarded and the sacred shrine there was looted and shattered, sending a traumatic wave across Iran and destroying any possibility of an understanding or genuine cooperation with Russian officials.

In May 1912 Abd al-Qasim, the regent, left for Switzerland and found excuses for not returning. According to the constitution his appointment as regent could only be terminated by the majlis and only he could convene it. The Russians and British brought many pressures on the ministers in 1913 and 1914 to grant major concessions for building railways across Iran, but no concession was valid unless approved by the majlis. Abd al-Qasim refused to come home to call it; the two powers were quietly frustrated by a classic Iranian stratagem.

The British discovery of oil in southwestern Iran increased their willingness to grant the Russians a free hand in the north. Among the constant stream of concessions granted at the turn of the century, one signed on May 29, 1901, gave to William Knox D'Arcy the exclusive rights to search for, obtain, exploit, develop, refine, transport, and sell natural gas, petroleum, and asphalt in all of Iran except the five northern provinces for sixty years. French archeologists in southwestern Iran had first reported the existence of oil there in 1892. A gusher was brought in at Masjid Sulayman in May 1908, and the Anglo-Persian Oil Company was organized the next year. The British bought one square mile of land on Abadan Island in the Shatt al-Arab to build a refinery and obtained rights of way for pipelines. All these negotiations with the local shaykh were carried on without the advice or participation of any official from Tehran. In this area the British were as independent as the Russians were in the north and had fewer obstacles and greater success. Britain was deeply concerned about oil and access to it; the British admiralty purchased a majority interest in the company in 1914 as the navy was turning from coal to oil.

Shah Ahmad was crowned on July 21, 1914, in the presence of many national and international dignitaries. Ten days later Europe was engulfed in war, and on November 1, 1914, the shah issued an imperial decree declaring strict neutrality for Iran. As Russia warred with the Ottoman Empire, Turkey said she wished to respect Iranian neutrality but could not as long as Russian troops remained in Azerbayjan, where attacks on Turkey could be easily mounted. Prince Hasan Khan, Iran's prime minister, requested a Russian withdrawal to obviate a Turkish invasion. Russia demanded promises from Turkey that no attack would be made should Russian troops be withdrawn. Such guarantees were not forthcoming. Kurds from Turkey invaded Iran in the vicinity of Lake Urumiyah and Russian troops poured into northern Iran. The third majlis opened on January 4, 1915, but Iran was no longer in control of her own affairs. A constitutional regime would have to await the end of the war.

REFERENCES: Chapter 29

Works cited at the end of Chapters 7, 15, 17, 18, 19, 20, 22, 23, 24, 25, 26, 27, and 28 are especially important for this chapter.

Algar, Hamid. *Mirza Malkum Khan: A Biographical Study of Iranian Modernism.* Berkeley: University of California Press, 1973. Malkum was an important, yet curious, political statesman of the last half of the nineteenth century. His call for popular representative government was an important influence leading to the Iranian constitutional movement of 1906.

Avery, Peter. *Modern Iran.* New York: Praeger, 1970. A very substantial, detailed work that begins with the mid-nineteenth century.

Browne, Edward G. *Materials for the Study of the Babi Religion.* Cambridge, England: University Press, 1918. Full of first-hand accounts of incidents and beliefs of the religion by a sympathizer.

————. *The Persian Revolution of 1905–1909.* New York: Barnes & Noble, 1966. A new impression of the 1910 edition. A full account of the revolution and the events of those years with eyewitness reports by a keen student of Iranian society.

Busch, Briton Cooper. *Britain and the Persian Gulf, 1894–1914.* Berkeley: University of California Press, 1967. A sprightly written study of the formation and execution of British policy toward the whole area. Makes extensive use of primary sources.

Huseyn of Hamadan, Mirza. *The Tarikh-i-Jadid or New History of Mirza 'Ali Muhammad the Bab* (trans. by Edward G. Browne). Cambridge, England: University Press, 1893. An account of the life and religious ideas of the founder of Babism by one of his followers. Browne's introduction is most useful in assessing the events.

Issawi, Charles (ed.). *The Economic History of Iran, 1800–1914.* Chicago: University of Chicago Press, 1971. Here is the documentary material needed for writing a coherent history of the Iranian economy.

Kazemzadeh, Firuz. *Russia and Britain in Persia, 1864–1914: A Study in Imperialism.* New Haven, Conn.: Yale University Press, 1968. A detailed chronicle and interpretation of diplomatic history, using primary sources.

Keddie, Nikki R. *Religion and Rebellion in Iran: The Iranian Tobacco Protest of 1891–1892.* New York: Humanities Press, 1966. An important work on mass movements against foreign concessions and the weakening of the authority of the shah prior to the constitutional movement of 1906.

McDaniel, Robert A. *The Shuster Mission and the Persian Constitutional Revolution.* Minneapolis: Bibliotheca Islamica, 1974. A thorough study of the revolution in Iran in 1906 and the failure of the Shuster mission in 1911. Considers the social, tribal, economic, and religious forces in Iran that brought on the revolution, as well as the international influences that foreshadowed the downfall of Shuster.

Shuster, W. Morgan. *The Strangling of Persia: Story of the European Diplomacy and Oriental Intrigue that Resulted in the Denationalization of Twelve Million Mohammedans: A Personal Narrative.* New York: The Century Co., 1912. The famous account of the experiences and work of Shuster in Iran in 1911.

Part Four

The Contemporary Middle East

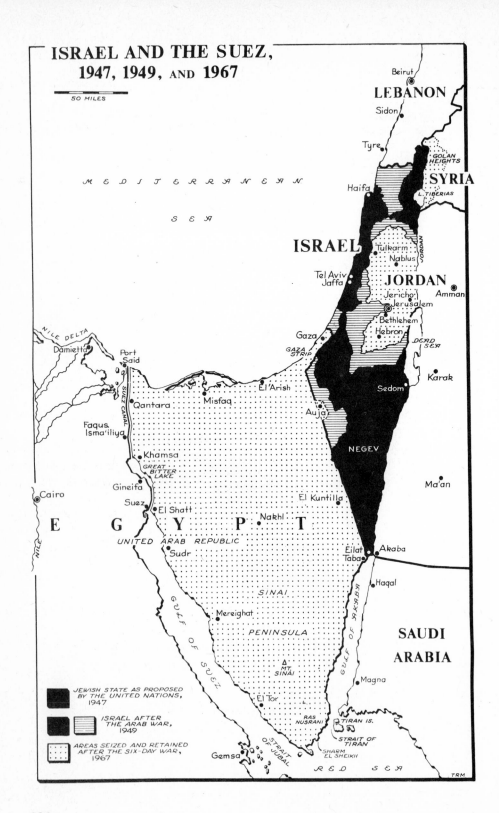

ISRAEL AND THE SUEZ, 1947, 1949, AND 1967

50 MILES

M E D I T E R R A N E A N

S E A

LEBANON

Beirut

Sidon

Tyre

GOLAN
HEIGHTS

Haifa

SYRIA

L. TIBERIAS

ISRAEL

Tulkarm

Nablus

Tel Aviv
Jaffa

JORDAN

Jericho

Amman

Jerusalem

Bethlehem

Gaza

Hebron

GAZA
STRIP

DEAD
SEA

NILE DELTA

Damietta

Port
Said

El'Arish

Sedom

Karak

Misfaq

Qantara

Auja

NEGEV

Faqus
Isma'iliya

Khamsa

Ma'an

GREAT
BITTER
LAKE

Cairo

Gineifa

Suez

El Shatt

El Kuntilla

E G Y P T

Nakhl

UNITED ARAB REPUBLIC

Sudr

Eilat
Taba

Akaba

Haqal

SINAI

SAUDI

Mereighat

PENINSULA

ARABIA

△
MT.
SINAI

Magna

El Tor

RAS
NUSRANI

TIRAN IS.

STRAIT OF
TIRAN

Gemsa

SHARM
EL SHEIKH

R E D   S E A

TRM

JEWISH STATE AS PROPOSED
BY THE UNITED NATIONS,
1947

ISRAEL AFTER
THE ARAB WAR,
1949

AREAS SEIZED AND RETAINED
AFTER THE SIX-DAY WAR,
1967

Chapter 30

Impact of World War 1 upon the Middle East

Turkey Enters the War

The shot at Sarajevo that killed Franz Ferdinand of Austria ricocheted around the world. It proved fatal as well to the Ottoman Empire. Sentiments in Turkey were mixed regarding the war. The great majority of influential Turks desired neutrality and believed that therein lay the best interests of Turkey, already torn, defeated, and impoverished by mediocre governments, revolutions, and the Balkan wars. Some leaders, trained in the liberal traditions of French and British political and university circles, inclined toward the Entente, although the inclusion of Russia, the traditional Ottoman enemy, disturbed them considerably.

A hard core of army officers, however, dominant in the committee for Union and Progress, had come under the spell of German military genius in their schooling by soldiers of the type of von der Goltz Pasha. Guided by Minister of War Enver Pasha who was confident that superior German arms assured victory, and spirited by Baron von Wangenheim, the German ambassador, the triumvirate of the Turkish cabinet signed with Germany on August 2, 1914, a secret alliance directed against Russia. Each engaged to assist the other, and Germany agreed not to withdraw her military mission from Turkey. Known to only five Turks, the alliance was reinforced a week later by the entry into the Straits and "purchase" of the German cruisers *Göben* and *Breslau*. The Turks used the entry as a lever against von Wangenheim to obtain six additional points in the alliance, the most significant being "assistance in the abolition of the capitulations." Purportedly, the purchase was made to replace two Turkish ships built and ready for delivery in England but sequestered by Britain on the outbreak of war. Renamed the *Sultan Selim Yavuz* and *Midilli (Mytilene)*, but still manned by their German officers and crews, these warships played an important role in relations between the two powers.

During the following eleven weeks military and diplomatic events in Europe and at the Porte moved rapidly. Turkish conversations with the Entente for an alliance raised questions about terminating the capitulations, Turkish mobilization on her eastern borders, and German concessions in Anatolia, Thrace, and the Aegean Islands. The Turkish price was too high. The Allies—Russia, England, and France—held the military strength of the Ottomans in low esteem and believed that a push through would be comparatively easy. They, therefore, decided that it would be more convenient to let Turkey join the Central Powers and to partition her after her defeat. How else would Russia ever obtain her coveted Constantinople and the Straits?

The policies of the extremists and adventurers in high Turkish circles prevailed, even though they were a small minority and completely out of touch with the masses. The executive committee of Union and Progress was closely divided between interventionists such as Enver and those who preferred neutrality. Berlin kept pressing Turkey to come into the war. Even Enver hung back, however, asking for more from Germany while protesting that Turkish mobilization was incomplete. On October 11, 1914, Enver, Talat, Jemal, and Speaker of the Assembly Halil met with von Wangenheim at the German embassy and indicated Turkey was nearly ready to join if Germany would shoulder a major share of the burden of war materials, transport, general supplies, and financing. As part of the bargain, Enver demanded a loan of £5 million in gold and promised that Admiral Souchon would have permission to attack Russia in the Black Sea as soon as £2 million in gold coin had been deposited to the Ottoman government's account in Istanbul. The next day £1 million was shipped from Berlin; it arrived on October 16; the second shipment reached Istanbul on October 21.

Enver was determined to have war so that he could also "liberate Egypt" as Napoleon had done. The government-subsidized press was in readiness; von Wangenheim had even bought one newspaper outright. Turkey closed the Dardanelles on September 26; "Ottoman" Admiral Souchon with the *Yavuz, Midilli,* and the fleet steamed up the Bosphorus into the Black Sea and on October 29 shelled Sevastopol and Odessa, mined sea lanes, and destroyed a number of Russian ships. Russia formally declared war on November 4; England and France followed the next day. The sultan pronounced a "holy war" on November 14. In the estimation of many Turkish leaders, the Ottoman Empire had begun to dig its own grave.

The great mass of Turks—Anatolian villagers—would fight for and support the sultan and his government with or without a "holy war" declaration. But perhaps calling for a holy war might induce Muslims under the French in North Africa, under the British in Egypt, the Sudan, and India, and under Russia in central Asia to rebel. Moreover, the war party of the Society of Union and Progress held illusions of recapturing Egypt and Libya and recognized the need for active Arab cooperation in the venture. But the call fell upon unreceptive ears. Revolts of even the slightest significance did not materialize, and the outright hatred generally felt among the Arabs for the Turks more than counterbalanced any Islamic tie. Furthermore, since the caliph was allied with the Christian powers of Germany and Austria-Hungary, the cynicism involved in the declaration of a holy war against the infidels escaped no one.

The immediate Arab reaction was twofold. One group looked upon the outbreak of a war involving Turkey and the imperialistic European states as a God-given opportunity to obtain a united and independent Arab national state. The other group, consisting of princely Arab families and their clients, regarded the war as a time to rebel against the Ottoman sultan and establish independent Arab kingdoms—each for himself and heaven protect the others.

With the formal entry of Turkey into the war Germany dominated Turkish actions and affairs. General von Sanders directed the army, and Admiral Souchon, the navy; British Admiral Limpus was, of course, "recalled." Though transportation, food supplies, finance, and many other highly important wartime problems were frequently left in Turkish hands, German officials regularly acted as they pleased. Turkey swarmed with Germans.

Gallipoli Campaign

A few days after the Turkish naval expedition into the Black Sea a British contingent bombarded the entrance to the Dardanelles, even before England declared war. In January 1915 the British War Cabinet acquiesced to the views of Winston Churchill and agreed to send a force to break through the Straits, take Turkey out of the war, and open a first-rate munitions supply route to Russia. The British army command, however, sabotaged the venture and greatly lessened its chances of success. After unsuccessful attacks in February and March by naval forces, an Anglo-French army began landing operations on the Gallipoli Peninsula in April 1915. The attackers met withering fire and stubborn defense by Turkish forces and some German officers under the command of General von Sanders. Suffering huge losses, the Anglo-French force, joined by the Italians in August, clung on, and twice nearly succeeded in a breakthrough. Lack of cooperation by the Russians at the Bosphorus end of the Straits, skillful tactics on the part of the Germans and Turks, and faulty intelligence work by the offensive forces led first to a stalemate and then to Allied withdrawal from the Straits in January 1916.

War Plans

The Russians were perturbed over the Dardanelles campaign for fear the British and French would take the Straits, capture Istanbul, and fail to relinquish them to the Russians. Nonetheless, they made the first overtures for some kind of a campaign to relieve the Turkish pressure in the Caucasus. The overall Ottoman war plan called for an attack upon the Russians in the east and an expedition to drive the British from Egypt. In the last months of 1914 Turkish forces moved east to take Kars and Batum, but the strategy was poorly conceived by Enver. After a few initial successes the Turks fell back—nearly 90 percent of the Third Army had been lost to frostbite, hunger, disease, and enemy action. Enver relinquished his command and returned to Istanbul. All news of the disaster was censored.

In the campaigns of 1915–1916, with the aid of Armenian revolutionaries and irregular forces, the Russians captured Erzerum, Van, Trabzon, Erzinjan, and other lesser cities in the east. In 1916 Mustafa Kemal Pasha, in command of the Second Army, joined the Third Army on the Caucasus front, but little was accomplished. Transportation was next to impossible; ammunition and supplies of every kind were scarce; and disease was rampant. In February 1917 forty-two Turkish army surgeons died of spotted typhus alone, and thousands of soldiers died of starvation and general debility. The dreadful casualties of Enver's first campaign and the considerable depopulation of the eastern areas as a result of the Armenian massacres and deportations in 1915 created such a weakness on the front facing Russia that it would have been fatal had not Russia been so hard-pressed in the European war theatres from 1915 to 1917.

The revolutions in Russia in 1917 affected the Caucasus front very markedly, especially the Bolshevik Revolution in the autumn. All the Russian troops except for the Armenian and Georgian divisions melted away. The Turks advanced rapidly to occupy Kars, Ardahan, and Batum, which the Treaty of Brest-Litovsk gave to Turkey. Georgian and German forces, however, retook Batum. Later, a Bolshevik-Armenian coup in Baku and the massacre of 10,000 Turks produced a concerted Turkish drive that led to the capture of the city in September 1918 and the killing of many Armenians. Germany deplored the Turkish inroads into the Caucasus and even went so far as to conclude a Bolshevik-German agreement, according to which German forces would protect the Caucasus and in particular Baku from attacks by a third party. However, at the end of war in 1918 the Caucasus area became an Allied problem.

The second ambition of Enver was the conquest of Egypt. In August 1914 Britain took precautionary measures there, and after Turkey's entry into the war Britain established a protectorate in Egypt on December 18, 1914. Khedive Abbas Hilmi was deposed and Husayn, his uncle, was appointed Sultan of Egypt. Jemal Pasha, minister of marine and one of the triumvirate, took command of the Fourth Ottoman Army and assumed responsibility for Syria, including Palestine. In February 1915 his forces made a surprise attack upon the Suez Canal, but possessing inadequate strength to hold the eastern bank, they retired to a line in the Sinai Peninsula with bases at Maan, Beersheba, and Gaza. Throughout 1915 small flying columns raided points on the Suez Canal. These raids compelled the British to maintain a large force there, but the morale of the Turkish and Syrian armies was depressed because they inevitably had to retreat.

A massive assault against the Canal was ordered for February 1916, but poor transport delayed the attack until the least opportune weather of midsummer. The assault proved a dismal failure, and from that moment until the end of the war Turko-German armies were on the defensive in this theatre of operations. Furthermore, the repressive and harsh policies of Jemal Pasha in Syria turned the diffident Arabs into a hostile population that began in 1916 to look upon the British as liberators. In March and April

1917 at the famous battles of Gaza Turko-German arms withstood heavy British fire and drove the enemy back to a line in Sinai. Later in that year a German-ordered-and-directed operation known as Yilderim, commanded by General von Falkenhayn, attempted to gain a favorable decision in Palestine. Again, failure of transport, sabotage of supplies en route, continuing harassment by Arab desert bands, and a buildup of British forces under General Allenby brought disaster.

The fourth area of major hostilities in the Middle East was Mesopotamia. British contingents from India seized Basrah even before the Turkish entry into the war and proceeded northward to the confluence of the Tigris and Euphrates. A sizable force under General Townshend captured Kut al-Amara in 1915, but it was defeated just south of Baghdad and fell back to Kut al-Amara, where the Sixth Turkish Army forced a surrender in 1916. However, Halil Pasha, Enver's uncle, failed to pursue his victory and permitted the British and Indian divisions to reestablish their hold on southern Iraq. A railroad was built and superior concentrations of men, artillery, and supplies enabled the British under General Maude to retake Kut al-Amara and capture Baghdad in 1917. Before the year was out the British were halfway between Mosul and Baghdad, but they had not yet reached the former at the time of the armistice in 1918.

The Armenians

While World War I was unfolding in the Middle East and shattering the Ottoman Empire, two national groups within the state, the Arabs and the Armenians, openly aided the enemy. Wealthy Armenians insisted that their people support the Ottoman government and the war, but the head of the Armenian Orthodox Church, residing in the Russian Caucasus, asseverated that the tsar was the protector of all Armenians. Thus, in Istanbul and the western cities of the empire Armenians complied with war orders, while in eastern Asia Minor the Armenian population, often following Westernized Armenian radicals such as Pasdirmajian, aided Russia by rebelling, and in the region of Van and Erzerum by open warfare. In April 1915 an Armenian government was proclaimed in Van. In some districts the entire Muslim population was killed.

These incidents touched off the unfortunate Armenian deportations and massacres of 1915 and 1916. An estimated 1,500,000 Armenians had lived in Turkey at the outbreak of war. The great preponderance were in Aleppo and the eight Anatolian vilayets of Erzerum, Van, Bitlis, Kharput, Diyarbakir, Sivas, Adana, and Trabzon. The basic order came in June 1915; it authorized the transfer of all non-Muslims away from points of military concentration and from lines of communication and required all non-Muslims in the military forces to be relegated to rear service units without arms. However, thousands of Armenians had already died.

The gravity of the action appeared when deportations occurred. Inadequate provisions in Syria, the general destination, led to the death of tens of thousands from exposure, exhaustion, and starvation. It seemed as if many were marched off into the desert to die. Everyone suffered, and the prosecution of the war on the Caucasus front was hampered from 1915 to 1917 because of the absence of the services normally provided by the Armenian inhabitants of eastern Anatolia. Many Armenians were set upon by marauding bands of Kurds and Turks, who perpetrated numerous atrocities. Representatives of neutral governments protested to the Porte, and German officials privately lamented the action. Talat, Enver, and the government, however, were deaf to all pleas, since influential individuals in the Turkish government were actually bent on exterminating the Armenian population in eastern Turkey. Perhaps a million Armenians perished. No doubt certain deportations were required, but the total action was entirely inconsonant with the need. Many Turks did shield and protect Armenian individuals and groups from the authorities; in general Turks considered the severity of the Armenian deportations and consequent loss of life as a blot on the Turkish record.

Arab Movements

The other pressing national problem confronting the leaders of the Ottoman government was the loyalty and aspirations of the Arabs. No open break occurred until June 1916, when Sharif Husayn of Mecca proclaimed his personal rule in the Hijaz. Prior to that move, Jemal Pasha as an Ottoman viceroy and commander of the Fourth Army maintained discipline and surface calm in Syria. Jemal supported pan-Islamism and sought to obtain the active support of the Arabs in the war. However, documents implicating numerous Muslim and Christian leaders in treasonable activities fell into his hands. Arrests were made, and in 1915 eleven persons were hanged in the main square of Beirut. When Enver called upon Jemal for troops for the Gallipoli campaign, an Arab division, including many leaders of *al-Ahd,* was sent in order that the more reliable Turkish troops might remain in Beirut and Damascus. In April 1916 about two hundred Arabs, including many well-known and influential men from the most prominent families in Beirut and Damascus, were arrested, tried, and sentenced; twenty-two were hanged. This act more than any other precipitated Husayn's declaration of Arab independence.

Before examining the moves for independence made by the western Arabs in Syria and the Hijaz, Arab-British relations should be placed in their proper setting. Petty Arab states existed along the western shore of the Persian Gulf and the southern coasts of Arabia. Almost every one had a treaty of friendship with Great Britain in which the latter exercised power over Arab foreign relations. In effect, protectorates were created. A British minister resident or an agent resided in the shaykhdom or the sultanate, advised on all governmental matters, and doled out gold sovereigns or Maria Theresa silver dollars to keep everybody happy.

When war became imminent, Captain Shakespear of the British Royal Navy, then attached to the India Office, visited Abd al-Aziz ibn Saud of the Nejd and entered into a standard Arab-British agreement: Ibn Saud placed his foreign affairs in British hands and accepted a generous subsidy. In regard to the Arabs as a whole and the question of a unified Arab nation, no reference was made and none was implied. Ibn Saud controlled an important segment of the interior of Arabia, and the India Office was merely assuring his neutrality, at least in the struggle between Briton and Turk in Iraq and the Persian Gulf area.

A more significant Arab development involved Husayn, whom the Young Turks had sent to the Hijaz as the Prince of Mecca. Early in 1914 Husayn's second son, Abdallah, in passing through Cairo had sounded out Lord Kitchener, British agent in Egypt, on the subject of British aid to Husayn, who desired to break with the Turks. After the advent of war, Kitchener recalled the conversation and instructed Ronald Storrs, British Oriental secretary in Egypt, to raise with his favorite chess opponent, Abdallah, the question of an alliance with the British and a declaration against the Turks.

Thus began the celebrated correspondence between Sharif Husayn and the British in Egypt. Husayn found himself in a delicate situation. His third son, Faysal, did not trust the British or French and felt that it would be better policy to cooperate with the Turks and win their gratitude. Abdallah, however, favored independence from the Turks and proposed, in cooperation with Arab secret societies in Damascus and Beirut, to take advantage of the world struggle in order to obtain British aid. Husayn postponed the decision until June 1916. Meanwhile, an exchange of letters between Husayn and Sir Henry McMahon, High Commissioner for Egypt and the Sudan, brought to a head the issue of Arab independence and an Arab state. Britain promised, upon the successful conclusion of the war, to agree to the creation of an Arab state. The area of the state was to be bounded on the north by a line drawn eastward from Alexandretta to the Iranian frontier and thence southward to the Persian Gulf and was to include the entire Arabian Peninsula. Excepted from this were British Aden and the districts of Syria west of Damascus, Homs, Hama, and Aleppo. The British refused to pledge the latter without the consent of France. Britain promised not to make a peace treaty that did not include this Arab state, and Husayn categorically stated that he would not consent to any part of Arabia becoming the possession of any power, by which he meant France. Also excluded from the Arab state were the small states, such as Kuwayt and Muscat, with which Britain had special treaty provisions.

Husayn, however, was not a free agent in dealing with the British. His son Faysal had conferred clandestinely in Damascus with leaders of the Arab movement, and in 1915 he presented the secret Damascus Protocol to his father. This document defined the Arab state's frontiers as Husayn later insisted upon them with McMahon, and it demanded abolition of the capitulations in return for economic preference to Great Britain. Its authors invited Husayn to forward their terms to the British as the basis on which the Arabs would revolt against the Ottoman Empire. Thus, the Husayn-McMahon correspondence should be regarded not as a negotiation entirely

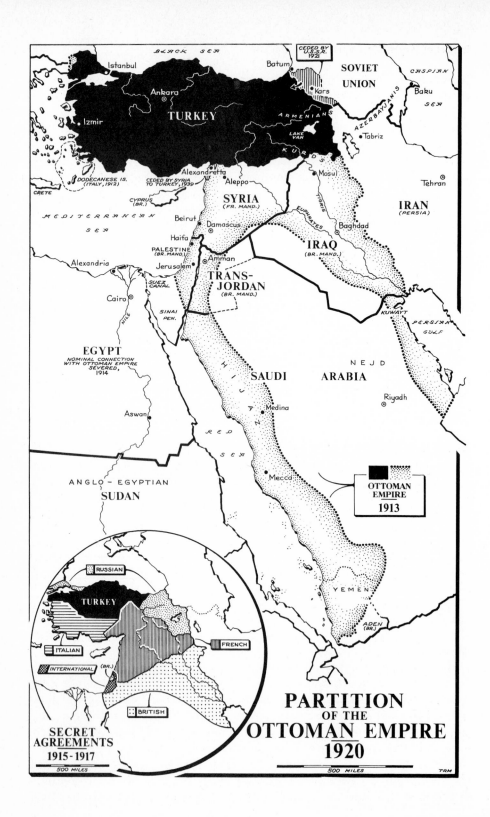

PARTITION
OF THE
OTTOMAN EMPIRE
1920

SECRET
AGREEMENTS
1915-1917

500 MILES

500 MILES

OTTOMAN
EMPIRE
1913

SECRET AGREEMENTS legend:
RUSSIAN
ITALIAN
INTERNATIONAL (BR.)
FRENCH
BRITISH

between two individuals but as a negotiation in part between representatives of two principals—the British government and the Arab people.

The Secret Treaties

While these negotiations with Husayn were in process, the Allies were engaged in formulating their notorious secret treaties, dividing among themselves both Turkish and Arab parts of the Ottoman Empire. As soon as war broke out in 1914 Russia pressed England and France for Istanbul as well as the Straits and considerable hinterland on each side. After many diplomatic exchanges Russia was reluctantly promised the object of her age-old quest. In exchange British and French rights in Asiatic Turkey would be defined by special agreement and the neutral zone in Iran would be included in the British sphere of influence.

Later the Pact of London was signed to bring Italy into the war. This pact promised Italy sovereignty over the Dodecanese Islands and the elimination of all rights of the Ottoman caliph yet remaining in Libya. Italian interests in Antalya were conceded and that area promised to her; in case Turkey was not dismembered Italy would be given recompense elsewhere.

The most far-reaching of the secret treaties—the Sykes-Picot Agreement of April 26, 1916—allotted to Russia the already promised Straits area, the vilayets of Erzerum, Trabzon, Van, and Bitlis, and Kurdistan. France was granted the coastal strip of Syria northward from Tyre, the vilayet of Adana including Mersin, and a vague area of Cilicia which comprised a triangle of Anatolia marked off by Adana, Sivas, and Mardin. Britain obtained an enclave about Haifa and Acre on the Mediterranean, and Mesopotamia from Baghdad to the Persian Gulf. Palestine west of the Jordan River and from Gaza to Tyre was, upon the insistence of Russia, cut from French Syria and promised an international administration because of the Holy Places and numerous Russian Orthodox establishments. The area of Syria from Damascus and Aleppo eastward through Mosul to the Iranian frontier was consigned to French protection, while the region from Kirkuk to Akaba and from the Mediterranean to the Persian Gulf became a British sphere. Alexandretta was designated a free port.

The secret Sykes-Picot Agreement was signed only a few months after agreements embodied in the Husayn-McMahon correspondence were concluded. Husayn did not learn of the perfidy until late in 1917, when the Bolsheviks published the secret agreements found in the imperial archives. Husayn requested an explanation. In January 1918 he received from Professor David G. Hogarth, an Oxford Arabic scholar who headed the British government's Arab Bureau in Cairo, an official statement virtually denying the existence of the Sykes-Picot Agreement and adding a cryptic remark about the consent of the populations concerned. Husayn trusted the British until after the war ended.

The Italians, however, learning of the Sykes-Picot arrangements, insisted upon a further delimitation of their ambitions. Thus, in a railway car on a siding at St. Jean de Maurienne in 1917 the prime ministers of England,

France, and Italy agreed that Italy should have the districts of Izmir, Antalya, and Konya, and all of southwestern Anatolia. A district north of Izmir also became an Italian prize. At the same time that Italy secured Izmir, Greece was promised Cyprus and the territory of western Asia Minor including Izmir as an inducement to join the war on the Allied side. Pledges and counterpledges with regard to the future of the Middle East were beginning to mount.

The Balfour Declaration

Zionism had yet to be heard. Zionism was a socio-political and nationalistic movement that developed among European Jews in the last quarter of the nineteenth century. Pogroms in Russia and anti-Semitism in the nationalistic states of Europe fostered political Zionism and provoked Theodor Herzl to establish the World Zionist Organization in Basle in 1897. Concessions were repeatedly sought from the Porte for a Jewish settlement company in Palestine, but the sultan refused, believing this would increase his already diffuse problems of nationalism. The Zionist Congress had declined a British offer in 1903 of a settlement in Uganda, for Zionism without Zion would be a paradox.

At the outbreak of war in 1914 Zionist activities were centered in Germany. Upon the division of Europe into two camps, however, another center arose in London, led by Dr. Chaim Weizmann. Opposition arose from the Anglo-Jewish Association and the Board of Deputies of British Jews, both of which were anti-Zionist. Weizmann, however, with the support of the *Manchester Guardian,* the Rothschilds, Lloyd George (whose private secretary was Sir Philip Sassoon), and Sir Herbert Samuel, won the favor of Lord Balfour. In the United States a cooperating Zionist committee was organized under the chairmanship of Justice Brandeis and supported by Rabbi Wise, Eugene Meyer, Nathan Strauss, Felix Frankfurter, and others.

The Zionists wanted an Allied commitment to create a Jewish commonwealth in Palestine upon the demise of the Ottoman Empire. Political pressure to this end was exerted, generally in the public press, and individually upon public and political figures. Slowly an influential group came to favor such a state, especially when the Zionists pledged that the new creation, so strategically placed with respect to Suez, would be in the British sphere of influence. Success came on November 2, 1917, when Lord Balfour wrote to Lord Rothschild:

His Majesty's Government view with favour the establishment in Palestine of a national home for the Jewish people and will use their best endeavours to facilitate the achievement of this object, it being clearly understood that nothing shall be done which may prejudice the civil and religious rights of existing non-Jewish communities in Palestine or the rights and political status enjoyed by Jews in any other country.

This letter, the famous Balfour Declaration, had the approval of the British Cabinet as well as that of President Wilson, who insisted upon adding the modifying clauses. Later, France and Italy accepted the declaration, and Wilson publicly acknowledged it in October 1918. The exact meaning of the declaration has been much debated in the last decades, but at the time of its writing there was no doubt of its intent. Also it was definitely contrary both to the Sykes-Picot Agreement and to the Husayn-McMahon correspondence. Reasons for its issuance have been advanced by those responsible. It was alleged that its pronouncement was required to gain support for the Allies from Jewish circles in Germany and Austria. There may be some basis to this, for in 1918 Germany and Turkey also offered the Zionists a charter for a Jewish settlement company in Palestine. It was constant political pressure and the winning of important men to their cause, for whatever reason, that brought success to the Zionists. They were disappointed, however, that the declaration did not read "recognizing Palestine as the national home for the Jewish people."

Husayn was dismayed when the news of the Balfour Declaration reached him, and quite naturally he requested an explanation. Professor Hogarth was sent to explain that Jewish settlement in Palestine would not be permitted to compromise "the political and economic freedom of the Arab population." Again, Husayn accepted Britain's word.

The Fourteen Points

One other Allied promise was made during the war. When Baghdad and Jerusalem fell to British forces, the victorious generals announced that any future settlement would be made with the consent of local populations. These utterances foreshadowed the broad concepts of Wilson's Fourteen Points, presented to the American Congress on January 8, 1918. In particular they foreshadowed Wilson's twelfth point, which stated that the Turkish parts of the Ottoman Empire should have a "secure sovereignty" and that other nationalities should be given "an undoubted security of life and an absolute unmolested opportunity of development." Greeks, Armenians, and Arabs felt that this point alluded to them and they built their hopes upon it. Arabs believed that Wilson's declaration recognized their aspirations as proposed by Husayn, and that the Fourteen Points nullified the Balfour Declaration and all secret treaties, agreements, commitments, understandings, and promises made under the duress of total war.

Allied Victory

Failure of the German-Turkish campaign in the summer of 1917 opened the way for the British in Egypt to move into Palestine. Jerusalem fell to General Allenby in December 1917. British forces, accompanied by French detachments, then proceeded northward along the coast, taking Tyre, Sidon, Beirut, and Tripoli. The Turks' interior lines of communication were continuously harassed by the Arabs under Faysal. The Arab revolution of June 1916 shattered the Turkish regime in the Hijaz, and Arabs under

Faysal east of the Jordan paralleled the actions of Allenby. Under the stimulus and encouragement of such British liaison officers as Colonel T. E. Lawrence, Colonel C. C. Wilson, and Sir Reginald Wingate, and receiving British equipment and gold, the Arabs captured Akaba and Maan and entered Damascus in October 1918, at the same time as did the British. The Seventh Turkish Army under Mustafa Kemal Pasha held the Arabs before Aleppo, as the armistice signed at Mudros between the Allies and the Turks ended all hostilities.

German failures on the Western Front in the summer of 1918 and the imminent collapse of Germany spelled the end of warfare in the Middle East. Without German matériel and general assistance the Ottoman Empire could not maintain effective resistance. Admiral Gough-Calthorpe, commander of the British Mediterranean Fleet, received representatives of the new Ottoman government of Izzet Pasha aboard the *Agamemnon* off Mudros on the island of Lemnos and on October 30, 1918, signed an armistice ending the war. It was not an unconditional surrender, but Turkish forces were to be demobilized, and the Allies were to have free access and control of the Straits. Opening the door to total Allied control was Article VII which stated: "The Allies have the right to occupy any strategic points in the event of any situation arising which threatens the security of the Allies." Under such an article any action was allowable.

The war, four years almost to the day, brought many changes to Turkish society, which disintegrated so fully under the terrible conditions of the war that Asquith declared "the Sick Man had really died this time." To describe the miserable conditions in Turkey to those who did not experience them or similar circumstances would require many pages. Suffice it to say that the larger cities were disturbed more than the villages, and Istanbul most of all. Shortages of every kind developed; war profiteers appeared; physical suffering among the masses became widespread; and the general low standard of living deteriorated rapidly, as inflation lifted the prices of everything without much change in wages. Most commodities were scarce. Foreign goods could not be imported, and domestic produce was largely requisitioned by the government. Worse still, the government proved entirely incapable of governing. Inefficiency, mismanagement, and malfeasance dominated every government office. The capitulations were abolished; the Ottoman Public Debt Administration was terminated; and the war-burdened government assumed control over many unaccustomed activities. The end of the Turkish state seemed obvious, and Asquith completed his declaration on the Sick Man with the pronouncement that "his resurrection was impossible."

The war generated many new and positive forces in society. As the power of the government waned, Arabs, Greeks, Armenians, and all subject nationalities of the empire gave more open expression to their nationalism. For the Armenians, it led to destruction. To the Greeks, it brought a temporary fulfillment of cherished dreams. And among the Arabs, it created the revolt and new Arab states. For the Turks the rapid decay gave to many liberals and democrats, such as Halidé Edib and Ahmed Emin, and to uncompromising nationalists, such as Mustafa Kemal, an opportunity to be heard and to have some heed paid to their demands for governmental leadership that would place the welfare of the nation above self-interest.

Of the other effects of the war, one of the more salutary for the Middle East was the presence of many British, French, Italian, and German soldiers, and their equipment. Thousands of Middle Easterners saw Westerners and their manner of living for the first time. Their machines opened a new world to Arabs and Turks. The impact of the West upon the Middle East in every facet of its living, from transportation to religion, was more profound and penetrating in these four war years than it had been in several centuries of contact through religious, commercial, and intellectual missions from the West. A new age for the Middle East was born.

REFERENCES: Chapter 30

Volumes cited in Chapters 7, 13, 18, 19, 22, 23, 24, 25, 26, 27, 28, and 29 have value for this chapter.

Bowman-Manifold, Michael G. E. *An Outline of the Egyptian and Palestine Campaigns, 1914 to 1918.* Chatham, England: Mackay, 1922.

Busch, Briton Cooper. *Britain, India and the Arabs, 1914–1921.* Berkeley: University of California Press, 1971. A detailed account of World War I in the Middle East from the viewpoint of the British in India, using Indian archives.

Djemal Pasha, Ahmed. *Memories of a Turkish Statesman, 1913–1919.* New York: Doran, 1922. The autobiography of one of the triumvirate in Turkey during the war.

Emin, Ahmed. *Turkey in the World War.* New Haven: Yale University Press, 1930. A basic and thorough study, by the leading editor in Turkey, of the political, economic, and social forces in Turkey during the war years. His name in the 1930s became Ahmed Emin Yalman.

Evans, Laurence. *United States Policy and the Partition of Turkey, 1914–1924.* Baltimore: Johns Hopkins Press, 1965.

Howard, Harry N. *The Partition of Turkey; A Diplomatic History, 1913–1923.* Norman: Oklahoma University Press, 1931. The most definitive work on the political, diplomatic, and international aspects of World War I in the Middle East.

Hurewitz, J. C. (compiler, tr., ed.). *The Middle East and North Africa in World Politics: A Documentary Record.* Vol. II, *British-French Supremacy.* 1914–1945: New Haven Conn.: Yale University Press, 19—. This volume will contain the significant documents for the area in this crucial period.

Ingrams, Doreen (ed.). *Palestine Papers, 1917–1922: Seeds of Conflict.* New York: George Braziller, 1973. Declassified British policy documents on Palestine taken from the Cabinet, Foreign Office, and Colonial Office, beginning with Herbert Samuel's memorandum of 1915.

James, Robert Rhodes. *Gallipoli: The History of a Noble Blunder.* New York: Macmillan, 1965. New interpretation.

Kedourie, Elie. *In the Anglo-Arab Labyrinth: The McMahon-Husayn Correspondence and its Interpretations, 1914–1939.* Cambridge, England: Cambridge University Press, 1976. A thorough examination of the correspondence and the conversations, followed by a full report of the various interpretations and histori-cal reports of it put out by the British Foreign Office, the British Colonial Office, the Arab Bureau, and others.

Lawrence, T. E. *Seven Pillars of Wisdom.* London: Jonathan Cape, 1935. The full account of the colonel's activities among the Arabs during the war.

Marder, Arthur J. *From the Dardanelles to Oran: Studies of the Royal Navy in War and Peace, 1915–1940.* London: Oxford University Press, 1974. The first chapter deals with the naval participation and activities at Gallipoli. This outstanding naval historian shows the lost opportunities in the early campaign and indicates that the Allies would have had a real possibility of success if their equipment had been better.

Moorehead, Alan. *Gallipoli.* New York: Harper, 1956. The story of the famous campaign.

Nevakivi, Jukka. *Britain, France and the Arab Middle East, 1914–1920.* New York: Oxford University Press, 1969. A new study making use of recently opened British archives for the period. Scholarly and sound.

Sachar, Howard M. *The Emergence of the Middle East: 1914–1924.* New York: Knopf, 1969. A well-documented account of the area in those years from a Eu-ropean rather than a Middle Eastern view.

von Sanders, Liman. *Five Years in Turkey.* Baltimore: Williams & Wilkins, 1928. The record of the German commanding general stationed in Turkey during the war.

Stein, Leonard. *The Balfour Declaration.* New York: Simon and Schuster, 1961. First good complete history.

Storrs, Ronald. *Orientations.* London: Nicholson & Watson, 1937. Storrs was the Oriental secretary to the British High Commissioner in Egypt during the war.

Townshend, Charles V. *My Campaign in Mesopotamia.* London: T. Butterworth, 1920. By the commanding general of the British forces.

Trumpener, Ulrich. *Germany and the Ottoman Empire, 1914–1918.* Princeton, N.J.: Princeton University Press, 1968. A detailed account largely from German sources. Discusses the alliance of 1914, the conduct of the war, financing, Ar-menian persecutions, German economic efforts, and political evolution of the alliance. An outstanding work, with many new interpretations.

Weber, Frank G. *Eagles on the Crescent: Germany, Austria, and the Diplomacy of the Turkish Alliance, 1914–1918.* Ithaca, N.Y.: Cornell University Press, 1970. Largely from German and Austrian archival materials. Another first-rate contri-bution.

Wilson, Arnold T. *Loyalties: Mesopotamia, 1914–1917.* London: Oxford University Press, 1930. A detailed record of the military occupation of Iraq by a British participant long active in that part of the world.

Chapter 31

The Middle East at the Paris Peace Conference

Allied Claims and Promises

Less than two weeks after the Mudros armistice halted World War I in the Middle East, Germany signed the armistice with the Allies and war officially ceased. The fate of the Middle East devolved then upon the several armies of occupation and, perhaps even more importantly, upon "the smoke-filled rooms" of Paris, where politicians, diplomats, statesmen, generals, journalists, and representatives of every special interest gathered to make peace. The Middle East, however, was only a small part of the total settlement. Problems with respect to Germany took precedence over all others, and decisions affecting France, Germany, and central Europe frequently compromised the verdict on the Middle East.

The prime conflict concerning the Middle East appeared in the frightful disparity contained in the assorted secret treaties, agreements, and letters exchanged among the Allies, to say nothing of contradictions in numerous pious, platitudinous, and public pronouncements by Allied leaders during the war. A recitation of a few illuminates the confusion: the London Pact of 1915, the Sykes-Picot Agreement, the Balfour Declaration, the Husayn-McMahon correspondence, the Fourteen Points, the liberation statements at Baghdad and Jerusalem, and the "make the world safe for democracy" slogan. Thus, the hopes of the many who traveled to Paris were high.

Lloyd George went to the conference professing friendliness and good will for the peoples of the Middle East and clamoring for their welfare and aspirations. But he had every intention of advancing the interest, power, and possessions of the British Empire. Egypt, Mesopotamia, Arabia, Palestine, Iran, Cyprus, and the Caucasus were considered British prizes, and under no circumstances were Istanbul and the Straits to be awarded to France. Lloyd George regarded the entire Middle East, with the possible exception of Syria and parts of Anatolia, as an economic adjunct of the British Empire. Clemenceau, on the other hand, stood for a French hold upon Syria and southern Anatolia, hoped to acquire or at least dominate the Straits, and dreamed of having a French adviser at the elbow of the sultan of Turkey who would exercise a role similar to that of the British adviser in Egypt. President Wilson, on his trip across the Atlantic aboard the *George Washington,* met daily with his advisers and sincerely discussed plans for peace in the Middle East that would fulfill the pledge made in his Fourteen Points. Since Allied governments concurred in that declaration, he believed it wiped away all previous "sins."

The big three held major decisions in their hands; hosts of others, however, had greater personal or national interests in the Middle East. Prince Faysal came to Paris to represent the Arabs, his father, and the Kingdom of the Hijaz, which had been a belligerent since June 1916. Faysal expected England to abide by her pledges given to the Arabs for their national state. Three groups of Armenians presented conflicting claims for their nation, and President Wilson sent out the Harbord Mission to ascertain the facts. Venizelos, the Prime Minister of Greece, used all of his charm and diplomatic blandishments to obtain Allied promises with respect to the Greek "Great Idea," that is, restoration of the Greek empire to include western Asia Minor, Constantinople, and the Straits. Prime Minister Orlando of Italy intended to receive the Dodecanese Islands, southwestern Asia Minor around Antalya, and an area in and about Izmir.

Bankers, oil men, exporters, bondholders, missionaries, churchmen, shippers, and humanitarians of sundry kinds also converged at Paris to lobby for their respective interests. Amid receptions, lively dinner dances, and weekends at rented chateaux within easy motoring distance of Paris, the future of the Middle East was sought. Everyone was there except the Turks. They did, however, have unofficial agents in Geneva, and Damad Ferid Pasha, the Grand Vizir, was permitted on one occasion to deliver a statement before the supreme council of the conference.

Dr. Weizmann, Judge Brandeis, Rabbi Wise, Professor Frankfurter, and Mr. Sokolov watched over and advanced the cause of Zionism by shepherding the Balfour Declaration through the negotiations to assure its incorporation in all final settlements for the Middle East. Opposing these ardent Zionists stood a few Jews, such as Edwin Montagu, Claude G. Montefiore, Jacob H. Schiff, Louis Marshall, Mayer Sulzberger, and Henry Morgenthau, Sr., former American ambassador to the Porte and treasurer of the Democratic Party's national committee. They felt that Zionism endangered the slow process of assimilation of Jews occurring in national states of the West. Morgenthau believed that creating a Zionist state in Palestine would raise the question of dual nationality. With 299 other leading American Jews, therefore, he signed a petition to President Wilson against the establishment of any Jewish state.

Nevertheless, a coterie of active Zionists won the support of Lloyd George, Balfour, Lord Milner, and Lord Robert Cecil, as well as the sympathy of President Wilson. The policy of self-determinism, however, seemed to be blocking Zionist aims. At the time, Jews constituted not more than 15 percent of the population of Palestine, and a policy of counting heads would have favored Palestine's inclusion in an Arab state as pledged to Sharif Husayn. Lloyd George was unimpressed by Zionist pleas, but he definitely opposed the idea of the Holy Places falling into the hands of "agnostic, atheistic France." More influential with the British was the concept of acquiring Palestine as a stronghold to protect Suez and other British interests in the Middle East. The Zionists reinforced this hope by declaring openly that Jews would opt for a British mandate and by talking of eventual home rule for a Jewish Palestine within the British Commonwealth of Nations. The Zionists' dreams were achieved as a paraphrase of the Balfour Declaration was included in the peace treaties and accepted by the League of Nations.

Out of the welter of claims and counterclaims for the Middle East was born the King-Crane commission. On the suggestion of President Bliss of the American University of Beirut, Wilson proposed to the supreme council that a commission of inquiry composed of American, British, French, and Italian representatives go to Syria, Palestine, Mesopotamia, and Armenia to obtain the information needed to implement the program of self-determination. At first the French, British, and Italians agreed, but later they refused to cooperate. Therefore, President Henry C. King of Oberlin College and businessman Charles R. Crane, the American appointees, proceeded alone in the spring of 1919 with a staff of experts. They visited Palestine, Syria, and Turkey, receiving petitions and local deputations. Having faith in Western democratic principles, the Arabs rejoiced in the coming of the commission. The King-Crane report was submitted in the autumn of 1919 but was suppressed as it ran counter to arrangements already dictated between England and France. Wilson's illness caused the issue to be shelved.

San Remo Agreement

No permanent decisions regarding the Middle East could be reached in Paris in 1919, and the signing of a peace treaty for the area seemed more uncertain than ever. Wilson became gravely ill. The American Senate and people were not favorably disposed to accept a mandate for any territory. Russia was out of the picture. Germany and Austria were broken. And Italy was suffering from internal dissension and disillusionment. Questions of the Middle East, therefore, lay squarely between England and France. Meanwhile, armies of occupation governed the Middle East and the peoples grew restless waiting for peace.

British forces under Allenby controlled Egypt, Palestine, and Lebanon; Faysal and the Arabs held sway over the Hijaz and the interior lines of Arabia including Damascus; and Britain was again master in Mesopotamia with an army from Mosul to the Persian Gulf. Official British policy was set to hang on to as much of the occupied area as possible and to make the Middle East a definite part of the British Empire.

But policy was not the chief concern of the soldiers in the armies of occupation. The British army in 1919 was still the civilian army created during the war, and the aim of the great majority of men was to be demobilized as soon as possible. As officers in the Middle East pulled every string to get out, the turnover in personnel grew serious. Officers newly assigned to the Middle East barely became acclimated before they arranged a transfer home or to some permanent part of the empire. Added to the confusion was the fact that there was little planning or thought for military government or occupation.

In the last months of 1919 British contingents in Beirut and along the Lebanese coast were replaced by French units, and under arrangements concluded in Paris General Gouraud became Allied administrator in Syria. These moves gave advance notice to the Arabs that settlement of the war in the Middle East would follow lines drawn in the hated Sykes-Picot Agreement. Anti-Jewish riots in Jerusalem and Jaffa, the election of Faysal as king of Syria and of Abdallah as king of Iraq by the Arab National Congress in Damascus, growing tenseness in Baghdad, insurrection in Egypt and the dispatch of the Lord Milner Mission to Cairo drove Britain to realize that a treaty for the Middle East was imperative.

One of the sensitive questions in the settlement between England and France revolved around the division of Mosul oil. The Turkish Pertroleum Company, 75 percent British and 25 percent German, had obtained in 1914, a few weeks before the outbreak of war, a concession to exploit the oil of Mosul. The Sykes-Picot Agreement, however, assigned Mosul to France. As early as December 1918, therefore, Britain began pressing the French to allow Mosul to be attached to Mesopotamia. In Paris in May 1919, after much haggling, the Long-Berenger Agreement was initialed: Britain and France would split equally all oil rights obtained in Russia, Rumania, and Galicia; France would be able to purchase 34 percent of all disposable oil in the British crown colonies and Britain to purchase 34 percent in the French colonies; France would receive 25 percent of the Turkish Petroleum Company; and England was given the right to build two pipelines across French-mandated areas from Mosul to the Mediterranean. Lloyd George stormily vetoed the arrangement when he learned of it, on the basis that political settlements would have to be agreed upon first. In February 1920 the Greenwood-Berenger Agreement, containing similar terms, was approved. Added were provisions that France could buy 25 percent of the crude oil from all Mesopotamian fields and 25 percent of any Anglo-Persian crude that might flow through pipelines across French-mandated territories to the Mediterranean. With this in hand the Allied negotiators journeyed to San Remo on the Italian Riviera, where on April 24, 1920, they reached an agreement on oil, pipelines, mandates, and united action with respect to the Turks and Arabs.

The Treaty of Sèvres

The San Remo Agreement prepared the way for a peace settlement with the Ottoman Empire, and the Treaty of Sèvres was signed on August 10, 1920. By this treaty the Ottoman sultan recognized the severing of Syria, Mesopotamia, Arabia, and Egypt from his empire. A British protectorate over Egypt was allowed and the independence of the Arab rulers and their states, subject to their treaties of friendship with Britain, was accepted. Provisional independence for Syria and Mesopotamia under the tutelage of some mandatory power was acknowledged. Syria, already assigned to France, included the cities of Alexandretta, Aleppo, Damascus, and Beirut. The vilayet of Mosul was attached to Baghdad and Basrah to form the State of Iraq under British supervision. Palestine, including the lands on each side of the Jordan and extending to the Gulf of Akaba, was given as a mandate to Britain, with the Balfour Declaration written into the authorization. In addition to the oil understandings, France was given a free hand to deal with Faysal and the Arab Syrian kingdom with force—to crush them if necessary.

The Treaty of Sèvres was obsolete before it was drawn, and because of various exigencies within Turkish portions of the Ottoman Empire it was never fully ratified. Theoretically, then, final arrangements in the Middle East awaited the Treaty of Lausanne in 1923; yet divisions, boundaries, and the disposal of non-Turkish parts of the Ottoman Empire in that final treaty varied only slightly from the transfer of legal authority that was proposed at San Remo and Sèvres. Provisional mandates bargained for at San Remo dictated Arab political and economic life for the following twenty years, and Britain and France immediately took action in their respective spheres.

There was one additional settlement in this era of treaties and engagements. In March 1921, Winston Churchill, who was then colonial secretary, held a lengthy conference in Cairo with most of the British Middle Eastern experts, including Sir Herbert Samuel and Sir Percy Cox, high commissioners for Palestine and Iraq, respectively. They hatched a scheme that put Faysal, ousted by the French from Damascus, on the throne of Iraq and carved from the part of Palestine east of the Jordan the state of Transjordan for Prince Abdallah, who originally had been promised Iraq. Since the British did not wish to be under any obligation to the French in getting oil out through Syria, a section of the Syrian desert was claimed for Transjordan. This created a British-controlled route from Mosul to the Mediterranean.

Allied Occupation of Turkey

The Allies were not faring too well in the Turkish parts of the Ottoman Empire. On November 13, 1918, a combined Allied fleet traversed the Bosphorus and dropped anchor in the Golden Horn. Ten days later an Allied army under a French general entered Istanbul. Soon thereafter, British, French, Italian, and American high commissioners arrived to assume responsibility for the four zones established in the city. Istanbul immediately attracted Western commercial interest, and imports into Turkey to satisfy the lack of goods in the war years gave the city many characteristics of a boom town, which the occupational forces did not dispel. Greeks and Armenians in Turkey welcomed the Allies as liberators, and foreign residents rejoiced that the war was safely over and their fellow Westerners were returning to control the situation. The Allies rolled back time to 1914: the capitulations were restored; the Ottoman Public Debt Administration functioned again; and concession hunting became once more the sport of the day.

At first the Turks were relieved that the fighting had terminated, since they were genuinely weary of war; there had been more than the usual share of orphans, refugees, invalids, and general victims. As the occupation proceeded, however, thoughtful Turks grew dismayed at the Allies' lack of justice, understanding, and political wisdom. It soon became apparent that Sultan Mehmed VI and his ministers were only convenient Allied puppets. (Following the armistice successive grand viziers were Izzet Pasha, Tevfik Pasha, and Damad Ferid Pasha.) It also became clear that Anatolia would be carved up, if the Allies could agree on a partition without fighting among themselves.

Britain moved northward from Mosul; France claimed Cilicia as an extension of Syria; and Italian forces landed at Antalya to assure that promises would be fulfilled. One of the tragedies of the time was initiated, when under cover of an Allied fleet Greek troops landed at Izmir to take possession of what the Greeks had been awarded in Paris. Supported by Britain and France, Venizelos had won Wilson over to the Greek occupation, which began on May 15, 1919. Small incidents of organized Turkish resistance occurred almost immediately, and a few atrocities committed by the Greeks, especially at the village of Menemen near Izmir, made Turkish acceptance of Greek rule in Asia Minor impossible.

Turkish Nationalists
The day following the Greek landing at Izmir, Mustafa Kemal Pasha, appointed as inspector general of the Third Army by the Allied high commissioners and the sultan, sailed for Samsun on the Black Sea coast with orders to commence demobilization and restore law and peace to Anatolia. Before the summer was over Kemal resigned his commission and convened rebellious national congresses at Erzerum and Sivas, calling for all patriotic Turks to join the Association for the Defense of the Rights of Turkey in Europe and Anatolia.

The Greek landing at Izmir produced extensive street demonstrations in Istanbul; resentment toward the Allies swelled. Ferid Pasha's government was dismissed in October, and a new cabinet was formed under Ali Riza Pasha, who, it was hoped, would reach an accord with Kemal and the nationalists of the Sivas congress. As the strength of the nationalists grew in Istanbul, many members of the Ottoman parliament in Istanbul openly supported the movement. In January 1920 they drew up a six-point program as the basis for a lasting peace. It proposed self-determination for the Arabs, western Thrace, and the eastern provinces of Kars, Ardahan, and Batum; complete political and economic unity and independence of Turkish areas; international protection of minorities; and internationalization of the Straits, if Istanbul were guaranteed as a secure residence for the sultan-caliph. The increasing popularity of the nationalists in Istanbul and the active collaboration of many leaders with them spurred the British in March 1920 to occupy the city of Istanbul with a strong military force. Ali Riza was replaced by Salih Pasha. Nationalist leaders and prominent Turks who were unable to hide or flee to Anatolia to Mustafa Kemal were seized and sent to Malta.

Heretofore, the occupation had been nominal. With the British in full control, patriotic Turks flocked to Kemal and his nationalists. In April 1920 a Grand National Assembly met at Ankara, adopted the six-point program, and elected Kemal as its president. Sultan Mehmed VI dismissed the parliament, and Damad Ferid Pasha became grand vizir for the second time. The Turkish resistance was now fully committed to fight for freedom and independence.

The Allies never imagined that the "sick man" of Europe, after the punishment he had taken during World War I, could ever rise from his coma. They reasoned that the noises and movements in the interior were only the sounds and twitchings preceding death. The San Remo Conference blithely beckoned the Powers to the Treaty of Sèvres and its unreality. Greece was given western and eastern Thrace, including Edirne and territory up to a line twenty miles from Istanbul. The district and city of Izmir would be administered by Greece for five years, after which a plebiscite would determine its future. Armenia was established as an independent state, whose frontier with Turkey would be arbitrated by President Wilson. Kurdistan, east of the Euphrates River, obtained local autonomy, which might be transferred to independence upon the consent of the League of Nations. Although Istanbul remained under Turkish sovereignty, the Straits area was to be controlled by an international commission. Turkey would maintain an army of 50,000 men, all armaments being under Allied supervision. Minority rights were respected. New, humiliating articles were added to the reestablished capitulations. And the Ottoman Public Debt Administration under British, French, and Italian direction was given almost absolute control over economic, financial, and budgetary matters. Equally galling to the Turks was the announcement of the Tripartite Agreement among England, France, and Italy, dividing what remained of Turkey into three spheres of influence almost exactly along the line marked by wartime secret treaties. The Treaty of Sèvres left Turkey prostrate, and no self-respecting Turk could countenance it.

It was little wonder that Mustafa Kemal and the nationalists in Ankara were alternately termed bandits and futile wild men and their movement often thought of as a hoax. They faced the British in Istanbul and the Straits, Greeks at Izmir, Italians at Antalya, French at Adana and in Cilicia, British in Kurdistan, and Armenians in the northeastern vilayets. Fortunately for Kemal, the enemy never presented a concerted attack, and he was able to meet them one by one.

Mustafa Kemal

Modern Turkish nationalism, conceived in the latter part of the nineteenth century and nourished by the poems and polemics of the Young Turk period, was born in 1919 and 1920. It first saw the light of day on the plateaus of central Anatolia, and its birth pangs were a series of wars for independence against the several enemies cited above. Mustafa Kemal, its military and political midwife, was born in Salonika in 1881. He belonged to the lower middle class and attended military schools in Monastir and Istanbul, where he distinguished himself in mathematics and oratory. As an officer he served in Damascus and Monastir and took an active part in the various revolutionary societies that honeycombed the army in the days prior to and after the Young Turk Revolution of 1908. He served in Libya in the war against Italy and participated briefly in the Balkan wars. The outbreak of war in 1914 found him military attaché to Sofia, but he soon effected his transfer and became one of General Liman von Sanders' most valued Turkish officers in the Gallipoli campaign. By 1918 he had commanded armies on every Turkish front.

Mustafa Kemal possessed a brilliant, razor-edged mind. He demanded first-rate performance by himself and those about and beneath him. An early teacher had given him the sobriquet *"Kemal"* (Perfection), a name he eventually came to use almost exclusively. Kemal was contemptuous of pomp and hollow ceremony, and sometimes gave the appearance of being vicious. Although a devoted nationalist with energy, an indomitable will, and an incorruptibility that was frightening to many, he was completely wild and licentious in his private life—usually to the total consternation of foreign statesmen and political analysts.

At Ankara in 1920 this great leader, tough and uncompromising, stood as a Turkish nationalist hopelessly defying the victors of World War I. He commanded the scanty resources of a dozen poor upland provinces of central Asia Minor, bedraggled veterans of several scattered armies, and an enthusiastic band of patriots trailing in from Istanbul. However, the crack, undefeated Turkish Ninth Army, which had operated in the Caucasus and marched to the Caspian Sea, served as a fine nucleus, and Kemal organized an undaunted force about them. In the spring of 1920 he drove the French back to Aleppo and signed an armistice removing them from the combat. Then the Turks under Kiazim Karabekir Pasha captured Kars and with the help of the Bolsheviks crushed the Armenian forces. The Treaty of Gümrü in December 1920 ceded Batum to Russia in exchange for the provinces of Kars and Ardahan. A few months later the Treaty of Moscow confirmed this new frontier and pledged Russian aid against the imperialists' aims in Turkey. In March 1921 Kemal reached an agreement whereby the Italians, for certain well-defined economic concessions, evacuated Antalya and Scala Nuova, south of Izmir. Consequently, by the opening of the summer of 1921 Kemal faced only the Greek army and some weak British occupational contingents on the Straits.

Turkish-Greek War

Since June 1920 the Allies, through British insistence, had assigned to the Greeks the task of protecting the Allied position in Turkey, "liberating" the country from the Kemalists, and enforcing the peace terms upon the Turks. Immediately, Greek armies advanced in Thrace and Anatolia. Over the following fourteen months they had remarkable success, taking Edirne in Europe and Afyon-Karahisar, Kutahya, Eskishehr, and Izmit in Asia Minor. The only victories Kemal could show were the two tactical battles of Inönü, where Colonel Ismet won lasting fame in 1921.

Time, however, was on Kemal's side. Britain and France quarreled over German reparations, the question of the Rhineland, and a host of other problems. These quarrels finally caused a break over Turkish policies. Franklin-Bouillon was sent to Ankara, where a secret treaty of peace and friendship between France and the nationalist government was concluded in October 1921. Evidently foreseeing Kemal's victory, France recognized him unofficially in order to get in on the ground floor in an economic reorganization that would include the development of the rich resources of Asia Minor. French munitions actually made their way to Ankara.

King Alexander of Greece died from the bite of his pet monkey in October 1920. He was succeeded by his father, Constantine, who was recalled from exile. The British distrusted Constantine, and when the Greeks refused to heed British advice against the Anatolian venture, the British decided to let them manage it on their own. King Constantine called for an advance upon Ankara, while Lord Curzon searched for an honorable way out for England. In February 1921 Bekir Sami, the foreign minister of the Ankara government, gladly accepted an invitation to a London conference. The Greeks, however, eschewed the conference, since Lloyd George was guardedly encouraging them to press on against the Turks. After the French and Italian reconciliations with Kemal and a second failure at peace by Curzon, the Allies officially declared their neutrality. Lloyd George could promise the Greeks only his political assistance. Although arms were denied the Greeks, the nationalists were obtaining war matériel from France, Italy, and Russia.

The Greek advance was checked by the three-week Battle of Sakarya, which ended in September 1921. Stubborn and heroic Turkish resistance and extended Greek lines of communication decided the issue, although the Kemalists needed a whole year to regroup their forces for the victorious rush upon Izmir. The Greek generals recognized their plight and informed the Allies that Greece would be unable to enforce the Treaty of Sèvres upon Turkey unless they could occupy Istanbul. This condition was abhorrent to the British, who hoped to incorporate Istanbul in their empire through the device of an international commission which they would control.

After the Turkish victory on the Sakarya lines on August 26, 1922, the rout became general: The Turks won the Battle of Dumlupinar on August 30; Greek General Tricoupis and his staff were captured September 2; Mustafa Kemal entered Izmir on September 11; and by September 19 all

Greek forces were cleared from Anatolia. The war with Greece had been won, but intense bitterness remained. The Greek army in retreat pursued a scorched-earth policy and committed atrocities against defenseless Turkish villagers in its path. Shortly after the occupation of Izmir fire broke out and destroyed nearly half of the city. Who started the fire has never been determined, but once under way explosions of hidden Greek bombs and ammunition supplies rendered it uncontrollable.

From Izmir the nationalists turned to the Straits. French and Italian forces at the Dardanelles crossed to the European side, leaving the British to hold the positions. Lloyd George called in vain upon the Dominions for reinforcements as the fleet stood by. General Harrington, in command of the Straits, recognized the hopelessness of his position without more troops. He arranged an armistice between the Allies and the government of the Grand National Assembly, which was signed at Mudanya on October 11, 1922. Eastern Thrace with Edirne was ceded to the Turks, and the proposition for a conference to negotiate peace was accepted. Kemal had won; the British postwar policy for Turkey collapsed, taking Lloyd George with it.

Lausanne Conference

Invitations to meet at Lausanne were issued on October 27, 1922. Kemal accepted on October 31. A similar invitation to the sultan's government compelled the Grand National Assembly to pass a law on November 1 deposing Mehmed VI and voiding all laws of his government. Refet Pasha took over control of the city for the nationalists on November 5, and Mehmed VI fled aboard a British cruiser for Malta. On November 18 the Grand National Assembly chose Mehmed's cousin, Abdul Mejid, as caliph. The Ottoman Empire had come to its end.

Convening on November 20, 1922, the Lausanne Conference had a stormy course and one adjournment before the final acts were signed on July 24, 1923. England, France, Italy, Russia, Japan, Bulgaria, Rumania, Yugoslavia, Greece, and Turkey participated in the deliberations and signed one or more of the several documents drawn up. The United States sent only unofficial observers, who did, however, from time to time take an active part in discussions. Lord Curzon, the British foreign minister, dominated the conference until it broke up; his imperious six-feet-four-inch figure was a sharp contrast to that of the Turkish delegate, Ismet Pasha, who was only five feet four inches tall. Few people had ever seen or heard of Ismet until this conference, and all predicted he could hardly be a match for the foreign minister of Great Britain. But Ismet proved to be a stubborn, inflexible, and skillful negotiator. After all, the Turkish people were willing to fight again to obtain independence, whereas the British had just sacked their prime minister rather than run the risk of further war. Frequently, when Lord Curzon would arrogantly deliver some advice and admonition, he would become infuriated almost to the breaking point when Ismet, who was a trifle deaf, would cup his bad ear and say: "Répétez-vous, s'il vous plaît?"

At the conference eastern Thrace with Edirne went with full sovereignty to Turkey. Of the Aegean Islands, Tenedos and Imbros went to Turkey, the Dodecanese to Italy, and the remainder to Greece. The settlement with regard to the Straits, in which the Russian delegate Chicherin participated, gave Turkey full sovereignty over the area. It was, however, stipulated that each shore be demilitarized to a depth of fifteen kilometers and that navigation of the Straits be regulated according to terms of a special international convention enacted concurrently with the Treaty of Lausanne. The Mosul frontier was left to be negotiated at a later date directly between Turkey and Britain, the latter acting for the kingdom of Iraq. In regard to the Armenian and Greek minorities Turkey accepted articles similar to minority clauses inserted in treaties with Austria, Hungary, and Bulgaria, and the Greeks agreed to a compulsory exchange of populations, excluding the Greeks of Istanbul and the Turks of western Thrace. The capitulations and the privileges of foreigners in Turkey were abolished entirely. Financial questions were settled by terminating the Ottoman Public Debt Administration in all of its manifestations and by a proportionate assumption of Ottoman debts by all successor states. Finally, the Allies accepted the cancellation of all prewar concessions and contracts, and Turkey agreed not to alter her tariff for five years after the Treaty of Lausanne came into force.

The conference broke temporarily in February 1923 over the last three points. Before the conference reconvened in April, the Grand National Assembly rejected any compromise on Ismet's stand, Lord Curzon was replaced, and the Turks threw a real scare into the Allies by granting a concession for the development of oil, railroads, and other resources to an American group headed by retired Admiral Chester. The United States government protested that it was not actively supporting the Chester group, but when the conference reopened, the new American listener, Joseph C. Grew, let it be known that the United States expected to share in any development of oil resources in Turkey and the Middle East. Such a declaration provided a salutary rein upon British and French ambitions and paved the way for a relaxation of demands upon the Turks.

Ismet went home to Ankara in the summer with the knowledge that Turkey was recognized as an independent free nation, except for the demilitarization of the Straits and the undefined border with Iraq. A modified version of the Lausanne Treaty was signed between the United States government and Turkey, but it was rejected by the American Senate in 1927. Since Turkey and the United States had never been at war, a peace treaty was really not necessary and regular diplomatic relations were resumed late in 1927, when Joseph C. Grew was received at Ankara as ambassador.

The exchange of populations between Turkey and Greece, begun in the summer of 1923 under the aegis of the League of Nations, proceeded over many months. One and a half million Greeks and half a million Turks were moved, at considerable hardship to the individuals involved. The impact upon Greece was most serious. Turkey lost a valuable merchant and commercial class, but Ismet argued at Lausanne that such a loss would be more than offset by the advantages of a homogeneous and united Turkish nation.

The Treaty of Lausanne and its various conventions was ratified during the summer of 1923. On October 29, 1923, just nine years after the Ottoman Empire entered World War I, the Grand National Assembly in Ankara declared Turkey a republic and elected Ghazi Mustafa Kemal Pasha president.

REFERENCES: Chapter 31

Works important to this chapter are cited in Chapters 7, 13, 18, 19, 22, 23, 24, 25, 26, 27, 28, 29, and 30.

Armstrong, Harold. *Turkey in Travail: The Birth of a New Nation.* London: Lane, 1925. The story of the Turkish Revolution.

Bovis, H. Eugene. *The Jerusalem Question, 1917–1968.* Stanford, Calif.: Hoover Institution Press, 1971. An absolutely invaluable source of information.

Busch, Briton Cooper. *Mudros to Lausanne: Britain's Frontier in West Asia, 1918–1923.* Albany: State University of New York Press, 1976. A study of British policy in the area between the Straits and Central Asia after the breakup of the Ottoman and Russian empires and the emergence of a new balance of power.

Cummings, H. H. *Franco-British Rivalry in the Post-War Near East.* London: Oxford University Press, 1938. Discusses the decline of French influence after World War I.

Edib (Adivar), Halidé. *The Turkish Ordeal.* New York: Century, 1928. Written by a Western-educated Turkish woman who participated in the Turkish struggle for independence.

Edmonds, C. J. *Kurds, Turks and Arabs: Politics, Travel, and Research in North-Eastern Iraq, 1919–1925.* London: Oxford University Press, 1957. A detailed record in the first person of the problems and settlement of the Mosul border region.

Grunwald, Kurt, and Joachim O. Ronall. *Industrialization in the Middle East.* New York: Council for Middle Eastern Affairs Press, 1960. After fine topical chapters, including ones on human and natural resources and financial problems, the authors have a chapter for each of the countries of the area except Saudi Arabia, Kuwayt, Yemen, and Libya, which are lumped together.

Hanna, Paul L. *British Policy in Palestine.* Washington: American Council on Public Affairs, 1942. The activities and interests of the British in the area.

Helmreich, Paul C. *From Paris to Sèvres: The Partition of the Ottoman Empire at the Peace Conference of 1919–1920.* Columbus: Ohio State University Press, 1974. A thorough examination of most of the sources for the war period, including the British archives. Objective and very well organized topically and chronologically.

Howard, Harry N. *The King-Crane Commission: An American Inquiry in the Middle East.* Beirut: Khayats, 1963. A definitive work by the leading authority on the subject, based on an examination and critical study of all the sources available.

Klieman, Aaron S. *Foundations of British Policy in the Arab World: The Cairo Conference of 1921.* Baltimore: Johns Hopkins University Press, 1970. A first-rate account of this historic and prestigious meeting, drawn from official sources.

Manuel, Frank E. *The Realities of American-Palestine Relations.* Washington: Public Affairs Press, 1949. Chapters IV, V, and VI provide great detail on Palestine at the Peace Conference.

Monroe, Elizabeth. *Britain's Moment in the Middle East, 1914–1956.* Baltimore: Johns Hopkins Press, 1963. A comprehensive and objective survey.

Sonyel, Salahi Ramsdan. *Turkish Diplomacy, 1918–1923: Mustafa Kemal and the Turkish National Movement.* London: Sage Publications, 1975. A very clear and sober study of the international diplomacy of the period centering around the diplomacy of the nationalists. Based on archival and primary sources in Turkish and Western languages.

Temperley, H. W. V. *A History of the Peace Conference of Paris.* Vol. VI. London: Henry Frowde & Hodder & Stoughton, 1924. By one of the British experts and historians at the conference.

Toynbee, Arnold J. *Survey of International Affairs, 1925.* Vol. I, *The Islamic World since the Peace Settlement.* London: Oxford University Press, 1927.

———. *The Western Question in Greece and Turkey.* London: Constable, 1922. An account of the events in Turkey after 1918.

Toynbee, Arnold J., and K. P. Kirkwood, *Turkey.* London: Ernest Benn, 1926. A survey of the background of the Turkish Revolution.

Chapter 32

The Turkish Republic Under Atatürk

Establishment of the Republic

On October 29, 1923, the Grand National Assembly voted approval of a declaration asserting that "the form of government of the Turkish State is a Republic." That same day it elected Ghazi Mustafa Kemal Pasha president of the republic. The idea of a republic, however, was not entirely novel, and its declaration only revealed an evolution proceeding naturally since the autumn of 1919.

The shift of power and representation of the Turkish nation from the sultan's government to Kemal's occurred in October 1919, when the nationalists proved strong enough to prompt the sultan and his supporters to dismiss the Ferid Pasha cabinet, call for the election of a new parliament, and induce the new cabinet of Ali Riza Pasha to seek an accord with them. Although Kemal failed to persuade the newly elected parliament to sit at Ankara, it adopted so much of his program that the British fully occupied Istanbul "to protect" the sultan. Kemal then called for the convening of an extraordinary Grand National Assembly. It met on April 23, 1920, at Ankara, recognized the prisoner-like status of the sultan, and declared that there was "no power superior to the Grand National Assembly." Kemal became its president and a council of state was elected to serve as the executive arm of the Ankara government, as it was called.

The Grand National Assembly, however, continued to debate whether it was a permanent or provisional government until January 30, 1921, when it passed ten fundamental articles of government as amendments to the Ottoman constitution of 1876. These articles established the assembly as a permanent institution, to be elected every two years. They also served as the basis of government until April 20, 1924, when a new constitution was adopted. Meanwhile, a second assembly was elected in April 1923, giving Kemal and his cohorts at the reopening of the Lausanne conference a strong mandate in their uncompromising stand for full financial, economic, and administrative independence. It was this second assembly in Ankara—something akin to a rump parliament—that proclaimed the republic and later adopted the constitution.

Meanwhile, Kemal's Association for the Defense of the Rights of Turkey in Europe and Anatolia changed into the People's party *(Halk Firkasi)* in 1922 and then in 1923 to the Republican People's party *(Cumhuriyet Halk*

Firkasi). Kemal as president of the People's party used frequent party caucuses for debate and formulation of policy; at these meetings, often continuing through the night, actual government policy decisions were made. While the Greek war was in progress goals were easy to determine, but after the Mudanya armistice Kemal used every wile and force at his command to carry through his points. When Ismet found Lord Curzon intractable at Lausanne, many Anatolian leaders of the party counseled direct military action against the British in Istanbul as the best solution. This step, which would have been highly successful initially, was skillfully countered by Kemal, who understood how the Allies would eventually react.

Before the constitution was adopted, a fundamental change had been made in the religio-political structure of the state. When Mehmed VI left Istanbul for Malta in 1922, the Grand National Assembly declared the caliphate vacant and elected to that office Abdul Mejid, who had never masked his sympathy for the nationalist cause. Certainly, Kemal and his associates were not prepared to shock the conservative majority of Turks by destroying the position precipitously. Moreover, the anomaly of a caliph without temporal power was not clearly understood, for in many Turkish minds he was equated to the pope. However, after the nationalists became aware of the power conflict they could not countenance a caliph who was responsible for the enforcement of Sacred Law and yet only a figurehead for certain temporal traditions.

When voices were raised in the Grand National Assembly on the topic of the caliphate, Kemal proposed that it be abolished and that ecclesiastical schools be closed. The proposal was thoroughly debated at a party caucus in March 1924 and enacted by the Assembly the following day. In addition, the Ottoman family was banished from Turkey, and the Sacred Law courts were abolished. The functions of the ministries governing pious foundations were transferred to a newly created presidency of religious affairs under the immediate supervision of the prime minister, who in a veiled sense became caliph.

Until the spring of 1924 the Turkish government followed the provisions of the Ottoman constitution of 1876 except where it had been modified. The widely anticipated Constitution of the Republic was promulgated on April 20, 1924. Drawn up without too much controversy, it stated that sovereignty resided in the Turkish nation, whose representative was the Grand National Assembly. It declared all Turks equal before the law and forbade special privileges for groups or individuals. A Turk was defined as anyone who is a citizen of the Turkish Republic, without distinction as to race or creed. Freedom of speech, thought, press, and travel were guaranteed. The religion of the state was declared to be Islam; the language, Turkish; and the seat of government, Ankara.

The government established by the constitution was in form a democracy but was in fact, at that time and for twenty years to follow, a one-party government controlled by Kemal and his close political associates. The Grand National Assembly was elected for a four-year term by universal male suffrage. (Women received the vote in 1934.) The president of the republic was elected by the Assembly from its membership for a similar term. The president appointed the prime minister, who selected his cabinet from the deputies with the approval of the president and consent of the Assembly. Until 1945 the machinery of government was almost entirely in the hands of the Republican People's party. Candidates for election as deputies from the various districts to the Grand National Assembly were nominated by that party, and only one slate of names was presented to voters. Party caucuses determined who ran for which office and from which province. Debates in the Grand National Assembly were largely perfunctory. Kemal made the final decisions.

Mustafa Kemal Pasha was correctly labeled a dictator: he determined high policy, selected high officials of state, and forced his will upon the party and nation. But in most matters affecting the nation and the public at large he was careful to prepare the people by skillfully organized speeches before action was taken. Kemal was convinced that he knew what was best for the Turkish people and also knew the best way to obtain it. His abiding ambition was for the Turkish people, not for himself. In this way he was a benevolent dictator and extremely popular. Had there been free elections in Turkey while he lived there can be little doubt but that he would have been elected and reelected president of the republic.

Following acceptance of the new constitution and regularization of the republican regime, further reforms came at a bewildering tempo. Whenever possible Kemal and other leaders toured throughout Anatolia, explaining the necessity of what was being done and publicizing new reforms about to be introduced. Kemal turned toward the West and its democratic traditions rather than to Soviet experiments then in progress on Turkey's northern and eastern frontiers. Turkey's leaders had been educated in the West or influenced by teachers who had received much of their training in the West. In this connection one of the more important schools was Galatasaray Lycée in Istanbul, where the language of instruction was French and traditions were definitely French and Western.

Reforms touched every aspect of life and society in Turkey in the 1920s and 1930s. In the earlier period change was rapid and followed no clear pattern of planned or coordinated development. Perhaps sensing the difficulty of keeping in mind the sequence of these reforms, Kemal terminated the uncoordinated and rather haphazard course of modernization in 1931. Terming the entire program "Kemalism," he defined his reforms along six broad classifications. These six became the party's campaign platform for the elections of 1935 and were adopted as the basic principles of the new Turkish nation when they were incorporated into the constitution by amendment in 1937. They were: republicanism, secularism, populism, nationalism, statism, and reformism.

Article 1 of the constitution reads: *The Turkish State is a Republic.* Kemal could have made himself king or sultan. He insisted upon a republic, though, because it was more Western and more democratic and because he believed it suited Turkey. But conservative elements, clients of the Ottoman family, the religious hierarchy, and the devout clung to the old order. Kemal ensured the permanence of the republic by instituting sweeping legal reforms in 1926.

Abolishing the caliphate and closing the Shariah courts did not change the basis of law in Turkey. Law reforms in the nineteenth century had Westernized the commercial and criminal laws, but civil law and legal procedures were still tied to Sacred Law, which hardly fitted a twentieth-century republic. In the autumn of 1925 a new law school opened in Ankara to instruct lawyers and judges in the fundamentals of Western laws. Then, early in 1926, the Grand National Assembly adopted the new Civil Code and Debts Law, based on Swiss law; the new Penal Code, taken from Italian law; and the new Commercial Code, which was a modification of the German Code. These went into effect later in the year, and since 1927 Turkish law has been an outgrowth of the European Napoleonic Code. With new codes of a Western and secular nature thoroughly installed, the old regime became such an outmoded way of life that any departure from the republic was unthinkable.

Secularization

The second most important reform movement was the secularization of the state and society. Islam pervaded all aspects of life in Turkey, and Kemal and many leaders subscribed to the theory, learned from their contacts with the West, that Islam's hold upon society retarded development and created the difference between West and East. Friday, the Muslim holy day, was made a compulsory day of rest throughout the land in 1924, in part to give the day another emphasis. In 1925 dervish orders were forbidden, and their tekkes, holy shrines, and mausoleums were closed. Most startling of all in that year was the law forbidding men to wear the fez and ordering all headgear to have a brim or a visor. Earlier, Kemal was photographed in a straw Panama, and the armed services were outfitted in Western-style military caps. The fez was considered a Muslim symbol, although it came from Europe at the time of Mahmud II. The veil was never outlawed, but its use was discouraged in every possible way.

Adoption of the Swiss Civil Code in 1926 brought many secular changes. The Muslim calendar for legal, official, and everyday use was abandoned and replaced by the Western Gregorian calendar. Everywhere the Muslim year of 1342 became 1926, although the Muslim calendar was still employed in calculating Ramazan, the month of fasting, and all other religious holidays.

A far-reaching effect of Western law was the end of polygamy and the new status of women. Since not very many men had been able to afford more than one wife, the prohibition against polygamy was not very drastic, but the altered condition of life for women began to change the whole fabric of Turkish society.

Progress in secularization went so far that in 1928 the constitution was amended, removing the statement that Turkey is an Islamic state and providing that government officials, on being inducted into office, would swear on their honor rather than before God to fulfill their duties. Later, in 1935, the day of rest was changed to Sunday, and the *vikend* (weekend) was established by law from Saturday at 1:00 P.M. to Sunday midnight.

Kemal probably was an atheist, but many about him were sincerely religious. Yet, all deemphasized the place of religion in national life. Fewer individuals observed religious days; in Istanbul and Ankara many persons paid no attention to Ramazan and many children were not taught their prayers. Religious instruction was removed from public and private schools. The faculty of theology at the University of Istanbul enrolled so few that it was consolidated in 1933 with the department of literature. By 1939 Turkey was a secular state, as typical in this respect as France, Germany, or the United States.

Populism

In the Ottoman Empire the capitulations and the millet system gave special privileges to foreigners and to many religious minorities. Moreover, some families and individuals had certain rights and immunities. In the republic, however, Article 69 of the constitution states that all Turks are equal before the law and that all "privileges of whatever description claimed by groups, classes, families, and individuals are abolished and forbidden." It was this idea that Kemal incorporated in the word "populism."

Early Turkish society was democratic in character; certain aspects of ghazi and akhi life were almost communal. Peasant villages in Anatolia still retained many of these traits. The new, free republic of Turkey was won by these peasants, and to them the new Turkish society was dedicated. Tax burdens upon them had always been inordinately heavy, so Kemal in an early speech promised them relief on this score in payment for their efforts in the national struggle. The Grand National Assembly in 1925 abolished the tithe upon their lands, and taxes upon agriculture were lightened in order to stimulate greater production.

Primary education in government-supervised schools became obligatory, as free and universal education was established as another expression of populism. In conformity with the constitutional law for universal education, schools were built by the thousands during this era of Turkish history. Emphasis at first was placed upon teacher training schools, since a lack of teachers handicapped the program's success. Each village was required to have a primary school of five grades. Secondary schools were constructed in the towns to prepare students for various vocations and for entrance to *lycées,* which were the equivalent of American senior high schools and junior colleges. Beyond the *lycée* was the University of Istanbul and, later, Ankara University and specialized schools.

With the illiteracy rate at an estimated 80 percent, the ability to read became a privilege that Kemal desired for all. The Arabic script was never satisfactory for the Turkish language, in which vowels play an important part in word formation. Writing and spelling were arduous exercises, and sometimes to read a specific passage was difficult unless one had some idea of what had been written. In 1928 the Grand National Assembly adopted a new, strictly phonetic Turkish alphabet based on Latin characters; it became compulsory January 1, 1929, and after that date all public signs, newspapers, books, etc., were in the new script. The work involved in the changeover was staggering. New textbooks had to be printed for every subject; in the autumn of 1928 schools opened several weeks late because books were unavailable. The literate had to learn to read and write all over again, and the government erected huge posters to show the new alphabet. Kemal and members of the Grand National Assembly traveled about the country giving public reading lessons in the Latin characters. Changing headgear was relatively easy in comparison to the alphabet transition. But the campaign was effective. Millions learned to read within the next decade, as the illiteracy rate was reduced to approximately 50 percent. Newspapers multiplied, typewriters became less complex, and a modern national life embracing a majority of the population was born.

Adult education has been exceedingly popular in republican Turkey. Beginning with the Young Turk movement in 1908 a program of public education was fostered by the government, first by an organization called the Turkish Hearth *(Türk Ocak),* and after 1932 by the Folk House *(Halkevi).* These organizations had public reading rooms and a staff of leaders who organized athletic, dramatic, musical, social, educational, and inspirational programs for the people. The several hundred such houses that were opened before Kemal's death proved most valuable in spreading the spirit of the new Turkey throughout the land and among all strata of the population.

Nationalism

The fourth point in the Kemalist program was the development of nationalism. The growth of nationalism in the nineteenth century was effected in the Ottoman Empire in diverse ways. Greeks, Serbs, Bulgarians, Armenians, and others were stirred toward autonomy and independence. Nationalist wars of liberation followed, bringing massacres, atrocities, and devastation to Turks as well as to others. Turkish Ottomans, when they were touched by nationalism, often were waylaid by pan-Islamism, pan-Turanism, or a peculiar kind of synthetic Ottoman nationalism. Kemal, almost instinctively, was a fiery Turkish patriot, proud of being a Turk. He set out in his program to make all Turks proud of their race and heritage.

Although all the reforms of the Kemalist regime were tinged with nationalism, none was more pointed than the new histories in the Latin alphabet for elementary and secondary schools. Though the books minimized the history of the Ottoman Turks, in order to forget the centuries after Suleiman I, they set out for the Turks a glorious and significant past. Sumerians and Hittites became Turks. Most non-Semites of Middle Eastern antiquity were claimed as Turks; indeed, all peoples who came from central Asia were classified as Turks. Since the Turkish word for man is *adam* and since Adam traditionally was the first man, it was popularly said that Adam was Turkish and, therefore, that all peoples are Turkish. Individuals who viewed these theories critically were berated, so most skeptics remained silent. Many Turks found genuine satisfaction in these theories, and there was no doubt of their value in generating a more dynamic Turkish national feeling.

For half a century Turkish literature and even newspaper Turkish had been filled with a heavy burden of words taken from Arabic. Since these words were not used in conversational Turkish, they made written Turkish unintelligible to the great majority. After the adoption of the new alphabet the drive to free Turkish from an Arabic vocabulary and even to resurrect Turkish words from obsolescence gained great headway. For a period of several years in the mid-1930s the government published every few weeks a list of new Turkish words and their old equivalents. Since all government publications used the new words and since communications to the government containing old words were often ignored, business concerns and foreign organizations frequently employed someone to keep up with the rapid language changes. As a result Turkish perhaps lost the richness and variety of the Arabic language, but an immeasurable gain came in giving Turks a written language closely resembling their vernacular.

One of the more dramatic and publicized events in Kemal's program of Turkish nationalism was the forced adoption and use of family names. Only a few of the old Turkish families had names, and many did not use them. The Grand National Assembly gave to Kemal the name of *Atatürk* (Father of the Turks); Inönü, to Ismet in honor of his two victories there; and other appropriate names to party leaders. The head of each family went to precinct police headquarters and selected the family name from a list of approved Turkish words and names, or a combination of these. No one else in that district could take that name. Most names had a meaning, such as Biyiklioğlu (son of the man with a mustache), Üstündağ (mountaintop), and Kirkağaçlioğlu (son of the man with forty trees).

At times nationalism seemed to engulf the Turks, and certainly it made them extremely sensitive even to objective and friendly criticism. Whether Atatürk believed in all the theories he supported is debatable, but he certainly believed in the necessity of not tolerating public debate about them. In any case they were efficacious, and Atatürk's slogan, Turkey for the Turks and the Turks for Turkey, was proudly accepted by the nation.

Statism
At Lausanne the most bitter wrangling had been over the capitulations and implications of economic and judicial imperialism. Turkish victory in these presaged the law reforms and the establishment of better court procedures. Economic independence was compromised by the promise not to tamper with the tariff for five years. Kemal's advisers desired to develop the eco-

nomic resources of Turkey and to inaugurate industrialization without too much foreign influence or participation. The unfortunate experience that the Ottoman Empire had suffered from foreign loans, capital, and concessions conditioned Kemal against any repetition for the republic. His idea was that Turkey would develop her own resources and industrialize behind a strong protective tariff that could become effective in 1929.

In view of the impending tariff merchants imported excessive quantities in 1929, raising the trade deficit for that year to over 100 million Turkish pounds. By November the demand for foreign exchange to pay bills began to force down the price of the Turkish pound. Fear and speculation played such havoc with exchange rates that the government introduced rigorous controls over foreign exchange that have never been relaxed completely. Within a short time the Turks discovered that imports and exports could be more easily regulated through exchange control than by tariffs and quotas and that a managed economy could be introduced.

With the depression, Turkey's exports dropped; in consequence there was a tightening on import permits. When, therefore, Herr Schacht proposed an attractive compensation trade agreement with Nazi Germany, the Turks readily accepted. Trade with Germany boomed, and in 1936 over 50 percent of Turkey's exports went to Germany. American tobacco companies found they could buy more cheaply in Hamburg than in Turkish markets. Although Turkey rejoiced that Germans paid higher than world prices for many commodities, she quickly learned that many manufactures of heavy industrial goods were either overpriced in the German market or impossible to buy with blocked marks. To counter this impasse Turkey limited the size of the clearing agreement with Germany and offered a premium in exchange rates for exports to the United States and other hard-currency countries. When World War II broke out, Turkey had clearing agreements with twenty countries and had just entered into a reciprocal trade agreement with the United States.

Kemal understood that agriculture was the principal occupation and resource of his nation and he strove to increase the output. He established a model farm near Ankara, where the latest techniques, modern machinery, and implements were demonstrated for all to see. Activities of the Bank of Agriculture, founded by the Ottomans in 1889, were greatly expanded; its loan service to small farmers was increased, and credit cooperatives were authorized in 1929. Agricultural prices began to be supported by the government in 1932, and in 1933 the Higher Agricultural School was opened in Ankara, later to become a part of Ankara University. With all these aids Turkish farmers improved their national position greatly under the Kemalists, even in the face of a worldwide depression in agricultural prices. When World War II broke out, they were relatively prosperous.

Kemal felt that advances in industry moved too slowly, in contrast to the progress in agriculture. Too few people had any industrial know-how, and those with capital tended to follow the traditional practice of investing in buildings or land. Private industry lagged. On the other hand, government monopolies in matches, tobacco and cigarettes, alcohol, and salt, and the government acquisition and government operation of railroads, harbor facilities, electric utilities, and coastwise steamers were highly successful. Expansion programs were effective, and railroad lines were extended in several areas. From state monopolies and public works Kemal turned to state enterprises. Under government direction the Bank of Affairs aided commerce and to a small degree sponsored industry, but its capital and resources were too limited to give the needed stimulus. Thus, in 1933 the government inaugurated a Five-Year Plan for the development of industry, and the Sümer (Sumerian) Bank was created to own and operate such enterprises. A score of factories were built to produce textiles, paper, glass, sugar, and steel. In 1936 the government established and financed the Eti (Hittite) Bank to do for minerals and the metal industry what the Sümer Bank was accomplishing in other lines.

In Turkey this policy of state enterprises, created and managed by the government, was called "statism" and gave rise to some debate. Some branded the course as a step toward communism and verified their charge by pointing to two substantial loans made by the U.S.S.R. to provide machinery for the Sümer Bank's textile factory at Kayseri. Others claimed it was a kind of autarchy as preached by Hitler and Mussolini and thus linked Atatürk with the two dictators. Still a third group supported it strongly, asserting that it was a type of state capitalism that would develop the nation without creating individuals of great power and wealth such as Rockefeller, Carnegie, Morgan, and Ford. Different views were held even in high places in the Republican People's party. And in 1937 when Ismet Inönü resigned as prime minister and was replaced by Celal Bayar, the minister of economy, a rumor circulated that Atatürk had brought in the latter because he was a more enthusiastic believer in statism.

Continuing Reform

The sixth and final arrow on the shield of Kemalism stood for reformism. By this Atatürk meant opposition to blind conservatism and a rigid adherence to the *status quo.* He did not believe in change for change's sake, but he knew all too well how reformers grow old and conservative, especially when they hold responsible government posts. Kemal wanted his revolution to evolve and expand, as a continuing process. The program with respect to women fell into this category. He wished more than just a change in their legal status and costume. He compelled wives of cabinet ministers to learn to dance; he encouraged girls to become airplane pilots; and he opened the way for women to become lawyers, doctors, bankers, and public officials. Of 399 members elected to the Grand National Assembly in 1935, 17 were women.

Another important change was in regard to sports. Early Ottomans were keen sports enthusiasts and had competitions in archery, polo, horse racing, wrestling, and many other sports. In the eighteenth century there was a complete reversal; physical exertion was looked upon as degrading and sports participation as undignified. Before Atatürk died in 1938 every city had several sports clubs. Turkey sent entries to the Olympics and to the Balkan Games. And soccer (*futbol*) became the new national sport, which boys and girls everywhere played with great enthusiasm.

The old Ottoman government was corrupt in almost every detail. Bribes and tips (baksheesh) were universal, and everyone knew that the magnitude of the service or permission governed the size of the baksheesh. Kemal was ruthless in his treatment of this custom; and although it did not disappear entirely, anyone in the government found guilty of it was speedily dismissed and prosecuted. When it was intimated that one of Kemal's secretaries of long service accepted a silver cigarette case for some service rendered, he was suddenly appointed ambassador to a foreign capital and soon thereafter recalled and dismissed.

One of the most fruitful reforms had to do with the idea of the role of destiny in human affairs. If some unpleasant circumstance developed or an unfortunate event occurred, the natural reaction was to shrug the shoulders and blame it on God and fate. Through persistent education and practical demonstrations in sanitation, orderly government, and mental attitudes, one heard it freely said that an individual's destiny rested in one's own hands, and the responsibility for mishaps should not be blamed on any supernatural force.

Turkish Politics

Even though there was only one political party under Kemal through most of this period, and all politicians supported the six points of Kemalism, it should not be assumed that there was no politics in Turkey. Ismet Pasha became prime minister on October 30, 1923, immediately after the proclamation of the republic and the election of Kemal as president, and remained in office for thirteen months, when he was replaced by Fethi Bey, another member of Kemal's party. At that time the Progressive party was organized by members of the nationalist movement in opposition to Kemal. They were a motley, disaffected group. Some were ultraconservatives who wished to restore the sultan-caliph; some were personally ambitious; and others were genuine liberal democrats who looked askance upon Kemal's forceful and dictatorial methods and hoped for true democratic procedures.

Fethi proved to be a poor administrator, and Ismet returned to power in March 1925. Immediately, he pushed through a law for the maintenance of order under which a Tribunal of Independence was set up. A few dissidents were tried as enemies of the state, still fewer executed, and others exiled. Newspapers were closed, and editors such as the illustrious Ahmet Emin were exiled for varying lengths of time. The liberal Halidé Edib and her husband, Dr. Adnan Adivar, left Turkey and lived in various places in Europe until the exile laws were repealed and political amnesty to all, even to Ottoman royalty, was declared in 1938. Needless to say, the Progressive party was disbanded. Disturbances among the Kurdish tribes in the southeastern provinces were attributed to these political events.

Elections for the Grand National Assembly took place in 1927, and Kemal was chosen president for his second term. At a nine-day Congress of the Republican People's party just before the meeting of the Assembly, Kemal made an historic six-day speech, reviewing in detail the events of the resurrection of the Turkish nation from its abject defeat and humiliation at the Mudros armistice in 1918 to the year 1927. Feeling more secure, Kemalists withdrew the laws for the maintenance of order in 1929; the following spring Kemal invited Fethi Bey, then ambassador to France, to return and form an opposition party. The Liberal party, as it was called, drew to its support many disgruntled persons from Istanbul and Izmir, where the worldwide depression and new tariffs were affecting commerce adversely. The Liberals called for more free enterprise and less statism, claiming that the Republicans were too slow in improving the national economy. They were successful enough to frighten the Republicans, and when a few political rallies ended in disorderly fights, Kemal judged that the time had not yet arrived when Turkey might have more than one party. Fethi's party was disbanded in 1930. The quadrennial elections, held in 1931, reaffirmed the Republican party's hold on the nation, as Kemal was elected to a third term. A few members were designated as "independents," but almost immediately thereafter new reforms such as the *Halkevi* program and the establishment of the Sümer Bank were undertaken to answer the charges advanced by the Liberal party.

Conditions improved; the Republican party went to the polls in 1935 without opposition; and Atatürk entered his fourth term. This time, thirteen "independents" were elected. In October 1937 Ismet Inönü resigned again as prime minister, to be replaced by Celal Bayar. Although Kemal and Ismet had worked together for seventeen years, basically they were of very different temperaments. Their mutual belief in party discipline, strong public authority, and central control kept them together. But differences in foreign affairs relating to Italy in the Mediterranean and France in Syria led to the break.

Atatürk died November 10, 1938. Excessive drinking and a profligate personal life eventually undermined his iron constitution. His death was a shock to the nation, and the emotional wave it unleashed demonstrated the love and devotion that he had won from the Turkish people. Inönü was elected president the following day, and the Republican People's party carried on with only a slight break. Bayar soon stepped down from the prime ministership, and more conservative steps were taken in government practices and directions. A new Grand National Assembly was elected in 1939, and Inönü became president again for a full four-year term. Europe and the world were entering into the stages preparatory to World War II. Inönü was faced with this as well as with additional problems of Turkish development.

International Affairs

The remarkable internal progress of Turkey and the relatively smooth sailing of Kemal's domestic politics were paralleled by success in the foreign field. The Treaty of Lausanne left the undetermined frontier with Iraq to be settled directly with Great Britain as trustee for Iraq. Negotiations dragged on and reached a highly inflammable point in 1925. Kemal became convinced, with considerable justification, that Britain was fomenting Kurdish revolts in the southeast. To stir the Kurdish tribes was not difficult; the Mosul province, the area in dispute, had a large Kurdish population whose leaders wanted an independent Kurdistan. Moreover, Kurds within Turkey resisted the centralization process and secularization program of the nationalists. On several occasions war over Mosul was debated in party caucuses in Ankara, but peace prevailed. In 1926 a treaty was signed and ratified by England and Turkey, giving Mosul to Iraq. The question of Mosul oil was raised, and allegations were hurled that oil was the real bone of contention. British interests controlled the Mosul concession, which under Turkish sovereignty might be lost. For a time American oil interests supported Turkish claims, but when American companies were allocated nearly a quarter of Mosul oil their fervor for Turkish possession cooled. The treaty did, however, give Turkey 10 percent of all oil royalties paid by the concessionaire to Iraq for the following twenty-five years. Turkey promptly settled for a cash payment of £500,000 from Iraq.

Relations with Greece after the exchange of populations improved rapidly. Venizelos made a state visit to Turkey and was received with much fanfare in Istanbul and Ankara. In 1930 conferences held in Athens led to friendly understandings among Turkey, Greece, Bulgaria, Rumania, Yugoslavia, and Albania. Such meetings were repeated annually; in 1934 the Balkan Pact or Entente was signed, guaranteeing all frontiers and pledging collective security for the Balkans. However, Bulgaria and Albania refused to adhere, because other members declined to discuss minority questions or territorial revision.

In July 1932 Turkey was admitted to membership in the League of Nations, and in 1934 was elected to a seat on the Council. For a small nation Turkey took an active part in league affairs. She cooperated with league efforts to control illicit traffic in narcotics and maintain collective security. She supported Republican Spain and recognized the full implications of Mussolini's policy of regaining the Roman empire for Italy.

Almost immediately after Italy's attack upon Ethiopia Turkey entered into diplomatic action for changing the demilitarized status of the Straits. Undeclared wars and the appeasement of military aggression left Turkey insecure at the Dardanelles and the Bosphorus. After much preparation the Lausanne signatories met at Montreux, where on July 20, 1936, Bulgaria, France, Great Britain, Japan, Rumania, Turkey, and the U.S.S.R. signed a convention governing the Straits. Because of Turkey's actions at the league regarding sanctions against Italy in her Ethiopian adventure, Italy refused to sign the convention until 1938.

Britain went to the conference with the intention of giving Turkey the right to fortify the Straits and administer the Straits regime. It was also the British intention, however, to keep the Straits relatively open to warships when Turkey was a nonbelligerent, thus maintaining an open channel for British naval forces to press upon Russia. The U.S.S.R. attended the conference to give Turkey full sovereignty over the Straits with a proviso limiting very markedly the entry of foreign warships into the Black Sea. Through the centuries Russia had desired the Straits open when she felt strong and closed when she felt weak; in 1936 she felt weak. At first the Turkish negotiators at Montreux followed the Soviet line, with every intention of swinging more toward British views at the propitious moment as a necessary compromise. In this way Turkey might come out victorious without offending any power too greatly. That Turkish policy succeeded cannot be doubted. Shortly after an international news broadcast announced agreement at Montreux, Atatürk in full dress attire was seen on the sands in front of his villa near the Sea of Marmara doing handsprings and cartwheels in full celebration of his triumph. Turkey thus gained a heightened sense of international security in a period of growing distrust of collective security and nonaggression pacts.

Two other notable achievements in international affairs followed. In 1937 Turkey entered into the Saadabad Pact with Iran, Iraq, and Afghanistan in much the same fashion as she had in the earlier Balkan Pact. It was Turkey's attempt to bridge the gap between Asia and Europe and maintain friendly relations with her neighbors on both continents.

Turkey's most troublesome frontier was that to the south with Syria. Until 1926 there were many border incidents with France, which charged Turkey with condoning and harboring bandits who raided across the border into Syria. And the situation with respect to the province of Alexandretta remained. In obtaining the mandate for Syria, France promised to give Alexandretta, where more than 90,000 Turks resided, a separate administration. When in 1936 France was apparently preparing to give Syria independence, Turkey was concerned about the future of Turks in Alexandretta. It was rumored that Kemal departed for Alexandretta to solve the matter dramatically and that only İnönü's hurried interception and convincing arguments induced him to stay his hand. In July 1938 a Turko-French condominium for Alexandretta was established, and later that year the population gave pro-Turks 22 seats out of 40 in the provincial assembly. Voting themselves autonomy, the deputies proclaimed the Republic of Hatay and immediately sought a union with Turkey. France, not without bitter protests from the Arabs of Syria, acquiesced in this action; Hatay was annexed to Turkey in June 1939.

In 1939, as maneuvering among the powers in the diplomatic prelude to World War II became more tense, Turkey's international position grew in importance. Hitler sent Franz von Papen as ambassador to Ankara to cement German relations and strengthen the ties that were built on the very sizable trade nourished by the clearing agreements of 1935. Britain and

France, however, countered more successfully with a military alliance and nonaggression pact. After the Mosul agreement relations with England improved, and when Edward VIII and Mrs. Simpson were cruising in the Mediterranean on the king's yacht in the summer of 1936, a rapprochement between Atatürk and England was consummated in the bar of the Park Hotel in Istanbul. Other Turkish leaders were impressed at the coronation of George VI in 1937, and three credit agreements in the spring of 1938 paved the way for a closer understanding between the two countries. In May 1939 a "declaration of mutual guarantee" was made that was generally recognized as a veiled alliance. At the same time military items and heavy industrial goods were validated for purchase through the credit agreements. Meanwhile, in connection with the annexation of Hatay Turkey signed a nonaggression pact with France and obtained an arms credit. Thus, when the von Ribbentrop-Molotov pact of August 23, 1939, touched off World War II, Turkish leaders found themselves in a neutral position between Germany and the West, yet more committed and more friendly to England and France.

REFERENCES: Chapter 32

Volumes already cited and valuable for this chapter are found in Chapters 12, 18, 19, 23, 24, 25, 26, 28, 30 and 31. Chapter 37 contains additional references.

Allen, Henry E. *The Turkish Transformation: A Study in Social and Religious Development.* Chicago: University of Chicago Press, 1935.

Armstrong, Harold C. *Grey Wolf, Mustafa Kemal: An Intimate Study of a Dictator.* London: Barker, 1932. Not always flattering, yet sympathetic.

Başgöz, Ilhan, and Howard E. Wilson. *Educational Problems in Turkey, 1920–1940.* Bloomington, Ind.: Research Center for Language Sciences, 1968. A search for an educational philosophy and structure relevant to the economic and social realities of modern Turkey.

Bisbee, Eleanor. *The New Turks: Pioneers of the Republic, 1920–1950.* Philadelphia: University of Pennsylvania Press, 1951. A spirited study of the many changes in Turkey in the latter part of the 1930s and during the 1940s.

Bodurgil, Abraham (compiler). *Atatürk and Turkey: A Bibliography, 1919–1938.* Washington, D.C. Library of Congress, 1974. All books and periodical articles in Western languages dealing with Atatürk and Turkey under his leadership. There are 1,338 entries in 191 different publications.

Cohn, Edwin J. *Turkish Economic, Social, and Political Changes.* New York: Praeger, 1970. Not much coverage of the role of the military in Turkish society but does emphasize that successive Turkish governments stressed expansion rather than reform.

Edib (Adivar), Halidé. *Conflict of East and West in Turkey.* 2nd ed. Lahore: M. Ashraf, 1935. A personal account of the Revolution.

——. *Turkey Faces West; A Turkish View of Recent Changes and Their Origin.* New Haven, Conn: Yale University Press, 1930. An interesting essay on why Turkey turned toward the West rather than toward Russia.

Ekrem, Selma. *Turkey, Old and New.* New York: Scribner, 1947. An informal yet valuable essay on the changes in Turkey.

Harris, George S. *The Origins of Communism in Turkey.* Stanford, Calif.: Hoover Institution on War, Revolution and Peace, 1967. A new view based on original sources and recent memoirs.

Kinross, Lord (Patrick Balfour). *Ataturk: A Biography of Mustafa Kemal, Father of Modern Turkey.* New York: Morrow, 1965. Full and well-documented from Turkish sources not yet available to the public.

Smith, Elaine Diana. *Turkey: Origins of the Kemalist Movement and the Government of the Grand National Assembly (1919–1923).* Washington D.C.: The author, 1959. The best account of this period.

Szyliowicz, Joseph S. *Education and Modernization in the Middle East.* Ithaca, N.Y.: Cornell University Press, 1973. A description of the educational systems of Egypt, Turkey, and Iran within their social and political settings.

Thomas, Lewis V., and Richard N. Frye. *The United States and Turkey and Iran.* Cambridge, Mass.: Harvard University Press, 1951. A concise and accurate analysis of American interests in these two states.

Thornburg, Max Weston, Graham Spry, and George Soule. *Turkey: An Economic Appraisal.* New York: Twentieth Century Fund, 1949. A detailed survey and study of Turkey's economic position and potential.

Trask, Roger R. *The United States Response to Turkish Nationalism and Reform, 1914–1939.* Minneapolis: University of Minnesota Press, 1971. Shows the evolution of United States attitudes from misinformed hostility to benevolent toleration to warm understanding.

Vere-Hodge, Edward R. *Turkish Foreign Policy, 1918–1948.* Ambilly-Annemasse: Imprimerie France-Suisse, 1950. Summarizes the main streams of foreign policy events without too much comment.

Webster, Donald Everett. *The Turkey of Atatürk: Social Process in the Turkish Reformation.* Philadelphia: American Academy of Political & Social Science, 1939. A detailed study of political and sociological developments in Turkey to 1938.

Weiker, Walter F. *Political Tutelage and Democracy in Turkey: The Free Party and Its Aftermath.* Leiden, The Netherlands: Brill, 1973. The period of "tutelage" was from 1923 to 1946, when there was but a single political party responsible for both modernization and democracy.

Yalman, Ahmed Emin. *Turkey in My Time.* Norman: University of Oklahoma Press, 1956. The autobiography of Turkey's outstanding newspaper editor.

Chapter 33

The Fertile Crescent Under the Mandate System

French Occupation of Lebanon and Syria

When Prince Faysal galloped at the head of his cavalry into Damascus on October 3, 1918, aspirations for a new Arab nation seemed assured of fulfillment. Political and intellectual leaders were deeply stirred by the thought of a modern state in which Arab peoples might work and achieve the regeneration of their culture and society in a modern independent setting. From the sincere-sounding promises and public statements made by Allied officials Arabs anticipated the creation and general recognition of an Arab national state. On the horizon, to be sure, were a few dark clouds such as the Balfour Declaration and the Sykes-Picot Agreement, but certainly the bright sun of peace would evaporate these wartime mists.

Faysal and his supporters advanced northward taking Homs and Hama and pressing upon Aleppo, while the British proceeded along the coast to Alexandretta. During 1919 the Allies (British) controlled the coastal regions of Syria, and Arabs held the interior. Since the Arabs inhabited that area they found it rather incongruous that they were supposedly occupying enemy territory.

After two trips to London and Paris with respect to the peace settlement, Faysal belatedly discerned his naïveté in accepting wartime commitments at face value. Learning at first hand the unreliability of Western leaders, he became the personal victim of slippery French diplomacy and shrewd British imperialism. The Arabs desired independence, and the Allies would not grant it.

Throughout 1919 little headway toward a satisfactory settlement developed. The Anglo-French agreement in September was a crushing blow, as it cut off Palestine and provided for a French military occupation of Syria. By December General Gouraud and French troops replaced the British in Beirut and along the Syrian littoral. Faysal's Arabs held the interior. The General Syrian Congress, composed of eighty-five members elected from all parts of Syria, including Palestine, met in Damascus in July and after considerable free discussion passed resolutions that defined Arab aims. Inspired by the newly formed Arab Independence party, the resolutions requested independence for Syria, including Palestine, with Faysal as king, independence for Iraq with Abdallah as king, repudiation of the Sykes-Picot

Agreement and the Balfour Declaration, and rejection of the mandate idea. Another resolution called for refusal of assistance from France in any form. In many ways actions of the Syrian congress resembled and paralleled those of the Kemalist nationalists, who at that moment were meeting in Ankara.

Obtaining no redress, the General Syrian Congress declared on March 8, 1920, the independence of Syria, including Palestine and Lebanon, as a constitutional monarchy under Faysal. The French declined to recognize the announcement; the meeting of the Allied supreme council at San Remo answered the Syrian action by acknowledging, informally yet firmly, a French mandate over Syria and Lebanon and separation of Palestine under the British.

Faysal was caught between the superior force of the Allies and the national patriotism of the Arabs. His wavering caused General Gouraud to fear an Arab buildup in Damascus, where the San Remo awards completely blighted faith in British and French integrity. When he obtained Senegalese reinforcements, Gouraud sent Faysal an ultimatum (July 14, 1920), demanding within four days unqualified acceptance of the French mandate, the end of Arab conscription, reduction of the Arab army, adoption of the new French-issued currency in Syria, control of Syrian railroads, and the arrest of persons guilty of acts hostile to the French. In the face of a French army advancing from Beirut to occupy Damascus, Faysal telegraphed his agreement. Obviously, the French did not foresee that the ultimatum would be accepted, as new conditions were added and the march proceeded. Faysal ordered the disorganization of the Arab army, but isolated groups opened fire on the French. A bloody engagement occurred at Maysalun Pass, and in the train of airplanes, tanks, and the rattle of machine-gun fire General Gouraud captured Damascus on July 25. Faysal left within a few days, and the French occupied the whole province of Syria in rapid order.

Although full legal title to the mandate did not materialize until the Treaty of Lausanne in 1923, and although America did not recognize the mandate authority until 1924, the actions of 1920 confirmed French possession. Detailed French administration began at once. General Gouraud, as high commissioner, issued a decree (September 1, 1920) dividing the mandate for Syria and Lebanon into four separate districts: greater Lebanon; Aleppo, including Alexandretta; Latakia; and Damascus. The latter comprised the Jebel Druze area in the south and all remaining interior regions. The plan seemed to be: divide and rule.

Mandate for Lebanon

The day before the mandate was splintered General Gouraud issued a decree that added the city of Beirut, coastal regions to the north and south including Tripoli, Sidon, and Tyre, and the Bika Valley and Baalbek to the old sanjak of Lebanon to form a new greater Lebanon. Since 1861 the sanjak had had an autonomous political existence under an elected central administrative assembly consisting of four Maronites, three Druzes, two

Orthodox Christians, and one member each for the Melkites, Matawilahs, and Sunnis. By extending the area the French intentionally reduced the preponderance of the Maronite sect by changing population proportions, increasing Sunni Muslims so that the Christians held only a slight overall majority.

After the high commissioner's decree, a provisional administrative commission for Lebanon was appointed to serve until local governmental authority could be created. A number of the commissioners were Lebanese from various religious groups, but the governor was French. A Lebanese governor, it was said, would cause too much jealousy and friction among the religions. The usual departments of government were formed and staffed by Lebanese, where competent and loyal individuals could be found. But of course each department had many French officers and advisers.

Above the governor of Lebanon stood the high commissioner, who had a government of his own to assist him. Separated into departments such as security, education, and public works, this administration was manned by Frenchmen and French colonials who served as the authority to which the Lebanese government looked. A most important group under the high commissioner was that of the information officers, who served in every district of Lebanon, reported developments to the high commissioner, exercised unlimited influence over local affairs, and stood as "tutors" to prepare the country and its people for full independence.

Certain functions of government such as customs, posts, telegraph, railways, public utilities, currency, and local troop levies were not divided locally by the four administrative units. And the high commissioner reserved for his own government full supervision of these "common interests." Income from the central operations paid common expenses, and the balance was apportioned among the four state units, always with bickering and dissatisfaction.

One bright point in favor of the mandate system was the allowance for two parallel governments: one held and admnistered by the mandatory power; one of completely local, in this case Lebanese, organization to be instructed by the other. In theory and in principle, the system was excellent. In actual practice, it allowed for a fully determined colonialism to operate more or less unmolested behind a semblance of local self-government.

French Imperialism in Lebanon

French imperialism manifested itself in Lebanon in many ways. In a number of districts martial law was established, and throughout the mandate period the French were quick to decree its use. The press was muzzled effectively; numerous papers accepted French subsidies and published accounts of all events in a version favorable to French interests. French investors largely owned and operated the railways, public utilities, and banks of Lebanon; the entire fiscal and economic policy was initiated by the French. New concessions and general contracts granted by the Lebanese government went to French concerns or to Lebanese firms with strong French connections.

In 1920 the *Banque de Syrie et du Grand Leban,* headquartered in Paris, was founded as the bank of issue. Stable Egyptian currency had been introduced with Allenby's army, but the French found it awkward to buy their monetary needs in Egypt. The new currency was tied to the French franc, one Lebanese pound being exchangeable for twenty francs. However, it had the disadvantage of fluctuating with depreciating French currency— the fall of the franc played an important role in uprisings in Syria and Lebanon in 1925.

French imperialists spoke of their "civilizing mission," a phrase that expressed the view that an area, region, or people would be permanently and indissolubly linked to France if French language and culture flourished in their midst. To gain this end French cultural missions visited Beirut and other cities and towns of Lebanon. But the chief work was accomplished through education and the use of French as a second language. French schools of primary, secondary, and *lycée* rank were opened in many communities, and these always obtained more funds and aid than schools in which Arabic or some other language prevailed. All schools taught French, and textbooks for history, social sciences, literature, and the humanities had a French coloration on every page. French newspapers were encouraged, and French was an official language in the courts, government offices, contracts, and every walk of life. Many Lebanese had French wives.

There were, however, many favorable aspects of French rule, a concrete indication of which was the higher standard of living and growth of the population. Schools improved and increased in number; food and clothing became more plentiful; roads were built; motorcars and transport became available; doctors were trained; disease was controlled; and sanitation and health standards were greatly raised. Striking changes came in the city of Beirut, but developments were widespread across the state. Emigration declined, as life in Lebanon grew more attractive. Populations and standards of living were, of course, on the rise around the world and Lebanon shared in this world trend; credit, however, must also be given to French administration, selfish and blind as it may often have been.

Local Lebanese Government
In Lebanon, as conditions of life flourished, the desire for independence and true self-government spread. In 1922 a representative council was elected and began meeting. General Weygand, the second high commissioner, instituted a Lebanese council of state and won Lebanese confidence and affection by his intelligent and judicious decisions. His sudden replacement in January 1925 by General Sarrail altered the peaceful developments almost immediately. The unfortunate move resulted from the electoral victory of the anticlerical Left in France. (Weygand was a "good Catholic.") General Sarrail's arrogant manners, unwise tactics, anticlericalism, inopportune appointments, and brusque officialism fomented quarrels with the

Maronite Church, the Druzes, and many Lebanese leaders. He insulted the representative council, abolished the old elective system that had recognized centuries-old religious divisions among the people, appointed an unpopular Frenchman as governor of Lebanon after first stating he intended to name a native Lebanese, offended the Christian patriarchs, and permitted his war with the Druzes of Syria to spread into Lebanon.

When the general uprisings of 1925 that General Sarrail provoked refused to burn themselves out, the general was recalled and replaced by Henri de Jouvenel, editor of *Le Matin* and French representative at the League of Nations. Henri de Jouvenel called upon the representative council to draft a constitution that would recognize the mandate and French responsibility for Lebanon's foreign affairs and give the high commissioner veto power and the right to dismiss the executive head of the state and to dissolve the legislature. Beyond those restrictions de Jouvenel readily surrendered to the Lebanese authority over their own affairs. On May 23, 1926, the Lebanese Republic was proclaimed. Charles Dabbas, an Orthodox Christian, was chosen president by the assembly, which consisted of the old representative council and a new senate of twelve appointed by the high commissioner in accordance with the constitution.

Although de Jouvenel resigned in July, his successor, August Ponsot, carried on tactfully. No major political problem arose until the acute world economic crisis and its repercussions on trade, unemployment, and finance in Beirut caused Ponsot to suspend the constitution in 1932. The president remained head of the government, and a new cabinet was appointed with instructions to supervise and regularize all expenditures more closely. A new constitution was promulgated in 1934 by a new high commissioner, Count de Martel. The power of the assembly was restricted, and the sectarian basis of election and membership in previous assemblies was ignored. Political life in Lebanon maintained an uneasy calm, until disturbances in 1936 in Syria forced France to reassess her position in her mandates and negotiate a treaty with Lebanon as well as with Syria.

The sheer weight of French military and naval forces in Lebanon kept political agitation under wraps. Moreover, the French insinuated to Maronite and other Christian leaders in Lebanon that their security against a Muslim tidal wave required full trust in France and cooperation with French rule. However, British concessions to nationalism in Iraq and Egypt incited the Syrian uprisings. These in turn enjoined France to initiate the treaty arrangements with Syria and Lebanon in 1936.

Syrian-French negotiations for a treaty forced similar actions in Lebanon. France could hardly be less generous to a more friendly Lebanon than she was to a recalcitrant Syria. Inhabitants in the Sunni Muslim parts of Lebanon, which the French had decreed to Lebanon in 1920, were divided in their sentiments and wishes in 1936. Many belonged to the Syrian National party of Lebanon and agitated for union with Syria. Others preferred the more stable political life and higher standard of living in Lebanon. The latter began openly to fraternize with Christian groups. Christians reciprocated by emphasizing their common interests, language, and general culture and by making much of the tacit arrangement by which the president of Lebanon was always a Christian and the prime minister always a Muslim. The Maronites wished to avoid the chances of greater Lebanon being dissolved, for they assumed that the old mountain Lebanon was too small to survive in the twentieth century.

Negotiations for the treaty were opened in October 1936 in Beirut and a twenty-five year Franco-Lebanese Treaty of Friendship and Alliance was signed November 13. The independence of Lebanon was recognized, and France pledged to support Lebanon's admission to the League of Nations within three years. Lebanon agreed to respect French interests and nationals and to maintain the established parity of the two currencies. French troops were permitted in Lebanon without restriction. In Beirut the Christians rejoiced, but many Muslims did not, as they hoped to reunite Lebanon with Syria. Despite some bloody fighting in the streets, the Lebanese assembly ratified the treaty in four days and independence seemed assured. In January 1937 the constitution of 1926 was restored, but difficulties loomed ahead. First, negotiations with Syria over economic matters and a settlement of "common interest" affairs dictated by the treaties with France hit a snag. Then, the Blum government fell in Paris; the insecure international position frightened French conservatives into refusing the treaties, which the conservatives believed would weaken France still further.

Badly disappointed, the Lebanese marked time while World War II was brewing. Local political parties continued their maneuvers, the conflict centering upon local matters and more often than not upon local personalities. The Unionist party, led by Emile Edde, was pledged to full independence for Lebanon separate from Syria, while the Constitutionalists under Bishara al-Khuri looked with favor upon close and friendly relations with the other Arab states and did not object to some ties to Syria.

Mandate for Syria

All other divisions of Syria created by the 1920 decree had a life during this period even more variegated than Lebanon's. When the decree was issued, native governments were ordered for Latakia, Aleppo, Damascus, and the Jebel Druze. With Alexandretta attached to Aleppo as a special province, Damascene Syrians felt that France was deliberately blocking them from the sea and never admitted the legality of the fragmentation. In June 1922 the independence of the Jebel Druze was proclaimed; the remaining states were grouped into a federation with an Antiochene Turk, Subhi Barakat, as president of the federal council. The following year each territory acquired a representative council "appointed by an indirect election." (Latakia had become the State of the Alawis.) In 1924, just before quitting Beirut, General Weygand laid the foundations for a treaty settlement with the mandate similar to that which the British gave Iraq. At the same time he terminated the federation by recognizing a separate government for the Alawis and amalgamating Aleppo into the state of Damascus, which then became Syria. Alexandretta, though a part of Syria, had its own administration.

Every action taken by General Sarrail seemed to be wrong. In the Jebel Druze he touched off a bloody uprising by supporting the French delegate, Captain Carbillet, who had been doing a splendid job in ramming through new roads, irrigation channels, and reforms of many types. Carbillet was, however, ignorant of the Druze character and wholly tactless; the more Carbillet did for them, the more they disliked him. Since the decree of 1920 called for a native governor, Druze leaders petitioned for Carbillet's removal. General Sarrail replied by inviting the Druze leaders to Damascus, where they were arrested. Revolt flared rapidly across the entire mandate. General Gamelin was given command of the French forces under General Sarrail in September, and severe fighting occurred in the Jebel Druze. In October, Druze columns appeared at Damascus, and the French bombardment of that city caused damages estimated at several millions of dollars and considerable loss of life.

This tragedy brought Sarrail's immediate recall. Henri de Jouvenel, his successor, called for elections in Latakia and Syria. Subhi Barakat, whom the Damascus faction hated because he wanted to move the capital of a united Syria to Aleppo, resigned the presidency. The presidency was then offered to Taj al-Din al-Hasani, chief judge of Damascus, but since his eleven-point program was unacceptable to the French, he refused the proffered post. Every succeeding Syrian request over the following two decades was based on Taj al-Din's platform. He demanded that Latakia and the Jebel Druze be joined to Syria; that areas within Lebanon be allowed to choose between Syria and Lebanon; that a treaty be negotiated and entered into with France; that Syria join the League of Nations; that French troops be evacuated; that a currency reform be enacted; and that Syria be entirely independent in her domestic affairs. When the high commissioner refused this program, a Circassian, Damad Ahmed Nami, was appointed president of Syria. Guerrilla warfare continued, and General Gamelin tried to pacify the territory. In May 1926 Damascus was again shelled. This time fighting was even more destructive and savage than in the previous October. Ponsot replaced de Jouvenel. Both France and the Syrian nationalists began to realize that some compromise was necessary. The latter asked France to forget the past, and Ponsot announced that a constituent assembly would be elected, a constitution drafted by Syrians, a Syrian government inaugurated, and a treaty of alliance with France concluded, in that order.

Local Syrian Government

Damad Ahmed Nami resigned in February 1928, and Ponsot appointed Taj al-Din president of a Syrian council of ministers to form a provisional government and hold elections. This was done in April, the constituent assembly of seventy members meeting in June. Fifty-two of the members were Sunni Muslims; a nationalist bloc under the leadership of Jamil Mardam, Hashim al-Atasi, and Faris al-Khuri began to take shape, while a more radical independence wing was led by Shukri al-Kuwatli, and Riyad al-Sulh. The constituent assembly entered into the task of drafting a constitution, which was presented to the assembly in August. It established a Western-type republic with a president, prime minister, cabinet, unicameral legislature, and high court. Syria was pronounced to include Lebanon and Palestine; the official religion was to be Islam; and no mention was made of France as a mandatory power. Since several articles violated French international commitments and were contrary to League of Nations stipulations, Ponsot found the constitution unacceptable. In a conciliatory speech he urged that five articles be withdrawn and a sixth redrafted. The assembly refused to comply and the quarrels were resumed.

In 1929 the assembly was prorogued, but debate over the constitution continued. In a surprise move in 1930 Ponsot unilaterally promulgated new governments for Alexandretta, Latakia, and the Jebel Druze; simultaneously, he established in Syria the constitution, including the five censured articles and the altered sixth. Elections were not decreed, however, until the spring of 1932, and when the chamber of deputies met in June it comprised fifty-four moderates and seventeen nationalists. A middle-of-the-road candidate was elected president of the Republic, while Hakki al-Azm, a moderate, accepted the prime ministership and selected his cabinet equally between moderates and nationalists. The latter soon took the lead and pressed for conclusion of a treaty of independence with France.

Throughout 1933 all political conversations centered about a treaty. The French insisted upon excluding Lebanon, Latakia, and the Jebel Druze. The nationalists demanded the end of all foreign privileges and the dismissal of French armed forces. Unfortunately, in May in the midst of bitter debate, Ponsot fell ill, and his successor, Count de Martel, did not arrive until October. While al-Azm did present the proposed treaty to the chamber in November, such a howl arose that the high commissioner suggested its withdrawal. Parliament was suspended and later dissolved, with the president governing by decrees which were recommended by his cabinet. In 1934 Taj al-Din became prime minister and held on for nearly two years.

From January 11 to March 1, 1936, Damascus and most of the towns of Syria became the scene of an organized strike against the French regime. In the midst of the strike Taj al-Din resigned as prime minister and was replaced by Ata al-Ayyubi, a moderate. The French sensed the handwriting on the wall even if they could not see it, and de Martel came to terms with the nationalist party leaders. Negotiations for a treaty were resumed in Paris on the basis of Alexandretta being a part of Syria and Lebanon being recognized as a separate state. The long discussions ended only after Delbos took over for the Blum government and agreed that the Jebel Druze and Latakia be incorporated into Syria. Rejoicing, Syria elected the nationalists to power in November 1936. Hashim al-Atasi became president of the republic and Mardam headed the cabinet. The Syrians ratified the treaty that would free them from French imperialism, but, as with the similar Lebanese treaty discussed above, the French government never did ratify it.

In 1939 the cabinet and president resigned, and the high commissioner suspended the chamber of deputies. Syria was back where she was in 1920 when the mandate began. At the outbreak of World War II, Syria was governed by an appointed council of directors under the immediate control and supervision of High Commissioner Gabriel Puaux, who had replaced de Martel in January 1939.

The bitterest event for the Syrians to swallow was the gift of Alexandretta to Turkey. In 1920 the French had declared a special administration for Alexandretta in view of the large Turkish population residing there. At first, it was attached to Aleppo but under separate rule. When Aleppo was joined to Damascus to form Syria, Alexandretta retained its own semiautonomous regime as part of Syria but was responsive directly to the will of the French high commissioner in Beirut. When questions over its status were raised by the Turks in 1936 and conversations initiated, the Syrians objected. As discussions proceeded to Franco-Turkish responsibility, to an independent Hatay, and to outright annexation to Turkey in 1939, Syrian nationalists protested every step of the way. With considerable justification and legality they declared that the terms of the mandate forbade France from any such action.

For two decades France tried to govern Syria but failed ingloriously. Policies dictated by Paris were high-handed, unwise, and based on an almost complete misunderstanding or disregard of the situation. To cap these mistakes French administrative personnel delegated to Syria were generally either pompous incompetents or officials transferred from North Africa, where at the time they were able to look upon the inhabitants as "natives" without starting a revolt. The Syrians did not want French rule or even French advisers in the first instance, and the French did little to endear themselves to the Syrians.

British Occupation of Iraq

Eastward, the British were having their troubles in Iraq. At the end of World War I the British were occupying Basrah, Baghdad, and Mosul and controlling much of the land in between and on the far sides of both the Tigris and the Euphrates. Many British administrators coming in at the end of hostilities brought their families, evidently understanding that this territory was not a temporary acquisition. Sir Arnold Wilson, acting high commissioner, made a virtue of efficient government, irrespective of sentiment, prestige, or local desires. Arab unrest grew from the uncertainties over an Arab state of Iraq. When the news from San Remo arrived, the rebellion burst. From May to October 1920 a real war, reportedly costing the British nearly £40 million, raged in Iraq, with resistance forces dominating the whole land except for the chief three cities.

Hurriedly, Sir Percy Z. Cox was recalled from the ambassadorship in Tehran and sent to Iraq as high commissioner. The affection and esteem in which he was held by Iraqis was attested to by the welcome showered upon him at his arrival on October 1, 1920, and by the rebellion's termination. Having been British political agent for the Persian Gulf for a number of years and civil commissioner in Iraq during the war years and immediately thereafter, Sir Percy gathered about him a star-studded galaxy of advisers and assistants such as Gertrude Bell, his Oriental secretary, and H. St. J. B. Philby. Quickly he organized a provisional council of state in which Sayyed Abd al-Rahman al-Gailani, Baghdad's *naqib* (official head of the Sunni Arab community), became prime minister. Other portfolios were distributed among influential families and religious sects from different parts of the state. Each minister had a British adviser, and in reality the council was supervised by these advisers. All were under the direction of the high commissioner; few Iraqis held any illusion that they had a true national government.

The Kingdom of Iraq

Sir Percy Cox proposed convening a national assembly to draw up electoral laws and establish an Iraqi government, but it was not called until 1922 and did not meet until 1924. The difficulty was the question of a ruler, and the British were fearful lest an assembly choose someone unresponsive to their suggestions. Although the Damascus congress named Abdallah king of Iraq, the British selected Faysal as king of Iraq in 1920 and Churchill's Cairo Conference nominated him. There were other candidates, but the return to Baghdad of several hundred Arab officers who had served with the British in the Hijaz and Syria gave the necessary weight to the acceptance of Faysal. Abdallah withdrew his name, and Faysal arrived in Baghdad at the end of June 1921. The council of state invited him to become king; after a referendum was held in various districts of the state, Faysal was enthroned on August 23, 1921. Sir Percy and his associates managed affairs wonderfully.

Faysal served until his death twelve years later. His charm, tact, and broad tolerance made him an admirable choice, as his knowledge and experience made him acceptable to desert shaykhs, bedouins, and the townsmen of Iraq. At the same time, Faysal recognized fully the British position of control and appreciated the fact that without British support he would never have become king. Through the winter and spring of 1922 a treaty was drafted by the British in conjunction with Faysal and al-Gailani. At the last stages the council of state was brought in, and after a serious crisis the treaty was ratified in October. It defined the special position of Great Britain in Iraq, actually giving the British military and economic control and, in a veiled manner, granting English nationals many immunities and privileges in the country. British advisers were accepted in all offices. Its many articles justified the objections by the nationalists (of which there were now three political parties: National, Renaissance, and Independent) that the treaty was only a sugar-coated mandate which, however translated, meant "subjection and colonization."

Anglo-Iraqi Affairs

Much uncertainty and agitation accompanied the elections for a constituent assembly in 1924. King Faysal in his speech from the throne urged the assembly to ratify the treaty with Great Britain, pass upon the constitution, and enact an electoral law for a parliament—all of which was done in 1924. A new treaty with England was signed in 1926 and yet another in 1927. The British pledged, with certain qualifications, that Iraq would be supported in 1932 for membership in the League of Nations; the qualifications, however, raised such doubt with respect to Britain's sincerity that the treaty of 1927 was never ratified.

Loopholes as to League support were removed, and the momentous Anglo-Iraqi Treaty of 1930 was achieved. This treaty, which became the prototype of the Anglo-Egyptian Treaty of 1936 and the treaties of France with Syria and Lebanon in the same year, established a twenty-five-year alliance between Iraq and Great Britain. The two countries agreed to follow a foreign policy not inconsistent with the treaty, which meant that Iraq assented to "full and frank consultation in all matters" of foreign affairs. Iraq concurred to the presence of British troops in Mosul and other districts for five years and gave a lease on several air bases. In return Britain contracted to defend Iraq in case of war. Attached to the treaty were annexes giving England considerable power in matters of finance, business, and education, and indicating that British advisers were to be employed rather than advisers of other nations. The signing of this treaty cleared the way for Iraq's membership in the League of Nations, which voted admission unanimously on October 3, 1932. The high commissioner became British ambassador; the mandate was terminated; and Iraq stood ostensibly as an independent state.

The Government of Iraq

The constitution placed executive administrative power in the hands of a cabinet headed by a prime minister and composed of at least six other ministers. The cabinet was jointly responsible to the chamber of deputies, which could force the cabinet to resign upon a vote of no confidence. The king, however, could dissolve the chamber. Parliament was bicameral. The chamber of deputies, elected indirectly by universal manhood suffrage, had one representative for every 20,000 male inhabitants, with a special provision that four Christians and four Jews were to be elected. (There were eighty-eight in the first chamber.) The first chamber was elected in 1925 and elections in 1939 were held for the ninth. The senate was appointed by the king and had a membership of not more than one-fourth that of the chamber. Senators were appointed for eight years; half were appointed every four years. Only the chamber could initiate legislation; in appearance the chamber, as representative of the people, held the dominant position in the government.

In practical application, however, the cabinet was the powerful body, and none ever fell from a vote of no confidence. The cabinet controlled elections and obtained the dismissal of the chamber when necessary. Yet, there were twenty cabinets from 1925, when the constitution came into force, until the outbreak of World War II in 1939. A cabinet would promise to obtain full independence from Great Britain, and when it failed, it invited the opposition to try its hand. Ministers moved about from post to post in succeeding cabinets. Nuri al-Said Pasha, four times prime minister in that period, appropriately quipped: "With a small pack of cards, you must shuffle them often."

Perhaps the political and ministerial ferris wheel would not have been so pronounced had King Faysal lived longer. In 1933 Faysal became worn with fatigue. His health broke, and he died in Switzerland, where he had gone for rest and medical care. He was succeeded immediately and without question by his twenty-one-year-old son Ghazi. Young and inexperienced, the new king followed a constitutional policy in the Western tradition. However, Iraq might have been spared some of her political confusion of those years had Ghazi been more mature and sufficiently concerned with government to play an advisory role in national affairs. Addicted to fast motor cars, he was killed in an accident in 1939. He was succeeded by his four-year-old son, who became the boy-king Faysal II under the regency of Prince Abd al-Ilah, the king's maternal uncle and son of Prince Ali, King Faysal I's oldest brother.

Minority Problems in Iraq

Iraq's problems were far from solved by the adoption of constitutional government, technical independence from Great Britain, and admission to the League of Nations. In the northern part of the state Kurdish tribes were preponderant, and with their fellow tribesmen in Turkey and Iran they hoped for the peace settlement to bring forth a Kurdistan. The Kurdish tribes were seminomadic and roamed the mountains and valleys of the eastern highlands, moving freely from country to country and resisting outside authorities. They had no desire to be taxed or organized. The Iraqi government took punitive measures repeatedly against uprisings in the neighborhood of Mosul and Suleimaniyah in the 1920s and early 1930s. Kurds were elected to parliament and served in Baghdad, but settling the Kurdish tribes was by no means completed in 1939.

During World War I a group of Assyrians (Nestorians living along the upper Euphrates) had joined with the British and fought against the Ottomans. Leaving Turkey at the end of the conflict and finding themselves a homeless minority in Iraq, many had accepted service in the British army stationed there. In 1933, after Iraq was free and a member of the League, incidents between Assyrians and Arabs led to bloody engagements, massacres in Assyrian villages, and a "pacification" by Iraqi forces commanded by General Bakr Sidki. Britain helped Iraq obtain a generous whitewash of the affair before the League in order not to jeopardize her position in Iraq.

The most serious religious problem in Iraq arose from the lasting Islamic schism between Sunnite and Shiite Arabs. The latter held a population majority; the former dominated the government and society. As long as Faysal I lived, little trouble developed, for many Shiites were fondly under the delusion that he secretly belonged to their sect. Shiite divines easily stirred their followers; Shiite preachers, entering Iraq from Iran, could easily retire across the frontier when asylum was needed.

Social Problems

In addition to minorities and varying religious sects there was a grave social and economic cleavage between the townspeople and the tribes. The government of Iraq was definitely in the hands of the townspeople; yet the tribes, and particularly their shaykhs, were powerful forces in the Iraqi nation. At least 80 percent of the population won their livelihood from the land, much of which was irrigated. But the science of irrigation had so degenerated over the centuries in Iraq that soils became salty and channels silted rapidly, compelling peasants to move frequently to new land. In the middle Euphrates area the tribes also engaged in stock raising, moving their herds from sparse pasturage as the cover was grazed. Thus the tribes had a constant tie with desert bedouins. The tribal shaykhs were recognized, perforce, by the British in their occupation of Mesopotamia as the responsible heads of the districts, thereby obtaining a quasi-title of ownership of the land. Every assembly and parliament in Iraq always had a goodly number of these shaykhs as members. They were invariably conservative and friendly to the British, in whom they saw a protection from town-dwelling Iraqi politicians. Since the tribesman was a good soldier, the tribes of the middle Euphrates were a force with which to contend until the Iraqi army was equipped with the strength and mobility of more mechanized weapons. General Bakr Sidki won his spurs of acclaim again in 1935 by leading an armed expedition to quell a rising of the tribes of the middle Euphrates.

Iraqi Oil

One of the jarring factors in Iraqi politics, domestic and international, has been the oil resources of the country and their exploitation. Before the war oil rights were granted by the Ottoman government to the Anatolian Railway Company and the Baghdad Railway Company, both German concerns. When the D'Arcy Exploration Company became interested in the Mosul fields, the Turkish Petroleum Company was formed in 1912 with German, Dutch, and British ownership. The San Remo conference turned over the German interests to the French. And during the Lausanne conference the British agreed very reluctantly that half of their holdings, which by this time were owned by the Anglo-Persian Oil Company, would be made available for purchase by America's Standard Oil Company of New Jersey and its associates.

The Mosul controversy between England and Turkey was partly over oil; when in 1925 it appeared likely that Mosul would be awarded to Iraq, that government gave a seventy-five-year concession to the Turkish Petroleum Company. Development, however, moved very slowly. Whereas the oil production by 1930 in Iran had increased to nearly 46,000,000 barrels, in Iraq it was only 909,000 barrels. Iraqi leaders charged that Western oil concerns were holding back in Iraq and exploiting their wells in other parts of the world. Although this might be good business for the companies, to Iraq it seemed entirely negligent, for she was losing revenue when it was sorely needed.

A gigantic gusher was struck at Baba Gurgur near Kirkuk in 1927. By 1929 the company had not taken up all the concession, but the government refused to extend the time. After consideration by the League and much negotiating a new concession was made in 1931 to the Iraq Petroleum Company, the company's name having been changed in 1929. The 1931 agreement gave an outright concession to lands in the Baghdad and Mosul provinces east of the Tigris, except for a few districts where the Anglo-Persian Company had historic rights. Furthermore, the company pledged to build before 1936 a pipeline system to Haifa and the Syrian coast and to begin annual payments of £400,000 against future royalties. Half of this sum would be nonrecoverable. Royalties were fixed at four gold shillings a ton for a period of twenty years. The pipeline was built from Kirkuk across the Tigris and the Euphrates. There it divided, one branch going to Haifa and one to Tripoli. Both branches began delivering oil in 1934.

Other companies showed an interest in Iraqi oil possibilities, and in 1932 a concession was given to the British Oil Development Company for lands west of the Tigris and north of the 33rd parallel. Payments of £100,000 began in 1933 and steadily mounted. Thus, by the time Iraq attained her independence she was fast becoming independent economically. This concession to the British Oil Development Company and another for a district in the south around Basrah were controlled by the Iraq Petroleum Company. Through further concessions in 1938 it held the oil production of all of Iraq in its hands.

While oil brought Iraq into touch with the great powers, border raids by nomads on the deserts and in the mountains led to interminable negotiations and difficulties with the smaller states upon her frontiers. Boundary settlements with varying degrees of permanence were made with Kuwayt, Saudi Arabia, Transjordan, Syria, Turkey, and Iran. As a further step in regulating the frontiers and relations with Turkey and Iran the Saadabad Pact was signed by the foreign ministers of Iraq, Iran, Turkey, and Afghanistan at the shah's palace near Tehran on July 8, 1937.

Politics in Iraq
Domestic politics from the very beginning in Iraq were heavily charged with personalities. Each dynamic figure gathered about him a clientele, published a newspaper, and organized a political party. Eagerness for per-

sonal power, prestige, and position, however, was sublimated in the struggle for independence from England. Parties emerged, flourished, and died quickly; members and even leaders went from one to another with considerable ease. In the 1920s the two most important and durable parties were the National and the People's parties. Each pledged to throw off the treaty-mandate subterfuge and obtain real independence. The People's party was headed by al-Hashimi, who in the 1930s led his followers into a collective party known as the National Brotherhood *(Ikha al-Watan)*. Prime minister twice, he was active in politics and held various portfolios in a number of ministries until a coup d'état in 1936 forced him into exile. Jafar Abu al-Timman, who participated in different ministries, organized the National party. Disillusioned by the acts of his political associates, he moved toward the left. In 1933 he joined the Reform party and took an active part in the 1936 coup.

In 1930 when Nuri al-Said Pasha concluded the Anglo-Iraqi Treaty of Alliance, he revived the prewar Covenanters party *(al-Ahd)*. But its members were soon swallowed up in the political confusion of independence. Nuri Pasha, an Iraqi who had served in the Ottoman army and then joined the Hijaz force supporting the Arab revolt, returned to Baghdad, where he worked for the kingship of Faysal and held office in many cabinets as foreign minister. Prime minister four times before the outbreak of World War II, he was a strong stabilizing force for better government.

Nuri's opponents in 1930 joined together under al-Hashimi and Rashid Ali al-Gailani to form the National Brotherhood party. This party dominated the government and the cabinets from 1932, when Iraq was admitted to the League of Nations, until it was overthrown by the 1936 coup. Meanwhile, a Reform party *(Ahali)* resulted from the meetings and discussions of younger Western-educated men who were liberal in their views and desirous of a more democratic and socialistic government. They were disgusted with the shuffling corruption of the conservative governments conducted by their elders. For a few years they gained wide influence through their party newspaper, but they soon succumbed to experienced politicians such as Hikmat Sulayman and Abu al-Timman.

Realizing that the power of the National Brotherhood government could not be broken and that the cabinet of al-Hashimi and Ali al-Gailani could not be removed without active assistance from the army, Hikmat Sulayman brought about a coalescence of the *Ahali* group with disgruntled army officers who felt that Iraq was not yet ready for full-blown Western democracy and its inefficiencies. The army "hero" proved to be Bakr Sidki.

The plot ripened, and in the autumn of 1936 Sidki Pasha moved on Baghdad. Rashid Ali al-Gailani, Nuri al-Said, and al-Hashimi escaped into exile; al-Askari Pasha, perennial minister of defense, was assassinated; and Hikmat Sulayman became the new prime minister. Parliament was dissolved and new elections were rigged so as to seat a great number of deputies who had never served in any previous chamber. The socialist predilections of the Ahali group led to quarrels with Sidki and his army officers. Other officers became jealous of Sidki, and in August 1937 he was assassinated. Another army coup d'état soon ended the first, and until 1941 one army coup followed another most methodically, while politics descended to personal vilification and vulgar invective. Iraq was deeply immersed in this national suffering when World War II began.

REFERENCES: Chapter 33

Important works for this chapter are in Chapters 2, 7, 8, 19, 20, 22, 23, 26, 28, 30, and 31.

Abouchdid, Eugenie Elie. *Thirty Years of Lebanon and Syria (1917–1947)*. Beirut: Soder Rihani Printing, 1948. Gives a Lebanese point of view.

Be'eri, Eliezer. *Army Officers in Arab Politics and Society*. New York: Praeger, 1970. A thorough survey of the Arab officers and armies from the Baghdad coup of 1936 to the June War of 1967.

Bonne, Alfred. *State and Economics in the Middle East: A Society in Transition*. London: Routledge & Kegan Paul, 1948. An excellent survey.

Bullard, Reader. *Britain and the Middle East*. London: Longmans, Green, 1951. The British point of view.

Cooke, Hedley V. *Challenge and Response in the Middle East: The Quest for Prosperity, 1919–1951*. New York: Harper & Bros., 1952. A good outline of the economic situation and the planning and development.

Cooper, Charles A., and Sidney S. Alexander (eds.). *Economic Development and Population Growth in the Middle East*. New York: American Elsevier, 1972. An intensive view of the economic conditions and population problems of Egypt, Israel, Syria, Jordan, Lebanon, and Iraq.

Davis, Helen Miller. *Constitutions, Electoral Laws, Treaties of States in the Near and Middle East*. Durham, N.C.: Duke University Press, 1947. An indispensable work although newer works have appeared.

Ellis, Howard S. *Private Enterprise and Socialism in the Middle East*. Washington, D.C.: American Enterprise Institute, 1970. An examination of the economic development of Egypt, Iraq, Turkey, Lebanon, and Iran and the special problems appearing in each state.

Foster, Henry A. *The Making of Modern Iraq: A Product of World Forces*. Norman: University of Oklahoma Press, 1935. A thorough work on the early period.

Frye, Richard N. (ed.). *The Near East and the Great Powers*. Cambridge, Mass.: Harvard University Press, 1951. The chapter, "The Scheme of Fertile Crescent Unity: A Study in Inter-Arab Relations" by Majid Khadduri is of special note.

Gendzier, Irene L. (ed.). *A Middle East Reader*. New York: Pegasus Press, 1969. A well-balanced selection of articles on society and politics in Israel and the Arab countries as well as a substantial sampling of important statements on the Arab-Israeli conflict.

Gulick, John. *Social Structure and Culture Change in a Lebanese Village*. New York: Wenner-Gren Foundation for Anthropological Research, 1955. A study of the changes in value systems relating to land, religion, and kinship.

Hindus, Maurice. *In Search of a Future*. Garden City, N.Y.: Doubleday, 1949. A study of Iran, Egypt, Iraq, and Palestine in the period immediately after World War II.

Hurewitz, J. C. *Middle East Politics: The Military Dimension.* New York: Praeger, 1968. An analysis of the way military and political functions interact in traditional Muslim societies; of how military modernization began in the area; and of how current regional and national politico-military factors and great power rivalries interact and condition affairs in the area.

Ireland, Philip Willard. *Iraq: A Study in Political Development.* London: Jonathan Cape, 1935. Especially good for the war years and the peace settlement.

Karpat, Kemal H. (ed.). *Political and Social Thought in the Contemporary Middle East.* New York: Praeger, 1968. A sixty-two-article anthology giving a cross section of the literature on the modernization in the Arab world.

Keen, B. A. *The Agricultural Development of the Middle East.* London: H. M. Stationery Office, 1946. An outline for the future coordination of the resources of the area.

Khadduri, Majid. *Independent Iraq: A Study in Iraqi Politics, 1932–1958.* 2nd ed. London: Oxford University Press, 1960. The best work on this subject.

———. *Political Trends in the Arab World: The Role of Ideas and Ideals in Politics.* Baltimore: Johns Hopkins Press, 1970. A work of objectivity and meticulous scholarship.

Leiden, Carl (ed.). *The Conflict of Traditionalism and Modernism in the Muslim Middle East.* Austin: University of Texas Press, 1968. Eleven outstanding papers on military, literary, social, political, legal, religious, developmental, and epistemological aspects of the general subject.

Lloyd, Seton. *Iraq.* New York: Oxford University Press, 1944. An official view.

Longrigg, Stephen Hemsley. *Four Centuries of Modern Iraq.* Oxford, England: Clarendon Press, 1925. A very substantial work giving an excellent background.

———. *Iraq, 1900–1950.* London: Oxford University Press, 1953. A fine continuation of his earlier work.

———. *Syria and Lebanon under the French Mandate.* New York: Oxford University Press, 1958. Covers the period from the end of World War I to the aftermath of World War II. A fair and judicious account with sound conclusions.

MacCallum, Elizabeth P. *The Nationalist Crusade in Syria.* New York: Foreign Policy Association, 1928. The rebellion of 1925 to 1927.

Main, Ernest. *Iraq from Mandate to Independence.* London: George Allen & Unwin, 1935. A full study of the early years of Iraq.

al-Marayati, Abid A. (ed.). *Middle Eastern Constitutions and Electoral Laws.* New York: Praeger, 1968. This is a very useful and necessary work that updates the work of Helen Miller Davis.

McFadden, Tom J. *Daily Journalism in the Arab States.* Columbus: Ohio State University Press, 1953. Gives an insight into the workings and reporting of the Arab press at the end of World War II.

Mikesell, R. F., and H. B. Chenery. *Arabian Oil: America's Stake in the Middle East.* Chapel Hill: University of North Carolina Press, 1949. Relates Iraqi oil to the situation at the end of World War II.

Musrey, Alfred G. *An Arab Common Market: A Study in Inter-Arab Trade Relations, 1920–1967.* New York: Praeger, 1969. A study of the direction and potential of Arab economic integration.

Patwardhan, Vinayak N., and William J. Darby. *The State of Nutrition in the Arab Middle East.* Nashville: University of Tennessee Press, 1972. The most authoritative and comprehensive review of the state of nutrition in Syria, Lebanon, Iraq, Jordan, Egypt, and Libya.

Petran, Tabitha. *Syria.* New York: Praeger, 1972. Analyzes cultural and social movements. Points out the sad state of education in Syria during the Mandate period.

Preston, Lee E., with Karim A. Nashashibi. *Trade Patterns in the Middle East.* Washington, D.C.: American Enterprise Institute, 1970. Concentrates on intraregional trade. Has much tabular data.

Seton-Williams, M. N. *Britain and the Arab States: A Survey of Anglo-Arab Relations, 1920–1948.* London: Luzac, 1948. Pro-British.

Shwadran, Benjamin. *The Middle East, Oil, and the Great Powers.* New York: Praeger, 1955. Gives much information about the impact of the oil companies on the peoples of the Middle East.

Speiser, E. A. *The United States and the Near East.* Cambridge, Mass.: Harvard University Press, 1950. American interests and relations in the area.

Suleiman, Michael W. *Political Parties in Lebanon: The Challenge of a Fragmented Political Culture.* Ithaca, N.Y.: Cornell University Press, 1967. A straightforward and informative work describing in detail the seventeen Lebanese political parties and two quasiparty groups. Most useful.

Tibawi, A. L. *Islamic Education: Its Traditions and Modernization into the Arab National Systems.* London: Luzac, 1972. Part I deals with the period from the rise of Islam to the nineteenth century. Part II traces the development of the educational systems in most of the Muslim states. Part III reviews educational and cultural problems common to all.

United Nations, International Bank for Reconstruction and Development. *The Economic Development of Iraq.* Baltimore: Johns Hopkins University Press, 1952. A complete study of the economic situation in Iraq.

———. *The Economic Development of Syria.* Baltimore: Johns Hopkins University Press, 1955. A complete study of the economic situation in Syria.

Vatikiotis, P. J. *Conflict in the Middle East.* London: George Allen & Unwin, 1971. A study of inter-Arab and intra-Arab conflicts as they are reflected in the perceptions of Middle Easterners, and an analysis of the causes of conflict, such as the weakness of political institutions and the lack of a political community.

Warriner, Doreen. *Land and Poverty in the Middle East.* New York: Oxford University Press, 1948. A useful work.

———. *Land Reform and Development in the Middle East.* New York: Oxford University Press, 1957. Excellent chapters on Syria and Iraq.

Ziadeh, Nicola A. *Syria and Lebanon.* New York: Praeger, 1957. A study of the complex political patterns in these states.

Chapter 34

Palestine and Transjordan

Zionists, Arabs, and the British

The British under General Allenby captured Palestine, including the Ottoman province of Jerusalem, in 1917. From then until July 1, 1920, it was occupied and administered by the British army. After the Balfour Declaration, but even before the armistice, the Zionist movement sent a commission to the area, headed by Dr. Weizmann, Major Ormsby-Gore, and Major de Rothschild. Its purpose was to establish a link between the British military and the Jewish population of Palestine, to assist in the return of Jews who fled during the war, and to coordinate the activities of Jewish organizations and institutions. The future of Palestine remained up in the air until the San Remo Conference in April 1920, when it was awarded to England. Till then, uncertainty nurtured every rumor and fear, and those who lived in Palestine experienced a restlessness that later events never did resolve.

At the close of the war the population comprised about 550,000 Muslims, 70,000 Christians, and 50,000 Jews. The Muslims and most Christians were Arabic-speaking natives. Some Jews were cultural Arabs, having lived there for many centuries. Some had resided there a generation or two, having immigrated to live and work in Jewish agricultural community projects typical of mid-nineteenth-century socialistic utopian societies. The great majority of Jews, however, were newcomers. They belonged to *Haluka* (distribution) communities living on charity from world Jewry, and included Jews of various nationalities who had emigrated to the Jewish Holy Land to pray and die. During the war immigration ceased, some Jews left Palestine, others were expelled by the Turks, and the Jewish population dropped to an estimated 20,000. Moreover, a normal percentage of the *Haluka* died without the usual influx of others who wished to die in Palestine.

The Balfour Declaration stated that Great Britain "viewed with favour the establishment in Palestine of a national home for the Jewish people." But Zionists had hoped for "Palestine as the national home of the Jewish people, and the right of the Jewish people to build up its national life in Palestine." Active Zionists were confident that with work and time a Jewish national state having all the rights and appurtenances of a typical European national state would be created. They worked toward that goal; many acclaimed it openly.

The Arabs of Palestine considered their land to be a part of Syria and placed their faith in promises made to Sharif Husayn with regard to an Arab state, in Wilson's Fourteen Points, and in the Anglo-French Declaration. The British denied the existence of the Sykes-Picot Agreement and suavely explained away the Balfour Declaration as providing only for a Jewish cultural and religious home. To this the Arabs had no objection, as British oriental experts well knew. Since the Arabs enjoyed a majority of 85 to 90 percent of the population, they hoped to become an integral part of the eventual Arab national state. The arrival of the King-Crane commission encouraged them to believe that the Arab view would prevail. The Zionist commission, however, disturbed them; and the return of Jews who fled during the war, accompanied by the immediate postwar agitation for Jewish immigration to Palestine raised a multitude of fears in their hearts.

The British wanted to incorporate Palestine into their empire because of its proximity to Suez, its suitability as an outlet for Mosul oil, and its strategic position with respect to Arabia. The British army was occupying Palestine, and there seemed to be no good reason for leaving. A Zionist alliance might serve Britain's imperial interests and prevent the French from holding the entire Levantine coast and from approaching close to Suez.

Obviously, had these British views been clearly focused by the cabinet, the military administration in Palestine would never have been slighted to the extent of having a succession of three chief administrators in 1919. Procrastination, intrigue, war weariness, faction, and strife plagued the British military administration and intensified public unrest throughout Palestine.

British Mandate

Reprisals and bloodshed first occurred in April 1920, when many Arab villagers flocked to Jerusalem to the Nabi Musa celebrations. Rumors turned into riots; Arabs who inflamed the villagers and Zionists with caches of arms were seized and sentenced by British military courts to penal servitude. That same month the Powers, meeting at San Remo, affirmed the British mandate over Palestine; on July 1, 1920, Sir Herbert Samuel, the first high commissioner for Palestine, including Transjordan, relieved the military authorities of their burden.

During the five years of Sir Herbert's civil administration four separate, yet parallel, governments were formed. Most important was the British executive government, composed of various administrative departments over each of which the high commissioner appointed a British director or secretary. These officials formed a cabinet, whose first chief secretary was Wyndham Deedes. Departments were established for public works, education, immigration, customs, excise and trade, antiquities, treasury, revenue, attorney general, police, health, agriculture and forests, posts and telegraphs, lands, and audit. An advisory council consisting of ten British officials, four Muslims, three Christians, and three Jews was appointed. An elective legislative council was projected, but it never came into existence because of disagreement over the ratio of representation between Arabs and Jews.

The Jewish community inaugurated the second government. In the fall of 1920 a Jewish national assembly was elected. It, in turn, appointed a Jewish national council *(Vaad Leumi)*, which the high commissioner recognized as representative of the Jewish community in Palestine. The national council governed the Jews of Palestine in personal, communal, and religious affairs and recommended actions to British authorities concerning matters affecting the Jewish community. Certain Jews of prewar Palestinian residence, however, clung to a theocratic concept of Jewish life and refused to be governed by the national council. Supported by *Agudath Israel,* they disclaimed all connections with political and nationalistic Zionism, but they proved too small a minority for the British Palestine administration to recognize in any formal way.

The third government was the international Zionist organization, with headquarters in London. It represented the more than thirty Zionist groups in many parts of the world that had sponsored the drive to obtain the Balfour Declaration. A number of its executives who lived and worked in Palestine between 1921 and 1929 were known as the Palestine Zionist executive. Each member was responsible for some department of work: political, immigration, education, industry, health, and public works. Sometimes referred to as a quasi-government, the Zionist executive followed the policies established by the Zionist organization in London and augmented the administration of the mandatory administration in Palestine. Frequently when the high commissioner's government and the Zionist executive were at odds, the Zionist organization proved more effective in persuading the British cabinet and House of Commons to follow the Zionist course than the foreign or colonial secretary was in obtaining support for the policies of the high commissioner.

These three "governments" represented imperialism, Jewish settlers, and world Jewry, respectively. The fourth government tried to represent the great majority of the people of Palestine—Muslim and Christian Arabs. Arab notables—of which the two most prominent families were the al-Husaynis and the Nashashibis—at first voiced the opinion that Arab Palestine was and should continue to be a part of Syria. But they had no love for the French and, therefore, dropped that contention after Faysal's defeat at Damascus. Following a large Arab congress at Haifa in December 1920 the Arab executive was born. Musa Kazim al-Husayni, former mayor of Jerusalem, was its chairman until 1934. Although the Arab executive attempted to parallel the activities of the Zionist executive, it never had the latter's extensive financial resources or wealth of personnel at its call. Without any effective political muscle or singleness of purpose, this fourth force could in no way compete with any of the other three.

In addition to the Arab executive the British created the supreme Muslim council in 1921 to deal with Muslim religious affairs, especially custody of religious endowments and administration of Muslim courts. Fines, fees, and patronage gave the supreme Muslim council considerable power; and its president, Hajj Amin al-Husayni, became the leading political Muslim figure in Palestine in the 1930s. Commonly known as the Mufti, Hajj Amin was chosen, with Sir Herbert Samuel's connivance, for that office in 1921. A position held for life, the mufti of Jerusalem, like muftis in other cities, gave legal opinions on Sacred Law for citizens and the courts.

With four governments in Palestine, each with several parties or groups, and with the eyes of the world upon the Holy Land of three religions, Sir Herbert found the task of governing the mandate a challenge to human ingenuity. He had to remember Britain's imperial concern for Palestine and the entire Middle East. He had to govern the mandate economically and peacefully. He had to fulfill the mission of the mandatory power in instructing the people, 85 percent of whom were Arabs, and in preparing the way for self-government and independence. And he had to follow the instructions of the cabinet in London, which was persistently dogged by political pressure to honor not only the letter of the Balfour Declaration but also its spirit as interpreted by the Zionists who were already building the foundations for a national state of Israel. The dilemmas posed kept the political scene in Palestine shifting, as first one faction and then another played the leading role.

Immigration Policies

No problem weighed more heavily upon Palestine than that of immigration and population. Zionist leaders, who wished to obtain a Jewish majority as quickly as possible, encouraged mass immigration. When a majority was achieved, Great Britain would be asked to relinquish her mandate, and Palestine would become an independent Jewish national state. Justice Brandeis dissented from this policy, believing that immigration should proceed slowly and only as rapidly as a secure economic basis for the immigrant's livelihood could be assured.

Sir Herbert Samuel upon assuming office in 1920 announced that Jewish immigrants would be permitted to enter Palestine at the rate of 1,000 per month; later that same year an annual quota of 16,500 was set. Under this program nearly 10,000 Jewish immigrants entered Palestine up to May 4, 1921, when immigration was suspended because of serious Arab riots in Jaffa. A month later immigration was permitted to continue; Winston Churchill, then colonial secretary, announced in a famous memorandum of July 1922, in answer to Samuel's demand for a policy statement, that Britain intended to honor the Balfour Declaration and to fulfill the pledge of allowing the Jewish community to increase its numbers through immigration. The pledge with respect to immigration, however, would be interpreted and regulated so that the volume of immigration should not exceed the economic capacity of Palestine to absorb new arrivals.

In actual practice middle-class families or anyone who had $2,500 could obtain an entry permit, and a skilled workman needed only half that sum. In addition the Zionist organization, through various funds collected in Europe and America, provided the necessary funds for carefully selected immigrants. Immigration increased rapidly, and nearly 35,000 Jews entered in the year of 1925. From 1927 until 1933 the number arriving in Palestine did not always offset those leaving. Beginning in 1933 entries rose sharply and in several years reached 40,000. Moreover, many Jewish visitors remained in Palestine illegally so that the precise number "ingathered" between 1920 and 1939 was unknown, but it was well over 300,000. The total Jewish population rose to 445,000 in 1939, not quite 30 percent of the total population.

Arab influx and natural growth were high, but did not keep pace with the Jews. There were 620,000 Arabs in 1918, and in 1939 the estimate tallied some 1,044,000. The high Arab birth rate accounted for natural growth of about 20,000 a year. The Jews, with 6,000 births a year, had to find 14,000 immigrants annually to keep pace in their desperate population race.

Whenever immigration reached high figures, riots between Arabs and Jews resulted. The gates would be barred for a few months. Then, political pressure in London resulted in the order being rescinded. Principles of economic absorptive capacity were constantly discussed, but how to apply them and by what standard they could be judged were never determined. To the Zionist organization any limitation upon "ingathering" smacked of heresy and appeared fatal to the whole nationalist movement.

Land Policies

A large majority of Jews settling in Palestine came from urban centers in Europe. Yet one of the underlying philosophies of Zionism called for an agricultural society in Palestine, and workers on the land enjoyed an honored position in Zionist society. Zionists pledged that Arab tenant farmers would not be driven from lands purchased by their Jewish National Fund, but this guarantee proved impossible to fulfill. Some of the very best lands in Palestine were purchased at inflated prices from Arab absentee landlords living in Damascus and Beirut. For centuries a regular land market had existed for investment purposes, and transactions rarely affected the tenant cultivator. However, land bought by the National Fund became the inalienable property of the Jewish community with express provisos that only Jews might work the land or be employed upon it. Tenant families who had lived in a village and tilled the land about it for a thousand years were evicted, sometimes summarily. Since rumors fly in the Middle East, each tenant farmer feared he would be the next and reacted vigorously against any Jewish immigration.

Land was expensive in Palestine, because the population was relatively dense already and because to expand the cultivable area required a considerable outlay of funds for irrigation, fertilizers, draining, flushing to counteract salinity, removal of stones, and so on. In the 1930s farm land cost on an average about four times what it did in the United States, and the wages of farm labor were so high that general agriculture on a commercial basis was not feasible. Very few private individual farms were set up. The Jewish National Fund purchased most of the farm land and rented it at nominal fees to farmers, who would live in a private village or colony *(moshavah)*, a cooperative village *(moshav ovdim)*, or a collective village *(kibbutz)*. Cultivation of citrus fruits was encouraged, and in the years before 1939 annual exports reached 10,000,000 cases. These exports provided Palestine with almost all of her earned foreign exchange.

The trend of agricultural development had a marked effect upon the Arab rural community. Living alongside the Jewish agricultural establishments, Arab farmers learned and followed the practices of their neighbors. This was attested by the fact that in 1936 at least half of the citrus production came from Arab lands. Hill-country land that could not be farmed by mechanized equipment and would not easily submit to intensified cultivation was shunned by the Zionist organization and left to Arab peasants. It was marginal farming at best, but the tax structure of the administration bore heavily upon the peasants who worked these lands, and their poverty was sharply depicted against the higher Jewish standard of living.

Industrial Progress

Although Zionist groups spent over $75 million on land for all types of farms and although society highly regarded work on the land, the majority of Jews settled in urban communities, the greatest of which became Tel Aviv. Other centers were Jaffa, Haifa, and Jerusalem. The overall Jewish urban population amounted to 75 percent of the Jewish community. At the end of World War I Tel Aviv was a small dingy town of 2,000 inhabitants on the outskirts of Jaffa; in 1939 it contained over 150,000 inhabitants and was called "the only purely Jewish city in the world." Much of the industry was located there, and it became the center of artistic and cultural life in Jewish Palestine. The Zionist organization had continual difficulties in persuading immigrants from European cities to settle in rural agricultural villages after they had been sheltered in Tel Aviv.

A relatively large amount of industry developed in Palestine, but up to 1939 it was directed to supplying the local market. Exports from Dead Sea potash and chemical industries were just beginning to show in the trade statistics. In 1935 the pipeline from Iraq began to discharge oil at its terminus in Haifa, but only a negligible amount was refined locally. Palestinians had visions of supplying the industrial needs of a wide area in the Middle East, but at that time they could not meet local requirements.

The industrial and labor picture in Palestine was dominated by the General Federation of Jewish Labor *(Histadruth)*. Owning and operating a number of industries, the Histadruth represented about three-fourths of the Jewish workers, whose wages were higher than those of non-members. Arab laborers were unorganized; and the obvious wage disparity and discrimination in favor of Jewish workers incited bitter feelings. Yet unemployment figures were low, and many regulations against hiring Arabs were ignored. For example, by 1935 only 28 percent of the labor on Jewish orange plantations was Jewish. Wages for Arab workmen were higher in Palestine than in neighboring states, but the higher cost of living held any increase in real wages to a minimum.

Social Developments

On social and cultural endeavors the Zionist organization and many individuals and groups, such as the Histadruth and *Hadassah* (the American Zionist women's organization), expended much time, effort, and money. From the outset, education was deemed most important. The cornerstone of Hebrew University in British-occupied Jerusalem on Mt. Scopus was laid July 24, 1918, even before the end of the war. Schools of every description —primary, secondary, teacher training, vocational, agricultural—came into existence, and before 1939 every Jewish child received at least a primary education. Hospitals, clinics, maternity and infant care, medical-research laboratories, and public-health campaigns also received much attention. Since public funds from the Palestine government for such uses were insignificant, the needs of the Arab population were unfulfilled. But contributions from abroad, particularly America, enabled the Jewish community to maintain a level of public services more comparable to those of Western society.

Finances

The activities of the Zionist organization in purchasing land, supporting new immigrants, building schools and hospitals, starting industries, and financing its myriad of projects were made possible by contributions from world Jewry. Estimates show that about $400 million was the cost of the Zionist development in Palestine between 1919 and 1939. Annual exports in the last years before World War II reached $4 million, most of which were receipts from the citrus industry. Annual imports rose to about $18 million. Other expenses came from the outlay for new land and its rehabilitation—$55 million in 1935—building materials, machinery, and arms and ammunition. A significant number of settlers brought capital with them in the form of foreign exchange, enabling Palestine to make purchases of machinery, capital goods of all sorts, and consumption goods necessary to maintain life. The Palestine Economic Corporation, an American concern, invested in ventures that had a sound economic outlook. Some of these were the King David Hotel in Jerusalem, the Palestine Electric Corporation, and the Palestine Potash Company.

Without the steady flow of money and resources into Palestine the Zionist achievement could not have been recorded. At any time after its inception the faltering of Jewish charity would have been disastrous. At no time in that period did Palestine ever approach a self-supporting status, and the bountiful gifts stabilized the society at a standard of living far above what any reasonable expectation of the exploitation of the country's resources could produce. To that degree the entire economy of Palestine was false. After the end of the first great surge of immigration, which came to 33,000 in 1925, the fall in the value of Polish currency, slackening of interest in the West, and then worldwide depression brought emigration from Palestine and severe economic crisis. Only the advent of Hitler and the accompanying sympathy toward the Jews saved the Zionist program for Palestine.

British Administration

Sir Herbert Samuel served as high commissioner for five years. Only one serious outbreak of violence (1921) between Jews and Arabs occurred during his term, and perhaps a recurrence of the riots was averted by Churchill's White Paper of 1922 which promised the Arab community that nothing would be done to jeopardize Arab rights. Outward peace reigned, and prosperity and activity dominated the Palestine scene. The Hebrew University in Jerusalem opened its doors; commerce and agriculture advanced; and political passions seemed to have cooled.

After considerable political controversy, and following the Churchill White Paper, the council of the League of Nations on July 24, 1922, approved the mandate for Palestine. In entrusting the state to Great Britain the League incorporated the Balfour Declaration in the preamble and recognized the historic association of the Jewish people with Palestine. The terms of conveyance instructed Great Britain to recognize the Zionist organization and in cooperation with it to facilitate Jewish immigration and "close settlement by Jews on the land" without prejudicing the "rights and position of other sections of the population." The mandatory instrument gave Great Britain authority with regard to all Holy Places and Muslim Foundations with the express injunction that they be administered according to religious law, existing rights, and public order. Free access to Holy Places and free exercise of worship were guaranteed. English, Arabic, and Hebrew were designated as official languages; all public inscriptions had to be written in Arabic and Hebrew. Article 25 of the mandate exempted all the land of Palestine east of the Jordan River from the execution of such provisions of the mandate as Great Britain deemed inapplicable to that area.

To say the least, the terms of the mandate were not easy to fulfill. Every high commissioner from 1920 to 1939 tried to comply with the instructions. But each one discovered how difficult—almost impossible—it was to follow the dictates of the colonial office in London, to "cooperate" with the Zionists, and to maintain the Arab rights and position. Sir Herbert attempted to have a constitution adopted and a legislature elected and convened, but found Arab leaders unwilling to cooperate. Through political boycott and threats to riot the Arabs hoped to obtain British recognition that their preponderant majority entitled them to control the institutions of self-government.

Field Marshal Lord Plumer, who came as high commissioner in July 1925, had been the administrator of Malta and a distinguished soldier in World

War I. He set out to inform everybody that he intended to pursue the instructions of the mandate, resisting pressure and threats from any and all sources. His three years were peaceful ones, and British armed forces were reduced as an unnecessary financial burden.

The Jewish Agency

In 1929 the Zionist organization in its work in Palestine was transformed into the Jewish Agency. This step followed the suggestion put forth in Article 4 of the mandate urging the Zionist organization "to secure the cooperation of all Jews who are willing to assist in the establishment of the Jewish national home." In 1925 Dr. Weizmann advanced the formation of an enlarged Jewish Agency to consist of an equal number of Zionists and non-Zionists and thus obtain support of all Jews for the development of Palestine. But differences over fund raising in America between Rabbi Wise and non-Zionists headed by Louis Marshall and Felix Warburg retarded its approval.

However, in 1929 at Zurich the sixteenth Zionist congress voted the enlarged Jewish Agency. The precarious world economic situation made it imperative for Zionists to win support from whatever source, and the announced objectives of the new Jewish Agency were: assist Jewish immigration to Palestine; foster the Hebrew language and culture; acquire land by the Jewish National Fund as inalienable property of the Jewish people; promote agriculture and colonization based on the principle of Jewish labor; and provide for religious needs of Jewish people. The president of the Zionist organization automatically served as president of the Jewish Agency, Dr. Weizmann becoming its first president. Zionists were hesitant about uniting with non-Zionists for fear that the program would be diluted and compromised. In actual practice the Jewish Agency drew in more and more Jews to support its ambitions, finally committing most Jews to the full program.

In addition to the non-Zionist Jews of the Western world who desired full integration into Western society in Western nation-states, two groups were opposed to the policies of the Jewish Agency. The more numerous was composed of the rigidly orthodox in Palestine and elsewhere, who felt that the Zionist program, being nationalistic, destroyed the religious basis of Judaism. The other group, led by Vladimir Jabotinsky, rebelled against the acquiescence of the Zionist organization to the Churchill White Paper of 1922. Calling themselves the revisionists, they demanded immediate fulfillment by the Palestinian government of the national home on both sides of the Jordan River, and condemned the inclusion of non-Zionists, whom they regarded as Jewish traitors.

The Passfield White Paper

The vocal outbursts of these rabid revisionists, along with disturbances in 1928 near the Wailing Wall, frightened the Arabs and actuated them to be more concerned with Muslim rights along the Wall, which was part of the enclosure around the area surrounding the Dome of the Rock. Muslim Arabs, agitated by many wild rumors, irritated worshippers and aroused Jewish ire by disturbing prayers and various religious services. Custom and precedent have always been powerful claims in religious law in the Middle East, and Arab acts, which to Jews and Westerners seemed intentional aggravations, were efforts to maintain legal rights and prohibit new rights from developing.

Hostilities broke out in August 1929. A group of young Zionists from Tel Aviv, in open defiance of orders from the acting high commissioner, sang the Zionist anthem and raised their flag at the Wailing Wall. The next day a Muslim ceremony took place at the same spot, with minor disturbances occurring. In Jerusalem a Jewish boy kicked his football into an Arab tomato patch, and a fight ensued in which the boy was stabbed. British police arrested the Arab, but were then mobbed by a Jewish throng. Rioting continued for several days, with a dozen assaults upon Arabs and seven on Jews. On August 23 Muslims attacked Jews in Jerusalem, and serious incidents followed in Hebron and Safed. Troops were called from Egypt and Transjordan. On August 26 Jews invaded a mosque in Jerusalem, killing the imam. Later the same day a Muslim shrine was damaged and the tombs of the prophets desecrated.

Sir John Chancellor, the high commissioner since 1928, returned from summer leave on August 29 and order was restored. He condemned the Arab leadership for the outrages. Over 130 Jews were killed and 339 wounded; 116 Arabs were killed and an unknown number wounded. Trials were held for over 1,000 persons—90 percent Arabs, 10 percent Jews—and 25 Arabs and 1 Jew were condemned to death.

Meanwhile, Whitehall sent out Sir Walter Shaw as head of a commission "to inquire into the immediate causes which led to the recent outbreak in Palestine and to make recommendations as to the steps necessary to avoid recurrence." The League of Nations also sent its own Wailing Wall commission to find some "solution of the problems relating to the question of the Holy Places of Palestine." Furthermore, the British government sent Sir John Hope Simpson to study and report on land settlement, immigration, and development in Palestine. Certainly information would not be lacking!

All the reports were submitted. In October 1930 Lord Passfield (Sidney Webb), the colonial secretary, issued his famous White Paper outlining British policy on Palestine. The Passfield White Paper repeated the same general view presented in 1922 by the Churchill White Paper and emphasized the equal responsibility of the Palestine government to the Jewish and non-Jewish populations. Attention was drawn to the "economic absorptive capacity" of Palestine, and again the statement differentiated between a Jewish national home and a Jewish nationalist state.

In a constructive vein, Lord Passfield indicated that additional armed forces would be stationed in Palestine to add greater security, especially for the more exposed Jewish settlements. He condemned the Arabs for non-cooperation in establishing a legislative council and promised that steps would be taken to give some self-government to Palestine with or without the help of any particular group in Palestine. The White Paper stressed the poor condition of Arab peasants and pointed out the need for Arab land development. It stated that the immediate task of the Palestine administration would be to assist agricultural progress of the Arabs and to close Jewish immigration if it prevented any Arab from obtaining employment.

The storm of protest which arose from the Zionist camp was serious. The tone and interpretation of British intentions expressed in the Passfield White Paper crushed the leaders of the Jewish Agency. Weizmann, Warburg, and Melchett resigned their positions. Because of Dr. Weizmann's policy of cooperation with Great Britain and his acceptance of the Churchill White Paper of 1922, he had been under constant pressure, led by Jabotinsky, Rabbi Wise, and Nahum Goldmann. In view of their attacks, the Passfield White Paper made Weizmann's position untenable among extreme Zionists.

Pressure upon the British government moved Prime Minister Mac-Donald to announce misgivings over the White Paper and to write a public letter in February 1931 to Dr. Weizmann, emasculating the White Paper on almost every position it had taken. Then the Arabs were up in arms, and the Palestine Arab executive denounced MacDonald's letter as a breach of faith. British indecision and wavering invited many leaders of the Middle East to reason that the Passfield White Paper resulted from the Arab outbreak of August 1929 and that the MacDonald letter stemmed from Jewish agitation against the White Paper. British prestige suffered; the rewards of violence and threats appeared consequential. Under such conditions a peaceful future for Palestine looked rather bleak.

Economic Advances

Although the political situation remained unsettled through the next several years, and British attempts at inducing some form of self-government proved as fruitless as the first overtures of Sir Herbert Samuel, the economic boom into which Palestine entered gave optimists an opportunity to assert that all was well. Lieutenant-General Sir Arthur Wauchope became high commissioner in November 1931, just when the boom was first accelerating. Jewish immigration picked up; agricultural and industrial production jumped; government revenue trebled and quadrupled; citrus cultivation spread; and new capital investments gave greater opportunities for labor, which in turn kept wages at a high level. After 1932 the arrival of German artisans and capitalists in flight from Hitler provided greater stimulus to the boom. Genuine international capitalists provided more optimism by discussing the role Palestine might assume as an entrepôt between East and West. Successful transportation routes between Baghdad and Damascus encouraged others to link Basrah and Haifa. The Anglo-Persian Oil Company proposed a pipeline to the Palestinian coast, and airlines planned to use Palestine as a major stop between Europe and India and the Far East.

Legal and illegal immigration swelled, and Zionist spokesmen (ignoring the high Arab birth rate) predicted a Jewish majority in Palestine within a decade. In consequence, the Arab executive during the month of October 1933, provoked a series of armed attacks upon the British, whom they accused of aiding the Zionists. Meanwhile, the revisionist Zionists continued to inveigh against the mild course of the Jewish Agency and its collaboration with the British. Dr. Arlosoroff, a leader of the Zionist Labor party and chairman of the political department of the Jewish Agency in Palestine, was murdered by revisionists, and the British suppressed their demonstrations. Commentators, in reviewing these outbursts, noted that the attacks were not by Jews or Arabs against the other and assumed unjustifiably that the two peoples were learning to live together.

The amazing growth of the Jewish community in the years between 1933 and 1936 affected even remote Arab villages in the hill country of Palestine. The great influx encouraged the leaders of the Jewish Agency to predict publicly that at the current rate of "ingathering" Jews would comprise a majority of the population by 1947. Arab political efforts and leadership coalesced into one united group, which called itself the Arab Higher Committee.

Evidence that the Zionists were acquiring arms through smuggling came to light when a shipment of "cement" inadvertently was discovered to be 359 drums of firearms and 400,000 rounds of ammunition. A double standard of wage rates developed in Haifa, Jaffa, and Jerusalem, much to the displeasure of Arab labor, and discrimination in hiring became obvious to all. Italian successes in East Africa and the appeasement of Mussolini lowered British prestige in the Middle East.

Peel Report

In the face of these ominous developments the Arabs in November 1935 petitioned the high commissioner to establish, among other things, "democratic government in accordance with the Covenant of the League of Nations and Article 2 of the Palestine Mandate." A month later Sir Arthur Wauchope presented details of a legislative council to be composed of 11 Muslims, 7 Jews, 3 Christians, 2 business representatives, and 5 British officials. Accompanying the announcement was the statement that the high commissioner would proceed with the establishment of the council whether or not any community refused to participate in the elections. The Arabs announced they would cooperate; the Jews declared they would not. Outnumbered, they feared they would lose on the immigration issue. Far better to delay self-government for a few years more until a Jewish majority was achieved. The Zionist cause was supported by the English House of Commons. In April 1936 the high commissioner acknowledged that plans for self-government were postponed.

Hebrew newspapers in Palestine rejoiced over the Jewish victory in the English Parliament, Arab leaders were dismayed. At a time when Arab strikes and disorders in Iraq, Syria, Lebanon, and Egypt forced England and

France to grant self-government, peaceful persuasion in Palestine failed to bring similar concessions.

The violence in Palestine came first from the population; only later was it directed by the Arab Higher Committee. Arab highwaymen held up a caravan of cars near Nablus, shooting two Jews. During the following days numerous Arabs in Tel Aviv and Jaffa were attacked by Jews. Then, Arab rioting began and continued in a sporadic way for many months. Strikes ensued; many groups refused to pay taxes; and before the end of April 1936 a general Arab strike spread to all Palestine. The Arab Higher Committee declared the strike would continue until the British agreed to grant self-government, halt Jewish immigration, and prohibit transfer of Arab lands to Jews. A peaceful strike was contemplated, but feeling ran so high among the Arab population that bombings and property destruction were frequent. There were as many attacks directed against the British as against the Zionists.

In May Great Britain sought to pacify Palestine by sending Earl Peel as head of a commission of inquiry. But an impasse developed: the Peel Commission would not leave England until the strike ended; the Arab Higher Committee would not end the strike until Jewish immigration was suspended; and the British refused to cancel the immigration schedules. Palestine had grown important to the British Empire with regard to air routes to Asia and Africa, sea lanes through Suez and the Mediterranean, and oil deliveries from Iraq. The security of these interests was presented to the British public as dependent upon the success of Zionism in Palestine. British difficulties and embarrassment mounted. Sentiment and pronouncements in Turkey, Iraq, Egypt, and India sided with the Arabs; Poland and the United States, each with large Jewish groups, pressed England to favor the Zionists.

In October 1936, upon pleas from the kings of Iraq and Saudi Arabia—both of whom were at that time subservient to Britain and British pressure—the Higher Committee called off the strike without obtaining its demands. Zionism and Britain won, but only by giving neighboring Arab governments an active hand in Palestinian Arab affairs (undoubtedly at British invitation). In November Lord Peel and his colleagues arrived in Palestine, made their survey, and in July 1937 published their report. Without too much difficulty the Peel Report concluded that an "irrepressible conflict" had arisen over the question: "Who, ultimately, would rule the country?" The report recommended the division of Palestine and proceeded to suggest frontiers and conditions of partition. Simultaneously, a White Paper was issued by the cabinet supporting the Peel Report as official policy.

The partition scheme was bitterly assailed by Zionists, non-Zionists, and Arabs. Non-Zionists ruled out a national state of any kind, and the partition plan established one. Zionists, while not entirely shutting the door on the idea of partition, argued that partition had already been enacted when

Transjordan was cut off and that further decrease of the national home was contrary to the letter and the spirit of the mandate. The Arab Higher Committee and Arab National Defense party denounced the principle of partition and noted that this particular scheme gave seven-eighths of the Arab citrus groves to Jewish Palestine while 77 percent of the land in that state would be Arab owned. The Arab state could never be solvent and would be dependent upon the Jewish state. Moreover, with unlimited immigration the Jewish state would become overpopulated and demand more space from the Arabs, who would be subject "to perpetual encroachments, political and economic." To Arabs any partition was unreasonable and in violation of the mandate and the Covenant of the League of Nations.

Pursuing the suggestions given in the Peel Report and White Paper, the Palestine administration took more positive action. Jewish immigration was curtailed and a firmer hand was directed against the Arabs. The Jerusalem offices of the Arab Higher Committee were searched. In September 1937, after the murder of a British official, Hajj Amin al-Husayn was removed from the presidency of the supreme Muslim council and five of the Higher Committee were deported to the Seychelles Islands. (Hajj Amin escaped to Lebanon.) These acts touched off an Arab rebellion and guerrilla warfare against the British, although numerous attacks upon the Jewish community also occurred. To defend themselves the Jews, with the approval of the authorities, greatly expanded their illegal force, the *Haganah*, which totaled over 10,000 men, well-trained and well-armed by the Jewish Agency.

Into this maelstrom was sent the Woodhead Commission in April 1938 to reinvestigate the partition scheme and to report on detailed frontiers for the two states. Published in October 1938 the Woodhead Report outlined three different possibilities. Plan A was the Peel Partition. Plan B left much of Galilee to the British permanent mandate and reduced the Jewish enclave south of Jaffa. Plan C suggested only small Jewish and Arab states, retaining most of Palestine in a mandated territory.

Civil War
But the plans fell on deaf ears. Palestine was in open revolt. Bands of Arab rebels attacked police stations, driving officials from town to town; by October 1938 even the Old City of Jerusalem was occupied by the rebels. The *Irgun*, an illegal and secret national military organization set up by the revisionists, perpetrated many attacks upon the Arabs, and the *Haganah* increased its membership and obtained many "opportunities for broader experience." Palestine was on the verge of civil war and rebellion.

The open revolt in Palestine coincided with the pressure of Hitler upon Czechoslovakia, the Munich accord, and the nadir of British prestige. Germany and Italy showered propaganda and courtesies upon the Arabs of Palestine, and England quickly realized how vulnerable her position with the Arab states had become. A new high commissioner, Sir Harold MacMichael, arrived in 1938, and the new colonial secretary, Malcolm Mac-

Donald, declared that plans for partition were being dropped and invited
Arabs and Jews to a conference in London.

Representatives of Egypt, Iraq, Transjordan, Saudi Arabia, Yemen, and
Palestine Arabs—Husaynis and Nashashibis—came from the Arab side.
Representatives of the Jewish Agency and Zionist and non-Zionist Jewish
groups from Great Britain, the United States, France, Germany, Belgium,
Poland, eastern Europe, and South Africa filled out the roster. The conference opened on February 7, 1939. In essence the British proposed (first to
the Arabs and then to the Jews, since the former would not sit down with
the latter) a considerable reduction in Jewish immigration and land purchases and the establishment of a single self-governing Palestine after ten
years. The Jews refused to discuss the question further and left, since the
terms ruled that Arabs would comprise two-thirds of the population and
Jews would forever be a minority in Palestine. Although definitely more
favorably disposed, the Arabs declined to accept the proposals because they
did not go far enough toward curbing the Zionist presence.

Rebuffed on both sides and with time running out in Europe, Great
Britain issued a White Paper on May 17, 1939, declaring her unilateral
solution of the Palestine impasse. Proposals followed the earlier scheme.
About 75,000 Jewish immigrants would be allowed to enter over the next
five years, after which the doors would be open only upon Arab consent.
Land sales from Arabs to Jews would be strictly regulated. Aften ten years
self-rule would be established on lines similar to those already prevailing in
Iraq.

The Arab Higher Committee rejected this solution, asking for independence at the beginning rather than the end of the ten-year period. Remembering distinctly how the Churchill and Passfield White Papers were
quickly disowned by British governments when Jewish pressure was applied, the Arabs could not believe that this White Paper would have a
different ending. Jews in Palestine and Zionists throughout the world denounced the White Paper as a treacherous document, and no sacrifice was
deemed too great to frustrate and defeat it. In Jerusalem there were shouts:
"Down with Weizmann!" and "Up with Jabotinsky!" A British policeman
was shot in Jerusalem; David Ben-Gurion, who had taken over from Weizmann as chairman of the Jewish Agency executive, announced that this
murder "marked the beginning of Jewish resistance" to the new British
policy. At the twenty-first Zionist congress at Geneva in August 1939 Ben-
Gurion urged that Jews defy Britain and act in Palestine as though the
Jewish Agency were the state. Rabbi Silver of the United States supported
Weizmann's more moderate position and pointed out how foolish it would
be to side with England in the coming war against the Nazis and at the same
time embarrass her in Palestine.

To what extent Great Britain would have moved to implement the White
Paper of 1939 cannot be judged. In the summer of that year she was too
weak and the crisis in central Europe too serious for any action to be initiated. When World War II broke out Zionists and Arabs alike recognized

that the ultimate outcome of the struggle among the great powers would probably be the determining factor in the future of Palestine. The decision might be made on the battlefields of Europe.

The history of Palestine in the two decades between the World Wars had three component parts. The Zionist society worked hard with great faith, courage, and determination to build the Jewish national home in Palestine. Any compromise from that goal was dishonorable. The diligence, the improvement of agriculture and land, and the spirit of society were laudable. The Zionists were blind, however, to the fact that they were intruders in another people's home and insensitive to the distrust, dislike, and fear they generated in Arab hearts. Arab society believed that an Arab independent state had been promised and that any infringement of that pledge was dishonorable. The lesser-organized Arabs in central Arabia, Kuwayt, the Hijaz, Yemen, Iraq, and Transjordan were independent, and the more developed Arabs of Egypt, Syria, and Lebanon had representative legislatures and considerable independence. Was it not strange that they, the Arabs of Palestine, did not have similar freedom? No peoples from distant places gave them hundreds of millions of dollars to develop their country. They felt the indictment that they did not utilize their land was disproved by the facts that their citrus grooves were as productive as those of the Zionists and that they were better grain farmers than the Jews. The Arabs, however, suffered from benighted leadership, which erroneously judged that violence would intimidate Jew and Briton into giving the Arabs independence. The third component, the British, acted administratively as though Palestine were a colony but economically as though the land belonged to someone else. British businessmen saw little profit in investing or settling in Palestine when its permanence within the empire was doubtful. Through those years Great Britain tried, usually unsuccessfully, to balance her budget; consequently, the idea of spending sums to raise standards of living in Palestine or increase productivity of the land for the benefit of native inhabitants had few supporters. Thus, England just muddled along, gaining enmity on all sides.

Transjordan

East of the Jordan River, however, British policy fell more into traditional patterns of imperial behavior. Since the area east of the river was promised to the Arabs and Sharif Husayn, the British found it good policy as well as convenient to grant the administration of that land to Prince Abdallah as a reward for not attacking the French in Damascus. Accordingly Transjordan was given to Abdallah in 1921. In 1922 the League council exempted it from many provisions of the mandate for Palestine, particularly those referring to Holy Places and implementation of the Balfour Declaration. The following year in Amman, capital of Transjordan, Sir Herbert Samuel announced the independence of Transjordan, which was also proclaimed simultaneously by Abdallah. England, nevertheless, remained in control until an understanding was concluded between the two governments. In actual practice from 1921 onwards Britain gave financial grants to Abdallah, and his administration was assisted by British officials.

In 1926 Abdallah convened a group of Arab notables to prepare the way for an elective legislative assembly. In 1927 petitions were submitted to him demanding a national representative council and freedom from British rule. To meet this pressure upon Abdallah, a treaty was concluded in February 1928 at Jerusalem between Great Britain and Transjordan, placing their relations on a firm basis. Legislation and administration in Transjordan was exercised by the prince under authority of the British high commissioner through the British resident stationed in Amman. The British were to control the budget, finances, army, economic development, and foreign affairs. Shortly thereafter, Abdallah issued a constitution providing for a legislative council, but Transjordanian notables refused to cooperate because they objected to the excessive control by the British.

Great Britain continued to dominate Transjordan between World Wars I and II, largely through annual financial support to Abdallah, support that increased from about $500,000 a year in the 1920s to $1 million in 1939. Britain had two military forces in Transjordan. First, there was the Arab Legion, organized in 1921 by Captain Peake of the Egyptian Camel Corps. It was planned as a police force, but it defended the frontiers from bedouin infiltration. Originally it had no desert section and no airplanes, but after 1930 it expanded and blossomed into one of the most significant military forces in the Middle East. Although under the command of the prince of Transjordan, it received five-sixths of its financial requirements direct from the British treasury. In the treaty of 1928 provision was made for formation of the Transjordan Frontier Force under the direct control of the high commissioner, since he was responsible for Transjordanian foreign affairs and the protection of her frontiers.

Both armies were instruments of the British government in the Middle East. They served to protect the frontiers of Palestine, Transjordan, and Iraq from raids by Ibn Saud and to maintain and police the corridor between Iraq and Transjordan through which ran the oil pipeline from Kirkuk to Haifa. Transjordan not only was an anchor for the British position in the Middle East but also stood as an important link in her empire. Prince Abdallah performed well for the British and they sustained him in a dignified manner.

REFERENCES: Chapter 34

Almost every volume discussing affairs of the Middle East in modern times bears some relationship to the events and movements presented in this chapter. Of special note, however, are those found in Chapters 7, 19, 23, 27, 28, 30, 31, and 33.

Abu-Lughod, Ibrahim (ed.). *The Transformation of Palestine: Essays on the Origin and Development of the Arab-Israel Conflict.* Evanston, Ill.: Northwestern University Press, 1971. Sixteen outstanding scholars discuss the resistance to Zionism among the Arabs from the time of the mandate. Includes four studies on the international aspects of the conflict. Generally sympathetic to the Arabs.

Antoun, Richard T. *Arab Village: A Social Structural Study of a Transjordanian Peasant Community.* Bloomington: Indiana University Press, 1972.

Aruri, Naseer H. *Jordan: A Study in Political Development (1921–1965).* The Hague: Nijhoff, 1972. Offers insight into the interdependence of domestic and international politics.

Ben-Horin, Meir. *Max Nordau: Philosopher of Solidarity.* New York: Conference on Jewish Social Studies, 1956.

Bentwich, Norman. *England in Palestine.* London: Kegan Paul, Trench, Trubner, 1932. Written by the mildly Zionist British official who served as head of the Department of Justice in Palestine until 1930.

Bowle, John. *Viscount Samuel: A Biography.* London: Gollancz, 1957. An objective study of the life of the first High Commissioner.

Cohen, Aharon. *Israel and the Arab World.* New York: Funk & Wagnalls, 1970. Covers Arab-Jewish relations from early times through 1967, but is best on the period from 1917 to 1948.

Cohen, Israel. *Theodor Herzl, Founder of Political Zionism.* New York: Thomas Yoseloff, 1959. A fine biography of the founder of Zionism.

Dodd, C. H., and Mary Sales (eds.). *Israel and the Arab World.* London: Routledge & Kegan Paul, 1970. A collection of official and semi-official documents on the evolution of the conflict since 1917.

Elon, Amos. *The Israelis: Founders and Sons.* New York: Holt, Rinehart and Winston, 1971. Well-written, stimulating, and provocative. Shows the personalities, ideology, and feelings behind the early and contemporary Zionist movement. Elon describes and analyzes Israel's diverse dilemmas frankly and honestly, without cant or self-serving argumentation.

Esco Foundation for Palestine. *Palestine: A Study of Jewish, Arab, and British Policies.* 2 vols. New Haven: Yale University Press, 1947. A vast work that includes all kinds of important information on the period of the mandate. Almost a source-book.

Furlonge, Sir Geoffrey. *Palestine is My Country: The Story of Musa Alami.* New York, Praeger, 1969. A study of Musa Alami's life and the work of his school.

Glubb, John Bagot. *The Story of the Arab Legion.* London: Hodder & Stoughton, 1948. Glubb was the commanding officer as well as a historian.

Goldmann, Nahum. *The Autobiography of Nahum Goldmann: Sixty Years of Jewish Life.* New York: Holt, Rinehart and Winston, 1969. A leader of the world Zionist organization and the world Jewish congress for many years. Clashed with and lost out to Ben-Gurion.

Graves, Philip P. (ed.). *Memoirs of King Abdullah of Transjordan.* New York: Philosophical Library, 1950. Covers the important events of the king's earlier life.

Halpern, Ben. *The Idea of the Jewish State.* Cambridge, Mass.: Harvard University Press, 1961. The most profound book on this subject.

Hattis, Susan Lee. *The Bi-National Idea in Palestine During Mandatory Times.* Haifa: Shikmona, 1970. An outstanding objective and scholarly study of this difficult problem. Much of the material comes from the Zionist Archives and the Israel State Archives. (The British Colonial Office has closed much of its archives on this subject until 2069.)

Hurewitz, J. C. *The Struggle for Palestine.* New York: Norton, 1950. A first-rate book by a careful scholar.

Hyamson, Albert M. *Palestine under the Mandate, 1920–1948.* London: Methuen, 1950. Follows the Zionist line.

Jarvis, Claude Scudamore. *Arab Command: The Biography of Lt. Col. F. G. Peake Pasha.* London: Hutchinson, 1942. Col. Peake organized the British forces in Transjordan.

Joseph, Bernard. *British Rule in Palestine.* Washington, D.C.: Public Affairs Press, 1948. Surveys the mandate period.

Katz, Samuel. *Days of Fire.* Garden City, N.Y.: Doubleday, 1968. An account of underground work in Palestine before 1948, written by a founder of the Irgun. Contemptuous of those Zionists who compromised with the British and the Arabs.

Khalidi, Walid (ed.). *From Haven to Conquest: Readings in Zionism and the Palestine Problem until 1948.* Beirut: Institute for Palestine Studies, 1971. Contains a lengthy introduction by Khalidi and eighty articles and documents by leading political figures concerned with Zionism and settlement in Palestine.

Laqueur, Walter. *A History of Zionism.* New York: Holt, Rinehart and Winston, 1972. This is a sympathetic but not uncritical account of the pre-state period.

Lowdermilk, Walter C. *Palestine, Land of Promise.* New York: Harper, 1944. Outlines and discusses irrigation possibilities in Palestine in glowing terms.

Luke, Harry C., and Edward Keith-Roach. *The Handbook of Palestine and Transjordan.* London: Macmillan, 1930. Semiofficial.

Main, Ernest. *Palestine at the Crossroads.* London: George Allen, 1937. Discusses the questions of partition and the future.

Marlowe, John. *The Seat of Pilate: An Account of the Palestine Mandate.* London: Cresset Press, 1959. A British view.

Moore, John Norton (ed.). *The Arab-Israeli Conflict.* Princeton, N.J.: Princeton University Press, 1974. A three-volume work of 3,459 pages sponsored by the American Society for International Law. It contains documents, government publications, a selected bibliography, and readings by well-known writers on international law.

Porath, Y. *The Emergence of the Palestinian-Arab National Movement, 1918–1929.* London: Frank Cass, 1974. A brilliant, indispensable monograph on the foundations of the Palestinian Arabs' rejection of Zionism and the Arabs' appeals to England for relief.

Quandt, William B. *Palestinian Nationalism: Its Political and Military Dimensions.* Santa Monica, Calif.: Rand Corporation, 1971. The author discusses the rise of the several liberation movements, their organizational and ideological problems, the nature of their leadership, and the results of their military and terrorist activities.

——, Fuad Jabber, and Ann Mosely Leach, *The Politics of Palestinian Nationalism.* Berkeley: University of California Press, 1973. Three essays that contribute to an understanding of Palestinian politics.

Schechtman, Joseph B. *The Mufti and the Fuehrer, The Rise and Fall of Haj Amin el-Hesseini.* New York: Thomas Yoseloff, 1965. Unfriendly account of the activities of the Grand Mufti.

Taylor, Alan R. *Prelude to Israel: An Analysis of Jewish Diplomacy, 1897–1947.* New York: Philosophical Library, 1959.

Vatikiotis, P. J. *Politics and the Military in Jordan: A Study of the Arab Legion, 1921–1957.* New York: Praeger, 1967. A detailed study of civil-military relationships.

Weizmann, Chaim. *Trial and Error: The Autobiography of Chaim Weizmann.* New York: Harper, 1949. The life of the leader of Zionism during the mandatory period.

Chapter 35

Egypt and the Sudan

The British Protectorate

On Decemeber 18, 1914 Great Britain unilaterally declared the establishment of a protectorate over Egypt. Although the announcement carried a pledge of ultimate self-government, a protectorate was humiliating to Egyptians. Its Arabic translation was the word used to refer to dependence of certain Christian minorities on European powers. The Egyptian ministry of foreign affairs was abolished, its functions appropriated by the British agent and consul general, who under the protectorate became high commissioner. Khedive Abbas Hilmi II, pro-Turkish and violently anti-British, had not returned from his summer palace on the Bosphorus when hostilities broke. He was deposed; his uncle, Prince Husayn Kamil, was proclaimed sultan of Egypt. Already the legislative assembly was prorogued, so the British could expect little opposition during the war. Rushdi Pasha remained as prime minister and concurred readily with British demands; in the face of troops and the disposition of the British government, he had no alternative.

Educated Egyptians were not overly concerned with these political developments. Egypt had been occupied by England for over a generation, and it appeared natural that in a world struggle Egypt should be aligned with her actual master rather than with any technical or legal overlord such as Turkey. The price of cotton, the problems of marketing a new crop, the importation of foodstuffs, and the issuance of legal tender notes by the national bank seemed matters of far greater importance than national politics.

For nearly four years, therefore, Egypt served as a military base for British forces. At one time there were three independent British commands located there. The price of cotton more than trebled, and wheat became scarce and high priced. Troops requisitioned supplies, taking camels and donkeys from peasants. Egyptians were drafted into an army which fought alongside the British, although Britain had promised to recognize Egyptian neutrality. Inflation was rampant, and fortunes were made by corrupt and illegal practices. The personnel of the British civil service deteriorated in quality. The military ignored Egyptian sensibilities; the stationing of so many troops in Egypt naturally caused many awkward situations and numerous unfortunate incidents. The public blamed the British for every ill that befell Egypt in the war years.

Rushdi Pasha bravely cooperated with Lord Kitchener, Sir Milne Cheetham, Sir Henry McMahon, and Sir Reginald Wingate. He did not openly press for commitments on the termination of the capitulations or for the steps toward self-government that were cited in the protectorate declaration. However, Rushdi instructed his judicial adviser, an Englishman, to prepare recommendations on these points. Drafted in the form of constitutional reform, the proposals called for a bicameral legislature, the dominant upper house to be composed of Egyptian ministers, British advisers, and representatives of the foreign communities of Cairo and Alexandria. As soon as its contents leaked to the public, no Egyptian leader could possibly support the document.

Apparently, British officials were out of touch with sentiment in Egypt. Their reports to London did not enlighten the Foreign Office with a true description of trends, but followed the traditional imperialistic philosophy of Lord Curzon, the foreign secretary. The presence of so many Westerners in Egypt, public declarations from Allied politicians, and the coming of age of a new generation hurried Egyptian nationalism forward with great strides in the years between 1914 and 1918.

Egyptian Nationalism and the Wafd

Two days after the end of the war in Europe Saad Zaghlul Pasha, an ardent nationalist who had been minister of education under Lord Cromer, presented the high commissioner with a list of demands. If allowed, these demands would have given Egypt independence. Informed that London would reply, Zaghlul asked permission to proceed with his delegation *(Wafd)* to London to discuss his independence program. Wingate urged London to grant the wish, but the Foreign Office refused, because Zaghlul had no organized party and in no sense represented the government of Egypt. Upon the approval of Sultan Fuad, Rushdi sought an invitation immediately to go to London to discuss the future status of Egypt. (Sultan Husayn died in 1917 and was succeeded by his brother.) Again Wingate urged that an invitation be tendered, but Downing Street, busy with preparations for the Paris conference, declined, and thus encouraged the deterioration of political conditions in Egypt.

Zaghlul and his delegation avidly organized committees throughout the country and stimulated vigorous nationalistic feeling against the British. Rushdi and his chief associate, Adli Yakan Pasha, resigned after their rebuff. Zaghlul threatened dire consequences should the sultan appoint a successor. At this juncture (March 8, 1919) Zaghlul and three other leading Wafd party members were arrested by the British military with Foreign Office approval (Egypt being under martial law) and deported to Malta. Egyptian reaction was spontaneous: Insurrection and violence spread to all districts within ten days. Military forces rushed to Egypt crushed the revolt by the end of the month.

Lloyd George suddenly awoke to the fact that something needed to be done. General Allenby was appointed high commissioner. Lord Milner was designated head of a commission of inquiry to investigate the situation and report on the nature of a constitution that would be best for Egypt under the protectorate. Zaghlul and his fellow internees in Malta were freed to lay their demands before the peace conference. They were bitterly disappointed, however, when the American delegation announced its recognition of the protectorate over Egypt.

In Egypt Wafd leadership was stirring the populace to impress the Milner mission with the strength of the national movement. It did its task so well that any Egyptian seen talking to the mission was branded as a traitor. Various acts of violence occurred against Englishmen. In March 1920 Lord Milner returned to London uncertain as to what the next step should be. Still in Europe, Zaghlul visited England to discuss the Egyptian question with Lord Milner. Zaghlul's prestige and nationalist standing were considered impeccable, and his following was so devoted that any solution or compromise he proposed would have been acceptable to the Wafd and all the nationalists in Egypt.

A memorandum containing the principles on which a treaty of alliance between Egypt and England might be drawn was composed in August 1920. It recognized Egypt as a sovereign independent constitutional monarchy with representative institutions. Britain would undertake to defend Egypt, and Egypt would offer all assistance within her borders to England. Egypt would have diplomatic representation abroad, but would coordinate her policies with those of Britain. Egypt would appoint British judicial and financial advisers and would permit Britain to maintain a military force in Egypt. The capitulations would be abolished but England would have the right to prevent the adoption of laws inconsistent with legislation enacted under the previous regime. The final point pledged Egypt to call a constituent assembly to ratify the treaty and to adopt a constitution.

Lord Milner signed the document as the basis for a treaty that he would be willing to recommend to the cabinet. But Zaghlul temporized, asserting that the memorandum would have to be approved by the people of Egypt before he could go ahead. Several of his party returned to Egypt, where the memorandum was published and Egyptian sentiment tested. The response was lukewarm, largely because Zaghlul gave out public declarations quite noncommittal in tone. At this point he informed Lord Milner that the memorandum was not clear on several points. The British, however, would bargain no further, and conversations were broken off completely.

Zaghlul returned to Egypt in April 1921, ready to prevent anyone from obtaining a treaty from the British. Adli Pasha, the new prime minister, spent the summer in England trying his hand at treaty-making. But with Zaghlul agitating at full force against him any treaty that was not preceded by the termination of the protectorate and martial law was foredoomed.

Egyptian Independence

In December 1921 Adli resigned. Sarwat Pasha, acting prime minister, formed a new cabinet on the premise that Great Britain would immediately recognize Egypt as an independent sovereign state. Zaghlul's activities were redoubled. Allenby, appreciating that no treaty that Britain would be prepared to sign would be acceptable to Zaghlul, deported him to the Seychelles. Still the British cabinet did not agree to recognize Egyptian independence; it took a personal trip to London by Allenby to impress upon England the necessity of accepting the quasi-commitments made in the Milner-Zaghlul memorandum and to Sarwat. On February 28, 1922, the day of Allenby's return to Egypt, he gave out the unilateral British declaration ending the protectorate and elevating Egypt to the rank of an independent sovereign state. Martial law, proclaimed on November 2, 1914, was to be terminated as soon as the sultan's government passed an act of indemnity. Until Egypt and England could conclude an agreement England reserved to herself the security of communications, defense, the protection of foreign interests and minorities, and the affairs of the Sudan. Egyptian nationalists were annoyed that their country's independence was declared by another state. Yet, England had assumed the protectorate by unilateral action and might relinquish it in like manner.

The price of cotton fell in Egypt from $187 a cantar to $18 during the worldwide collapse of prices in 1920. Had the depressed situation persisted for any length of time, political anarchy in Egypt might have been attributable to economic difficulties. As it was, the fall from exorbitant heights had beneficial effects upon the fellaheen. Pressure to grow cotton was lessened, and more foodstuffs were raised. In 1922 a price recovery allowed the government, under the British declaration of independence, to develop in a more favorable economic climate. Sultan Fuad became king of Egypt, and a succession of men passed through the chambers of the prime minister. Politics became a three-way embroilment among nationalists, the king, and the residency (as the British high commissioner's office was termed).

The Constitution of 1923

The residency pressed Fuad to appoint a prime minister who would present a constitution for the new sovereign state. Egyptian leaders feared such a step, lest it ruin them politically; the king insisted upon an article naming him king of Egypt and the Sudan, thus taking a stand that he knew the British would not tolerate. Finally, a constitution was drawn up and promulgated on April 21, 1923; martial law was withdrawn in July; elections for a parliament were held in September; and agreement was reached in October concerning the service of Britishers in the Egyptian government.

The constitution gave to the king considerable powers. He could dissolve or adjourn parliament. He called parliament, and he could veto acts of parliament. (A two-thirds majority of the membership of each house could, however, override his veto.) The king appointed and dismissed ministers, and could issue decrees in the absence of parliament. The king was commander in chief of the armed forces. In reality a determined king could be chief executive of the state. Ministers were responsible to parliament; but since they held office at the pleasure of the king, they found it difficult to serve two masters. Two-fifths of the senators were appointed by the king; three-fifths were elected. Senators held office for ten years, and membership was restricted to men of considerable property or to persons who had held office or a prominent position in the state. Members of the chamber of deputies held office for five years; one deputy was elected for every 60,000 inhabitants. The chamber of deputies alone had the right to dismiss the cabinet or a minister by a vote of no confidence and could try ministers for malfeasance in office. Nowhere in the constitution was Great Britain mentioned. But with British troops and many British advisers in Egypt and with an Englishman as *sirdar* (commander in chief) of the Egyptian army, Egyptians were fully justified in doubting that independence had been attained.

Egyptian Politics

Zaghlul was released from detention in March, and, together with other Wafd leaders who had also been freed, he returned to Egypt in September in time for elections. The Wafd gained 188 seats out of 215 in the chamber of deputies. When parliament convened the next January, Zaghlul promptly accepted Fuad's invitation to form a ministry upon the condition that as prime minister he would not compromise the program of the Wafd, of which he remained president.

The assumption of office changed Zaghlul's political life almost completely. Heretofore he had devoted his energies to ousting the British and thereby maintaining his leadership of the Egyptian people. But under his leadership the Wafd had been a party of agitators, and seemingly it could not change its tactics. His Wafd program had not been completed: British troops and advisers must go; the Sudan must be "returned" to Egypt; and any British claim to share in protecting the Suez Canal must be abandoned. These goals called for the continuation of intimidation by demonstrations against the British and veiled invitations to violence. Similar stirrings, to which the British reacted strongly, were "encouraged" in the Sudan. The situation was anomalous. As prime minister, Zaghlul was responsible for the maintenance of law and order in Egypt; as head of the Wafd, he was in open defiance of law and order.

In the summer of 1924 at Ramsay MacDonald's invitation Zaghlul went to London, ostensibly to negotiate a treaty of alliance. What he did was to present his entire program as unequivocal demands. No treaty was signed, yet Zaghlul returned triumphantly to Cairo. He made a pretense of resigning but, of course, his resignation was refused. Four days later, on November 19, 1924, Sir Lee Stack, governor-general of the Sudan and commander in chief of the Egyptian army, was assassinated on the streets of Cairo. Zaghlul immediately, officially, and publicly, expressed his horror at the crime and pledged swift and thorough action to bring the culprits to trial.

Nevertheless, the deed was the logical and indirect result of open invitations to violence instigated by Zaghlul and the Wafd. Subsequent judicial proceedings demonstrated that leading Wafdists, including two members of Zaghlul's cabinet, were implicated.

The British cabinet decided to take vigorous action. On the afternoon of November 22, escorted by a regiment of British cavalry and in full military attire, Lord Allenby called at the offices of the council of ministers, read in English two communications to Zaghlul, handed him copies in French, and departed. Allenby was angry, and he took every opportunity to display force and humiliate Zaghlul. The note placed blame for Sir Lee Stack's murder upon Zaghlul's "campaign of hostility to British rights and British subjects in Egypt and the Sudan" and asserted that the Egyptian government was held in contempt by all civilized peoples. Egypt was given about thirty hours to meet the following demands: apologize for the crime; punish the criminals; forbid and suppress public political demonstrations; pay a fine of £500,000; recall all Egyptian officers and army units from the Sudan; notify the competent departments that the Sudan would increase irrigated areas of the Gezira to an unlimited figure; and withdraw all opposition to British wishes in regard to the protection of foreign interests in Egypt.

The demands were stiff. Zaghlul discussed them with the cabinet and Fuad and laid them before the chamber of deputies that evening in secret session. Compliance was voted for the first four demands. Upon refusal of the last three, Allenby notified the Sudan government to take all necessary actions and ordered the British army to occupy the Alexandrian customs offices. Zaghlul resigned; Fuad appointed Ziwar Pasha, who speedily came to terms with the British concerning the role of British advisers in the Egyptian government.

Parliament was dissolved in December and new elections were held. The Liberal party, led by elder politicians who were descended from Ottoman Turkish families long resident in Egypt, and a new Unionist party, made up of the king's friends, combined with numerous independents from the provinces to defeat the Wafd. Nevertheless, the chamber of deputies elected Zaghlul its president in March 1925. This act led the king to dismiss parliament immediately. He was now determined to crush Zaghlul, who seemed to be growing more prominent than the king.

New elections were not held until May 1926. In the meantime Fuad appointed several new ministers from among his friends, so that the cabinet was controlled by Nashat Pasha and the Unionist party. Allenby retired, and Lord Lloyd, formerly governor of Bombay, became high commissioner. He made common cause with the Wafd to force the king to call for elections, in which the Wafd again obtained a sweeping victory. Despite the victory Lord Lloyd persuaded Zaghlul to step aside, and Adli Pasha of the Liberal party headed a ministry of three Liberals, six Wafdists, and one Independent.

The three-cornered struggle among Wafd, palace, and residency eventually exhausted Adli's strength; in April 1927 he resigned, to be replaced by Sarwat Pasha, another Liberal. During that summer negotiations for a treaty of alliance were opened again in London, this time between Sarwat and Sir Austen Chamberlain, but Sarwat did not expect to persuade the Wafd to accept the treaty. In August Zaghlul died and was succeeded as Wafd leader by Nahas Pasha, who at that time was hardly more than a figurehead. Discussions regarding the treaty broke down in March 1928 over the question of British troops in Egypt. Nahas refused to compromise on that issue, and Chamberlain stated that Britain could make no further concessions than those contained in the draft treaty.

Upon the failure of the discussions Sarwat resigned, and Nahas formed a ministry. But Fuad, always eager to discredit possible rivals, forced Nahas to resign by publishing a questionable document disclosing that Nahas and two of his associates had received £130,000 for agreeing to transfer certain estates from the king's hands to other management. The next prime minister was Muhammad Mahmud Pasha, an original Wafdist exiled to Malta with Zaghlul but in 1928 supported by residency and palace. Mahmud dissolved parliament and suspended the constitution for three years, thereafter governing as a mild dictator with bitter opposition from the Wafd. Mahmud reached agreement with the British over the Nile waters, the old Ottoman debt, and other financial matters. But desire for a treaty with Great Britain remained paramount, and in 1929 while on a holiday in England Mahmud judged the right moment had arrived.

The Labourites replaced the Conservatives, and Arthur Henderson took over the Foreign Office. Lord Lloyd was publicly dismissed for being too autocratic and out of step with the times. In June 1929 negotiations began, and the Labour cabinet made sweeping concessions with respect to Egyptian national feelings. British troops would remain only around the Canal, the capitulations would be abolished, England would relinquish her right to protect foreigners, and the Sudan question would be considered a subject for further negotiations. However, England would only recognize a treaty ratified by a freely elected Egyptian parliament. The draft treaty was a great victory for Mahmud, but upon his return to Egypt his position became untenable. Since the Wafd refused to accept his treaty and since the British insisted upon elections, Mahmud resigned.

Elections returned the Wafdists to power, and Nahas Pasha again came to power as prime minister—as a protégé of the British Labour party. But his position was impossible. He had denounced the draft treaty obtained by Mahmud, and the British declared that they had reached the "high-water mark" of concessions. Treaty negotiations were dropped temporarily. Fuad, fearing the apparent alliance of the Wafd and the residency led by Sir Percy Loraine, the new high commissioner, engineered the resignation of Nahas and appointed Ismail Sidki Pasha as prime minister.

The Constitution of 1930

Parliament was prorogued; Nahas incited riots; the British sent warships. Sidki, protesting against foreign intervention, restored order. In this coup d'état of June 1930 Sidki appeared as the strong man. The constitution of 1923 was abrogated and a new constitution with a new electoral law rigged to keep Wafdists out of office was quickly adopted. Sidki organized a new political party, the People's party. In coalition with the Unionists and Independents the People's party defeated a Wafdist-Liberal united front, which boycotted the election. Sidki was able to establish his dictatorship only through the ineptitude of the British Labour government, which maneuvered both Liberals and Wafdists into indefensible positions. Sidki sent the students back to their studies; politicians muttered rather meekly; and the wealthy landowners gladly supported the new rule, for they were surfeited with the petty quibbling, jealous vindictiveness, and political arrogance of the nationalistic Wafd lawyers whom they had largely created. No treaty with England was attempted; prime ministers who tried always fell from office, and both Sidki and Fuad preferred British troops in Egypt to the Wafd. Furthermore, Sidki must have understood that the British government would not interfere in Egyptian domestic politics as long as British imperial interests were not directly jeopardized.

Fuad again did not intend to permit a potential rival to remain in office very long. Sidki fell from power in September 1933 on the issue of a minor scandal, although a paralytic stroke had reduced his command of affairs several months earlier. A procession of ineffectual prime ministers followed, some of them being the same weak figures who occupied the post ten years earlier after the crisis provoked by the British declaration of Egyptian independence. Power rapidly gravitated to the king, who was also amassing a great fortune. The controller of the royal estates, al-Ibrashi, also grew in influence, as Fuad's ill health rendered him less able to handle his own affairs.

The Anglo-Egyptian Treaty of 1936

The deterioration of domestic affairs prompted the residency in 1934 to advise the dismissal of al-Ibrashi, whom most Egyptians detested. Even the nationalist furor which this intervention incited did not stem the popular tide against palace government. In November 1934 the 1930 constitution was abrogated in favor of the 1923 constitution. The latter was not reissued, however, because the British secretly vetoed it.

At this juncture a crisis of an entirely different order appeared—the Italian adventure in Ethiopia. Britain increased her military establishment in Egypt—in Alexandria, Cairo, Suez, and Port Said—with the knowledge and consent of Prime Minister Nessim Pasha. An election campaign speech in England in October 1935, however, gave Egyptians their first inkling that British naval headquarters in the Mediterranean were to be transferred from Malta to Alexandria. This startling information had the instantaneous effect of throwing Nahas, Sidki, and Mahmud into a united front and laying Nessim open to the charge of being subservient to the British. A few days later Sir Samuel Hoare, British foreign secretary, heaped more coals on the fire by publicly stating that the Egyptian constitutions of 1923 and 1930 were ill-adapted documents, and government-inspired London editorials advised the Egyptians not to manipulate the Ethiopian crisis by blackmailing England into promises that were "manifestly inopportune."

Anti-British riots were spontaneous; November 21, 1935, was declared an official day of mourning. In an attempt to soothe Egyptian feelings Sir Samuel delivered a public speech a month later. But this speech brought tempers to a white heat by stating that at some future time Egyptian wishes and freedom would be considered but that at the moment Great Britain was too busy with other matters. Fortunately, Anthony Eden soon took over the reins of the Foreign Office, and communications and advice from Sir Miles Lampson, the high commissioner, were given some heed. Strangely enough, the last of Hoare's ineptitudes goaded the united front to declare that its leaders would support the negotiation of a treaty with England on the basis of the draft treaty that Egypt had rejected in 1930. Also, the constitution of 1923 was reissued, elections were set for late spring, and the return to more responsible parliamentary government was envisaged.

In April 1936 King Fuad died. His only son, Faruk, ascended the throne. Since the constitution provided that parliament should meet within ten days of the king's death, elections were moved up to make compliance possible. The Wafd party won 166 seats out of 232 in the chamber of deputies and obtained a majority in the senate. With such a solid backing Nahas became prime minister with a Wafd cabinet. Since he named the regency, the power of the Wafd was supreme. For several months already he had been chairman of the all-party delegation negotiating the treaty with England. Without fear of recrimination or charges of treason, Nahas consummated the Anglo-Egyptian treaty on August 26, 1936. A landmark had been achieved.

Beyond the malice of internal Egyptian politics the chief stumbling blocks to such a treaty had been: the Sudan, British armed forces, and the capitulations. In 1930 negotiations foundered on the Sudan question; in 1936 all predicted failure when Britain announced that disposition of her forces in Egypt needed reconsideration. Between 1930 and 1936, however, the military evolution became obvious to politician and public alike. When, therefore, the British asked for a wider area in the Canal Zone and more facilities on land, sea, and air, Egyptian objection was only nominal. The occupation was changed to a twenty-year military alliance. Sir Miles Lampson won over the British cabinet and the British public to an appreciation that defense of the Canal and imperial communications could never be solved by British "unilateral action except at an utterly prohibitive cost and in the teeth of bitter resentment." The Sudan settlement permitted again unlimited Egyptian immigration to the Sudan and use of Egyptian troops in the Sudan. The end of the capitulations, actually arranged by the Montreux convention of 1937, proved of the utmost consequence to Egypt. The abolition of mixed tribunals and curtailment of consular courts were not abrupt, but the end was set for 1949. Henceforth, foreigners and foreign companies would be subject to Egyptian laws, especially taxation and financial legislation.

The treaty was immensely popular in Egypt. Parliament ratified it by a vote of 202 to 11, and the unprecedented happened when British troops were cheered on the streets of Cairo. But Nahas Pasha's popularity waned when Faruk reached his majority in 1937 and the palace again became a political force. Even the treaty was no longer popular, probably because the Italian conquest in East Africa was legitimized and the threat of war in the Mediterranean subsided. Nahas resigned at the end of 1937; Mahmud then headed a coalition cabinet of Liberals, Saadists (a new party of disaffected Wafdists) and Independents. A new election, arranged in 1938, defeated the Wafdists of Nahas, and the palace government gained ascendancy. Just before World War II broke out Mahmud stepped down and Ali Maher Pasha, the Saadist leader, became prime minister of a cabinet from which both Liberals and Wafdists were excluded. The wheel turned; Faruk and his palace officials won full power.

Social and Economic Problems

Internal politics and the problem of getting rid of the British consumed the energies and attention of Egyptian leaders between World Wars I and II, and these were the topics eternally discussed in Egypt. However, other problems, certainly basic and significant for the Egyptian nation and perhaps even more difficult to solve, did exist. Foremost was the increasing population pressure. The population increased from 12,718,000 in 1917 to 15,721,000 in 1937, although the cultivated area remained constant. Increased agricultural yields, improved irrigation techniques, and intensive cultivation—three crops per year instead of two—met the situation in part, but there was a general lowering of the standard of living among Egyptian peasantry. Sanitation and health conditions were poor, and the death rate was very high. Yet, the birth rate was higher. These factors, coupled with a lack of coal and industrial development, gave the waters of the Nile an importance that other national societies found difficult to appreciate. This dependence on the Nile explained the critical blow to Egypt intended by Allenby's ultimatum to Zaghlul regarding unlimited irrigation in the Sudan. Although heightening the Aswan Dam and the construction of dams in the Sudan and Uganda augmented water supplies in Egypt, such developments barely kept pace with the growing population (which at the end of the period was increasing at the rate of 1.73 percent per annum).

Tied to this pressure of population were many economic, financial, and commercial problems. Cotton was king, and the government and landowners subverted the entire economy for the benefit of cotton culture. Agricultural experimentation, types of irrigation, industrialization, trade practices, tariffs, bank loans, tenant farm policies, and land reform—all were considered in the light of their relationship to the production of cotton. Taxation in general rested lightly on agriculture and landowners and bore heavily upon imports, industry, and commerce. Abolition of the capitulations following the Anglo-Egyptian treaty of 1936 and the Montreux convention in 1937 altered the commercial world of Cairo and Alexandria. A general exemption from taxation had given British, French, Italians, Greeks, Armenians, Levantines, Jews, and even Syrians and Lebanese with passports in their pockets advantages that enabled them to dominate Egyptian finance and commerce. If Egyptians and their Ottoman-descended compatriots wished to participate in business in their own country, they found it almost necessary to form a partnership with a foreigner. Furthermore, native businessmen evaded taxes because their foreign counterparts did not pay taxes. After 1936 the situation was rapidly reversed. Foreigners suddenly found it advantageous to have Egyptians as partners, and more corporations engaged in business in Egypt were registered there. For the first time since the age of the Pharaohs, Egyptian nationality ceased to be a badge of inferiority.

Education

A third big development in the period between the two wars was in education. In 1914, with a budget of slightly more than half a million pounds, the ministry of education had 15,000 students in primary, secondary, and higher schools in all of Egypt. By 1939 the budget rose to four and a half million and the number of students to 232,000. But there was still much to do. Illiteracy was high, and the size of the task ahead was staggering. Planning and direction were often ill conceived. The stress was upon literature, language, and the humanities. The needs of Egypt at the lower levels of sciences, shop work, simple foundries, forges, and vocational training as well as at the higher levels of doctors, engineers, scientists, and industrial managers were ignored.

Since the constitution of Egypt declared that free education must be provided for children between the ages of seven and twelve, elementary schools to teach the four R's—reading, writing, arithmetic, and religion— were organized in many villages. By 1939 nearly 1,000,000 children were enrolled. Unfortunately, after children had finished a village school they were not prepared to enter a vocational or secondary school. Elementary schools attempted only to stamp out illiteracy. However, two parallel systems grew in the 1920s and 1930s and were preparing Egypt for a fuller national life beyond anything imaginable by the average British colonial official of the period prior to 1930. The educational system was slowly creating a national consciousness among the masses, as the Wafd was doing among the middle and upper classes. Education was helping to ready the masses for the national determination and political democracy for which Wafd leaders were striving.

The Anglo-Egyptian Sudan

Whenever Egyptians considered severing British ties, the Sudan loomed impressively in their thinking. In the nineteenth century the Sudan had been important to Egypt because of the border warfare and slave raids that so frequently disturbed their relationship. In the twentieth century fitting solutions to controversies over Nile water, dams, barrages, irrigation projects, and immigration became vital for Egypt and her burgeoning population.

Shortly after the close of World War I the interrelationship of the Sudan and Egypt came to the fore with the setting up of the Gezira project, the operation of which began in 1925. The scheme went back at least to 1900 and Kitchener, who envisaged the irrigation of the triangular stretch of land south of Khartoum between the Blue and White Niles. Much preliminary work was done in pilot projects, soil testing, and general planning. World War I delayed the building of the Sennar Dam on the Blue Nile, and its completion did not come until 1925. Under Allenby's direction the Gezira commission recommended irrigating 300,000 acres of the possible 2,000,-000 acres by gravity flow, with management in the hands of the Sudan Plantations Syndicate, a British organization. Land tenancies were established at forty acres each, two-thirds of which could be planted to vegetables, grains, and fodders, which would be the tax-free property of the tenant. The remaining one-third had to be planted to cotton, of which the tenant, the Syndicate, and the Sudan government received 40 percent, 25 percent, and 35 percent respectively. The government rented land at about fifty cents an acre from the original owners and then assigned forty-acre tracts to applicants. By 1939 the tenants were on the average receiving about $250 as their share from the sale of the cotton crop.

The Gezira scheme was highly successful, and in the last years before World War II the area had reached an annual production of 60,000 tons of cotton and 75,000 tons of cottonseed. Since, however, almost the entire cotton crop was exported to Great Britain and since Sudan cotton was giving the British textile industry a greater independence from Egyptian staples, Egypt grew sensitive to any expansion of irrigated tracts in the Gezira.

Egyptian leaders never abandoned their claim that Sudan and Egypt were indissoluble, chiefly because of the water and the expectation that the undeveloped Sudan would serve as an escape valve for growing population pressures in Egypt. Fears and tensions were, however, diminished by the treaty arranged in 1929 between Lord Lloyd and Mahmud Pasha to govern and allocate the water of the Nile. Instead of being able to irrigate only 300,000 acres of land from the water of the Blue Nile, the Sudan was allotted nearly 1 billion cubic meters of water by the agreement. The Nile projects commission, which was examining the entire Nile with a view toward building dams and reservoir basins and regulating drainage, siltage, and annual flow, estimated that this Nile water agreement would leave for Egypt a guaranteed annual irrigation water supply of about 22 billion cubic meters. After 1929 Egypt seemed assured of all the water she could use, and control of the Sudan ceased, at least for the moment, to be a major political matter.

In the months and years immediately preceding 1939 the Egyptian nation looked with pride upon the accomplishments of the previous two decades. The Anglo-Egyptian treaty of 1936 gave political freedom and sovereignty; the constitution assured political democracy and responsible government; the Montreux convention of 1937 removed the bonds of economic servitude and set the stage for industrial, commercial, and financial independence; and the Nile water agreement of 1929 allayed the fears of the Egyptians, rich and poor alike, that a foreign power would be able to force a thirsty Egypt into submission. Native Egyptians believed that they now controlled their own lives and destinies for the first time in over 3,000 years. The wealth of their country would be their own. Great days lay ahead.

REFERENCES: Chapter 35

Numerous volumes already cited contain material of value to this chapter, especially those in Chapters 7, 15, 17, 19, 20, 21, 22, 23, 24, 26, 27, 28, 30, 31, 33, and 34.

Beshir, Mohamed Omer. *The Southern Sudan: Background to Conflict.* New York: Praeger, 1968. An explanation of the natural and ethnic character of the southern Sudan. Traces its political, social, and economic history.

Davies, Reginald. *The Camel's Back.* Hollywood, Fla.: Translantic Arts, 1958. Describes service in rural Sudan.

Fernea, Elizabeth Warnock. *A View of the Nile: The Story of an American Family in Egypt.* Garden City, N.Y.: Doubleday, 1970. A colorful and realistic account of the life of a family living in a village in Egyptian Nubia, in Cairo, and weekending at a landed estate in the Nile delta.

Frank, Gerold. *The Deed.* New York: Simon & Schuster, 1963. An account of the assassination of Lord Moyne and the trial of the conspirators.

Galatoli, Anthony M. *Egypt in Midpassage.* Cairo: Urwand & Sons, 1950. Important discussion of Anglo-Egyptian affairs and political developments in Egypt.

Harris, Christina Phelps. *Nationalism and Revolution in Egypt: The Role of the Muslim Brotherhood.* The Hague: Mouton, 1964. An excellent monograph giving important views of the Muslim Brotherhood and the society in Egypt that produced it. Carries the story of the Brotherhood up to its suppression by Nasser in 1954.

Heyworth-Dunne, James. *Religious and Political Trends in Modern Egypt.* Washington, D.C.: The author, 1950. Another volume that is particularly good on the Muslim Brotherhood.

Issawi, Charles, *Egypt: An Economic and Social Analysis.* London: Oxford University Press, 1947. A competent economic study by a British-trained Syrio-Egyptian who is the outstanding scholar on the economy of the area in this century.

———. *Egypt at Mid-Century: An Economic Survey.* New York: Oxford University Press, 1954. A revised edition of the above with later material added and a slightly different outlook.

Jackson, H. C. *Sudan Days and Ways.* New York: St. Martin's, 1954. Written by a British official in the Sudan from 1907 to 1931.

————. *Behind the Modern Sudan.* New York: St. Martin's, 1956. A continuation of the above.

Landau, Jacob M. *Parliaments and Parties in Egypt.* Tel Aviv: Israel Oriental Society, 1953. A thorough study of political parties in Egypt from the late nineteenth century to World War II. The author is strong in discussing and detailing the developments before and after World War I, especially in the early 1920s.

Little, Tom. *Modern Egypt.* New York: Praeger, 1967. An updated version of his 1958 volume. The approach of a careful and perceptive reporter. A well-written account of Egyptian affairs, especially since 1918.

MacMichael, Harold. *The Sudan.* London: Benn, 1954. Emphasizes development under British rule.

Mitchell, Richard P. *The Society of the Muslim Brothers.* London: Oxford University Press, 1968. The most exhaustively researched and complete treatment of the subject to date.

Quraishi, Zaheer M. *Liberal Nationalism in Egypt: Rise and Fall of the WAFD Party.* Delhi: Alwaz Publishers, 1967. A full-scale study from the Wafd's inception in 1918 to its end in 1953. Strongest in the early period.

Royal Institute of International Affairs. *Great Britain and Egypt, 1914–1951:* London: Oxford University Press, 1952.

Ziadeh, Farhat J. *Lawyers, the Rule of Law, and Liberalism in Modern Egypt.* Stanford, Calif.: Hoover Institution, 1968. Traces the role of liberal tradition, national independece, and constitutionalism in the work of lawyers in Egypt.

Chapter 36

Shah Reza's Iran

Imperialism in Iran

When World War I burst upon the Middle East, Iran was experiencing chaotic problems involving internal political and constitutional developments, financial and economic turmoil, and intense imperial rivalry among Russia, Great Britain, and Germany. After Shuster left for America at the end of 1911, democratic nationalists believed that the German blandishments offered the only hope of avoiding an impending partition of Iran by British and Russian imperialists. In the few years prior to 1914 German activities in Iran had been fruitful, and during the first months of the war Prince von Reuss concluded a secret treaty with the Iranian government promising arms, ammunition, money, and independence in return for cooperation with Germany.

Britain and Russia, aware of these agreements, acted swiftly to hold Iran in their power. Russian troops moved from Qazvin, which they had been occupying for several years, to the outskirts of Tehran. Supporters of the Central Powers then fled to Kermanshah, where an anti-Allied Iranian government was formed. Shah Ahmad remained in his capital with his cabinet, and technically Iran maintained her neutrality. The German consul, Wassmuss, stirred the Qashqai and Bakhtiyari tribes in southern Iran and threatened British oil operations in Khuzistan. To counter this danger and protect the wells, the British weakened their Mesopotamian drive and eventually sent Sir Percy Sykes to organize the South Persian Rifles. In 1917, in cooperation with Russian cossacks from the north, they occupied Kerman, Isfahan, Shiraz, and most of Fars. Russia's collapse, however, left the northern provinces open; for a time German and Ottoman troops held Azerbayjan, but they were recalled at the end of the war and the British remained dominant in Iran.

Postwar Problems

Lord Curzon had dreams of a British Empire from the Mediterranean to Singapore. With Iraq and Palestine already pledged, Iran was the missing link. Sir Percy Cox was sent from Baghdad to Tehran to escort Iran into the British Empire. An Iranian delegation went to Paris, but being anti-British it was not permitted to attend the peace conference or to state Iran's case, though Iran did secure an invitation to join the League of Nations. A less hostile delegation negotiated and signed on August 9, 1919, an Anglo-Iranian treaty. Though the words were friendly, it virtually transformed Iran into a dependency of the British Empire, and public opinion throughout the world rightly judged it in that light. Iranian government departments, finances, public services, and the army would be in British hands. Iran received a 7 percent loan of £2 million; in return, her tariffs would be adjusted and customs controlled by the British as collateral against the loan.

The Iranian Assembly *(Majlis)* refused to ratify the treaty; and general worldwide British military retrenchment effected a withdrawal of British forces and the demobilization of the South Persian Rifles. Bolshevik Russia, on the other hand, pursued a more beguiling course by denouncing tsarist treaties with Iran. In pursuing tsarist General Denikin, Soviet forces landed troops in 1920 at Pahlevi on the Caspian, occupied Iranian territory north of the Elburz Mountains, and refused to depart until all British military were evacuated. A Soviet Republic of Gilan was established at Resht under the nominal leadership of Kuchuk Khan, over whom, Moscow alleged, she had no authority.

Iran protested to the League of Nations. There she was given quantities of sympathy but informed that better results could be obtained by direct negotiations with the Bolsheviks. Taking these words to heart, she concluded at Moscow on February 26, 1921, a treaty of friendship. The frontiers and independence of each were to be respected; Iranian debts to Russia were canceled; all concessions were relinquished, except the Caspian Sea fisheries, since even Communists had to have caviar; neither would harbor enemies of the other; and if a third power menaced or occupied any part of Iran, Russia might send troops to Iran. Also, Iran promised not to cede to any other power or national thereof any privilege or concession being relinquished by Russia. Shortly thereafter, Russia withdrew her troops and her support of the Soviet Republic of Gilan, which promptly succumbed to an Iranian military expedition.

Thus, rejection by the majlis of the Anglo-Iranian treaty of 1919, the subsequent withdrawal of British troops, and the Soviet-Iranian treaty of 1921 confirmed the independence of Iran. However, she did not possess sufficient leadership for political democracy and was torn with strife and economic disorder. Disease, poverty, corruption, and debased public morality prevailed everywhere throughout the land. The areas encompassing the installations of the Anglo-Persian Oil Company were the only flourishing districts of the country, and they were fully under the thumb of the British government. World War I left Iran in a seemingly hopeless state with little outside interest able and willing to lend a helping hand.

Reza Khan

Five days before the signing of the Russo-Iranian treaty in Moscow, Reza Khan, an officer of the Iranian cossacks, led his men into Tehran and with a coup d'état took over the reins of government. A self-educated trooper with a keen nationalist feeling, Reza rose from the ranks of the Russian-officered Iranian cossacks and became one of its leaders when the Russian officers were ousted in 1920. On his march on Tehran he was advised in part by British officers; consequently, opponents charged, though quite incorrectly, that Reza was a pawn in British imperialistic ambitions.

For the following two decades Reza Khan and his army controlled the Iranian government, although following the coup d'état a fiery crusading journalist, Sayyid Ziya al-Din Tabatabai, became prime minister. Several others succeeded to that post, until Reza assumed office in 1923 and invited Shah Ahmad to take "an extended and prolonged tour" of Europe. Republican sentiment was astir as Reza looked westward to pattern his state after Kemal's Turkey. But in 1924 when the stage was virtually set for a republican declaration, the Turkish assembly abolished the caliphate and advanced along its progressive secular path. Frightened Iranian divines raised such a storm that Reza met with a group of religious leaders at Qum. Thereafter, public mention of a republic was forbidden. In 1925 Reza Khan Pahlevi became shah, and the throne was vested in male members of the Pahlevi family born of Iranian mothers.

The problems facing Reza Shah in Iran were similar to those before Kemal in Turkey, only far more difficult. The two most pressing were reestablishment of a recognized central governmental authority and reform of national finances. The former was largely a matter for Reza and the army to resolve; the latter remained the work of an American, Dr. Arthur C. Millspaugh, formerly economic adviser to the secretary of state. Employed by the Iranian government in 1922 as administrator-general of finances, he held the power and authority of a cabinet minister. By his contract, which ran for five years, no commercial or industrial grant could be made without his consent, no financial decision could be taken without his approval, and no expenditure or contracting of any financial obligation could be assumed without his agreement. With such vast powers and the staunch support of Reza's military force Dr. Millspaugh balanced the budget by reorganizing the tax structure and enforcing the collection of taxes, current and in arrears. State enterprises were inaugurated and economic conditions improved gradually. However, Dr. Millspaugh was frequently tactless and too rigid in his manners for a proud and sensitive people in whom through centuries of personal government pliability had become deeply ingrained. In 1927 he and his American staff departed after he refused to renew his contract except on the same terms of power and authority as before.

One stipulation between Reza and Dr. Millspaugh provided that the budget of the ministry of war would always be met, for Reza understood the source of his power. By 1926, when Reza crowned himself Shah of Shahs of Royal Iran, he had personally led his army to end rebellions in Azerbayjan and Khurasan and had partially tamed the nomadic tribes. His greatest success was achieved in ending the independent rule of Shaykh Khazal of Mohammerah, with whom the British had a "working agreement" with respect to the operations of the Anglo-Persian Oil Company. The imposition of Reza's authority over the distant provinces, peoples, and governors of Iran upped state revenues and made Dr. Millspaugh's policies more effective and widespread. This in turn assured a more certain execution of royal government.

According to the constitution of 1906, which was still in force, the power of the nation was vested in the shah, the senate, and the assembly, which by 1926 was filled with Reza's supporters. The senate was appointive, but Reza never called it and never made any appointments to it. The assembly nominated a prime minister who was appointed by the shah. Reza Shah's greatest work, perhaps, was the instilling of an enthusiastic attitude toward work among the personnel of the ministries. Sometimes he would appear at a government office early in the morning to see if the officials were on duty and on time.

Reforms

Public veneration given to religious leaders had proved a stumbling block to many Iranian governments. Reza, therefore, attempted to relegate religion, its institutions, and its leaders to a less influential position in national life, particularly after the Shiite divines raised such an effective furor over republicanism in 1924. Dervishes were forbidden to appear on the streets or along the roads of the countryside. Public parades and presentations of the passion play in memory of the deaths of Ali, Hasan, and Husayn were prohibited. Other overt acts showed the supremacy of Reza over the clergy. In 1928 when a religious leader in the mosque at Qum digressed from his sermon to admonish the queen for unveiling her face, Reza hurried there with two armored cars, entered the mosque without removing his boots, and publicly whipped the offending preacher. Veils were outlawed in 1935; at the same time the shah and other officials took to removing their hats and caps in public buildings.

Equally significant and more pointed was the confiscation of religious property and endowments, the income from which went to the support of schools, hospitals, state industries, and other state enterprises. No longer were religious teachers and leaders *(mullahs)* independent, and their schools were closed. Their livelihood henceforth came from the state, and their hold over the population through education was shattered. Furthermore, secularization of the law was speeded. The French judicial system was introduced in 1927, and decisions affected by opinions rendered by mullahs were declared void and without force. Even religious law over marital status was limited. In 1929 religious courts exercised jurisdiction only over domestic relations, personal status, and notarial acts. Many new laws were promulgated. In 1928 the capitulations, which granted rights to foreigners concerning courts, trials, and legal privileges, were abolished. Theological students were subjected to military conscription, and education became a public responsibility under the supervision and regulation of the central government.

One of Reza Shah's permanent contributions stemmed from his need for better communications to bring the more distant parts of his realm within his power. There may have been 2,000 miles of roads in Iran on the day of his coup d'état; by the outbreak of World War II the road system had been extended to over 17,000 miles. In view of Iran's role in the supply line to Russia in World War II, perhaps Reza's most far-reaching achievement was the construction of the Trans-Iranian railway from Bandarshapur on the Persian Gulf to Bandarshah on the Caspian Sea, a distance of 865 miles. Completed in 1938, it was an engineering marvel, consisting of 224 tunnels and passing from sea level to an altitude of nearly 9,000 feet and then down to below sea level. The route pleased neither Russia nor Britain; from their points of view it began nowhere, passed through Tehran, and again ended nowhere. But as the Iranians saw it, the railroad connected the northern fertile provinces with the south and by passing through nomad country facilitated the movement of the shah's military strength.

Like Kemal in Turkey, Reza felt the need of industrialization and economic development. Fundamentally, Iran had an agricultural economy, and thoroughgoing reforms should have been undertaken in that direction. Improved systems and means of irrigation were proposed, and better agricultural methods were studied. Some beneficial results were obtained. Yet, progress fell far short of the envisaged goals, largely because two-thirds of the arable land was held by absentee landlords who were satisfied with the old techniques and who demanded an immediate high return on their investment.

Industries were built for refining sugar; spinning and weaving cotton, silk, and wool; canning fish, meat, fruit, and vegetables; soap and vegetable oil processing; manufacturing cigarettes and cigar and pipe tobacco; and making bricks, cement, steel products, and various chemicals. Most of these were state enterprises and varied widely in efficiency and capacity. Prices for the goods produced were high, but a state monopoly over most frontier trade rendered competition with imported goods negligible. Nonetheless, since Iranian industry suffered from a lack of technicians and plant managers, the industrial development under Reza proved unsatisfactory. In part to combat Russian trade practices, Reza created a state trading mechanism under which much of the foreign trade was managed by the government. Various other monopolies were instituted for special purposes; monopolies on sugar and tea, for instance, helped finance the building of the Trans-Iranian railway.

Oil Developments

By far the most important industrial enterprise in Iran during the period of Reza Shah's rule was the Anglo-Persian Oil Company, which by agreement paid Iran 16 percent of the profits. During World War I the company property, installations, and pipelines had been protected by a light infantry force organized, equipped, financed, and officered by the British. After the war the question of what profits to include while calculating the Iranian government's 16 percent was bitterly debated, until a settlement was proposed in 1920 by Sir Sydney Armitage-Smith, the Iranian government's financial adviser. The basis for computing profits was described, and in lieu of past royalties and claims a payment of £1 million was made by the company. The agreement was never ratified by the assembly, although the £1 million was accepted; and in 1932 Iran canceled the concession.

The difficulty originated from the fact that Iran had no control over the quantity of oil produced and no guaranteed annual income from the concession. With the complexity of oil operations and the multiplicity of companies, Iran lost confidence in the integrity of the company's bookkeeping practices. Fluctuations in the amounts received by Iran—£411,000 in 1923; £1,400,000 in 1926; £502,000 in 1927; £1,437,000 in 1929; and £307,000 in 1931—left the finances and the budget of the government completely at the mercy of the company, which could shut off the oil wells in Iran at will and obtain the necessary crude oil for its markets in other fields. Furthermore, in 1931 Great Britain went off the gold standard, and Iran's sterling balances were depreciated. The rumor spread that oil products were sold to the British navy at cost. If true, this meant that there would be no percentage of profits for Iran on those sales. Finally, a new concession was negotiated in 1931 by the Iraq Petroleum Company giving more favorable terms to Iraq. Since Anglo-Persian was one of the principal owners in Iraq, the Iranian government felt it should have treatment equally favorable.

After bitter wrangling, sharp notes, and the dispatch of British warships to the Persian Gulf, England took the case to the League council and tried to submit it to the Permanent Court of International Justice at The Hague. Neither body took action; Iran protested that neither had jurisdiction, the case being between a private company and the Iranian government. Iran did, however, inform the company that she was agreeable to the granting of a new concession, provided that its terms were more favorable to Iran than those in the previous concession.

The new concession, which was signed in Tehran in April 1933, included the following provisions: The area covered was immediately reduced by half, and after 1938 to 100,000 square miles, to be selected by the company. The company relinquished its exclusive right to build and operate pipelines in Iran. Iran would receive four shillings per ton on all oil sold in Iran or exported. Iran would be paid 20 percent of all dividends over £671,250, and the company guaranteed that total annual payments to Iran would never be under £750,000. Iran would be secured against any depreciation of sterling. The company was exempt from taxation, but in lieu of such charges the company agreed to pay the government nine pence per ton on the first 6 million tons exported and six pence per ton above that, the minimum annual payment to be £225,000. The Iranian government oil commissioner was to be paid £2,000 annually by the company, and he had the right to examine the books and attend directors' meetings. Gulf of Mexico or Rumanian oil prices, whichever was lower, should be the price used in calculating the price of oil in Iran, such price to be 10 percent lower than the basic price and 25 percent lower to the government. Finally, the concession could not be transferred without Iran's consent, and in 1993 all properties within Iran would revert to the Iranian government.

Undoubtedly, the winning of this agreement by Reza Shah was his finest economic and diplomatic victory. Some observers at the time believed that Iran, by this stroke, obtained her independence. Certainly her oil income was placed on a more sustaining basis, even though it seemed clear that the British admiralty was still able to purchase Iranian oil more cheaply than the Iranian government.

International Affairs

Shah Reza in his foreign affairs maintained friendly relations with his neighbors. Visits were exchanged, and in 1934 he was entertained in Ankara. The crowning achievement was the signing of the Saadabad pact in 1937 with Turkey, Iraq, and Afghanistan at Reza's Garden Palace in the mountains near Tehran. The pact provided for mutual cooperation, consultations, and nonaggression.

In addition to the concession of the Anglo-Persian Oil Company, which became the Anglo-Iranian Oil Company in 1935, when Reza insisted on the use of the word "Iran" to denote his country, the Anglo-Iranian treaty of 1928 helped to settle affairs with England. Imperial Airways was allowed to fly planes over Iran; Britain recognized the end of the capitulations; British support for Shaykh Khazal of Mohammerah was terminated and Reza took over the shaykh's role in protecting the oil pipelines; British consuls and agents were still permitted to deal directly with tribes such as the Lurs, Bakhtiyaris, and the Qashqais; and Iran recognized British rule in Iraq. Except for Iran's claim to the Baḥrayn Islands all outstanding matters were considered, and the anti-British feelings in Iran became quiescent temporarily. Such feelings could, however, easily be brought to the surface, for twisting the British lion's tail was a sporting event for all Iranian nationalists.

Shah Reza's relations with Soviet Russia were more complicated, especially since Iran and Russia had a long common frontier. Iran was traversed by Soviet agents of all kinds, and rebellions occurred in Azerbayjan and Khurasan. When the rebellions were suppressed, all communist activities went underground. In the Russo-Iranian treaty of 1921 Russia had formally renounced all concessions and Iran was forbidden to grant these concessions to other foreigners. Thus, in the 1920s and again in the 1930s, Russia protested vehemently when Iran granted oil concessions in her northern provinces. Since northern Iran's export market was almost exclusively Russian, Russia could and frequently did exert great pressure on Iran by closing her frontiers to Iranian goods. This weapon was invoked in 1926 to obtain a fishing agreement for the Caspian Sea. For political ends Russia dumped goods on Iran and by 1931 had all but ruined Iranian exporters. Sensing the inability of private traders in Iran to challenge the Soviet state trading companies, Reza placed all foreign trade in Iran under state monopoly and control. This device and Germany's return to the Iranian scene with the advent of Hitler gave Iran some freedom from economic domination by the colossus to the north.

Caught between the British in the south and the Soviets in the north, Iran turned to Germany as a counterpoise. German technicians were invited in great numbers, advising the various ministries and aiding in scientific agriculture, communications, engineering works, and industrial enterprises. When compensation and bank-clearing agreements were concluded after Dr. Hjalmar Schacht's visit in 1935, the volume of trade between the two countries jumped. In 1939 over 40 percent of Iran's foreign trade was with Germany. Iranian schools hired German professors and numerous Iranians took advanced degrees in German universities. Modern Iranian architecture showed strong German influences. Large numbers of Germans visited Iran for various reasons and on diverse pretexts. Nearly a thousand a year came in the period before 1940 and many remained. Germany was making a valiant bid for Iran; had peace continued a few more years beyond 1939, Iran might well have been closely tied to Germany. The rapid events after 1939 quickly changed the picture. Within two years Soviet Russia and Great Britain were partners in the drive to destroy Germany, and Iran was forced to cooperate. The entire focus of government and life in Iran was reoriented. A new era was ushered in.

Shah Reza

Shah Reza Pahlevi was an uneducated soldier who had a soldier's respect for authority and expected his will to be followed implicitly. The subterfuges of traditional Iranian officialdom frustrated him into direct and ruthless conduct. Discovering that the minutiae of governing frequently were not accomplished when his back was turned, he consumed too much of his time with the details. There was a vast amount of work that needed to be done in Iran and too few to do it, and Reza became immersed in a welter of programs too numerous for him to carry through alone. Taking so much responsibility on his own shoulders discouraged initiative in those about him; in consequence the promising projects for agricultural reform, educational and secular development, and state industrial enterprise fell far short of their goals. Reza's lack of education did, however, make it possible for him to discard many traditions of Iranian society that a man trained in the niceties and subtleties of Iranian culture and its long history would have been incapable of ignoring. Westernization in Iran had a stout ally in Reza Shah. His resolute will and toughness, despite the religion, the great landowners, and the traditional dissimulation of the Iranian people, would not let the regeneration of Iran and her people fail.

In the end Reza became interested in acquiring a great personal fortune in estates and funds in foreign accounts. He grew tired, his temper rose, his sensitivity to criticism mounted, and his power became more absolute. Ignorance lured him into many traps and unfortunate decisions regarding policies and men. His forced abdication in 1941 and the Allied intervention in Iranian affairs probably saved much of the Westernization program begun by Reza in his early days on the throne.

REFERENCES: Chapter 36

See works already cited in Chapters 4, 6, 7, 8, 9, 10, 15, 17, 18, 19, 20, 22, 23, 26, 27, 28, 29, 30, 31, 32, and 33. Chapter 37 contains additional references.

Amuzegar, Jahangir, and M. Ali Fekrat. *Iran: Economic Development Under Dualistic Conditions.* Chicago: University of Chicago Press, 1971. A fine analysis of the reasons for slow economic growth prior to 1950 and of the conditions that led to rapid development after 1954.

Banani, Amin. *The Modernization of Iran, 1921–1941.* Stanford, Calif.: Stanford University Press, 1961. After an introductory historical summary, this study, based largely on Iranian sources, gives a detailed survey of the impact of Shah Reza on his country.

Bharier, Julian. *Economic Development in Iran, 1900–1970.* London: Oxford University Press, 1971. Bridges very neatly the gap between the historical and the analytical studies of modern Iran.

Binder, Leonard. *Iran: Political Development in a Changing Society.* Berkeley: University of California Press, 1962. One of the most important studies of contemporary Iran.

Cottam, Richard W. *Nationalism in Iran.* Pittsburgh: University of Pittsburgh Press, 1964. A comprehensive, systematic, and stimulating study emphasizing the interrelated themes of liberal nationalism and the policy of the United States toward Iran.

Elwell-Sutton, Lawrence P. *A Guide to Iranian Area Study.* Ann Arbor, Mich.: J. W. Edwards, 1952. An important bibliography.

————. *Modern Iran:* London: Routledge & Kegan Paul, 1941.

Fatemi, Nasrollah S. *Diplomatic History of Persia, 1917–1923: Anglo-Russian Power Politics in Iran.* New York: R. F. Moore, 1952.

Groseclose, Elgin. *Introduction to Iran.* New York: Oxford University Press, 1947.

Haas, William S. *Iran.* New York: Columbia University Press, 1946. Useful for the modern period to the end of World War II.

Kamshad, Hassan. *Modern Persian Prose Literature.* Cambridge, England: The University Press, 1966. Accounts of the authors' lives, summaries of important works, and many translated excerpts. Points out that the major theme of most twentieth-century Persian prose is social protest against government tyranny and corruption, opportunism in all classes of society, the position of women, and the clergy. Another theme is the readjustment problems of foreign-educated Iranians upon their return home.

Lambton, A. K. S. *The Persian Land Reform, 1962–1966.* New York: Oxford University Press, 1969. The most comprehensive account of the subject. The author has collected first-hand data on many villages in different parts of Iran.

Lenczowski, George. *Russia and the West in Iran, 1918–1948, A Study in Big Power Rivalry.* Ithaca, N.Y.: Cornell University Press, 1949. A first-rate study.

Millspaugh, Arthur C. *The American Task in Persia.* New York: Century, 1925. An account of his first tour of duty in Iran.

———. *Americans in Persia.* Washington, D.C.: The Brookings Institution, 1946. A personal account by the American adviser to the shah.

Ramazani, Rouhollah K. *The Persian Gulf: Iran's Role.* Charlottesville: University of Virginia Press, 1972. A meticulously researched analysis of Iran's role in the area and her relationship with other Persian Gulf states and with the Powers. The author uses Persian, Arabic, and Western sources.

Sykes, Christopher. *Wassmuss, "the German Lawrence."* London: Longmans, Green, 1936. The fascinating story of the German agent in Iran during World War I.

Wilber, Donald N. *Iran: Past and Present.* 7th ed. Princeton, N.J.: Princeton University Press, 1975. A classic summary of Iran's history and development, largely since 1921.

———. *Riza Shah Pahlavi: The Resurrection and Reconstruction of Iran, 1878–1944.* New York: Exposition Press, 1975. An account of the shah's life almost week by week, blow by blow, by an outstanding scholar. It records the dynamism of Iran in a stage of transition.

Wilson, Arnold T. *Persia.* New York: Scribner, 1933. Was an excellent survey at its time and is still useful for the earlier period of modernization.

Zonis, Marvin. *The Political Elite of Iran.* Princeton, N.J.: Princeton University Press, 1971. An in-depth view of the most powerful political decision-makers in Iran.

Chapter 37

World War II and the Middle East

Turkish Neutrality

Upon the outbreak of World War II Turkey declared her neutrality. Yet, her position was not clear-cut. In the fifteen months before the actual rupture of peace and even as early as 1936, Turkish foreign policy had been veering toward Britain and France. In September 1939 Turkey was joined to England and France by several pacts regarding credits, chrome, and nonaggression. On the other hand, almost 50 percent of her trade was with Germany. Furthermore, the Nazi-Soviet pact of August 1939 gave Turkish leadership every reason for caution, since Russian power and objectives in the Black Sea area and eastern Asia Minor were difficult to assess.

In such a situation Turkish relations with Russia appeared of paramount importance. Shukru Saracoğlu, Turkish foreign minister, spent nearly a month in Moscow in an attempt to formulate a mutual assistance pact with the U.S.S.R. Molotov set the price: a proviso that the Straits be closed to the British and French and a proviso that Turkey under no circumstances become involved in hostilities with the Nazis. The Turks would not agree. On October 19, therefore, they signed a formal fifteen-year treaty of alliance with France and the United Kingdom. Its terms held that in the event of an act of aggression upon Turkey her allies would come to her assistance, that Turkey on her part would enter the war should it come to the Mediterranean, but that under no circumstances would Turkey be drawn into a conflict against the U.S.S.R. At the same time loans and credits of £43.5 million were made to Turkey to bolster her financial position and speed the flow of arms. Britain also had an all-important agreement, which ran until January 1, 1943, whereby she could, if she so desired, purchase and export the entire output of Turkish chrome ore.

Upon the fall of France, the entry of Mussolini into the war, and the loss of British armor at Dunkirk, the Turkish government quickly reassessed its international position. It was suspected that Russia, surely having been awarded Istanbul and the Straits by Hitler, might soon move to seize the prize, as she was already doing in Finland, the Baltic, and Bessarabia. Turkey had bravely cast her lot with Britain and France, but the likelihood of a German defeat was far removed in the summer of 1940 and the winter of 1940–1941. War came to the Mediterranean upon Italy's declaration, but

Turkey maintained her neutrality and continued in that course through the Italian campaign against Greece, the German conquest of Yugoslavia and Greece, and the occupation of Bulgaria.

British naval and air personnel in civilian garb were numerous in Turkey, and the British urged Turkish entry into the war at the time of the debacle in Greece. Steadfastly, the Turkish leaders refused. They pointed out that Britain was no more prepared to give planes and heavy armor to Turkey than to Greece and that recklessness on Turkey's part would invite German retaliation. Also, if Turkey could maintain a neutral role, she would serve as a land barrier to Syria, Suez, and the Persian Gulf. Furthermore, the leaders could see no purely Turkish reason for joining in the war.

Hitler's invasion of Russia acutely disturbed the orientation of Turkish neutrality. The Turks clearly foresaw that a German defeat would leave Soviet Russia the dominant continental power of Europe. Since the British had promised Russia the Straits in World War I and since the appeasers had been so free with other nations' territories, England might easily concede the Straits to Russia to seal the sudden new alliance between them. Moreover the Straits might be safe from German aggression as long as German arms were engaged deeply in Russia. As American lend-lease began to rebuild British strength, it became possible for the Turks to envisage a negotiated peace without victory that might eventually safeguard Turkish frontiers and leave the Straits in their hands.

The might of Germany from the middle of 1941 to the spring of 1943 awed Turkish leaders, while Franz von Papen, the crafty German ambassador in Ankara, played on the fears and suspicions of Saracoğlu, who as a loyal Turk could only rejoice at the prospect of the crushing of Russia. Turkey signed a ten-year nonaggression pact with Germany in June 1941, although the Turks insisted on a statement that this pact did not contravene any previous Turkish commitments. In October a trade agreement was concluded, providing for the shipment of various raw materials to Germany, among which would be chrome ore. After January 1, 1943, when the chrome agreement with Great Britain would expire, Germany would be enabled to purchase 90,000 tons of ore in exchange for war equipment valued at L.T. 100 million, most of which would have to be delivered to Turkey before the chrome ore could be exported. Although it was a hollow German victory, the Turkish press played it up as a concrete evidence of Turkish neutrality to parallel the argument of Menemencioğlu, who took over the foreign ministry when Saracoğlu became prime minister, that Turkish neutrality benefited the Axis since it kept "British shipping out of the Black Sea!"

Toward the end of 1942 a wavering became noticeable in the Turkish position. German casualties in Russia weakened the contentions of von Papen; meanwhile, the flow of many millions of dollars worth of American lend-lease goods to Turkey permitted her to give some evidence of her natural sympathy for England and the United States. Although Sir Hughe Knatchbull-Hugessen and Laurence A. Steinhardt, British and American ambassadors, worked hard to bring about friendly relations between Turkey and Russia, President Inönü and others entertained serious doubts about the future good will of Stalin with regard to the Straits.

Throughout 1943 the great discussion centered on opening a second front and the possibility of Turkish cooperation and open participation. The topic was raised early in 1942 in a general way; in 1943 it was again considered and debated at Casablanca, Adana, Quebec, Moscow, Cairo, Tehran, and Cairo. Churchill repeatedly pressed the case for Turkish entry and for a concerted attack upon Germany through the Balkans as the best way to defeat Germany and save central Europe and the Balkans from the Bolsheviks. Russia, on the other hand, believed that Turkey should declare her position against the Axis and shoulder some of the real burdens of the war. But Turkey steadfastly refused to abandon her neutrality, recognizing that German bombers from bases in Bulgaria, only twenty minutes from Istanbul, could pulverize that fair city almost at will. The decisive veto on Churchill's plan was exercised by General Marshall. No arms would be spared from the cross-channel attack upon Europe, for the Americans at that moment were demanding a frontal attack upon Germany. Without aid, Turkey would not enter the war. She did, however, permit British and American officers to circulate quite freely "incognito." And American airmen, downed in Turkey on the return from bombing Rumanian oil installations and other Balkan targets, were frequently allowed to escape from their internment.

In April 1944 chrome shipments to Germany were halted; in August, following British and American promises that they would take adequate measures to prevent the collapse of the Turkish economy, Turkey severed diplomatic and economic relations with Germany. Finally, in February 1945, in order to become a charter member of the United Nations and attend the San Francisco conference, Turkey declared war upon Germany. But for all practical purposes the war was over, and Turkey entered the tense postwar period.

During the war years the Turkish economy was subjected to constant pressure from all sides. At times more than 1,000,000 men were under arms, and the Turkish budget called for vast military expenditures. Deficit financing brought inflation, price controls being either absent or ineffective. Moreover, large sums were thrown about by agents, spies, and "tourists" from the belligerent powers. Extensive German purchases of mohair, olive oil, hazelnuts, chrome ore, tanning materials, and tobacco, in addition to tobacco and chrome exported to England and the United States, gave Turkey great purchasing power at a time when the importation of consumer articles and capital goods was exceedingly difficult.

Another cause of inflation was the policy of preclusive or preemptive buying pursued by England and the United States in Turkey. Several hundred million dollars-worth of low-grade chrome ore, mohair, hazelnuts, olive oil, and valonia were bought and stored in Turkey for the sole purpose of keeping these goods from Germany. An active market in these commodi-

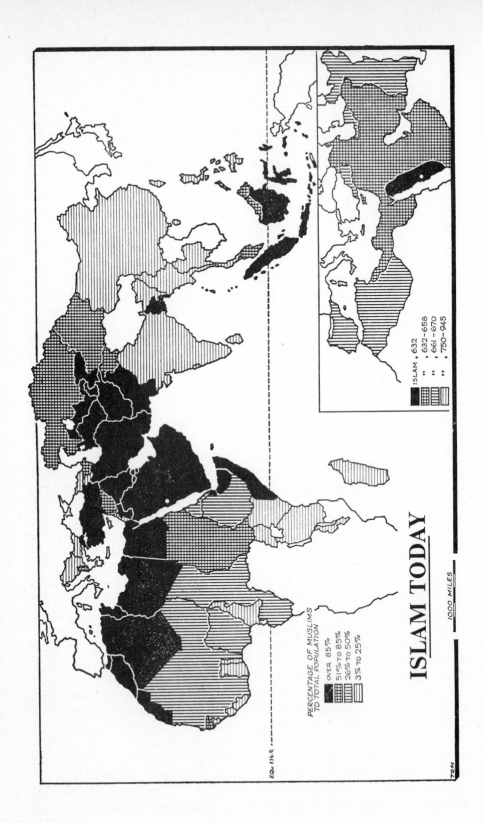

PERCENTAGE OF MUSLIMS
TO TOTAL POPULATION

OVER 85%
51% TO 85%
26% TO 50%
3% TO 25%

ISLAM, 632
" , 632-658
" , 661-670
" , 750-945

ISLAM TODAY

1000 MILES

EQUATOR

TRM

504

ties forced prices up and increased production. Valonia, used in tanning and derived from an acorn from trees that grow wild in Turkey, was a good example. As the demand for valonia rose, more peasants gathered more acorns from the woods to increase their income and, incidentally, to lead the Allies to purchase more. From time to time shiploads of goods were dumped in the Black Sea to eliminate storage charges. The end of the war found Turkey with a sizable fund of foreign exchange acquired from exports and sales that were never balanced by imports.

The general shipping shortage of the Allies and the difficulty of importing goods into Turkey through the Mediterranean created many other abnormalities in Turkish trade. Furthermore, since Turkey was a neutral power, all exports from the United States and the British Empire were carefully screened to make sure that goods would not be reexported to the Axis. An informal Anglo-American coordinating committee was established in Ankara from the staffs of the British and American embassies, and no goods were cleared for export to Turkey from Allied ports without the approval of this committee, which also passed upon some $125 million worth of American lend-lease goods.

Inflation and mounting deficits induced Inönü in 1942 to experiment with a capital levy tax in hope of lowering prices, balancing the budget, and absorbing some of the abundance of money. A law *(Varlik Vergisi)* authorized the creation of a special committee in each province to levy a tax on all persons according to their capital and in varying percentages on the assumption they were evading their proper income taxes. Particularly in Istanbul, gross inequalities developed. Greeks, Armenians, Jews, and foreigners were hard pressed, some being assessed sums nearly equal to their total capital. Those who did not pay were sentenced to hard labor on railroads in eastern Anatolia. Representatives of the Allied governments protested to Inönü, but the situation with regard to Turkish neutrality was so delicate that all news of the capital tax was censored in Western presses until the spring of 1943. Upon official pressure at the highest levels in wartime conferences in 1943 the tax was abolished and those who had not paid were released. The experience, however, left an unpleasant residue of insecurity on the part of non-Turkish citizens, who regarded the tax as an expression of unbridled nationalism.

When Turkey broke with Germany in August 1944, it was feared that a sudden termination of preclusive buying and the cessation of German purchases of strategic raw materials along with comestibles such as figs, raisins, and fish would be a ruinous shock to the Turkish economy. However, no crash occurred. Shipping became more plentiful, Turkish ports were opened, and Turkish products found a ready market in a world apparently short of almost everything.

For Turkey the period of the war from September 1, 1939, to February 23, 1945, had marked a difficult course of neutrality. Turkey wished to live in peace with the victorious powers, but during the course of the war it was not always clear who would win. Furthermore, at first Russia and Germany were opposed to England and France; then, at one stroke, in 1941 Russia and England were combined to crush Germany. Those five and one half years seemed endless to President Inönü and the leaders of Turkey.

Egypt and the War

In other areas of the Middle East World War II brought armies, shortages, inflation, political strain, economic opportunities, and a variety of social and intellectual upheavals. At the very outset Egypt held a pivotal position. Ali Maher, the prime minister and a person with great influence over King Faruk, induced the government to sever diplomatic and economic relations with Germany as soon as Britain declared war. Martial law was declared; ports were placed under the authority of the British navy; and censorship of posts and telegraph was established. When parliament convened in November the speech from the throne indicated that Egypt would give active and willing cooperation to England in defense of Egypt. Some concern arose over the price and market for cotton, particularly since nearly 20 percent of Egyptian cotton exports had gone in the previous year to Germany and countries under her control. Demand, however, was brisk, and open-market prices climbed higher than those guaranteed by the government. When Mussolini entered the war, Egypt broke off relations with Italy, but notified him that war would not be declared unless Italy attacked Egypt. As a result of British pressure, Ali Maher, recognized as anti-British, was replaced by Hasan Sabri, an independent. The latter formed a broad national government, including Ahmad Hasanayn, a pro-Britisher, in the very influential post of chief of the royal cabinet.

The Italian declaration brought the war to Egypt's doorstep. In September 1940 Italian forces advanced some fifty miles into Egypt toward Alexandria, resting at Sidi Barrani until December, when General Sir Archibald Wavell drove them west of Benghazi. Then, in April 1941, after contributing heavily to the support of Greece, British forces reeled toward the Egyptian frontier, although the fortress of Tobruk held. From then until May 1942, Germany's General Rommel and his Afrika Korps fought a see-saw battle against the British, pushing the front to al-Alamayn, only seventy miles west of Alexandria. In October 1942 a two-week battle at al-Alamayn broke the German army, which continued to fall back, as General Bernard Montgomery at the head of the British Eighth Army followed in full pursuit. British and American forces, which landed in Morocco and Algeria on November 8, 1942, under the command of General Dwight D. Eisenhower, met General Montgomery in Tunisia at the end of March 1943, and the war in North Africa came to its end.

As war raged in the western desert, life in Egypt changed rapidly. Although a few British continued their afternoon cricket matches at the famed Gezira Sporting Club, most found the tensions of war pressing upon them. When the Mediterranean was virtually closed to shipping, a glut of cotton loomed ominously, but Britain solved the problem by agreeing to buy the entire crop at a price all Egyptians admitted was generous. Husayn Sirri, a nonparty civil engineer, succeeded to the prime ministership upon the death of Hasan Sabri in November 1940; his policies continued a similar course. Wafdists and Saadists refused to participate in the cabinet. The following spring, when the general situation appeared very black a number of seditious or suspect individuals, such as Ali Maher, General Aziz Ali al-Misri, and Hasan al-Banna, leader of the extreme Muslim Brotherhood, were confined to residence in rural areas.

Shortages of cereals, inadequate price regulations, and the lack of import and export controls created hardships for the population of Cairo and Alexandria. These developments furthered political disintegration and made the anti-British intrigues of King Faruk and the palace clique more effective. The German capture of Benghazi and the Japanese victories in south Asia emboldened Faruk and his cronies. The students were called out, and Husayn Sirri resigned on February 2, 1942. The following day the British ambassador, in an audience with the king, complained that Sirri's cooperation with the British had been thwarted at every step, urged that a new government commanding the support of a majority of the country be formed without delay, and suggested that Nahas Pasha and the Wafd be called to head the government. On February 4 an ultimatum, supported by the American minister, demanded that Faruk make the appointment or accept the consequences. On the advice of the palace clique, Faruk refused. That evening the British ambassador, accompanied by General Stone and a tank force, called on Faruk at Abdin Palace and offered him the alternative of appointing Nahas Pasha or boarding a British warship at Suez and spending the remainder of the war period on the Seychelles or Mauritius. Faruk chose the former course, and Egypt remained fully loyal to the war effort. Corruption and inefficiency increased; patronage to "deserving" Wafdists became rife; but the Allies no longer had a troublesome, uncooperative Egyptian government with which to cope.

Nahas held office until October 1944. In the meantime corruption and favoritism grew, and the hatred between Nahas and Faruk became notorious. Nahas weakened his position and his party by succumbing to unabated nepotism, especially with respect to his wife's family. He quarreled with prominent supporters, many of whom left the Wafd and formed a new party, the *Kutla*. His dismissal was a foregone conclusion. As soon as the theatres of the war were removed to a distance far from Egypt, British insistence upon retaining the Nahas government could no longer be valid. Pledging cooperation with Britain against Germany and Japan, Saadist Ahmad Maher formed a government composed of Saadists, Liberals, and members of the Kutla. On February 24, 1945, he informed the chamber of deputies of his intention to declare war upon Germany in order that Egypt might become a charter member of the United Nations. As he left, he was assassinated by a young Egyptian fascist. Al-Nukrashi, the second in command of the Saadist party, assumed the prime ministership, and a formal declaration of a defensive war against Germany and Japan was issued on February 26. Strangely enough, Egyptian entry into the war opened the postwar period and its many problems for Egypt.

Independence of Lebanon and Syria

The probability of war in Europe stiffened the French goverment's attitude toward Syria and Lebanon, and appropriate measures were taken by Gabriel Puaux, the high commissioner. His delegate in Damascus took over control of the police from the minister of the interior. In July 1939 Hashim al-Atasi, president of Syria, resigned in protest over the gift of Alexandretta to Turkey. Puaux thereupon dissolved the chamber of deputies, suspended the constitution, placed foreign affairs and defense directly in French hands, established a council of five to govern Syria, and again formed separate regimes for Jebel Druze and Latakia.

Upon the outbreak of war General Weygand was sent from France as commander in chief of French forces in the Levant. The appointment cheered the Syrians and Lebanese, since Weygand had been exceedingly popular as high commissioner. In September the Lebanese constitution was suspended and the powers of the cabinet transferred to a Lebanese secretary of state, assisted by French advisers. However, the fall of France left the situation uncertain. General Weygand had been recalled, and General Mittelhauser elected to remain loyal to General Pétain and the Vichy government.

In August 1940 Italian officers arrived in Beirut to supervise an armistice for the Axis, but were frustrated by Puaux and General Fougeres. Many French officers found it possible to slip away to Palestine, where they proceeded to join the Free French forces of General de Gaulle. Others were arrested and imprisoned in Syria and Lebanon. When General Dentz appeared in November as high commissioner, collaboration with Vichy and the Axis became even more open. From the Hotel Metropole in Beirut German agents who flocked into the French mandate began to prepare the states for German control. Economic difficulties and the collapse of the French franc, to which Syrian and Lebanese currencies were tied, led to strikes and political demonstrations. General Dentz attempted to soothe local feelings by establishing new governments under Khalid al-Azm in Syria and Alfred Naccache in Lebanon.

The new arrangements only partially settled the atmosphere, because the leaders of Syria and Lebanon were plotting to acquire complete independence at this moment of French embarrassment and did not relish the thought of falling into the orbit of Germany or Italy. In the spring of 1941 infiltration by German "tourists" and the use of Syrian airfields for German aid to Iraq posed a serious threat to the British position in the Middle East. The French states were blockaded, and England declared that the use of Syria or Lebanon as a base by any hostile power would not be tolerated. Because of incipient dangers in Lebanon and Syria, British and Free French forces under General Sir Henry Maitland Wilson and General Catroux entered the French mandate from Palestine and Transjordan in June. Resistance by General Dentz was unexpectedly strong, and the Allied forces battled their way into Beirut and Damascus. An armistice was signed in July at Acre. Those French who wished to be repatriated were permitted to leave, but many remained at their posts, since French cultural institutions were respected and their work was unimpaired.

On the first day of the invasion of the French Levant, General de Gaulle designated General Catroux delegate general and plenipotentiary of Free France in the Levant. He appointed Alfred Naccache president of Lebanon and Taj al-Din al-Hasani president of Syria, and recognized these two states as independent and free republics. Meanwhile, Britain sent General Sir Edward Spears as head of a British mission to the Levant, incorporated the "republics" into the sterling bloc, and brought the supplying of their requirements under the machinery of the Middle East Supply Center in Cairo.

These provisions did not satisfy the nationalists, who complained that the people had no hand in them. Under such pressures the suspended constitutions were reestablished in 1943 and elections were held for legislative bodies. In Syria the leader of the National Bloc, Shukri al-Kuwatli, became president of the republic. In Lebanon Bishara al-Khuri was chosen president and Riyadh al-Sulh prime minister; the newly elected Chamber had thirty Christian and twenty-five Muslim members. The French, however, found it extremely difficult to relinquish prerogatives such as issuing decrees and maintaining special troops and agents in the states. Lebanese and Syrians objected to the continuation of these forms of colonialism and adopted resolutions dropping all references to France from their constitutions. When al-Khuri and the Lebanese cabinet were arrested, a general strike and spontaneous anti-French riots forced the French to give in. When the National Bloc in Syria also demanded the withdrawal of French controls, General Catroux agreed (December 1943). In 1944 the U.S.S.R. and the United States gave full diplomatic recognition of the independence of the two states, which declared war upon the Axis on February 27, 1945, and thereby became charter members of the United Nations. The actions of the Russians and Americans compelled the reluctant British and the weakened French to accept Syrian and Lebanese delegates at the San Francisco conference and to respect the free position of these two republics of the Levant.

Unrest in Iraq

World War II found Iraq weak economically and in a highly charged political atmosphere. In 1939 Britain loaned Iraq nearly £4 million for armaments and railroads, and the Iraq Petroleum Company advanced £3 million to cover ordinary governmental expenses. Nuri al-Said, the prime minister, broke relations with Germany, took over German property, and interned all Germans who remained in Iraq. Although the government declared it would live up to its treaty obligations with Britain, most leaders quietly rejoiced over the embarrassment of England and France and expected that their fellow Arabs in Palestine, Syria, and Lebanon would secure independence during the struggle. Hajj Amin al-Husayni, the Jerusalem mufti, took up residence in Baghdad in October 1939 and from there directed his campaign to obtain an Arab state in Palestine.

Early in 1940 because of local politics Nuri al-Said resigned his office in favor of Rashid Ali al-Gailani, who was a "hard worker, a persuasive speaker, a passionate nationalist, ambitious and reckless." Unfortunately Rashid Ali had little knowledge of the world outside of Iraq and thus judged the results of his actions in a narrow local perspective. In July 1940 he offered to join the war openly on the side of Great Britain if Palestine would be established as a state immediately. At that time an Arab state would have resulted, since Jews comprised only one-third of its population. Churchill's refusal split the Iraqi government right down the middle. Nuri led the moderates; Rashid Ali championed the uncompromising nationalists, who succumbed easily to Axis flattery and thought to use German and Italian arms and money to achieve their nationalist goals.

In November the British ambassador suggested to the regent that a more amicable prime minister be found, an overture which prompted Rashid Ali to look to the Axis for material aid. In December, after refusing the regent's request to resign, he publicly stated that Iraq's foreign affairs were being strengthened with "friendly states" other than Britain. As clandestine relations with the Axis developed, Nuri, Taha al-Hashimi, minister of defense, and three other ministers resigned. When a parliamentary vote of no confidence loomed before Rashid Ali, his plea for the dissolution of parliament was denied by the regent, who then left Baghdad to be free from pressures. In the face of such opposition Rashid Ali resigned, and the regent appointed Taha al-Hashimi upon the insistence of Rashid Ali's army friends who were known as the Golden Square.

Taking office February 3, 1941, Taha al-Hashimi failed to curb the power of the Golden Square. Rashid Ali grew desperate and worked incessantly to return to power. On the night of April 1, 1941, supported by the army, Rashid Ali returned to power in a kind of coup d'état. The regent was smuggled out of the country by the American minister. The British, fearing the worst, landed an Indian army brigade at Basrah to protect an important air assembling base. Discussions between Rashid Ali and Sir Kinahan Cornwallis, the British ambassador, did not improve matters. When more forces were landed at Basrah, the Iraqi army threatened the meager British units stationed at the air base at Habbaniyah in the vicinity of Baghdad. Bombings and artillery attacks by the Iraqis lasted from May 2 until May 30, when the British and the Arab Legion from Transjordan relieved Habbaniyah and occupied Baghdad. Rashid Ali and his allies fled to Iran and Turkey; German planes, which had just arrived, flew off to Syria; the regent returned; and Nuri al-Said eventually became prime minister at the head of a new government.

For the remainder of World War II relative political peace reigned in

Iraq, and Nuri al-Said devoted much time and energy to building the Arab League and promoting Arab unity. Iraq declared war on the Axis in January 1943 and signed the United Nations Declaration the same month. It was the first Middle Eastern state to qualify for membership in the United Nations.

Iraq became greatly involved in the process of supplying goods to the U.S.S.R., and vast numbers of British and American troops were stationed there. In 1942 Iraq was made eligible to receive lend-lease aid, and quantities of military and necessary civilian goods were dispatched. Inflation disrupted her economy in many ways, as British and American expenditures introduced great purchasing power over a wide segment of the population without a concomitant importation or production of consumers' goods. Iraq's economic requirements were screened by the Middle East Supply Center in Cairo. Since Iraq was a member of the sterling bloc, Britain also had an effective instrument for controlling and channeling Iraq's foreign trade to British Empire sources, often to the great discomfiture of American and Iraqi business interests. As World War II came to an end Iraq attempted to break the economic domination that London had effectively maintained since the end of World War I.

Occupation of Iran

At the outbreak of World War II Iran under Shah Reza was deeply involved economically with Germany. Large percentages of imports and exports were German, and German technicians were assisting in the development of the industry and the natural resources of Iran other than oil. Although Iran declared her neutrality, official Iranian attitudes were pro-German until the Nazi invasion of Russia in 1941. Shah Reza was decidedly anti-Russian and anti-British, largely because of the time-worn imperialism of those powers in Iran. The British closed the sea routes to Germany and did not permit Iranian goods to pass to Germany through neutral states. The Soviet Union opened her ports, and a treaty of March 1940 allowed Iranian goods transit through the U.S.S.R. to states having treaty relations with Russia.

Iran swarmed with Axis officials and agents of every sort. S.S. *Oberfuhrer* Ettel became German minister in Tehran, and the legation served as headquarters for German agents operating in Iraq. Although Russian hands were partially tied because of the Soviet-Nazi agreement, communist activities flourished in the northern provinces in expectation of the U.S.S.R.'s taking over Iraq and Iran in accordance with her understanding with Germany.

Hitler's invasion of Russia in June 1941 changed the situation in Iran almost overnight. On June 26 the Soviets informed Shah Reza that the Germans planned a coup d'état in Iran and that the U.S.S.R. could not ignore the presence and unfriendly activities of Germans there. In July, after the Anglo-Soviet agreement for mutual assistance, the two governments initiated joint pressure on Iran to force the unusually large number of Germans in Iran to depart. Shah Reza was furious at such requests, and no action was taken.

Arrangements were rapidly developing whereby Russia would be supplied from Britain and the United States through Iran. Of necessity, Iran could not be permitted to become a tool of Germany. British and Soviet troops, therefore, began their occupation of Iran on August 25, 1941. Token resistance was offered for two days, until a new government under Muhammad Ali Furuki ordered submission and British-Soviet contacts were made at two different points northwest of Tehran. Since Shah Reza was still defiant, Allied forces approached Tehran with the intention of occupying the capital. Instead, the shah abdicated on September 17 because of "failing health," and his twenty-one-year-old son, Mohammad Reza, was proclaimed shah. Reza was taken first to Mauritius and then to South Africa, where he died in 1944. A roundup of Axis agents and friends bagged several hundred, but the mufti of Jerusalem, Iraqi rebels, and notorious agents such as Franz Mayr and Roman Gamotta escaped the net.

For the remainder of the war Iran cooperated with the Allies. At the famous Tehran conference the Big Three, at Roosevelt's suggestion, complimented Iran on her service in the supplying of Russia. The quantities of goods that passed to Russia over the Trans-Iranian railway and by motor truck through Iran were so vast the figures of tonnage are incomprehensible. The operations influenced life in the country markedly. In time more than 30,000 American troops were stationed there along with many British and Russians. Their expenditures brought quantities of foreign exchange. But the Iranians found little to purchase with these sums, as imports were held to a minimum by the Middle East Supply Center, which controlled Iranian foreign trade. Inflation became very serious with prices for scarce items soaring to such an extent that truck tires sold for £450 each and one aspirin tablet for $2.50. Before the end of the war the general price level had increased 1000 percent over 1939, and the dislocation of the Iranian economy became general.

As was so frequently the case, the Allied ousting of Shah Reza also removed the strong hand at the helm of internal governmental affairs. The various elements in Iranian society that Reza ruthlessly controlled immediately reared their heads, weakened the government, and played havoc with the centralizing and nationalizing processes that Reza had engendered. Nomads secured rifles and arms; Shiite divines returned to do battle against a secular state; wealthy landowners ignored taxation; and communist agitators were released from jails. Dr. Millspaugh was invited again to administer Iran's finances; Colonel Norman Schwarzkopf, another American, reorganized the police; and an American military mission advised the army. German undercover activities continued for many months after the forced reversal of Iranian policy. The German military penetration of Russia and the British retreat to al-Alamayn encouraged a restlessness among Iranian leaders. Franz Mayr came out of hiding and helped organize a group called Nationalists of Iran. General Zahedi joined the movement and aided in the revolt of the Kurds and the southern tribes. All these activities faded quickly, however, when the Germans faltered at Stalingrad.

In 1942 a tripartite treaty of alliance was signed by Iran, Great Britain, and the U.S.S.R. Iran recognized the foreign troops as in no sense an occupying force, while the other two parties to the treaty acknowledged the independence of Iran and agreed to a withdrawal of their forces not later than six months after the end of the war with the Axis. The supply route to Russia was the major concern. Russia, nevertheless, utilized this golden opportunity to further her imperialistic and communistic interests in Iran. She aided the *Tudeh* (Masses) party, protected their rallies with Soviet tanks, published communist newspapers, intrigued with Armenians and Kurds, and finally in 1944 demanded an oil concession. Britain tried to counter such moves with her own propaganda, but it was only partially successful. The United States did little at all, although lend-lease was made available in 1942. Iran declared war on Germany in September 1943, thus qualifying at an early date for membership in the United Nations.

The Middle East Supply Center

World War II brought many innovations and organizational devices to the Middle East. None was more encompassing than the Middle East Supply Center. As the volume of supplies for General Wavell poured in, tonnage for civilian use did not abate. Ports and docks were so choked with goods, many of them luxuries, that at times it seemed certain the war would be lost for want of anchorage and unloading space. Out of this chaos was born, in April 1941, an executive agency that grew and spread its effective control everywhere in the Middle East except Turkey. It allocated available shipping for the several areas; it ascertained the types and quantity of goods to be imported and it passed upon import permits; it determined from which country imported goods should come; it guaranteed the Middle East at least minimum requirements of scarce and rationed articles and commodities; and it maintained in the Middle East common stocks of wheat and other bulk items for emergency use.

In the beginning the Middle East Supply Center was operated entirely by the British. But in 1942, when lend-lease goods went to the Middle East and more and more shipments originated in the United States, American officials participated in the direction of policy at the Cairo headquarters, and an operational office was established in Washington. However, representatives of Middle Eastern governments did not sit on any of the boards or have any voice in determining policy. Officers of the Middle East Supply Center grew to regard their work and the functions being performed not only as an indispensable contribution to the war effort but also as a benevolent tutelage in techniques of economic planning, area coordination, and development of resources. Middle Easterners questioned the advantages and benefits of the Middle East Supply Center, and as the war drew to a close its original justification disappeared.

As early as 1944 it became manifest that Britain, through control of imports, use of the sterling area pool, and the denial of dollar exchange, was employing the center as a restraint of trade and as an instrument for maintaining the economic colonialism of the British Empire. Since such acts were contrary to American foreign trade policies, the United States withdrew from the operations in 1945 and the center wound up its affairs. Undoubtedly many of its regional activities would have been advantageous to perpetuate, but nothing had been done to bring in Middle Eastern governments or train local personnel to maintain the work. Thus, when the center was abandoned, its possible peacetime usefulness did not materialize, and the Middle East returned to divisive and national economic policies. For many states of the Middle East the demise of the Middle East Supply Center more accurately announced the termination of World War II than did armistices, treaties, or the birth of the United Nations.

REFERENCES: Chapter 37

Reference items in Chapters 19, 22, 27, 28, 29, 30, 31, 32, 33, 34, 35, and 36 are useful for this chapter.

Beaton, Cecil. *Near East*. London: Bateford, 1943. A British view during the war.

Eagleton, William, Jr. *The Kurdish Republic of 1946*. New York: Oxford University Press, 1963. The story of the Soviet attempt to penetrate this area in World War II.

Hirszowicz, Lukasz. *The Third Reich and the Arab East*. London: Routledge & Kegan Paul, 1966. A study of the relations of Germany with Arab movements in Saudi Arabia, Iraq, Turkey, Syria, and Egypt, and of German relations with the Grand Mufti and others. Translated from Polish.

Howard, Harry N. *Turkey, the Straits and U.S. Policy*. Baltimore: The Johns Hopkins University Press, 1974. Covers the years from 1830 to the 1970s. Is especially good on the August 1946 crisis resulting from Turkey's rebuff of the U.S.S.R.'s suggestion for establishing Soviet bases on the Straits. The author was at that time an officer in the Department of State and prepared most of the background papers during the crisis, as well as for U.S. negotiators at Yalta and Potsdam.

Kirk, George. *The Middle East in the War, Survey of International Affairs, 1939–1946*, Vol. II. London: Oxford University Press, 1953. A standard work by an outstanding author. Thorough, inclusive and objective.

————. *The Middle East, 1945–1950. Survey of International Affairs, 1939–1946*. London: Oxford University Press, 1954. Another indispensable work.

————. "Turkey," in Arnold Toynbee and Veronica M. Toynbee (eds.), *The War and the Neutrals. Survey of International Affairs, 1939–1946*. London: Oxford University Press, 1956. An excellent chapter on Turkey from the outbreak of the war, her entry into it, and her position during its course.

Knatchbull-Hugessen, Hughe. *Diplomat in Peace and War*. London: J. Murray, 1949. By the British ambassador in Ankara during much of the war.

Paiforce. *The Official Story of the Persia and Iraq Command, 1941–1946*. London: H. M. Stationery Office, 1948. A detailed report from official sources.

Sachar, Howard M. *Europe Leaves the Middle East, 1936–1954*. New York: Knopf, 1972. The last five chapters deal with the Palestine problem.

von Papen, Franz. "Postscript," in L. C. Moyzisch, *Operation Cicero.* (Constantine Fitzgibbon and Heinrich Fraenkel, trans.) New York: Bantam, 1952. The famous story of the German spy in Ankara during the war.

Weisband, Edward. *Turkish Foreign Policy, 1943–1945: Small-State Diplomacy and Great Power Politics.* Princeton, N.J.: Princeton University Press, 1973. A pointed account of Turkey's responses to the war and the policy-making process in Ankara.

Wilmington, Martin W. *The Middle East Supply Center.* Albany: State University of New York Press, 1971. An amazing story of British and American cooperation at a difficult and sensitive time.

Young, Desmond. *Rommel, The Desert Fox.* New York: Harper, 1950. An interesting study of the Nazi general who led the German drive in North Africa.

Chapter 38

Turkey Becomes a Democracy

The Powers and the Straits

In 1938, when Kemal Atatürk died, his great prime minister and negotiator of the Lausanne Treaty, Ismet İnönü, was elected president by the Grand National Assembly. At the same time he acquired the leadership of the Republican party, the one legal political party in Turkey. Almost immediately, Turkey was caught in the maelstrom of World War II. Though İnönü preserved the neutrality of his country until 1945, Turkey found an independent policy exceedingly difficult and at times of doubtful value.

In the winter of 1939–1940 Russia tried in vain to gain an advantage in eastern Anatolia and at the Straits, and throughout the war she repeatedly indicated dissatisfaction with Turkey's inactive role. In March 1945 Russia terminated, as obsolete, the Turkish-Soviet treaty of neutrality and nonaggression. In June, with the war in Europe ended and the United States still facing Japan, with the expected prospect of bitter and large-scale engagements in the Far East for another eighteen months, Russia demanded the cession of Kars and Ardahan and the granting of Soviet bases on the Straits. Courageously the Turks replied with a categorical "No."

At Potsdam the three powers agreed that the Montreux convention of 1936 governing the Straits should be revised and that each should discuss the question directly with Turkey. The United States then presented a note to Turkey in November 1945, stating that the United States would participate in a conference to revise the Montreux convention. Four principles were declared worthy of consideration: that the Straits be open to merchant ships of all nations at all times; that the Straits be open to the transit of warships of the Black Sea powers at all times; that the Straits be closed to the passage of warships of non-Black Sea powers at all times, except for an agreed limited tonnage, except for the consent of the Black Sea powers, and except when acting for the United Nations; and that certain changes be made to bring the Montreux convention up to date.

Great Britain supported the American view, and Foreign Minister Bevin and President Truman publicly announced their adherence to such a course. Not until August 1946 did Russia reveal her views. In a note to Turkey the Russians declared five points. The first three were essentially identical to the first three of the American note. Point four, however, called for a regime for the Straits controlled only by Turkey and the other Black Sea powers. Point five invited Turkey to organize with Russia a joint defense of the Straits to prevent their use by other countries having aims hostile to the Black Sea powers.

Britain and America reacted strongly against the last two points and repeated their willingness to consider a revision. Turkey replied in a like vein, stating that Russia's points four and five were "not compatible with the inalienable rights of sovereignty of Turkey" and could not be considered. The Soviets presented another note in September; England, the United States, and Turkey replied in October. This second round of notes showed no fundamental change. Following these exchanges the subject was dropped, and no revision or alteration of the Straits regime was effected.

In the 1970s, with the development of a Soviet presence in the Mediterranean, Soviet warships passed through the Straits in great numbers. Small- and medium-sized aircraft carriers, guided-missile submarines, and destroyers of various types were permitted passage, as ships of these classes were either not mentioned or not prohibited in the Montreux convention.

The Truman Doctrine and American Relations
The Soviets maintained strong pressure on Turkey by deploying sizable army groups in areas from which attacks upon Turkey could be launched. Turkey, in turn, considered it expedient to keep under arms nearly 1,000,000 men, even though such a force could only delay by a few weeks a Russian conquest. The United States showed interest by sending the S.S. *Missouri* to Istanbul in March 1946 on the pretext of returning the body of the Turkish ambassador, who had died in Washington in 1944.

Continued Soviet pressure on Turkey in the immediate post-war period had an adverse effect upon the Turkish economy. Government leaders understood Russia could maintain the pressure almost indefinitely and sought a way out of their dilemma. The solution was found in the Truman Doctrine, proclaimed to the American Congress in March 1947; $100 million was requested, along with $300 million for Greece, to bolster Turkey to be more self-sustaining in her long-range resistance to Russia.

The plan was conceived and worked out by Turkish and American military, economic, and political leaders. It entailed two primary objectives. The first was to mechanize and modernize the Turkish army, so that the effectiveness and firepower of each unit would be doubled; this would allow a proportionate cut in the size of the army without a reduction in strength. The other objective called for an improvement in the systems of communication and transportation, to give the army greater maneuverability. A large portion of the first grant to Turkey appeared in the form of military equipment, but a significant $5 million was set aside for a public road-building program.

From 1947 until the United States Congress cut off military aid to Turkey in 1975, between $6 and $7 billion dollars had been expended by the United States on the program for Turkey. The army was reorganized from top to bottom; tanks, trucks, new artillery, and sophisticated equipment of every description were brought into Turkey accompanied by teacher-technicians. A new air force was created, and a steady flow of the latest planes, including 400 F-100 interceptor jets in 1970 and a promise to sell 40 Phantom F-4 jets in 1972—to maintain a balance with Greece—kept the Turkish air force an important modern power. American military missions were everywhere, especially along the northern coast where the most modern eavesdropping and electronic stations were located. By 1970 some 23,000 American military personnel were based in Turkey. The navy was enlarged and warships of most classes were added. Ports were updated, and hard-surface all-weather roads connecting major cities were built. With new harbor facilities, Iskenderun (Alexandretta) became a major terminus in the south, from which new roads extending northward and eastward toward the Russian frontier were constructed. A major airfield was built near Adana and others in eastern Anatolia were laid. Hydroelectric projects were undertaken; irrigation was advanced and dams were built; and internal national strength grew by leaps and bounds.

When war broke out in Korea in June 1950, Turkey sent a brigade of 5,000 men to support the United Nations position. In the ensuing battles the Turkish forces distinguished themselves and received world acclaim. Simultaneously, Turkey applied for membership in the North Atlantic Treaty Organization and in September 1951 was admitted along with Greece. Izmir became NATO headquarters for the eastern Mediterranean and developed into an important naval base for NATO powers. After the Soviet Union's action in Czechoslovakia in 1968 Turkish President Sunay reaffirmed Turkey's adherence to NATO. In 1975, when the American Congress voted an arms embargo against Turkey because of the action in Cyprus, the status of some American bases was changed and Turkish forces occupied them. Later there was an easing of the embargo and some bases were reopened to American personnel though overall Turkish authority was not relinquished.

After an estimate in 1970 that nearly 80 percent of the heroin illegally sold in the United States was manufactured from Turkish opium, the Turkish government banned the growing of poppies in twelve of the twenty-one producing provinces and the United States agreed to aid the farmers switch to other crops. A request for $400 million in aid went to Washington along with a reduction of the producing provinces to four. The American Congress appropriated $35 million and cut the amounts of military aid and various program credits. As some 300,000 farmers were involved in opium cultivation and enjoyed a profitable market in edible poppy seeds and oil, the elimination of their crop wrought hardships. Becoming a political issue, the opium question was debated during the elections of 1973; the two leading contenders, Süleyman Demirel of the Justice party and Bulent Ecevit of the Republican People's party, pledged to repeal the ban, arguing that Turkish farmers should not be punished because Americans could not control the drug traffic. In June 1974, poppy production was resumed and the United States cut military aid to $180 million and general economic aid to $27 million.

Greece and Cyprus

Turkey sought to be not only a land bridge but a military, political, and friendly link between Europe and the Balkans. In February 1953 the treaty of Ankara was signed by Turkey, Greece, and Yugoslavia, drawing those three into a cooperative alliance. The value of this pact was sorely tried in 1955 and 1956. The most serious problem developed on the island of Cyprus where Greece was working in conjunction with the Greek Cypriots to effect the union of Cyprus with Greece. Since 20 percent of the population was Turkish and since Cyprus is close to the southern Turkish shore, the Turkish government took a firm stand in opposition to the proposed union. Turkey argued that she gave the island to England to administer in 1878, and that if England relinquished control the island should be returned to Turkey. Believing that Cyprus held strong strategic importance for the Turkish ports of Antalya, Mersin, and Iskenderun, Turkish spokesmen threatened that Turks would fight to prevent Cyprus from joining Greece. The British in 1957 broached partition as the only possible peaceful solution. Ankara accepted this course reluctantly, but Athens rejected the proposal, thus burying the Balkan alliance. Greece also weakened the eastern bastion of NATO by recalling Greek officers from Izmir and declining to discuss NATO affairs with the Turks.

In 1959, as the only apparent recourse, the three involved powers, Greece, Turkey, and Britain, signed three treaties in London establishing and guaranteeing a Republic of Cyprus. Coming into being in August 1960, Cyprus became the ninety-fifth member of the United Nations. Archbishop Makarios, head of the Greek Orthodox Church in Cyprus and leader of the Greek Cypriot community, and Dr. Fazil Küçük, leader of the Turkish Cypriot community, accepted this settlement. According to the constitution, partition or union (enosis) with Greece was barred. The Greek Cypriots would elect the president and the Turkish Cypriots the vice president, and both officials would have to sign acts to make them law. There was provision for a council of ministers and a house of representatives, with membership set at a 70 to 30 ratio of Greeks to Turks. In addition separate Turkish and Greek Cypriot communal chambers were set up to control education, religion, social welfare, and personal affairs, almost like the millets of the Ottoman Empire. The above ratio was also to hold in the civil service and police, whereas in the army a ratio of 60 to 40 was to prevail. In the ensuing elections in 1960, Archbishop Makarios became president, defeating his leftist rival 2 to 1, and Dr. Küçük was elected vice president. Britain retained 2 large bases and 19 other posts including an airfield and radar stations. Greece was allowed a military force of 950 and Turkey one of 650 on the island with the right of periodic rotation of personnel.

In 1963 Archbishop-President Makarios touched off a new crisis by decreeing the end of separate Turkish and Greek municipalities in the cities and proposing thirteen constitutional changes, one of which would terminate the requirement that the vice president approve all legislation. This meant the end of any Turkish veto power. Makarios asserted that the present constitution was unworkable, but his opponents declared he had never intended that it succeed.

Bloodshed occurred between the communities in December 1963, with Greece and Turkey supporting their respective nationality groups. Terrorism developed and the issue went to the United Nations, where a mediator was appointed and the Security Council sent a peace-keeping force. Greece and Turkey privately arrived at various compromise solutions, but Makarios vetoed them as well as the settlement formulated by the United Nations. Prime Ministers Inönü of Turkey and Papandreou of Greece restrained the hotheads from leading their countries into war. At one time when it appeared Turkey would intervene militarily, United States President Johnson sent a stiff note to Inönü warning him of the dire consequences of such an act. Later that summer both Inönü and Papandreou visited Washington.

By 1964 the situation in the Eastern Mediterranean was grave. Greek security forces on the island jumped from 20,000 to 40,000, with volunteers coming from Greece. Supplies came from the U.S.S.R., which looked with favor on Makarios' stand for independence immediately and enosis later. Greek Cypriot forces attacked ports on the north side of the island where supplies were being landed from Turkey. The Turkish air force strafed Greek Cypriot positions, and Turkey threatened to invade the island. Apparently the Greek government decided there was too much flirting with Moscow and too much independence of action. General George Grivas, the hero of the Cypriot struggle in the 1950s and an advocate of instant enosis, was returned to Cyprus to control the irregulars.

Fighting erupted again in Cyprus in November 1967, and both Greece and Turkey ordered partial mobilization. Representatives from the U.N., NATO, and the United States converged on the area, prevailing upon Athens to recall Grivas and upon both governments to draw down all forces in Cyprus to the levels allowed by the 1960 treaty. In February 1968, Makarios was reelected president by over 96 percent of the Greek Cypriots and Dr. Küçük was unopposed as vice president. Progress for peace seemed to be a reality and signs of economic improvement appeared. However, Grivas clandestinely returned to Cyprus in 1971 and by January 1974, when he died, had reconstituted an old terrorist group, the National Organization of Cypriot Fighters.

With Grivas gone, Makarios was emboldened to grapple with the guerrilla bands fighting for immediate enosis, and in July 1974 wrote a sharp letter to the military junta in Athens demanding the recall of 650 Greek officers in Cyprus. In quick reaction, the Greek Cypriot National Guard with the approval of the junta in Athens overthrew Makarios, appointing a notorious terrorist, N. G. Sampson, as the new president. Makarios escaped with the aid of the British to plead his case at the U.N. On July 20 Turkey, to prevent enosis, landed 40,000 troops on the northern coast of

Cyprus and seized Kyrenia and a ten-mile-wide strip to Nicosia. The Greek government mobilized but, recognizing the overwhelming superiority of the Turkish forces, agreed to a cease-fire on July 22. The following day the Athens junta handed over power to a civilian government under former Prime Minister Constantine Caramanlis, who flew back from exile in Paris. That same day Sampson was removed and Glafkos Clerides became acting president of Cyprus. Talks took place in Geneva among the British, Greeks, and Turks, but no solution could be found. A second Turkish drive on August 14 ended with 40 percent of the island in Turkish hands. Some 200,000 Greeks and 20,000 Turks became homeless refugees. Greek Cypriots murdered the American ambassador and both Turkey and Greece denounced the United States for not being impartial. Makarios returned to Cyprus in December, granting amnesty to those who overthrew him but declaring partition unacceptable.

Prime Minister Ecevit gained immense popularity throughout Turkey for his bold actions in Cyprus. He resigned in September, expecting to force a general election in which the Republican People's party would gain a working majority in the National Assembly. An election did not materialize and timid caretaker ministers held office until April 1975, when Demirel formed a weak coalition government, calling for a bizonal federal solution in Cyprus. After more talks, Rauf Denktaş, vice president of Cyprus since the 1973 elections, called in February 1975 for a separate Turkish state in northern Cyprus. Approved in Ankara by Demirel, the idea led to a constitutional vote in June by Turkish Cypriots and discussions between Clerides and Denktaş, both moderates, who secretly agreed to the bizonal federation under a weak central government. This interim understanding was a signal for all parties to make concessions, but since none felt sufficiently secure for such a deviation, the Cypriot impasse remained.

With no solution in sight, Denktas organized a National Unity party and fostered the idea of separate and autonomous Greek and Turkish Cypriot states linked together in a federal union. Elections in June 1976 in the Turkish area gave Denktaş the title of President of the Turkish Federated State of Cyprus, and his National Unity party won 30 of 40 seats in the state assembly. He was sworn in as president in July, and a cabinet was appointed. At the same time Ankara declared that no effort to partition Cyprus would be made and Denktaş reaffirmed earlier stands that his step did not divide Cyprus into two sovereign states. General elections for the assembly in the Greek areas were held in September, with supporters of Makarios winning 34 of 35 seats. Negotiations between Makarios and Denktaş continued. However, in April 1977 Makarios suffered a heart attack and died on August 3, 1977. Spyros Kyprianou, leader of the assembly, became acting president, and promises of a settlement between the Turkish and Greek factions had to be postponed.

In the regular Turkish quadrennial elections for the assembly in June 1977 the Cyprus question was downplayed by Ecevit and Demirel. Turkish troops on the island were being recalled, and at election time their number had been reduced from 40,000 to 27,000. When Demirel became prime minister in August he vowed to help establish an independent, nonaligned, bicommunal, bizonal federal system of government for Cyprus. Discussions between the two Cypriot factions were resumed.

In addition to the tension over Cyprus, Turkey and Greece found themselves in a controversy over oil. Foreign companies had been prospecting for oil for the Turkish government in Thrace and offshore since 1970. In 1974 Turkey and Greece disputed the location of the continental shelf in the Aegean, Greece claiming rights to territorial waters to a distance of twelve miles. With so many Greek-held islands in the Aegean in shallow water close to the Turkish coast, the rights and claims of the two countries overlapped everywhere. In May they agreed to try to settle the oil dispute by negotiation. However, with the imbroglio on Cyprus, the oil matter remained unsolved. In the summer of 1976 Turkey sent an oil-exploring ship on several missions into the Aegean, an act that Greece declared illegal and a violation of international law. Greece took the matter to the United Nations Security Council, but it soon became recognized that only negotiations and compromise between the two countries could resolve the issue. Demirel, in taking office in 1977, promised to try for a negotiated solution to the controversies over the Aegean continental shelf and the Aegean air space.

The Democrat Party
The Turkish constitution always stated that Turkey is a democracy, and references to this were made frequently in speeches and in schoolbooks. However, only one political party existed, and various electoral and press laws were adopted that could hardly be classed as democratic in principle or in practice. In 1945, in discussing the charter of the United Nations, a number of deputies in the Grand National Assembly pointed out that by subscribing to the charter and joining the United Nations Turkey would be obligated to practice "genuine democracy." A motion to modify all laws of a dictatorial and unconstitutional nature failed to pass, and violent discussion ensued.

President Inönü in opening the Grand National Assembly in 1945 recommended a change in the electoral law to provide for direct election of deputies. Articles in the press appeared immediately criticizing the government on many issues. Leaders of a new group, the Democrat party, began to formulate a program and organize. The four principal advocates were: Celal Bayar, the last prime minister under Atatürk; Adnan Menderes, Republican deputy for Aydin; Refik Koraltan, deputy and one-time governor of Artvin; and Fuad Köprülü, scion of the famous family of seventeenth-century Ottoman grand viziers, deputy, internationally known historian, and professor at the University of Istanbul.

The Democrat party subscribed to the six points of the Republican party —after all they were incorporated into the constitution. But the war years had brought many economic dislocations producing inflation, shortages, wealth, hardship, and corruption. The Democrats capitalized on these and attracted to their banner all who had any grievance with the government. They asserted that the Republicans sacrificed private enterprise in the interest of government ownership and promised that they, if elected, would undertake to turn state industries over to private ownership and would operate the government more efficiently.

Elections for the Grand National Assembly were scheduled for the spring of 1947, and the Democrat party favored that date. Republican leaders, however, became worried over the obvious successes of the opposition and called the election for July 1946. When the results were announced Republicans held 391 seats and Democrats 65. The Democrats questioned the election of 300 Republicans, claiming stuffing of ballot boxes, faulty counting of ballots or no counting at all, and all manner of irregularities. Nevertheless, the election stood as announced and the Democrats began to plan for 1950.

After 1946 several other parties were formed by disgruntled deputies, and the Democrats proclaimed they would not participate in another election until concrete election reforms were introduced. Election booths were adopted, and regulations for nonpartisan election boards were passed. Democrat leaders toured the country and gathered into their party young, energetic men and women from the provincial towns and cities. In the elections in May 1950 the Democrat party presented in each district local candidates who had prestige and a local following. They won a resounding victory. Totals in the new Grand National Assembly were: Democrats 408 and Republicans 69. Almost 90 percent of the electorate went to the polls; in popular balloting, the Democrats obtained 53 percent against 40 percent for the Republicans. On May 22, Celal Bayar was elected president of the Republic to succeed Ismet Inönü, who gracefully relinquished the office and power he had held for nearly twelve years. Refik Koraltan became president of the Grand National Assembly. Adnan Menderes assumed the office of prime minister and formed a new cabinet of fourteen ministers, including Fuad Köprülü as foreign minister. The triumph was complete. Of the former leading Republicans, only Inönü and the last prime minister won election to the Grand National Assembly.

During the following four years the first effects of American aid programs were felt in Turkey, and the Turkish economy surged forward. The Democrat party reaped the benefits of that prosperity. Although there were numerous cabinet shifts and two new cabinets, Adnan Menderes retained his position of prime minister under Bayar's presidency. In the elections of May 1954 more than 80 percent of the registered electorate returned 503 Democrats and 31 Republicans, with 58 percent of the popular vote going to the Democrats and 35 percent to the Republicans. The four principal founders of the Democrat party retained their respective positions in the government and looked forward to another four years of leadership.

Almost immediately, however, weaknesses in the Turkish economy put the Democrats in a bad light. The Democrat leadership reacted vigorously.

Radio stations were not allowed to broadcast criticisms of government policies and newspaper editors were imprisoned for "inciting" public opinion or for "insulting" the prime minister. In 1955 the Republican party refused to take part in local elections, charging that the Democrats would not allow free elections. The secretary general of the Republican party was arrested when he claimed that the Democrats had stolen the election in 1954.

Restrictive press laws were passed; at one time in 1955 five of the leading newspapers of Istanbul were suspended by government order. Even some Democrat deputies of the Grand National Assembly were expelled from the party for criticizing the new press laws. A number of deputies resigned from the party to form a new Freedom party, which in 1956 gathered greater strength and some illustrious names, such as that of the son of Fuad Köprülü, the Democrat foreign minister. The popularity of the Democrat party in Turkish cities sank in 1956 to a low point, and Republican leaders began to take heart that victory might be won in 1958, if they could gain greater support in rural areas. To this end a Republican leader visited the Black Sea coastal region in the summer of 1956. However, he found his activities curtailed at every turn by government action. Many began to fear that the prized democracy of the Turkish Republic was withering on the vine.

Suddenly, in September 1957, Menderes moved up the elections seven months to October. The Democrats won 424 seats in the Grand National Assembly to 178 for the Republicans. Menderes inaugurated a new cabinet in November. In January 1958 twenty members of the Freedom party were jailed for holding an illegal meeting, an indication of the confidence and strength of the Democrat administration. Victory gave Menderes a new lease on the prime ministership.

Military Coup of May 27, 1960

Droughts, beginning in the middle of the 1950s, turned wheat surpluses into shortages, further upset the balance of payments, and undermined the entire economy. Debts mounted, and though Menderes still refused to adhere to any planning, he vigorously and heedlessly pursued developments in every sector of the economy. With returns from most of these investments many years away, inflation and its attendant ills were aggravated and went unchecked. Efforts to curtail luxury imports, black-market activities, and rising prices proved futile. In the summer of 1958, in order to obtain a new loan from the International Monetary Fund and the United States, Menderes agreed to a stabilization program, which included devaluation of the lira, rigorous import controls, investment regulations, an end of deficit financing, and the curtailment of domestic credit. The shock to the urban economy was intense. By the spring of 1959, unemployment, business failures, and shortages had developed everywhere, but still there was no planning. Vocal opposition to the Democrat regime became commonplace among the educated and articulate urban classes who were most affected by the economic dislocation.

General carping at governmental ineptitude turned to outright criticism. In those years politics between the Democrat and Republican People's parties was passionate and angry. Legal actions for libel were almost unknown, and the party in power usually exercised control over the press and radio to suppress opposition. In the spring of 1959, while on a speaking tour in southwestern Turkey, Inönü was set upon by a rough pro-Democrat crowd and fell to the ground when hit in the head by a stone. Blank columns in the newspapers enforced official silence but stimulated inquiry. Rumors flew that President Bayar had ordered house arrest for his bitter opponent. Furious accusations were hurled about the National Assembly in Ankara and Republican leaders interpreted from a few of Menderes' remarks that new elections might be called in 1960.

Such speculations induced Inönü and his party to step up the pressure and to be prepared should the call be suddenly announced. Menderes was indifferent to the attitudes of the urban elite as long as he retained the support of the villagers, who comprised 70 percent of the electorate. In 1959, on an airplane trip to London to sign the Cyprus treaties he had quite miraculously walked away unscathed from a crash that killed most of the passengers. From that moment Menderes' followers loudly proclaimed that he had been saved by an Act of God in order to lead his country, and many Republicans began to despair of ever defeating him. Early in 1960 several sessions of the National Assembly ended in fistfights. Menderes and Inönü continued to make speeches throughout the country, and political tension mounted.

Turkish law forbade political campaigning except for forty-five days preceding an election. No election had been called, but the leaders were acting as if it had. In April Inönü and some of his party deputies were on their way to Kayseri to participate in a political meeting, when their train was stopped by the army acting on orders from the government. Inönü refused to give way, claiming that the constitution guaranteed freedom of travel to Turkish citizens and that the penal code prohibited interference with a deputy carrying out his duties. He was allowed to proceed to Kayseri. The uproar from this action and the involvement of the army in politics had not abated when the National Assembly voted to establish the extralegal Committee of Fifteen to Investigate the Activities of the Republican People's Party and a Section of the Press. References to the committee were banned in the press, and Inönü was expelled from the Assembly for the next twelve sessions.

Within a few days, on April 28 and 29, university students marched in the streets until they were suppressed by military action and gunfire. Demands for Menderes' resignation were shouted at him whenever he appeared. On May 21 a thousand cadets of the Military College in Ankara marched on the presidential residence to sing martial songs. On May 25 the National Assembly recessed, and Menderes announced that the investigating committee would soon report its findings. Then, on May 27, 1960, at 4 A.M. the army struck. President Bayar, Prime Minister Menderes, the entire cabinet, and Democrat deputies of the National Assembly were arrested, government offices were seized, and within four hours a bloodless revolution had been accomplished. The military curfew was lifted that afternoon and joyously wild celebrations occurred in Ankara and Istanbul.

The National Unity Committee

The day of the coup, the army flew General Cemal Gürsel to Ankara where he was installed as Head of the Provisional Government. Earlier that month General Gürsel, Chief of the Land Forces, had publicly criticized the investigating committee and retired. A father figure at the age of sixty-six, he was a necessary link between the senior officers, the older politicians, and the public on the one hand, and the colonels, majors, and captains who had instigated the coup. The military body formed to govern the nation was known as the National Unity Committee, but for several days the identity of its members, other than General Gürsel, was not revealed. At a public ceremony in Ankara at the National Assembly hall each of the thirty-eight NUC members stepped forward, pledged to be loyal, to serve the Turkish nation, and to "work for nothing else than the welfare of the nation and its sovereignty," as well as for the creation of a "new Constitution, and transferring power to the new Parliament."

Who were these thirty-eight officers? Five held the rank of general, six were captains, and the rest were colonels and majors; most of them at the time of the coup held key posts. Twenty-two were born after the end of World War I and all but a few had been educated in the 1920s and 1930s during the heyday of Kemalism. None came from a prominent family. In various public interviews each one declared that he had participated in the revolution to put the reforms of Atatürk back on the tracks.

The day after the coup NUC appointed a cabinet, most of whom had not been identified with any political party; only four army officers were included. In June, a provisional constitution was promulgated providing for a head of state, commander in chief, and cabinet. Laws were proposed by the cabinet, approved by NUC, and decreed by the head of state within ten days. In July, NUC announced the government's program to balance the budget and end inflation, to free imports and exports of all controls, to devise a constitution on a democratic basis following the United Nations Charter, to reorganize state enterprises and gain entry into the European Common Market, to improve education and health, to undertake land reform, to restrict public works to need only, and to establish a nonpartisan administrative force in government. There was something for everyone in this program.

To reorient the government was a large order, but to reform the armed services was a task more manageable. In August, 235 generals and admirals were retired; the next day nearly 5,000 colonels and majors were retired with two years' severance pay and full pension. One NUC general, who was sixty-two, put himself on the list as an example of the rejuvenation of the army, certainly a prime motive in the mass retirement. However, it was also apparent that a great many conservative and pro-Menderes officers had been specifically included. There was no public pressure to have this order rescinded, but in October when 147 university professors were ousted there was a loud outcry. In time the various university senates reviewed each case and many were reinstated.

Within NUC a division arose with one group under the leadership of Colonel Alpaslan Türkeş, who advocated pushing through the entire program of the revolution forcefully and quickly. In November wrangling ended in physical attacks over the establishment of a governmental cultural union to oversee all intellectual life in Turkey. Coupled with the known desire of Türkeş radicals to postpone indefinitely elections and the return to civilian rule, this proposal raised the specter of dictatorship. In the predawn hours of November 13, fourteen members of NUC received messages of their dismissal and were ordered not to leave their homes. In a few days all were sent abroad as counselors of embassies; Türkeş was sent to New Delhi. Since one member of NUC had been killed in an accident, there remained twenty-three.

Seven Istanbul University professors, headed by university president Onar, a professor of administrative law, were flown to Ankara the morning of the coup and at noon were commissioned by Gürsel to draft a new constitution within a few weeks. By the time the Onar constitution was submitted to NUC, considerable public debate and a remarkable series of constitution seminars, attended by politicians, journalists, and many members of NUC, had produced feelings that a Constituent Assembly was needed. On January 6, 1961, this Assembly was convened in two houses: the Senate, made up of NUC; and a 272-member House of Representatives elected from the provinces, the Republican People's and the Republican Nation parties, and such groups as university faculties, the press, the judiciary, teachers, trade associations, labor groups, and 44 appointed by General Gürsel and NUC. Members of the Republican People's party dominated the Assembly.

A committee of the House was selected to draft a new constitution, under the able chairmanship of Enver Ziya Karal, professor of the history of Turkish revolution at Ankara University. The Karal Constitution, a more political document, was accepted by the Constituent Assembly on May 27, 1961, the anniversary of the coup. In July a national referendum approved it by a 62 percent vote, with 83 percent of the electorate participating. That such a large number cast a negative ballot was fair warning that many voters still gave their devotion to Menderes.

From the autumn of 1960 until the end of the summer of 1961, the attention of the nation was in large part focused on Yassi Island in the Sea of Marmara where Bayar, Menderes, the cabinet, governors, police officers, and Democrat members of the Grand National Assembly, 592 defendants in all, were being tried. NUC chose a thirty-one-member High Investigation

Commission, a nine-judge tribunal, and a team of prosecutors. Fat dossiers were compiled for each case, and prosecutors strove to show violations of law and the constitution, personal use of state funds, acts bordering on treason, and a great variety of peccadilloes, in an attempt to obtain convictions or at least to destroy these politicians in the eyes of the nation. But the trials were not very successful. They were filmed and broadcast, the Yassi Hour became popular, and Menderes was not permitted to be forgotten. Many came to believe the tale that each night he mounted his white horse and rode over the water to pray at a famous mosque on the Golden Horn! Most of those who had voted Democrat in the past were unconvinced by these trials, regarded the charges as trumped up, and the evidence as fraudulent. The trials closed in September 1961 with 15 receiving the death sentence, 31 getting life imprisonment, and 133 acquitted. Prime Minister Menderes, Foreign Minister Zorlu, and Finance Minister Polatkan were hanged. President Bayar's death sentence, because of his age and poor health, was commuted to life imprisonment.

About a month after the hangings, the electorate went to the polls to choose 150 senators and 450 members of the Assembly. The constitution provided for a two-house parliament—in addition to the elected senators, the president of the republic could appoint fifteen and the remaining twenty-two (one refused) members of NUC were given life membership. The two houses meeting together as the Grand National Assembly would elect a president for a seven-year term. Upon the successful referendum on the constitution political parties expanded their activities. Ismet Inönü, as the respected leader of the Republican People's party, expected to win a majority in each house and thus to become the new prime minister. Since the Democrat party had been outlawed two new parties were formed with the hope of attracting former Bayar-Menderes followers. The Justice party selected its name to signify the need to assure justice to the former national political leaders; it openly asked for Democrat votes. The New Turkey party pitched its campaign to attract intellectuals who had been Democrats in 1950 but who had withdrawn from the party after the election of 1954. The fourth party to contest the election was the Republican Peasants' Nation party which had been a minor conservative party since 1946; in 1961 under new direction it hoped to profit from the military turn of events.

Over 81 percent of the electorate voted. In the Senate the division by majority vote was: Justice, 70 seats; Republican People's 36; New Turkey, 28; and the Nation, 16. For the Assembly, where there was proportional representation, the count was: Republican People's, 173 seats; Justice, 158; New Turkey, 65; and the Nation, 54. In the popular vote, the Republican People's party won about the same number of votes it had in the elections of 1950, 1954, and 1957, and no one could deny that the Justice party had inherited most of Menderes' votes. No party held a majority in either house so that there was no question over the election of Cemal Gürsel as president on October 26, 1961, by the Grand National Assembly. He promptly resigned from the army and was sworn in as fourth president of the Turkish Republic.

The Second Turkish Republic

President Gürsel's first obligation was to appoint the prime minister, but a corollary to this task was to find someone who could form a cabinet that would obtain the support of the House of Representatives (Assembly). The election showed that a coalition was the only choice. Gürsel picked Inönü as the most likely to succeed as prime minister under such conditions. After political maneuvering for two weeks Inönü induced the Justice party to join with his Republican People's in forming a coalition cabinet in which each party held eleven posts, although the major ones were occupied by his party. In the Justice party program one of the major attractions was an implied pledge to obtain amnesty and the release of Democrat political figures held since the day of the coup. Inönü discovered that an amnesty for Bayar and all of the others was a daily plea of Justice leaders.

In the first months little was accomplished, and critics openly challenged Inönü's regime to act or resign. In February 1962 nearly seventy officers led by Colonel Aydemir, Commandant of the Ankara Military Academy, staged a revolt to overthrow Inönü, but it was easily suppressed. The officers were gently retired from the forces and placed under house arrest. In May, when a bill granting amnesty to these officers was passed, the Justice party demanded in vain that the bill be expanded to include imprisoned Democrats. They withdrew from the coalition, but Inönü was able to form a new cabinet with the support of the New Turkey and Republican Peasants' Nation parties.

Early in 1963 a law was approved granting amnesty to many Democrats, and Bayar was freed for six months for medical treatments. Massive demonstrations against his release occurred, and Justice leaders accused the Republicans of having fomented these protests; the tension touched off another attempted army coup, again led by Colonel Aydemir. These incidents, coupled with a general economic stagnation, brought a reaction favorable to the Justice party, which then won 65 percent of the popular vote in local elections and carried victories in 42 of Turkey's 67 provinces. Consequently, Inönü was deserted by his allies and resigned. But, when the Justice leaders were unable to find a majority, Inönü put together a third cabinet by obtaining the support of the independents in the Assembly. He won a vote of confidence by 225 to 175.

Massive loans from the United States and other NATO nations, from a European Consortium for Aid to Turkey, from the European Investment Bank, and from the International Monetary Fund created an improvement in Turkish economic conditions, and fine harvests of wheat, cotton, and tobacco gave Inönü a base on which to hope for a successful administration.

A new and extensive five-year development plan was enacted in 1963. It called for government expenditures of $2 billion and private investments of more than $4 billion to increase the gross national product by 40 percent.

Whatever chances Inönü had to maintain the Republican People's party in office were ruined by affairs in Cyprus in 1964, however. The grievances of the Turkish Cypriot minority incensed the Turkish nation; many Turks felt that their government had the right to intervene overtly and blamed Inönü for being too subservient to American exactions. He was condemned for going to Washington when Johnson called; his support in the Assembly on Cyprus narrowed to 200 to 194 with several abstentions.

In the opening weeks of 1965 Süleyman Demirel, the Justice leader, announced a campaign to take over the government. On February 13, 1965, the budget bill was defeated 225 to 197, the cabinet resigned, and President Gürsel invited an independent senator to serve as the head of a caretaker government until the October elections. However, Demirel was appointed his deputy and ten Justice men were in the cabinet. Demirel declared that the Justice party wanted to prove to the military and to the voters that it could govern peacefully and successfully.

According to the electoral law, primaries in eligible parties for the 450 Assembly seats are held forty-two days before the election; official campaigning among the parties is not allowed until two weeks before the election and lasts for only ten days, permitting a four-day respite until the day of balloting. Elections for the six-year Senate seats are staggered by having one-third elected every two years; the first Senate election had been held in 1964. All through the spring and summer the campaigning among six distinct parties accelerated. Great interest was aroused and keen competition developed in the primaries for places on the party tickets.

Over 1,100 candidates in the Justice party contested for the 450 places. Demirel pledged support of the May 27, 1960, coup and its six-point program and advocated continued alliance with the United States and NATO, an understanding of Russia, and an honorable settlement of the Cyprus problem. He called for an orderly and progressive advance in industry, agriculture, and education. Cleverly, he adopted a gray horse as the party symbol, plainly bidding for those still loyal to Menderes and his "white horse."

Inönü, the Republican People's leader, now eighty-one years old, appealed to those in governmental circles, the older established families, dedicated Kemalists, army officers, and many intellectuals to return his party to office. As the campaign progressed, he turned more toward the U.S.S.R. and asserted that his party was neither an American stooge nor a capitalistic pawn and was, in fact, somewhat left of center.

The New Turkey party struggled to find a middle course between socialism and capitalism, but its suggestions for a mixed economy fell on sterile soil. Former Colonel **Türkes** and some of his army friends took over the Republican Peasants' Nation party at a party caucus early in 1965; in the campaign he stressed the need for scientific planning for the most effective development of the nation's resources, and stated that private enterprise should be clearly limited in its activities. That party's former leader formed a new Nation party, opposing all leftist tendencies and maintaining the more conservative traditions of Turkish society. On the left of all these, Mehmet Ali Aybar established the Labor party, which contended that land reform should be immediate; that foreign trade, banking, and insurance be nationalized; and that all industry be conducted solely by the state.

In spite of acute differences, the election was held in an orderly manner. Only 60 percent of the electorate exercised their rights, and it was apparent that a million of Inönü's party had remained at home rather than vote left of center. The Justice party won 240 seats and a clear majority; the Republican People's garnered 134; and the new Labor party won only 15. President Gürsel invited Demirel to form a new government; within a few days an entire Justice cabinet was announced and was given a vote of confidence by the Assembly.

The Justice Party

The dire predictions concerning the advent to power of the Justice party were unfounded. Prime Minister Demirel steered a middle course between East and West. Soviet Premier Kosygin visited Turkey in 1966, and his call for the withdrawal of all foreign troops from Cyprus was well received. Many nationals from Western Europe and the United States entered into industrial and economic ventures in Turkey, and Demirel initiated the construction of the Keban Dam, 670 feet high, on the Euphrates River.

In March 1966 President Gürsel, who had been in a coma for some weeks, was declared incapable of carrying out his duties. In his place, General Cevdet Sunay, conveniently appointed to the Senate, was elected as the fifth president of Turkey. Senate elections in June 1966 brought the Justice party 65 percent of the popular vote and 35 of the 52 seats up for election, indicating general approval of Demirel's conduct. The Republican People's party had not given up hope, as was shown in its partial rejuvenation by the election of Bulent Ecevit, a vigorous young member of the Assembly who had been minister of labor from 1961 to 1964, as secretary general and leader of the party. Since both Ecevit and Demirel were American-educated, the vocal anti-American forces gravitated to the other parties.

Following Justice party successes in Senate elections, President Sunay, succumbing to Demirel's petitions, pardoned Bayar. The Assembly granted amnesty to members of Menderes' government and then a month later extended it to 50,000 prisoners in Turkish jails. A euphoria seemed to engulf the nation as tensions lessened and the economy moved forward with yearly increases in the gross national product, expanding markets in Europe, many Turkish workers sending back income from good jobs in Germany, and the widening development of industry and resources at home.

In April 1967 the desertion of forty-eight parliamentary members of the leftward-moving Republican People's party to form the Reliance party was viewed by the Justice party as a favorable omen indicating the correctness of its policies. Senate elections in 1968 brought Justice's total to 101 of the 150 elective senators. The following year in the nationwide Assembly election, Justice garnered 252 seats to 143 for the Republican People's party.

Both parties had gained in the Assembly at the expense of the others since both were moderate in their approach to foreign affairs and general programs, leaving extreme positions such as withdrawing from NATO and closing down American military bases to splinter groups on the left and the right. Many remarked that Demirel would be in for another four years.

But the world malaise of the years between 1968 and 1972 affected Turkey as well. There were vast numbers of unemployed; galloping inflation and devaluation; miserable shanty towns in Istanbul, Ankara, Izmir, and smaller cities; student disturbances; labor unrest; and many unsatisfied wants in education and land distribution. In February 1970, when Demirel's budget was defeated in the Assembly because many Justice members voted against it, he resigned, formed a new cabinet, and expelled twenty-five Assembly members from the party, leaving him with a margin of two. With disorders mounting, martial law was established in Istanbul in June.

Opposition became more open, however. In the first months of 1971 students rioted repeatedly. Terrorist activities by the extreme left and right grew apace, including bank robberies, bombings, and kidnappings. Demonstrators called for withdrawal from NATO and CENTO. Anti-Americanism appeared everywhere. Early in March four U.S. airmen were kidnapped and held for several days. On March 12, 1971, the four leaders of the military forces, extremely fearful of the trend of events, issued a statement that they would take over governmental authority if the situation did not improve immediately.

Coup by Communique
The memorandum blamed parliament and the government for driving the country into "anarchy, fratricidal strife, and social and economic unrest," leading the public "to lose all hope" of rising to the levels set as goals by Atatürk, and failing "to realize the reforms stipulated by the Constitution." It called for an end to politics and for the forming of a "strong and credible government" to halt the "anarchical situation" and to implement "reformist laws." Demirel resigned immediately; President Sunay viewed the military demand as a constitutional requirement; editorial writers and leaders of the other political parties were dubious about ending anarchy quickly and bringing unity. They were not even in agreement on what Atatürk's principles were.

President Sunay invited Nihat Erim, a senator, professor of law, and a former member of the Republican People's party, to form a nonparty government and stabilize the nation. Erim presented a program for land reform, more education at every level, and improved government services in agriculture and finance. Martial law was imposed in eleven critical provinces; in June, 2000 terrorists and members of the self-styled Peoples' Liberation Army were arrested. To alter the mood throughout the land was a herculean task, not one for a weak caretaker, nonpolitical administration. As one Turkish political analyst noted, unless the holders of the levers of political and economic power in a community change hands, nothing changes.

For thirty-four months the three successive caretaker prime ministers and cabinets who tried to govern barely held affairs together. Erim put through a constitutional amendment restricting the autonomy of universities and the freedom of the press and radio. This caused five Justice party members to resign from the cabinet. Erim tendered his resignation but stayed on until April 1972. Meanwhile fifty-seven army officers had been dismissed and arrested for passing arms to leftist terrorists; other extremists had been executed; and the Peoples' Liberation Army kidnapped three British radar technicians working for NATO to exchange for three imprisoned terrorists. Police found their hideout but the hostages were killed before the terrorists were.

In May 1972 former Defense Minister Ferit Melen formed a cabinet composed of eight Justice party members, five from the Republican People's party, two Reliance party members, and nine technocrats. This was a mix to satisfy the military and the politicians. In October thirteen leaders of the outlawed Labor party, including Behice Bovan, a woman who was the party's head, were sentenced to fifteen years in prison. In November, when the Republican People's party moved further to the left, its five cabinet officers resigned their positions. Inönü lost control to Bulent Ecevit and left the party, taking twenty-five parliament members with him. The military leaders again cautioned that they would not tolerate another descent into political chaos. In March 1973 President Sunay's term expired and the military pressed to have the constitution changed to allow him two more years. When this was refused, voting for several candidates went on and on, ballot after ballot, in the Grand National Assembly. The military warned Demirel, and on the fifteenth ballot a compromise resulted in the election to the presidency of Fahri Korutürk, a former admiral and one-time ambassador to the U.S.S.R.

Ferit Melen was replaced as prime minister in April 1973 by Naim Talu, who formed another nonpolitical administration. The next day a trial began for 256 persons accused of subversive activities. Soon thereafter sixty members of the secret Marxist-Leninist Turkish Communist party were arrested for planning guerrilla warfare. This was followed by the arrest of forty-two members of an alleged underground "United Front." Martial law was maintained until September, when it was lifted to permit campaigning for the October quadrennial elections for the National Assembly.

Under Bulent Ecevit the Republican People's party waged a vigorous campaign, urging state control of the economy, amnesty for political prisoners, reduced interest rates and better credits for small industries and farmers, real land reform, revision of agreements with the European Economic Community, and greater interest in Eastern-bloc nations and the Third World. Ecevit stressed that his party was no longer the party of the elite, and that Demirel and the Justice party represented the rich and stood for stagnation. Other legal parties were: the National Salvation party, which went along generally with Ecevit's program except that it stood for a return to rigid Islamic practices; the Democrat party, which opposed Demirel's expansionist budget; the Reliance party, made up of conservatives who did not follow Ecevit to the left; and the small ultra-conservative Nationalist Action party. When the vote was in, the Republican People's party had won 185 seats, the Justice party 149, National Salvation 48, the Democrats 45, the Reliance party 13, and others 10. None achieved a majority. President Korutürk asked Ecevit and then Demirel, but neither was able to form a cabinet, so Talu stayed on in office.

How long could such a stalemate continue? Another general election did not seem to be the answer. At the end of January 1974 Ecevit formed a weak coalition government with the right-wing National Salvation party. Progress, or even political movement, proved difficult until the July coup on Cyprus, after which Ecevit directed the Turkish military landings and occupation of the northern 40 percent of the island. In the face of Greek and American opposition and condemnation, Turkish success redounded to the favor of Ecevit, whose popularity soared at home. In September, at the peak of his triumph, he stepped down, stating that his domestic program had not been achieved; in fact, he resigned to get rid of the National Salvation party, force a new general election, and ride (he expected) to a solid majority on his Cyprus and foreign policies. To call for general elections required a positive vote in the Assembly and this he could not obtain. Demirel and the other leaders, recognizing that Ecevit might win a smashing victory were elections held immediately, decided to put them off until the regular date in 1977.

Ecevit had overplayed his hand. For two months he and Demirel unsuccessfully attempted to put together a coalition. Then, President Korutürk tried in vain to form a nonpolitical government. Finally, Demirel threatened the small right-wing parties, saying he would form a coalition with Ecevit unless they joined with him to stave off the elections until a time when Ecevit's popularity had waned.

On April 12, 1975, the new Justice-right wing coalition was put to the test in the Assembly and won 222 to 218, with two abstentions and four absentees. There was actual fighting on the floor of the Assembly, and the Republican People's party accused Justice leaders of locking the four absentees in their hotel rooms so they could not vote. Demirel had pledged to extend health and unemployment benefits, to enact plans for workers to acquire ownership of factories, to develop the eastern provinces, to support the bizonal policy for Cyprus, to be tough in the Aegean oil negotiations, to keep NATO membership, and to reassess relations with the United States. Demirel maintained his narrow majority after the Senate elections in October, although the Republican People's party made a gain of seventeen seats. Since it won 44 percent of the vote to Justice's 41 percent, Ecevit called upon Demirel to resign. Demirel, naturally, refused.

Throughout 1976 there were strikes, machine gun battles between rival student political groups, kidnappings, airplane hijackings, and many demonstrations. Calls for law and order were heard amidst much unemployment, poverty, and two-digit inflation. In September a seven-day strike by the Revolutionary Trade Unions Confederation, in alliance with municipality and petroleum industry workers, was ended by the arrest of seven leaders, but the methods of breaking it only heightened the tension. Shortages of various commodities were daily occurrences, largely because the balance of payments deficit had emptied the treasury. Finally, Demirel proposed that elections for the assembly be moved up from October to June 1977.

Campaigning was vigorous. Ecevit was stoned in Erzincan and, in a leftwing demonstration in Istanbul in May, 39 were killed and 200 wounded when a gun battle suddenly erupted among the several groups in the crowd. In his campaign Ecevit pledged to stop extremist violence, to reconcile social justice, democracy, and development, and to maintain high economic growth without inflation and balance of payments deficits. When the final returns were tabulated the Republican People's party under Ecevit had gained a plurality with 213 seats. Justice won 189, Erbakan's National Salvation 24, Nationalist Action under Turkeş 16, and others 8. By law President Korutürk had to invite Ecevit to form a government, but he lost his first vote of confidence in fifteen days. Demirel, with Erbakan and Turkes, put together a coalition, which the assembly approved on August 1 by a vote of 229 to 219. Demirel assured the nation that he would work realistically with NATO, the United States, and the U.S.S.R., that he would seek industrial and technological assistance from the European Economic Community and Islamic nations, and that he would negotiate in good faith with Greece with regard to Cyprus and the Aegean.

Through the remaining months of 1977 inflation continued, unabated by a 20 percent devaluation of the currency, and the economy was on the verge of collapse. Disorders were not curbed and pessimism prevailed. Ten Justice party members of the National Assembly deserted Demirel in December and joined Ecevit and a few independents in passing a vote of no confidence in the government (228 to 218). On January 1, 1978, after President Korutürk's invitation, Ecevit accepted and declared that with the aid of the dissident Justice members he would not need to form a coalition cabinet.

The Middle East

In April 1954 Turkey signed a pact of mutual cooperation with Pakistan— a pact that was hailed as the nucleus for the building of a defense line against the Soviet bloc. In February 1955 Turkey and Iraq joined in a five-year pact to consult in all matters of defense. In an exchange of letters the countries agreed to cooperate "in resisting any aggression directed against either of them." The Baghdad pact provided that other nations of the Arab League and any other nation concerned with the Middle East might join. In April the United Kingdom signed; and later Pakistan and Iran became the fourth and fifth members. The Turks believed that these treaties bolstered their flanks and enabled them to play an important role in the Middle East as a link to NATO and the West.

The Iraqi revolution and withdrawal from the Baghdad pact in 1958 led the members to reorganize it as the Central Treaty Organization (CENTO), and to enhance Turkey's position in it. Airfields at Adana facilitated the airlift of American troops and supplies in their occupation of Lebanon, thereby committing Turkey more overtly to the power struggles in the Middle East. In April 1963, however, Turkey announced the abandoning of her Jupiter missile bases and the return of all the NATO-based nuclear warheads to the United States.

In general, Turkey maintained friendly relations with the Arab states. Starting in 1973 a more progressive relationship with Syria and Iraq was undertaken. Turkey and Syria began negotiations for a treaty covering cultural exchanges, transit and tourism arrangements, and questions of land dispute. Beginning in 1974 the most vexatious issue was that of the water flow in the Euphrates River. The great Keban dam, 205 meters high, was started in 1966. It was to create a lake 115 kilometers long and produce for Turkey 1.2 billion kilowatt hours of electric power annually. The lake was to be one-third filled by July 1974. When the cost of imported oil jumped suddenly in 1973, Turkey decided to store sufficient water by July 1974 to begin producing more of her own energy. Because 60 percent of Turkey's energy came from petroleum, two-thirds of which was imported from the Arab states, Ecevit felt compelled to act. In the spring of 1974, when Turkey reduced the Euphrates' flow below previously agreed levels, Syria complained bitterly and wanted the flow doubled, because the level was so low that dams in Syria were reducing the flow into Iraq to a mere trickle. Turkey remained steadfast and did not increase the flow until midsummer, when Saudi Arabia mediated the quarrel between Iraq and Syria.

A 975-kilometer oil pipeline from Kirkuk in Iraq to Iskenderun in Turkey, with an annual capacity of 35,000,000 tons, was completed in 1977. Each country paid for the costs within her borders (for Turkey about $350 million). It was agreed that Turkey could buy ten million tons and would be paid transit fees of 35 cents per barrel. Also, a Turkish-Arab bank was established; five agreements were signed with Libya, covering oil, industry, finance, and military operations; and Iran, Pakistan, and Turkey signed the Treaty of Izmir, which set up a free-trade zone and a joint investment and development bank, and opened channels for further cooperation over roads, railroads, and telecommunication systems. Traffic was already flowing over the CENTO highway between Istanbul and Tehran. Support from the Arab states over the Cyprus issue greatly strengthened Arab-Turkish ties; at the Islamic conference in Istanbul in May 1976 Turkey gave unreserved support to the Palestinian cause and allowed the Palestine Liberation Organization to set up an office in Turkey.

The U.S.S.R. and Eastern Europe
With the failure of Soviet pressure to gain some kind of advantage over the Straits, Turkish relations with Moscow though proper were not warm. After the withdrawal of the NATO nuclear warheads in 1963 Khrushchev informed Turkey that Stalin had been wrong in 1946 to demand changes in the Straits regime; there was no need to revise the regulations. In 1966 Kosygin visited Turkey and called for an "active detente" between the two neighbors. The following year Demirel returned the visit, saying that the "last traces of hostility" were removed. In Moscow he obtained a loan for the construction of a third steel plant, to be located at Iskenderun. Built with the aid of 600 Soviet technicians, it was opened by Soviet Premier Kosygin in 1975.

President Sunay, cordially received in the U.S.S.R. in 1969, entered into a new $84 million Turkish-Soviet trade agreement. In 1972 Soviet President Podgorny in Ankara offered to renew the nonaggression pact that had been canceled so abruptly in 1945. Sunay showed little interest as party politics precluded any such move. In 1974 the U.S.S.R. supported the Turkish action on Cyprus and began to offer Turkey military arms and equipment when supplies were cut off by the American Congress. Turkey purchased sixty helicopters from the Soviets in 1975 and entered into new economic and industrial agreements in 1976 amounting to $1.23 billion for 1977 and $7 billion over the next decade. The Turks were lenient in permitting Russian warships to pass through the Straits to bolster the Soviet fleet in the Mediterranean.

Economic Progress
In 1944 Turkey severed economic relations with Germany, on the understanding that the Western Allies would not permit her economy to founder. She based her fears of economic collapse on the knowledge that she would no longer be able to sell quantities of goods to Germany and that the Allies would cease their preclusive buying programs. However, no decline was apparent, and inflation forced prices upward. The continued unbalanced budget over the next years maintained economic activity at a high level. With vast American aid beginning to flow in 1947 the economic development of Turkey progressed rapidly.

Criticism of state monopolies and business appeared as soon as curbs on the press were relaxed in 1945. With the encouragement and aid of the government a new private bank, the Industrial Development Bank of Turkey, set out to make funds available for private business and serve as a bridge between the needs of businessmen and the conservatively held savings of the ordinary Turk.

In the years after 1946 Turkish industry grew by leaps and bounds. The purchasing power of the peasants, who constituted the great majority of Turks, was sustained at a high level by the government, and suddenly the wants of the peasant burgeoned to an unprecedented degree. New industries, often founded by foreign capital in partnership with Turkish capital, were sprouting in all regions of the country. Yet, the expansion was not entirely healthy. Many accused Menderes of wasteful activities and found fault with his rapid rebuilding of parts of Istanbul; in fact when a building was summarily torn down, it was said to have been "Menderized." Still he forged ahead. His energies and ambition were indefatigable.

On the other hand, the Democrat party did not find it easy to dispose of state-owned enterprises, and long-range planning did not take into account many short-range problems. By the beginning of Bayar's second term the Turkish economy was in serious jeopardy. Foreign exchange was scarce, commercial payments abroad were months in arrears, and business obligations were mounting. The American government refused to grant a sizable loan on the basis that the Menderes cabinet ignored the principles of sensible economic growth. Imports of many commodities such as coffee were strictly limited, and their scarcity created unfriendly attitudes toward the government. The Turkish pound, whose official rate was eighteen cents, fell to seven cents on the black market, with repeated rumors of devaluation and repeated official denials.

Menderes appeared oblivious to difficulties, and faced mounting inflation with increased activities. The national budget in 1957 reached $1.4 billion, and passed $1.65 billion in 1958. A 40 percent duty was levied on most imports; 30 percent of the budget went for capital development, 25 percent for defense. Sizable trade agreements were negotiated with Yugoslavia and Soviet bloc states, which were particularly interested in Turkish tobacco. New sugar factories were built, and in 1957 the Krupp interests of West Germany agreed to invest over a billion marks in a new blast furnace that would add 800,000 tons of steel to Turkish production. Menderes' confidence in Turkey's future was boundless, even though the economy was passing through the kind of "growing pains" that Western economies had experienced repeatedly in the nineteenth century. Perhaps his audacity sprang from his assurance that the United States would bail him out if conditions became serious.

In 1958 grants and loans were obtained from the United States and Western Europe to prevent a collapse. As already indicated, however, the shock of the stabilization program was so severe that it was an important factor in bringing on the coup of 1960. Menderes had found an increasing majority clamoring for an ever larger share of the national product for immediate consumption; after he was gone NUC and the leaders of the Second Republic experienced the same pressures.

When NUC took over, the Menderes regime was branded as economically incompetent and dishonest. It was revealed that the total public debt was over $1 billion and the nation's foreign debt stood at $965 million, a sum so vast that it crushed any hope for solvency and posed an intolerable burden on future foreign exchange earnings. These findings led many business people, even those who had profited from and strongly supported Democrat policies, to acquiesce in NUC restrictions and to appreciate the attempts of Inönü and Demirel to proceed with economic plans and an orderly development.

Nevertheless, the foreign debt continued to grow and by 1966 stood at approximately $2.4 billion, taking about 40 percent of Turkey's foreign earnings to service the debt. The gross national product, however, increased markedly during these years, from $6 billion at the time of the coup to over $9 billion by 1967 and more than four times that figure a decade later. Government budgets jumped 10 to 30 percent yearly, with sums for capital investment often amounting to a quarter of the total. The momentum to develop the economy, set in the Menderes years, was irresistible, and though Inönü, Demirel, Ecevit, and others might deplore its effects on inflation, deficits, interest rates, and social unrest they did not halt it. Many contended that the extraordinary economic activities and innovations of the controversial 1950s were only now bearing fruit. Loans were made to support a copper producing complex in the Samsun area, hydroelectric installations in many provinces, a super phosphates plant, a new tractor factory, aluminum mills, lignite and borax mines, steel mills, and refineries, to mention a few. In addition to these, many companies from Europe, the United States, and Canada built plants to manufacture products of all kinds, including automobiles, drugs, and machinery. In spite of inflation and devaluations of Turkish and world currencies, the Turkish economy grew 8 to 10 percent a year.

By the end of 1962 all needs for refined petroleum were being met by local refineries, but in succeeding years oil production did not keep pace with energy demands. Despite the building of new dams and a constant increase in domestic oil production, 60 percent of local petroleum needs still were being met by imports in 1976. The cost was draining Turkey's economy; the only likelihood of salvation lay in the possible discovery of oil offshore in the Aegean or the Black Sea.

Exports were needed to earn foreign exchange to pay the bills. Turkey began earnestly in 1964 to seek European tourists to visit her beaches, to explore her cities and countryside, and to view her antiquities. To attract these tourists, roads, hotels, transportation, and numerous other facilities had to be furnished; along the way the Turkish economy and social fabric began to be transformed.

Similarly, in the 1960s more and more Turkish workers found jobs in western Europe, principally in West Germany. In 1965 there were about 200,000 remitting about $100 million; in 1971 about 600,000 sending home $500 million; and in 1973, the peak year, 1,200,000 returning over $900 million. It was also estimated that there was a list of 800,000 who had applied to go abroad for work. Many of these arrived in Istanbul from distant provinces and camped there, idle for months, creating a social problem. In 1974, with 2 million Turks unemployed, the European recession closed the door on further emigration, and European labor forces demanded that Turkish workers be sent home. With population in Turkey increasing at a rate of 2.5 percent a year, passing 40 million in 1976, unemployment and the lack of capital investment to create jobs bred political and social instability.

One of the persistent criticisms hurled at Menderes was his distaste for planning. In 1963 the Grand National Assembly passed the first five-year plan; a second was approved in 1968, a third in 1972, and a fourth in 1978 calling for expenditures of $70 billion. Covering industry, agriculture, and trade, the plans allocated resources and attempted to generate development. Usually they emphasized industry, in which new investments have run from 25 to 30 percent of the total, because industry provides the most new jobs and produces goods to alleviate market shortages. Meeting the plans has been hampered by world recession and inflation, skyrocketing oil prices, weak labor markets in Germany, inadequate rainfall, problems in Cyprus, restrictions on poppy harvests, and aid cutbacks by the American Congress. Turkey's currency was devalued three times in 1975, twice in 1976, and nearly 20 percent more in 1977, but these have been only palliatives. Major developments in every aspect of national life must be undertaken before general production and the standard of living rise to meet the expectations of all.

One major advance was the completion in 1973 of the great suspension bridge across the Bosphorus. Situated north of the center of Istanbul, and designed to carry 21,000 vehicles per day, it had exceeded that target by 10 percent in its second year of operation and by 1977 revenue from tolls had paid for it. Connecting with another heavy-duty bridge over the upper reaches of the Golden Horn, it became the final link in an outer-belt superhighway that bypasses the traffic congestion of Istanbul and makes practical the trucking of produce from the garden areas of Anatolia to the metropolitan centers of western and northern Europe. Prior to the building of the bridge, unrefrigerated trucks laden with tomatoes had been known to stand in line for three or four days waiting for the ferry to cross from Asia to Europe.

Agriculture

Starting in the days of Atatürk the government patronized the peasants and did not impose taxes on farm income. Unbalanced budgets and, to some degree, the ills of the economy resulted from the lack of such taxes. The government established a soil office, which bought grain, tobacco, and other farm produce at established prices, frequently above world prices. Production was stimulated, and after the road-building program opened up many new areas in Anatolia and greatly reduced the costs of transportation, the quantities of wheat delivered to the soil office soared. This program, coupled with bountiful rains and the importation of tractors, plows, and harvesters, led in 1952 to an exportable surplus of 1.5 million tons of wheat. Cotton culture advanced in the Adana plain; markets were excellent for tobacco; and new areas were opened for the growing of sugar beets to supply Turkey's fifteen sugar refineries. Between 1951 and 1956 Turkey exported over 16 million tons of grain for an income of $550 million. Part of this surge in agricultural production may have resulted from land-distribution programs, which were approved after bitter debate in 1945 and slowly implemented, beginning in 1947. Almost 5 million acres of land were slated to be distributed among 200,000 peasant families. After 1950, however, the Democrat party so reduced and inhibited the program that little redistribution occurred. The large, wealthy landowners remained powerful allies of Menderes and his commercial and industrial friends.

Unfortunately, droughts in 1956 and 1957 changed the wheat surpluses to deficits, and in each of these years over 600,000 tons of wheat were obtained through American aid grants. To stimulate greater production higher prices were set for wheat in 1957, although a scarcity of consumer goods and other price controls still deterred farmers from bringing their crops to market. A devaluation in 1958 sought to offset the effect of Turkish inflation, which had forced the American tobacco companies to curtail their purchases in Turkish markets.

The well-being of the farmers in Anatolia and their staunch support of the Democrat party were significant factors in the strength of Menderes after 1954. Although crises in foreign trade and in finance shook the faith of the inhabitants of the larger cities in Menderes' leadership, his following in rural provinces enabled him to enact restrictive press laws silencing his urban critics without offending his wealthy agricultural friends, who re-elected him in 1954 and again in 1957.

As would be expected, the leaders of the coup in 1960 treated the agricultural sector of the economy most carefully. A land reform policy was prominently included in the initial program proposed by NUC; thereafter, agricultural investments continued to hold a high priority, especially under Justice party rule. In 1961 an income tax was levied on agricultural incomes for the first time. This touched the wealthier farmers and the largest producers, whose tax free incomes under Menderes had been under attack by economists and merchants.

Improved conditions lifted annual exports of cotton and tobacco to $100 million each in 1965, as agriculture accounted for 85 percent of Turkey's exports and about 40 percent of the gross national product. New, Mexican wheat varieties were introduced, and in 1968 cereal production reached 19 million tons. New dams and irrigation systems and the expanded use of fertilizers and farm machinery continue to increase the total output.

A continuous question in Turkey ever since the eighteenth century has been who owns and controls agricultural lands. At times vacant tillable lands were assigned by the government to nomads and Turkish peasants returning to Anatolia from the frontiers of the shrinking empire. When there were no more vacant lands, the only solution was to take land from large holdings and parcel it out to those who had none, and various reformers over the years have sought to do this. Leaders of the 1960 coup spoke warmly of land redistribution. Later, a prize-winning Turkish novelist took the life of landless peasants as his theme.

Some 380,000 acres were transferred in 1967, and 277,000 more in 1968.

Some reformers estimated that over 8 million acres ought to be redistributed, and some leaders such as Türkeş pressed to have it accomplished in a bold stroke. The Justice party, supported by large landholders, followed the policies of Menderes and moved slowly. Republican People's party leaders advocated a vigorous program as part of an overall solution to the disorders of 1971. Demirel was opposed to such a sweeping change, whereas Ecevit urged its rapid implementation in hopes of solving unemployment, slowing the drift of villagers to the city, and lessening the need to export workers. He asserted that it was social injustice to have 4 percent of the farmers tilling 34 percent of the land, leaving 96 percent to work the remaining 66 percent. Prime Minister Erim in 1971 pledged land reform; when he was forced to water down the program, eleven ministers left his cabinet, bringing about the fall of his government.

In the election campaign of 1973 Ecevit proposed that the holdings of all absentee landlords be nationalized and that the owners be compensated; that maximum acreage holdings be set by the Assembly; that no partnerships be established to circumvent the intent of redistribution; and that recipients of land be required to participate in farm cooperatives. His inability to meet these promises when he became prime minister was cited as a reason for his resignation in September 1974.

Religion and Education

One of the greatest changes in Turkey brought about by the advent of democracy was in religion and education. The rural population never really subscribed to Atatürk's program of deemphasizing Islam. As soon as the peasants had a voice in affairs, they insisted that religion be restored to some semblance of its former position in society, although they did not insist that the separation of state and religion be undone. Many serious-minded leaders concluded that much of value would be gained by reinstating the spiritual and ethical values of Islam, and lay teachers were permitted to give religious instruction in the schools. In 1949 the College of Theology, which had been closed at the University of Istanbul by Atatürk, was reopened as a part of Ankara University, and a new Institute of Islamic Studies was founded at the University of Istanbul. Study of the old script became possible; the mausoleums of holy men and the caliphs were once again open to the public; a few new mosques were built; religious days of fasting and feasting were more widely observed, and the muezzin's call to prayer was again sounded in the traditional Arabic. Radio Ankara programmed readings from the Koran, and attendance at mosques increased.

Traditional Islam entered politics when İnönü permitted a multiparty system in 1946. The Democrat party of Bayar and Menderes, including in its program strong attractions for the conservative and simple Islam of the Anatolian villagers, was successful to a degree never possible for the heirs of Atatürk. The Republican People's party was never able to erase from the villagers' minds the incessant Kemalist line that "they were primitive and nasty and superstitious" and that to participate in modern Turkey they would have to abandon their ancestral ways and become "civilized." The Democrats, by contrast, built 15,000 mosques in ten years and subsidized Koran reciters for mosques in every village. On the other hand, of the 60,000 "men of religion" in the country barely 8 percent had as much as a primary school education (five grades).

Educated and Westernized Turks, especially Republicans, deplored what they called an abuse of religion in order to win votes, and officers of NUC cited this tactic as one of the most significant in moving them to revolt. They were particularly infuriated by and at the same time ashamed of the Democrats' use of Menderes' escape from the airplane crash in England in 1959. Every radio in the land blared forth the view that God had saved him to lead his country, and henceforth a vote against Menderes was a vote against God. Moreover, when he returned to Istanbul over 100,000 loyal followers were at the airport to greet him. As Menderes stepped from the craft a score of sheep had their throats cut to satiate the evil force that had sought his blood; this ceremony was repeated twice before he reached his hotel, and reports and pictures of the demonstrations and rites were circulated to every village, to the dismay of secularized Turks. Against this kind of religio-political campaigning, opponents felt helpless.

Although leaders of the Republican People's party and NUC delivered scathing rebukes to Menderes for pursuing this policy, they too were following a like practice within a short time—6,000 mosques were built between 1960 and 1964, and NUC gave sizable sums to religious training schools. NUC also advocated the advancement of village education; it sought to meet the ever-difficult problem of teachers for the villages by changing the obligatory two-year military service as reserve officers for all *lycée* graduates to a like term as teachers in village elementary schools.

In the 1965 elections many villagers voted for Justice party candidates, recognizing in them the heirs of the Democrats. When Inönü moved his party left of center, Justice campaigners equated this with atheistic Russian communism. Turkish peasants have hated Russians for generations; to this was added the word *communist,* which replaced the word *infidel* as the common insult to hurl at opponents.

Conservative religion was still a strong political force, as the new National Salvation party demonstrated in the election of 1973. Winning slightly over 10 percent of the seats in the Assembly, it was the party of ultraconservative Islam in regard to education, culture, and religious practices, while supporting leftish approaches to many socio-economic problems. Islam pervades Turkish society and is a political force demanding to be recognized as a valid component of Turkish thought and culture.

In the schools a real awakening in the study of Ottoman history occurred. Atatürk, to strengthen Turkish nationalism and to forget the unhappy seventeenth- and eighteenth-century Ottoman experiences, hurdled all of Ottoman history and found glory for the Turks in earlier epochs. After World War II the writings on early Ottoman history were rediscovered, and a more systematic and scholarly investigation into the origins of Ottoman institutions and the foundations of Turkish life in Asia Minor began. Higher education was advanced by the opening of Atatürk University in 1958 at Erzerum and by the founding of the Middle East Technical University in Ankara.

Following the 1960 coup education at all levels received heavy emphasis. By the end of the decade Middle East Technical University had a faculty of more than 600 and a student body of over 6,000. Hacettepe University in Ankara, begun in 1958, had grown to have full faculties in the social sciences, medicine, and hygiene. New universities were founded, Seljuk University and Ege University, among them, in widely separated districts of Anatolia. Part of Robert College, an American school, was given to the government in 1971 and renamed Boğaziçi (Bosphorus) University.

In the election campaign of 1973 both Demirel and Ecevit promised to establish universities throughout the land to enable every student who wished to do so to attend. At the elementary level there were nearly 5 million children in 30,000 schools, 200,000 students in 900 vocational schools, and 100,000 in the universities. The number of *lycées* increased dramatically, with every province possessing at least one. This permitted all qualified students to enroll. A number of these schools used a foreign language, often English, as the language of instruction. Turkey was entering slowly into a modern world of universal education. The flood of articles and monographs from the pens of Turkish scholars in almost every field presaged a flourishing intellectual development. Professional journals publishing articles in these disciplines attested to the arrival of Turkish learning and society upon the world scene.

On the other hand, this major development did not produce a more stable and balanced society. There were still wide gaps between the levels of Turkish life, and university and educational circles were painfully aware of these almost bridgeless chasms. Beginning with the several years preceding Menderes' fall, student and faculty demonstrations, riots, and disorders were common events. In June 1968 students occupied part of the University of Ankara, insisting upon the removal of a dean and demanding changes in the curriculum. When the government failed to enact reforms the rector and eleven deans at the university resigned in protest. Most universities were closed in the autumn of 1968 and remained shut until spring. In 1971, 220 students at Hacettepe University were arrested after a five-hour gun battle; in 1972 the dean of the Ankara University Law School was sentenced to six years in prison for supporting illegal student activities. A law passed in 1973 gave the government the right to take full control of a university in the event of student disorders, but the government soon discovered its only recourse was to close the university and shut its gates. Disruptions of every kind continued.

Most modernized Turks have looked upon their country as the bridge between the West and the Middle East; they have frequently objected to the inclusion of Turkey in the concept of the "Middle East." Turkish leaders in 1953, at the time of the celebrations of the 500th anniversary of the

Turkish capture of Constantinople, presented the thesis that the Ottoman occupation of the Balkans and the holding of the Straits, at a time when the peoples of Western Europe were disorganized and weak, had preserved Western Europe, the entire Mediterranean area, and Western civilization itself from destruction by the barbarians of the East. In the minds of Turkish leaders NATO and CENTO were the logical continuations of this age-old role of western Turks. However, Western attitudes at the time of the Cyprus troubles in 1974 and since have led many Turks to wonder how well Western peoples appreciate the Turkish contributions.

REFERENCES: Chapter 38

Additional references for this chapter are found in Chapters 7, 12, 23, 24, 26, 28, 32, 37, 44, and 45.

Adams, T. W. *AKEL: The Communist Party of Cyprus.* Stanford, Calif.: Hoover Institution Press, 1971. The development, workings, and significance of the communist movement in Cyprus.

Ahmad, Feroz. *The Turkish Experiment in Democracy, 1950–1975.* London: C. Hurst & Co., 1977. The most thorough study of Turkish politics from the end of World War II to 1975 to have appeared.

Bahrampour, Firouz. *Turkey: Political and Social Transformation.* Brooklyn, N.Y.: Theo. Gaus' Sons, 1967. A valuable contribution from a non-Western viewpoint.

Benedict, Peter. *Ula: An Anatolian Town.* Leiden, The Netherlands: Brill, 1974. The story of a small town's response to the social and economic changes that have been eroding its importance.

Benedict, Peter, Erol Tümertekin, and Fatma Mansur (eds.). *Turkey: Geographic and Social Perspectives.* Leiden, The Netherlands: Brill, 1974. Focuses on patterns of settlement in rural areas, villages, towns, and cities.

Fisher, Sydney Nettleton (ed.). *The Military in the Middle East: Problems in Society and Government.* Columbus: Ohio State University Press, 1963. Essays by different authors on six countries, including Turkey.

Frey, Frederick W. *The Turkish Political Elite.* Cambridge, Mass.: M.I.T. Press, 1965. A survey of contemporary Turkish rulers and their social and educational backgrounds.

Harbottle, Michael. *The Impartial Soldier.* New York: Oxford University Press, 1970. An account of the U.N. forces in Cyprus from 1966 to 1968.

Harris, George S. *Troubled Alliance: Turkish-American Problems in Historical Perspective, 1945–1971.* Stanford, Calif.: Hoover Institution Press, 1972. A study of the alliance as seen from the Turkish end.

Hinderink, Jan, and Mubeccel B. Kiray. *Social Stratification as an Obstacle to Development: A Study of Four Turkish Villages.* New York: Praeger, 1970. A case study in rural change.

Karpat, Kemal H. *Turkey's Politics, The Transition to a Multi-Party System.* Princeton, N.J.: Princeton University Press, 1959. A penetrating work by the outstanding scholar on modern Turkish politics.

Karpat, Kemal H., and contributors. *Turkey's Foreign Policy in Transition, 1950–1974.* Leiden, The Netherlands: E. J. Brill, 1975. Individual chapters on Turkish policies with NATO, the United States, the U.S.S.R., Israel and the Arabs, and Cyprus. The last one presents the Cyprus conflict from the Turkish viewpoint.

Kinross, Lord (Patrick Balfour). *Within the Taurus.* London: J. Murray, 1955. A trip across Asia Minor with an outstanding observer.

Landau, Jacob M. *Radical Politics in Modern Turkey.* Leiden, The Netherlands: E. J. Brill, 1974. A study of the radical parties of the right and left. Shows that radicalization has been the most important influence on Turkish politics since 1960.

Makal, Mahmut. *A Village in Anatolia.* Wyndham Deedes (tr.). London: Valentine, Mitchell, 1954. An important insight into village life in Asia Minor by one who grew up in such a village.

Ozbudun, Ergun. *Social Change and Political Participation in Turkey.* Princeton, N.J.: Princeton University Press, 1977. A study of Turkey's development, with major stress on parties and voting patterns in relation to modernization.

Robinson, Richard D. *The First Turkish Republic: A Case Study in National Development.* Cambridge, Mass.: Harvard University Press, 1963. A judicious apologia for the Menderes regime.

Stirling, Arthur Paul. *Turkish Village.* London: Weidenfeld and Nicolson, 1965. A case study by an eminent sociologist.

Szyliowicz, Joseph S. *A Political Analysis of Student Activism: The Turkish Case.* Beverly Hills, Calif.: Sage Publications, 1972. A study of student participation in Turkish politics over the last century, with emphasis on the period since World War II. Important for an understanding of the current scene in Turkey.

———. *Political Change in Rural Turkey: Erdemli.* The Hague: Mouton, 1966. A comparative study of the southwestern Turkish town of Erdemli in 1941 and in 1957.

Tamkoç, Metin. *The Warrior Diplomats: Guardians of the National Security and Modernization of Turkey.* Salt Lake City: University of Utah Press, 1976. A study that reveals the interplay between foreign and domestic policy and the determining role of the political elite.

Vali, Ferenc A. *Bridge Across the Bosporus: The Foreign Policy of Turkey.* Baltimore: The Johns Hopkins Press, 1971. Helps in understanding the complex processes of Turkish foreign affairs.

———. *The Turkish Straits and NATO.* Stanford, Calif.: Hoover Institution Press, 1971. A short but thorough study.

Weiker, Walter F. *The Turkish Revolution, 1960–1961: Aspects of Military Politics.* Washington, D.C.: The Brookings Institution, 1963. A detailed account of the military government, and a discussion of the participants, their policies, and their aspirations.

Xydis, Stephen G. *Cyprus: Conflict and Conciliation, 1954–1958.* Columbus: Ohio State University Press, 1967. Largely based on the papers of the Greek foreign minister during this period. A lucid discussion of the relations between Colonel Grivas and Archbishop Makarios.

Chapter 39

Iran–Nationalism Versus Imperialism

U.S.S.R. and Azerbayjan

The treaty of alliance signed on January 29, 1942, by Great Britain, the U.S.S.R., and Iran provided that Allied forces would be withdrawn from Iran within six months after an armistice with Germany and Japan. At the Tehran conference in 1943 Roosevelt, Stalin, and Churchill signed a statement suggested by Loy Henderson, United States ambassador to Iran, that their governments desired to maintain "the independence, sovereignty, and territorial integrity of Iran," and that Iran's economic problems would receive their full consideration.

After the armistice with Japan on September 2, 1945, Iranian nationalists looked forward to March 1946, when all foreign troops would be evacuated. Their high hopes were soon dashed; in December the Soviets engineered and supported a communist revolution in Tabriz. Although the Communist Tudeh party had been dissolved in Azerbayjan, a new Democrat party under the leadership of Comintern agent Jafar Pishavari had established the autonomous Republic of Azerbayjan. During the war this province was under complete Russian control, and officials of the Iranian government from Tehran were even denied entry there. Taxes could not be collected, and local officials usually discovered that orders from Tudeh party leaders carried more authority than their own.

Almost immediately government troops were sent from Tehran to quell the rebellion, but Soviet troops blocked the roads with Sherman tanks. Open interference by the U.S.S.R. was charged by Iran, and in January 1946 an appeal was made to the United Nations. Russia pursued delaying tactics there, evidently hoping to bring additional troops into Iran and in the end present the West with an accomplished deed. A week later, when the Iranian parliament by a margin of only one vote chose Ahmad Qavam as the new prime minister, the Western press assumed that Iran was on her way behind the Iron Curtain, since Qavam had befriended the Tudeh party.

March 2, 1946, passed without any sign of the withdrawal of Soviet troops. The American troops had gone before January 1 and the British left in February. But additional strength for the Russians entered Iran in March, and the cold war began.

Qavam's first task was to cajole the Russians into removing their troops. He encouraged the Tudeh party leaders in Tehran to hold mass demonstrations in front of the parliament building to prevent parliament from meeting and thus ensure its automatic and legal termination. This allowed Qavam to rule by decree until a new parliament would be elected. He closed down anti-Soviet newspapers and arrested rightist political and army leaders. Meanwhile, the Iranian ambassador to the United States, Husayn Ala, laid a complaint before the Security Council of the United Nations and pursued a vigorous policy to secure Soviet withdrawal.

At the Security Council Soviet Ambassador Gromyko walked out as a stalling device to gain time for a bilateral settlement in Tehran. Stalin had evidently decided, in the face of strong British and American statements in support of Iran, and the worldwide publicity flowing from the United Nations' first large problem, not to use force in Iran. On March 24 Russia announced that the evacuation of Soviet troops would begin immediately and be completed in five or six weeks. As a part of the bargain Qavam agreed to allow an autonomous regime in Azerbayjan and to form a Soviet-Iranian Oil Company, 51 percent Soviet owned, to exploit oil in northern Iran. Cleverly, Qavam obtained an admission from Russia that Azerbayjan was an internal Iranian problem with which the Tehran government would deal "benevolently." Qavam received Azerbayjani communist leaders in Tehran and appointed one who had been educated in Russia as Iranian governor-general in Tabriz.

Feeling that Iran was in the bag, Russian troops departed on May 6, 1946. Qavam played his cards well. The Tudeh party and Azerbayjan Democrats held huge demonstrations in Tehran, and a vociferous attack was launched against the Anglo-Iranian Oil Company. Three Tudeh members and a fellow-traveler were included in a new Qavam coalition cabinet, composed of Qavam's new Iran Democrats, the Tudeh party, Azerbayjan Democrats, the Socialist party, and two other left-wing groups. The Soviet position reached its high point; to the world it appeared that Iran had been won by Russia, since the process that proved so successful in eastern Europe and the Balkans seemed well advanced in Iran.

However, Qavam may have been cautiously leading the Russians into a trap. He talked of reform, undoubtedly quite sincerely. Yet the Russians and the Tudeh party could hardly work against the rapid growth and popularity of a reforming Iran Democrat party, which by the end of the summer had political control and could dominate any forthcoming election for parliament.

At this point Qavam may have overplayed his hand, for the young shah demanded his resignation, informing him that the army had agreed to support the shah if trouble occurred. Qavam pledged his loyalty to the shah and was reinstated after he promised to fire the three Tudeh members of the cabinet, liquidate the autonomous Azerbayjan province, and organize a real party to face Tudeh. Parades and demonstrations of Qavam's Iran Democrats suddenly outshone those of the Tudeh party, and Qavam won the shah's support. He also won a majority for his party in the parliamentary elections that winter. Since Qavam declared that elections in all provinces, including Fars and Azerbayjan, would be held under the supervision of government forces, the Soviets were presented with a difficult choice. Only if Qavam's Iran Democrats won the election could the new parliament be expected to vote an oil concession to the Soviet-controlled company. Only if an election were held could an oil concession be submitted to an Iranian parliament. But no national elections could be held so long as the Soviet-supported autonomous province of Azerbayjan existed. Tehran troops entered Azerbayjan in November, and fighting developed. United States Ambassador George V. Allen quickly declared that his government favored Iranian sovereignty and territorial integrity as provided for in the United Nations Charter and adhered to the principle that it was entirely normal and proper for the Iranian government to send its security forces into the provinces to preserve order during elections. Since Russia did not wish to send in troops, she stood by and witnessed the collapse of the communist regime in Azerbayjan. The Tudeh party in Tehran disintegrated and refused to participate in parliamentary elections.

Elections were held in a leisurely fashion throughout the country during the winter months. Qavam's coalition won handily and the shah opened the new parliament in July 1947; a few weeks later it gave to Qavam a vote of confidence. Almost immediately the Soviets pressed for ratification of the oil concession to the Soviet-Iranian Oil Company that Qavam had initialed in the spring of 1946. Qavam, at this juncture, informed the Soviet ambassador that the oil agreement was unsatisfactory. Russian reaction was sharp, and Qavam was accused of treacherously violating his agreement and returning to the policy of hostility and discrimination practiced by Shah Reza and previous reactionary governments.

The Iranian government took heart from the decisive stand and support of the United States. Qavam's new cabinet included three graduates of the American College of Tehran, and the United States extended a military credit of $25 million. Princess Ashraf, the shah's twin sister, visited the United States. And General Norman Schwarzkopf, American adviser to the Iranian gendarmery, assisted in the establishment of order and governmental control in Azerbayjan.

As it became more apparent that the Iranian parliament would rebuff the Soviets, the British became fearful that a categorical refusal might lead also to the nationalization of the Anglo-Iranian Oil Company. The English ambassador advised Qavam not to slam the door in the face of the Russians but to leave it somewhat ajar. Sentiment in parliament was inflamed, however, and Mosaddeq reminded Qavam of the law of 1944, sponsored by that fiery nationalist, forbidding an Iranian government from granting or even negotiating an oil concession with a foreign state without parliament's consent. U.S. Ambassador Allen, speaking before the Iranian-American Cultural Relations Society, reiterated America's respect for Iranian sovereignty and said: "Iran's resources belong to Iran. Iran can give them away free of charge, or refuse to dispose of them at any price, if it so desires ... The American people will support fully their [Iranians] freedom to make their own choice." With this public support and an agreement by the United States to send a military mission to raise the efficiency of the Iranian army, parliament on October 22, 1947, voted 102 to 2 to void Qavam's agreement with the U.S.S.R., to exempt Qavam from penalties under the 1944 law, and to authorize the government to enter into negotiations to regain Iran's rights with respect to oil in areas where the British held concessions.

The U.S.S.R. fumed, hurled charges at Qavam, and stated that Russia would consider Iran a bitter enemy. But the crisis passed. Iranian leaders breathed easier; Iranian politics returned to normal. At the same time Qavam's coalition evaporated. In December he failed on a vote of confidence, and within two weeks his parliamentary opponents accused him of embezzlement, ordering improper arrests, and governing by decree without parliamentary approval. He was arrested and allowed to go to Paris for "his health."

Iran Looks to the United States

Shortly after returning from the Tehran conference, Roosevelt argued that Iran would be the ideal place to show the world what an unselfish American policy of economic and technical assistance could do for a less-favored friendly nation. When America had supported Iran staunchly in her stand against the Soviets, American prestige had soared and Iranian leaders had anticipated all manner of benefits and assistance. The needs were titanic and endless: irrigation, agricultural methods, improved seeds and stock, tools, land ownership, health and sanitation, education, dams, and many other items. American assistance in providing capital and technical and managerial know-how was acceptable to the Iranians, because the United States seemed less imperialistic than other powers and was not associated with Iran's past struggles against Russia and England.

In the 1930s Reza Shah had made plans for modernizing Iran. Though the war disrupted these plans completely, they were not abandoned, and in 1946 Qavam gathered fifty notables and experts to draw up at the shah's insistence a seven-year development plan for Iran. Time passed, more plans were drawn and studied, but nothing happened. Truman launched the Point Four Program in 1949, and there was considerable talk in Iran about aid from the United States under that project and in arms grants under the Mutual Defense Assistance Act. Although American leaders were sympathetic to Iranian needs, they believed that Iranian politics were unstable and that funds, either loans or gifts, would be largely wasted and lost. Cabinets came and went in Tehran. Between Qavam's ousting and the appointment of Mohammad Mosaddeq on April 28, 1951, Iran had six prime ministers, some for only a month or two.

In 1949 the shah decided to take a hand in obtaining aid and visited the United States. For six weeks he observed, talked, and listened. A joint statement was issued by the shah and President Truman to the effect that the United States would support the Iranian application for an International Bank loan and would aid Iran under the Point Four Program. The shah stated that Iran would welcome such assistance as well as the investment of private capital in the Iranian economy. He promised that appropriate measures would be taken to encourage such investment.

When the shah returned he lent enthusiastic support to reform. A new American ambassador, Henry F. Grady, gave Iranians great hope that aid would be forthcoming. A commission was appointed to ferret out, publicize, and punish corruption in government, but conditions grew even worse. Then, the outbreak of the Korean War ended any prospect of obtaining American aid, and a member of parliament formally asked the government to explain why Iran should "bother" anymore with the United States. The shah announced that a program of land reform in Iran was being inaugurated by splitting up his royal estates into small farms that would be sold to peasants on long-term installment payments. But the program moved slowly, and other landowners failed to follow suit.

Iran's economy floundered seriously. The end of World War II and the evacuation of foreign troops had halted a sizable influx of foreign exchange, and a general decline in world trade in 1948 and 1949 depressed the economy still further. Receipts from oil payments slumped under the administration of the British Labour party because of its general restrictions upon dividend payments. Although the deterioration threatened a collapse of the government and a likely victory for a resurgent Tudeh force, the upper class appeared supremely indifferent. Corruption continued unabated; land reform was quietly opposed; the wealthy and influential ignored their income taxes; and prestige politics remained the sport of the great landowners. Pressures, however, developed to reconsider the concessions held by the Anglo-Iranian Oil Company as commanded by parliament in 1947.

Oil Problems

Ever since 1940, voices had been raised over the question of oil concessions and in particular with respect to royalties. In 1944 Mosaddeq, almost single-handedly, pushed through parliament a law forbidding further oil concessions or even their discussion with foreigners. Following the resolution of 1947, cabinet leaders started to consider the position of the Anglo-Iranian Oil Company and the income from oil. The income was never enough and did not compare favorably with receipts of Latin American countries. As finances grew desperate and American aid did not materialize, eyes turned more and more toward the prospering Anglo-Iranian Oil Company, which had every appearance of possessing greater wealth and income than the Iranian government.

For the public the oil crisis began June 1, 1948, when the company announced that payments would remain the same as in 1947, even though the company's net profit after taxation jumped from $26.9 million in 1947 to $52.1 million in 1948. In 1947 the Iranian government received $19.9

million in royalties and taxation, whereas the British government received
$56 million directly in dividends and taxation. When these figures were
presented to the Iranian public, the outcry was sharp. Then the announcement followed that the British government was limiting dividends, which
according to the royalty formula would keep payments at the 1947 level.

Another galling feature of the old 1933 agreement was a stipulation that
petroleum would be sold in Iran at only 10 percent below world prices
which the Iranian public felt was unreasonable, particularly since the company sold oil to the British navy at a still lower price. In addition, the Iranian
public believed that substantial profits were concealed by the selling of
petroleum products cheaply to affiliated concerns. In this way higher profits
would flow to stockholders, but would not be reflected in higher royalties
to Iran.

In view of the dissatisfaction in Iran, officials of the Anglo-Iranian Oil
Company visited Tehran in the summer of 1948 and received a memorandum asking for an agreement similar to that which Venezuela had with
American companies. In particular, this meant 50 percent of the company's
profits. Furthermore, employment of fewer foreigners and training more
Iranians for technical and managerial positions in the company were demanded. Moreover, the prime minister informed the company negotiators
that a 50-50 sharing of profits was being discussed at that moment in Saudi
Arabia by the Arabian-American Oil Company.

After considerable delay the Gass-Golshayan supplementary agreement
was signed in 1949 by the company and the Iranian government. It increased the discount on oil sales in Iran to the same figure given to the
British navy and arranged payments to double those stipulated in the old
1933 schedules. However, for prosperous years such as 1947, 1948, and
1949 payments fell short of 50 percent. In lean years, as the company
pointed out, they might be better than that. Just at that time the company's
1948 report was published, showing that Britain received $79.2 million in
taxes and Iran $37.8 million in royalties. The uproar was deafening and
parliament took no action on the agreement.

When the new parliament met in 1950 the question of the agreement fell
to a newly created oil committee. Headed by Mosaddeq, who now led a
National Front party with eight members in parliament, the committee
refused to act. The prime minister was unable to induce the company to
consider a 50-50 split, although in this plea he had the support of the
American ambassador. Another prime minister urged the company to
make some concessions, but it was obdurate, pointing out that had Iran
accepted the agreement in 1949 she would have received over $64 million
instead of $37.8 million.

The United States warned Great Britain that some appeasement would
be necessary. Since the company refused to take any action until the government brought the agreement to parliament, debates were held and the
oil committee rejected the agreement. Almost immediately the company
urged the prime minister to reopen negotiations to seek a 50-50 split of the

profits. But it was now too late. Mosaddeq had presented a resolution demanding nationalization of the oil industry and calling upon the prime minister to find out whether such a step was feasible. After consultation the prime minister reported publicly on March 3, 1951, that nationalization was impractical; he was assassinated four days later.

Nationalization of Oil

Within a week parliament passed a bill nationalizing the oil industry, although it was not signed by the shah until May. Britain objected, and the new prime minister rejected the protest. Riots, strikes, and wild demonstrations affected the area of the oil installations. British cruisers appeared in the Persian Gulf, and refineries at Abadan shut down. When the prime minister did not move to take over the properties of the Anglo-Iranian Oil Company, parliament forced his resignation, and Mohammad Mosaddeq, hero and chairman of the oil committee, became prime minister on April 28, 1951. The following day a law was passed to evict the company, and Mosaddeq ousted it on October 1, 1951.

In May, as soon as the Mosaddeq government took steps to implement the nationalization law, the company and the British government proposed arbitration applying to the International Court of Justice at The Hague for a decision. Mosaddeq declared the Court had no jurisdiction over the case, which was a dispute between a private company and the sovereign state of Iran. When the British complained that the Iranian government had not responded to requests for negotiation, and admitted that they were prepared to consider a settlement that would involve some form of nationalization, Mosaddeq supposed that the main battle had been won. He was now ready to begin negotiations with the company.

But negotiations proved arduous. Each side believed it possessed the stronger bargaining weapons to back up its legal position. In addition, each had to be mindful of powerful psychological, political, and economic forces in its own nation. Finally, each side either ignored or was misinformed about the views, intentions, and strength of its opponent.

The company asserted that only it could operate the intricate industry and the Abadan refinery; that only it could provide the great outlay of capital needed; that production in Kuwayt could within one year replace any loss in Iran if the company were dispossessed; and that the tanker fleet could be easily shifted to other routes, thus leaving to the National Iranian Oil Company only the small domestic market in Iran.

The company believed that the tottering Iranian economy could not withstand the added shock of a loss of royalties and that political leaders who had benefited from the oil income would quickly force Mosaddeq to come to terms. Also, the company held that the action of the Iranian government was illegal, since it contravened the 1933 agreement.

On the other hand, the company and the British government failed to read the signs of the times in Tehran or to comprehend that nationalization of the Anglo-Iranian Oil Company united the various divergent classes in

Iran as nothing had done since the Tobacco Concession two generations earlier. Nationalization suddenly meant independence, and Mosaddeq not only had twisted the British lion's tail—something all Iranians had been longing to do for a long time—but had pitted the Iranian lion against the British lion and had won. A recent prime minister had faltered on that point and was murdered. Mosaddeq always understood that a like fate could be his.

Mosaddeq encouraged the Iranian populace to assume that income from the oil industry would enable them to live in ease and comfort. But he did not realize the complexities of the international oil industry or the difficulties involved in selling Iranian oil without world cooperation. Furthermore, he did not take into account that neighboring countries such as Iraq, Kuwayt, and Saudi Arabia might object if oil companies restricted production in their fields to provide a market for Iranian oil.

Mosaddeq believed that Britain and Western Europe required Iranian oil for the continuance of their economies and thus would be forced to come to terms. He also expected that the United States would support Iran in her struggle with the company, because American ambassadors were friendly and had warned Britain of the serious consequences of the loss of Iranian oil. Moreover, he fully anticipated that the United States would give aid to Iran for fear that Iran would drift behind the Iron Curtain if her economic position became more chaotic than it was already.

Iranians perhaps misjudged British tempers and failed to understand that neither Labourites nor Conservatives wanted to liquidate the empire. Thus, the role played by Iran in World War II as the provider of oil for the British navy and high-octane gasoline for the Royal Air Force was overlooked entirely, and the relationship of Anglo-Iranian oil to British dollar earnings and sterling oil was ignored. Iran's leaders had studied the legality of the nationalization of industry in Great Britain; they assumed that England would recognize the legality of the same process in Iran. Moreover, they failed to perceive that Britain's acceptance would invite nationalization in Iraq, Saudi Arabia, Bahrayn, and Kuwayt—a thought that gave nightmares to oil officials the world over.

In the ensuing debate between the company and Iran the position of Prime Minister Mosaddeq was exceedingly strong. Although his National Front party had a delegation of only 8 out of 136 in parliament when he became leader of the government, his following and influence were widespread. One of his staunchest supporters was a leader of the Shiite divines, Ayatollah Sayyid Abd al-Kasim Kashani. He hated the British, who had interned him as a German agent during World War II. In 1949, after an unsuccessful attempt upon the life of the shah, Mullah Kashani was suspected of inciting the Devotees of Islam *(Fidaiyan-i Islam)* to commit such assassinations and was exiled. Elected to parliament in 1950, he returned to take his seat and was no doubt implicated in the death of the preceding prime minister. As long as Mosaddeq was uncompromising with the British,

Kashani worked with the government and used his position to excite popular religious fervor in support of Mosaddeq.

Oil Stalemate

From the moment of Mosaddeq's entry into office and the beginning of the drive to eject the Anglo-Iranian Oil Company, until his unsuccessful coup d'état in August 1953, the drama of the nationalization of oil in Iran had many scenes, a large cast of players, and a constant shift of location. There were five proposals made by the British, the United States, or international groups to effect a settlement; all failed. In June 1951 the company agreed to the principle of nationalization and proposed the formation of a new company with British and Iranian directors to handle the production and distribution of petroleum products for Iran. In July Truman entered the controversy and sent his personal ambassador, W. Averell Harriman, who supported the company's proposal. Mosaddeq refused, on the basis that some understanding on compensation should first be reached.

By the end of the summer of 1951 the oil industry in Iran was shut down; the tanks were full, and no oil was being loaded. When the Security Council of the United Nations considered the question at the request of Great Britain, Mosaddeq came to New York to state again that this was not a subject for United Nations concern since the Charter forbade acts that impair the sovereignty of any member. While in the United States Mosaddeq discussed the question with high American officials, but no meeting of minds occurred. The United States government and American oil men reassured the British that America would not take on the job of running the oil business for the Iranian govenment. At the same time the American government made available over $300 million to England to enable her to buy oil in the Western Hemisphere. With this aid and encouragement the British position with Iran remained obdurate. Still further, the United States refused to grant loans to Iran to offset losses from royalties, although $24 million was granted in 1952 for Point Four projects. Production was hurriedly upped in other Persian Gulf oil-producing states, since the situation appeared to be critical.

After these failures the issue was reduced to the amount of compensation. In August 1952 Truman and Churchill sent a joint proposal that the question be submitted to the International Court. In October Iran severed diplomatic relations with Great Britain, while Mosaddeq said that he would agree to an International Court adjudication of compensation if the bases used were those employed by the British government when it nationalized properties in the United Kingdom. In February 1953 a revised proposal, supported by the Eisenhower administration, was forwarded to Mosaddeq, but it was declined with the statement that Britain must first state her claim.

Each time exchanges were made tempers became worse, and charges and countercharges, repeated in all of the presses of the world, grew bitter and exaggerated. Mosaddeq asserted that the British were asking compen-

sation for future expected profits now to be lost and that he would, therefore, demand payment by the company of all royalties that Iran should
have, but had not, received in the past.

As the controversy dragged on, Britain and the West adjusted to the loss
of Iranian oil. By the spring of 1953 there was a glut of oil on the world
market, and many oil companies were actually worrying about what they
would do with Iranian oil and where they could market it if it suddenly
became available again.

Governmental Crisis

In Iran affairs were descending rapidly to a state of chaos. The loss of
royalties was beginning to pinch. Thousands of Iranian oil workers were
transferred to the public payroll. And scarcity of foreign exchange and the
absence of any great earning power destroyed Iran's foreign credit. Since
the great mass of Iranians, however, were not dependent upon or affected
by royalty payments or foreign exchange, life did go on. Nevertheless,
Mosaddeq was not nearing any solution. The nationalists were becoming
frustrated; the army was short on supplies; and the wealthy landowners who
governed the country soon discovered that the loss of the royalty revenues
on which their corrupt governmental practices battened was forcing them
to change their ways.

A crisis developed in July 1952 upon the opening of the newly elected
seventeenth parliament. Before Mosaddeq would accept the prime ministership, he demanded absolute power for six months to inaugurate governmental, economic, and social reforms. Many members of his own party
objected. So did the shah, when he was asked to allow Mosaddeq to become
minister of war as well as prime minister. Thereupon Mosaddeq resigned,
and the shah appointed Qavam to form a cabinet. Qavam publicly branded
Mosaddeq a demagogue and Kashani a hypocrite, and stated that he would
settle with the British. Quite understandably, he was forced to resign. But
first there were four days of bloody rioting led in Tehran by Mosaddeq,
Kashani, and a resurgent Tudeh party.

To avoid civil war the shah sent for Mosaddeq, whereupon Kashani
through his influence over the Devotees of Islam halted the violence in
Tehran. Kashani was elected speaker of parliament. In August Mosaddeq
became minister of war and was granted unlimited powers. He had reached
the pinnacle of his career; soon the cracks in his structure began to appear.
Quarrels within his own party arose over appointments, and in January
1953, when he obtained a continuation of his personal rule for another year,
Kashani deserted him. Demonstrators attacked Mosaddeq's home, forcing
him to flee for safety to the United States Point Four office. In July Kashani
failed to be reelected speaker. Thereafter, many members of Mosaddeq's
National Front party resigned their seats in parliament. Mosaddeq was
gathering more and more power into his own hands, and even those of his
party who were members of the oil committee deserted. In July, having
been guaranteed personal safety, General Fazullah Zahedi, one of the pop-

ular strong men in the army and Mosaddeq's open opponent, left the parliament building where he had been taking sanctuary for ten weeks.

When Mosaddeq announced that a popular referendum would be held on the question of the dissolution of parliament, the storm began to break. Only the shah could dissolve parliament. Kashani placed a religious boycott on the referendum, but voting proceeded, separate polling places being provided for those voting for and those voting against the measure. Mosaddeq won with 99.93 percent of the vote. On August 12, 1953, he announced his intention to dissolve parliament.

Mosaddeq's Fall

By this time the government of Mosaddeq had lost the support of every political and social group in Iran except a small number of bazaar merchants of Tehran and the communists, who throve on the disorders. The mobs of Tehran could be swayed easily to demonstrate for almost anyone. Mosaddeq had tried for too long to make political capital from his nationalization of oil, without adding any new funds to this original capital, and now he faced political bankruptcy. He did not understand the world ramifications of the oil industry. He did not have the personality, organization, or real courage to become a dictator. His playing with fire with the communists failed to smoke out any assistance or sympathy from the United States. Lacking any solid support from Iranian nationalists, the army, landowners, religious groups, or the shah, Mosaddeq lost out completely.

Many Iranians believed that Mosaddeq would be able to obtain aid from the United States, and encouragement for this view was fostered by promises made by President Truman. In the spring of 1953 Secretary of State Dulles changed the American tune and helped to pull the rug from under Mosaddeq. In May Dulles visited every capital in the Middle East from New Delhi to Athens with the exception of Tehran, ostensibly because time did not permit—but Iran understood. In July much publicity was given to Eisenhower's letter to Mosaddeq declaring that aid would not be given to Iran unless the oil dispute was settled or arbitrated. A few weeks later Dulles stated that aid would be withheld from Iran because Mosaddeq openly countenanced and apparently cooperated with the illegal Tudeh party.

Allen Dulles, the secretary's brother and head of the CIA, and Princess Ashraf, the shah's twin sister, visited each other in Switzerland. General Schwarzkopf, who had organized the Iranian gendarmery and was a friend of the shah and General Zahedi, visited Iran as a tourist in August. On August 13, after Mosaddeq had usurped the shah's power by deciding to dissolve parliament, the shah dismissed Mosaddeq. He appointed General Zahedi as prime minister. Mosaddeq refused to be dismissed and remained in office through the use of troops. On August 16 the shah fled by plane to Baghdad and Rome, and Zahedi escaped to the provinces. But on August 19 crowds in the streets of Tehran began to shout: "Long live the Shah." Zahedi's men attacked Mosaddeq. A minor tank battle decided the issue in favor of Zahedi, who appeared before nightfall. The shah returned on August 22; Mosaddeq was caught and arrested; a new cabinet under Zahedi was approved; and on September 5, Eisenhower granted $45 million to Iran on an emergency basis.

The new government began to ferret out communists and crack down on opponents. Mosaddeq was found guilty of attempted rebellion and sentenced to three years' imprisonment. His foreign minister was tried and shot for inciting rebellion. In October 95 percent of the shops in the bazaar closed in protest against the vocal attacks on Mosaddeq. Several merchants were arrested. When a second attempt at closing was tried, government workmen demolished the vaulted roofs over the alleys in four areas of the bazaar, which brought the merchants quickly to support Zahedi.

The Oil Settlement
The grant from the United States was made on the condition that the oil dispute be terminated. Herbert Hoover, Jr., spent two weeks in Tehran in October discussing a settlement, which still could not be effective in Iran if it appeared to revive any aspect of colonialism. In February 1954 a consortium of eight major world oil companies met to debate the complex problem of getting Iranian oil swirling into world markets and royalties flowing into the desperate Iranian treasury. On August 5, 1954, Iran signed an agreement whereby the consortium would extract, refine, and market petroleum for the National Iranian Oil Company (NIOC). The Iranian company would receive half of the profits and pay $70 million a year for ten years as compensation for nationalization. Parliament ratified the agreement in October, and oil began to gush immediately. The pivotal problem was solved. After that date the world demand for oil products expanded rapidly, enabling the sale of Iran's oil without market dislocations, and yearly payments to Iran rose sharply to approximate $300 million by 1960.

In 1956, NIOC took over the Russian oil concession east of Tehran, thus controlling the oil resources of the entire nation. In August a team of consortium engineers brought in a prodigious gusher in a new field near Qum. Capacity production for this single well was estimated at 80,000 barrels daily, three times greater than the most productive well in Iran heretofore. The bidding for exploitation of the Qum strike was intense. In 1957 an agreement was reached between NIOC and the Italian firm AGIP Mineraria by which Iran would receive 75 percent of the profits.

Exploration for other oil fields continued apace, and in 1958 concessions were granted for $25 million to Pan-American International Oil (PAIO), a subsidiary of the Standard Oil Company of Indiana, and to AGIP, both as partners of NIOC to explore offshore fields in the Persian Gulf. The Island of Kharg in the gulf was chosen as a convenient base for oil operations, including those of the consortium, and pipelines were laid between Kharg and the mainland in 1960. NIOC acquired tankers and began to find markets for its oil in Argentina, India, and Japan. In 1965 an additional port for refined petroleum products, with pipelines, refineries, and docks was begun at Bandar Mashut, some 550 miles south of Abadan, and in 1966 NIOC signed an oil agreement with Entreprise Française des Recherches et d'Activitées Petrolières (ERAP), whereby ERAP was neither partner nor concessionaire but only a contractor to NIOC. Schemes for the piping and utilization of the seemingly limitless quantities of natural gas in the oil fields, burned off and wasted for decades, turned into a reality in 1965 with the founding of the National Iranian Gas Corporation (NIGC). A mill was shipped from the United States to roll pipe for the line, Great Britain agreed to help finance it, and the U.S.S.R. signed an arrangement to aid in the engineering and construction of the line to the Caspian Sea area in the U.S.S.R., completed in 1970, and to receive payment in natural gas deliveries. Another innovation was the launching of a petrochemical industry under the control of the National Iranian Petrochemical Corporation (NIPC), with a $170 million complex appearing at Bandar Shapur in partnership with Allied Chemicals of New York, and a $21 million petrochemical plant at Abadan with the B. F. Goodrich Company participating.

In 1950, the last year of normal oil activities before nationalization, the average daily production had been about 660,000 barrels. Not until late in 1956 was this rate achieved again; after 1956 increases reached over 13 percent annually, until 3,750,000 barrels were produced daily by 1970. Oil and gas income to the government soared and in 1970 it stood at $1.1 billion. The shah, complaining regularly to the consortium that it was not upping production fast enough, kept pressing for larger payments. In 1969 the energetic Manuchehr Eqbal was appointed to head NIOC. He applied new pressures to the consortium and all concessionaires to expand production and increase payments to the state. In 1970 the consortium agreed to a small increase in the posted price of crude oil from Iranian wells and to raise the Iranian share of the profits to 55 percent. This action signaled the entry of a new age in the production and pricing of petroleum, not only for Iran but for the entire world.

Iran and OPEC

In 1960, at a meeting in Baghdad, representatives of Iran, Iraq, Kuwayt, Saudi Arabia, and Venezuela formed the Organization of Petroleum Exporting Countries (OPEC) to try to coordinate oil policies regarding levels of production, export prices, percentages of profits to be paid in taxes and royalties, and concession policies in the hiring and training of nationals of the host countries. Over the ensuing decade meetings of OPEC were held regularly without much world impact. As other oil producing states—Abu Dhabi, Algeria, Ecuador, Gabon, Indonesia, Libya, Nigeria, and Qatar—joined OPEC, more and more of the petroleum needs of the world were being met from OPEC resources.

In Tehran in February 1971, during an OPEC meeting, representatives of some twenty-two of the world oil companies capitulated to a threatened embargo and agreed that 55 percent of the profits would accrue to the producing countries. The companies also agreed to a sizable increase in the posted price of crude oil (the base from which profits are calculated), and to a set formula for changing the posted price in accordance with fluctuations in the value of the dollar. OPEC, with Iran playing a significant role, by this action established its leverage over petroleum markets. By the end of 1972 crude oil was selling for $3 per barrel, almost double the price in early 1970.

Iran's oil revenues reached $2.5 billion in 1972. In July of that year the consortium agreed that oil prices would be indexed to follow the prices of Western capital goods. The consortium agreed also to increase Iran's oil production by 100 percent, to pass 8 million barrels per day by 1976. In 1971 production had averaged 4.5 million barrels per day; in 1972 it was running over 5 million per day. Furthermore, the shah announced that Iran would take over the entire operation of the consortium and other oil companies by 1979 were these quotas not achieved.

World demand for oil appeared insatiable. In 1973 world consumption jumped more than 4 million barrels per day, most of the increase coming from expanded output in the Persian Gulf area. OPEC raised the price of oil twice in 1973; by the end of the year the posted price was set at $11.65 per barrel, and Persian Gulf oil was frequently bringing $18 per barrel at auction. Iran did not join the Arab states in their embargo or reduction of output during the October 1973 Arab-Israeli War, and Iran's average daily production topped 6 million barrels. Budget revenues jumped far beyond estimates, since oil income provided nearly 90 percent of Iran's annual budget. 1973–1974 revenues, originally set for $7 billion, were increased to $11.7 billion. Budget revenues for 1974–1975 moved up to $30.8 billion. For 1977–1978 they were estimated at $49 billion. However, a pinch was felt in 1975 when prices softened and production dropped 15 percent as a result of the world economic recession. Nevertheless, OPEC raised prices by 10 percent in October 1975 and by another 10 percent at the end of 1976. Iran, along with other populous members of OPEC, pressed for larger increases as the needs of the budget and five-year plan (1973 to 1978) were almost limitless. That plan had called for $16 billion but was raised in 1973 to $27.6 billion and then more than doubled in December 1974 to $69.6 billion. By the end of 1976 the world economy had adjusted to the higher oil prices and Iran's output was again over the rate of 6 million barrels per day.

It was widely estimated that Iran's oil resources would be diminished very significantly within twenty years unless new discoveries were made at an accelerated pace, and that they might be nearly depleted by the end of the century. The shah, therefore, was greatly concerned that the oil income be used to generate a balanced economy and to develop other mineral resources and a self-sustaining industry. His first goal was to boost non-oil revenues so that they would equal oil revenues by 1985. His hope was to industrialize Iran and make his empire the equal of any Western European country. He spoke of Iran as another Japan. Had not Mosaddeq died in 1967 he would have rejoiced at Iran's prodigious oil income in the mid-1970s and would have seen some of his dreams coming true. He might even have felt that the shah was fulfilling his program and obtaining for Iran a just return from the nation's heritage.

Affairs of Government
The second compelling situation after Mosaddeq's downfall was the restoration of constitutional government. In December 1953 the shah dismissed parliament and called for elections to begin that month. Zahedi's followers and the shah's friends won in the elections and dominated the new parliament. In April 1955 Zahedi retired as prime minister and the shah appointed Husayn Ala to the post. Husayn Ala had been prime minister, foreign minister, minister of the court, and ambassador in Washington and was recognized as friendly to the West. Elections were held again in 1956. This time the lists of candidates and the manner of the elections insured a victory for conservatives, landowners, and friends of the shah. Former members of the National Front party protested; Allah-Yar Saleh, Mosaddeq's ambassador in Washington, took sanctuary in the parliament building and went on a hunger strike to call attention to the injustice and mockery of the election.

Early in 1957 Ala resigned to become minister of the court, and the shah appointed Manuchehr Eqbal as prime minister of a new cabinet. He organized a Nation party to support his policies and to combat a new opposition party (People's), led by the shah's friend, Assadollah Alam, who coalesced groups interested in agricultural reform, the division of large estates, labor, and equality for women. The shah divorced Queen Soraya in 1958 because she had not borne him a son; the following year he married Farah Diba, who gave birth to a son and heir to the throne in 1960. A second son was born in 1966.

Beginning in 1961 Mohammed Reza Shah exercised his influence and power for what came to be termed the "White Revolution," or "Revolution from the Throne." He appointed an independent, Dr. Ali Amini, prime minister, who formed a completely independent cabinet. Income from oil was on the increase but the state coffers were empty. Dr. Amini was a sensitive, well-educated, and honest aristocrat with a keen feeling for social responsibility and the welfare of the masses. Within a few days parliament was dismissed and the shah and Dr. Amini set out to reform the nation. Five generals were arrested on charges of corruption and embezzlement, and many civilian officials were investigated and discharged. The cabinet issued a land law decree requiring all landowners to sell to the government all land holdings in excess of one village and stating that the government would sell such land to landless villagers. In March 1962 the shah presided at such a distribution in Azerbayjan. In Tehran the students rioted when scholastic requirements were raised and tightened. Dr. Amini was unmoved and the demonstrations were suppressed.

In July 1962 Dr. Amini's health failed and, disappointed in not getting the grants-in-aid he expected from the United States, he resigned. The shah appointed Assadollah Alam, the leader of the People's party, who pledged to continue the reforms. At a meeting of 5,000 village representatives in Tehran the shah presented a six-point program: (1) The break-up of large estates held by religious foundations and individuals and the distribution of these to landless peasants; (2) The nationalization of forest areas; (3) The sale of some 200 government industries to privately owned companies to obtain funds to compensate the landlords and to establish agricultural cooperatives; (4) The compulsory payment of 20 percent of industrial and business profits to the employees; (5) The forming of a literacy corps from those in military service to go into the villages to teach the illiterate; and (6) The enacting of new electoral laws to eliminate corruption in the elections. Alam supported this program wholeheartedly and in January 1963 a referendum approved it by a vote of over 5.5 million to 4,000. Shiite religious leaders protested vehemently, but their censure had been expected because their income came largely from the landed estates of the foundations.

The promised elections came in September 1963, not only for the Majlis but for the thirty elective seats of the Senate; the old parties were not permitted to present candidates. The New Iran party was organized by forty-year-old Ali Mansur particularly to support the shah's six-point program. Mansur's party handily controlled the Majlis, which now was dominated by agrarian reformers and city dwellers, rather than the great landowners, as had been true in the past. The shah appointed thirty new members of the Senate, including two women. For the first time in Iranian history women voted, and in the cities they went to the polls in great numbers. (In the referendum earlier that year, women had gone to the polls and put ballots in the boxes but these were not counted.)

With the backing of New Iran the shah appointed Mansur prime minister in March 1964; he won a unanimous vote of confidence in the Majlis and 51 of 60 votes in the Senate. Mansur agreed to dissolve the state sugar monopoly and submitted a new bill limiting land holdings from 75 to 300 acres, depending upon the type and use of the land. Unfortunately, Mansur was assassinated in January 1965; in his place, the shah put the former finance minister, Amir Abbas Hoveyda, a New Iran member, who declared he would fulfill Mansur's programs. The land reform measures did not progress as rapidly as many had hoped, and by the end of 1965 only 14,000 peasants had received titles to their lands.

With Prime Minister Hoveyda working closely with him, the shah believed he had attained political stability. Amidst a gathering of national leaders and international figures at Gulistan Palace in Tehran, he celebrated his forty-eighth birthday on October 26, 1967, by placing the crowns of the empire upon his head and that of Queen Farah. Parliamentary elections followed one after the other, and the shah and Hoveyda managed them handily.

To enhance the international stature of the shah and the state, the "Feast of the Last Twenty-Five Centuries" was celebrated for four days in October 1971. At Persepolis, surrounded by all the pomp and circumstance that

$100 million can generate, royalty, religious dignitaries, and governmental figures from more than 100 states gathered to mark the 2,500th anniversary of the founding of the Persian Empire by Cyrus the Great. Many criticized the great cost, in view of the poverty suffered by most Iranians, but it was pointed out that the new roads, new hotels, and other facilities were permanent constructions, and that added tourism would more than pay for these luxuries.

The pageantry failed to impress various elements in Iranian society who viewed the shah's worldwide travels and self-acclaim and Hoveyda's political structure as idle theatricals. With society and the economy evolving rapidly, Iran's unchanging cultural patterns of individuality, religious idealism, and contempt for government, of family privilege, and of tribal and provincial loyalties produced many incidents of unrest. Communists, socialists, democratic intellectuals, religious dissidents, disloyal tribal leaders, republican sympathizers, disaffected army personnel, and alienated students, found open opposition to the government difficult and any united action impossible. Some turned to terrorism.

Attempts were made on the life of the shah and his family, and a number of ministers, generals, and leaders were assassinated. Terrorist activities increased in 1972. There was a violent student strike at the University of Tehran, and several bombs exploded there. Eight alleged terrorists were executed in 1973; a few weeks later, supposedly in retaliation, terrorists killed an American military officer. SAVAK, the secret police, energetically rounded up suspects, and reported killing 200 or more terrorists.

When direct campaigns against terrorists proved unsuccessful the shah inaugurated other programs to combat the violence. Early in 1973, on the tenth anniversary of the "White Revolution," the shah unveiled plans for private and government-owned companies to sell shares of stock to the general public, including workers. Two years later, after little movement in this direction, another public announcement was made indicating that several hundred companies would place $1.5 billion worth of shares, representing 49 percent of their stock, on the public market. Government-owned operations, except for oil, steel, copper, and transportation, were included in the package, though it was noted that management would be retained in government hands.

The two political parties did not appear to possess any allure or dynamism. In 1975 they were dissolved and one political party was formed—*Rastakhiz,* or National Resurrection party, with Prime Minister Hoveyda as its secretary-general. Still, there was low voter turnout in the elections that year. As long as SAVAK agents seemingly were everywhere—even when Iranian students congregated abroad—and had jailed several thousand supposed terrorists, political participation, even voting, appeared futile to many Iranians and inordinately dangerous to some. Since politicians enjoyed almost no initiative, the shah found only timid responses to his solicitations.

In the summer of 1977 when drastic power shortages developed and widespread blackouts cut industrial production, public clamor for relief was loud and clear. Iranians suddenly realized that the nation's rush for development had gone too rapidly. They also learned that oil production for several years in the future had already been committed for a variety of imports. The shah summarily fired Prime Minister Hoveyda, who had held that office for twelve years, and seven other cabinet ministers, and appointed Prime Minister Jamshid Amuzgar who had been petroleum negotiator and minister of the interior. Amuzgar favored a much slower pace of economic expansion and set out to curb inflation and balance the budget.

Between East and West

Soon after Zahedi assumed power, relations improved with the U.S.S.R. A trade agreement doubling the amount of goods previously exchanged was signed, and the Soviets indicated a desire to settle outstanding boundary and financial controversies. In 1954 a new commercial protocol was concluded with the U.S.S.R., whereby Iranian imports of machinery were permitted, and Russia agreed to return to Iran eleven tons of gold and $8 million in goods held for safekeeping in Russia since the early days of World War II. At the time of the gold transfer the shah was invited to visit Moscow; it appeared that the Kremlin had decided to win Iran by a more friendly attitude. It was nearly a year, however, before the visit was made. Meanwhile, Iran had joined the Baghdad pact on October 11, 1955. This move brought two notes from the U.S.S.R., declaring that adherence to the pact violated Iran's treaty obligations. These notes were viewed as thinly veiled threats to implement clauses in other treaties giving Russia the right to intervene or enter into the northern provinces of Iran if the latter's independence were threatened.

The shah's trip was planned to improve relations between Iran and the U.S.S.R. in line with the settlement in 1954 of a number of irritating problems. The signing of the Baghdad pact and the favorable reception of the Eisenhower Doctrine in certain government circles did not help. The Kremlin protested but the many friendly gestures toward Iran continued. Direct rail service was opened between Moscow and Tehran in 1958 and negotiations got under way for a nonaggression pact. After the revolution in Iraq in 1958 and the transformation of the Baghdad pact into CENTO, Iran suddenly seemed to have greater strategic value for the United States, and in 1959 Iran signed a bilateral agreement with the United States, the latter to render aid in case of any aggression upon the former. Khrushchev, furious, broke off all negotiations with Tehran but shortly realized he should not write off Iran without another attempt to neutralize the Caspian area. In 1960 Moscow suggested that aid for the development of oil, natural gas, and heavy industry, specifically a steel industry, would be available from the U.S.S.R. in exchange for a nonaggression pact and a pledge that Iran would not allow foreign bases or rocket launching sites on her soil. In 1962 Iran agreed that no rocket bases would be permitted. This cleared the way for friendlier relations; the next year President Brezhnev visited Iran and was warmly applauded when he addressed parliament. Definite aid projects moved slowly but a number came to be fulfilled in 1966 when the U.S.S.R. agreed to help build a natural gas pipeline from the oil fields of southern Iran to Astara, a U.S.S.R. port on the Caspian sea, and to take natural gas as payment. Credits were advanced for development of the iron mines at Baft and the coal mines at Kerman, and for building machine-tool plants and a steel mill at Isfahan.

When the United States declared that aid programs, technical assistance, and grants would terminate in 1968, on the grounds that the Iranian economy had reached the level at which it could progress on its own, the shah began to look elsewhere for trade and arms. Although military assistance from the United States, directly and through CENTO, continued, the shah announced in 1967 the purchase of $110 million in Soviet arms to be paid for within eight years by the delivery of natural gas, cotton, and other commodities. A trade agreement for $540 million was signed the next year. The shah returned to Moscow in 1972 to sign an agreement augmenting trade by 1,000 percent within five years. In 1970 the U.S.S.R. made a loan to the Iranian State Railways for improving the roadbed and communications. That year the natural gas pipeline was opened from Qum to Baku. As funds began to flow to Iran from higher oil prices and greater production, foreign loans and credits tapered off, but in 1975 when money became tight again a $3 billion trade agreement was concluded with the U.S.S.R. The following year a five-year trade agreement, covering an additional $3 billion was negotiated in the hope of facilitating greater Soviet-Iranian exchange which in the first nine months of 1976 had amounted only to 315 million rubles, almost evenly divided between exports and imports. Likewise, conventions were arranged with Poland and Czechoslovakia bartering Iranian oil for their industrial and agricultural machinery and products.

The United States and the West
Friendly relations with the United States were continued by Zahedi, Ala, Eqbal, and the prime ministers who followed. An American military mission was established to train the Iranian army, and sizable quantities of military equipment were received under mutual defense arrangements until 1966, when the United States declared that the Iranian economy had become strong enough to support its army. In addition to equipment $30 million was expended annually to subsidize the army; in the two decades from 1946 to 1966 over $700 million in military aid and matériel had been given by the United States. By 1966 nonmilitary aid—grants for technical aid, loans from the World Bank, and outright gifts from the United States —totaled over $550 million.

Beginning in the late 1960s, the shah, who always loved to travel abroad in the manner of his nineteenth-century predecessors, led missions to many Western capitals to negotiate diplomatic, military, financial, and economic development matters. He visited Washington almost yearly beginning in 1968. In 1975 he consummated arrangements for marketing oil and obtained promises of nuclear reactors and very large quantities of military items.

In 1969, when Britain's intention to withdraw her military presence from the Persian Gulf area became known, the shah proclaimed an increased role for Iran there. After 1970 Iran's expenditures for new armaments skyrocketed; it is estimated that from 1973 to 1976 Iran bought or contracted for $12 billion in ships, tanks, planes, guns, and support equipment from the United States alone. In the 1976–1977 budget Iran allocated $8.2 billion for defense, including an item of $3.4 billion for the purchase of 160 F-16 jet fighters. In addition two American oil firms agreed to lift 300,000 barrels of oil daily for several years to pay for more F-16s. In 1977 the United States met Iranian requests for early warning planes by agreeing to sell five planes to bolster Iran's radar capabilities. Thousands of American technicians accompanied the weapons to train Iranians in their use. Vast amounts were also spent in Western Europe for military goods. In 1976 the American Congress questioned the wisdom of selling huge quantities of the most advanced weapons to Iran, but the shah was determined to acquire what he considered necessary for the defense of Iran, her astonishing resources, and her trade routes.

In 1966 Iran began industrial development and trade talks throughout the world. In the following decade trade missions flocked to Tehran to participate in Iran's industrialization. New enterprises ranged from aluminum plants to fish-meal factories. By 1975 trade with the United States alone reached an estimated $15 billion. World banking groups loaned Iran large sums. The shah was in a hurry to industrialize and to exploit fully the vast resources of Iran before the oil gave out. In OPEC meetings he urged higher oil prices to ease Iran's weighty debt.

Arab Affairs

Throughout the first half of the twentieth century, relations between Iran and the Arab states were not particularly warm. The age-old antagonisms between the Arab and Persian cultures and peoples were exacerbated by the running controversies between Sunni and Shi'a Islam. After World War II the international oil companies played off the Arab oil producers against Iran and drove the wedge still deeper. In 1965 increasing friction with Iraq over respective rights in the Shatt al-Arab and Iranian rebels harbored at Karbala led to the severing of diplomatic relations. Affairs with Egypt and Syria were strained, and Lebanon expelled the Iranian ambassador. During the June 1967 war Iran adopted a very mild pro-Arab stance at the United Nations and continued to supply oil to Israel.

Though King Faysal of Saudi Arabia made a state visit to Tehran late in 1965, the shah postponed his return courtesy call because of Saudi Arabia's stand on a proposed confederation of the Trucial Arab Amirates on the Persian Gulf. The threat of a new Arab state, including Bahrayn, Qatar, and possibly even Kuwayt, with immense oil resources across the Gulf, which might be a Saudi Arabian satellite or a great power client, gave the shah new worries. After an agreement was signed with Saudi Arabia on the demarcation of the Gulf shelf, with Kuwayt and Qatar concurring, the shah went to Riyadh and Kuwayt in November 1968.

When in 1970 Bahrayn sought to become an independent state, and it became clear that the amirate group would be formed without Kuwayt or Qatar, Iran relinquished her claim on Bahrayn and acquiesced in the independence of the United Arab Amirates. However, the shah announced that Iran would prevent Abu Musa and the two Tunb Islands from falling into "hostile" hands. Iran declared that these islands had been seized from her eighty years ago, when she had been weak, and now that she was strong she would protect them. These islands occupy a strategic position just inside the Strait of Hormuz, and any unfriendly power holding them could deny passage to tankers laden with Iranian oil. On November 30, 1971, one day before the British abandoned them, the shah occupied the islands. The shah proposed to the amir of Sharjah that the latter fly his flag over Abu Musa and retain sovereignty over the 800 inhabitants, and that any oil found there be divided evenly between the two states. Iran would give Sharjah £1.5 million annually until oil revenues for Sharjah reached £3 million. The amir of Ras al-Khaymah, however, objected to the Iranian landing on Greater and Lesser Tunbs, and five persons were killed in the fighting that ensued. Iran continues to occupy the two Tunbs; complaints against Iran and against Great Britain for permitting the take-over, made by Iraq, subsided. In Ras al-Khaymah, the resentment continues and Iranians remain very unpopular.

Iran's feud with Iraq was aggravated by the fact that both states front on the Shatt al-Arab. Abadan and Khorramshahr, two of Iran's vital ports, are located there, and Ahwaz is on the Karun River only a short distance upstream from the Shatt al-Arab. When Iraq began to erect significant fortifications at the entrance to the Gulf, the shah protested. Iraq bitterly condemned Iran's occupation of Abu Musa and the Tunbs in 1971 and severed diplomatic relations, deporting 60,000 Iranians from Karbala and Najaf. The shah, in turn, extended military aid to the Kurds, who were in rebellion in northern Iraq, and gave sanctuary to 70,000 fleeing Kurds. At the outset of the Arab-Israeli War of October 1973 Iraq, uneasy, offered to resume diplomatic relations. The shah welcomed the request, and stated that Iraq need not worry about her frontier with Iran. Early in 1975 a detente between the two was reached and Iranian support for the Kurds suddenly ended, leaving many of them in very precarious positions. Through the good offices of Algeria a treaty was signed by Iran and Iraq in June 1975, which included a comprehensive delineation of the border based on the 1913 Constantinople Protocol. Later that year good-neighbor agreements were concluded concerning the Shatt al-Arab and an understanding to allow 12,000 Iranians per year to visit their holy shrines in Iraq.

Beginning with the Tehran OPEC meeting in 1971, relations with the Arab states were meliorated by common oil interests. After the massive oil price increases in 1973, the shah's concern for the Arab states grew perceptibly. Generous loans for economic development went to Syria and Egypt, and help was tendered in the rebuilding of Port Said and the widening of the Suez Canal. The shah stated that Israel should return to her pre-1967 borders.

Above all, the shah was striving for a "Pax Irana" in the Persian Gulf and Gulf of Oman. In 1973, at the request of Sultan Qabus of Oman the shah sent a military force to Dhufar to assist in defeating a rebellion aided by leftist agents from China and South Yemen. When the shah, who had good relations with China, entered the fray the Chinese advisers were replaced by Cubans. Some 2,000 Iranian troops were in Dhufar by the end of 1974. By 1976 most of the rebellion had been quelled. In additional regional activity, in November 1974 the Iranian navy staged massive naval exercises in the Gulf of Oman and Arabian Ocean, and Iran settled her differences with Afghanistan over the waters of the Helmand River.

Dams and Plan Organizations
At the end of World War II it was anticipated that the natural resources of Iran, in addition to oil and gas, could be developed. As soon as the oil crisis was settled Zahedi announced the inauguration of a second five-year development plan to be financed by oil revenues and, it was hoped, by the World Bank. The plan, beginning with the budget year 1954–1955, concentrated on building dams, hydroelectric power plants, irrigation systems in arid regions, and on draining land in swampy areas. Recognizing that the vast majority of Iranians were farmers and that the well-being of the nation would be served best by improving their property and increasing their productivity, the bank made loans to finance agricultural transportation, industries, social services, and electric power development. In 1956 the plan was extended to seven years; projects costing $1 billion were outlined; and the oil consortium announced that it intended to spend $140 million in developing the various oil centers. A five-year contract to develop the resources of Khuzistan in southern Iran was signed by the American Development and Resources Corporation, which agreed to start construction of a 660-foot high dam on the Dez River in 1958.

Beginning in 1960 planning permeated Iranian society. Sixty percent of Iran's oil revenues had been earmarked for Zahedi's plan, and much had been poured into the building of dams, which through irrigation, flood control, and electric-power generation would change the economy of Iran. In 1961 the great Karaj Dam, northwest of Tehran, was completed. In 1962 the 352-foot high Manjil Dam on the Sefid Rud River in Gilan was opened. Built at a cost of more than $100 million by French contractors, it irrigated about 375,000 acres and produced 132,000 kilowatts of electric power. The new Mohammed Reza Dam on the Dez River was dedicated in 1963, and the contract with the Development and Resources Corporation was renewed for an additional $140 million. It was intended that this dam would irrigate 360,000 acres in the province of Khuzistan in southwestern Iran, provide 520,000 kilowatts of electricity, and serve as the key project of a

Dez River Authority to transform Khuzistan into the rich agricultural producing area it had been in the past. In 1967 contracts were let with British and French concerns for the Shah Abbas Dam on the Zaindeh River in the south. In 1971 the Cyrus the Great Dam in western Azerbayjan was dedicated.

Great interest developed in 1962 in a third development plan, this one to run seven years, from 1962 to 1968. As originally drawn, the plan carried a budget of $1.87 billion, five-sevenths of which was to be financed within Iran. It called for an annual growth rate of 6.5 percent in productivity—10 percent in fact, but the lower figure was adjusted to the increase in population. Hardly under way, the plan's budget and scope were expanded to $2.72 billion to cover new communications systems and extended agricultural programs. Many pessimists saw their fears justified when there was only a 3 percent increase in 1965 and a welter of faltering half-finished projects. Many of these were completed, however, and a boom in 1966 generated great optimism. The gross national product increased by 12.5 percent, with a per capita national growth of 10 percent. There was good weather for agriculture and many industries surpassed the planners' expectations. Development activity was so promising that capital began to flow into Iran from every direction.

Economic Independence

Iran's oil production in 1966 was almost three times what it had been ten years earlier. Prices had not risen greatly and income, therefore, went up nearly 300 percent. Annual budgets and the gross national product reflected these riches. When the budget for the fiscal year, 1967–1968, reached almost $1 billion, the United States announced that her aid programs would end in 1968. Low-interest loans from the World Bank and the United States Export-Import Bank were continued, one from the latter to help American companies participating in a $172.5 million petrochemical complex at Bandar Shahpur. Other credits provided for electric power development, as the shah laid grandiose plans for an atomic reactor center at Tehran University. In 1967 a pipe-rolling mill was opened at Ahwaz, most of the initial production of which would go into the trans-Iranian gas pipelines. When high-grade copper ore was discovered in the Kuhpalagi area, government officials talked of Iran becoming one of the world's major copper producers.

The fourth economic development plan, covering 1968 to 1973 reflected unlimited optimism. Totaling $10.8 billion, 90 percent of which was expected from domestic revenues, the plan allocated 23 percent to agriculture, 20 percent to industry and mining, 16 percent to communications, and generous amounts to education, housing, and social services. Industrial production would be doubled, agricultural output increased by 25 percent, and 1 million new nonfarm jobs created to eradicate unemployment, a troublesome urban problem.

Simultaneous with this new five-year plan the Iranian economy took off.

The budget for 1968–1969 was established at $3.6 billion, a staggering 270 percent rise over the previous year. In each of the following four years the budget leaped 20 percent or more to reach $7.3 billion in 1972–1973. Allocations for development and defense were doubled year after year, and the annual gross national product topped $12 billion in 1972. The World Bank loaned $300 million to Iran's Industrial and Mining Development Bank; nineteen international banks put together a five-year loan of $100 million in Eurodollars to the Central Bank of Iran; German money developed an aluminum smelter; loans from Japan, together with funds from NIOC financed a $350 million petrochemical complex at Bandar Maashar on the Persian Gulf; British companies began to work an open-pit copper mine; and Rootes Motors in 1968 launched a program to build Hillman cars in Iran, expecting to turn out 140,000 before 1973. Wherever one turned new projects and developments appeared. Iran even participated in developing a $275 million petrochemical complex in India. No wonder the shah had the courage to invite the world's leaders to Persepolis in 1971 to celebrate the rebirth of the Persian Empire; he believed he was propelling his people from the sixteenth to the twenty-first century, when Iran would once again be one of the world's powers.

A second economic transformation began to overtake Iran in 1973 with the quadrupling of oil prices. The budget for fiscal 1973–1974, announced for $7 billion, was expanded to $11.7 billion, and the budget for 1974–1975 rose to $30.8 billion by the year's end. The budget for 1976–1977, puffed up by inflation, soared to $45 billion. Expenditures quickly were extended beyond revenues, and Iran returned to the borrowing pattern of previous years. At the December 1976 OPEC meeting Iran voted for a 15 percent increase in oil prices.

The fifth five-year development plan went into effect in March 1973; it lay out $32 billion for new investments and gave a high priority to agriculture and social welfare in an attempt to reduce the frightening gap between rich and poor. As the plan unfolded it became inadequate, and in December 1974 the level of capital expenditures was reset at $69.6 billion. One aim of the plan had been to raise the annual gross national product 233 percent, to $28 billion, at its conclusion in 1978; after twenty months, however, the gross national product had already far exceeded its goal, and a new target of $60 billion was fixed.

Greatly increased income in 1974 changed the direction and type of Iranian commercial and industrial development activities. In 1973 a steel mill with an annual capacity of 700,000 tons had been opened at Aryamehr. Soviet aid had been required to complete the mill. In 1974, however, when orders were placed in France as part of an agreement calling for the purchase of $4 to $5 billion in French goods and services over ten years, Iran made an advance payment of $1 billion to help France meet her oil bills. Among other things the French were to build in Iran were five nuclear reactors, an automobile factory, and the Tehran subway system. Industrial projects worth $2.2 billion were contracted for in West Germany, while

Iran purchased 25 percent of a Krupp subsidiary. Germans also agreed to construct two nuclear power plants. A loan of $1.2 billion also went to Great Britain to bolster her sagging economy, to be repaid with future trade deals.

The year 1975 repeated the previous year. In addition to Iran's many contracts with American concerns, trade with western Europe continued apace. A $5.5 billion agreement signed with West Germany and an economic understanding with the Netherlands encompassed such diverse aspects of Iranian life as shipping, agriculture, electrical equipment, and the utilization of natural gas. Iran indicated to Turkey that she would advance $1.1 billion over several years to enhance cooperation between the two neighbors in matters of energy, tourism, agriculture, and defense communications. The shah vowed in a speech that development would progress so rapidly and Iran's vast natural resources would be so thoroughly exploited that non-oil revenues would reach 50 percent of oil revenues by 1985 and would equal them a decade later.

The quadrupling of oil prices had brought on a world economic recession, which greatly affected affairs in Iran. The demand for petroleum products slumped badly while the prices of imported goods and services, especially military hardware and capital items, continued to mount, bringing on a $4 billion trade deficit in 1975. Though the shah turned again to borrowing from the West, development advances did not halt: the British Steel Corporation laid the foundations of Iran's third steel mill at Isfahan, to cost $1 billion; and West Germans started construction on the first of four nuclear power generating units after Iran accepted international nuclear inspection. Still, Iran had funds for capital investments. The Pahlavi Foundation bought B. F. Goodrich's 58 percent holding in an Iranian tire and tube plant and the government purchased 25 percent of West Germany's Krupp Industries. In October 1976 President Valéry Giscard d'Estaing of France visited Tehran and promised to build two nuclear power centers, a railroad, housing, a major highway, a conventional power station, and other projects. Cost to Iran: $12 billion.

For the year ending in March, 1976, Iran's nonmilitary imports were $12.4 billion, more than triple what they had been only two years earlier. With ever-increasing amounts of weapons, sophisticated equipment, and accompanying technicians, and the eagerness of multinational corporations to participate in development projects, the modernization of Iran was rapidly underway. The predictions of the shah seemed attainable.

REFERENCES: Chapter 39

Important readings for this chapter are also found in Chapters 20, 29, 30, 32, 33, 36, and 37.

Amuzegar, Jahangir. *Iran: An Economic Profile.* Washington, D.C.: Middle East Institute, 1977. A four-part work covering: economic structures and forces; production and distribution patterns; economic plans and policies; and performance and prospects.

Baldwin, George B. *Planning and Development in Iran.* Baltimore: Johns Hopkins

Press, 1967. A discussion of Iran's first three development plans and of land reform.

Bill, James Alban. *The Politics of Iran: Groups, Classes, and Modernization.* Columbus, Ohio: Charles E. Merrill, 1972. Shows how new groups and classes are challenging traditional political arrangements. Contains a good analysis of the White Revolution.

Chubin, Shahram, and Sepehr Zabih. *The Foreign Relations of Iran: A Developing State in a Zone of Great-Power Conflict.* Berkeley: University of California Press, 1974. A very useful handbook on the day-to-day operations of foreign policy.

Elwell-Sutton, Lawrence P. *Persian Oil: A Study in Power Politics.* London: Lawrence & Wishart, 1955. A discussion of the oil dispute in Iran.

Fatemi, Nasrollah S. *Oil Diplomacy: Powderkeg in Iran.* New York: Whittier Books, 1954. Written by the brother of Mosaddeq's foreign minister.

Ford, Alan W. *The Anglo-Iranian Oil Dispute of 1951–1952.* Berkeley: University of California Press, 1954. Thorough and detailed review of the events.

Hamzavi, A. H. *Persia and the Powers: An Account of Diplomatic Relations: 1941–1946.* London: Hutchinson, 1946. By the Iranian press attaché in London. Especially valuable for the documents in the appendix covering incidents from 1942 to 1946.

Irwin, Pollock. *A Tar Heel in Iran.* Charlotte, N. Carolina: Heritage House, 1957. An interesting account of an American in Iran.

Kemp, Norman. *Abadan: A First-Hand Account of the Persian Oil Crisis.* London: Allan Wingate, 1953.

Lambton, A. K. S. *Landlord and Peasant in Persia.* New York: Oxford University Press, 1953. The most scholarly and challenging work on this subject. Gives an historical account of land tenure, the oppression of the villagers, and the problems of the peasants.

Laqueur, Walter Z. *Soviet Russia and the Middle East.* New York: Praeger, 1959. A penetrating description of many aspects of communist activity in the Middle East, especially in Iran, and the U.S.S.R.'s dilemma over whether to help communists or to try to establish friendly relations with governments that persecute communists.

Motter, T. H. Vail. *The Persian Corridor and Aid to Russia.* Washington, D.C.: Department of the Army, 1952. An official history of the work of the Persian Gulf Command in forwarding lend-lease supplies to Russia during World War II.

Ramazani, Rouhollah K. *Iran's Foreign Policy, 1914–1973: A Study of Foreign Policy in Modernizing Nations.* Charlottesville: University Press of Virginia, 1975. Shows the triumphant emergence from the desperate 1941–1946 period to the power and position of 1973.

Roberts, Norman S. *Iran, Economic and Commercial Conditions.* London: H. M. Stationery Office, 1948. A good evaluation of the first seven-year plan at its outset.

Smith, Anthony. *Blind White Fish in Persia.* New York: E. P. Dutton, 1953. An excellent study of village life in Iran.

Upton, Joseph M. *The History of Modern Iran: An Interpretation.* Cambridge, Mass.: Harvard University Press, 1960. A philosophical essay on developments in modern Iran.

Warne, William E. *Mission for Peace: Point 4 in Iran.* New York: Bobbs-Merrill, 1956. Warne directed the mission for many years.

Zabih, Sepehr. *The Communist Movement in Iran.* Berkeley: University of California Press, 1966.

Chapter 40

Oil and Saudi Arabia

The collapse of the Ottoman Empire and the withdrawal of Turkish forces from the Arab provinces following the Mudros armistice in 1918 created in the Arabian peninsula a partial political and power vacuum. Within two years the French had taken over Syria and the British Palestine, Transjordan, and Iraq in accordance with their prearranged agreements. For the remainder of the peninsula the situation was quite different. London did not doubt that it was to be a British sphere of influence.

Long before World War I the Persian Gulf had become an English lake; official British residents and agents controlled the foreign affairs and advised the rulers of the petty states on the eastern Arabian shore from Kuwayt to Muscat. On the southern shore Britain held her colony of Aden and protected or had treaty rights with the various sultans, imams, and amirs. And even Abd al-Aziz ibn Saud, ruler of the Nejd, admired the British. But along the western coast communications from Istanbul by sea via Suez, by land routes from Damascus, and by the Hijaz railway enabled the Ottoman Empire to maintain more than a shadow of control. From this coast and from Syria and Iraq the Porte found it profitable and possible to keep a hand on the precarious balance among the marauding Arab tribes of the interior deserts and to sway decisions favorable to Turkey's allies.

Sharif Husayn of Mecca

In essence the British inherited the Turkish role in 1916, when they subsidized Sharif Husayn of the Hijaz on the western coast and recognized and subsidized Abd al-Aziz ibn Saud in central and eastern Arabia. Sharif Husayn was given nearly $1 million in gold each month and supplied with arms to captain the Arab rebellion against the Turks. Husayn proclaimed himself king of the Arabs, and was promised a united Arab state at the end of the war. When the mandate system was established and Syria, Palestine, and Iraq were taken by France and England, he was disillusioned and provoked. In 1921, after the Cairo Conference, the British proposed a treaty that recognized Husayn as the sovereign of the Hijaz, and continued his subsidy indefinitely. Yet, he refused; his pride and honor would not permit him to accept the clauses that mentioned Britain's "special position" in Iraq and

Palestine. The payments of gold ceased and Husayn was on his own, although negotiations were attempted in 1923 and again in 1924.

Without British protection and assistance Sharif Husayn of the Hijaz, even though he styled himself king of the Arabs, reverted to being only one of five independent Arab rulers, and not the strongest of these. His position was not enviable. He had taken the lead in the discussions with the British regarding Syria and Iraq; now, the onus of failure was his, even though he always acted as if his sons Abdallah and Faysal in Transjordan and Iraq were only his viceroys in those "Arab provinces." Unfortunately for his son Ali, heir in the Hijaz, his viceroys had taken with them most of the veteran army built up during the war.

Husayn was not, however, an Arab of the tribes or the desert. Having lived in Istanbul at the court of Abdul Hamid II for fifteen years, he looked down upon such individuals as Abd al-Aziz ibn Saud as uneducated bedouins, and certainly he did not know how to talk with them. They, for their part, considered Husayn an effeminate town-dwelling Europeanized Arab who had lost genuine Arab characteristics. Husayn offended the Arabs of Arabia at every turn and insulted their chiefs in unforgivable language. During the war, when he was trying to get the cooperation of all Arabs against the Turks, he rejected a draft agreement proffered by Abd al-Aziz ibn Saud with the remark that it must have been "penned by a madman or a man in his cups."

In addition, Husayn was a miserable administrator. Almost the sole income of the Hijaz was derived from the annual pilgrimage. Husayn mismanaged it, offended the Egyptians over ceremonials, and permitted pilgrims to be fleeced by the merchants until it became a scandal throughout the Muslim world. His final mistake was the assumption of the title of caliph in 1924 after the Turkish Republic abolished the Ottoman caliphate and exiled the last caliph.

Abd al-Aziz ibn Saud boiled in rage that that "sinful man" should so desecrate the position held by Abu Bakr and Umar. Moreover, Ibn Saud had several old scores to settle with Husayn and he needed the income from the pilgrimage. Most important of all, however, was Ibn Saud's natural Arab inclination to unite the Arabian peninsula under one rule—his rule!

Ibn Saud

Abd al-Aziz ibn Abd al-Rahman ibn Faysal Al Saud, better known in the West as Ibn Saud, was born in 1880 to the Saud family of Riyadh in the Nejd. Since the middle of the eighteenth century his family had been the political mainstay of the puritanical sect of Islam originated by Muhammad ibn Abd al-Wahhab, and the Saudis aided in the propagation of Wahhabism throughout Arabia. Ibn Saud's ancestors battled Muhammad Ali and Ibrahim, who invaded Arabia from Egypt. The most serious and persistent rivals and enemies, however, were the Ibn Rashid family of the Shammar tribe to the north, centered upon the town of Hail. Ibn Saud's uncles lost out in the constant warring, and at an early age Ibn Saud lived in exile in Kuwayt and other Arab towns. His father renounced any right to rule, but the son was of a different character. In 1902, against seemingly impossible odds, Ibn Saud, in the kind of derring-do so much loved and admired by the Arabs, led forty young Arab bloods up tilted palm trunks over the walls and roof-tops of Riyadh to recapture the city for himself and family.

In the years that followed he was able to ward off the declining Bani Rashid. In 1913 he captured from the Turks the valuable province of al-Hasa on the Persian Gulf, not knowing then that al-Hasa was practically floating on oil. When World War I descended upon the Middle East, Ibn Saud was visited by British officers and finally came to terms with Captain Shakespear, sent there by Sir Percy Cox, who for years had been chief British resident in the Persian Gulf. Ibn Saud agreed to accept $25,000 a month not to join with the Turks against the British and not make any foreign commitments without informing the British. Upon the defeat of the Turks in Arabia during the war, and with the knowledge of the provisions of the Mudros armistice as well as the Sykes-Picot agreement, Ibn Saud was as anxious to extend his rule as any other Arab potentate.

In 1911 Husayn captured Ibn Saud's brother and forced Ibn Saud to acknowledge Turkish overlordship to obtain his brother's release. No Arab chieftain could have done otherwise and retained his honor; yet the humiliation rankled in Ibn Saud's breast. In 1916 Ibn Saud agreed to follow Husayn's leadership in the resistance movement against the Turks, but he thought of the Arab grouping as an alliance of equals. Ibn Saud held as preposterous and vainglorious Husayn's claim to be king of the Arabs.

The first blow in retaliation was struck in 1919. Abdallah, Husayn's second son, led a column of armed men to seize the oasis of Khurma. Ibn Saud held Khurma, but the British Foreign Office had ill-advisedly awarded it to Husayn. Ibn Saud fell upon Abdallah at Turaba and annihilated his army; Abdallah barely escaped with his life, and the British informed Ibn Saud that he could keep his conquests but must not invade the Hijaz.

When in 1920 and 1921 Britain installed Abdallah in Transjordan and Faysal in Iraq, Ibn Saud felt that he was being surrounded by Husayn and the Hashimite clan. The apparent encirclement spurred Ibn Saud to move outward. He sent his son Faysal in 1920 with a force of 5,000 men across 700 miles of difficult trails to defend the highlands of Asir and the realm of the Idrisi family, which was being squeezed by the tactics of Husayn and Imam Yahya of Yemen.

Forging a strong bond of friendship with the Idrisi and obtaining their allegiance, Ibn Saud sensed that this was the moment to settle his family feud with the Bani Rashid. In a series of swift and daring expeditions Ibn Saud captured Hail in the autumn of 1921 and incorporated the land of the Shammar tribes into his Kingdom of Nejd. A number of the Bani Rashid resided as his "guests" at Riyadh, and Ibn Saud became the sole power in the interior expanses of Arabia. A provisional settlement was made with the British with regard to their "protected" areas. Sir Percy Cox in 1922 drew up with Ibn Saud the protocol of Ukair, loosely defining areas and districts.

Two neutral zones were set up on the boundaries of Ibn Saud's kingdom —one facing Iraq and the other next to Kuwayt. These neutral zones served as buffer regions, so that wandering tribes would not create incidents.

The extension of his realm, however, led to serious economic problems. The annual income of the kingdom (Ibn Saud's income) at the time was about $750,000, to which was added a $30,000 subsidy from the British. For a state that had just doubled its responsibilities, however, the income was patently insufficient, and to augment it in Arabia seemed exceedingly diffi-cult. In the winter of 1923 Ibn Saud went again to Ukair to meet with agents of the Anglo-Persian Oil Company and the Eastern General Syndicate. They bid against each other for an oil concession in Ibn Saud's lands. He was not much impressed, but needing money desperately he gave the conces-sion to the Eastern General for a rental of $10,000 a year. Interestingly enough, only two years' rental was paid, then, upon the advice of geologists who explored the al-Hasa desert, the concession was abandoned.

King of Saudi Arabia

In the autumn of 1923 Great Britain held a conference at Kuwayt of all the Arab amirs, shaykhs, and sultans under her subsidy. They were told that payments would stop at the end of March 1924; a lump-sum full payment was handed them forthwith. From that moment they became free agents. But at the same conference the British delineated the frontiers among the several Arab states, insisting among other points that Ibn Saud must relin-quish Khurma and Turaba to Husayn. Ibn Saud left the conference refusing to accept the frontier decision.

Ibn Saud had hardly reached Riyadh when Husayn arranged to be pro-claimed caliph. The announcement shocked Ibn Saud, who felt that the Holy Places of Islam were being defiled by a presumptuous person. At the same time it undoubtedly revealed to him a sure escape from his poverty. Drive Husayn from the Hijaz and obtain the pilgrimage income for himself! In August Ibn Saud struck his second blow against Husayn. The battle was at al-Taif, and in October Ibn Saud occupied Mecca. Husayn fled to Jidda and abdicated in favor of his eldest son, Ali. Husayn then took up residence in Akaba until the British conveyed him to Cyprus. There he suffered a stroke and lived on, a broken man, until he died in 1930 in Amman at the court of his son. Ibn Saud could have pressed on easily and defeated Ali at Jidda, but he realized that this might involve the powers. Obtaining no aid from England, Ali surrendered to Ibn Saud in 1925 and went to Baghdad to live at his brother's court.

Ibn Saud was now master of all of Arabia except for Aden, Yemen, Asir, and the various shaykhdoms of the Persian Gulf area. The people of the Hijaz declared him King of the Hijaz, a title which he added to that of Sultan of Nejd. The Wahhabis in taking Mecca destroyed a number of the shrines that they considered the works of the devil, and Ibn Saud refur-bished the Holy Places Husayn had permitted to fall into disrepair. In 1926 he held an Islamic congress in the Hijaz. This congress had a double role:

to bring Islamic leaders of all schools of thought from all parts of the Muslim world to see him and the administration he was inaugurating in the Hijaz, and to allow his own Wahhabi theologians to rub elbows with Muslim divines of other training and experience. The congress might also popularize the pilgrimage, which now became Ibn Saud's greatest source of income.

Abd al-Aziz ibn Saud was a born leader. He inspired confidence. He was just and honorable in his administration and prompt in his decisions and actions. Arrogance was foreign to his character. He observed the Wahhabi code; yet social innovations were not blindly obstructed just because they were novel, but carefully appraised and judged accordingly. The introduction of the telephone and the radio into Arabia, for instance, was bitterly opposed by the archconservatives among his Wahhabis, who argued that these instruments must be agents of the devil since they could carry the voice so far. Ibn Saud neatly disputed that contention by pointing out that these instruments would bring the word of God and that one would be able to hear worthy divines of the al-Azhar read the Koran. The telephone and the radio came to Arabia.

Life around Ibn Saud, whether he was at al-Taif, Mecca, Medina, or Riyadh, was simple, democratic, and direct. He lent a sympathetic ear to the troubles of the poorest of his subjects. The business of government was dispatched with simplicity and efficiency. A trusted friend of long standing, Abdallah Sulaiman, served as finance minister, treasurer, and paymaster, and on most occasions kept the state's money in his bedroom at the palace in Riyadh. At one time he commented on his anxiety over the risk involved when the balance rose to $50,000 in cash.

The military power of Ibn Saud rested on a combination of factors, the chief of which was the organization of the *Ikhwan* (Brotherhood). In Muslim history such groups were important in Morocco, the Sudan, Iran, Turkey, and many other places. Ibn Saud's founding of Ikhwan communities starting in 1912 proved most significant in his rise to power. The first brotherhood was established around the desert wells of Artawiya, where the fighting bedouin were partially settled. Its motive was partly economic. Ibn Saud provided funds for a mosque, religious schools for reading and writing, wells, agricultural irrigation, arms, and ammunition. The settlement was a religio-socio-military camp and became the prototype of several hundred such towns. From the brotherhoods Ibn Saud received his most devoted soldiers and the necessary stiffening for the regular bedouin levies and volunteers that made his army and expeditions to Yemen, Asir, and "the frontiers" of Iraq and Transjordan so feared and so successful.

Of equal significance was the extension of Ibn Saud's power over the bedouin tribes of the Hijaz and other provinces coming under his rule. Traditionally independent and subject only to their own tribal customs, they rebelled against Ibn Saud's justice, military conscription, peace, and taxation. When Ibn Saud learned of a particularly serious raid committed by the Bani Harb, he fell upon their encampment and subdued them completely. He tied other tribes to his rule by the holding of suitable hostages at his court and by judicious marriages for himself and his sons. In 1932 the official name of the state was changed from the Kingdom of the Hijaz and of the Nejd and its Dependencies to the Kingdom of Saudi Arabia. At that time it comprised most of Arabia.

After the occupation of Jidda Ibn Saud in 1925 arranged with Sir Gilbert Clayton the treaties of Bahra and of Hadda, which defined on paper the frontiers with Iraq and Transjordan. However, no mention was made of Maan and Akaba, which Ibn Saud claimed since they had heretofore been incorporated in the Hijaz, but which the British joined to Transjordan. In 1927 Sir Gilbert returned to Arabia and the treaty of Jidda was signed. Great Britain recognized Ibn Saud as a sovereign and independent ruler. He pledged "to maintain friendly and peaceful relations" with Kuwayt, Bahrayn, Qatar, and the Oman Coast—all of which were under the protection of Great Britain. The treaty of Jidda set a precedent, and within a few years Ibn Saud was recognized by and had similar treaties with Italy, France, Russia, Turkey, Iran, and other states that had Muslim subjects.

The problem of Asir troubled Ibn Saud for many years. After the death of Muhammad Idrisi in 1923 the heirs mismanaged affairs and quarreled continually. Already Ibn Saud had won victories in the highlands of Asir, and when Imam Yahya of Yemen took the port of Hodeida and the region of Tihama, the Idrisi called upon Ibn Saud for help. Having become a protectorate in 1930, while virtually an integral part of Ibn Saud's Arabia, Asir was divided. Imam Yahya's failure to curb his aggression in Asir brought hostilities in 1934, and Ibn Saud won a quick and crushing victory. In the treaty of al-Taif peace was established magnanimously on the basis proposed before the fighting. Imam Yahya retained the plain of Tihama and the valuable port of Hodeida; there were no reparations, indemnities, or payments. Ibn Saud had shown his authority and his power; he had also proved to the Arabs his leniency, his honor, his generosity, and his wisdom. He now had stature among the Arabs.

Discovery of Oil
Life in Arabia might have gone along smoothly and comfortably almost indefinitely, had not the world-wide depression of the early 1930s upset Ibn Saud's economy. The scale of government operations and Ibn Saud's personal expenditures depended upon the pilgrimage traffic, which in the late 1920s had amounted to over 100,000 visitors each year. In 1931, however, the traffic dropped to 80,000; in 1932, to 40,000. The Kingdom of Saudi Arabia could no longer meet its bills.

Through the advice of H. St. John B. Philby, an English Arabist, a convert to Islam, and after 1930 a member of Ibn Saud's privy council, Karl S. Twitchell, an American mining engineer who had been exploring in Yemen, was employed to search for oil and other mineral resources in Saudi Arabia. His expenses were paid by the American philanthropist Charles R. Crane, of World War I King-Crane Commission fame. First visiting Jidda in 1931, Twitchell examined the Hijaz for water resources and returned a pessimistic report. However, he suggested the possibilities of oil and minerals. While Twitchell was exploring the breadth of the country in 1933, Ibn Saud gave a concession to the Standard Oil Company of California and received an advance of 30,000 gold sovereigns. The concession ran for sixty years, and a royalty of four gold shillings per ton of oil would be paid to Saudi Arabia.

Almost immediately the California Arabian Standard Oil Company (CASOC), owned equally by Standard Oil of California and the Texas Company, was formed. Mapping, geologic surveying, and drilling in al-Hasa province were initiated by engineers who came across to the mainland from Bahrayn, where oil had been found in 1932. No oil in commercial quantities was found at the depth at which oil had been discovered in Bahrayn. However, with the deepening of well number seven at Dhahran in 1938 oil was found in quantity. The first oil was shipped in November to Bahrayn. In accordance with the concession Ibn Saud received another £50,000 in gold. Piers were quickly constructed, and the first tanker was filled directly at Ras Tanura in May 1939, Ibn Saud turning the first valve. Exploration spread. Before World War II other producing wells were located north of Dhahran and another forty miles west of Abqaiq. When the war came 12,000 barrels were going daily to Bahrayn, and Saudi Arabia was considered as a future important oil-producing state. However, oil production was not expanded in Saudi Arabia during the war for lack of men and equipment.

At the time Twitchell was looking for oil he had, as a good mining engineer, his eye out for minerals, especially gold. After trials and disappointments gold was found between Mecca and Medina at Mahab Dhahab. A company was established in 1934 to work the mine, probably one of King Solomon's. Called the Saudi Arabian Mining Company, 15 percent was owned by Saudi nationals, and the rest by the American Smelting and Refining Company, the American Cyanamid Corporation, and several Britishers. The government received as royalties 5 percent of the gross value of all metals recovered. At the outbreak of the war Ibn Saud was receiving several hundred thousand dollars a year from the gold mines.

World War II

With the outbreak of World War II and the fall of the pilgrimage trade after Italy entered the war Ibn Saud was reduced to desperate financial straits. In 1940 CASOC advanced several million dollars against future royalties. In 1941 Ibn Saud requested a further advance of $6 million, declaring that without the sum the state he had built would disintegrate. Since the future of CASOC was obviously at stake, a proposal was made to the American government to grant the sum against future oil deliveries. President Roosevelt directed the bid to the British government, which began advancing sizable sums to Saudi Arabia in 1941. By the spring of 1944 Ibn Saud was over $50 million in debt to London, and the end was not in sight. After a great deal of debate in Washington $34 million in American lend-lease was made available to Saudi Arabia.

In 1944 the American army requested the building of a refinery at Ras Tanura; compliance strained the finances of the company, which by now had changed its name to Arabian American Oil Company (Aramco). In 1945 an underwater pipeline was built to Bahrayn, enabling the flow of oil in Saudi Arabia to be increased. Royalties paid by Aramco to Ibn Saud began to obviate the need for the subsidies from the West.

The total income of the Saudi government jumped from about $7 million in 1939 to over $200 million by 1953. Because of inadequate banking facilities and Wahhabi views on loans, much of the cash journeyed to Cairo, where it was turned into luxury articles of small bulk that could be easily shipped by small dhows to the Arabian coast. Lavish living and excessive incomes for the family of Ibn Saud and his friends became the custom, and a great part of the income of the state was squandered.

Expansion of Oil Production

In the postwar era Saudi Arabia became entirely dependent upon oil royalties. Toward the end of the war the demand for petroleum products in the Mediterranean became staggering, and the need for a pipeline from Dhahran to the Levant coast prompted the American government to suggest that it buy into Aramco and finance the pipeline. Private oil companies raised a violent storm, but it appeared that the European market for oil in the recovery period would be insatiable, and it was imperative that more pipelines be built from the oilfields to the Mediterranean. Aramco was compelled to seek additional capital for the construction; in 1946 arrangements were made for Standard Oil of New Jersey and Socony-Vacuum to acquire 30 and 10 percent, respectively, of Aramco stock.

French petroleum interests brought suit against this action. They alleged that it violated the Red Line agreement of 1928, which stipulated that oil companies participating in the Iraq Petroleum Company would not engage separately in oil production in Arabia. Nevertheless, work on the pipeline was started, and steel pipe began to be shipped in 1947. All work on the line ceased during the Palestine War. Syria, Lebanon, and Jordan declared that the line would not be permitted as long as the United States supported the partition of Palestine and the creation of Israel. Ibn Saud, however, announced that he would not revoke the American oil concessions, and work was resumed. The oil companies reached a settlement with the French, and thereupon organized the Trans-Arabian Pipe Line Company. Over half a billion dollars was expended between 1948 and 1953 in constructing the TAP-line and developing new fields and facilities for Aramco. In 1950 the 1,068 mile TAP-line was completed, and 300,000 to 500,000 barrels a day began to flow from Dhahran to Sidon. New production was brought in every year; by 1955 oil was being produced at a daily rate exceeding one million barrels. In 1943 the daily rate had been 15,000 barrels; in 1946, 165,000 barrels; in 1950, 500,000 barrels.

The original concession to Aramco provided for royalties of four gold shillings per ton of oil produced. During the war and in the years immediately following gold sovereigns commanded a high premium in the Middle East, and the question of the equivalent of four gold shillings was hotly debated. At the official exchange rate a gold sovereign was worth about $8.25, which made the royalty 22 cents per barrel. But sovereigns were bought and sold in the open markets in the Middle East at twice the official rate. In 1948 Aramco agreed to value the gold sovereign at $12.00, which raised the royalties to 32 cents per barrel.

As production increased and Aramco profits began to swell, Ibn Saud pressed for greater returns. At the end of 1950 a new concession was signed. It gave Saudi Arabia: four gold shillings, at the official $8.25 rate, per ton; a 20 percent tax on Aramco profits before United States taxes; and certain customs duties and taxes or 50 percent of Aramco profits after United States taxes, whichever sum was the greater, an arrangement first devised by Venezuela. Made retroactive to January 1, 1950, the new formula increased the 1950 royalties from $60 million to $90 million. By 1956 the payments topped $250 million annually. The announcement of these terms led to the breakdown of oil discussions in Iran and a change in the rates in Iraq. In fact, the Aramco-Saudi Arabia concession terms in 1950 established the general pattern of royalties throughout the Middle East.

For the next several years oil policies and arrangements remained steadfast, except for a 40 percent increase in production in 1951. By 1954, largely as a result of a near shutdown in Iran, oil exports were 75 percent above the 1950 level. The rising income posed many new problems to government leaders who, at this critical juncture, no longer had the accustomed stern hand over them.

Ibn Saud's Sons

Abd al-Aziz ibn Abd al-Rahman ibn Faysal Al Saud died on November 9, 1953, and was immediately succeeded by the eldest of his thirty-five living sons, Saud ibn Abd al-Aziz Al Faysal Al Saud. For a number of years the aged Ibn Saud had been afflicted with arthritis and was approaching blindness. In 1933 Prince Saud had been declared heir apparent and began to participate in governmental activities. Other sons shared duties of administration; the most prominent of these was the second living son, Prince Faysal. In the king's last years definite ministries of government were established, and a formal cabinet was organized. The new King Saud served as his own prime minister. Prince Faysal was declared heir to the throne and continued his work in foreign affairs.

Various developments revealed that a new man was king. In 1954 Abdallah Sulaiman resigned. He had been Ibn Saud's closest adviser for a quarter of a century on all matters; as finance minister he had restricted expenditures by the princes. Shortly thereafter, H. St. John B. Philby, an adviser to Ibn Saud since 1930 and a special friend of Prince Faysal, was expelled from

Saudi Arabia for "unfriendly" acts. Corruption spread rapidly, especially in the awarding of contracts. Many Saudi officials were able to buy estates in Egypt or apartment houses in Beirut, and the construction of palaces in al-Taif and other spots in Arabia proceeded apace.

Problems of finance, bitter Arab rivalry, intense Arab nationalism, internal social upheaval, international politics, traditional nepotism, and the impact of modern living produced such dire conflicts in King Saud's mind that he became unequal to the task of governing. Suddenly, in March 1958, after a family conference in Riyadh, King Saud assumed the role of a "constitutional" monarch. The reins of government were awarded to Prince Faysal, who was generally acknowledged as a firmer and more talented administrator than his brother.

Faysal ibn Abd al-Aziz Al Faysal Al Saud was born in Riyadh in 1904 and grew up in the household of his maternal grandfather, where he was toughened in the ways of desert warriors. As early as 1919 he undertook various missions for his father, becoming viceroy of the Hijaz and foreign minister in 1926. Ibn Saud once likened Faysal to the desert and commented that just when you thought you had dominance over him he slipped through your fingers like a handful of sand. Though Faysal had traveled widely, he remained austere and simple in his personal tastes. He was known for his fairness, integrity, and dependability.

Prince Faysal, once in power, dismissed the new minister of finance; removed Prince Fahd, King Saud's son, who was defense minister; and fired five of the king's foreign advisers. A stronger hand was at the helm.

The question of highest priority for Faysal was how to cope with the ineptness and prodigality of King Saud in a society in which the king's wish was law. Faysal had promised his father many years before that he would never raise a hand against his older brother. When, in December 1960, King Saud reasserted his authority, Faysal dutifully stepped aside. The drastic measures adopted by Faysal to end corruption and waste, to institue efficiency and tighten authority, and to modernize the state and society had irritated many influential figures and depressed the economy.

King Saud's return did not meliorate the situation. Numerous pro-Nasser groups were coalescing into substantial factions, and in 1962 Prince Talal and three other brothers left for Beirut publicly censuring King Saud for idleness and mismanagement. The revolt in Yemen in September opened the eyes of even the most conservative elements as to what could happen at home and they called for Prince Faysal to run the government. Refusing to be king, he again took over as prime minister, forming a new cabinet, and removing from office all of King Saud's sons. In an address to the nation Faysal outlined a new program calling for: the drafting of a body of fundamental law; the organization of a consultative council; the establishment of a ministry of justice; the abolition of slavery; and rapid economic and social development. Faysal began to establish a more progressive regime, and Prince Talal and the others returned to Riyadh in 1963, forgiven for their defection.

King Saud failed miserably in a second bid to regain his powers. On November 2, 1964, he renounced his right to rule and left Saudi Arabia. Reported to have very large sums on deposit in Swiss banks, and continually in need of medical attention, Saud lived in Vienna, Paris, Cairo, and Athens, where he died in 1969, a pitiful figure. Faysal was recognized as king. In 1965, the popular fifty-two-year-old Prince Khalid, another son of Ibn Saud, was named deputy prime minister, crown prince, and first heir to the throne.

For a decade King Faysal managed the affairs of Saudi Arabia astutely. In spite of the billions that began to pour into the treasury in the 1970s and the undreamed of budgetary surpluses, King Faysal stood fast in the conservative management of affairs. Faysal gathered his brothers about him and drew heavily on family talents. In 1967 Minister of the Interior Prince Fahd, a brilliant administrator and facile negotiator, was named second deputy prime minister and second in line to succeed to the throne. Prince Sultan, with Prince Turki as his deputy, was named minister of defense and aviation, and Faysal's son Prince Saud was appointed vice governor for planning affairs.

Following the death of Egypt's President Nasser in 1970, King Faysal became the dominant figure among the Arabs as well as the leader of Islamic society. An avowed enemy of communism and Zionism, he was ready to use his influence, power, and resources against both. His assassination on March 25, 1975, at the hands of a disgruntled nephew, saddened the Arab peoples and shocked the world. The trial of the unhappy prince uncovered no conspiracy; three months later he was beheaded publicly, as tradition demanded.

Within hours of Faysal's murder the council of royal princes installed Prince Khalid ibn Abd al-Aziz Al Faysal Al Saud as king, prime minister, and foreign minister of Saudi Arabia. Prince Fahd became crown prince, first deputy prime minister, and minister of the interior; Prince Abdallah was named second deputy prime minister and commander of the national guard; Prince Sultan remained minister of defense and aviation; and Prince Saud, Faysal's son, was given the important post of minister of state for foreign affairs. King Khalid, now the oldest of Ibn Saud's living sons, was born in Riyadh in 1912. Khalid's mother was from the Jiluwi branch of the Saud family, which made him doubly royal. Shunning public life as much as possible and loving the desert, he was one of the lesser-known princes. Many assumed he would be overshadowed by his aggressive brother Prince Fahd, but King Khalid, extremely popular with the Arab tribesmen, rapidly learned to wield his power in a quiet but forceful manner. Shortly after he ascended the throne he granted amnesty to all political prisoners. Then, in May 1975, he delegated to Fahd authority over the daily affairs of government. A few months later he appointed a consultative council, a kind of parliament, and in October he formed a new cabinet of twenty-five ministers, including five of his brothers as leaders and his nephew Prince Saud holding the foreign affairs portfolio. The skill he and Prince Saud demon-

strated in bringing Syria and Egypt together in 1976 over the volatile
Lebanese question gave rise to the belief that King Khalid was firmly on the
throne.

The Oil Boom and OPEC

Each year after 1956 the production of oil increased beyond all predictions.
At first a daily average of 1 million barrels was a yearly goal frequently
reached; in 1962 it soared to 1.5 million barrels daily; and in 1966 topped
2.5 million barrels a day, making Saudi Arabia then the fourth largest world
producer, after the United States, the U.S.S.R., and Venezuela. Offshore
discoveries, added to continuous exploration and new finds, more than
maintained the quantities of proven oil reserves, which were 50 billion
barrels in 1960, 81 billion by 1967, and 175 billion ten years later. In the
1950s Aramco surrendered its claims to the western half of the country, and
in 1963 gave up additional areas at the request of the government, which
wanted to negotiate with other interests.

Aramco held the concession for the exploitation of oil in Saudi Arabia's
half of the neutral zone adjoining Iraq and the Getty Oil Company possessed rights for the neutral zone facing Kuwait, where operations produced significant quantities of oil and royalties for Saudi Arabia. In order
not to give Americans a monopoly, King Saud granted in 1957 to the
Arabian Oil Company of Japan the right to explore for oil in the waters of
the Persian Gulf off the shores of the neutral zone, with Saudi Arabia to
receive 56 percent of the profits. This concession raised serious questions
because the states bordering on the gulf had established no understanding
with respect to territorial limits and offshore claims. In 1965 the several
Persian Gulf states accepted the idea that offshore rights could be extended
to the middle of the gulf.

One of the difficult problems for Saudi Arabia as well as for the oil companies has been the vagaries of supply and demand, made more complex by
new discoveries of oil in many new regions, and subject to the wish of each
nation to be self-sufficient in petroleum products, becoming if possible an
exporter to earn foreign exchange. Though increases in world oil consumption have not always kept pace with production, any reduction in exports
has hurt Saudi Arabia's budget, since it is tied to oil exports (which often
account for over 90 percent of revenues). Moreover, larger exports from
one country too frequently meant that the international oil companies
would curtail production in another country. To meet this challenge Abdallah al-Tariqi, director of petroleum and mineral affairs of Saudi Arabia,
initiated in 1960 at Baghdad the Organization of Petroleum Exporting
Countries (OPEC), composed of Iran, Iraq, Kuwait, Saudi Arabia, and Venezuela. OPEC sought to stabilize world prices, obtain reasonable profits for
oil companies, assure a voice in all oil decisions, guarantee that consumers
would not be cut off from supplies, and boycott companies not cooperating
with OPEC. Since its formation, Libya, Algeria, Indonesia, Qatar, Nigeria,

Abu Dhabi, Gabon, and Ecuador have joined, making it by 1973 a powerful force in the world.

Initially, OPEC attempted to protect its members, each one a weak developing nation, against the machinations of an informal cartel of the international oil companies, sometimes referred to as "the seven sisters." In the mid-1970s, however, the tables were turned. The oil companies, through the nationalization or purchase of oil-producing resources by the host country, had become subservient to the OPEC members, while the petroleum importing states were reeling from OPEC price fixings and increases that were sucking billions of dollars from their economies into the treasuries of the oil producers.

In 1968 Kuwayt, Libya, and Saudi Arabia joined together in the Organization of Arab Petroleum Exporting Countries (OAPEC), with the stipulation that membership was reserved to Arab states whose oil production constituted a major part of the nation's economy. Because of their almost total dependence upon their petroleum resources, they saw the need to enter into the oil business on their own. Immediately, Shaykh Ahmad Zaki Yamani, Saudi oil minister, pressed for Aramco to accept active participation by Saudi Arabia in producing, refining, transporting, and marketing oil and its derivatives. OAPEC had deemed 20 percent a prudent beginning. Five years later the Saudi government bought 25 percent of Aramco. With the purchase of another 40 percent in 1974, the government owned 60 percent of Aramco at a cost of $1.2 billion. Negotiations to obtain the remaining 40 percent for an additional $800 million were concluded in 1976. The settlement allowed the former owners of Aramco to market 80 percent of the Saudi oil production, receiving a fee of 21 cents per barrel for their services. Furthermore, they would, for a consideration, continue their role in exploration and expand facilities for refining, pumping, loading, and shipping petroleum products.

Except for 1967, when oil revenues faltered and the markets were dislocated because of the June War, the closing of the Suez Canal, and a temporary freezing of shipments to Great Britain and the United States, Saudi oil production broke one record after another. World economies were prospering and their petroleum requirements mounted. By the end of 1971 output was over 5 million barrels per day and in 1973 reached 6 million. Already the year before in Washington, Yamani had announced the ability and willingness of Saudi Arabia to produce 12 million barrels a day to supply the needs of the United States. In 1974 Saudi Arabia passed the U.S.S.R. and the United States and became the world's leading producer, averaging 8.3 million barrels a day. Despite the record production, proven reserves increased each year as exploration brought in new fields.

Oil consumption rose rapidly throughout the world, and demand was outrunning supply. Pressure on prices brought seventeen oil companies in February 1971 to a historic meeting in Tehran to meet the demands of OPEC to pay to the six Persian Gulf members an additional $10 billion over the next five years. After the devaluation of the dollar that summer, OPEC called for upward adjustments of prices and an 8.5 percent increase went into effect early in 1972. With no end of the seller's market in sight, OPEC raised prices about 12 percent in June 1973. During the Arab-Israeli war, in mid-October 1973, Saudi Arabia, four other Arab countries, and Iran jacked up the price of crude oil another 17 percent; in December the posted price for Saudi Arabian light crude, the universal standard, was raised 11 percent more. Another 10 percent was levied in 1975. When at the end of 1976 OPEC voted 10 percent more, Saudi Arabia balked, and Yamani declared that the Saudis would up the rates only 5 percent and would boost production to 12 million barrels per day, if necessary, to prevent world prices and those of other OPEC members from exceeding that figure. In 1977 rates went up another 5 percent to keep Saudi prices in line with other OPEC members. However, Yamani declared that oil prices would remain frozen until the end of 1978.

At the end of 1974 the average posted price of Saudi Arabian crude oil stood between $11 and $12 a barrel, and the auctioned price often went higher. The astonishing leap in prices disturbed world economic and financial relationships, spurring a world-wide recession. Oil demand softened and Saudi exports declined; yet with the heightened prices, Saudi Arabian budgets escalated accordingly, jumping from $2.5 billion in 1971–1972 to $32.5 billion in 1976–1977. Unallocated surpluses rose to $12 billion or more each year.

Financial Problems
One of the vexing problems in Saudi Arabia was that of finance and currency. Since there was no paper money, the medium of exchange had been foreign gold coins and local silver coins, and Ibn Saud failed to establish any stable ratio of value between the two. Gold coins were almost exclusively English George V sovereigns, which were the generally recognized standard of value in Saudi Arabia. Silver riyals were first circulated in 1933, and a concerted attempt was made to maintain a parity between gold and silver. However, the world decline of silver prices and the abandonment of the gold standard by England and the United States played havoc with the exchange rates. World War II raised black-market rates of gold from $35 to over $85 an ounce.

In 1952 an American financial mission reorganized the currency situation at the request of Ibn Saud. New Saudi gold sovereigns of $8.24 value were issued, a monetary agency was established, and an exchange rate of forty silver riyals to a Saudi sovereign was fixed. The great value of the monetary agency rested upon its ability to stabilize the value of the currency by buying and selling riyals and foreign exchange on the money markets in Jidda and Dammam. Furthermore, after the new royalty rates were fixed in 1950 more of Saudi Arabia's income was received in sterling and other soft currencies, the disposal of which was more easily arranged by the agency, which took on the aspects of a central bank.

The agency was also able to assist in the preparation of a budget. The first budget, of $55 million, was drawn up for the fiscal year 1948, but Ibn Saud ignored it, and no budget was published again until 1952. Budgets have been presented each year since. In 1956 the budget approximated $300 million, but there is no certainty that the government adhered to it, since a distinction between the public treasury and the private purse of the king and the royal family had not been finely drawn. The accounts of the government were usually balanced by the following year's royalties and normally ran a deficit in the neighborhood of $50 million.

In 1957 Saudi Arabia, troubled fiscally, joined the International Monetary Fund and the International Bank for Reconstruction and Development. Deficits and the irresponsible spending habits of the royal family brought matters to a climax in March 1958. At a full family council Prince Faysal, nominal first minister, was handed complete authority over the internal, foreign, and financial policies of the state. Spending was curbed, and national budgets were expected to have more significance in the future.

Faysal ran the state along tight financial lines. He decided that his first task was to observe the balanced budget and retire the debt. Luxury imports including automobiles were forbidden and the civil list for the royal family was greatly reduced. Princes complained and King Saud, unable to curb his style of living or proverbial generosity, saw his personal debts rise in 1959 from $8.4 million to $31.6 million. King Saud rejected Faysal's budget at the end of 1960, when he reassumed his full powers of personal rule. Again budgets were ignored and debts mounted. How long this situation could have prevailed is difficult to guess, for the civil war in Yemen brought many of the princes and the tribal leaders to their senses. When Faysal was forced upon Saud again, he set the 1963 budget at $550 million and promised to have the public debt fully discharged by the end of that year. As king, his budget remained in balance.

Currency in circulation reached unprecedented levels—over a billion riyals in 1964, a figure that had doubled in five years. Faced with inconveniences from the sheer bulk of coins, the government had for a number of years allowed the Saudi Arabian Monetary Agency to sell receipts to pilgrims in meeting local expenses. In a very short time, these pilgrims' receipts came to serve as a medium of exchange, and the monetary agency issued them as currency. Still, the gold and foreign exchange cover was maintained and the value of the riyal held firm on world exchanges at 4.5 to the U.S. dollar.

After the temporary reduction in oil shipments at the time of the June 1967 war, income turned up, and the usual yearly gain in the budget of 10 to 12 percent was maintained until 1971, when the budget jumped to $2.4 billion, more than 60 percent over the previous year. An income tax had been introduced by 1970. Better oil prices allowed more spending for education, public health, communications, economic development, and defense, which usually was allocated 25 percent of the budget. The new wealth changed Saudi Arabia's standard of living almost beyond recognition.

In 1972 income ran far ahead of budgeted expenditures; most of the surpluses were invested or held on deposit in the West. The budgets for 1975, 1976, and 1977 reached $32 billion, and such large amounts flowed into the monetary agency that Saudi Arabian reserves were, after those of West Germany, the largest in the world. Aid to foreign countries at the end of 1975 stood at nearly $5 billion. Saudi Arabia's enormous bank deposits and investments in the United States, West Germany, Great Britain, Switzerland, and other Western nations concerned world money managers about the effects of sudden transfers of capital. Saudi Arabian leaders became fearful that some European industrial economies would collapse. To forestall this, Saudi Arabia in December 1976 held fast at the OPEC meeting in Qatar for only a 5 percent oil price increase.

Military Forces

For all of Ibn Saud's character and personality, he never for a moment dropped his guard or forgot that his position rested on military power. In 1947 a British army mission came to train his forces in the use of more modern weapons. And in 1951 Saudi Arabia signed a mutual-defense assistance agreement with the United States for various types of equipment, including eighteen tanks. The most powerful military base in that part of the Middle East was located at Dhahran. Here, toward the close of World War II, the United States constructed a mighty airfield and installations from which planes could control much of the Middle East and bomb strategic spots in the U.S.S.R. American rights to the base were discussed in 1949 and extended until June 1951, when a five-year lease was signed. In 1956 Saudi Arabia requested that the United States pay an annual rental of $50 million for Dhahran; in 1957, during King Saud's visit to Washington, a five-year renewal was authorized. In exchange the United States promised to train a small Saudi navy, organize and instruct a Saudi air force at Dhahran, and expand the army school at al-Kharj. However, King Saud informed the United States that the lease for the base would not be renewed. In 1962 the Dhahran base was relinquished to Saudi Arabia and another vestige of World War II was removed.

The outbreak of civil war in Yemen in the autumn of 1962 reemphasized the military aspects of life in Saudi Arabia, as the United Arab Republic supported the Yemeni republican forces under al-Sallal while Imam Muhammad al-Badr and the royalists sought protection from Saudi Arabia. In the northeast, Kuwayt looked to Saudi Arabia to help ward off the danger of invasion from Iraq. Jet fighters were quietly invited back from the United States in 1963, American paratroopers participated in training the Saudi Paratrooper Corps, and a British military mission arrived to advise the Saudi army. Antitank missiles were acquired from England, arms from France, and a modern air defense system complex was installed. Aid went to al-Badr, more arms came from the United States, and a new military base was built in the southwest near the Yemeni border after Egyptian air raids in 1965 on the Saudi towns of Jizan and Najran. The military seriousness of the civil war in Yemen and Nasser's involvement there, in Aden, and in the South Arabian Federation were impressed upon King Faysal, especially by the frequent bombing of Saudi towns and by Nasser's accusation that Faysal was supporting a reactionary regime in Yemen.

Saudi Arabia felt weak and vulnerable. The value of her oil and the size of her proven reserves were a great temptation to many. King Faysal relied on his brother Prince Sultan, the minister of defense and aviation, to obtain arms wherever possible to protect against internal enemies or outside attacks. Upon the British withdrawal from the Persian Gulf in 1971 and the opening of diplomatic relations between the Soviet Union and the newly established United Arab Amirates, King Faysal became doubly concerned over potential leftist actions in the region. He had been aiding Sultan Qabus of Oman against Chinese-supported guerrilla rebels in Dhufar, reportedly channeling CIA money to Qabus. In 1972 intensive military maneuvers were held in the southwest. Preparedness against attacks or coup attempts anywhere in the region was the constant aim; as Iran, Israel, and other possible enemies acquired vast supplies of sophisticated weapons an arms race began. In 1973 Saudi Arabian military purchases topped $1 billion.

After King Khalid succeeded to the throne in 1975, Prince Fahd flew to England and France where he pledged $1 billion to each to bolster their faltering economies as advance payments for arms shipments. Going on to Washington, he paid $750 million for jet planes, parts, and training. By the spring of 1976 Saudi Arabia had in the previous twelve months spent $4 billion in the United States for military goods; in the following year more than $4 billion was scheduled for military expenditures in the United States. Not to be dependent on one source, Saudi Arabia in 1977 sealed a four-year arms contract with Great Britain, at a cost of £500 million, for training and support service for the Saudi air force and for building runways, hangars, and radar sites. It seemed that the military could escalate its requirements to almost any heights, especially when similar amounts of arms were flowing to Iran, Iraq, and Israel, and the Soviet Union still evidenced great interest in the Persian Gulf region.

Saudi Relations in the Middle East
Saudi Arabia's wealth and her control of the Muslim Holy Places on her soil guaranteed respect from the other Middle Eastern states. That esteem was promoted even more widely by Ibn Saud's remission of taxes and special charges upon those making the pilgrimage to Mecca. In 1953 the number of visitors rose to 120,000. There had been a time, not too remote, when the fees from these pilgrims kept the state solvent. What a change the oil made!

Saudi Arabia, one of the first members of the Arab League, steadfastly participated in its deliberations, although she never took until 1973 the leading role that her wealth, prestige, and position as custodian of the Holy

Places might warrant. During the Palestine war, Saudi Arabia, not having a frontier contiguous with Palestine, did not send troops or take an active part. She cooperated in the boycott of Israel, however, and for many years did not permit Jews to land at the Dhahran airport. In 1946 Ibn Saud protested to President Truman against the American position on the partition of Palestine, and the president tried to assuage the Saudi Arabians by awarding the Legion of Merit to Ibn Saud and Crown Prince Saud. In 1948 Ibn Saud became so incensed over the American recognition of Israel and the dishonoring of the pledge given him that he refused a $15 million Export-Import Bank loan.

In 1953 a serious dispute arose with Great Britain over the possession of the Buraimi oases. Britain contended that the Buraimi oases were a part of Trucial Oman, but Ibn Saud also claimed them, and Saudi forces held the oases. The question remained unsettled until 1974 when a division was made between Saudi Arabia and Abu Dhabi of the newly formed United Arab Amirates.

Saudi Arabia supported Egypt in her nationalization of the Suez Canal Company, although halting the flow of Saudi oil via the canal was a serious blow to Saudi finances. During the Sinai war, Saudi Arabia ordered a general mobilization and called on all Arabs to oppose the attack. Diplomatic relations with the aggressors were severed, and King Saud took a strong stand in favor of Arab nationalism. Yet, through the entire Suez affair Saud was vexed that Egypt had seized the canal without consultations with other Arab states. He feared, however, to take a position in opposition to Nasser, since a growing number of Arab nationalists in Saudi Arabia equated Arab nationalism and Nasserism.

Throughout the period of the union of Egypt and Syria in the United Arab Republic, and the vagaries of Nasserism in Iraq, Jordan, and Syria, Saudi Arabia pursued a neutral course, adhering to the principle that one Arab state must not interfere in the internal affairs of another. King Saud protested to Iraq over her threats against Kuwayt in 1961, and dispatched troops there to safeguard Kuwayt's newly declared sovereignty.

In 1962 Saud and Faysal, condemning the United Arab Republic's intervention in Yemen on the side of the republican regime, broke diplomatic relations with Nasser. Faysal stoutly believed that the republican regime in Yemen would collapse within a few hours if Egyptian forces were withdrawn. Faysal initiated costly and decisive steps to strengthen his own military forces to show Nasser he could not be cowed into abandoning his neighboring Arab state. A military stalemate soon resulted in Yemen. Faysal met twice with Nasser in 1964 and again in 1965, but ceasefires, conferences between the rival parties, and arbitration efforts by Kuwayt were unsuccessful. When Great Britain announced in 1966 that her withdrawal from Aden was fixed for 1968, Nasser could not bring himself to pull his troops from nearby Yemen. Faysal maintained that the Yemeni people should determine their own future. Only in the aftermath of the June 1967 war was Nasser forced to withdraw his forces and permit a compromise.

Saudi Arabia, however, refused to recognize either the Yemen Arab Republic or the Peoples Republic of South Yemen. Relations with both remained strained and border incidents kept the frontiers closed until 1970, when agreements were reached with the Yemen Arab Republic and diplomatic relations were established. Questions were raised about uniting the two Yemens, but King Faysal would agree only on the impossible condition that they become an Islamic state. Under Khalid loans of $420 million were given to the Yemen Arab Republic for development projects and budget balancing. King Khalid and Prince Fahd, wishing to pacify all Saudi borders, in 1976 normalized relations with the Peoples Republic of South Yemen and gave that state a grant of $100 million.

In 1968, when Great Britain announced her intention to give up her bases on Bahrayn and Sharjah and her special privileges in the Persian Gulf, Saudi Arabia understood the need to secure the gulf's stability and peace. She denied Iran's claim to Bahrayn, but after the shah visited Riyadh, Faysal did agree to divide the continental shelf in the gulf with Iran. The seven shaykhdoms of the Trucial Coast began to discuss forming the United Arab Amirates, and King Faysal urged Qatar and Bahrayn to join. He sent his brother Prince Nawaf to tour the amirates to promise aid and encourage their cooperation, even though Saudi Arabia's border with Abu Dhabi was still contested. When the United Arab Amirates was launched in 1971 Saudi Arabia maintained cordial relations. And, since the Amirates did not oppose the move, Saudi Arabia voiced no objection to Iran's occupation of the Tunb islands and Abu Musa. In OAPEC and OPEC the United Arab Amirates supported Saudi Arabia's insistence in 1976 that an oil price increase be limited to 5 percent. Saudi Arabia has also maintained friendly relations with Qatar and Bahrayn.

Saudi Arabia's friendship with Kuwayt goes back to the nineteenth century. Saudi Arabia stood firm when Kuwayt felt threatened by Iraq. In 1970 Saudi Arabia and Kuwayt arranged to divide the Neutral Zone equally into what each termed the "Partitioned Zone." In 1975, after King Faysal's assassination, Prince Fahd flew to Baghdad to mediate the border problems between Kuwayt and Iraq and agreed with Iraq on dividing the Neutral Zone between Saudi Arabia and Iraq.

Saudi Arabia began to take an active role in Arab affairs at the Arab meeting in Khartoum in 1967, when she agreed to give $140 million a year to Egypt and Jordan for their expenses as states facing Israel. In 1969 Faysal emerged as a recognized Arab leader and attended the Arab summit at Rabat and after Nasser's death in 1970 Faysal was active in all Arab matters. He received Yasir Arafat, the Palestinian leader, in Riyadh for conversations in 1970, and declared publicly in 1971 that there could be no peace in the Middle East without Israeli evacuation of Muslim Holy Places in Palestine, withdrawal from 1967 conquests, and recognition of Palestinian rights. In 1973 Faysal was one of the leaders of the oil embargo, reducing Saudi Arabia's production levels and signaling his solidarity with the Arab cause against Israel. Faysal's prestige rose, and Arab leaders found that political decisions not favored with his approval had little appeal. Saudi support for Egypt, Syria, and Jordan was continued in 1974, and an extra $300 million was pledged to Egypt. At the Arab summit meeting in Morocco that year Faysal accepted the Palestine Liberation Organization (PLO) as the representative of the Palestinian people and declared again that there could be no peace in the Middle East until the Arabism of Jerusalem was recognized.

Faysal's policies were continued after his death. In 1975 Prince Fahd resolved Saudi controversies with Iraq and helped to settle the Euphrates water dispute between Syria and Iraq, giving Syria $150 million to help cover expenses in her confrontation with Israel. Massive aid from Arab countries for the relief of Egypt amounted to $2.5 billion with Saudi participation coming to 40 percent. King Khalid and Prince Saud, his foreign minister, brought Syria and Egypt together in 1976 over the civil war in Lebanon, inducing Egypt, Syria, Lebanon, Kuwayt, Saudi Arabia, and the PLO to agree to the creation of an Arab peacekeeping force of 30,000 in Lebanon. Egypt, Syria, and Saudi Arabia managed also to align their positions on a possible settlement with Israel, indicating they would accept the existence of Israel if Israel would recognize Palestinian rights, would withdraw to her pre-1967 frontiers, and would accept Arab control of Islamic Holy Places in Jerusalem.

The strong Islamic traditions established in Saudi Arabia by Ibn Saud were preserved by Faysal, who expressed sorrow at the annexation of the Muslim parts of Jerusalem by Israel in 1967 and who repeatedly avowed his desire to pray at the Holy Places there. Believing that the 375,000 pilgrims from eighty countries who came to Mecca in 1969 testified to the strength of Islam, Faysal organized the First Islamic Conference, a summit of all Muslim nations and peoples, which met in Rabat to consider the consequences of the burning of the Al Aqsa Mosque in Jerusalem. The following year the conference was held in Jidda where an Islamic secretariat was established to promote political, economic, and cultural cooperation among the members to regain East Jerusalem.

Development in Saudi Arabia

The considerable influx of money following World War II generated many plans for the improvement of Saudi Arabia. In 1947 a four-year plan to cost $270 million called for the building of railroads, highways, ports, airfields, schools, hospitals, electric-power plants, irrigation systems, and conduits and canals for supplying water to Jidda, Mecca, and other cities. Aramco proved an interested ally in these programs and located able engineers for many of the projects. The railway between Dammam and Riyadh was completed, and in 1955 work was begun on the line to connect Riyadh and Jidda by way of Medina. Plans for an asphalt highway from Jidda to Dammam by way of Mecca, al-Taif, Riyadh, and al-Hasa materialized in 1955; in later years other highways, some built by Italian firms, were restored to facilitate pilgrimage routes from Iraq. The port of Dammam was reconstructed, and three small ports on the Red Sea were improved. To serve as a gateway to Medina the port of Yanbu was developed on the Red Sea; it was opened in 1966 by Prince Khalid.

In 1957 King Saud University in Riyadh was opened, and former palaces in Jidda, Medina, and Riyadh were converted into schools. The Islamic Sharia College was opened in Medina, and the Petroleum and Mining College at Dhahran graduated its first class in 1972. With the assistance of UNESCO a College of Education was begun in Riyadh. Elementary schools appeared in all parts of the kingdom in great numbers; in 1963 alone there were 100 new schools for boys and 62 for girls. The budget for 1968 carried a line of $136 million for education. New construction in Riyadh turned the capital into a bustling city; the spectacular Nasriya Palace was inaugurated in 1957; and all offices of the government were moved there from Jidda. Hospitals were built in numerous places. Each year transportation and communications were vastly improved, financed by ever larger budget appropriations, thereby extending the power of the central government over all sections of the state.

Under Faysal economic development had the highest priority, receiving 40 percent of the budget. Surveys had revealed sizable and commercially valuable deposits of iron, copper, and silver, and the amounts of sulphur obtained from oil were vast. A steel-rolling mill not far from Jidda was opened in 1966. A glass industry was established at Riyadh, and plants for producing sulphur, paint, ammonia and its derivatives, petrochemicals, fertilizers, carbon black, and other products were built in Dammam by British, Italian, and American firms. Engineers studied the laying of natural-gas pipelines to deliver the wasted trillions of cubic feet of gas from the oil fields of al-Hasa to every part of the land or to liquify and export it to the West.

The government issued a Five Year Development Plan for the years 1970 to 1975. The goal was to raise the gross national product by an annual rate of 9.3 percent. Exploration for uranium, iron, copper, gold, and silver was undertaken, and an agreement was signed with Yemen, Ethiopia, Egypt, and the Sudan to cooperate in exploiting the mineral deposits on and under the seabed of the Red Sea. Construction boomed everywhere. Ships in the harbor at Jidda waited for days and weeks to unload their cargoes.

In 1975 a second Five Year Development Plan was announced; it would cost the staggering sum of $150 billion. One-sixth was allocated to industrialization; other allocations were for paved roads, new housing units, irrigation projects, and agricultural expansion. The Saudis hoped that foreign capital would also participate in the nation's development, which would bring technological skills and insure sound economic management.

One of the most significant developments of the early 1950s was the al-Kharj agricultural program. At al-Kharj deep wells were cleaned; pumps were installed; and more than 8,000 acres of land, almost miraculously, produced fine alfalfa, vegetables, melons, and fruits in great abundance. Begun in wartime under American stimulus, the al-Kharj project served as an example of what could be done to increase the local food supply. The scarcity of water hampered agriculture, except in some of the great free-flowing oases in al-Hasa, and its lack began to pinch the industrial plans of King Faysal. Schemes for bringing water from the Euphrates to Riyadh were not too far-fetched, and Saudi Arabia engaged in several desaliniza-tion projects. In 1962 it was noted that there was more drilling for water than for oil. Each water find was widely celebrated. Intensive hydrological surveys were carried out in several areas. In 1965 Aramco announced the discovery of a reserve of fresh subsoil water, estimated at 20 trillion gallons, and struck another extensive fresh-water reserve sixty miles east of Riyadh. However, the supply of water in the capital became more and more critical, and in 1966 a Finnish concern won a contract to build and deliver water-purification equipment for the city while Dutch and American firms were building a desalinization plant near Jidda. In 1971 a project to irrigate 20,000 hectares in al-Hasa province, where 15 percent of the population lives, by building canals and improving the drainage systems was started. Dams were built wherever water resources justified the conservation and the investment. The availability of fresh water could be more crucial for the future of Saudi Arabia than the presence of oil.

REFERENCES: Chapter 40

Significant works for this chapter are also found in Chapters 4, 7, 18, 19, 20, 22, 23, 24, 27, 28, 30, 31, 33, 34, 36, and 38.

Aldington, Richard. *Lawrence of Arabia: A Biographical Enquiry.* London: Collins, 1955. A more recent assessment of this controversial figure.

Ali, Sheikh Rustum. *Saudi Arabia and Oil Diplomacy.* New York: Praeger, 1976. The use of the oil weapon in 1973.

Armstrong, Harold C. *Lord of Arabia, Ibn Saud: An Intimate Study of a King.* London: Berker, 1934. An early and friendly biography.

Brown, Edward Hoagland. *The Saudi Arabia-Kuwait Neutral Zone.* Beirut: Middle East Research and Publishing Center, 1963. An excellent, detailed volume on the origins and terms of the tangled concessions for the oil beneath the Neutral Zone and its adjacent islands and territorial waters.

de Gaury, Gerald. *Faisal, King of Saudi Arabia.* New York: Praeger, 1967. A per-ceptive study of a complex and intelligent ruler.

Dickson, H. R. P. *The Arab of the Desert.* New York: Macmillan, 1949. A sociological study of the nomads of Arabia.

Finnie, David H. *Desert Enterprise: The Middle East Oil Industry in Its Local Environment.* Cambridge, Mass.: Harvard University Press, 1958.

Hamilton, Charles W. *Americans and Oil in the Middle East.* Houston: Gulf Pub-lishing, 1963. Describes how the Americans negotiated for concessions and exam-ines the changes wrought in the life of the people by the influx of oil money.

Howarth, David. *The Desert King: Ibn Saud and His Arabia.* New York: McGraw-Hill, 1964. A well-researched, sympathetic, and very readable account of the colorful founder-king of Saudi Arabia. Written from the British viewpoint.

Knauerhause, Ramon. *The Saudi Arabian Economy.* New York: Praeger, 1975. A handbook of Saudi Arabia's economic development.

Lebkicher, Roy, George Rentz, and Max Steineke. *The Arabia of Ibn Saud.* New York: Russell F. Moore, 1952. An excellent study by three experts.

Leeman, Wayne A. *The Price of Middle East Oil: An Essay in Political Economy.* Ithaca, N.Y.: Cornell University Press, 1962. In this frank and controversial book the author asserted that the price of Middle East oil was too high and that the oil companies in the Middle East were forming an oligopolistic structure.

Lenczowski, George. *Oil and State in the Middle East.* Ithaca, N.Y.: Cornell University Press, 1960. Describes the political and social impact of the massive oil discoveries and recounts the negotiations for payments during the decade of the 1950s.

Longrigg, Stephen H. *Oil in the Middle East: Its Discovery and Development.* 3rd ed. New York: Oxford University Press, 1968. Updated, thorough study of oil development and its effect on politics and life in the Middle East. By one of the individuals involved in the process.

Lutfi, Ashraf. *OPEC Oil.* Beirut: Middle East Research and Publishing, 1968. An assessment of the international oil business, and the role of the Organization of Petroleum Exporting Countries.

Mikdashi, Zuhayr. *The Community of Oil Exporting Countries: A Study in Governmental Cooperation.* Ithaca, N.Y.: Cornell University Press, 1972. Traces the evolution, administration, structure, and achievements of OPEC and OAPEC. Constitutes a history of the changing relations between oil-producing countries and producing companies.

Monroe, Elizabeth. *Philby of Arabia.* London: Faber & Faber, 1973. A vivid picture of the man, the times in which he lived, and the journeys by which he most deserves to be remembered.

Mughraby, Muhamad. *Permanent Sovereignty over Oil Resources: A Study of Middle East Oil Concessions and Legal Change.* Beirut: Middle East Research and Publishing Center, 1966. A monumental handbook.

Page, Stephen. *The USSR in Arabia: The Development of Soviet Policies and Attitudes Towards the Countries of the Arabian Peninsula.* London: Central Asian Research Center, 1971. One of the best books to appear recently on the area. Drawn from Soviet press reports and radio broadcasts.

Philby, H. St. John B. *Arabia.* New York: Scribner, 1930. Philby was a British Muslim who served as adviser to Ibn Saud for several decades and was one of the outstanding Arab scholars of his day. It was Philby who suggested the name "Saudi Arabia" to Ibn Saud. A fine survey of the early period.

———. *Arabia of the Wahhabis.* London: Constable, 1928. Tells of Ibn Saud's conflicts with the Rashids.

———. *Arabian Days.* London: Robert Hale, 1951. An excellent account of the life of Ibn Saud.

———. *Arabian Highlands.* Ithaca, N.Y.: Cornell University Press, 1952. Travels in Arabia and particularly in Asir.

———. *Arabian Jubilee.* London: Robert Hale, 1951. An excellent account of Ibn Saud and his dynasty.

———. *Arabian Oil Ventures.* Washington, D.C.: The Middle East Institute, 1964. Philby was the focal point of nearly all the early negotiations between the oil interests and the king. He relates the three oil ventures—two ill-fated attempts followed by the third one by Aramco.

———. *The Empty Quarter.* London: Constable, 1933. An account of travels through southern Arabia.

———. *Forty Years in the Wilderness.* London: Robert Hale, 1957. An account of Philby's life and travels in Arabia.

———. *The Heart of Arabia,* 2 vols. London: Putnam, 1923. Geography.

———. *The Land of Midian.* London: Ernest Benn, 1957. Travels in northwest Arabia.

———. *A Pilgrim in Arabia.* London: Robert Hale, 1942. A description of the pilgrimage to Mecca.

———. *Saudi Arabia.* London: Benn, 1955. A history of that state by one who helped found it.

Stocking, George W. *Middle East Oil: A Study in Political and Economic Controversy.* Nashville, Tenn.: Vanderbilt University Press, 1970. A prediction in 1970 that the downward price of oil since early in 1960 would soon be reversed.

Thomas, Lowell. *With Lawrence in Arabia.* New York: Grossett, 1955. An account by one of the first to make Lawrence well known.

Toriguian, Shavarsh. *Legal Aspects of Oil Concessions in the Middle East.* Beirut: Hamaskaine Press, 1972. From the beginning to 1970.

Troeller, Gary. *The Birth of Saudi Arabia: Britain and the Rise of the House of Sa'ud.* London: Frank Cass, 1976. Of particular value for the period from 1910 to 1926.

Twitchell, Karl. *Saudi Arabia.* Princeton, N.J.: Princeton University Press, 1953. A fundamental work by a mining and hydraulic engineer who did much of the original work in exploring Arabia.

van der Meulen, Daniel. *The Wells of Ibn Sa'ud.* New York: Praeger, 1957. Rise of the Saudi family and the development of the state.

Vicker, Ray. *The Kingdom of Oil.* New York: Scribner, 1974. An objective introduction to the Middle East, keeping in mind the global energy and geopolitical situation.

Vidal, F. S. *The Oasis of al-Hasa.* New York: Arabian American Oil Company, 1955. The geography and economy of this province of Saudi Arabia.

Winder, R. Bayly. *Saudi Arabia in the Nineteenth Century.* New York: St. Martin's Press, 1966. A valuable, comprehensive, well-organized, scholarly study.

Chapter 41

Smaller Arabian States

The great central mass of the Arabian peninsula consists of the Kingdom of Saudi Arabia which also controls the province of al-Hasa facing the Persian Gulf and the provinces on the eastern shore of the Red Sea from the Gulf of Akaba southward through Asir to Yemen. All of the other coastal areas of the peninsula are divided into numerous smaller Arab states. On the east, along the Persian Gulf, are Bahrayn, Kuwayt, Qatar, and the United Arab Amirates (formerly the Trucial States of Oman). Oman is on the southeastern and southern shores. In the south and southwest are the former Imamate of Yemen, the British colony of Aden, and the Hadhramaut, all of which are now divided between the Arab Republic of Yemen and the People's Democratic Republic of (South) Yemen.

Bahrayn

Bahrayn is an amirate composed of several islands totaling 200 square miles and standing about twenty miles off the coast of Saudi Arabia and the Qatar Peninsula in the Persian Gulf. Inhabited largely by Arabs and ruled by Iran for more than a century, Bahrayn was taken by Arabs from Iran and became a British dependency through naval action in 1820. Except for pearl fishing, smuggling, slave trade, and the breeding of white donkeys, Bahrayn was quite unimportant until the presence of oil was suspected in the 1920s.

In 1930, after three other concerns had held oil concessions, Standard Oil of California and The Texas Company formed the Bahrayn Petroleum Company (Bapco), a Canadian corporation, and obtained the concession. Oil in commercial quantities was discovered in 1932, and Bahrayn oil entered the world markets in 1934. A refinery was constructed to handle Bahrayn's output of 30,000 barrels a day and, later, an additional 125,000 barrels coming from Saudi Arabia by an underwater pipeline. In 1952 Bapco entered into an equal profit-sharing agreement with Bahrayn's ruler, which gave him about $8 million a year in royalties to add to his $3 million income from taxes. Bapco signed an agreement with the amir in 1974, turning over 100 percent of the company to the government in two stages. In 1976 the Bahrayn National Oil Company was formed by the government to hold the oil rights; Bapco, however, continued to manage the business. Bahrayn's oil reserves are limited, but improved production techniques have increased output in the 1970s to about 66,000 barrels daily.

Bahrayn's financial condition remained stationary until oil prices jumped in 1973 and Bahrayni oil revenues topped $100 million a year. Bahrayn became a member of OAPEC, honored the 1973 embargo against the United States and the Netherlands, and participated in the Persian Gulf production slowdown. OAPEC decided in 1972 to spend $250 million to build a tanker drydock in Bahrayn to service ships of up to 350,000 tons. In 1969 a £2 million satellite station was built in Bahrayn, which with the OAPEC drydock and a British naval base provided income and more jobs. When the British left in 1971, the United States assumed responsibility for the base until the lease was terminated in 1977.

Bahrayn has been ruled by the Al Khalifah family for more than a century, the ruler in 1977 being Amir Isa ibn Salman Al Khalifah who succeeded his father in 1961. The Al Khalifah family has been noted for its leniency. Life on the islands has been secure and not too harsh, and the appeal of political agitators has usually been temporary. A nineteenth-century treaty with Great Britain placed the foreign relations of the state in British hands, exercised from 1926 to 1956 by Sir Charles Belgrave, the ruler's adviser. During the Suez crisis and Sinai War in 1956, when a rising, Nasser-inspired Arab nationalism among younger Bahraynis threatened refinery installations, Bahrayn turned to Saudi Arabia and Kuwayt for protection. After the immediate danger passed the nationalists concentrated on building Arab socialism in Bahrayn. From time to time the Arab Nationalist Movement instigated strikes, but the nationalists were confronted with a just and generous labor code that had been operative in Bahrayn since the 1950s.

Great Britain dropped a bombshell in January 1968, when she announced that her special treaty position with the states of the area would be abrogated at the end of 1971. Bahrayn, Qatar, and the seven small amirates of the Trucial Coast discussed a federation. Encouraged by Saudi Arabia and Kuwayt, numerous conferences were held to draw up the structure of such an entity. To the dismay of Arab leaders everywhere, however, Iran reasserted her old claim to Bahrayn. When a mission from the U.N. in 1970 ascertained that Bahrayn desired independence, Iran indicated that Bahrayni wishes would be honored. After the proposed federation rejected Bahrayn's demand for representation according to population, Amir Isa on August 14, 1971, declared Bahrayn an independent and sovereign state. A treaty of friendship was signed with Great Britain, and Bahrayn's applications for membership in the Arab League and the United Nations were accepted.

In 1972 the amir convened a constituent assembly of 44 members, half appointed and half elected. By mid-1973 the constitution was approved by the amir and by popular referendum. It declared that Bahrayn is an Arab and Islamic state; that men and women are equal; that any concessions must have parliamentary approval; that labor unions are sanctioned; and that the government should strive for Arab political and economic unity. When elections for 30 seats in the National Assembly were held in December, political parties were banned; still, ten young "leftists" were elected and a number of older established figures were defeated.

At the time the parliament was convoked a new cabinet of twelve members was appointed. Parliament elected its speaker and formed committees. Though there were labor difficulties over the employment of low-paid foreign workers, all seemed to proceed smoothly. Then, in August 1975, the amir dissolved parliament, refused to schedule the election of a new parliament, and transferred its responsibilities to the cabinet, which he expanded to seventeen members. A number of leftists were arrested, allegedly for conspiring with avowed Marxists and popular front groups.

Late in 1976 two new laws were promulgated in an attempt to lessen the tensions arising from labor difficulties and the recession. One stipulated that Bahraynis were to be hired before foreigners; the other established a fund into which employers paid 14 percent and employees contributed 7 percent of their wages for national insurance covering old age, accidents, disability, and termination of employment, and providing death benefits for survivors. Though these laws somewhat assuaged popular unrest there were no indications that elections for a new parliament would be held.

Kuwayt

North of Bahrayn on the mainland of Arabia near the head of the Persian Gulf lies the Amirate of Kuwayt. Long a port and the seat of a profitable shipping trade from Basrah to Zanzibar, Kuwayt first came to world attention during the Berlin-to-Baghdad railroad epic. Lord Curzon brought it under British protection in 1899 to prevent the German imperialists from obtaining a suitable terminus for their road to the east. Thereafter, Kuwayt lapsed into oblivion, except to the British colonial office, until the end of World War I. Ibn Saud tried to seize it for his growing kingdom, but British guns turned him away.

After oil was struck on Bahrayn, the world oil companies sought concessions in Kuwayt. The Kuwayt Oil Company, Ltd. (KOC), a British corporation owned equally by the British Petroleum Company and the Gulf Oil Company, received a concession in 1934 for the entire 5,800 square miles of the state. Oil was not found until 1938, when the Burghan field was tapped and proved to be the largest known pool of oil in the world. Commercial production, however, was stalled during World War II and did not begin in earnest until 1946. Even then operations went slowly. In 1950, as troubles loomed in Iran, production was increased rapidly.

The original concession had provided for a royalty payment of 7 cents a barrel; a new agreement in 1951, following the examples of Saudi Arabia and Venezuela, called for equal sharing of company profits. In 1955 production soared over 1 million barrels a day, and royalty payments to Kuwayt's ruler, Shaykh Sir Abdallah al-Salim Al Sabah, exceeded $250 million. In addition, the shaykh gave a concession for his half of the neutral zone to the American Independent Oil Company and the Paul Getty Oil Company for a down payment of $7 million and a royalty guarantee of 35 cents a barrel.

In 1961 concessions were given to the Arabian Oil Company of Japan for the neutral zone offshore rights at a 57 to 43 division of profits, favoring Kuwayt, and to the Royal Dutch Shell Company for the Kuwayt offshore areas. The Kuwayt National Petroleum Corporation (KNPC) was founded, with 60 percent held by the government and the remainder held by Kuwayti nationals; KNPC was given an option to buy 20 percent of Shell's concession. Oil production passed 2 million barrels per day in 1960; royalties stood at $600 million; and petroleum exports at well over $1 billion.

Kuwayt could hardly spend all her oil income; nevertheless, in 1968 the amir urged the oil companies to increase production and royalties, even though KOC had recently paid $90 million to cover back royalties. In 1969 the companies were again warned they might lose their concessions if they increased production elsewhere at the expense of Kuwayti production. Oil revenues rose about 7 percent a year until 1971, when KOC agreed to raise the posted price from $1.59 to $1.68 a barrel and to boost the tax paid by the company from 50 to 55 percent of the profits. By the end of 1973 OPEC won a posted price of $11.65 for Persian Gulf crude. In the mid-1970s, concerned about the effects of worldwide runaway inflation and fearing that she was depleting her proven reserves too rapidly, Kuwayt began to limit her oil production. To leave much of the oil safe in the ground rather than bring it to the surface had considerable appeal. Though oil at auction brought $12 to $19 a barrel, the government forced production down to 2 million barrels daily in 1975; yet in 1976 oil revenues were nearly $8 billion.

In the late 1960s OPEC members at their meetings pressed a program of nationalization of oil and urged each member to take 20 percent at the first opportunity. In 1974, KOC agreed after long negotiations to accept $112 million from Kuwayt for 60 percent of the company. By the time similar terms were hammered out with the Arabian Oil Company, the National Assembly was clamoring for it all. The assembly voted for full nationalization in 1975, with Kuwayt guaranteeing to sell the companies 950,000 barrels per day for five years.

With a population of less than 200,000 before 1950 and about 800,000 by 1977, less than half of whom were native born, the wealth pouring in changed the life of the people rapidly. Shaykh Sir Abdallah used half his royalties to build schools, roads, hospitals, electrical plants, and the other requirements of a modern community. Kuwayt University opened in 1966 with faculties in arts, sciences, and education. Because Kuwayt's water resources are negligible, large sea-water conversion plants were built in the 1950s; new plants doubled the supply every decade.

KOC had constructed three oil refineries, and in 1958 construction on modern port terminals was launched. By 1960 Kuwaytis were saying that everything needed had been completed and the city and state had been constructed. But when new building slowed down and government land purchases stopped, everyone complained of a recession. Government leaders realized that continued expansion was essential. Massive five-year plans were devised to stimulate the gross national product, raise the per capita income, generate an "equality in distribution," and guarantee "equality of opportunity for those with limited incomes." The five-year plan initiated in 1976 called for the expenditure of $12 billion dollars to alleviate economic stagnation.

The surge in oil income beginning in 1973 increased the per capita income dramatically; by 1976 it reached $11,500, the highest in the world. Nevertheless, in 1974 non-Kuwayti Arab workers were leaving at the rate of 3,000 per month because they could find better pay and greater opportunities elsewhere. Moreover, a substantial strain of Kuwayti nationalism has arisen. As far back as 1969 foreigners had to have an invitation or a permit. The government began to deport non-Kuwayti Arabs for "subversive acts," and enacted stringent laws on the obtaining of Kuwayti citizenship. One of the perplexing problems in Kuwayt has been how to maintain a dynamic economy in the face of the high tide of oil revenues.

The city of al-Kuwayt, with the highest per capita income in the world, became a modern town within a decade, with more automobiles and more hard-surfaced roads per capita and more air conditioners per habitation than any other city in the world. Its wealth attracted people from many parts of the world, especially from other Arab areas. The influx of Egyptians and Palestinians was relatively high, a factor which sensitized most Kuwaytis to Arab nationalism.

The Amirate of Kuwayt was declared free and independent on June 19, 1961, after discussions with Great Britain led to a peaceful termination of the treaty of protection. In less than a week Amir Abdallah was threatened by Iraq, and called upon Great Britain for protection; three warships and a contingent of marines arrived to stay until August, when troops from Saudi Arabia, Jordan, and the United Arab Republic replaced them. Kuwayt joined the Arab League, but her entry into the United Nations was delayed until 1963 by the U.S.S.R.

At Amir Abdallah's behest a constituent assembly drafted a document in 1963 calling for an elected fifty-member National Assembly. The majority of those elected supported the rule of the Sabah family; eight, however, belonged to the Arab Nationalist Movement. The amir's brother Sabah al-Salim Al Sabah was named prime minister and heir to the throne, and became the new ruler when Abdallah died in 1965. The family occupied eleven of the sixteen places in the first cabinet. The new amir chose his cousin Jabir al-Ahmad al-Jabir Al Sabah as prime minister and heir to the throne. When Amir Sabah al-Salim died on December 31, 1977, Jabir al-Ahmad Al Sabah was recognized immediately as Amir of Kuwayt, and the several princes of the ruling family began to maneuver for the dual position of crown prince and prime minister.

During the 1970s there were three National Assembly elections. Of the members elected in 1975 half had not served before. They were younger, better educated, and less conservative than those they replaced. The new National Assembly chose to be active; this irked the ruling family, so on August 29, 1976, Amir Sabah dissolved it, suspended the articles of the constitution guaranteeing freedom of the press, and declared he would rule by executive decree.

Kuwayt's tremendous wealth and oil resources are constant temptations to aggression. To provide a buffer Kuwayt's rulers initiated a policy of granting and loaning significant sums to other Arab states. In 1962 the Kuwayt Fund for Arab Economic Development (KFAED) was established. By 1977 it had given out more than $1 billion to Arab states for a great variety of enterprises. In 1974 the capital of the fund was increased to over $3 billion, giving it in the eyes of the Arab states a status almost equal to the World Bank. Kuwayt took a new and unprecedented step in 1977 by granting $240 million for aid to black Africa.

After Great Britain announced she would withdraw from the Persian Gulf in 1971, Kuwayt began to buy defensive weapons. In 1973 $1.5 billion was allocated for defense expenditures over the next seven years. But Amir Sabah recognized that a state as small as his could not hope to withstand the armed might of any of the world powers. His only hope was to conduct a foreign policy that would guard his independence and maintain friendly relations with all, offending none.

Kuwayt declared war against Israel in 1967. Later, Kuwayt joined in contributing over $100 million to Egypt to offset the loss of Suez Canal earnings. Also, Amir Sabah annually sent $130 million to Egypt and Jordan. In 1970 Palestinian Liberation Organization leader Yasir Arafat received $14 million for the PLO, and $180 million in the Kuwayti budget was designated for the support of "Arab steadfastness." In 1973 $344 million was given to the Arab countries fighting Israel. Yet, Palestinians, as are all foreigners, were not permitted to settle permanently in Kuwayt.

Kuwayt's relations with Iran have always been in a delicate balance. An agreement was struck in 1968 on offshore oil rights in the Persian Gulf. Amir Sabah was so furious, however, when Iran occupied the Tunb islands and Abu Musa in 1971, that he refused for twelve months to accept a new Iranian ambassador. Crown Prince Jabir, urging the nine smaller Arab states in the Persian Gulf to unite in some kind of federation, gave his blessing to the new United Arab Amirates in 1971. Seminars were organized in Kuwayt for the training of UAA personnel to fill diplomatic posts around the world.

In 1971 Kuwayt's rulers were vexed by Iraq's occupation of two nearly uninhabited Kuwayti islands near the mouth of the Shatt al-Arab, which dominate the sea lanes to the Iraqi port of Umm Qasr. The Arab League acted to settle the dispute, and Saudi Arabia sent 15,000 soldiers to protect Kuwayt. Iraq claimed the islands are of vital importance to her, one for use as an oil terminal for the Rumaylah fields in the south, the other as a protective military base, and stationed her forces on each of them. A solution was reached upon Saudi Crown Prince Fahd's visit to Baghdad in 1975. It is believed that Kuwayt gave Iraq a ninety-nine-year lease on the islands in exchange for a recognized demarcation of the Kuwayti-Iraqi frontier, although Kuwayt officials have claimed that reports of the leasing of the islands are "incorrect."

In Kuwayt education is free, from elementary school through university; medical attention and hospital care are free; there are no taxes; there is no poverty; and there are more millionaires per thousand of population than anywhere. Nevertheless, curbs on the press and the dissolution of the National Assembly even concomitantly with the world's highest per capita income, presage difficulties in the years to come unless skillful hands are in control and wise judgments prevail.

Qatar

Few had heard of Qatar before the discovery of oil there in 1950. Under a treaty with the British in 1916 the ruling shaykh pledged to prevent piracy along his coasts and recognized a perpetual truce with Great Britain that virtually controlled all of Qatar's foreign relations. Occupying a barren peninsula of 4,000 square miles jutting eastward into the Persian Gulf, the shaykhdom had one principal town, Doha, and was ruled absolutely by the Al Thani family. The Qatar Petroleum Company, a subsidiary of the Iraq Petroleum Company, held the mainland concession and exploited its major well at Dukhan, about sixty miles from Doha. Offshore rights were held by Shell Qatar, which began producing in 1961, and which was reorganized in 1967 to include Ente Nazionale Idrocarburi of Italy. By 1966 Qatar was receiving over $100 million annually in royalties, and production stood at 276,000 barrels daily. A decade later annual income was over $2 billion, oil production had doubled, and the population had increased tenfold to 220,000, about 80 percent of whom lived in Doha.

Qatar, admitted to OPEC in 1968, agreed with Abu Dhabi to divide the revenues from the rich Bunduq field that straddled the line separating them. Thereafter, four Japanese firms were given rights to an offshore area of 2,800 square miles. In 1972 Saudi Arabia began the negotiating process whereby Qatar would acquire ownership of the operating oil companies; in 1974 a general agreement was initialed by which the government would buy 60 percent of Qatar Petroleum Company and Shell Qatar. In 1977, Qatar Petroleum Company relinquished all control of its oil operations to the government but continued to provide services, managerial assistance, and trained personnel.

The shaykh gave half of the revenues to his family which, with retainers, was estimated to number 20,000; used one-fourth to cover the expenses of government and the public services; and kept the remainder for himself. A religious scholar of Arab history and Islamic law, Shaykh Ali ibn Abdallah ibn Qasim Al Thani acceded to rule in 1949. He found the problems of oil development and riches so vexing that he retired in 1960 to his villa in Switzerland, abdicating in favor of his son Shaykh Ahmad ibn Ali Al Thani, who also preferred Switzerland.

The British departure from the Persian Gulf in 1971 gave birth to a federation of Gulf states. As proposed the first prime minister would have been Shaykh Khalifah ibn Hamad Al Thani, cousin and heir of Qatar's ruler and actual ruler while Shaykh Ahmad was in Switzerland. The plan foundered, and on April 2, 1970, Amir Ahmad ibn Ali Al Thani declared he was independent and a sovereign. Shaykh Khalifah was named prime minister; nine of the other ministers were from the Thani family as well. On September 1, 1971, Amir Ahmad proclaimed Qatar's separation from the British. Later that month Qatar was admitted to the Arab League and the United Nations.

On February 22, 1972, with Amir Ahmad vacationing in Switzerland, Khalifah ibn Hamad Al Thani staged a bloodless coup. He pledged to modernize the administration, cut consumer prices, and raise civilian and military salaries by 20 percent. Amir Khalifah, a member of the more vigorous and managerial Hamad clan of Al Thanis, began to take an active role in Arab affairs, proposing a Persian Gulf common market and a single currency which, he hoped, would rival the dollar and pound by 1985. He made loans or grants to Arab states for military preparedness against Israel and for economic development. In 1977 Qatar also gave $45 million to a fund for black Africa. In addition, he arranged for an earth satellite communications system centered at Doha to carry thirty international telephone lines and TV and radio transmissions. In 1975 per capita income in Qatar rose to $8,320, behind only Kuwayt and the United Arab Amirates. Dr. Hasan Kamil, an Egyptian serving as Director of Government, outlined a program for improving communications systems, developing a water and sewage system, and providing housing for indigent families. Under Amir Khalifah transformation of traditional society is being effected "with a minimum of chaos and upheaval."

Trucial States of Oman

Lying along a four-hundred-mile strip of the coast of Arabia on the Persian Gulf south from the Qatar Peninsula to the Straits of Hormuz and along the Gulf of Oman to the territory of the Sultan of Oman are seven Arab shaykhdoms. For centuries they won their livelihood from the sea by pearl diving and piracy; when not thus engaged they raided each other. In 1820 a British naval expedition from India in collaboration with a land force from Muscat caught them in a vise and forced a treaty upon each of the seven rulers by which they agreed not to make war on each other, not to raid shipping, not to permit or traffic in slavery, and not to make treaties with other powers. Great Britain in return agreed to protect them from outside aggression. It proved difficult for England to enforce the treaty and equally distasteful for the seven shaykhs to abide by a rule so contrary to habits and patterns of life established over centuries of fighting. In 1853 a Perpetual Maritime Truce was signed, giving the name "Trucial States" to the group. These seven are: Abu Dhabi, Dubay, Sharjah, Ajman, Umm al-Qaywayn, Ras al-Khaymah, and Fujayrah. Each was hardly more than a small coastal town with a desert hinterland, although Abu Dhabi held several of the settlements in the inland Buraimi oases. Dubay had the largest town; Sharjah was the location of the British political resident agent, a small military force, and an airstrip; Abu Dhabi was the largest. In 1960 the total population of all seven states was estimated at 86,000. The seven shaykhs met twice a year in a kind of council, but no formal organization or federation developed.

When piracy and slave trading were no longer possible or profitable, the shaykhs turned to smuggling and shipping gold to India. Pearling reached its peak about 1925, at which time the revenue in the pearl trade for all of the Persian Gulf area including Kuwayt and Bahrayn was about $10 million. Less than a tenth of this came to the seven rulers of the Trucial States. The marketing of cultured pearls hurt the trade, and then the development of even less expensive synthetic pearls, followed by the depression, finished it off. After World War II, as the total value of the pearling industry in the Persian Gulf dropped to $250,000, the towns of the Trucial States were in the doldrums. Their shaykhs seemed to be enjoying idleness and were unconcerned about the oil wealth of their neighbors. Abu Dhabi in 1961 was still insignificant, with a population of about 15,000 and a total revenue of a little under $150,000 for its ruler Shaykh Shakhbut ibn Sultan ibn Zayd Al Nuhayyan, who had acceded to his position in 1928.

For more than a decade Petroleum Development (Trucial Coast) Ltd., later named Abu Dhabi Petroleum Company, a subsidiary of Iraq Petroleum Company, held the concessions for the seven shaykhdoms. Oil had been struck in 1960 in commercial quantities at Murban and Umm Shaif, both in Abu Dhabi. Offshore concessions had been given by Abu Dhabi and Dubay to Abu Dhabi Marine Areas Ltd., two-thirds owned by British Petroleum Company and one-third by Compagnie Française de Petroles, and a strike had been made near Das Island offshore from Umm Shaif. In 1962 Shaykh Shakhbut received $20 million in royalties; by 1966 royalties had reached $84 million. Production jumped rapidly to reach 367,000 barrels daily, more than in Qatar or Rumania. Proven crude reserves were estimated in 1967 to be about 12.5 billion barrels.

What to do with all this money? Shaykh Shakhbut's wants were simple and inexpensive. His major recreation was hawking. At times he voiced the wish that the oil companies would take their half and leave his half in the ground where it would be secure and less bothersome. He baffled British oil executives by putting off arrangements for a new contract more favorable to him until 1965 when he accepted the fifty-fifty split. Immigrants brought diseases unknown to the local Arabs; there was an unsought emphasis on speed and education; prices soared; visitors came and left without his knowledge or permission. Disconcerting changes were everywhere: a new twenty-five-room air-conditioned hotel, water distillation plants, and plans for an international airport. He was not convinced that all was for the betterment of his people.

Developments were slow and difficult to wheedle from Shaykh Shakhbut. With British blessings a family council sent Shakhbut to Bahrayn in 1966, placing his youngest brother, Shaykh Zayd ibn Sultan Al Nuhayyan, in control. Shaykh Zayd, ebullient, lighthearted, and possessed of great physical strength, was brought up in the informal nomadic life of the desert. He announced a $42 million development plan with a British consortium, which would build a covered market, a seawall, sewage works, one hundred miles of dual highway from Buraimi to Abu Dhabi, and seventy miles of water pipelines from Buraimi.

Zayd began with a substantial income of $170 million, more than double that of Shakhbut's last year; ten years later, after production had quadrupled and OPEC and OAPEC had upped the prices tenfold, revenues were nearly $8 billion. At the 1976–1977 rate of production, oil reserves were expected to last for a century at least. Meanwhile, the population had jumped to 100,000, only a third of whom had been born in Abu Dhabi. Zayd arranged with Qatar to delimit their common border in order to divide the Bunduq field, which began producing in 1976. He also settled a long-standing feud with Saudi Arabia over the Buraimi oases, agreeing in 1974 to divide the promising Zararah oil fields.

With other OPEC members Abu Dhabi pressed her oil companies for a transfer of ownership. But little progress was achieved until 1972 when 25 percent was obtained; this was increased in 1974 to 65 percent. Zayd, concerned about any slackening of production, in 1975 threatened the companies with a takeover if they did not raise production immediately from 700,000 barrels to 1.2 million barrels daily.

In 1967 the Abu Dhabi Investment Board was established to invest the surplus funds, which each year became greater; in 1976 they were estimated at roughly $6 billion. Shaykh Zayd has a most generous nature, and no one requesting help went away disappointed. Millions were given or loaned to less affluent Arab states, and uncounted sums handed out to the members of his extended family, to neighboring shaykhs, and to bedouin chiefs. Still, what to do with the mounting cash balances has created a controversy in governing circles. A director of planning was appointed in 1968 to draw up a five year National Plan to invest $100 million in local projects; this was soon increased to $621 million; by 1971 it was over $1 billion.

In 1969 Shaykh Zayd named his eldest son, Shaykh Khalifah, as his heir, and began to assign prime ministerial tasks to him. With the 1971 British pullout and the apparent failure of a Persian Gulf states federation, Zayd declared Abu Dhabi to be an independent amirate. On July 1, 1971, he appointed a full-fledged cabinet, with Khalifah as prime minister. This gave Abu Dhabi the only governmental cabinet among the seven Trucial states, but it withered and was dissolved after the United Arab Amirates became a reality.

Northeast of Abu Dhabi along the Persian Gulf coast toward the Strait of Hormuz lies the small amirate of Dubay. With 120,000 people, Dubay is the most populous of the seven amirates. Based on an estuary of the gulf, Dubay has been the main commercial and smuggling center on the coast for more than a century. Her merchant and gold-smuggling multi-millionaires have over the years established solid connections in Europe, Asia, and Africa.

Dubay's ruler, Amir Rashid ibn Said Al Maktum, who succeeded his father peacefully in 1958, has considerable knowledge of foreign trade and international finance, skills acquired from his mother, the real power in Dubay for fifty years. He became chief executive officer and principal owner of the Dubay Electricity Company and the Dubay State Telephone System. Rashid has demonstrated great acumen in the political advancement of Dubay, especially within the growing structure of the United Arab Amirates.

Oil was discovered in commercial quantities in 1967 by the Dubay Petroleum Company in the offshore Fatah field. Oil was first exported in 1969, at which time Dubay attained membership in OAPEC. By 1977 daily exports neared 300,000 barrels and yearly revenues exceeded $1 billion. Many millions were spent to enlarge the airport to accommodate jumbo jets, to build a new air terminal complex, to construct the biggest deep water port in the Persian Gulf, and to establish a free port.

When OAPEC decided in 1972 to locate a large drydock in Bahrayn, Dubay, outraged, resigned from OAPEC and spent $225 million to erect one on her estuary, completing it ahead of OAPEC's. Dubay remained the chief business center for the entire coast, and by the mid-1970s twenty banks handling capital from two dozen countries had joined the British Bank of the Middle East, long the sole banking house in Dubay. Amir Rashid set up small departments of government, each responsible to him, and each operating on its own income, like a business.

The amirate of Sharjah, population 2,000, lies contiguous to Dubay on the north and east. Included in Sharjah's territory is the strategic island of Abu Musa in the Strait of Hormuz, with its offshore oil fields. The amirate's fine municipal government, developed over many decades, has served as a model through the entire region. In 1969 Sharjah granted onshore oil concessions to Shell Oil and offshore rights to a Shell-West German consortium.

Until 1971 the British located their military and air bases in Sharjah, which was the headquarters of the Trucial Oman Scouts. Egyptian support of Sharjah's Amir Saqr ibn Sultan Al Qasimi irritated the British, and his flirting with Nasser who was stirring up trouble in Aden was not appreciated. When the British suggested in 1965 to Amir Saqr's six brothers that he be replaced, Saqr retired to Cairo. His cousin Khalid ibn Muhammad Al Qasimi, at that moment successfully operating a paint store in Dubay, became amir. Although Khalid had the full support of the ruling family, he found running the government more difficult than he had supposed.

The day before the British withdrew their forces from Sharjah and before their treaties with the amirs, including Amir Khalid, became invalid, Iran occupied Abu Musa with no interference or objections. An arrangement was made whereby the inhabitants of the island would remain under Sharjah rule, offshore oil revenues would flow to Sharjah, and Iran paid $7.5 million for the military bases.

Soon thereafter, former Amir Saqr staged an unsuccessful coup with the aid of the Arab Socialist Action party. Khalid was killed but the rebels were captured by troops of the recently organized United Arab Amirate. Khalid's brother Sultan ibn Muhammad Al Qasimi then became the new Sharjah ruler. Amir Sultan, an engineering graduate of the College of Agriculture at the University of Cairo, with an interest in education and agriculture, also became minister of education in the UAA cabinet.

The easternmost amirate, adjacent to the tip of the peninsula is Ras al-Khaymah, with a population of 50,000. Without any known oil resources Ras al-Khaymah depends on agriculture, fishing, and shipping for her income. Amir Saqr ibn Muhammad ibn Sultan Al Qasimi, who seized power in 1948, is a strong-minded leader, though sensitive to the positions of the wealthy and powerful amirs of Abu Dhabi and Dubay. For a long time Amir Saqr kept in close touch with Arab nationalist circles in Iraq and Egypt. He objected loudly to the Iranian occupation of his Tunb Islands and has refused to accept their loss. In 1971 he declined to join the United Arab Amirates, but swallowed his resentment in 1972. As it turned out many of his supporters were appointed to important UAA offices, one becoming UAA ambassador to the United States. Amir Saqr's heir, Shaykh Khalid ibn Saqr Al Qasimi, the only heir in the seven amirates to be educated in the United States, became vice-chairman of a commission to reorganize the UAA's governmental structure.

The other three amirates, Ajman, Umm al-Qaywayn, and Fujayrah, are small—their combined territory is smaller than that of Ras al-Khaymah, the smallest of the larger four—and are sparsely populated. Their incomes will remain meager unless oil is found on or off the shores of their territories. At the time of the formation of the UAA Ajmah was ruled by Amir Rashid ibn Humayd Al Nuaymi, Umm al-Khaymah by Amir Ahmad ibn Rashid Al Mualla, and Fujayrah by Amir Muhammad ibn Hamad Al Sharqi, who died in 1974 and was succeeded by his son Amir Hamad ibn Muhammad Al Sharqi who had been UAA minister of agriculture and fisheries.

United Arab Amirates

Early in 1968 the rulers of the nine petty states in the Persian Gulf region under British protection began to think about forming some kind of a federation. They sought the reactions of Iran, Iraq, Kuwayt, and Saudi Arabia. Iraq called it a British subterfuge for continued control, but Kuwayt and Saudi Arabia were very encouraging. Iran, claiming ownership of Bahrayn, termed it an intolerable outrage. Abu Dhabi and Dubay then announced that they intended to federate. With the wealthiest and the most populous of the seven smaller amirates leading the way the others found refusal difficult, though Bahrayn, Qatar, and Ras al-Khaymah did decline to join. On July 18, 1971, six of the amirates formed the United Arab Amirates and accepted the drafted constitution, which allows other amirates to apply for membership. Officially coming into being the day after the British treaties lapsed, the UAA was within a week admitted to the Arab League and the United Nations. Ras al-Khaymah joined the UAA in 1972.

The UAA constitution recognized the independence of each member, each with her own flag and in full control of local affairs. It provided for a Supreme Council, consisting of the rulers of the states, each of whom had one vote. Decisions on procedural matters were to be reached by majority vote, while substantive issues required a five-vote majority that had to include Abu Dhabi and Dubay. Policies of state, federal laws, budgets and financial reports, decrees, treaties, and the appointment of high officers of the government had to be approved by the Supreme Council.

Amir Zayd of Abu Dhabi was chosen president and Amir Rashid of Dubay vice-president, each for a five-year term; both are eligible for reappointment. Amir Maktum ibn Rashid Al Maktum, heir to the amir of Dubay, was named prime minister, and Amir Khalifah, heir to the ruler of Abu Dhabi, became deputy prime minister. An eighteen-member cabinet was sworn in (five more were added when Ras al-Khaymah joined). A forty-member council consisted of eight members each from Abu Dhabi and Dubay, six each from Sharjah and Ras al-Khaymah, and four from each of the others. The Trucial Oman Scouts were taken over from the British and proved their worth shortly in quelling the coup in Sharjah.

As time passed the UAA government under the amirs of Abu Dhabi and Dubay won the approval of most of the political and business leaders in the area and acceptance by states around the world. The U.S.S.R. accorded it full diplomatic recognition at an early date. In 1973 local cabinets were disbanded, and education, public works, industry, agriculture, and justice were added to the responsibilities of the federal cabinet, its membership now at twenty-seven. Abu Dhabi's OPEC membership was transferred to the UAA. Except for the rulers of Abu Dhabi and Dubay, however, the heads of state were reluctant to surrender much of their power and revenue or allow any diminution of their prestige. There was an absence of overall planning as the rulers attempted to outdo each other's construction programs. In 1976 agreement could be reached only to extend the interim constitution of 1971 for another five years and to establish a border patrol. Even Amir Zayd's threat not to accept another five-year term did not move the smaller states.

Oman
The Sultanate of Oman, sometimes referred to as Muscat and Oman (Muscat was the official residential town of the sultan) has been inhabited since antiquity and is situated at the southeastern corner of the Arabian Peninsula. By the Treaty of Sib in 1920, the sultan recognized that the interior of the country would be governed by an elected imam who would have political and religious authority. No great difficulties or problems arose until 1954, when Ghalib ibn Ali was elected imam against the strong wishes of Sultan Said ibn Taymur ibn Faysal, who had held this power since his accession in 1932. Warfare broke out between the two in 1955, with Imam Ghalib supported by the Arab League including both Egypt and Saudi Arabia, and Sultan Said aided by British troops. For many years the sultan's

foreign relations were managed unofficially by Great Britain, a practice obtained through treaties of commerce and navigation in 1939 and 1951. By 1959 the imam and his followers had been routed from their mountain strongholds and fled into neighboring Saudi Arabia, and from there had made their way from one Arab capital to another, receiving red-carpet treatment but no substantial help.

On July 23, 1970, Sultan Said ibn Taymur was overthrown by his English-educated twenty-eight-year-old son Qabus, who exiled his father to England. Sultan Qabus indicated that he planned to establish a representative government, remove irksome rules such as restrictions on smoking, dancing, and the wearing of eyeglasses, and end Oman's isolation. Qabus also invited his uncle Tariq to return from European exile to become prime minister. Oman was admitted to the Arab League and the United Nations in 1971. Hampered by the massive expenses incurred in fighting a rebellion in Dhufar and a decline in oil revenues, Tariq resigned "for health reasons" in 1972. Qabus took over the reins himself, declaring that Oman was not yet prepared for responsible ministerial government.

In 1963 oil in commercial quantities was discovered by Petroleum Development (Oman) Ltd., owned jointly by Shell Petroleum Ltd. and the Gulbenkian interests. In 1967 the latter sold most of their share to Compagnie Française des Petroles. That same year a new agreement was reached with Sultan Said, giving him 12.5 percent of the royalties and splitting the profits on the usual 50-50 basis. Oil production averaged 300,000 barrels through the 1970s. Though not a member of OPEC, Sultan Qabus followed oil prices carefully, and government revenues soared from $5.6 million in 1966 to $1.4 billion in 1976. In 1974 Oman acquired 60 percent of the oil company. That same year Prospection Limited of Canada discovered sizable deposits of high-grade copper ore and traces of other valuable metals in northern Oman. This find has led to speculation that deposits may be hidden in the unexplored mountains of Oman.

The greatest problem facing Sultan Said and his son Qabus over the years has been the guerrilla warfare and open rebellion in Dhufar province in the southwest. After the British left Aden in 1967, left-wing activists from South Yemen formed the People's Front for the Liberation of the Occupied Arabian Gulf (PFLOAG), which clashed with Said's forces near Salalah. When Qabus became sultan he offered amnesty to the Dhufar rebels who were being trained in Iraq by Chinese officers supplied with Russian arms obtained from South Yemen. Rejecting his offer, they took control of much of the southern regions of Dhufar.

In 1971 King Faysal recognized Qabus' regime and gave him substantial sums, some of which allegedly came from the American CIA. The struggle began to go the sultan's way in 1972, when most of the hill tribesmen gave their allegiance to Qabus. Qabus went to Amman to marry King Husayn's daughter, and arranged for a Jordanian military mission to "Omanize" the army. Appeals were sent to the Arab League and the UN to seal the border with South Yemen and to force the South Yemeni regular army units to leave. Much to the annoyance of Arab leaders, Qabus received substantial aid from Iran in 1973. Immediately, Algeria and Libya offered to send troops to replace the Iranians. When Iran entered the action, the Chinese withdrew and the U.S.S.R. told PFLOAG to go underground. Egypt advised the South Yemenis to desist. Qabus gave permission for the United States to use Masirah island as a base from time to time, and was permitted to buy helicopters and antitank missiles. Oman then signed a naval agreement to allow Iran to patrol the Omani side of the Strait of Hormuz.

Convinced that the rebellion had been crushed, Qabus began in 1976 to devote more than half of his budget to development and services for the people. The Supreme Planning Council issued a five-year plan to expend $8.2 billion for education, harbors, roads, and the development of resources. Qabus confessed, however, that it would be fifteen or twenty years before most of the projects would have an impact on his society.

Aden and the Federation of South Arabia
The port of Aden is located seven hundred miles west of the Dhufar border on a rocky peninsula jutting out from the south coast of Arabia into the Indian Ocean about one hundred miles east of Bab al-Mandeb, the narrow strait controlling the southern entrance to the Red Sea. Aden, the sole port in the entire area, has been important for trade between East and West, including Africa, since antiquity. A local shaykh seized Aden in 1735 and occupied it until the British came in 1839. After the opening of the Suez Canal, Aden grew rapidly into one of the great British coaling stations, a submarine cable center, and, as a free port, a trading entrepôt. From the Crown Colony of Aden the British spread their influence along the entire southern Arabian coast, and by treaties with local rulers established what came to be known as the Eastern Aden and the Western Aden protectorates. The former comprised five independent sultanates and two shaykhdoms; the two largest sultanates together were usually called the Hadhramaut, from which originated many of the prosperous Arab merchants of Indonesia. In Western Aden, which surrounded the city of Aden, there were seven sultanates, six shaykhdoms, two amirates, and one confederation of tribes.

After World War II social and political attitudes in Aden and the protectorates changed markedly. During the war, the mountains of supplies on their way to Middle East theaters of war raised Aden to the third-ranking port, after London and Liverpool, in the British Empire. In 1954 the Anglo-Iranian Oil Company erected a $150 million refinery there and almost overnight created a new city, Little Aden, to support it. The contrast in living conditions and public conveniences with Aden proper made many residents of Aden wonder why if improvements could be made so easily they did not enjoy them too. In the protectorates a new generation of rulers wanted more independence. Aden governors were dependent directly upon London, and the individual princes longed for home rule.

Talks in London led to the creation in 1959 of the Federation of the Arab

Amirates of the South, comprising six of the states of the Western Aden Protectorate. Later others joined to make a total of seventeen. The name was changed in 1962 to the Federation of South Arabia. Aden became a member in 1963. A new capital, al-Ittihad, at Bir Ahmad not far from Aden, was completed and occupied in 1961. The federation was governed by a seven-member Supreme Council elected by a Federal Council composed of six members from each state except Aden, which had twenty-four. Yemen refused to recognize the federation because she had claimed the territory ever since 1735. In Aden many Yemeni workers and refugees mounted a Free Yemeni Movement. As long as Imam Ahmad ruled in Sana they did not want a union, but the revolution of 1962 and the birth of the Republic of Yemen altered conditions. President al-Sallal claimed Aden and the Federation of South Arabia, and was strongly supported in this demand by Nasser. Leaders of the various states who cooperated with the British or participated in federation matters were subjected constantly to threats of violence and assassination. Great Britain promised independence for 1968, and announced that troops would be withdrawn. Agitation grew worse as competition developed in Aden and the federation states among Arab nationals for the role of the successor to the British. One important group was the National Front for the Liberation of Occupied South Yemen (FLOSY), sponsored by the United Arab Republic. Among the others only the National Liberation Front (NLF) survived. All were aiming at 1968, but each had its eyes on the others. Through coups and kidnappings in the shaykhdoms and sultanates in 1967, NLF gained control of all the states of the federation, whose officials declared the union to be at an end. With Nasser's need to cut his commitments abroad, NLF showed that it had more muscle of its own than did FLOSY. As the position of the British grew untenable the date of withdrawal was moved up to November 1967. NLF appeared to have the upper hand, and Qahtan al-Shabi, NLF's leader, formed a group that assumed office when the British left.

People's Republic of South Yemen
The NLF controlled all the states, but only a small minority of politically minded individuals felt any national pull for South Yemen or any devotion to a socialist society. Rebellions against the NLF and its edicts broke out in every part of the state. Within the NLF there was constant bickering and rivalry over programs and positions. Saudi Arabia refused to recognize the new regime and gave asylum to former rulers of the federation. A score or more of the former leaders of the small states were executed, and FLOSY continued to operate in the Yemen Arab Republic, serving as a magnet for all the malcontents. Though loyalties were not established, attacks originating in Saudi Arabia or the Yemen Arab Republic were repulsed.

Qahtan al-Shabi, the leader of NLF, became the president, prime minister, and commander in chief of the armed forces of the People's Republic of South Yemen. The thirteen-man high command of NLF, soon expanded to forty-one, served as the executive council and a cabinet took office. All were inexperienced in administrative matters. Before the end of 1967 South Yemen had been admitted to the Arab League and the United Nations, and later joined the World Bank and the International Monetary Fund. Great Britain, the United States, and the U.S.S.R. recognized South Yemen. The new defense minister hastened to Moscow for aid and arms at the same time as al-Shabi was proposing complete harmony with the Yemen Arab Republic.

The Suez Canal had been blocked just before the republic was formed, and it was not reopened until June 5, 1975. In modern times the chief reason for the development of Aden, and the main source of its income, was the servicing and repairing of ships in connection with the canal. The cessation of traffic produced economic disaster, compelling the new regime to adopt austerity measures, which aroused considerable discontent among the populace. In 1969 al-Shabi made the fatal mistake of dismissing Muhammad Ali Haytham, the minister of the interior. Five days later, young leftists removed al-Shabi, accusing him of "one-man dictatorial rule." A five-man presidential council under the chairmanship of Salim Rubay Ali, with Muhammad Ali Haytham as prime minister, took power. Later, the al-Shabis were arrested; they were shot "while trying to escape." The cabal drafted a constitution in 1970, which provided for a Peoples Supreme Assembly. Salim Rubay Ali remained securely on top, however.

The new administration could not alter the basic difficulty: the collapse of trade and the resulting massive unemployment. Stringent economic measures were adopted, including the raising of tariffs to 300 percent to inhibit imports. The new leaders sought funds in Moscow, and Salim Rubay was given $33 million in Peking for a five-year road-building venture. Salim Rubay attended the Arab summit meeting in Rabat in 1969 and there mended relations with liberal Arab states, which gave him enough money to wipe out a $2 million budget deficit and still have $1.6 million for health centers and schools. Peaceful relations, however, could not be arranged with Saudi Arabia and the Yemen Arab Republic.

People's Democratic Republic of Yemen

Late in 1970, after the publication of the draft of the new constitution, the name of the state was officially announced as the People's Democratic Republic of Yemen (PDRY). The People's Supreme Assembly, numbering 101 members, elected Ali Nasir Muhammad Hasani prime minister. Rubay and Hasani remained the controlling figures of the government.

Conditions did not improve. Whereas at least 500 ships a year dropped anchor in Aden harbor before the Suez stoppage there were fewer than fifty in 1972. When Libya suspended aid the outlook grew even bleaker. Higher taxes were imposed on sugar, flour, and other foods, bringing insurrection in many rural areas. With NLF extremism and ineptitude aggravating the economic difficulties and inciting more rebellions, other Arab countries began to question NLF policies and leadership. The government's week-long celebration of Lenin's birthday contrasted against no acknowledgment of Muhammad's engendered dismay.

Poverty did not halt military ambitions. China set up a military mission in Aden alongside Moscow's, which was arming the PDRY forces. The arms often went to PLOAG'S guerrilla war in Dhufar against Oman; most, however, were used in attacking exiles and FLOSY "mercenaries" in Saudi Arabia and the Yemen Arab Republic (YAR). More and more it seemed to be a conflict of southern dissidents against the Marxist Aden regime. In 1972 a group of more than forty exiled leaders, invited to a conference with NLF, were shot on arriving. PDRY then lost all her friends except China, the U.S.S.R., and Iraq. When the YAR massed 50,000 troops ready to march south, the NLF began to consider seriously plans to unite the two Yemens.

After secret meetings the prime ministers of both Yemens signed a document pledging to halt acts of hostility and to pull back troops from their borders. Over the next two years the negotiations on unity revealed only that each side was ready to absorb the other.

During the October 1973 Middle East war, PDRY declared the Strait of Bab al-Mandeb a war zone and consented to the stationing of other Arab troops there. PDRY leased Perim island in the strait to Saudi Arabia for ninety-nine years for $150 million. Relations improved with Egypt and Saudi Arabia. Salim Rubay Ali then pronounced a policy of coexistence with all Arab states.

The Suez Canal was reopened for traffic on June 5, 1975, and life began to stir in Aden. Plans were made to recondition harbor facilities to repair four ships a month and provide mooring for twenty. Relations with Saudi Arabia were normalized, eased by a Saudi grant of $100 million. Saudi financial help in building an oil terminal in Aden to complement the refinery was approved and plans to link it by pipeline to oil fields in the Persian Gulf area were drafted. British Petroleum in 1977 transferred title to its large refinery in Aden to the government and agreed to continue its operation. In 1976 the PDRY and the Saudis agreed that ambassadors should be exchanged. PDRY leaders realized that moderation was the only course open to them.

The Imamate of Yemen

The Imamate of Yemen was in 1948 one of the most remote and isolated spots in the world. In 1934 Ibn Saud had forced peace upon the ruler of Yemen, Sayf al-Islam Yahya Hamid al-Din. Charles R. Crane visited the country in the 1930s, and Karl Twitchell built bridges there to connect Sana with ports on the Red Sea. The British had a running quarrel with Imam Yahya over the frontier of the Aden protectorate, until a British-Yemen treaty of friendship was signed in 1934.

In the period between the two world wars the imam turned to Italy for support. A ten-year treaty was signed and a Yemeni mission visited Mussolini to obtain arms and munitions. In 1937 the treaty was renewed for twenty-five years, and Italian doctors and technical people appeared in Yemen. During World War II Yemen remained neutral, but ousted Germans and Italians from her territory. Diplomatic missions were received, and Colonel William Eddy in 1946 negotiated a United States-Yemen treaty of friendship and commerce with Imam Yahya. Yemen was admitted to the Arab League in 1945 and to the United Nations in 1947.

Society changed slowly in Yemen; Imam Yahya remained the despot, holding the line as he had for forty-three years. Many of the younger generation and leaders of the rival princely family—the Wazir family— plotted to remove him. The former group, known as "Free Yemenis," were led by Imam Yahya's sixth son, Prince Ibrahim, who settled in Aden. In 1948 Imam Yahya was assassinated, Prince Ibrahim flew in from Aden, and an Al Wazir became imam. To counter this coup d'état, Yahya's eldest son, Ahmad Hamid al-Din, received aid from Ibn Saud and overthrew the insurgents. Many rebels were beheaded; Prince Ibrahim died in prison from a "heart attack."

The development of Yemen proceeded at a snail's pace, and the forces for change attempted a coup against Imam Ahmad in 1955. The revolt was led by his brother Prince Abdallah, who had traveled in the West and represented Yemen at the United Nations. It was crushed by the imam's eldest son, Prince Muhammad al-Badr, who freed his father and hanged Prince Abdallah.

The attempted coup, however, did stir up action in Yemen. Imam Ahmad took over the post of prime minister; he appointed al-Badr deputy prime minister, foreign minister, and minister of defense. A thirty-year concession was granted to the American Yemen Development Corporation to prospect and exploit the mineral resources of Yemen on a 50-50 basis. A trade mission from the Soviet bloc arrived in Taizz, the imam's favorite residence and thus the capital, and negotiated trade agreements for the U.S.S.R. and East Germany, a treaty of friendship with Czechoslovakia, and recognition of Communist China. The U.S.S.R. loaned Yemen $60 million, and China signed a five-year trade agreement and provided credits to build a 300-mile road from Hodeida to Sana. During the war in Sinai Yemen offered to permit volunteers to go to Egypt, and Soviet-bloc arms shipments arrived in Yemeni ports.

Complaining of the Baghdad pact, Yemen signed the Jidda pact with Egypt and Saudi Arabia, which established a five-year military alliance. After the formation of the United Arab Republic Crown Prince al-Badr visited Cairo where he signed a pact creating the United Arab States, a vague federation of Yemen and the United Arab Republic.

In 1959 Imam Ahmad went to Italy for medical treatment. He left his son and crown prince, Muhammad al-Badr, as regent. Seizing the opportunity, al-Badr immediately liberalized the rule, abrogated the absolute authority of the imam, removed many tyrannical officials, and instituted an eight-man advisory legislature. Imam Ahmad rushed home, placed al-Badr under house arrest, and beheaded, mutilated, or imprisoned al-Badr's closest partners. Yemen remained frozen until Imam Ahmad's death in 1962, whereupon his son became Imam Sayf al-Islam Muhammad al-Badr. The new ruler appointed Soviet-trained Colonel Abdallah al-Sallal army chief of staff, and promised that Yemen would begin to move into the twentieth century. A week later al-Sallal and a military junta bombarded the royal palace at Sana, declared that Imam al-Badr had been killed, and formed a Republic of Yemen. However, al-Badr was not dead, and about ten days later he held a large news conference in the mountains of northern Yemen.

Yemen Civil War: Royalist vs. Republican

At the very outset al-Sallal arranged a five-year military defense pact with Cairo; between 20,000 and 70,000 Egyptian troops were sent to Yemen to insure al-Sallal's position and to ensure control by Nasser over republican Yemen. The modernized Egyptian army, finding it impossible to fight in the mountain areas, restricted its activities to the plains and larger towns. The royalists were supplied with arms and ammunition by Saudi Arabia; their fighting forces were almost entirely made up of hill tribesmen who fought willingly against the Egyptian foreign invaders. Furthermore, they were always eager to capture automatic weapons, and stores of ammunition. No one doubted that they would conquer the plains within hours after the departure of the Egyptian troops. As the war dragged on it cost Nasser more than $500,000 a day.

Toward the end of 1962, after the Republic of Yemen had been recognized by the U.S.S.R. and the United Arab Republic, the United States proposed the withdrawal of all foreign troops from Yemen. On this basis the United States recognized the republican regime, which was admitted to the United Nations. Not until the June 1967 fiasco, however, did Nasser give his word to King Faysal that Egyptian troops would depart from Yemen and that support for al-Sallal would be terminated. When the British announced that they would be leaving Aden in 1968, Nasser declined to remove his troops; from Yemen he could occupy Aden and hold both ends of the Red Sea.

Under the rule of Imam al-Badr royalist Yemen remained unchanged, but as the struggle wore on al-Badr agreed to accept a constitution and a state council, and to create a modern legislature. Saudi Arabia gave him $20 million annually pressing him to form a coalition with a "Third Force" grouping of anti-Egyptian republicans. Many royalists despised the Third Force, but al-Badr agreed to form an anti-Egyptian front, including one Third Force adherent in a new cabinet in 1967.

Republican Yemen had more difficulty. As well as being a hard man to please, al-Sallal was in poor health and was forced to remain in Cairo for medical treatments for protracted periods. Amid jealousy and distrust one prime minister would be turned out to escape to Cairo with his life, often to return when his replacement fled. After an attempted coup, al-Sallal reassumed the post of prime minister and reestablished his absolute authority. As Nasser's puppet, al-Sallal, if his health permitted, would hold Yemen, it was hoped, until the British departed from Aden. Abandoned by Nasser at Khartoum, al-Sallal vowed to fight on alone. On November 5, 1967, on his way to Moscow, he was overthrown in a bloodless army coup.

Yemen Arab Republic

With al-Sallal gone, the last Egyptian troops departing in December, and King Faysal demanding moderation, the civil war lost its drive. The army turned over the government to a group of civilian Third Force republicans under Abd al-Rahman al-Iryani; within a few weeks a new war cabinet under Major General Hasan al-Amri replaced it. Royalists made a desperate, unsuccessful stand by besieging Sana. After considerable maneuvering, al-Badr rose from his sick bed, returned to Sana as ruler, and declared he would negotiate with the republicans without prior conditions. When Saudi Arabia halted the flow of arms and money, al-Badr, with his brothers, uncles, and cousins, gave up the struggle and left.

At the first session of a new republican government on March 17, 1969, Abd al-Rahman al-Iryani declared that the royalists had been defeated and the war was over. The new National Assembly at its first meeting reelected al-Iryani president and chose General al-Amri prime minister. Twelve of the fifty-seven seats in the Assembly remained empty, reserved for members from South Yemen, a gesture on the part of the Yemen Arab Republic (YAR) toward union of the two Yemens.

Society in Yemen was in chaos, the economy was in a shambles, famine stalked a land devastated by a three-year drought. The moderately socialist government was staffed by relatively able and earnest people. But governments were only temporary. Early in 1970 Muhsin al-Ayni, an experienced politician, took over the leadership of the cabinet and went to Saudi Arabia, the key to peace and progress for Yemen. He agreed to discontinue the friction along the frontier, to promote reconciliation among all the factions within YAR, and to accept back all exiles except al-Badr. After thirty royalist leaders returned to Sana, regained their property, and had one of their number elected to the presidential council, Saudi Arabia recognized YAR and exchanged ambassadors. That autumn it rained for thirty consecutive days, breaking the drought, but not in time to alleviate the famine. With 40 percent of the people near starvation, the United Nations issued a general appeal; it received a generous response. General al-Amri resumed his role as commander in chief.

The permanent constitution was presented to the National Assembly in 1971. It stated that YAR is an Islamic state in accord with the "principles of Muslim social justice." The large, elected Consultative Assembly chose al-Iryani as president of the council and Ahmad Muhammad Numan as prime minister. Burdened by the chronic deficit and administrative anarchy Numan resigned and General al-Amri moved in again. Two weeks later al-Amri murdered a photographer in a quarrel and was forced into exile. The government was given back to al-Ayni and the politicians.

The war with the People's Democratic Republic of (South) Yemen superseded all else in 1972 and 1973. In 1972 the prime ministers of the two Yemens approved detailed agreements to unify, the heads of state signed a unification document, and the YAR Consultative Council approved it. Yet, al-Ayni accused it of obstructing unity. He resigned and was replaced by a member of the presidential council. In 1973, though the talks with South Yemen continued, so did the border raids and assassinations. The Arab League's bid in 1973 to devise a formula for unification proved futile.

One prime minister followed another, until al-Iryani, in poor health and frustrated, resigned the presidency. The next day, June 13, 1974, the army staged a bloodless coup, suspended the constitution, dissolved the assembly, and removed the prime minister and cabinet.

Leading the coup was a Ruling Command Council of seven members under the hand of Colonel Ibrahim al-Hamadi, who became chairman and head of state. A new cabinet was installed under Prime Minister Muhsin al-Ayni, also a member of the council. The new chief announced that the state would now tilt toward Saudi Arabia. Within a short time sizable grants began to flow from Arab capitals. These sums, added to the $160 million coming in yearly from Yemenis working in Saudi Arabia, buoyed the economy.

Early in 1975, al-Hamadi and the ruling military junta fired al-Ayni for trying to improve relations with Marxist South Yemen, and appointed Abd al-Aziz al-Ghani, an economist and former governor of the central bank, to head a new cabinet. Reputedly "a man who talks very little but works much," al-Ghani set out for Riyadh and obtained a loan of $273 million, half of which was to be spent on roads, and a third to cover the budget deficit. The advance was made on the condition that all Soviet military advisers were to leave the Yemen Arab Republic. With military relations with the U.S.S.R. frozen, al-Hamadi sought arms and advisers from the United States. In 1976 the United States agreed to sell $139 million in arms to Yemen. A joint Saudi-YAR Coordination Council was created to establish educational projects, to build hospitals and new mosques, and to renovate historic mosques. Saudi Arabia made new grants of $160 million. The military junta and Colonel al-Hamadi seemed in firm control; the return of representative government was uncertain.

On October 11, 1977, Colonel al-Hamadi and his brother were assassinated by three unknown assailants. Lt. Colonel Ahmad al-Ghashmi, head of the first armored brigade, member of the command council, and al-Hamadi's closest friend and associate, took control; al-Ghani remained prime minister; and both declared al-Hamadi's policies would prevail.

REFERENCES: Chapter 41

Significant works for this chapter are also found in Chapters 1, 4, 7, 19, 22, 23, 24, 27, 28, 30, 31, 33, 34, 35, 37, 39, and 40.

Adamiyat, Fereydoun. *Bahrein Islands.* New York: Praeger, 1955. Geographical and historical.

Anthony, John Duke. *Arab States of the Lower Gulf: People, Politics, Petroleum.* Washington, D.C.: The Middle East Institute, 1975. An up-to-date analysis of the politico-economic and socio-tribal structure of the amirates. It begins with the independence of the amirates in 1971 but gives historical background.

Belgrave, Charles. *Personal Column, An Autobiography.* London: Hutchinson, 1960. Belgrave was adviser to the shaykh of Bahrayn for many years.

Bujra, Abdalla S. *The Politics of Stratification: A Study of Political Change in a South Arabian Town.* Oxford: Clarendon Press, 1973. A study of Hureidah, an independent city-state of 2,000 people until it was absorbed in 1940 into the Quaity Sultanate.

Calverly, Eleanor F. *My Arabian Days and Nights.* New York: Thomas Y. Crowell, 1958. A report on medical work in Kuwayt. By the wife of one who lived there from 1909 to 1929.

Chisholm, A. H. T. *The First Kuwait Oil Concession Agreement.* London: Frank Cass, 1975. The record of the commercial and political negotiations of the oil concession agreement in 1934.

Daniels, John. *Kuwait Journey.* Luton, England: White Crescent Press, 1971. Describes the development of Kuwayt from the discovery of oil in the 1930s to the 1970s.

Demir, Soliman. *The Kuwait Fund and the Political Economy of Arab Regional Development.* New York: Praeger, 1976. A sketch of the fund and its uses.

Dickson, H. R. P. *Kuwait and her Neighbors.* London: George Allen & Unwin, 1956. A lengthy survey of statistics, history, travel, and life.

Hawley, Donald. *The Trucial States.* New York: Humanities Press, 1971. Draws on a number of unpublished sources. The first third gives an historical overview of the states.

Hay, Sir Rupert. *The Persian Gulf States.* Washington, D.C.: Middle East Institute, 1959. Author served eight years as British political resident in the Persian Gulf. Gives up-to-date information on geography, climate, and history of the amirates.

Key, Kerim K. *The State of Qatar: An Economic and Commercial Survey.* Washington, D.C.: The author, 1976. Oil, industry, finance, social services, tourism, and economic facilities. Maps, charts, and statistics.

Landen, Robert Geran. *Oman since 1856: Disruptive Modernization in a Traditional Arab Society.* Princeton, N.J.: Princeton University Press, 1967. An outstanding work on diplomacy, imperialism, and political development in the Persian Gulf area.

Mann, Clarence. *Abu Dhabi: Birth of an Oil Sheikhdom.* Beirut: Khayats, 1964. The impact of the discovery of oil in an undeveloped state.

Philby, H. St. John B. *Sheba's Daughters.* London: Methuen, 1939. Accounts of trips by an old Arab hand to the interior of Arabia and to the Hadhramaut.

Phillips, Wendell. *Oman: A History.* New York: Morrow, 1967. A survey of the history from ancient times to 1961.

Rihani, Ameen. *Around the Coasts of Arabia.* London: Houghton Mifflin, 1930. A description of the Arab states in the Persian Gulf region.

Scott, Hugh. *In the High Yemen.* London: J. Murray, 1942. A good insight into the days of Imam Yahya.

Stark, Freya. *The Southern Gates of Arabia.* New York: Penguin Books, 1945. The experiences of a seasoned and perceptive traveler.

Townsend, John. *Oman: The Making of a Modern State.* New York: St. Martin's Press, 1977. Author gives a first-hand account of recent developments in Oman.

Tritton, Arthur S. *Rise of the Imams of Sanaa.* London: Oxford University Press, 1925. An excellent historical study.

van der Meulen, Daniel. *Aden to the Hadramaut: A Journey in South Arabia.* London: J. Murray, 1947. An account of a journey in South Arabia in 1939 by a civil servant from the Dutch East Indies.

Waterfield, Gordon. *Sultans of Aden.* London: J. Murray, 1968. The story of Captain Stafford Bettesworth Haines of the Indian Navy, who governed Aden from 1839 until 1854 and made it into a city.

Wenner, Manfred. *Modern Yemen.* Baltimore: Johns Hopkins Press, 1967. The best concise history of Yemen.

Chapter 42

The Arab Crescent and the Arab League

French Evacuation

Undoubtedly with quite different motives, the U.S.S.R., China, and the United States recognized the unconditional independence of Syria and Lebanon in 1944. Shortly thereafter, both declared war against Germany in accordance with the Yalta program and joined the United Nations as charter members. The presence of British troops on their soil antagonized only the more uncompromising Syrians and Lebanese. But the French symbolized the previous mandate-colonial status; fear of the permanence of French control governed emotions in Beirut and Damascus.

General de Gaulle understood that the troops would have to be withdrawn, but he evidently hoped to retain a strong French influence in the Levant by means of treaties with Syria and Lebanon that would be at least as favorable as the British treaties with Iraq and Egypt. He particularly desired that the French language be accepted and taught in all schools and that French schools be entirely free from Lebanese and Syrian control. Naval, military, and air bases for the French would be held indefinitely, and assurances would be given that the Levant would remain a French sphere in economic matters.

Syria and Lebanon indicated a willingness to discuss these points and negotiate treaties, but only after departure of the troops. The landing of additional French soldiers in Beirut was interpreted as military pressure. Open resistance to the French erupted, and the French shelled Damascus in May 1945. This goaded Churchill into serving an ultimatum upon de Gaulle to cease fire and detain his troops in their barracks while British forces restored order. The U.N. Security Council, prodded by the U.S.S.R. and the United States, recommended that foreign troops leave Syria and Lebanon as soon as practicable. The last French troops departed from Syria in April 1946, but remained in Lebanon until December. The two countries of the Levant had achieved independence.

Republic of Lebanon

In Lebanon the nationalist-minded leaders who had controlled the quasi-independent regime since 1943 remained unchanged. The confessional aspect of the state was upheld, as was the tradition that the president be a Maronite Christian and the prime minister a Sunni Muslim. At that time the Lebanese chamber of deputies included 30 Christians and 25 Muslims.

Elections for the chamber were held in 1947. The Constitutional party, the one in power, continued in office. The problem of Palestine, the economic detonations resulting from independence, the postwar relaxations, and the East-West crisis gave Lebanese politicians ample opportunity for disagreement. Perhaps the smallness of the country, the paucity of its natural resources, and the diversity of religious affiliations—the customary attribute of national distinction in the Middle East—bound together all the political leaders except the extremists. Among themselves they quarreled over favors, prestige, position, and power, but they usually closed ranks on foreign crises. Cabinets changed frequently, but the leaders shuffled the various ministerial posts among themselves. In the three decades following the departure of the French fifteen different men occupied the position of prime minister, many of them on several occasions. Bishara al-Khuri was overthrown in September 1952 by a bloodless public strike, mismanagement, corruption, and arrogance being the charges against him. Camille Shamun, leader of the Progressive Socialist party, was elected president. A new electoral law enacted in 1952 decreed that the chamber be composed of 13 Maronites, 9 Sunnites, 8 Shiites, 5 Greek Orthodox, 3 Druzes, 3 Greek Catholics, 2 Armenian Orthodox, and 1 collectively to the minor groups such as Protestants, Jews, and Roman Catholics.

Fringe parties did not succeed in winning many supporters, but they did have considerable nuisance value and kept the leaders in office more alert to their responsibilities. The largest of these parties—the Nationalist Bloc, at one time led by Raymond Iddah (Edde)—believed that Lebanon's destiny, and certainly her independence, rested upon close relations with France. This party declined after the French departed. Kamal Jumblat, a Druze, pursued a utopian socialist doctrine, whereas Antun Saada, who refused to accept the partition of Syria, formed the Syrian National party, a pro-fascist group that strove incessantly and often violently for the reunion of Lebanon with Syria.

Beirut and the other Lebanese towns on the coast had prospered greatly during the mandate period, mainly from commerce. During the war Beirut, which served as a port and base for operations in the Levant, became Westernized to a remarkable degree. National independence gave Beirut the opportunity to become one of the great markets in the Middle East. Her merchants proved equal to the responsibility, and Beirut evolved rapidly into a great Middle Eastern commercial and financial center. Shortly after 1948 Lebanon established a free money market that attracted Middle Eastern moneys to her banks.

Although the Lebanese rejoiced over the departure of the French, they were not bitterly anti-French. The many business connections precluded a complete break. And Lebanese-Syrian currency remained tied to the French franc until 1948, when France devalued the franc by 44 percent without increasing the cover for the Syrian-Lebanese pound, as had been

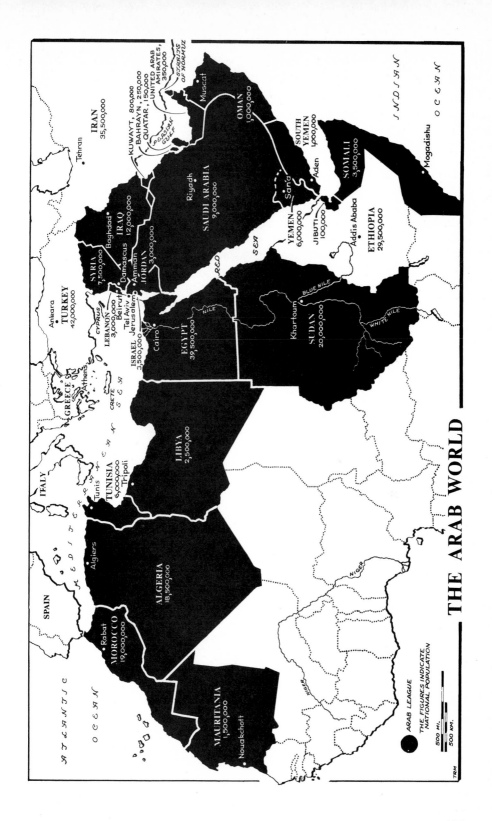

THE ARAB WORLD

ARAB LEAGUE

THE FIGURES INDICATE
NATIONAL POPULATION

500 MI.
500 KM.

TRM

ATLANTIC OCEAN

SPAIN

ITALY

MEDITERRANEAN SEA

GREECE
Athens

CRETE

TURKEY
42,000,000
Ankara

CYPRUS

IRAN
35,500,000
Tehran

STRAITS OF HORMUZ

PERSIAN GULF

Muscat

OMAN
1,000,000

KUWAYT, 800,000
BAHRAYN, 250,000
QUATAR, 150,000
UNITED ARAB
AMIRATES, 350,000

Riyadh

SAUDI ARABIA
9,000,000

IRAQ
12,000,000
Baghdad

SYRIA
7,500,000
Damascus

Beirut
LEBANON
3,000,000
Tel Aviv
ISRAEL
3,500,000
Jerusalem
Amman
JORDAN
3,000,000

RED SEA

Sana
YEMEN
6,000,000

SOUTH
YEMEN
1,000,000
Aden

JIBUTI
100,000
Addis Ababa

SOMALI
3,500,000

Mogadishu
INDIAN OCEAN

ETHIOPIA
29,500,000

BLUE NILE

Khartoum

SUDAN
20,000,000

WHITE NILE

NILE

Cairo

EGYPT
39,500,000

LIBYA
2,500,000

TUNISIA
6,000,000
Tunis
Tripoli

Algiers

ALGERIA
18,500,000

MOROCCO
19,000,000
Rabat

MAURITANIA
1,500,000
Nouakchott

NIGER

ATLANTIC OCEAN

623

agreed in 1944. France offered to make up the balance in properties claimed by France in Lebanon, in European currencies, in credit for purchases in France, and in additional French francs. Lebanese leaders protested vigorously but in the end accepted the offer, fearing a breakdown in trade. The financial settlement, rearranged and improved upon again in 1959, smoothed relations with France, and trade between the two countries was maintained at its customary level. In 1964 the charter of the French-owned Banque de Syrie et du Liban expired and the new state Bank of Lebanon was established to take over the issuing of currency and to conduct banking for the government. French control and the mandate period were finally concluded by the termination of this last visible instrument of power.

Every year after World War II Lebanon had a sizable unfavorable balance of trade that was more than redressed by commercial services, tourism, remittances from Lebanese emigrants, and investments of foreign capital. In 1958 just a day or two before the formation of the United Arab Republic, large capital sums flowed to Beirut from Syria. Wealthy individuals in Arab countries and from many other parts of the world found Lebanon a suitable haven for their funds. In 1965, for example, it was estimated that $150 million from Syria, Saudi Arabia, and Kuwayt was deposited in Lebanese banks. When such moneys were invested in local apartment houses or in new industry, the balance of payments was aided, but it endangered the liquidity of these accounts. The closing of the doors on October 15, 1966 of the Intra Bank of Beirut was a rude shock to the Middle East. A bank holiday was declared; the Bank of Lebanon guaranteed the solvency of all other banks in the country; but it took a full year for the reorganization of Intra Bank. Meanwhile, orders had been issued that all banks must keep with the Central Bank 25 percent of their demand deposits and 15 percent of time deposits. Since banking was one of the leading businesses in Lebanon and the principal occupation of many of the political figures and cabinet members, the security and integrity of banking was a prime concern of the government.

For some years business and political leaders in Lebanon deplored the nation's dependence on commerce and banking as too uncertain in times of world recession or tension; they advocated taking measures to direct the economy toward industry and scientific and specialized agriculture. Difficult as this was where consumer prices were high and natural resources few, considerable progress was achieved. Except for a recession in 1961 each year seemed more prosperous and auspicious until in 1967 the tightening of money, the June war, and the closing of the oil pipelines from Iraq slowed the economy.

From 1968 until the civil war in 1975 the Lebanese economy showed growth rates in some years up to 20 percent; in other years it stagnated, especially at those times when the border with Syria was closed or oil stopped flowing through the pipelines from Iraq and Saudi Arabia. Seventy-three percent of the Lebanese economy stemmed from commerce, and any restraint on the movement of goods was felt immediately in most sectors of the society. When incomes in the oil-producing states of the area began moving up in 1972, money was more plentiful in Beirut, prices rose, and massive strikes became common. Teachers at Lebanese University struck for higher pay and better working conditions. After more than half were forced to resign, students took to the streets demonstrating for them and getting the government to grant higher salaries. In the early 1970s the imbalance in Lebanon's economic life was inescapable. Wealth was piling up in the hands of merchants and bankers while unemployment and poverty were spreading through the cities and villages. Strikes and student demonstrations were manifestations of an escalating revolt against the worsening quality of life.

In 1948, in the early days of the republic, when Syria refused to accept the French offer to offset some of the losses to the Lebanese-Syrian pound resulting from the sudden devaluation of the franc, a new and separate Lebanese currency was established. Within a few weeks the currency break with Syria presented difficulties of payments, exchange rates, and trade balances. An agreement extended the economic unity of the two countries for an additional three years and arranged that 44 percent of the aggregate customs receipts at all frontiers would be credited to Lebanon. However, the divergent economic interests of the two countries caused one storm after another, and in 1950 precipitated an economic break and the closing of the frontier for nine months. In 1952 an economic agreement with Syria provided that no duties between the two countries would be levied on agricultural produce or livestock.

Hardly a year went by without border incidents that temporarily closed the Syrian border and interrupted travel and trade. The period from the Sinai War in 1956 to the dissolution of the union of Syria and Egypt in 1961 was unusually troublesome. Again in 1968 border relations deteriorated, this time over the actions of al-Saiqah, a Syrian-based Palestinian commando group. In 1971 Syrian Prime Minister Assad assured Lebanese leaders that Syria and al-Saiqah would not interfere in Lebanese affairs. But promises were impossible to enforce along mountainous and irregular borders inhabited on each side by people for whom frontiers are unnatural.

The Trans-Arabian pipeline, carrying oil from the Saudi Arabian fields to the Mediterranean, had its terminus near Sidon in southern Lebanon. In 1947 Lebanon forced work to cease on the line because of the American position on the partition of Palestine. Construction, however, was resumed in 1949, and oil began to flow in 1950. A refinery was built in Sidon to process petroleum, and a second was erected in 1955. On the coast north of Beirut the Iraq Petroleum Company's (IPC) pipeline touched the sea at Tripoli, and after World War II two new parallel lines were laid to offset the disuse of the Haifa line and to market the increased Iraqi production. The lines and refineries brought very welcome income. But in 1956 a new law was passed, aimed at Iraq Petroleum and TAP-line, imposing heavy taxes retroactively to 1952 on foreign oil companies having pipelines in Lebanon.

IPC immediately objected, dropped its plans for an additional pipeline to Tripoli, and discharged employees in the Tripoli area. Not until 1958 did IPC agree to pay Lebanon back transit fees and to raise the rate so that yearly royalties jumped from $1 million to $3.5 million. In 1962 IPC built a modern refinery at Tripoli and agreed to make available to Lebanon all of her domestic needs in local currency. At the same time a similar settlement was concluded with TAP-line, giving Lebanon "payments in arrears" and setting a new rate that increased annual revenues from $1.25 million to $4.5 million.

Although Lebanon had no oil of her own, she began to benefit directly from Middle Eastern oil resources to a small degree. As oil prices moved up due to OPEC pressures, Lebanon sought increased payments for the flow of oil across her land. Rates were adjusted in 1973, raising Lebanon's income to $12 million a year from IPC. When Iraq nationalized IPC Syria wanted to acquire IPC rights in Lebanon, but in accordance with a 1931 agreement Lebanon took over the IPC pipeline and the Tripoli refinery. Iraq retaliated by banning all goods from Lebanon, and Syria closed the border for three months during the summer. Eventually, Syria recognized Lebanese ownership of IPC installations in return for improved conditions for Syrians resident in Lebanon, including a provision giving them equal pay for equal work.

Although the U.S.S.R. recognized Lebanon in 1944, the Soviets gave her only passing interest. In Beirut the communists were extremely active in the trade-union movement. Street demonstrations were so frequent that they bored the public; but communists enjoyed such success organizing parades and protests among the students at the American University that government officials closed it temporarily in 1954. Yet, in the 1953 elections all communists and their sympathizers failed miserably at the polls.

After 1954 the U.S.S.R. signed an economic agreement with Lebanon; a similar trade pact was initialed in 1955 with East Germany. Russian technicians surveyed Lebanon in 1956 for various economic and industrial possibilities, and trade agreements were negotiated with Communist China and Bulgaria in 1957. Rapidly expanding population (about 3 percent a year), limited land resources, and unemployment offered fertile fields for Soviet activities. Lebanese officials recognized the challenge and initiated various projects, the most promising being the Litani River irrigation and hydroelectric power plan. Beginning in 1960, the leaders of all groups adopted a policy of nonalignment and used this term repeatedly in public pronouncements. Officials too closely identified with American or French circles had to step aside. Non-Lebanese Arab Communists were deported. But trade was encouraged with the Soviet bloc.

Lebanon in the main remained a Western-oriented nation, though she could not deny her position on the Mediterranean, her past history, and her cultural associations. Relations between Lebanon and the United States generally were cordial until the early 1970s. The American University of

Beirut created much good will, as did the presence in the United States of numerous Lebanese emigrants.

By far the greatest difficulty for Lebanon after World War II arose from the partition of Palestine and the birth of Israel. Lebanon joined the Arab League at its inception. She argued in the United Nations against the partition of Palestine and halted work at Sidon on the pipeline. However, Lebanon's part in the Palestine war was very small, and she suffered only a handful of casualties. Public demonstrations in Lebanon definitely indicated sympathy for the Palestinian Arabs.

Lebanon, however, found no difficulty in subscribing to the various truces declared in the Palestine war and easily entered into armistice negotiations. Israeli forces withdrew from four Lebanese villages that they had occupied. In 1949 an armistice was signed, recognizing the previous Palestine-Lebanon frontier and adding demilitarized zones on each side. Lebanon refused to recognize Israel and adopted the boycott practices of the Arab League. Since unemployment was widespread in Lebanon, the influx of over 100,-000 Arab refugees, equal to almost 10 percent of the total population of Lebanon, injected an explosive factor into the Palestine settlement. The refugees were located in fifteen camps scattered from Tripoli to Tyre, though mainly in the south, and were supported by United Nations grants; but their continued presence and natural increase to 185,000 by 1973 tilted Lebanon's religious and political balances toward the Muslims and the poor.

From 1968 on, the Palestinian specter jarred Lebanon's precarious equilibrium repeatedly, as the level of violence rose steadily. In December 1968 Palestinian commandos from Beirut attacked and severely damaged an Israeli plane at the Athens airport, killing one passenger. Two days later the Israeli air force raided the Beirut airport, destroying planes valued at $40 million. The United Nations Security Council censured Israel, condemning the foray as "premeditated military action" and ordering Israel to pay damages to Lebanon.

Already, students had been demonstrating and after the airport affair 25,000 students struck, protesting the inefficacy of the armed forces and demanding universal conscription in Lebanon. Palestinian actions against Israel were intensified, though the government tried to prevent Lebanon from becoming a base for such attacks. The Lebanese army moved to crack down on Palestinian activities, but guerrilla forces seized control of most of the refugee camps in the country. Bloody riots in Tripoli, Beirut, and other places compelled the government to attempt a ceasefire, the first of many over the ensuing years.

Palestinian guerrilla operations throughout 1970 brought repeated retaliatory raids from Israel. Over 15,000 Lebanese abandoned their homes in the south. Christian and Shiite Muslim leaders demanded that the government act to curtail the Palestinians; Sunnite Muslims supporting the Palestinians called on the government to strengthen the army and urged that outside aid be found. Armed clashes occurred in Beirut between Palestinians and Pierre Jumayyil's Christian Phalangist private army. A nationwide strike drew attention to the need for protection and economic assistance to south Lebanon. Signs of incipient civil war were everywhere.

Palestinian forces poured into Lebanon after their defeat in Jordan in 1970 in such numbers that they took full control of a thirty-five kilometer strip along the southern border. Martial law was invoked in the entire country. PLO leader Yasir Arafat, headquartered in Beirut, reached an agreement in 1972 with Prime Minister Salam whereby the guerrillas would consult with the government, which would hold ultimate veto power over any action. Large sections of the population, however, subscribed to the Palestinian aims; sympathy strikes were frequent; to many university students Palestinian activists were neither guerrillas nor terrorists but heroic national freedom fighters.

Then, in 1972, came the bloody massacre by Japanese terrorists at the Tel Aviv airport and the killing of Israeli Olympic contestants at Munich. Asserting that each of these had been plotted by Palestinians in Beirut, Israeli authorities retaliated with air and land strikes in south Lebanon. In April 1973 Israeli raiders landed by boat south of Beirut, entered the city, killed three Palestinian leaders, destroyed their headquarters, and got away unscathed. The uproar against the government forced Salam and his cabinet from office; they were replaced by a cabinet dominated by Shamun's rightist bloc. Soon, hostilities erupted outside Beirut between Palestinians and the Lebanese army. With daily shelling of south Lebanon a commonplace in the spring of 1974, many offered to send aid but President Franjieh rejected all except Russian surface-to-air missiles. At this juncture Shamun's rightist military units began to cooperate with Jumayyil's Phalangists, and the many contesting and conflicting forces in Lebanese society entered the fray. The fighting polarized until by 1975 a civil war was raging in Lebanon.

Lebanese Politics

The relative calm of post-World War II Lebanese political life was shattered by the 1956 Suez crisis. President Shamun supported Egypt in her nationalization move, and mass rallies and strikes condemning Western pressures on Egypt took place in Beirut and other cities. When the Sinai war began, Lebanon declared a state of emergency and Shamun invited the heads of all Arab governments to Beirut to determine what action should be taken. Lebanese leaders spoke vigorously in the United Nations and in other forums, lamenting the aggression upon Egypt and urging the speedy withdrawal of Israeli forces from Gaza and the Straits of Tiran.

As soon as the Sinai war ended, Lebanese leaders engaged in a bitter parliamentary election. A National Union Front announced its opposition to Prime Minister al-Sulh and President Shamun. Collecting around several disgruntled former prime ministers such as Salam, al-Yafi, and Uwayni, the front was against a constitutional amendment permitting Shamun to succeed himself, and advocated close and impartial cooperation with other Arab states. Clashes occurred, but the elections were conducted in July. The government won 50 seats, the National Union Front 8, and the Independents 8. Significantly, Salam, al-Yafi, Jumblat, Karami, and other prominent politicians failed to win election, and in August Sami al-Sulh reshuffled his cabinet.

The politicians who found themselves frozen out of office commenced a battle to regain power and discovered eager allies in Syria and Egypt. Arms smuggling from Syria became commonplace, and Lebanese frontier police were shot in attempts to halt the illicit traffic. Terrorists bombed the parliament building and Government House. Lebanon's public acceptance of the Eisenhower Doctrine became a prime target of the opposition. Foreign Minister Charles Malik reiterated that Lebanon would side with the Arabs in any dispute with the West involving legitimate Arab rights and aspirations. He warned, however, that Middle Eastern conflicts could not be solved by alliances with communists.

When the United Arab Republic increased pressures surrounding Lebanon, her leaders announced immediately that Lebanon would not join. Arms and men from Syria and Egypt began to flow into Lebanon, but Malik confirmed a report that he had received a promise of unlimited military and economic aid from the United States to maintain Lebanon's independence.

In March 1958 a reorganized cabinet under al-Sulh won a vote of confidence. At the same time eighty-two Lebanese leaders, including the heads of several of the religious communities, signed a statement warning President Shamun against amending the constitution and seeking reelection when his term expired in September. Political demonstrations and outbreaks of violence erupted in Tripoli and Beirut. Soon designated as rebels, politicians out of office extended independently their sway over specific areas: Salam in the Basta quarter of Beirut; Jumblat in the Druze mountain area; Karami in the sector north of Tripoli; and others in two or three isolated regions. Syria and Egypt helped the rebels, but matters remained stalemated, as General Shihab refused to commit the army to either political camp and acted only to maintain public order.

Shamun, pressured by Dag Hammarskjöld of the United Nations, agreed not to try for reelection, and General Shihab acquiesced to a quiet demand that he accept the presidency. Civil strife had subsided when revolution broke out in Iraq. The possibility of sizable Syrian intervention in Lebanon became so frightening that Shamun called upon President Eisenhower for urgent relief. The landing of American marines in Beirut heightened the quarrel among local politicians to the level of the cold war between East and West. Many blustered, but it was evident that no one would seriously challenge the Americans, who asserted that the marines would be withdrawn as soon as a peaceful solution to Lebanon's political problems could be devised. As was expected, the presidential election resulted in the choice of General Fuad Shihab, and the rebels declared they would be satisfied if and when the American troops left. Most Lebanese political leaders hoped that genuine neutrality would descend upon Lebanon so she could become "the Switzerland of the Middle East."

President Shihab was inaugurated September 23, 1958, three days after Sami al-Sulh had left for France and self-imposed exile; American troops departed October 25th; and the United Nations observers were gone by November. The president designated Rashid Karami as prime minister of a cabinet that in a few days was reduced to four members, the others being Uwayni, Raymond Iddah, and Jumayyil. The Chamber voted to give Karami authority to rule by decree for four months. Some of the open wounds of the battles began to heal and calmer relations with the United Arab Republic alleviated much of the bitterness. Shihab and Nasser met for a warm exchange at the Lebanese-Syrian border, and in Cairo Karami signed a beneficial economic pact. Karami skillfully avoided involvement in the heated quarrels between Nasser and General Kassim of Iraq, and so satisfied the domestic and foreign policy inclinations of the Lebanese factions that he remained at the helm until the spring of 1960. Then he stepped aside for the formation of a caretaker cabinet in preparation for the summer elections for a new ninety-nine-member Chamber. (The number of members in Lebanon's Chamber was usually divisible by eleven so that the accepted ratio of six Christians to five Muslims could be easily maintained.) No official census had been taken since 1932 as the ruling majority did not wish to test this proportion. The membership breakdown, which remained unchanged until the 1975 civil war, was: 30 Maronites, 20 Sunnites, 19 Shiites, 11 Greek Orthodox, 6 Druzes, 6 Greek Catholics, 4 Armenian Orthodox, 1 Armenian Catholic, 1 Protestant, and 1 other Christian.

The elections were orderly. Fourteen parties participated and Karami's won eleven seats. Forty-one independents were elected. With such a peaceful situation President Shihab felt he was no longer needed and announced his resignation. When the new Chamber urged him to reconsider he acceded to their pleas. Saib Salam formed a large cabinet to try to unite all parties and shades of opinion; but after bitter quarrels he relinquished the post to Karami who skillfully steered a neutral course until the 1964 elections.

Shihab refused to consider the suggestion that the constitution be amended to allow him a second term. Fifty-one-year-old Charles Hilu, the minister of education, was elected fourth president and took office in September 1964. Karami, with the strong approval of President Hilu and a cabinet of experts, set out to purge public life and the government of gross inefficiency and corruption. Their patronage ebbing away, party leaders became so piqued they forced Karami out in 1966 and installed Abdallah al-Yafi. With the failure of the Intra Bank that autumn Karami and the technicians were returned to office.

In Arab affairs Karami and most of the political leaders adhered to Arab League policies. In May 1967 he requested that the United States Sixth Fleet not make its scheduled call at Beirut, for fear that such a visit might be interpreted as Lebanese bowing to non-Arab pressures. When the June 1967 war broke out President Hilu declared a state of emergency; Karami withdrew Lebanon's ambassadors from Washington and London and forced the recall of theirs from Beirut. Lebanon branded Israel as the aggressor at the Security Council and made one brief air foray over Israel. After the fighting was halted Lebanese politics returned to the usual competition for position and influence. Karami gave up the prime ministership in February 1968 as was customary before an election, and al-Yafi headed a caretaker government.

The election campaign quickly became a heated contest between what were termed "right" and "left" groups. A rightist coalition of Shamun's National Liberal party, Jumayyil's Phalange, and Iddah's National Bloc won thirty seats; Karami's Democratic Bloc took twenty-four; most of the remaining forty-five places were filled by independents. Actually the balance in the new Chamber was about equally divided between the two sides. Al-Yafi and his new cabinet remained with great difficulty until January 1969. At that time Karami was called upon to form a wide coalition cabinet in an attempt to solve the problem of clashes between security forces and Palestinian activists. Without a representative of Shamun's party in the cabinet, conservative Christians withdrew. Karami offered to resign in April and again in November, but stayed on until after the presidential election late in 1970.

The unwritten national pact that the president be a Maronite, the prime minister a Sunnite, and other officials belong to other religious groups was reaffirmed by all leaders, assuring a peaceful election. Sulayman Franjieh, minister of economy, was elected president. Supported by Shamun and Jumayyil, he received 50 votes; Ilyas Sarkis, governor of the Central Bank, Karami's candidate, received the remaining 49. A political truce was declared, as a cabinet headed by Salam won a 78 to 1 vote of confidence, promising to battle corruption and to concentrate on economic and social problems. Salam was forced to resign when public opinion turned against him during intensive Israeli military raids in the spring of 1973.

With many young leftists in the Chamber for the first time in 1972, President Franjieh saw one cabinet after another founder amid intense controversy over the strength of the army, support of the Palestinian cause, reforms in health and education, and foreign policy.

During the October 1973 war Lebanon maintained an official neutrality, to the disgust of most Palestinian groups. As clashes multiplied in 1974 and the Palestinian armed forces grew to 10,000, Shamun's National Liberal party and Jumayyil's Phalange formed independent militias. In September, after armed battles and political assassinations, two ministers, followers of Jumblat, resigned, claiming the government was ignoring the issue of law and order and had allowed huge arms shipments for the militias to be landed on the coast.

Lebanese Civil War

On April 13, 1975, a busload of Palestinians was massacred by Phalange militia, just at the time Prime Minister Rashid al-Sulh was suggesting a reform of the parliamentary representative system to give greater military and political muscle to Lebanon's Muslims. These actions accelerated the polarization of Lebanese society. The Palestinians joined the leftist parties, largely Muslim in composition, while Shamun's National Liberal party co-operated with Jumayyil's Phalange in supporting President Franjieh, to form a Maronite-dominated coalition of the Christian right. Five hundred were killed in the first encounter. Rashid al-Sulh was forced to resign and Franjieh tried to form a military government. Lasting only five days, it gave way to the experienced Karami, who formed a six-man Christian-Muslim cabinet, omitting followers of Jumayyil and Jumblat. But calls to end the national pact insured the continuation of the civil war.

Bitter fighting continued through 1975 and most of 1976. The Lebanese army, which for a time had remained aloof, entered the war in September 1975 in the battle between the Muslims of Tripoli, Karami's home, and the Christian town of Zgharta, Franjieh's residence. The bloodshed spread to Beirut, where house-to-house fighting devastated sections of the city. It was calculated that $3.4 billion in damages was incurred in 1975 alone, as 3,500 businesses were bombed, burned, or looted. Many international companies moved their headquarters from Beirut to Athens, Amman, Cairo, or Dubay. Beirut ceased to be the financial center of the Middle East. Though a half dozen ceasefires were agreed upon none lasted more than a few days. Muslims and others called repeatedly upon President Franjieh to resign.

The causes of the civil war lay in part with the personal rivalries and antagonisms endemic in Lebanese political, social, economic, and religious life. Added to this were the growing involvement of Lebanese and Palestinians in each other's affairs, and the inflexibility of Lebanon's political and governmental structures. The war was exacerbated by the participation of foreign powers desiring to determine its outcome.

Most Lebanese supported the aims of the Palestinians and viewed their plight with sympathy, but as Lebanese they did not wish to share directly in the struggle. They refused to accord citizenship to them and hoped they would go away. Above all, the Lebanese abhorred the idea that the Palestinians might somehow have an overriding voice in Lebanon's political future. Thus, they were greatly distressed as the Palestinians increased their use of Lebanon as a base of operations against Israel, fearing especially that Israel might seize south Lebanon up to the Litani River.

The Palestinians for their part saw in Lebanon a staging area for incursions into Israel; they used Beirut as a convenient spot for plotting action against Israel throughout the world. Christian conservative militants like Shamun, Jumayyil, and Franjieh, finding their government supine in the face of the Palestinian menace, organized to combat them privately. Leftist groups in Lebanon, especially those who were Sunnites, accepted their

Palestinian co-religionists as useful allies in the contest against the well-armed and wealthy Christian rightist minority.

Quite apart from the Palestinians, the political structure of Lebanon was askew. No census had been taken since 1932, as those in power were afraid of what it might reveal. Most knowledgeable observers judged that the ratio of six Christians to five Muslims in parliament and the civil service no longer reflected Lebanon's demography; it might even have changed to a ratio of four Christians to six Muslims. Tampering with the original ratios would alter the power lines within the state, and any suggestion of this infuriated Shamun, Jumayyil, Franjieh, and their confreres. Jumblat, the Druze social-ist, demanded equal representation of Christians and Muslims and proposed completely secular elections in which religion would be ignored. Furthermore, the Christian rightist minority was considered the party of the wealthy while the Muslim leftist majority was the party of the poor and underprivileged. Separated by religion, political philosophy, and econom-ics, the two sides seeking power had drifted into civil war.

After a short lull intense fighting was resumed in December 1975; by March 1976 it was reported that between 15 and 20 percent of the heart of Beirut had been destroyed and perhaps 10,000 people had died. Franjieh continued to refuse to step down and the Lebanese army began to experi-ence massive defections. The perplexing situation in the army revolved around the fact that most of the 18,000 men and many of the junior officers were Muslims, while the senior officers were almost all Christians. Franjieh had hesitated to call upon the army, fearing that the men might shoot their officers. Then, army defectors formed the Lebanese Arab Army and united with leftist Muslims and Palestinians. Franjieh and Karami, deeply con-cerned, met with Syria's President Assad in February 1976 to initial the Damascus Agreement. In it, Assad pledged to withdraw the Syrian-based Palestine Liberation Army and Franjieh promised to call for equal number of seats in parliament for Christians and Muslims, to revise the electoral law to give genuine representation to the people, and to provide real social reforms. Back in Beirut he announced the "new foundation," which modi-fied the national pact only for parliament and the civil service but not for high government officials.

As the fighting wore on it began to look as if victory for the leftist Muslim-Palestinian coalition was only weeks away. Then, on March 29, 1976, Assad cut off all supplies going from Syria to the Palestinians. It seemed that he had suddenly changed sides. He may not have relished the idea of a Pales-tinian-dominated Lebanon that would have been able to jeopardize Syria's relations with Israel and could have involved him in war at a time he did not choose. He may not have wished to see the Maronite minority crushed in Lebanon, since he and many of his colleagues belonged to the Alawite sect, a distinct minority in Syria. Also, many of the leftists were members of the Iraqi branch of the Baath party, bitter enemies of the Syrian branch. Assad certainly did not wish his country to be squeezed between Iraq and Lebanon. Furthermore Iraq, Libya, and other more radical states were sending arms and supplies to the leftists. All seemed to add up to the old adage of divide and rule.

The Christian militias and the Syrian army were now aligned against the Palestinians and Muslim leftists. Neither side was prepared to compromise. Syrian troops entered Lebanon in April, and along with Jordan were opposing victory for any Lebanese party.

Throughout the spring of 1976 maneuvering for the election of a successor to Franjieh consumed the attention of all the factions. Arafat and Jumblat pushed the candidacy of Raymond Iddah; the Phalange group, with the approval of Assad, obtained the necessary votes for Ilyas Sarkis, who had lost out by only one vote six years earlier. Elected in May, Sarkis assumed office on September 23, 1976, but the war continued. When Syria ordered the bombing of refugee camps, Iraq shut off the flow of oil to Syria. The strain of the military operation began to tell on the Syrian economy, especially when Saudi Arabia and other Arab states cut off aid. At the same time, Israeli naval units were preventing arms shipments from reaching the Muslim leftists and were supplying arms to the Christian militias. By October there were more than 20,000 Syrian troops in Lebanon, occupying nearly half the country.

With the internationalizing of the Lebanese civil war the Arab League called for a joint Arab force to police a ceasefire. Major resistance ended when the Tel al-Zaatar refugee camp fell to Syrian and Christian guns. Meeting in Riyadh under pressure from King Khalid, Egypt, Syria, Kuwayt, the PLO, Lebanon, and Saudi Arabia called for an Arab peace-keeping contingent of 30,000, under the command of President Sarkis. Composed mainly of Syrian troops, the Arab force was warned by Israel not to enter the area south of the Litani River. The war was not over, however, for the shelling, bombing, ambushing, and killing continued through 1977.

Rashid Karami had relinquished the office of prime minister in December 1976, and President Sarkis appointed a Muslim banker, Salim al-Huss, to the difficult post. No parliamentary election had been held in 1976 as required by the constitution, and the question of representation in the Chamber, one of the roots of the civil war, had not been broached. Until it was, peace for a united Lebanon could only be temporary and illusory.

Toward the end of 1976 the Arab peace-keeping troops took control of Sidon and Tripoli and opened the highways between them and Beirut. An American bank reopened and in January 1977 all banks resumed full domestic and foreign services. Peace, however, was fleeting. Pro-Iraqi Palestinians battled al-Saiqah (Syrian) Palestinians in Beirut. Raymond Iddah and Shamun were attacked by gunmen who were driven off by bodyguards: Jumblat, however, was assassinated in March 1977.

Most of the fighting occurred in Lebanon in the sensitive area south of the Litani River along the Israeli frontier where Muslim and Maronite villages and enclaves are juxtaposed in an irregular pattern. Israel had already advised Arab peace-keeping forces not to enter the region; without the presence of the Lebanese army there, battles between Palestinian forces and Christian militia were resumed. Early in 1977 the Christians captured a small Muslim town in south Lebanon. Although Palestinian troops went to support the Muslims another village fell to the Christians. By the end of March heavy shelling took place almost daily and the Christian militia was receiving Israeli support. The frontier was opened; supplies and armed forces moved back and forth. The Israeli foreign minister declared Israel would not tolerate attacks on Lebanese villages near the Israeli border. Long range artillery duels erupted, Palestinians supported by Syria and the Christians by Israel. A cease-fire was arranged in August to be broken by twelve days of heavy fighting in September. American diplomacy negotiated a cease-fire on September 26 among the five contestants: Lebanon, Syria, Israel, the PLO, and the Maronites. Though no documents were signed it was agreed that Maronite enclaves in the south were to be safe and unmolested; that the border was to be open for the passage of people and goods as long as Maronites and Israelis wished; that Christian troops would be sent to Christian barracks and Muslim troops to Muslim barracks; that PLO guerrillas would pull back; that Lebanese troops, supervised by the Arab peace-keeping forces, would police the area; that the safety of all refugee camps would be guaranteed; and that the 1969 Cairo accord would be fulfilled.

How long the cease-fire would hold was uncertain. Without vast amounts of aid Lebanon would be socially and politically unstable and to build a respected Lebanese army would be unlikely. But Arab countries would not give financial aid to Lebanon as long as Maronites continued to traffic with Israel. An American aid program of $50 million was useful as a stopgap. Fundamental questions in Lebanon were difficult to resolve until an overall peace settlement in the Middle East could be reached. By October 1977 the Christian and Muslim militias were larger than ever and public recruitment had lifted the number of trained and armed soldiers to an estimated 45,000, ten times the size of the Lebanese army. Shamun's Christian Tigers and the Muslim Ambushers, equal in strength and composed of commandos, nurses, frogmen, and teen-agers, parade without interference and demonstrate before dignitaries and foreign correspondents.

On March 11, 1978, eleven Palestinian commandos landed on the Israeli coast with the idea of entering Tel Aviv, seizing hostages, and demanding the release of some of their brethren. They were apprehended, however, and most of them were killed; but thirty-four Israelis were also killed in the incident. Three days later, in retaliation, the Israeli army in its largest engagement since 1973 invaded south Lebanon to a depth of six miles, hesitated briefly, and then occupied all of Lebanon south of the Litani River. Arabs everywhere were indignant and many Western leaders demanded Israeli withdrawal. U.N. peacekeeping forces were assembled quickly and began to take up positions there on March 22. Considerable fighting continued in scattered areas between Israelis and Palestinians and between Lebanese Christian militias and Lebanese Muslim and army groups. World opinion obliged the Israelis to pull back, which they did in stages; insisting that Palestinian forces be controlled before withdrawal, the Israelis completed their operation in mid-June. Meanwhile, over 100,000 Lebanese villagers had become homeless and any hope for internal peace in Lebanon was pushed far into the future.

Republic of Syria

When World War II ended, the Syrian political leaders who had battled for complete independence in the mandatory period were in control and had the satisfaction of forming the first fully sovereign Syrian republic. Shukri al-Kuwatli held the presidency, Jamil Mardam was prime minister, and a new chamber of deputies was elected in 1947.

National feelings in Syria ran high. The actions of the French had been more drastic in Damascus and the interior provinces of Syria than in Beirut. Three times in recent memory the French had wantonly shelled Damascus, which had been the site of the Arab congresses as well as the capital of Faysal's short-lived Arab kingdom in 1920. All French schools in Syria were closed in 1945, and when France devalued the franc in 1948, Syria issued her own separate Syrian pounds. French offers of reconciliation were refused, and any official who appeared friendly or compromising toward the French was digging his own political grave.

The dream of a united Arab state to include Lebanon, Syria, Transjordan, Palestine, and Iraq had not died in Syria. As Syria emerged independent at the close of the war, the value of union appeared greater than ever; many Syrians regarded it as almost a necessity. Each state separately was weak; together they would have strength. Yet, an arrangement to accomplish even partial federation required political genius of a high order. Fertile Crescent unity was not a new idea, but after the area had been divided between England and France unification had been impossible.

The fall of France in 1940 whetted Abdallah's ambitions to join Syria to Transjordan. But in 1947 President al-Kuwatli of Syria publicly stated that in any uniting Transjordan would be annexed by Syria. Syrian political leaders had no intention of being governed from Amman by Abdallah. Indeed, they did not relish the thought of surrendering position and power in Syria to any group or person. Others within Syria looked forward to the merger of Iraq and Transjordan, the two Hashimite kingdoms, and the eventual inclusion of Syria and Lebanon. Leaders in Iraq and Syria discussed the union of their two states into a Fertile Crescent union. The Syrians believed that they possessed a more advanced population and that though slightly smaller, they would dominate Iraq. On the other hand Iraqis recognized that their country contained greater wealth, both developed and potential, and felt certain that Iraq would lead the combined state.

Syria played an active part in the formation of the Arab League, attended its conferences, and promised to cooperate militarily against the formation of a Zionist state. In 1947 the Palestine liberation committee obtained over 27,000 volunteers in Syria, and Druze chiefs notified the government they could furnish 10,000 men for the fight. In the spring of 1948 various Syrian army officers, including Colonel Adib al-Shishakli, participated in the Palestine war, but in the actual fighting Syrian forces proved to be ineffective. There was no great enthusiasm for shedding Syrian blood so that Abdallah in Transjordan or Faruk in Egypt might have more territory to rule.

On March 30, 1949, Chief of Staff Husni al-Zaim carried out a bloodless coup d'état. Learning that President al-Kuwatli was planning his dismissal, al-Zaim arrested the president and the leading political figures. The public approved for a number of reasons: the Palestine war was a failure; corruption was not reduced; the constitution had been amended to permit the president to succeed himself; and al-Kuwatli opposed the Fertile Crescent unity plan. A new cabinet was formed; al-Zaim as prime minister also held the portfolios of defense and interior. Political parties were outlawed, and a new constitution was planned. In June al-Zaim, "The Leader," was elected president; on August 14 General Sami al-Hinnawi arrested al-Zaim, who was immediately shot.

Husni al-Zaim had started out strongly, arranging a cease-fire agreement with Israel and obtaining assurances from Nuri al-Said that Iraq would come to the assistance of Syria if attacked by Israel. Husni proposed unity with Iraq "on the basis of a full autonomous state for each country," and military figures journeyed between Damascus and Baghdad. Fearing Hashimite rule in Syria, Egypt and Saudi Arabia rushed diplomatic and financial support to al-Zaim, causing him to abandon unionist policies and become president of a new Syrian republic. Worst of all, he showed an inclination to restore to France some aspects of her cultural influence. French, for instance, became an official language, along with Arabic.

Upon the execution of al-Zaim, General al-Hinnawi called upon Hashim al-Atasi, an elder statesman, to form a new government. A constituent assembly was elected, and al-Atasi was chosen head of state. (Women voted for the first time.) Meanwhile, discussions with Iraqi officials produced a draft framework for a common regime; Syria and Iraq would have a common army, a supreme cabinet including foreign affairs, defense, finance, and economy, and a customs and monetary union. But the Republican Bloc, enemy of union, stirred the army to move. On December 19, 1949, Colonel Adib al-Shishakli arrested al-Hinnawi, who was charged with treason and conspiracy with a foreign power (Iraq).

Colonel al-Shishakli did not at first rule directly. The constituent assembly declared Syria to be a republic, and al-Atasi was elected president. No one, however, doubted who was the real power in the government. Colonel al-Shishakli desired sincerely to return Syria to civilian government; the cabinet reflected that intention except for the minister of defense, who kept the army's hand on political affairs. A liberal constitution adopted in 1950 contained articles with respect to education, labor, land ownership, and the rights of the citizen.

The new constitution and the new government, however, did not alter the fundamental weakness of Syria or usher in a new flourishing economic order. Syria began to look to the Soviet bloc. Attacks were made upon

American activities, and Syria was urged to sign a nonaggression pact with the U.S.S.R.

One cabinet succeeded another in 1951; in November a prolonged cabinet crisis ended with the leader of the Islamic Socialist Front as prime minister. The philosophy of this group, as one member described it, was "a Marxist drink in a Muslim cup."

Colonel al-Shishakli acted swiftly. Most of the cabinet was jailed, President al-Atasi resigned, political parties were outlawed, and plans for a new government and a new constitution were initiated. The new constitution was not presented until 1953, at which time al-Shishakli became president and prime minister. He arrested many leading political figures and declared martial law in Damascus and Aleppo.

But al-Shishakli had overreached himself. The army revolted, forcing him to flee. Hashim al-Atasi became president again; the 1950 constitution was reinstated; and the 1949 chamber of deputies was recalled until a new parliament could be elected. Khalid Bakdash, leader of the Communist party, became the first Arab communist duly elected to an Arab parliament on a Communist party ticket. Ex-president Shukri al-Kuwatli returned from five years of exile in Egypt and was elected president in August 1955. A succession of prime ministers battled with the complex economic, social, and political problems of Syria, but none found a constructive program, largely because of virulent nationalism and the submergence of Syrian interests to those of Egypt and Saudi Arabia.

The political instability in Syria in the decade after World War II was extremely detrimental to economic planning and development. Excellent plans for the division and distribution of large tracts of land among poor and landless peasants were enacted into law, but were not implemented to any great extent. Moves in that direction antagonized the large landowners and led in part to the demise of the al-Shishakli regime in 1954. After the breakdown of economic relations with Lebanon, Syria took steps to improve the port facilities in Latakia and to channel more of Syria's foreign trade through that point. But Latakia did not have the geographical advantages of Tripoli, Beirut, Sidon, and other Lebanese ports.

Raids and counterraids occurred frequently on the border of Israel. In 1955 Israeli forces mounted a massive attack on Syria. Since the Western powers, and particularly the United States, were identified with the foundation of the Zionist state, the West bore the onus of the Syrian defeat and frustration. Only then did the Syrian political leaders turn more directly to the Soviet bloc and begin to put into effect the old axiom that my enemies' enemies are my friends.

The signing of the Baghdad Pact in March 1955 moved Syrian politicians into the Egypto-Saudi camp. The Syrians were already suspicious of the series of treaties of friendship among Turkey, Iraq, and Transjordan in 1946; the Baghdad Pact, especially after the ready adherence given to it by Britain, was anathema to Syrian nationalists and incited most of them to join the Egyptian camp.

Syria quickly closed ranks with Egypt and Saudi Arabia, declaring that Syrian armed forces would be joined with those of her friends under a unified Egyptian command. In October 1955 the Damascus Pact was signed, pledging mutual assistance and establishing an alliance among the three states. In 1956 the pact was consummated by a generous loan to Syria by Saudi Arabia and by the arrival of Soviet war matériel from Egypt. Syria signed trade agreements with the U.S.S.R. and Red China in 1955 and with Rumania in 1956. Syria also joined in denouncing the United States, and the pronouncements of the Syrian representative to the United Nations became more bitter and more fiery.

Shukri al-Kuwatli, who was elected president in 1955, had lived in exile in Egypt from 1949 to 1954, where he had witnessed the exciting successes of Colonel Nasser. In Damascus any role other than that of a friend to Egypt was unpardonable and impossible, since the new, young army staff officers were ardent supporters of Nasser and his revolution. Thus, when Nasser nationalized the Canal, Syrian demonstrations were more open and enthusiastic than those of other Middle Eastern states. Syrian spokesmen swore that the oil pipelines would be sabotaged should the West commit aggression against Egypt. After Israel, Britain, and France invaded Sinai, Syria did not permit the repair of the pipelines until Israeli forces withdrew from the Gaza Strip.

To distract the attention of the masses from internal political sniping, a running series of plots, accusations of treason, scandals, and political witchhunts were offered in Damascus. Israel, the United States, Iraqi royalty, Turkey, and al-Shishakli were the most convenient whipping boys. Forty-seven prominent politicians were courtmartialed on charges of fomenting a revolution. Most were tried *in absentia*, but many who appeared confessed meekly to the charge. Incidents such as these abetted the drift toward the left.

The regime needed arms to prevent an internal coup, to strengthen Syria's position vis-à-vis Israel and Iraq, and to influence affairs in Jordan. Furthermore, the army was moving rapidly into the political arena and had a natural desire for quantities of improved weapons. Following Nasser's example, Syria applied to Moscow and received about $60 million in tanks and other matériel in 1956. President al-Kuwatli visited the U.S.S.R., and a dozen MIG-17 jet fighters appeared in Syria. Soviet-bloc ships unloaded their cargoes at Latakia. In 1957 Soviet activities in Syria led Western leaders and sympathizers to believe that Syria was almost irretrievably on her way behind the Iron Curtain.

Each frustration drove the Syrians further to the left, strengthened Soviet bargaining, and emboldened the Pan-Arabists. It also brought to a head a rivalry brewing in the army for a decade. The young army graduates of the Homs Staff College were fiery Arab nationalists who pointed to the defeats in Palestine and the weakness of Syrian policies as proof of the senior officers' incompetence. Lt. Col. Abd al-Hamid Sarraj, chief of army intelligence, emerged as the leader of the junior officers; in 1957 the issue was joined when the older officers tried to isolate him by sending him to a post in Cairo. He refused to go, and General Afif Bizri, the new chief of staff, was surrounded by Sarraj's friends.

Northern Region of the United Arab Republic

Meanwhile the hope of uniting Syria and Egypt germinated. In 1956 Syria appointed a committee to negotiate a federal union with Egypt, and the various steps toward the union's consummation were outlined. Resistance was expected in Aleppo from officers opposed to the youthful clique. To drown all possible opposition in a bath of emotional nationalism, conspiracies jeopardizing national integrity were unearthed and ordinary frontier incidents involving opium smugglers and cattle rustlers along the Turkish border were magnified into crises. Turkish acts of aggression were imputed to the machinations of Western imperialists.

The resulting tension not only silenced internal opposition, but also served as a screen for the arrival of Egyptian troops to forestall a likely coup d'état of the 1949 variety. The insubstantiality of the crisis was disclosed, but the Egyptian regiments remained in Syria. In February 1958 the union was officially declared by the Syrian government and Nasser, though Nasser was somewhat cool to the haste in which the union was effected. A few days following the announcement, Khalid Bakdash, leader of the Arab Communist party, enplaned from Damascus with his family for Moscow. There was also considerable flight of capital to Beirut. Nasser became president and al-Kuwatli vice-president of the United Arab Republic, which was divided into two regions, Egypt and Syria.

To effect the union of two sovereign states has always been a most difficult, perplexing, and sometimes painful experience. In the case of Egypt and Syria, with no common frontier, separated by nearly 600 miles, and with such disparate economies and social customs, it was a daring step but one that had to be rigorously enforced. In a few weeks Syrian foreign affairs were thoroughly submerged by Egyptian policies. Nasser as president of the United Arab Republic directed all activities and appointed all officials. Trade and economic measures were to conform as soon as possible, and in each case Egyptian patterns were to be imposed upon Syria. Unity in other matters moved more deliberately. Budgets, finances, and currency were to remain separate for five years, at least. Egypt's austere economy of the post-Sinai War period was placed on Syria, and all imports were rigidly licensed. Merchants grumbled and permits for expensive luxury goods were denied. Egyptian land reform ideas were extended to Syria; all holdings over 740 acres were to be distributed to landless peasants.

All this might have been acceptable had there not been severe droughts and crop failures in 1958, 1959, and 1960. Syria's barley crop was wiped out in 1958, and there was only a 40 percent yield of wheat in 1959. Famine was avoided by shipments of grain from the United States in 1959 and 1960, all for nontransferable Syrian pounds. Export trade with Lebanon, Syria's best customer, was shattered in part by the difficulties and border closing of 1958, in part by the shift to Soviet orientation and Egyptian controls, and in large part by the scarcity of commodities. Syria survived by receiving Egyptian budgetary support, aid from the United States, a credit from the International Monetary Fund, development loans from the U.S.S.R., and by having relatively normal cotton crops.

It was not possible politically to govern Syria like an Egyptian province. Nasser announced the appointment of the first United Arab Republic cabinet in March 1958 and named four vice presidents, two of them from Syria. Most regular cabinet posts had two heads, one for Syria and one for Egypt. All political parties in Syria were dissolved; political figures lost their power bases and found themselves isolated in Cairo or eased out of position, sometimes not so gently. With political parties and leaders gone and the Syrian army immobilized and demoralized by control from Cairo, real power in Syria fell to Colonel Abd al-Hamid Sarraj and his intelligence forces. The task of governing Syria fell to an executive council of eleven, later eighteen, and a moribund legislative council, both hand-picked by Nasser. Under the chairmanship of Nur al-Din Kahalah, a nonpolitical technician and an engineer, the executive council prepared budgets, planned industrial development and irrigation projects, and carried on the usual administrative functions of government.

The major weakness of this arrangement was the lack of sufficient authority to crack heads together and get things done. To remedy this Nasser in the autumn of 1959 sent Field Marshall Abd al-Hakim Amer to Damascus as chief of government. The Syrian military resented his presence and looked to Colonel Sarraj as the leader of Syrian factions. A year later Sarraj assumed the chairmanship of the executive committee and Kahalah took over the preparation and administration of a new five-year plan for industrial and public works. As head of the executive, the police, and military intelligence Sarraj's position in Syria rivaled that of Nasser in Egypt. The ten-year development plan drawn up in the early 1950's moved forward. The Rastan Dam on the Orontes, irrigating 62,500 acres, was completed in 1961, and the great Euphrates Valley Project, to cost nearly $300 million was initiated. Under the supervision of Kahalah a dam was to be built to add 1.5 million acres to cultivation, avert disastrous floods, and produce enough electric power to satisfy the needs of the country for the foreseeable future. In 1960 a Syrian delegation in Moscow signed agreements for twenty economic development projects totaling another $300 million. Industries of many kinds began, and the production of textiles, cement, and glass increased remarkably. At the new petroleum refinery at Homs a problem even arose over how to market the surplus gasoline.

The new social and economic forces at work in Syria freed the imaginations of Syrians who had been suffocated by politics since the end of World War I. However, the better-established groups and families involved in land, trade, finance, politics, and the army discovered that the union relegated them to less prominent positions and infringed upon many of their accustomed prerogatives. Land reform sapped their privileges and power;

trade quotas, import licenses, and nationalization hampered their business opportunities; banks were nationalized or "Arabized"; and army officers were frustrated and divided by their loyalties to the uncertain power of Field Marshall Amer and the clandestine intelligence apparatus of Colonel Sarraj.

Acute rivalry and controversy between these two officers quietly waxed through 1961. In Damascus Sarraj called together all governors and important officials to outline future steps in the growth of Syria and to receive their loyalty to him. Amer objected violently; Nasser called them to Cairo to settle the dispute. Sarraj evidently got the worse of it for he resigned his vice-presidency and returned to Damascus. However, with both Amer and Sarraj absent for nearly a week, the army, banding together with all the dissident groups, staged a successful coup on September 28, 1961. Nasser's first reaction was to order purely Egyptian cadres of the army to seize the rebels, naval units to occupy Latakia, and paratroopers to drop on Damascus. Informed that these would be unsuccessful, he declared the next day that Arab should not fight Arab and recognized the fait accompli. A month later the Syrian Arab Republic was by unanimous vote readmitted to the Arab League.

The Syrian Arab Republic
Perhaps if Nasser had granted regional autonomy to Syria within the United Arab Republic, Syrian nationalism and pride would not have been so outraged at being ruled by Egyptians. Syrian officers resented their second-rate positions, and the stifling of political activity was more than the Baath party leaders had bargained for. The military council placed a civilian group at the head of the government. It pledged to reverse the nationalization process launched that spring and to reestablish a free economy although it declared that the land reform measures and the law requiring that 25 percent of the profits in an industry be distributed to the employees would stand. Activity on the part of political parties was prohibited. Amer escaped to Egypt the morning of the coup; Sarraj was arrested and imprisoned four days later; Kahalah was appointed head of the Euphrates Valley Project. Syria was readmitted to the United Nations and all the major powers recognized the new state.

National elections were held for a parliamentary body that would serve until the constitution was readied. Moderate conservatives held a majority in this body and elected Nazim al-Kudsi as president of the state. He asserted that his government would pursue a policy of nonalignment in foreign affairs and a course of "constructive socialism" at home. Parliament voted to cancel all nationalizations effected under the United Arab Republic, but did retain some control over big business. In five months Syria appeared to have adjusted to the new order.

However, everyone was not satisfied. Officers of the armed forces overthrew the government on March 28, 1962. Four days later there was a countercoup in Aleppo by "free" officers who appealed to Nasser for intervention. The commander in chief of the army resolved the impasse at a conference in Homs. President al-Kudsi resumed his office, the rebellious officers left Syria, and a new cabinet ordered the renationalization of al-Khumassia, a large business-holding company controlling sizable sections of Syrian industry, especially in textiles, cement, and detergents. All foreign banks were nationalized, and a stabilization fund from the United States, West Germany, Italy, and the International Monetary Fund, along with a bumper crop said to have been the best since 1932, made it possible to liberalize foreign exchange controls. Internal dissension proved more than the cabinet could handle, and in September Khalid al-Azm, sometimes called "the Red millionaire," became prime minister and ruled by decree after dissolving the parliament.

Every successive coup made the government weaker and more imperious and deepened the rifts within the body politic. The Baath party with each change profited from its better organization and from its well-defined and articulated objectives. Baath ("Renaissance"), developed during World War II by Michel Aflaq, a French-educated Christian Arab, stressed nationalism, unity, and socialism as the three forces Arab society should embrace in order to rejuvenate the Arab world and to restore its once-famed brilliance and affluence in commerce, industry, and culture—a full-flowered Arab renaissance. The Baath's main opposition was lodged in the pro-Nasser elements of the army and among those who believed that only under Nasser's leadership could the cherished dream of Arab unity be achieved. Nasserite and Baathist ministers in al-Azm's cabinet quarreled repeatedly, and when a Baathist coup in Baghdad on February 8, 1963, overturned and executed Kassim, a similar blow was expected in Damascus. It came on March 8.

Led by young officers, the National Council of the Revolutionary Command seized the government and placed the Baathists in control. Salah al-Bitar became prime minister, and seventy-four business, political, and military leaders were deprived of their civil rights. On March 14 al-Bitar announced that steps were being taken to form a tripartite union with Iraq and the United Arab Republic. Conferences were held in Cairo and, with much fanfare, on April 17 a charter uniting the three states was proclaimed. It was dead, however, before it was published, because Syria and Iraq insisted upon equal votes whereas Nasser demanded that voting should depend upon population, probably because Egypt's population was greater than that of the other two combined. As it became public knowledge in May that union talks had failed, Nasserites staged demonstrations and riots in Aleppo and Damascus to exert pressure on the Baathists. Two hundred and fifty were arrested, as General Amin al-Hafiz, a staunch moderate Baathist, assumed the post of deputy prime minister. At the end of June he was pushed aside by a pro-Nasser general who lasted ten days, when the Baathists seized full power again and reinstalled General al-Hafiz, who retained command of the Syrian government until he was ousted on February 23, 1966, by a radical left-wing branch of the Baathists.

While al-Hafiz ruled, al-Bitar served as prime minister part of the time and al-Hafiz held the position himself at other times. As long as the Baathists also dominated the government in Iraq the two states cooperated in many affairs, and the pan-Arab executive of the Baathist party directed policies. Syria sent 5,000 soldiers to help Iraq quell Kurdish revolts; in 1963 an Iraqi-Syrian Supreme Defense Council was created. This was abrogated after the Baathists were eased from power in Iraq. Relations with the United Arab Republic were normalized, and Syria joined with Lebanon, Jordan, and the United Arab Republic in plans for diverting water from the Banyas River to the Yarmuk and thence to Jordan. Nationalization, industrialization, and development proceeded rapidly. After five large textile factories were taken in 1964, business leaders ordered a general strike that al-Hafiz broke by threatening to nationalize all retail businesses in Hama and Damascus. In 1965 he nationalized all major manufacturing and processing plants, public utilities, domestic and foreign oil companies, and many export-import firms. A French group received a contract to build an international jet airport in Damascus and a West German consortium was the successful bidder on the Euphrates Dam. But al-Hafiz was too conservative for some, too radical for others, too cool toward Nasser, or too friendly.

During 1965 an extreme left-wing pro-Chinese group among the Baathists reached for power. General Salah Jadid became chief of staff and brought in a new prime minister and minister of defense. Their plot was uncovered in December, when al-Hafiz noticed that some of the loyal officers on his staff were being reassigned to distant posts. Key army units were brought in line, each declaring loyalty to al-Hafiz. The Syrian executive of the Baath party that had fallen into the hands of dissidents and radicals was dissolved and its offices and functions taken over by the more moderate pan-Arab executive body controlled by al-Hafiz, al-Bitar, and Aflaq, while a new cabinet of moderates was formed on January 1, 1966. It lasted fifty-four days. General Jadid and the extreme army wing of the Baath party arrested and imprisoned the moderates. Jadid became the chief executive of the Baath party and chairman of the National Revolutionary Council; Nur al-Din al-Atasi, chief of state; Yusuf Zuayyin, prime minister; General Hamad Ubayd, chief of staff; General Hafiz Assad, minister of defense; and Dr. Ibrahim Makhus, deputy prime minister and foreign minister. Jadid, Assad and Makhus were members of the Alawi minority group of north Syria, and Ubayd was from the Druze minority. Not belonging to the mainstream Syrian religious and social groups, they found satisfaction in pressing their Arab nationalism and socialism.

This extreme faction declared that it wanted to maintain a "permanent struggle" on all fronts, and coupled Nasser with "traitors in the Arab world" who compromised with "imperialism" and reaction. It assailed him for abandoning the Yemenite Republic to the "jaws of reaction" at the Jidda agreement with Saudi Arabia and for the unfulfillment of his obligations to Palestine. It complained that the U.S.S.R. talked but did nothing, whereas Communist China understood the needs of the Arabs and was prepared to help them. At home, Dr. Makhus, the chief ideologist of the group, called for a "developing and deepening social experience" for everyone.

Throughout 1966 and into 1967 many delegations from the new regime visited the Soviet bloc countries, seeking trade pacts, cultural missions, industrial aid, and major development loans. The arrangement with West Germany for the Euphrates Dam was dropped, and in 1966 the U.S.S.R. granted $157 million for the first stage of the dam that would double the cultivable area of Syria. When requests for greater royalties from the transit of oil of the Iraq Petroleum Company failed, IPC pipelines were closed, not to be reopened until Syrian demands were met in the spring of 1967.

Border incidents on the Israeli frontier increased in number and seriousness in 1966, especially as action on the water-diversion plans commenced. In July Israel attacked in considerable force the earth-moving machinery employed and some of the foundations of the project. In January 1967 acts of violence became so numerous that the United Nations brought about a temporary ceasefire. Raids that included mine explosions and the shooting of Israeli soldiers and police were frequently carried out by members of al-Fatah, a society of Palestinians dedicated to the regaining of their homeland. Many units of this society were based in Syria, but raids often came from Lebanon or Jordan. In November 1966 Israel attacked and destroyed the village of al-Samu in Jordan to warn that al-Fatah raids should be stopped. Syria called for the deposing of King Husayn for not having prevented the raid or retaliating in like measure. A crisis flared in May 1967, when Syria believed that she had evidence that Israel was preparing an attack in such depth that even Damascus might fall. Sensing that this might be similar to the Israeli war on Suez in 1956, Syrian leaders called on Egypt and the other Arab states to make good on their pledges to come to her assistance and protection.

The Aftermath of the June 1967 War

When the Israeli-Arab war broke out on June 5, 1967, the main fighting occurred in Sinai and Jordan, and not until the fourth day did Syria feel the full brunt of the Israeli forces. By the time the cease-fire became effective Syria had lost the Golan Heights above the Sea of Galilee and the Israeli army had occupied the city of al-Quneitra. It was rumored that the road from al-Quneitra to Damascus was wide open and only the cease-fire kept the Israelis from attacking the Syrian capital. President al-Atasi, attending the meetings of the U.N. Security Council and the General Assembly, repeated his nation's stand that no direct negotiations with Israel were possible until the Israeli forces had fully withdrawn from Arab lands she had occupied in the war. Syria refused to attend the Arab summit meetings at Khartoum in August in any official capacity because she was unprepared to accept a political solution to the Israel-Arab quarrel.

The full political effects of the loss of the Golan Heights were felt in the autumn of 1968 when Syria's prime minister and foreign minister were toppled from office. A group of moderates within the Baath party, allied with Baath pragmatists in the military, seized control, and President al-Atasi became prime minister as well. General Jadid, as al-Atasi's deputy, and General Assad, as minister of defense, retained their hold on government and party affairs.

Through 1969 and 1970 General Assad moved carefully into a position of dominance in the Baath party and in the Syrian government. Less concerned than Jadid with doctrinaire ideology, Assad stressed the Arab and nationalist aspects of Baath principles. He urged more cooperative ventures with Iraq and Egypt, pushed preparations for war with Israel, but demanded greater independence from the U.S.S.R. At a stormy Baath party congress Assad took charge and arranged compromises favorable to his positions. In May 1969 an interim constitution was issued under his aegis. The constitution declared that Syria was a democratic, popular, socialist republic. It authorized a People's Assembly to elect the chief of state and ratify all laws. Assad remained defense minister, but as regional commander of the Baath party he was the most powerful person in the government.

Following a Baath party congress in October 1970, al-Atasi resigned as prime minister and Assad seized control in a bloodless coup. Hafiz al-Assad, now prime minister, headed a new twenty-six member cabinet, half of whom were Baathists. At this time Assad, born near Latakia, the son of a peasant, was about forty years old. An Alawi, he was a member of a Muslim minority sect, and had found an opportunity for education and advancement only in the military. As a leading officer and minister of defense he had visited the U.S.S.R. and many of the countries of Europe; he now felt ready to lead his country. Early in 1971 a constitutional change made the president the highest official of the state, and Assad was sworn into this office in March. He asserted he would return the Baath party to the masses. Michel Aflaq, one of the founders of Baath, Amin al-Hafiz, and others were tried *in absentia* and given death sentences, which Assad commuted to life imprisonment.

A People's Council of 170 members was appointed: 85 Baathists; 12 Socialist Union Movement members; 12 Arab Socialist Unionists; 8 Arab Socialists; 8 Communists; and 45 representing trade unions, peasants, doctors, lawyers, artisans, and religious men. The new cabinet had members from all the political parties. In April the council ratified the decision to join with Egypt and Libya in the Federation of Arab Republics.

In 1972 Assad was able to consummate a National Progressive Front to which all political parties adhered. Only the Baath had the right to engage in political activity in the army and among students. Front policies were based on resolutions of Baath party congresses. Assad hoped the parties would merge with Baath, but only the Socialist Unionists agreed to consider; the Communists refused vehemently. Conservative forces still were powerful in Syria, and in the elections for local administrative councils the Baathists won only 10 percent of the Damascus slate.

The permanent constitution was ready and approved by the council in March 1973. It stated that Syria was democratic and socialist, with sovereignty belonging to the people, and that laws were to be based on the Sharia. The Baath was declared to be the leading political organization; the economy was socialist; personal and religious freedoms were sacred; the president was elected to seven year terms; and the legislature was to be a 186-member elected National Assembly. In May 1973 elections the Baath party obtained 122 seats with 70 percent of the vote, and Assad was chosen president. When it was learned that a shipment of tanks was on its way from Algeria to al-Saiqah, the Palestinian commandos based in Syria, Assad confiscated them, protesting that tanks were unsuitable for commando raids. Assad was firmly in control.

The defeat in the June war and the loss of the Golan Heights did not fragment Syrian economic life or greatly injure its infrastructure. The destruction of Syrian war matériel was significant, however, and the influx of 70,000 persons displaced from Golan created problems. Good crops during these years eased the situation considerably. In 1968 the first earth was moved for the Euphrates Dam at Tabqa, renamed Madinat al-Thawrah ("Revolution City"), and the first phase was completed in July 1973. The dam, 65 meters high, over 4,500 meters long, and backed up an 80 kilometer reservoir, Lake Assad, would irrigate 1.5 million acres of fertile lands and, with eight giant turbines, would create 800,000 kws. of electric power. Once in use the dam brought acute problems with Turkey and Iraq over amounts of water flow. Agreement was reached with Turkey, which was building her own giant dam on the river at Keban. Iraq complained that Syria's new dam and reservoir had reduced the water coming into Iraq to a trickle. The dispute remained unresolved until 1975.

Assad benefited also from the beginning of Syrian oil production. Largely on her own, Syria organized the General Petroleum Organization (GPO) to exploit oil resources discovered in the northeastern areas of the country in what was called the "Karachuk" field. In 1968 a 644-kilometer pipeline from Karachuk through Homs to Tartus on the Mediterranean was completed and oil began to flow. By 1971 production topped 100,000 barrels daily and Syrian crude replaced Iraqi oil at the Homs refinery. Agreements were made with TAP-line and IPC officials to use those facilities. Syria was admitted to OAPEC in 1972. Prices for Syrian oil followed those of OPEC, but since Syria had developed the fields and brought the oil to market without the participation of the international oil companies, she found selling it difficult until 1973, when other producing nations began to dispose of their oil at auction.

In 1970 all large industrial firms that had not yet been nationalized were taken over. The economy, however, was not booming, for Syria was experiencing difficulties in selling oil, sagging cotton production, and trade deficits. A sweeping economic liberalization program was instituted; individuals were encouraged to participate in and stimulate the private sector of the economy.

Syria had broken diplomatic relations with the United States and several Western European countries at the time of the June 1967 war, and they

remained severed for a number of years. Lines to the U.S.S.R. were open
and strengthened. Soviet arms shipments of all types continued to arrive
and many Soviet experts were assigned to the Euphrates Dam project.
Syrian officials were warmly welcomed in Moscow. The U.S.S.R. moved her
Mediterranean fleet base from Egypt to Latakia in 1972, and transferred to
Syria massive quantities of arms valued at $700 million, including surface-
to-air missiles.

The July 1968 coup in Baghdad placed Baathists unfriendly to Syria in
control of Iraq. Baghdad began to give sanctuary to Syrian Baathists out of
favor in Damascus, and Assad castigated the Iraq Baathists for murdering
and imprisoning progressives. He did recognize that Arab states must cooperate militarily were they ever to end the menace from Israel, so in 1969
he worked to establish a joint army command among Syria, Iraq, and Jordan. King Husayn's bloody contest with the Palestinians in 1970 aborted the
collaboration. Syrian tanks rushed to support the Palestinians but had to be
recalled five days later when Assad refused them air support.

More promising was the 1970 proposed linkage of Egypt, Libya, and the
Sudan that Assad asked to join. The Federation of Arab Republics, consisting of Egypt, Libya, and Syria, became an official body in September 1971,
organized to coordinate policies and to merge at some distant future date.

The most immediate tasks facing Assad, however, were what to do with
the Palestinians within his borders and how to regain the Golan area. When
Assad took power he shared the Baath party's credo that a "war of popular
liberation" was the only way to get the Israelis out. Syria became a haven
for Palestinian commando groups; the Syrian army even helped train one,
al-Saiqah. The cease-fire line stayed relatively quiet until 1969 when air
clashes occurred frequently with Israeli planes penetrating deeply. The first
half of 1970 saw tank battles, massive air actions, and an Israeli attack on
a Syrian army camp only forty kilometers from Damascus. Though Assad
spurned a cease-fire later that year the combat subsided considerably. Assad
then ruled that Palestinian groups must not involve Syria in their operations. In 1970 he outlawed al-Saiqah interventions in Lebanon. Eventually
he curbed al-Saiqah's independence, arresting its civilian Baathist leaders
and placing it under Syrian army control. Assad may have been planning
war against Israel, but he had no intention of giving al-Saiqah or any other
Palestinian body the opportunity to select the place or time.

October 1973

In conjunction with Egypt, Syria launched a massive attack upon Israel on
October 6, 1973. With more than 1,000 tanks, the Syrians crossed the Golan
cease-fire line, captured Mt. Hermon, and encircled the town of al-Quneitra. Israel counterattacked, bombed key military and economic targets
throughout Syria, and by October 10 had pushed to within forty kilometers
of Damascus. Within two weeks immense quantities of arms and munitions
were being airlifted to Syria from the U.S.S.R. and to Israel from the United
States. After a trip to Moscow by American Secretary of State Henry Kis-

singer, the two great powers forced a cease-fire upon the three belligerents on October 23, under the auspices of the U.N. Security Council.

In May 1974 Syria and Israel agreed to the establishment of a U.N. neutral zone on the Golan Heights, which included giving to Syria the town of al-Quneitra and all the area taken by Israel in the recent fighting. The U.N. force was to remain for six months, when a more permanent settlement was expected. Assad's stand continued to be that Israel must give up all the lands taken in 1967.

Israel in bombing Syria during the fighting destroyed a new electric power system, the oil refineries at Homs and Banyas, much of the port facilities at Latakia, and various industrial plants. The cost of war damage to Syria was set at $2.4 billion. Czechoslovakia agreed to supply $35 million to rebuild the Homs refinery; England built a $30 million textile mill at Latakia; sizable contributions came from oil-producing Arab governments; encouragement was given to the private economy in the hope of attracting the investments of Middle East oil money.

In 1974 President Nixon visited Damascus; shortly thereafter diplomatic relations with the United States were resumed. Assad established relations with West Germany, as the tempo of his diplomacy quickened. In 1975 Kissinger shuttled repeatedly among Damascus, Tel Aviv, Jerusalem, Cairo, Riyadh, and Amman in futile efforts at arranging a deeper pullback of forces as a part of his bid to bring peace to the Middle East through a step-by-step process. One difficulty seemed that Assad had little to offer in exchange for a partial Israeli withdrawal.

The longer President Assad retained power the more stable the economy became. Oil production increased by 30 percent in 1975, reaching 150,000 barrels daily. Large-scale prospecting, with Soviet help, was pressed in 1976, while an American group was invited to explore for offshore oil fields. Syria, like most Middle East countries, had development plans, but with the ephemeral condition of political life after World War II her ambitions were always altered or sabotaged except for projects fostered and protected by dedicated persons, such as the Euphrates Dam. Even there, international tensions reached explosive levels in 1975 and were only settled by the firm finesse of Crown Prince Fahd of Saudi Arabia who shuttled between Baghdad and Damascus to soothe feelings and bring a compromise. Now, evidence of economic advancement was everywhere. Cotton crops were excellent, trade with Jordan and other neighboring countries was improving, and imports from the United States leaped from $40 million in 1974 to $128 million in 1975 to $300 million in 1976. A generous five-year trade agreement was signed with the U.S.S.R. in 1976, as vast quantities of Soviet war matériel, including the latest MIGs, were being delivered. Syria's gross national product jumped 25 percent between 1973 and 1975. Assad would not permit domestic politics to jeopardize Syria's prospects for prosperity. He persuaded the Social Unionists to merge with the Baath party and engineered a drive against the Communist party, arresting nearly three hundred. Local opposition grew quiescent.

The shifting sands of Arab diplomacy created a constant challenge for Assad. He denounced President Sadat after Egypt signed a disengagement pact with Israel in 1975. Though both Syria and Egypt had recognized the PLO in 1974, it was Assad who led the drive among the Arabs at Rabat to recognize the PLO as the legitimate representative of the Palestinians. Assad then moved to repair his relations with King Husayn. Normal diplomatic channels were reopened, and the two leaders agreed to coordinate all policies toward Israel and the PLO. Assad visited Amman in August 1975, where he and Husayn established the Supreme Syrian-Jordan Command Council, a step toward a military integration of their forces.

Assad at first mildly favored Palestinian aspirations in Lebanon and permitted al-Saiqah units to operate almost openly there. By the spring of 1976 he began to understand that any victory in Lebanon could well be hollow. The prime ministers of Syria, Egypt, Lebanon, Kuwayt, and Saudi Arabia met in Riyadh in June 1976 with PLO leaders to formulate a way to end the strife in Lebanon, enforce cease-fires, and prepare for a later conference of the heads of state to seal an agreement. To police Lebanon they designated an Arab League peace-keeping force of 30,000, most of whom were Syrian soldiers already in place, under the nominal command of President Sarkis of Lebanon.

Through the good offices of Crown Prince Fahd of Saudi Arabia the bitterness between Assad and Sadat was partially assuaged at their September 1976 meeting in Riyadh. Assad announced the creation of a unified political command with Egypt to shape policies toward Israel (Sudan asked to join in February 1977). They tried to formulate an integrated program for relations with the Palestinians and for a course of action in any proposed reconvening of the Geneva conference for peace in the Middle East. Syrian Foreign Minister Abd al-Halim Khaddam met with President Carter in Washington to advance Syrian views on steps that might lead to Geneva and Assad in Moscow discussed these issues with Soviet leaders. President Carter and Assad conferred in Geneva in May on procedural and substantive matters for a Middle East peace, and later in the summer Khaddam returned to Washington for further negotiations. The role, if any, to be played by the PLO at Geneva was the thorny issue.

On August 1, 1977, elections for the 195-member People's Council were held. Only 51 percent of eligible voters went to the polls. The ruling coalition obtained 159 seats (the Baath party won 125) and all the others elected were independents. What caused the widespread apathy was not ascertained and some leaders remarked that in Syria people were not forced to go to the polls as was the case in some countries. However, within a few weeks Assad attacked profiteering and corruption in Syria and scores were arrested, including the heads of five state organizations. Certainly the economy was not booming, and the balance of payments deficits were in the hundreds of millions of dollars. The budgets of the 1976–1980 five-year plan were slashed 13 percent and aid was sought from all sources. The United States gave $90 million.

One of Assad's continuing concerns and efforts was to prevent the renewal of civil war in Lebanon. He had taken the Syrian leadership of the Arab peace-keeping troops in Lebanon as a means of controlling Palestinian operations while a Lebanese army could be reconstituted and could assume control. The outburst of fighting in south Lebanon in September 1977 and the Israeli participation with the Christians against the Palestinians and Muslim villagers tested his skills. Though some Syrian units of the Arab peace-keeping forces did appear in south Lebanon near the frontier, Assad took great care in stationing Syrian soldiers in areas close to Israeli borders since their presence in large numbers might invite a full-scale invasion. Even in 1978 at the time of the Israeli incursion into south Lebanon, Syrian units were ordered not to confront the Israelis. It appeared that at least for the time being Assad preferred peace to war.

Kingdom of Iraq
From the declaration of war against the Axis in January 1943 until the revolution of 1958 Iraq underwent twenty-one changes of prime minister, with thirteen different men holding the office. On six different occasions Nuri al-Said Pasha occupied it; and at all times he was the most powerful political leader in Iraq. When he was not prime minister, he served as minister of defense or from his seat in the senate pulled the strings to direct the policies followed by others.

Elections for the chamber of deputies were usually well managed by Nuri al-Said. All political parties were dissolved in November 1952, and again in 1954. These moves were instigated to force parties to reorganize or to reapply for party licenses, some of which might be denied. The Communist party remained underground and worked assiduously through other groups and parties. In Iraq the communists found their following in the educated youth of the lower middle class in Baghdad, Basrah, and other large cities, and in those who adhered to the Rashid Ali movement from 1935 to 1941.

In 1939, when King Ghazi was killed in an automobile accident at the age of twenty-seven, the throne had passed to his four-year-old son Faysal II. King Ghazi's cousin Abd al-Ilah became regent and heir to the throne. The authority of the palace was prescribed by the constitution; yet the regent's influence was felt in all quarters through the difficult years of World War II and the Palestine war. In 1953 King Faysal II reached his eighteenth year and nominally assumed full power.

The experience of the British with the Rashid Ali episode during the war opened their eyes to the necessity of revamping their attitude toward Iraq. Iraqi leaders, indirectly encouraged by growing American interest in the area, pressed for a new treaty to replace the one of 1930. Negotiations led to the signing of an Anglo-Iraqi treaty at Portsmouth, England, in 1948, wherein Britain retained the right to send troops in the case of war or threat of war. Almost immediately students rioted in Baghdad, and the regent declared that the new treaty did not "realize the national aims of Iraq." The treaty was never ratified, and the 1930 treaty remained in force until Britain joined the Baghdad Pact.

In 1947 Senator Nuri al-Said tried to bring about a union with Transjordan. In the end he settled for a treaty of friendship and brotherhood providing for mutual consultation in matters of foreign affairs. Although criticized in parliament, it was ratified in June and served as the basis for joint operations in the Palestine war. Iraq's treaty of friendship with Turkey, ratified in July, brought an even stronger protest, since it implicitly recognized the Turkish possession of Alexandretta. More significantly, the Egypto-Saudi camp within the Arab League viewed the Turkish treaty as strengthening the Hashimites, and therefore detrimental to interests of the Arab League.

Iraq, however, did not consider her actions as violating the letter or the spirit of the Arab League. Actually, the movement for the formation of the league had some of its roots in Baghdad, and Iraqi leaders heartily supported league actions except when they adversely affected Iraq. In 1947 Iraq protested the partition of Palestine and sent nearly 20,000 soldiers to fight alongside the Arab Legion of Transjordan.

Although the geographical position of Iraq precluded any appreciable number of Arab refugees from Palestine locating there, sympathy for them ran high. Iraqi officials declared they would not open any negotiations with Israel until the plight of the refugees was relieved. Ill feeling toward Jews in Iraq mounted in proportion to the misery of the refugees and the general disillusionment over the war's outcome. Nuri al-Said made the suggestion that Iraq would welcome 100,000 refugees if she could send 100,000 Iraqi Jews to Israel. Public acts against Jews in Iraq multiplied. In March 1950 a law was passed permitting Jews to renounce their Iraqi citizenship and in the following months thousands left. In May over 50,000 were flown to Israel; before the year was out almost all Iraq's Jews had left.

Frustration and unrest mushroomed in Iraq. This was especially true in Baghdad, whose population was expanding rapidly. Lack of full independence from Britain, the Palestine war fiasco, political corruption, nationalization of oil in Iran and the new 50-50 profit-sharing arrangement in Saudi Arabia, the high cost of living, ownership of land, and the disastrous annual flooding of sections of Baghdad were the concern of many Iraqis. Since the political structure hardly touched the ordinary Iraqi, "grass roots" stability in government was quite absent. An explosion occurred in 1952 over some examinations given by the dean of the School of Pharmacy. Demonstrations turned to general riots, which were exploited by the communists. The regent declared martial law and appointed the chief of staff prime minister. He abolished political parties, jailed right- and left-wing party leaders, closed the schools and all but one newspaper, and placed a curfew on Baghdad.

The lid was clamped on just in time, but professional politicians were frightened and realized that reforms of many kinds had to be initiated. Fortunately, new financial resources were at hand. Oil production, because of a closedown at Abadan, had been expanded; more important, the Iraq

Petroleum Company agreed in 1952 to a new schedule of royalties, increasing them to 50 percent of the profits before taxes. The treaty was retroactive to 1951; as world petroleum requirements spurted, royalties mounted until in 1955 they were estimated at $250 million.

By a law passed in 1950, 70 percent of all oil royalties were devoted to economic development, especially flood control and irrigation projects on the Euphrates, the Tigris, and the Diyala rivers. Aided by a loan in 1950 from the International Bank, the development board began flood control and irrigation works at Samarra on the Tigris and at Ramadi on the Euphrates. Completed in 1956, the Samarra barrage prevented serious flooding in Baghdad in 1956, and the waters from the lake created made it possible to reclaim valuable land by irrigation. Since a survey made in 1950 revealed that nearly 80 percent of Iraq's cultivable land was state-owned and unoccupied, the development board attempted to improve the lot of poverty-ridden sharecroppers.

Other programs cleared vast slum areas in Baghdad and built public-housing projects. Schools were extended to push down illiteracy rates. A large government-owned oil refinery was opened in Basrah in 1952. In Mosul a cotton-spinning factory was opened that would supply one-third of Iraq's requirements. A five-year development plan to run from 1956 to 1960 was to expend $1.1 billion for flood control, industry, electric power, roads, schools, hospitals, public housing, and bridges. Even the great reduction in oil production for several months in 1956 and 1957 during the Sinai war did not curtail the program of the development board, which announced that it held over $280 million in unspent funds. Many Iraqi leaders looked into the future to see a great and prosperous Iraq, provided there was internal peace and no attacks from the Soviet bloc. Others were extremely impatient and believed that the government of Nuri al-Said moved too slowly, too inefficiently, and too indifferently to achieve a better life for Iraqis.

Because of the proximity of the U.S.S.R. Iraqi leaders had a discerning respect and fear of Russian power. Consequently, it was expedient to favor cordial relations with Turkey, Great Britain, and the United States. Although the public attacked these three foreign states from time to time, the concerted policy of the Iraqi government advanced friendly relationships with each.

In 1955, however, the situation changed rapidly. Iraq signed the so-called Baghdad Pact with Turkey. In general, this pact repeated the terms of the treaty of friendship, but it added military cooperation and coordination. Britain adhered to the pact by signing an important agreement with Iraq. Among other things, this agreement wiped out the treaty of 1930, provided for Britain to evacuate her troops and air force from the Habbaniya and Shuayba airfields, and gave fuller sovereignty and independence to Iraq. An improvement over the draft treaty of 1947, this instrument brought Britain into the Baghdad Pact and gave Iraq her wishes. Soon Iran and Pakistan joined the Baghdad Pact, making a chain of allied states separating the

Soviet bloc from the strategic areas of the Middle East. Although the United States did not join the pact, she sent military missions to the area, provided military equipment for member states, and affiliated officially with the pact's military and economic committees.

Egypt viewed the Baghdad Pact as a threat to her control over the Arab League and her leadership in the Arab world. Nuri al-Said was accused of being the tool of Great Britain and restoring colonial status to Iraq. Syria at first tried to mend the quarrel between Cairo and Baghdad, but in the end succumbed to Egyptian oratory and Saudi money, and participated in the Damascus Pact. Calling Nasser a dictator and declaring that the Baghdad Pact was Iraq's concern, Nuri al-Said held firm to his course. He was confident that peace and security from fears of Russia, as well as economic development, an increased standard of living, and a cultural and social renaissance would create in Iraq a life and society to parallel the modern rejuvenation of Turkey combined with the medieval splendor and wealth of the days of Harun al-Rashid.

Although Nasser was regarded as his rival for leadership in the Arab world, Nuri al-Said adjured that Western threats of force when Nasser nationalized the canal violated the United Nations Charter. When Israel, France, and England invaded Egypt in 1956, Iraq was in an embarrassing position. Her army, poised on the Jordanian border to counter an Israeli military build-up, entered Jordan; and she broke diplomatic relations with France. There was great clamor in Baghdad against Great Britain, and from November 1956 to March 1957 Iraqi officials boycotted meetings of the Baghdad Pact in which Britain was represented. Syria complained so insistently over the presence of Iraqi troops in Jordan that they were recalled. A semblance of normalcy was not attained until March 1957, when the pipelines in Syria were repaired.

With the coming of spring, the return to relative peace, and the resumption in the flow of oil, Nuri al-Said turned over his office to close friends. The government ceased to jam radio broadcasts from Cairo and Damascus, and Nuri al-Said visited several European capitals and Washington to discuss wider support of the Baghdad Pact and a solution to the Israeli problem. As the United Arab Republic began to form, political tension in Baghdad mounted. The possibility of a union between Iraq and Jordan had been discussed for many years, and the annexing of Jordan had been openly proposed in 1956. The union of Syria and Egypt forced the issue in Jordan, where the government of King Husayn could not endure as a solitary force. In February 1958 Iraq's King Faysal went to Amman, and after visits there by Nuri al-Said and Crown Prince Abd al-Ilah, the real power in Iraq, an Arab federation of Iraq and Jordan was proclaimed. King Faysal was recognized as chief of state and King Husayn as second in leadership. Defense, foreign affairs, finance, and education were consolidated, but the treaties, laws, budgets, and local administrations of each state retained their validity and were not binding upon the other. In March a federal council was named and a constitution was drafted and proclaimed. In Iraq Nuri al-Said resumed the post of prime minister.

Upon hearing the news Nasser congratulated the two kings; in a few weeks, however, his friendly remarks turned into violent condemnations and open invitations to Arab nationalists in each state to remove the kings, by assassination if necessary. In May elections Nuri al-Said's supporters were returned to parliament which ratified the constitution of the federation; King Husayn supposed that he had found someone who would protect him.

Republic of Iraq

Iraqi troops were ordered in July to march into Jordan to be ready to safeguard Lebanon's Shamun administration. But the Iraqi commander, General Abd al-Karim Kassim, in a swift coup d'état on July 14, 1958, overthrew the king and Nuri al-Said, both of whom lost their lives in the revolution. Mobs in Baghdad became delirious with excitement, sacked the British Embassy, and seized a few Europeans and Jordanians. Order, however, was quickly attained. The reverberations from the revolution were felt around the world.

General Kassim proclaimed the Republic of Iraq and became prime minister of the state. Oil production did not stop; the pipelines were undamaged. Neutrality was pronounced as the policy of the state. Within less than a month the new government was recognized by the United Arab Republic, the U.S.S.R., the states of the Baghdad Pact, and the United States. Kassim declared that Iraq would honor her international obligations, and did not formally resign from the Baghdad Pact. When King Husayn announced he was assuming the position of chief of state of the Arab federation, Kassim renounced the union.

The completeness of the revolution and its full acceptance by the general populace throughout the state amazed only those unfamiliar with Iraq's social and national conditions. Nuri al-Said was thoroughly disliked and the crown prince was hated. The same government had been in power too long and had failed to satisfy the aspirations of the majority. Land reform, poverty, and the low standard of living, Israel, social advances for the urban masses, sanitation and health, and the depressed state of the educated middle class were but a few of the problems the people of Iraq felt pressing upon them, and the belief was widespread that Nuri al-Said and the Hashimites had not tried to cope with them adequately.

In the minds of the populace the old regime had built too many palaces and had allocated too much of the oil royalties to dams and less useful capital works. Many of these were still in the construction stage and their returns were yet to be enjoyed by the public. General Kassim announced that a new development board would receive 50 percent of the royalties and would work to establish Iraq as a welfare state based on practical socialism. Under a five-year agricultural program holdings larger than 500 acres of nonirrigated lands or 250 acres of irrigated lands would be expropriated and distributed to landless peasants in plots from 7.5 to 30 acres. The new board would set up government-owned basic industries in steel, machinery, and petrochemicals. The U.S.S.R. agreed to furnish credits of $140 million for technical assistance in constructing and operating plants for steel, tractors, textiles, nitrates, and hydroelectric power.

Coming so soon after the birth of the United Arab Republic, General Kassim's revolution raised expectations of an immediate fulfillment of Arab unity by joining Iraq with the United Arab Republic. Colonel Abd al-Salam Muhammad Arif, second in rank among the revolutionaries and assistant commander in chief of the armed forces, led the group that soon came to be called Nasserites. Watching the trend in Syria, Kassim and other leaders, however, had no desire to be puppets of Cairo. The fundamental Iraqi nationalism of these leaders forced Kassim to dismiss Arif as deputy prime minister and minister of the interior and to designate him ambassador to West Germany. A revolt by his regiment was crushed, and he was arrested on the charge of having attempted to murder Kassim. At a trial in 1959 he was found guilty and sentenced to death; at a later date the death sentence was lifted.

On the last day of 1959 Kassim revealed a four-year economic plan totaling $1.1 billion to change the face of the nation. A steel mill was planned near Khadhimaya and large sums were allocated for other industry, housing, public welfare, land reclamation, transportation, and communications. Over 150 agricultural and industrial projects were initiated in 1961, and over 60 percent of the cultivated lands had been divided into smaller plots.

But there was no real peace in Iraq. Until Kassim was overthrown and executed in a coup in 1963 his regime was constantly beset by a three-way struggle among communists and pro-communists on one side, pan-Arab nationalists, usually Nasserites, on another, and Iraqi nationalists on the third. There was street fighting in Baghdad at the slightest provocation. In 1959 a revolt broke out in Mosul led by the tribes and pan-Arabists. Blaming the United Arab Republic for plotting it, the army loyal to Kassim crushed the revolt with the aid of Kurdish forces. However, Iraq did return in 1960 to Arab League meetings, political parties were allowed again, and tension with other Arab states was dissipated to the extent of having a meeting of the Arab League Council in Baghdad. Then, in 1961 Kassim laid claim to Kuwayt. Because of the return of British forces and the quick adverse reaction by the other Arab states, especially Saudi Arabia and the United Arab Republic, Kassim did not press his diplomatic blunder. Iraq walked out of the Arab League meeting that admitted Kuwayt to membership, and broke relations with states recognizing her independence. Except for improved relations with Syria after the demise of the United Arab Republic, Kassim generally remained isolated from the other Arab states throughout 1962.

Iraq had had persistent difficulties with the Kurds in northern Iraq since the end of World War I. The Kurdish tribes wanted independence or at least autonomy in a federalized or decentralized Iraq. The British and Nuri al-Said discussed, negotiated, fought, and left the Kurdish problem unsolved. Under the leadership of Mulla Mustafa Barzani, Kurdish resistance increased in 1961. Although temporarily subdued, it exploded in 1962 into a full-scale revolt, placing all of northeastern Iraq except for the cities and towns entirely in Kurdish hands. Because major oil resources of the state were in this region the government was unwilling to tolerate secession or total local control. The army had attempted to subdue the Kurdish provinces but had never succeeded. Each time a government in Baghdad hinted at some accommodation with Barzani the generals showed their disaffection. The people in Basrah and Baghdad, on the other hand, chafed at the continuing conflict and the percentage of the national budget consumed in the struggle.

Added to the factionalism brought by Nasserism, communism, and Iraqi nationalism, the Kurdish dilemma set the stage for a successful Baath party coup on February 8, 1963. Kassim lacked charisma; he had been unable to articulate an appealing ideology. The Iraq executive, dominated by the pan-Arab executive of the Baath party, mostly from Damascus, engineered the coup in collaboration with the army, and immediately organized a National Council of the Revolutionary Command. Colonel Arif was appointed president and General Ahmad Hassan al-Bakr became prime minister. An overnight roundup of communists indicated the nationalist orientation of the Baathists, who preached Arab unity. From his redoubt in the north Barzani welcomed the Baath coup. Little changed, though. The new regime, pressed by the soldiers, resumed Kassim's campaigns, remaining at odds with the Kurds, the communists, and Nasser. The Baath leaders canceled the ambitious development plans as being ineffective and drew up their own, although projects already initiated went unchanged.

The U.S.S.R. protested vigorously to Prime Minister al-Bakr about the treatment that Kurds and communists were receiving from the Baathists, and Nasser began to assail the Baghdad regime for treachery to the Arab cause. In May most of the non-Baathists were ejected from the cabinet and a small Nasserite revolt was broken ruthlessly while talks for complete economic union with Syria were in progress. The problems facing Baghdad and the continuous discussion within the Baath hierarchy deterred unanimity of purpose or direction. By autumn abeyant Iraqi nationalists in Baathist circles resented the domination by the international or Syrian Baathists in every policy dispute. In November 1963 all non-Iraqis were forced out of positions of influence, and President Arif assumed full power, appointing General Tahir Yahya as prime minister. Two months later Arif removed all extreme Baathists from office and went on to form his own Iraqi Arab Socialist Union. A Baathist coup in 1964 was foiled and its leaders imprisoned. Later cabinet shifts added more of the pro-Nasser coterie.

From 1963 until 1968 Iraq was under the personal rule of one or another Arif. When Abd al-Salam Muhammad Arif lost his life in a helicopter crash in southern Iraq on April 13, 1966, his elder brother, General Abd al-

Rahman Arif hurried home from Moscow to be elected president, and carried on with the same fundamental program and political orientation.

From the time the Baathists established themselves in Baghdad, Barzani had refused to bargain for anything short of Kurdish autonomy and a statement in Iraq's constitution that "Iraq is a federative state of Arabs and Kurds." With the inability of the first Arif to meet this condition Barzani asserted *de facto* autonomy for Iraqi Kurdistan and established a parliament and a legislative supreme revolutionary council. The fighting continued, and in 1966 the second Arif launched an offensive with 65,000 troops and coordinated heavy bombing by the air force. The offensive failed, and the Kurdish forces scored some notable victories over the Iraqi armies. For many months Iraq's prime minister had been advocating a moderate stand on Kurdish rights; when the military approach failed again, as he had predicted, he announced that the government was prepared to recognize "Kurdish nationality, language, and tradition." Kurdish delegates were received in Baghdad and a twelve-point program for the Kurds was announced. Among other things, it promised general amnesty for Kurdish rebels; recognition of Kurdish cultural and political autonomy; decentralization of the government; proportionate Kurdish representation in the cabinet, the army command, and the diplomatic corps; economic redevelopment in the north; and the appointment of Kurdish officials in Kurdish areas. Barzani accepted these proposals, but pan-Arabs and the army were so incensed at the implied surrender to the Kurds that President Arif was pressed into appointing a general as prime minister.

The following spring students at Baghdad University went on strike, criticizing Arif for ineffectual leadership and accusing the prime minister and others of incompetence and corruption. They demanded immediate elections and a constitutional regime. Even retired army officers joined the protests. Arif refused to comply, and on July 17, 1968, was removed by a coup and packed off to London.

Inter-Arab relations, particularly those with Cairo, always had been difficult for Iraqi leaders. When Colonel Arif was first in command under Kassim, he was ousted for being too pro-Nasser. As a figurehead under the Baathists in 1963, President Arif showed no public inclination toward Egypt. When he became president in his own right, he approached Nasser for a reconciliation and made cabinet shifts to bring in more Nasserites. Most of these resigned in 1963, charging Arif and his ministers with being dilatory in implementing Arab socialism and in effecting a union with the United Arab Republic. At the onset of the 1967 Israeli crisis Arif sent 30,000 Iraqi troops to Jordan, to reinforce and encourage King Husayn to take a firmer posture toward Israel and the Western powers. Arif maintained a middle course in the debates of the Arab summit meetings at Khartoum. As it turned out, Nuri al-Said, Kassim, and the two Arifs all experienced similar problems with other Arab states in the period after World War II.

Iraq Under General al-Bakr and the Baathists

The July 1968 coup was plotted by a group of young, nationalistic army officers in collaboration with the right wing of the Baathist party. They coalesced temporarily under a group of leaders calling themselves the Revolutionary Command Council (RCC). Controlled by the Baath, it named Baathist General Ahmad Hassan al-Bakr president and a Nasserite general as prime minister. This conflict in leadership soon proved unfeasible; within two weeks the prime minister was shipped off as ambassador to Morocco, and the RCC named al-Bakr president, prime minister, and commander in chief of the armed forces. Restrictions against communists were relaxed; a wave of political arrests followed; puritanical laws regarding such things as hair styles and marriages to foreigners were enacted; and a new provisional constitution was promulgated giving all power to the RCC. Few changes were made in 1969, though the constitution was amended to abolish the office of prime minister and to add two vice presidents. The activities of Palestinian commando groups were sharply curbed on the grounds that they were abetting domestic enemies of the state.

Political existence was so fraught with frustrations that Iraq's leaders constantly saw themselves confronted by spies, saboteurs, and antigovernment plotters. In the first eight months of 1969 at least six public hangings occurred, in which fifty-four people were executed for spying for the United States, Israel, or Iran, or for seeking to overturn the administration. Arrayed against the regime were conservative and anti-Baath forces on one side and ardent communists and left-wing Baathists supported by Syria on the other. In addition the Kurds in the north constantly were fighting for independence or full local autonomy, while Shiites in the south sought religious support from Iran.

In 1972 a new strong man appeared, Saddam Husayn al-Taqriti, who became assistant secretary general of the Baath party, vice-chairman of RCC, and vice president of Iraq. There were constant rumors that al-Bakr was not well. But it was clear that al-Bakr and his chief deputy Saddam controlled all political and governmental actions and made all important decisions. Saddam moved to the fore; the political clout of the military wing of the Baath party ebbed rapidly. For the next several years there were no challenges to their rule.

Since the end of World War II the economy of Iraq has been linked to and dependent upon oil. Under al-Bakr there was no change. In 1969 Iraq National Oil Co. (INOC) invited thirteen west European and Soviet-bloc companies to bid for the rights to the North Rumayla fields, but then withdrew the opportunity when the Soviets loaned Iraq $70 million to enable INOC to develop the fields on its own. A contract was awarded in 1970 to a French company to build a pipeline from the fields to Fao on the Persian Gulf, and harbor facilities at Fao were greatly improved. Petroleum exports remained fairly constant in 1968, 1969, and 1970, and increased by 11 percent in 1971. Posted prices of crude were jumped twice in 1970 from $2.21 to $2.50 a barrel and to $3.21 in 1971. With royalties and taxes raised from 50 to 55 percent, Iraq garnered substantial oil income: $549 million in 1970 from IPC; $914 million in 1971. And with Czechoslovakia building and financing a $62 million refinery near Basrah, Hungarians and INOC drilling new wells, and the strength of OPEC, Iraqis harbored justifiable expectations of swelling treasury receipts.

Following OPEC policy, Iraq's oil minister in 1971 demanded acquisition of 20 percent of IPC and received an affirmative reply early in 1972. However, a 44 percent cut in IPC production during the first half of 1972 led to bitter arguments, and Iraq nationalized IPC on June 1, 1972. After nine months of bargaining, an agreement was reached whereby IPC would pay Iraq $367 million in back taxes and arrears on royalties, Iraq contracted to deliver to IPC at Mediterranean terminals 50 million barrels of crude in 1973 and 60 million in 1974, IPC waived all claims on the North Rumayla fields and agreed to increase production in the Basrah field. New oil fields were discovered near Baghdad in 1975, and at the same time the Basrah Petroleum Company was fully nationalized. Volume continued to mount, bringing in unbelievable sums—$9.25 billion in 1976. An oil pipeline from the Kirkuk area northward and then across Turkey to a terminal near Iskenderun was completed in 1977. With the pipeline to Fao it gave Iraq outlets on the Persian Gulf and through Turkey, Syria and Lebanon, assuring her continuous access to world markets and a certain independence.

Iraq's other economic concern, after petroleum, has been agriculture. Under Nuri al-Said great emphasis was laid on irrigation projects and dams, since a large majority of the population won its livelihood from the land. Though the Baathists were more concerned with finding income for the inhabitants of the teeming slums of Baghdad, the several five-year plans also carried development programs for irrigation. In 1971 the World Bank loaned $27.5 million and the U.S.S.R. advanced $20 million to dig and equip the twenty-five mile Tharthar Canal, which would link the Tigris River to the Euphrates and channel surplus water to irrigate central Iraq. With the completion in 1973 of Syria's Euphrates Dam, peasants in Iraq began to grumble about low water levels; in 1975 70 percent of the winter crops were ruined, cultivation in some areas being reduced to 4 percent of normal. Iraq stepped up her schedule for the great dam being built on the Euphrates near Haditha. Begun in 1966, largely under the supervision of Soviet engineers, its cost was estimated at $709.8 million. It was supposed to supply 80 percent of the irrigation and industrial needs of the region, and electric power produced from the dam would exceed 1.5 billion kilowatts annually.

The Kurds continued to press for independence. Mustafa Barzani led sporadic military actions in 1969, often against IPC installations at Kirkuk. In the autumn Baghdad launched a full-scale military campaign against Barzani who, reputedly, was aided by Israel and the American CIA. In 1970 al-Bakr guaranteed that Kurdistan within the Iraqi state would become an autonomous area where Kurdish would be the official language and that in Iraq as a whole Kurds would enjoy proper proportional representation in the army, the civil service, the national legislature, and the cabinet, including a Kurdish vice president. Five months later Barzani accused the government of inaction and bad faith. Serious fighting resumed and lasted until 1974. The leftist Kurdish Revolutionary party, which fought with the Baath against Barzani, merged with the Kurdish Democratic party to form an alliance with the Baath to counter Barzani. Barzani's forces maintained a stout resistance, supplied with arms and funds from Iran, Israel, and the CIA. The detente arranged in 1975 between Iran and Iraq spelled disaster for the Kurds. Iran abandoned them and drove out most of the 100,000 Kurds who had fled to Iran as refugees, while the Iraqi army mounted an offensive that killed many Kurds and gave Baghdad control of the areas of the north. The government uprooted thousands of Kurds from their homes and scattered and transplanted them in the south.

During the summer of 1976, however, the resettling of Kurds in central and southern Iraq had to be halted because the program was stirring Kurdish groups in the north to resume open fighting. Then, Kurdish commandos captured a number of Polish technicians in northern Iraq and agreed to release them in April 1977 only when Baghdad issued permission for 40,000 Kurds to return to their homes in the north. Obviously, the Kurdish problem in Iraq had not been solved.

Relations with Iran during most of the period after 1968 had been bad. Besides the Kurdish irritant, the two states quarreled over the Shatt al-Arab and the Persian Gulf. Iraq refused to renegotiate the 1937 treaty, insisting in 1969 that Iranian ships using the Shatt strike their colors and not carry Iranian navy personnel. The Iranian ambassador was expelled from Baghdad in 1970; the next year diplomatic relations were cut when Iran occupied Abu Musa and the Tunbs Islands. Over the years numerous Iranians had visited the Shiite pilgrimage holy places in Iraq, many residing indefinitely. In 1972 more than 60,000 pilgrims were deported to Iran, causing a horrendous uproar. At last, in March 1975, at an OPEC meeting in Algiers, the shah and Saddam struck a reconciliation. In a formal treaty of detente signed in June in Baghdad, Iraq relinquished exclusive control of the Shatt and the shah deserted the Kurds. Subsequently, Iraq consented to visits by 12,000 Iranians a year to the Muslim shrines in Iraq.

The Baath regime acted to enhance relations with the U.S.S.R., which generally supported Iraqi interests and policies and supplied large loans for the Euphrates Dam and other undertakings. These loans were repeated year after year; one for $1 billion was arranged in 1976 to support four irrigation projects. When a fifteen-year treaty of friendship was signed in April 1972, a number of Arab states objected and likened the treaty to Nuri al-Said's Baghdad Pact. Iraq offered Basrah as a port for Soviet warships, and that summer the U.S.S.R. sent a naval squadron on an official visit to Umm Qasr, where it was agreed that the Soviet navy would have priority bunkering and resupply rights.

Prior to the great oil price rise in 1973 and the flood of hard currency pouring into her treasury, Iraq had looked to the Soviet bloc for help in her economic projects. Beginning in 1974, however, Iraq turned to Japan and the West. Still unaccustomed to the oil wealth, the government sought and obtained credits for many of its purchases. Japan provided $1 billion on account against future shipments of 1.2 billion barrels of oil. With cash in Iraqi hands Western officials and businessmen began to be seen in Baghdad. Iraq loaned France $1 billion to help her pay for oil imports and diplomatic relations were resumed with Great Britain. Iraq's trade climbed rapidly; in 1976, Iraqi imports, largely from the West and Japan, totaled $6.5 billion. One Iraqi leader, questioned about this shift in trade patterns, replied that the regime's intention was "not to sacrifice technology for ideology." West German interests were very energetic in pursuing industrial and commercial possibilities and in 1975 replaced the Soviets as the chief supplier of Iraqi imports. Japan stood second and the United States and France were tied for third place. The U.S.S.R. fell far behind. In 1977 France moved ahead when her prime minister on a visit in Baghdad agreed to sell to Iraq Mirage F-1s, helicopters, missiles, and armored vehicles valued at $1.5 billion.

Iraq's new affluence seemed to alter Saddam's attitudes toward other Arab states. Even before the settlement with Syria over the Euphrates waters a broad agreement had been made with Assad. Crown Prince Fahd of Saudi Arabia came to Baghdad in 1975 not only to try to settle the problems brought on by Syria's Euphrates Dam but to delimit the Iraqi-Saudi border, split the neutral zone between them, and lay out the route of a hard-surface highway from Najaf to Medina. President Sadat was feted in Baghdad while advisers and experts drew up a trade agreement covering oil exports from Iraq and the importation of electrical appliances and 3,000 automobiles from Egypt. Plans were also made to move 500 Egyptian farm families to lands near Baghdad. Loans were extended to many Arab governments, including Tunisia, Yemen Arab Republic, Egypt, and Syria, and the dispute with Kuwayt over offshore islands was allowed to remain dormant. Old rivalries were not easily forgotten, but by 1977 none was being openly pressed.

The Arab League
The notions of Arab unity, cooperation among Arab states, even one federated or national Arab country were not novel when Anthony Eden, British foreign minister, said in 1941 that Britain would give "full support to any scheme that commands general approval." In 1942 Nuri al-Said circulated his "Blue Book," which suggested the "reuniting" of Syria, Lebanon, Palestine, and Transjordan into one state (Syria) and the formation of an Arab League to include any Arab states that might desire to join. Egypt and Saudi Arabia were lukewarm, fearing the Greater Syria embodied in his idea. After Eden commented again that the initiative of an Arab League "would have to come from the Arabs themselves," Nahas Pasha put forth other suggestions in 1943 and discussed them with the Arab prime ministers. In 1944 a committee representing the Arab states, including Palestine, pre-

sented the Alexandria Protocol to the various Arab governments. In essence it was the draft charter of the Arab League. Following discussions within each Arab government, representatives of Iraq, Syria, Lebanon, Transjordan, Saudi Arabia, and Egypt signed the Arab League pact at Cairo in March 1945. Other members joined later: Yemen, 1945; Libya, 1953; Sudan, 1956; Morocco, 1958; Tunisia, 1958; Kuwayt, 1961; Algeria, 1962; Somalia, 1967; South Yemen,1967; Bahrayn,1971; Qatar,1971; Oman, 1971, United Arab Amirates, 1971; Mauritania, 1973; the Palestine Liberation Organization, 1976; and Jibuti, 1977. The pact provided for a council, composed of a representative of each member state, and a secretariat-general, whose permanent seat was to be in Cairo. The council was to hold two ordinary sessions each year, in March and October, and extraordinary sessions whenever two members made a request.

The purpose of the league was to seek cooperation of member states in economic, cultural, social, and health affairs, in communications, and in matters affecting nationality. It embodied a guarantee of the sovereignty of each member and a promise to respect the systems of government established in other member states and to abstain from any interference in internal affairs of other member states. No collective-security or mutual-defense articles were included in the pact; no separate defense arrangement developed until 1950, when a loosely constructed security pact was accepted.

Although Great Britain had called the Arab League into being in hopes of obtaining greater security in the Middle East, the Arab states found in the league a promise of unity against the partition of Palestine and the birth of a Zionist state. In this connection six Arab rulers pledged their cooperation in opposing Zionist claims to Palestine. To implement the promise, the Arab League council in extraordinary session voted to send notes to Great Britain and the United States protesting the recommendations of the Anglo-American committee of inquiry. If notes proved unsuccessful, the council agreed to discuss diplomatic and economic (oil) measures that might be taken.

Egypt, Saudi Arabia, and Iraq each wanted the Arab League based in her country. From the league's inception, however, Egypt had the upper hand. The league's second and longtime secretary-general was Abd al-Khalik Hassunah, former Egyptian foreign minister. When the partition of Palestine became certain, the league urged its members to resist and later exhorted them to go to war against Israel. Saudi Arabia and Yemen, however, gave only token aid; Syria and Lebanon proved ineffective; and the Egyptian army was poorly equipped and mismanaged. Only Abdallah's forces of Transjordan, the Arab Legion, and the Iraqi troops showed any capacity for the fight, and only on their center front was there any success. Although each Arab state signed an accord that no part of Palestine would be annexed to another Arab state, none intended to uphold that agreement. Agents of the Arab League refused arms to other Arabs in Palestine if they were supporters of Arab families known to be inimical to Hajj Amin al-Husayni, the ex-mufti of Jerusalem who looked upon himself as the future ruler of Arab Palestine.

As defeat was experienced in Palestine, the Arab League declared that any member who made peace with Israel would be expelled. It also voted to oust Jordan, which annexed the remaining Arab portions of Palestine. In 1950 a treaty of joint defense and economic cooperation was inaugurated, obligating all to take up arms if any one became the victim of aggression. Actually designed to prevent the Fertile Crescent unity program, but purporting to strengthen the Arab states against Israel and satisfy the clamors of Arab nationalists in the streets, the treaty was signed by five states. Two more states, Iraq and Jordan, acceded to it in 1951 and 1952, respectively.

Beginning in 1950 the Arab League expanded its activities. An Economic Council was created to coordinate and unify economic policies, commerce, trade, and financial developments. In 1964 it set up an office in Brussels to serve as a liaison with the European Economic Community (EEC). Councils and federations for education, science, communications, public relations, labor, the practice of law, and aviation were also formed. Conferences and congresses were sponsored on a wide variety of subjects as medicine, Islam, Arab history, banking, chemistry, pharmacy, law, dentistry, tourism, and engineering. These meetings were valid steps in the direction of real unity and effective means of drawing leaders in Arab society together for the exchange of ideas and the comparison of problems.

Ministers and high officials met with their counterparts from Arab League countries to correlate policies and to formulate plans for joint ventures of every kind. It had become obvious that it was unwise for each country to have one of everything and pragmatism took precedence before pride and unwarranted duplication. A sampling of conferences includes the Arab Ministers of Labor in 1967, the Arab Chambers of Commerce in 1973, the Governors of Arab Central Banks in 1975, and a Congress sponsored in 1971 by the Arab Lawyers Foundation. Yet, the resistance of particular groups and states to many of the suggestions often proved strong, as the participants found it difficult to surrender their own national interests and special advantages.

International diplomacy and politics, however, were the Arab League's underpinnings. The league declared its sympathy for Arab independence struggles in Morocco and Algeria, supplied funds to nationalists there, granted asylum to the leaders, and urged that economic measures be taken against France. When Morocco and Algeria had acquired independence they were duly admitted to full membership in the league. Egypt was supported in her struggle with Britain over Suez Canal bases; Yemen and Saudi Arabia were aided in their disputes with Britain over Aden and the Buraimi oases; and West Germany was invited to reconsider her reparations agreement with Israel. In 1965 the league asked all Arab states to recall their ambassadors from Bonn after West Germany exchanged ambassadors with Israel; some Arab states went on to recognize East Germany. After

Lebanon, Algeria, and the Sudan recognized West Germany in 1972, the Arab League voted to nullify its stand.

The United Nations in 1960 officially accepted the Arab League as a regional organization, which facilitated agreements between the league and such U.N. bodies as the World Health Organization. Furthermore, it made possible the opening of Arab League offices with full diplomatic status in non-Arab capitals.

Early in 1955, when Iraq announced her intention of entering into a military arrangement with Turkey, the Arab League almost foundered. Egypt threatened to resign from the "Collective Security Pact," and Saudi Arabia and Yemen promised to follow Egypt into a new pact that would exclude Iraq. After the signing of the Baghdad Pact, however, Egypt did not walk out. Instead she moved quickly to form the Damascus Pact and to attract to her banner all the other Arab states. It seemed that the old Egypto-Saudi rivalry with the Hashimites had returned. Egypt was concerned lest Iraq, with her potential wealth and significant military and economic aid from the West, become suddenly as strong as Turkey and therefore the natural military leader among the Arab states. Lebanon refused to commit herself in this struggle. Jordan, torn by internal strife between the partisans of the two camps, also remained unpledged. The crisis over the Egyptian nationalization of the Suez Canal Company tended to restore unity to the Arab League, at least for the moment, for Iraq, Lebanon, and Jordan declared their concurrence in Egypt's actions. The Arab League drew up a plan for an Arab Investment Bank, but it was modified in 1968 to become the Arab Development Fund. An Arab Bank for social and economic development in Africa, with a capital of $206 million, was incorporated in 1974. The Arab Monetary Fund, headquartered in Abu Dhabi, was created in 1976, with a capital of $875 million to cover balance of payments problems among the Arab states.

In intra-Arab affairs the league tried to use its good offices to keep peace but usually acted only after one or both parties to an argument invited it to do so. In 1972 the league's representatives were stationed on the border between Oman and the People's Democratic Republic of Yemen; later the league appointed a committee to observe the frontier between the two Yemens to prevent armed incursions. Neither league venture proved very successful, and the hostilities were resolved in other ways. In 1975 the league was asked to mediate at a technical but not at a political level the Euphrates water dispute between Iraq and Syria. Within a few weeks, however, Syria withdrew from the talks, preferring a settlement arranged by Saudi Arabia.

The Arab League has been bypassed on matters so portentous that they have required heads of state to meet directly to make commitments and decisions. One such Arab summit meeting was held in Khartoum in the summer of 1967 to assess the disastrous June war. The conferees pledged to unify their diplomatic and political actions "to ensure the withdrawal of

Israeli forces from the occupied Arab territory," as well as to speed the liquidation of foreign bases, to consolidate military preparedness, and to employ oil policies as a weapon to achieve these goals. Saudi Arabia, Kuwayt, and Libya agreed to give financial aid to the United Arab Republic and Jordan to ease their war losses. Another summit was held in Rabat in 1974, where the important decision was reached to make the Palestine Liberation Organization the sole legitimate representative of the Palestinians and to remove King Husayn of Jordan from any role in the Palestine movement. At one summit meeting schemes for Arab utilization of Jordan basin waters were reviewed and plans were adopted to divert some of the headwaters of the Jordan, such as the Hasbani and Banyas rivers, to the Yarmuk where the Mukheiba Dam would regulate the water in Syria and Jordan. Promises were given to provide air cover for the building of all aspects of this scheme from attack that Israel had threatened.

The Arab boycott of Israel was shaped at summits and Arab League meetings. Each country was pledged to cease trade and all dealings with firms and individuals in all countries that had financial, business, or personal connections with Israel. Pressure was applied, at first with little effect, to obtain the cooperation of foreign firms, and a regular "blacklist" was maintained. In 1963, with the rising markets in the Trucial States after the exploitation of oil there, boycott offices were opened in Abu Dhabi, Dubay, and Sharjah.

Undoubtedly the best-known and certainly the most influential Arab alliance is the Organization of Arab Petroleum Exporting Countries (OAPEC), formed in January 1968 by Saudi Arabia, Kuwayt, and Libya. Prior to this several Arab Petroleum Congresses had been held. OAPEC's structure includes a council of ministers, an executive bureau, a secretariat, and a court; its purpose is to "determine ways and means of safeguarding the legitimate oil interests of its members." At OAPEC's first ministerial council meeting in 1968 Ahmad Zaki Yamani, Saudi Arabia's oil minister, was named secretary-general.

By 1969 other Arab states began to see how the organization could influence prices, regulations, oil flow, and every aspect of the relations between the giant oil companies and the producing countries, which at that time felt desperately in need of protection from the powerful and often arrogant international oil company executives. Algeria, Abu Dhabi, Dubay, Qatar, and Bahrayn were accepted as members, with the last four having no votes. When Iraq asked for admittance in 1970 the debate within OAPEC was furious, for Iraq was considered a radical state that in policy decisions would probably vote with Libya and Algeria against Saudi Arabia and Kuwayt. After many heated arguments Iraq, Syria, Egypt, and Oman were allowed to join in 1972, and OAPEC's charter was altered to permit membership to any oil-producing Arab state, not just to those whose oil income constituted more than 50 percent of its total revenues, as had been the case. When oil prices began to double and quadruple in 1972 and 1973 OAPEC and OPEC worked in tandem, the OAPEC countries with membership in

OPEC often forming a nucleus of opinion around their able spokesman Yamani.

The Arab League played a decisive role in Lebanon's civil war. When it seemed the country was about to be destroyed, the league, opposed to any partitioning of Lebanon, as well as the participation of Israel and other non-Arab states, held a meeting in Cairo in June 1976, at which Saudi Arabia suggested organizing Arab peace-keeping forces to supervise a cease-fire. At a partial summit meeting in Riyadh in September, attended by the heads of state of Saudi Arabia, Syria, Egypt, Jordan, Kuwayt, and Lebanon, and the leader of the PLO, arrangements were made for a cease-fire policed by an Arab military presence composed of contingents from several Arab states, though most were Syrian soldiers already in Lebanon. It was financed by contributions from various Arab states, and was to remain in Lebanon for six months so that Lebanese officials could reestablish the authority and legitimacy of government. The force remained on when the six months expired, as the Lebanese army had not yet reconstituted itself.

Though the Arab peace-keeping force did its job reasonably well, in general such demonstrations of Arab unity have been unusual. The persistent question of an Arab federation or a federal union, and how it is to be led (or dominated) remains to be resolved.

REFERENCES: Chapter 42

Important references for this chapter are also found in Chapters 21, 22, 23, 25, 26, 27, 28, 30, 31, 33, 37, 40, and 41.

Abu Jaber, Kamel S. *The Arab Ba'th Socialist Party: History, Ideology, and Organization.* Syracuse, N.Y.: Syracuse University Press, 1966. A descriptive and analytical study gathered from printed material in Arabic and English. It contains a noteworthy account of the organization and structure of the party as outlined in its manual of internal rules, constitution, and political platforms, and from the resolutions of its congresses.

Agwani, M. S. (ed.). *The Lebanon Crisis, 1958: A Documentary Study.* New York: Asia Publishing House, 1965. A collection of interviews with the leading personages during the crisis and extracts from speeches, with an introduction to each piece placing it in perspective.

Alnasrawi, Abbas. *Financing Economic Development in Iraq: The Role of Oil in a Middle Eastern Economy.* New York: Praeger, 1967. A study of the years 1950 to 1964, covering Iraq's six development plans.

Barakat, Halim. *Lebanon in Strife: Student Preludes to the Civil War.* Austin: University of Texas Press, 1977. Sociological survey of student attitudes.

Birdwood, Lord. *Nuri al-Said: A Study in Arab Leadership.* London: Cassell, 1959. A political biography that covers Nuri al-Said's military education and career in the Ottoman army, his involvement in Arab secret societies devoted to Arab independence, his participation in the Arab revolt, and close relations with King Faysal I.

Boutros-Ghali, B. Y. *The Arab League, 1954–1955.* New York: Carnegie Endowment For International Peace, 1955. Historical background followed by sections on political and nonpolitical activities. Appendices contain the texts of the Arab League Pact and the Treaty of Joint Defense and Economic Cooperation.

Childers, Erskine B. *Common Sense about the Arab World.* New York: Macmillan, 1960. Legacies of the past, Western myths about the Arabs, Arabism in revolt, and the economic and social reforms brought in by the several revolutionary regimes.

Dann, Uriel. *Iraq under Qassem: A Political History, 1958–1963.* New York: Praeger, 1969. An account of the regime's early impetus for social and political reform, the personal power struggles, and the conflicts between nationalists and communists.

Devlin, John F. *The Ba'th Party: A History from Its Origins to 1966.* Stanford, Calif.: Hoover Institution, 1976. A detailed account of origins, doctrine, and political fortunes of the Baath.

Entelis, John P. *Pluralism and Party Transformation in Lebanon: al-Kata'ib, 1936–1970.* Leiden, The Netherlands: Brill, 1974. A comprehensive study of the largest, best organized political organization in Lebanon.

Fisher, Sydney N. (ed.). *Social Forces in the Middle East.* Ithaca, N.Y.: Cornell University Press, 1955. Essays on various occupational groups in the Middle East and their points of view.

Glubb, Sir John Bagot. *A Soldier with the Arabs.* New York: Harper, 1958. The memoirs of a professional soldier with experience in Iraq and Jordan who served as chief of staff of Jordan's Arab Legion until 1956. Indispensable.

Haddad, George M. *Revolutions and Military Rule in the Middle East.* Vol. II: *The Arab States.* New York: Robert Speller & Sons, 1971. Discusses the thirty-nine coups in Syria, Iraq, Lebanon, and Jordan between 1936 and 1969. Best on Syria.

Hammond, Paul Y., and Sidney S. Alexander (eds.). *Political Dynamics in the Middle East.* New York: American Elsevier, 1971. Searches beyond the immediate issues to examine underlying behavior and attitudes.

Hudson, Michael C. *The Precarious Republic: Political Modernization in Lebanon.* New York: Random House, 1968. A fine analysis of governmental institutions.

Hurewitz, J. C. *Middle East Dilemmas.* New York: Harper, 1953. The difficulties existing as the United States entered into Middle East affairs.

Ionides, Michael. *Divide and Lose. The Arab Revolt, 1955–1958.* London: Geoffrey Bles, 1960. By an hydraulic engineer interested in the waters of the Jordan.

Ismael, Tareq Y. *The Arab Left.* Syracuse, N.Y.: Syracuse University Press, 1976. Covers the Baath, the Arab Nationalist Movement, Nasserism, and the "New Left" after 1967.

Jalal, Ferhang. *The Role of Government in the Industrialization of Iraq, 1950–1965.* London: Frank Cass, 1972. A good examination of Iraq's development policies.

Kazziha, Walid. *Revolutionary Transformation in the Arab World: Habash and His Comrades from Nationalism to Marxism.* New York: St. Martin's Press, 1975.

Kerr, Malcolm. *The Arab Cold War, 1958–1964: A Study of Ideology in Politics.* New York: Oxford University Press, 1965. A balanced, comprehensive study of the factors that contributed to Syrian-Egyptian unity. Examines the struggles between the Baath and the Egyptian elites.

Khadduri, Majid. *Arab Contemporaries: The Role of Personalities in Politics.* Baltimore: Johns Hopkins Press, 1973. A survey of the personalities of twelve modern Arab political leaders, including Nuri al-Said, Nasser, Jumblat, Aflaq, and Bakdash.

———. *Republican Iraq: A Study of Iraqi Politics since the Revolution of 1958.* New York: Oxford University Press, 1969. Detached and objective, with painstaking attention to detail and accuracy. Based on primary sources and many personal interviews. By the outstanding student of modern Iraq.

Khalil, Muhammad. *The Arab States and the Arab League: A Documentary Record.* Vol. I: *Constitutional Developments.* Vol. II: *International Affairs.* Beirut: Khayats, 1962. Valuable reference work of over 600 documents.

Kimball, Lorenzo Kent. *The Changing Pattern of Political Power in Iraq, 1958–1971.* New York: Robert Speller & Sons, 1972. Good on the military politics of the period.

Koury, Enver M. *The Crisis in the Lebanese System: Confessionalism and Chaos.* Washington, D.C.: American Enterprise Institute, 1976. Examines the Lebanese system of power-sharing.

———. *The Patterns of Mass Movements in Arab Revolutionary-Progressive States.* The Hague: Mouton, 1970. A study of the revolutionary process in Syria, Iraq, Egypt, Algeria, and Tunisia.

Langley, Kathleen M. *The Industrialization of Iraq.* Cambridge, Mass.: Harvard University Press, 1961. A thoroughgoing analysis of Iraq's prerevolutionary economic growth.

Laqueur, Walter Z. *Communism and Nationalism in the Middle East.* New York: Praeger, 1956. An excellent, encyclopedic treatment of communists, their fronts, and their endeavors in the Middle East.

Macdonald, Robert W. W. *The League of Arab States.* Princeton, N.J.: Princeton University Press, 1965. An examination of the accomplishments of the league in its first twenty years.

Malone, Joseph J. *The Arab Lands of Western Asia.* Englewood Cliffs, N.J.: Prentice-Hall, 1973. An analysis of events in the Middle East, concentrating on the period since World War II. Presents a sharp picture of the religious-ethnic-family structure of Lebanese and Iraqi politics.

Al-Marayati, Abid A. *A Diplomatic History of Modern Iraq.* New York: Robert Speller & Sons, 1961. An examination of Iraq's preparations within and outside the League of Nations for effective participation in the United Nations.

Nuseibeh, Hazem Saki. *The Ideas of Arab Nationalism.* Ithaca, N.Y.: Cornell University Press, 1956. The growth and development of nationalism in the Middle East.

Polk, William R. *The United States and the Arab World.* 3rd ed. Cambridge, Mass.: Harvard University Press, 1975. Suggests a possible solution to the Arab-Israeli impasse.

Qubain, Fahim I. *Crisis in Lebanon.* Washington, D.C.: Middle East Institute, 1961. A comprehensive, fair-minded account of the 1958 crisis.

———. *The Reconstruction of Iraq, 1950–1957.* New York: Praeger, 1958. A picture of change induced by rising oil earnings, by the interest of Nuri al-Said, and by public investment as planned by the Development Board. Very useful.

Rabinovich, Itamar. *Syria Under the Ba'th, 1963–1966: The Army-Party Symbiosis.* New York: Halsted Press, 1972. Carefully scrutinizes successive Baath party congresses. Analyzes political changes, tensions, and armed conflicts during the Baath's first years of rule.

Salem, Elie Adib. *Modernization Without Revolution: Lebanon's Experience.* Bloomington: Indiana University Press, 1973. Examines the stability, durability, and modernization capability of the Lebanese polity.

Salibi, Kamal S. *Crossroads to Civil War: Lebanon, 1958–1976.* Delmar, N.Y.: Caravan Books, 1976. Deals with the complex elements.

Sayegh, Fayez A. *Arab Unity: Hope and Fulfillment.* New York: Devin-Adair, 1958. Arab unity seen as a response to the political fragmentation of the Arab world during the nineteenth and early twentieth centuries.

Sayigh, Yusif A. *Entrepreneurs of Lebanon: The Role of the Business Leader in a Developing Economy.* Cambridge, Mass.: Harvard University Press, 1962. A study of the background, education, attitudes, and ambitions of 200 men who make the decisions in Lebanon's major firms.

Seale, Patrick. *The Struggle for Syria: A Study in Post War Arab Politics, 1945–1958.* London: Oxford University Press, 1965. Advances the thesis that whoever wishes to dominate the Middle East must control Syria, where the Baath party has successfully drawn together the elements of Arab nationalism in language, culture, history, and aspirations. A careful analysis of events leading up to the union in 1958 of Egypt and Syria.

Shwadran, Benjamin. *The Power Struggle in Iraq.* New York: Council for Middle Eastern Affairs Press, 1960. A description of the political events immediately following the 1958 revolution.

Smith, Wilfred Cantwell. *Islam in Modern History.* Princeton, N.J.: Princeton University Press, 1957. A thoughtful, philosophical study of the position of religion in the present-day Middle East.

Smolansky, Oles M. *The Soviet Union and the Arab East under Khrushchev.* Cranbury, N.J.: Bucknell University Press, 1974. An account of relations between 1958 and 1964.

Stewart, Desmond. *Trouble in Beirut.* London: Wingate, 1959. A first-hand account of the civil strife in 1958.

Suleiman, Michael W. *Political Parties in Lebanon: The Challenge of a Fragmented Political Culture.* Ithaca, N.Y.: Cornell University Press, 1967. A solid, straightforward, and informative work. Describes the history, organization, ideology, and role of seventeen parties and two quasi-party groups in Lebanon.

Torrey, Gordon H. *Syrian Politics and the Military, 1945–1958.* Columbus: Ohio State University Press, 1964. A thorough study of the various political parties in post-World War II Syria, and the position of the military toward and within each.

Trevelyan, Humphrey. *The Middle East in Revolution.* Boston: Gambit, 1970. Sir Humphrey was British Ambassador in Cairo, Baghdad, and other spots from 1955 on.

Yamak, Labib Zuwiyya. *The Syrian Social Nationalist Party: An Ideological Analysis.* Cambridge, Mass.: Harvard University Press, 1966. Examines Antun Saadah's doctrine of Syrian nationalism, his political philosophy, and the organizational structure of the party.

Yaukey, David. *Fertility Differences in a Modernizing Country.* Princeton, N.J.: Princeton University Press, 1961. From interviews with 900 Lebanese women on the subject of their fertility and their sexual practices.

Yodfat, Aryeh. *Arab Politics in the Soviet Mirror.* Jerusalem: Israel Universities Press, 1973. A survey of what the Soviet press wrote about internal affairs in Egypt, Syria, and Iraq from the 1950s to June 1967.

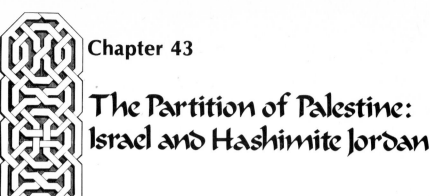

Chapter 43

The Partition of Palestine: Israel and Hashimite Jordan

The Jewish Refugees

The British White Paper of 1939 supposedly placed the future of Palestine on ice for the duration of World War II. Land transfers from Arabs to Jews were halted, and total immigration for the next five years was fixed at 75,000. For the moment the Jewish Agency and the Arab Committee acquiesced to these terms, but few believed that the Palestine problem would not demand a solution immediately at the end of the war. The Jewish Agency and the neighboring Arab states were girding themselves for the eventual struggle.

The official Zionist position was drawn up in 1942 by a Zionist conference at the Biltmore Hotel in New York City. Ratified in Jerusalem by the inner general council of the Jewish Agency, the Biltmore program called for the establishment of a Jewish commonwealth in all of Palestine, and for unlimited immigration under the control of the Jewish Agency.

As the war in Europe drew to a close, the drive to fulfill the Biltmore program was intensified by pressures from all sides. Jews from Germany, Poland, and eastern Europe fled their homes and found temporary refuge in German and Italian displaced-persons camps. World Jewry in the West, in memory of the Jews massacred by the Nazis, felt a "divine impatience" over the procrastination in finding homes for these displaced persons. Illegal immigration to Palestine multiplied, and thousands filtered through the lines held by the Jewish brigade in Italy. Others came by ships of every description. Crises arose when British authorities would not permit them to land, turned them back, or interned them in Cyprus or Mauritius. The S.S. *Patria,* crowded with visaless refugees, was sunk off Haifa; its surviving passengers were allowed to land and remain. All but one of the 769 visaless passengers on an old cattle boat, the S.S. *Struma,* were lost when she sank in the Black Sea. Incidents such as these heightened the irritation at the delay in opening the gates of Palestine to the homeless.

To the new leader of the Jewish Agency, David Ben-Gurion, the refugees, if settled in Palestine, would provide the needed majority to assure a dominant position for the Zionists. The Jewish Agency, therefore, insisted that the refugees come to Palestine, and urged the continuance of immigration quotas in the United States to prevent their departure for America, the destiny which most preferred.

An influx of Jews into Palestine found ready opposition from the Arab governments. Britain, in the midst of war, had her hands full with internal security in the Arab states. Thus, any policies for Palestine had to remain quiescent in order not to incite an Arab uprising, which the British believed to be certain if Jewish immigration stood at a high level. Since the Zionists feared that time might be against them, they urged the attainment of their program in 1945. They rejoiced at the Labour victory at the polls, because Labour leaders, in opposition and out of power, had made promises favorable to Zionist aspirations.

Ben-Gurion had already warned that the reply to the British government, should it return to the 1939 White Paper, would be "bloody terror" and "constant and brutal force" in Palestine. Likewise, Rabbi Silver, president of the Zionist Organization of America, condemned the moderate diplomacy used by Weizmann as old-fashioned, and inspired the Jewish masses to maintain their fighting spirit and prepare for any emergency. Sir Stafford Cripps and British Foreign Minister Ernest Bevin learned, however, that there was an Arab as well as a Jewish question. Consequently, all the ministries of the government concerned with the Middle East "sang the same refrain. . . . nothing should be done that would further antagonize the Arabs." The Labour government postponed any new departure and left the 1939 White Paper in effect. In the United States, President Truman, who bore no responsibility for the problems of the Middle East, supported the immediate granting of 100,000 immigration certificates requested by Ben-Gurion and entreated British Prime Minister Attlee to act quickly in the matter. To this the British declared that no radical change in policy toward Palestine could be made unless the United States would share in the maintenance of security in Palestine by providing U.S. troops. Attlee knew Truman would refuse to consider this move.

Zionist Guerrilla Tactics and Terrorism

Delay brought terror to Palestine. Ben-Gurion gave his approval of overt actions by the three illegal Zionist armed forces in Palestine. Haganah ("Defense"), with a membership of about 60,000, had been organized in 1920 to defend isolated Jewish settlements from Arab attacks; in the 1930s it spread, with winks from the British, to every Jewish community in Palestine. During World War II it acquired by various illegal means weapons of every description from small sidearms to tanks. In 1945 the "brilliant and biting" Moshe Sneh, aged thirty-seven, assumed command of Haganah and worked out arrangements to coordinate efforts with Menachem Begin, leader of Irgun Zvai Leumi ("Zionist National Military Organization"), and Nathan Freidman-Yellin, leader of the Stern Gang ("Fighters for the Freedom of Israel"). All three men had resided together at the Jewish Academicians House at the University of Warsaw. Irgun and the Stern group were right-wing semi military organizations dedicated to obtaining a Zionist political state that would include all of Palestine. They fought against the

Arabs in the 1930s and were fascist in character, in sharp contrast to Zionists of the Jewish Agency and Haganah, who were more likely to be socialists.

The British were caught between urgent Zionist and American demands and a categorical refusal of the Arab states to countenance any abrogation of the 1939 White Paper. Upon the stalling of the Labour government Sneh suggested that "one serious incident" should occur as a warning of what would erupt unless Zionist policies obtained. On October 10, 1945, the Palmach (Haganah commandos) raided a British detention camp at Athlit and freed 208 illegal immigrants. On the night of October 31 the Palmach sank three small British naval ships and tore up the tracks of the Palestine railway in 153 places; Irgun attacked the Lydda railway station; and Sternists sabotaged the Haifa oil refineries. Late in December Irgun raided a military arms depot in Tel Aviv, killing nine men of the security forces. Although conferences were held between leaders of Irgun and the Jewish Agency every fortnight, Ben-Gurion and Moshe Shertok (later Sharett), head of the political department of the Jewish Agency, denied all cognizance of these affairs and feigned helplessness in preventing them.

The Jewish resistance movement against British authority operated in the same way as had the guerrillas whom the British had aided, only months previously, in Nazi-occupied Europe. Upon rumors that British delays would continue until further investigations were made, Zionist leaders reminded all: "Six million Jews died in Europe while we waited for the democratic powers to act. Thousands more of the remnant will die if we sit here with hands folded during the winter, while they investigate again." The situation in DP camps in West Germany was being aggravated intentionally by the clandestine operations of Haganah in bringing in Jews from central Europe—notwithstanding public accusations by Weizmann, Walter Winchell, and Eddie Cantor that all who made such charges were anti-Semitic or the remark by Rabbi Wise that such statements reminded him of the forged Protocols of the Elders of Zion.

Anglo-American Committee of Inquiry
Since Britain hesitated to act because of Arab pressures and since the United States was insisting on action without any willingness to shoulder the responsibility of maintaining order in Palestine, an Anglo-American committee of inquiry of six Britons and six Americans was appointed to study the question. The committee was to meet in Washington, London, Europe, Palestine, and the Arab states and recommend steps to achieve a solution. In the early months of 1946, while the committee questioned individuals in Palestine, terrorist deeds continued. Haganah publicly boasted of its participation. The report of the committee recommended granting 100,000 immigration certificates to European Jews. It recognized, however, that hostility between Jews and Arabs made the establishment of an independent Palestine impossible at the moment, and advised that Britain retain the mandate until a trusteeship agreement under the United Nations could

be arranged, that steps be taken to raise the Arab standard of living in Palestine, and that all laws discriminating against Arabs be removed.

British leaders were provoked when President Truman suggested 100,000 visas be given at once. The Labour government was faced with a dilemma. Approval of a loan to Britain was before the American Congress, where the Zionists had many friends; negotiations were in process for a treaty with Egypt; Soviet pressures upon Turkey, Iran, Kurdistan, and northern Iraq were increasing day by day. The cost of maintaining a sizable force—at least 100,000 men— in Palestine was a heavy charge on a tight budget for a state on the verge of bankruptcy. Furthermore, if Britain were to evacuate her troops from Egypt, as seemed likely, the need of a strong base in Palestine became imperative.

As the British cabinet weighed the dilemma, violence spread in Palestine. Munitions thefts, explosions, sabotage, bank robberies, killings of English soldiers, and destruction of bridges were an open declaration of war by the Jewish resistance movement. Jewish leaders in Palestine reasoned that outrages would obtain concessions from a fearful England. As part of the British reaction Jewish Agency leaders were arrested and their offices occupied; members of the Palmach were rounded up; British military authorities imprisoned numerous suspected terrorists; and great caches of arms were seized. In retaliation Irgun, with the connivance of Haganah, blew up the King David Hotel in Jerusalem, British military headquarters, killing ninety-one people and wounding forty-five others.

To resolve the impasse a new Anglo-American suggestion, called the Morrison-Grady plan, was presented. This plan advocated the creation of separate Arab and Jewish autonomous provinces under a central government that would control Jerusalem and the Negev. Similar provincial autonomy plans had been rejected by the Anglo-American committee of inquiry, and even before that such plans had gathered dust in the colonial office for years. Rejected by both Arabs and Zionists as unsatisfactory, the plan was then modified by the leaders of the Jewish Agency, who by this time had abandoned the Biltmore program and indicated a readiness to accept a separate state in Palestine. It was insisted, however, that the state include the Negev desert area.

Hope for a solution was in the air as Weizmann's moderation gained ascendancy—only to be shattered beyond repair by President Truman's announcement in October 1946, just before the congressional and the New York gubernatorial elections, that the United States strongly supported the immediate entry of 100,000 Jews into Palestine. Furthermore, at the world Zionist congress at Basle in December Weizmann was elected president by only 51 percent of the vote, and the activism of Ben-Gurion and Rabbi Silver carried political resolutions against the moderation of Weizmann, Shertok, and Rabbi Wise. Rabbi Silver's prescience assured the congress of American support, politically and financially, for the establishment of an independent state of Israel. At the same time he predicted that an independent state could never be achieved by a policy of "gradualism."

Terrorism revived in Palestine. A British officer and three sergeants were seized by Irgun and flogged. In January 1947 a Jew was sentenced to death for his part in an attack upon a police office where a policeman was killed. Irgun abducted a British judge and a civilian from the Tel Aviv district court and did not release them until a stay of execution of the condemned man was signed.

Palestine Before the United Nations

In February 1947 the British made one last desperate offer, but each side refused it. Consequently, Bevin decided to refer the question to the United Nations. During debate in the House of Commons it was intimated that England would give up her mandate shortly and in the meantime would take no action to prejudice the eventual United Nations decision.

At British request a special session of the U.N. General Assembly was called to consider Palestine. The U.N. Special Committee on Palestine (UNSCOP) was authorized to investigate any question relevant to Palestine and report by September 1. UNSCOP visited Palestine in June and July, during which time Zionist terrorists attacked the prison in Acre and freed many prisoners. The British hanged three Jews apprehended in the attack; in reprisal Irgun hanged two British sergeants. In another incident, the S.S. *Exodus 1947,* boarded at Marseilles by 4,554 Jewish passengers with passports and visas for Colombia, was seized at Haifa by British authorities and turned back to France.

The situation remained tense as all awaited the UNSCOP report being drafted at Geneva. All eleven members agreed that the mandate had proved unworkable. Three approved a binational federal state; the other eight favored a partition plan envisaging an economic union. The report recommended partition lines forming three sections of territory for Jews and three for Arabs, with northern and southern points of intersection and communication. Jerusalem and Bethlehem were to be internationalized. The Arab and Jewish states would become independent only when they signed a ten-year economic union pact compelling the stronger Jewish state to assist the poorer Arab one. As proposed, 45 to 50 percent of the population in the Jewish state would be Arab, and 1 percent in the Arab state would be Jewish. Referred to as "death by a thousand cuts," the partition plan was as improbable and impractical as the signing of a ten-year economic union between the two was unthinkable. UNSCOP called for establishment of the states before October 1, 1948, while Britain declared her mandate would be terminated May 15 and her troops evacuated before August 1.

The General Assembly reached a vote on the UNSCOP report on November 29, 1947, approving it by a vote of 33 to 13, with 11 abstentions. Several days before the vote was taken it appeared that the partition plan might not obtain the necessary two-thirds majority of those voting, but several postponements gave the Zionists and their sympathizers among United

States officialdom opportunity to put pressure on five states that had intended to vote against partition.

The Palestine War

The U.N. partition plan touched off a civil war in Palestine. Thereafter, Haganah, Irgun, and Sternists openly attacked the British when in need of arms, and Arab forces grew in numbers with volunteers and arms coming in surreptitiously from neighboring Arab states. As more and more British soldiers were killed, there arose a clamor from the British public to pull out fully and quickly. Zionist arms were smuggled in from New York and Czechoslovakia. No day passed without violence. On December 15, 1947, the Palestine government relinquished the policing of Tel Aviv to the Zionists and Jaffa to the Arabs. Attack and counterattack brought savagery to new heights in Jerusalem and Haifa. Trained and well-equipped Syrian volunteers with a few officers from the Syrian army entered north Palestine in January 1948; by mid-March they numbered about 5,000. Under the leadership of Fawzi al-Kawukji, a Lebanese soldier of fortune and Arab patriot, the Arab liberation army in the upper Jordan Valley reduced the fear and anarchy spreading through Arab villages.

Nearly 100 British soldiers perished in Palestine in the three months after the U.N. partition vote. In February 1948, since the partition plan appeared unworkable, the United States proposed that the five permanent members of the U.N. Security Council should consider a temporary trusteeship for Palestine under the U.N. Trusteeship Council. The Jewish Agency protested at this "shocking reversal" of American policy and declared that even a temporary trusteeship could not be accepted. The United States, then, suggested a truce, but Shertok replied there could be no delay in the achievement of independence.

While the United States was seeking to escape from the dilemma she had fostered, full-scale war descended upon Palestine. The Arab liberation army, augmented by Iraqi and Egyptian contributions and dignified by the blessing of the Arab states, together with detachments of Palestinian Arab units, became engaged in April with the Zionist military organizations in many sectors of Palestine. The Jews took Tiberias and Haifa, which were in the area assigned to a Jewish state by the partition. Heavy mortar attacks by Irgun and the Sternists upon Jaffa and Acre, which had been reserved for the Arab state, accelerated the flight of Arabs from those cities. Arabs threatened the line of communications between Haifa and Tel Aviv and the New City of Jerusalem. On April 9 Irgun units attacked the Arab village of Dair Yasin near Jerusalem and killed about 250 villagers, half of them women and children. Three days later the Arabs attacked a Jewish convoy bound for beleaguered Hebrew University and Hadassah Hospital on Mount Scopus, killing 77 doctors, nurses, university teachers, and students. As war spread and its outrages multiplied, civilians tried to escape. Zionist authorities were vigilant and allowed no Jew to leave without an exemption from military service issued by Haganah and a receipt for taxes paid for

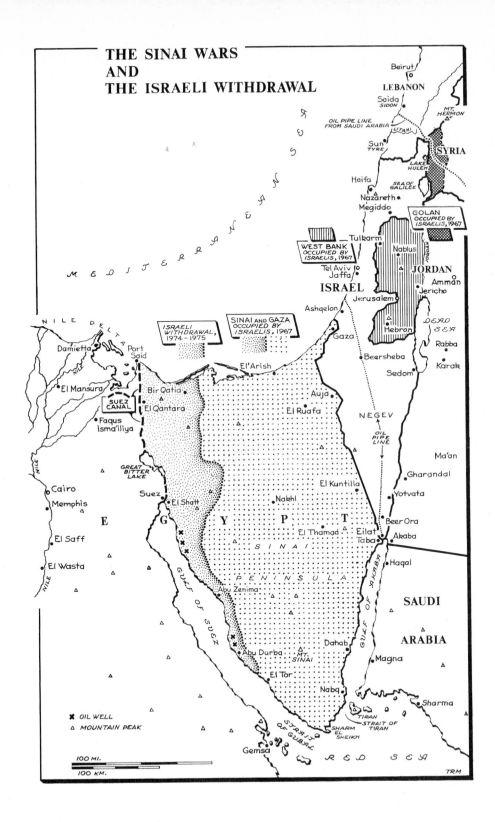

THE SINAI WARS
AND
THE ISRAELI WITHDRAWAL

Beirut

LEBANON

Saida
SIDON

OIL PIPE LINE
FROM SAUDI ARABIA

MT.
HERMON

LITANI

Sur
TYRE

SYRIA

LAKE
HULEH

Haifa

SEA OF
GALILEE

Nazareth

Megiddo

GOLAN
OCCUPIED BY
ISRAELIS, 1967

Tulkarm

WEST BANK
OCCUPIED BY
ISRAELIS, 1967

Nablus

Tel Aviv
Jaffa

JORDAN

ISRAEL

Jerusalem

Amman

Jericho

Ashqelon

MEDITERRANEAN SEA

NILE DELTA

ISRAELI
WITHDRAWAL,
1974-1975

SINAI AND GAZA
OCCUPIED BY
ISRAELIS, 1967

Gaza

DEAD
SEA

Rabba

Damietta

Port
Said

El'Arish

Beersheba

Karak

El Mansura

Bir Qatia

Sedom

SUEZ
CANAL

El Qantara

Auja

NEGEV

Faqus
Isma'iliya

El Ruafa

Ma'an

GREAT
BITTER
LAKE

OIL
PIPE
LINE

Gharandal

Cairo

Suez

El Shatt

El Kuntilla

Yotvata

Memphis

Nakhl

Beer Ora

E

G

Y

P

T

Eilat

Akaba

El Saff

El Thamad

Taba

SINAI

Haqal

El Wasta

PENINSULA

SAUDI

Abu Zenima

ARABIA

Dahab

MT.
SINAI

Magna

Abu Durba

El Tor

Nabq

Sharma

TIRAN
STRAIT OF
TIRAN

GULF OF SUEZ

GULF OF AKABA

X OIL WELL

△ MOUNTAIN PEAK

SHARM
EL SHEIKH

STRAIT
OF
GUBAL

100 MI.

Gemsa

RED SEA

100 KM.

TRM

military financing. Arab refugees did not find such barriers; it was estimated that by the middle of May 1948 Arab civilian refugees from thirty exposed villages and from Tiberias, Haifa, Jaffa, and other occupied cities totaled about 150,000.

On May 14, 1948, at Tel Aviv, in the midst of such anarchy, Ben-Gurion, flanked by his twelve fellow ministers of the national council of the Jewish state, proclaimed the establishment of the Jewish state in Palestine, to be called Israel. President Truman announced *de facto* recognition of Israel by the United States minutes after Ben-Gurion's proclamation in Tel Aviv.

The Arab League had previously declared that it would not recognize the State of Israel and that league members would be encouraged to intervene in Palestine. On May 15, 1948, the Palestine war began. Two Egyptian forces entered Palestine. One proceeded along the coast (in the area assigned to an Arab state) to Isdud, twenty miles south of Tel Aviv, where it was halted by an Israeli force; the other crossed the Negev, through Beersheba, to Bethlehem and the southern suburbs of Jerusalem. A Palestinian Arab force held the Lydda airfield, and an Iraqi force crossed the Jordan and advanced to Tul Karm, ten miles from the Mediterranean. A small Lebanese token force crossed into Palestine from southern Lebanon, and an army of a few thousand Syrians served to pin down a few Israeli forces in the north. The Arab Legion of Transjordan held the center of the line, occupied areas in the Arab portion of Palestine, and defeated Israeli attacks upon Jerusalem.

Although the Arab radio and press claimed victory after victory and described excursions through Arab-held areas as triumphant advances in Palestine, the Arab leaders knew that success had not been theirs. Arab soldiers found their equipment obsolete or defective; officers were incompetent in staff work; the zeal of the Arab soldier was cool. Moreover, the Arab Legion was under orders not to move into territory awarded to the Jews by the U.N. partition plan. On the other hand, Israeli activity and ardor were highly stimulated. In the early days of the war bitter controversy developed between Haganah and the extremist groups, but Ben-Gurion became official commander in chief of the army, and direct leadership was given to Yigal Yadin and Yigal Allon.

The Palestine war distressed the powers. On May 20 the U.N. Security Council appointed Count Folke Bernadotte of Sweden mediator for Palestine, giving him a free hand to bring about an end to hostilities. A truce was arranged that ran from June 11 to July 8, and a second truce began on July 19. In October Israeli forces drove the Egyptians from most of their positions in the Negev, including Beersheba; cleared northern Palestine; drove al-Kawukji and his Arab liberation army into Lebanon and Syria; and occupied fifteen Lebanese villages. In December Israeli mechanized forces, supported by a cover of planes, drove the Egyptians into a narrow corridor at Gaza and invaded Egyptian territory in the Sinai Peninsula, compelling the Egyptian government to sue for a cease-fire arrangement on the promise of agreement to an armistice.

Without question the Israeli army won the Palestine war. To a very marked degree during those months Israel was a nation in arms fighting for her independence and her very existence, and this spirit pervaded the fighting units. Pride in the courage of the Jewish soldier and his feats in the face of great danger aroused soldiers to extraordinary accomplishment. A singleness of purpose permeated all levels of society and eliminated most problems of discipline. Early in the struggle the independence of the Sternists and Irgun was largely curbed, even with force on several occasions. In contrast, the diversity of aims, personal jealousies, and national self-interest of the Arab states and their leaders deprived the Arab armies of the cooperation and coordination necessary for victory.

In the spring of 1948 the Arab states, taken as a whole, were better supplied than the Zionists; Iraq, Transjordan, and Egypt had arms treaties with England. But by the autumn of 1948 the situation was reversed. Numerous shipments of smuggled arms from the United States arrived in Israel, and dollar gifts collected in the United States purchased quantities of first-class arms from Czechoslovakia. Bombers were obtained in the United States and England. The British forces illegally disposed of all types of supplies; two staff sergeants received £20,000 from Haganah for several tanks. Frequently officials from the U.N. mediators' team watched Jewish stevedores unload crates of arms and ammunition. The arms embargo to the area hindered the Israeli effort very little, but the Arabs were not so successful in circumventing it.

Then, too, truces worked to the disadvantage of the Arabs. Delays gave greater opportunity for the ambitions of the leaders to erode the Arab effort. The Arab soldiers by training and experience were good fighters when aroused, but equally ready to return home when the fighting was over. To kindle their ardor a second and a third time proved difficult, and to explain to Arab soldiers the reason for a truce was a fruitless task.

Armistice

During the first truce Count Bernadotte made several suggestions for a basis on which peace could rest. A fundamental point incorporated the Arab portion of Palestine into the state of Transjordan, a development which Israelis rightfully recognized would alter the balance of power in Palestine. As the end of the truce approached, Israel rejected the mediator's offers, but went along with Lebanon, Transjordan, Iraq, and Saudi Arabia to prolong the truce. But not Syria and Egypt. They were so involved in a press build-up to destroy Israel, that the governments hardly dared to postpone the battle. The second truce was never well observed, and the Israelis, who conquered three times more Arab territory in the second stage of the war than they had in the first, were difficult to contain. Count Bernadotte continued to search for a peaceful solution, and in one suggestion placed Jerusalem in the Arab sector. But Israel without Jerusalem was an emotional impossibility to Zionists; the head of the Sternists in his newssheet wrote: "The task of the moment is to oust Bernadotte and his observers. Blessed be the hand that does it." A few days later Bernadotte was murdered by a Sternist soldier.

In the autumn of 1948 several cease-fire agreements were arranged. Ralph Bunche, the acting mediator, at his headquarters on the Island of Rhodes obtained an armistice between Israel and Egypt in February 1949. The important article pertained to the temporary frontier between the two states: the Gaza strip was left to Egypt, but the line was so drawn that many Arab villages were separated from their farmlands; the al-Awja area was demilitarized on the Israeli side, and Egyptian forces were withdrawn fourteen to seventeen miles.

An armistice between Israel and Lebanon was signed in March, and the old frontier was recognized and demilitarized on each side. The question of a settlement with Syria was delayed by the coup d'état of Husni al-Zaim; in July Ralph Bunche obtained agreement and an armistice. The frontiers remained as they were drawn in 1920; the upper Jordan River and the Sea of Galilee were wholly in Israel, but a small part of the Lake Hulah marsh area was recognized as a demilitarized zone.

With Transjordan the settlement was far more complex. Debates at the U.N. in the autumn of 1948 revealed that the Western powers agreed that King Abdallah of Transjordan might take over what was left of Arab Palestine, an annexation perfectly agreeable to him. Although such a step was definitely in opposition to the ex-mufti's government-of-all-Palestine plan, proclaimed at Gaza, the main area left to Arab control was occupied by the Arab Legion of Transjordan. Israel refused to consider surrendering her award of the Negev in the partition plan for western Galilee, which she had conquered shortly before the cease-fire. Israeli forces ignored cease-fire agreements in Jerusalem; later they ignored the armistice with Egypt and pushed south, hoping to establish themselves on the Gulf of Akaba, open a route to the Orient for the new state, and bypass Suez. British troops occupied the port of Akaba to prevent its fall to Israeli forces, but Israeli troops reached the gulf at a small port, renamed Elath.

In central Palestine the position of the Arab Legion grew precarious. Israeli commanders told King Abdallah to withdraw to a depth of two miles on a fifty-five mile front, or Israel would resume hostilities. Such an expansion was necessary to the state of Israel, as the Arab lines blocked the main road connecting Tel Aviv with Galilee; but for Transjordan it left many villagers destitute since their lands were on the other side of the line. With these concessions the armistice was signed in April between Israel and the new state of Jordan, which had been announced in December 1948. Iraq came under this armistice, since she had declared she would recognize any armistice entered into by her fellow Hashimite ruler.

Arab Refugees
After the several armistices defined the temporary boundaries of Israel, the greatest question remaining was that of the Arab refugees. The number of Palestinian Arabs from the area incorporated in Israel gathered in camps

in surrounding Arab states totaled some 700,000 in 1949. The camps were located in the Gaza strip held by Egypt, and in Jordan, Syria, and Lebanon. Egypt and Lebanon had serious overpopulation problems; east Jordan was quite barren; and west Jordan, the portion of Palestine annexed to Transjordan, did not have the resources to support a large influx of destitute people. Also, many inhabitants of Jordan were without means of support because the new frontier line had put their lands in Israel.

The refugees had left their homes for a variety of reasons. In Haifa blaring loud speakers manned by Jews circulated through the city building up fear in the minds of Arab residents until they broke and fled. In other cities Arabs were expelled when the Israelis took over. And in a number of Arab villages Israeli forces demolished the houses so the Arabs could not return. The massacre at Dair Yasin and the numerous outrages and reprisals of previous years frightened the Arabs. Hearing over the radio optimistic broadcasts and news reports that Arab armies from Egypt, Syria, Iraq, and Transjordan would be victorious in a week or two, many Arabs in towns and villages turned the key in the door, pocketed it, and walked away, fully expecting to return with the victorious armies in a few days.

The refugee question was also a main stumbling block to any peace settlement. Most refugees believed that they wished to return, although very few would have felt at home had they been allowed to do so. Conditions, and even the surroundings, had changed. But lands, buildings, and bank accounts required compensation, if refugees stayed away. Arab leaders had not the political courage to tell the refugees they could not return; and Israel agreed to discuss compensation and aids to resettlement only in an overall peace arrangement with the Arab states.

Late in 1948 the U.N. set up a disaster-relief operation to care for refugees, whose numbers were growing rapidly. The United Nations Relief for Palestine Refugees (UNRPR) was organized January 1, 1949, to operate for nine months until the next harvest. Extended until May 1950 UNRPR worked through the Red Cross and the American Friends' Service Committee. When refugee work appeared to be a long-range rehabilitation task as well as straight relief the United Nations Relief and Works Agency for Palestine Refugees in the Near East (UNRWA) was created. Work-relief projects and reintegration schemes were developed, but the refugee camps continued as an irritant in the Middle East and acted as breeding grounds for frustration and social revolution. Israel remained adamant about taking back any of the refugees, and in 1957 declared that even to mention the subject was illogical since there was so much land available in Syria and Iraq. One positive step to alleviate tension, however, was taken in October 1956, when Israel released 80 percent of the funds in blocked accounts of the refugees.

Another issue of contention was the status of Jerusalem. The partition plan of 1947 had called for internationalization of the Holy City. The armistice between Israel and Jordan left Jerusalem divided with barbed wire cutting across it. (The eastern part and most of the Old City were held by

Jordan.) Although the United Nations declared that Jerusalem must remain an international zone, it became two cities. Israel refused to demilitarize her sector, asserting that it was surrounded by Arab territory on three sides, and Jordan refused to permit Jews access to their holy places in the Old City. In 1949 a number of Israel's ministries were moved from Tel Aviv to Jerusalem, and in December the *Kneset* (Parliament) met there. In January 1950 it was proclaimed that Jerusalem had been the capital of Israel since her founding. All government offices moved there except the ministry of foreign affairs, which remained in Tel Aviv to keep in touch with foreign diplomats. (Many governments, including the United States, forbade their diplomats to move to Jerusalem and refused to recognize it as the capital.) In August 1966 the Kneset moved into a luxurious palace, constructed as a permanent home for the Kneset by gifts from the Rothschilds. Many Israelis complained that it was too costly and so remote that the Kneset "would no longer function in public view in downtown Jerusalem." In 1958 the chief military parade commemorating the founding of the state was held in Jerusalem. Although its proximity to Jordan caused much apprehension in many capitals, Ben-Gurion insisted upon the demonstration, and over 250,000 people flocked to Jerusalem to participate in the joyous occasion.

King Abdallah proceeded formally to incorporate the Arab portion of Palestine into his state, renaming Transjordan the Hashimite Kingdom of Jordan. An election was held in April 1950, and a new cabinet was formed composed of six ministers from Transjordan and five from Palestine. Israel refused to recognize the incorporation, but the Arab League states grudgingly permitted King Abdallah his expansion, even though they threatened to expel from the league any state that took any part of Palestine.

In 1950 the American, British, and French foreign ministers, meeting in London, signed a tripartite agreement affirming that their states would take action to prevent any violation of frontiers or armistice lines. They also declared that they were prepared to forestall an arms race between the Arab states and Israel. This meant lifting the arms embargo and accepting the armistice lines and the *status quo* in the Middle East.

The State of Israel

When the state of Israel was proclaimed in 1948 by Ben-Gurion, a provisional government was organized. The ministers were leaders of the former semiofficial departments of the Jewish community, and their tasks were coordinated to the war effort. In January 1949 elections were held for a national parliament and constituent assembly (Kneset). Mapai (Workers party), a socialist center group, received almost 36 percent of the vote and obtained the largest bloc of seats in the Kneset. Although a committee was directed in 1950 to bring in a written constitution for the state, Ben-Gurion, the prime minister, was predisposed to an unwritten constitution in the British manner, and desired that the constitution be built up law by law. One of the very first laws (the Law of Return) provided for unlimited ingathering of Jewish people, the immigrants automatically becoming Israeli citizens upon their entry.

The Kneset was composed of 120 members elected by proportional representation from national party lists. In addition to the initial election in 1949, elections have been held in 1951, 1955, 1959, 1961, 1965, 1969, 1973, and 1977, and in every one except the last Mapai won a commanding plurality and easily formed the government with a coalition of one kind or another. Thirteen parties were represented in the Kneset elected in 1951. Ben-Gurion's Mapai won 45 seats; General Zionists (a center bourgeoisie party), 20; Mapam (Social Democrats), to the left of Mapai, 15; Herut (Irgun and right wing), 8; and Maki (Communists), 5. The other seats were scattered among the remaining parties. The election of 1955 showed gains for the extremes and losses for Mapai and the General Zionists. In 1959 some of the religious parties gathered in a National Religious Front and obtained 12 seats. Mapai more than recovered its losses of 1955, with Mapam and the General Zionists declining badly. In 1961 Ben-Gurion resigned over the Lavon affair and called for a new election when he could not fashion a coalition to form a government. The party lineup in the new Kneset remained about as it had in 1959, except for a new Liberal party under the leadership of Nahum Goldmann, a former American citizen who became an Israeli. A merger of the General Zionist and Progressive parties, the Liberals won 17 seats, equaling that of Herut and second to Mapai's 42 seats. Ben-Gurion, with difficulty, put together a shaky coalition and held on until 1963, to resign in favor of Levi Eshkol. When Eshkol refused to reopen the Lavon affair and appeared weak in handling Arab and domestic problems, Ben-Gurion called for his resignation. Eshkol did resign, in December 1964, opening the way for elections in 1965. Disputes within Mapai ended in Ben-Gurion and six of his associates leaving the party in 1965. They established a new party, Rafi (Israeli Workers' List), and entered the election contests of that year. Herut and the Liberals coalesced for the election as did Mapai and a few minor parties. Seventeen parties presented candidates, and with Ben-Gurion in the fray heading Rafi, it was a spirited election, with 83 percent of the electorate casting ballots. Eshkol and his Mapai and associates won 45 seats, however. Following the election, Ben-Gurion declined an invitation to rejoin Mapai and asserted he would continue fighting the "stupid and corrupt regime of Eshkol." (After the Six-Day War in June 1967, politics and the affairs of the occupied areas interacted upon each other so fully that later elections should be considered separately.)

Chaim Weizmann was elected to Israel's presidency, an honorific office, for a five-year term in 1948, and served until his death in 1952. After Albert Einstein refused the offer, the honor of the presidency went to Itzhak Ben-Zvi, who was reelected in 1957 and again in 1962. Upon his death in 1963, Zalman Shazar was elected president and reelected in 1968. He retired in 1973, and Ephraim Katzir, a distinguished biophysicist and Mapai's nominee, was chosen over the National Religious party's candidate to succeed to the office.

Ben-Gurion served as prime minister from 1948 until January 1954, when he retired to a kibbutz in the Negev. He was followed as prime minister by Minister for Foreign Affairs Moshe Sharrett, a leader of Mapai. However, as the situation within and around Israel became more serious, Ben-Gurion returned to the cabinet as minister of defense in February 1955, and as prime minister in November. In 1956 Sharrett was relieved of the foreign ministry because he did not favor reprisal attacks upon Egypt, Syria, and Jordan. Golda Meir, minister of labor, took his place. After the Sinai war Ben-Gurion remained as prime minister until he resigned in June 1963. Eshkol, his successor, had been the minister of finance and a prominent member of the powerful Histadruth, the Israeli Federation of Labor.

The Lavon affair that caused so much turmoil in the government started in 1954. Bombs planted in books in the United States Information Agency library in Cairo exploded killing several persons. Egyptian investigators traced the act to Israeli agents who were caught and tried. Egypt claimed that the plot had been an Israeli attempt to anger Americans against Egypt and to effect the cutoff of American support for the Aswan Dam. Lavon, Israel's minister of defense at the time, was blamed for the act and forced to resign in 1955. In 1960 he was exonerated by the cabinet, which accepted the evidence that Lavon's signature to the documents and orders had been forged. (Government censorship of stories about Lavon was not lifted until 1971, however.)

Although Ben-Gurion had not been prime minister when many of these arrangements were said to have been made but had been closely associated with Moshe Dayan and other individuals involved, he felt the blame was being shifted to him. Ben-Gurion, with the support of Moshe Dayan, formed his own party, Rafi, and presented a slate of candidates for the election of 1965. The majority of Mapai supported Eshkol, and Rafi placed only ten members in the Kneset. Eshkol formed a new coalition cabinet, made up of members of Mapai, the National Religious Front, Mapam, and Independent Liberals. The most important change was in the foreign ministry, where Abba Eban replaced Golda Meir. When the crisis developed in late May 1967 over the Straits of Tiran and war was imminent, Eshkol gave the portfolio of the defense ministry to General Moshe Dayan.

Real authority rests in the hands of the prime minister. Ben-Gurion usually held the post of defense minister as well as prime minister; the concentration of power was considerable, especially because there was no effective committee in the Kneset to review affairs of the ministry of defense. Sharrett was foreign minister and prime minister, whereas Eshkol followed the custom of Ben-Gurion and headed the defense ministry along with the prime ministry. Every cabinet after the first election of the Kneset until 1977 was a coalition centered around the Mapai party which Ben-Gurion and Eshkol headed. Various parties joined with Mapai, and these have changed through the years except Mapam was a constant partner. The National Religious Front consisting of middle-of-the-road parties with a religious basis supported Mapai after 1959 until 1977. Several cabinet crises occurred over Jewish dietary beliefs and the question of women serving in the armed forces. There were important discussions over the question of who was a Jew. In 1960 it was decided that a Jew is a person born of a Jewish mother who does not belong to another religion or is a convert according to law; still later in 1970 it was ruled that non-Jewish spouses, children and grandchildren of Jews come under the Law of Return to become Israeli citizens but they would not be accepted as Jews.

Open immigration into Israel had been the goal of Zionist leaders from the beginning of the mandate, and the great debate over the 100,000 quota in the years after World War II made it imperative that unlimited immigration be a cardinal principle of the new state. In the first decade after independence at least 800,000 immigrants swelled Israel's population rapidly; 700,000 came in the first four years. Since 55 percent of these postindependence immigrants were Sephardic Jews of Oriental origin, their assimilation presented new problems for Israel. Furthermore, because the birth rate in this group was much higher than in others, there was the distinct likelihood that in time Sephardic Jews would outnumber the dominant Ashkenazi, or European Jews. It became necessary to Westernize these Oriental Jews as soon as possible after their entry, so that their presence would not strain the economy of the new state to the breaking point. At the same time, however, the government issued appeals for greater immigration to build the nation. In May 1958, at the time of the tenth anniversary celebrations, Ben-Gurion announced that the population of Israel had reached 2 million.

Economic difficulties in Israel, resulting from a widening trade gap, greater military expenditures at the expense of development, and a sharp dropping off of capital investments, reparations, bond sales, and charitable gifts, brought unemployment, devaluation, and belt-tightening pressures. Furthermore, more than 40,000 Oriental immigrants were housed in makeshift camps, and riots occurred in Haifa, Beersheba, and other cities over the discriminatory practices of government in housing, jobs, and education for the Oriental Jews. Consequently, Israelis began to emigrate in worrisome numbers. On August 2, 1966, the Law of Return was amended by the Kneset to curb the practice of residing in Israel long enough to acquire citizenship and a passport and then departing. At the time of the 1967 war, with the population at an estimated 2.65 million, several thousand foreign Jews came to aid in the emergency.

Israeli Economy

The economy of Israel has been exceedingly precarious ever since her birth in 1948. Many inhabitants expected and obtained a standard of living comparable to that of central Europe, although Israel was a small and poor country of the Middle East. Their standard of living was made possible by gifts and loans from foreign governments and individual Jews in many countries. The United Jewish Appeal set a goal of raising approximately $250 million in each of the early years, which contributed greatly to maintaining a balance in Israeli finances.

Imports for several years ranged from four to five times the value of exports. Although the Israeli pound was devalued in 1962 by 40 percent and Draconian measures were taken to cut consumer spending by 30 percent, the situation deteriorated. In the five years from 1961 to 1965, the average yearly unfavorable balance was $371 million, and in the year before the 1967 war Israel had an unfavorable balance of payments of over $600 million. A new economic policy had to be found, as critical reports were issued on the inefficiencies of the kibbutzim, the question of agriculture versus industry, planning for the productive employment of immigrants, luxurious living, high wages, and the general standard of living. Because Histadruth, the Israeli Federation of Labor, controlled Mapai, and Mapai dominated the government, there was considerable doubt as to how strong a check Eshkol could maintain on wages, prices, and the standard of living. In 1967 wages and prices continued to rise at their usual rates until the outbreak of war in June when the entire economy was disrupted to such an extent that it marked a watershed in the Israeli economy.

The burden of the immigrants upon the economy hampered capital development in many ways. New houses were built by the tens of thousands, and the newcomers had to be fed and clothed for many months before they were integrated and absorbed into Israeli society. Some Israeli economists suggested that immigration be limited, but such a policy was anathema to leaders who had heard the British and Arabs mouth such proposals for a quarter of a century. In 1950, in anticipation of 600,000 additional immigrants in the following three years, Israel organized a drive to raise $1.5 billion to settle the new people. After the Sinai war, as the number of new immigrants dropped off, the building trades in Israel suffered a slump, with mass dismissals. The conclusion of German reparations in 1965 and the serious decline in charitable gifts from world Jewry made the economic crisis of early 1967 more acute. One cause of that crisis was frequently attributed to the great mass of immigrants over the previous twenty years, the rapidity of their integration into the economic life of the state, and the lack of any critical evaluation of the productiveness of these immigrants, and usefulness of the work in which they were engaged, and the general criterion used in planning their employment.

The need for capital funds for irrigation projects, industry, communications, and exploration for natural resources exceeded most expectations. Too often a new development project was considered worthy if it would aid immigrants, and frequently the cost was thought unimportant. In January 1951 a $500 million bond issue for capital development was launched in the United States, but sales were disappointing. Moreover, the economic plight of Israel became so grave and consumption goods so scarce that proceeds of the bond sales had to be used to buy food and other essential imports. In 1952 relief came in the form of an agreement with West Germany, whereby Israel would receive $822 million in reparations to be paid in goods over the next fourteen years.

During her first ten years Israel received more than $2.55 billion as imports of capital. Much of this foreign exchange had been spent for consumer goods, producing an artificial standard of living that demanded a continuation of this stream of foreign capital and "spending money." The shock of the termination of West German reparations was so great that a loan of $40 million was arranged in 1966, and considerable dismay was shown in Tel Aviv when there was no indication that it would be repeated in subsequent years. The pinch became painful in 1966. As industry advanced, many Western firms set up subsidiaries in Israel that brought in considerable capital. However, all understood there was a limit to this type of growth, given the political and economic isolation of Israel in the Middle East.

One of the gravest burdens upon the Israeli economy was imposed by the economic boycott by the Arab states. The proclivity of Israelis was for industry or mechanized and specialized production, which would complement the raw materials and agricultural produce of Arab countries. Iraq shut off the flow of oil in the pipeline to Haifa, forcing Israel to buy higher-priced petroleum from Iran and the Gulf of Mexico. This pressure stimulated a drive to become more independent of the Arab states in matters of transport as well as in oil. Elath on the Gulf of Akaba was pushed as the gateway to the east: a railroad connecting Elath with the national network in the Negev was begun in 1956; an oil pipeline from Elath northward was completed as far as Beersheba in 1957, to Ashkelon in 1968, and enlarged in 1971; and the highway from Elath to Beersheba was opened in 1958. After exploratory talks with Asians and Africans Israeli leaders felt that their industry and commerce had a propitious future in those continents, and Elath was the key as long as free passage through Suez was denied to them.

Interest in Elath, however, did not blind the Israeli planners to their dependence upon the West and Mediterranean contacts. In 1960 a loan was negotiated for the construction of a deep-water port at Ashdod, eighteen miles south of Tel Aviv. When the port was completed in 1965 the ports of Jaffa and Tel Aviv were closed, and Ashdod and Haifa were the only two Mediterranean ports. In the 1967 crisis the closing of the Straits of Tiran by the United Arab Republic to Israeli shipping and other flags carrying strategic goods to or from Elath on the Gulf of Akaba affected Israel vitally and was a cause for war.

The prospect of irrigating the Negev and utilizing its land inspired Israeli engineers and planners to build gigantic canals from the north, circumventing Jordan, to the barren southlands. Syria and Jordan protested this unilateral use of Jordan waters, but settlement and irrigation in the Negev remained a promising and exciting development in Israel. May 5, 1964, when water from the Jordan began to flow southward through the channels and pipes was a day of great celebration. Within a few years two other water intakes from the Sea of Galilee were in operation.

The Eichmann Trial

On May 23, 1960, Ben-Gurion startled the world by announcing that Adolf Eichmann, head of the German Gestapo Jewish Affairs Bureau during World War II, had been captured and was in Israel, where he would be tried for his war crimes against the Jewish people. Located in Argentina and abducted by Israeli agents, he had been flown directly to Israel in an Israeli plane used to transport an Israeli official to a conference in Buenos Aires. The trial opened before three distinguished Israeli judges on April 11, 1961, and Eichmann was ably defended by Robert Servatius of West Germany. He declared that the kidnapping of the prisoner in Argentina made the trial illegal, that Israel and Israeli law did not exist during World War II, and that no Israeli court could be objective in this case. Gideon Hausner, Israeli attorney general, as the chief prosecutor, stated that the manner of bringing the prisoner to trial was irrelevant to the legality of the trial; that no court could be objective in view of the enormity of his crimes; and that there was no international or other national tribunal available for the trial. Eichmann entered a plea of not guilty and a fifteen-count indictment was pressed against him. The trial ended August 14, 1961, after an almost daily procession of gruesome photographs, letters, diaries, and witnesses portrayed the dreadful events perpetrated against the Jews for which Eichmann was held responsible, either directly or indirectly. He was judged guilty by the court on December 11, 1961, sentenced to death by hanging on December 15, and executed on May 31, 1962, after the president had denied his plea for mercy.

The extensive publicity given to the trial and the horrible details contained in the evidence and accusations served to remind the world of the terrible suffering experienced by Jews and to bolster flagging sympathy and support for Israel in terms of gifts, loans, bond sales, and diplomacy. Within Israel, the trial spurred comfortable and lagging spirits to make greater efforts to build the state.

Foreign Affairs

Israel looked to the United States for political and financial support. Each year Israel sought grants and loans from the American government, and the minister of finance always submitted a large budget to the Kneset. In 1958 he asked for $640 million; in 1966 it was set at $1.1 billion; and in 1977 the budget stood at $15 billion. But these figures did not give a true picture of the state's economy, for various other expenditures and receipts from United Jewish Appeal and other sources were not included in the regular budget. In the face of mounting armament in Egypt, Syria, and other Arab states Israel turned to the United States, England, and France for arms of the most recent manufacture and type. In 1958 she obtained Mystère jets from France; in 1962 the United States supplied Hawk missiles and in 1966 offensive weapons such as Skyhawk bombers able to bomb the Aswan High Dam on the Nile. Since the cost of such weapons if purchased in an open market was prohibitive, Israel urged that arms be supplied at prices more commensurate with her ability to pay. Israeli leaders believed that their favorable press and many sympathetic coreligionists in the United States would make it difficult for any American administration to act for long in a manner unfriendly to Israel. It was largely this support and confidence that gave the Israeli government its courage in the face of the surrounding hostile Arab states.

After the British evacuated their army and officials from Palestine in 1948 the Israeli attitude toward England grew less tense and more friendly. Britain unfroze most of the Jewish sterling balances, and trade between the two countries improved. From time to time criticism was leveled at Britain's supplying of arms to the Arab states, and British withdrawal from Suez Canal zone bases was recognized as increasing Egyptian power and Israeli insecurity.

In the early days of the state of Israel relations with the Soviet bloc were cordial, and sizable shipments of arms from Czechoslovakia in 1948 were instrumental in winning the Palestine War. Maki (the Communist party) was active, and Mapam subscribed to Marxist philosophy. Mapai, the largest party, followed a left-wing political ideology and was not antagonistic to advanced socialist concepts. However, most Israelis were fiery nationalists and found it difficult to subordinate their aims to those of the U.S.S.R. Moreover, there was evidence that Stalin in his last years became anti-Semitic. After publicity over the trial of the Jewish doctors and attacks upon representatives of Mapam in Russia, a serious bomb explosion occurred in 1953 at the Soviet legation in Tel Aviv, and the Soviets severed relations. Following Stalin's death, however, anti-Semitism was eased, and relations were resumed. In 1955, when the Soviet bloc began cultivating the Arabs and arms deals were made, Israeli feelings toward the U.S.S.R. took a sharp turn for the worse. Nonetheless, since the Arab states did not permit their oil to be delivered to Israel, arrangements were concluded in 1956 to import oil from the U.S.S.R., the price being considerably less than dollar oil from Iran or the Western Hemisphere. After the Sinai war the Arab states complained so bitterly to the U.S.S.R. over the oil affair that deliveries were discontinued, but no break occurred.

Relations remained cool, and in the 1960s as Israel looked more to the West for trade and support and sent her technicians to aid developing African and Asian countries, thus competing with Soviet engineers and agents, the U.S.S.R. grew more critical of Israel. In 1964 all outstanding commercial agreements with Israel were canceled, and Israel on her part complained of the treatment of Jews in the U.S.S.R. and the limitations placed on their cultural development as Jews. In the crisis of 1967 the Soviet delegate to the U.N. Security Council attacked Israel bitterly and severely as an imperialist and a tool of the imperialists.

After the armistice agreements came into effect in 1949, hopes for peace remained unsatisfied. The growth of Arab nationalism, particularly in Egypt and Syria, gave Israeli leaders cause to look to the defenses of the state. The most common expression of Arab leaders in this respect was contained in the idea of a "second round" in which the Israelis would be driven into the sea. On the other hand, some political leaders in Israel, frequently of the Herut party, spoke of the need to expand and to take Akaba to the south and to incorporate all of Palestine, even Transjordan, into the state of Israel. To many Arabs across the frontier the likelihood of expansion being forced upon Israel by the swarms of immigrants seemed very real. Border incidents occurred every few days. Israel was not always blameless in these affairs and was censured or reprimanded for several. In 1953 about 250 well-trained Israeli troops attacked the Jordanian village of Kibya, destroyed the houses and one school, and killed fifty-three people.

Until 1956 Israel felt considerable security because of the support of the United States and world Jewry. Her military posture with respect to her neighbors was excellent; jealousies and rivalries among the Arab states, notwithstanding the Arab League, appeared to be her salvation. In 1956, however, there seemed some danger that the balance might be changing in favor of Egypt. The Soviet-bloc arms deals of 1955, the inability of the West to act in the face of Nasser's nationalization of Suez, and Nasser's success in aligning Syria, Jordan, and Egypt in a military pact under one command, thus tightening the noose around Israel, led Ben-Gurion to undertake a military build-up in 1956. To allay obvious fears in Damascus, Amman, and Cairo, as well as in Washington and perhaps in Moscow, Ben-Gurion declared in June that Israel would refrain from war even if provoked. Reprisal raids fell under a different category; a punitive drive went into Jordan on October 10, so worrisome in fact that the British warned Tel Aviv that aggression against Jordan would activate the Anglo-Jordan security treaty. Later, in October, Israeli delegates at the U.N. asserted that a preventive war would never be launched against their Arab neighbors.

The Sinai War

Three days after the statement at the U.N., Israel mobilized. The following morning, October 29, she invaded Egypt. The army moved quickly, and by November 7 most of the Sinai peninsula had been occupied. Sharm al-Shaykh, guarding the Straits of Tiran and the entrance to the Gulf of Akaba, was taken. British and French troops then seized the Suez Canal by heavy bombing and captured Port Said and the northern half of the canal on October 31. Israel's announced war objectives were: to weaken the Arab positions and destroy their arms; to unseat Nasser by administering a swift military defeat; to open the Suez Canal to Israeli use; to control the passage of ships into the Gulf of Akaba; and to free the port of Elath.

From the very beginning world opinion was so shocked by the action that achievement of the war aims was doubtful. Eisenhower had telephoned Eden some days before the outbreak to dissuade him from engaging in such measures. The day preceding the attack Eisenhower had warned Ben-

Gurion against taking any overt action; and immediately after the attack an emergency meeting of the U.N. Security Council denounced the invasion and demanded a cease-fire. England and France entered the fray with the avowed purpose of keeping the canal open for traffic. Egypt, however, found it easy to block the canal by sinking ships in the channel. With the United States, the U.S.S.R., Canada, India, and most of the world ranged against the three invaders, the cease-fire was accepted on November 7. Withdrawal from Suez by the English and French and from Sinai by the Israelis started within a few days. U.N. forces were gathered and came in to prevent incidents. But Israel refused to surrender the Gaza Strip and Sharm al-Shaykh. Ambassador Eban in Washington and Foreign Minister Meir at the U.N. tried to hold these two key points and offered to yield only if guaranteed freedom from Egyptian raids and open use of the Straits of Tiran. Eisenhower denounced any such promise and castigated the idea of permitting gain from aggression. Finally, in March 1957 Ben-Gurion, in the teeth of violent opprobrium from the Herut in the Kneset, agreed to withdraw from both points on the "assumption" that border incidents would halt and that the Gulf of Akaba would be open to Israeli shipping. The troops pulled back, Egyptian civil administrators took over in the Gaza Strip, and the U.N. Emergency Force (UNEF) was permitted to patrol only the Egyptian side of the frontier, including Sharm al-Shaykh. In many observers' eyes the situation returned fully to the conditions prevailing upon the outbreak of the incident.

Almost immediately after the British and French invasion of Port Said, Hugh Gaitskell in the House of Commons questioned his government about its collusion in planning the Sinai war. In reply Selwyn Lloyd, the foreign secretary, said, "There was no prior agreement between us about it," and Eden a few weeks later added, "There was not foreknowledge that Israel would attack Egypt—there was not." Finally, after a decade, with the publication of General Dayan's diary and other studies, as well as interviews with some of the principals involved in 1956 such as French Foreign Minister Pineau and Selwyn Lloyd, Gaitskell's suspicions were vindicated.

Israel, England, and France, it turned out, all had been harboring grievances against Egypt, and during the summer had been plotting an attack. The nationalization of the Suez Canal, the denial of its use to Israeli shipping, the Egyptian possession of the Straits of Tiran, and its closure to the Israelis almost strangled Israeli trade with Japan, Asia, and East Africa. A direct attack upon Egypt seemed the only way out, but Ben-Gurion held that such a unilateral move would open Israeli cities to bombing by Egypt's Ilyushins, against which he had little defense. Dayan wrote that if they did not succeed at the very outset in surprising the Egyptians, the Israeli plan would fail. Israel needed the collaboration of the British and the French, especially the former with their Canberra bombers based on Cyprus. Britain was seriously provoked by the nationalization of the canal, and France was furious over the help Egypt was affording to the rebels in Algeria. At first England and France wanted to make the assault without Israeli participation, but Israel declared they were engaging in the enterprise willy-nilly. On October 10 France and Israel were in agreement over the plans for French naval support and air cover as well as air-dropped supplies. On October 16 Eden and Lloyd went to Paris and held top-secret meetings with Premier Mollet and Pineau at which time the British pledged to participate, and a French telegram (picked up by American intelligence) alerted Ben-Gurion: "You can depend absolutely on the British." Then, on October 24 or 25 at Sèvres, outside Paris, Ben-Gurion, with Dayan at his side, Mollet, and Patrick Dean, a British Foreign Office official, signed an Anglo-French-Israeli agreement to attack Suez.

The plan was for Israel to start the attack on October 29, 1956 as though it were a typical border-reprisal raid, and for two days her air force with undercover French assistance would confine itself to protecting Israeli skies and ground forces. This ruse was set so that Egypt would consider it a raid and not bomb Israeli cities. Then, England and France would enter the war, bomb Egyptian air fields, seize the canal, and cut off Egyptian forces in the Sinai peninsula where they could be utterly destroyed. It all went as planned except that the Anglo-French force did not act quickly enough, perhaps in an attempt to conceal the collusion. It gave time for world opinion, and the actions of the U.S.S.R. and the United States to force the cease-fire and eventual evacuation.

The aggressive nationalism of Zionism was disclosed by the Sinai war, and many Zionist sympathizers the world over were keenly chagrined by the revelation. The Arab states experienced defeat again and, amazed at the deftness of England and France and the might of Israel, felt the urgent need for more military equipment, organization, and cooperation. The Gulf of Akaba remained open, with UNEF occupying Sharm al-Shaykh, and though Egypt and Saudi Arabia protested its use, they made no move to block the Straits of Tiran.

That Egypt would not some day seek revenge for this humiliation no one could gainsay, but Nasser's first reaction was to seek greater influence throughout the Arab world and to disregard Israel. When turmoil developed in Jordan later in 1957, Israel warned against Iraqi or Syrian troops occupying Jordan. It was an open secret that Israel would feel compelled to seize all of Palestine west of the Jordan River if Jordan was annexed to another Arab state. When the revolution in Iraq in 1958 shook confidence in the future of Jordan, Israeli leaders again warned that Israel would move to the west bank of the river if Syrian or Iraqi troops entered Jordan. Since worldwide tremors would follow in the wake of such a move a special session of the U.N. General Assembly was hurriedly called in hopes of finding a more permanent solution to Israel's position in the Middle East. In any case, the future of Israel seemed assured. But questions of permanent frontiers, relations with her Arab neighbors, and her influence with the world powers remained to be settled.

Israel and Her Arab Neighbors After Sinai

Following the Sinai war, Israel proceeded with her plans to build a natural uranium nuclear reactor in the Negev to develop rockets and missiles and perhaps an atom bomb, although she insisted that all such scientific activity was for peaceful purposes.

With UNEF stationed on the Egyptian side of the frontier, clashes after 1957 were rare there. Israel would not permit this group on Israeli soil so that UNEF was unable to control Israeli movements. For the most part, Israel's clashes with her Arab neighbors centered on Syria. The border was not drawn but had a neutral demilitarized zone, with both sides asserting the rights of its owners to cultivate it. Each spring there were raids by Arabs upon Israelis who were cultivating land in the demilitarized zone, to which Israel frequently answered with reprisals. In 1960 Arabs tried to cultivate some of the area, and Israel wiped out a Syrian base at Tawafik in a large operation for which she was condemned by the U.N. Syria-Israel Mixed Armistice Commission (UNSIMAC).

The most serious Israeli reprisal of 1966 occurred against the village of al-Samu, Jordan. The Security Council censured Israel for the deed and King Husayn of Jordan was bitterly criticized by the Arab League and by large numbers of his own subjects for not having replied to the Israeli forces. Some feared he might lose his throne as a result of the incident, and even Israel was worried over this possibility, for any new group in Amman would be less friendly to Israel than Husayn had been. Within Israel there was grave concern lest Eshkol's government had gone too far.

The problem of the infiltration of the Israeli frontier by Arab individuals and Arab terrorist societies such as the Palestinian al-Fatah, the planting of mines, arson, and the shootings of soldiers, police, and farmers continued and grew in rates of incidence, the amount of destruction, and loss of life. The solution seemed as far away as ever, though some Israelis doubted that reprisals were the answer. In the spring of 1967 incidents again occurred, and in April five Syrian villages were shattered by bombs dropped from airplanes; investigations by UNSIMAC blamed Israel for violating the armistice.

The Six-Day War, June 5–10, 1967

Tensions mounted and Israeli cabinet members, under great pressure from the public for action against mines, bombs, and killings, spoke out on the possibilities of a penetration in depth in Syria, which was regarded as the base of the al-Fatah operations. The Syrians believed they had evidence that an Israeli move was scheduled for May 17, 1967. Alarmed, they called upon the United Arab Republic to make good on her mutual-defense pact. This led Nasser to request U Thant, Secretary General of the U.N., to remove UNEF from the United Arab Republic. This he promptly did— some thought too promptly—and since Israel had refused in 1957 to accept any UNEF groups on her soil the frontier was suddenly alive with military forces on each side. With UNEF leaving Sharm al-Shaykh, the United Arab

Republic took over the guns there and announced the closing of the Straits of Tiran to Israeli shipping. Egypt had never renounced her claim that these straits were territorial waters, and had never recognized the Israeli possession of Elath. The loss of free navigation to and from Elath through the Gulf of Akaba and the Red Sea to the markets of Japan and the East, and to the oil fields of the Persian Gulf was so menacing that Israel declared she would fight rather than acquiesce in this closure. This was the difficult problem facing the Security Council in 1967.

When it became apparent that neither the United States nor the U.N. was able to effect an immediate opening of the Straits of Tiran, Israel launched an attack upon the United Arab Republic in order to seize the straits and to control the Sinai peninsula. Although Israel warned Jordan and Syria to stay out of the quarrel, they joined with the United Arab Republic to form a united front. Israel believed, however, that the most serious challenge would come from the United Arab Republic. Furthermore, Nasser had begun to mobilize his troops in Sinai even before the U.N. Emergency Force withdrew. Coupled with his bellicose public speeches and the tone of Cairo Radio, the concentration of Egyptian forces east of the Suez Canal compelled Israel to act. General Dayan, the hero of the Sinai campaign of 1956 and a co-founder of the Rafi party, was brought into the cabinet as minister of defense. On June 5, Israel, in a series of surprise attacks, destroyed the air capabilities of the United Arab Republic, Jordan, and Syria. With complete mastery of the skies and superb coordination of all branches of the military, Israeli forces within six days occupied all of Sinai to the east bank of the Suez Canal, all of Jordan west of the Jordan River, and the Golan Heights and the city of al-Quneitra in Syria. When they captured the Old City of Jerusalem, Israelis poured into the streets to rejoice at the seizing of their holy city. They then agreed to a cease-fire called for by the U.N. Security Council.

Throughout the summer and autumn of 1967, at numerous sessions of the U.N. Security Council and General Assembly, Israel's Foreign Minister Abba Eban stated repeatedly that there could be no peace until the Arab states sat down and negotiated directly with Israel, even though Eban knew full well that no Arab leader felt sufficiently secure to do this. Israeli demands, in addition to recognition by the Arabs, were the establishment of definite boundaries, the guaranteed use of the Suez Canal and the Straits of Tiran, and the end of raids and terrorism. Within a few days of the cease-fire, the Arab part of Jerusalem was incorporated into the Israeli sector; General Dayan and others categorically stated that this act was permanent and not negotiable. Structures before the Wailing Wall were bulldozed away so that the many thousands who came there to pray could be accommodated.

As the summer passed it became doubtful that the Arab leaders would negotiate with Israel, especially after the Arab summit meeting at Khartoum in August where any such step was vigorously condemned. The Israeli government now was faced with the problem of what to do with the occupied territories. Some thought of establishing the Palestinian Arab state envisioned by the 1947 U.N. partition decision. Others proposed an autonomous Arab state federated with Israel. Neither was embraced by the Israeli government. In the autumn of 1967 the Israeli destroyer *Eilat* was sunk off Port Said by sophisticated seek-and-destroy missiles from a United Arab Republic ship; a few days later the oil installations at Port Suez were destroyed in retaliation by Israeli gunfire. These acts strengthened the hands of those in Israel who demanded a hard line against the Arabs. The large number of Arabs in these territories augmented Israel's existing refugee problem, however. In addition, former trade patterns across the Jordan River were upset as a result of the war. Israel, victorious in war, found herself troubled by new human and economic problems. Each day that no settlement was achieved, the status quo became more difficult to dislodge.

No resolution of the tensions in the Middle East appeared remotely possible. The U.N. seemed helpless and Israel ignored it. The General Assembly passed by an overwhelming vote a resolution calling upon Israel not to unify Jerusalem, but Israel disregarded it. On November 22, 1967, the Security Council passed unanimously a British-sponsored measure, Resolution 242, authorizing U Thant to send to the Middle East a special personal representative to negotiate peace between Israel and her Arab neighbors. Resolution 242 implicitly recognized Israel's right to exist, and called for the establishment of permanent borders, withdrawal of Israeli troops from occupied lands, Israeli use of the Suez Canal and the Straits of Tiran, and a just settlement for the Arab refugees. Gunnar Jarring of Sweden was appointed for this mission, which had no chance for success because Nasser declared that he would not recognize Israel and that the Suez Canal would not be open to Israel as long as Israel occupied Arab lands. At the same time, Israel repeated that there could be no substitute for direct negotiations. Many believed that Israel's leaders took this stand to avoid having to commit themselves on what they would accept as the state's new frontiers, since they were not sure that the Israeli public would condone any withdrawal from lands won in the June war.

No Peace, No War

Israel's economy was disrupted throughout most of 1967. Trade losses were large but wages were maintained for all workers. Contributions from world Jewry, especially from the United States, for and because of the war, poured into the country. These monies, amounting to hundreds of millions of dollars, eased Israel's financial plight. Still, the expenses of the war and of maintaining the occupied territories left Israeli finances in a weak position.

Before the war the balance of payments deficits had been instrumental in keeping the level of unemployment high. The unfavorable trade gap of $200–$300 million a year was met from gifts and loans by foreign governments and individuals. The expectation of such annual sums made it possible to live with large budgetary deficits, at a time when defense spending took half the entire budget. In 1968 it was estimated that nearly 60 percent of the budget was raised by bond sales in the United States and Canada. Meanwhile, the trade gap did not disappear: in 1969 it was over $700 million; by 1973 it had soared to $1.5 billion. Drives to curb imports, high taxes on all luxury items, tariffs, and liberal gifts from abroad did not seem to suffice. In 1970 the European Economic Community agreed to a preferential trade arrangement that would, over a three-year period, reduce European tariffs on Israeli goods by 50 percent, hopefully opening up new markets to Israeli producers. But the advent of another war in 1973, followed by world-wide inflation and economic recession, and the quadrupling of energy costs, so altered conditions that the EEC arrangement could not be tested properly. Israel's trade gaps persisted; the military and defense expenditures did not permit otherwise.

During the six-year interlude between the wars of 1967 and 1973 the development and industrialization of Israel proceeded rapidly, though not as swiftly as many wished. However, economic growth did increase substantially, with per capita income going from $1,011 in 1967 to $2,806 in 1973. Production climbed in most sectors of the economy, and capital investment from overseas was impressive. A new refinery at Ashdod brought a 50 percent increase in domestic oil production, and the output of wells in occupied Sinai met nearly all of Israel's petroleum needs.

In 1970 the economy took a sharp upward turn; unemployment vanished, and soon more than 10,000 Arabs from the occupied areas were being bussed to work daily into Israel proper. Many civic leaders shuddered at what would happen should that labor supply suddenly be terminated if Israel were to withdraw from the West Bank and Gaza. With prosperity, strikes became incessant, affecting every occupation from hospital attendants and electric power plant workers to doctors and civil servants.

Inflation grew rampant. To stem it wage and price controls were tried, but they proved unworkable and ill-suited to an economy in which a preponderance of goods were imported. The budget and that portion of it allocated to defense increased dramatically until 1972 when defense demands fell below 30 percent. Still, enormous defense costs were a crushing burden on Israelis who accepted them as the price of survival.

In these years cynics began to assert that Israel was losing her special character and becoming like other societies. They cited as evidence a growing materialism. The utopian idealism of the kibbutz, the agricultural commune, was waning. Moreover, there was an astounding rise in the nation's crime rate. Socialists pointed out that too much poverty existed in Israel, especially among Jews of non-European origins, who demonstrated frequently in the streets against discrimination. Though some spirits did flag, Israel's military victories and ensuing self-confidence generated widespread ebullience and produced advances in business enterprise, art, literature, scientific discovery, and archeology. Individualism was so prevelant that a number of Jews who had emigrated from the U.S.S.R. asked to return there because they could not cope with the unstructured life in Israel. Life in Israel in 1973 was vibrant but, as the continual rash of strikes showed, many were dissatisfied with the present. And many were apprehensive of the future.

After the Arab part of Jerusalem was proclaimed an integral part of Israeli Jerusalem, plans were developed to reconstruct the old Jewish quarter inside the medieval walls, evicting Arabs who had lived there since 1948, when the Jewish inhabitants were evicted. In 1969, after a fire raged for two hours in the very holy al-Aqsa mosque in Jerusalem, the Islamic states in a meeting at Rabat accused Israel of careless surveillance. Authorities in Jerusalem apprehended a foreign Christian who was adjudged the arsonist and found to be mentally deranged. Incidents of various kinds occurred repeatedly and Israeli officials reacted by expelling Arabs—teachers, shop-keepers, religious leaders, and notables—to Jordan and sometimes confis-cating or bulldozing shops and homes. The physical and economic aspects of the city were greatly enhanced but the Arab inhabitants never felt secure as citizens with rights equal to the others.

In much of the rest of the occupied territories life went on as before. After the Israeli economy had been righted trade between Israel and the occu-pied lands began to provide a substantial market for West Bank produce; in addition, the previous markets in Amman and on the East Bank re-mained accessible to the West Bank, as bridges over the Jordan River were reopened. Yet, the Arabs deeply resented having to live under an occupy-ing force. This brought incidents of violence, anti-Jewish reactions, and stern Israeli reprisals. Each one of these, such as the killing of an Arab judge in Gaza by Israeli soldiers in 1968, fired the resentment of the Arabs, making it more difficult to administer them without the use of the military.

Soon after the end of the fighting in 1967, Jewish settlers moved into places near Hebron and Jericho from which Jews had been forced to leave in 1948. New settlements were made in the occupied lands as Dayan ad-vocated that new settlements be made in any occupied area from which Israel did not intend to withdraw. In 1971 Dayan urged that the govern-ment "plan and implement" without waiting for a peace that might be ten to fifteen years distant.

The cease-fires arranged in June 1967 were never fully observed, and Resolution 242, though accepted in principle by all parties, could not be implemented as no agreement could be reached on the meaning and extent of Israeli withdrawal. By 1968 air raids and artillery duels on the Golan Heights and over Suez were commonplace. All semblance of peace disap-peared in 1969. In one fifty-day period Egypt flew 100 sorties against the Israelis in Sinai and the Israelis countered with 1,000 over Egypt. After an Arab attack on Elath, Israeli bombers knocked out Jordan's East Ghor irrigation system. Air encounters over Syria and Golan were daily occur-rences. In the first three months of 1970 Israel made air raids deep into Egypt; these were curtailed when losses inflicted by newly installed Soviet surface-to-air missiles made the missions too costly. On August 7, 1970, a ninety-day cease-fire between Israel and Egypt arranged by U.S. Secretary of State Rogers went into effect. Though both sides engaged in a military buildup along the canal, the cease-fire was extended an additional three months, and peace talks that included Jordan were resumed at the U.N. No progress resulted, and the official cease-fire ended in March 1971.

The tempo of the struggle along the canal never rose to the 1970 level. On the Syrian front artillery duels and even tank battles occurred and air engagements often over the Mediterranean kept all on constant alert. One battle in November 1972 lasted eight hours and to many it seemed that all-out war must be imminent. After King Husayn defeated and drove all armed Palestinian forces from Jordan in 1970, they settled in Lebanon and began to harass Israel from south Lebanon, which many began to call "Fatahland." By 1973 peace in the Middle East was as elusive as ever.

In the six years following the 1967 war Israel felt compelled to allocate over $6 billion for defense expenditures; several billion dollars more came in the form of gifts and marked-down sales of matériel from the United States. General Bar Lev, Israel's chief of staff, directed the construction of a strong defense, named the Bar Lev line, east of the Suez Canal to serve as a forward wall against attack. When France halted the shipment of military supplies, Israel turned to the United States and obtained agreement on the delivery of fifty Phantom jets and the promise of more in the years ahead.

Because of her ignoring of many adverse U.N. votes, Israel found herself increasingly dependent on the United States. Her diplomatic relations with many nations, especially in Europe, took on a formal, often frosty, tone; by the end of 1969 Israel found herself isolated at the U.N. and unwelcome in many European capitals. Israel enjoyed good relations only with West Germany, the Netherlands, Rumania, Great Britain, and the United States. In 1972 Uganda severed diplomatic relations with Israel, and most other central African states followed soon thereafter.

After the June 1967 war Dayan remained as minister of defense; his splinter Rafi party, along with another centrist party, Ahdut Avodah, were gradually reintegrated into Mapai. General Itzhak Rabin, chief of staff and one of the architects of the 1967 victory, was appointed ambassador to Washington in 1968. Though there were significant political divisions on ideas regarding peace, Mapai was united for the election of 1969, joining with Mapam to form a Labor Alignment, and achieving a majority with a total of sixty-three seats in the Kneset. Prime Minister Eshkol died suddenly on February 26, 1969, and Yigal Allon was named interim prime minister. On March 17 the party chose seventy-year-old Golda Meir to become Israel's fourth prime minister.

Sixteen parties participated in the October 1969 elections for the seventh Kneset. The Labor Alignment won fifty-six seats, and after much political maneuvering Meir enticed the right-wing Gahal party, the National Religious party, and some others to join a coalition commanding ninety-eight seats in the Kneset. Showing great skill in pouring balm on open political wounds, she formed a cabinet that included Allon as deputy prime minister and minister of education, Dayan at defense, Pinhas Sapir as finance minister, Abba Eban at the foreign office, and Begin, Galili, and Peres as ministers of state without portfolios. To hold together such a galaxy of prima donnas was not easy, and it was said frequently that only Golda Meir had the ability to manage them. In August 1970 Gahal withdrew in protest over the cabinet's acceptance of the American-sponsored cease-fire at Suez. In 1973 Gahal joined Herut and the Liberals to form a new right-wing bloc, Likud, in preparation for the October elections, which many political figures thought would be narrowly contested.

The Yom Kippur War of 1973

War broke out again on October 6, 1973, as Egypt and Syria, in a surprise, coordinated campaign, attacked Israel on Yom Kippur, Judaism's Day of Atonement. Egyptian forces crossed the Suez Canal at five points, shattering the Bar Lev line, while Syrian troops occupied Mt. Hermon and retook much of Golan. Within a few days the highly trained, well-organized, and spirited Israeli forces were able to beat back the attacks and go over to the offensive. They contained the Syrian drive and directed air attacks at Latakia, Banyas, Tartus, and Homs, where the oil refinery was destroyed and new industrial plants were leveled. A few districts in Damascus were bombed and Israeli troops reached Sasa, about 35 kilometers from the capital. On the southern front Israeli forces had crossed to the west bank of the Suez Canal and were driving to surround the Egyptian Third Army on the east bank, when a cease-fire was arranged. The quantities of weapons deployed and destroyed on all sides were enormous. Five days after the war started the Soviets were airlifting weapons, tanks, and airplanes to Egypt and Syria in astounding numbers. Israel called upon the United States for help, and began to receive massive shipments on the eighth day of fighting. In all it was estimated that Israel lost 500 tanks and 120 aircraft and suffered 2,400 killed and as many wounded; the Arabs lost 1,500 tanks and 450 airplanes, while their numbers killed and wounded exceeded Israel's. The cost to all the combatants was staggering; it has been estimated that Israel spent $7.2 billion.

The magnitude of the war shocked the world, and when the U.S.S.R. and the United States became indirectly involved as suppliers the full impact of the war was frightening. The U.N. Security Council could do nothing to stop the fighting, so on October 20 Secretary of State Kissinger flew to Moscow and reached an understanding permitting the adoption of U.N. Resolution 338 which called for a cease-fire on October 22. The cease-fire did not hold, and the U.S.S.R. suggested to the United States that the two take action to enforce it. When the United States rejected this the Soviets seemed as if they would intervene unilaterally, whereupon President Nixon ordered a partial alert of American forces. The specter of a world war loomed until the passage of U.N. Resolutions 339 and 340, calling for a cease-fire and providing for a United Nations Emergency Force (UNEF), which began to arrive on the lines between the Egyptian and Israeli armies on October 27.

Tensions eased on November 11 when Israeli and Egyptian officers met on the road to Cairo and signed an agreement freeing the trapped Egyptian Third Army and providing for the immediate exchange of prisoners, an end to the Arab blockade at the southern end of the Red Sea, further negotiations on cease-fire lines, negotiations on an overall settlement, and U.N. enforcement of the cease-fire. A conference on an overall peace settlement was convened in Geneva in December but it was adjourned after one day. Amid continual cease-fire violations Egypt and Israel, prodded by the United States, signed a disengagement in January 1974. Israel agreed to pull back her troops 20 kilometers east of the canal and allowed limited numbers of Egyptian soldiers to be stationed on the east bank, separated from Israeli forces by UNEF detachments.

The cease-fire on the Syrian front was abrogated repeatedly until May 1974. After Kissinger engaged in several rounds of shuttle diplomacy between Jerusalem and Damascus, all additional territory on the Golan seized by Israel in the Yom Kippur War, as well as the city of al-Quneitra taken in 1967, was relinquished to Syria. U.N. Disengagement Observer Force units were placed between the two antagonists on a three-month, renewable basis. Rather than return to Geneva, Israel and the United States preferred a step-by-step approach to peace. Kissinger shuttled between Jerusalem and Cairo, with side trips to Damascus, Riyadh, Amman, and Aswan, until Israel and Egypt signed a Sinai disengagement pact in Geneva in September 1975. Israeli forces withdrew eastward in Sinai for 50 kilometers, yielding the strategic Mitla and Giddi Passes. UNEF units were stationed between the Israeli and Egyptian zones with an early-warning electronic system erected at the passes and manned by 200 American civilian technicians. Israel agreed to return the Abu Rudeis oil fields in the Sinai to Egypt and Egypt promised to permit nonmilitary cargoes bound for Israel to pass through the canal, which had been reopened in June.

Israel had been preparing for a parliamentary election when the war broke out. The platform of the Labor Alignment had been more "dovish" than before. Postponed until the end of December 1973, the election, in which twenty-two parties and splinter groups presented candidates, brought diminished strength for the Labor Alignment. It won just under 40 percent of the popular vote, and its seats in the Kneset were reduced from 56 to 51, while Likud, the more "hawkish" coalition, received more than 25 percent of the votes and increased its position in the Kneset from 32 to 39 seats.

Shortly after the elections, the Agranat Commission that had been appointed to investigate the conduct of the war issued its report blaming Elazar, the army chief of staff, along with Defense Minister Dayan and Prime Minister Meir for Israel's unpreparedness and early setbacks. Golda Meir resigned, and the Labor Alignment chose Itzhak Rabin to head a new government. Chief of staff from 1963 to 1967 and ambassador to Washington from 1968 to 1973, Rabin appointed Peres minister of defense and chose Allon to replace Eban at the foreign ministry. At first Labor commanded only sixty-one seats in the Kneset, a majority of one, but in October the National Religious party returned to the coalition to provide a comfortable margin.

The exceptional cost of the war dislocated Israel's economy. Then, OPEC's quadrupling of oil prices brought worldwide inflation and recession. Israel's budget moved up to $8.4 billion in 1974, with over 40 percent for defense, to $11.5 billion in 1976, and to $15 billion in 1977, $4 billion of which went for defense. The Israeli pound underwent almost constant devaluations. Taxes jumped until it was estimated that Israelis paid about 70 percent of their income to the state. Compulsory loans led to riots and protests but with balance of payments deficits nearing $4 billion a year the government had no other choice. In 1975 at one time when the recession momentarily engulfed Israel the government resorted to printing money to support the unemployed. Discouragement was so prevalent that the rate of emigration rose to equal that of immigration, and industrial productivity fell markedly. Some wondered if the earlier idea of sacrifice to build the state was becoming outmoded. A former minister of finance was sentenced to fifteen years in prison for corruption and eight former officials of the defense ministry were arrested for corruption, bribe taking, and financial kickbacks.

Affairs turned a bit better in 1976. Unemployment was reduced to 5 percent and the trade and balance of payments deficits were lessened. A great boon to the economy was the development and rapid growth of the armament industry. Not only did it help to reduce imports of weapons and dependence upon foreign sources, but it provided export revenues. In this industry Israel showed great skill and ingenuity in redesigning foreign models or in using foreign parts and engines in original Israeli designs. The list of countries purchasing Israeli weapons had become impressive by 1977 and gave every indication of contributing significantly to the economy.

After the cease-fires and withdrawals stabilized the fronts in Sinai and Golan, at least for the time being, the major point of conflict shifted to the border with Lebanon, where shellings or incursions from one or another side occurred daily. Many Palestinian camps in south Lebanon served as staging areas for raids into Israel. In 1974 Palestinian commandos attacked the towns of Kiryat Shemona and Maalot, killing a great many, and in 1975 Palestinians seized a small hotel in Tel Aviv and killed eighteen before they were subdued. Israel retaliated for these and scores of other raids by shelling the camps and villages where the raiders were based and sending punitive missions of armored detachments, often to a considerable depth into Lebanon, to try to destroy the potential for such actions. The eruption of the Lebanese civil war in 1975 gave Israel a temporary respite on her northern border. Israel assisted Lebanese rightist Christian groups, and asserted that she would never again permit south Lebanon to come under the control of the Palestinians.

In the spring of 1978 in a retaliation for a bloody raid coming from south Lebanon, Prime Minister Begin made good on this declaration by invading

Lebanon and occupying all of the area south of the Litani River. He agreed to withdraw Israeli forces only after U.N. forces arrived and Palestinian fighters appeared chastened.

Who would control the lands in Gaza, the West Bank, and Golan captured in 1967 became an increasingly troublesome problem for Israeli leaders. The pressure of ultranationalist political and religious groups such as Gush Emunim (Faith Bloc) to establish Jewish settlements in the territories, even in defiance of authorities, was relentless. The U.N., with the United States concurring, condemned such settlements as obstacles to peace. Within the occupied Arab territories and in Arab-inhabited regions of Israel, the respectable showing made by the Arab armies in the Yom Kippur war stirred the population's latent Arab nationalism. Sabotage and internal resistance had begun shortly after the Six-Day war; these dangers increased after the Yom Kippur war. Added to them were open anti-Israeli demonstrations and incidents in West Bank towns and in Arab areas of Israel. Authorities gave more power and autonomy to West Bank mayors, and in local elections in 1976 for councils and mayors pro-PLO candidates won sweeping victories. In Nazareth, a Christian Arab town, the communists elected a mayor and took a majority of the council seats. Fighting broke out in the Galilee when a plan was revealed to appropriate 1500 acres of Arab-owned land for urban housing, and a storm of protest broke over a leaked report from the interior minister that suggested ways to curb or reduce Israel's growing Arab population.

The Yom Kippur war left Israel more isolated than ever. Cuba and most of the black African nations severed diplomatic relations. UNESCO ostracized Israel in 1974, asserting that she was altering the historical features of Jerusalem, and in 1975 the U.N. Social Committee declared Zionism to be a form of racism and the General Assembly passed a resolution to the same effect, although the United States government vehemently denounced these stands.

Begin's Likud Comes to Power

The political timetable in Israel called for the election of the Kneset in the autumn of 1977, but scandals in the government and various challenges to Prime Minister Rabin's policies and leadership forced him to resign and schedule elections for May 17. New parties began to appear. Arieh Eliav, a "dove," headed a party called Yaad (Challenge). Yigal Yadin, a former general turned archeologist, founded the Democratic Movement for Change, a party whose position on the Arabs seemed similar to that of Labor, but which advocated massive structural reforms in Israel's government. Remaining as interim prime minister in a caretaker government, Rabin won the leadership of Mapai by a very narrow margin over Defense Minister Peres. A bare five weeks before the election Rabin was forced to withdraw from the leadership position in favor of Peres when he lied over the disclosure that he and his wife kept illegal bank accounts in Washington.

On May 17, 1977, the Israeli voters gave Likud 43 seats in the new Kneset, an increase of only four from the election in 1973; but the Labor Alignment fell from 51 to 32 and, thus, no longer held a plurality. The law required the president to invite Menachem Begin, head of the Herut party and leader of Likud, to form a government. With the aid of several religious parties and a few independents and the defection of Moshe Dayan from Labor to become foreign minister, Prime Minister Begin welded a coalition of 61 of the 120-member Kneset. Yigal Yadin, leader of the Democratic Movement for Change (DMC), refused to add his party's fifteen seats to the Begin government because he believed Israel should agree to a more lenient policy for the occupied territories. In October, however, the DMC came into the government and Yadin became deputy prime minister, an important position in view of Begin's poor health.

Since early in 1976 living conditions and life in general in Israel had deteriorated. Inflation was running at 38 percent a year and the annual trade deficit was nearly $3 billion. Devaluations every few months had little effect. Unemployment crept up to 5 percent, reflecting the shift in the economy from homebuilding and domestic needs to exports. Business and industry felt shackled by the red tape of a controlled economy and a semi-authoritarian regime. A combination of wealthy entrepreneurs, poor and disenchanted Oriental Israelis, right-wing hawks, and discontented shopkeepers threw out the Labor Alignment to support Likud, which had promised to cure the social, economic, and financial problems weighing upon Israel.

At the end of October, the government abandoned socialism. Finance Minister Simha Ehrlich, a disciple of Nobel prize-winner Milton Friedman, lifted restrictions of the buying and selling of foreign exchange and the freeing of the Israeli pound from controls; its value dropped 40 percent overnight. A conservative free economic system was announced with import and export subsidies ended and many taxes raised sharply. Dock workers struck immediately, kibbutzim and farm laborers were shocked, and leaders of the Labor Alignment and Histadruth attacked the policy. Earlier Professor Friedman had visited Israel as an economic consultant and had observed that socialism and Judaism are inherently in opposition. The Begin government with many powerful and wealthy Liberal party members participating intended to cure Israel's economic ills by trying his remedies.

On coming to power Begin sent his longtime confidant, Shmuel Katz, to the United States to acquaint American Zionist leaders with the views of the new leader and to arrange a July meeting between President Carter and Prime Minister Begin. Katz also declared the new government accepted the U.N. Resolution 242 and would attend a Geneva conference on Middle East peace. The July meeting of the two leaders appeared friendly but no basic issues were debated. Upon Begin's return to Israel three new settlements were placed in West Bank territory and again three more in

August. He asserted that these were not occupied territories but Judea and Samaria, inseparable parts of Israel, that had been liberated in 1967. President Carter indicated disappointment over the developments and called them obstacles to peace. The European Economic Community declared that peace in the Middle East must provide for a Palestinian homeland and Palestinians must participate in the peace-making process. In September a joint U.S.-U.S.S.R. declaration called for the reconvening of the Geneva conference with the statement that the Palestinian problem must be considered. Foreign Minister Dayan in Washington and leaders in Israel reacted vehemently against the reentry of the Soviets into the negotiations and the American demarche in the need to involve the Palestinians. Begin asserted that Israel under no conditions would negotiate with the PLO and would not agree to the establishment of a Palestinian state on the West Bank. These opposing stands made the convening of a Geneva conference unlikely. With all the fanfare and public euphoria in Israel associated with President Sadat's visit to Jerusalem in November 1977, the question of peace and the future status of the Palestinians and the West Bank were widely debated and strained all political ties in Israel.

Transjordan

East of the Jordan River Prince Abdallah ruled his semidesert domain and seminomadic people under the tutelage of Great Britain. The strength of his position was anchored to the financial and diplomatic contributions of the British and was buoyed up by the Arab Legion and the Transjordan frontier force, the strongest Arab armies in the Middle East. The British found them useful in Iraq and Syria during World War II. Abdallah was the staunchest friend of the British in the Middle East.

Abdallah's rule and his governmental machinery were uncomplicated until 1949. A new treaty was drafted and signed in 1946, recognizing Abdallah as king of Transjordan and giving him greater independence from Great Britain, which was permitted to keep a military mission and various training facilities in the country. A constitution was promulgated and became effective in 1947, providing for a chamber of deputies to be elected for a five-year term and consisting of 20 members: 12 Muslims, 4 Christians, 2 bedouins, and 2 to represent the Circassian and Shishan communities. The other house of the parliament was a council of notables composed of ten members appointed by the king.

King Abdallah was strongly criticized in the Arab League for agreeing to such a subservient position as the treaty established, and Transjordan's application for membership in the U.N. was blocked by the U.S.S.R. on the grounds that Transjordan was not independent. Consequently, another treaty was signed in 1948, specifying "co-operation and mutual assistance" between Transjordan and Great Britain. Prime Minister Samir Rifai Pasha called for elections, and only one political party (the Government Revival party) presented candidates for the chamber of deputies, although a few independents were returned. Aside from Abdallah's relations with the British and the annual subvention received from them, his main attention politically centered upon the Arab League. Because of Abdallah's everlasting dream of a greater Syria over which he would rule, Egypt and Saudi Arabia were always unfriendly.

During the Palestine war in 1948, the Arab Legion defended Jerusalem and successfully held the fortress of Latrun from a desperate Israeli attack. Together with Iraqi troops, Abdallah's forces held the lines from the Gulf of Akaba to north central Palestine near Janin and bore the main brunt of Israeli drives. Abdallah favored the Nashashibi, Tukan, and other Palestinian Arab families as opposed to the al-Husayni family and the ex-mufti Hajj Amin. When the defeat of the Arabs could no longer be denied, Abdallah acted to incorporate what remained of Palestine into his state, and in June 1949 renamed it the Hashimite Kingdom of Jordan.

Hashimite Kingdom of Jordan
Almost overnight King Abdallah's problems became exceedingly complex. The small state of an estimated 400,000 inhabitants suddenly burgeoned into a kingdom of 1,360,000 people. More than half of the Arab refugees flocked into Jordan. Those who had means of support, an education, or a skill either integrated themselves into Jordanian life or migrated to other Arab lands or to the far corners of the earth; nearly 500,000 did not and continued to live in refugee camps. A serious problem arose in those villages of Arab Palestine whose lands and support were cut off by the armistice lines of 1949.

Grave as the refugee situation was for Abdallah, the Arabs, and the world, the most significant aspect of this influx and the annexation of Arab Palestine to Transjordan sprang from a transformation in the character of the state. West Jordanians and refugees after 1950 comprised more than half of the population. On the average they were better educated, more politically minded, more ardent in their Arab nationalism, and more unremitting in their desire to have a "second round" with Israel and regain mastery in their own state. Abdallah doubled the size of the chamber of deputies in 1950, and half of the members were elected to represent each side of the Jordan. The council of notables was also increased to a membership of twenty, seven of whom were Palestinian.

The Palestinian Arabs, accustomed to blaming their woes on the Jews and the British, turned their venom on King Abdallah and the Amman government. Although Abdallah was not greatly interested in economics, an irrigation project to provide arable land for refugee families was inaugurated. Musa Alami founded an Arab development society which built several model villages near Jericho. And UNRWA contributed to a number of productive programs that benefited the state. But none was enough, and the king bore the brunt of the attack. Abdallah was sane and shrewd, as well as moderate and realistic. For these attributes he was despised. In 1951 he was murdered in Jerusalem by an adherent of the ex-mufti, Hajj Amin al-Husayni.

King Husayn

The king's eldest son, Talal, was proclaimed king. His emotional stability was highly questionable, and in 1952 he departed for Europe, leaving the kingdom to his son Husayn. The latter became king on his eighteenth birthday, in 1953. The post of prime minister became more important, but until 1956 the position shifted from one old-time political friend of Abdallah to another: Samir al-Rifai, Tawfik Abu al-Huda, Fawzi al-Mulky, Said al-Mufti, Haza al-Majali, and Ibrahim Hashim.

All authorities agreed to the need for development in Jordan, and recognition of the potential of Jordan waters led to many schemes. The difficulty of achievement stemmed from the conflicting interests of Lebanon, Syria, Jordan, and Israel and from the absence of peace in the Middle East. Division of the water proved a stumbling block, especially as the natural storage reservoir, Lake Tiberias, was wholly located in Israel. In spite of failure to come to terms on a regional system Syria and Jordan drew up a pact to build a hydroelectric-irrigation dam on the Yarmuk River. Other plans were made to construct roads, reforest considerable areas, and build a cement factory. The U.N. Technical Assistance Administration allocated sizable sums for Jordan, and in 1954 the United States gave over $12 million to Jordan. Britain continued her support of the Arab Legion and subsidized the government to the extent of several million pounds annually.

The signing of the Baghdad and Damascus pacts in 1955 and the formation of power rivalries in the Middle East placed Jordan in a critical position. Her dynasty belonged to the same family as that of Iraq, and her financial ties to England favored a closer relationship to the Baghdad pact. But the bitter denunciations of the pact from the other Arab League states, led by Egypt and Syria, warned Jordan of the dangers in allying herself with Britain, Turkey, and Iraq. Furthermore, Palestinian Arabs, in their campaign to regain possession of the whole of Palestine, were very skeptical of a pact that included or was under the patronage of any Western state, for it was generally understood that the West would not easily permit the destruction of Israel.

Thus, in 1955 when pressure was exerted upon Jordan to join the Baghdad pact, Prime Minister al-Majali, who was amenable to such a move, was forced out of office after five days of riots, attacks upon British and American diplomatic offices, and a final declaration of neutrality. Saudi Arabia announced her willingness to contribute to the support of Jordan's government and the Arab Legion on the condition that the British be ousted. John Bagot Glubb Pasha, the English head of the Arab Legion, was dismissed summarily in March 1956 and was replaced shortly by Colonel Ali Abu Nuwar, the military aide and long-time companion of King Husayn. Abu Nuwar became chief of staff, head of the Arab Legion, and a contender for complete power in Jordan. Britain continued financial support, but sympathizers of President Nasser rapidly gained in strength and position in Jordan. King Husayn was young and inexperienced. Abu Nuwar, young and exceedingly ambitious, looked upon himself as the Nasser of Jordan, and gathered together a band of young and ardent nationalistic officers seeking power.

Jordanian Crises

In June 1956 Prime Minister al-Mufti admitted that he planned to negotiate a revision of the treaty with Britain, but parliament was dissolved the day before it was to debate the subject. With the nationalization of Suez, accompanied by Nasser's rages, Abu Nuwar flitted from Beirut to Damascus to Cairo to Riyadh, receiving assurances of military assistance from Syria, Iraq, Egypt, and Saudi Arabia in case Jordan were attacked.

With that backdrop for an election campaign, pro-Egyptian candidates were assured victory. About 50 percent of the qualified voters cast ballots, as the National Socialists under Sulayman Nabulsi won eleven seats in the 40-member chamber. Nabulsi's cabinet was installed the day Israel invaded Egypt, and Syrian and Iraqi troops moved in to safeguard Jordan from Israel —and from one another.

Nabulsi frequently suggested that Jordan should ask for arms and aid from the Soviet bloc. Passionately anti-British, he reminded Syria, Egypt, and Saudi Arabia of their offer to assume the annual subvention Jordan received from Great Britain and declared that Jordan was ready to terminate her treaty with Great Britain. Fulfillment came with the Arab solidarity pact in 1957; Egypt and Saudi Arabia each promised to contribute £5 million and Syria promised £2.5 million for support of the Jordanian army.

Many Jordanians rejoiced as the British troops departed in 1957. Nabulsi, in collaboration with Abu Nuwar, appeared ready to form a closer political, economic, and military union with Syria. However, King Husayn dismissed Nabulsi, and Abu Nuwar fled to escape arrest. Syrian troops moved to occupy north Jordan. The fate of King Husayn hung in the balance. Showing real courage, Husayn rallied his bedouin troops about him at Zarka and reestablished peace and his authority.

Jordan's finances were in serious condition. Saudi Arabia paid her first installment on the Arab solidarity pact in May, but nothing was forthcoming from Egypt or Syria. Husayn, therefore, asked for aid from Iraq and the United States; the latter contributed $20 million. Arms from the United States were airlifted to Amman in September. Feeling more secure, Husayn convened parliament in October and denounced U.S.S.R. sympathizers. The Baath and Communist parties were outlawed, and the conspiracy to merge Jordan with Syria was driven underground.

The next crisis arose when Syria and Egypt formed the United Arab Republic. Husayn begged his cousin in Iraq to visit Amman and protect Jordan by establishing some type of federal union. As a result the Arab Federation was consummated in February 1958. Provisions were included in its constitution to insure separate treaty obligations, as Husayn did not believe Syria would countenance his adherence to the Baghdad pact. King Husayn became an alternate to the chief of state, and procedural steps for closer federation were undertaken. A joint budget was fashioned, with Jordan's share being set at 20 percent. Although Nasser fumed at Husayn for betraying the Arab nation to "imperialists," and assailed him as a decadent weight upon Arab nationalism, Husayn believed he had weathered the storm and that union with Iraq would protect him from Syria and strengthen his stand against Nasserism.

But still another and more serious crisis fell on Husayn in July 1958, with the revolution in Iraq and the murder of King Faysal, of Arab Federation prime minister Nuri al-Said, and of two Jordanians in the federation's cabinet. Left, technically, head of the federation, Husayn proceeded to assert his authority, but Iraq abrogated the union, abruptly throwing Jordan adrift in a turbulent storm of Arab nationalism. Abu Nuwar, now Husayn's sworn enemy, was lodged in Cairo plotting his overthrow. He might have succeeded had not British paratroopers been flown in from Cyprus. The bedouin troops rallied to Husayn's side, and his throne seemed secure as long as the British troops remained in Jordan.

With Egypt and Syria bound together in the United Arab Republic, with General Kassim riding a wave of popularity in Iraq after having ousted the monarchy and destroyed the Hashimite family there, with the Saudi family maintaining its perpetual feud with the Hashimites, with Israeli expansionists talking of annexing all of Palestine west of the Jordan River, with several thousand British soldiers in Jordan causing Arab nationalists everywhere to call King Husayn the tool of the imperialists, and with half of his own subjects wishing for a different state and a different regime, retreating to a villa in Lausanne must have seemed tempting to Husayn. To make matters worse, nearly 75 percent of Jordan's total revenues in 1958 came from grants and subsidies from Great Britain and the United States. Imports were more than eleven times the amount of exports. Local capital was virtually nonexistent and exploitable natural resources were unknown. But King Husayn was tough and tenacious. He enjoyed the loyalty of his army, which was regarded as the best-trained and best-equipped force among the Arabs. The British troops left in November, and Husayn set out to keep his throne. His program consisted of internal economic growth and development, aimed at making Jordan economically self-sufficient by 1970; of democratizing the government, progressing as rapidly as the several elements in Jordan's society could be brought into accord; and of steering an artful course among the jealousies, rivalries, ambitions, and ideologies of his Arab neighbors, while retaining his independence from the great powers.

In 1959 the Jordan Development Board was established to coordinate and sponsor efforts to increase the productivity of the state. A major project was the East Ghor Canal, which was to channel off water from the Yarmuk River and carry it parallel and east of the Jordan River for more than forty miles toward the Dead Sea to irrigate tens of thousands of acres of dry but fertile lands. The first stage was finished in 1961 and the second in 1962. The total cost was more than $25 million, and at that point 40,000 acres were irrigated. The banks of the canal would be heightened as more water became available; at two Arab summit meetings in 1964, plans for diverting water from the Hasbani and Banyas rivers to the Yarmuk and for building dams on the Yarmuk were designed to augment the flow into an enlarged East Ghor Canal. The Jordan Phosphate Company received loans from the U.S. government to enlarge its facilities for exploiting the vast chemical deposits in the Dead Sea. Tourism became a growing industry as Jordan began to capitalize on her wealth of archeological remains.

In 1959 there was relative political calm within Jordan. General Kassim's reorganization in Iraq, and the difficulties of merging Syria and Egypt into the United Arab Republic occupied the full attentions of Husayn's covetous neighbors. The radio invectives from Cairo and Baghdad reached such a crescendo that it was recognized that for Jordan's survival there had to be a greater sharing of responsibility. Elections held in 1961 turned out only 10 percent of the electorate. To counter this discouraging apathy the king appointed as prime minister Western-educated Wasfi al-Tal, who selected an entirely new cabinet. Parliament was dissolved and new elections were held in 1962. This time 70 percent voted for the 166 candidates for the sixty seats.

After the revolution in Yemen in 1962 Husayn turned more toward King Faysal in Saudi Arabia. Relations with the Saudis did not mend until 1964, however, when Arab summit meetings were held in Cairo and Alexandria. There the several Arab states pledged $200 million for the Jordan water diversion to the Yarmuk River. Also at the Cairo gathering it was voted to create an Arab political entity for Palestine and to draft a constitution for it. Arab refugees from Palestine were to elect delegates to a national assembly, which would meet every two years, alternating between Jerusalem and Gaza. Known as the Palestine Liberation Organization (PLO), it was to raise an army that would have a separate identity but be a part of the army in each of the Arab host states. In 1966 Husayn agreed that PLO might conduct elections in Jordan for the national assembly, but he refused to accept its armed forces or PLO leader Ahmad al-Shuqayri's suggestion that the capital of Jordan should be transferred to Jerusalem.

Vilification of Husayn from some Arab capitals continued, and Damascus suggested that the Syrian army would gladly supply arms to those who wished to overthrow him. Yet, in May 1967, at the height of the crisis with Israel, Husayn flew to Cairo where Nasser embraced him at the airport. They proceeded to sign a five-year mutual defense pact, and Jordan pledged her army, should war come with Israel. Husayn believed fully that his throne would be lost and he assassinated if his army did not move promptly and with full vigor on the center front in any Arab-Israeli confrontation.

Consequences of the June 1967 War
Within a few hours after the beginning of hostilities on June 5, 1967, the Jordanian air force had been destroyed by Israel. Complete mastery of the air over Jordan gave Israel such an advantage that King Husayn's army was

ineffective. The entire area west of the Jordan River, including Jerusalem, was lost, and about 200,000 refugees fled eastward across the river. The most productive part of Husayn's kingdom was gone, his finances were in shambles, and his armed forces were without equipment. Throughout the summer various moves were made to enable the new refugees to return to their homes or to the camps. Israeli officials allowed about 14,000 who had homes to return, but none were accepted back in the camps. Husayn assumed virtual command of all branches of his government. At an Arab summit meeting in Khartoum, Saudi Arabia, Kuwayt, and Libya agreed to aid Jordan financially. Thirty thousand Iraqi troops remained in Jordan to protect the king as well as to strengthen his position against Israel. In the autumn Husayn visited Moscow to explain the Arab position and to sound out the possibilities for replacing his lost military equipment. In November 1967 he visited Washington and the U.N., where he indicated that he and other Arab leaders might be able to find a path that might lead to recognition of Israel.

The Hashimite Kingdom of Jordan was now confined to the East Bank of the river. Israel was holding some 5,600 square kilometers of Jordan which had had a population of 650,000. During the few days of fighting or soon thereafter more than a third had fled, most ending up in Jordan, and very few ever returned to their homes. Israel permitted the civil administration of the West Bank to remain Arab, and since the salaries of most officials had come from Amman, Husayn continued to pay them.

Jordan served for the next several years as the staging area for Palestinian attacks upon Israel. Very soon after the close of the war, Husayn declared his opposition to any attack upon the occupied areas, reminding all that such incursions would be injurious to their fellow Palestinians living there. He objected strongly to the use of Jordan as a base for training and launching guerrilla actions against Israel—not that he was unsympathetic to the goals. He had no intention of transforming Jordan into a guerrilla state, and he fully supported the U.N. Resolution 242 for ending the state of war and bringing peace to the area. His interpretation of 242 required Israel to return all his lost territory to him.

Since more than half of Husayn's subjects were Palestinians, many of them recent arrivals, his policies were condemned by many as traitorous to the Arab people. Even some of his ministers were not opposed to Palestinian actions from Jordan. In any case, throughout 1968, 1969, and 1970 there were countless assaults on Israel, followed by reprisals on Jordan. The Israeli attack on the village of Karameh was particularly grave. Over fifty Jordanians were killed and the U.N. Security Council censured Israel for it. Destructive Israeli retaliation upon Jordan did not deter Palestinian guerrilla deeds on Israel and the Security Council denouncings never dampened the Israeli determination to punish the invaders.

Husayn decreed that the commandos were not to wear Jordanian army uniforms nor to carry arms in Jordan's towns, but enforcing the rule was next to impossible. In general, Jordan suffered more than Israel did in these exchanges. Early in 1969 King Husayn met Yasir Arafat, leader of al-Fatah and the PLO, in a fruitless attempt to come to an understanding over the activities of the Palestinians in Jordan. The radical Popular Front for the Liberation of Palestine (PFLP) and al-Fatah were training commandos and launching attacks from Jordan almost at will. Israel's retaliations were crippling Jordan's economy. When Palestinians shelled Elath the Israeli air force bombed the East Ghor Canal, causing the irrigation of 36,000 acres in the Jordan valley to cease. Through American mediation, Jordan agreed to curtail commando operations and Israel permitted the restoration of the canal. In June 1970 fighting between Palestinians and Jordanian army units broke out. After some 200 were killed a precarious compromise brought a lull in the hostilities.

After the 1967 war Husayn's relations with other Arab leaders and with Europe and the United States were friendly and cooperative. In the last half of 1967 and in 1968 and 1969 he traveled prodigiously, seeking the funds and economic assistance necessary to keep Jordan afloat. He tried to acquire arms and military equipment to maintain some semblance of security and independence. He also spoke publicly to explain the role of Jordan in the Middle East and to declare his position and policies relative to the Middle East and to world affairs. His success was evident—he was still king.

The forced migration of many "new" personages to the East Bank after the 1967 war brought a growth of radical political parties to parallel the influx of Palestinian commandos and patriots. A National Front was formed in 1968 as an umbrella for the Communists, the Baath, the Muslim Brotherhood, the National Socialists, and the Independent Socialists. They united under the leadership of Sulayman Nabulsi, a National Socialist whom King Husayn had dismissed from the post of prime minister in 1957. Early in 1969 Husayn named Abd al-Munim al-Rifai prime minister in order to calm relations with the Palestinians and to provide a period of quiet for the United States and the U.S.S.R. to work together to break the Arab-Israeli deadlock. When they failed to act Husayn adopted a more militant stance toward the Palestinians; in August he sent al-Rifai back to the foreign office and installed al-Talhuni, an anti-Palestinian, as prime minister. Nevertheless, in June 1970 when the activities of the commandos threatened to overthrow his kingdom, Husayn not only reappointed al-Rifai prime minister to please the Palestinians, he brought back Abu Nuwar as his counselor. When Husayn accepted the American proposal for a Middle East cease-fire in July 1970, the Palestinians declared they would not "tolerate such treason" and prepared for a showdown with Husayn. Husayn at this point acted decisively, removing the civilian government, establishing military rule, and personally taking control of his armed forces.

"Black September"

Peace negotiations in New York in August aroused the commandos for battle. Iraq announced she would aid the Palestinians. Then, al-Saiqah, Syrian-based Palestinian commandos, moved into Jordan. On September 6,

1970, Palestinians hijacked three airliners—Swiss Air, Pan Am, and TWA—
and failed in their attempt to capture an El Al plane. Two days later a
BOAC plane was taken. All were flown to the Middle East; after the passengers were evacuated the four were blown up, three of them in Jordan. A
week later Husayn appointed a cabinet made up entirely of military officers,
with Brigadier Muhammad Daud as prime minister. On the following day,
September 17, 1970, Husayn launched a full-scale campaign against the
commando groups. Syrian tanks crossed the border to support the hard-
pressed Palestinians, but withdrew upon warnings from Israel and the
United States. After a week Husayn had the upper hand. Under pressure
from the Arab League, Husayn and Arafat signed in Cairo a fourteen-point
peace agreement. Guerrilla actions in Jordan were clearly defined and
attacks upon Israel were not to be launched from Jordan. The Palestinians,
angered by their defeat, began to refer to the time as "Black September."

Toward the end of October 1970, feeling relatively secure, Husayn appointed al-Tal again as prime minister, with instructions to enforce the
Cairo agreement. Since all its points could not be fully implemented without destroying the state, a step Husayn would not countenance, al-Tal
became a likely target for Palestinian patriots. Jordanian officials met in
Beirut in 1971 with West Bank leaders and commando officers on the issue
of a Palestinian state as Palestinian strongholds in the northern hills of
Jordan were being besieged and eliminated. In July the Jordanian army
killed about 300 commandos and took 2,500 prisoner. Resumption of hostilities distressed all the Arab leaders, who angrily charged Husayn with violating the Cairo agreement. The nub of that accord was Husayn's acceptance
of the clause, "free movement of Palestinians" in Jordan. In November,
as al-Tal was entering a hotel in Cairo for more discussions, gunmen of
the PFLP cut him down. A shocked and grieving Husayn appointed
Ahmad al-Lawzi to succeed al-Tal. Later, Husayn juggled the cabinet to
include three Palestinians, hoping for improved and widened political
support.

Having driven most of the commandos from Jordan to Lebanon, Husayn
was freer to arrange his own affairs. In March 1972 he issued a twelve-point
plan for peace with Israel. It proposed the creation of the United Arab
Kingdom, a federated state of two autonomous regions—the East Bank and
the West Bank—with Amman and Jerusalem as the two capitals. Israel was
not enamored of the proposal. Arab leaders fumed; many who had not
already cut diplomatic ties with Jordan did so, leaving Husayn isolated
among the Arab states. By the end of the year, however, relations were
partially restored with Syria and Egypt, Husayn recognizing the patched
amity by freeing 700 political prisoners, among whom was Abu Daud, a
leading Palestinian commando, whose death sentence had previously been
commuted to life imprisonment.

The internal strife cut Jordan's gross national product for 1970 by 25
percent. The United States and West Germany together nearly made up
Jordan's $25 million budget deficit, though, and the United States promised

to replenish Jordan's expended stock of military equipment and to provide aid for reconstruction. Husayn's Middle East neighbors withheld their subsidies again in 1972 when he unveiled his twelve-point peace plan. The economy turned down in 1972, but loans from Saudi Arabia, West Germany, and the United States kept Jordan solvent.

As a crisis atmosphere arose in 1973, Husayn observed that in case war should break out in the area, Jordan would not act "impulsively and naïvely." In September full diplomatic relations were renewed with Egypt, then with Syria; Kuwayt restored her subsidy soon after.

After the October 1973 War

Syria and Egypt initiated the war against Israel on October 6; Husayn did not participate, but held his forces on full alert until the 13th, when he sent a token force of 1,000 to join the Syrians. They returned to Jordan at the initial cease-fire. In January 1974 Husayn passed to Kissinger a confidential ten-point proposal for disengagement between Israel and Jordan, including the West Bank. The second world Islamic conference, held a few weeks later in Lahore, named the PLO as the sole legitimate spokesman for the restoration of Palestinian rights and territories. Again, at the Arab summit meetings in Rabat in October, Arab foreign ministers in one vote and twenty kings and presidents in another reaffirmed the Lahore declaration. Husayn could only acquiesce; Saudi Arabia gave Jordan $300 million to soften the blow, as Husayn agreed that he would be the first to recognize Arafat and a PLO government-in-exile. Then, vexed, he announced that he would cease paying salaries to West Bank officials, since they were no longer under Jordan's jurisdiction. This stirred up such angry remonstrances that he relented, resumed the payments, and continued to pour considerable sums from Jordan's development plan into West Bank projects. Legislation in 1974 stripped the West Bank of its half of the seats in parliament and of its half of the posts in the cabinet.

The October 1973 war (the Arabs called it the Ramadan War, since it began during the Muslim month of fasting) left few economic traces in Jordan. The immense surge in oil revenues brought untold wealth to the oil producing Arab states. The sudden affluence of Jordan's neighbors spilled over until Jordan's budget, climbing year by year, reached $1 billion in 1977. In 1975 a five-year development plan for $2.5 billion was adopted, and aid money from the United States and the Arab countries topped $500 million.

Because of the Lebanese troubles most international companies vacated their offices in Beirut; many moved to Amman, thereby adding to Jordan's revenues. As a member of the World Institute of Phosphates, a sort of OPEC organized by Morocco for phosphate producers, Jordan saw the price of her exports of 1.3 million tons jump from $15 to $60 a ton. Income from tourism also increased sharply. All these revenues, coupled with a growing amount of remittances from Palestinians working in countries throughout the world, produced a boom in Jordan. In 1976 the development plan budget was doubled to include the groundwork for the projected Maqarin dam and expanded programs in agriculture, transportation, mining, industry, and phosphates.

Shortly after the Ramadan War certain contingents in the army requested the resignation of the prime minister and demanded higher pay; Husayn, refusing to heed their demands, summarily retired ten senior officers. Parliament was dissolved in 1974, and Husayn and the cabinet governed without it. After the Rabat decision on the roles of Jordan and the PLO, Husayn postponed elections indefinitely and resurrected the old parliament.

In 1977, as the civil war in Lebanon wound down, the Palestinian guerrillas not only were weakened by their losses of men and weapons but were controlled to some extent by Syria. Arafat's power and position were diminished, and the role of the PLO in Arab conclaves seemed less commanding. It seemed possible that Husayn might once more have a voice in any settlement between the Israelis and Palestinians. In 1977 the federation he had proposed earlier, drawing together Palestinians on the West Bank with those on the East Bank, began to arouse interest again. In Cairo at the March meeting of the Palestine National Council its executive committee, headed by Arafat, asked for a normalization of relations with Jordan. Husayn and Arafat, supported by their political advisers, discussed at length the need for a link between Jordan and a proposed independent Palestine state.

Political and diplomatic friendships in the Middle East are mercurial. In 1975 Sadat and Assad were royally entertained in Amman and Husayn was warmly received in Cairo and Damascus. In the latter capital the two leaders, with full support of their governments, formed the Supreme Syrian-Jordan Command Council, which would act to coordinate their states' foreign policies, military plans, economic matters, and cultural, educational, and information affairs. Later, when Syria and Egypt again declared that steps would be taken to lead to a federal union between them, Jordan felt included. However, Husayn viewed his relations with Washington and Moscow as even more important than those with the Arab states. Repeatedly he spoke of the United States as the power that would make the final decisions on the Middle East.

REFERENCES: Chapter 43

The number of books covering this subject is very large and is growing rapidly. Of special significance are items in Chapters 28, 30, 31, 33, 34, 37, and 42.

Abdallah, King. *My Memoirs Completed.* (Harold Glidden, tr.) Washington, D.C.: American Council of Learned Societies, 1954. A continuation of the reference edited by Philip P. Graves in Chap. 34.

Abidi, Aqil Hyder Hasan. *Jordan: A Political Study, 1948–1957.* New York: Asia Publishing House, 1965. Scholarly, well-researched and documented, and readable.

Abu-Lughod, Ibrahim (ed.). *The Arab-Israeli Confrontation of June, 1967: An Arab Perspective.* Evanston, Ill.: Northwestern University Press, 1970. Nine essays by Arab scholars, most of whom are professors in American universities.

Allon, Yigal. *The Making of Israel's Army.* New York: Universe Books, 1970. Allon, who has been deputy prime minister of Israel, was a commander in the Palmach and one of the architects of the Israeli defense forces.

Avnery, Uri. *Israel without Zionists: A Plea for Peace in the Middle East.* New York: Macmillan, 1968. Says Israel must take account of the national aspirations of the Arabs.

Beaufre, Général d'Armée André. *The Suez Expedition, 1956.* New York: Praeger, 1969. Beaufre was the key French officer in the planning and execution of the Suez operation.

Begin, Menachem. *The Revolt: Story of the Irgun.* New York: Schuman, 1951. A fascinating story by the Irgun's leader, a legendary figure who became prime minister in 1977.

Bell, J. Bowyer. *Terror out of Zion, Lehi and the Palestine Underground.* New York: St. Martin's Press, 1977. The story of Irgun and the Sternists.

Ben-Gurion, David. *Israel: Years of Challenge.* New York: Holt, 1963. An account of the founding of the state and the accomplishments of the first decade.

Bernadotte, Folke. *To Jerusalem.* London: Hodder & Stoughton, 1951. By the U.N. mediator who was assassinated while attempting to bring peace to Palestine.

Bernstein, Marver H. *The Politics of Israel: The First Decade of Statehood.* Princeton, N.J.: Princeton University Press, 1957. The best study of Israel's early government, administration, and politics.

Brecher, Michael. *Decisions in Israel's Foreign Policy.* New Haven, Conn.: Yale University Press, 1975. It contains an analysis of decision making in Israel on critical issues, including the Sinai war of 1956 and the June war of 1967.

————. *The Foreign Policy System of Israel: Setting, Images, Process.* New Haven, Conn.: Yale University Press, 1972. Meticulous research, comprehensive use of documentary sources and interviews, and impressive marshalling of data.

Buehrig, Edward H. *The U.N. and the Palestinian Refugees: A Study in Nonterritorial Administration.* Bloomington: Indiana University Press, 1971.

Burns, E. L. M. *Between Arab and Israeli.* London: Harrap, 1962. By the Canadian general who headed the U.N. Truce Supervision Organization after 1949.

Chaliand, Gerard. *The Palestinian Resistance.* Middlesex, England: Penguin Books, 1972. A serious analysis of a revolutionary phenomenon.

Cooley, John K. *Green March, Black September: The Story of the Palestinian Arabs.* London: Frank Cass, 1973.

Crosbie, Sylvia Kowitt. *A Tacit Alliance: France and Israel from Suez to the Six-Day War.* Princeton, N.J.: Princeton University Press, 1974. Traces the rise of Franco-Israel friendship from its beginnings through the Suez Crisis to its abrupt end in 1967.

Dayan, Moshe. *Diary of the Sinai Campaign.* New York: Schocken Books, 1967. A first-hand account by the commanding general of the Israeli forces.

Eban, Abba. *Autobiography.* New York: Random House, 1977. A full story of his public life.

Eytan, Walter. *The First Ten Years: A Diplomatic History of Israel.* New York: Simon and Schuster, 1958. By the director-general of the Israeli Foreign Office.

Fishman, Aryei (ed.). *The Religious Kibbutz Movement.* New York: Jewish Agency, 1957. The ideology of the religious settlements, their religious and festival celebrations, and a brief history of each of ten settlements.

Gabbay, Rony E. *A Political Study of the Arab-Jewish Conflict: The Arab Refugee Problem (A Case Study).* Geneva: Librairie E. Droz, 1959. Written with perception and balance.

Golan, Galia. *Yom Kippur and After: The Soviet Union and the Middle East Crisis.* New York: Cambridge University Press, 1977. An Israeli analyst reconstructs the Soviet role in the October 1973 war.

Halevi, Nadav, and Ruth Klinov-Malul. *The Economic Development of Israel.* New York: Praeger, 1968. A macroeconomic analysis of the period since 1947.

Isaac, Rael Jean. *Israel Divided: Ideological Politics in the Jewish State.* Baltimore, Md.: Johns Hopkins University Press, 1976. An assessment of Israeli extremist movements.

Jabber, Fuad. *Israel and Nuclear Weapons: Present Options and Future Strategies.* London: Chatto & Windus for the International Institute for Strategic Studies, 1971. An examination of Israeli capabilities and an analysis of Israeli military doctrine.

Janowsky, Oscar I. *Foundations of Israel: Emergence of a Welfare State.* Princeton, N.J.: D. Van Nostrand, 1959. Good on political and constitutional development.

Jiryis, Sabri. *The Arabs in Israel.* (Inea Bushnaq, tr.) New York: Monthly Review Press, 1976. Deals especially with the effects of the military government on Arab Israelis.

Kanovsky, Eliyahu. *The Economic Impact of the Six-Day War: Israel, the Occupied Territories, Egypt, Jordan.* New York: Praeger, 1970. Concludes that the occupied territories constitute an economic liability for Israel.

Katz, Samuel. *Days of Fire: The Secret History of the Irgun Zvai Leumi and the Making of Israel.* New York: Doubleday & Co., 1968. Written by one of Begin's close associates, and in 1977, as Shamuel Katz, Begin's chief emissary to the U.S.

Khouri, Fred J. *The Arab-Israeli Dilemma.* Syracuse, N.Y.: Syracuse University Press, 1976. Scholarly and comprehensive portrayal of the views, politics, and actions of the contending parties.

Kiernan, Thomas. *Arafat: The Man and the Myth.* New York: W. W. Norton, 1976.

Kimche, Jon. *Seven Fallen Pillars.* New York: Praeger, 1953. An account of the first Israeli-Arab war.

———, and David Kimche. *A Clash of Destinies: The Arab-Jewish Wars and the Founding of the State of Israel.* New York: Praeger, 1960. A fine piece of contemporary history.

Kurzman, Dan. *Genesis 1948: The First Arab-Israeli War.* New York: World Publishing, 1970. A very detailed account, including much material on the period before 1948.

Leslie, S. Clement. *The Rift in Israel: Religious Authority and Secular Democracy.* New York: Schocken Books, 1971. An examination of a problem in Israeli life and in Israel's foreign relations.

Litvinoff, Barnett. *Ben-Gurion: The Biography of a Statesman.* New York: Praeger, 1954. Based largely on interviews with people close to Ben-Gurion.

Love, Kenneth. *Suez: The Twice Fought War: A History.* New York: McGraw-Hill, 1969. A monumental work on the 1956 conflict, based on interviews, published sources and documents, and the Dulles and Eisenhower papers.

Luttwak, Edward, and Dan Horowitz. *The Israeli Army.* New York: Harper & Row, 1975. Luttwak is a defense consultant in Washington and Horowitz is a reserve officer in the Israeli army.

McDonald, James G. *My Mission in Israel.* New York: Simon and Schuster, 1951. The experiences of the first American ambassador to Israel.

Medding, Peter. *Mapai in Israel: Political Organization and Government in a New Society.* London: Cambridge University Press, 1972. One of the most important works on Israeli party politics.

O'Ballance, Edgar. *The Arab-Israeli War, 1948.* New York: Praeger, 1957. An excellent military study.

———. *The Third Arab-Israeli War.* Hamden, Conn.: Archon Books, 1972. A fine military account of the 1967 war.

———. *Arab Guerrilla Power: 1967–1972.* Hamden, Conn.: The Shoe String Press, 1973. Follows the Palestinians from their initial concept—a Chinese-Algerian style people's war—to their retrenchment after the 1970 defeat in Jordan, and then examines the future prospects of the Palestinian movement.

Peretz, Don. *Israel and the Palestine Arabs.* Washington, D.C.: Middle East Institute, 1958.

———, Evan Wilson, and Richard J. Ward. *A Palestine Entity?* Washington, D.C.: Middle East Institute, 1970. An exploration of a number of options that could produce a settlement of the Palestinian issue.

Perlmutter, Amos. *Military and Politics in Israel: Nation-Building and Role Expansion.* New York: Praeger, 1969. Describes the strong influence of army leadership since 1948 in determining the path of Israeli foreign policy.

Roberts, Samuel J. *Survival or Hegemony?: The Foundations of Israeli Foreign Policy.* Baltimore: Johns Hopkins Press, 1973. Asserts that Israel follows the principles of *Realpolitik.*

Rubner, Alex. *The Economy of Israel: A Critical Account of the First Ten Years.* New York: Praeger, 1960. An estimate of the economic damage caused by the deliberate suppression of market forces and the market mechanism.

Safran, Nadav. *The United States and Israel.* Cambridge, Mass.: Harvard University Press, 1963.

Schechtman, Joseph B. *The Arab Refugee Problem.* Philosophical Library, New York: 1952. More favorably disposed to Israelis than Arabs.

———. *Rebel and Statesman—Early Years.* New York: Thomas Yoseloff, 1956. A biography of Vladimir Jabotinsky, founder of the Revisionist movement among the Jews in Palestine.

Schleifer, Abdullah. *The Fall of Jerusalem.* New York: Monthly Review Press, 1972. Describes the capture of Jerusalem in 1967 and shows how this was the main prize, along with the West Bank, sought by the Israelis in 1967.

Schmidt, Dana Adams. *Armageddon in the Middle East.* New York: John Day, 1974. An account of the Arab-Israeli conflict from the beginning to the October 1973 war. Also describes the whole area, country by country, showing how the conflict affects each.

Schwarz, Walter. *The Arabs in Israel.* London: Faber and Faber, 1960. Contends that Israel has not dealt fairly with the Arabs in her midst.

Segre, V. D. *Israel: A Society in Transition.* London: Oxford University Press, 1971. A sociological survey of Israel's development.

Selzer, Michael. *The Wineskin and the Wizard.* New York: Macmillan, 1970. A profound study of what it means to be a Jew, and an explanation of the Jewish mission and its relation to the State of Israel.

Sharabi, Hisham. *Palestine and Israel: The Lethal Dilemma.* New York: Pegasus, 1969. An incisive analysis of Arab psychology and the Palestinian militant perspective.

Sicron, Moshe. *Immigration to Israel, 1948–1953.* Jerusalem: Falk Project for Economic Research in Israel, 1957. A study of the effects of immigration on Israel's economy.

Spiro, Melford E. *Kibbutz: Venture in Utopia.* Cambridge, Mass.: Harvard University Press, 1956. An intimate study of a kibbutz.

Vlavianos, Basil J., and Feliks Gross (eds.). *Struggle for Tomorrow: Modern Political Ideologies of the Jewish People.* New York: Arts, 1954. A listing and description of the ideology of the political parties in Israel.

Weingrod, Alex. *Reluctant Pioneers: Village Development in Israel.* Ithaca, N.Y.: Cornell University Press, 1966. A study of a settlement of Moroccan immigrants in the Negev.

Wilson, Evan M. *Jerusalem: Key to Peace.* Washington, D.C.: Middle East Institute, 1970. An account of the city from 1945 to 1967 by the American consul general in Jerusalem from 1964 to 1967.

Chapter 44

The Advent of the Egyptian Republic

Anglo-Egyptian Affairs

The murder of Ahmad Maher in 1945 raised Mahmud al-Nukrashi, second in the Saadist party, to the prime ministership and highlighted the long-standing questions that clouded the relations of Egypt and Great Britain. Having declared war against Germany, Egypt entered the United Nations as a charter member. There, she confronted Great Britain with the allegation that provisions of the Anglo-Egyptian treaty of 1936 infringed upon Egyptian sovereign rights beyond a point tolerable for an independent state.

When Attlee replaced Churchill, Egyptians believed that an enlightened and generous British government had come to power and that the moment was propitious for a thorough renovation of relations with England. Nukrashi asked England for a reexamination of the treaty, but did not urge his demands in the face of British preoccupation with Soviet pressure upon Azerbayjan and the Turkish straits. The Wafd, in opposition, along with the fascist Young Egypt, the Muslim Brotherhood, communists, and nationalist student groups, rioted in February 1946, protesting Nukrashi's supineness toward the British, and forcing his resignation. Faruk appointed to the prime ministership Ismail Sidki, who permitted some demonstrations as salutary but clamped down sternly when they seemed to get out of hand.

Negotiations with the British were now a political necessity. Sidki formed a team to discuss revision of the 1936 treaty. The Wafd refused to participate unless Nahas Pasha was designated chairman of the delegation, and this Sidki could hardly accept. Through the summer the debate centered on three issues: evacuation, joint defense, and the Sudan. Despite good will and an earnest desire for a trustworthy accord on each side, basic desiderata kept the two parties poles apart. Egypt held that the British military occupation must end everywhere in Egypt and that foreign troops must leave. If war broke out or if Egypt felt threatened by war, she would call upon England to come to her aid. With respect to the third issue, the unity of Egypt and the Sudan under the Egyptian crown must be recognized. Attlee confirmed that Britain was willing to withdraw her forces from Egypt after ratification of an alliance specifying terms for the return of troops and use of bases in Egypt. But Soviet demarches against Iran, Turkey, and Greece led London to fear for the safety of the Suez Canal. Churchill, in opposition, put his finger on the sensitive spot when he warned that if Britain withdrew Egypt would surely refuse permission for British troops to reenter the Suez Canal zone, even in time of danger.

Nonetheless, there might have been a solution had not statements about the future of the Sudan provoked a complete breakdown of the discussions. Agreement was reached that the British would leave Cairo, Alexandria, and the Delta in 1947, and the canal zone in 1949, and that the reentry of British troops would become operative if aggression were committed against Egypt or one of her immediate neighbors. If some other Middle Eastern state were the victim of an aggression, discussions would be mandatory. Agreement on the Sudan left the rule as established in 1899, but mentioned "unity between the Sudan and Egypt under the common Crown of Egypt." Sidki claimed success in achieving the desired union, whereas Bevin confided to his opponents in parliament that the *status quo* remained and assured the Sudanese that no step would be taken to prejudice their desire for independence. Sidki promptly resigned, and treaty revision reached a stalemate. Nukrashi returned to office and took the dispute to the Security Council of the U.N. At Lake Success in 1947 no proposals could obtain sufficient votes to pass. The British refused to budge on the Sudan, stating bluntly that they did not intend to appease Egypt by compromising the right of the Sudanese for self-determination. The Egyptians could not give up their contention with respect to the unity and oneness of the people of the Nile Valley. Furthermore, since British troops had departed from Cairo and Alexandria, part of the Egyptian protest no longer pertained.

Egypt and the Sudan
The future of the Sudan loomed large in the minds of Egyptians. The water of the Nile passed through the Sudan, and the possibility of dams and water diversion frightened Egypt. The Sudan was underpopulated and contained vast areas where the expanding population of Egypt might earn a livelihood. Moreover, cotton culture in the Sudan was considered an unnecessary and threatening competition for the cotton of Egypt. In view of these factors Egypt desired to control the Sudan and force the Sudanese economy into a role complementary to her own. To foster such a development, Egypt at every opportunity mouthed the cliché: the unity of the Nile Valley and her peoples.

Another consideration for Egypt was the utilization of the Nile for electric power and wider irrigation. Egypt's swelling population presented an awesome and relentless specter to her politicians. Industrialization required power, which was available if the Nile could be harnessed. Bids for the development of hydroelectric generating stations at the old Aswan Dam were entertained in 1947. Fertilizer plants to produce more than half of the nitrates so vital for Egyptian high-yield agriculture were specified; and a steel mill to exploit the high iron content of hematite ore deposits in the Aswan vicinity was contemplated. The foundation stone of the Aswan hydroelectric plant was laid in 1948, and contracts for machinery were awarded to a number of European firms. Work progressed slowly, and in 1952 completion of the project was still estimated to be five years away. Other projects for increasing the water supply were advanced. Discussions were held to consider a dam at Marawi, and it was agreed that the Sudan might raise by one meter her dam at Sennar.

The Palestine War

Soon after Prime Minister Nukrashi returned from his futile attempt at the U.N., the partition of Palestine and war against Israel engulfed Egypt and dissipated the resources of the nation. Having had an active hand in the creation of the Arab League and aspiring to dominant leadership among Arab states, Egypt sent two forces into Palestine in May 1948. One advanced through Gaza along the coast; the other pushed inland to Bethlehem and the outskirts of Jerusalem. In October the Egyptian forces suffered several reverses from Israeli surprise attacks in the Negev, which left the Egyptians discredited. Egypt signed the armistice in February 1949, leaving her in possession of the narrow Gaza strip and recognizing the demilitarization of the al-Awja area on the Sinai frontier. The armistice was a humiliation for the leader of the Arab League and an experience the soldiers would not soon forgive the politicians in Cairo, whom they were sure were responsible for the defeat. Over 200,000 refugees were huddled in the narrow, barren Gaza strip, solemn testimony of the defeat of the Arabs and a vexatious problem for Egypt.

The Muslim Brotherhood

The inflamed nationalism, rampant during the Palestine War, provided the perfect climate for the further growth of *al-Ikhwan al-Muslimin* (the Muslim Brotherhood). Founded in 1929 by Hasan al-Banna, then a youthful teacher in Ismailia in the Suez Canal zone, the Muslim Brotherhood grew under the founder's fiery oratory and positive approach to a personal and social religion. He exhorted his followers to return to the Islam of the Prophet, which meant an acceptance of the Koran as divine revelation and the law of society. He desired to re-create Egypt, as well as other Muslim lands, as an Islamic theocracy and to thwart the trend toward a secular state. But the true strength of the Muslim Brotherhood lay not so much in its ideology as in the energy, devotion, fanaticism, ruthlessness, and singleness of purpose of the leaders and in the tightness of its organization.

In its earlier years the Muslim Brotherhood maintained an active program of social welfare and agricultural cooperatives, but in later years it dedicated its workers in a militant spirit reminiscent of fascism. Its goal became the remaking of society into a manifestation of Hasan al-Banna's mystical concept of early Islamic life. No compromise from the "right way" could be tolerated. In the Palestine war the fearlessness of Brotherhood units at the front occasioned many heroic acts, which, however, in no way changed the outcome of the war. Reprisals, pressure, assassination, and armed gangs gave the Muslim Brotherhood power, and its actions attracted the youth who yearned for a positive course to follow.

The Egyptian government found the Muslim Brotherhood a serious threat and took punitive measures against it. In 1946 fifty-seven members were arrested in Alexandria; in 1948, after the murder of the chief of police, thirty-one were arrested in Cairo, and Prime Minister Nukrashi ordered the Brotherhood dissolved. A few days later Nukrashi was assassinated by one of the Brethren. In 1949, when Hasan al-Banna was murdered, the government took no serious steps to ascertain his assailants. In 1951 permission was given to reactivate the Brotherhood on condition that its semimilitary activities be discontinued. Hasan al-Hudaibi, elected supreme guide in 1951, did not have the unrelenting zeal of al-Banna, and the movement appeared to lose its drive and spirit.

Postwar Economy

Postwar Egypt found herself in a curious economic situation. Price levels were still high, employment full, and commodities scarce. But over £E450 million in funds loaned to Britain during the war were held in blocked sterling assets in London. For the first time in the memory of man Egypt became a creditor state—and almost overnight. Egypt clamored for machinery, machine tools, industrial and capital goods, and consumer articles. Bankrupt Great Britain could only allow a few purchases and promise the rest in the future. Formal negotiations were opened in 1947 over the balances, and a schedule for the release of old funds was established. By 1950 the balance had been reduced to £E270 million, with plans to wipe out the balance by 1961.

But sterling balances only spotlighted the economic needs of Egypt. Schools, health facilities, industry, fertilizers, and better markets for her cotton, arms, and communications were required in an increasing volume. Land reform to break up the concentration of arable acreage in the hands of a few and revision of the tax structure to lighten the inordinate tax burden on commerce and industry and to increase taxes on income and land became a necessity. No country in the Arab Middle East was better prepared to accomplish these changes than Egypt. She had a progressive society, with an educated group that understood the needs and saw many of the ways in which they could be met. But political power remained in the hands of those who preferred to check the inevitable social and economic revolution in Egypt.

Faruk and Politics

The corruptness and vagaries of King Faruk and his palace entourage made politics unstable in Egypt. With immense wealth in land at his disposal, his political influence was considerable; no one could foretell what might capture his fancy. For a time he even subsidized Hasan al-Banna and the Muslim Brotherhood. His control of appointments, government contracts, policies of all kinds, land sales, and every aspect of society smothered any nascent political responsibility or democratic action and tended to corrupt wealthy landowners, ambitious journalists, lawyers, and politicians. Public morals were at a low ebb.

Following the assassination of Nukrashi, the question of the withdrawal of British troops from the Suez Canal zone dominated the national scene. Since the British strongly intimated that a secure settlement could not be achieved unless Egyptian leaders had the solid support of the Egyptian nation, a free election that Wafdists would not boycott was a necessity. Although charges of corruption and cooperation with the British during the war were leveled at Nahas Pasha, the elections held in January 1950 demonstrated Wafd supremacy and Nahas' hold upon Egypt. Returns for the chamber of deputies showed: 228 Wafdists, 28 Saadists, and 26 Liberal Constitutionalists. Nahas Pasha assumed the prime ministership again and formed a Wafdist cabinet that remained in power until the riots of January 1952.

Before considering developments under Nahas Pasha's new administration, one solid accomplishment in 1949, the termination of the mixed courts, should be mentioned. Mixed courts were established in 1876 to handle cases involving foreigners, and their demise had been fixed by the 1937 treaty of Montreux. The transfer of cases and jurisdiction to Egyptian courts occasioned no difficulties, mainly because of the excellence of Egyptian courts, the availability of Egyptians who had been sitting as judges in the mixed courts, and the admission of most of their lawyers to the Egyptian bar. Egypt celebrated their ending, but paid tribute to the great public service rendered over the years by the mixed courts and openly recognized the "high tradition of judicial administration" left to Egypt as an invaluable legacy. However, these courts had become an anachronism, and their passing removed another vestige of the hated imperialism of the West.

Suez Canal Zone

Reestablishment of a Wafdist party government under Nahas Pasha immediately brought the Suez Canal and its British control into prominence. In part, the Suez Canal Company had agreed to terms regarding companies engaged in business in Egypt. The Suez Canal Company employed Egyptians for 80 percent of the technical positions and 90 percent of the administrative jobs. The number of Egyptian directors of the company was raised from two to seven out of a total membership of thirty-two. And 7 percent of the company's profits, not to be less than £E350,000 annually, were paid to Egypt. But foreign troops in the canal zone still caused friction. After a few conversations with the British, Nahas Pasha requested them to leave the Sudan and the Suez Canal zone, but formal talks were not initiated until 1951.

By October 1950 pressure within Egypt and the intractability of the British impelled Nahas, after innumerable warnings, to abrogate unilaterally the Anglo-Egyptian treaty of 1936 and the Anglo-Egyptian agreements of 1899 establishing the condominium over the Sudan. This drastic declaration brought forth within five days the British suggestion and invitation that Egypt become one of the founders, along with England, France, Turkey, and the United States, of a Middle East defense command similar in scope to the North Atlantic Treaty Organization. Britain announced she was ready, if Egypt would form such a command, to abandon the Anglo-Egyptian treaty of 1936 and her rights therein to military establishments and troop bases in the Suez Canal zone.

Demonstrations, riots, and limited military engagements broke out at several points in the canal zone. Egypt protested that a Middle East defense command could not be accepted, since it would inevitably mean the presence of foreign troops in Egypt. Britain, on her part, stated frankly that troops and officials would remain in the Sudan and in the Suez Canal zone regardless of Egypt's unilateral denunciation of her international commitments. Incidents became more frequent, and on January 25, 1952, an engagement at Ismailia involved 1,500 British troops. More than forty Egyptians were killed.

Riots and Revolution

The following day, "Black Saturday," Cairo exploded with riots and demonstrations against the British, foreigners, and authority. Damage ran into the tens of millions of pounds; Shepheard's Hotel was destroyed; and subversive elements tried to overturn the government. Martial law was declared, and King Faruk replaced Nahas Pasha with Ali Maher Pasha, directing him to maintain security and order. Ahmad Husayn, the leader of Young Egypt *(Misr al-Fatah)*, which had turned from its fascism of the 1930s to socialism, was arrested for plotting the demonstrations and abetting the riots.

After Black Saturday the situation remained tense. Ali Maher notified fifteen nations that his government regretted the losses and injuries sustained by their nationals, and a £E5 million fund was created to cover damages to shops and property. He transferred the military-training programs for volunteers in the Muslim Brotherhood and Young Egypt to the ministries of war and navy. But his actions did not solve the immediate problems and were considered only half measures. In March another took his place; Parliament was suspended for thirty days, and new elections were postponed. Conversations with the British over the Sudan and the canal zone were abandoned when the British declared they would recognize the king of Egypt as king of the Sudan only if the Sudanese likewise recognized him as their king. On July 23 the government was overthrown by an army coup, ostensibly led by Major General Muhammad Nagib.

In a broadcast to the nation General Nagib attacked corruption and bribery as the "main reason for our failure in the Palestine war; they are the main reason for troubles in Egypt's political and economic life." He went on to say that his group of officers sincerely believed that steps "were necessary to inspire the Egyptians with a new spirit and determination to go ahead and work toward fulfilling Egypt's national aspirations." These few words, whether his own or prepared for him, contained the significant principles of the revolution. King Faruk was forced to abdicate on July 26, 1952, in favor of his infant son, Prince Ahmad Fuad.

The army had always refused to shoulder the blame for the defeat in Palestine, contending that the war had been lost in Cairo. When Cairo tried to make the army the scapegoat, the officers revolted, adopting the popular theme that the economy and political life of the state had to be cleansed thoroughly before Egypt could become a modern state or hope to stand up against Israel. Revolution would lead to a full reformation of the state. Ali Maher was invited to form a civilian cabinet; all civilian titles were revoked; secret political-police sections of the royal and provincial governments were abolished; political prisoners were released; corrupt officials were arrested; censorship of the press was terminated; elections for parliament were announced for February 1953; and a land reform program drawn up by army leaders was submitted to the prime minister.

That measures for land reform came from army sources indicated that the Revolutionary Command Council (RCC), about which little was heard in the first weeks of the revolution, played a powerful role in the events of the day. The RCC assumed that the disproportionate size of land holdings by a few was the primary cause of the abject poverty of the masses. The RCC was comprised of less than a score of officers from various branches of the services. Each officer of the council held the support of other officers, and thus the RCC acted as the governing body of the revolution. The most powerful leader of the RCC was Lt. Colonel Gamal Abd al-Nasser. General Nagib did not belong originally to the RCC but was picked by the officers to serve as their "front man." Both the right wing (Muslim Brotherhood) and left wing (Communists, Socialists, and the renovated Young Egypt group of Ahmad Husayn) had their supporters among the officers and voices in the RCC.

In September 1952 Ali Maher resigned as prime minister and Nagib took over, at the same time arresting fifty "former associates" of ex-King Faruk. The new cabinet decreed that all political parties be purged of corrupt leaders and reorganized within a month. At first the Wafd refused to comply, but later arranged to do so by elevating Nahas to honorary president. Four hundred fifty army officers were dismissed, and a steady housecleaning began in the various ministries and bureaus of the government. Raids were made on homes of "hostile elements" in Cairo and Alexandria, and quantities of documents to use in prosecuting officials for inefficiency or malfeasance were carried off. The rector of al-Azhar University was replaced by a theologian friendly to the revolution. In November Nagib was voted dictatorial powers until January 1953; his powers were then extended another six months.

In September 1952 the cabinet decreed a new agrarian law, restricting landownership to 200 acres and stating that the government over the ensuing five years would expropriate excess lands, beginning with the largest estates. Compensation in the form of 3 percent thirty-year government bonds would be at the rate of ten times the rental value of the land. Until lands were seized by the government, owners would be taxed at a rate of five times their normal rates, although owners might sell lands in five-acre lots to farmers owning less than ten acres. Land taken by the government was to be sold in two- to five-acre tracts to farmers owning less than five acres. The price was fixed at 15 percent above the compensation price and was to be paid over a thirty-year period at 3 percent interest.

The Republic of Egypt

It soon became obvious that the RCC had no special plans or program outlined when the revolution began. The RCC was publicly noticed first in 1950, when parliament censured its existence. Acting before King Faruk destroyed it, the RCC believed that if it "turned the rascals out" all of Egypt's troubles would be ended and the whole nation would come forward and usher in a glorious regime for a better Egypt. Nasser wrote in his account of the revolution that the RCC soon learned, after waiting briefly for the Egyptian people to unite in such a task, that vigorous leadership was necessary to prevent chaos and accomplish its dream. The RCC revolution in Egypt was three revolutions in one: a "French Revolution," to get rid of a king and form a republic; an "American Revolution," to drive out the British; and a "Kemal Atatürk Revolution," to transform and regenerate the social and economic facets of an old civilization. For purposes of clarity and to avoid a chronological discussion of events on almost a day-to-day basis, each revolution will be examined singly. Yet the interplay of the revolutions and the basic complexity of the situation should never be overlooked in assessing the forces at work in Egypt in the period beginning in 1952.

Once the power of the army was established by the coup d'état, even though it worked through a civilian government, the influence and authority of the king vanished. The deposing and exile of King Faruk were simple matters of informing him that he had to go. Six weeks later army officers discovered that politicians were relatively unconcerned about the revolution, and Nagib became prime minister. A national committee suggested the formation of a republic, which was declared on June 18, 1953. Nagib was acclaimed president and prime minister, and Nasser became deputy prime minister and minister of the interior of the parliamentary Egyptian republic.

The RCC announced that it would rule for a transitional three-year period, at the end of which parliamentary government would be established. In Cairo and Alexandria a large group of politically conscious citizens, conditioned by years of national agitation, were apprehensive of military dictatorships. They accepted the need for army action to rid the country of Faruk, but feared that soldiers would be loath to step aside once they learned to enjoy political power.

Nagib and Nasser

Nagib and Nasser heeded these susceptibilities. The numerous problems pressing for a solution afforded displaced politicians a fine opportunity for criticism. The Muslim Brotherhood was a powerful group capable of organizing "spontaneous" demonstrations, and it frequently made common cause with communists, socialists, fascists, and Wafdists. Communists were arrested from time to time, and new parties were created to evade the law requiring old parties to reorganize their leadership. The government instituted a new revolutionary tribunal to try enemies of the state and particularly to crack down on an alliance formed by communists, Wafdists, Saadists, and confederates of ex-King Faruk. Nahas, his wife, a former Saadist prime minister, the former chief of the royal cabinet, and others were arraigned before the tribunal and sentenced to long prison terms.

Extremists, however, did not surrender so easily. In January 1954 serious fighting broke out between a group of the Muslim Brotherhood and the Liberation Rally, the party organization sponsored by the RCC. A six-day state of emergency was declared, the Muslim Brotherhood was dissolved, and seventy-eight of the members, including Hasan al-Hudaibi, were arrested. More communists were jailed. On February 25, 1954, the first showdown occurred between Nagib and Nasser. It appeared that Nagib was willing to make peace with the Brotherhood and some of the old political groupings, proceed immediately with the calling of parliamentary elections, and reinstitute civilian government. Nasser and his followers believed that such a course would surely return the old crowd to power, defeat the revolution, and hurry the social and economic principles of the new order to an early grave.

Nasser, for the RCC, announced that Nagib had "resigned" from the presidency and the prime ministership "three days ago" and was confined to his house. Nasser became prime minister; but this development did not please the socialists, the Muslim Brotherhood, the Wafd, or any of the extreme political forces in Egypt. On February 27 Major Khalid Muhi al-Din, an avowed socialist, member of the RCC, and commander of the tank corps, appeared before Nasser and demanded that Nagib be reinstated. When Nasser ordered his arrest, the major coolly remarked that his officers at the tank park were at that moment preparing to launch an assault upon the RCC headquarters if their major was not back in their midst with an affirmative response within two hours.

Nasser gave in when an officer brought word that Muhi al-Din was not joking. The tanks were manned, the motors were running, and the ammunition was in place. Nagib returned to the presidency, but Nasser remained as prime minister. Sentiment for a civilian government was very strong, even in the army. Students demonstrated against the military regime; and the Egyptian bar, in a memorandum signed by one hundred leading Egyptian lawyers, asked for a return to civil rule. Nagib and Nasser called in Ali Maher, who after proper consultation announced on March 4, 1954, that a constituent assembly to which the military regime would turn over its authority would be called within three months. Nagib became prime minister again and chief of the RCC, which declared that power would be transferred to a civilian government on July 23, 1954. Nahas, leaders of the Muslim Brotherhood, and other politicians were released from arrest.

At the end of March the RCC threatened to resign, and Nasser and Major Salah Salim absented themselves from RCC meetings. The pressure was on, and Nasser emerged victorious. It was announced that the RCC would not relinquish its power and that elections would not be held until 1956, when the three-year transitional period terminated. In April, after Major Muhi al-Din went to Paris "on business for the RCC," Nasser averred that Nagib had become the tool of dishonest politicians of the old regime. Nasser again became prime minister; he brought eight members of the RCC into the cabinet. In June nine officers of the tank corps were sentenced to fifteen-year prison terms; in September five leaders of the Muslim Brotherhood were stripped of their Egyptian citizenship.

In October 1954, following the signing of the agreement with the British on the evacuation of the Suez Canal zone, Nasser narrowly missed being assassinated by a member of the Muslim Brotherhood. The treaty was not tough enough for them. An angry mob immediately burned the Brotherhood headquarters, and 400 Brethren, including Hasan al-Hudaibi, were arrested. President Nagib was relieved of his office and placed under house arrest; it was charged that he had cooperated with the Muslim Brotherhood and with communists in the attempt to overthrow Nasser and the RCC. A list of 133 "wanted" members of the Muslim Brotherhood was published, as the faculty at al-Azhar University denounced religious terrorists. Hasan al-Hudaibi and others went on trial; six were hanged for complicity in the attempt on Nasser's life.

Shortly thereafter Nasser became acting president. He declared that parliamentary government would be restored as promised in 1956. When that time came Nasser introduced a draft constitution, which was submitted to a national plebiscite. Following its approval, the national assembly met and elected a president as the constitution provided. The public then voted its approval of the president, also as outlined in the constitution. These events transpired without any hitches; President Gamal Abd al-Nasser was duly elected and inaugurated as head of the Islamic Arab Republic of Egypt. The constitution contained a full bill of rights and obligations for the individual and guaranteed the economic, physical, legal, and moral welfare of Egyptian citizens. It provided for a national assembly, elected for a term of five years, and a president, who could dissolve the assembly, propose, veto, and promulgate laws, and appoint and dismiss civil, diplomatic, and military officials.

The transition from military rule to constitutional government appeared complete. However, the constitution of 1956 was drawn to place extraordinary power in the hands of the president. Thus, the change altered Nasser's title, but not his power. On the surface the wishes of a large segment of the populace of Cairo and Alexandria for civilian constitutional government were met. The popularity of Nasser in his heroic acts of the summer of 1956 belied, at least for some time, doubts regarding the success and permanence of the transition.

The Sudan and Suez

The second aspect of the Egyptian revolution was, as one American observer aptly phrased it, "Turning out the Redcoats." It had two phases: freeing the Sudan, and obtaining full sovereignty over the canal zone. Prime Minister Nagib was especially favored to accomplish the former. His mother was Sudanese; no one dared accuse him of being negligent in pressing Egyptian interests in the Sudan. In 1952 Nagib held conversations with various Sudanese leaders and signed an agreement approving the establishment of self-government in the Sudan. Great Britain subscribed in principle to Nagib's arrangement, and on February 12, 1953, an Anglo-Egyptian agreement was entered into in Cairo ending the condominium of 1899. Although Nagib gave the Sudan the opportunity of choosing not to become federated with Egypt, the minister of national guidance, Major Salah Salim, included Sudanese affairs in his responsibility and by several excursions to Khartoum endeavored to develop a course advantageous to Cairo.

The signing of this Anglo-Egyptian agreement served as a step in solving Suez difficulties. Negotiations with the British were reopened in April but were broken off summarily, again over conditions upon which British and Allied troops might return. After Nagib returned from a pilgrimage to Mecca, a sixth meeting was held and agreement was reached on four points: an Egyptian would command the bases in the canal zone; his deputy, a technical adviser, would be a Britisher and would receive orders from London as well as from the commander; 4,000 British technicians would remain until Egyptians were trained to take over; and the British garrison would depart from the zone eighteen months after full agreement was ratified.

In July negotiations moved to high-level discussions in Cairo. President Eisenhower sent a letter to President Nagib stating that "simultaneously" with the signing of an Anglo-Egyptian accord on the Suez Canal zone the United States would enter into "firm agreements" with Egypt for economic assistance to strengthen the Egyptian armed forces. An agreement in principle was made on July 27, 1954, although the formal arrangement was not signed until October. There were five main points: British troops would be withdrawn by June 18, 1956; the Anglo-Egyptian treaty of 1936 was abrogated; Britain or her allies would be afforded facilities for the entry of troops into Egypt in case of an attack upon Arab League states or Turkey; each party pledged to uphold the Constantinople Convention of 1888 guaranteeing freedom of navigation of the canal; and the duration of the agreement would be seven years. The American role in bringing a settlement between Cairo and London was generally recognized, and three weeks after the signing of the formal Suez documents Egypt and the United States entered into an arrangement whereby Egypt would receive a grant of $40 million for the modernization of her economy. The United States also consented to consider proposals concerning construction of a high dam at Aswan, an offer which started quite a different chain of events.

Arms for Egypt

When Egypt entered into the Suez agreement with England, Nasser expected to arm and operate the military establishments in the zone. Modern military machines, however, were so costly that only a nation with a large heavy-industrial capacity could afford the matériel unless purchases could be made at only a fraction of the real cost. Nasser undoubtedly recognized this, for Egyptian officials in conversations in Washington revealed that Eisenhower's letter was interpreted as the prelude to an arrangement between the United States and Egypt similar in character and scope to the American program in Turkey, where nearly $1 billion had already been spent by the American government.

Requests for arms aid, specific and general, were forwarded to Washington. But no action was taken. Prior to the settlement over the Suez Canal zone the United States had granted specific sums for land reclamation and small irrigation projects; after the signing of the agreement an offer of $40 million was made for improving the general economy. But little was forthcoming for the army; Israel and her American friends objected strenuously. Moreover, Nasser was unable for internal political reasons to enter into agreements such as Turkey had with the United States.

Receiving little military aid from the West, Nasser turned to the Soviet bloc. Because of the success of Israeli raids along the frontier, Egypt felt insecure. Moreover, Nasser's power rested on army officers who demanded first-rate equipment. If he could not satisfy them, they would turn to someone else who would promise to get them arms. Unless Egypt had arms of sufficient quantity and quality she could not expect the powers to believe that she could operate the bases along the canal. The solution: Egypt would control and man the defenses of the zone; the powers would furnish the money and matériel.

Nasser announced on September 27, 1955, that an arrangement had been concluded with Czechoslovakia to obtain arms in exchange for cotton. (Later he admitted that the agreement was with the U.S.S.R.) The first deliveries came from Europe and the Far East and were unloaded in October at Alexandria and Suez. Egyptian and neighboring Arab nationalists rejoiced over the news, since they interpreted the turn of events to mean that they were more independent of the Western imperialist powers and could at their own convenience attack Israel, the satellite of those same powers.

Nasser Seeks to Dominate the Middle East

Peace between Israel and Egypt remained unattainable under Nagib and Nasser, as it had under their immediate predecessors. The pattern of infiltrations, border raids, reprisals, bombings, protests, threats, accusations, and denunciations was unchanged. Israeli boats and ships of other nations laden with cargo for Israel were denied passage through the canal; Egypt asserted that any goods that would aid an enemy could legally be denied transit through the canal insofar as it was a part of Egyptian territory.

The most serious incident occurred on the night of February 28, 1955, when Israelis at half-battalion strength fell upon Egyptian positions near the outskirts of Gaza, killing thirty-eight and wounding thirty-one. The attack had the effect of forcing Nasser to obtain arms somewhere, regardless of price or strings. This act above all others drove Egypt to the Soviet arms deal.

With regard to the other states of the Middle East Nagib and Nasser looked upon themselves as natural leaders and sought to augment the dominant role of Egypt. Egypt had the largest population and, with the exception of Lebanon, was by far the most Westernized Arab state. Her newspapers, movies, radio, universities, industry, and commerce outstripped those in other Arab countries. Naturally, Arabs turned to Nasser for leadership. "Free Officer" or "RCC" groups sprang up in Syria and Jordan, and Nasser gave their leaders encouragement and assistance.

With the Arab League's headquarters and staff located in Cairo and most of its council meetings held there, the natural tendency of Arab political leaders to gravitate to Egypt encouraged Nasser's aggressive stand. The Cairo newspapers and radio exercised a powerful influence throughout the Arabic-speaking world. Nationalism, sponsored and disseminated by those media, always was Arab in scope, rarely Egyptian. In fact, Egyptian nationalism and Arab nationalism were equated; if a Syrian or an Iraqi national proposed a course of action in the interests of his own nation that might run contrary to the interests of Egypt, he was immediately branded, even in his own country, as opposed to Arab national interests.

Nasser and the Arab League looked with sympathy upon the actions and aspirations of Arab nationalists in Morocco, Algeria, and Tunisia, and funds were collected and sent to help them achieve their goals. In the Sudan, once the Sudanese attained self-government and release from Great Britain, the experience of freedom was so sweet they hesitated to exchange it for Egyptian control. Political parties favorable to federation with Egypt cooled their ardor, and political leaders enjoyed the prerogatives of cabinet offices. In 1955 no agreement was reached over the division or use of Nile water for power and irrigation, and in the program concerning the construction of the high dam at Aswan no discussions were undertaken over the creation of the lake that would inundate a considerable area in the Sudan.

Nasser's most caustic wrath was reserved for Nuri al-Said, his archenemy and the architect of the Baghdad Pact. More than rivalry between Nuri and Nasser was involved. It was a rivalry between Iraq and Egypt for leadership in the Arab world—a competition extending back through history to medieval and early Muslim times and into antiquity. The Middle East had become more power conscious than ever before, as all looked with appreciation and understanding to what the American aid program was accomplishing in Turkey. Nasser evidently expected an "Eisenhower-Dulles Doctrine" for Egypt as a reward for signing the treaty with the British in 1954, a treaty which he entered into at great personal risk. His enemies were ready to murder him for signing any treaty with Britain, and they referred to him scathingly as Gamal Abd al-Dulles. Suddenly he feared the tables were turned. Nuri al-Said had aligned with Turkey and the West, and the military aid program would strengthen an Iraq already witnessing national exhilaration from development programs and oil royalties. Cairo broadcasts vilified Nuri as a British agent and invited Iraqis to rejoin the Arab nation, which of course meant under Egyptian leadership.

Egyptian Affairs

Many Egyptian leaders under Nagib and Nasser contemplated establishing a secular government, but discovered that they had to proceed cautiously toward such a goal because of the power of the Muslim Brotherhood. Individuals among them spoke privately of the need for a Muslim reformation, and after the curtailment of the Muslim Brotherhood in 1954 a more open policy was pursued. Muslim and non-Muslim religious courts in Egypt were abolished in 1956, and cases pending in those courts and all others of similar nature were heard in secular courts. The decree did not repudiate Sacred Law, but henceforth precepts of Sacred Law were to be interpreted by civil judges.

The revolution also brought benefits in social welfare for the masses. A minimum wage for agricultural workers was set, and relief programs for the destitute were inaugurated. Village schools were built, teacher training extended, health services widened, and many projects for agricultural improvement instituted. In industrial areas social workers were employed to begin the monumental task of aiding new factory workers to make the adjustment from village life to the strange ways of an urban center.

When Nagib announced his coup d'état, he blamed corruption and bribery for the ills that beset Egypt. Inefficient and corrupt officials were dismissed, and a special court was established to try cases of corruption. Much publicity was given to these trials and proceedings, mainly to demonstrate the sincerity and fervor of the revolution and to reduce the natural tendency toward corrupt governmental practices.

The population in Egypt in 1956 numbered about 22 million and was increasing by 500,000 every year. Without a parallel increase in economic output the standard of living remained so low as to constitute a political danger. Thus, the most pressing problems for Nasser were economic. The marketing and world price of cotton, the great cash crop of Egypt, had concerned every Egyptian government since the end of World War II. In 1948 when cotton prices were high, Egypt bartered 38,000 tons of cotton for 211,000 tons of Russian wheat. The Egyptian government supported the cotton market at levels frequently above world prices and thus resorted to the expedient of exchanging cotton for foodstuffs, which were likewise priced above the world market. Rather than grow wheat and other edible

crops which peasants might surreptitiously eat absentee landlords preferred to produce cotton, control its marketing, and be easily assured of full
delivery of the crops on the part of the peasants.

So eager on the question of land distribution were the new leaders that
after the departure of King Faruk they rushed forth with land reform
measures. Implementation, however, progressed slowly; in four years less
than 200,000 acres were appropriated by the government and put into the
hands of the peasants. Landowner opposition and the likelihood of reduced
production on broken estates deterred a government already hard pressed
by the realities of politics and economics.

In 1953 a five-year development plan was announced. A newly created
permanent national resources development board called for $60 million to
irrigate 37,000 acres of new land and distribute better wheat and hybrid
corn seeds. The greatest plan of all, of course, was the great dam at Aswan,
which would take years to construct, cost hundreds of millions of pounds,
and would irrigate approximately two million acres. It was obvious, however, that the economic situation in Egypt could not wait for the completion of such a project.

Egypt needed power for industry, irrigation pumps, and modern machinery. The discovery of oil in commercial quantities had long been hoped
for in Egypt, and in 1954 a thirty-year concession was granted for the
exploitation of oil in the western desert to the Coronada Petroleum Corporation of New York, which agreed to spend a minimum of $8 million for
exploration within six years. Another concession was awarded to the Egyptian Oil Exploration Company, a subsidiary of the Cities Service Company
of New York. Oil was found in 1955 in the Sinai Peninsula, where the
National Petroleum Company brought in a well for which it claimed a
production of 3,000 barrels a day. It was hoped that wider and continued
exploration would locate enough oil to satisfy Egyptian needs.

Reforms, social measures, expanded government services, strengthening
of the army, and irrigation and hydroelectric programs increased the size
of annual budgets, even when longer-range capital-improvement projects
were excluded. Income from taxes and other sources, though not fully
published, obviously fell behind spending. Nasser resorted to loans rather
than to increased tax collections. Finding opposition from the National
Bank of Egypt to extensive borrowing, Nasser issued a decree in 1955
requiring all directors over sixty years of age to be dismissed from the
boards of Egyptian companies. This law was designed to remove from the
bank those opposed to his financial policies. Thereafter the government
borrowed £E300 million to support the cotton market, then bartered some
of the cotton for wheat and arms. Other sums went for various projects and
to commence work at Aswan. Money in circulation jumped by 30 percent.
Inflation appeared, gold balances dropped, and wealthy Egyptians turned
their cash into any goods that could be purchased. By 1956 the weakened
economy of Egypt had become subject to wide fluctuations.

The economic pressures in Egypt, which the old regime largely ignored and which in the absence of any national or moral inspiration brought its downfall, were still present to crowd in upon Nasser and his government. He described himself as a "man in a hurry" and warned that "the longer I take to do things the less time I will have to accomplish them." Many things that Nasser, the RCC, and the dedicated men about them wished to do were long-range affairs requiring twenty or forty years to effect. But the peasants and the poor in the cities would not wait for the better life unless they could have some concrete assurance that it would come; they needed a least a small down payment on it immediately. Also, the old ex-pashas and wealthy landowners, who found their income diminished, the bulk of their lands seized, the cotton market no longer rigged in their favor, their taxes collected, and their names reviled, distrusted the new order as long as they could not see an obvious and irrefutable national good resulting immediately from their discomfiture.

High Dam at Aswan

It behooved Nasser to give an earnest demonstration of the "promised future." Construction of the high dam at Aswan was carefully and gloriously pictured as the rational step to revolutionize the Egyptian standard of living. Two million acres of new land would be made available for cultivation and almost limitless kilowatt hours of electricity generated. Upper Egypt would become industrialized and the population pressure would be relieved. Arable land would increase 30 percent. This would give Egypt a balanced and healthy economy. At a cost of $600, $700, perhaps even $900 million over a period of ten to fifteen years the dam could be built.

The Egyptian economy was too poor to finance the dam itself. A charge of $70 or $80 million a year taken from the living of the people would lower the standards beyond endurance. Furthermore, an estimated $200 million in foreign exchange would be required in the early stages of construction to import the necessary equipment and materials. The United States government admitted an interest in 1954, and the possibility of a loan from the International Bank was investigated.

Talks on these subjects were held in Washington in 1955. The arms deal with the Soviet bloc had already been announced and shipments had begun. These events gave rise to fiery denunciations of the West. Nasser defiantly warned that his acquisition of arms must not lead to Western shipments of arms to Israel. At the same time Egyptians and the Arab world were treated to bitter harangues against the Western powers when the Baghdad Pact was signed and the members invited Jordan to join.

Nasser's government already had trade pacts or barter arrangements with Czechoslovakia, mainland China, East Germany, Hungary, Rumania, and the U.S.S.R. The West looked upon these as economic necessities for Egypt and regarded Nasser's ranting against Great Britain and the United States as bombast for domestic consumption. In spite of these factors, therefore, the United States offered in December 1955 to grant $56 million and Great Britain agreed to release £5 million to Egypt to strengthen her internal economy, on the assumption that work on the high dam would begin. Although the American Congress refused to consider the proposal that the Egyptian grant be made annually for the ensuing ten years, there was an understanding that such a course was more than likely. With the American grant it also became apparent that Egypt's economy would be considered strong enough to warrant a $200 million loan from the International Bank, which approved the Egyptian application in February 1956.

At this juncture Nasser appeared to have been triumphant. He had obtained from the U.S.S.R. the arms his soldiers were demanding and was offered approximately $900 million over a ten-year period to build what every educated Egyptian dreamed of. Egypt stood where Turkey had stood in 1947, and the promise of the future was even brighter.

But Nasser failed to grasp the opportunity. His basic ignorance of the West, his inexperience in politics, economics, and foreign affairs, and the weakness of his advisers led him astray. It was announced that the U.S.S.R. was also offering to finance the building of the high dam at Aswan "with no strings attached." Although the authority for this notice became uncertain, Nasser continued to deliver emotional diatribes against the West, complaining of the humiliating "strings" demanded by the United States; he then consummated new trade pacts with China, Bulgaria, and North Vietnam. To the West it appeared that Nasser was courting the Communist bloc in order to increase the grants from the West. Public discussion of the high dam financing and the pledge of cotton crops to the Soviet bloc in payment for arms created doubts in the minds of Western leaders as to the wisdom of proceeding with the construction. Political and economic conditions in Egypt deteriorated.

On June 18, 1956, the last contingent of British soldiers departed from Suez in accordance with the treaty of 1954. Foreign Minister Shepilov of the U.S.S.R. was the honored guest of the three-day celebration. In his speeches and those of Nasser opprobrium was heaped upon the West; Shepilov declared that the U.S.S.R. was happy to see the end of political and military imperialism and encouraged Nasser to work to remove economic colonialism—the oil companies—from the Arab world.

These attacks by Nasser, and his embrace of the Soviet bloc, paralleled a further worsening of the Egyptian economy. Expenditures continued to exceed income, charges for sustaining the expanding military establishment mounted, and gold balances dropped sharply. The situation in Egypt was growing tense, and Western leaders began to entertain doubts about the ability of Nasser and his close coterie of friends to maintain their authority. In 1956, when the Egyptian ambassador to Washington returned from Cairo with instructions to notify the American government of Egypt's readiness to accept the American offer to build the high dam at Aswan, Secretary of State Dulles first informed the press, then coldly told him on July 19 that times and conditions had changed and that the United States had withdrawn the offer.

Nationalization of the Suez Canal

The manner in which the notice was given advertised the fact that a calculated rebuff was intended, perhaps to downgrade Nasser's reputation as Washington had downgraded Mosaddeq's in 1953. Immediately the attacks upon the West grew more scurrilous. Nasser struck back by nationalizing the Suez Canal Company on July 26, 1956. He had raised great expectations in Egypt about the building of the dam. Without some dramatic move he was lost. The Suez Canal provided the answer. In his declaration on the canal Nasser stated that Egyptian officials had taken over the company offices in Egypt, ordered all employees to stay on the job, asserted that the canal would remain open and would operate as usual, and explained that nationalization would provide Egypt with a $100 million annual profit to use in building the Aswan Dam.

The boldness, excitement, and drama of the action were heady fare for the Arabs and a much-needed tonic for Nasser's prestige. When England and France threatened to use force against Egypt, all the Arab states, as well as the U.S.S.R. and India, rallied to Nasser's support. Workers in Iraq, Kuwayt, Jordan, Syria, and Lebanon pledged to cut the oil pipelines if the West attacked Egypt.

Nationalization of the Suez Canal Company had been contemplated in previous years by other Egyptian governments. At the end of World War II Egypt unsuccessfully offered to buy, with some of her blocked sterling, the canal shares held by Britain. The 1949 agreement guaranteed Egypt £E350,000 annually from the company, or 7 percent of the gross profits, whichever was greater. In 1955, although gross revenues in tolls from the canal operations were nearly $100 million, the figure cited by Nasser, profits were only $31 million; the Egyptian share was $2,170,000.

According to terms of the concession, the ownership of the canal would revert to the Egyptian government in 1968, at which time the government would purchase the assets of the company. The company held in reserve large sums accrued from past profits. In May 1956, upon pressure from Nasser, the company agreed to invest some $60 million of reserves in Egyptian development projects.

The canal had been the subject of the international Constantinople Convention of 1888, in which passage through it was guaranteed in peace and war to all ships. Egypt, however, was held to be the custodian of the canal's security, and Article X stated that the provisions of the convention "shall not interfere" with steps Egypt "might find it necessary to take for security . . . the defense of Egypt and the maintenance of public order." Until 1954 it was recognized that Great Britain was the protector of the canal; since 1948, however, Egypt, using Article X of the convention, had acted to deny passage of the canal to Israeli shipping, and by inaction on this point the powers condoned the Egyptian interference with Israeli use of the canal.

Reaction in the West, especially in England and France, to the nationalization was precipitous. Naval units were moved to the eastern Mediterranean, troops were readied, and paratroopers were rushed to Cyprus. In

London and Paris government leaders pointed out that Nasser by the seizure was assuming a position along the vital artery of world commerce; he
would be able to close the route at his whim and thus subject western
Europe to economic blackmail. The bulk of the oil consumed in western
Europe was Middle Eastern oil, 60 percent of which passed through the
canal. It was charged that Nasser violated international treaties and ignored
the international character of the canal.

The issue resolved itself into four main points. Paramount was the ability
of Egypt at some unforeseen moment to close the canal, raise rates, or deny
entry to ships of a single state and thus jeopardize the security and well-
being of any nation. As Nasser had been able to do that for quite some time,
nationalization of the canal hardly changed the status or the international
conditions of the waterway or its transit. Secondly, genuine concern was felt
in many quarters over the question of whether Egypt could manage the
intricate operations of the canal and maintain its efficiency. Expert opinion,
however, held that Egypt would be able to run the canal with a modicum
of cooperation and good will. A third and very significant factor involved
prestige. It appeared to the Western public that Nasser had, with support
from the Soviet bloc and neutralist India, gained a diplomatic victory. The
fourth and most telling component of nationalization arose from its avowed
purpose of obtaining a munificent income and from the invidious inference
that the canal company had reaped exorbitant profits. In 1955 slightly over
31 percent of the gross revenues showed as profits, a percentage exceedingly high in comparison with most companies. Two-thirds of the profits,
however, were set aside for improvements on the canal. Therefore, unless
Nasser could run the canal more economically than the company and was
willing to forego capital expenditures, profits from the canal would not go
far in building the high dam.

Under nationalization, operation of the canal continued and ships passed
through as usual. Egyptian funds were frozen in England, France, and the
United States, and Egypt permitted British and French companies to pay
tolls for their ships into Suez Canal Company accounts in Paris and London.
Hurriedly, a twenty-four nation conference in London devised a plan
whereby Egypt would own the canal, but an international body in accordance with an international treaty would operate and control it. Although
agreeing to maritime states advising on the operations of the canal, Nasser
politely rejected the proposal and insisted on "the sovereign right of Egypt
to run the canal." Thereupon, England and France applied further pressure
by inducing many British and French canal pilots to quit their jobs, hoping
thereby to prove that Egypt could not run it. Next, the London group, led
by Secretary Dulles, formed a Suez Canal Users' Association (SCUA), which
would employ its own pilots, navigate its own boats, pay for all upkeep of
the canal, and give Egypt a fee for its use. Nasser vehemently declared that
imposition of SCUA would mean war.

As time passed, and the boats were still going through the canal, the
opportunity grew for a reasonable settlement. It was illogical to deny that

Egypt had the sovereign right to nationalize the Suez Canal Company, and no action was being taken in violation of the Constantinople Convention of 1888. Moreover, as Arab opinion cooled, Nasser became less bold. Iraq, Kuwayt, and Saudi Arabia were suspicious of references in his speeches to "Arab oil" as if it belonged to Egypt. They resented the fact that he took this step without conferring with other Arab League states and were apprehensive lest oil production would be curtailed and their royalties reduced. Nasser's canal coup appeared less startling and less successful, and it became apparent to all that revenue from the canal would never build the high dam at Aswan, which still appealed to most as the only first-rate project for solving Egypt's problems. In October 1956 each side to the dispute brought the matter to the Security Council of the U.N., where agreement was reached on six basic principles for the canal's operation. Accepted by England, France, and Egypt, these six principles were an equitable compromise devised as a face-saving program for all.

The Sinai War

The emotionalism aroused by the keen disappointment over the Aswan Dam fiasco and the obvious success in the Suez triumph waned, and diplomats believed that "reason," through the six principles drafted at the United Nations, would prevail. The calm, however, was rudely upset by the Israeli invasion of Sinai on October 29, 1956. Many aspects of this event, including the British and French plot, using the Israelis as a willing foil, have been discussed in the preceding chapter. As surprising as was this attack to the world public, many foreign offices and military intelligence units were well aware that forces were being mobilized by England, France, and Israel, perhaps with the expectation that if they attacked Nasser's regime would collapse and Egyptian sovereignty would again become the weak reed it had been under Faruk. Britain and France had agreed at their secret conclave at Sèvres to enter the war in not less than four days after the Israeli attack, and the ultimatum that they delivered to Egypt and Israel on October 30 calling for a halt to the war and insisting that each withdraw to positions ten miles from the canal was a ruse, in part to cloak their collusion and in part to enable them to occupy the canal area without Egyptian resistance. Aware of the French air force participation in the war from the start and the build-up of British contingents in Cyprus, Nasser early in the war ordered his troops to fall back to positions west of the canal, grounded some of his planes, and sent the rest to bases in Saudi Arabia. Nasser refused the ultimatum and the powers entered the fray. Air attacks on November 2 shocked the entire world and brought about meetings of the U.N. Security Council, which called for an immediate cease-fire. Cooperation by naval forces and paratroopers brought the fall of Port Said, whereupon the U.S.S.R. warned that she was prepared to use force if need be to obtain the withdrawal of Western and Israeli troops from Egypt. In the face of sharp words from the United States and the U.S.S.R. a cease-fire was ordered on November 7, and U.N. observers entered the canal area the next day. The British and French commenced their evacuation in December upon the arrival of the United Nations Emergency Force (UNEF), and Israel withdrew from Sinai in January. Only after severe pressure from the United States in March did Israel give up her hold on the Gaza strip and the Straits of Tiran. U.N. salvage crews cleared the canal, which Egypt had blocked in several places during the war, and shipping was resumed in April.

Upon Egypt the effects of this episode were incalculable. A large part of the arms recently acquired from the Soviets was lost in Sinai, and the Egyptian army was again said to be weak and unprepared. The Western world and the Middle East were blanketed with accounts of the rapidity and apparent ease with which the tough and highly trained Israeli army had occupied Sinai, and much was made of the phrase, "one hundred hours to Suez," without examining the role the expected British and French invasions had upon Egyptian strategy. The destruction in Port Said, the damages in Sinai, and the loss of revenue from Suez operations were severe blows to the national economy. Had not the United States and the U.S.S.R. rescued Egypt, Nasser might have fallen after the British, French, and Israeli attack; Egyptian and Arab pride would have suffered enormously; Israel would have held Sinai, including the Straits of Tiran, and England would have returned to her position astride the canal, and armed aggression would have been shown to be profitable.

Nasser, however, assumed a bold posture and emerged from the disaster stronger than ever. All the Arab nations rallied publicly and diplomatically to his side, and in January 1957 he arranged an Arab solidarity pact, whereby Jordan could throw off her British financial shackles to become the ward of Syria, Saudi Arabia, and Egypt. Though he eventually lost out in Jordan Nasser grew more popular with the Arab masses throughout the Middle East.

During the crisis Britain and the United States froze sterling and dollar balances, which imposed a hardship on Egyptian trade and industry and drove Nasser more firmly into the Soviet economic orbit. Simultaneously, Nasser decreed the "Egyptianization" of seven banks and seventeen insurance companies owned by British and French interests. Stockholders and directors, henceforth, must be native-born Egyptian citizens.

After Israeli troops left Gaza relations between Egypt and the West improved. During negotiations for compensating Suez Canal Company shareholders, agreement was reached for a payment of £E28.3 million. Egyptian authorities operated the canal efficiently, and the International Bank explored the economic feasibility of widening the canal to permit constant two-way traffic. Egyptian bank balances were released. The high dam at Aswan again came under discussion; the International Bank agreed to reconsider the project, and in 1958 British engineers considered the complexities of its construction. West Germany advanced credits of 400 million marks to develop Egyptian industry, the first realization of which appeared in the German-constructed steel mill at Helwan. That the numerous Soviet barter deals had fettered Egyptian exports to the West was implied in a 1958 decree allowing a discount of 23 percent on cotton export prices to hard-currency countries.

Following the Sinai war Egyptian politics remained unsettled. Pressure for some show of democratic action gave rise to a call for elections to a national assembly having 350 seats. Only one political party, the National Union, was permitted, and Nasser became its head. However, 5 million voted in July; the contests were so close that runoffs were required in about two-thirds of the constituencies.

The United Arab Republic

In Arab politics, the year 1958 was one of remarkable developments. Provisions of the various pacts Egypt had entered into with other Arab governments stipulated that unified military command rested in Egyptian hands. Thus, in 1957 when the Syrian-Turkish crisis arose, Egyptian troops were sent to Syria. Their presence in Syria insured a peaceful birth for the United Arab Republic. Certain Syrian groups had long favored a merger with Egypt, and Nasser's Radio Cairo carried to every Syrian village vigorous propaganda for uniting all Arabs. Communist influence over Syrian political life advanced so rapidly that Syrian leaders recognized their only salvation lay in combining with Egypt. The rush of events carried Nasser pell-mell into the union, obviously more hastily than desired, but he could hardly refuse the fruits of his own propaganda. The United Arab Republic was declared with little deliberation on February 1, 1958, and several days later Nasser presented to a cheering throng in Damascus a seventeen-point program for the new state. He declared that a new assembly would be appointed, composed of 300 Egyptians and 100 Syrians. A cabinet for the U.A.R. was also selected. Significantly, twenty of the thirty-four members were Egyptians, and Egyptians held, among others, the portfolios for defense, foreign affairs, education, and national guidance.

As the months passed, many north Syrians acted displeased over the merger. Nasser revealed that Syria was not as rich as he had supposed and that the union would take a number of years to perfect. Nevertheless, its creation upset the balance of power among the Arab states and gave the U.A.R. genuine hegemony in the Middle East. The imam of Yemen sent his son to Cairo to seal the establishment of the United Arab States. Although only a nominal merger, it gave lip service to the ideal of Arab unity, showed the imam's respect for Nasser's position, and afforded the imam freedom from having Radio Cairo beamed at his country. Movements similar to Nasserism in Iraq, Saudi Arabia, Kuwayt, and Jordan were encouraged, and Jordan and Iraq formed a joyous union. Nasser reacted swiftly to the challenge to his dominance and condemned that federation as the evil doings of "imperialists." Elements in every Arab state looked to him for inspiration and sought to attach themselves to his political coattails. Nasser could hardly disappoint them. Radio Cairo invited Arabs in Baghdad, Beirut, and Amman to revolt against their rulers. Syrians found the Lebanese borders easy to infiltrate, and Nasser's agents abetted the civil disturbances that racked Lebanon in 1958. He inspired the men who led the Iraq revolution in July 1958, and his brand of Arab nationalism conditioned the masses in Iraq to accept the new leaders with open arms. Nasser apparently had no direct hand in the revolution, but he quickly welcomed General Kassim's acquisition of power and successfully gathered considerable credit among Arabs by rejoicing over the victory. Had not American marines and British paratroopers landed in Lebanon and Jordan, those states might have fallen to Nasser's partisans. The shaykh of Kuwayt and Prince Faysal of Saudi Arabia recognized his power and hastened to make their peace with Nasser before their dynasties followed the Hashimites of Iraq into oblivion.

The appointed assembly of 400 for the United Arab Republic was looked upon as a preliminary body that would take some of the first steps in consummating the union. Elections in Syria were too normal a process to ignore, and in Egypt elections were a long tradition. The problem was how to bypass the politicians and get through to the people. Machinery for obtaining an elected national assembly had been devised to eliminate political parties and politicians. The Baath leaders in Syria were so opposed to it that Nasser dropped Hurani and al-Bitar as vice presidents. President Nasser took his constitutional oath of office, and the fiction was maintained that the people ruled through a hierarchy of committees, councils, unions, and assemblies. A month before, however, an executive council of fifteen had been designated as a kind of super-cabinet to make decisions, but even here most questions of any weight were referred to the Supreme Council of three—President Nasser, Field Marshall and Vice President Amer, and Vice President (Syria) Abd al-Latif al Baghdadi. In 1961 the skilled, disgruntled Syrian politicians collaborated with disaffected soldiers, merchants, and landowners to lead Syria out of the union.

The United Arab Republic Without Syria
The Syrian secession caused only a slight shock to the Egyptian region of the United Arab Republic because most of the adjusting had been on the Syrian side. President Nasser called for new elections in 1962 for the National Union (sometimes called Congress), which would represent the "genuine popular forces—peasants, workers, artisans, industrialists, etc."—of the nation.

Ali Sabri, a socialist, was selected as prime minister. The government promised that a national assembly would be elected, some political activity would be permitted, and a new constitution would be forthcoming. The Arab Socialist Union under Nasser's presidency was launched as the U.A.R.'s sole political party, to gather into its fold all political activists and would-be leaders from the nation's various social and economic sectors. A great deal of hard work at the grassroots level produced sufficient understanding to hold elections for the National Assembly in March 1964. A Nasser-approved list of 1,748 candidates, all members of the Arab Socialist Union, filed for the 350 seats. The normal life of the Assembly was set at five years, although the president could dissolve it and call for new elections in sixty days. The Assembly could give a vote of no confidence in the cabinet as a whole or single out individual ministers for its disapproval. What would happen if a cabinet received a negative vote was not elucidated. Nasser remained president and was elected to a third six-year term in March 1965. Field Marshall Abd al-Hakim Amer was chosen first vice president and Ali Sabri remained as prime minister. In October 1965 Vice President Zakariya Muhyi al-Din was sworn in as prime minister with an altered cabinet; Ali Sabri was appointed vice president and was given the post of secretary-general of the Arab Socialist Union. There had been alleged plots against Nasser and the government by the communists and the Muslim Brotherhood, and Muhyi al-Din was delegated to clamp down more rigorously on these groups. At the same time economic conditions had worsened and relations with the West were at a low point. The new prime minister was known as a moderate and more adept at resolving economic dilemmas.

Arab Socialism

European communism, because of its emphasis on dialectical materialism and its atheism, had difficulty in making an appeal in Egypt. This foreign ideology, supported by one of the great powers of the world, was an easy target for the deep-rooted and almost timeless Egyptian xenophobia. Governmental control over agriculture and commerce had been traditional in historic times, and in the monolithic structure being devised by Nasser any different pattern was unthinkable. The state held a responsibility for the economic well-being and advancement of its citizens, and whether it was called state capitalism or state socialism really made no difference. Arab socialism had all the right connotations, did not conflict with Islam or the past, and with such a name it was a commodity exportable to neighboring states.

Steadily the government increased its hold over commerce, industry, and finance by nationalizing many types of businesses. By 1961 all banks and insurance companies had been nationalized in what was deftly called "Arabization," and all newspapers and periodicals were placed under the control of the National Union and later the National Assembly. In 1962 estimates showed that 90 percent of all major businesses had been "Arabized," including flour mills, transportation firms, and seventy-seven bakeries in Cairo. In 1963 foreigners were forbidden to own farmlands in Egypt. Over $1 billion in property was sequestered when the property of Egypt's richest citizens, "422 millionaires and reactionaries," was confiscated. A highly progressive income tax was enacted, and 25 percent of net profits in all businesses had to be distributed to the employees.

The United Arab Republic had development plans too. The second five-year plan, drawn up for 1960 to 1965, called for a total expenditure of about $4 billion to raise the national income by 40 percent. The Pan American Oil Company brought in commercially productive wells in the Gulf of Suez and the Red Sea; natural-gas strikes were made in the delta area; and several rich seams of coal were discovered.

The greatest single venture was the building of the new dam at Aswan, now formally designated the Aswan High Dam. At the end of 1958 the U.S.S.R. loaned the U.A.R. $100 million to get it under way, and open construction began in 1960. Prime Minister Khrushchev, who attended the celebrations in May 1964, when the first stage was completed, promised to see it through to completion. Water began to back up in 1965.

The second most dramatic development project was the improvement of the Suez Canal. In 1958 a record number of ships, 17,842, used the canal, but already the size of oil tankers, nearly half of the ships passing through, was increasing to the point where many were unable to navigate the narrow and shallow course. Once shipbuilders reached the tonnage that was too great for the canal, they would likely start building much larger tankers suitable for rounding Africa. In 1959 three American firms had contracts for $18 million to deepen and widen the canal to permit ships of 37-foot draft to pass. But this was recognized as only a temporary palliative; Nasser planned to spend $270 million over a ten-year period to enable supertankers of 47-foot draft to navigate the channel. In 1966 the canal earned $197 million on the passage of 20,285 ships. However, new tankers of 300,000 to 2 million tons aroused concern in the United Arab Republic that even after the completion of the extensive improvements, oil shipments from the Persian Gulf to Europe would not be able to pass through the canal.

Through the years industrial development in the United Arab Republic moved rapidly forward. Agreements were reached with Soviet-bloc countries and mainland China for financial and technical aid to industry of every sort. The same was true for Western nations. West Germany in 1963 loaned the United Arab Republic $57.5 million to assist in twenty-five development projects. In this decade the United States gave large amounts of aid, and almost every year shipments of American wheat and other foodstuffs, paid for in nonconvertible currency, arrived at Alexandria.

The continuing problem of the population explosion was a counterbalance to these advances. In 1958, at the time of the formation of the United Arab Republic, Egypt's population was estimated at 24 million; by 1966 it was slightly over 30 million, an increase of 25 percent in only eight years. The annual increase in population was rapidly approaching the 1 million mark, and when the impounded waters of the Aswan High Dam became available to expand the irrigated lands in Egypt, they would hardly feed the numbers added after the project was begun. Any improvement in the standard of living had to come from improved agricultural methods and industrial production.

Nasser and the World
Following the Soviet agreement to aid in building the Aswan High Dam, the U.A.R.'s relations with the U.S.S.R. and the Soviet bloc continued on a friendly government-to-government level. Large quantities of military

goods were supplied, ostensibly in exchange for future cotton shipments, but arrangements were shrouded as were the actual military deliveries. Soviet technical assistance, equipment, and machinery in some years reached a figure of $175 million. Leading U.A.R. figures visited Moscow and other Soviet-bloc capitals to sign trade agreements and obtain support in world affairs. In addition to Khrushchev's visit in 1964, Chou En-lai came to Cairo in 1963, Walter Ulbricht in 1965, and Alexei Kosygin in 1966. In spite of these visits and the massive aid for the Aswan High Dam and other programs, Nasser actively suppressed communists. Several hundred were jailed at various times, and special crackdowns were conducted almost yearly, much to the annoyance and embarrassment of Soviet leaders, who admonished Nasser publicly for his treatment of the left. The Soviet Union, nevertheless, upheld its position of general support and in the May 1967 crisis between Israel and the U.A.R., the U.S.S.R. strongly supported the latter in discussions at the U.N. Security Council.

Nasser's relations with the West were always somewhat fragile because of past European imperialism and the difficulty that Europeans and their governments had in throwing off the concepts on which that imperialism had been based. In 1959 a general settlement was reached with Great Britain, and diplomatic relations were resumed. England released £50 million in frozen sterling and remitted payment of £50 million for installations at Suez; the U.A.R. waived payment for damages inflicted by the 1956 bombings and invasion and returned sequestered property. With Nasser's growing interest in Aden and the Federation of South Arabia, relations became strained with London. Diplomatic relations were severed in June 1967 over the crisis in the Middle East.

France in 1958 agreed to pay the U.A.R. $57.4 million for the release of French property sequestered during the 1956 episode, but relations remained delicate. In 1967 President de Gaulle took a neutralist stand on the Middle East crisis and would not involve France in the meetings of several maritime powers that were considering the means of forcing the Straits of Tiran and breaking the blockade of Elath.

West Germany gave many loans and considerable aid to the U.A.R. for industrial development, and many West German scientists were employed in missile and rocket endeavors in the western desert. After Ulbricht's visit to Cairo and the raising of the U.A.R. mission in East Berlin to the level of a consulate, Bonn protested. Diplomatic relations were broken, and Nasser declared that these actions resulted from West German arms shipments to Israel.

Relations with the United States fluctuated widely in the period after 1956. Suspicious of the close relations between the United States and Israel and mindful of America's great wealth and power, the U.A.R. was wary in her attitudes toward the United States. The U.A.R. needed vast amounts of wheat and other farm products, aid for industrial and public-works developments, and from time to time simple loans to sustain her budget. The yearly variations in help and its magnitude were startling. In 1962, for example, about 500,000 tons of wheat were shipped to the U.A.R., and the United States indicated the likelihood of making $100 million available in various forms each year for the next five years. When the United States strongly requested that the U.A.R. cease sending arms shipments to the Congo, Nasser's reply was sharp and defiant. The American library in Cairo was sacked and burned. In the crisis with Israel in 1967 the U.A.R. was angered by American leadership in trying to break the blockade of Elath. Accusing the United States of participating with Israel in the war against the Arab states, the U.A.R. broke diplomatic relations with the United States on June 6, 1967.

The United Arab Republic tried to establish friendly relations with the new states of Africa. In 1961 Nasser attended the African Congress at Casablanca, after which he recognized the pro-leftist Gizenga as the rightful ruler of the Congo. Later that same year he hosted the All-African Peoples Congress in Cairo in the hope of establishing leadership in this movement. Nasser had frequent meetings with Nehru of India and Tito of Yugoslavia in which the three hoped to form a third force of uncommitted nations. Many of their problems were the same, but as developing nations they did not attract a following among the other new and underdeveloped nations, for they had little concrete aid to offer.

The greatest role and the greatest hope for leadership of the U.A.R. in the world was in the Middle East and among the Arab nations and peoples. Nasser was cast as the hero of the modern Arabs, and he had a large and devoted following in every Arab country from the southeastern tip of Arabia to Morocco on the Atlantic. They kept the political pot boiling in Syria and Iraq, and those who desired a change in Saudi Arabia, Kuwayt, Yemen, Aden, and Jordan were in his camp. In 1962, at the outset of the revolution in Yemen, the U.A.R. was the first among the Arab states to recognize the republican regime of al-Sallal; Nasser signed a joint defense agreement with al-Sallal and sent 12,000 soldiers to fight against the forces of al-Badr. Although Nasser agreed to withdraw his forces to induce American recognition of the new Yemeni regime, they never left, and the U.A.R. sustained the republicans and controlled them to the point where Cairo dictated policies and named the officeholders in Sana. Saudi Arabia began to shelter the monarchists and funnel arms and ammunition to them, producing a stalemate. Estimates were made that the U.A.R. had expended about $1 billion in the effort, and Nasser sought to end the cost and cut the casualties. Truce meetings and cease-fire agreements with King Faysal were of no avail. After England announced her planned withdrawal from Aden in 1968, Nasser not only decided to stick it out in Yemen but also encouraged his supporters to acts of violence and terror in Aden and throughout the Federation of South Arabia to secure a regime favorable to the U.A.R. The Baathist coups in 1963 in Baghdad and Damascus were supposed to be first steps in the recreation and extension of the United Arab Republic. Conferences to effect these steps proved that Arab peoples might want Arab unity, but Arab leaders were not prepared to sacrifice local interests and personal positions to Egyptian dominance.

Arab leaders recognized that Saudi Arabia, Kuwayt, Iraq, and Libya had wealth in oil royalties; they looked to these states for economic leadership. However, the United Arab Republic, the most populous, the most modernized in industry, education, and transportation, and, with Soviet aid, the best equipped in modern weapons, was regarded as the natural military leader. Nasser had been successful in standing up to the powers in 1956, and the propaganda effort from Cairo had succeeded in making Nasser the outstanding charismatic figure in the Arab world. With Arab summit meetings in Alexandria and Cairo, with the headquarters of the Arab League located there, it was natural that the Arab states would follow the lead of the U.A.R. in general world affairs and in matters of joint military action and defense against Israel. President Arif of Iraq joined in a mutual military command with the U.A.R. in 1964 and Syria followed in 1966. They were pledged to join with each other in a war against Israel, and each agreed to accept Palestine Liberation Organization armies as adjuncts to their own forces.

In May 1967 Syria called upon Nasser to make good his pledge to come to Syria's assistance should Israel attack. Feeling that he would have a serious problem at the Israeli frontier because of the presence of the United Nations Emergency Forces, Nasser requested U Thant to remove these troops from their places along the Gaza strip, the Sinai peninsula, and the Straits of Tiran. The U.A.R. immediately reinstituted the blockade of Elath she had enforced up to 1956. Israel reacted angrily. As the tension mounted, and as each side prepared for war great solidarity appeared among all the Arab states; each one gave her support to the United Arab Republic as the strain between Syria and Israel shifted southward toward the Israeli-Egyptian frontier.

The Six-Day War

When war came in June the United Arab Republic bore the main brunt of it, but other fronts were opened between Israel, Syria, and Jordan. At meetings of the U.N. Security Council in New York delegates from Lebanon, Syria, Iraq, and Morocco spoke eloquently for the U.A.R.; people in most Arab capitals attacked American and British embassies; and Iraq, Syria, Sudan, and Algeria joined with the U.A.R. in breaking diplomatic relations with Great Britain and the United States on June 6, 1967. The cease-fire of June 10, 1967, called for by the Security Council and arranged by General Odd Bull of Norway, left Israeli troops holding Sinai and virtually the entire east bank of the Suez Canal. In general the line was the center of the canal, and for several weeks thereafter occasional spurts of gunfire erupted when one side or the other launched a small boat, apparently to test the vigilance and determination of the other. The U.A.R. lost most of her air force and a large part of her tanks and other war matériel.

Several thousand soldiers, mostly officers, remained as prisoners of war in Israeli hands.

Nasser publicly assumed the blame for the disastrous defeat and resigned his office. The general reaction against his resignation was so overwhelming he rescinded his decision and subsequently enjoyed greater popularity and esteem than ever. The quality of the military leadership and the lack of organization and commitment were blamed for the infamy, and several thousand officers were relieved of their commands. It was reported that many officers had deserted their posts and men in the face of the enemy and that the planning of offense and defense had been exceedingly faulty. It was asserted that only the sons of the influential had been accepted for the air force. The disgruntled officers were kept under close surveillance. At the time that Nasser went to Khartoum for summit meetings Field Marshall and Vice President Amer was arrested. Shortly thereafter Amer committed suicide, and it was announced that he had been involved in a plot to overthrow Nasser.

As soon as the cease-fire became effective, various Arab leaders indicated the need for a conference of leaders of Arab states to arrive at a unified position. The prime minister of Sudan arranged to have an Arab summit meeting at Khartoum. The meeting's final resolution, announced on September 1, 1967, affirmed Arab solidarity and the necessity for joint efforts to eliminate all traces of Israeli aggression. In addition, the resolution called for liquidating all foreign bases in Arab countries, consolidating military preparedness, considering oil as a diplomatic weapon, and upholding of the rights of the Palestinian people to their land. This meant refusing to recognize Israel or to have negotiations with her. At the summit meeting Saudi Arabia, Kuwayt, and Libya promised the equivalent of $100 million to the U.A.R. to offset the loss of revenue from the Suez Canal.

In addition, Nasser and King Faysal of Saudi Arabia agreed to end their intervention in the Yemeni civil war. This understanding led to the overthrow of al-Sallal in November and so weakened the forces of FLOSY in South Arabia that its rival party, NLF, gained the upper hand and received the power and symbols of government when the British evacuated Aden and the surrounding area on the last day of November 1967.

On the international scene the U.S.S.R. supported the position of the U.A.R. at the United Nations and began to replace much of the military equipment lost or damaged in the Six-Day War. By the end of the summer it was estimated that nearly 80 percent of the air strength had been restored and new additions had been made to the navy. The port of Alexandria became a base for Soviet ships, enabling Moscow to station more of her fleet in the Mediterranean. For the first time Nasser surrendered to the U.S.S.R.'s demands that Soviet military personnel be stationed in Egypt to train U.A.R. officers in the use and maintenance of Soviet equipment and to aid in the organization of a more effective armed force.

After the Khartoum conference the U.A.R. quietly turned to repairing her relations with the United States and Great Britain. The charges that the

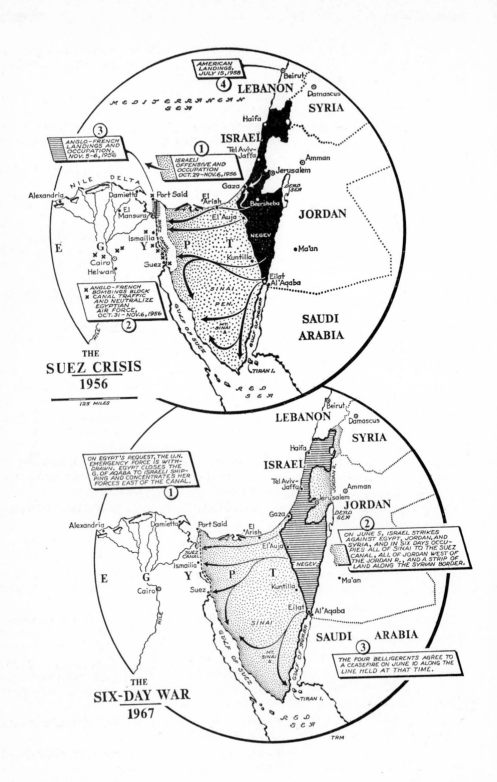

AMERICAN
LANDINGS,
JULY 15, 1958

④ LEBANON
● Beirut
● Damascus
SYRIA

MEDITERRANEAN SEA

Haifa

③ ANGLO-FRENCH
LANDINGS AND
OCCUPATION,
NOV. 5-6, 1956

ISRAEL

Tel Aviv-
Jaffa

① ISRAELI
OFFENSIVE AND
OCCUPATION
OCT. 29-NOV.6, 1956

● Amman

NILE DELTA

Alexandria

Damietta
Port Said

● Jerusalem

Gaza

● El
Mansura
El 'Arish

DEAD
SEA

Beersheba

El 'Auja

JORDAN

E
G
Ismailia
Y
P
T
NEGEV

Cairo
● Ma'an

Helwan
Suez
Kuntilla

✕ ANGLO-FRENCH
BOMBINGS BLOCK
✕ CANAL TRAFFIC
AND NEUTRALIZE
EGYPTIAN
AIR FORCE,
OCT. 31-NOV.6, 1956

②

SINAI
PEN.

Eilat
Al'Aqaba

SAUDI
ARABIA

GULF OF SUEZ

MT.
SINAI

GULF OF AQABA

THE
SUEZ CRISIS
1956

TIRAN I.

RED
SEA

125 MILES

● Beirut
● Damascus

LEBANON
SYRIA

Haifa

ISRAEL

Tel Aviv-
Jaffa

● Amman

ON EGYPT'S REQUEST, THE U.N.
EMERGENCY FORCE IS WITH-
DRAWN. EGYPT CLOSES THE
G. OF AQABA TO ISRAELI SHIP-
PING AND CONCENTRATES HER
FORCES EAST OF THE CANAL.

①

● Jerusalem
JORDAN

Gaza

DEAD
SEA

Alexandria
Damietta
Port Said

El
'Arish

El 'Auja

② ON JUNE 5, ISRAEL STRIKES
AGAINST EGYPT, JORDAN, AND
SYRIA, AND IN SIX DAYS OCCU-
PIES ALL OF SINAI TO THE SUEZ
CANAL, ALL OF JORDAN WEST OF
THE JORDAN R., AND A STRIP OF
LAND ALONG THE SYRIAN BORDER.

SUEZ
CANAL

Ismailia

E
G
Y
P
T
NEGEV

Cairo
● Ma'an

Suez
Kuntilla

Eilat
Al'Aqaba

SINAI

SAUDI
ARABIA

③ THE FOUR BELLIGERENTS AGREE TO
A CEASEFIRE ON JUNE 10 ALONG THE
LINE HELD AT THAT TIME.

GULF OF SUEZ

MT.
SINAI

GULF OF AQABA

THE
SIX-DAY WAR
1967

TIRAN I.

RED
SEA

TRM

two powers had aided Israel with air cover during the war were dropped, and shipments of oil to Great Britain by other Arab states went unnoticed. Many American diplomats returned to Cairo, and the American University was permitted to reopen for the fall term. When Gunnar Jarring, the Swedish ambassador to Moscow, was appointed special U.N. representative to the Middle East to aid in the negotiation of a settlement as outlined by the British-sponsored Resolution 242, passed unanimously by the Security Council on November 22, 1967, Nasser was careful not to be too enthusiastic over the terms.

Cease-Fires and Stalemate

There were hopes that Ambassador Jarring by shuttling back and forth between Cairo and Jerusalem would be able to implement Resolution 242 and convert the rather ephemeral cease-fire into a more permanent accord, maybe even a peace treaty. Both Israel and the U.A.R. subscribed publicly to the resolution, but each interpreted it differently. Nasser, insisting that Israel withdraw from the Sinai and all Arab lands, refused to negotiate face-to-face with the Israelis, as they were demanding, until they had pulled back to the pre-1967 borders; Israel refused to consider doing so until a peace agreement was signed. Jarring made several efforts, but each time he had to announce that the positions of the sides were irreconcilable. Muhammad Hasan al-Zayyat, a leading Egyptian political figure, stated officially, late in 1967, that the U.A.R. guaranteed the "right of Israel to exist" on the basis of Resolution 242. Nasser himself, however, never used these words.

Within days after the cease-fire began, the inevitable incidents along the canal began to occur. Any unusual movement invited shots, and before long artillery shells were cascading onto enemy positions. In the autumn of 1968 Israeli artillery gravely damaged Port Tawfik; U.A.R. commandos made a temporary crossing of the canal; Israeli paratroopers and airplanes destroyed a number of installations on the Nile near Aswan. Nasser declared that the U.A.R. could not be bombed into submission and would fight back until Israel was prepared to abide by Resolution 242. In 1969 250 U.A.R. commandos again crossed the canal; Israeli tanks then raided across the Gulf of Suez. Artillery duels and air raids became so commonplace that the smaller ones went unreported. In April Nasser no longer recognized the cease-fire as being in force.

In 1970 the duels involved such advanced weapons that it appeared that full-scale war would be resumed. An Israeli air raid on an industrial plant near Cairo killed many civilians, which hastened the Soviets in sending and helping in the setting up of SAM-3s (surface-to-air missiles) in the canal area. Israeli planes could no longer fly over U.A.R. territory at will. A six-month truce went into effect on August 8; though each side accused the other repeatedly of violations, the serious shooting stopped for six months.

President Podgorny of the U.S.S.R. made a four-day visit to Cairo soon after the fighting stopped in June 1967. A short time later the U.A.R.'s foreign minister received the red-carpet treatment in Moscow. These expressions of goodwill increased over the next few years. After the Soviets installed short-range surface-to-air missiles in the U.A.R. they began to deliver tanks and supersonic jets. By mid-1970 such large amounts of war matériel had been received by the U.A.R. that it was estimated Nasser's forces were better armed than they had been in 1967.

The arrival of Soviet military advisers and technicians brought welcome technical assistance, but problems of personnel relationships lowered morale in the U.A.R. The number of Russians shot up to 10,000; they were piloting aircraft over Cairo and manning some of the missile sites; six were killed by Israeli shells, a factor that abetted the American push for the cease-fire in 1970. The U.S.S.R. aided in many other developments as well, giving $800 million for an industrial complex in Helwan and providing two new generators at Aswan. President Nasser was in Moscow twice in July 1968, once for extended medical treatment, which was repeated in 1970.

In the last half of 1967 Nasser's friends rallied to his side. Large subsidies from Saudi Arabia, Kuwayt, and Libya kept the economy afloat despite bad economic conditions. Oil from the Sinai was not available, the canal was closed, tourists did not come, and the cotton worm infestation was the worst in fifty years. Blueprints for another deepening and widening of the canal were shelved, but drilling by American companies for oil in the Gulf of Suez and in the western desert near the Qattara depression proceeded, with several promising strikes. Plans were advanced for the Suez-Mediterranean pipeline (SUMED). The Aswan Dam was completed without much fanfare in midsummer 1970, at a time when crops were greatly improved and the forecast of production rosy indeed. By 1970 the U.A.R. had adjusted from the shock of 1967; recovery was on the way. Trade agreements were signed with Czechoslovakia, Turkey, India, Yugoslavia, and various African states including Sudan; talks were proceeding favorably with the EEC; Iraq was bartering oil for automobiles; and Soviet trade balances were approaching half a billion dollars. The 1970–1971 budget, totaling $5.5 billion, with only 10 percent for defense, augured for a balanced economy as a minimum.

Though Nasser offered his resignation upon the defeat in 1967, the populace refused to accept it, and the politicians and soldiers concurred. He assumed the office of prime minister and head of the only political organization, the Arab Socialist Union (ASU), until that post went to Ali Sabri. Trials and arrests continued, and students rioted over the leniency of a fifteen-year sentence to the former commander of the air force. These demonstrations strengthened Nasser's position sufficiently to permit him to arrest forty other officers, giving life sentences to some. Though many universities around the world were experiencing troubles and riots at this time, the closing of U.A.R. universities twice in 1968 was connected with local developments—one being the new decree no longer exempting students from military service. A national referendum was held to endorse Nasser. Ninety-eight percent of those eligible voted, and Nasser won 99.98 percent of the votes cast. With this massive support he dissolved the National Assembly and called for new elections in 1969, at which time Anwar al-Sadat, one of the original members of the Revolutionary Command Council, became vice president.

It was obvious at the Khartoum meeting that Nasser still was strong; soon, leaders of most of the Arab states came to Cairo to display their support. Nasser felt so secure he even walked out of a summit meeting at Rabat when Saudi Arabia and Kuwayt declined to increase his subsidy. In 1970, conversations were held and much interest advanced by Libya and Sudan for a federation of the three states. Syria, which had suggested some type of union the previous year, asked that provisions for a four-part federation be studied.

Anwar al-Sadat

Many wondered how the disaster of 1967 could have left Nasser more popular than ever and his leadership so compelling. The only answer could be that he was the most charismatic figure to appear among the Arabs in his century. He was, however, to leave them at the age of fifty-two, for on September 28, 1970, Nasser died suddenly of a heart attack. The U.A.R. and the entire Middle East were stunned. Heads of state and dignitaries from around the world attended his funeral and paid their respects to the creator of the Egyptian republic. Vice-President Anwar al-Sadat automatically became interim president. Sadat was nominated president by the National Assembly, elected overwhelmingly by national referendum, and sworn in on October 17. Supported wholeheartedly by the Arab Socialist Union, Sadat chose Mahmud Fawzi as prime minister and minister of war, appointed a national defense council, and supported Ali Sabri for vice-president.

Sadat, a devout Muslim graced with a warm personality and a devoted family man of modest tastes and habits, was born in 1918 in a village in the Nile delta. Attending a military academy in 1936, he formed a secret group of twelve along with his classmate Nasser to work for the liberation of Egypt from Faruk and the British. Jailed by the British during World War II as a German sympathizer, he participated with Nasser, Ali Sabri, and others in the 1952 coup and acted as its first spokesman. He wrote an account of the coup and held positions as speaker of the National Assembly and secretary-general of the National Union, the first political party of the revolution.

On assuming the presidency Sadat chose to show the continuity of the republican regime. He gathered about him many of Egypt's proven leaders and pursued and confirmed many of Nasser's undertakings. In December 1970 the Geneva peace meeting opened, but the Israelis withdrew on the second day. In February 1971 Sadat agreed to an extension of the six-month cease-fire for an additional thirty days. When that expired he refused to prolong it but made no move to resume the fighting. He declared that when Israel returned all the Arab lands she was occupying, Egypt would recognize the right of Israel to exist and would allow open passage of ships to Israel in the Gulf of Akaba. President Nixon pledged his friendship to Sadat. Soviet President Podgorny visited in Cairo in January 1971 and journeyed with Sadat up the Nile for the formal dedication of the completed Aswan Dam.

Before Nasser died Libya and Sudan had discussed with him the idea of a tripartite federation. Sadat pursued this vigorously; in 1971 the creation of the Federation of Arab Republics was announced. Sudan, one of the original instigators of the move, held back because of protests from her non-Arab southern provinces. Instead, Egypt, Libya, and Syria agreed to federate, with one flag, one capital, one cabinet, and a joint military command.

Arab Republic of Egypt

The new federation made the name United Arab Republic incongruous, and on May 1 Sadat pronounced the formation of the Arab Republic of Egypt, calling it a socialist democracy. Meeting dissidents head on, Sadat removed Ali Sabri from his office and arrested him along with Fawzi and several other high officials, accusing them of plotting a coup. Four alleged plotters, including Ali Sabri, were condemned to death, a sentence Sadat commuted to life imprisonment. Later, he dissolved the National Assembly, reorganized the ASU, scheduled new elections for the assembly, and brought forth a new constitution. Under this, Islam was declared the state religion, civil rights were strengthened, seizure of property was banned, and women were given equal rights. Sadat had taken full power in his own administration.

President Podgorny returned to Cairo in May 1971 to sign a fifteen-year treaty of political, economic, and military cooperation under which the Soviets agreed to provide training for the army and to furnish weapons. On return visits to Moscow Sadat boldly stated Egypt's policy of resistance to communism anywhere in the Arab world; he was not very successful in obtaining more arms. He and the Soviet leaders did agree, though, to a "further strengthening of military cooperation" in order to recover Arab lands.

Within a few weeks, however, Nixon was in Moscow and the Soviet-American policy of détente was proclaimed. Sadat decided that he could no longer rely on Moscow to support him actively in regaining the lands from Israel or on Washington to pressure Israel to withdraw. He openly stated that the United States plan for "proximity talks" with Israel was a "dead horse" and that the cease-fire and stalemate only benefited Israel. On July 18, 1972, he ordered all Soviet military advisers and experts to leave Egypt, a move popular with the Egyptian people, who had had many unpleasant experiences with them. By autumn, Sadat began to have second thoughts about alienating the Soviets; through Assad of Syria a rapprochement was made and arms shipments were revived, though the number of Russians in Egypt was kept small.

Oil strikes in the Libyan desert not far from the Egyptian border gave hope of finding commercial quantities of oil in Egypt. New discoveries in 1971 and 1972 helped Egyptian production to rise to over 200,000 barrels daily and enabled Egypt to become a member of OAPEC. The Mobil and Exxon oil companies joined in 1973 with Phillips Petroleum and Amoco in drilling and searching for oil, Exxon agreeing to spend $50 million in exploration within a twelve-year period. The Egyptian economy was sustained only by the regular remittances from Saudi Arabia, Kuwayt, and Libya, plus occasional one-time grants such as $250 million from the Persian Gulf states and 260,000 tons of wheat from the United States.

Sadat's relations with other Arab states were not easy. More conservative than Nasser, he steered a course further to the right, especially after Ali Sabri's attempted coup. The coordination of policies with the more radical leaders of Syria proved difficult, leading to the early demise of the Federation of Arab Republics. Its end was sealed by a week's sojourn in Cairo by Saudi Arabia's King Faysal, who found Sadat a congenial and harmonious host. The rapprochement effected by this visit was most significant in Sadat's ouster of the Russians. In the following year Saudi Prince Fahd announced in Cairo that his country would contribute "men, money and weapons" in their common cause. With the foundering of the federation, Sadat and Libya's Muammar Qaddafi made plans for a merger of their two countries, even uniting the two ASUs. But before long that idea was dead and Libya had closed her embassy in Cairo. Sadat broke diplomatic relations with King Husayn of Jordan after Husayn made proposals for peace with Israel and for a Palestine-Jordan federation. To the south, Sadat had so many controversies with Sudan that he requested Sudanese troops to leave the Suez Canal battle area. In 1973 Sadat mended his fences, visited Saudi Arabia, Qatar, and Syria, and smoothed over differences with Sudan. Both Assad and Husayn were in Cairo in September 1973, and diplomatic relations were restored with Jordan. Several months earlier Sadat had taken over the positions of prime minister and military governor-general, placed Egypt on a war footing, and announced a war budget. As the days passed and as Sadat drew closer to his Arab allies, tension mounted; many sensed that Egypt was moving toward a confrontation with Israel.

The Ramadan War, 1973

Early in 1973 Sadat, unable to tolerate the stalemate with Israel any longer, sent his national security adviser to Washington and then to Moscow. His reception was cool. Without any new ideas or advancement toward peace, Sadat coordinated military operations with Syria and sent Egyptian forces across the Suez Canal on October 6, 1973, in the midst of Ramadan, the Muslim holy month of fasting. Prime Minister Kosygin of the U.S.S.R. visited Cairo on October 17 and evidently indicated Soviet support. South Yemen sent word that the Bab al-Mandeb Straits were at the disposal of the Egyptian command, which imposed a blockade at that point. The main battle terminated on October 25 with a temporary cease-fire on the 22nd, as called for by the Security Council Resolutions 338, 339, and 340. Egypt insisted that the Israelis return to the October 22 cease-fire line before prisoners could be exchanged.

After the exchange of prisoners Sadat accepted an American invitation to attend a peace conference in Geneva in December, but it lasted for only a day. After many trips by Kissinger between Jerusalem and Cairo or Aswan, an interim withdrawal was agreed upon on January 18, 1974; Israel pulled back her forces 20 miles east of the canal, Egypt was allowed limited armed units on the east bank of the canal, and U.N. Emergency Forces patrolled the area between. Sadat declared that he would keep Egypt under arms until all Arab lands were freed from Israel.

A New Egypt

Sadat's exuberance at Egypt's initial successes in the war, though dampened by the Israeli counterthrusts, left him confident enough to modify the severity of his control over Egypt's political processes. Former powerful military, political, and press figures were released from jail in 1974; censorship was lifted; and even a plot to overthrow Sadat did not deter him from asking Egyptians to endorse a liberalization of the government. A turnout of 8 million voters convinced Sadat that the masses supported him in his shift to more democracy. Giving up his post as prime minister, Sadat installed a civilian cabinet. He instigated the formation of two groups within the Arab Socialist Union, a leftist one and the Social Democratic Platform, headed by his brother-in-law, whose goal was the encouragement of industrial development and the investment of foreign capital. Sadat was reelected in 1976 to another six-year term as president. In the elections for the Peoples Assembly, many of the seats were contested; embryonic political parties could be seen, though they were tightly circumscribed: There were centrists, rightists, leftists, and independents in the new body.

President Nixon's visit to Egypt in June 1974 gave Sadat a great boost in morale. Months before, during Kissinger's shuttles, relations with the United States had been resumed. Nixon focused world attention on the Nile. He promised a nuclear reactor, $250 million in general aid, and 100,-000 tons of wheat. Already Americans were helping to clear the canal, and four large American banks opened branches in Egypt.

War losses to Egypt since 1967 were calculated at $38.8 billion; her needs seemed astronomical. In 1974 Sadat received millions from Iran, West Germany, Japan, France, and the World Bank, $1.7 billion from Saudi Arabia and the Persian Gulf states. At Rabat in 1974 the Arab leaders pledged an extra $1 billion a year for four years for Egyptian recovery.

In June 1975, without any concessions by Israel, the Suez Canal was officially opened to traffic, a peace gesture that did not go unnoticed in Jerusalem. Though rates were double what they had been when the canal was closed in the Six-Day War, usage reached the 1967 level by autumn. Japan loaned Egypt $140 million for widening and deepening the canal. Nevertheless, it was realized that many years would pass before tolls amounted to the hoped-for $450 million a year.

As debate became freer in Egypt the Aswan Dam turned out to be a favorite topic for disagreement. Its electric power generation had fallen short of what had been promised; a number of land reclamation projects had failed; each year many tons of rich silt were being blocked from the Nile delta and profitable fishing was being ruined in the Mediterranean; and new currents were causing severe erosion along the coast. On the other hand, defenders of the dam pointed out that electric power had been quadrupled; flooding had been curtailed; and the water supply and control system had saved crops in 1972 and 1973, when water levels in the Nile, without the dam, would have been ruinously low. Such public discussions, though frightening to some, assured others that democracy was on the way.

The Sinai Pact

In June 1975 Sadat met United States President Ford at Salzburg to serve notice of his earnest desire for peace. Kissinger, taking heart from these conversations, as well as from the opening of the canal and a surprise pullback of some Israeli troops, succeeded on September 4 in getting Egypt and Israel to sign at Geneva an interim agreement called the Sinai Pact. Israeli forces retired 50 additional kilometers, surrendering the strategic Mitla and Giddi passes and giving up the Abu Rudeis oil fields. Egypt agreed that Israeli nonmilitary cargoes might pass through the canal. The U.N. accepted a larger buffer zone, and the United States consented to monitor an early-warning electronic complex and to relay the signals received to both sides. It was agreed that the Sinai Pact was "not a final peace agreement" and that each side promised "not to resort to the threat or use of force or military blockade."

With the Sinai Pact in hand, Sadat in October visited Washington, where Ford gave him a warm reception. Addressing a joint session of the Congress, Sadat articulated his friendly feeling for the United States, his acceptance of the special relationship between the United States and Israel, and his hope that Americans would come to understand the Arab peoples and would appreciate the need for justice for the Palestinians.

Sadat's adherence to the Sinai Pact infuriated Syria's Assad, who likened Sadat to a traitor for freeing the enemy to concentrate all her power on the Syrian front. Other Arab leaders were slightly less vindictive, but Sadat quietly protested that Egypt's economy was woefully weak and that the country's miserable standard of living demanded peace. Relations with Libya fluctuated month by month, but usually they were not pleasant; Qaddafi looked upon Sadat as a weak reed. Sudanese affairs were much warmer; tentative joint-defense plans were drafted, though the idea of any union was shelved.

The Soviet Departure

As early as 1974 Sadat announced that Egypt would not rely solely on the U.S.S.R. for arms, though he did concede that Soviet friendship would be an active factor in Egyptian policies. Despite Sadat's expulsion of Russian personnel in 1972 the fifteen-year Treaty of Friendship and Cooperation of 1971 was upheld and arms shipments were continued. U.S.S.R. Foreign

Minister Gromyko promised arms and general aid when he was in Cairo in 1974, while Sadat assured him that the U.S.S.R. was important to Egypt. More fighter planes arrived in 1975, but Sadat looked for military goods elsewhere. He obtained bombers in France, and Saudi Arabia funded purchases of $1 billion in arms from Great Britain. Relations with the Russians turned chilly again, as talks in Cairo for the reengagement of large numbers of Soviet advisers were unsuccessful.

Frustrated, Sadat abrogated the Treaty of Friendship and Cooperation on March 14, 1976. Nevertheless, a favorable trade protocol signed three months previously remained intact, and a similar trade pact in 1977 provided for a variety of Egyptian exports to the U.S.S.R. and imports of machinery and other products. Part of Egypt's problem was the huge debt of more than $14 billion to the Soviets and others. In September 1977 Sadat postponed indefinitely all debt payments. Still, believing that trade with the Soviet bloc would continue, not fully satisfied with the arms being received, and convinced that the United States, not the U.S.S.R., held the cards for peace, Sadat opined that the Soviet treaties hampered his diplomatic moves and tied Egyptian policies too closely to the Russians, especially in view of American-Soviet détente.

Sadat Veers Toward the West

With a crushing debt and the insatiable interest charges, constant unfavorable balances of trade, and a population burgeoning beyond 38 million, Sadat's most pressing needs, besides peace, were loans, credits, and capital for development. The oil-rich Arab states, Western Europe, and the United States were his hope. In the wake of his Washington trip in 1975 and a visit with President Carter in 1977 he obtained grants and promises of about $1.85 billion in American aid for the years 1976 and 1977. In 1977 the International Monetary Fund loaned Egypt $140 million following riots in Cairo over food price increases. American oil companies were drilling for oil in several districts in Egypt and offshore, bringing in hard currencies. Sadat made a productive diplomatic and trade promotional tour of Western Europe in 1976. British firms agreed to dig the first tunnel under the Suez Canal for $100 million, to be paid on a long-term basis. France indicated she would permit the sale of 200 Mirage F-1 flight bombers for $1.2 billion; more than half of them would be assembled in Cairo as part of the Arab arms industry that the Arab states had decided to develop. There was also a trade agreement with mainland China and $750 million pledged to Sadat on a February swing around the Persian Gulf. Adding up all their sources of income Egyptian leaders felt that the economy could survive.

This belief was greatly bolstered by the Arab oil states and by Egypt's own development plans. A five-year plan supported by the Egyptian Development Fund was inaugurated in 1976 before Sadat cut his Soviet ties. Set at $20 billion, it was budgeted from expected loans from the United States, Japan, West Germany, France, the Netherlands, and Arab lands. In 1976

Saudi Arabia offered $1 billion in cash and the other Arab oil states came up with $1.5 billion. Then, all of them together guaranteed Sadat annual grants of $2.5 billion, assuring him sufficient financial security to remain independent of the Soviets. To complement these hopes and endeavors, states bordering the Persian Gulf created a $2 billion Gulf Fund for Development in Egypt. Similar to the Kuwayt and OPEC funds, it would make loans at low interest rates for feasible projects.

Saudi Arabia had no little influence on Egypt's decision to void her treaty with the U.S.S.R. With Saudi support Sadat disengaged Egypt from Soviet dominance but discovered thereafter the need to pursue policies generally favored in Riyadh. This became clear in June 1976, when the Egyptian and Syrian prime ministers were informed in Riyadh that Egypt, Syria, and Saudi Arabia henceforth must work in unison in their foreign policy. This was interpreted to mean that they would make peace with Israel on the basis of U.N. Resolution 242, that they would oppose any Arab states and groups that rejected the eventual recognition of Israel, and they would induce the PLO to give up its military role. In October 1976 Sadat was called to Saudi Arabia, where the decision was reached that the Lebanese civil war must be concluded and that Arab League forces, including Egyptians, must go there to stop it. At the end of 1976 Sadat announced that Egypt and Syria were preparing to form a "united political leadership" and to study the necessary steps to bring about the union of the two countries. The attraction was powerful enough to entice Sudan to link her policies to the Egypto-Syrian joint political command in 1977.

Sadat's major difficulties, however, lay in domestic economics and finances. Though industrial output rose 11 percent in 1976 and the development plan anticipated a greater increase than that for each year, the economy was in real trouble. Even with the massive injections of cash from Arab friends ends just did not meet. Belt tightening was tried again in January 1977. When prices were increased on basic commodities the worst riots since 1952 broke out in Cairo; they were quelled only with difficulty by the militia. Demonstrations and strikes were outlawed immediately; communist groups were accused of fomenting the disturbances. But the cries of the people calling, "Nasser, Nasser," must have sent chills through Sadat. It showed those pressing Sadat to restrict government spending that there were limits to what they could expect him to do. The government bread subsidy was figured at $250 million yearly, any sudden removal of which could bring rebellion. Even so, there could be no doubt in 1977 that Sadat had moved away from Nasser's path; indeed, he may have reversed directions completely. One could observe that Sadat now favored a more open economy in place of a highly centralized regime; his eye looked first to Egypt rather than to Pan-Arabism; his policies veered to the right, not to the left; and his ear was attuned to Riyadh and Washington instead of Moscow.

Sadat's Peace Offensive

On November 9, 1977, in addressing parliament in Cairo, President Sadat declared his readiness to discuss peace with Israeli leaders and to go anywhere to do so, even to Jerusalem and to the Kneset. Two days later Prime Minister Begin invited him to come to Jerusalem. Many considered these only rhetorical gestures but Sadat astonished the world by flying to Jerusalem on November 19, accompanied by a large Egyptian delegation and prominent world figures from the media whose interviews with Sadat aboard the plane were beamed instantaneously by satellite around the world. Greeted at the airport by President Katzir, Prime Minister Begin, and all important Israeli leaders, Sadat was showered with warm enthusiasm on the drive to Jerusalem. In his speech to the Kneset on the following day Sadat boldly announced that he recognized Israel as a state in the Middle East and was ready to make peace. He stated that Arab lands seized by Israel in 1967 must be returned and the right of self-determination for the Palestinian people recognized.

By this audacious trip Sadat demonstrated in full view of the world his sincere desire for peace with Israel and gambled that this action would compel Israel to make an equal compromise or show her intransigence to all. To maintain the momentum won by his television diplomacy, Sadat invited Syria, Jordan, Lebanon, Saudi Arabia, Israel, the U.S.S.R., the United States, and the PLO to send delegates to Cairo two weeks later to work on plans for the proposed Geneva conference. Over and over Sadat repeated his stand that he had no intention of making a separate peace, that self-determination for the Palestinians was the crux of the issue, and that the Cairo meeting would arrange procedural matters. Israel accepted immediately, to be followed a few days later by the United States; the others declined.

The rump conference at the historic Mena House at the foot of the Great Pyramids was very photogenic but could do nothing. Meanwhile, the other Arab leaders, irked by Sadat's unilateral move and fearful lest Egypt's desperate economy force him to entertain thoughts of a separate peace, met in Libya and Iraq to condemn Sadat for his treachery. Undaunted by their calumnies, Sadat asked Begin to meet with him at Ismailia on the banks of the Suez Canal on Christmas Day to present the Israeli proposals. On a hurried trip to Washington, Begin failed to obtain full endorsement of the plans and President Carter intimated that Sadat would not be likely to accept them. At Ismailia Begin outlined his ideas of granting local self-rule to the Palestinians in the occupied areas which, however, would still have an Israeli military presence. At the end of a five-year period residents would opt for either Israeli or Jordanian citizenship. Sadat found the proposals unacceptable but the momentum was sustained by the establishing of two Israeli-Egyptian ministerial committees for military and political matters, meeting in Jerusalem and Cairo, to further the negotiations.

Egypt's terms were revealed on December 31, 1977, by the foreign minister. He declared that Israel must accept two principles: one, that Israel must withdraw from the West Bank and Gaza; and two, that Israel must recognize the "inalienable rights" of the Palestinians to self-determination. Once these principles were accepted he stated that negotiations then could focus on the matter of security for all parties and on the manner and time period for the achievement of self-determination and troop withdrawal. Sadat also induced President Carter to stop briefly at Aswan on January 4, 1978, to urge him to press Israel to moderate her stand with regard to the Palestinians and to suggest that the United States become a more active participant in the negotiations. But negotiations of such sensitive details were slow, and Begin had the difficult and laborious job of securing Kneset approval of every point. However, Sadat realized that positive steps toward a peace that he could accept as just had to come soon if the slide toward chaos were to be averted.

Independence of the Sudan

At the end of World War II the growing sentiment in Egypt for the unification of the Nile and the absorption of the Sudan left the British unmoved, but it attracted the support of Ashiqqa party leaders in the Sudan, largely because they sought to play Egypt off against Great Britain. In 1947 the British announced that, even without any agreement or confirmation from Egypt, steps would be pursued to form a separate Sudanese elected legislative assembly with an executive council at Khartoum. The new governor-general, Sir Robert Howe, proceeded slowly, and elections did not materialize until November 1948. The Umma party, which gathered its inspiration from the famed nineteenth-century Mahdi, incorporated in its platform a program of independence and won the election. The Ashiqqa party showed friendship for Egypt and boycotted the election. However, all the parties in 1950 demanded that Great Britain and Egypt grant the Sudan the right of self-government and self-determination as early as 1951.

Within a few months after the revolution in Egypt, General Nagib met with many Sudanese leaders. He reached an agreement with the Umma party approving the establishment of self-government in the Sudan by the end of 1952. For a three-year period the administration, police, and army were to be Sudanized, after which time the right of self-determination would be exercised by the peoples of the Sudan. Anthony Eden announced that Great Britain subscribed in principle to this arrangement, and an Anglo-Egyptian agreement was entered into in Cairo ending the condominium of 1899 and accepting the self-government statute formulated by the Sudan government. After it became official on March 21, 1953, preparations for the election of a two-chamber parliament were launched.

Two prominent parties opened their campaigns. The Umma party declared that it favored the founding of a republic. The head of the party was Sir Abd al-Rahman al-Mahdi, spiritual leader of the Ansar sect of Muslims. The Umma group favored a slow process of separation from England; to ardent nationalists, therefore, Umma was a stronghold of the conservatives and the *status quo*. The Ashiqqa party in 1953 posed as the sponsor of separation from Great Britain and the end of the condominium. Sir Ali al-Mirghani, head of the Khatmiya sect, served as titular head of the party, which now took the name of National Unionist party (NUP). The active leader was Ismail al-Azhari, a graduate of the American University of Beirut and teacher of mathematics at Gordon Memorial College in Khartoum, who espoused a close tie with Egypt.

Elections were held in November 1953. Of the ninety-two seats for the house of representatives NUP won forty-seven, and Umma nineteen. In the senate of thirty elected and twenty appointed members NUP obtained thirty-one places; Umma, only seven. Parliament was convened by Sir Robert Howe, the governor-general. NUP organized the houses. Ismail al-Azhari became prime minister and minister of interior, and formed a cabinet of twelve. Sudanization proceeded rapidly; in August eight Sudanese became provincial governors, replacing the customary British civil servants.

Early in 1955 the NUP started to splinter over the question of the tie to Egypt. Three members left the cabinet to establish a new Republican Independence party, which presented a platform of unfettered sovereignty for the Sudan, but pledged cultural and economic cooperation with Egypt. By June Ismail al-Azhari took the same position and ousted from the cabinet the advocates of union with Egypt.

In August leaders of NUP and Umma requested Egypt and Great Britain to withdraw their troops from the Sudan—which they agreed to do. This action led Sir Ali al-Mirghani and Sir Abd al-Rahman al-Mahdi to effect a compromise. On December 19, 1955, the Sudan house of representatives declared Sudan an independent state and requested recognition from Egypt and Great Britain. The senate passed the same declaration; Egypt and Great Britain granted their approval and recognition on January 1, 1956; Sudan became the ninth member of the Arab League on January 19; and on February 6 Sudan was admitted to the United Nations as the seventy-seventh member.

In February Ismail al-Azhari formed a new coalition cabinet of sixteen members. In March a resolution was passed, adopting "The Republic of the Sudan" as the official name of the state. The new government was thrown almost immediately into the choice of support and adherence to the East or the West. In March a Soviet mission arrived to establish an embassy at Khartoum and offered to give economic and technical assistance. Some military equipment arrived from Egypt, and a Czech mission agreed to sell arms.

Nearly 50 percent of Sudan's trade had been with Great Britain, less than 10 percent with Egypt. Cultural ties with Egypt were firm; a great number of Sudanese were educated in Cairo and Alexandria, where they came under strong Egyptian influences. The problem of the Nile waters was a vital one for Sudan, but doubly so for Egypt. Negotiations between the two states ended in stalemates and in feelings of suspicion and distrust on the part of Sudanese for high-sounding Egyptian phrases. With these complex and diverse forces at work upon Sudan, a policy of complete independence and an honest neutralism attracted general support. In June Sir Ali al-Mirghani and his Khatmiyah followers resigned from NUP and founded the People's Democratic party. They favored the continued independence of Sudan, peace, neutralism, support of the Bandung conference resolutions, a better standard of living for all in Sudan, and the convocation of a constituent assembly to draft a permanent legal basis for the state. As twenty-one deputies and fourteen senators were members of the new party, Ismail al-Azhari's cabinet lost its majority. A coalition of Umma and the People's Democratic party (PDP) elected Abdallah Khalil to the prime ministership by a vote of 60 to 32.

Khalil took office as events in Suez, Egypt, and the Middle East assumed worldwide significance. Sudan was a member of the Arab League, denounced the use of force, declared that SCUA violated international law, and, later, condemned England, France, and Israel for their aggression against Egypt. The blocking of the canal hurt Sudan's trade more than that of any other state. Three times within a year Khalil flew to Cairo for talks with Nasser to discuss the relationship of the two countries and to impress upon Egypt that Sudan's problems were separate from those of Egypt. Khalil believed in true neutralism and notified Nasser that Sudan would obtain economic aid and military equipment wherever she could. Accordingly, Khalil accepted aid from the U.S.S.R., gave contracts to West German firms to construct irrigation canals, and welcomed financial, economic, and agricultural assistance from the United States.

Throughout 1957 the NUP called for a general election, but Khalil postponed it because of Middle East tensions. The election was held in 1958, at a time when Egypt was forming the United Arab Republic with Syria. Sudan evidenced no desire to federate in any way with Egypt, for Khalil's coalition won a working majority in each house. A new cabinet was installed with much the same membership as before, and Sudan pursued her course of neutralism in Arab affairs and in the world at large.

Undoubtedly one of the factors giving Khalil such a generous mandate was a preelection quarrel with Egypt over the territory north of the twenty-second parallel. Egypt had claimed this land for many years, but it had been occupied and administered by the Anglo-Egyptian Sudan. Egypt objected to Sudanese elections in the area, sent an army detachment up the Nile, and presented Sudan with an ultimatum to withdraw her armed forces. Khalil refused and asked the U.N. Security Council to order Egypt to halt her aggression. The Arab League could not take action against Nasser, but Haile Selassie intervened quietly. Egypt agreed to postpone the issue until after the election in Sudan; this decision virtually conceded the disputed region to Sudan, since elections in the area would give a legal sanction to Sudanese sovereignty.

Military Government

If there were no quarrel over the territory there were differences over the use of the Nile's water. In 1958 Nasser publicly asserted that Sudan had violated the 1929 Nile Water Agreement by undertaking the new Managil Project, a plan similar and contiguous to the Gezira Scheme, whereby a significant part of the Nile's water was to be taken without any prior consultation with Egypt. Certainly he contended Sudan could not expect any solution to the flooding of the Nile Valley and the city of Wadi Halfa unless the needs of Managil were included. A week later, at the time of the Baghdad coup, rumors began to circulate that PDP was about to withdraw from its coalition with Umma and join with NUP to force Khalil's resignation because they objected to his pro-Western policies and his failure in coming to an agreement with Egypt over the Nile. Fearing that this would move Sudan into the Egyptian camp, General Ibrahim Abboud, commander of the army, in an easy military coup, suspended the constitution on November 17, 1958, turned out the cabinet, dissolved parliament, and declared a state of emergency. A thirteen-member Supreme Council of the Armed Forces proclaimed that it held constitutional authority and that its president, General Abboud, would exercise all legislative, judicial, and executive powers and remain commander in chief of the armed forces. Three attempted coups against Abboud in 1959 failed. Again in 1961 disorders in Khartoum led to the arrest of a number of former political and government leaders, including Khalil of Umma and Ismail al-Azhari of NUP. However, with improved economic conditions and apparent progress in developing resources, political stability induced Abboud to take the first step toward more responsible government. Khalil, al-Azhari, and others were released, and Abboud announced that a Central Council of State would be formed, a majority of whose members would be chosen by elected provincial councils. Six million voters cast their ballots in 1963 to elect rural and municipal councils, which in turn would choose the provincial councils. This exercise in democracy occurred without any widespread disorders, although the response in the three southern provinces was accompanied by the rumblings of nationalist and separatist movements.

A factor in Khalil's failure in 1958 had been the near collapse of the economy, largely due to a poor cotton crop and low world prices. In 1956 the Managil Project had been drafted as a $100 million attempt to bring under irrigation 830,000 acres as an extension to the million-acre Gezira Scheme. Other development plans, costing $280 million over five years, emphasized the building of railways, roads, hydroelectric plants, and telegraph services. Almost half was expected to come from the World Bank, with other assistance coming from the United States, Great Britain, West Germany, the U.S.S.R., and Yugoslavia. Abboud made no changes in these policies, and the Managil Project was completed in 1962. Work on two other dams, the Roseires Dam and the Khashm al-Girba Dam was speeded up. The former would irrigate an additional 870,000 acres in the east-central region of Sudan, and in part it was being financed by West Germany, the World Bank, and the International Development Association. The Khashm al-Girba, on the Atbara River in the northeast, was designed to provide lands for the villagers in the Wadi Halfa region who would be displaced by the waters behind the Aswan Dam. In 1963 a new Sennar Dam was being constructed to furnish more electric power.

Abboud approved long-range economic development plans in 1961 and had them incorporated in 1962 into a ten-year plan, which was expected to increase the gross national product by 63 percent. Abboud also tackled the long-standing argument with Egypt over the Nile waters; in 1959 he accepted $43 million from Egypt to help resettle those in the Sudan who would lose their lands and homes from flooding caused by the new Aswan Dam. A general agreement was also reached whereby in the future Sudan would be authorized to take 18.5 billion cubic meters of water annually from the Nile, leaving some 55.5 billion for Egypt. There was genuine satisfaction in Sudan over this division, for it was far more than she had previously.

Return to Civilian Rule and the Southern Provinces

On October 30, 1964, rioting and bloodshed erupted in Khartoum as a result of many frustrations, the greatest of which were the continuing unrest and disorders throughout the southern provinces. Sudan's political leaders compelled Abboud to step aside for a civilian-caretaker government under Sirr al-Khatim al-Khalifah, an independent. Al-Khalifah appointed a five-man council to assume the presidential function—one chair, reserved for a southerner, was unfilled. Elections for a constituent assembly were called in 1965 but were held only in the northern provinces. In June 1965 a coalition government of Umma and NUP members was formed by Muhammad Ahmad Mahjub of Umma and Ismail al-Azhari, the NUP leader, who was elected president of the Supreme Council.

In 1966 the assembly voted a censure motion against Mahjub's rule charging corruption and failure, and elected Saddiq al-Mahdi, the new leader of Umma, as prime minister. It signaled the arrival of a new political force in Umma. In a fifteen-man cabinet, Saddiq al-Mahdi placed eight members of NUP, three independents, and only four from Umma, but these four held the portfolios of prime minister, information, defense, interior, labor, and health. Saddiq was thirty years old when he took office; he was an Oxford-educated economist and a modernist who had broken with his uncle, the leader of the Ansari sect, over the question of conformity with past religion-oriented and traditionalist governments. This great-grandson of the Mahdi advocated neither capitalism nor communism, but a "clear-cut form of socialism" to harmonize the efforts of government capital and individual effort. He said, "We must shape Sudan in accordance with the modern world or perish." He set out to restore confidence among the international community in Sudan's stability, position, and responsibility. He declared adherence to Sudan's commitments to the U.N., the Arab League, and the Organization of African Unity. He also set out on a tour of the southern provinces to try to end the long rebellions there. As for the economy, Saddiq placed a prohibition on imports of nonessential goods and eliminated extravagant borrowing from the central Bank of Sudan, established in 1960. With no overpopulation and no food shortages to worry about, Saddiq was optimistic about Sudan's future.

Sudan needed political tranquility, however, and this would depend on Saddiq's skill in solving the southern problem. After the declaration of Sudan's independence and the departure of the British, strife erupted between the pagan and Christian blacks inhabiting the southern provinces and the northern Arab Muslim regions. Self-rule, autonomy within a loose federation, secession, and independence—each of these schemes had supporters who mistrusted the government of Khartoum and the Arab politicians and generals. To centuries of distrust and fear was added the new African nationalism. In 1964 large-scale fighting broke out. Government forces were successful, and tens of thousands of rebels and secessionists fled into Uganda, Kenya, Tanzania, Ethiopia, and other African states. Over 300 Christian missionaries active in the south were deported, and three of the rebel leaders were sentenced to be hanged. William Deng, leader of the Sudan African National Union (SANU), from his exile in Uganda pleaded the southern cause, but others who believed his organization to be too soft and ineffective organized Anya-Nya, a terrorist society pledged to kill Arabs in Sudan's Equatorial Province. Although al-Khalifah went to Uganda to negotiate with SANU, and conferences were held in Khartoum, no solutions were reached. Later in 1965 SANU leadership passed to Aggrey Jaden, but he, too, was unable to find satisfactory answers to the difficulties. A new separatist group, the Azania Liberation Front, was born, and the stream of exiles and refugees widened. In the decade from 1956 to 1966 bloodshed in the southern provinces pulled down one government after the other.

Muhammad Ahmad Mahjub

Saddiq al-Mahdi felt that there was a real basis for national cohesion in Sudan, and the activist southern leaders had more confidence in him than in his predecessors. Though violent clashes in Equatoria early in 1967 between Sudanese army units and Anya-Nya guerrillas claimed one hundred lives Saddiq went ahead with the first elections in ten years in the south to fill their seats in the assembly. Umma won fourteen and SANU ten, forming a rather conservative Southern bloc in the assembly. In April Saddiq swayed the vote in a popular referendum on the philosophy of the new constitution, producing a document more secular than Islamic. Saddiq's uncle, Imam al-Hadi al-Mahdi, leader of the Ansar sect and head of the conservative wing of Umma deserted him; the Umma-NUP coalition collapsed. Muhammad Ahmad Mahjub was asked again to be prime minister and to head a coalition government comprised of al-Hadi's Umma followers, NUP, PDP, and the Southern bloc. Saddiq and his Umma contingent aligned with others as the New Forces Congress.

When the crisis between Israel and the Arab states developed in May 1967 Sudan supported the United Arab Republic; after war broke out Sudan severed relations with Great Britain and the United States. In order to achieve a firmer union of the Arab states Mahjub called for an Arab summit meeting in Khartoum. The meeting condemned Israel as an aggressor and reaffirmed Arab solidarity. In an attempt to heal the most disruptive force among the Arab states, Sudan arranged a compromise between Saudi Arabia and the U.A.R. over Yemen, and succeeded in inducing foreign forces to leave.

Early in 1968 Mahjub dissolved the assembly and called for new elections. Saddiq protested, and his followers flocked to Khartoum in his support. Troops loyal to Mahjub occupied government buildings; the elections were held and Mahjub enjoyed a smashing victory. Throughout the year there was much student unrest, with communist, Muslim Brotherhood, traditional, and Nasserite groups fighting each other, until the universities were closed. Late in the year Mahjub suffered a severe stroke and was flown to London, not to return until February 1969. In his absence political affairs stagnated, the economy drifted, and no solution for the southern provinces was found.

After the June 1967 war Mahjub had found it convenient to improve relations with the U.S.S.R., the Soviet bloc, and mainland China. The U.S.S.R. sent a military delegation to examine Sudan's defenses and agreed to train Sudanese students and officers and to provide planes and weapons. Prime Minister Mahjub, however, was more closely tied to the West, despite his break with Great Britain, West Germany, and the United States, at the time of the 1967 war. Until his stroke he had been successful in getting sizable loans from the Arab states and the West, largely for internal improvements.

Mahjub continued to fail to pacify the south. With southerners in the cabinet and amnesty offers to the rebels in 1968, he still could not end the civil war. Fighting in the south involved Zaire and Uganda, where exiles formed a provisional government. At one time government troops opened the roads in Equatoria and secured the towns, but the countryside was fully in the hands of the Anya-Nya guerrillas.

Jaafar Muhammad al-Numayri

On May 25, 1969, Colonel Jaafar Muhammad al-Numayri and a band of young officers seized the government, deposed al-Azhari and Mahjub, and established a Revolutionary Command Council to rule. Numayri's cabinet, composed of officers and Nasserite socialists, offered a policy of "freedom and socialism" and pledged to find a solution for the south. Former leaders were arrested, all salaries and fringe benefits were cut 20 percent, press censorship was abolished, offenders from the old order were tried, and the poll tax was dropped. In the autumn the cabinet was reorganized; civilians were placed in most posts and Numayri became prime minister as well as head of the RCC. Communists were dropped from the RCC and all political parties were outlawed. At this juncture Numayri set off for Moscow to explain his actions and seek help.

Since the rift in the Umma party had been healed before it had been outlawed, Imam al-Hadi al-Mahdi as Ansar leader and his nephew Saddiq retained considerable power. In March 1970 they tried to overthrow Numayri, but the army easily defeated them; al-Hadi was killed and Saddiq was expelled to Egypt. As the communists had aided al-Hadi, Numayri seized their leader and exiled him to Cairo. The Communist party, however, had a very strong and active membership, estimated at between 5,000 and 10,000; denouncing it and punishing its leader hardly rendered it impotent.

The Soviets accorded Numayri every courtesy—except arms and economic assistance. Later, in Peking, he found a much warmer welcome and more substantial aid. Numayri sought to align his ideas with those of Nasser and the U.A.R. Upon the proclamation of the Federation of Arab Republics in 1971 Numayri declared that Sudan would be unprepared to join until a new Sudanese constitution had been drafted, the communists subdued, the southern question settled, and a strong internal political party organized.

Numayri was driven to seek some way out of the impass in the south. The south itself was seemingly so divided that Numayri hardly knew to whom to talk. A southerner was brought into his cabinet as minister for southern affairs, with a budget of $7.2 million for reconstruction, but he was found to have little influence in the south. Numayri extended amnesty to all rebels, announced that a provisional government for the south would be established, developed intensive social, economic, and cultural programs, and began a school to train southerners for leadership roles. Yet, the battles went on. Failing in these schemes, Numayri offered regional autonomy to the three southern provinces, but he could find no hand to grasp. As the most power resided in the leadership of the Anya-Nya National Armed Forces, Sudan launched an offensive against it; the only result was a steady increase in the insurgency.

In 1970 Numayri produced a five-year economic development plan intended to raise the gross domestic product by 8.1 percent annually. All banks and cotton exporting firms and some foreign companies were nationalized. Newspapers had already been taken over. Numayri's brand of socialism meant an end to foreign and domestic private companies of any size. A number of small loans from other nations and international organizations helped Sudan's economy. Numayri, however, needed immediate results, and these would not be forthcoming for a decade or more.

National Democratic Front Coup

In July 1971 the leader of the Communist party escaped from jail. On July 19 his followers, under Major al-Ata, captured Numayri and sixty army officers. A new seven-man RCC was formed, claiming to represent a National Democratic Front, "an alliance of workers, peasants, intellectuals, soldiers, the Free Officers, and national capitalists." They stood for agrarian reform and autonomy for the south. Pro-Numayri organizations were banned and four communist ones were reactivated. However, two leaders of the coup were in London. When they flew to Sudan their British plane was forced to land in Libya where they were detained. The Sudanese people and the army did not rally to support the communists, and the army, loyal to Numayri, took control, arrested the instigators of the coup, and reinstalled Numayri on July 22. Fourteen of the coup leaders, including al-Ata, were tried and executed.

Democratic Republic of Sudan

Leaders of the coup had charged that Numayri was squeezing out leftists and communists and drifting to one-man rule; that the economy was stagnating; that the southern rebellion was dragging on; and that Sudan had not joined the Federation of Arab Republics. Numayri recognized the validity of these accusations, and in August 1971 the RCC produced a provisional constitution for the Democratic Republic of Sudan. Numayri ran for president in September and received 98.7 percent of the vote. After his inauguration the RCC resigned and Numayri formed a cabinet with himself as prime minister. He appointed three vice-presidents: the general and chief of staff who had rescued him in July; a former leftist civilian chief judge who had been allied with the communists; and Abel Alier, a loyal and influential southerner.

For twenty years the southern civil war had hampered every action in Khartoum. Numayri realized he could not defeat the rebellion so he opened negotiations in London with Major Joseph Lagu, the Anya-Nya leader, and Abel Alier met in Ethiopia with a southern executive council of the South Sudan Liberation Union. Six separate peace documents were signed in March 1972 in Addis Ababa, giving local autonomy to the south and amnesty to all; arranging for a cease-fire, the return of refugees, and the transition of the guerrillas into the southern army; and paving the way for the higher executive council of SSLU to become the council for South Sudan. By the end of the year the three southern provinces had been united into South Sudan, which had an elected assembly, a chief executive answerable to it, and an executive council responsible for all government except defense, currency, and foreign affairs, which remained under the control of Khartoum. Six thousand guerrillas and a like number of regular soldiers became the southern command under General Joseph Lagu, whose military rank equaled that of Numayri. Abel Alier became president of South Sudan, still holding the rank of vice-president for Sudan. One of the greatest problems facing these new leaders was that of resettling the 180,000 refugees returning from Uganda, Ethiopia, and Zaire and the 250,000 who had fled to the bush. Autonomy turned out to be real, as English rapidly replaced Arabic in southern government affairs, though Arabic was supposed to be the official language.

At the end of 1973 Numayri opened the first People's Regional Assembly of South Sudan, an act that finally marked the end of rebellion and the achievement of autonomy from Khartoum. A few incidents occurred afterward, but they stemmed largely from local events. There was some rioting in 1974 when it was rumored that 2 million Egyptians were to be settled in the Jonglei Canal region, and fighting broke out in 1975 against southerners based in Ethiopia. Most observers, remembering the bitter feuds and the blood shed for two decades, marveled at the arrival of peace.

Shortly after the failure of the communist coup in 1971, 1,800 Soviet military advisers were held under detention; most were soon sent home. Numayri was furious that the Soviet mission in Khartoum had interfered in Sudan's domestic affairs by trying to negotiate an understanding between him and the secretary-general of the Sudanese communists. The ambassadors to the U.S.S.R. and Bulgaria were asked to leave. Relations with the Soviets, though made formal again in 1972, remained distant.

Numayri's paramount foreign relations concern was with Egypt and other Arab states, for they exercised the most influence over affairs in Sudan. Sudanese troops were on their way to Suez two days after the outbreak of the war in 1973. Within months an unusual arrangement was consummated whereby a Sudanese minister was placed in charge of all Egyptian matters in Khartoum and an Egyptian minister looked after Sudanese affairs in Cairo. The Sudanese Socialist Union, Sudan's sole political party, followed the programs of the Arab Socialist Union in Egypt and began to cooperate with the Syrian Baath. In 1974 Numayri met with King Faysal, whom he affectionately called "our senior brother," and concluded an accord on the minerals on the Red Sea bed, offshore rights in the Red Sea, and the security of that region. Later Numayri persuaded the presidents of Somalia, North Yemen, and South Yemen to meet together to discuss Red Sea security and support for the Arab secessionists in Eritrea. He encouraged Saudi Arabia to counter the Soviet moves in Somalia and the new Republic of Jibuti, to ensure Arab control and dominance in the Red Sea and East African areas.

Numayri shifted to the right in domestic politics after the aborted 1971 coup. After the election in 1972 for a new People's Assembly he held the offices of president, prime minister, and minister of defense. A permanent constitution was drafted and the Sudanese Socialist Union took an active role in the task. In addition to approving the constitution and autonomy for South Sudan, the SSU urged agrarian reform, equal rights for women, a socialist Sudan, and better health, education, and social services. In May 1973 the new constitution was promulgated. Some groups, fearing Numayri's obvious power, had been opposed to it—and a small coup had been stifled in January—but the new apparatus for government won popular acclaim; even university students and the Muslim Brotherhood praised it.

In response to the worldwide inflation that also affected Sudan, Numayri raised prices on many consumer goods such as sugar, gasoline, and cigarettes. The protests were so vehement and popular reaction so violent that

Numayri resigned. Immediately the masses demonstrated and demanded that he return, which he dutifully did. By 1974, feeling more secure in his position, Numayri released large numbers of political prisoners, including most former leaders. Probably this was a mistake as in September 1975 they staged a serious coup. Rebels seized the radio station in Khartoum, but troops loyal to Numayri mounted a tank assault and captured them. Numayri blamed the Muslim Brotherhood, communists, and Libya for financing and training the group. Less than a year later, Numayri survived another coup attempt, the tenth against him. Eighty-one of those involved were executed. Saddiq al-Mahdi, in London, admitted he had organized it, again with Libyan support. Numayri told all Libyan diplomats to leave, denied Libyan planes overflight privileges, blocked automobiles with Libyan license plates at the frontier, and forbade Sudanese workers to go to Libya. It appeared that Numayri's susceptibility to coup attempts derived from an inability to provide inspiration in a highly pluralistic body politic. But his durability indicated that he had sufficient following among the troops and the masses to keep him in power.

Numayri's retreat from the left became clear in 1972, when he appointed a government committee to reexamine nationalization and to decide which companies to return to former owners and how much added compensation should be paid for those retained. The report was presented in 1973, and the takeover of many companies was rescinded. Obviously Numayri desired to attract foreign capital investments and to open the door to the oil moneys flowing into the Middle East. In a joint venture with Saudi Arabia an oil refinery was located at Port Sudan; Kuwayt agreed to build a pipline from there to Khartoum. Saudi Arabia, Kuwayt, Qatar, Abu Dhabi, and Iran advanced sums for trade and development. Prospecting for oil was widespread along the Red Sea coast and in central Sudan, 645 permits being issued in 1974. The Chase Manhattan Bank opened a branch in Khartoum.

Since the end of the nineteenth century explorers and agriculturalists have seen Sudan's potential as one of the great food producers of the world. In 1904 the British proposed cutting a channel for the White Nile to bypass the Sudd swamp area, where every August the Nile floods about 5,000 square miles. Such a canal would save some 4 million cubic feet of water for irrigating 200,000 acres of rich farm land. Called the Jonglei Canal, it would be about 175 miles long. In 1975 a French consortium was contracted by Egypt and Sudan to build it at a cost of $175 million. Estimates show that eventually it may be able to irrigate nearly 4 million acres and will open up a vast area to cultivation. Satellite photographs showed that only 10 percent of Sudan was under cultivation, but that 100 to 200 million acres were fit for farming. The Arab Fund for Economic and Social Development considered that Sudan could produce amounts equal to 35 to 40 percent of the Middle East's food imports by 1985. Numayri hoped that oil money and Western technology would develop Sudan into a "food power."

REFERENCES: Chapter 44

Important references for this chapter are also found in Chapters 7, 20, 22, 23, 27, 28, 33, 35, 37, 42, and 43.

Adams, Michael. *Suez and After: Year of Crisis.* Boston: Beacon Press, 1958. Dispatches of the *Manchester Guardian* correspondent.

Ammar, Hamed. *Growing Up in an Egyptian Village.* New York: Grove Press, 1954. A description of the life and culture of the fellahin.

Bechtold, Peter K. *Politics in the Sudan: Parliamentary and Military Rule in an Emerging African Nation.* New York: Praeger, 1976.

Beling, Willard. *Pan-Arabism and Labor.* Cambridge, Mass.: Harvard University Press, 1960. An excellent study describing the relationship between the unions and politics.

Berger, Morroe. *Bureaucracy and Society in Modern Egypt: A Study of the Higher Civil Service.* Princeton, N.J.: Princeton University Press, 1957.

———. *Islam in Egypt Today: Social and Political Aspects of Popular Religion.* Cambridge, England: Cambridge University Press, 1970. Shows that the long-held autonomy of certain religious institutions has been lost in today's Egypt.

Childers, Erskine B. *The Road to Suez: A Study of Western-Arab Relations.* London: Macgibbon & Kee, 1962. A provocative study.

Cremeans, Charles D. *The Arabs and the World: Nasser's Arab Nationalist Policy.* New York: Praeger, 1963.

Dekmejian, H. Hrair. *Egypt Under Nasir: A Study in Political Dynamics.* Albany: State University of New York Press, 1971. Covers material to May 1971. The product of considerable scholarly research and close attention to the Egyptian scene.

Fakhouri, Hani. *Kafr El-Elow: An Egyptian Village in Transition.* New York: Holt, Rinehart and Winston, 1972. A study of the manner in which industrialization and urbanization have affected social institutions in Egyptian villages.

Fawzi, Saad El Din. *The Labor Movement in the Sudan, 1945–1955.* New York: Oxford University Press, 1957. The development of the movement and its role in the new state.

Gilsenain, Michael. *Saint and Sufi in Modern Egypt: An Essay in the Sociology of Religion.* Oxford: Clarendon Press, 1973. An important study of economics, sociological problems, and religion in contemporary Egypt.

Glassman, Jon D. *Arms for the Arabs: The Soviet Union and War in the Middle East.* Baltimore, Md.: Johns Hopkins University Press, 1975. Emphasizes the periods of 1956, 1967, and 1973.

Haddad, George M. *Egypt, The Sudan, Yemen and Libya. Revolutions and Military Rule in the Middle East: The Arab States.* Part II, Vol. 3. New York: Robert Speller & Sons, 1973. Contends that the military started out socialists and ended up fascists.

Heikal, Mohamed. *Nasser: The Cairo Documents.* Garden City, N.Y.: Doubleday, 1973. An account by the editor of *al-Ahram,* who was a confidant of Nasser's.

———. *The Road to Ramadan.* New York: Quadrangle, 1975. The 1973 war and the planning that went into it.

Hopkins, Harry. *Egypt: The Crucible: The Unfinished Revolution in the Arab World.* Boston: Houghton Mifflin, 1969. The revolution of 1952, the development of Arab socialism, the newly emerging society, and the Palestine problem.

Issawi, Charles. *Egypt in Revolution: An Economic Analysis.* New York: Oxford University Press, 1963.

El-Kammash, Magdi. *Economic Development and Planning in Egypt.* New York: Praeger, 1968. A discussion of the economic problems coming from population pressures and an examination of the changes in the economy arising from the revolution of 1952.

Lacouture, Jean. *Nasser: A Biography.* New York: Knopf, 1973. By a distinguished French journalist.

Lebon, J. H. G. *Land Use in Sudan.* Bude, England: Geographical Publications, 1965. Important for its insight into agrarian reform movements.

Lotz, Wolfgang. *The Champagne Spy.* London: Vallentine, Mitchell, 1972. Lotz, an Israeli spy in Egypt from 1961 to 1967, gives an interesting picture of the country during those years.

Mabro, Robert. *The Egyptian Economy, 1952–1972.* New York: Oxford University Press, 1974. Fine survey of land reform, the Aswan Dam, and industry.

Manzalaoui, Mahmoud (ed.). *Arabic Writing Today: The Short Story.* Berkeley: University of California Press, 1968. An anthology of short stories, mostly from Egypt, that paint a sharp portrait of Egypt and Egyptians today.

Mayfield, James B. *Rural Politics in Nasser's Egypt.* Austin: University of Texas Press, 1971. A discussion of the relations between Egyptian peasants and towns-people and an analysis of village institutions and the social groups that cluster around them.

Abd al-Nasser, Gamal. *Egypt's Liberation.* Washington, D.C.: Public Affairs Press, 1955. A blueprint of the revolution. First issued in Cairo in 1954 under the title *The Philosophy of the Revolution.*

Neguib, Mohammed. *Egypt's Destiny.* London: Gollancz, 1955. By the Egyptian general who headed the revolution in 1952.

Nutting, Anthony. *I Saw for Myself.* New York: Doubleday, 1958. The Suez crisis described by the British Minister of State in the Foreign Office, who broke with Eden and resigned from his government post.

O'Brien, Patrick. *The Revolution in Egypt's Economic System: From Private Enterprise to Socialism, 1952–1965.* London: Oxford University Press, 1966. A study of the political, legal, and institutional ramifications of the change from private enterprise to socialism.

Robertson, Terrence. *Crisis: The Inside Story of the Suez Conspiracy.* New York: Atheneum, 1965. An authoritative work drawing upon classified and private sources.

Rubenstein, Alvin Z. *Red Star on the Nile: The Soviet-Egyptian Relationship Since the June War.* Princeton, N.J.: Princeton University Press, 1977. A comprehensive study. Reflective.

El-Sadat, Anwar. *Revolt on the Nile.* New York: John Day, 1957. Sadat's description of the Free Officers organization and the events leading to the 1952 revolution.

Safran, Nadav. *Egypt in Search of Political Community.* Cambridge, Mass.: Harvard University Press, 1961. A very well written analysis of the political thought that shaped modern Egypt.

Samaan, Sadek H. *Value Reconstruction and Egyptian Education.* New York: Columbia University Press, 1955. A discussion of new forces and ideas in Egypt, especially in the training of teachers.

Shibl, Yusuf. *The Aswan High Dam.* Beirut: Arab Institute for Research and Publishing, 1971. A very useful account, with tables and a good bibliography.

Sid-Ahmed, Mohamed. *After the Guns Fall Silent.* New York: St. Martin's Press, 1977. By a prominent Egyptian journalist on the role of the 1973 war in removing obstacles to a negotiated peace.

Stephens, Robert. *Nasser: A Political Biography.* New York: Simon & Schuster, 1972. A thorough biography by a *London Observer* correspondent.

Stone, Julius. *Aggression and World Order.* Berkeley: University of California Press, 1958. A legal case study of the 1956 crisis.

Vatikiotis, P. J. *The Egyptian Army in Politics: Pattern for New Nations.* Bloomington: Indiana University Press, 1961. The workings and role of the army in the UAR.

Wai, Dunstan M. *The Southern Sudan: The Problem of National Integration.* London: Cass, 1973. Covers the wide spectrum of views on the Sudanese conflict.

Wheelock, Keith. *Nasser's New Egypt.* New York: Praeger, 1960. A careful study of his early administration.

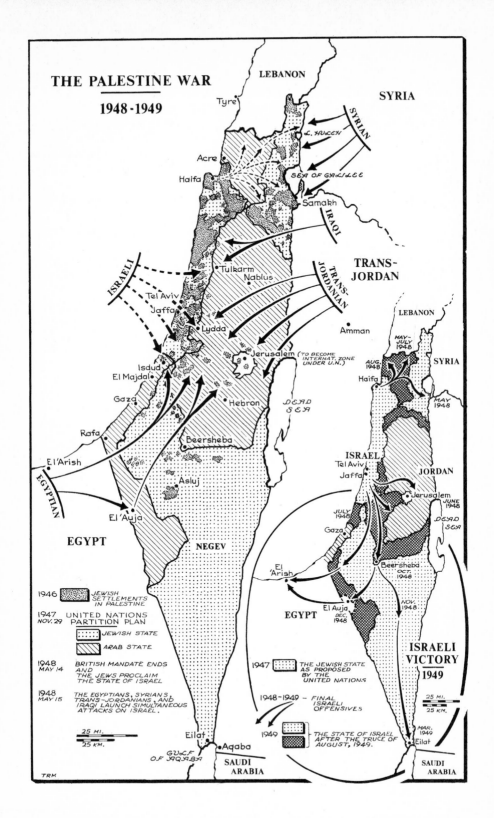

THE PALESTINE WAR

1948-1949

LEBANON

SYRIA

Tyre

L. HULEH

SYRIAN

Acre

Haifa

SEA OF GALILEE

Samakh

IRAQI

ISRAELI

Tulkarm

Nablus

TRANS-JORDANIAN

TRANS-JORDAN

Tel Aviv

Jaffa

Lydda

Jerusalem (TO BECOME INTERNAT. ZONE UNDER U.N.)

Amman

Isdud

El Majdal

Gaza

DEAD SEA

Hebron

Rafa

Beersheba

El'Arish

EGYPTIAN

Asluj

EGYPT

El 'Auja

NEGEV

LEBANON

MAY-JULY 1948

AUG. 1948

Haifa

SYRIA

MAY 1948

ISRAEL

Tel Aviv

Jaffa

JORDAN

Jerusalem

JUNE 1948

JULY 1948

DEAD SEA

Gaza

Beersheba

OCT. 1948

El 'Arish

EGYPT

El Auja DEC. 1948

NOV. 1948

ISRAELI VICTORY

1949

1946   JEWISH SETTLEMENTS IN PALESTINE

1947 NOV. 29   UNITED NATIONS PARTITION PLAN

    JEWISH STATE

    ARAB STATE

1948 MAY 14   BRITISH MANDATE ENDS AND THE JEWS PROCLAIM THE STATE OF ISRAEL

1948 MAY 15   THE EGYPTIANS, SYRIANS, TRANS-JORDANIANS, AND IRAQI LAUNCH SIMULTANEOUS ATTACKS ON ISRAEL.

1947   THE JEWISH STATE AS PROPOSED BY THE UNITED NATIONS

1948-1949   FINAL ISRAELI OFFENSIVES

1949   THE STATE OF ISRAEL AFTER THE TRUCE OF AUGUST, 1949.

25 MI.
25 KM.

25 MI.
25 KM.

MAR. 1949

Eilat

Eilat

Aqaba

GULF OF AQABA

SAUDI ARABIA

SAUDI ARABIA

TRM

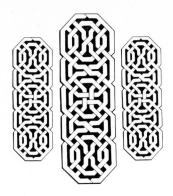

Index

About the Author

Sydney Nettleton Fisher was born in Warsaw, New York, in 1906 and attended Oberlin College (A.B., M.A.) and the University of Illinois (Ph.D., 1935). He has been a member of the faculty of the Ohio State University since 1937, except for leaves of absence to accept visiting professorships and grants for foreign travel and study. In addition, Professor Fisher has worked with various branches of the government as a specialist in Middle Eastern problems and has frequently been asked to deliver public lectures on world affairs and the Middle East.

Professor Fisher is a member of Phi Beta Kappa, a Fellow of the Royal Historical Society, and a member of the Accadèmia del Mediterràneo. He has served as Director of Publications of the Middle East Institute and as editor of *The Middle East Journal* and has contributed articles to numerous journals and encyclopedias. He is the author of several books, among them *Foreign Relations of Turkey, 1481–1512* (1948), *Social Forces in the Middle East* (1955), and *The Military in the Middle East* (1963).

DATE DUE			

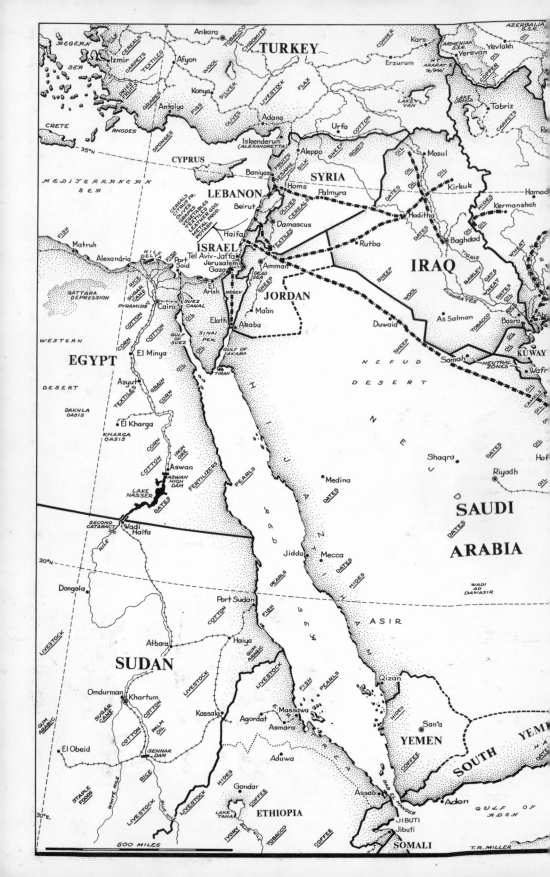

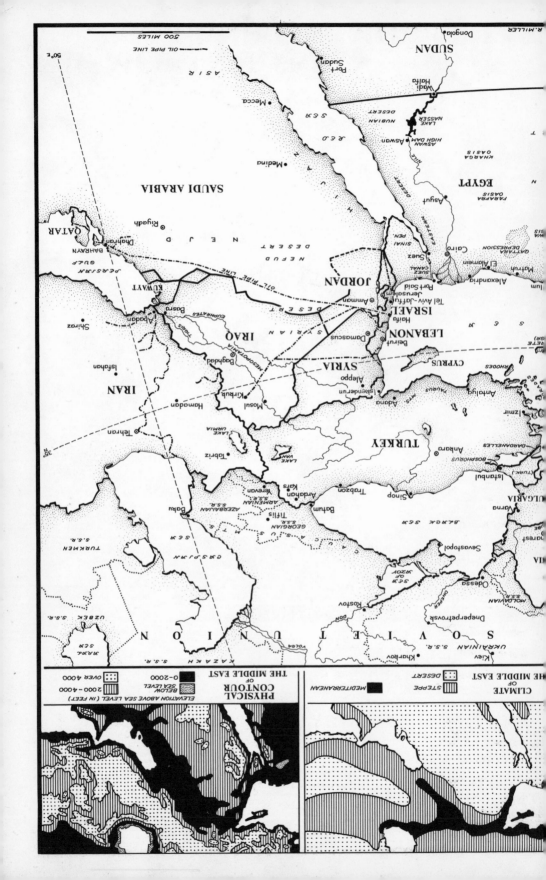